"Very few books on any subject can be truly called
indispensable; this is one of the few."
St Petersburg Times, Florida

"A handbook it isn't! You could use this massive paperback instead of barbells
… bedded in a wonderfully clear, contemporary design, it's a treat for the
armchair traveler and a passionate confirmation for the world music aficionado."
The Beat

"One of the best books on music I have seen. It must rank as
one of the ten music books one would take to a desert island
… absolutely a must have – the music book of the year."
Passion

"The only reference book world music lovers will ever need."
Berkeley Express

"Heaven on a stick … the chapter titles seduce you
into wanting to read more and more."
dB Magazine

"*The Rough Guide to World Music* maps out its territory in detail and
celebrates diversity … enhances the joy of stumbling on someone whose
name you cannot pronounce, from somewhere you have scarcely heard
of, playing music more wonderful than you could ever imagine."
David Honigman

"Truly excellent … easily the most accessible publication in its field, it's
an essential book for anyone with an enquiring ear to the world."
New Internationalist

"A great book … excels in that it covers a plethora of music
scenes and the cultural differences between them."
The Voice

"The most comprehensive survey yet undertaken, and as complete a reference
work as you'll find, with the added bonus that it's written by knowledgeable
enthusiasts, which keeps the scholarly elements easily digestible."
Tower Records Magazine

"It seems like every page of this amazing resource, The Rough Guide
to World Music, sends me out to yet another record store trying
to find something new that was described so interestingly."
David Harrington, Kronos Quartet

THE ROUGH GUIDE to

World Music

Africa & Middle East

compiled and edited by
Simon Broughton, Mark Ellingham
and Jon Lusk

with Duncan Clark

ROUGH GUIDES

www.roughguides.com

Credits

In-house editors: Duncan Clark, Peter Buckley,
Matthew Milton, Joe Staines, Ruth Tidball, Tracy Hopkins
Layout: Duncan Clark, Peter Buckley, Dan May
Picture research: Mark Ellingham
Proofreading: Jennifer Speake
Production: Aimee Hampson, Katherine Owers
Reference Director: Andrew Lockett

Publishing Information

This third edition published September 2006 by
Rough Guides Ltd, 80 Strand, London WC2R 0RL
345 Hudson St, 4th Floor, New York 10014, USA
Email: mail@roughguides.com

Distributed by the Penguin Group:
Penguin Books Ltd, 80 Strand, London WC2R 0RL
Penguin Putnam, Inc., 375 Hudson Street, NY 10014, USA
Penguin Group (Australia), 250 Camberwell Road, Camberwell, Victoria 3124, Australia
Penguin Books Canada Ltd, 90 Eglinton Avenue East, Toronto, Ontario, Canada M4P 2YE
Penguin Group (New Zealand), 67 Apollo Drive, Mairongi Bay, Auckland 1310, New Zealand

Printed in Italy by LegoPrint S.p.A

Typeset in Minion and Myriad to an original design by Duncan Clark

© Rough Guides Ltd
672 pages; includes index

A catalogue record for this book is available from the British Library

ISBN 13: 978-1-84353-551-5
ISBN 10: 1-843-53551-3

1 3 5 7 9 8 6 4 2

Contents

Part 1: Africa

map of countries and styles covered 3

Algeria | Rai 5
rocking the casbah

by Andy Morgan and Chris Nickson

Oran: Where It All Began 6; Chaabi in Algiers 7; Women, Dock-Workers and Street Urchins 7; Cheikha Remitti 9; Independence and the Jazz Age 10; Hick Music Goes Pop 11; Cassette Chebs 13; Khaled, the King of Rai 14; Rachid Taha 16; Courage Under Fire 16; Rai Today 17

Algeria | Kabylia 22
berber spring

by Andy Morgan and Catherine Elias

Exile and Protest 23; Women on the Verge 24; Celtic Connections 24; Another Tribe, Another Mountain 24

Angola 27
unstoppable rhythms

by Bram Posthumus

The Early Years 28; The Shattering of Dreams 29; Bonga: the Voice of Angola 29; Waldemar Bastos: the Heart that Spans the World 30; New Styles 31; Victor Gama 31

Benin & Togo 35
afro-funksters

by François Bensignor

Benin Rockers 36; Traditions 37; Beninois Music Abroad 37; Angélique Kidjo: Keep On Moving 38; Music Market Woes 39; Togo 39

Botswana 43
khoisan to pop

by Rampholo Molefhe

Traditional Sounds 44; The Dawn of Popular Music 44; The Modern Era 45

Burkina Faso 47
hidden treasure, hip-hop hopes

by François Bensignor

A Multitude of Traditions 48; Urban Music 49; Festivals 49

Cameroon 52
the awakening lions

by Jean-Viktor Nkolo, Graeme Ewens and Alain Marius Mouafo Wemba

Recording Roots 53; Manu Dibango: Cameroon's Musical Ambassador 54; Makossa 55; Bikutsi's Essential Thrust 55; Cameroon Today 57; Richard Bona: a Bona Fide Star 58

Cape Verde 62
music of sweet sorrow

by Osvaldo dos Reis, Susana Máximo, David Peterson and Jon Lusk

The Morna 63; Cesaria Evora: the Barefoot Diva 64; Coladeira 65; Funana 65; Eugénio Tavares 66; Batuco and Finaçon 67; International Stars 67; Simentera: Return to Roots 68; Cape Verdeans in the USA 69; Festivals 69

Congo 74
heart of danceness
by Graeme Ewens

Soukousemantics 75; Rumba Roots 76; The Belle Époque 77; Francofile 78; Riding the New Wave 79; Papa Wemba: God Sees All 80; Party Time in Paris 81; Kinshasa in the 1990s 82; New Directions 83; Ndombolo and Beyond 83

Côte d'Ivoire 91
zouglou to cut'n'run
by François Bensignor, Brooke Wentz and Soro Solo

Live and Local 92; Ziglibithy 93; Zouglou 93; One-Way Ticket to the Top 93; Reggae and Rap 94; Cut'n'run 95

Equatorial Guinea 99
malabo blues
by Manuel Dominguez

Fang Traditions 100; Pop Styles 100; The Diaspora 101

Eritrea 103
songs of the patriots
by Dawit Mesfin

MaTA 104; Party Time 104; Guayla Royalty 105; Ambassadors and Icons 105; Love's Labour's Lost 106

Ethiopia 108
land of wax and gold
by Francis Falceto

Trad/Mod and the Golden Age 109; Wax and Gold 110; New Styles 111; Live in Addis: Azmaris 111; Ali Tango 111; The Harp of King David 112; Future Shock 113; Music Shops in Addis 113

Gabon 117
cranning the night away
by Philip Sweeney

Cults and Traditions 118; Congolese Rumba and Army Bands 118; Renovation Cha Cha and Zouk 119; Pierre Akendengué: Ethnomusicology as Art 119; Patience Dabany and the Bongo Dynasty 120; Cranning the Night Away 120

Ghana 123
from highlife to hiplife
by John Collins and Ronnie Graham

Highlife Roots 124; Dance-Band Highlife 124; Palm Wine Music: Buy the Man a Drink 125; Concerted Efforts 126; Guitar-Band Highlife 127; E.T. Mensah 127; Osibisa 128; 1970s Afro-Fusions and Back-to-Roots 128; Economic Collapse and the Highlife Diaspora 129; Ghanaians Abroad 129; Gospel and Reggae since the 1980s 130; The Hiplife Boom 131; Sankofa: Back to the Roots 131; Who's the Daddy? 131; "Classical" Highlife Survives 133

Guinea 136
move over mali
by Katharina Lobeck

The Kings' Singers 137; The Futa Jallon 138; Modern Music Begins 139; The Independence Era 140; Bembeya Jazz 141; Syliphone Records 142; New Identities: the 1980s and 90s 144; Guinea in the World 146; Mory Kanté 147; The Music Scene Diversifies 148

Guinea-Bissau 153
backyard beats of gumbe
by Guus de Klein and Bram Posthumus

Backyard Beats 154; Ethnic Traditions 154; Music and Independence 155; The 1980s on a Shoestring 156; The 1990s: Survival and War 156; Bidinte 157; Manecas Costa and the Gumbe 158

Indian Ocean 163
a lightness of touch
by Graeme Ewens, Alain Courbis and Werner Graebner

The Comoros 164; Mauritius 165; La Réunion 165; Granmoun Lélé: Pure Dynamite 166; The Seychelles 166

Kenya 171
the life and times of Kenyan pop
by Doug Paterson

Kenya's Tribal Music 173; The Early Days 174; Finger-Pickin' Good 174; Benga Wizards 175; Luhya Legends 176; Kikuyu: Prayers for the Country 176; Kamba Calliope 177; Congolese & Swahili: Big-Name Bands 178; Immigration Department 178;

Wanyika Dynasty 180; Hakuna Matata... 181; Ndiyo Hiyo Video! 182; New Directions 182

Liberia 188
music from the ashes
by Bram Posthumus

Traditions and Choirs 189; Sweet Liberia: Pre-War Songs 189; War and Exodus 190; Back on its Feet? 190; One Producer's Story 191

Libya 193
a cultural crossroads
by Robert Nurden

From Folk to Progressives 194; Politics and Pop Songs 195; Ma'luf 195; Desert Blues 196

Madagascar 197
a parallel universe
by Ian Anderson

Highland Hitmakers 198; Half-Green and Salegy 199; Traditional Instruments 200; Sounds of the South 200; Famadihana: Reburial Parties 202; Malagasy Guitar: a Word With Bouboul 203; Where to Find Music in Antananarivo 204; Westernization and Back to Roots 204; Music Under Ravalomanana 206

Malawi 211
sounds afroma!
by John Lwanda

Banjos, Jazz and the Malawi Beat 212; From Kwasa Kwasa to Nyambo 213; Ethnographer's Corner 213; Live in Malawi! 214

Mali 219
gold dust by the river
by Lucy Duran

Music for Sundays 220; Sumu and Sandiya 220; Girl Power, Mali Style 221; Kandia Kouyaté 222; Mande History 223; Mande's Hereditary Musicians 223; Jeli Languages and Instruments 224; From Mali to Mississippi ... and Back 225; Regional Styles and Repertoires 226; Dance Bands and Cultural Authenticity 227; The Rail Band vs Les Ambassadeurs 227; Old Music, New Era 228; Salif Keita: Mali's Superstar 229; Current Trends 230; Wassoulou 231; Ali Farka Touré: the Donkey That Nobody Climbed On 231; Hunters' Music 232; Birth

of the Kamalengoni 232; Wassoulou Women 233; Oumou Sangaré: the Songbird 233

Mauritania & Western Sahara 239
the modes of the moors
by Matthew Lavoie

Moorish Music 240; The Birth of Modern Music 241; Sahrawi Sounds from the Refugee Camps 241; Jakwar 242; The Current Scene 243; Haratin Music 243; Malouma Mint Meidah and Mauritanian 'Pop' 242; Afro-Mauritanians 243; Pulaar Music 244; Sounds of the Soninke 244

Morocco 248
a basic expression of life
by David Muddyman, Andy Morgan and Matthew Lavoie

Berber Music 249; Festivals in Morocco 250; Rwaïs 251; Andalous Music 251; The Nuba 251; Milhûn 252; Gharnati 253; Moussem Madness 253; Sufi and Gnawa Music 254; Gnawa 254; Chaabi and Fusion 254; Al'aïta 255; Roots-Fusion 255; From Egypt to Morocco ... and Back 255; Najat Aatabou 256; Berber Power 257; International Fusion 257; Moroccan Cassettes 258; Rai, Rap and Rock 259; Sephardic Music 259

Mozambique 265
a musica continua
by Celso Paco and Tom Bullough

Coastal Music: Timbila 267; Marrabenta Pulse 267; Dilon Djindji: King of Marrabenta 268; Jazz-Fusion 269; Sounds Today 269; The Musical Diaspora 271

Namibia 275
little brother struggle
by Minette Mans

'Patches' of Practice 276; Imported Sounds 277; Looking for a Revolution 278; Festivals 278

Niger & Touareg 280
sounds of the sahel
by François Bensignor

A Map of Niger 281; Cultural Policy 281; Touareg Rockers and Desert Blues 282; Hopping Youth Clubs 283

Nigeria 287
africa's stumbling giant
by Andrew Frankel

Nigerian Uniqueness 288; Nigerian Peoples 288; Instruments 289; Juju 290; Nigeria's Record Industry 291; Highlife Nigeria Style 292; Traditional Pop and Apala 293; Fuji Fever 294; Waka 295; Fela Kuti and Afro-beat 295; From Kalakuta to Kakadu: Shanties, Shrines and Nite-spots 296; Praise Singing the Big Boss 297; Nigeria Abroad 298; Reggae, Hip-hop, Rap and Beyond 299; In a Suburb Near You… 300; Future Grooves 300

Pygmy Music 304
forest songs from the congo basin
by Dave Abram and Jerome Lewis

Pygmy Polyphony 306; Music in Forest Life 307; Listening to the Forest 307; Beyond the Forest 308; Pygmy Fusion 308; The Baka Music House 309; Survival 310

Rwanda & Burundi 313
echoes from the hills
by Dorian Hayes and Karengera Eric Soul

Traditional Music 314; The Drummers of Burundi and Ballet Inganzo 315; Cécile Kayirebwa and the Rwandan Diaspora 316; Contemporary Music in Rwanda 317; New Music in Burundi 318

São Tomé & Príncipe 321
island music of central africa
by Caroline Shaw and Emile Chabal

Rhythms and Dance 322; Modern Music 323

Senegal & The Gambia 326
a tale of two countries
by Mark Hudson, Doudou Sarr, Paul Hayward and Lucy Duran

Mande Senegambia 327; Wolof Traditions and Negritude 327; Dance Music: the 1960s and Star Band 328; Gambian Traditions and Developments 328; Orchestra Baobab: Still Growing 330; Dakar Superstar: the Rise of Youssou N'Dour 331; Jazz, Funk and the Faye Brothers 331; The Ups and Downs of Youssou N'Dour 332; Seck and Lô 333; The Man from the North: Baaba Maal 334; Baaba Maal 335; A World Apart: Casamance Hothouse 336; Female Performers 336; Rap and New Directions 336; Sene-Rap 339

Sierra Leone 345
from palm wine to protest
by Bram Posthumus, Ed Ashcroft and Richard Trillo

Palm wine and Milo 346; A Brief Golden Era 347; Exile and Revival 347

South Africa | Popular Music 351
nation of the voice
by Rob Allingham and Gregory Mthembu-Salter

Deep Roots 352; The West, Urbanization, Marabi and Jive 353; A Music Industry 353; The Producers 354; Pennywhistle Jive: the Kwela Boom 355; From Sax Jive to Vocal Mbaqanga 356; Zulu Acapella: Mbube and Iscathamiya 358; Ladysmith Black Mambazo 359; Neo-Traditional Styles 360; Sotho and Pedi-Traditional 360; Zulu-Traditional 360; Shangaan/Tsonga-Traditional 361; Local Soul 362; White South African Music 363; Bubblegum 364; Brenda Fassie – Africa's Pop Goddess 365; Kwaito Kulture 366; The Divas 367; Urban Roots 368; Cape Hop 369; Reggae 370

South Africa | Jazz 377
hip kings, hip queens
by Rob Allingham and Gwen Ansell

Swing 378; The Jazz Singers 379; Progressive Jazz: the 1960s 379; Mama Africa 380; Still Grazin': Hugh Masekela 381; Meanwhile, Back Home… 382; … And Today? 383; Zim Ngqawana 384

South Africa | Gospel 389
I've got the power
by Gregory Mthembu-Salter

Star Voices 390; Live Witness 391

Southern Africa | Archives 393
hugh tracey: pioneer archivist
by Mark Hudson

Looking Back 394

Sudan 397
still yearning to dance

by Peter Verney, Helen Jerome and Moawia Yassin

The North 398; Early Days and Jazz 398; Players and Poets 399; Women Singers 401; Southern Sudan 402; Southern Survivals 402; The Nuba 402; Where Next? 403; Dance & Trance: Sufi Dervishes 403

Tanzania & Kenya | Taarab 408
the swahili coastal sound

by Werner Graebner

Taarab Roots 409; Ikhwani Safaa Musical Club 410; Lamu and Mombasa 411; Zanzibar Culture Club 412; Modern Taarab 413; The "Little Granny" of Zanzibar 413; Tanga: Black Star 414; Dar es Salaam 414

Tanzania | Popular Music 418
the land of use-your-brain

by Werner Graebner

Muziki Wa Dansi 419; The Morogoro Jazz Band 419; No Sweat from Congo: Maquis and Matimila 422; Hotel Pop 423; Bongo Flava 423; Tradition & Innovation 424; Mchiriku Madness 425; Jagwa Jive 425; Reggae and Ragga 426

Uganda 430
strong roots and new shoots

by Andy Cooke and Sten Sandahl

The Kampala Scene 431; Kadongo Kamu 431; Traditional Music 431; Royal Court Music 431; Village Music 432

Zambia 436
evolution and expression

by Ronnie Graham, Simon Kandela Tunkanya and Kennedy Gondwe

From Independence to Zam-rock 437; Kalindula Arrives 438; Emmanuel Jaggari Chanda 438; Zambian Music in the 1990s 440; Tribal Music, Dance and Instruments 440; Mondo and the Re-emerging Music Industry 441; The 21st Century 441

Zimbabwe 444
mbira, sungura and chimurenga: play it loud!

by Banning Eyre and Tom Bullough

Tough Times 445; Beerhalls and Biras 446; The Mbira 446; Mapfumo: Chimurenga Man for All Seasons 447; Tuku Music 449; Oliver Mtukudzi 450; Jit Hits the Fans 451; Rumba-Sungura 452; Praise the Lord and Pass the Sadza 453; Ndebele Pop: the Bulawayo Sound 453; New Directions 455

Part 2: Middle East

map of countries and styles covered 461

Arab World/Egypt | Classical 463
music, partner of poetry

by David Lodge, Bill Badley and Neil van der Linden

Classical Arab Music 464; Shared Roots 464; Koranic Recitation: the Basis of Islamic Music 465; Theory, Scales & Rhythm in Classical Arab Music 466; Emerging Traditions in the Twentieth Century 466; Superstars of Cairo 468; Sayed Darwish 468; Farid el-Atrache and Asmahan 468; Umm Kulthum 469; Umm Kulthum's Composers 470; Mohammed Abdel Wahab 470; Leyla Murad 470; Abdalhalim Hafez 471; Warda al-Jaza'iriya 471; Festival of Arabic Music 471

Arabesque 475
oriental fusion

by Phil Meadley

The West Looks East 476; The French Connection 476; Back to Morocco 477; The London Equation 477; Arabesque Moderne 477; The Istanbul Express 478

Armenia 481
the singing apricot tree
by Simon Broughton

Religious Music 482; The Massacres and the Diaspora 482; Folk Music 483; Ashoughs 484; Classical Music, Cabaret and Pop 484; Djivan Gasparyan and the Duduk 485

Azerbaijan 489
in the mugham
by Razia Sultanova and Simon Broughton

Meyxana: Wedding Rap 490; The Aşiq Bard Tradition 490; Mugham 491; Alim Qasimov 491; Mugham on the Move 492

Egypt | Popular/Street Music 495
satellites of love
by Reda el Mawi, Sam Farah, David Lodge and Bill Badley

Sufi Music and Trance 496; Rural Folk Music: the Nile, the Desert and the Copts 497; New Nubian, Old Nubian 498; Bride and Home 498; Music of the Youth 499; Shaabi: Art from the Workers 499; Shababi 500; Shaabi Superstars 501; New Media, New Values 502

Georgia 505
a musical toast
by Simon Broughton

Table Songs 506; Polyphony 506; Professional Choirs 507; Booking a Band Georgian-Style 507; Urban Songs 508

The Gulf 510
khaleeji comeback
by Bill Badley

Saudi Arabia 511; Bahrain 512; United Arab Emirates 512; Qatar 513; Kuwait 513; Yemen 513; Oman 515

Iran 519
the art of ornament
by Laudan Nooshin and Simon Broughton

Classical Iranian Instruments 520; Classical Music 520; From Courts to Cassettes 521; Post-Revolutionary Revival 521; Mohammad Reza Shajarian 522; Modes and Improvisation 522; Listening to Classical Music 523; Folk Music 524; The Bakshi of Khorasan 524; Kurdish Tanbur Players 524; Other Regional Highlights 525; Iranian Pop 525; Kayhan Kalhor 526; Pop Artists 526

Iraq 533
mesopotamia forever
by Neil van der Linden

Maqam 534; Baghdad's Roaring Fifties 535; The Assyrians 535; Rural Sounds 535; Jewish Musicians in Iraq 535; The Great Iraqi Oud Tradition 536; Popular Music 536

Israel 539
narrow bridge/global village
by Dubi Lenz

Songs of the Good Old Land 540; Yemenite Songs 540; Chava Alberstein: Shadow of Israel 541; Roots and Fusions 542; Yair Dalal: Israeli Oud 543

Jewish Music | Sephardic 551
ladino romance
by Judith Cohen and Hilary Pomeroy

Origins and Evolution 552; Key Figures 552; The Levy Legacy 553; Spaniards and Fusions 554; Song Preservation 555

Jordan & Bedouin Music 559
camel steps and epics of the sheikhs
by Bill Badley

Music of Movement 560; Bedouin Instruments 561

Kurdish Music 563
songs of the stateless
by Eva Skalla and Parwez Zabihi

Bards, Minstrels and Songs 564; Instruments and Rhythm 564; Partition States 565; Kurdistan of Turkey 565; Federal Kurdistan of Iraq 566; Kurdistan of Iran 567; Syrian and Armenian Kurdistan 567; The Diaspora 567; The Kamkars 568

Lebanon 572
the rising star in the middle east
by Bill Badley

Diverse Cultures, Diverse Styles 573; Doing the

Dabke 574; Fairuz and the Rahbanis 574; Female Stars 575; Male Pop Singers 575; Sacred Sounds 576; The Diaspora 576

Palestinian Music 580
sounds for a new state
by Andy Morgan, Mu'tasem Adileh and Bill Badley

Rural Songs: Dabke and Qawaali 581; Songs of Partition 581; The Intifada 582; Beginnings of a State 583; El Funoun – Palestinian Art-Music 584; New Opportunities 585

Syria 589
sufis and superstars
by Roger Short

Silk Roots 590; The Sultan of Tarab 590; Super-divas 591; Abdullah Chhadeh, the Qanun and the Hookah 591; Sufi Nights 592; Country Music, Syrian-style 592

Turkey 595
sounds of anatolia
by Martin Stokes and Francesco Martinelli

Turkish Folk 596; Saz Music and the TRT Sound 596; Regional Folk 597; Aşık Music 597; Classical Traditions 598; Classical Fasil and Later Developments 599; Classical Stars 600; The Whirling Dervishes and Sufi Music 601; Dede's Dervish 602; Gypsies and Fasıl Music 602; Western-style Art Music 603; Minority Musics 603; Kurdish Music 603; Greek–Turkish Music 604; Jewish Traditions 604; Arabesk 604; Oriental Roots 604; Arabesk Goes Big-Time 605; Pop and Anatolian Rock 606; Sezen Aksu 607; Turkish Rap in Germany 608

Introduction

Since **The Rough Guide to World Music** first appeared in 1994, the World Music scene has grown dramatically. Vast numbers of CDs are released each month, artists from across the world perform regularly in major concert halls in the "West", and the BBC has created the annual Awards for World Music (The Planets). In addition, ease of travel makes it feasible for those in Europe and America to go and experience the music of the world, in person, in situ. Now African music enthusiasts don't just hang out around Sterns record shop in London and listen to Andy Kershaw on the radio – they go to the Essaouira Festival in Morocco, which has become a sort of Gnawa Woodstock attracting 400,000 people each year, or to the celebrated Festival in the Desert near Timbuktu. Music can be a window on and a passport to the world.

This third edition of *The Rough Guide to World Music* reflects the music's burgeoning popularity – most obviously in its size. The book has grown to fill three volumes, with this first instalment, **Africa & Middle East**, to be followed by **Europe, Asia & Pacific** and **The Americas & Caribbean**. All in all the guide will be around three times the size of the original edition: close to a million words and in excess of two thousand pages. But then the *Rough Guide* has earned the tag of being the 'World Music Bible'.

We have strived in this new edition to chart the changing scene, including coverage, for instance, of African hip-hop, which has swept across the continent in recent years and is the music of choice for young Africans, often in genuinely local forms. Also represented are the club and DJ scenes, which have been energized by global sounds, with dynamic fusions based on everything from Afro-beat to Sufi music. We have also addressed omissions in the last edition, with brand new chapters on Botswana, Namibia, Liberia, Libya, Lebanon and Iraq – as well as musical styles that have become particularly dynamic in the last few years, such as Touareg music and Arabesque.

In this volume, our (impossible) aim is to cover African and Middle Eastern music of every style – popular and classical, religious and secular, new and traditional. It's music you can buy on CD, see at festivals and concerts, and hear in villages, in clubs, at celebrations and on the radio around the world. The book attempts to represent all of these contexts, with nods to key venues, festivals, producers and record labels as well as singers and instrumentalists.

How the Book Works

This first volume of *The Rough Guide to World Music* is divided into two sections: **Africa** and the **Middle East**. Within each section the chapters are arranged alphabetically by country or sometimes by ethnic group – for instance with Kurdish, Sephardic or Pygmy music. There are running heads and an index to help you find your way.

Each chapter consists of an article, discography and playlist. The **articles** are designed to provide the background to each country's musical styles, explaining the history, social background, politics and cultural identity, as well as highlighting the lives and sounds of each country's musicians. The **discographies** begin with reviews of compilation CDs and then move on to individual artists, each of whom gets a brief biography and recommended recordings. Please note these are selective and not comprehensive discographies, which we hope will lead you into an artist's best work. The ⊙ symbol denotes

CDs, ▥ cassettes (which are still prevalent in some regions) and ◉ LPs. Our top recommendations for each country or genre are highlighted by a ★ symbol.

A new feature of this edition are the **playlist** boxes at the end of each discography. These are intended as an alternative way into the music, giving a representative cross-section of the very best tracks that you might want to load onto an iPod or other MP3 player. They are not necessarily available on iTunes yet, but a trawl around the Web (on sites such as *www.calabashmusic.com*) will often unearth downloadable files.

Enjoy…

Part 1

Africa

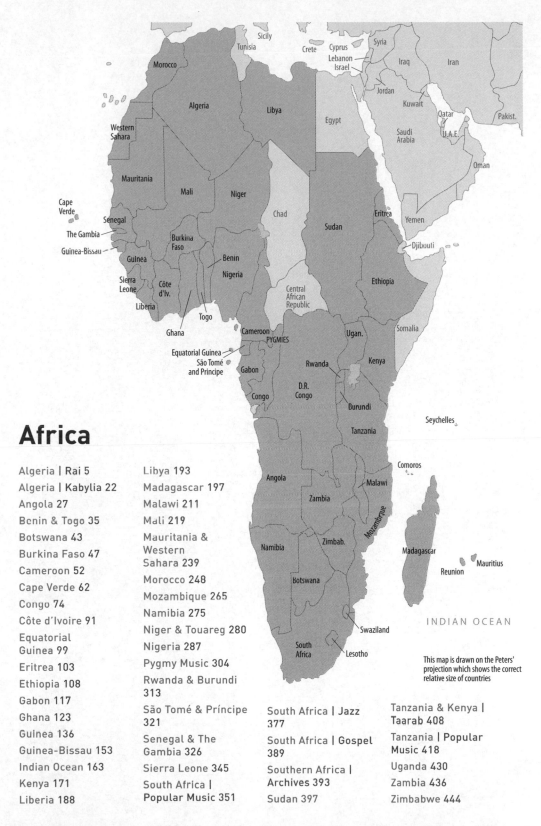

Africa

Algeria | Rai 5
Algeria | Kabylia 22
Angola 27
Benin & Togo 35
Botswana 43
Burkina Faso 47
Cameroon 52
Cape Verde 62
Congo 74
Côte d'Ivoire 91
Equatorial Guinea 99
Eritrea 103
Ethiopia 108
Gabon 117
Ghana 123
Guinea 136
Guinea-Bissau 153
Indian Ocean 163
Kenya 171
Liberia 188

Libya 193
Madagascar 197
Malawi 211
Mali 219
Mauritania & Western Sahara 239
Morocco 248
Mozambique 265
Namibia 275
Niger & Touareg 280
Nigeria 287
Pygmy Music 304
Rwanda & Burundi 313
São Tomé & Príncipe 321
Senegal & The Gambia 326
Sierra Leone 345
South Africa | Popular Music 351

South Africa | Jazz 377
South Africa | Gospel 389
Southern Africa | Archives 393
Sudan 397

Tanzania & Kenya | Taarab 408
Tanzania | Popular Music 418
Uganda 430
Zambia 436
Zimbabwe 444

This map is drawn on the Peters' projection which shows the correct relative size of countries

Algeria | Rai

rocking the casbah

Rai's enduring legend, Khaled
David Browne

For much of recent history, being a musician in Algeria has meant taking your life in your hands. Many singers and producers of the heady, controversial style known as *rai* were cold-bloodedly murdered, along with writers, politicians and others trapped in the ongoing battle between the military regime and Islamic fundamentalist terrorists. Yet even the possibility of death didn't silence the voices, and this powerful music continued to pour out of Algeria – and the Algerian community in France. Even today the struggle continues, as Andy Morgan and Chris Nickson explain.

t's easy to draw parallels between Algerian **rai** and that other successful style of late twentieth-century urban music with which it shares all but one letter. American rap and Algerian *rai* are both styles born out of a strong local culture which use the language of the street to express opinions about street life. They value lyrical improvisation and 'borrow' musical ideas from many sources if and when necessary. They antagonise the values of 'decent' society and the cultural mainstream. They are the musical styles most favoured by the dispossessed in their respective countries, by those who have little to lose and a lot to say. And for both, their paths to international fame have been littered with controversy and misunderstanding. Just as folk who live comfortably within the cultural pale in America wince when they hear words like 'bitch' and 'uzi' coming from the mouth of a rap artist, so the cultural muftis of the Maghreb turn red when they hear tales of drunkenness, despair, sex and hedonism from the lips of a teenage *cheb* (youth).

As the genre has found a global audience, the biggest stars have moved up from the seamy cabarets of Oran to concert halls around the world. Along the way, the music has lost a lot of its defiance (today, the favoured music of modern Algerian youth is angry hip-hop), but it's retained a lot of its power.

Oran: Where it all Began

Wind your way back in search of the roots of *rai* and you'll find yourself in the west of Algeria, with its lush cultivated coastline and harsh arid interior, peppered with the towns whose names echo throughout the history of the genre – Ain Temouchent, Relizane, Saida, Tlemcen, Mostaganem, Sidi bel Abbes, Mascara and, of course, the city where it all started and whose name is synonymous with *rai* itself, **Oran**.

Oran is a modern seaport and the capital of the colonial province of Oranie in western Algeria. Known as the 'little Paris' of North Africa, it has had a reputation for being one big fun-house ever since the Spanish invaded it centuries ago and kept women there to entertain the troops. Before Algeria won its independence from France in 1962 (after eight years of armed struggle), the city had been divided into separate quarters – French, Jewish, Spanish and Arab – each with its own atmosphere and music.

The Jewish quarter – known as the Derb – was where Jewish musicians like **Saoud L'Oranais**, **Larbi Bensari** and **Reinette L'Oranaise** performed each night in the cafés and cabarets. The Span-ish quarter, Sidi El Houari, was mostly the home of fishermen, but in 1939 many refugees arrived from Spain following the Civil War, and Spanish music became an important part of Oran's musical framework.

The French lived in the best accommodation the old town had to offer and went to the Jewish cafés to get their shot of oriental dancing and maybe a little something else. The old Muslim quarter was known as Medina Jdida (new town). Muslims were forbidden by the French administration to sell alcohol in their own cafés so they crossed to the Jewish and Spanish quarters to get it. The various communities – between whom music was often the best point of contact – coexisted relatively peacefully, hustling for their daily bread, watched over by their French colonial rulers.

At the end of World War I, Arabic music in western Algeria was dominated by two main strands. The strictly regulated 'classical' style known as *al-andalous*, and the more popular styles. Andalous music was imported into North Africa from southern Spain after the expulsion of all Muslims and Jews, following the Christian reconquest of Spain in 1492.

Of the original 24 *nubas* (suites of music and songs) that form the foundation of the strictly regulated andalous music only eleven remain intact and seven of these are fragments. For a long time this was the state's 'official music', performed by musicans who went through a rigid, exacting schooling. There were three distinct schools – *san'a* in Algiers, *gharnati* in Tlemcen and *malouf* in Constantine in eastern Algeria. The structures used by all three bear a strong similarity to the *maqams*, or modes, of Arab classical music, and they all use sung poetry, but with regional differences.

Inevitably, where you have classical styles, you'll also find folk styles, and in Algeria the main ones are *hawzi* and *aaroubi*. Both have their musical roots in the classical *san'a* style of Algiers, but began to develop a strong identity of their own in the late nineteenth century.

Hawzi flourished between the wars, and many of its stars were women such as **Maâlma Yemna**, **Cheikha Tetma**, **Myriam Fekkai**, **Fadila D'zirya** and the great Jewish diva **Reinette L'Oranaise**, who was beloved by both Jews and Muslims alike. In fact many of hawzi's prewar stars were Jewish, since respectable Muslim women were not expected to sing in public.

Meanwhile out in the streets, music with its roots in the age-old rural chants of the local Bedouin tribes was being performed for the masses. Dressed conspicuously in long white jellabas and turbans, the *cheikh*s (the word 'cheikh' is a venerable title meaning something like 'honourable sir') used a more populist form of poetry known as *melhûn*, set to a very basic two- to three-chord rural music with strong pounding beats. While they sang the long epic sagas of the melhûn canon they would bang out the beat on a small metallic drum called the *guellal*, accompanied by two players of a hard rosewood desert flute called the *gasba*. Their stage was any café in the Arabic quarter (the *Café Bessarhraoui* was a favourite haunt), a marriage, a circumcision ceremony or any busy marketplace such as the *tahtaha* of Medina Jdida where they performed among magicians, story-tellers, political agitators, beggars, teeth-pullers, snake-charmers and the rest of the motley crew that frequented such places.

The music of the cheikhs was known as *bedoui*, *gharbi* (meaning 'from the West') or *folklore Oranais*. The cheikhs guarded their skills jealously and their circle was a hard one to enter. The works of the great melhûn poets like Zenagui Bouhafs or Mestfa ben Brahim were long, complex and difficult to learn. The aspiring bedoui artiste would have to suffer a long apprenticeship under the strict supervision of a 'master' and then pass a test before he could grace his name with the title 'cheikh'. The cheikhs, men such as **Cheikh Hamada**, **Cheikh Khaldi**, **Cheikh Mohamed Senoussi** (who made the first bedoui recording in 1906), **Cheikh Madani** or **Cheikh Hachemi Bensmir** were somewhat stuffy and retro. They were from society's 'guardian' class, men with strong standards of morality and decency. Despite the fact that the French authorities distrusted melhûn, with its eulogies to the great Muslim saints and freedom-fighters of yesteryear, they looked benignly on the activities of the cheikhs, whom they considered to be a healthy bulwark against lewd talk in the local arts.

Many cheikhs were refined city-dwellers who led a comfortable coexistence with their French overlords and were even collaborators, generally loath to step out of line. Hamada, to be fair, was an exception, and became a stern critic of the colonial administration. One of his sons was executed by the French. The cheikhs were popular but their language was not populist.

Chaabi in Algiers

Along the coast in the capital, Algiers, a new form of popular music was emerging. *Chaabi* means 'of the people', and it's very definitely the people's music, even in a country where *rai* rules. It's a catch-all term in the same way as rock and pop in the West, covering a multitude of styles. Two of the biggest are *chaabi-melhûn*, which evolved in the 1940s, and a modern, more contemporary sounding chaabi.

Chaabi-melhûn can be traced directly to **Hadj Mohamed el Anka**, who used the dialect of Algiers to sing the work of poets – many of them Moroccan – and bring a more local flavour to the music. Chaabi-melhûn uses a system called *bayt wa çiyâh*, offering melodic and rhythmic choices, to accompany songs that can last anywhere from fifteen to forty minutes, allowing time for improvisation by both singer and musicians.

Although it's still widely played, chaabi-melhûn was largely overtaken in the 1950s by modern chaabi, also called *aasri* (or contemporary), which brought in melodies that derived less from the classical and folk traditions and took a more direct – rather than poetic – approach to lyrics. As it evolved, the songs became shorter. It's popular at wedding and circumcision ceremonies, where it sits cheek by jowl with *hawzi*. As a style it's produced some stirring music, such as the classic song "Ya Rayah", whose definitive version by **Dahmane El Harrachi** was reinterpreted by Algerian rebel rocker **Rachid Taha** on his *Diwân* album.

Women, Dock-Workers and Street Urchins

The early decades of the last century were a time of great change and social upheaval in Algeria. The traditional patterns of society, based on land and tribal allegiance, had been broken down by the land-grabbing policies of the colonists which resulted in a new urban underclass of poor factory workers, for the most part illiterate and rootless.

The venerable cheikhs seemed unprepared to sing about the stresses of poverty, rural immigration, colonial misrule, unemployment, overcrowding, crime, prostitution and other daily concerns of this new group of people. This job was left to the street poets who sang *zendanis* (from *zendan* meaning 'cellar') or bar songs which stitched together snippets of melhûn, bawdy rhymes and patches of improvised street wit covering every topic of momentary concern in the community of the dispossessed.

The musicologist Jules Rouanet, writing for *La Revue Musicale* in 1905, described these forerunners of *rai* music in these damning terms: "The zendani are the musical airs which can be found right at the bottom of the Arabic musical repertoire. Any self-respecting musician does not sing the zendanis. He leaves them to women, dock workers and street urchins, and the people take their revenge by giving themselves whole-heartedly to the culture of this pariah style. They pepper these short melodies with all kinds of lyrics, fugitive improvisations and, in moments of inspirational weakness, with 'ahs' and 'ya lallas' … sufficient to fill the gap."

He might also have mentioned that these inspirational hiatuses were often filled with the cry 'ya rai' or 'errai errai'. The word 'rai' covers a vast expanse of meaning and loosely translates as an opinion, choice, advice or point of view. Momentarily stumped for the right phrase or rap with which to continue, the singer would simply intone this all-encompassing word as if to say "This is how I see the world."

In the topsy-turvy society of 1920s Oran, **Muslim women** were the exploited of the exploited. If you had the misfortune to be born poor and female you had to learn survival in hostile surroundings. The constant struggle to preserve female honour was lost by many unsuspecting young women and social ostracism was the usual result. If a young female had a mind to pursue a career in singing or dancing then polite society would usually turn its back on her. Traditionally, a women who had lost her ticket to social respectability, for whatever reason, or who simply craved the opportunity to sing for a living, could join one of the groups of itinerant female singers who sang the *medh* – popular poetic songs in praise of the Prophet performed on a bed of basic pounding percussion and sometimes accompanied by a flute or violin. The *meddhahates* would tour the region, strictly supervised by their leader, or *m'allma*, and perform to female-only audiences at marriages, Ramadhan gatherings and circumcision feasts.

For a woman who found herself on the dangerous periphery of society, membership of a meddhahate group offered companionship, support and a meagre means of survival. Although most meddhahate groups kept a low profile, only performing 'standards' and never their own material, some medh singers, like **Soubira bent Menad**, **Les Trois Filles de Baghdad** and the great poetess **Kheira Essebsadija**, did acquire notoriety in the interwar years. Meddhahate groups still exist today, and at the last count (1988), more than three hundred were registered with UNAC (Union Nationale des Arts Culturels) in Oran.

The crucial link between the 'low-life' zendani songs and modern *rai* however is not the meddhahates but the **cheikhas**. These women were generally the daughters and wives of peasants or manual labourers, or orphans who had survived the harshest of upbringings and opted for the life in music as the only way to keep on living with some kind of dignity. They were known as the 'women of the cold shoulder' because of their revealing clothing which put them beyond the pale of 'decent' society. Adopting the rural bedoui style of the cheikhs, they mixed it with the style of the meddhahates and came up with a truly individual, rough-neck, free-speaking and generally 'shocking' approach to poetry and music.

Whereas the meddhahates performed only for women, the cheikhas would sing for all and sundry and especially for men, in the steamy world of hash dens, cantinas, Moorish cafés, bars and bordellos in Oran and other towns. Quickly ditching the classical and poetic language of the cheikhs, which was purely men's talk anyway, the cheikhas adopted a patchwork of Oranian street slang, interwoven with bits of French and clichés of the melhûn canon.

The music of the cheikhas is considered to be as far removed from what might be politely described as 'family entertainment' as is feasibly possible. When they 'went public' they severed all ties with their previous existence and gave up their family name. They shrouded themselves in a carefully woven veil of mystery and anonymity, never allowing their images to be portrayed on the covers of records or cassettes, adopting colourful nicknames which often alluded to their place of origin and travelling from village to town to village with their male retinue of *gasba* players and a *berrah*, a kind of MC who performed the introductions and shouted dedications to members of the audience in return for money.

Cheikha Remitti El Reliziana from Relizane (see box) was the most notorious, outspoken and

Cheikha Remitti

Cheikha Remitti, the grandmother of **Algerian rai music** spent most of her bitter-sweet, eighty-four years walking on the wild side of life. She was already a school-of-hard-knocks graduate when she recorded the infamous "Charrag Gatta" for Pathé Marconi in 1954. The title of the song means 'Tear, lacerate!', a completely unveiled message to female virgins to do the deed.

Remitti's orphaned childhood in the western Algerian town of Relizane not only taught her how to survive, but to do it with style and panache, sleeping rough in *hammam*s (local Arabic bath-houses) and the tombs of local marabouts, singing with groups of itinerant female musicians called *meddhahates*, or dancing past exhaustion through until dawn at all-night *wa'adat*, the local marriage or saint's-day feasts. The young Saadia (The Blessed or Happy One), as she was then known, earned her nickname in a bar-tent at the annual festival of Sidi Abed. When her entourage suggested that she buy a round for her assembled fans, many of whom were French, the singer overcame her dire ignorance of the language of the colonial masters by singing the words of a popular tune to the bewildered French barmaid "Remettez panaché madame, remettez!" (Another shandy barmaid. Another!). The result was a new name – Cheikha Remitti El Reliziana.

Remitti, who died in 2006, was the greatest of all the *cheikhas*, the women singers of western Algeria who sing and improvise their raunchy lyrical snapshots of daily low-life in a thick, highly flavoured dialect unique to the country around the great sea-port of Oran. Her notoriety was founded on her remarkable skill with words, her acute improvisational abilities and her fearlessness. Only those ears tuned in to the cheeky and comical patois of Oranie can appreciate her razor-sharp talent for satirical improvisation. Inspiration came to her at night, and, in her words, "like a swarm of bees attacking my head." She sang about the pleasures of booze ("Some people adore God. I adore beer"), the repugnant attitude of old men towards their young brides ("Who would bring repugnant old saliva together with sweet young saliva"), the pleasures of sex ("He scratched my back and I gave him my all"), about cars, telephones, the TGV and the homesick agonies of the emigrant.

All this verbal wizardry was belted out in a voice that could grate the hide off a rhinoceros, a deep souful rasp that pulsated to the raw rhythmic trance of the metallic *guellal* drums, interweaving with the swirling barren wail of the *gasba* (a rosewood desert flute). On stage, Remitti flirted outrageously with her audience, distilling all the sexual power of an Elvis groin thrust into the rhythmic hike of her eyebrows and the flutter of her shimmying shoulders, the glint of her gold teeth vying with the wicked sparkle in her eyes.

Even though she enjoyed a respect and love that still unites Algerians in the recent era of murder and political chaos, official recognition was painfully slow in coming. Remitti maintained that her "lust for life" sat easily with heart-felt religious convictions, and in 1975 she performed the sacred duty of pilgrimage to Mecca, earning herself the respected title of *hadja*. But official acceptance of her music didn't arrive until 1994 when she performed at the temple of all things culturally acceptable in the Arabic music world, the Institut du Monde Arabe in Paris. Later that year her collaboration with Robert Fripp and Flea (of the Red Hot Chilli Peppers) on the album *Sidi Mansour* proved that her mojo didn't just work on her fellow Arabs, but a much wider range of cultures and ages. In 2001 she played several dates in the US, and although she did not record or perform after that, she remained an icon. If *rai* is the blues of North Africa, then Cheikha Remitti is the Bessie Smith of the genre.

Collection Maurice El Médioni

Maurice El Médioni (on piano) with Lili Labassi, c.1935

oldest surviving member of the cheikhates and claimed to be *el ghedra* (the root) of modern *rai*. She was the visible tip of the cheikha phenomenon, which is peculiarly Oranian and much misunderstood, even maligned in other parts of the country. Behind her are other great cheikhas, like the comparatively young **Cheikha Djenia** (from the word *djinn*, or evil spirit), **Cheikha Kheira Guendil**, **Cheikha Grélo** (cockroach) **el Mostganmia** (from Mostaganem), **Cheikha Bachitta de Mascara** (from the town of the same name) who caused a scandal in the forties by wearing trousers and a cap, **Cheikha el Ouachma** (tattooed) **el Tmouchentia** (from Ain Temouchent) and **Cheikha Zohra el Reliziana**.

At the inspirational source of the cheikhates' art is the concept of *mehna* which has close affinities to the elusive *duende*, so cherished by the great singers of flamenco. Cheikha Djenia gives this definition of mehna: "Mehna is hard and terrible. Mehna is strong and dangerous. She who has never experienced it is lucky. It's better for her, for her peace of mind. Mehna is the love that hurts, the love that sickens. Mehna, God preserve us, is like a tumour, an evil that envelopes your being. That's mehna, that's suffering, that's life. A woman's mehna is different from that of a man. A man, even if he suffers from it, will never show it."

Independence and the Jazz Age

In the 1930s, the underground agitators and mujaheddin of the emerging independence movement considered the *rai* of the cheikhas anti-revolutionary and apolitical, drugging the people with retrograde thoughts of debauchery and alcoholic oblivion. Remitti and others could not have cared less and continued defiantly to expound the everyday woes and occasional pleasures of the workers and peasants who flocked to the cafés where they performed. Around this time, too, 78rpm records by the great Egyptian artists Umm Kalthum and Mohammed Abd el-Wahab were beginning to find huge popularity all across the Maghreb and new styles of city music were evolving.

In Oran, the Egyptian sounds were blended with a little classical andalous and a measure or two of *rai* and the result was *wahrani*, a new urban hybrid whose greatest exponent was **Blaoui Houari**. Sailors fresh in port would come and sell records in Houari's father's café featuring the latest French pop tunes by the likes of Edith Piaf, Tino Rossi and Josephine Baker. These sounds became very popular with young urbanites and this popularity grew stronger in the period when American troops were stationed in Oran during the World War II. Seduced by the music and culture of the jazz age, Houari and a group of talented contemporaries including **Ahmed Wahby**, **Djelloul Bendaoud**, **Maurice El Médioni** and **Mohammed Belarbi** incorporated Western instruments like the piano and accordion into the local musical language. Wahby's song "Ouahrane Ouahrane" (Oran Oran), became a classic anthem of the new Oranian folklore, or *bedoui citadinisé* as it was also known.

Ever since the early 1930s, the battle for an independent and free Algeria had been gathering pace. In the mid-1950s the volcano of revolutionary fervour erupted and insurrection gripped the country. The cheikhas and the urban wahrani stars were quick to add their voice to the protesting chorus. Some, like Blaoui Houari and the outspoken **Ahmed Saber**, ended up in jail whilst others like Ahmed Wahby escaped to Tunisia to join the FLN (Front de Libération National) in exile.

In the words of Remitti: "The FLN didn't have to contact me. Straight after the uprising of November 1, 1954 I began to sing about the armed struggle. For we, the generation of cheikhs Hamada and Madani, were prepared for the armed struggle." In the bitter heat of the war of independence many *rai* artists managed to make their first records. The French company Pathé, who seem to have dominated the music industry in Algeria until the late 1950s, gave Blaoui Houari, Ahmed Wahby and Cheikha Remitti their first breaks during this period.

Hick Music Goes Pop

With the eventual capitulation of the French under De Gaulle and Algerian independence in 1962 there was a brief period of nationwide jubilation, street partying and riotous merrymaking. Very soon, however, a cloud descended on the young nation. The Marxist theoreticians of the Boumédienne regime were not partial to outspoken libertine musicians championing sexual freedom and the good life. Their cultural policy was to promote a respectable 'national' musical genre and not surprisingly they opted to place the classical andalous style mixed with a little of the local chaabi music of Algiers on this lofty pedestal. *Rai* was, after all, hick music, sung by a bunch of hooligan yokels with stiff Oranian accents who were unworthy of any role in the sacred Algerian patrimony.

In Oran, things were seen a bit differently. One artist in particular, **Ahmed Saber**, continued to parody the shortcomings of the new government in songs like "El Khaïne" (The Thief – a diatribe against official corruption) or "Bouh bouh el khedma welat oujouh" (Oh, oh, you get a job by pulling strings) which mixed *rai*, *wahrani*, jazz and a little rumba. He dared even to criticize Ahmed Ben Bella, Algeria's first president and the hero of the revolution, and spent several periods in jail, eventually dying in poverty in 1967. Boumédienne, Ben Bella's successor, shut the regional TV station of Oran, prohibited alcohol and put a ban on large concerts or gatherings of *rai* musicians. *Rai* was locked behind closed doors.

This was not an unfamiliar place for *rai* to find itself. *Rai* was always most comfortable in small gatherings such as marriages, circumcision feasts or simple family get-togethers in which the singer would improvise stories about the lives of the people present, all of whom she or he knew personally, and the berrah would go around cajoling tips out of the audience. In these surroundings *rai* could be poured out uninhibited without fear or recrimina-

Jak Kilby

Bellemou Messaoud

tion. Apart from anything else, the *gasba* flutes and *guellal* drums of the traditional *rai* orchestra were totally unsuited to large concert halls.

This fact hadn't escaped the attention of the younger generation and especially of two young musicians from Oran, multi-instrumentalist (but mainly trumpeter) **Bellemou Messaoud** and singer **Belkacem Bouteldja**. Independently, both dreamed of updating the *rai* sound to make it more suitable for the youth of the mid-1960s who were getting hooked on the latest sounds from Europe and America. The French *beau mec* Johnny Halliday played the Regent cinema on Oran's corniche or seafront strip and dozens of hopeful 'rocker' combos – with names like The Students or The Vultures (the latter fronted by the Ahmed brothers, later key *rai* producers) – began boogying to the beat of The Beatles, James Brown and Otis Redding. This was the hey-day of 'Yé Yé', that particularly French twist on beat-mania and the youth of Oran, Algiers and other big cities were rolling and shaking with the rest of the world.

Rai had to be made danceable to retain its appeal. Bouteldja, alias 'Le Joselito', hit the big time in 1964 at the tender age of 14, taking songs from

Jak Kilby

Chaba Fadela and Cheb Sahraoui, original superstars of *rai*

the cheikhates and melhûn repertoire and spicing them up with modern instrumentation and arrangements. Messaoud started experimenting by substituting the *gasba* with sax or trumpet and the small *guellal* with the much larger, booming tabla drum. Around the same time, Bouteldja was customizing an accordion so that it could play the quarter-tones so characteristic of Arabic music in general.

The post-revolutionary generation of young musicians, which included Bellemou, Bouteldja, **Boutaïba Sghir** and **Benfissa** started to formulate a modern **pop-rai**. Their influences ranged from rock to flamenco, from jazz to bedoui and the *rai* of the cheikhas. Spanish artists had been visiting Algeria for decades to play for the large Spanish community of Oran. Their music was very popular, especially with the young Bellemou who had studied at the Spanish music school in his hometown of Ain Temouchent.

After a few years testing their new sounds on the Oran wedding, cabaret and café circuit, Bellemou and Bouteldja had achieved local fame, not to say notoriety. Trumpets, saxophones and accordions in *rai* music? They left audiences speechless. Cheikha Remitti, jealous and proud by nature, was furious at her baby being stolen from her. "I built the house and they stole the keys and moved right in," she declared angrily.

In the slip-stream of Bellemou's and Bouteldja's success a new generation began turning to the *rai* hybrid to provide a soundtrack to their lives.

Among these 'midnight' children were two child singers from Oran who were becoming a popular attraction at wedding and circumcision feasts – the singers who were to become known as *rai*'s first big stars, **Chaba Fadela** and **Cheb Khaled**.

Fadela Zelmat's family house in the seedy former Jewish quarter was a stone's throw from the municipal theatre and she had always had her heart set on a stage career. Nicknamed 'Remitti sghira' (little Remitti) by the theatre's director, the young Fadela starred in Mohamed Ifticène's 1976 film *Djalti* at the green age of 14, where she played the role of a smoking, drinking, bikini-and-miniskirt-wearing local girl. She also performed as a backing vocalist on various recordings by Boutaïba Sghir and Cheikha Djenia.

Khaled Brahim came from the Echmuhl district in Oran's new town where his father was a mechanic in the local police garage. Like all his contemporaries, Khaled was mad for the sounds of the Moroccan new wave, groups like Nass el Ghiwane and Jil Jilala who were busy moulding a hard, modern style of Arabic music and becoming popular all over the Maghreb. With his Nass el Ghiwane sound-alike group **Noujoun el Khams** (The Five Stars), Khaled would play anywhere and everywhere, beginning the evenings with Moroccan- and rock-influenced songs and later, when only the intimates were left in the house, finishing off with some down-home *rai*.

The 1970s were a bad time for the youth of Algeria. The previous decade had exacerbated the problems of poverty, homelessness and unemployment which had plagued the country since independence. When President Chadli took over from the long-standing leader Boumédienne in 1977, corruption became almost endemic. The young people of cities like Algiers and Oran, too old for school and too young for military service, existed in an aimless limbo, denied sexual freedom or the chance to travel abroad and continually preached to about religion and morality by the authoritarian central government. Frustrated as they were, they were not oblivious to the general radicalization of Third World culture which was implicit in the music of Bob Marley, the Moroccan new wave and the plight of the Palestinians.

The mid-1970s also witnessed another development that was to be crucial to the pop-*rai* boom of the 1980s. For decades, record producers in Algeria had released their material on 45rpm vinyl singles which were relatively expensive to produce. After 1974 cheap cassette recorders became available and the vinyl era rapidly ended. Producers, or *éditeurs* as they're known in French, sprang up like flowers after a freak flood, ranging from two-bit sharks with a microphone and a beaten-up cassette player, to the likes of brothers **Rachid** and **Fethi Baba Ahmed** who ran a studio and production centre in Tlemcen, or the talented arranger-producer **Mohammed Maghni**, all survivors of 1960s rock groups who strove to develop new sounds and styles.

Cassette Chebs

For the emerging generation of chebs and chabas, royalties were unheard of. Candyfloss contracts were confected and then ignored. When Cheb Khaled eventually hit the big time, a number of producers claimed to have an exclusive deal with him. His reply was: "My only contract is with God."

The cassette revolution allowed *rai* to circumvent the traditional uninterest and elitism of the state-run media giant RTA (Radio Télévision Algerienne) with whom many of the young *rai* singers had a love-hate relationship. On the one hand they despised the haughty indifference of the media cadres far away in Algiers, and on the other they craved the fame and potential fortune which might result from TV coverage.

According to Bouziane Daoudi and Hadj Miliani, the authors of *L'aventure Rai*, one of the few books on the subject, it was a desire on the part of the musical scene in Oran to be considered on a par with the lucky few who appeared on television that the title **'cheb'** – meaning 'young' or 'charm-

ing' – was adopted. The presenters of musical shows on TV would intone a formula to introduce the next act which consisted of the anodyne phrase "Wa el an nouqadim lakouni éch-cheb…" (And now please welcome the young …). The *éditeurs* in Oran, in a calculated game of one-upmanship – and also, it must be said, to differentiate their young recording stars from the cheikhs and cheikhas of old – persuaded and cajoled all and sundry to become cheb this and chaba that.

The modern *rai* era was born when Chaba Fadela recorded **"Ana ma h'lali ennoum"** (Sleep doesn't matter to me any more) in 1979. The song was a hit, and more importantly, a hit all over the country. It was the first time that *rai* had really gone out beyond its western Algerian stronghold and seduced the whole nation. All the elements that had made the *rai* of the cheikhas so controversial – the plain speaking, the realism, the love of life, the lack of concern for accepted mores – were at its heart.

Not every singer was prepared to jump on the cheb bandwagon, however. The silver-tongued exponent of 'clean' *rai*, **Houari Benchenet**, whose popularity rivalled that of Cheb Khaled's in the early 1980s, resolutely refused to adopt the cheb moniker and preferred the more socially palatable and elegant wahrani style to the new *rai*.

One of the first Khaled cassettes

Jak Kilby

Cheb Mami, still one of the great voices of *rai*

Nevertheless, without any official sanction from government or media, *rai* continued to grow in popularity. In 1983, Chaba Fadela teamed up with the talented classically trained musician and arranger **Mohamed Sahraoui** to record "**N'sel Fik**" (You're mine), one of the anthems of modern *rai*, under the supervision of producer **Rachid Baba Ahmed**. Shortly afterwards the pair got married and became the most famous man-and-wife team in Arabic music. **Cheb Hamid**, whose singing style owed a lot to flamenco, scored huge hits in the early 1980s with "El marsam" and "Maandiche maa" before going back to his job as a hospital technician.

Another burgeoning star was **Cheb Mami**, who was only 14 when he burst onto the scene in 1982 after coming second in a televised talent contest and went on to blaze a trail of firsts – first to move to France in 1985, first to play at Paris's most prestigious rock venue L'Olympia in 1989, first *rai* singer to perform in the US three months later and first to record an album outside France or Algeria (*Let me Rai*, 1990, produced by Hilton Rosenthal in Los Angeles).

1986 was the year when *rai* became a truly international phenomenon. The more progressive organs of the French cultural media like the magazine *Actuel* or Radio Nova had been giving the phenomenon some scant coverage in the early years of the decade. Meanwhile back home, the Algerian establishment had finally relented (in summer 1985) and the first-ever official **festival of rai** was staged in Oran. Cheb Khaled, already a superstar in his own country, was crowned King of

Rai. In the summer of 1986 the cultural organization Riadh el Feth, led by the ubiquitous Lieutenant Colonel Hocine Snoussi, staged a Festival of Youth in Algiers at which many of the emerging Algerian 'World Music' stars performed. *Rai* was represented at the festival by the group **Raina Rai**, from Sidi bel Abbès, a weak choice in the eyes of the hardcore *rai* cognoscenti at the time who considered the group to be a pale imitation of the 'real' *rai* – although these days their album *Hagda* is now universally included amongst the great recordings of the genre.

With World Music becoming a force in the French and international music scene the stage was set for *rai* to join the party. In January 1986, the working-class Parisian suburb of Bobigny staged a festival of *rai* which showcased the talents of Cheb Khaled, Chaba Fadela and Cheb Sahraoui, Raina Rai, Cheikha Remitti and others to an intrigued and delighted audience of North African immigrants and French journalists. The word was out and the word was *rai*.

Khaled, the King of Rai

In spite of the successes of Cheb Mami, Fadela and Sahraoui, Cheb Tati *et al.*, no one has achieved fame and fortune on the international stage to rival **Khaled**. When still known as Cheb Khaled he was signed in 1991 to a worldwide recording deal by the legendary French label and Polygram subsidiary, Barclay.

When Barclay took on the challenge of spreading the *rai* gospel throughout the world, the idea of investing large amounts of cash in the career of an Algerian singer was viewed as a huge risk by many. In the event, the pay-off was handsome. Their first album release, *Khaled* (1992), produced by Don Was and featuring the smash hit "Didi", went gold in France (over 100,000 sales) and sold respectably in many other countries. The follow-up, *N'ssi N'ssi* (1993), featuring songs from the soundtrack of Bertrand Blier's film *1-2-3 Soleils,* sold less well but compensated by earning Khaled a *César* (the French equivalent of the Oscar) for best soundtrack album.

In 1996 Khaled released his third Barclay album, *Sahra*, which featured a song co-written with France's answer to Neil Diamond, Jean-Jacques Goldman, entitled "Aïcha". This innocuous love-ballad, dedicated to the younger of Khaled's two daughters, was a huge hit in France, far outselling anything the stars of variété Française had to offer at the time.

Since *Sahra*, Khaled's international progress has been patchy; for every step forward there seems to have been at least one back. The huge success of *1,2,3 Soleils* cemented his French status as *rai*'s leading figure, and he became an unlikely star in India.1999 saw him poised to make a greater global leap with the release of *Kenza* (named after his other daughter). Employing former prog-rocker **Steve Hillage** (Rachid Taha's producer), Khaled brought in swirls of Cairo strings, whilst keeping the melodies strong. For a while it looked as though he might even crack the American market, which had largely remained immune to his charms, but 9/11 may have put paid to that.

Even so, Khaled became the first Arabic artist to tour the US in the wake of the disaster (in early 2002). Later that year he returned to play his hometown of Oran – only his second Algerian concert since leaving the country in the 1980s.

From the outside, it looked as if the first few years of the new millennium were a period of consolidation. He left Barclay, accusing them of incompetence, and found himself in French courts twice on personal matters, including a paternity suit. Within the *rai* community, rumours began to circulate that the King was losing his touch.

Then came *Ya-Rayi* in 2004, an album that silenced the doubters. There was a

more rooted feel to much of the material (including Khaled on accordion on a couple of tracks), and it even included collaborations with old-timers, **Maurice El Médioni** and **Blaoui Houari**. It wasn't a complete return to basics, however, as Khaled threw in an unusual piece of *rai-zouk* fusion, uniting Algeria and the Antilles, and also worked with his former producer **Don Was** on the title cut.

It's as if there was only ever room for one North African to become a name in French households (and beyond) and Khaled, with his radiant smile and happy-go-lucky unthreatening demeanour, earned himself the job. The other big names of the genre, Mami, Fadela and Sahraoui have had to content themselves with fame amongst the World Music cognoscenti – in addition, of course, to their huge and abiding popularity amongst North Africans.

Universal, France

Khaled in the late 1990s

Rachid Taha

Neatly sidestepping any genre, **Rachid Taha** symbolizes the children of the North African diaspora who've slowly come back to their roots. He was born in Oran in 1958 and his parents migrated to Lyon in France when he was 10. Caught up by punk, he founded the band Carte Séjour (Residence Permit) in the early 1980s, causing a stir with an abrasive, ironic version of the patriotic standard "Douce France".

Richard Dumas/Barclay

Eventually going solo, he teamed up with producer Steve Hillage on a trio of albums that blended dance beats and Arabic melodies. But he really found his feet with 1997's **Diwân**, where he revisited older Arabic songs, turning in a stunning reworking of the classic "Ya Rayah". He called the disc "my version of John Lennon's *Rock'n'Roll* album; covers of the Arabic singers and writers that inspired me to make music when I was young. I chose songs for their strong rhythms and the political poetry of their lyrics. Arabs in France are like blacks in the U.S., integrated yet separate. Music may be the best way we have to come to a real understanding of each other."

The album made him a household name among the *beurs* (second-generation immigrants) and led to him being part of the historic *1, 2, 3 Soleils* concert with Khaled and Faudel. But while his music bowed to both *rai* and chaabi, the undercurrent of punk still ran strong. He was rediscovering his roots, and beginning to find a way to balance his past and present.

Made in Medina in 2001 came much closer to realizing his vision of Arab-based rock, with the all-female **Bnet Marrakech** providing backing vocals for Taha's raw voice and powerhouse band. A live album bought time, but with *Tékitoi* he completely nailed the sound in his head, including a cover of "Rock The Casbah", by one of his inspirations, The Clash, that turns the song upside down with frantic percussion and Arabic lyrics.

Quite how far he can take his particular fusion remains to be seen, but he remains an important force in French and Algerian music.

Many people back in Algeria who had followed and idolized Khaled throughout the 1980s felt that he lost touch after his departure for France and seemed intent on fuelling his rapid rise to international fame with rehashed versions of old worn-out standards rather than producing a new and exciting material. His departure left a vacuum which was eventually filled to overflowing by the Casanova of *rai*-sentimentale, **Cheb Hasni**. Hasni's sweet-as-syrup language of love proved to be even more popular than Khaled, and his cassettes sold in their tens of thousands. Ironically, two of his most famous songs, "Baraka" which launched his

career in 1989, and "N'châf Lhaziza", also known as "Visa", are amongst the most crude and real of pop-*rai*. However, his fame rests on his seductive celebrations of love and women. Together with Cheb Nasro and Cheb Tahar, he dominated the *rai* scene in the early 1990s.

Courage Under Fire

This is where the story of *rai* crashes into the tragedy that is modern Algeria in a terrible and dramatic head-on collision. On 29 September 1994, **Cheb Hasni** was gunned down by commandos of the Armed Islamic Group near his home in Oran. His death, and that of the legendary producer **Rachid Baba Ahmed** in similar circumstances a few months later, dealt a blow not only to *rai* but to Algerian culture in general that many continue to feel deep inside.

The irony of these events is painful. Here was a young singer, at the height of his fame, who preached in the language of earthly love and paid for it with his life. In many ways Hasni's death symbolizes the struggle that *rai* has been engaged in throughout its existence. Intensely hedonistic and apolitical by nature, *rai* has always been ensnared in politics despite itself. Whilst the zendani crooners, the cheikhas, the masters of wahrani and the chebs have concentrated on singing truthfully and passionately about the life which they lead, warts and all, a cultural polemic has raged all around them led by the self-appointed guardians of tradition, morality and the 'spirit' of Islam.

Speaking only months after the riots which shook Algeria in 1988, Cheb Sahraoui put *rai* in its proper perspective: "There's absolutely no connection between *rai* and the violence of last October. *Rai* does not incite revolt. It's just a youth thing designed to let you have fun and forget your troubles. *Rai* is all about partying and nothing to do with politics." But in a country like Algeria – torn between religious fundamentalism, social traditions and the glare of modernity – having fun can all too often be in itself a political act and a singer of *rai* can, without intention, be considered a political animal, suitable for brutal and senseless elimination.

Considering the horror of Hasni's death, it is extraordinary that *rai* continues to be performed and recorded in Algeria. New stars like **Cheb Hassan**, who performs in a suave tuxedo to rapturous

audiences, accompanying himself on a single solitary synth-keyboard, or the latest female *rai* sensation, **Kheira**, are keeping the genre alive and the cassette vendors in business. Nevertheless, there is a sense of crisis in the scene. The generation of Khaled and Fadela are now in their forties, long past their "cheb" phase and struggling with the mundane realities of surviving and rearing families in the suburbs of Oran, Algiers, Paris, Lyon and Marseille. The next generation, born and bred in France, have little time for the record-em-quick-and-sell-'em-cheap philosophy of the *éditeurs* in Barbès, the African 'ghetto' of Paris. They're too busy getting down to the break-beats of the French rap explosion and, more importantly, they expect to buy well-produced and well packaged music on CD.

Faudel, a *rai* sensation in France, is typical of this new generation. Born and bred in the charmless Parisian suburb of Mantes-la-Jolie, he demonstrates a concern for quality, in terms of both recording and musicianship, totally out of keeping with the old values of the *éditeurs*. "I grew up in the *quartiers* of funk and rap, which changes everything," he says. "The Barbès circuit doesn't interest me. It's a closed world which caters only for North Africans." His debut album, *Baïda*, was released to huge critical acclaim in 1998 before he'd even reached his twenties.

The old-style producers thus face a change-or-die ultimatum which few show signs of heeding. Ask any of the Arab cassette-shop owners in Paris how business is going, and you get bowed heads and tales of woe. Nevertheless, it is with the few younger *beur* (children of North African immigrants) producers and musicians who are aware of the need for change – who can adapt *rai*'s sound to the tastes of the new generation, and take on board the notions of proper investment in recording, marketing and publicity – that hope must lie. As one prominent *rai* producer said recently: "The beurs are *rai*'s best hope."

Rai Today

However, arguably, the *beurs* haven't really delivered. Faudel has headed firmly towards the middle of the road, trying to blend *rai* with other genres, generally without great success. Even Cheb Mami hasn't made the outstanding album he's capable of, opting for a safer, more commercial route. An album of collaborations between *rai* and Jamaican artists had some promise, but ultimately fell short. And Cheikha Remitti, soon after performing in the US, sadly died in 2006 – just a few months before her slated debut at London's Promenade Concerts.

Cheb Hasni
Lover's Rai

At least Khaled has returned with an excellent new disc and, judging from the compilations of older material appearing, Algeria is starting to do some soul-searching and rediscovering its past.

But where's the young, emerging talent? Turning to rap, it seems. Down on Oran's Avenue Larbi-Tébessi or on Mohamed-Khémisti Street, today's youth – banned from the coffee and tea shops – hang out. To many of them, *rai* is music for a distant, older generation. Algeria has become a leading light in North Africa's hip-hop scene, with about sixty groups in Oran alone, and another hundred in Algiers. While hip-hop had long since turned the heads of North African youth in France, now it's hit big at home, with bands like **MBS** and **Intik**. And although it started as the preserve of middle-class kids speaking out about repression, it's filtered down to the working classes, effectively supplanting *rai* as the voice of rebellion and frustration. So, even in the home of *rai*, hip-hop has become the global language.

To remain credible and relevant, what *rai* desperately needs now is a musical revolution, similar to the one it experienced in the 1980s. Whether it happens in France or Oran, the music is waiting for a much-needed shot in the arm.

DISCOGRAPHY Algeria | Rai

There's a fair amount of *rai* available on CD these days, though many of the latest releases still appear first (and in some cases only) on cassettes issued in France or Algeria. If you want to track these down, get yourself to Paris and scour the cassette shops near the Barbès Rochechouart metro station, or the shops Bouarfa (32 rue de la Charbonière) and Laser Video (1 rue Caplat).

⊙ **Pop-Rai and Rachid Style**
⊙ **Rai Rebels**
Earthworks, UK
These two compilations feature the work of the late Tlemcen-based producer Rachid Baba Ahmed, whom many hoped would prove to be the Lee Perry of *rai*. Although he didn't fulfil his early promise before his tragic and untimely death, there are some seminal tracks here including Fadela and Sahraoui's *rai* standard "N'sel Fik" (on *Pop-Rai*) and excellent contributions by Cheb Khaled and Cheb Anouar.

⊙ **Spirit of Rai**
Wagram, France
Budget-priced, but pretty comprehensive trawl through the history of *rai*, from the early cheikhs and cheikhas to pop-*rai* and some of the sounds of the French diaspora. It includes "Trig Lycée", the song that first brought (Cheb) Khaled to prominence, and plenty of other excellent material.

★ **Trésors de la Musique Algérienne**
Institut du Monde Arabe, France
A fine compilation culled from the archives of Algerian Radio, this captures the full range of Algerian music in a first golden age of growth, with everything from early chaabi to hawzi, malouf, aasri and Kabyle music. An indispensable introduction to Algerian roots.

⊙ **Wahrap**
Atoll, France
It's not *rai*, but it's the music that the young are making in Algeria. The title says it all – Wah (short for Wahran, or Oran) and rap. Some good, some amateurish, but all quite heartfelt and a sign of the times.

Cheb Anouar

The young Anouar – whose contribution to the Earthworks' compilation *Pop-rai and Rachid Style* (above) stood out a mile – has always been among the most promising artists from Rachid's stable.

⊙ **Laaroussa**
Étoile d'Evasion, Algeria
A charged recording, on which Anouar's husky singing style is aptly accompanied by a simple violin-driven backing-track.

al-Djazaïriya al-Mossiliya

The group, a traditional orchestra playing classical Algerian Andalusian music, was founded in the 1930s. They are currently led by the brilliant mandolin player Nacer Eddine Ben Merabet.

⊙ **Musique Andalouse d'Alger**
Institut du Monde Arabe, France
A live CD with some stunning improvisations, especially from Nacer Eddine Ben Merabet. A deep listening experience, but well worth the effort.

Cheb Djellal

Djellal is a much underrated Moroccan *rai* singer from Oujda, close by the Morocco–Algeria border.

⊙ **Le Prince de la Chanson Maghrebine**
Boualem, Algeria
This set demonstrates to full effect Djellal's pared down and menacing Moroccan-*rai* style with its hypnotic call and response vocal arrangements, without a tacky synth sound in earshot. Absolutely captivating.

Chaba Fadela and Cheb Sahraoui

This husband-and-wife team was one of the most enduring names in pop-*rai* and was responsible for many classic recordings of the genre. Now separated, they are both still active on the international concert circuit.

Faudel, 1990s boy wonder, now established star

⊙ You Are Mine
Mango, UK

The best of a pair of albums recorded by the duo for Mango in the UK. On this solid collection the duo perform one of their many versions of "N'sel Fik". The other Mango disc is Fadela's *Hana Hana*.

Faudel

Born of Algerian parents and brought up in the grim Parisian suburb of Mantes-la-Jolie, Faudel inherited the mantle of '*rai* boy-wonder' in the 1990s. Shunning the ways of the traditional *rai* 'ghetto' in France, he aimed instead to seduce "le grand publique" in the manner of his childhood hero, Khaled.

⭐ Baïda
Sankara/Mercury, France

"To warn people of the worst, that's my mission", declares the young and precocious Faudel who reaped plaudits from both the French and North African media with this, his first release. The musicianship and arrangements here are excellent and Faudel's voice, nurtured from an early age on both North African and Western influences, is a joy to hear.

Cheikh Hamada

One of the greatest, if not THE greatest of all the roots *rai* male vocalists, Cheikh Hamada made his first recording in the 1920s and continued to record in Algeria, Paris and Berlin until his death in 1968. He has left a rare and priceless body of material which is one of the best examples of modern pop-*rai*'s ancestral roots.

⊙ Le Chant Gharbi de l'Ouest Algérien
Les Artistes Arabes Associes, France

Roots *rai* in all its rough-and-ready glory. Hamada's raucous wail jerks along over the rhythmic wail of the *gasbu* flutes and the *guellal* drums. This is no slick hi-fi experience and one for people who like their *rai* raw, rootsy and unadulterated.

Cheb Hasni

Hasni Chekroune was the leading figure of so-called 'soft rai', featuring amorous and romantic lyrics directed at female and family-oriented audiences. Hasni had released a prolific 150 cassettes before being gunned down by fundamentalists in 1994.

⊙ Lover's Rai
Rounder, US

An excellent 'best of' collection with translations of lyrics and full notes.

(Cheb) Khaled

Khaled was crowned 'King of Rai' when he was still a cheb, at the first *rai* festival in Oran in 1985. Since then he has continued to extend his dominance, not only over the *rai* genre, but also over Arabic music in general. He is *rai*'s only true crossover star, loved and respected both by North Africans and by the wider French and international public.

⊙ Hada Raykoum
Triple Earth/Sterns, UK

This is pop-*rai* in its raw mid-1980s state with Khaled singing like the rebel he was reputed to be. Although the sound of his music became slicker in his later productions, the raw sound of the Maghreb blues was never better showcased than on this seminal release.

⊙ Fuir mais où?
MCPE, France

Recorded in 1991, when tensions in Algeria were reaching dangerous new levels, this album found Khaled in a fiery and thought-provoking mood.

⭐ Khaled
Barclay, France

Produced by Don Was, this album blew *rai* wide open for thousands of non-Maghrebis throughout the world. Featuring the bombastic bass-driven "Didi", which was *rai*'s first international hit.

⊙ N'ssi N'ssi
Barclay, France
Although many of the songs are old *rai* standards, the production of Don Was and Philippe Eidel is of the highest quality with beautiful lush string sections recorded in Cairo.

⊙ Ya Rayi
Wrasse, UK
After a dubious opening track, this takes off like the clappers and is Khaled's best and most rooted album in years, with the man himself playing accordion on several cuts. Lots of funky, slinky grooves and the inclusion of two old Algerian heroes (Maurice El Médioni and Blaoui Houari) make this feel like a homecoming.

WITH CHABA ZAHOUANIA

⊙ A Ya Taleb
MCPE, Algeria
The King of Rai has often teamed up with the genre's most durable and impressive female star for a quick cassette release or two. Zahouania is one of the rare singers who has successfully mastered both the folk-*rai* style of the cheikhas and the pop-*rai* of the chebs and chebas. This duo recording is fantastic, rootsy, raw *rai*, featuring a great tribute to one of Algeria's all-time heroes "Sidi Boumédienne".

WITH RACHID TAHA & FAUDEL

★ 1, 2, 3 Soleils
Barclay, France
The King, the Revolutionary, and the Young Pretender shared a stage at the Bercy Stadium in late 1998 for a gargantuan celebration of *rai*, peace and Algerianité. The three nabobs put on an unforgettable show, backed by an orchestra of more than forty musicians, including a 28-piece Egyptian string section, all under the musical direction of (Taha's producer) Steve Hillage.

Cheb Mami

Since causing a sensation, aged 14, on the Algerian TV talent show *Alhan wa Chabab* (Melodies of Youth) in 1982, Cheb Mami has fought hard to earn international recognition with a string of well-produced releases. His lyrics have always been less crude and abrasive than those of many *rai* contemporaries, making him popular with young women and their anxious parents. Universally acknowledged as one of the greats of the genre.

⊙ Let Me Rai
Totem/Virgin, France
The superb voice of Mami is at times here hi-jacked by bland production: at others it's done full justice by subtle use of violins and accordion. A mixed bag, but significant for the fact that it reveals the musical ambitions of the most realistic pretender to Khaled's throne.

⊙ Meli Meli
Totem/Virgin, France
An older and maturer prince of *rai* explores various eclectic avenues on this 1998 release which features fusions of *rai* and rap, *rai* and flamenco and *rai* and funk. A collection of fine well-produced tunes.

Maurice El Médioni

As a young Jewish piano-player in pre-independent Algeria, Médioni made the clientèle of a pied-noir bar in Western Algeria swing. He is now an esteemed veteran living in Marseilles.

★ Café Oran
Piranha, Germany
Marvellous revival of the post-World War II hey-day of El Médioni with his captivating blend of indigenous Andalusian music and *rai*, Cuban rumba, and North-American jazz and boogie-woogie.

Bellemou Messaoud

The trumpeter Messaoud is one of *rai*'s pioneers, having updated it from folk to pop form in the 1960s.

⊙ Le Père du Rai
World Circuit, UK
As an example of Messaoud, this album should be included in any self-respecting *rai* collection, though its fine moments are sadly accompanied by a rather flat production.

Reinette l'Oranaise

After Independence in 1962, Reinette fled the anti-semitic new regime and settled in Paris, where she lived in obscurity until in her 80s, when a French journalist tracked her down and she relaunched her career. She recorded several discs and continued to perform until her death in 1998.

★ Mémoires
Blue Silver, France
Reinette's final recording distils both the dark and radiant memories of a long, eventful life into five songs full of dignity, passion and soul. Accompanied by the great Algerian pianist Mustapha Skandrani, and playing *oud* herself, she pours out her wistful words in a voice too rough for sentimentality and too sweet for bitterness. North African blues at its best.

Cheikha Remitti

The diva of folk *rai* (and mother of ten children), Cheikha Remitti was still strutting about the stage, singing deeply suggestive songs, well into her 70s. She is a nut with an acquired taste – but hypnotic once cracked.

⊙ Rai Roots
Buda/CMM, France
This compilation features Remitti in all her lustful, rasping, pounding glory.

⊙ Sidi Mansour
Absolute Records, France
Who could have imagined this? Remitti – at 70 – recorded in Paris and LA with youngblood Algerian producer Houari Talbi,

along with Robert Fripp, Flea (Red Hot Chilli Peppers), and a host of LA sessionmen. Absurdly out of print now, but worth hunting down, it remains the best fusion of rock and *rai*.

Rachid Taha

The first French-Algerian rock star intelligently blends brilliantly produced rock music (thanks to his pal Steve Hillage) with chaabi and other North African popular music.

★ Diwân
Barclay, France
Taha's bold and brilliant 1998 masterpiece, produced by Hillage. The blend of technology and tradition reaches maturity here with a myriad of styles from Morocco, Algeria, Egypt and the Sahara, unified by a single overriding approach but keeping their individual charms and flavours.

⊙ Tékitoi
Barclay, France
Includes an intriguing contribution from Brian Eno and a version of The Clash's "Rock The Casbah". Taha seems less angry than in the past but the Casbah is still rocking beautifully.

Cheb Zahouani

Grim-faced Zahouani has a 'local hard man' look and sings in a suitably rasping no-nonsense style.

⊙ Moul El Bar
Bouarfa, Algeria
Hardcore *rai*, set to hard bass-heavy rhythm tracks.

PLAYLIST
Algeria | Rai

1 **THE RINGDOVE El Hadj Mohamed El Anka** from *Trésors de la Musique Algérienne*
The father of chaabi in a glorious performance with a band and chorus that seems to glitter.

2 **YAH RAYAH Dahmane El Harrachi** from *Trésors de la Musique Algérienne*
One of the classic Algerian songs in its definitive performance that rocks as hard as anything a *rai* singer – or Algerian rocker – has managed.

3 **QUM TARA Reinette L'Oranaise** from *Mémoires*
The blind Queen of hawzi, recorded late in life, but still with a voice that tingles the spine on a lulling yet intense track.

4 **NEDIHA GAOURIA Bellemou Messaoud** from *Le Père du Rai*
Maybe he's not quite "the Father of Rai," but he changed its course in the 60s. Traces of Spain, spaghetti westerns and wailing trumpets are all part of the mix.

5 **MAGHBOUN Cheb Khaled** from *Pop-Rai and Rachid Style*
Before global fame beckoned, young Khaled sang his heart out for producer Rachid Baba with a bottle of wine in his hand. This is the result.

6 **SIDI MANSOUR Cheikha Remitti** from *Sidi Mansour*
The ultimate rock-*rai* mix? In her seventies, Remitti collaborates with Robert Fripp, and Zappa alumni for one of the most adventurous tracks ever.

7 **ROCK EL CASBAH Rachid Taha** from *Tékitoi*
Taha takes The Clash to Oran, cranks up the percussion and strings and brings in a football terrace chorus. The perfect reinvention.

8 **YA RAYAH Cheb Khaled, Rachid Taha & Faudel** from *1, 2, 3 Soleils*
The three modern champions of Algerian music together, bringing the music full circle.

Algeria | Kabylia

berber spring

Singer-songwriter Souad Massi
Khalil

Between 1992 and 2002, a quarter of a million Algerians were killed in a civil war born of an unresolved identity question: would the country be an Afro-Mediterranean secular Islamic state or an Arabo-Islamist state? In the middle of this struggle, another emerged: a fight for the survival and recognition of the language, culture and identity of the Amazigh (Berber) people – the indigenous Algerians. Imazighen (plural of Amazigh) represent 30% of the Algerian population and the largest tribe are the Kabyles, who live in the remote and beautiful mountains of Kabylia, to the east of Algeria's capital, Algiers. Andy Morgan and Catherine Elias take a look.

The people of Kabylia are descendants of the tribes who inhabited the whole of North Africa from around 3000 BC – or even earlier. They speak Taqbaylith, a dialect of the broad Berber language called Tamazight, and their history is a continuous struggle for the survival of their culture and language against a torrent of invaders: Byzantines, Romans, Vandals, Arabs, Turks, French and, most recently, both the socialist leadership of independent Algeria and their violent Islamic fundamentalist enemies.

In pre-colonial times, music in Kabylia was tied to the ebb and flow of village life. Songs and dances were performed on a powerful rhythmic bed comprising *t'bel* (tambourine) and *bendir* (frame drum) with added colour from the *ajouag* (flute) and *ghaita* (bagpipe).

The French colonizers realized that it would be easier to do business with the traditionally liberal and democratically minded Kabyles than with their Arab neighbours, and practised a policy of divide and rule, favouring Kabyles in education, the civil service and emigration to France. Indeed, the earliest North African émigrés in France were Kabyles, and by the 1980s 46% of all Algerian immigrants in France originated from the Kabyle provinces of Setif and Tizi Ouzou.

Exile and Protest

The story of **modern Kabyle music** starts in 1930s Paris, where a small Kabyle community was well established and a network of cafés run by Kabyles provided places for the exiled musicians to perform.

Slimane Azem, a young Kabyle singer who arrived in Paris in 1937, was inspired by the great nineteenth-century Kabyle poet **Si Mohand Ou Mohand.** Azem tackled the pain and homesickness of his immigrant countrymen in plain, simple language which expressed deep, intense emotion. He was a passionate supporter of the struggle for Algerian independence and his song "Gegh Ay Ajrad Themourthiou" (Locusts, Leave my Country) was a barely veiled message to the French colonial overlords in Algeria, bringing him into direct conflict with the French police.

In the 1950s, Egyptian music took over the Arabic world and Kabyle singers began to accompany their songs with lavishly orchestrated scores. Singers and composers such as **Cherif Kheddam**, **Alloua Zerrouki** and **Akli Yahiatene** all released hit records and their popularity lasted well into the 1970s. Also during the 1950s, the careers of three female Kabyle singers took off, despite considerable hostility on the part of some of their families, who considered singing ignoble and an anathema to womanhood. **Cherifa**, **Hanifa** and **Djamilla** all made a lasting impression on Kabyle song, and paved the way for contemporary female artists like **Malika Domrane**, the group **Djurdjura**, **Iness Mêzel** and **Souad Massi**.

The music of the 1960s cultural revolution – Dylan, Baez, Brassens, *et al.* – was an inspiration for many young Kabyle singers, including a geology student named Hamid Cheriet, who took the name **Idir** ("he shall live" in Taqbaylith) and recorded a track called "A Vava Inouva" (My Little Father) in 1973. This was Kabylia's first international hit, selling previously unheard-of quantities in both Algeria and Europe. Together with his contemporaries **Aït Menguellet** and **Ferhat**, Idir is a cornerstone of modern Kabyle pop. While Idir is the thinker, Aït Menguellet is the poet, inheriting the mantle of Si Mohand Ou Mohand. He still lives in the village of his birth in the Djurdjura mountains, stubbornly refusing to leave Algeria despite the tragic fate of many of his fellow musicians.

In the early 1980s, after the momentous events of 1980 when the whole of Kabylia rose up against the Arab socialist government in Algiers in what became known as the *Tafsut Imazighen* (Berber Spring), other artists like **Matoub Lounès**, **Djamel Allam** and **Abdelli** stepped into the limelight with ever-more ambitious fusions of progressive Western pop and traditional Kabyle music. In 1986 *rai* music exploded on the scene with its brash hedonistic stance and stole the limelight. Suddenly the cultural and political radicalism of Kabyle music seemed unfashionable.

A Kabyle singer named **Takfarinas** (born Ahcen Zermani) managed to adapt to the new ethos and his tale of teenage love pangs "Weytelha" (She's beautiful) was a big hit in the 1980s. He has since

become a Kabyle superstar, complete with girl singers and dancers, marrying Kabyle lyrics, both romantic and political, with a wide range of musical styles.

For Kabylia, one of the hardest-hitting incidents of the 1990s (a decade that was full of them) was the assassination of **Matoub Lounès** on his return to his home in Djurdjura after years of exile in France. He had been attacked before, and kidnapped before, but on June 25, 1998 he was savagely murdered in broad daylight in front of his family. His death sparked widespread riots throughout the region and many suspected that the government, which was preparing to pass a new Arabization law to further curtail the freedoms of the Berber minorities, was responsible for this senseless act of brutality. At his burial service, his sister Malika said, "The face of Lounès will be missed but his songs will dwell in our hearts forever…"

Women on the Verge

Since the late 1990s, Kabyle women in exile have begun to cover some new ground. **Iness Mêzel** started as a sister duo in France. **Fatiha** and **Mali-**

ka Messaoudi** won two Kora awards for their 1998 disc *Berber Singing Goes "World"*, melding poetic Taqbaylith lyrics with jazzy, breezy modern arrangements. Fatiha continued on her own with 2005's *Lën* (There is…) – more poetic Kabyle lyrics and jazz-inflected cabaret-style accompaniment. Both discs address the status of women in Algeria, and by extension in France, where the government honours Algeria's Family Code, which denies basic rights to women.

Meanwhile, **Souad Massi** (who has Kabyle roots but doesn't speak Taqbaylith) abandoned a musical career in Algeria and fled to exile in France where her Darja (Algerian-Arabic) and French original songs caught the world's ear and opened many hearts. Her vulnerable yet determined voice and steady acoustic guitar (plus a cast of excellent sidemen) produced her hit debut *Raoui* (Storyteller) in 2001.

Celtic Connections

A trend that began with Idir is the exploration of commonality between Celtic melody and folklore and those of Imazighen. On *Identité*, a reworking of some of his classic songs in duet with varied singers from Europe and Africa, Idir joined with Karen Matheson of Capercaille on "A Vava Inouva", and with Breton Dan Ar Braz on "Awah, Awah".

Since then, the Celtic-fusion torch has been successfully picked up by two other artists. **Akli D**'s debut in 2001, *Anefas Trankil* (Let Him Be), embroiders Celtic melodies onto Berber beats and Taqbaylith lyrics telling of the pain of exile (in non-poetic everyday language). Hocine Boukella, in his alter-ego **Cheikh Sidi Bemol**, displays his biting wit and innovative "gourbi rock" style (a *gourbi* is a shack in Kabyle) on *El Bandi* (The Bandit). The lyrics are in Taqbaylith, Darja, French and even English, and Boukella's singing brings to mind a Kabyle cross between Tom Waits and Mark Twain.

Another Tribe, Another Mountain

To the east of Kabylia, in the Aures Mountains, live the **Chaoui** tribe of Imazighen, who speak the Tachiwit dialect of Tamazight. The great Hungarian classical composer **Béla Bartók** heard Chaoui performers in Paris in the early 1900s and was intrigued, later visiting Biskra in the Aures to further explore their music – which, he found, bore similarities with the Magyar folk melodies of the Carpathian Mountains. The 2003 double disc *Treasures of Algerian Music* (Institut du Monde Arabe) offers a rich sampling of the Chaoui melodies that beckoned Bartók. More recent examples of the tribe's sounds can be found on two discs by **Markunda Aures**: *An Algerian Woman of Passion* (1999) and *Chants de femmes des Aures* (2002).

Les Maîtres de la Chanson Kabyle:
⊙ **Vol 1 Slimane Azem**
⊙ **Vol 2 Cheikh El Hasnaoui**
⊙ **Vol 3 Cherif Kheddam**
⊙ **Vol 4 Alloua Zerrouki**
Les Artistes Arabes Associes, France
This extensive series covers the roots of modern Kabyle music. The artists featured on the first four volumes were all crucial players in the development of the music and the CDs collect their most important tunes, delivered in the heavily Egyptian-influenced style that prevailed in the 1950s.

Akli D

Born in Kabylia, now living in France, this relative newcomer is called the "Kabyle Bob Marley" – not only for his hair, but also for the way his songs of exile can reach across all borders, much as the reggae legend's did.

⊙ **Anefas Trankil (Let Him Be)**
Al Sur, France
Celto-Kabyle songs of exile, mostly in Taqbaylith, with some French and English added. Akli D nails the feelings of the diaspora, especially on "Azal Izilan" (Heatwave) and "Ay Azdayri" (The Algerian), whose plaintive, biting refrain is: "O child of this country / What is the pain gnawing at you? / Does the wind bring it to you / Cold from the west?"

Cheikh Sidi Bemol

In this guise – which loosely translates as Sheik Saint B-flat – Hocine Boukella (also a brilliant cartoonist drawing under the name Elho) serves up a tasty stew of musical ingredients from the Paris headquarters of his mini-empire. Check him out at www.louzine.net.

⊙ **El Bandi (The Bandit)**
M10 Records, France
"Gourbi rock" from 2003 with a big dose of slinky, lazy blues. The title-track, which begins "My teeth were unemployed, like me / They don't work no more", demonstrates Hocine Boukella's clever approach to common Kabyle (and Algerian) themes, such as unemployment, bad government and bad luck – all set to refreshing roadhouse rock/blues/jazz sounds.

Idir

Idir's gentle and lyrical style was a complete revelation when he emerged on the scene in the 1970s. It owes more to French singers such as Brassens than to the Egyptian models that had dominated Kabyle music in previous decades.

⊙ **A Vava Inouva**
Blue Silver, France
It was the title-song of this album that launched Kabyle music onto the international stage. A thinly veiled parable about the precarious state of Kabyle culture and language, "A Vava Inouva" describes a scene in the Djurdjura Mountains, where a group of villagers huddle around a fire contemplating the still, snow-bound night and the dangers that threaten their existence. The song takes centre stage on this compilation.

⊙ **Identité (Identity)**
Sony International, France
A 1999 album reworking previous Idir classics with varied world talents such as Manu Chao, Geoffrey Oryema and Gnawa Diffusion – each with their own "identity" issue.

Matoub Lounès

Lounès was one of the big names of Kabyle music from the 1980s until his assassination in 1998. He had an uncompromising commitment to the struggle of the Berber people for democracy and tolerance in a bitterly divided Algeria.

⊙ **Tigri G-Gemma**
Blue Silver, France
The list of song-titles on this album ("The Revolutionary", "The Widow's Revolt", "Remorse and Regret", "The Spoils of War") testifies to Matoub Lounès' commitment to the struggle. The music is an intelligent blend of Kabyle melodies and rhythms with Western rock and funk.

Souad Massi

Bringing new meaning to the expression "runaway success", this young singer-songwriter has carved out a highly successful career in her adopted home of France.

⊙ **Deb (Brokenhearted)**
Wrasse Records, UK
Massi's second album is full of Darja and French love songs, dance songs and protest songs, presented in her lovely clear alto. It's marvellously genre-crossing stuff, with heavy doses of Spanish and African rhythms. Despite the pink packaging, Massi displays courage in tackling the political and social demons of Algeria and the heartache of exile.

Iness Mêzel

After splitting with her sister Malika to pursue a solo career, Fatiha Messaoudi kept on the duo's name – Iness Mêzel, which means "tell them never to despair". The child of a Kabyle father and French-Italian mother, her music combines diverse influences into something vibrant and fresh. You can find samples of her music (and that of other artists discussed here) at www.azawan.com.

⊙ **Lën (There is…)**
Silex, France

This 2005 disc combines glorious poetics with musical forays into such disparate styles as polyphonic African jazz, minimalism, smart cabaret combos and the intimate folk ballad "Yemma" (The Mother I Left), a wrenching attempt to process the need to leave Algeria due to its lack of basic rights for women.

Aït Menguellet

Born in 1950, Lounis Aït Menguellet came to fame aged 17 via a TV talent contest and quickly made a name for himself with his heartfelt poetic lyricism and cultural insights. Despite the tragic fate of many of his contemporary musicians, he still lives in the village of his birth, high in the Djurdjura Mountains, though he refuses to perform live in Algeria, fearing his appearance might provoke a massacre. A huge figure not only amongst Kabyles but North Africans as a whole.

★ **Chants & Poesie de Kabylie**
Blue Silver, France

This compilation features many of the most important tracks by this iconic figure – the songs that have inspired Kabyles for the past three decades. Aït Menguellet's moody, bluesy voice and rasping single-string guitar plucking are given an excellent showcase, and Kamel Hamadi, another big name in the Kabyle scene, adds *oud* and bouzouki to some songs.

⊙ **Yenna-d Umghar (The Old Sage Speaks)**
Izem Editions, France

There's a strong Celtic influence on this 2005 album, with a bit of country thrown in for good measure. Menguellet sings about the wise old men of his village and Kabyle values in a typically poetic style. "Dda Yithir" is the standout.

Takfarinas

When he was 6 years old, in the Kabyle village of Tixeraine above Algiers, Takfarinas made a guitar from a gasoline can and the wire from a bicycle brake. Since that day, the so-called "Vidette" (Motorboat) Kabyle, hasn't stopped making music.

★ **Tagmilt I Tlawin (Honor of Women)**
RCA Records, France

The songs on this 2004 release are so nice that Tak recorded them twice – once in Taqbaylith and again in French. They run the gamut from samba ("Torero") to rap (the title-track), while "Ay Delaali" (It's So Beautiful) is a steamy love ballad with a killer saxophone bridge and soul-singer acrobatics.

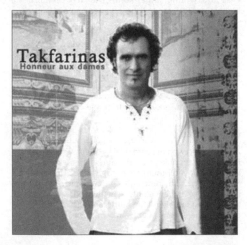

Takfarinas
Honneur aux dames

1 TAMETOT (WOMAN) Iness Mêzel from *Lën*
Mêzel's voice is strong and sweet as it swoops and soars in this poetic tribute to Kabyle women and their dance tradition.

2 MA KAYEN WALOU KIMA L'AMOUR (THERE'S NOTHING LIKE LOVE) Cheikh Sidi Bemol from *El Bandi*
This catalogue of the ills of the world – and Algeria in particular – is balanced by the declaration that "there's nothing better than love!"

3 RÉVOLUTION (TAGRAWLA 2) Idir from *Identité*
Amazigh Kateb Yacine, lead singer of Gnawa Diffusion and son of Algerian literary luminary Kateb Yacine, adds jarring and vibrant harmony to Idir's classic "Tagrawla".

4 AZUL (GREETINGS) Akli D from *Anefas Trankil*
Akli D courses through musical styles from chaabi and Gnawa trance to backbeat in his husky, well-travelled voice. We're all invited to this party.

5 CCNA N TEJMILT (SONG OF HOMAGE) Aït Menguellet from *Yenna-d Umghar*
Menguellet at his toe-tapping, organic, authentic Kabyle best. The refrain proclaims: "You think you're great, but you're not higher than God."

6 ECH EDANI (I SHOULDN'T HAVE FALLEN IN LOVE WITH YOU) Souad Massi from *Deb*
Aided by a chorus of Spanish men, Massi rocks on this wild flamenco-flavoured anthem. Great Spanish guitar riffs.

7 ALAROPLANE AWIYI (AIRPLANE TAKE ME) Takfarinas from *Tagmilt I Tlawin*
This raucous, infectious clarion call to the diaspora makes everyone want to go back to Kabylia – no matter where they're from.

8 A VAVA INOUVA (MY LITTLE FATHER) Idir from *A Vava Inouva*
This is the song that started it all, and it never stops evoking the warmth, sweetness and safety of a Kabyle hearth in winter.

9 AVRID N' TDUKLI (ROAD OF UNITY) Matoub Lounès from *Tighri G-Gemma*
Long before the troubles started, Matoub was warning the people to unite and take action to save their beautiful country in this catchy classic anthem.

10 AFROUKH IFILELES (SWALLOW) Slimane Azem from *Les Maitres de la Chanson Kabyle*
This bird glides above Kabylia, viewing all the beauty and wonder of the place for the homesick exile in Azem's timeless poetic song.

Angola

unstoppable rhythms

Angolan standard-bearer, Bonga
Lusafrica

For decades, Angola was cut off from the rest of the world by a brutal civil war and a xenophobic Stalinist government. Awash with oil and diamonds and blessed with some of the most fertile soil in the world, the country was incomprehensibly destroying itself. Little surprise, then, that the exquisite music from Angola remained unknown, except to a few diehard connoisseurs. But today, the war is over, the country is opening its doors, and the strong, gripping, danceable sounds are emerging. Regular visitor Bram Posthumus is drawn back once again.

If you're heading for Angola's capital, Luanda, expect chaos: cars driven at breakneck speeds, a glitzy 4WD parked next to a beggar who may be sleeping or dying in his filthy blanket, landmine victims holding out their stumps to cars, stumbling through the long potholed streets lined with hideous blocks of overcrowded flats built in the 1960s by the Portuguese…

Everything is mixed up here, and the same is true of the country's music. Angola has a wealth of traditional styles, many of which remain intact in the interior, where brave farmers work the immense expanses of rolling savannah land. But in the cities you're most likely to hear crossbreeds of Congolese, Portuguese and Brazilian genres, with jazz, blues, R&B, soul and 1960s pop thrown in for good measure. A *kissange* (Angolan thumb piano) is served up with a guitar imported from Europe; a mournful local voice is backed by jazz piano; and a rasping *reco-reco* (bead-wrapped cylinder) accompanies bass and thumping beats.

Distinctly Angolan elements include artful call-and-response, with a chorus that can sound joyous, mournful or even sexy in its rejoinder; memorable and incisive melodies; and exceptionally good vocals – especially in the country's searing *lamentos*. Best of all, however, are the irresistible rhythms, whether it's a syncopated, accordion-driven **rebita** (invented on an island not far from Luanda, and a specialty of **Banda Maravilha**) or a lively *semba*, as sung by local heroes **Carlos Lamartine** or **Paulo Flores** over bursts of guitars or horns and abundant percussion. The latter belongs to the same family as samba: Angolan slaves took an early version with them to Brazil, and rhythms have been going back and forth ever

since. The term "semba" comes from an Angolan word for "navel" – a reference to the erotic belly movements men and women make during the accompanying dance.

The Early Years

Back in the nineteenth century, people were experimenting with styles, writing songs, ballads and waltzes both traditional and contemporary. Brazilian influences were much in evidence, reflecting the fact that Angola was colonized on behalf of European powers (first Portugal, then Holland, then Portugal again) from Brazil. Throughout the first half of the twentieth century, brass bands made the rounds of Luanda, and there were semi-professional singers, accompanied by guitars, *kissange*, congas, drums, shakers and the **hungo**, a highly percussive one-string instrument shaped like a bow. They sang in Portuguese and in Kimbundu, the language of the coast.

The first group that turned all these disparate influences into an all-encompassing Angolan sound was **N'gola Ritmos**, founded in the 1940s. They made a point of playing original material and singing in Kimbundu. The Portuguese audiences, used to fado from the motherland and perhaps a hint of semba, didn't like it at first. But lead singer **Liceu Vieira Dias** was determined to make his cultural statement. Coming from a musical family and especially influenced by his aunt, he travelled into Angola's interior, mixing what he heard with Portuguese melodies and American jazz. Eventually, N'gola Ritmos won over the public, but not the colonial authorities: Vieira Dias was jailed with a few other members of his band on suspicion of fomenting a conspiracy. The band played on without him but never recovered.

Former N'Gola Ritmos singer **Lourdes Van Dúnem** carried on and started her own group, **Trio Feminino**. Others, like **Kituxi** (who began his career in the 1950s) decided to remain closer to the traditional style. But the big movement happened when groups and singers started coming out of the deprived parts of Luanda known as *musseque*. What followed was an explosion of recording from the likes of **Artur Nunes**, **David Zé**, **Os Kiezos** and **Orquestra os Jovens do Prenda** (Prenda is one such poor suburb). Following the defiant road taken by their musical parents, these artists blended traditional styles with salsa, jazz and Congolese rumba. The influence of global stars like The Beatles was also pervasive, leading to the take-up of the electric guitar, used with almost reckless abandon in Luanda and elsewhere. For their part, Orquestra os Jovens do Prenda (one of

ORQUESTRA OS JOVENS DO PRENDA

The Irresistible Kizomba Beat of Angola

BERLIN FESTA!

recorded live at Heimatklänge

Bonga: the Voice of Angola

Freedom fighter, champion athlete and maker of one of the most powerful albums in the history of African music – *Angola 72* – **Bonga** (like Bono or Madonna) is known by just the one name. Characterized by percolating acoustic guitars, fluid bass lines and hypnotic percussion, his music has much in common with the styles of Portugal's other former colonies, including morna of Cape Verde. Indeed, Bonga recorded "Sodade" back in 1974, long before the song was made famous by **Cesaria Evora**. For good measure, the two joined voices on a recent recording of the song.

Bonga does ballads, mournful lamentos and, yes, semba. 'Semba is the music that defines Angola but if you go to Brazil you will also find semba in Bahia. It's the roots of samba,' he says. 'You'll also hear a solidarity with musicians from Cape Verde. We have a two-step rhythm called *coladeira* and a style called *rebita*, which uses accordion and harmonica. But semba is the heartbeat of our music.'

Born José Adelino Barcelo de Carvalho in 1943, Bonga grew up surrounded by traditional music. 'There were a lot of groups playing folk music and it became part of the resistance. It was a way for our culture to survive,' he says. In 1966 he emigrated to Portugal, where he joined the anticolonial resistance movement, taking the "underground" name Bonga Kuenda (meaning "he who is looking and is always ahead and moving"). When the Portuguese secret police issued a warrant for his arrest, he fled to Rotterdam, where he recorded *Angola 72*, an album that sits alongside such other insurrectionary musical manifestos of the times as Sly & The Family Stone's *There's a Riot Going On* and Bob Marley & The Wailers' *Catch A Fire*.

'Artists have a duty to speak out,' he insists. 'For me it was an obligation and the politics were even more important than the music. The record was banned in Angola and when sailors from Cape Verde took some copies there, they were sent to jail.' But radio stations in countries bordering Angola played it constantly, ensuring it became the soundtrack of the liberation movement.

The equally impressive *Angola 74* followed two years later, by which time the liberation of Angola was just around the corner. But independence was followed by a long and bloody civil war that kept Bonga in exile in Europe. Since peace was achieved in 2002 he has been a regular visitor to Angola again, although he is not overly optimistic about the future. 'There's a lot of corruption and I wish I could be more upbeat. But it's down to the musicians to try and build a better Africa."

Nigel Williamson

the first bands to make an impact abroad) imitated the sound of the traditional two-player marimba using four guitars – solo, "contra solo", rhythm and bass – augmented by unison fanfares on trumpets and saxophones and piles of rhythms. Their style became known as **kizomba**.

The Shattering of Dreams

By this time, the war of independence against the Portuguese was in full swing, and music became a part of it – most notably in the remarkable work of **Bonga**, recorded in Europe (see box).

After independence in November 1975, the war degenerated into senseless slaughter, with three armed groups fighting each other, thousands of South African and Cuban troops pouring in and the two superpowers using Angola as their battleground. Two years after independence, an event took place that sent shockwaves which still reverberate today. Nito Alves, a young revolutionary firebrand of the ruling Marxist party, who felt that the new rulers were betraying the trust of the

poor Angolans, staged an uprising. The ruling party's response was swift and merciless: thousands were killed in Luanda and elsewhere in a campaign ominously named the *limpeza*, the clean-up. Musicians were not spared: **David Zé, Artur Nunes** and **Urbano de Castro** all lost their lives, as did intellectuals, journalists and anyone else considered an accomplice of Alves, who himself was found in the mountains close to Luanda and executed. Many artists, including **Carlos Lamartine** and a young **Waldemar Bastos** (see box overleaf), decided that they had had enough and left.

Independence, so eloquently praised by the sweet voices of the **Kafala Brothers** – one of the first Angolan groups to tour Europe – had become a nightmare. The ruling party's political intolerance brought about a suffocating police state, and the civil war (which would last until February 2002) intensified. At first a mostly rural affair, in 1992–93 it came to almost all the major towns in the interior, including Kuito, Huambo and Malange, causing widespread destruction there.

By this point, the Angolan dream was also

Waldemar Bastos: the Heart that Spans the World

Like Bonga, **Waldemar Bastos** has spent much of his life in Europe and, also like his compatriot, he believes that musicians have a unique role to play in building on the recent peace. Born in 1954, he was surrounded by all kinds of music: traditional, religious, Congolese, European and Brazilian. He started singing at an early age and was imprisoned by the Portuguese colonial police while still at school. In the early 1980s, after the high hopes of independence had turned to bitter disappointment, he defected from a cultural delegation visiting Portugal and initiated a long trek around the world – to Brazil, eastern and western Europe and finally to Portugal, where he now lives.

His breakthrough came in 1997 with the album *Pretaluz* (Blacklight), which was superbly produced by Arto Lindsay for **David Byrne**'s Luaka Bop label after Byrne had chanced upon one of Bastos's records in a Lisbon store. Bastos says of *Pretaluz*, 'It was born out of profound anxiety about my country. It was a plea: let this war finally be over.' Peace didn't arrive for another five years, but even during that dark time, Bastos managed to score impressive hit records back home. It is rumoured that one of them, "Pitanga Madura", was danced to by the two main protagonists of the civil war: President José Eduardo dos Santos and (now slain) rebel leader Jonas Savimbi. The story does not relate whether they danced together.

In 2003, Waldemar returned to Angola for the first time in twenty years, to perform at the national stadium in celebration of the end of the war. 'It was the first time I had seen peace in my country and a belief in the future on peoples' faces,' he recalls. The experience informed his latest album, *Renascense*. Produced by Jamaican veteran Paul "Groucho" Smykel, it literally spans the world, as it was recorded in Malaga, Istanbul, Berlin and London, and incorporates African, Latin and Asian musical strands. *Renascense* is driven by the twin themes of hope and reconciliation. 'It expresses my dream of harmony between individuals and nations. We have to build bridges between people and songs are the best tools we have to do that.'"

Nigel Williamson & Bram Posthumus

comprehensively destroyed, and this is reflected in the lyrics and tone of the music of the period. Artists both inside and outside the country recorded desperate, heartbreaking pleas for peace, tolerance and unity. Listen, for example, to **Waldemar Bastos**'s "Velha Chica" or his searing version of "Muxima"; to the melancholic lamentos recorded in Paris by exiles such as **Bonga** or **Teta Lando**; or to "Minha Angola" by **Sam Mangwana** (who was born in Kinshasa but considers himself as Angolan as his parents).

Some of the fine musicians forced out of their country found a receptive audience in their new European homes.

New Styles

In spite of the conflict and dispersing talent, Luanda managed to remain a musical powerhouse. There are few live venues, but studio facilities have improved and recordings of Angolan music are widely heard on radio and in night clubs, especially the slick new sound of *kizomba* – a lazy *zouk*-like beat that has little to do with the earlier style of the same name. In this style, artists such as **Paulo Flores**, **Eduardo Paim**, **Filipe Mukenga** and **Carlos Burity** – almost completely unknown internationally – have built solid followings and released regular albums. Some of the better titles include Flores's *Xé Povo*, Paim's *Foi Aqui*, Mukenga's *Kianda Ki Anda* and Burity's *Massemba*. While Flores and Paim have sentimental tendencies, all these titles have a pleasant mix of semba and more traditional rhythms, ballads and tunes that fall somewhere between jazz, Cape Verde and the Caribbean.

Another genre to catch on in a major way is hip-hop. **SSP** (South Side Posse) pioneered it in the 1990s with the album *99% de Amor* and has used its popularity to help combat drug use and AIDS. **Tony Amado** uses a traditional beat called *kilipango*, smashes it with hard-as-nails techno and calls it *kuduro*, literally "hard ass". His two albums include *Angolano, Abre Olho* (Open your eye, Angolan) and *Bailumdu*. However, much of the most politically hard-hitting rap – discussing issues such as poverty, unemployment, corruption and crime – is produced outside the country by groups such as Cape Town-based **Army Squad** and **Matu Moxy**, and Lisbon-based **Conjunto Ngonguenha**.

As for links to the past, Orquestra os Jovens do Prenda finally disbanded after various break-ups and reformations, but **Carlos Lamartine** – who started his career in the 1950s and lost almost all his friends in the 1977 slaughter – has soldiered on. So has the tireless **Kituxi**, who has made a career out of playing strictly traditional material and recently joined one of **Victor Gama**'s projects (see box). Liceu Vieira Dias's son Carlos, meanwhile, plays with **Banda Maravilha** (Miracle Band) and their illustrious guests such as legendary accordionist **Mestre Geraldo Morgado**.

Also worthy of mention is **Lourdes Van Dúnem**, who made one album in the 1990s (*Ser Mulher*) and appeared on Wally Badarou's anti-war *So Why* project, alongside Youssou N'Dour and Lágbájá, but has been silent since. She told an Angolan newspaper that she would gladly record again if she could find someone to pay her expenses.

Victor Gama

Born in Angola but resident in Portugal, **Victor Gama** is a unique figure. Not only a composer and performer, he's also a designer of extraordinary new instruments based on those of Angolan traditions. With their evocative names, such as Vibrant Rings, Spiralphone and Southern Cross, the new instruments can be played by several people at the same time, resulting in anything from gentle waves of sound to hypnotic repeating patterns.

Gama was also the brains behind the Odantalan project. Convinced that the Congolese/Angolan music of old has left its mark all over the world, he illustrated the point by bringing together musicians from Brazil, Cuba, Colombia and Angola. They explored a shared musical universe and the result is fascinating and somewhat disorientating at the same time.

As if all that wasn't enough, Gama also works with local and international groups to record the traditional music of Angola's interior. He started in the southern Cuando Cubango province, getting village elders, composers and musicians together and recording the results on a laptop. A demo CD called *Tsikaya* gave a taste of things to come, as Gama hopes to cover other parts of Angola too. Part of the plan is to set up small archives in cities across Angola, musical libraries that anyone can access. The first is in Benguela and run by a cultural collective called BISMA.

Recordings by the big names of Angolan music, and a number of excellent compilations, are widely available internationally, but other discs are harder to dig up. Lisbon is the most obvious port of call, with the gigantic Fnac in the centre and the market at the Praça de Espanha being good starting points. And if you ever happen to be in Luanda, don't miss the one tiny record store. When walking along the Marginal towards the National Bank, turn left at Antonio Ole's multi-coloured sculpture in front of the Air France office.

In addition to the CDs discussed below, the documentary *O quintal do Semba* (Semba's backyard) is worth investigating. It's available on DVD from *www.maianga.com.br*.

⊙ **Angola 60s**
⊙ **Angola 70s (vols 1 & 2)**
⊙ **Angola 80s**
⊙ **Angola 90s**
Buda, France

All of these are excellent collections of what was hot in any of the four decades covered. If you want to get a flavour of Angolan music from a certain era, this is the best place to start. The sound quality of the earlier decades isn't great, but the warmth, exuberance and defiance of the music shines through. Good liner notes accompany each volume.

⊙ **Soul of Angola**
Lusafrica, France

This is how urban Angolan music sounded between 1965 and 1975, with twangy guitars and great rhythms. Some of the more influential name featured (Oz Kiezos, Artur Nunes, Jovens do Prenda) get more than one track. The highly informative notes are a bonus.

⊙ **Semba da minha Terra**
Sons d'Africa, Portugal

A great showcase of the names of the 1990s, featuring just about every single popular figure: Carlos Burity, Paulo Flores, Carlos Lamartine, Gaby Moy. Top party music.

Banda Maravilha

This group unites some of Luanda's leading musicians around guitarist Carlos Vieira Dias, and in the 1990s was responsible for some of the most infectious dance music on the planet. Since the album listed below, however, their releases have been more electronic and disappointing.

⊙ **Angola Maravilha**
Kanawa, Portugal

A shaking, snaking, trilling mix of semba, rebita and other styles. The first track, "Rebita", is a remake of a tune by Os Merengues in true *axiluanda* style of the fishermen from Luanda's harbour island. A great band at its peak.

Waldemar Bastos

Born in 1954, exiled in 1982 and now based in Portugal, Bastos has never lost his yearning for the country of his birth. He's a truly cosmopolitan star, and his music moves effortlessly from one Angolan style to another, and across borders too.

★ **Pretaluz**
Luaka Bop, US

Bastos's dramatic, tremulous voice is captured beautifully on this largely acoustic CD. The fantastic mix of vocals, guitars, percussion and bass was lovingly produced by New Yorker (and honorary Brazilian) Arto Lindsay.

⊙ **Renascense**
World Connection, Netherlands

A gentler, calmer Waldemar Bastos celebrates the return of peace to his country on an album that radiates hope. Bastos likes to enlarge the simple pleasures in life, such as the wonderful effects of drinking natural water ("Agua do Bengo"), seeing fishermen going about their business ("Um Dongo") or dancing with unadulterated optimism ("Paz, Pao e Amor").

Bonga

Standard-bearer of Angolan music, political activist and all-round entertainer, Bonga has been in the business for three and a half decades. His output hasn't always been consistent, but features some glorious moments. In recent years he has returned to his best form. In addition to the discs listed blow, top albums include *Roça de Jindungo* and *Mulemba Xangola*.

★ **Angola 72**
Lusafrica, France

Still widely available, this classic collection of songs proves that you can write political material and make excellent music at the same time. An album that effortlessly stands the test of time.

⊙ Kaxexe
Lusafrica, France

This 2003 release finds Bonga in very fine form, mixing the sounds of Angola, Brazil, Cape Verde and Portugal with typical flair. He takes you from a killer ballad to a foot-tapping rebita, via the dance-floor showstopper "Turmas do Bairro". Glorious.

⊙ Swinga Swinga: the Voice of Angola 102% Live
Piranha, Germany

Bonga has stage cred aplenty and this 1996 release is still his best live album. The gruff vocals convey great variety of expression, and the Brazilian influences and counter-influences blend seamlessly thanks to a superb backing band. A real showcase.

Carlos Burity

The suave Burity has been steadily building his audience by skilfully performing great semba, poignant ballads and some material loosely based on traditional dances. He has a wonderful tenor and an uncanny ear for catchy tunes.

⊙ Ginginda
Melodie, France

Burity's only international release is his best album to date, containing the searing ballad "Nzumbi Dia Papa" and the unstoppable "Ojala Ye Ya" alongside the big Angolan hit "Congalia". An excellent introduction.

Conjunto Ngonguenha

This is an outfit made up of friends who got together in Lisbon in 2001. Keita Mayanda, Ikonoklasta, L and Conductor (the bandleader) mix rap and studio wizardry with references to Angolan classics.

⊙ Ngonguenhação
Matarroa, Portugal

This debut album mimics a radio broadcast, interspersing street beats with snippets of imaginary announcements. The rapping, in Portuguese, is ingenious and fast (perhaps a bit too fast for some), and the music and beats are inventive.

Paulo Flores

Possessing a mournful voice that's slightly rough around the edges and an on-stage style comparable to those of the smoothest European crooners, Paulo Flores has a collection of interesting and varied songs to his name. All the usual suspects show up, from semba and lamento to ballads and Cape Verdian morna.

⊙ Xé Povo
Maianga, Angola

A lovely selection of songs recorded in Luanda in 2003 and showcasing all those artistic traits that have made Flores an Angolan household name. As well as guitar-led ballads and smooth morna-like songs, there are some pretty good dance tunes.

Victor Gama

Composer, instrument builder and retriever of musical treasures, Victor Gama's output runs the gamut from traditional songs of the most isolated Angolan villages to modern soundscapes.

⊙ Pangeia Instrumentos
Rephlex, UK

The compositions are long and spacious, and the instruments are new, but a traditional feel is never far away. Think of an orchestra of thumb pianos playing original compositions. A fascinating journey through an unexplored sound-world.

⊙ Odantalan02
Pangeiart, Portugal

Recorded in Luanda, this album features Gama's collective of artists from Angola (including Kituxi), Colombia, Brazil and Cuba. Traditional sounds are key here, and marimba, hungo and percussion are all prominent. An interesting experiment.

The Kafala Brothers

The sons of a pastor assassinated by the Portuguese, these two brothers started singing in the church choir that their mother conducted. Their cultural roots are in the Kimbundu region but they have picked up music from all over Angola. They made one album that was swiftly adopted by the anticolonial movement but have faded since.

⊙ Ngola
Anti-Apartheid Enterprises, UK

Backed by acoustic guitars, the brothers use their honey-dripping voices to convey poetic and heavily political lyrics in gorgeous harmony. The title-track is the lament of someone whose family was killed by the South African army. A document of times past.

Kituxi

The career of Kituxi – musician, composer, arranger and multi-instrumentalist – spans half a century. He was in various bands that emerged in the wake of the cultural wake-up call of N'Gola Ritmos and has been with his own ensemble since 1980.

⊙ Grupo Kituxi: Dingongena
Zona Musica, Portugal

A production steeped in Angolan traditions. Hungo, marimbas and other percussion intertwine with voices in a celebration of diverse styles. From percussion-laden dances to call and response vocals, it's all here.

Carlos Lamartine

A major figure on the Angolan music scene since the 1950s, Lamartine only released his first album (Angola Ano 1) in 1975 and his second (reviewed below) in 1997. After many years of exile, he has now returned to Angola.

★ Memórias
Kanawa, Portugal

A masterful compilation, bringing together a rich variety of Angolan languages, instruments and genres – semba, kilipanda, ballads, Angolan merengues and Afro-Cuban beats, to name just a few.

Teta Lando

Originally from northern Angola, Lando became one of the musical political activists in the 1960s, resulting in his exile to Paris. He returned to Luanda after many years and now runs a production company in his own name.

⊙ Memórias (1968–1990)
Teta Lando Produções, Angola

An impressive collection of songs spanning more than two decades. Sung in Portuguese, Kimbundu and Kikongo, the tracks are initially quite sparse – with strumming guitars and percussion – but later on the arrangements become more elaborate, featuring keyboards and the like.

PLAYLIST
Angola

1 M'BALA M'BAIXA **Grupo Kituxi** from *Dingongena*
A call-and-response feast with traditional percussion.

2 SEMBA DA ILHA **Orquestra os Jovens do Prenda** from *Soul of Angola*
The first in a long line of great dance tunes from this legendary outfit.

3 MONA KI NGI XICA **Bonga** from *Angola 72*
An absolute killer lamento, even after three and a half decades.

4 MUXIMA **Waldemar Bastos** from *Pretaluz*
A heart-rending guitar-and-voice version of Angola's best-loved traditional song.

5 OJALA YE YA **Carlos Burity** from *Ginginga*
After a quiet opening, this track explodes into an irresistible semba.

6 MWANA WA KUMBUA **Nani** from *Angola '80s*
One of the rare female voices of Angolan music in fine form.

7 ECOS & FACTOS **Conjunto Ngonguenha** from *Ngonguenha Çao*
Inventive and infectious rap with a street beat mix.

8 A GUERRA DOS HOMENS REPTEIS **Victor Gama** from *Pangeia Instrumentos*
Intricately interwoven tones from one of Gama's own instruments. Mesmerizing.

9 POEMA DO SEMBA **Paulo Flores & Carlos Burity** from *Semba da Minha Terra*
The signature Angolan dance tune of the 1990s.

10 NGONGO YA BILUKA **Lourdes van Dúnem** from *Angola '70s*
An early showcase of a fine voice. If only someone could give her that record deal…

Carlos Lopes

Born in Benguela, Lopes is a relative newcomer. Since appearing in Luanda's annual song festival, organized by the LAC radio station, he has made two albums: *Filipa de Angola* in 1998, dedicated to his late mother; and the following, released four years later.

⊙ Angola, noites e luas
Gravisom, Portugal
A diverse, highly agreeable set of songs, starting with a very danceable semba ("Uadibale"), continuing with slightly over-the-top sentimental ballads (not at all unusual in Angola) and following them up with dance tunes, some of them with a traditional feel and others with that distinctly Angolan mix of Latin America and Cape Verde.

Lulendo

Lulendo comes from the northern town of Maquela do Zombo but like so many of his fellow artists he has spent close to two decades in Paris. He first was widely noticed with an album titled *A qui profite le crime*.

⊙ Angola
Nola Musique, France
Lulendo's most recent offering is as eclectic as they come, assembling Congolese-style ballads, some funky stuff partly based on the music from his home province and a few rather questionable ballads.

Filipe Mukenga

Composer and arranger Filipe Mukenga released a crop of swinging albums in the 1990s, the best of which is reviewed below. In other capacities, he's written songs for various artists, as well as film music and a rather odd "peace song" sponsored by an international NGO.

Kianda Ki Anda
Lusafrica, France
Put on your dancing shoes! This is a pulsating, entertaining and intelligent album of exquisitely well-arranged tunes. Mukenga takes you from the opening title-track through to the festive and nostalgic "Eu Vi Luanda" (I Saw Luanda), via a bluesy tribute for a friend and a loving jazzy rendition of "Humbi Humbi", a popular traditional song. Brilliant stuff.

Benin & Togo

afro-funksters

Angélique Kidjo – Benin's World Music force
Jak Kilby

The music of Benin and Togo has been affected by politics in very different ways. While Benin was one of the frontrunners in Africa's democratic movement of the early 1990s – later re-electing former dictator Mathieu Kérékou as head of state – Togo was ruled for 38 years by the tyrant Gnassingbe Eyadéma, recently replaced by his son. During dictatorial regimes, music has not had a high profile in either country, but fifteen years of democracy in Benin has helped to strengthen an enthusiastic new tradi-modern sound, whereas Togo's musical creativity seems to have been stifled. François Bensignor investigates both countries, with guidance from Eric Audra, François-Romain Dumont and Jean-Baptiste Miel.

Togo and **Benin**'s present-day music scenes could have been completely different. In the mid-1980s, the Togolese capital of **Lomé** could boast one of the most sophisticated 24-track recording facilities in Africa at its **Africa New Sound** studio, where records by **Abeti** and **Dr. Nico** were produced. But life became a struggle under President Eyadéma's regime, with social unrest destroying any semblance of a music scene at home.

Things aren't so bad for musicians in Benin these days, but ironically, the nation's stars –**Wally Badarou**, **Nel Oliver**, **Tohon Stan** and the superstar **Angélique Kidjo** – owe something to Mathieu Kérékou's dictatorship (1972–90), insofar as it encouraged them to seek work abroad and leave a homeland where artists were expected to praise those in power.

Benin

From 1960 to 1972, in the first years of independent Dahomey (as Benin was called before Kérékou changed its name), the music scene was quite vibrant – strongly influenced by Ghanaian and Nigerian highlife, Cuban music, Congolese rumba, American soul and French *chanson*.

At that time, the late **Ignacio Blazio Osho** and his **Orchestra Las Ondas** could fill any club they played. **G.G. Vickey** was the first Benin musician known on the international scene, thanks to the recordings he made in 1964 for Pathé Marconi while studying economics in France. During his working life, he ran two parallel careers as a singer and as a public revenue inspector. Founded in the 1960s, **El Rego et ses Commandos** played Théophile do Rego's famous Play Boy Club in Cotonou, paving the way for the Afro-Cuban direction taken by **Gnonnas Pedro y sus Panchos.**

Each big city had its own group: **Picoby Band d'Abomey**, **Super Star de Ouidah**, **Anassua Jazz de Parakou**, and so on. But two groups based in the capital city of Cotonou were the breeding ground for new talent: **Black Santiago** and **Orchestre Poly-Rhythmo**. Black Santiago was founded in 1966 by Ignacio de Souza (d. 1988) and still plays the Sheraton Hotel; **Sagbohan Danialou** was the group's drummer for several years. Founded in 1967, Poly-Rhythmo have gained an international reputation and cut more than a hundred singles. But with the Kérékou government, the scene ground to a halt. There was no more wild nightlife, as clubs and bars were forced to observe a strict curfew. Musicians, when they could, moved abroad to play, settling in Paris and elsewhere.

Benin Rockers

The first Benin musician to emerge with an international reputation was **Nel Oliver**, who debuted in France in 1976. He absorbed a range of Afro-American influences to create a powerful "Afro-*akpala*-funk", and continues to pound away a message: "Démocratie" was the title-track of his 1997 album, sung in Yoruba, Goun, English and French. He has become an important producer in the 1990s, with a studio and record company in Cotonou. His success, however, does not even compare with that of **Angélique Kidjo** (see box, overleaf), who started out her career in Holland before going solo at the end of the 1980s and cracking the international dance market with "Ayé" in 1994. Currently living between New York and Paris, she goes from strength to strength.

Among other Benin artists, **Gnonnas Pedro** stood out, as is obvious from the public reaction to his death at the age of 61 in August 2004. National mourning was declared by the head of the state and all the government ministers went to his funeral. After a lengthy solo career he had gained an international profile after joining Afrosalsa supergroup **Africando** in 1995, following the death of lead singer and founder Pape Seck.

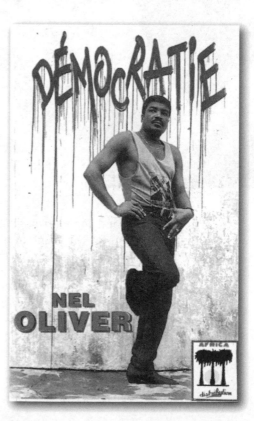

Beninois Music Abroad

A European African-music fan travelling in Benin would probably be surprised to discover that names like **Gangbe Brass Band** or **Denagan Janvier Honfo** are hardly known in Cotonou. Based in Germany, Honfo takes his inspiration from Benin's percussion tradition. His three CDs – *Aziza*, *Bolo Mimi* and *Kini Kana* – are a highly sophisticated take on voodoo rhythms, using a wide and colourful range of traditional percussion instruments, including numerous rattles, gourds, water drums, bells and the *guidigbo* thumb piano.

Though still living in Benin, Gangbe Brass Band have deliberately targeted the European and international markets. Their mix of big-band jazz sounds and traditional percussion patterns has won the public's attention at many European festivals, thanks to Michel Debock from Contre-Jour, who has produced their tours and albums since 2001. Numbers such as "Remember Fela", the intriguing version of Afrobeat on their third album *Whendo*, are slowly but surely broadening their international audience.

Contre-Jour

Gangbe Brass Band

Other Benin musicians like **Cella Stella**, **Vivi l'Internationale**, **El Rego**, **Ambroise Coffi Akoha** and **Bluecky d'Almeida** have followed a more mainstream Afro-pop direction, easing their way onto radio and TV playlists in various African countries. Among several young talents, **John Arcadius** has cut a good album, *Agada*, for his own Comlan Productions label in Belgium.

Outside influences hit Benin in the 1990s, with **Yaya Yaovi** launching a **reggae** group after a visit to Bob Marley's Tuff Gong studio. Recently, **rap** has also found a niche market. Most groups have a rather derivative US style (with French lyrics), though **Ardiess Posse** have a different approach, with **Logozo**, one of five rappers in the group, rapping in the Fon language. Their success has paved

the way for a new Afro-rap generation, adapting voodoo rhythms to accompany socially engaged lyrics. Among many emerging groups, **H2O** boasts rap "made in West Africa".

Traditions

But where are the real and original Benin sounds to be found? Perhaps the one good thing that came out of Kérékou's "Marxist-Leninist" regime was that artists were encouraged to seek their own traditions and make something out of them, albeit for the government's benefit. Thus **Tohon Stan** created his **Tchink System**, a musical style that derives from the local funeral music known as *tchinkoumé*, traditionally played with "water

Angélique Kidjo: Keep On Moving

Most successful World Music artists, having served their time on the fringes of the global recording industry, settle more or less permanently in Europe or America, reaping the rewards of hard work and talent and generally giving short shrift to purists who pick holes in their widely acclaimed crossover productions.

If any female artist embodies this kind of world music, it's **Angélique Kidjo**. The diva from Benin, who signed to Island Records in 1989, has done more to popularize African music than any other woman. Her music combines a broad spectrum of genres from soul to funk-rock, always with high-tech production by Parisian producer (and husband) **Jean Hébrail**. The common factor is Kidjo's angelic voice – not so much honeyed as darkly caramelized, and given full rein on every album. It is a staggeringly powerful instrument, coached by jazz training in Paris and the influence of *zilin* – a blues-like vocal technique from Abomey, the Fon heartland in central Benin. She still sings almost exclusively in Fon, a tonal language, like the closely related Yoruba.

Kidjo's albums range widely in style, from her debut *Pretty*, which used Beninois rhythms like the *gogbahoun*, tapped out with a coin on a bottle, to *Parakou* (her first international release), to *Logozo* and *Ayé*, dancehall fusions tearing away from her roots, and then the innovative masterpiece *Fifa* (1996), incorporating field recordings from Benin and ranging from taut-muscle dance tracks to heart-dissolving ballads.

Born in 1960, Kidjo was brought up in an artistic household in Ouidah (the voodoo capital of Benin) by the kind of parents who helped create a Latin Quarter image for the country, as the seat of Africa's intellectual and creative avant garde. She performed from the age of 6 as an actor and dancer in her mother's theatre group. As a child, she listened to James Brown and The Beatles, singing her own Fon lyrics to the tunes, and when she joined her brothers' band, Santana and Simon and Garfunkel were her favourites (Carlos Santana was later to take a guest spot on *Fifa*).

By the time Kidjo was 20, she was already working as one of the country's very few professional female singers. She moved to Holland to sing with the Afro-jazz-weirdness fusioneers **Pili Pili**, led by Jasper Van t'Hof, and then to Paris, where she first recorded as a solo artist. Unlike most Benin or Togo musicians based in Paris, who tend to produce discs of largely roots appeal with Ivoirian and Gabonese artists, Kidjo went for a crossover music from the outset. She put her remarkable vocal talents to work with a loose and eclectic community of French, Caribbean, African and American musicians, and over the years she has travelled between Paris, London and America to record, with musicians of the calibre of Manu Dibango and Branford Marsalis in support.

Although Kidjo keeps a strong note of social concern in her lyrics – hunger, homelessness, AIDS, injustice – she always denies being a political person. In Africa's new, multiparty states, most artists are anxious to avoid any suggestion of political ambition. Pan-African idealism is more her style. She still rates Miriam Makeba as a role model, and, fittingly, one of her best songs is a haunting rendition of "Malaika", the love-song that helped make Miriam Makeba famous.

With her internationalist outlook, close-cropped hair, unique voice and exhausting on-stage dynamism, Kidjo has become by far the most popular African woman singer. She has an inspired realism, rejecting roots purists who would have music stay within its borders, yet continuing to draw inspiration from Africa as well as Europe and the US.

Her most recent album *Oyaya* (2004) represents the final instalment in a trilogy tracing the African diaspora from her part of West Africa across the Atlantic. The story began with *Oremi* (1998), which focused largely on R&B. *Black Ivory Soul* (2002) took her to the beaches of Bahia, where she encountered amazing resonances, not just in the music but the food, language and manner of the people she met. Finally she explored the fantastic diversity of roots styles in the Caribbean. She sums up what this odyssey taught her in the following simple conclusion: "There's only one humankind … there's no need to say 'they' and 'we'. We are all one."

percussion" – half-calabashes sitting in water-filled larger half-calabashes which are whacked with a sandal or other handy item.

Tohon Stan's "tchink" master, Anatole Houndeffo a.k.a. **Le Roi Alokpon**, is one of the most respected artists in Benin. His knowledge of traditional music goes as far as knowing how to grow the perfect type of *gota* calabashes that are used in *tchinkoumé*, and Tohon Stan buys them from him. Le Roi (king) Alokpon has been leading a double life for forty years. On the one hand, he is the wealthiest farmer in the Savalou region (200km north of Cotonou), growing cashew nuts, igname and manioc, and producing palm wine. On the other hand, he has recorded some sixty albums and spends his weekends playing celebrations, feasts and concerts with his fifteen- to twenty-piece band. He explains that *tchinkoumé* derives from *zinli*, which used to be played only for royal funerals within the Abomey king's court.

Alakpéhanhou is an interesting artist based in Cotonou, who works the *zinli* heritage with his group, where the *zin* jar-drums, which gave their name to the *zinli* style, play an important role. Alokpon's and Alakpéhanhou's recordings, among others can be heard on the *Sonorama* CD/DVD (see recommendations). Like a journey through southern Benin, this work guides us through the main "tradi-modern" styles that have become popular over the past ten years. It shows the *akonhoun* music from Abomey, originally made by using the player's chest as a drum. From the southeast region, the voice of the late Amagnon Koumagnon introduces the *massé-gohun*, one of the Yoruba styles like *fuji* and *akpala* that you can hear in Porto Novo.

Among the great names in the traditional music of southern Benin, **Sagbohan Danialou** comes from the village of Ekpe, between Porto Novo and Cotonou, where funeral ceremonies take place every Thursday, gathering musicians of all kinds from gospel to brass bands, whether traditional street groups or big names. A former drummer with Black Santiago, Sagbohan has gained great respect and local success with his intense *kaka* rhythms. Working on the rich Goun tradition, he takes *hongan* and *kakagbo* percussion, ritually used by the "Zangbeto" guardians of the night, creating new patterns to give them expression in the modern world.

The southwest is known for its modernized version of fishermen's *agbadja* music, which has become very popular during the last decade due to the likes of **Gbessi-Zolawadji** (a.k.a Albert Bessanvi). He was named Best Traditional Artist at the Kora All Africa Music Awards 2001 and decorated

by the State of Benin in 2004. Among the finalists for the Kora award in 2003, **K-Sim** (Alassane Kassim) was born in Parakou to a mother originating from northern Sahel. Drawing on soul, jazz and hip-hop and using traditional instruments and rhythms from Sahel cultures – mostly Fulani – his music relates more to new styles from Niger than the new sound of southern Benin.

Music Market Woes

Since the legal election of former dictator Kérékou in 1996, the Benin music market has taken some interesting turns. Initially there was a boom in privately owned music radio stations, but nowadays, most people living in towns have also got CD and video players. Three TV channels show musical programmes, with the leading private channel LC2, launched by ex-professional football player Christian Lagnidé, producing video clips and showing mainly music-based programmes. Even if these are dominated by the stars of *coupé-décalé* and *ndombolo*, this has inspired many Beninois artists to make video clips in order to promote their albums on TV.

Lately, the government has begun to crack down on pirates, who may sell two million copies of a successful album, while the legitimate producers only shift 50,000. It is now their responsibility to build legal distribution networks so that the music market becomes more viable and attractive.

Togo

It is much too early to tell whether the death of President Eyadéma, after 38 years of undivided rule, will mark a turning-point for Togo. Since the beginning of the 1990s, social unrest and military violence have shaken the country, hitting Togolese youth in particular. People who once loved to celebrate now think twice before having a party at their home, fearing the militia's punitive expeditions. The situation has hindered the careers of talented musicians on the national scene, many of whom have moved to Europe, or, in recent years, across the border to Benin or to Cameroon.

The best-known contemporary Togolese musician is **King Mensah**, who in the early 1990s joined the Ki-Yi M'Bock Theatre in Abidjan. He toured as an actor and a singer in Europe and Japan between 1992 and 1993, then created his own show in French Guiana and finally settled in Paris, where he formed his own group, **Favaneva**, and cut two records before heading to Benin, the country his mother came from. He won the "Best Traditional Artist" award at Kora 2000 for his album *Mensah, Mensah*.

It is impossible to avoid the legacy of the Togolese singer, **Bella Bellow**. Often compared to Miriam Makeba, her West African career began in 1966, when at the age of 20 she represented her country at the Dakar Arts Festival. Her soft voice, made for love songs, had a strong seductive power, at its best on slow ballads. With the release of her first single, produced in 1969 by the Togolese Paris-based producer, Gérard Akueson, she was invited to perform on French national radio's most prestigious musical programme, which in turn led to her appearance at the famous Paris music hall Olympia. Bellow then travelled and performed as far afield as Rio. Her death in a car accident in

1973, having just recorded the hit "Sango Jesus Christo" with Manu Dibango, made her a legend.

Bella Bellow's success story inspired many Togolese female singers, such as **Ita Jourias**, **Mabah**, the 1980s "sentimental queen" **Afia Mala** and the voice of the 1990s, **Fifi Rafiatou**, who has had some international success singing in Ife and Ewe dialects.

Another Togolese voice is that of **Jimi Hope**, who has forged his own heady mix of rock and tropical rhythms. Always a rebel, he is not afraid to denounce power abuse whenever necessary through his extremely cutting lyrics. An artist in every sense of the word, his strange paintings and surreal sculptures express this same desire to break the bounds of convention and explore new ground.

It seems that **hip-hop** is the movement that is about to really shake the young music scene in Togo. Launched in 2003, the Togo Hip-Hop Awards ceremony was backed by the first **Africarap** festival on its second staging in December 2004. Who will make it among the young groups that recently emerged? Will it be **Djantakan**, who was invited to play the Ouaga Hip-Hop festival in Burkina Faso? Or **Dzoku-Kay**, young pioneers on the rap-ragga scene, formed in 1998, who take their inspiration from northern *goumbe* music and traditional southern *agbadja* to form their own *goumbeja* style? Or young stars like **Small Poppy**, **Eric MC** and **Wedy**, promoted on TV and radio? Or **RX Patou**, who instead of copying American rappers, uses elements from his own culture in his style, and was thus named "Best Traditional Rapper" in 2004? Only time will tell.

DISCOGRAPHY Benin & Togo

Benin

⭐ **Sonorama Sud Bénin (CD & DVD)**
Available from www.cosmonote.net
Put together by François-Romain Dumont and Jean-Baptiste Miel, two of the contributors to this chapter, this is a unique and wonderful interactive documentary on the most popular dances and music in southern Benin: *zinli*, *kaka*, *agbadja*, *tchinkoumin* and so on. Videos, interviews and recordings of great artists who have never been to Europe – such as Le Roi Alokpon, Alekpéhanhou, Amikpon and Gbétchéou – take you into the heart of contemporary musical life, including voodoo ceremonies, village rehearsals and outdoor live shows.

⊙ **Yoruba Drums from Benin, West Africa**
Smithsonian Folkways, US
Drum ensembles of *bata* and *dundun* (hourglass tension drums) demonstrate the rapid-fire ritual percussion – includ-

ing "talking drums" – of the Yoruba religion. Detailed notes and analysis.

Gangbe Brass Band

With their original brass arrangements, this ten-man band showcases many different rhythms and styles, in particular Benin's voudoun music. They marry this with influences from neighbouring countries and echoes of African military bands and European brass bands. Better known abroad than at home as a result of their long association with French fusionists Lo'Jo, they've built up a growing international fanbase through memorable appearances on Europe's summer festival circuit.

⊙ **Whendo (Roots Racines)**
Contre-Jour, Belgium
This 2004 release includes a reprise of "Remember Fela" from

the band's 1998 debut. "Glessi" nods at Nigerian juju and both "Awhan-Ho" and the spiritually themed "Jesu Ohun" demonstrate their great voices. "Oblemou" wouldn't sound out of place at a New Orleans Mardi Gras. Go figure.

Denagan Janvier Honfo

Probably because he lives in Europe, far from his beloved country, Honfo takes Benin's percussion tradition very seriously and lifts it to a level of exquisite refinement.

⊙ Bolo Mimi
DJH, Germany

This is Honfo's second, very nicely self-produced CD, adding some vocal polyphonies to the subtle polyrhythmics he had developed on his previous outing, *Aziza*.

⊙ Kini Kana
DJH, Germany

The formula of blending percussion and voice is bolstered here with the addition of saxophone, trumpet and trombone on some pieces, though the sensitive approach of the singer ensures that the spirit of the original music is preserved intact.

Angélique Kidjo

Brought up in an unusually supportive family environment, Kidjo first made her name in Paris, and is now probably the most popular woman singer on the World Music stage (see box on p.38).

⊙ Logozo
Island, UK

On her second international CD, Kidjo showed the extent of her vocal range, and, with tributes to Miriam Makeba ("Malaïka") and Bella Bellow ("Sénié"), that she is up there with the greats.

⊙ Oremi
Island, UK

A remarkable exploration of the music of the African diaspora, especially American R&B. Kidjo covers Jimi Hendrix's "Voodoo Chile", employs jazz saxophonist Branford Marsalis and generally funks things up big time. With South African backing vocals adding timbre and texture, her art has seldom been more mature and sweetly inspired.

⊙ Black Ivory Soul
Sony, UK

The second of her African diaspora trilogy, this album takes us into the Brasilian favelas under the guidance of Carlinhos Brown, and with some final touches from Bill Laswell.

⭐ Oyaya!
Sony, UK

The final part of Kidjo's Black Atlantic trilogy is also the most diverse and satisfying. Appropriately, the title means "joy" in Yoruba, and the singer certainly seems to be having fun on this musical journey through the Caribbean. Her distinctive voice is perfectly at ease as she works her way through Cuban bolero, *changui* and conga, Puerto Rican *bomba* and *plena*, Haitian *compas*, Trinidadian calypso, Jamaican ska and more.

Cella Stella

Born in Cameroon, Stella built her career as a mainstream 1970s-African-style vocalist in Benin.

⊙ Sensationelle Cella Stella Charme & Voix
Nelric's Production, France

Produced in Paris by fellow-Cameroonian Toto Guillaume,

PLAYLIST
Benin & Togo

1 **GENDAMOU NA WILI WE GNANNIN** T.P. Orchestra Poly-Rythmo from *Kings of Benin, Urban Groove 1972-80*
Bernard Papillon's psychedelic lead guitar and the rhythm lend this a feel not unlike Senegal's Orchestra Baobab on a Cuban tip.

2 **REMEMBER FELA** Gangbe Brass Band from *Whendo (Roots Racines)*
A warm, loping tribute to Fela Kuti – the king of Afro-beat – with multi-layered brass, chugging percussion and smooth vocals.

3 **MISTER LOVE** Angélique Kidjo from *Oyaya!*
On this gentle bolero, Angélique sings of love with a voice like silky velvet.

4 **ALIHO** Denagan Janvier Honfo from *Kini Kana*
A spellbinding rhythm of bells, insistent drums and seductive voices; the melody twists and turns and works its way under the skin.

5 **MA WA NU DOGBÉ MÈ** Le Roi Alokpon from *Sonorama*
The powerful rhythms of *tchinkoumé* funeral music, a piercing flute, and the voice of Alokpon keeping the spirits at bay.

6 **NÉNÉ** King Mensah from *Mensah, Mensah*
Mensah's heartfelt words ring out over a mellow, pulsing beat.

7 **UNTITLED** Kpalandao Yurijao from *Kabiyé Orchestra and Lithophones*
Striking five flat stones of different lengths with two oval-shaped stones, Kpalandao produces an amazingly pure, crystalline sound.

this album goes from speedy dance tunes to very melodic songs. No special Benin blend, but a very professional and slick sound.

Stan Tohon & the Tchink System

Tohon's wild stage act has helped make his band popular all over West Africa since the late 1970s.

⊙ Tchink Attack
Donna Wana, France

This may lack some of the spontaneous power of the Tchink System's stage performances, but it's a vibrant disc nonetheless, with some very interesting rhythms on the hit song "Dévaluation".

T.P. Orchestre Poly-Rythmo

Now into their fourth decade, this charming but littleknown big band are a Beninois institution.

⊙ **The Kings of Benin, Urban Groove 1972–80**
Soundway, UK
This excellent 2004 compilation does a sterling job of covering the band's grooviest decade. Afro-soul, Afro-beat, *soukous*, Cuban sounds and funk are mixed up in a joyful and engaging gumbo.

Togo

⊙ **Kabiyé Orchestra and Lithophones**
Ocora Radio, France
The traditional music of the Kabiyé, from northern Togo, reflects the different phases of the agricultural year. Particularly striking here is the sweet sound of the *hila* (wooden flute), punctuated by short blasts on the *nondoou* (transverse horn), made from deer antler. The swinging rhythms are played on drums and an extraordinary collection of bells. Five tracks feature the *pinchanchalassi* lithophone (a percussion instrument made of stone). These wonderful 2001–04 field recordings give some idea of the wealth of Togolese music that remains to be discovered.

King Mensah

Mensah has performed on stage since he was 9 years old. A singer with Les Dauphins de la Capitale, he is also a storyteller and actor, and the most popular musician in Togo today.

⊙ **Madjo**
Bolibana, France
Driven by powerful percussion deeply rooted in African traditions, King Mensah's music, moving from Afro-beat to reggae, is also strongly influenced by jazz and jazz-rock.

⊙ **Mensah, Mensah**
Africa Productions, France
This album confirms King Mensah as one of the leading Afro-pop musicians in Europe. His music has a distinctive style, honed through years of extensive touring and contact with different influences. He doesn't forget his love of reggae either, or the rhythms of his native country.

Botswana

khoisan to pop

Khoisan boy playing a musical bow
Peter Johnson/Corbis

The landlocked southern African country of Botswana, with a population of approximately 1.7 million people, is renowned in the region for its political stability and economic success. Less well known is its cultural mix, which features the 20,000-year-old civilization of the Khoisan – also known as the Bushmen or Basarwa – as well as the Tswana-speaking inhabitants who arrived later. Rampholo Molefe surveys three generations of music.

The term **Batswana** describes all the various peoples of Botswana. That includes the Tswana-speaking majority – who dominate the popular music scene – as well as various minority groups whose music is based largely on traditional forms. Between them, these minorities speak more than twenty languages, and they've had to fight hard for land rights and cultural recognition.

Traditional Sounds

The music of the **Khoisan Bushmen**, with its intricate *stinkane* thumb piano, was once a mainstay of the district agricultural shows in the western and central parts of the country, where the Bushmen lived as indentured farm labourers (akin to serfs in many instances) and squatters. Today, however, Khoisan music fights for survival on the fringes of the country's mainstream culture – a situation made worse by the government's decision to relocate them outside the Central Kgalagadi Game Reserve, initially established in the 1960s to protect and preserve San culture. Heightened political awareness among the Basarwa and empathy from some Christian societies has helped keep the traditions alive – partly via the **Kuru Development Trust**, which sponsors music festivals and craft production.

In other areas of the country, there are the **Ikalanga** people, who settled mainly in the northeast of Botswana, and whose music relies more heavily on the drum. In the southwest, meanwhile, the influence of Afrikaans is noticeable – in the language, song and dance – as the indigenous inhabitants came into regular contact with the Dutch settlers of South Africa.

The **Balete**, **Batlokwa** and **Bakgatla** of southeastern Botswana are of the politically dominant Tswana stock, but they've maintained (until recently, at least) many elements of traditional culture, including singing, dance, poetry and the "Bogwera" and "Bojale" initiation schools for young men and women. The Balete, in particular, have kept alive their pipe orchestras, though with metal instruments replacing the traditional river-reed designs.

The survival of many of these traditional musics – in reality and/or recordings – is in no small part down to **Batho Molema**, a keen follower of traditional poetry and music at Radio Botswana. Molema inspired a Swedish-sponsored team to go out and make pioneering recordings of various ethnic groups.

The Dawn of Popular Music

The beginnings of Botswana's modern entertainment industry grew along the railway line that Cecil John Rhodes planned to run from Cape Town to Cairo. Early names from this era, such as **Blackie Selolwane** – reputed for his singing, saxophone and compositions – never fail to arouse interest among the generation that voted at independence in the mid-1960s. He and **"Blind" Toteng** toured the then Bechuanaland Protectorate from the southern town of Lobatse to Francistown in the north with musical friends from Nyasaland (modern-day Malawi), spreading a taste for modern dance and popular culture.

Things really took off, however, with the jazz scene. The **Metronomes** spearheaded this movement, playing at the independence celebrations of 1966–67 in newly established capital of Gaborone. Several of the band's founders were exiles from South Africa's toughening apartheid system. They bemused audiences with their upright bass, piano and a full frontline of trombones, trumpets and saxophones – more instruments than most people in their audiences had ever seen in one place. Their repertoire included jazz-swing standards like "Tuxedo Junction" and tunes by the likes of the Benny Goodman and Tommy Dorsey big bands. The music was popular with the ballroom dance community that attended state functions at the newly opened Town Hall, where Seretse Khama, the first president, was often a guest of honour.

Younger audiences, however, were thirsty for more modern styles (especially after a successful visit to the country by a band from Ireland). The **Scarers** provided these more contemporary sounds, often performing songs they heard on the radio the previous day. The group collapsed in the mid-1970s, but left behind one of the earliest recordings of Botswana pop – *Swabisa Satane* (Shame the Devil). They also inspired younger artists to consider music not just as a hobby but as a vocation. Among these was **Louis Mhlanga** – now based in South Africa, where he leads the group Musik ye Afrika – and **Socca Moruakgomo**, a protege of South African trumpeter Hugh Masekela who has played alongside legends such as Miriam Makeba. Socca's composition "What's Happening (Africa)" is one of the best-known songs by an artist from Botswana, addressing Africa's vulnerability to natural disaster, war, disease and unscrupulous politicians.

Moruakgomo, along with many others looking for a career in music, joined the army (the Botswana Defence Force), which offered musical facilities as well as military training. Similar opportunities were snapped up in the police and prison services. The bands of these various institutions – mainly five- and six-piece touring groups – included artists such as **Peter Molatlhgegi**, **Michael "Malombo" Mmereki**, **Tsilo Baitsile**, **Sebene Morolong** and several members of Mahalapye-based **Demote**. None of these musicians has released solo recordings, despite their local popularity.

Other artists to leave a strong imprint on the popular music scene were **Whyte Kgopo**, **Livingstone "Dollar" Paledi**, **Chreiser Matlhoko Lefatshe**, **Buster Mothupi** and **Tsholofelo Giddie**. All of these died without making a record, but many recall their heydays in the social clubs in Francistown and Gaborone, in bands such as Afro Sunshine, Imagine, Mother, Mofufutso, Ngwao, Kgwanyape, Kalahari, Shakawe, King Beat, Makgadikgadi and Serengeti.

The Modern Era

The influence of South Africa on Botswana's music scene reached its peak at the end of the 1970s when trombonist **Jonas Gwangwa** settled in the country, first joining **Dashiki** and later forming **Shakawe**. He and **Mphoeng Khama** combined music and corporate money for the first time, organizing a promotion by the new German brewery Prinz Brue (now Kgalagadi) which toured the whole country. Around this time, hotels also became musical hotspots, and nightclubs cropped up all over the country. There was the New Yorker and Ritzmar in Francistown, while in Gaborone the musicians and DJs entertained crowds at the Blue Note, Cameo, Woodpecker, Club 500, Club 585 and Nightshift.

With the South African Defence Force raid on Gaborone, on June 14, 1985, most of the South African artists living in Botswana left the country, leaving something of a leadership vacuum in the entertainment industry – a vacuum that local artists soon rose to fill. Around this time, individual artists starting taking over from bands as the dominant names on the scene. **Alfredo Moss** (tutored by Zairean Lawi Somana) found success with his *rumba*, while **Skizo Molosi**, **Vee**, **Brown Sugar** and several others created a local version of South African *kwaito* and R&B. **Maxi**, meanwhile, embraced the language of the Bushmen and the more traditional nuances of Tswana song to create a unique sound that has since caught the attention of South African recording studios.

Alongside the more modern electronic sound of the popular groups, there has also been an upsurge of traditional and folk artists. **Machesa** have been successful with their amplified versions of traditional folk songs, while **Ditholwana**, long-standing exponents of traditional song and dance, won a Kora award in 2004. Another example is **Stiger's Sister**, one of the few successful female artists from the country. Hailing from western Botswana, she sings a blend of Herero and Tswana lyrics.

Duncan Senyatso stands out among the luminaries who have integrated traditional song with a modern electronics. His latest album, *Kgeleke tsa Pina* (Heroes of Song) attempts to build bridges between the African and European sounds. In a slightly different vein, **Canny Ndaba**, first heard with Makgadikgadi over twenty years ago, mixes traditional sounds with jazz.

DISCOGRAPHY Botswana

Good recordings of the traditional music of Botswana are few and far between, but *www.botswanacraft.bw* sells a few relevant videos and has links to the Gantsi curio shop, which stocks indigenous music and crafts.

Socca Moruakgomo

Popularly known as "Mr Rain", trumpet player and singer Socca Moruakgomo graduated from the Defence Force bands and has since made a name for himself as a solo artist.

⊙ **Kalahari**
Own label, South Africa
Socca said that he "found his sound" with this second album.

"Missed Flight" features South African hero Hugh Masekela, a mentor to whom Socca has often been likened.

Canny Ndaba

Founder of the Makgadikgadi band, and a veteran of the music scene of northern Botswana, Canny Ndaba merges influences of the Ikalanga and Tswana traditions with American and South African jazz.

⊙ **Ke Botshelo (Such is Life)**
Own label, Zimbabwe
Ndaba's second offering is a philosophical album contemplating, among other things, the 9/11 terrorist attacks on New York.

Citie Seetso

Educated in jazz performance at the University of Natal in South Africa, bassist Citie Seetso combines compositional coherence with impressive solos. His innovative music could be a vision of things to come.

⭐ **Initiation**
Own label, Botswana
A great album, though hard to track down. The songs combine typical southern African styles with Afro-American-esque harmonies.

Duncan Senyatso

Duncan Senyatso – who typifies Setswana song better than any other – is from a family of musicians, all of whom played in the group Kgwanyape. That band used to play with visiting friends from Europe on violin and banjo, and Duncan has subsequently incorporated Celtic influences into his solo work.

⊙ **Kgeleke Tsa Pina**
Own label, UK
A tribute to the heroes of Setswana song – including Ratsie Setlhako, Sheleng and Speech Madimabe – this album integrates the mandolin and violin sounds of Scotland, where it was recorded, with the rhythms of southern Africa.

Skizo

David Molosi, aka Skizo, first caught the public eye as a member of the vocal and dance group Tribal Monks, who have since disbanded. He has worked with Don Laka, who has achieved celebrity status in the *kwaito*-jazz circles in South Africa.

⊙ **Afro Blue**
David Molosi Publishing, Botswana/South Africa
Excellent youthful dance tunes.

Stiger's Sister

Stiger's Sister's music is inspired by the ethnic groups of western Botswana (Setswana) and also by gospel. Her songs touch on issues such as the scourge of AIDS. She is one of the few women in Botswana to have recorded in her own right.

▦ **Amaherero**
Stiger and Sister Music Production, Botswana
Available on cassette only, and with slightly dodgy recording quality at that, this album nonetheless offers good examples of the rhythms of northwest Botswana.

PLAYLIST
Botswana

1 **KALAHARI Socca Moruakgomo** from *Kalahari*
A wonderful song about Botswana's dry, sparse, yet stunningly beautiful countryside.

2 **O MO LEBILENG Canny Ndaba** from *Ke Botshelo*
An entertaining song about a jealous man who believes he is contributing to the beauty of a woman by giving her gifts.

3 **KGELEKE TSA MMINO Duncan Senyatso** from *Kgeleke Tsa Pina*
A tribute to the veterans of Setswana folk, among them Ratsie Setlhako and Sheleng. The title means "Icons of Song".

4 **TUPUNDU Skizo** from *Afro Blue*
As this track show, Botswana-style *kwaito* is fantastic party music. The title refers to the endowments of a well-built African woman.

5 **AMAHERERO Stiger's Sister** from *Amaherero*
A tribute to the cattle-herding Herero people of western Botswana and Namibia.

Burkina Faso

hidden treasure, hip-hop hopes

Magic System

The new millennium has seen exciting new musical developments taking place
in Burkina Faso. Overshadowed until recently by the rich output of neighbouring
countries, especially the Ivory Coast and Mali, Burkinabé music is currently
benefiting from a new, dynamic climate in tune with the contemporary scene.
François Bensignor explores the country's traditional musics and profiles its
new leading lights.

The recent upsurge in homegrown talent in Burkina Faso is due to a number of favourable factors. Back in 1998, the capital Ouagadougou had only two 24-track studios – a busy one owned by **Désiré Traoré**, leader of **Dési et les Sympathiques** (at the time the best-known backing group for afro-pop artists), and another built by local star **Nick Domby**, equipped with new technology. Today artists can choose from a wide range of both professional and home studios. The establishment of the country's first duplication unit and first decent national distribution network at the end of 1998 by live music promoters Seydoni Productions had a great impact on the development of Burkina Faso's music business, combating the flood of pirate tapes.

Many kinds of traditional music were championed by pioneering labels such as **Bazar Music** (founded in 1989 by **Kaboré Moussa**) and those who followed suit, like **Sika Sound**, **Africa Musique** or **Faso Ambiance**, and this music is now available on cassette and even CD. Additionally, other labels such as traditional music specialists **Hakili Productions** and **Djongo Diffusion** – which nurture young, up-and-coming talent – have become much more professional. And thanks to the numerous radio stations and the private TV channel, Canal 3, artists from the younger generation are now getting good exposure. Broadcasting out of Ouagadougou and second city Bobo-Dioulasso, Canal 3 has helped boost the explosion of an energetic **hip-hop** movement, making Ouagadougou one of West Africa's major trend-setters in this genre. Finally, there's another important factor: the country has begun to throw off the once dominant cultural influence of Abidjan – the *de facto* capital of Côte d'Ivoire – in response to the hostile attitude of the authorities of southern Ivory Coast towards the Burkinabés.

A number of talented young artists look set to benefit from these new developments. One such artist is **Bil Aka Kora**, who won the Kundé d'Or (Burkina Faso's most prestigious music prize) in 2002 and 2005 and is acclaimed for his energetic and sophisticated style, which incorporates the traditional *kassena* rhythms of the Gurunsi. Another promising young talent, **Tim Winsé**, who started out as a dancer in international troupes, became a musician in order to promote the *lolo*, the traditional musical bow of the Samo, though he sings accompanied by modern instruments. These two singers have a better chance of reaching a larger audience than their elders, who despite their rich output, were hardly known at all outside their own country: **Simporé Maurice**, **Kaboré Roger**, **Georges Ouédraogo**, **Tall**

Farafina

Mountaga and **Black So Man**. One of them, **Amadou Ballaké** (Traoré), did manage to make a name for himself in the West by joining Africando All Stars in 2000. Other Bukinabé groups, such as **Farafina** (supported by WOMAD), **Badenya Les Frères Coulibaly**, (promoted by the Ateliers d'ethnomusicologie de Genève) and singers such as **Gabin Dabiré**, based in Italy, have carved out successful careers abroad, but would ring few bells back home. Another musician, **Zêdess**, has won both enemies and friends for his songs criticizing the government.

A Multitude of Traditions

Talking about "cultural diversity" is no cliché in relation to Burkina Faso (the former Upper Volta – renamed after the 1984 revolution of Thomas Sankara). This is a country of some sixty different ethnic groups.

West and southwest Burkina Faso is mostly under the influence of **Mande culture**, which is shared with both Mali and Côte d'Ivoire. The Dioula people settled their capital there, in Bobo-Dioulasso, still a strategic commercial and cultural centre. Musically, its strongest traditions are those of **balafon** (xylophone) and percussion.

The balafon tradition is shared by the **Bwaba**, **Lobi**, **Dagara**, **Wara**, **Siamoux**, **Bobo** and **Toussian** peoples. Ensembles internationally renowned for their performances of this music include Farafina, Badenya Les Frères Coulibaly, **Djiguiya**, **Kady Diarra** and **Sabounyouma**.

Burkina Faso has also produced some distinguished **djembe players**, such as **Adama Dramé**, known worldwide, and **Désiré Ouattara**, director of the ensemble **Saramaya**.

Living in the centre of the country, the **Mossi people** represent half of Burkina's population and have a strong *griot* tradition. The **Larle Naaba**, traditional head of all the Mossi griot musicians, still retains his traditional function vis-à-vis Mossi kings as a genealogist, counsellor, historian and musician. He has his own troupe and teaches musicians in his own royal court.

Numerous musicians carry on the Mossi traditions, content with the success they enjoy among their own people; **Zoubna Zanda**, for example, can fill a stadium without needing any publicity. Others, such as **Prince Balzac**, descended from the Tenkodogo royal family, are trying to modernize the music, as are the **Soeurs Doga**, whose vocal mastery and traditional rhythms have inspired young Burkinabé rappers.

The northern part of Burkina is the home of the **Fulbe people** (also called Fula and Peul), **the Bella** and **Touareg**, who are closely linked to their cousins across the Mali and Niger borders. Their traditional music is splendid, with incredible voice techniques and fabulous hand-clapping rhythms. There are also strong musical traditions among the **Senoufo**, **Gourounsi**, **Bissa** and **Nankana people** in the **south** along the borders of Côte d'Ivoire, Benin and Ghana.

Several times award winners at the Semaine Nationale de la Culture held in Bobo-Dioulasso, the **Wuzzi** group freely makes use of the *djeka* rhythm from the Bissa tradition. **Sami Rama**, meanwhile, also a Bissa but born in Abidjan, is set on pursuing an international career after winning the 2002 Kundé d'Or Best Singer award.

Urban Music

Ouagadougou's young people are eager for any music that gets them dancing, such as **Magic System**'s "Bouger Bouger". The Congolese *ndombolo* was overtaken by the Ivorian *mapouka*, then the *coupé-decalé*, which gave rise to a new style of music based on synthesizers. There followed a series of DJ-produced hits in rapid succession, all the rage one day, forgotten the next. Sadly, their simplistic, unsubtle rhythms have ended up driving out the live groups that used to perform in the *maquis* (open-air bar restaurants).

Reggae has hit Burkina Faso, heralded by Alpha Blondy and Tiken Jah Fakoly – both considered "Northern Ivorians", aligned with the *Forces Nouvelles* in their home country. But so far the country hasn't managed to produce any noteworthy reggae artists of its own. **Zêdess**, **Black So Man**, **Jean-Claude Bamogo** and **Solo Dja Kabako** have recorded some – but not exclusively – reggae music. Young artists, such as **Ben Jah Verity**, **Razo Star**, **Yiriba** or **Founy Faya**, who features on the compilation *Le Gang Rebel du Faso*, fall more squarely within the Afro-reggae tradition.

Without a doubt, it's **rap** that has really caught on in Burkina Faso. The **Ouaga Hip Hop Festival**, first held in 2000, has become an unmissable rap fixture. Every year, young Burkina Faso artists welcome their opposite numbers from numerous countries – Togo, Guinea, Niger, Mali, Ivory Coast, Senegal, Cameroon, Uganda, France, Belgium – to take part in two weeks of workshops, exchanges and concerts. Organized by **Ali Diallo**, founder of the Umané Culture Association, the festival succeeds in fulfilling its aims: to take into account the expectations and needs of African professional musicians and to work towards raising the standards of the profession as a whole.

Festivals

This multitude of musical traditions has had its profile raised through a variety of different festivals. Every two years since 1983, the **Semaine Nationale de la Culture** is held in Burkina's second city, Bobo Dioulasso, where traditional and modern musicians from all over the country come to compete for awards. In March–April the **Ouaga Jazz Festival**, created in 1992, puts on an eclectic programme in the capital Ouagadougou, and also in Bobo and Burkina Faso's third town Koudougou. Each year in November, Kougougou hosts its own festival, the **Nuits Atypiques**. This non-competitive international festival mixes traditional and modern acts. It was launched in 1996 by **Koudbi Koala**, founder of the dance and percussion troup, **Saaba**, with support from French and Dutch World Music festivals.

Well supported by the media, the hip-hop movement in Burkina Faso already has its stars, such as **Yeleen**, **Smockey**, **Sofaa**, **Kas Boven**, **Kouman Kan**, **Tere Pirattack** and especially **Faso Kombat**, who's very popular with the young. There is also a young rap protégé, **Madson Junior**, who, at the age of only 10, picked up the Most Promising African Artist award in the 2004 Kora Music Awards.

DISCOGRAPHY Burkina Faso

⭐ **Burkina Faso – Bisa, Gan, Lobi, Mossi**
Prophet/Universal, France
Magnificent recordings made by the musician and musicologist Chares Duvelle, featuring some of the most representative music of a number of ethnic groups, as well as their instruments, such as the xylophone used by the Lobi and the Gan musical bow.

⊙ **Burkina Faso – Savannah Rhythms**
⊙ **Burkina Faso – Rhythms of the Grasslands**
Nonesuch, Explorer Series, US
Recorded in the field by ethnomusicologist Kathleen Johnson, these two CDs are a good introduction to the traditional music of the major ethnic groups in Burkina Faso: Mossi, Peul, Dioula, Gourmantché, Hausa, Bwa, Samo, etc.

⭐ **Burkina Faso – The Voice of the Fulbe**
Le Chant du Monde, France
These recordings made by ethnomusicologist Sandrine Loncke in different locations of northern Soum province in 1992–93 and 1994–95 present the extraordinary voice techniques of *doohi* and *gude worbe* sung by men and *jimi rewbe* and *gude rewbe* sung by women. A very interesting and detailed booklet accompanies the wonderful music.

⊙ **Le Gang Rebel du Faso**
Vent d'Echange/Mosaic Music Distribution, France
This recording was the idea of the Vent d'Échange association and features thirteen groups from Burkina Faso. Most fall within the reggae tradition and African-style ska: Bingui Jaa Jammy (of Congolese origin), Ben Jah Verity, Founy Faya, Razo, King Zion, Terry Yiriban, Yoro Masa and Alassane Baguia. But here you will also find other styles: easy-listening by Awa Melone, interesting *tradi-moderne* by Sana Bobo and Z.Mo and the excellent Soeurs Doga, playing purely traditional music. www.mosaicmusicdistribution.com

Bil Aka Kora

One of the most respected young artists in Burkina Faso, Bilgo Akaramata Kora, alias Bil Aka Kora, was born in 1971 in Pô, in the province of Nahouri, in the south of Burkina Faso. He takes his inspiration from the Gurunsi tradition, and especially the *kassena* rhythms, to create original and modern sounds, dubbed "djongo music".

⊙ **Dibayagui**
Djongo Diffusion, Burkina Faso
This third album, allying melody and energy, affirms the artist's place in World Music. Reggae and jazz influences don't obscure the originality of the music, while the songs in Kassena and French are intelligently written and are served by a powerful and beautiful voice.

Gabin Dabiré

Based in Europe – currently Italy – since the mid-1970s, this veteran singer-songwriter has been a revelation.

⊙ **Kontômé**
Amiata Records, Italy
Some of Dabiré's work sounds like Uganda's Geoffrey Oryema in folksy mode, but his more complex choral arrangements, such as "Mariam a në Awa", have a carefully architectural beauty entirely their own.

Farafina

The musicians of Farafina have been touring Europe and America since the mid-1980s, driving the public to dance to their complex but clearly structured polyrhythms. Members have changed through the years but the music is still enjoyable.

⭐ **Faso Denou**
Real World, UK
Feel the percussive power of the two *balafons* (xylophones), bara-skinned open calabash, *doumdou'ba* tall drums and voluble *djembe*.

⊙ **Nemako**
Intuition, Germany
An interesting short but effortlessly lively set from the consummate performers, with a high-tech studio sound. There's more to please here than skilful percussion, including *kora*, some delicate arrangements and striking vocals.

WITH JOHN HASSELL

⊙ **Flash of the Spirit**
Intuition, Germany
An interesting encounter between the talented British trumpet player and this strongly rooted percussion troupe.

PLAYLIST
Burkina Faso

1 KANKARMA BOW Diotouré Hien from *Bisa, Gan, Lobi, Mosi*
A love song in which the singer accompanies himself with the *kankarma*, a large musical bow traditionally used by hunters.

2 DOOHI AND JIMI REWBE OF THE WAAL-DE OF FILFILI Unknown artists from *The Voices of the Fulbe*
A wedding song in which the voices of nine men and eight women draw the listener into a giddy swirl of sound.

3 KARA MOGO MOUSSO Farafina from *Faso Denou*
The combination of *balafon*, percussion and *djembe* is guaranteed to set your foot tapping. A perfect introduction to the different facets of Farafina's music.

4 FASO DENOU BE MIN Les Frères Coulibaly from *Anka-Dia*
This track, exhorting Burkinabés to work for their country, is a beautiful dialogue between the *donso ngoni* and the *balafon*.

5 DOUDOU Gabin Dabiré from *Kontômè*
This ballad is very nicely served by the warm voice of Gabin accompanying himself on the guitar, with African birdsong in the background.

6 DIBAYAGUI Bil Aka Kora from *Dibayagui*
The backing vocals sing a catchy tune, while Bil Aka Kora's slightly gravelly voice is accompanied by pleasing harmonies.

Badenya Les Frères Coulibaly

Formerly known as Les Frères Coulibaly, this *griot* family belongs to the Bwa people living in the north of Burkina. Brothers Souleyman, Lassina and Ousséni lead a standard percussion orchestra with *djembe*, *bara*, *tama* and *kenkeni* drums, *barafile* rattle, *balafon* xylophone and *kamele ngoni* harp-lute. Their albums of course don't fully capture the spectacle of their stage shows.

⊙ **Musiques du Burkina Faso & du Mali**
Musiques du Monde/Buda, France
This features brother Lassina Coulibaly with his traditional acoustic group Yan Kadi Faso. Beautiful *kora* playing is the standout, but there's also a great *balafon* duo "Massoum pien", complete with wooden "buzz", a spookily vocal fiddle (the *soukou*) on "Bri kamaye" and a flute solo on the affecting final track, "Ba mana sa" (The Death of a Mother).

⊙ **Séniwè**
Trace, Switzerland
This album from 2000 includes plenty of ferocious *djembe* and *dundun* action, *balafon* and tight call-and-response vocals. There's even some digital beats on a couple of tracks, but it's otherwise pretty standard fare from the brothers.

Cameroon

the awakening lions

Coco Mbassi
Philip Ryalls/Redferns

With over 250 ethnic groups and as many languages and dialects, Cameroon has one of the most diverse cultures in Africa. Music has always been an integral part of everyday life: songs and dances are performed at births, circumcisions, funerals, enthronings and other rituals, and even today some rural areas communicate using traditional instruments. The modern music scene of the country of the "Indomitable Lions" mostly draws on rhythms originating from this ancestral way of life in the various regions. Jean-Viktor Nkolo, Graeme Ewens and Alain Marius Mouafo Wemba explore the legacies and the latest sounds.

⏩ **Pygmy music** *Cameroon is also home to the Baka pygmies, who are featured in the Pygmy Music chapter.*

Cameroon is the homeland of several artists who have carved out high-profile international careers as musical ambassadors abroad. Most notable among these are saxophonist **Manu Dibango** (see box, overleaf) and the late **Francis Bebey**, who collaborated with Dibango while the two were living in Paris in the late 1950s. Bebey made his name as a novelist, story-teller, film maker and musicologist, though primarily as a guitarist and composer.

Aside from these two, the Cameroonian diaspora includes numerous talented instrumentalists who have performed or continue to do so in well-known bands all over the world. Among them are bass players like **Armand Sabal Lecco** (Paul Simon, Herbie Hancock, Peter Gabriel, Jaco Pastorius, etc.), **Etienne Mbappe** (Ray Charles, Ultramarine, Michel Jonasz, etc.), **Richard Bona** (Tito Puente, George Benson, Queen Latifah, Paul Somon, Herbie Hancock, etc.) and drummers like **Brice Wassy**, **Denis Tchangou** and the promising young **Conti Bilong** (Manu Dibango). However, this superficially positive image of the Cameroonian scene disguises numerous problems, and the country has not had a very significant share of the international market since the beginning of the 1990s.

There are certainly enough indigenous music and rhythms in Cameroon for a multitude of popular styles to surface. Among those already in the pop sphere are the **tchamassi**, made famous by the blind singer **André Marie Tala**, and the **mangambe**, a Bamiléké folk rhythm popularized in its modern form by the *sanza* player **Pierre Didy Tchakounte**, who had a string of album releases during the 1970s. In recent years mangambe has been the pulse of a new jazz-fusion championed by Brice Wassy, who spent several years at the core of Manu Dibango's always-impressive rhythm section. Then there is the Bassa people's **assiko** on the coast and a **fast**, guitar-based street music called **ambasse bey**. Many Cameroonian musicians also play highlife, *soukous* or juju music – styles imported from neighbouring Nigeria and Congo/Zaire.

Travel around the country and you will find further traditional elements still very much alive. There are traditions of **kalimba** (*sanza*/thumb piano) music; talking drums; the **balafon** (xylophone) and **accordion**; **Islamic music**; huge **religious choirs**; **acapella**; traditional **horn trumpeters** in the Bamoun country. And then there are those Pygmies.

Recording Roots

In the 1930s, various record companies such as Pathé imported primitive equipment and persuaded local musicians to record. After briefly introducing themselves, the artists had to perform in one take. These recordings are so bad it's difficult to tell who's playing what or to make out the lyrics. You hear something like: "It's me, Thimothé Essombé, from Yabassi, near Douala, and I am happy, today, in the year nineteen-something or other, to sing this song for my loved one. La la la Jules et Mambo …" And the whole thing is all over in less than two minutes.

Back then, Cameroon's urban pop music was American, French or British, and eventually artists such as James Brown, The Beatles, Chuck Berry, Johnny Haliday and Sylvie Vertan inspired an internationalism. But in the 1950s the fledgling music industries in Nigeria and Congo had an important influence as 78rpm discs by **highlife** and **rumba** artists were being broadcast across Africa on the radio. Following behind came the traders who supplied original discs and later made licensing agreements to reissue popular records.

The only developed city in Cameroon at the time was the port of **Douala**, and it was low-key compared to its neighbours. Prevailing musical styles included the frenetic guitar action of **ambasse bey**, while **accordion** players bridged the gaps between folk songs and French chansons. In the international hotels, white clients expected to hear the latest American swing, or local versions of it.

Singer/guitarists were the first to create something approaching a local sound, with artists such as **Lobe Lobe**, **Ebanda Manfred**, **Nelle Eyoum** and **Ekambi Brillant** among the pioneers. A musically progressive artist, Brillant more or less created **makossa**, and his single "N'Gon Abo" was such a hit that to this day in Cameroon it'll have everyone on the dance floor in seconds, shaking their waists.

In those days, music was not as politicized or tribalized as it has become. Just as Brillant did a song in the Ewondo language of the Beti people from the Yaoundé district, so **Messi Martin** also made attempts to sing, quite beautifully, in the Douala language, thanks to the collaboration of Nellé Éyoum, himself from Douala and another of the fathers of modern *makossa*.

Before independence in 1960 there were no recording opportunities, although some Cameroonians did appear on Congolese and Nigerian labels – such as **Herbert Udemba**, whose songs were released on the Nigerphone label as "Ibo minstrel style". The opening of a radio station in Douala

Cameroon's Musical Ambassador

With fifty years of professional life behind him, **Manu Dibango** is almost uniquely qualified for the role of African musical standard-bearer. "Between palm wine and Beaujolais," commented a French newspaper about the music of France's longest resident African artist. Honoured there as Commandeur des Arts et Lettres, Manu is also a grandee at home. His 70th birthday celebrations in Cameroon in December 2003 included a big reception in the capital Yaoundé with massed government ministers, while in Douala, his home town, there were pirogue races, dinners and a concert at the stadium at which his mother's old choir sang.

Jak Kilby

Manu Dibango

The son of a civil servant, Manu was sent to boarding school in France in the late 1940s, where he began studying piano and saxophone, often heading for Paris to jam in some of the earliest black nightclubs. Moving to Belgium in 1956, he rapidly graduated to bandleader at **Les Anges Noires**, the smartest black club in a Brussels. It was the time of the negotiations for the independence of Belgium's major colony, the Congo. Among the entourage brought to Brussels by Patrice Lumumba, the Congo's tragically fated first premier, was African Jazz, the dance band led by **Joseph Kabasele** ("le Grand Kalle") – the father of Congolese rumba. Kabasele had a recording session booked and his sax player was ill, so Manu won an entrée to Africa's first pan-continental pop. With his new Belgian wife, a dancer named Coco, he moved between Brussels and the Congolese capital, where he opened a club called the Tam Tam and mixed with the founding fathers of Congolese pop.

By the mid-1960s, Manu had made his way back to Paris, where he fell in with a Yugoslav bandleader who had the bright idea of forming the first black band to tour the Saturday night bals of la France profonde. Manu's ye-ye phase climaxed as chef d'orchestre for Nino Ferrer, creator of the whacky hit "Les Cornichons" (The Gherkins), and as sax player for Gilbert Becaud, "Monsieur 100,000 Volts", France's answer to Johnny Ray.

By the end of the decade, an African music scene was forming in Paris, nurtured by companies like Decca. Manu was soon at the centre of it, arranging for everyone from **Francis Bebey** to **Ernesto Djédjé**. In 1972, Manu used the Cameroonian *makossa* rhythm as the basis of his "**Soul Makossa**", dashed off as the b-side of a theme song for the 1972 Africa Cup football championship. This became a worldwide hit, allowing Manu to move to New York, where African roots rediscovery was then hot. Approached by **Jerry Masucci**, of the all-conquering salsa label Fania, he spent a couple of years gigging with the **Fania All Stars**, the charanga group that helped make salsa a global phenomenon.

After a period as head of the State Television Orchestra of the Ivory Coast, Manu returned to Paris in the early 1980s, and was soon central to the newly emerging crossover scene. In 1984, Manu's "Abele Dance" became one of the first hits of the phenomenon soon to be christened World Music, and a year later he was co-ordinating Tam Tam Pour l'Ethiopie, a charity super-concert.

Since then, things have continued in the same vein, Manu's sound mutating with the changing fashions, and his own taste. In the 1990s, the UK rapper **MC Mello** came on board, followed by excursions into negro spirituals, and back to Cuban standards in the company of **Cuarteto Patria**. The new millennium saw Manu embroiled in musical politics, as president of the Cameroon Music Corporation, where he became much involved in training programmes and anti-piracy campaigns. Another sideline was honorary presidency of the municipal talent competition of his old school town in France. 'It's curious', he commented, 'young people nowadays are as likely to be playing djembe as piano' – a revolution for which Manu is as responsible as anyone else alive.

Philip Sweeney

finally made recording possible. In 1962, **Eboa Lotin**, "The Lion", made his recording debut for Philips. His style, based on guitar and harmonica riffs, was a precursor of *makossa*, named after a children's dance. He was followed by **Misse Ngoh**, a member of Los Calvinos band, who developed a more flamboyant finger-picking style.

The most popular form around the time of independence was **assiko**. Played on acoustic guitar accompanied by percussion and bottle, this was a local variant of **palm wine music** (see Sierra Leone) with an up-tempo beat. Leading protagonists were **Dikoume Bernard** and **Jean Bikoko**, who recorded a national hit "A ye pon djon ni me" in 1960 for the Samson label and went on to form a forty-strong troupe of assiko dancers. The fifty-year-old **Oncle Medjo** also found fame with a similar line-up.

Makossa

The Douala-based style of **makossa** has dominated Cameroon's pop scene since the 1960s, and with Manu Dibango's funky hybrid "Soul Makossa" in 1972 (see box opposite) it briefly reached an international audience. In its earliest form, it was a folk dance and music, evolving out of the mission schools of Douala, where it was played on guitars and accordions. Perhaps the best early exponent was **Eboa Lotin**, who has been much anthologized on cassette in Doula.

In the early 1970s, *makossa* became an increasingly urban, electric style, with a dance rhythm precisely cut for the nightclubs. Then in the 1980s it was transformed into **pop-makossa**, and produced largely from Paris. Most of the effective music of this new style was played by the so-called **National Team of Makossa** – a clique of Paris-based musicians directed by bassist **Aladji Touré** with **Toto Guillaume** and **Ebeny Wesley**.

The best singers of this era were the group **Black Styl** with famous singers such as **Nkotti François** and **Emile Kangue**, who achieved gold status with his album *Dikom lam la moto*. There are others like **Moni Bilé**, **Alexandre Doualla** (a.k.a. **Douleur**), **Ngalle Jojo**, **Jeannot Karl Mandenge**, **Marcel Tjahe** and the duo **Tim & Foty**. For a flavour of the early 1980s, and some spine-tingling, high note vocals, "Ami" (a remake of Ebanda Manfred's hit), the international smash by Bébé Manga, is highly recommended. It has recently become available on the *Golden Afrique* compilation CD (Network, 2005). It's also worth seeking out material by *makossa* artist **Ben Decca**, the elegant mix of the group **ESA**, **Tom Yom's** or **Prince Eyango**'s 1987 hit "You must calculate", as well as **Misse Ngoh**.

Other must-hears for the full Cam *makossa* treatment are: **Sam Fan Thomas**, whose *African Typic* collection made him the biggest Cameroonian name abroad after Dibango; guitarist **Toto Guillaume**, who has backed just about everyone (including Miriam Makeba) and was one of the main engineers of the explosive affair between Antillean *zouk* and African music; and **Lapiro de Mbanga**, who achieved fame with his anti-ruling-party, pidgin-English vitriol in song.

Graeme Ewens

Makossa singer Moni Bilé

Bikutsi's Essential Thrust

Cameroon's dictatorial President Paul Biya (since 1982) is a great aficionado and dancer of the rival musical style of **bikutsi**, which has its power-base in the city of Yaoundé. With his patronage, it has flourished on the (heavily state-censored) radio and TV.

K-Tino has become one of the leaders of the new generation of bikutsi singers. Her songs are often crude, pornographic and anticlerical. But such themes are the essential thrust of **bikutsi**, a style whose origins lie in a blood-stirring war rhythm – the music of vengeance and summoning to arms, sounding through the forest. Traditionally, it used rattles and drum and the *njang* xylophone or *balafon*. And, for decades, if not centuries, Beti women tricked the Christian Church, as well as their own men, by singing bikutsi using complex slang phrases reserved for women. While clapping out the rapid-fire rhythm, they sang about the trials and tribulations of everyday life; they discussed sexuality; and they talked about sexual fantasies and taboos. In the middle of the song, a woman would start a chorus leading to a frenzied dance of rhythmic foot-stamping and shaking: shoulders-back-bottom-clap-clap-clap-clap-clap. The whole thing was accompanied by strident screams and whistles.

Many women still perform the old folk dances across the sprawling hills of Yaoundé city and beyond to the south. One of the stalwarts of bikutsi was **Anne-Marie Nzié**, "The Queen of Cameroonian music" who kept the form popular from the 1940s until the 1980s, recording on the Pathé Marconi label. She made a brilliant comeback in 1999 with a new CD issued by Label Bleu in France and followed this up with three years of international touring. Another historic group was the **Richard Band de Zoetele** – which employed a six- to eight-piece *balafon* orchestra.

The inventor of "modern bikutsi", as a staple of mainstream Cameroonian pop, was **Messi Me Nkonda Martin**, founder of the band **Los Camaroes**, whose tunes were played incessantly on provincial radio stations in the 1960s and 70s. Messi Martin came up with an idea that translated the sound and magic of a traditional *balafon* to a new era, linking together some of the strings of an electric guitar with lengths of cotton cord, to give a damper tone and a slight buzz. Other bikutsi performers soon followed his example, notably the singer **Maurice "Elamau" Elanga**.

If bikutsi's sound is characterized by screaming, clapping, stamping, and *balafon*-playing (or *bala*-style guitar), its acclaimed superiority over *makossa* lies in its heavily charged content: where there's bikutsi, there must be dance, controversy, social debate and sex, either implied or explicit. The mellow-voiced Messi Martin has excelled at all of these, with his liberal doses of social commentary and ongoing womanizing. When he stopped composing and performing, his younger brother **Beti Joseph** took over. His "N'Son Anyu" was a rant against the unscrupulousness of local journalists. **Mbarga Soukous** and a handful of others also found momentary fame with overtly "pornographic" lyrics.

Gradually, bikutsi musicians improved the technical quality of their music and began to challenge the commercial success of *makossa*. Maurice Elanga shrewdly added brass in the 1970s. **Nkondo Si Tony** used electronic keyboards and synthesizers, and brought state-of-the-art production to bear. His output on the local cassette market was impressive, and he acquired something of a cult status among Yaoundé youth. Later, the long-established bikutsi/rumba big band, **Les Veterans**, began to make themselves heard in Europe with some bikutsi album releases. It was a man called **Mama Ohandja**, however, who truly popularized the bikutsi in the 1970s, with a string of releases on the French Sonodisc label and a touring band called **Confiance Jazz**.

Stern's

Les Têtes Brulées

In the 1980s, Ohandja's success was followed and surpassed by **Les Têtes Brulées**.This was a band who looked great, and whose stylish (almost easy-listening) appeal soon won them festival slots in Europe and the US. There's no doubt that they took bikutsi to a new audience, just as Manu Dibango had done with *makossa*, but the death in 1989 of their sensitive lead guitarist **Théodore Epémé** (aka Zanzibar) was a real blow, and by the mid-1990s the "Hot Heads" had well and truly burnt out. A "best of" album, *Bikutsi Fever*, appeared in 2000.

More roots bikutsi performers in the 1980s and 90s included the experienced musicians **Uta Bella**, **Marilou & Georges Seba** and **Jimmy Mvondo Mvelé**. All of them grew up in the Yaoundé area, and found work as producers and session and concert musicians in Paris and New York. Others included **Sabbal Lecco** and **Vincent Nguini** – who made huge (and undervalued) bikutsi contributions to Paul Simon's *Rhythm of the Saints* album – and the singer **Sissi Dipoko**.

The new generation of bikutsi singers includes the popular singers **Govinal**, **Zele**, **Racine Sagath**, **Bisso Solo**, **Tanus Foe** and others based abroad like **Chantal Ayissi**, **Sally Nyolo** and **Richard Amougou**.

Cameroon Today

In the 1990s, the lack of a music infrastructure, economic decline and the inability of musicians to maintain working bands combined to mute the production of homegrown music. However, that's not to say that nothing new emerged during that decade. **Bend-skin** is a recent kind of street-credible percussion-led folk music, pioneered as a pop music by **Kouchouam Mbada**, **André Marie Tala** and **Isidore Modjo**.

Another style which owes something to folk roots, and something to bol (from "bal" accordion-playing), is **Bantowbol**, championed by **Gibraltar Drakus** with Nkondo Si Tony. And then there's a lesser-known rhythm from northern Cameroon – the **nganja** – which was exposed in Britain during the mid-1980s by the eccentric dancer/singer **Ali Baba** and got a new contemporary run-out from **Le Groupe Kawtal** under the name Goumba balewa. The Baka Pygmies music was also popularized in the meantime by the **Patengue** and **Baka** Bantu groups from the southeast.

There is also a kind of Congo/Zairean **"new rumba"**, and a **makossa-soukous** fusion, popularised by **Papillon**, the late **Kotto Bass**, **Jean Pierre Essome**, **Benji Matéké** and **Petit Pays** who has been the most popular singer locally for almost

a decade. A dance called zengé was introduced in the mid-1990s by **Sergeo Polo** and **Njohreur** to accompany this recent beat.

There is moreover a new wave of Cameroonian singers who emerged abroad in the mid- and late 1990s and introduced a kind of revival in Cameroonian music. **Richard Bona** (see box overleaf) is undoubtedly the most popular artist of this new generation. Based in New York since 1995 this excellent bass guitar player and singer followed in the footsteps of **Manu Dibango** by mixing in his own way jazz and pop into *makossa* and various other Cameroonian rhythms. His charming voice has been compared to both **George Benson** and **João Gilberto**. The four albums he has so far released were very successful in Cameroon as well as in jazz clubs all over the world. In the 2004 edition of the "Victoires du Jazz" Awards, he won Best International Artist.

Sally Nyolo, on the other hand, has brought new colours into bikutsi music. This former Zap Mama group member based in France since the age of 13 was "discovered" in Cameroon thanks to her

Sally Nyolo

first album, *Tribu*, released in 1996. In that album she evoked the daily life in the equatorial forest, telling stories in the amazingly pure language of the Eton – one of the Beti tribes – with vocal polyphonies of the Pygmies and sounds from nature. *Tribu* found a great success in the US where over 100,000 copies were sold (out of 300,000 overall).

A Bona Fide Star

Born in 1967 into a family of musicians – his grandfather was a *griot* and drummer, and his mother sang in choirs – bass guitarist **Richard Bona** began playing (and building) instruments from an early age. Concentrating on *balafon*, guitar and flute, he first started performing professionally when he was 11, soon after moving to Douala with his father. A turning point occurred when Richard was recruited to play jazz in a local hotel: knowing little about it, he listened to hundreds of records, taking particular inspiration from "Portrait Of Tracy" by legendary bass guitarist Jaco Pastorius.

Following the death of his father, Richard had a brief spell in Germany before moving to Paris. Here he continued his musical studies, but also found time to play bass guitar with such jazz luminaries as **Manu Dibango**, **Mario Canonge**, **Jacques Higelin** and **Didier Lockwood**.

New York was Richard's next port of call, after the French authorities refused to renew his residence permit. Arriving in 1995 (with virtually no English), he quickly managed to establish himself on the jazz scene, where he was noticed by **Jack Holmes**, sometime songwriter for **Harry Belafonte**. An introduction to Belafonte followed, and before long he was working as his bandleader. He also played with **Joe Zawinul**'s band on its 1997 world tour (contributing to two albums) and collaborated with such famous artists as Paul Simon, Queen Latifah, Tito Puente and Herbie Hancock.

In 1998, following a good word from saxophonist **Brandford Marsalis**, Richard signed for Columbia Jazz, who issued his debut album *Scenes from My Life* a year later. *Révérence* (2001) featured some starry guest artists, including guitarist **Pat Metheny** and saxophonist **Michael Brecker**, while his third album *Munia – The Tale* (2003) was a tribute to Miles Davis with an appearance by **Salif Keita**. By this time he had left Columbia Jazz (who had tried to restrict him to MOR material) and the new album was released by Universal Jazz, France.

Just before being awarded the trophy for the Best International Artist of the year 2003" in the "Victoires du Jazz" awards, Bona collaborated with **Lokua Kanza** and **Gerald Toto** on an album simply entitled *Toto, Bona, Lokua*. He released his own fourth album, *Tiki,* at the end of 2005.

Alain Marius Mouafo Wemba

In 1997, she won the Prix Découverte RFI and has since issued three more albums: *Multiculti* (1998), *Beti* (2000) and *Zaïone* (2002), in the meantime touring various European and African countries, in the US and Japan.

In 1998, having previously worked with Deep Forest, **Wes Madiko** emerged in France, with his first album *Welenga* shifting 200,000 units. The single "Alane" sold an astonishing 1.3 million copies but unfortunately this success had very little influence on the popularity of *makossa* and Cameroonian music as a whole.

Others like **Henri Dikongue**, **Etienne Mbappe**, **Gino Sitson** (a highly talented New York-based vocalist and former singer in the Soul Makossa band of Manu Dibango) and the London-based gospel singer **Coco Mbassi** helped to give Cameroonian music a new identity which fused jazz, pop and local traditional rhythms.

Increased exposure to international music media inevitably, by the end of the 1990s, led to the development of rap music in Cameroon. Though the **Bantu Pô Si** group can be considered as the forerunner of the rap movement in the country – and indeed the most popular of all – there are others like **Thierry Olemba**, **Koppo** and **Krotal** who have developed rap in a Cameroonian style and gained a huge youth followings.

Cameroonian artists are battling to recover the leading place in the African musical scene they had occupied till the mid-1980s. But even today they are not helped by the governmental authorities who continue to show very little interest in fostering the development of a music industry infrastructure nor in the fight against piracy.

☉ Fleurs Musicales du Cameroun
FMC/Afrovision, Cameroon
An authoritative and comprehensive 3-album boxed set, produced, arranged and musically directed in the early 1980s for the government by Manu Dibango, to showcase the country's musical vitality. One disc of folksongs and two of *makossa*, mangambe, bikutsi and assiko – and a 12" booklet. Long since deleted but one to scour the record fairs for.

☉ Makossa Connection Vols 1–4
TJR, France
Four-hour *makossa* celebration, with everyone you know and many you won't – Guy Lobé, Emile Kangué, Manulo, Moni Bilé, Ben Decca, Salle Jean, Lapiro de Mbanga, Hoigen Ekwalle, Epée et Koum, Ndedy Dibango and Gilly Doumbé.

☉ Mvet ai Mendzang. Beti-Cameroon
Wergo, Germany
This CD brings together two major aspects of the culture of the Beti tribe (central and southern Cameroon): the hypnotic *mvet* (a sort of zither with notched bridge) of the storytellers for those nights around the fire, and the more muscular *mendzang* xylophone, used for various celebrations. Recorded live in Cameroon during 1984 and at Berlin's Ethnographical Museum in 1989.

Chantal Ayissi

The "pretty diva" of bikutsi is a great dancer and one of the genre's main stars.

☉ Passion
Claudia Sound, France
Apart from bikutsi, Chantal also sings *makossa* and explores Ivorian new beats.

Kotto Bass

The late Kotto Bass was a popular, witty and engaging artist whose *soukous* fusion provided an antidote to straight *makossa*.

☉ Best of Kotto Bass
Kouogeng & Fils, Cameroon
Apart from the very best tracks from the two albums he has released, this CD includes old tracks with Sam Fan Thomas's orchestra MBC and the previously unreleased "Africa Rumba".

Francis Bebey

By the time of his death in 2001, "Africa's Renaissance Man" had worked his way through jazz and most of his country's roots music. A multi-instrumentalist and musicologist, his music defies ready categorization.

☉ Nandolo/With Love: Francis Bebey Works 1963–94
Original Music, US
This retrospective features Bebey on bamboo flute, kalimba and acoustic guitar. It is highly, and frequently, recommended.

Moni Bilé

Smooth, suave but excitable, Bilé really maximized the enjoyment potential of *makossa*. He was the most influential artist of the 1980s, whose hi-tech productions outsold all others; he achieved gold status in France for his album *O si tapa lambo lam*.

☉ L'intégrale de Moni Bilé: 20th Anniversary
MB Production/Monthia, France
This 5-CD box set (with a total of 61 tracks) contains some of Bilé's greatest successes like "O si tapa lambo lam", "Chagrin d'amour" and "Esoua bwanga" among others.

Richard Bona

Currently one of the best bassists in the world, Richard Bona is becoming one of the most influential Cameroonian singers both at home and abroad with his jazzy way of playing *makossa* and other Cameroonian rhythms.

★ Révérence
Columbia Jazz/Sony Music, US
Richard Bona opens his second album with an "Invocation" for a peaceful world and follows up with poetic lyrics related to love, the protection of the planet, etc. On the whole it is still a blend of Afro Cuban salsa, jazz and various Cameroonian rhythms.

☉ Tiki
Universal Music Jazz, France
In his latest (fourth) release Richard Bona opens himself to Brazilian music and mostly to samba. Also featuring some West African and Arabic music grooves.

Manu Dibango

The "makossa man" has maintained his output into the late 1990s and has about a dozen CDs on the market. The perceived "African" content ebbs and flows but, call it what you will, Manu's music always swings.

☉ CubAfrica
Celluloid/Melodie, France
Really mellow versions of Cuban classics, accompanied on acoustic instruments by Cuarteto Patria and Manu's eternal guitar partner, Jerry Malekani. As sweet as can be.

☉ B Sides
Soul Makossa/Melodie, France
This is certainly the only album of Manu Dibango without a note of sax on it. The main instruments here are the marimba and vibraphone, bringing a new groove to mostly rare tracks of the 1970s.

★ Long box Manu Dibango
Universal Music, France
This 3-CD set contains 47 of the most significant tracks of Manu Dibango's career. Chosen by the man himself, the material covers all the styles he has dabbled in over the years in various locations.

Henri Dikongue

With the release of his first album *Wa* in 1995, the previously unknown Henri Dikongue swiftly became championed as the finest folk singer in Cameroon thanks to his subtle lyrics and soft melodies.

⊙ Biso nawa
Buda Musique/Melodie, France
The main attractions on this fourth album are, once again, the thrilling lyrics and captivating melodies. There's little accompaniment apart from Dikongue's own understated guitar playing.

Isnebo & Faadah Kawtal

Since Ali Baba died, Isnebo Haman has become the main representative of the *Fulbe* (in French known as Peul and in English as Fulani) music from the arid savannah in the north of Cameroon. In 1995 he composed with his former colleague Sali Gondjeh the soundtrack of the French movie *Le maître des éléphants.*

⊙ Divine
Label Bleu/Indigo, France
The piercing voice of Isnebo and the sound of traditional instruments such as talking drum, *garaya* (a sort of two-stringed lute) and *gouma* (a two-metre-high drum) make this 2002 album a genuine blend of traditional and modern music.

Guy Lobe

Lobe arrived on the Paris scene in the mid-1980s just as Antillean musicians were "zouking" up *makossa.*

⊙ Dix Ans Vols 1 & 2
Tandem/Blue Silver, France
A double-barrelled collection of straight-ahead, no-nonsense *makossa* that takes you dancing through a decade.

Benji Matéké

Benji is one of the best singers of the new generation of *makossa* men. The track "Rosy Muna" from his second album made him very popular in Cameroon, and since then he has released two others.

⊙ Boulot c'est boulot
Simon Music, France
Benji Matéké's fourth and most recent album has proved popular with *makossa* fans. Benji brought together one of the masters of the old generation – Toto Guillaume – and the best current *makossa* producer – Jean Philippe Tamba – to help him with his best effort yet.

Lapiro de Mbanga

A master of political rap, Lapiro was hugely controversial – a tough blend of politics, rhythm and hot language made him a big name in Cameroon.

⊙ Ndinga man again: na you
JPS Production, France
After almost a decade of misunderstanding with his fans Lapiro comes back with a highly competitive hard *makossa* album in which he criticizes the corrupted ruling authorities in caustic pidjin-English.

Charlotte Mbango

A serious *makossa* singer who can work just as well with other rhythms, Mbango was introduced to international audiences in the early 1990s as part of the Manu Dibango roadshow.

⊙ Konkai Makossa [Makossa New Form]
Touré Jim, France
Backing Mbango, you hear Sissi Dipoko, Aladji Touré and Toto Guillaume. If you want to know what hi-tech, 1990s *makossa* means, venture no further.

Coco Mbassi

The music of Coco Mbassi stands at the crossroads between African gospel, jazz and acoustic soul music.

★ Sisea
Conser Prod/Tropical Music, UK
Music of the soul: Coco Mbassi praises the Lord with her charming voice and sweet melodies.

Sally Nyolo

Sally Nyolo came out of the Belgium-based, world-babes band, Zap Mama, and has been the first of the group to make a solo breakthrough.

⊙ Tribu
Lusafrica, France
Her first solo release: twelve songs which showed off her superb voice and individual treatment of bikutsi.

⊙ Zaione
Lusafrica/BMG, France
A very varied CD from 2002, which includes numerous duets and some delightful acoustic tracks as well and guests such as Les Nubians, Princess Erika and Nicoletta. Sally Nyolo remains bound to Cameroon roots music with bikutsi, assiko and mvet, for instance, but also explores other beats like reggae.

Anne-Marie Nzié

Known as "The Golden Voice of Cameroon" and the "Queen Mother of Bikutsi", Anne-Marie Nzié is still pumping out some pretty robust music with her quavering Edith Piaf-like voice. She made her recording debut in 1954 on the Congolese Opika label, playing Hawaiian guitar, but had only released one album of her own, *Liberté*, on the Pathé Marconi label, between then and 1998.

⊙ Beza Ba Dzo
Label Bleu, France
Produced by, and featuring, the drumming of Brice Wassy, Anne-Marie's second album renders her folklore-based material with power and energy. Her semi-acoustic amalgam of traditional and modern instrumentation makes a welcome change from *makossa.*

Papillon

Papillon is a popular new *makossa* singer, bringing a *zengé*, *zouky, soukous* shake-up to liven up the scene.

⊙ Homme Fort
Gazon Synthetique/TJR, France
Sounds more zouky than *makossa*, and thus a rather too manufactured sound for some tastes.

Petit Pays

As a young artist, PP (Moundy Claude) gave the *makossa* scene one of its best successes with his second work *Ça Fait Mal*, a great local cassette release.

⊙ **Avant Gout**
Melodie, France
With his band Les Sans Visas, PP gets down a *zouk/soukous/makossa* blend, complete with shouted animations.

⊙ **Le CV de Petit Pays (10 Ans, 10 Hits)**
Melodie, France
Another decade under the bridge on this fine compilation.

Sam Fan Thomas

"Mr Makassi" had a truly phenomenal success with "African Typic Collection" – what many don't know is that the closing refrain [words and music] is lifted straight from a song by Franco, called "Boma l'Heure".

⊙ **The Best of Sam Fan Thomas**
TJR, France
Thomas ran out a string of sound-alike records following that first big hit and tried to trademark makassi. Here we have an hour and a quarter of bright, perky, singalong tunes.

SAM FAN THOMAS & CHARLOTTE MBANGO

⊙ **African Typic Collection**
Virgin Earthworks, UK
Four Cameroonian songs (and one stray Cape Verdean number via Paris) packaged around the mega-hit title song.

Gino Sitson

Gino Sitson is a vocal virtuoso with a unique technique, capable of reproducing percussion and miscellaneous other effects with his voice. He deftly combines African polyphonies with jazz, blues and gospel.

★ **Bamisphere**
Polyvocal Records, US
A masterclass in vocal wizardry: this CD presents many rhythms from Cameroon such as assiko, bend skin and *makossa* with a completely different orchestration dominated by "vocal instruments" created by Gino himself.

Brice Wassy

Manu Dibango cohort, Brice Wassy is a consummate session drummer and a producer with a pan-African CV. His own material, like Dibango's, is jazz fusion.

⊙ **Shrine Dance**
M.E.L.T. 2000, UK
Brice draws on a full palette of textures for his second album with an international jazz line-up. The set includes everything from a bikutsi version of Miles Davies to the *mangambe* and *mevum* – yet another dance rhythm.

Tom Yom's

Yom's (yes – that's his name) is a revolutionary part-bikutsi artist with an exceptional, high, clear voice, singing compositions by, among others, Eboa Lotin.

⊙ **Tom Yom's and the Star's Collection, Sunny Days**
TJR, France
Ignore the naff packaging and a few duff numbers: Yom's is a singer and musician of real power and range.

Thanks to Prince Eyango for help
with this chapter

PLAYLIST
Cameroon

1 **BESOKA ON SALSA Manu Dibango** from *B Sides*
This is a remastered version of a 1970s favourite in which Manu Dibango plays marimba, vibraphone, piano and organ … but no sax!

2 **SWEET MARY Richard Bona** from *Révérence*
Acoustic *makossa* beat, with Richard Bona playing the acoustic guitar and percussion as well as telling the story of a woman trying to escape from an arranged marriage.

3 **SARAH Anne Marie N'Zié** from *Beza ba dzo*
The evergreen "Queen of Bikutsi" rides an enchanting bossa nova groove featuring Mario Canonge, Jean Philippe Rykiel and Manu Dibango.

4 **BAMISPHERE Gino Sitson** from *Bamisphere*
A beautiful example of Gino Sitson's vocal orchestra – mixing conventional harmonies and vocal polyphonies.

5 **RETOUR AUX SOURCES Chantal Ayissi** from *Passion*
Chantal Ayissi features Ambroise Messi, a renowned player of the *mvet* (zither with notched bridge), providing this bikutsi track with an original twist.

6 **MY SOUL'S LOVE Coco Mbassi** from *Sisea*
A blend of Afro-jazz and gospel song, with charming voices all praising the Lord.

7 **OVER DONE Lapiro de Mbanga** from *Ndinga man again: Na you*
This track is the sort of hard *makossa* that is very much appreciated in the clubs of Douala. It features the hoarse voice of Lapiro, known ever since as an advocate for the poor.

8 **GOUMA Isnebo & Faadah Kawtal** from *Divine*
An Afro-rock number which includes many traditional instruments such as the bull horn and the huge drum that gives its name to this track.

9 **NGAM-NGAM AMWENE OBAM, MAAN YEMISON (NGAM-NGAM AMWENE, SON OF OBAM) Ndeng Joseph** from *Mvet ai Mendzang*
Tales and epics of the African equatorial forest from the fireside, by a storyteller who accompanies himself with his *mvet*.

10 **LAISSEZ MON MARI Benji Matéké** from *Boulot c'est boulot*
New wave *makossa* with a very lively beat. With his thin voice, Benji Matéké evokes a wife defending her spouse despite rumours of his infidelities.

Cape Verde

music of sweet sorrow

Island icon Cesaria Evora
Joe Weurfel

Until the early 1990s, few outsiders knew Cape Verde for much beyond its airport, a stopover connection on many flights between Europe, South America and Africa. In music circles, at least, a great deal changed with the huge success of the "barefoot diva" Cesaria Evora, who topped the mainstream charts in France and Portugal. These days, there's an emerging tourist industry, and travellers who prolong their stay can enjoy the astonishingly rich music of this small archipelago. Osvaldo dos Reis, Susana Máximo, David Peterson and Jon Lusk take an extended tour.

the music of Cape Verde has gained quite a high profile in recent years through the success of **Cesaria Evora**, the unlikely "barefoot diva". She mainly sings the bluesy **morna**, and its more upbeat derivative, the **coladeira**. Following in her footsteps, a number of other artists have subsequently made it clear that these are just two of the more obvious examples of a diverse array of styles unique to her island archipelago home.

The Republic of Cape Verde is a group of ten islands of volcanic origin, 600km off the coast of Senegal. An Atlantic world apart, Cape Verde is a former Portuguese colony, independent since 1975 – not quite African, but scarcely European. Named after Cap Vert, the peninsula of Dakar, this small country is anything but green; in fact, for ten months of the year, it is dry, dusty and windy, essentially a maritime extension of the Sahel. It is prone to catastrophic droughts, which, together with the islands' isolation, and lack of opportunities, have driven very large numbers to emigrate.

The islands were uninhabited when the Portuguese arrived and settled in 1462, but with the arrival of African slaves and sailors, they became quite racially mixed. The bulk of the modern population is composed of the descendants of African slaves; the everyday language is Kriolu – a creole language which blends old-style Portuguese with West African languages. In the five hundred years of its occupation, Portugal almost totally ignored the islands' development. Thousands perished in famines, went to São Tomé as plantation workers or emigrated overseas. Of a million people who call themselves Cape Verdean, only about a third actually live on the islands. The remainder are scattered in the US (mostly New England), Europe (mainly Portugal, France, Italy and the Netherlands) and Africa (Dakar). There is even a flourishing community in Cardiff, Wales. Almost every family has relatives overseas.

The islands' music is coloured by this history of separation and longing, by the creole culture and by the mix of Europeans and Africans. Cape Verdean music is influenced both by the waltz and the contre-dances of the old continent and by rhythms from Africa, Brazil and the Caribbean. There is a variety of unique styles, some of which have changed little over the centuries. Some, such as the **morna**, sound quite European, while West African elements are more to the fore in **batuco** and **funana**.

Music is an essential cultural expression of the life of Cape Verdean communities, an integral part of family and social celebrations, and of popular festivals. Each island is proud to have its own music. Brava sees its men emigrate, thus the morna there is sad and slow; in Santiago people dance as on the African continent, demonstrating their African roots; in São Nicolau, a very religious island, people sing above all at funerals and for their saints.

The Morna

What tango is to Argentina, or fado to Portugal, the **morna** is to Cape Verde. This national song form, the most popular of the archipelago, is at least a century and a half old and is part of nearly every Cape Verdean band's repertoire. It represents the soul of the people.

Hovering on the borderline between music and poetry, the morna is both a lyrical song with a profoundly melancholic flavour and a dance. Almost always written and sung in Kriolu, mornas are slow and have minor-key melodies. The lyrics are the heart of the matter and can stand alone as a poetic form. They speak of love and longing for one's distant *cretcheu* (beloved), of the beauty of the archipelago, of departure and separation and sufferings in the new land, of death. It is the music of *sodade* – an intense melancholy – of a people who want to stay on in their island home, yet must leave to survive.

As one of the oldest musical genres of the archipelago – it developed in early-nineteenth-century dance halls – the morna's origins are a subject of ongoing debate. There are theories that it was influenced by the Luso-Brasilian *modinha*, the Portuguese *fado* or perhaps African rhythms from Angola. The fado-modinha-morna triangle is so clearly drawn that it is obvious they are all interconnected.

In its earliest form, on the island of Boavista, the morna was cheerful and satirical. It developed its classic themes of love, emigration and nostalgia in the hands of the Brava-based composer **Eugénio Tavares**, (see box on p.66) who composed many of Cape Verde's best loved mornas and was the first to do so in Kriolu instead of Portuguese. Later, in São Vicente, with **B. Leza** and **Manuel d'Novas**, it changed its tone once again into a lively, happier form. The great mornas sung today are by Tavares, but the form is still actively composed.

Until the advent of electric instruments in the 1960s, mornas were performed by a solo singer accompanied by string ensembles of different sizes. These consisted of at least one guitar, often a fiddle, and sometimes bass, and a piano or accordion. The high-pitched strumming that is an identifying feature of many

The Barefoot Diva

Lusafrica

She's single-handedly put her tiny nation on the musical map, sold millions of CDs and spurned Madonna's requests to sing at the superstar's wedding and parties. All of this achieved while barefoot and puffing on strong cigarettes. Yet **Cesaria Evora** ('Cize' to her own people) never appears in the least phased by her international fame.

'You have more resources than we do in Cape Verde, beyond that we are the same,' Evora tells interviewers who may imagine she's impressed to be singing in London or Paris.

From living in a dirt floor hut to selling out grand theatres is a long journey and Evora has traversed it like few others. Born in Mindelo on the island of São Vicente, she began singing with her mother (a cook) and father (a musician and cousin of morna composer B. Leza). When her father died when she was seven, Ceasaria spent time in an orphanage and went on to sing on the streets and then in bars. The opportunity to represent Cape Verde in Portugal in 1985 saw Evora travelling to Europe for the first time. By then she was a 44-year-old grandmother and inured to the disappointments of life. An instant hit, she's now hailed as one of the world's great singers.

'I'm pleased that people like my singing,' says Evora, 'but for a long time I found it impossible to make any money. It was only when **José da Silva** came into my life that things became good.'

Da Silva, a Cape Verdean émigré based in France, became her producer/manager/promoter. Initially, interest was slow – Evora's first two albums found her singing over electro-pop backings – but 1991's *Mar Azul* was acoustic and showcased her voice at its most winning, impossibly languid, bruised by hardship and heartbreak. 1992's *Miss Perfumado* won over the French market (300,000+ sales of every album since) and international prominence.

Evora's albums are always professional affairs and over the 1990s Da Silva paired her with Cuban string sections, Brazilian musicians, Spanish pop stars and Bonnie Raitt. Yet for 2003's *Voz D'Amor* Evora returned to singing in front of a small Cape Verdean band to record her best album in recent years.

Evora's concerts depend on her mood: she can sing beautifully yet appear indifferent to the event – this is played up on stage by her sitting down for a fag during an instrumental – or she can find a great joy in performing for her public. One thing's for sure, Cesaria Evora has the voice of a siren. Long may she continue to bewitch.

Garth Cartwright

mornas was provided by the **cavaquinho**, an instrument popular in Portugal and Brazil, from where it was introduced to the islands. The cavaquinho is much like a ukulele, with four strings, tuned like the top four strings of a guitar. Another instrument used was the twelve-stringed Portuguese or tenor guitar called the **viola**, which is a little shorter than a standard guitar. Its rhythmic role was supplanted by the maracas, but it is still used on occasion. Contemporary mornas make use of trumpet, sax, clarinet or electric guitar – which often state the melody or play an instrumental break – backed by a piano, synths, a string section and maybe a jazz drum kit.

Among the most famous performers of morna are **Cesaria Evora** (see box opposite), **Djosinha**, a great musician and talented violinist who died a few years back, and **Bana**. The last is a singer with a magnificient voice from Mindelo, the town of São Vicente. He worked for many years with the disabled composer **B. Leza**, whom he transported from gig to gig. After stints in Rotterdam and Paris, he is now based in Lisbon. He has released a number of albums of varying quality since coming out of retirement in 1997 and despite health problems, he still performs occasionally at clubs like B. Leza, EnClave and his own bar/restaurant.

Bana, Cape Verde's voice in Lisbon

Other well-known morna singers include **Ildo Lobo**, one-time leader of the group Os Tubarões, and the female singers **Nancy Vieira**, **Mariana Ramos**, **Maria Alice**, **Celina Pereira**, **Titinha** and **Sãozinha**. Among instrumentalists, the great virtuoso was the late **Travadinha** (Antonio Vicente Lopes), who was a legendary performer on cavaquinho.

Coladeira

At the more African end of the Cape Verdean musical spectrum is the **coladeira**, faster in tempo than the morna, less involved lyrically and melodically, but generally more rhythmically complex. The form probably derived from the morna, with some South American input, in the 1930s.

Coladeiras are mainly songs of humour, joy and sensuality, more whimsical (and sometimes satirical) than the morna, with a tight, sexy rhythm. They are usually performed late in the evening, when the atmosphere heats up and dancers call for the band to play something faster. The term itself refers to the manner of dancing – man and woman move as if glued together ("cola" being the Portuguese word for glue).

The creators of modern coladeira were **Ti Joy** (Gregório Gonçalves), **Djosa Marques**, **Luis Morais** and – above all – **Frank Cavaquim** and **Manuel de Novas**, whose texts have enriched this São Vicente music genre. The best-known coladeira group was **Os Tubarões**, a six-piece outfit fronted by the vocalist **Ildo Lobo**. They recorded eight albums, and played in the US and Europe, before finally splitting in 1994. Other popular performers include the group **Mendes Brothers** (currently living in the US), **Cabo Verde Show**, **Gardenia Benros** and **Tito Paris**.

Funana

Closer still to African mainland roots is **funana**, an accordion led music and dance in which the rhythm plays a central role. Unlike the morna and coladeira typical of São Vicente, funana is mainly a rural art, typical of **Santiago**, the most African of the islands. It conveys a strong eroticism through exaggerated dance rhythms, though it can also be just as expressive as any morna. The words are often about special events in local everyday life or the past. Like Cape Verdean poetry, these texts are based on double entendres and allusions.

Again the origins of this music are uncertain. It was possibly imported at the beginning of the twentieth century from São Tomé (where a similar musical form exists), along with the accordion. Originally, the accordion was accompanied by just a metal scraper (*ferro* or *ferrinho*), and this traditional funana bears a very strong imprint of West African traditions, particularly in terms of rhythm and vocal technique.

Funana was for a long time looked down upon by both the Church and the colonial government. Exposed to contempt and prohibitions because of its "primitivism", it was forced underground until independence. Since then, however, it has been incorporated, revitalized and in some

Eugénio Tavares

Morna composers are as important to Cape Verdeans as their singers, and there is huge respect for the likes of **Luis Rendall**, **Olavo Bilac**, **Abilio Duarte**, **Manuel de Novas**, **Teófilo Chantre**, **Ramiro Mendes**, and especially for **B. Leza** (Francisco Xavier da Cruz), who died in the 1980s, having written some 1700 songs.

But the truly great figure is **Eugénio Tavares**, the composer of many of Cape Verde's best-loved mornas. Born in 1867, Tavares was a native of Brava and is a romanticized figure in Cape Verdean lore. Working most of his life as a journalist and civil servant, he was a champion of Kriolu language and culture, and one of the first to compose poetry in Kriolu instead of Portuguese.

Most of his mornas dealt with the pain and spirituality of romantic love. One of his most popular, "O Mar Eterno", is the tale of his romance with a wealthy young American woman who was visiting Brava by yacht. She was impressed by Tavares' poetry, and the two fell in love, but her disapproving father doused the affair by setting sail one night. Tavares found out the next morning that she had gone, and set down his sadness in a morna that is still often performed.

A number of his compositions also portray the sadness of those emigrating from the islands, such as "Hora di Bai" (The Hour of Leaving), his most famous song. It is a morna traditionally sung at the little dock at Furna, in Brava, as people boarded America-bound ships, and it is also often sung to signal the end of an evening's festivities.

On his death in 1930, Tavares' body was accompanied to its resting place by crowds of people singing and playing his mornas. He was the interpreter *par excellence* of the soul of Brava's inhabitants, poignantly exploring the aspirations and feelings of his people. *Mornas e Manijas*, edited by Osorio de Oliveira, is a collection in Portuguese of many of his morna lyrics, and *Sãozinha Canta Eugénio Tavares* is a fine recent recording of his songs, available on the MB Records label.

---

cases "modernized" by many of the pop bands of the islands in a movement similar to those in other African countries.

The band who started this was **Bulimundo**, who studied the rhythms and melodic structure of funana and succeeded in adapting it to electronic musical instruments, bringing it from the experience of rural peasants to the towns. In the following decade, many bands followed their lead, notably **Finaçon**, formed in Santiago in the late 1980s by brothers Zeca and Zeze di Nha Reinalda. The band is no longer around, but it is remembered for an album produced in Paris with the ground-breaking Congolese musician Ray Lema, and for the creation of *funacola*, a mix of coladeira and funana. Another very successful group from Santiago is the **Ferro Gaita**, a trio playing accordion, ferrinho and bass.

The major singer of rural, traditional funana is acknowledged to be **Kodé di Dona**. Born in 1940 in the heart of Santiago, the first years of his life coincided with the country's worst famine which lasted until 1947, and his song "Fomi 47", which has been covered by many other groups, is his own testimony to a tragedy ignored by Portugal, which saw people dying at the roadside. A working farmer today, Kodé is a remarkable composer with an ability to turn his own experience into song. His sense of poetry illustrates perfectly the allegorical tradition of the *badiu* peasant culture of Santiago island. His voice seems broken with the misery which is described in his songs: hoarse with alcohol abuse, it ranges from mumbled pain to lively mockery. He released his first album, *Cap Vert*, in 1996, following it up with *Kodé di Dona* in 1997 and *Djan-Bai* in 2001. These days he performs only at special events in Cape Verde, Portugal and other European countries, usually with his sons. Numerous

Susan Maximo

Kodé di Dona

Cape Verdean artists such as Tito Paris, Zéca di Nha Reinalda and Albertino continue to record his compositions.

Batuco and Finaçon

The **batuco** is primarily a form of women's music from the Santiago countryside. Another legacy of Africa – there are similar forms on the mainland – it fulfils a ritual role, and is traditionally performed at the ceremonies of the *tabanka* (a processional festival dance), and at weddings and christenings. A female soloist sings the verse, a group of women sing the refrain and when the music becomes more animated everyone present repeats a line.

Batuqueiras (women who perform batuco) need to possess both wit and a gift for poetry. They tend to be older women, though a noted exception is **Nacia Gomi** who at the age of 10 demonstrated an extraordinary talent. A key figure of Cape Verdean culture, she has been selected as her country's representative at international events such as the 1992 World Exhibition in Seville.

The batuco performance is made up of songs (usually improvised) with verses satirizing or criticizing social or personal events. A performance includes keeping time by clapping and beating a rolled-up cloth (the *tchabeta*) placed between the legs to form an acoustic box, and the *torno*, a typical African dance involving the wriggling of the buttocks in a simulation of the sexual act. The **finaçon** is the critical moment of a performance, when the *cantadeiras* (women singers) convey their particular message.

The batuco and the finaçon, though different forms, complement each other – essentially batuco is the rhythm and finaçon the text. The latter can involve compliments to party-givers, matrimonial advice, condemnation of loose behaviour, comments on political issues, criticism against those in power, maxims and advice on social issues and even saucy allusions.

The rhythmic support for finaçon is provided only by hand-clappers. The style of singing is both mumbled and shouted, and the songs are often of substantial length. It requires a very special lead singer, combining musical talent with considerable philosophical and poetic qualities. Among its most famous performers, alongside Nacia Gomi, were the late **Nha Gida Mendi** and **Bibinha Kabral**.

There is one man known as **Denti d'Oro** (Gold Teeth) who performs finaçon, with a group comprising women, men and children. Having had permission from his mother to perform a music mainly confined to women, he claims he became a finaçon singer in order to keep the tradition alive. Although his texts are shorter and less witty than Nacia Gomi's, he is well known in Santiago. He recorded his first album at the age of 70 and his most recent recording is a joint album with Gomi and members of Ferro Gaita.

International Stars

In addition to the major star **Cesaria Evora** (see box on p.64), there are a number of groups and singers in Cape Verde who regularly release recordings on labels in Portugal, France and Holland, where most of the music is recorded. Many of them divide the year between Cape Verde and either Portugal or New England, playing to large audiences at

Simentera: Return to Roots

In 1992, a number of professional artists and musicians gathered together in the capital of Praia, united by a passionate interest in Cape Verde's traditional music and musical history. The result was the establishment of a permanent cultural group, **Simentera**, which began investigating traditional forms. Since the very beginning, the organization was characterized by its innovative work – new concepts of composition, new techniques for musical arrangement and elaborate research into Cape Verdean music, rescuing musical genres and styles almost forgotten.

The group can now look back on a number of successful performances in their own country and widely acclaimed international tours. In 1994, they recorded an album *Music from Cape Verde* with other Cape Verdean artists, and a year later recorded their first solo album, *Raiz* (Root) on the Lusafrica label. It was followed by a second solo album *Barro e Voz* (Clay and Voice) in 1997, a disc which **Mario Lucio de Sousa**, the group's leader, described as music which "mirrors the music of our islands in its various rhythms and origins, calling up old folk-songs with both African and European roots. Through the different Cape Verdean musical types, one is telling the history of Cape Verde's identity formation itself."

Simentera

Mario Lucio grew up as an orphan after losing both parents at the age of 12. Born in Santiago, he first picked up a guitar in an army barracks as an 11-year-old soldier. While educating himself in his teens, he decided to leave music as a hobby. He studied law in Cuba and became an independent lawyer upon his return to the archipelago. But after holding a key position in the government, he decided to return to his original passion – music.

When listening to Simentera's music, one of the group's astonishing six lead singers immediately stands out: **Tété Alhinho**, whose warm contralto always seems to sparkle with enthusiasm. Having also penned songs on all of Simentera's album, it was obvious that she had the potential for a solo career. Her debut album *Voz* duly appeared in 2003, re-released the following year with additional tracks after she was signed to the Dutch label World Connection.

Tété Alhinho

Terezinha Araújo's voice is more of an acquired taste, best described as a wobbly, almost child-like soprano. However, her debut solo CD *Nôs Riqueza* (2004) is a revelation, with arrangements featuring *balafon* and kora alongside traditional Cape Verdean instruments. Terezinha's parents were exiled to Guinea Conakry in the 1960s, where the child star was "discovered" by Miriam Makeba. She now has a repertoire rich in influences, ranging from Cape Verde and Angola to Guinea-Bissau.

independence festivities held in the Cape Verdean enclaves.

Sax-player and clarinettist **Luis Morais** died in 2003 but multi-instrumentalist **Paulino Vieira** is still active. Both have produced and played on many albums by Cape Verdean artists, as well as their own projects. Vieira, in particular, is a musical explorer who has brought together various overseas influences (reggae, country, R&B) and merged them with home-grown rhythmic and instrumental roots. A long-established group of artists that have achieved big success in Paris is **Cabo Verde Show**, a dance music vehicle for musicians and singers Manu Lima, Luis da Silva, Serge da Silva and René Cabral. Often labelled as *zouk*-derivative, they have said their music was a precursor of Jacob Desvarieux's Antillean sound, and claim it was he who was influenced by the sounds of the islands, rather than the reverse.

This legendary band last recorded a studio album *Santa Catarina* in 1998. However, two "Best of …" compilations were released in 2005. Manu Lima and René Cabral have also been very active, Lima in particular has established himself as a leading producer on the Parisian *zouk* scene.

Among other musicians and groups living abroad in Holland and Lisbon are **Gil & the Perfects**, **Dina Medina**, **Grace Evora**, **Djoy Delgado**, **Os Rabelados Splash**, **Dany Silva**, **Tito Paris**, **Maria Alice** and **Bana**.

Other current popular musicians on the islands include **Bau** (an excellent violinist and guitarist who plays in Cesaria Evora's band but who has released several solo albums), **Vasco Martins** and **Simentera** (see box opposite).

Cape Verdeans in the USA

Throughout the nineteenth century, many Cape Verdeans escaped poverty by fleeing to New England on whaling ships, and the number of emigrants increased from the start of the twentieth century. There are now more Cape Verdeans and their descendants in the US than in the islands themselves. California and Hawaii both have sizeable communities but the largest concentration is in **New England**. With the decline of the whaling era, many of the old ships were bought by Cape Verdeans and sailed back and forth between the US and the islands, delivering supplies and transporting emigrants to America.

Festivals

The **Baia Das Gatas** (Bay of Sharks) Music Festival, scheduled every in August on the island of São Vicente, is the oldest in Cape Verde and the place where Cesaria Evora made one of her earliest public appearances. Over the years, many other artists have used this festival as a springboard to success. About 150,000 fans from all over the country and the world, more than the island's population, come to this bay to mount their tents on the beach, which becomes an authentic village of *morabeza* (fun).

The **Gamboa Festival**, scheduled in May in Praia, the capital city of Cape Verde, is a two-day festival which features renowned local and international artists, mostly from the Cape Verdean diaspora. Over 80,000 people turn up every year to the main harbour of Santiago island, Gamboa Beach.

The **Santa Maria Festival** takes place around the first half of September on the Island of Sal. Santa Maria, also the name of one of the most beautiful white-sand beaches in Cape Verde, where the stage is mounted, is known for its splendid hotels located near the festival. Attracting a large number of tourists from all over the world and people from other islands, this festival has recently begun to challenge Gamboa and Baia Das Gatas.

The **São Felipe Festival**, on the island of Fogo, was initially known for its famous horse race. However, the organizers have recently expanded this event by making music the main attraction. There's also a prominent soccer tournament, culinary shows and an usual religious ritual. The emphasis on music has truly boosted its quality and attendance, and it now attracts many well-known artists.

The large Cape Verdean community in Rotterdam, Holland, celebrates the **San João Festival**. During the last weekend in June, Cape Verdeans overflow the famous Praçinha De Quebradu (downtown of Rotterdam) to enjoy two days of cultural activities including dance, plays and music.

Cape Verdean Independence Day Festival In Providence, Rhode Island, where many Cape Verdean/Americans first landed, community leaders, sponsored by the local government, organize a festival to celebrate the independence of Cape Verde. This illustrious festival features musicians from the US, Europe and Cape Verde.

The new arrivals brought their music with them, playing it at social gatherings and on special occasions. Early **Cape Verdean string bands** included the **B-29s**, the **Cape Verdean Serenaders** and groups led by **Augusto Abrio** and **Notias**. Cape Verdeans also contributed to the Big Band era, with orchestras such as Duke Oliver's **Creole Vagabonds** and the **Don Verdi Orchestra**. These groups played mostly the swing music of the day, but also included their arrangements of Kriolu songs.

Today there are many musicians playing in New England, notably **Zé Rui de Pina** who grew up making drums and singing in and around Boston. Influenced by Ildo Lobo and Zeca di Nha Reinalda, Pina's first album, *Tchika* (1985), was backed by the Guinea-Bissauan group **Tabanka Djaz**, while his 1992 release, *Irresistible*, included contributions from another Boston-based artist, **Norberto Tavares**. A native of Santiago, Tavares and his group Tropical Power play both Cape Verdean and Brazilian music. Also based in Boston is singer-songwriter **Frank de Pina**. Born in Cape Verde in the 1950s, he and his brothers formed his first group, Os Vulcanicos, in 1971. Also New England-based are the **Creole Sextet**, who specialize in the older Cape Verdean styles, and have been playing parties, benefits and dances in the area for many years.

Perhaps the leading names on the US-based Cape Verde scene are **The Mendes Brothers**, João and Ramiro. Ramiro is a veteran strings arranger and producer, having worked on most of Cesaria Evora's releases and for many other Cape Verdean artists. The Mendes Brothers display an eclectic mix of styles, including explorations of the Luso-African music of Angola, semba in particular.

The brothers also run their own label, MB Records, whose Cape Verdean roster boasts **Gardenia Benros**, a relatively young singer based in Rhode Island, the very danceable **Mirri Lobo** and the morna-singer **Sãozinha**, with whom they released a CD of beautiful old Eugénio Tavares songs. Other rising MB hit-makers include **Kalú Monteiro** and **Djim Djob**. The twosome, formerly members of the Jamm Band, have produced several albums including the latest from Bana, Maria de Barros, Belinda and Grace Evora.

DISCOGRAPHY Cape Verde

★ Cape Verde: Anthology 1959–1992
Buda Musique du Monde, France

A splendid historic 2-CD compilation, ranging from the first professional recordings in 1959 to the post-Cesaria boom of the early 1990s, featuring morna, coladeira and funana. It runs more or less chronologically from early tracks by Fernando Quejas, through early Bana and Voz di Cabo Verde to the romantic violin of Travadinha, the funana of Zéca and Zeze di Nha Renalda and classics from Cesaria, Bana and Finaçon. Great photos and notes on the history of the music.

⊙ The Soul of Cape Verde
BMG/Lusafrica, France

A great introduction to some of the best names in Cape Verdean music. It opens with a soft, sultry track from Cesaria and follows up with Maria Alice, Bana, Celina Pereira, the bird-like voice of Titina, the exquisitely out-of-tune violin solo of The Mindel Band, guitar playing by Bau, Voz de Cabo Verde and lots more. Melancholy, seductive and highly recommended.

⊙ The Rough Guide to the Music of Cape Verde
World Music Network, UK

Important figures like Tito Paris, Ferro Gaita, Ildo Lobo and Simentera are all covered, with Bana particularly well represented on the lovely "Africa Um Dia". The emphasis is on lush, accessible studio creations, with only Grupo de Batuque da Cuidade Velha to illustrate the folk-roots side of things on their cushion-and-voice batuku excerpt. The one disappointment is that (due to licensing restrictions), Cesaria Evora is represented only by a lame live track.

Tété Alhinho

As the most instantly recognizable vocal talent to emerge from the great Simentera, Alhinho was the most obvious candidate for a solo career.

⊙ Voz
World Connection, Netherlands

Despite her dependably husky voice, this solo debut doesn't live up to the high expectations generated by her dazzling performances with Simentera. The simple acoustic guitar accompaniment does showcase her voice, but exposes the lack of strong material apart from the delightful "Tema" – predictably penned by Márlo Lúcio. And the three tracks with fuller arrangements tacked on the end sound out of place, especially the Afro-Cuban closer.

Bana

Bana is one of the most amazing voices from Cape Verde, and a father figure for artists like Cesaria and Tito Paris. He settled in Portugal in 1975 and invited musicians to perform with him there giving them international exposure. Now in his late sixties, he still performs at the café B. Leza in Lisbon.

⊙ Bana chante la Magie du Cap Vert
Lusafrica, France
In this 1993 recording Bana exercises his vocal chords around a sweet, classic selection of mornas and coladeiras with a band that understands the old style.

⊙ Gira Sol
Iris, France
Songs about life in Cape Verde. After a few years of recording inactivity, Bana released this acclaimed CD in 1997.

Maria de Barros

Born in Mauritania, this California-based singer grew up in Dakar, Senegal. Despite this, many are claiming her as the perfect heir to Cesaria Evora, her godmother. Maria's repertoire derives from the rich musical traditions of Cape Verde as well as drawing on the sounds of Africa, Europe and South America.

⊙ Dança Ma Mi
Narada World/EMI, US
A powerful traditional record that showcases some great songwriting flair and Maria's outstanding voice. Filled with up-tempo dance songs, and handsomely produced.

Bau

A frequent performer in Cesaria's band, Bau is a top instrumentalist on cavaquinho, guitar and violin (many of which he makes himself).

⊙ Jaílza
Lusafrica, France
Beautiful playing, if slightly soft-centred, on fourteen instrumental tracks with that unmistakable sighing Cape Verdean melancholy.

Cordas do Sol

Deep in the island of Santo Antão, there's a place called Vale do Paul, home of Cordas do Sol, a group that examines the life, language and traditions of Cape Verde's second largest island through music.

⊙ Terra de Sodade
Lusafrica, France
A compilation of their first two albums; Linga d'Sentonton (2000) and Marijoana, released in 2002. Even though the lack of any serious songwriting or vocal talent is apparent, their penchant for Cape Verde's rustic acoustic stringed instruments gives their music (mainly coladeira, morna and kolas-anjon) an undeniable appeal.

Cesaria Evora

Cape Verde's barefoot musical ambassador is the best-known Cape Verdean artist in Europe. In 1975, with the disappearance of nightlife after independence, she gave up singing and raised her children as a single mother. In 1987 she was invited to Portugal by the singer Bana and went on to record a series of discs which, with the release of Miss Perfumado in 1992, brought international late-flowering fame in which she seems to revel.

★ Miss Perfumado
BMG/Lusafrica, France; Nonesuch, US
The album which swept Cesaria to international attention. Its appeal lay partly in its acoustic approach, which allowed the chanson-like mornas to emerge in sharp focus, backed by some wonderful piano and guitar playing.

⊙ Cesaria
BMG/Lusafrica, France; Nonesuch, US
This 1995 album was Cesaria's follow-up to Miss Perfumado, and many rate it even higher. "Petit Pays", which opens, is a delicate love song for Cape Verdean music and, apart from one dud track ("Flor na Paul"), the rest of the disc complements it splendidly with some great musical arrangements.

⊙ Voz D'Amor
BMG/Lusafrica, France; Nonesuch, US
A back-to-basics treat that came after a period of collaboration, which at times threatened to obscure the barefoot diva's subtle charms. The few guests who do grace this understated collection of mornas and coladeiras are more subtly integrated than ever before, and Cesaria sings as well as she ever has.

Ferro Gaita

Founded in 1996, six-piece band Ferro Gaita enjoyed early success with their debut album Fundu Baxu (1997). Since then they have worked at the cutting edge of the more African-influenced aspect of traditional Cape Verdean music and have won an international reputation.

⊙ Rei di Funana
Harmonia/France
If you think of Cape Verdean music as gentle and easy-going, check out Ferro Gaita's rootsy, hard-driven funana dance music. Dominated by the charismatic presence of accordionist and lead singer Eduino, this is music to set the pulse racing.

Jorge Humberto

Known as the poet from Mindelo, Cape Verde, Humberto has a subtle and distinctive way of expressing the culture of his native island. Inspired by poets like Euqénio Tavares and B. Leza, he has provided many hits for singers such as Ana Firmino, Biús, Maria Alice and Dudu Araujo in recent years.

⊙ Identidade
Morabeza Records/France
The missing link between the generation of Cesaria and that of younger artists like Fantcha and Biús, Humberto lays bare his soul on this album through his appealing and poignant lyrics.

Ildo Lobo

For a long time overshadowed by Bana and Cesaria Evora, Ildo Lobo first made a name for himself as a vocalist with Os Tubarões. Known for his extraordinary voice and charisma, this native of Sal, Cape Verde, finally reached international fame with Nos Morna (1996) and Intelectual in 2002. Sadly, in 2004, one month before the release of Incondicional, he died of a heart attack at the age of 50.

⊙ Incondicional
Lusafrica, France
Dominated by clarinet, acoustic guitars and cavaquinho, this album opens with the last morna Lobo wrote: "Nha Fidjo Matcho", the advice of a father to his son. Perhaps not his overall best album, but it has certainly a depth that grows on you.

Doçura/Harmonia Mundi

Tchéka

Mario Lucio

This traditionalist and exceptional instrumentalist/songwriter is one of the founders of the outstanding band Simentera. He is also the man behind the success of many Cape Verdean artists, including the late Ildo Lobo and Tété Alhinho.

⊙ Mar e Luz
Melodie, France
This album highlights the rare musical vision Mario Lucio has been demonstrating over the years, and reveals his love for his traditional roots.

Lura

Born to Cape Verdean parents in Lisbon, Lura has emerged as a name to watch in recent years. She started out as an R&B/jazz singer, with an appealing alto voice, who made sporadic allusions to her roots. After two so-so albums, she finally delivered something special with her third.

⊙ Di Korpu Ku Alma
Lusafrica, France
A strong set drawing heavily on the songbook of the late Orlando Pantera, with a couple of numbers by Manuel Lopes Andrade (Tchéka) and some songwriting from Lura herself. Features morna, coladeira, funana and in particular the batuku rhythm of Santiago island.

Mariana Ramos

Daughter of Toy Ramos (former guitarist of the legendary Voz de Cabo Verde), Ramos was born in Dakar, Senegal. Highly influenced by jazz, blues and French *variété*, Mariana began singing Cape Verdean music later as an adult.

⊙ Bibia
Lusafrica, France
A soul-drenched album, propelled by the mixture of acoustic and electric guitar playing, and showcasing a distinctively silky and sensual voice.

Simentera

A renowned group of musicians living in Santiago, Simentera have been instrumental in rediscovering the country's musical history. Now on an extended sabbatical while various members pursue solo careers, they cultivate the traditional forms, playing only acoustic instruments.

★ Tr'adictional
Melodie, France
The group's fourth album, released in 2003, is easily their most consistent and one of the finest Cape Verdean albums of the last decade. Though remaining true to their philosophy of championing roots musics, there's plenty of zestful experimentation going on, with guest appearnces by Manu Dibango, Toure Kunda, Paulinho Da Viola *et al*.

Tchéka

Born in the port of Ribeira Barca, a district of Santiago, Tchéka (Manuel Lopes Andrade) began performing alongside his father, Nho Raul Andrade, a popular violinist. After making his mark at local dances, weddings, baptisms and so on, Tchéka developed a more personal style, based on *batuku*. He has since established himself as one of the most promising young songwriters and composers of the archipelago.

⊙ Nu Monda
Lusafrica/France
On this album Tchéka experiments with the *batuku* rhythm by transposing it onto his guitar. The highlight track is "Nu Monda", Tchéka's masterpiece.

Lena Timas

A native of the island of Santo Antão, Lena started taking music seriously around six years ago alongside her husband and producer, Zé Timas. After touring the United States as a back-up singer for several local artists, she decided to step into limelight.

⊙ Magia D'Morna
Zemanu Productions, US
This album masterfully emphasizes Lena's distinctive and compelling vocals, which drift over cosy tracks backed by traditional instrumentation, all courtesy of Zé Timas and Manu "Kat" Santos.

Os Tubarões

A group from Santiago known for its coladeiras, its wonderful vocalist and lively concerts. Unfortunately, they stopped performing and recording in 1994.

⊙ Os Tubarões ao vivo
EMI Valentin de Carvalho, Portugal
Perhaps the best of the band's eight albums, this is a recording of a live concert in Lisbon in 1993.

Nancy Vieira

Born to Cape Verdean parents, Nancy grew up in Lisbon, where in 1995 she won a TV singing contest. A sociologist by training, she decided to become a professional singer by popular demand. Her sweet and sturdy voice, has earned her countless invitations to perform on stage with Bana, Tito Paris and Boy Gê Mendes, among others.

★ Segred
PraçaNova, Portugal
This is one of the most diverse traditional albums released in recent years. Nancy shows her great range singing popular tunes from all corners of Cape Verde.

PLAYLIST
Cape Verde

1 PETIT PAYS Cesaria Evora from *Cesaria*
On this yearning morna, Cesaria fondly lists the good things about her island home, backed by the gentle sway of her excellent acoustic band. Mesmerizing stuff.

2 BOAS FESTAS Luis Morais from *The Soul of Cape Verde*
A sweetly soulful instrumental cut by the late saxophonist and composer, who was a revered and much loved figure of Cape Verdean music.

3 AFRICA UM DIA Bana from *Glrasol*
The grand old man of Cape Verdean song, who interprets this lovely morna with enormous pathos, shadowed by some sinuous clarinet and flute.

4 DANÇA MA MI CRIOLA Tito Paris from *The Rough Guide to the Music of Cape Verde*
A very danceable coladeira by this well-respected singer, who runs the famed B. Leza club in Lisbon. A cool horn arrangement, fine gravelly vocals and a memorable tune.

5 FALSO TESTEMUNHO Maria Alice from *The Soul of Cape Verde*
This Lisbon-based singer's most famous track.

6 FUNDO BAXO Ferro Gaita from *The Rough Guide to the Music of Cape Verde*
Ferro Gaita are specialists in the hard dance style called funáná. This is a typical example.

7 FLADU FA Simentera from *Tr'adictional*
Lead singer Tété Alhinho gives an amazingly sensual performance, and the arrangement is to die for. This one speeds up into a carnival blur of sound.

8 BATUKU Lura from *Di Korpu Ku Alma*
One of several examples of songs on her latest album featuring the batuku rhythm.

9 VELOCIDADE Cesaria Evora from **Voz D'Amor**
Another Luis Morais song, this time one of his upbeat, bouncy coladeiras. Taken from the fine, stripped-down album Cesaria made in 2003, after a series of high-profile collaborations.

Congo

heart of danceness

Franco and OK Jazz
Graeme Ewens

The *rumba* of Congo was a musical form that hit a nerve throughout Africa, animating dancers of all ages and social classes in a way that no other regional style, not even Ghanaian highlife, has come close to matching. With its spiralling guitars and hip-swinging rhythms, *soukous*, as it's commonly known to the rest of the world, has also had a bigger cumulative effect on Western dance floors than any other African music. Graeme Ewens explores the streams and tributaries of Central Africa's musical powerhouse, so at odds with the country's tragic war-torn political history.

n any discussion of the Congo, it pays to clear up the geography at the outset. Confusingly, there are two countries called Congo. The bigger of the pair was colonized by the Belgians and over the years has been known as **Congo-Kinshasa**, as **Zaïre** (during the aberrant three-decade regime of President Mobutu Sese Seko) and as **DRC** (Democratic Republic of the Congo). The other, smaller Congo was colonized by France and is known as **Congo-Brazzaville** or simply the Republic of the Congo. The two nations are separated by the Congo River, and their main cities – Kinshasa and Brazzaville respectively – are the only two capitals within eye-shot of each other anywhere in the world. Musicians from Brazzaville have been heavily involved in the musical developments of the last few decades, but DRC – and Kinshasa in particular – has provided most of the Congolese superstars.

Indeed, for much of the mid-twentieth century, Kinshasa (known as Léopoldville in colonial days) was Africa's undisputed musical heart, pumping out an endless flow of life-giving dance music. Great bands such as **African Jazz**, Franco's **OK Jazz** and **African Fiesta** led the way, and were followed up by stars such as **Zaïko Langa Langa**, **Papa Wemba** and, later, **Koffi Olomide** and **Wenge Musica**. Each generation brought its own style, but they all played music known in the West as **rumba** or **soukous** – albeit inaccurately (see box below). By the 1990s, the glory days of Congolese music were over, but there are still a number of impressive artists on the scene and young Congolese still turn out in their droves to dance to their country's music – which remains the top crossover genre on the African continent.

Despite severe social, political and economic difficulties the Congolese have maintained a reputation for knowing how to enjoy themselves, and music and dance have always been a key element of this. Early rumba dances such as the *maringa* and *agbwaya* were expressions of physi-

Soukousemantics

The Congolese have no generic term to identify their music. People speak of *miziki na biso* (our music) to distinguish it from imported sounds, but even that phrase relies on the French word *musique* rendered into Lingala. Over the years, various styles of Congolese music have been called by the names of the dances from which they sprang or which they generated, but none has ever applied to the whole, expansive genre.

The global entertainment industry can't abide this sort of thing. Its publicists and salesmen seem unable to function without names to label their products, and journalists and DJs are equally dependent on these tags. Their first attempt at a catchy moniker for Congolese music was *rumba rock* in the 1980s. There was some rationale for this: in the 1950s and 60s Congolese musicians had ardently embraced Cuban styles such as rumba, and indeed they referred to some of their original compositions as "rumbas". At the same time, the Congolese sound was quite distinct from anything played in Cuba, thanks in large part to electric guitars – instruments associated with rock. The problem was that "rumba rock" implied that Congolese music was an artificial fusion of two foreign forms, which it most definitely was not, and it was never a term that local musicians or fans used.

Hence *soukous*, the tag that has gained most recognition in Europe and America since the late 1980s. A sinuous, almost onomatopoeic word, it is uniquely Congolese – though, like *miziki*, it's a corruption (or should we say redemption?) of a French word. The problem with this one is that it's applied much too broadly. In Congo, "soukous" refers to a particular dance style popular in the late 1960s, and more recently it's been a football term to describe a cunning feint when dribbling the ball. Using the word to identify music as different as Kallé Kabasele's classics and Koffi Olomide's latest is like referring to everything from "Mystery Train" to "She Bangs" as twist.

Since the turn of the century, Congolese artists in their fifties and sixties such as Sam Mangwana, Papa Noel, Mose Fan Fan and the group Kékélé have revived the sounds of their youth and with them an old name, rumba. While acknowledging Cuban influences, they insist their music is indigenous to Congo and so, in fact, is the name. Rumba, they say, is the Spanish mispronunciation of *nkumba*, the KiKongo word for "waist". Afro-Cubans of Congolese ancestry had taught successive generations a social dance from the old country, a style in which a man and a woman held each other by the waist. That was the rumba that returned to Congo on records and radio waves in the twentieth century.

But that doesn't mean that rumba is a correct term for all Congolese dance music. After all, Congo is the original Land of a Thousand Dances.

Ken Braun

cal grace – subtle hip moves and shifts of balance – rather than fancy footwork and pirouettes, and this understated style has remained the basis, seasonally adjusted with a few new gestures or arm movements. And though there have been many great hits over the years, the passing of time can be more easily measured by memories of seductive rhythms such as the *rumba-boucher, kiri-kiri, cavacha, kwassa-kwassa, madiaba, sundama kibinda nkoi* and *ndombolo* rather than particular song titles.

Rumba Roots

The dance format that stormed West and Central Africa before and after World War II was the **Afro-Cuban rumba**. Itself a new-world fusion of Latin and African idioms, the rumba was quickly reappropriated by the Congolese, most notably by adapting the piano part of the *son montuno* to the guitar and playing it in a similar way to the *likembe* or *sanza* thumb piano. Although Ghana's highlife pipped it to the post as the first fusion dance music with pan-African appeal, Congolese music was less influenced by European taste than highlife and it was in many ways more African, even though Western instruments were used.

The forefathers of Congolese popular music included the accordionist **Feruzi**, often credited with popularizing the rumba during the 1930s, and the guitarists **Antoine Wendo Kolosoyi**, **Jhimmy** and **Zachery Elenga**. These itinerant musicians entertained in the African quarters at funeral wakes, marriages and casual parties. In more bourgeois society, early highlife, swing and Afro-Cuban music were the staples of the first bands to play at formal dances where the few members of the elite "evolués" could mix with Europeans.

A few early greats, such as **Jean Bosco Mwenda** from Katanga – who was recorded in the field by the South African musicologist Hugh Tracey and later made his career in Nairobi – blazed a trail in Congo's eastern regions. But most of the key developments took place in Kinshasa, whose population swelled after World War II, with huge numbers of Congolese attracted to the city by well-paid work, public health and housing – and by its reputation as a "town of joy". In Kinshasa, life was cosmopolitan: French-style *variété*, or **cabaret music**, made its mark, while other ingredients which combined to form the classic Congolese sound included vocal harmonic skills learned at church and, later, a tradition of religious fanfares played on brass-band instruments.

Beside its inherent musical appeal – not least its ability to sound both mellow and highly charged

Joseph "Le Grand Kalle" Kabasele

at the same time – the cross-border popularity of Congolese music was boosted by a number of practical factors. First, it was "non-tribal", making use of the interethnic (and very melodic) trading language of **Lingala**. Second, the distinctive guitar style was an amalgam of influences from the Central African interior and the continent's west coast. Third, the music also appeared in the right place at the right time. The postwar Belgian Congo was booming and astute Greek traders in Kinshasa saw the commercial potential of discs as trade goods to sell alongside textiles, shoes and household items – including, of course, record players.

Inspired by the success of the GV series of Cuban records distributed by EMI, the **early Congolese labels** – Ngoma, Opika, Esengo, CEFA and Loningisa – released a deluge of 78rpm recordings by semi-professional musicians of local rumba versions alongside releases of folklore music. Radio Congo Belge, which started African music broadcasts in the early 1940s, provided the ideal promotional medium. While live performance remained more informal, the record companies maintained their own house bands to provide backing for singers. The CEFA label employed Belgian guitarist and arranger **Bill Alexandre**, who brought the first electric guitars to the Congo and is credited with introducing the finger-picking style. The rival Loningisa label recruited Henri Bowane from the Equatorial region, who injected even more colour into the style.

The Belle Époque

The Congolese music scene really came alive in 1953 with the inauguration of **African Jazz**, the first full-time recording and performing orchestra, which was led by **Joseph "Le Grand Kalle" Kabasele**. In the same year, 15-year-old prodigy "**Franco**" Luambo Makiadi (see box overleaf) first entered the Loningisa studio to play with his guitar mentors Dewayon and Bowane. Three years later Franco and half a dozen colleagues from the studio house band branched out to form Orchestre Kinois Jazz (a Kinois is someone from Kinshasa), which soon became known as **OK Jazz**.

Kalle's African Jazz, which included the guitar wizards **Nicholas "Dr Nico" Kasanda** and his brother **Dechaud**, alongside singer **Pascal Tabu Rochereau** and the Cameroonian saxophonist and keyboard player **Manu Dibango**, ensured themselves musical immortality with the release in 1960 of "Independence Cha Cha Cha", which celebrated the end of colonial rule in the Belgian Congo and became an anthem for much of Africa. Kalle was a showman as well as composer and arranger, and he created an international-sounding fusion, which gradually re-Africanized the popular Latin rhythms. Franco and the school of OK Jazz also started from the same points of reference but their music was rootsier, drawing on traditional folklore rhythms and instrumental techniques, and the songs were more down to earth.

During the 1950s and 60s there was a constant movement of musicians between the Belgian and French colonies, where the proliferation of "Congo bars" and a mood of optimism gave the region its good-time reputation. The fabled group **Rock'a Mambo** contained musicians from both schools and from both banks of the Congo River – notably **Papa Noel Nedule**, **Jean Serge Essous**, **Nino Malapet**, **Rossignol** and **Pandi**. Eventually, the first three of these settled in Brazzaville under another name which was to become legend: Bantou Jazz, later **Bantous de la Capitale**. In the decade following independence in 1960, both cities spawned hundreds of dance bands, releasing 45rpm singles on dozens of labels.

Among these groups were Orchestre Cobantou, Diamant Bleu, Beguen Band, Cercul Jazz, Negro Band, Negro Succes, Conga Succes, Afrizam, Vox Africa, Orchestre Revolution, Orchestre Jamel, Los Angel, Les Maquisards, Vedette Jazz, Kin Bantous, Conga 68, Les As, Les Zoulou and African Soul (a vehicle for Manu Dibango). As more and more oldies are revived by retrospective record labels some of these names are sure to resurface.

By the 1970s, the music had evolved a stage further and, thanks largely to the extended playing time of 7" discs, more emphasis was placed on the exciting instrumental section known as the **seben**, when the slow rumba breaks, singers stand back and the multiple guitars go to work on the dancers. Franco was a master of the seben and his style was mimicked (though never matched) throughout Africa.

For several years the careers of African Jazz and OK Jazz ran parallel, but the former disbanded in the mid-1960s after recording some four hundred compositions. Band member **Pascal Tabu Rochereau**, who later took the name "Tabu Ley", went on to set up **African Fiesta** with Dr Nico, whose rich, florid, solo style gained him a huge following of his own. What came out of the relationship was something slightly experimental, with a greater diversity of rhythm and melody and occasional hints of Western soul and country music. African Fiesta rapidly garnered a rather urbane audience, but they separated after two years. Nico went on to lead **African Fiesta Sukisa**, while Tabu Ley formed **Afrisa**, which maintained the allegiance of a "sophisticated" audience and for some time was the only serious rival

Jak Kilby

Tabu Ley Rochereau

Francofile

The continuity of Congolese music was broken in 1989 with the death of **Franco Luambo Makiadi**, leader of **OK Jazz** and the last surviving giant of the Belle Époque. As well as being a stunning guitar stylist – with a hard, metallic urgency to his sound – Franco had a relationship with his audience that remains unmatched. More than any other public figure he accompanied his country's progress from the colonial repression of village society through independence and statehood to the constricts of military rule and the first murmurings of democracy.

Born in 1938, Franco grew up alongside his mother's market stall, among the "Yankees" and "'bandits", so he was always in tune with the street people of Kinshasa, who liked their music hard and their songs to deal with day-to-day realities. His first instrument was a homemade, tin-can guitar with stripped electrical wire for strings, but at the age of 11 he was given a real guitar and came under the tutelage of **Paul Dewayon**, an early recording artist who also moved among the market people rather than the intellectual *évolués* (literally, "evolved") classes.

Franco's fancy finger-picking, his street-cred and boyish good looks made him an almost instant success. He was quickly hailed a "boy wonder" and, by the age of 15, was a popular recording star and member of the **Loningisa** label house band, in demand for modelling the latest clothes and a heart-throb for the women of Kinshasa. In 1956, he helped found OK Jazz and, although he was only third in seniority, his organization and commitment, combined with his star quality, made him very much the leader.

When independence came to the Belgian Congo in 1960, the founder of the first dance orchestra and acknowledged "father" of Congo-rumba music, **Joseph Kabasele**, set up a recording deal for OK Jazz in Europe, and through the 1960s the band evolved into the biggest and most effective music machine in Africa. By then known as the "Sorcerer of the Guitar", Franco re-Africanized the Afro-Cuban rumba by introducing rhythmic, vocal and guitar elements from Congolese folklore. Although primarily a dance band, OK Jazz was also a vehicle for Franco's observations and criticisms of modernizing society, and his songs had great information and educational value. His sternest morality lecture was "Attention na Sida" (Beware of AIDS) in 1987.

Like many African superstars, Franco had an ambivalent relationship with the state. He was a true patriot, but he also felt compelled to speak his mind and, while he was an essential element in Mobutu's *authenticité* (authenticity) programme, he was also reprimanded and jailed more than once and several of his records were banned. Although he was a stern moralist, he could slip quite easily into obscenity in his declared mission to provoke and tell the truth. The meanings of his songs are often opaque, with layers of allusion covering a subtext or hidden agenda. His own constituents, however, have always known exactly who and what Franco was criticizing.

Franco also pumped out standard African praise and memorial songs, and covered a whole range of topics from football to commercial endorsement. But the theme to which he constantly returned was the conflict between men and women, and he couched many of his messages in a soap-opera style. The format reached a peak in 1986 with the episodic "**Mario**", about a lazy but educated young man and the older woman he lives with and exploits (until she eventually gets fed up and kicks him out).

More than any other African musician, Franco transcended the boundaries of language, class, nationality and tribal affiliation. His music was as hugely popular in Anglophone Africa as in the French-speaking countries, and OK Jazz records have been licensed almost worldwide. He also had considerable international success, though he played only once in Britain and once in America. During a career which lasted nearly forty years, he released over 150 albums and composed some thousand songs, while the band's complete repertoire was closer to three thousand. In mid-life, he developed the bulk to match that reputation, weighing around one hundred and forty kilos (300 pounds) at his peak. The band too was massive, with up to forty musicians on call.

When Franco died in October 1989, after a long illness, Zaïre spent four days in national mourning, while the radio played non-stop OK Jazz. His long-time rival, Tabu Ley Rochereau, described him at the time as "like a human god", while Sam Mangwana talked of a combination of Shakespeare or Mozart with Muhammad Ali or Pelé.

Graeme Ewens

to OK Jazz. Both Kalle and Nico faded during the 1970s and died in the early 1980s.

Key figures who emerged from the growing ranks of these great dance bands included the raucous, honking sax player **Verckys Kiamanguana**, who spent six years with OK Jazz before setting up **Orchestre Veve** and other groups of the New Wave. Others also found varying levels of solo fame after working in both camps, notably the erstwhile co-president of OK Jazz, **Vicky Longomba**, as well as **Ndombe Opetum**, **Dizzy Mandjeku** and **Sam Mangwana**.

Mangwana's smooth, sympathetic vocal style endeared him to followers of both camps and to listeners of all ages. He started out in the early 1960s with **Vox Africa** and Festival des Maquisards before joining Tabu Ley's Afrisa. In 1972, he controversially switched allegiance to OK Jazz for three productive years before returning to Afrisa. Eventually he set up a splinter group in West Africa called **African All Stars**, with whom he developed a pan-African sound with pop and Caribbean rhythmic undertones – the basis of a successful globe-trotting solo career.

A one-time colleague in OK Jazz, guitarist **Mose Fan Fan** was Franco's deputy and co-soloist for several years, introducing a tougher, rock inflection to the OK Jazz rumba. In 1974, he took his fate in his hands and moved to East Africa with **Somo Somo**, where he fed the craze for Congolese music before settling in Britain in the mid-1980s.

Many other Zaïrean musicians also appeared in other parts of the continent in the 1960s and 70s. Among the first wanderers was **Ryco Jazz**, founded by Bowane, who brought Congolese rumba to West Africa and the French Antilles. In East Africa, meanwhile, the likes of **Baba Gaston**, **Real Sounds**, **Orchestra Makassy**, **Orchestre Maquis** and Samba Mapangala's **Orchestre Virunga** all enjoyed more acclaim outside the Congo homeland than they might have done in Kinshasa. Musicians from the Brazzaville side of the river were more likely to move west, with artists from Les Bantous de la Capitale such as Pamelo M'ounka and Tchico Thicaya establishing a fan base in Abidjan.

Riding the New Wave

The classic Congolese sound was a rich tapestry of vocals, guitars and rhythm instruments, embellished with full-blown horn arrangements that became more prominent after **James Brown** visited Kinshasa in 1969 and 1974. During that time, however, a new stream of pop music had sprung from the students at Gombe High School, who had picked up on the Western rock-group format and started doing their own thing. One group of graduates known as **Los Nickelos** was able to experiment and record in Brussels, while their juniors back home formed **Thu Zahina**, which influenced a whole generation during its brief existence. Their early recordings, which have recently come to light, showcase a band that really took rumba to the edge.

The new music, of which Thu Zahina was a leading exponent, was raw and energetic, with emphasis on spiralling, interactive guitars and rattling snare drums during the seben, and hardly a horn to be heard (at least not in their live performances). Taking elements of the *animation* (shouting) from strident forms of shanty-town music, and also from the wordplay used at Bakongo funerals, the new bands brought an extra vitality to the music, adapting traditional dances like the *soukous* and inventing new ones, such as the *cavacha*, to accompany the extended seben.

The groups which capitalized most on the New Wave were **Stukas** (aka Stukas Boys), led by the outrageous showman **Gaby Lita Bembo**. The latter played with a frenetic intensity and brought a new dynamism to the scene (with theatrical performances that included stage props such as a crucifix and chains), but his music was also something different from the largely Kongo culture which informed most of the Kinshasa bands. Lita was from the Ekonda people of the equatorial region and he exploited their wailing choral style, which was driven by a relentlessly fast, machine-like, finger-picking guitar style (or, in the case of Bongo Wende, a teeth-picking guitar technique).

However, it was **Zaïko Langa Langa** that was to lead the way for the whole post-independence generation. This group was founded by conga player **D.V. Moanda** and lead singer **Nyoka Longo**. The name was a contraction of "Zaïre ya Bakoko" (Zaïre of our Ancestors) plus Langa Langa, the name of a people in the equatorial region. They also added the prefix Tout-Choc-Anti-Choc.

Within months, the band had expanded to take in a line-up of singers and guitarists who helped to redefine *soukous*. Among the early members were **Papa Wemba** (see box overleaf), who eventually formed Viva La Musica; **Evoloko Jocker** of Langa Langa Stars; **Bozi Boziana**, who joined Choc Stars before setting up rival Anti-Choc; **Pepe Feli Manuaku** of Grand Zaïko Wa Wa; and dozens more. Unlike other bands, Zaïko was not the personal property of one leader. It was always a group, totalling over twenty musicians. However, following a serious rupture in 1988 – by which point Zaïko was a national institution – the situation changed. One group remained with Nyoka Longo, who

Papa Wemba: God Sees All

The first years of the new century were not kind to Congolese music legend **Papa Wemba**. Separated from the Real World label and divorced from his international management, he was exploited by sensationalist UK film-makers and even jailed for alleged people-trafficking into France and Belgium. But the international legend of Congolese music lives on.

Although Papa's 1990s Real World recordings lack the true substance to justify any of them as great works, he learnt well from his experiences and songs like the sensual "Pourquoi tu n'es pas là" (from *Bakala Dia Kuba*, 2001) show how he cleverly reworked earlier attempts at global fusion into something genuinely able to transcend borders.

During Papa's six-month imprisonment – while awaiting trial in France in 2002 – he underwent a spiritual awakening, re-embracing Christianity and claiming God as his guide. This was confirmed musically with the inclusion of religious songs on his 2003 CD *Somo Trop*. In the end, he was found innocent of all serious charges, but his reputation remains tarnished and he has been consistently refused work visas for the UK and US since his release.

Jak Kilby

Back in his home market, the core of Congolese pop music had changed during the previous decade. With the decline of the two once-great schools of rumba (typified by Franco and Tabu Ley), their replacement has been one single school: that of **Wenge Musica**. What Wenge began, everyone else followed – including Papa. It was a necessary music transition from third- to fourth-generation Congolese rumba, but one which many of Papa's old friends failed to make.

Today, in the two bands that he leads, Papa tends to surround himself with much younger musicians. This has fuelled speculation that the great man is bored with the popular music that once captivated and inspired him. His own music is still strong and sells well, but he seems more removed with each passing year. However, his status as a visionary and an eccentric is set in stone.

Vincent Luttman

adopted an old ZLL slogan **Nkolo Mboka** (Village Headman), while the defectors set up **Zaïko Langa Langa Familia Dei** (Family of God), which also splintered soon after.

A host of rival New Wave groups had appeared in the early 1970s, including **Lipua Lipua**, **Bella Bella**, **Shama Shama**, **Empire Bakuba** and **Victoria**. Their music had a rough, sweaty feel, while most of the singers, with the exception of husky-throated Pepe Kalle, compensated with honey-toned vocals. Many of the New Wave bands were promoted by Kiamanguana Verckys, who turned to record production and created a kind of Kinshasa "garage-band" sound. From the ranks of these bands and their subsequent offshoots came Kanda Bongo Man, Nyboma, Pepe Kalle and Emeneya.

Soukous really took hold in international markets during the mid-1980s, when musicians began recording in Europe and the cleaner Paris sound edged out the less polished Kinshasa variants. Among the early successes were the **Four Stars** (Quatres Étoiles), whose smooth arrangements and streamlined presentation offered a direct challenge to the more ornate big bands – although the top two orchestras were still thriving, with Franco and Tabu Ley releasing international albums at a prolific rate.

During the mid-1980s Tabu Ley boosted the effectiveness of Afrisa with the introduction of **Mbilia Bel**, an attractive young singer with a dreamy, creamy voice who became one of Africa's first female superstars. Bel had started her career as a dancer with **Abeti Masekini**, a powerful performer, who, along with Vonga Aye, had paved the way for female singers a decade before. While the male bands were obliged to stick to their winning dance formulas, women artists were able to experiment with European-style ballads and a variety of

Iman/fRoots Archive

Mbilia Bel with the prodigious guitarist-arranger Rigo Star

regional and international rhythms. One of the most versatile and charming was **M'Pongo Love**. Until her untimely death in 1990, Love enjoyed a glittering career, despite the disabling effects of polio, which left her lame in one leg.

Female Congolese music has been headed up more recently by **Tshala Mwana**, who debuted as a dancer in M'Pongo Love's band Tsheke Tsheke before finding fame as the queen of **mutuashi**, the funk-folk rhythm of the Baluba people. A whole string of young women singers was later introduced through Bozi Boziana's Anti-Choc, notably **Jolie Detta** and the angel-voiced **Deyess Mukangi**. Kinshasa was also home to **TAZ Bolingo**, one of Africa's rare all-female bands, who played a particularly languid, smoochy *soukous* under the slogan "self-control". Others who achieved a degree of international success during the 1990s include the *soukous* dance queen **Yondo Sister** and **Nana ad Baniel**, who came to light in OK Jazz.

An aspect of the New Wave phenomenon which brought *soukous* to international attention was the **fashion** ingredient. Inspired by Papa Wemba, the cult of *kitende* celebrated cloth and promoted style consciousness to the rank of a religion. Wemba's followers – the *sapeurs* – took their name from an informal but highly competitive group of poseurs who called themselves the Société des Ambianceurs et des Personnes Elegants (the Society of Cool and Elegant People). Reminiscent of eighteenth-century dandyism and of the 1960s British mod scene, the *sapeur* movement was viewed as the antithesis of scruffy, informal hippiedom.

Although any new-rumba music provided the soundtrack for the sapeurs' fashion battles, the main style icons were individuals such as Wemba, Emeneya and Koffi Olomide, while the deities were Japanese and European designers such as Yohji Yamamoto and Jean-Paul Gaultier.

Party Time in Paris

By the end of the 1980s the "classic" era was over and the Zaïrean music business had fragmented. Of the big three, Franco was dead, Tabu Ley was semi-dormant (with Afrisa having partially disintegrated) and Verckys' business influence was waning. The Zaïko generation still appealed to Congolese who weren't even born when they started, but international listeners favoured the more minimal studio sounds coming out of Paris.

There were more pressing, non-musical reasons, too, for a shift of scene, as Zaïre lurched deep into anarchy and economic chaos amid the death throes of President Mobutu's corrupt regime. Many bands quit a muted Kinshasa, going on extended foreign tours or settling in the US, London, Brussels, Paris or Geneva.

The spearhead of the new **Parisian soukous** scene was **Kanda Bongo Man** who, with commercial foresight, cut back on the fancy choral parts and architectural arrangements to create fast-track party music which he has since brought to audiences around the world. Other key Paris players included **Pepe Kalle**, Empire Bakuba and the guitarist **Rigo Star** (who came out of Wemba's Viva la Musica in the early 1980s). Star, with his clean, crisp guitar sound, accompanied Kanda on tour from 1983 and then appeared on countless records, often as arranger, with a galaxy of star

Dave Peabody

Kanda Bongo Man

Olomide started as a song-writer for Papa Wemba, and by the end of the decade had become the most popular singer in Africa. His unique style known as "Tcha-Tcho" was aimed at a female audience who adored his romantic vocalizing. Koffi was the master at switching from his syrupy and ornate rumba into a seben in which his Quartier Latin group would let rip on an extended guitar and animation work-out complete with sexy dancing girls and swivel-hipped male chorus.

names including Wemba, Olomide, Madilu System and Mbilia Bel.

Another guitarist in Kanda's first touring group, **Diblo Dibala**, went on to form **Loketo**, whose crossover sound, packaged for young, pop-wise Western audiences, made them dance-floor darlings. In 1991, Diblo regrouped with **Matchatcha**, in which his devilish licks featured even more prominently. Lokassa Ya Mbongo's **Soukous Stars** offered a similar fast-food version of the Congolese recipe. This type of easy, sleazy medley package was advanced somewhat by the drummer and showman **Awilo Longomba**, son of OK Jazz original Vicky, who brought guest singers into his line-up and has won a series of Kora awards for his techno-*soukous* style and amusing videos. For all his throwaway comedic style, Awilo has pedigree. He started out playing with Lita Bembo's Stukas, later joining Wemba in Viva la Musica and then taking a key part in Nouvelle Génération. In recent years he has stepped out from behind the drum kit and has taken on vocal duties himself.

One of the few new bands to make a real go of it in Europe was **Nouvelle Génération**. Comprising several defectors from Wemba's Viva clan, the new boys created a dynamic, danceable sound around voices and upbeat rhythms. They didn't move the music forward a full generation, but did give a pointer to new possibilities. Their recordings hit the spot, but the band found it hard to grind out a living in Europe, and faded back into the shadows.

Kinshasa in the 1990s

Back in Kanshasa, the most popular names of the 1990s were **Koffi Olomide** and **Wenge Musica**.

Wenge Musica, meanwhile, was formed by former university students at the end of the 1980s and by the 1990s had become the most promising and creative of a new breed of young musicians. Driven by the phenomenally talented guitar of **Alain Makaba** and the sublime voice of **J.B. Mpiana**, the original Wenge Musica also featured a singer/animator called **Werrason** and several co-vocalists. The band gave themselves the full name of Wenge Musica BCBG ("Bon Chic, Bon Genre", a reference to their highly fashionable appearance) and as their personnel changed and the numbers swelled they eventually split into several factions. J.B. led the **Wenge BCBG** group while Werrason called the main rival outfit **Wenge Musica Maison Mère**.

Also active in the early 1990s were Zaïko Langa Langa, **Rumba Ray**, **Bana OK** and Zaïko veteran **Dindo Yogo**. But overall, the music scene was suffering on account of the socio-political upheavals, with studio facilities scarce and the number releases dropping. In December 1993, a showcase event in Kinshasa demonstrated that the music had not been silenced. The remaining big bands were brought together with artists such as Papa Wemba and Koffi Olomide, who had been recalled from Europe to show that *soukous* was alive and well.

A few subsequent festivals helped keep the old *flambeau* burning, but further upheavals in the mid- to late-1990s set Congolese music back in many ways. DRC was no longer stable, and for a while during the post-Mobutu civil war, the capital was policed by foreign soldiers, which helped break down the cultural integrity that had underpinned the music. There was no more political patronage and little promise of an income from music. Curfews shut down many of the clubs and several of

Ndombolo and Beyond

In the late 90s, the **ndombolo** dance was to become almost as ubiquitous as the term *soukous* or rumba had been to earlier generations. During 1997 *mobondo*, *kitisela ya maman* and, most significantly, *kibinda nkoi* were the dance moves that accompanied the seben section of most of the big-name Congolese artists. *Kibinda nkoi* – 'the footsteps of the leopard' – replicated the movements of the big cat stalking its prey and was understood to refer to the impending demise of Mobutu, "the Leopard of Zaïre".

By the end of 1997 Mobutu's 32-year rule was over, and the tentative footsteps of the leopard dance had relaxed into a spread-leg position with arms dropped at the side and a provocatively rotating backside. This new dance, named *ndombolo*, spread to every African dance floor. Performed by the troupes of nubile female dancers that accompanied each major Congolese orchestra, the dance was the embodiment of raw sexual

Martin Sinnock

energy. The male chorus lines made it even more exaggerated, strutting around the stage imitating ape mating rituals.

Since then, cutting-edge groups have moved on to new dances. The civil war prompted one called **position de tir** (shooting position), a simple step culminating in a crouched position with arms emulating the jerky movements of a machine gun. Others continue to emanate from the Kinshasa streets, usually created by the *chegués* – the young and mostly homeless kids living rough in the city. Some of these new dances have been assimilat-

Koffi Olomide leads the line

ed by major groups; in some cases the groups even act as benefactors to the *chegués*. King Kester Emeneya, for example, is quick to give credit to the boys who have shown him new dance steps and has even brought them to Europe as part of his spectacular stage show.

Martin Sinnock

them became churches – notably those temples of rumba, Vis-A-Vis and Kimpwanza in the district of Matonge. Many musicians also succumbed to "long illnesses" which saw no fewer than five Zaïko guitarists and a keyboard player die in a couple of years. Singers such as Lengi Lenga, Dindo Yogo and Pepe Kalle also passed on, and few others appeared to replace them.

New Directions

In the absence of a vibrant, commercial and regenerative music scene, many stars turned to religion. The music stayed much the same but the lyrics praised God rather than patrons or fashion houses. One of the first to drop out of the game and take this route in the late 1980s was **Bimi Ombale**, a sweet-voiced original of Zaïko, whose church was within singing range of the Vis-A-Vis, along with

some other great vocalists including ex-Choc Star **Debaba**. The latter released a series of impressive evangelical discs with a conventional guitar-led backing which proved that religious rumba could be as exciting as any non-Christian music. Ex-colleague **Carlito** soon followed suit and other well-known singers like **Djo Nolo**, **Mavuela Somo** and **Mopero** all tried their hand at religious music.

A number of women singers also took up the Bible, including Jolie Detta (previously of OK Jazz), **Mama Feza**, **Théthé Djungandeke** and Tabu Ley-protégée **Faya Tess**. Some say the women were given more of a chance to express themselves in church, although few acquired the power or the income of the male priests. However, much of the arranging and some of the instrumentalizing was, and is, provided by well-known musicians, working quasi-anonymously. As is now common throughout Africa, fundamentalist religion and private churches

Graeme Ewens

Konono No. 1

derive great momentum from spiritually cleansed popular music. Surprisingly, the ex-OK Jazz and Veve veteran, Verckys Kiamwangana, spent a couple of years at the turn of the century living in Britain, and could be heard playing his sax every Sunday morning in a north London church.

Religion was not the only replacement for the fading rumba, however. Other artists reverted to folklore – following, ironically, the example of Mobutu's "Recourse to Authenticity" programme. The neo-folklore movement first came to light in 1989 with **Swede Swede** who were a rhythm revelation of the early 1990s, using a variety of drums, percussion, vocals and harmonicas to created a postmodern, neotraditional sound that recalled the raw, rhythmic charge of pre-electric music.

The Swede Swede phenomenon might have remained hidden in Kinshasa if a Belgian music engineer called Vincent Kenis had not been on hand to record them and bring the band to Europe. Kenis had played keyboard with Franco and Olomide among others, but his real interest was in the neotraditional shanty-town bands of the local quartiers, which are now known as tradimoderne. During the early years of the new millennium, Kenis recorded dozens of these informal bands in the working-class neighbourhoods of Kinshasa. He eventually brought one group – **Konono No. 1** – to Belgium and released a fantastic and fascinating album, *Congotronics*, in 2005, followed by

a compilation of various other artists. The tradi-modernists turn the whole *soukous* genre on its head. Their instruments are homemade, crudely amplified likembe thumb pianos accompanied by frenzied percussion and raucous vocals broadcast via old-fashioned speakers.

Another route taken by some of the more mature old-school professionals was to unplug the amplifiers. One of the first and finest examples of the **acoustic revival** was guitarist Mose Fan Fan's UK-produced CD *Congo Acoustic*, which reinforced the mellow, swayful mood of the grand old rumba, but delivered it in a gentle, minimal style. This stimulated the formation of a rival acoustic supergroup under the leadership of Papa Noel, called **Kékélé**. When their first release came out there was hope of an African equivalent to the phenomenally successful Cuban revival band, Buena Vista Social Club. That didn't happen but the new genre was soon firmly established. Another grand master of the old school, Sam Mangwana, joined the flow with an acoustic set of his own and the old hero Antoine Wendo Kolosoyi returned from forty years of obscurity with exellent international releases in 1999 and 2002.

In other developments, a handful of iconoclastic solo musicians have emerged and cracked the international music scene. These include **Ray Lema**, working in a jazz-funk-rock fusion mode, and the unclassifiable vocalist **Lokua Kanza**. As everywhere, rap music has also stamped its inevitable mark on Congolese youth culture. The massive success of hip-hop collective **Bisso na Bisso** in 1998–99 laid the foundations for this, but the success has not been repeated.

There have also been disco playback acts, funk bands and even punk-metal thrashers to come out of both the Congos, but the rumba remains supreme – even if it is a shadow of its former self. The *soukous* line continues unbroken with the Wenge family, **Felix Wazekwa** (a Koffi Olomide

protégée) and a bunch of local acts. From Brazza, the **Extra Musica** line-up has managed to survive, while others such as **Les Coeurs Brisé** and the American exile **Ricardo Lemvo** have kept their end up.

Congolese musicians tend to perform for their own constituents, rather than new audiences, and their music sells much better through DVD, cable TV and underpublicized community performances than in the mainstream. Congo rumba had its fifteen years in the international limelight and in many ways it is now an underground artform.

DISCOGRAPHY Congo

⊙ **Congo Compil**
Syllart, France; Stern's, UK
Part of the *Rendezvous* series, this compilation contains good examples of Kinshasa kitsch, mostly licensed from other labels so not the typical Syllart fast-food (though many tracks share a synthetic keyboard sound). Eleven tracks from the likes of Koffi, Zaïko, Kalle, Madilu, Wenge, Wemba and Defao put the emphasis on vocal expression. It's good to hear people like ex-OK Jazz guitarist/composer Simaro and Choc Stars charmer Carlito get another outing, while Emeneya's "Nzinzi" still stands proud.

⊙ **Congotronics Vol. 2**
Crammed Discs, Belgium
This CD/DVD double-disc package captures more of Kinshasa's street bands performing their raunchy dance music on an ingenious selection of homemade instruments. By including electric guitar on some of the tracks, the music becomes slightly more accessible than Konono No. 1's first *Congotronics* collection and the splendidly atmospheric film footage really brings the music to life.

★ **Golden Afrique Volume 2**
Network Medien, Germany
Subtitled "Highlights and Rarities from the Golden Era of African Pop Music (1956–1982): the Great Days of Rumba Congolaise and Early Soukous", this 2-CD set is a beautifully packaged and lovingly annotated reissue. The emphasis is firmly on the rumba greats, including Franco, Le Grand Kallé, Tabu Ley Rochereau, Sam Mangwana and Dr Nico, and it serves as a tremendous introduction for the novice.

⊙ **The Rough Guide to Congolese Soukous**
World Music Network, UK
It's impossible to represent the Congo on one disc but this collection manages to include the big names Franco, Rochereau, Zaïko,

Pepe Kalle, Wemba and Olomide plus some *soukous* from Kanda Bongo Man and others.

⊙ **Ngoma: Souvenir ya l'Indépendance**
Pamap, Germany
Ngoma was one of the earliest and most influential labels in post-World War II Léopoldville – now Kinshasa. This is the second of three compilations from the German label containing the melodies, instruments and grooves that moved the nation through the 1950s: folk ballads, early urban fusions and proto-rumba as well as a soul number from Manu Dibango.

⊙ **Revue Noir à Kin, Zaïre '96**
Revue Noir, France
Recorded "in the field" during the last dark days of Mobutu's reign, this release is a compilation soundtrack for issue no. 12 of the prestigious French art magazine. With less emphasis on rumba but more of the shanty-town sound, this shows how life was bubbling away despite restrictions and repression. Raw, urgent and refreshingly unsophisticated.

⊙ **Soukous Paris**
Syllart, France; Stern's, UK
Collection of hot snacks, best taken with a couple of cold drinks, a cement dance floor and some heady atmosphere. Although the fast, curly guitar action, simple melodic mantras and whipcrack drum machines sound a bit dated now, the line-up includes Lokassa, Dally Kimoko, Diblo, Kanda, Kass Kass, Nyboma, Yondo Sister and the late lamented Mpongo Love.

Bantous de la Capitale

The Brazzaville band Les Bantous was formed by ex-members of OK Jazz in the late 1950s to become virtually the official Congo-Brazzaville state orchestra. There is a series of Bantous CD compilations which documents this great Congo orchestra.

⊙ Les Grands Succès des Bantous de la Capitale, Vol. 3
Anytha Ngapy/FDB, France
The third in the five-volume CD series of the Bantous' greatest hits includes the LP *El Manicero*, a showcase for Essous and Malapet originally subtitled "The Best Saxes in Central Africa". There's mellow, big-band backing and some actual "Latin" rumba from 1970 as well as the classic "El Manicero" (The Peanut Vendor).

Mbilia Bel

Mbilia Bel rose to fame with Tabu Ley's Afrisa band and as a solo singer became one of Africa's first women superstars.

⊙ M'bilia Bel & Tabu Ley Rochereau avec L'Afrisa International – Loyenghe
Sonodisc, France
This disc reissues the entire 1982 Loyenghe double-LP, which shows the duo of Bel and Tabu Ley performing at their peak. There is also a series on the Syllart label which collects all of their marvellous collaborations.

Gaby Lita Bembo & Stukas

Gaby Lita Bembo & Stukas were contemporaries of Zaïko Langa Langa and if anything they were even more raunchy.

⊙ Kita Mata ABC
RetroAfric, UK
This captures some of their spectacular showmanship with dazzling guitars and spaced-out echoing vocals.

Bisso na Bisso

The most successful Congolese hip-hop act, Bisso na Bisso are a group of Brazzaville/Parisian 20-somethings brought together from different crews under the direction of top French rapper Passi.

⊙ Racines
V2, France
Cool Parisian hip-hop beats, soulful voices and meaningful lyrics, blended with samples and reworkings of classic African pop hits and delivered with panache. High production values and a classy guestlist lifted this debut well above the norm. Three or four of the fifteen tracks here are all-time greats, and there are only a couple of duds. The album scored in a big way in France and quickly inspired a new generation of African-language rappers.

Bozi Boziana & Orchestre Anti-Choc

After quitting the Zaïko Langa Langa offshoot Choc Stars, Bozi Boziana created Anti-Choc to provide a faster power source for his energetic compositions. He combined his own melancholic voice with a succession of feisty female singers and sparkling instrumentalists.

⊙ Bozi Boziana – Bana Saint Gabriel
Sonima SM 1197
Bozi reunited with old Zaïko pal Evoloko Lay-Lay and Anti-Choc female singer Deyess Mukangi for this exquisite album that helped win him a Kora Award.

⊙ Bozi Boziana featuring Jolie Detta & Déesse, Vol. 1
⊙ Bozi Boziana featuring Déesse, Scola Miel & Betty, Vol. 2
Ngoyarto, France
Two CDs that collect a total of twenty of Bozi's greatest tracks performed with his Anti-Choc female vocalists.

Choc Stars

Founded in 1984 by Ben Nyamabo with musicians from Zaïko and Langa Langa Stars, Choc Stars developed a sound that was mellow yet passionate. The songs are generally slower than those of the other bands, but the arrangements add up to a cool, seductive *soukous* sound. They faded out in the early 1990s but singer Defao's Big Stars now carry the flag.

⊙ Les Merveilles du Passé, Choc Stars Vol. 3
FDB, France/Zaïre
Verging on the sleazy side of good taste with the right amount of studio ambience and production values that sustain the camp delivery, this collection does the group proud. "Celio" is particularly fine.

Kester Emeneya

As one of the original New Wave singers, Emeneya was a first generation *sapeur*, playing florid modern Congolese music as leader of Victoria Eleison.

⊙ King Kester Emeneya & Victoria Eleison Dream Team Dream Band – Mboka Mboka, Vols 1 & 2
BH Electronic, France
King Kester re-invents himself on this double CD by re-recording seven tunes including the magnificent "Kimpiatu" in a extended but stripped-down modern style that confirmed his status as one of the most exciting and creative bandleaders of the day.

Luciana & Ballou Canta

For ten years Luciana de Mingongo was a singer in Papa Wemba's Viva la Musica prior to founding the spectacular breakaway group Nouvelle Génération de la Republique Democratique. Ballou Canta has been a regular member of the internationally successful Soukous Stars and is one of the best-known Paris-based session singers.

⊙ Luciana & Ballou Canta – Rumba Lolango
Deux Rives Productions, France
In a similar way to how Kékélé have revived the classic rumba sound, *Rumba Lolango* brings together Cuban sounds with vintage Congolese rumba and subtle touches of *zouk* and funk.

Mose Se Sengo "Fan Fan"

A few decades ago, Fan Fan was playing guitar with Franco, writing some material and filling in for the big man at rehearsals and when Franco was unavailable. Following some hits of his own, he headed east to conquer Tanzania and Kenya. He moved to England in 1984.

⊙ The Congo Acoustic
Triple Earth, UK
On this album, the usual attitude is moderated and a more relaxed Fan Fan delivers contemplative, mellow music with an unplugged warmth. "Sikulu" pays urbane homage to Fela Kuti's Afro-beat, with horns chirruping politely

⊙ Bayekeleye
LAA, UK
Maintaining the gentle approach, this self-produced album offers relaxed guitar-picking and familiar-sounding repertoire in a less familiar style. There are vocal contributions from the great Josky (also one of Franco's frontmen) as well as Deyess, Ballou Canta and Luciana, and some smoky vibrato-laden saxophone.

Franco and OK Jazz

Franco – Le Grand Maître – is the outstanding figure in Congolese music, and perhaps even Africa's greatest ever star. His career encompassed more than 150 record releases and, since his death in 1989, there have been more than sixty compilations issued on Sonodisc alone, many of them bearing the titles of original discs but with completely different tracks. Following are just a few of the highlights.

⊙ Le Folklore de Chez Nous
Glenn, France
A twelve-track 72-minute collection reflecting Franco's Bakongo ethnicity with great songs ranging from the mid-1960s to the late 1980s.

⊙ Likambo Ya Ngana
Sonodisc, France

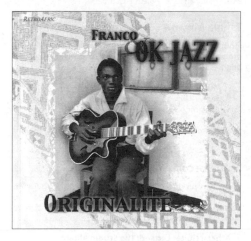

A classic 1971 release in which Franco reprises the 1940s accordion sound of Feruzi before grinding into some classic big-band rumba. Packed with exemplary guitar-picking.

⊙ Mabele
Sonodisc, France
A folklore treatment dating from 1974, including the classic title-track ballad composed by "vice-president" Simaro Lutumba and sung by Sam Mangwana.

Originalité
RetroAfric, UK
A terrific re-release of the very first recordings of OK Jazz. This was the point where classic rumba began the long journey into soukous. You enter OK, you leave very KO'd.

⊙ The Rough Guide to Franco
World Music Network, UK
This enjoyable dip into the massive Franco back-catalogue ranges from zippy 1950s merengues through dreamy 1960s and 70s rumbas up to 1980s OK Jazz big-band classics such as "Mario".

⊙ The Very Best of the Rumba Giant of Zaire
Manteca, UK
This compilation takes a similarly chronological approach, with less emphasis on biography and more on grooves. Includes the full quarter-hour version of Franco's opus "Attention na SIDA".

Evoloko Jocker

A classy singer with a taste for theatricality, Evoloko was one of the true eccentrics of the Zaïko Langa Langa family, making his mark with Langa Langa Stars.

⊙ Mingelina
FDB, France
A vocal curiosity so sweet it sticks to you, this was a fine, if belated, comeback release in the early 1990s.

Pepe Kalle

Pepe Kalle, "The Elephant", brought Empire Bakuba to the verge of true stardom during the 1980s. One of the most "typical" Kinshasa bands, Bakuba combined Kalle's husky voice with the stage antics of his dwarf friend, Emoro, and requisite wild guitars. Kalle is a crowd-pleaser, who remains, as they say, big in Africa.

⊙ Gigantafrique
GlobeStyle, UK
A collection that packs a double ration of Kalle dance tracks. Now somewhat dated, but it includes the original and biggest kwassa kwassa hit, "Pon Moun Paka Bougé".

Le Karma Pa

A former singer from Felix Wazekwa's band, Le Karma Pa is one of the bright new stars of modern Congolese music.

⊙ Le Karma Pa – Je M'Appelle Toi (Love Moi)
JOK Music, France
On this debut album, Le Karma Pa performs in a similar lush and romantic rumba style to that of Koffi Olomide. His second album is eagerly anticipated.

Kékélé

The lure of an African version of Buena Vista proved hard to ignore, and Kékélé came closest to achieving a global crossover hit with Rumba Congo on the Sterns label.

⊙ Congo Life
Sterns, UK
Their second album carries on the momentum of the first, even without Papa Noel. Syran Mbenza takes on the guitar master's role with style and polish in what is in effect an acoustic Four Stars project. The series of releases is set to continue.

Wendo Kolosoyi

The venerable Antoine Wendo Kolosoyi is one of Congo music's original maringa/rumba heroes, though he lay dormant for decades. He co-wrote and recorded "Marie Louise" with Henri Bowane and both went on to develop the song in totally different directions. Wendo's comeback album appeared almost fifty years later, on the Indigo label.

⊙ Amba
Marabi, France
This follow-up to the Indigo release is a collection of timeless new songs and more nostalgic reminders of Congo music's past glories.

Konono No. 1

Founded more than 25 years ago, but only now gaining wider recognition, this amazing group draw on traditional Bazombo trance music.

⊙ Congotronics
Crammed, Belgium
This ground-breaking album has to be heard to be believed. The rough, scratchy, homemade urban trance music has a unique charm and boundless energy. Crudely amplified likembes and scrapyard percussion generate the momentum while vocalists call up their ancestors through rusty old Tannoy speakers. This is typical of the neotraditional sound that echoes off corrugated iron and breeze blocks in Africa's biggest shanty town.

Alain Makaba

He was the original guitarist and musical arranger of Wenge Musica but when that group started to split up into different rival factions he withdrew from live performance and eventually moved into production.

⊙ Alain Makaba – Ya Ku Dominer
Simon Music, France
In 2004, Makaba recorded his second solo album, which was a classy comeback disc with melodic and straightforward guitar-led rumba.

Sam Mangwana

Sam Mangwana formulated his own "international" sound in Abidjan after quitting the Rochereau/Franco nexus. With his African All Stars he took on the world with *soukous*-based pan-African pop.

Maria Tebbo
Stern's, UK
From the first excited guitar licks, your feet will want to move. This is delightful, positive, enduring music of the first order, recorded in the optimistic late 1970s.

Les Maquis de Maison Mère

This group of breakaways from the Werrason faction of Wenge Musica is fronted by Fere Gola, Bill Clinton and Serge Mabiala.

⊙ Faites vos prieries miracles
Simon, France
This double CD is the group's first and maybe only release, as they are thought to have folded soon after. The album offers quality songs, precision vocals and sharp guitars with superb production and a great live sound – all of which made it stand out from the competition in the mid-2000s.

Defao Matumona

A former member of Grand Zaïko WaWa and Choc Stars, this classy singer and exceptional dancer broke away to lead his own group Big Stars, where he became the king of the *ndombolo* style.

⊙ Senchal Defao – Nessy de London
JPS, France
A fabulous millennial release from one of the Congo's most controlled vocalists. Includes his tribute to the late Pepe Kalle.

Antoine Moundanda

A consummate master of the giant thumb piano, from Congo-Brazzaville, Antoine Moundanda learnt the instrument as a therapeutic device for chasing evil spirits out of the afflicted.

⊙ Likembé Géant
Indigo, France
A live showcase for Moundanda's agile thumbs and those of his elderly accomplices. It's fascinating to hear these lush, equatorial sounds – which, adapted to guitar, were a key ingredient in the birth of *soukous*.

J.B. Mpiana

This Wenge Musica leader now calls his group Wenge BCBG. His main rival Werrason leads another great outfit called Wenge Musica Maison Mére.

⊙ JB Mpiana & Wenge BCBG – Anti-Terro
Badive, France
It took J.B. three years to come up with a follow-up to his *Internet* CD – and the result is a double disc with plenty of sweet guitar and some great ensemble vocals.

Tshala Mwana

From dancing girl to queen of *mutuashi*, Tshala's career progressed smoothly during the 1980s, making her the brightest female lead in the country.

★Mutuashi
Stern's, UK
An outstanding set of *mutuashi* songs with an irresistible driving pulse that pushes the funk-folk rhythm of the Baluba people into the Afro-Cuban realm. It's a whole lot different from the steam-rolling guitars of *soukous*.

Jean Bosco Mwenda

Bosco was picking out delicate melodies on his guitar in his own two-finger style in the Katanga province of the Belgian Congo in the late 1940s. It is cleaner cut and more reflective than the Kinshasa style.

⊙ African Guitar Legend: The Studio Album
Rounder, US
This great release includes "Masanga", the song that introduced Bosco to an international audience via an early WOMAD compilation cassette. Listen and melt.

Nouvelle Génération

These ex-Wemba musicians kept the New Wave rolling on. The band was short-lived, but their perky, confident handling of Kinshasa street rhythms brought a blast of fresh air in the mid-1990s.

⊙ Porokondo
FDB, France
The group's hot second album still swings the feet into action.

Koffi Olomide and Quartier Latin

Since learning his trade in Papa Wemba's Viva la Musica, Koffi has combined a distinctive, smoochy style of singing with dynamic arrangements that are instantly recognizable. During the 1990s he grew to become probably the most popular artist in Central Africa.

V-12
Sonodisc, France
Koffi's *tour de force* – he even announced it in 1996 as his last release before retiring (a wind-up, of course). Here he concentrates on vocal delivery and smooth arrangements with less emphasis on the frenzied sebens served up by his band Quartier Latin. The only frustration is that these great

songs have been truncated so as to squeeze a dozen tracks on the CD.

Tabu Ley Rochereau

Ley's voice shone out from African Jazz, African Fiesta and Afrisa, making him the country's favourite singer for a time. But his career slumped following his bust-up with Mbilia Bel and subsequent problems with the old regime. He has since reopened contacts with the new Congo, but so far no comeback has been forthcoming.

⊙ Rochereau & L'Afrisa International – 1971–77
Sonodisc, France

Much of Rochereau's best material remains unreleased on CD, but this collection includes six tracks from the famous Festac 77 disc in which Tabu Ley's Afrisa was augmented by leading youth band Zaïko Langa Langa, plus five earlier Rochereau hits.

Ryco Jazz

Founded by Franco's first bandleader, Bowane, Ryco Jazz left Congo in 1959, just before independence, for a tour of West Africa and stayed on the road as a quartet or quintet for eleven years. The band combined Congolese music with rock'n'roll and Latin/Caribbean grooves.

⊙ Rumba'round Africa
RetroAfric, UK

Ringing guitar and jive action with catchy songs in French, Spanish, Lingala and pidgin English.

Swede Swede

For a while, in 1989, it looked as if a whole new folk-loric genre was about to re-define Congolese music – with Swede Swede at the forefront. But the group fell into the familiar trap of splitting up once too often, then hanging out in Europe for too long. One of the few Congolese bands without guitars.

⊙ Toleki Bango
Cramworld, Belgium

The band's first CD on the Belgian label. It doesn't quite capture the rowdy energy of a live show, but it marks an interesting attempt to take Congolese music in a new direction.

Papa Wemba

As a member of the original Zaïko line-up, Wemba helped set the pace of modern Congolese music. Then, with the establishment of Viva la Musica, he refreshed it with hardcore folkloric rhythms and churning guitars, before setting a smoother course with his solo career, accompanied by Molokai, a band assembled with the international market in mind.

★ Papa Wemba
Stern's, UK

Wemba's unique, yearning, almost hymn-like voice is his greatest asset. On this stylish 1988 outing, still one of his best albums, Rigo Star's guitar work bursts through.

⊙ Dernier coup de sifflet/Epeak Ekomi na Douzieme Espiode
Americano/ FDB, France

A mellow foray with the late Stervos Niarchos (the *sapeur* crown prince to Papa's king), who composed a couple of tasty rumba ballads for the occasion. Recommended but hard to find.

PLAYLIST
Congo

1 COOPERATION Franco & Sam Mangwana from *The Rough Guide to Congolese Soukous*
A classic, from the first bars of the rousing guitar intro to the pure joy of the pair's vocal duelling and the passion of the seben.

2 MABELE Franco & OK Jazz from *Mabele*
A long, slow-talking blues written by "le Poet" Simaro Lutumba and sung emotionally by Sam Mangwana.

3 EL MANICERO Bantous de la Capitale from *El Manicero*
The all-time classic "Peanut Vendor", reprised here by two of Congo's finest saxophonists and co-founders of this Brazzaville institution.

4 L'UNION Bisso na Bisso from *Racines*
It's rap, but not as we know it. This mature, melodic and respectful track sums up the quality of Passi's Parisian posse.

5 SENTIMENT AWA Zaïko Langa Langa from *Sentiment Awa – Essesse*
Fine melody, great harmonies and wild passion.

6 TWIST WITH THE DOCTEUR Ry-Co Jazz from *Rumba'round Africa*
A Congolese take on 1960s rockabilly which adds humour to the Dr Nico-esque export rumba.

7 CELIO Choc Stars from *Les Merveilles du Passé, Choc Stars Vol 3*
Sweet and soft, this marks the high spot for a formidable team of *soukous* crooners.

8 LUFUA NDONGA Konono No. 1 from *Congotronics*
Smash-bang low-tech interpretation of timeless ancestral music – for shaking up preconceptions.

9 MALI YA MUNGU Mose Fan Fan from *Bayekeleye*
Gentle, introspective, semi-acoustic treatment of a typical Kikongo ballad by the one-time hard man of Congo guitar.

10 SAMBA Lita Bembo from *Kita Mata ABC*
Lita goes wild at the mike, while Stukas crank up the excitement level to fever pitch.

⊙ Mwana Molokai
Sterns, UK

When Stern's released Wemba's first international album in 1983, the eccentric entertainer was already a major star in Africa. Here the UK label provides a double CD packed with twenty years' worth of Viva la Musica, one of the most awesome groups ever to come out of Kinshasa.

Wenge Musica

Wenge Musica came to prominence in 1988 under the musical direction of multi-instrumentalist Alain Makaba but never improved on the excitement of their original release. Moving to Europe, where the band split in two, was part of their downfall.

⊙ Bouger Bouger
Natari, UK

Their debut album, since remastered in England. It's high-grade modern Kinshasa music with classy segues, synths and a nice line in shouting.

⊙ Alain Makaba – Ya Ku Dominer
Simon Music, France

The former guitarist and musical arranger with Wenge Musica made this classy 2004 comeback album with melodic and straightforward guitar-led rumba.

Thu Zahina

The New Wave started here. Formed in 1967 by a group of high-school students, Thu Zahina was the first "pop group" to challenge the big Congo bands. As wild as they were young, the boys bent rumba into a pop format.

⊙ Coup de Chapeau
RetroAfric, UK

Guitars wail and reverberate, stretching the confines of classic rumba, and the recently discovered snare-drum rattles like a calabash of cowries. Seminal, soul-stirring stuff.

Zaïko Langa Langa

From the end of the 1960s, the Zaïko extended family was the driving force of the guitar-powered "new generation".

⊙ Sentiment Awa – Essesse
Ngoyarto, France

Collection of 7" tracks from 1975–81 – the second Belle époque of Zaïko, in which they refined their old raunchy sound into a new "velvet chorus" style. The album includes the voices of Nyoka Longo, Evoloko, Bozi Boziana, Bimi Ombale and Lengi Lenga.

⊙ Jetez L'Éponge
Carerre, France

A Kinshasa classic from the *madiaba* era – 1989 – this is Nyoka Longo's response to the Zaïko split-up. Probably their strongest album yet, with hard guitars, thoughtful arrangement and powerful ambience.

Côte d'Ivoire

zouglou to cut'n'run

Dobet Gnaoré, a rising star in France
Contre Jour

The city of Abidjan, a modern metropolis with the rough, grey Atlantic on one side and cocoa plantations and savannah on the other, was once the capital of West Africa's recording industry. Those days are gone, even though Côte d'Ivoire still hosts the biennial MASA festival. Civil war hastened the decline of the economy, and although a fragile peace accord is currently in force, many of the country's leading musicians remain based amid the expatriate commmunity in Paris. François Bensignor, Brooke Wentz and Soro Solo recall past glories and report on the latest developments.

For many years after the wave of independence that swept the continent in the 1960s, Côte d'Ivoire was the musical crossroads of West Africa. After a heady period during the 1970s, when artists from all over the continent came and settled here, the country gradually began to decline, and it has been some time now since it was an obligatory stopover for African artists.

The major record labels such as Ebony Records, DC Productions, S.I.D (Société Ivoirienne du Disque) and SACODIS, as well as large distributors such as Maison du Disque, Ludo Musique, Studio 33, Shakara Musique and Badmos Record, have withdrawn one by one since the mid-1980s. And yet the country has given birth to movements such as *zouglou* and nurtured artists of world standing such as **Alpha Blondy**, **Tiken Jah Fakoly** and **Magic System**. Despite these individual success stories, the home market has withered.

As if this wasn't bad enough, the outbreak of war in September 2002 really spelt the death knell for the Ivorian music industry. Koné Dodo from Alpha Blondy Production says that the business has lost sixty percent of its market share, while Constant Anagonou of Showbiz, the biggest cassette producer, estimates a loss of around seventy percent. **Piracy** has increased sharply, and it's estimated that an appalling eighty percent of the national output is being pirated. A good number of respected recording studios such as **Néfertiti** have disappeared, giving way to home studios, which thrive in popular neighbourhoods in Yopougon, Marcory and Abobo-Gare. **JBZ** is the only studio from the old days that has managed to survive. Located in lush, palmy Cocody, it is one of the oldest studios in West Africa. A one-room facility, JBZ has been responsible for some of the best African recordings, including releases by Nahawa Doumbia, Pepe Kalle, Sam Mangwana and Lokassa.

A number of other factors have also contributed to Côte d'Ivoire losing its position as the epicentre of the West African music industry. These include the opening of studios in Senegal and Burkina Faso, the establishment of distribution networks in Mali, Benin and Togo and the growth of the market in many other West African countries – as well as changes in fashion.

Live and Local

Côte d'Ivoire is home to more than sixty native ethnic groups, and more than a hundred others that have migrated here. Among them, some have distinctive musical traditions. In the centre of the country, the **Baoulé**, who came from Ghana, developed a characteristic **vocal polyphony**, famous all over Côte d'Ivoire. Northeastern **Lobi** have strong **xylophone** traditions. In the north, **Senoufo** have intense initiation and funeral ceremonies, from which **Aïcha Koné**, a long-time local star, has borrowed and modernized the **poro** rhythm.

Rising star **Dobet Gnaoré** is a Marseille-based artist who sings in eight languages including Dida, Dioula and Baoulé. She was trained in the artists' village of Ki-Yi Mbock in Abidjan, where in 1996 she met Colin Laroche de Féline, with whom she formed the group **Ano Néko** ("Let's create together" in Dioula). Ki-Yi's artistic focus has always been accompanied by the cultivation of moral values and an acute awareness of the continent's ills. The community's teaching puts great emphasis on addressing African identity, the condition of women, the horrors of war and social inequalities. Such matters provide the inspiration for Gnaoré and her partner's lyrics.

In the west of the country the **Dan** have a very impressive mask tradition. From the southwest traditions, **Zagazougou** borrowed **gombe polyrhythmics**. On the southeast coastal area, **Appollo** people use **edongole talking drums** for their annual ritual *abissa* purification dance. The musician **Meiway** (see box opposite) has taken up *abissa* from his people's coastal traditions as well as *grolo*, *fanfare* and *sidder*, to create his sweet and sensual white-handkerchief **zoblazo dance** – one of the most impressive stage acts from the Ivorian scene. But these attempts to bring authentic Ivorian traditional sounds into modern music continue to be subverted by mainstream Afro-pop and Afro-*zouk* productions with drum machine and synthesizer backing.

In the 1960s, with Côte d'Ivoire newly independent, **Baoulé artists** were heard from transistor radios in every bar. The twin vocal sounds of the **Soeurs Comöé** were partly driven by the local *gbégbé* rhythm. Then, in the 1970s, the new dynamism of **Sery Simplice** and his **Frères Djatys** bubbled up, based around the same heavy-duty *gbégbé* rhythm. Today's veteran of the local scene, **Bally Spinto**, still plays a modern music strongly rooted in *gbégbé*.

Some of these first-generation artists still make good music, like **Anoman Brou Félix**, **François Lougah** or composer **Jimmy Hyacinthe**, who created the *goly*. Another celebrity of the 1960s, **Mamadou Doumbia**, toured all over West Africa and even the US. Today, he prefers to live the poor life of the simple people in Abidjan, rather than use his vocal skills to serve the new rap trend, as some producers urge him to. He has set up a home

One-Way Ticket to the Top

Meiway, a.k.a Frédéric Désiré Ehui, lives in Grand-Bassam, a coastal town east of Abidjan. He is from the N´Zema ethnic group (also known as Appollo), which is dominant in the southwest of Côte d'Ivoire. From an early age, he was steeped in the music of Bassam folk bands that his parents were involved with, learning how to play percussion and joining different choirs. As a student, he moved to Abidjan, joining several bands of young musicians in the bustling neighbourhood of Treichville. It was with the band **Les Génitaux**, who were named Best Young Ivorian Band in 1981, that he first met with fame.

In 1985, he arrived in Paris and created the **Défense d´Ivoire Groupe**, which won a prize in 1987. Then, in 1989, Meiway recorded his first album, *Ayiibebou* ("Swing one´s hips" in the Appollo language), which contains the early beginnings of **zoblazo**, a music and a groove inspired by traditional Grand Bassam rhythms. In 1990, this album won him the "Best Ivory Coast Singer" award, but it was only with his second CD, *200% Zoblazo* (1992), that Meiway became a star outside his native country.

If you haven´t seen a whole stadium audience standing up as soon as the first chords of "200% Zoblazo" are played, dancing like crazy, waving white handkerchiefs and singing the chorus until they are hoarse, you don´t know what "vibes" means. Now ten albums into his career, Meiway shows an ever-increasing degree of professionalism, consolidating his position as Côte d'Ivoire's most popular artist.

Soro Solo

Lusafrica

---

studio and continues to help young musicians get started, charging ten times less for a demo tape than most other outfits around town.

Ziglibithy

The real father of modern Ivorian pop is the internationally renowned **Ernesto Djédjé**. He consciously took a traditional rhythm of the Bété people as a base on which to build the frenzied guitar sound of his **ziglibithy**, putting dancers in a joyous trance all around Africa and further afield. Everyone in Côte d'Ivoire thanks him for giving the country its first modern musical identity.

Djédjé's teacher, local 1960s star **Amédée Pierre**, had himself used a strong Congolese rumba flavour in his self-titled **dopé** style. But seven years after he had left Amédée's band Ivoiro-Stars, Djédjé declared in a radio interview in 1975, that he didn't like the "Congolization" of Ivorian music. In 1977, Djédjé's album *Gnoantre-Ziboté*, recorded in Nigeria, was an instant hit throughout West and Central Africa, and crossed the oceans to Paris and Montréal. His early hit "Ziboté" resurfaced on the excellent 2005 compilation *Golden Afrique Vol. 1*. Djédjé's sudden death at the age of 35, while recording his sixth album, made him a legend.

A great many musicians have tried to follow in his footsteps, but none of them has achieved quite the same sucess. The late **Gnaore Djimi**'s *polihet* style, or **Luckson Padaud**'s *laba laba* – both deriving directly from ziglibithy and keeping up its traditional Bété spirit in today's society – can still be a great experience for any listener or dancer trying to get close to that deep African feeling. If you want to hear this music live in Abidjan, you'll find it in the far northern suburb of Yopougon, where it gave birth to the fresh **zouglou** rhythm.

Zouglou

Zouglou emerged in the early 1990s during a university crisis brought about by the aged President Houphouët-Boigny – the man who spent US$200m building a Vatican-style church as a gift for the Pope while students were turned into squatters on the university campuses. In the Baoulé language, they say "Be ti le zouglou" (stacked like a rubbish heap) to describe student life in **Yopougon**, where four people share one miserable single student room.

This is the place where the satirical and ironic zouglou music began, danced as a form of appeal to some fictitious god, crammed with humorous lyrics exposing the harsh reality of student life. **Didier Billé**, the unrivalled zouglou leader, soon became the focus of his generation with his caustic, witty songs. Fellow students raised money to enable him to record with his band **Les Parents du Campus**, who met with dazzling success when they appeared on the "Podium" TV programme.

The most interesting thing in zouglou is that it has created a new language that combines French, pidgin and Baoulé words given special meanings. Students have a lot of fun developing their own dictionary: *caillou* or *peeble* – to vandalize property; *coco* – a student who lives off his friends; *koun* – drunk; *libérer* – to liberate, or in other words, to dance zouglou.

The zouglou craze was at its peak in the mid-1990s, spreading to Burkina Faso and even to Mali.

Although it was overtaken first by mapouka and subsequently *coupé décalé* in Côte d'Ivoire, it is still very popular, mostly because of its sharp lyrics. Didier Billé remains a major figure, but with his move to Paris he has loosened his grip on zouglou jive. Zouglou has been an outlet for protest and disaffection among Ivorian youngsters for fifteen years and its leading exponents are now **Les Garagistes**, **Soum Bill** and above all, consistent chart-toppers **Magic System**.

Reggae and Rap

For the past two decades, reggae has played a leading role in Côte d'Ivoire's music scene. **Alpha Blondy**, who like many Ivorian artists sings in Dioula, the Mande trading language, was the first on the African scene to use reggae as a means to express his concerns to African urban youth. Born Seydou Koné, his life is something of a legend. He never knew his natural father, and grew up playing French pop and rock as a teenager. He discovered reggae when he was 20 at a Burning Spear concert in New York and began to experiment with the music and Rastafarianism. Taken back to Côte d'Ivoire, he was locked up by his stepfather, but

Jak Kilby

Ivorian dread, Tiken Jah Fakoly

managed to escape and change his name to Alpha Blondy. In 1983, Fulgence Kassy turned him into an instant urban star when he invited Blondy to appear on his TV programme *First Chance*. Signing with EMI France in 1984, he recorded in Jamaica at the Tuff Gong studio with the Wailers, then gained international recognition with some powerful stage performances with his band **The Solar System**.

Based in Paris for years, Blondy settled back in Abidjan in the mid-1990s. His flourishing record and stage career boosted reggae's appeal in Côte d'Ivoire, with many reggae singers attempting to emulate his success. Some, like **Ismaël Isaac**, have achieved a certain international success; others, like **Serge Kassy**, are well received on the local scene. **Tiken Jah Fakoly**, the most popular new reggae singer in Abidjan, is now making his presence felt abroad with messages of unity and good acoustic arrangements. Together with Alpha Blondy, Fakoly is the driving force behind African reggae, having acquired an ever-growing international following and a number of awards since the runaway success of his third album, *Mangécratie*, released in 1996.

Tiken's music is inspired by the Yagba of the Malinké in Odienné in northern Côte d'Ivoire, where he grew up. His work bears witness to the suffering of his fellow citizens and is rooted in the reality of a country torn apart by strife. He addresses the general malaise in Africa and roundly condemns the iniquities of globalization. Tiken is a non violent rebel who denounces the ineptness of African despots, their Western masters and the multinationals who pillage the continent. The sharpness of his lyrics and the thorny issues he tackles have made him the mouthpiece of young Africans, who have been waiting for some sort of concrete action from African politicians for over forty years.

As for **rap**, despite the fact that hip-hop was growing among Côte d'Ivoire's youth from the mid-1990s on, local producers showed little interest in making albums. Until that is, a sell-out concert at one of Abidjan's biggest venues, the Palais des Congrès, where the two local leaders of the rap scene met in a challenge. After this event, rap was taken more seriously by the local music businessmen, with artists like **All Mighty**, **Angelo** and **RAS** among the more prominent stars. However, in recent years, Côte d'Ivoire's rap scene has been all but eclipsed by another local phenomenon...

Cut'n'run

Coupé-décalé music burst onto the scene in a war-torn Côte d'Ivoire and is all about having a good time and a flash lifestyle. In *Noushi*, the language invented by street kids in Côte d'Ivoire, "coupé-décalé" means to "get rich quick by any means and then do a runner". Given the somewhat dubious nature of the phenomenon and the outlook of its creators and devotees, this new Ivorian movement has had a rather wary reception. The music is neither poetic nor militant and makes no claims for itself. Its sole aim is to entertain and offer fans the chance to show off their designer-label clothes and flash their money about in public.

In spite of this extremely frivolous and unconventional image, coupé-décalé has been all the rage on the dance floor since the summer of 2003, is growing all the time and is popular throughout West Africa. It's purely a nightclub invention. Under **DJ Jacob**, who is credited with starting the craze, the phenomenon took off in the Nelson in 2000 and then caught on in the Atlantis and the Alizée – all black nightclubs in Paris.

Coupé-décalé consists of a computerized circular beat coupled with Ivorian rhythms, rounded off with samples of *ndombolo*, the popular Congolese style. The lyrics, essentially a stream of Noushi onomatopoeia and metaphors, are inspired by the *griot* tradition and celebrate those nightclub customers who throw the most money about. A group of these Ivorian clubbers, well known on the Paris scene, formed a club calling itself the **Jet-Set** – a sort of collective of prominent consumers and "donors" who go to all the coupé-décalé evenings, flinging into the air twenty- and even fifty-euro notes. It's similar to the 1980s **sapeur** phenomenon (see Congo chapter).

It was **Douk Saga**, one of the members of the Jet-Set, who made the first coupé-décalé recording in 2003, called "Sagacité", stealing a march on DJ Jacob in Paris and his alter ego, DJ Kaloudji in Abidjan. Today there are more than twenty coupé-décalé DJ-singers and the genre represents around forty per cent of Côte d'Ivoire's musical output. Congo and the Democratic Republic of Congo have their own leading coupé-décalé DJs: DJ Zidane and TV Cinq, respectively.

The best-known DJs are **DJ Jacob**, **DJ Kaloudji**, **Douk Saga**, **Serpent Noir**, **DJ Arafat**, **Innocent Versace** and the **Résistance DJ collective**, each selling in the tens of thousands. The first coupé-décalé compilation appeared in 2005 and the first big-venue outing was at the Bataclan in Paris in April that year. This was followed by a tour of France, Switzerland, Italy and Germany.

⊙ **Anthology of World Music: the Dan**
Rounder, US
Rare insight into the music of one of the country's most culturally exciting ethnic groups – part of the southern Mande language group, famed for their exhilarating mask dances. Originally released on vinyl by Bärenreiter Musicaphon, the detailed booklet documents their music culture as it was in the early 1960s. Songs, percussion and an amazing orchestra of six ivory trumpets.

⊙ **Ivoir' Compil Vol. 9 "Spécial DJ Côte d'Ivoire"**
Africa Productions, France
Entirely devoted to coupé-décalé, this brings together fourteen tracks from the best-known DJs and is particularly good for clubs and parties.

★ **Maxi Ivoire**
Déclic, France
A 2-CD compilation released in 1997, showing a wide panorama of Abidjan's productions at that time. Moving from Afro-*zouk* star Monique Seka to king of *polihet* Gnaore Djimi, it also includes music from popular young zouglou band Les Poussins Chocs.

Angelo

Angelo is Côte d'Ivoire's main rap star, and presenter of the local hip-hop TV show.

⊙ **Represent**
Showbiz, Côte d'Ivoire
Accomplished rap and ragga sung in English and French, plus some more interesting material in Adioukou using some deep traditional percussion and singing styles.

Nyanka Bell

With her splendid voice, Bell – half-Corsican, half-Touareg – was nicknamed the "African Barbara Streisand" as a teenage singer in the Orchestre Radio Télévision Ivoirienne (RTI).

⊙ **Visa**
Sonodisc, France
Bell has always been influenced by American soul and soft funk, but this well-produced album, recorded in Paris and sung in a variety of different languages, shows her wide range.

Alpha Blondy

After his first record, "Brigadier Sabari", was an instant hit in 1983, Blondy became the leader of a powerful West African reggae movement and the voice of a generation. He is still, with South Africa's Lucky Dube, the best known African reggae star.

Jak Kilby

Alpha Blondy

☉ Akwaba: The Very Best of Alpha Blondy
EMI International, France

This 2005 album features sixteen of the greatest hits from thirteen albums spanning Alpha Blondy's career. Blondy invited UB 40 and young musicians, including Magic System, to join him.

Les Garagistes

It wasn't until their third album *Titrologie* sold around 100,000 copies that Les Garagistes found success, but they have been one of the most popular zouglou groups for fifteen years now.

☉ Tapis Rouge
Showbiz/Melodie, France

This second album from the garage mechanics of Yoougon, a working-class neighbourhood in Abidjan, is in praise of zouglou, the protest music that evolved among young Ivorians in the early 1990s.

Dobet Gnaoré/Ano Néko

Gnaoré has a beautiful voice and also dances and plays several acoustic instruments. Ano Néko ("let's create together") is the duo formed with her husband, guitarist Colin Laroche de Féline.

☉ Ano Néko (Créons Ensemble)
Contre-Jour, Belgium

This 2004 album is both urban and traditional. Socially concerned lyrics are set to arrangements featuring electric and acoustic instruments, gourds, *balafon*, *aoko*, bells and percussion.

Ismaël Isaac

Inspired by Alpha Blondy, the sweet-voiced Isaac has gone on to develop a style of his own.

☉ Treich Feeling
Misslin, France

After three local cassettes, Isaac recorded for the Sylla label in 1990 and Island in 1993. With a third CD in 1996, this is evidence of his increasing popularity and talent.

Aïcha Koné

Koné sang in the 1970s with the RTI Orchestra, initially under the leadership of Boncana Maïga, then Manu Dibango, becoming one of the first international female pop singers from Côte d'Ivoire.

★ Adouma
Bolibana, France

Recorded in 1983 under the artistic guidance of guitarist Jimmy Hyacinthe, this album shows a mature artist achieving fulfilment as one of the great performers of African song.

Magic System

Magic System was formed in 1996 during a school sports competition. The beautiful voice and biting lyrics of A'Salfo lend this group a distinctive character. They are zouglou's leading band.

☉ Cessa Kiè La Vérité
Virgin, France

The most recent release by the four Abidjan musicians is a cocktail of zouglou, reggae, dancehall and tropical-style electro. Singing in their native language and in French, the group

PLAYLIST
Côte d'Ivoire

1 **ATALAKU MÉGA** DJ Jacob from *Ivoir'Compil Vol. 9 "Spécial DJ Côte-d'Ivoire"*
In Ivorian-French creole, DJ Jacob sings the praises of the men who give their money away and eggs them on to even greater largesse.

2 **N'SIELÉ** Dobet Gnaoré from *Ano Néko (Créons Ensemble)*
Profoundly affected by the civil war in the Congo, Dobet Gnaoré and Colin Laroche de Féline wrote this song to denounce all the wars tearing Africa apart.

3 **IVOILIEN** Les Garagistes from *Tapis Rouge*
Using French lyrics, Les Garagistes sing fondly about their country, sadly destabilized by the war that broke out in 2002.

4 **PETIT POMPIER** Magic System from *Cessa Kiè La Vérité*
The story of a peasant who finds himself a mistress in the capital, only to get back to his village to discover his wife has also been cheating on him and has gone off with a younger man.

5 **KKMOU PRUDENCIA** Meiway from *Golgotha*
Despite claiming there is no war in Côte d'Ivoire, Meiway sides with the powers that be and denounces the rebels.

6 **MONDIALISATION** Soum Bill from *Terres des Hommes*
Soum Bill criticizes the globalization that is sapping Africa of its vitality and makes it poorer and poorer while the well-off are getting richer and richer.

7 **PLUS RIEN NE M'ÉTONNE** Tiken Jah Fakoly from *Coup de Gueule*
A heartfelt cry of indignation at how the Western powers have divided the world and keep Africa disunited and fragmented.

8 **BANANA** Alpha Blondy from *Akwaba: The Very Best of Alpha Blondy*
A cry to the African peoples to produce more food crops than cash crops in order to make sure they have enough to eat.

protests against the indifference of big business and pokes fun at several local figures.

Meiway

Meiway created *zoblazo* in the early 1990s, borrowing traditional Appollo dance rhythms, but making abundant use of digital instruments. He has created a powerful stage act with his group Zo Gang.

⭐ **200% Zoblazo**
Sonodisc, France

Released in 1991, *200% Zoblazo* was a hit all over West Africa and still remains some DJs' favourite track for waking up sleepy dancers. Play loud, dance and wave a white handkerchief!

⊙ **Golgotha**
Lusafrica, France

The tenth album in a career that has lasted fifteen years.

Monique Séka

Making her first appearance on the Abidjan scene in the mid-1980s with her Afro-*zouk* style, Séka's fame now extends not only to Africa but also the Caribbean and other African diasporas.

⊙ **Okaman**
Déclic, France

Released in 1995, this album earned Séka an African Music Award, a best performance award at Ngwomo 1996 and platinum sales in her home country.

Soum Bill

Soum Bill started out as the lead singer and composer of the group Mini-Choc, then Les Garagistes, and finally Les Salopards before launching his own solo career in 2000 with the album *Zambakro*.

⊙ **Terre des Hommes**
Africa-Productions, France

Soum Bill's second solo album won the "Prix Spécial du Jury" at the Kora Awards in South Africa. The lyrics deal with social problems and plead with Ivorians to work to improve their country.

Tiken Jah Fakoly

Tiken has made a name for himself as a protest singer. With his powerful and sharp reggae songs, he sees himself as the mouthpiece for young Africans, let down by the continent's politicians.

⊙ **Coup de Gueule**
Barclay, France

His second album sings out against all forms of injustice, American imperialism and the disaster that is African politics, calling for a united Africa.

Equatorial Guinea

malabo blues

Las Hijas del Sol
Marc Masschelin/fRoots

The problems facing musicians in Equatorial Guinea, isolated by thirty years of corrupt dictatorship and blighted by extreme poverty, are countless. There are few places to perform, a severe lack of instruments and recording equipment and no real market for cassettes, while the only radio station is run by the president's close family. Sadly, the discovery of oil in the 1990s has only led to an increase in corruption and a greater divide between the ruling elite and the poor majority. Nor has it translated into an improvement in the conditions for cultural expression – it's still the Equato-Guinean diaspora in Madrid and elsewhere that is most active as far as recordings are concerned. Spanish record-label chief Manuel Dominguez surveys the scene at home and abroad.

There is no doubt that Equatorial Guinea, formerly Spain's only colony in sub-Saharan Africa, has a rich selection of musics. You can hear them on the compilation cassette *Calles de Malabo*, which showcases the music of the country's dominant ethnic groups. And you can hear it in the capital city, Malabo, where people ease the pain of a repressive regime with a thriving nightlife based around beer and music. After 10pm, music of all kinds thumps out from the city's social thoroughfare, Calle Nigeria, which throngs with bars, cafés and stalls. Discovering just what it is that you're hearing, however, is a little trickier: this is one of the world's less-documented musics, and, come to that, nations.

Equatorial Guinea is a rather strange construct, comprising three formerly Spanish-owned areas of sub-Saharan Africa: Bioko (formerly Fernando Pó), a lush little volcanic island off the coast of Cameroon; Rio Muni, a strip of mainland Africa sandwiched between Cameroon and Gabon; and the tiny island of Annobón, far out in the Atlantic. For the most part, the territories consist of thick rainforest. All in all, they have a population of 400,000, governed (if that's the word) from Malabo, on Bioko island.

The Spanish handed over power in 1968 to Macias Nguema, a mild-mannered civil servant who rapidly degenerated into a murderous dictator. By the late 1970s, a third of the population had fled the country, disappeared or been killed. After a coup in 1979, Nguema senior was replaced by his nephew Lt-Col Obiang Nguema, who, while not exhibiting the same genocidal tendencies, has nonetheless starred in a number of Amnesty International reports. (He was also the focus of the infamous 2003 coup attempt in which the CIA, M16 and the Spanish government were all implicated.)

Fang Traditions

There are many distinct languages and cultures in Equatorial Guinea, including Ndowe (on the mainland coast), Annobónese (from Annobón island), Combe, Bujeba and Bisio. However, the largest ethnic group is the **Fang**, who originally lived only on the mainland but have emigrated to Bioko in such numbers that their language and culture now dominate the island, while the **Bubi**, the island's indigenous language group, are in decline.

The Fang have a vigorous song tradition, in which the main accompanying instrument is the **mvet**, a harp-zither fashioned from a gourd, a palm-leaf stem and, for the strings, woven plant fibre. *Mvet*-players have evolved a musical notation disclosed only to initiates of the *bebom-mvet* society, a kind of fraternity of *griots* responsible for maintaining folk traditions. Like the *kora* in Mali, the *mvet* has a two-sided bridge, is plucked with both hands and is used to accompanying epic history songs.

Another important form of traditional music is that of **chorus and drum groups**. Most villages, plantations and urban barrios have such an ensemble. Dressed in traditional, two-piece straw outfits, the members sing in an engaging call-and-response style.

Pop Styles

The dominant popular genre in Equatorial Guinea is Cameroonian **makossa**, though Congolese **soukous** is also popular, as is Western-style rock. But the country does have homegrown styles, too. The colonial heritage has left its musical mark in the form of acoustic hybrids of local and Spanish musics in which guitars play an important role. The finest exponents of this style are **Desmali y su Grupo Dambo de la Costa**. Hailing from the remote island of Annobón but now based in Malabo, they are legendary throughout the nation. Desmali's voice is delightful – sweet but with a ragged edge – and he's a great guitar player to boot. Percussion and vocal harmonies complete the formula. Another good acoustic group is **Dambo de La Costa**, whose particular version of the recipe includes a *pandero* frame drum.

There are many other active artists in the country. They range widely in terms of their musical goals (**Luna Loca**, from the backwater of Bata, mix song with theatre, while artists such as **Elvis Romeo**, from Annobón, combine local rhythms with modern styles such as hip-hop, merengue and reggaeton). They range equally widely in terms of style and subject matter (from **Samuelin**'s delirious song about polygamy to **Chiquitin**'s version of Jimmy Cliff's "The Harder they Come"). And they range widely, too, in terms of their ethnic group: **Maruja and Yoli Miski** are Fang, **Ngal Madunga** is Bisio, while **Luisira**, **Sita Richy** and **Chucunene** are Bubi.

Ultimately, though, despite the best efforts of the *Centro Cultural Hispano Guineano* (CCHG), based in an old colonial building in the centre of Malabo, there are still few opportunities for musicians in Equatorial Guinea. Hence many of those artists who have had a chance to do so, have looked abroad to make a living.

The Diaspora

In the 1980s, a few artists – among them **Maele**, **Bessoso** and **Efamba** – made albums in Paris, but the most significant Equato-Guinean exile community, musically and otherwise, is based in the outskirts of **Madrid**, where a small suburb has been named **Malabo Dos** by its inhabitants.

Figureheads of this Madrid-based scene have included **Mascara** and **Las Hijas del Sol** (Daughters of the Sun). The former group, consisting of the Zamora brothers, originally from Annobón island, had a hit back home in the early 1990s with their album *Bimole* but haven't made a splash since. The latter, with their harmonious voices, made music of a unique beauty, their songs dealing with themes such as immigration, racism and the environment. They released three successful albums: *Sibèba*, a sparse production with just voices, drums and guitar; *Kottó*, which follows Bubi tradition of acapella singing while incorporating reggae, *makossa* and other rhythms; and *Kchaba*, which featured the cracking Afro-beat *Grito Libre* ("Freedom Cry"). However, their subsequent work was disappointing, and they disbanded in 2004.

Another disappointment was the premature split of the supergroup **Malabo Strit Band**, which was formed in 2002 by some of the most prestigious Guinean musicians. The band featured Muana Sinepi (vocals), David Owono (bass and vocals), Pepe Dougan (keyboards and vocals) and Alex Ikot (drums and vocals). Coming with them from Malabo to Madrid to guest-star on their debut CD were Yolanda Avomo, Cecilia Nchama and Fausto Dougan. In the end, however, this promising band failed to gel as a unit and split after just one album.

More tenacious is Fang musician **Baron Ya Buk-Lu**. A favourite on the Malabo Dos disco scene, he's managed to release five CDs as well as an autobiography. Other artists worth a listen include **Cheri Male**, a native of Basakato, who released a disc called *E betapano*, and **Mastho Ribocho**, from Bioko, whose output includes *Chikela-Chikela* and *Hukalalee*. Also worthy of a mention is singer **Concha Buika**, raised in the Balearic Islands by Guinean parents, though her music owes more to jazz and flamenco than her African roots.

Over in Barcelona, meanwhile, **Louis M'Bomio** produced *Wayi*, twelve songs and the same number of videoclips, with music as danceable as it is diverse (including *makossa*, *ndombolo*, rumba, *mapouka* and house). But the cheap and incessant eroticism of his lyrics palls quickly.

Njbenegra

Muana Sinepi and the short-lived Malabo Strit Band

EQUATORIAL GUINEA

★ Calles de Malabo
Nubenegra, Spain
Though hard to track down, this compilation cassette introduces a whole generation of Equato-Guinean musicians – Chiquitin, Nona de Macha, Sindy, Elvis Romeo, Pola, Yoli Miski, Luisira, Nuresu, Samuelin, Aniobe and Charlot Zemba – and a wide variety of styles.

⊙ CAS Revelations 2000
Eko Music, Cameroon
A production by ICEF and CICIBA featuring Apolonio Mba, Jose Siale, Paco Bass, Kouki, Isabel Idjabe, Gady Bass and Hijas del Sol.

⊙ Mbayah
Nubenegra, Spain
A CD-ROM of traditional music performed by amateur musicians and singers from the Fang, Ndowe and Bubi peoples, mostly using indigenous instruments. Guest players include Hijas del Sol, Muana Sinepi and Baron Ya Buk-Lu.

Baron Ya Buk-Lu

This Fang pop artist, based in Spain, has played in a variety of styles since the 1990s. The following is probably the best of his various albums.

⊙ B.B. Project
Ngomo, Spain
Energetic disco music with strong Fang-roots flavours.

Las Hijas del Sol

Their name means 'daughters of the sun', but this duo of Piruchi Apo and Paloma Loribo are really aunt and niece. They are Bubi-speakers – native Bioko islanders – and their songs are very different from those of the other tribes due to the isolation of the island from the mainland.

⊙ Sibèba
Nubenegra, Spain
This brilliant debut, from 1995, showcases the Hijas' voices against a jungle of percussion and a little electric guitar (the latter supplied by Armando 'Super' Momo, who died the year after its release). Extensive liner notes, in Spanish.

★ Kottó
Nubenegra, Spain
Highly inventive and constantly surprising in its shifts of rhythm and colour, Kottó is a minor masterpiece. Traditional rhythms are mixed with reggae, makossa and bikutsi, and the lyrics, in Bubi and Spanish, are pointedly political: "You, who changed my paradise [by drilling for oil] have a desert in your heart. Stop to listen to my song before making any decisions."

Malabo Strit Band

This promising but short-lived outfit, based in Madrid, imploded after making their one and only album, released in 2003.

⊙ M.S.B
Nubenegra, Spain
There are flashes of greatness here, and the sensual, poppy voice of Muana Sinepi impresses, but the hotchpotch of styles – including soukous, reggae, R&B, bikutsi, makossa and local bangante – fails to cohere, and the sax and keyboards can get cheesy.

PLAYLIST
Equatorial Guinea

1 SIBEBA Hijas del Sol from *Sibèba*
The little-known music of the Bubis presented by two voices in wonderful harmony.

2 KARGAYAH from *Mbayah*
A death ritual from the Fang tradition.

3 TIRSO DE MOLINA Hijas del Sol from *Sibèba*
The song that made Hijas del Sol popular in Spain tells of the immigrant hassles of police and papers.

4 BISILA Muana Sinepi from *Mbayah*
This deservedly popular song is Muana Sinepi's best-known number in Equatorial Guinea.

5 KOTTO Hijas del Sol from *Kottó*
An original reggae tune – danceable, joyous and uninhibited.

6 AFROPOP Malabo Strit Band from *M.S.B.*
A jaunty celebration of the African influence on Spanish New Year rituals, with a strong hint of Manu Dibango's influence.

7 NOBAY Baron Ya Buk-lu from *Dumu aye 'ku*
Typical Bùk-lu: a melting pot of everything he could lay his musical hands on.

Eritrea

songs of the patriots

Faytinga, voice of independent Eritrea
Colbalt/Bellarosa

Africa's youngest nation, Eritrea, sits on the northern part of the Horn of Africa, bordered by Sudan in the west, Ethiopia and Djibouti in the south and Saudi Arabia across the Red Sea, for which it is named. The story of modern Eritrean music – which reflects the influences of successive colonial powers and the experience of emigration and war – is inextricably bound up with this small country's long struggle for independence. As Dawit Mesfin explains, rebellion, hope, despair and, above all, the thrashing out of an Eritrean identity, are recurring themes.

The story of the music with which Eritreans most readily identify starts with the Ethiopian occupation. After centuries of rule by the Ottomans, Egyptians, Italians and British, a UN resolution to federate Eritrea with Ethiopia went into effect in 1952. Almost immediately, however, Eritrea's autonomous rights were violated, sparking an armed struggle against the Ethiopian masters which lasted until Eritrea won independence in 1993. During these long decades, music assumed a special meaning to Eritreans. It was used to inspire the youth to join the struggle and to raise the political consciousness of the civilian population; to revive patriotism and shape identity.

Of course, Eritrea also has older, folkloric musics. The country's estimated four million people fall into nine ethnic groups – Afar, Bilen, Hedareb, Kunama, Nara, Rashaida, Saho, Tigre and Tigrinya – each of which has its own distinct culture, language and music. The Bilen and Tigre, for instance, share a beautiful dance called *shelil*, in which women dancers throw their braided hair left and right to an alluring rhythm. But even these older styles have a confrontational element: almost all Eritrea's ethnic dances feature the waving or brandishing of sticks, swords or daggers.

MaTA

During the 1950s, the sense among many Eritreans that their country was slowly being swallowed by its bigger neighbour was expressed through music and conversation in the tearooms and secret drinking holes of the capital, Asmara. A musician playing a **krar** – a handheld five-string harp-like instrument – would start singing songs about life under foreign occupation, and those gathered around would clap and join in.

Before long, these protest singers began forming musical groups with the aim of challenging the foreign culture that was engulfing their country. The most significant of these was the **Mahber Theatre Asmara** (aka Asmara Theatre Association or MaTA), which was established in August 1961, just a few weeks before the Eritrean independence struggle reached a point of no return. Within a very short period, MaTA gave birth to modern Eritrean music, turning out powerful protest songs and expanding its ranks to include many now-legendary musicians. Songs such as "Shigey Habuni" (Hand me my Flambeau) took the city by storm, and soon attracted the attention of the censors. Others, such as "Eti Ghezana Abi Hdmo" (Our Big Family Unit) and "Adey Adi Jeganu"

(My Home, Land of Heroes) were engraved in the hearts of many of the youngsters who later flocked to join the frontline. Every bar and tearoom in major towns played MaTA music.

MaTA's leading "actors" included **Tewelde Redda**, who broke new ground by introducing the electric guitar to the Eritrean scene in the 1960s. His contribution as a soloist, especially, was monumental, and many people still hum his songs, such as "Seb mKwaney" (Being Human) and "Ney Fi Tretna Yigermeni'" (The Mystery of Our Creation). Rèdda's songs contributed to the development of the liberation movement, which he eventually joined in the 1970s. He faded in exile and has not always received the recognition he deserves, but Eritreans of his generation regard him as an icon.

Another key player was **Alamin Abdeletif**, who represented the Tigre culture and became something of a lowlands figurehead. In the late 1960s and early 70s he was jailed for protest songs such as "Seb nKebdu Tray Aikonen Zinebr" (A Man Does Not Only Live to Eat). Today, after four decades of continuous performance, he is still actively involved in the scene. And his songs in Tigre and Tigrinya, such as "Yima" and "Abay Abashawul", remain ingrained in people's hearts.

Other important MaTA members included **Atoweberhan Segid**, **Osman Abdelrahim** and **Teberèh Tesfa Hunègn**. The latter, although she didn't write her own songs, was the best vocalist and most colourful Eritrean entertainer of the 1960s and 70s. She is remembered for the audacious performances of provocative songs – such as "Nsu Msai Ane Msti" (He is with Me but I am with the Other) and "Eti Gezana Abi Hdmo, tiKwan Qunchi Meli'omo" (Our Big House is Filled with Fleas and Lice) – that she would give to cheering university crowds. Like many other artists, Tebereh joined the liberation front in the late 1970s and sustained several wounds in the battlefield. Sadly, she never fully recovering from a head injury, but her legacy has been picked up by another ex-fighter: diva **Helen Meles**.

As well as turning out ground-breaking music, MaTA also paved the way for groups such as **Rocket**, **Merhaba** and **Zeray Deres**. Today there is an avenue in Asmara named after the organization and the old MaTA songs are still played, inside and outside Eritrea.

Party Time

Guayla, literally party music, is the most popular form of music for entertainment's sake, though even this can become politicized. A traditional dance originating in the highland villages, guayla takes different forms in different areas. In the villages, it features in weddings, engagements and other festivals, but can also break out any time and anywhere: a person starts singing and those gathered around will join in, clapping their hands and singing in a call-and-response style.

Guayla is played in two stages: *kudda* and *sbra*. During the kudda stage, the dancers move in a circle to a drum played slightly faster than one beat per second. There is not much shaking of the shoulders, nor twists and turns: the dancers just move along slowly, shuffling their legs in time with the booming drumbeat. Half way through the dance, the singer, usually the *krar* player, or the *abo guayla* (leader) tells the drummer to speed up with the instruction "Derb!" At this stage, sbra kicks in and the tempo is doubled. The dancers crouch, shrug their shoulders and get wilder, and the women begin to ululate more loudly and more frequently. Shaking their shoulders, the dancers pair up, gyrate, jump and occasionally rub back to back.

The drum used in guayla, the *keboro*, is made out of hide wrapped and tied around a big tin can, and strapped around the shoulder. Other traditional instruments, if available, give the whole affair more zest. These include the *chira waTa* (single-string violin), *embelta* (deep, monotone horn) and *shambuQo* (traditional flute). A more modern guayla version, with band accompaniment, is found in the cities.

Guayla Royalty

If guayla has a king, it has to be **Bereket Mengisteab**, a legendary musician who operated from Addis

Bereket Mengisteab

Ababa, the Ethiopian capital. He dominated Eritrean music for over four decades, starting in the mid-1960s with melodic, apolitical songs recorded in Ethiopia. In his time, he was the only Eritrean artist to be played on the radio. His beautiful compositions, stage presence, deft *krar* playing and use of the Tigrinya language assured his popularity. In the mid-1970s, Mengisteab joined the liberation movement, but he continued to entertain and inspire fighters with music. Today, a civilian once again, and nearing 70, he is still one of the most sought-after Eritrean artists.

The genre's queen, meanwhile, is 60-something **Tsehaytu Beraki**, generally considered the mother of Eritrean soul. She encouraged Eritreans to unite around their cultural background and values with memorable songs such as "Abashawul", "May Jahjah" and "Mejemerya Fikri", touching their hearts and fuelling their patriotism. Tsèhaytu personified guayla music for more than three decades and, with her elegant, smooth *krar* sound, earned the undying affection of a huge audience.

Ambassadors and Icons

Born in Asmara in 1970, **Abraham Afewerki** left Eritrea in 1979 and, like many Eritreans at the time, went to the Sudan, where he was active in the Children's Cultural Group. While still there, in his early teens, he wrote his first songs. He later spent time in Italy but now lives and works in Washington DC. He writes his own songs and plays *krar*, guitar, percussion and keyboards, and his music reflects the influences of all the countries in which he has lived and travelled. His live performances (especially his dance routines) have mesmerized Eritreans all over the world, helping him to become the country's best-known musician internationally. Unusually for Eritrean music, his lyrics are not at all euphemistic when it comes to love.

Afewerki may be Eritrean music's greatest ambassador, but the ultimate icon is **Yemane Baria** (Yemane Ghebremichael), widely considered to be the country's greatest-ever singer. Although he did not venture onto the international scene, the sheer power of his traditional and modern ballads made him a hero among Eritreans, his music epitomizing their personal and collective struggles. Though Eritreans have long been divided between government supporters and opponents, Baria somehow bridged this gulf – and the gulfs between young and old, highlanders and lowlanders, diaspora and locals. He was loved for his soothing voice, unusually slow guayla rhythms and his powerful, straight-to-the-heart lyrics.

Abraham Afewerki

Love's Labour's Lost

The predominant theme that guided Eritrean musicians from the 1950s was love of the motherland. *Hagerey* ("my country") could very well be the most frequently used word in Eritrea's musical vocabulary. Some artists, such as **Tesfai Mehari**, **TeKle Kiflemariam** and **Gual Ankere**, were literally raised in the battlefields.

As such, a preponderance of songs about freedom, unity, heroism and comradeship has meant that other emotions – such as love and heartache – have long taken a back seat. And the resistance was not always healthy for the music in other ways, too. Bands sometimes split due to their members' political affiliations, and many artists who went into exile, like **Tsèhaytu Beraki**, did not resettle in Eritrea after independence because of an excess of bloody memories.

Unfortunately, in the post-independence era Eritrean musical culture has not really broadened and developed. It scope is still narrow, and few of today's songs reflect the reality of life in the country. There's a sense that Eritrean artists need to put nationalism behind them and move on.

Thanks to Francis Falceto for assistance with this article.

Baria was most musically active in the 1970s and 80s, before Eritrean independence. Ironically, his capacity to express himself freely was somewhat restricted in post-independence Eritrea, though he managed to produce two memorable CDs in the 1990s, which can easily be found in any Eritrean community shops abroad, or on Eritrean websites such as Asmarino.com. He remained true to his humanist roots until his death in 1997.

DISCOGRAPHY Eritrea

⊙ **The Best of 2000**
Afro Sound, Canada
An authoritative collection, produced and arranged to show-case Eritrea's musical vitality and variety. Fighters and civilians, men and women, Muslim and Christian, young and old – all are represented on a tracklist featuring the likes of Alamin Abdeletif and Elsa Kidane.

⊙ **Éthiopiques 5: Tigrigna Music**
Buda Musique, France
Made in 1970–75, these recordings from Tigray (northern Ethiopia) and Eritrea include tracks by a number of resistance fighters. There are early cuts by Tsehaytu Beraki and Tèwèldè Rèdda, plus three from Eritrean drummer/singer Teklé Tefsa-Ezighe (which were suppressed in the 1970s and got their first airing on this 1998 CD). Typically of the *Éthiopiques* series, the notes are excellent.

Abraham Afewerki

Eritrea's leading musical ambassador, Abraham Afewerki was the first person from the country to release a CD internationally (his *Kozli Gaba* album, from 1991). A compelling singer and natural innovator, he has a unique style – an update of the traditional guayla sound.

⊙ **Hadera (Entreaty)**
Negarit Productions, US
This album from 2000 combines the subtle flavour of the *krar* with beautifully arranged electric and acoustic sounds. The songs (one of them written as a teenage exile in Sudan) feature touching lyrics, danceable grooves and a few melodies that seem to be borrowed from neighbouring Sudan and Ethiopia.

Faytinga

Faytinga developed her extraordinary musical talents between 1977 and 1991 – while she was fighting for Eritrea's liberation – and recorded her debut album, *Numey*, for the French label Cobalt in 2000. Her mixed ethnicity (Kunama, Bilen and Tigrinya), ties to the independence movement, striking looks and high, girlish voice have ensured broad appeal.

 Eritrea
Cobalt, France
Faytinga's second international release is a pleasantly varied selection of her own compositions, steeped in various Eritrean traditions but also reflecting the influence of neighbouring countries. The lyrics celebrate Eritrea's birth, the bravery of its fighters and everyday village life. *Krar, wata*, flute

and percussion – plus unobtrusive programming and guitar – are topped by Faytinga's soaring voice.

Helen Meles

Helen Meles is an Eritrean diva whose music encompasses a wide range of styles, both local and international. As well as her own compositions, she's known for her recordings of songs by the legendary Tebereh Tesfahuney – especially on the album *Ti gezana Abi hdmo*.

⊙ reseAni (Forget Me)
Sembel Multimedia Productions, US
Meles' third CD, from 2004, mixes traditional Tigrinya styles with European, Arabic and African influences. For instance, "mnAs teTari" puts a gospel-like accompaniment behind South African beats.

Tsehaytu Beraki

Like other popular artists of her day, Tsehaytu Beraki became increasingly politicized as the independence struggle intensified, and she eventually joined the liberation front. She's now based in the Netherlands.

⊙ Selam (Peace)
Terp Records, Netherlands
Produced with the avant-garde Dutch band The Ex, this double CD comes with an 86-page booklet full of historical and biographical notes, archive photos and lyrics translations. It features recordings of seventeen songs drawn from different periods of Beraki's life. Though not greatly varied – expect plenty of blues-like ballads backed by *krars*, *keboro* and a few additional instruments – this is an invaluable document.

PLAYLIST
Eritrea

1 ALEMUYE Faytinga from *Eritrea*
A melodic love song based on Kunama music, with subtle *krar* and flute, surging rhythm and a commanding vocal.

2 NSHA FQRI (LOVE CONFESSIONS)
Helen Meles from *ResAni*
A melancholic guayla track that shows off Helen's extraordinary vocal range. The beautiful lyrics are straight from the heart.

3 SELAM Tsehaytu Beraki from *Selam*
A powerful tribute to old comrades.

4 SHIKOR (SWEET) Abraham Afewerki
A compelling love song with a driving rhythm.

5 MILÈNU Tewelde Redda from
Éthiopiques 5: Tigrigna Music
A meandering bluesy piece recorded in 1972, combining *krar* and electric guitar.

Ethiopia

land of wax and gold

Gigi
Jak Kilby

Ethiopia is one of Africa's most fascinating countries, musically and in every other respect, and is once again open and welcoming to foreign visitors. An ancient mountain kingdom, it has expanded considerably in the last two hundred years, but it remains Christian at its Amharic heart (the Amhara are the dominant language group, powerful in trade and government). Long-time aficionado Francis Falceto tours the land of Ras Tafari and double entendre and offers suggestions for listening and buying in situ.

Before a brand-new Addis Ababa airport was recently inaugurated, as you got off the plane at the former airport, you were greeted by a sign that read: "Welcome to Ethiopia, Centre of Active Recreation and Relaxation". It was a sentiment sublime in its optimism, but perhaps no more or less true than all of the disaster-laden clichés that have been the currency of Ethiopian reportage for the last two or three decades. With the new millennium, the ancient land of Ethiopia could just be in line for rehabilitation. The recent war with Eritrea (1998-2000) and ongoing dispute about a border (dis)agreement that still sporadically simmers into conflict continue to cast a pall, but the country has come a long way since it shed its Stalinist dictatorship in 1991 and brought to an end thirty disastrous years of civil war.

The civil war – and Mengistu's seventeen years of dictatorship (1974–1991) – have had a profound effect on Ethiopia's cultural and musical life. For most of the Mengistu years, a continuous curfew deprived a whole generation of Ethiopians of any kind of nightlife. To these restrictions was added a censorship of nightmarish pedantry that picked through song lyrics before recording sessions could be licensed, and put overseas visitors through painstaking inspections of locally bought cassettes before allowing them to leave the country. Little surprise then, that those musicians who could emigrate did so, opting for a precarious exile in the US, Sudan, Saudi Arabia or Europe. Their number included **Girma Beyene**, **Teshome Meteku**, **Muluken Mellesse**, **Getatchew Kassa**, **Menelik Wossenatchew**, **Aster Aweke**, **Ephrem**

Tamru, **Kuku Sebsebe**, the producer **Amha Eshete** … a roll-call of the leading artists of the day.

All this has changed, and in the middle of the noughties, music feels omnipresent in Addis Ababa, the capital, honking out of battered tape decks in buses and taxis, drifting from stores and markets and pumped out loud at the innumerable little restaurants (*tedjbet*s or *bunnabet*s), guesthouses and semi-private drinking parlours. These nerve-centres of national vitality were always abuzz throughout the years of dictatorship, and they too have multiplied since its demise.

Trad/Mod and the Golden Age

Traditional music forms the basis of all Ethiopian styles. Even the most famous modern singing stars like **Tlahoun Gessesse** or **Mahmoud Ahmed** have two repertoires, one modern, the other rooted in tradition. Ethiopians buy modern and traditional cassettes with equal enthusiasm, and the modernity in question is essentially that of the "modern" Western instruments which have been introduced.

The first Western imports were **brass bands**, brought in by the military under Haile Selassie. Performers tried out their instruments on traditional material and by the late 1940s there were full **orchestras** to accompany fashionable singers. The first among them were the **Imperial Bodyguard Band**, the **Army Band**, the **Police Band**, the **Municipality Band** and the **Haile Selassie Theatre Band**, trained initially by European professionals,

Frew Haylin and The Imperial Bodyguard Band

Collection Francis Falcetto: Éthiopiques

often Armenians, but gradually private orchestras were formed.

The special characteristic of Ethiopian music is the use of a five-note, pentatonic scale with large intervals between some of the notes, giving an unresolved feeling to the music, like waiting for a stone to hit the bottom of a well and not hearing it. These modes create an intensity of performance not unlike soul music – especially in the hands of a singer like the Miami-based exile **Aster Aweke**. The limping asymmetrical rhythm of much of the music is also highly characteristic.

Shopping around for cassettes and CDs, you can occasionally come across the odd back-street shop full of old 45s from the 1970s. A good bunch of the recordings of the 1960s and 70s pioneers are worth getting hold of. Premier league names include **Tlahoun Gessesse**, **Bezunesh Bekele**, **Hirut Bekele** (no relation), **Mahmoud Ahmed**, **Ali Birra**, **Alemayehu Eshete**, **Muluken Mellesse** and **Ayalew Mesfin**. Try to get your hands on the five *Ethiopian Hit Parade* LPs, extraordinary compilations which comprise, apart from the stars mentioned, forgotten meteors like **Seifu Yohannes**, **Teshome Meteku**, **Tebereh Tesfahunegn** or **Tewolde Redda**. Old vinyls of traditional musicians like **Kassa Tessema**, **Mary Armede**, **Ketema Makonnen** and **Asnaketch Worku** are also pure gems to dig for.

Instrumental music also has its key figure in the shape of **Mulatu Astatqé**, promoter and sole exponent of **Ethio-jazz** and the king of arrangers through this golden, pre-revolutionary age. Jim Jarmusch's movie *Broken Flowers* (2005) used Mulatu's music extensively on its soundtrack, giving it worldwide exposure. Another superb figure, though seemingly forgotten these days, was **Getachew Mekurya**, a brilliant saxophone and clarinet player, and an innocent precursor of Albert Ayler and Archie Shepp.

The main body of Ethiopian records was produced in just one decade, from 1969-1978, when some five hundred singles and

Aster Aweke

just thirty LPs were released. Pressed first in India, then in Lebanon, Greece and finally Kenya, up to three thousand copies were produced for big hits – serious numbers at the time. These collectors' items represent the golden age of Ethiopian music, and are now mostly available in the *Éthiopiques* CD series (Buda Musique). By the end of this period, with the advent of a local cassette industry, there were tape pressings of 20–30,000, while the biggest hits sold more than 100,000.

It used to be possible to find cassette copies of these old standards, but since 2004 new regulations about copyright and repression of piracy have limited these facilities. A lot remains to be done to effectively protect Ethiopian musicians' rights.

Wax and Gold

During the dark years of the dictatorship in the 1980s, the cassette industry continued, and new singers emerged besides the veteran artists. Most stayed in the country, as it had become virtually impossible to emigrate. The top local stars of the decade included **Ephrem Tamru**, **Aster Aweke**, **Kuku Sebsebe**, **Netsanet Mellesse**, **Teshome Wolde** and **Amelmal Abate**, who shared three professional orchestras for recording sessions: the **Wallias Band**, the **Roha Band** and the **Ethio Stars**.

From 1985 on, one figure emerged forcefully: the singer **Neway Debebe** became an idol, bringing a freshness reminiscent of the vocal prowess of the early Tlahoun Gessesse. Alongside a generation of young singers, Debebe renewed interest in the poetic style of **sem-enna-werq** (wax and gold), an old tradition of double entendre to fool the censors, or at least enable them to turn a blind eye without incurring the wrath of the military chiefs.

Wax and gold meanings were expressed through apparently innocuous love songs. Here, for instance, is "Altchalkoum" (Can't Stand Any More), created by Tlahoun Gessesse on the eve of an abortive coup against Haile Selassie (it was performed by him with the backing of The Imperial Bodyguard Band, implicated in the coup attempt). Fooling nobody, it was quickly banned – and was banned again by Mengistu:

How long are you going to make me suffer?
I can't take any more, I've had enough.
I'm up to here with it,
I'm more than up to here.
I can't take any more,
How can I put up with it?
I can't put up with your torments
I don't know what more I can do.

New Styles

In the early years of the new millennium, with the establishment of a fragile democracy and the return of freedom of expression, it's not unreasonable to hope for a creative renewal for Ethiopian music: less of the one-two beat immediately danceable stuff, and a renewal of inspiration from the old style, rhythmically formidable *tchik-tchik-ka*, with its unfettered lyrics, controlled synthesizers and supreme horn sections. New talents are already jostling in an exciting field – **Fikreaddis Nekatibeb**, **Tigist Bekele**, **Tsedenia Gebre-Markos**, to name but three. And **Afrosound**, the **Express Band**, the **Medina Band** are waiting in the wings.

Don't expect too much from Ethiopian reggae. It really didn't exist until the recent fame of **Teddy Afro**, following in the footsteps of Alpha Blondy or Lucky Dube. It's true the word "rastafari" comes from Ras Tafari Makonnen, the title and surname of Haile Selassie, the last emperor of Ethiopia, but rasta fetishism has no special meaning in Ethiopia, despite the admiration for Bob Marley common to the whole of Africa. There is a community of Jamaican rastas at Sheshemene, 200km south from Addis Ababa, but they're viewed as an imported phenomenon. Nor is there any discernible relationship between Ethiopian music and reggae. At a pinch, the unusual beat of neighbouring Eritrea bears some comparison, but there's really no genuine historical or musical link, as this part of the world has never fuelled the African diaspora.

Live in Addis: Azmaris

It is a matter of fact that the modern music scene in Addis Ababa is very weak nowadays. It cannot be compared to the golden age of the 1960s and early 70s. Nightclubs tend to imitate Western trends and you will find very little Ethiopian music in them. The **Coffee House** (Egyptian embassy area) is an exception, hosting the most interesting jam sessions to be heard in town. Also try the **Imperial Hotel**.

Ali Tango

Every taxi driver in Addis knows the location of Tango Music and Video Shop, in the heart of the Piazza, the base of **Ali "Ali Tango" Kaifa**, who has played an essential role in the Ethiopian music scene over the last quarter-century. The shop is now managed by his son Adil Kaifa.

A smart talent scout and an inventive producer, Ali Tango pioneered the cassette industry after having produced some fifty records, including cult classics like Mahmoud Ahmed's "Ere Mela Mela", Muluken Mellesse's "Iemereqne", Alemayehu Eshete's "Wededkuh Afkerkush" and Ayalew Mesfin's "Gunfan". He also "discovered" Aster Aweke, Amelmal Abate, Neway Debebe and, most recently, the teenage singer Hebiste Tiruneh, the first great success of the post-dictatorship era. An enthusiast for technology, Ali Tango was the first to use digital recording equipment and he has opened a private studio – a high-performance set-up, even if it's not up to European standards.

The respected and envied godfather of a passionate industry, Ali Tango has always defended the freedom of expression of singers and independent orchestras – sometimes with great cunning during the dictatorship. He enthuses over all the regional rhythms of Ethiopia – Gurague, Tigrinya, Gondar, Kotu, Oromo – and even takes an interest in Yemenite and Somali music – a rather unusual path in such a culturally self-sufficient country.

Ilpo Saunio/Piranha

Krar, drums and washnit from the Tukul Band

The Harp of King David

Humming, buzzing and generally sounding like it comes from the centre of the earth is the Ethiopian harp known as the **begena**, aka The Harp of King David. Looking like a cross between a harp and a lyre, its strange and unique tone sounds not unlike an old analogue synthesizer. It is clearly a very ancient instrument, if not quite as old as its nickname, conjuring up Old Testament era origins, suggests. Formerly played by the members of the nobility (both men and women, including emperors), it is primarily a religious instrument these days, and is used to accompany psalms during Orthodox Christian celebrations.

Since the end of the Mengistu dictatorship, which suppressed religious practice, the *begena* has been slowly making its way back into the national consciousness. **Alemu Aga** is one of the foremost contemporary exponents of this sacred instrument, and performs regularly at home as well as in venues round the world. He has been teaching it privately for the last three decades. 'When I was a child of twelve years, I had lessons', he tells me in his soft tones. 'What made it easy was that the teacher was our neighbour. Especially on Sundays, we go to church and the teacher, he goes there to play and I carry the instrument for him. He plays first, then I follow and this is how I started.'

The *begena* itself is striking to look at. Standing on average about 4ft high, the base is a hollowed-out box, covered with either cow or sheep hide. Attached to the box is the zegba wood frame, often ornately carved with Coptic designs. Its ten strings, made of sheep intestine, are stretched between the box and the frame, and tuned to a pentatonic scale by a series of pegs on one end, and small hoops of leather on the other. The hoops allow the strings to lightly touch the bridge, creating the unique "buzz" peculiar to the *begena*. The strings are plucked or strummed with a horn plectrum.

'This instrument it has a special power,' says Alemu. 'When people listen, it will make them concentrate to keep quiet and listen attentively. For us it is food of the thought, you know.'

Certainly anybody who has heard the *begena* first-hand can attest to its strange meditative pull. In Belgium, where I first met Alemu, a lively crowd of expats quickly went quiet as he began his recital.

As for the King David reference, the Bible itself offers some clues. Ethiopia has oft-forgotten links with Judaism: 'The Queen of Sheba, who was a famous queen of Ethiopia, she heard about the wisdom of Solomon (son of King David)', explains Alemu. 'She went to visit him, and she stayed there for some time. (When) she came back, she gave birth to a child who became Menelik the First (the first emperor of Ethiopia, from which the royal family is said to be descended). He went also to visit his father. When he returned, it is believed that this instrument came to Ethiopia at that time.' Whether this tale is apocryphal or not, you are warmly recommended to seek out recordings of this most ancient of instruments. They seem to take you back to the roots of music itself.

Chris Menist

But the most interesting phenomenon for fans of Ethiopian music remains the incredible flowering of *azmaribet*s (hole-in-the-wall clubs). They're to be found absolutely everywhere and you can just look in to see if you like the atmosphere. Apart from a dozen or so main roads, the streets of Addis have neither names nor street numbers, and to give directions people refer to a district, then to a handy point of reference, like the post office, a pharmacy, a garage or an embassy. It's difficult, therefore, to be precise about addresses: but the taxi drivers know nearly all the music places (book a taxi for the whole evening). As Ethiopians are absolute strangers to even the music of the rest of Africa, they're invariably amazed when foreigners show interest in their music. You can be sure you'll be adopted and guided and introduced to all the best sounds and experiences.

You'll meet all sorts of musicians in azmaribets – players of *krar* (lyre), *masenqo* (one-string fiddle), *washnit* (flute), and *kebero* (percussion), even accordionists. These musicians are **azmaris**, equivalent to the *griots* of West Africa or the wandering *taraf* musicians of Romania, privileged carriers of popular music, mediators of collective memory. They have an ambivalent reputation among Ethiopians – a mix of suspicion of their bohemian life and respect for the power of the word.

Azmaris depend on tips – given to sing what one feels deep down, be it sadness, nostalgia, praises or veiled criticism. As such, they had a particularly hard time during the dictatorship. But since the end of Mengistu, they – and the azmaribets – have had a spectacular return. The clubs sprang up throughout the capital, with concentrations in the areas of Kazentchis and Yohannès Sefer (also called Datsun Sefer because local bar-owners were the first to swan about in Japanese cars). A whole new generation of talented, non-conformist, sarcastic azmaris burst upon the scene. Most arrived in the capital for the first time from their distant provinces, and the style of this new wave became known as **bolel** – literally "car exhaust fumes", the putt-putt-putt of jabbering and nonsense. Bolel is a mix of azmari traditions (praise or sarcasm at will, depending on the tip) and of modern urban culture (the country/city divide, TV, international references). For good examples of azmari musicians at work, try *Éthiopiques 2* and especially *Éthiopiques 18*.

In the Kazentchis area, you will meet the greatest Ethiopian voices and characters of bolel: **Abbebe Fekade**, **Iyerusalem Dubale** and her sisters **Yeshimebet**, **Enana** and **Bertukane**, **Betsat Seyoum**, **Adaneh & Malefya Teka**, **Tedje**, **Mimi**, **Tigist Assefa**, **Mandelbosh "Assabelew" Dibo**, to name a few of the hippest. In Yohannès Sefer, you'll find musicians in every house on the street. **Etenesh Wassie** is the queen of this area, the blues herself. Also pay a visit to **Gennet Masresha** and her son **Essoubalew Adugna**, who is becoming the best *masenqo* player in town.

Whether you find the atmosphere in your azmaribet bluesy or not, the alcohol flows freely and the atmosphere gets very hot, very quickly. Better put on your seat belt when they unleash the **eskista** – a dance style in which the shaking of shoulders and chests would melt a statue. **Heywet Demissie** (who performs at Yewoddal, the successful cabaret of Adaneh and Malefya Teka) and **Yèshiwork** (in her own cabaret in Kazentchis) are among the most impressive *eskista* dancers.

Future Shock

Ethiopian musicians are still in many ways reeling from the effects of the changes since the flight of Mengistu and the onset of democracy in 1991. The end of the civil war resulted in a new country on their northern border – Eritrea – and the first taste of personal freedom for a whole generation. Travel is much easier than before, so musicians and bands are able to play and record overseas (and return without a problem), and the opportunity to listen to other African and European music is beginning to have an effect on their own.

Contemporary bands are also influenced in the same direction by the demands of Addis Ababa teenage culture, keen to make up for lost exposure to global youth fashions over the last two decades. Western music, reggae, rap and

Music Shops in Addis

If you're looking for recorded music in Addis Ababa, you'll find the city full of **"Music Shops"** where you can get cheap tapes (the standard price for a cassette is about 1 euro). CDs are now increasingly available.

At the entrance to the Mercato quarter, near the Great Mosque, the noteworthy **Electra Music Shop** and **Ambassel Music Shop** stand out, in an area where music stores run to dozens. Not far from Mercato, the Piazza quarter is also the base for a number of bigger centres for music production, in particular **Alpha Music Shop**, and **Mahmoud Music Shop**, on the corner of Cunningham Street and Adwa. Close by, on the other side of the square, is **Ayalew Music Shop**, owned by Ayalew Mesfin, a singer who was a big star in the 1970s (now based in Colorado, but the shop is still there). His group, the Black Lion Band, had one of the most rapid-fire horn sections on the pre-Mengistu nightlife scene.

the sounds of Kenya and Congo (Zaire) are all increasingly popular.

As musician Abiyou Solomon (of **Abyssinia Band**) remarked: 'We don't exactly want to be westernized – we're just trying to produce music of equal quality to the rest of the world. We're working hard to make the sound richer and change the traditional arrangements a bit to make them more modern.' They are now experimenting with bubbling guitar tunes and writing songs in the seven-tone Western rather than the traditional pentatonic scale. Ironically, of course, it's pentatonic, polyphonic music that the global audience is really attracted to. If Abyssinia Band and their like can bridge the divide, that would be some success to sing about. But in the meantime, Abiyou has settled in Washington, DC.

The *Broken Flowers* soundtrack and the recent response from non-Ethiopian artists inspired by Ethiopian music (Either/Orchestra from Boston, Susheela Raman from UK/India, The Ex from Amsterdam, The Kronos Quartet from California and Yasuaki Shimizu from Japan) have done much to promote Ethiopian music abroad, to the great astonishment of Ethiopians themselves. This surprising phenomenon is changing the terms of the challenge: the future of Ethiopian music is no longer in the hands of Ethiopian artists only, which is a source of controversy as well as hope in Ethiopian communities.

113

If your local record store can't help, the best place to find recorded Ethiopian music – and have an unusual meal at the same time – is your local Ethiopian restaurant. For shops in Addis Ababa, see box on p.113.

Contemporary

⊙ Éthiopiques 1: Golden Years of Ethiopian Modern Music 1969–1975
Buda Musique, France
The first of the superb compilation series executive-produced by the author of this article, this features Muluqen Mellesse, the great Mahmoud Ahmed, Seyfu Yohannes, Teshome Meteku and a track from Gétachew Kassa.

★ Éthiopiques 3: The Golden Age of Modern Ethiopian Music 1969–75
Buda Musique, France
Volumes 1 and 3 of Buda's series feature bands and artists of the early 1970s – the years of flares, Afros and African unity, before the relatively healthy turmoil of Haile Selassie's reign was replaced by Mengistu's brutal military dictatorship in 1974.

⊙ Éthiopiques 13: Ethiopian Groove
Buda Musique, France
This diverse and satisfying mid-1970s sampler covers the final few years of the golden age of Ethiopian music and is drawn from Kaifa Records, founded by Ali Abdella Kaifa, aka Ali Tango. It features groups such as the Wallias, Black Lion, Dahlak and Sensation Band(s) backing popular singers, including the veteran Alèmayèhu Eshètè as well as lesser-known figures such as the racy vocalist Ayaléw Mèsfin and several distinctive female singers such as Bzunèsh Bèqèlè.

★ The Rough Guide to the Music of Ethiopia
World Music Network, UK
Compiled by the author of this chapter, and leaning heavily on the Éthiopiques series (for which there is no overall sampler), this is a solid, well-sequenced collection covering most

of the big names from the music's golden age (Alèmayèhu Eshètè, Mahmoud Ahmed, Mulatu Astatqé etc) when funk, soul, jazz and more were given a uniquely Ethiopian twist. Rootsier and more recent recordings such as Alèmu Aga's begena harp and the rough-and-ready sounds of asmari are also showcased, as is expat diva Aster Aweke.

Abyssinia Infinite

Whether it's a one-off project or not, this group effort is the best vehicle yet for Ejigayehu "Gigi" Shibabaw's thrilling voice. Bill Laswell takes an unusually restrained role as co-producer and various Ethiopian and international musicians are featured.

★ Zion Roots
Network, Germany
From 2003, and superior to her somewhat overcooked solo debut, this is a seamless combination of original and traditional songs. The sparse, largely acoustic arrangements are enhanced, rather than swamped, by effects, and Gigi's singing is sublime. Essential.

Mahmoud Ahmed

One of Ethiopia's greatest voices, Ahmed has been at the top for thirty years. His sound is beautiful, sad and always danceable. Elvis Costello is a notable fan.

★ Éthiopiques 7: Mahmoud Ahmed
Buda Musique, France
Recorded in Addis in 1975 with The Ibex Band – most of whose members went on to found The Roha Band – this was the first modern Ethiopian recording to be released in the West, and became something of a cult album, remastered here with four extra tracks. A classic: one hit and you're hooked. Two further volumes of Éthiopiques (6 and 19) are also devoted to Mahmoud Ahmed.

⊙ Soul of Addis
Earthworks, UK
A good compilation of Ahmed's work.

Mulatu Astatqé and Ethio-Jazz

As a teenager in the early 1960s, Astatqé studied music in England and the USA. No other musician in Ethiopia is anything like Mulatu, and it looks like his style will die with him.

⊙ Éthiopiques 4: Ethio-Jazz et Musique Instrumentale 1969–1974
Buda Musique, France
From the same early-1970s era as vols 1 and 3, but the sound here is very different, with two lps' worth of instrumental tracks from the superbly brooding and – uniquely in Ethiopia – Latin-influenced tones of Astatqé (on keyboards) and his Ethio-Jazz Band.

Aster Aweke

The first Ethiopian artist (after Mahmoud Ahmed) to cross-over into the Western market, Aster Aweke has a voice that kills you. She emigrated to the US in the late 1970s but remains hugely popular at home.

Jak Kilby

which Eshèté has built his reputation. Listen to the pianist Berhane Kidane, whose keyboard style is unique in Africa. Guest clarinettist is big Ivo Papazov from Macedonia.

⊙ Éthiopiques 9: Alemayehu Eshete
Buda Musique, France

This collection of rockers and crooners from the wild man of Addis is culled from his prolific 1969–74 recordings, with backing from the All Star Band and the Alem-Girma Band. Whether inspired by Little Richard, Elvis or Nat King Cole, the man is always entertaining.

Tlahoun Gessesse

Less obviously influenced by American pop vocalists than colleagues likeAlemayehu Eshete, Tlahoun's mixed Amhara/Oromo heritage gave him very broad appeal to the Ethiopian public, though foreigners may take some time to "get" him. He first made his mark with The Imperial Body Guard, whom he joined in 1958, and he still sings occasionally in Addis.

⊙ Éthiopiques 17: Tlahoun Gessesse
Buda Musique,France

Recordings made between 1970 and 1975 with The Body Guard Band, All Star Band, Exhibition Band and Army Band. The genius "modernist" touch of Mulatu Astatqé adds appeal in the arrangements on seven cuts, and Gessesse hums, moans and shrieks his way through them all.

Tsegué-Maryam Guèbrou

This conservatoire-trained pianist's original compositions for solo piano somehow combine the pensive melancholia and playfulness of Eric Satie, the virtuosity of Chopin and a distinctly Ethiopian lyricism all her own.

⊙ Éthiopiques 21: Emahoy Tsequé-Maryam Guèbrou, Ethiopia Song
Buda Musique, France

An astonishing retrospective taken from four of the albums Guèbrou recorded in sporadic bouts of creativity between 1963 and 1996. The breathtaking beauty of her playing is a revelation, as is the tragic story behind it. The good news is that she's still around.

The great voice – Mahmoud Ahmed

⊙ Aster
Triple Earth, UK; Columbia, US
⊙ Ebo
Barkhanns/Stern's, UK

These CDs, recorded in the US and London between 1989 and 1993, are notably Westernized in the brass-section arrangements, but still a formidable introduction to the Ethiopian feeling. If you can find it, *Kabu* is of comparable quality.

Alemayehu Eshete

Eshete introduced the languid poses of rock into Ethiopian music, but it's his home-grown soul/blues style that knocks out his fans.

⊙ Addis Ababa
Dona Wana/Musidisc Stern's, UK; Shanachie, US

Recorded in Paris, this CD introduces some of the hits with

Netsanet Mellesse

One of the younger artists who have emerged over the past decade, Mellesse's soulful voice has made him a top star.

⊙ Dodge
Dona Wana/Stern's, UK; Shanachie, US

Mellesse's exceptional voice is perfectly served by the sophisticated arrangements of bandleader and trumpeter Yohannes Tekola.

Getachew Mekurya

This remarkable master of the tenor saxophone began playing in 1948 and was a colleague of singer Alemayehu Eshete in the Police Orchestra before he made the recordings presented here in 1972.

115

⊙ **Éthiopiques 14: Getachew Merkurya, Negus of Ethiopian Sax**
Buda Musique, France
An instrumental set showcasing Getachew's unique melismatic style, which transposes the battlefield *shellèla* vocal style onto sax, and is also influenced by his background of playing the *masenqo* and *krar*. The sparse, jaunty and atmospheric backing on trumpet, keyboards, drums and bass superbly complements his horn on this left-field treat.

Yared Tefera

One of the most dynamic musicians of the post-Derg generation, rare for the care with which his music is produced.

⊙ **Park Center Mood**
Ethio-Grooves Records, US
Recorded in the US in 1997. The pieces "Antchi Hoyé Lèné" (with the amazingly innovative piano of Abegaz Kebrework Shiota) and "Ambassel" (featuring the historical veteran clarinettist Merawi Sitot) are simply masterpieces.

Teshome Wolde

Following in the footsteps of Mahmoud Ahmed, Wolde sings traditional and self-penned songs over a modern backing.

⊙ **Ethiopian Soul Revue**
Rags Productions, UK
Backed by the famous Ethio Stars band, Wolde's first CD release presents love songs in various arrangements, from jazz to funk and rock, but always with a hypnotic, swinging beat.

Folk & traditional

⊙ **Éthiopie: Love Songs**
Inédit, France
Two male singers and one female (none other than the great Gigi) perform exquisite songs accompanied by *krar* (lyre) and *masenqo* (fiddle). Traditional material compellingly recorded in Paris.

⊙ **Éthiopie: Polyphonies of the Dorze**
Chant du Monde, France
This discography would be incomplete without an example of one of the most outstanding forms of Ethiopia's many tribal musics.

⊙ **Music from Ethiopia**
Caprice Records, Sweden
Recordings made in Addis with Swedish assistance, bringing together traditional and modern songs. Includes some beautiful traditional examples and unusual ceremonial flute music from Tigray, in which each flute plays only certain notes of the melody. The modern songs aren't representative of the best of Ethiopia, but are still a reasonable showcase for what's around. Good accompanying booklet.

⊙ **Music of Wax and Gold**
Topic, UK
Field recordings by the late, respected ethnomusicologist Jean Jenkins, now reissued on this wonderful CD.

PLAYLIST
Ethiopia

1 SELÉ SENÈ SEQLET Alèmu Aga from *The Rough Guide to the Music of Ethiopia*
Alèmu Aga backs his own meditative vocals with the weird rustic buzzing of the *begena*. Putting this on is like opening a window on the past.

2 GELA Abyssinia Infinite from *Zion Roots*
A spooky *kirar* intro gives way to a great booming groove and the wonderful of voice Ejigayehu "Gigi"Shibabaw, answered throughout by hypnotic chorus vocals and accordion.

3 TITESH (DON'T WORRY/FORGET IT) Mahmoud Ahmed from *Soul of Addis*
A typical triple time Amharic rhythm drives this 1980s classic, a fine showcase for Ahmed's distinctive tight vibrato. Do you hear an echo of Stevie Wonder's "Master Blaster"?

4 KABU Aster Aweke from *Kabu*
A sparse, almost ghostly arrangement spotlights Ethiopia's most famous singer. The title can be roughly translated as "You are my rock".

5 YÈWÈYN HARÈGITU Alemayehu Eshete from *Éthiopiques 9: Alèmayèhu Ashèté*
Most active in the late 1960s and early 70s, this singer acknowledges the influence of Pat Boone, Elvis Presley and Little Richard, the latter especially evident on this 1971 cut.

6 MOTHER'S SONG Tsegué-Maryam Guèbrou from *Éthiopiques 21: Emahoy Tsegué-Maryam Guèbrou*
Dating from her first recording sessions made in Germany in 1963, this impossibly beautiful solo piano piece by the reclusive nun will take your breath away.

7 SHELLÈLA Getatchew Mekurya from *Éthiopiques 14: Getatchew Mekurya, Negus of Ethiopian Sax*
Backed by a warped, skanking riff of organ, rhythm guitar and squeaking trumpet, the tenor saxophonist gets wiggy and war-like, mimicking a traditional battlefield shellèla singer.

8 ANTCHI HOYÉ LÈNÉ Yared Tèfèra from *Park Center Mood*
Suave and swinging instrumental Ethio-jazz from this important post-Derg musician and his excellent ensemble.

Jon Lusk

Gabon

cranning the night away

First Lady Patience Dabany

A small nation with a population of just over a million, Gabon was linked colonially to other Congo Basin territories as part of French Equatorial Africa until independence in 1960. Its popular music has never achieved the distinctiveness and exportability of that of its great neighbours, the Congo and Cameroon, and due to oil wealth discovered soon after independence, Gabon's ability to import goods, immigrants and fashions has tended to militate against its own production. Nonetheless, the country has a remarkably rich patchwork of ethnic sub-divisions – with around fifty languages and dialects – and similarly diverse local colouring tints the world of Gabon's popular music. Philip Sweeney surveys the scene.

Much of Gabon's tribal music remains unexplored by ethnomusicologists and record labels. French pioneers such as the late Gilbert Rouget and Pierre Sallée, and current practitioners such as Silvie Lebomin, have produced a good deal of documentation on certain ethnic groups, such as the Fang – who are noted xylophone constructors and players – and the various **Pygmy** communities whose polyphony, shared with their Cameroonian counterparts, is so striking. Aside from these, however, Gabon's traditional music remains largely ignored, overshadowed by the country's various popular strands.

Cults and Traditions

Gabon's traditional instruments include the common families of flutes, membrane drums, bells, **balafon** (xylophones) and **sanza** (Congolese thumb piano), but also two instruments unique to Gabon, though not without cousins elsewhere. The first is the **mongongo**, a musical bow played like a giant Jew's harp: the mouth acts as a resonator for the plucked string, with the player humming to select the pitch. The second is the **ngombi**, a sort of seven-stringed harp with an animal-skin resonating box.

Both instruments, but especially the *mongongo*, are featured in the ritual music of the **Bwiti religion**, another Gabonese speciality. Bwiti is a syncretic animist cult, centred around the ritual ingestion, and subsequent purifying vomiting, of the hallucinogenic roots of the *iboga* plant. A Bwiti ceremony includes long nights of dancing around resin-burning braziers, during which the male dancers, draped in raffia-strand robes, swirl over the fire, their accoutrements flaring and spreading sparks over the congregation. Bwiti folklore troupes exist, though they are at a very early stage of transformation into entertainment, given the almost total lack of tourists Gabon has so far received.

In the 1980s, Bwiti music undertook its first step into the popular realm, when the singer and television presenter **Vickos Ekondo** produced a blend that he christened **tandima**. Ekondo's stage act featured traditional animal-skin costumes, barebreasted, painted female dancers, and a sufficiently authentic ritual Bwiti content that the entertainer was summoned before Bwiti elders to account for his breach of sacramental confidence. He had to absolve himself by the payment of a major tribute and the intercession of elders of the traditional Mwiri cult, who maintain customary, as opposed to official State, law and order, and who could,

it's widely accepted, have ordered a transgressor's death *in extremis*.

Congolese Rumba and Army Bands

Gabon's early popular music scene was dominated by **Congolese music**, with minor parts filled by the **ekoda** style from neighbouring Spanish (nowadays Equatorial) Guinea, played on accordion and drums, and by mission choirs (still popular today). Gradually, however, homegrown bands began to operate in Libreville *dancings* such as the Joyeux-Palace, the Bonga-Jazz and the Gabon-Bar, and the local **soulevé** rhythm became popular.

Soon after independence, a group of former students of Libreville's Bessieux College began to forge careers as musical leaders. Chief among them was **Pierre Akendengué** (see box opposite), whose composition came second in the competition for a national anthem, but who left Gabon for France in 1965. However, it was **Hilarion N'Guema**, a singer, guitarist, composer and humorous social commentator, who made the greater mark, founding the important guitar-and-percussion band **Afro-Succès**, whose repertoire of beguine, rumba, tango, French chanson and the **mvet** rhythm of the northern Gabonese Fang made its home bar, the Canne A Sucre, the most popular in Libreville.

The third major figure from this period – like Akendengué and N'Guema, still active today – was Christian Makaya, better known as **Mackjoss**, whose band **Negro-Tropical** was resident at the Gabon-Bar.

By the end of the 1960s, a political change of profound importance was under way. In 1967, Albert Bongo became President, and shortly afterwards decreed his newly created Parti Démocratique Gabonais the country's sole political party. Music-making was henceforth channelled into the hands either of a new series of military or police bands, or neighbourhood and community associations set up under PDG auspices. Mackjoss's Negro-Tropical dissolved and various members joined the **Diablotins**, the newly created band of the national police, though one with a mighty swing for a bunch of *flics*. Hilarion N'Guema briefly joined **Ekweza**, the *gendarmerie* band, which also absorbed the best musicians of the lately popular rock'n'roll-influenced bands **Les Sphinx** and **Les Sorciers Noirs**. N'Guema didn't remain a gendarme for long, moving to Paris, where he is still based.

Pierre Akendengué: Ethnomusicology as Art

Gabon's premier songwriter and performer, **Pierre Akendengué** has based his career on an interplay between his own quite modern tastes – including jazz and the European song movements – and the traditional music and storytelling of his country. He has also maintained a creative tension between cooperation with, and opposition to, the Bongo regime. Akendengué left Gabon at the age of 22 to study psychology in Orléans (he eventually obtained a doctorate) and simultaneously enrolled in the Petit Conservatoire of the influential chanson star Mireille. A meeting with singer-songwriter **Pierre Barouh** led to a deal with Barouh's successful avant-garde label **Saravah**, and burgeoning success in France, though Akendengué rapidly realized he could not achieve true originality without keeping to the fore the Gabonese roots of his musical personality.

During the 1970s and early 80s, his criticism of the Gabonese regime kept him in de facto exile in France, but in 1985 he returned and was welcomed into the establishment, with a post as **cultural adviser** to the President.

In Gabon he continued to make his own records, mixing lyrics in French and his first language **Myéné** with complex arrangements including modern and local instruments; his 1966 album *Poé* had been the first modern popular recording to feature the sound of an *ngombi* (mimicked in fact by Akendengué's acoustic guitar). While initiatives such as his **Carrefour des Arts** have encouraged young Gabonese singer-songwriters, Akendengué has also acted as an energetic **field collector**. In 2004 and 2005, with the backing of the Wildlife Conservation Society of the Bronx Zoo and the Moore Foundation, Akendengué undertook two major tours of the National Parks of Gabon, recording rich traditional music such as the polyphony of the **Pygmies** of the northern Minzoul region, and rare and threatened finds such as a variety of **pluriarch** of which only two players are left, and a once-common ritual song for young virgins that is now known to a single old village woman.

Although the epoch of the single party ended in 1990 and the militarization of bands a decade earlier, it's still common to find Gabonese musicians with military day jobs: if you want news of the *zouk* star **Etienne Madama**, for instance, you're likely to find it in reports of appointments in the Armed Forces, where Colonel Madama spends most of his time.

Renovation Cha Cha and Zouk

The 1980s saw a diversification of Gabonese music-making. The educational institutions instead of the army became important cradles of production. Bessieux College had given birth to **Les Stones**, one of whose members was **Alexandre Sambat**, later a government minister, record producer and lynchpin of the Gabonese *zouk* movement. Omar Bongo University became the *alma mater* of the **Orchestre M'Bala**, still going strong today,

and the Lycée Technique of Libreville created **Le Capo-Sound**, whose luminaries included **Oliver N'Goma**, later to become one of the country's biggest international stars.

As a new crop of musicians entered the fray, Gabon's musical infrastructure began to mature. This was due partly to the patronage of the omnipotent presidential family (see box on p.120). President Bongo, now renamed Omar after conversion to Islam, endowed Libreville with the **N'Koussou and Mademba recording studios** (two state-of-the-art facilities superior to anything else in the region) and one of Africa's most powerful radio stations. **Africa No. 1**, based in Libreville and transmitting from Franceville, near Bongo's home town in the south, established a continent-wide profile as a leading broadcaster of popular music.

These facilities began to attract regional stars to Libreville, including names such as the Zaïreans Zaïko Langa Langa and M'Pongo Love, Lapiro de Mbanga and Manu Dibango from Cameroon, and the South African diva Miriam Makeba. *Zouk*

Patience Dabany and the Bongo Dynasty

The career of **Albert Bernard Bongo**, later El Haj Omar Bongo, president of Gabon for almost four decades, embraces a swath of the country's musical history. In 1959, then a young civil servant, Bongo married **Josephine Dabany**, a girl from the Haut-Ogooué province. Her parents had brought her up in Brazzaville, across the Congolese border. Bongo was always a music-lover – once famously flying James Brown's band into Libreville for a party – and, as his relatives began to be placed in positions of power, the music scene was not ignored.

Bongo's brother-in-law was put in charge of the state-financed Mademba Studio, and a sister-in-law was on the board of the extravagantly equipped radio station Africa No. 1. Madame Josephine Bongo, meanwhile, set up women's *groupes d'animation culturelle* in Libreville and acted as *eminence grise* (behind-the-scenes influence) on her husband's musical decision-making. The Bongos' son **Alain** (later Ali Ben) **Bongo** performed as a singer with the **Jimmy Ondo** band, and wrote songs, before taking up his current position of minister of defence.

When Josephine Bongo decided to leave her position as First Lady and set up as the singer **Patience Dabany**, she was able to install herself in a large complex – including villa, shopping centre and her Ilouba recording studio – beside the gigantic Omar Bongo sports complex, with a second studio in Los Angeles, where she continued to see friends such as **James Brown** and **Thelma Houston**. Dabany's voice, her surprising prowess as a traditional percussionist and her choice of good songs and arrangements allowed her to produce some excellent records, mixing a big echo-y version of the Congolese *soukous* sound with influences from folklore and catchy songs in a wide variety of Gabonese dialects (as well as the Congolese lingua franca, Lingala). Dabany's early *soukous* hits – "Gaëlla", "Associe" and "Article 106" – are often interpreted as veiled reprimands to her former husband, but she remains close to the Presidential Palace and a major figure in the country.

stars such as Kassav (who passed a catastrophic week in Libreville in 1986, stranded by the disappearance of their would-be promoter) also paid visits, because this French Antillean style was by now spreading like wildfire in Gabon. The most successful exponent of **Afro-zouk**, as the Congo-adapted version of the genre came to be known, was **Oliver N'Goma**, who pursued a career in TV production while also creating huge hits such as "Bané".

Two other artists carried the flag for Gabon internationally. **Patience Dabany**, the former First Lady (see box above), used her position and money to move into top-level showbusiness in 1986, and her talent to make a success of it. Meanwhile **Pierre Akendengué**, who returned from French exile in 1985, re-established his position as musician of great individuality, and also proved an indefatigable promoter and producer of other artists. His album *Lambarena* was a landmark of ambitious, internationally minded production, with the nascent World Music movement firmly in its sights.

Cranning the Night Away

For a country of its size, present-day Gabon enjoys quite a diverse music scene, though not exactly a booming one. Africa No. 1 continues to broadcast internationally, including nowadays a new emphasis on Gabonese records, but its popular-

ity is diminished and a crop of newer rivals such as Emergence compete for its audience. The great Mademba and N'Koussou studios are derelict, but a dozen small-scale studios and production companies, of which the market leader is Jean-Yves Messan's Mandarine, have sprung up.

It continues, however, to be difficult for a musician to survive without either rich relatives or day jobs. Medium- to large-scale live concerts are scarce, restricted to lavish and expensive galas at the **Intercontinental Hotel** and private parties, plus the occasional stadium gig. Small bar shows and play-back sessions in discotheques exist, but don't pay enough to live on, while Gabonese record sales, with rare exceptions, are equally inadequate. Nonetheless, there is still plenty of Gabonese music. Pierre Akendengué continues to be regarded as its elder statesman, and his influence, exercised between 1988 and 1992 through the Carrefour des Arts concert and workshop programme he set up under the umbrella of the French Cultural Centre, has been considerable on a number of songwriters with both traditional and international influences. The most prominent of these is **Annie-Flore Batchiellilys**, a Punu-speaking country girl who, boosted by Akendengue's patronage, lived, studied music and worked the metier in France for thirteen years before returning to Libreville, where her second album, *Diboty*, was a major success in 2002, paving the way for her

Most Promising Female Artist prize at the Kora Awards in South Africa.

Apart from Akendengué, a considerable number of the senior stars continue to work, either from home or Paris. Oliver N'Goma commutes between the two, juggling dates with holiday leave from his TV post, while Patience Dabany oscillates between Paris (where she gives a couple of major shows a year), Libreville and Los Angeles.

A variety of new trends in dance music have emerged over recent years. There are, of course, Gabonese reggae and rap performers, notably **Didier Dekokaye** for the former and **Professeur T** the latter. The *mvet* rhythm of the Fang epic fables re-emerged in the late-1990s work of **Alexis Abessolo**, a former member of M'Bala. **Landry Ifouta**, a veteran showbusiness figure from Port Gentil, had huge success from 2001 onwards with a Latinized Congolese and *soulevé* mix. And more recently still came two crazes: **cranning**, which you dance to with hands in pockets, in a parody of cool nonchalance, and **riengo**, a variation on the classic Congolese pelvic thrust action deemed obscene and banned from TV after President Bongo saw his young son mimicking the dance (or so it's rumoured). The latter style's chief exponent was **Kacky Disco**, an army warrant officer and ex-member of the **Massako military band**. The *riengo* controversy thus neatly encapsulates modern Gabonese music: a lively dance rhythm, a mix of regional trends with local touches, a state-employed artist and the omnipresent eye of the presidency.

DISCOGRAPHY Gabon

⊙ Xylophone Fang
Philips, France
Wood-block pyrotechnics recorded live in 1976 in Bitam, northern Gabon, with a nucleus of backwoods Paganini and sundry villagers weaving an intricate if long-drawn-out spell over three 22-minute tracks.

⊙ Chants Atégés
Harmonia Mundi, France
An interesting collection of field recordings made between 1946 and 2003 in the villages of the high plateaux of southern Gabon, demonstrating a heartening degree of continuity of tradition, and a continued abundance of raucous voices and unrestrained percussion.

⊙ Music of the Bibayak Pygmies "Epic Cantors"
Ocora, France
The Pygmy polyphony found in Gabon and Cameroon is pure, striking and remarkably sophisticated. This fine recording showcases the soundworld of the Bibayak group.

Pierre Akendengué

The grand old man of Gabonese music is never going to be a dancefloor filler, but his blend of Europe and Africa was ahead of its time, and remains highly distinctive.

⊙ Lambarena
Sony, France
⊙ Ekunda-Sah!
Taxi Records, France
Separated by two decades, these records demonstrate the Akendengué recipe at its most classic and entertaining.

Annie-Flore Batchiellilys

Imbued with traditional sounds from her southern Gabonese village childhood, poetic ambition from her "spiritual father" Pierre Akendengué and European know-how from her years in France (with her French husband), Annie-Flore Batchiellilys also has the vision and determination required to forge a serious musical career.

⊙ Diboty
AFB Music, Gabon/France
This set of rather mannered ballads shows off Batchiellilys' musical preoccupations well.

Patience Dabany

The former First Lady of Gabon justifies her high profile via an arresting voice – steeped in the sound of Congolese village funeral singing, despite her LA proclivities – and excellent taste in arrangers and musicians.

⊙ Obomiyia
PADA International, Gabon/US
★ Article 106
PADA International, Gabon/US
Two relatively recent albums, both successes, and both endowed with a great Kinshasa wall of sound (complete with excellent, low-key solo guitar by Sylvain Kalibi) and some good songs, including one by Dabany's son, the Gabonese defence minister.

Vickos Ekondo

TV presenter, entrepreneur and another of the president's advisers on cultural affairs, the self-styled King of Tandima is also one of Gabon's most internationally travelled artists, his colourful pop-folklore troupe a feature of festivals around the world.

⊙ Lost Voices
Sounds And Lyrics, France
Recorded in Paris in 2003, this is a rather tamer version of the *tandima* sound, but it's easier to find than the old stuff and features important titles such as "Bovinga" and "Njobi Kawata Nde".

Oliver N'Goma

Born in 1959 in southern Gabon, Olivier, as he was christened, gradually moved up the ranks both in television and music until he achieved his breakthrough as the first star of Afro-*zouk* in 1990.

⊙ Bané
Lusafrica, France
Still his biggest hit, with 50,000 sales in Gabon alone, *Bané* was a major achievement. It shows N'Goma at his best: a competent, soulful singer more than capable of living up to a catchy song.

Hilarion N'Guema

Born in 1943 and active as a singer and songwriter since 1958, N'Guema's substantial body of work contains social commentary, often humorous, on many of the significant events and developments of African life.

⊙ Sida
Haïssam Records, France
Like the great Franco's "Attention na Sida", but produced before it, this text on the perils of AIDS combines stern warnings with sweet music.

Landry Ifouta

A honey-voiced crooner reminiscent of the late Franco, Ifouta shot to prominence in 2001 with the album *Aurore* and went on to launch the "cranning" craze of 2004–5.

⊙ Sans Commentaire
RAO Productions, Gabon
A pleasant set including a lovely Franco-esque opening love duet and slightly underwhelming soundtrack to said dance craze, complete with chuckling animateurs, a synthesized accordion part and sundry badinage.

Kacky Disco

W.O. Disco (Kacky means "thunderbolt", incidentally) graduated from the Armed Forces band to form his own quartet, the Codos (meaning army boots) and hit the medium-sized time in 2001 with his album *Raid in the South*.

⊙ Les Meilleurs Tubes 2001 a 2005
Iris Com, Gabon
This greatest hits comprises a dozen romping dance tracks, including the only track to segue into after a hectic cranning session: "Petit Modèle", the song that launched the *riengo* craze.

PLAYLIST
Gabon

1 **DIEU AIE PITIÉ** Pierre Akendengué
from *Lambarena*
Akendengué at his most commercial: a nice mix of rumbling percussion, twanging *mondongo*, female chorus and faint *zouk* shading.

2 **YANGA YANGA** Patience Dabany from *Article 106*
Classic mid-period Dabany, a mix of Congolese *pleureuse* and the Ronettes gone equatorial.

3 **IKOKU** Patience Dabany from *Obomiyia*
Atmospheric late Dabany, abandoning the *soukous* guitars but finding instead an excellent balance between Brazzaville roots and LA polish.

4 **EBENGUE BENGUE** Vickos Ekondo from *Lost Voices*
A slicker, sweeter version of his earlier work, nonetheless demonstrating the *tandima* sound tolerably well.

5 **BANÉ** Oliver N'Goma from *Bané*
Gabon's biggest hit for a decade and a half, and a good exposition of Afro-*zouk* wares.

Ghana

from highlife to hiplife

Alex Konadu – classic highlife
Jak Kilby

The quintessential Ghanaian music is highlife – the hugely popular dance style that dominated the country's scene for more than half a century. But over the years, and especially after the economic collapse of the 1970s and 80s, highlife has had to compete with local rock, reggae and gospel, and has mutated into new strains such as disco-influenced "burgher" highlife and rap-style hiplife. John Collins and Ronnie Graham tell the story.

ighlife – Ghana's urban dance music – has had enormous influence throughout West Africa, but its roots are firmly embedded in the clubs and dance halls of the colonial Gold Coast. Here, in the early years of Ghana's independence in the late 1950s, it effectively became the national music, and over the last half-century has proved to be one of the most popular, enduring and adaptable African styles.

Highlife Roots

The highlife story begins in the early years of the twentieth century, when various African and European influences – including church music, military brass-band music and sea shanties – were combined with the Gold Coast's own local rhythms and idioms. These included *osibisaba*, a Fante rhythm from southwest Ghana; various types of guitar music from Liberia; and *asiko* and *gombe* from Sierra Leone, though the latter originated among freed Maroon slaves from Jamaica in the early nineteenth century.

Instrumentation depended on what equipment was available, and out of a welter of neotraditional variations there gradually emerged a form known generically as **highlife**. The term was coined in the 1920s and referred to the high-class, top-hat-and-tails dance evenings that had become fashionable among the Ghanaian elite, with music provided by ballroom and ragtime bands such as **Excelsior Orchestra**, **Jazz Kings**, the **Accra Orchestra** and **Cape Coast Sugar Babies**.

However, two other proto-highlife forms had already appeared in Ghana's coastal towns and ports. A local **brass-band music** had evolved in Cape Coast and El Mina after 1870, when several thousand West Indian colonial soldiers were stationed in Ghana. The Afro-Caribbean music they played in their spare time resonated with Ghanaians, who went on to create their own local *adaha* music. This spread into southern Ghana, and during the 1930s, those Akan towns and villages who couldn't afford expensive brass instruments created *konkoma* (or *konkomba*) marching bands that used local drums and voices instead.

A fourth form of early highlife known as **palm wine** – named after the drink made from fermented palm-tree sap – evolved from the Fanti *osibisaba* and cross-fingering guitar techniques introduced by visiting Liberian Kru sailors. The most famous of the Fanti guitarists were **George William Aingo** and **Kwame Asare** (see box opposite). In the 1950s, guitar bands began to go electric, and pioneered by **E.K. Nyame**, they became linked to a popular theatre known as the **concert party** (see box on p.126).

Dance-Band Highlife

The already exuberant dance-band style was further enriched during World War II by elements of

King Bruce (on trumpet) with his highlife big band

Palm Wine Music: Buy the Man a Drink

Palm wine music is a retrospective term for various early twentieth-century music styles that combined local West African instruments with the portable ones of visiting seamen: the concertina, harmonica and particularly the guitar. It was played in working-class dockside bars and palm wine bars and included subgenres such as the *osibisaaba* and *annkadaamu* of the local Fanti fishermen, Sierra Leonian *asiko* music and the *dagomba*, "fireman" (i.e. ship coal-stoker) and "mainline" guitar-styles of visiting Liberian Kru sailors and stevedores.

Kru seamen had been working aboard European sailing ships from Napoleonic times and developed the distinctive West African two-finger plucking guitar technique, which spread along the West African coast from World War I on via Kru-town settlements. It was a Kru who, in the 1920s, taught Ghana's famous pioneer highlife guitarist **Kwame Asare** (or Jacob Sam), whose **Kumasi Trio** made the first highlife recordings (including the famous "Yaa Amponsah") for Zonophone in London in 1928 (re-released on CD by Heritage, UK).

When coastal palm wine music moved inland, it incorporated features of the traditional Akan *seprewa* harp-lute, creating the more rootsy *odonson* or Akan "blues" style of palm wine music. During the 1930s and 40s guitar (and concertina) records of these Akan "blues" were being distributed in southern Ghana by HMV and Parlophone, featuring artists like **Jacob Sam**, **Kwesi Pepera**, **Appianing**, **Kwame**, **Mireku**, **Osei Bonsu**, **Kwesi Menu**, **Kamkan** and **Appiah Adjekum**. These groups were all small, consisting of no more than a guitarist or two plus a percussionist, although Appiah Adjekum also used an array of *konkoma* frame drums, with his Liberian wife accompanying him on slide guitar.

Collection of John Collins

After World War II the palm wine groups expanded into guitar bands by borrowing instruments, such as standing double-bass, clarinets and Afro-Cuban bongos, from the highlife dance bands of the period, such as **E.T. Mensah's Tempos**. The most important of these postwar guitar bands was that of **E.K. Nyame** (with his falsetto singer **Kobina Okai**) who had trained with Appiah Adjekum. Other leading guitar bands of the 1950s were those of **I.E. Mason**, **Kwaa Mensah**, **Kakaiku**, **Onyina**, **Yamoah** and **Ampoumah** (T.O. Jazz). The 1950s bands were acoustic, but during the 1960s they went electric. However, since the late 1960s a number of bands and artists have gone back to the older, "unplugged" format. One is the Ashanti guitarist **Koo Nimo**, who began to revive the old palm wine style, using acoustic "box" guitar and traditional percussion instruments. He also sometimes teams up with the *seprewa* player **Osei Kwame Korankye**.

Some of the guitar-band old-timers have also moved back from amplified to acoustic guitar. For instance during the 1970s and 80s the late **Kwaa Mensah** performed and recorded some acoustic highlifes. Then there is **Kwabena Nyama** from Kumasi, who since 2000 has released several albums and toured Europe. Another is the late **T. O. "Jazz" Ampoumah** who, together with his singer **Kojo Menu**, worked and recorded with the Ghana University-based Local Dimension band. A few musicians of a younger generation also play in the palm wine mode, such as the Kwahu guitarist and singer **Kwadwo Tawia** (see the *Highlife Allstars* CD, p.134) and the group of guitarist **Papa Baah** and *seprewa* player **Kyerematen Baffour**.

Kwaa Mensah in regal mode

Concerted Efforts

The Ghanaian "**concert party**" evolved out of local renditions of vaudeville and music hall performed for the Ghanaian elites in the early twentieth century. In those days, well-to-do Ghanaians were entertained by local dance orchestras and variety programmes at high-class venues. The variety sketches consisted of tap-dancing routines, ragtime and short comedies in English performed by black-face comics, such as **Teacher Yalley** and **Williams and Marbel**. Sometimes visiting artists would also perform, such as the African American couple **Glass and Grant** who performed in Accra in the mid-1920s.

However, around 1930, the Fanti comedian **Bob Johnson** hijacked the concert party from the elite and took it to the rural hinterland. Consequently the first steps in the indigenization of this local tradition took place when Johnson's **Versatile Eight** (and later the **Axim Trio**) incorporated motifs from traditional Akan Ananse-the-Spider stories. In fact, Johnson's combination of American black-face with the mischievous Ananse character was so successful that from then on most Ghanaian comedians have called themselves "Bob".

During World War II, **Bob Vans** and some other Ghanaian servicemen fighting in Burma even set up a concert party to entertain troops of the West African Frontier Force. On returning to Ghana in 1946, Vans and his friends set up the **Burma Jokers**, changing the name to the **Ghana Trio** in 1948 after an upsurge of nationalism in Ghana. Indeed many of the concert parties (the Axim Trio and **Bob Ansah**'s group) supported Nkrumah and the nationalist cause; Ansah was even arrested by the British.

A further indigenization of the concert party took place in 1952 when **E.K. Nyame** formed the **Akan Trio**, which attached a concert party to his guitar band. This resulted in a comic highlife opera format that was used by practically all 1950s guitar bands: **Kakaiku**'s, **Yamoahs**, **Jaguar Jokers**, **Bob Cole**'s group, **Onyina's Royal Trio** and **Dr Gyasi's Noble Kings**. These all constantly toured Ghana, performing musical plays at even the tiniest villages. Because of the rough life on the road the women's roles were taken by female impersonators. Recognizing the contribution of the concert parties performers to the independence struggle, President Kwame Nkrumah established state-run Workers Brigade concert parties. He also encouraged the entrance of women into the concert profession.

By the mid-1970s there were at least seventy concert parties/guitar bands operating, the most important being the **African Brothers**, **Okukuseku**'s, **Happy Stars**, **Parrots**, **Kumapim Royals**, **F. Kenya**'s, **Alaji Frempong's Cubanos Fiesta**, **K.K.'s No. 2**, **Station Master** (Joe Eyison), **Alex Konadu**, **Osofo Dadzie** and then **Obra**, which had a long-running TV series.

Very few of these bands survived the collapse of the Ghanaian economy in the late 1970s and the subsequent political turmoil, night curfews and massive duties on imported band equipment. Today just a handful of concerts survive, like the **African Heroes**, **Teacher and his Afrikana**, **Paa Bobo** and **Bob Okalla**. Few still go on rural tours – an exception being the **City Boys** formed by **J.A. Adofo**, popularly known as the "Black Chinese". However, new avenues have opened up for concert performers. Some appear on television (such as the **Cantata** group), while others feature at the Unilever Keysoap concert party programme at the National Theatre in Accra, and some concert actors and actresses have found a new outlet with the upsurge of low-budget local video productions since the late 1980s.

swing and jazz, introduced by British and American servicemen, to produce what many consider to be classic highlife. These dance bands emerged from the prewar dance orchestras and flourished during the rapid process of urbanization and social change unleashed by the nationalist struggle of Kwame Nkrumah.

With independence in 1957, Nkrumah's social-ist-aligned government actively encouraged indigenous music. Apart from funding dozens of state bands, the president frequently travelled to neighbouring countries with a full dance band in his retinue. The music reflected the assertive self-confidence of Ghana at the time – newly indepen-

dent, reasonably prosperous and widely respected in the pan-African struggle. The top highlife bands composed original material in English and all the local languages, incorporating traditional rhythms into new arrangements. This framework was augmented by forays into "Congo" music, calypso and any other style which grabbed the bandleader's fancy. The result was a lilting, relaxed, sophisticated dance style with enduring appeal.

E.T. Mensah (see box opposite) led the charge with his talented Tempos band. A consummate musician, equally at home on sax or trumpet, he brought a new level of professionalism to African dance music and popularized it throughout West

Africa. Mensah had taken over as bandleader in the late 1940s from the master drummer **Guy Warren** (a.k.a. Kofi Ghanaba), a precocious talent responsible for introducing **Afro-Cuban percussion** into the highlife groove. Following a trip to London, where he met Caribbean musicians, he was also responsible for the introduction of **calypso**, playing it live with the Tempos while widening its appeal on his radio programmes. In 1953, he began to redirect his efforts and moved, via Liberia, to the US where he released a series of legendary albums that aimed to reintroduce black Americans to their African roots by combining modern jazz with African percussion.

Another major figure in classic era big-band highlife was **King Bruce**, who died in 1997, a trumpeter with a taste for jazz and swing. Bruce established a stable of dance bands, which included his own Black Beats, and later the Barbecues, the Barons and five other groups, all beginning with B and mostly playing "copyright" (i.e. cover-versions). An unrelated "B" band – the Broadways, led by the guitarist Stan Plange – went on to become the **Professional Uhuru Band** in 1965.

The other big highlife dance band was Jerry Hansen's **Ramblers International Dance Band**, formed in 1962 by Hansen and nine other Black Beat members and eventually consisting of a fully professional, fifteen-man line-up. Almost uniquely, they made a living from their shows and records for nearly twenty years, and a second-generation incarnation, led by Peter Manfo, is still going strong.

By the late 1970s, however, dance-band highlife was on the way out, having been undermined by new, imported pop styles and the near-impossibility of maintaining large, full-time groups in a declining economy.

Guitar-Band Highlife

After World War II, palm wine bands evolved into bigger guitar-based bands that borrowed dance-band instruments and then went electric in the 1960s. A key figure here was **E.K. Nyame**, who was in the vanguard of the early 1950s guitar-band scene and developed its repertoire by adding jazz elements, including double bass and Latin percussion. As leader of **E.K.'s Band**, the most popular guitar group, he also grafted highlife onto Ghana's popular vaudeville concert shows, or "**concert parties**" (see box). From the 1950s to the 1970s scores of similar outfits were formed in the wake of his success. In 1975, Nyame recorded a set of old

E.T. Mensah

Mensah, the pioneer of 1950s dance-band highlife, was born in Accra in 1919 and began his career with Teacher Lamptey's Accra Orchestra. During the 1940s Mensah joined the **Tempos**, originally formed by Arthur Harriman and Adolf Doku to play swing-jazz music for the thousands of British and American troops stationed in Ghana during World War II. Mensah took over the band after the war, and with help from

Ghanaba (Guy Warren) and **Joe Kelly**, created a brand of highlife strongly influenced by swing, as well as Afro-Cuban music and calypso. He was so successful that numerous Ghanaian bands followed suit, such as the **Red Spots**, **Rhythm Aces**, **Black Beats** and **Broadway**. Through trips to Nigeria he also sparked off an interest in highlife there, performed by the likes of Bobby Benson, Victor Olaiya, E.C. Arinze and Rex Lawson. After a period of semi-retirement, Mensah was called back into recording action in the late 1970s: first an Afrodisia release, then the *Highlife Giants* album with Olaiya in 1983 and finally in 1986 a European tour and CD releases of his old hits by Sterns/RetroAfric (*All For You* and *Day by Day*). When he died in 1996, Mensah was given a state funeral.

Jak Kilby

E.T. Mensah (right), with a reward for his labour

numbers to preserve for posterity what had previously only been available on 78s. On his death in 1977, like E.T. Mensah twenty years later, he was given a state funeral.

1970s Afro-Fusions and Back-to-Roots

During the 1960s Ghanaian music was influenced by Congolese music, pop and above all soul, whose "black and proud" message and Afro fashions led to a new era of experimentation in the early 1970s, with the creation of Afro-rock, Afro-beat and Afro-funk. Apart from London-based **Osibisa**, this new wave included pop bands like **Magic Aliens**, **Big Beats**, **Boombaya**, **Sawaaba Sounds** and even some highlife guitar bands, such as the **African Brothers** with their "Afro-hili beat". Producer **Kwadwo Donkor** also started working on Afro-beat with flautist Oscar Sulley, singer Eddie Ntreh and the Uhuru big band. This explosion of Afro music was reinforced by the Soul to Soul concert in Accra in 1971, featuring artists such as Wilson Pickett, Ike and Tina Turner, Santana, Les McCann and Eddie Harris.

The forward-looking entrepreneur **Faisal Helwani** was particularly important in this turn towards "Afro-roots" music. He supported innovative fusion groups like **Hedzolleh** ("Peace-Freedom" in Ga, the language of Accra), **Basa-Basa** ("pandemonium") and the **Bunzus**, who dug into Ghanaian culture and presented it in a sophisticated package. Helwani also repackaged giants of the past, promoting E.T. Mensah, the Uhurus and the palm wine acoustic guitarist Kwaa Mensah in a series of weekend variety shows.

Another initiative came in the form of the **Ga cultural revival** spearheaded by the neotraditional cultural troupe **Wulomei** (Ga for "traditional priest"), which sought to encourage young people 'to forget foreign music and do their own thing', in the words of band leader Nii Ashitey. They toured with Kwaa Mensah and were soon followed by other Ga bands such as **Dzadzeloi**, **Blemabii**, **Abladei**, **Agbafoi Bukom**, **Ashiedu Keteke** and **Suku Troupe**. These groups were characterized by powerful Ga drumming, female harmonies and exciting floor shows, yet they were as comfortable in hotel cabarets as they were in downtown Accra compounds. The Ga cultural troupes still play in Accra and it is worth checking **Bukom**, led by Big Boy Nii Adum, formerly of Wulomei, who remain active themselves, led by Nii Ashitey.

Highlife guitar was revitalized by Daniel "Koo Nimo" Amponsah. After absorbing his fingerpicking, palm wine guitar style from Kwame Asare, Kwaa Mensah and E.K. Nyame, Amponsah learnt classical guitar in his late twenties, and brought in all kinds of European classical and American jazz influences. He has been a source of inspira-

Osibisa

In Britain at the end of the 1960s, pop audiences were presented for the first time with African music: the "criss-cross rhythms which explode with happiness" of Osibisa. Formed in London in 1968 by Ghanaians **Teddy Osei**, **Mac Tontoh** and **Sol Amarfio**, and with a mixed African and Caribbean line-up, Osibisa's Afro-rock singles climbed the British charts and in the 1970s three of them – "Dance the Body Music", "Sunshine Day" and "Coffee Song" – made it into the UK Top Ten (still almost unheard of for African musicians).

Osibisa took their name from *osibisaba*, the prewar proto-highlife rhythm, which they chose to reflect the coming together of African roots and foreign pop. They were, for many years, the world's best-known African band and they made a lasting impact throughout Africa. As the situation deteriorated back home in Ghana, Osibisa became a beacon of hope for musicians struggling to keep body and soul together.

Between 1995 and 1997 the Red Steel label reissued all eight of Osibisa's innovative and influential albums. Mac Tontoh is now back in Ghana, where he is a member of the National Commission on Culture and runs his Kete Warriors group, while Gregg Koffi Brown released his debut solo album *Together As One* in 2005 after 22 years with the band.

tion to Ghanaian musicians trying to graft new musical stock onto old roots, and continues to perform regularly with his all-acoustic Adadam Agoromma band. He also incorporated the Akan *seprewa* harp-lute into his group and arranged for this almost extinct instrument to be taught at the University of Ghana's School of Performing Arts.

Economic Collapse and the Highlife Diaspora

For almost two decades – the golden era of the Nkrumah revolution – Ghana was the very heart of Africa and African music. However, with Nkrumah's overthrow in 1966 the country began a downward spiral of political instability, corruption and economic collapse. Musicians suffered alongside everyone else and their livelihoods were in jeopardy when the clubs and dance halls began closing, the instruments and equipment broke down and the beer dried up.

Many musicians left to seek work abroad. The nucleus of **Osibisa**, for instance, who were the most prominent African band in Europe in the 1970s (see box opposite), left Ghana shortly after the 1966 coup. Through the 1970s, and particularly during the economic lowpoint of the early 1980s, many others joined them, moving to Europe or **Nigeria**, which was enjoying a period of booming oil prosperity.

Many Ghanaian highlife bands flourished in Lagos and in Nigeria's eastern, Igbo regions. **Okukuseku** became the best known, but dozens of others – among them The Canadoes, The Opambuas, Odoywewu, The Kuul Strangers, The Beach Scorpions, The Golden Boys and Citystyle – also made their mark in Nigeria, often recording only one album before returning to Ghana. One example of a well-travelled professional musician was **Mr T.O. Jazz** (of Ampoumah's Guitar Band) who spent seven years in what was then Zaïre, and two years in the 1970s in Onitsha with Stephen Osadebe, the late Igbo highlife guitar master.

Ghanaians Abroad

Ghana's relationship with **Britain** was, of course, long-established. The folk musician Kwame "Sam" Asare had sailed to England as early as 1928 to make the first-ever highlife recordings, and during the 1930s all the country's top musicians made the pilgrimage to Decca's London studios. Ghanaians also started to put down roots in Britain: many arrived as students and seamen and ended up settling as musicians. An early arrival in the 1930s was **Cab Quaye**, who joined Billy Cotton's Big Band; in the 1940s **Guy Warren** played bongos with Kenny Graham's Afro-Cubists. By the 1960s, a new generation was arriving, while British tours by E.T. Mensah, Jerry Hansen's Ramblers and even the Gold Coast Police Band served to keep expat Ghanaians in touch with home.

In the early 1980s scores of talented Ghanaian musicians arrived in Britain to add momentum to the burgeoning interest in African music, making their presence felt as sessionists, teachers and bandleaders. Important contributions were made by Kwabena Oduro-Kwarteng, Kofi Adu, Herman Asafo-Agyei and Sam Ashley, the core members of **Hi-Life International**, a successful London-based band who put out two albums on Stern's. Other Ghanaian arrivals became core members of busy touring and recording groups like **Orchestra Jazira** and **Kabbala**, while **Dade Krama** ploughed a lonelier furrow with an innovative, more arty approach. And there were dozens of other Ghanaian musicians on the session music scene, like guitarist **Alfred Kari Bannerman**, the late keyboard specialist **Jon Kay** and vocalist **Ben Brako**.

In the early 1980s, due to changes in British immigration laws, Ghanaians began to focus their attentions on **Germany**. Here, highlife was being fused with funk and rock to produce a new, harder-edged, studio sound. **George Darko** led the way and his song "Akoo Te Brafo" (recorded in Berlin but a big hit in Ghana) gave rise to the term "**burgher highlife**". He returned to live in Ghana in 1989. Meantime, members of his band had formed **Kantata** in Berlin, releasing a successful album of dancefloor highlife including the song "Slim Lady", which was a huge success back in Ghana. In the 1990s, electronic "burgher" highlife took a huge slice of the Ghanaian popular music market; leading exponents included **Daddy Lumba** (ex-Lumba Brothers) and **Nana Acheampong**.

During the 1980s, **Canada** – in particular Toronto, where there was an established expatriate community – started to attract Ghanaian musicians. **Herman Asafo-Agyei**, the bass-player, composer and leader of the Afro-funk outfit **Native Spirit**, led the way and he was later joined by drummer **Kofi Adu** and star vocalists **Pat Thomas, A.B. Crentsil** and **Jewel Ackah**. Pat Thomas, one of Ghana's premier highlife vocalists, sang with many of the country's great dance bands in the 1970s before going solo in the following decade. He gained international recognition with 1980s albums such as *Highlife Greats* and in the late 1990s "Sika Ye Mogya"(Money is Blood) on the *In Retrospect* album. A.B. Crentsil's band, the **Sweet Talks**, was one of Ghana's top highlife groups, and in 1978 they went to Los Angeles to record the classic *Hollywood Highlife Party*. Soon after the group's split, Crentsil formed the new **Ahenfo Band**, which again won international acclaim with albums like *Tantie Alaba*.

Other artists with overseas connections include **Sloopy Mike Gyanfi** in Holland; **Mustapha Tettey Addy**, who for years commuted between Ghana and Germany before finally settling in his home country; the Swiss-based **Andy Vans**, and **Obo Addy** in the US. More musicians who went abroad include **Alfred Bannerman**, **Afro Moses**, **Okyefema Asante**, **Bob Pinado**, **Eddie Omensah** and **Nana Tsiboe**. Everywhere they go, Ghanaians have planted deep roots in host communities through their work in schools, clubs and social centres.

Jak Kilby

The prolific A.B. Crentsil

Gospel and Reggae since the 1980s

Back in Ghana, music entered the 1980s in much the same shape as the country itself – hungry, revolutionary and weakened by a decade of neglect. Only two studios had survived the 1970s, and cassette piracy undermined the motivation to record. Those musicians remaining at home began, with some success, to organize and lobby for government support, leading to copyright protection and the criminalization of tape piracy. Musically, meanwhile, **gospel** and **reggae** were the new forces.

With economic decline came a rise in religion, and especially Pentecostal and evangelical churches, and as secular nightlife took a dive, many musicians were hired by churches to promote the message. By the 1990s, there were an estimated eight hundred gospel groups, many of them playing variants of highlife. While few records are made, cheap cassettes are ubiquitous. Top groups include the wonderful **Genesis Gospel Singers**, one of seven bands of the Christo Asafo mission.

Ghana's local gospel music now represents around sixty percent of the country's commercial pop output and airplay. Many churches have their own recording studios, and in 1987 a **Gospel Musicians Union** was established. One effect of the gospel revolution was that, for the first time, a substantial number of women entered the popular dance music arena. The result was the rise to prominence of such great voices as **Helen Rhabbles**, **Mary Ghansah**, **Diana Akiwumi**, the **Tagoe Sisters** and the **Daughters of Glorious Jesus**.

Reggae, with its strong appeal for the disenfranchised underclass, understandably struck a chord throughout Ghana in the late 1970s and 1980s, boosted by stadium gigs from Côte d'Ivoire's reggae star **Alpha Blondy**. The reggae boom shows no signs of abating. **Kojo Antwi**, originally a singer with Classique Vibes, is now a successful solo singer specializing in soft reggae songs sung in Twi. **K.K. Kabobo** sings a kind of reggae highlife, also in Twi. Another name to listen out for is **Rocky Dawuni**.

Another reggae-highlife artist is **Amekye Dede**. Through the 1990s, Dede rose through the ranks to become the single most popular musician in Ghana. He started his career with the **Kumapim Royals** before moving to Nigeria in the early 1980s to play with the Apollo High Kings. In 1987 he returned home and released the sensational *Kose Kose*, which established a truly national reputation for the young guitarist. Playing in an idiom that seemed to capture the country's musical mood,

Who's the Daddy?

Reggie Rockstone is the godfather of local Ghanaian rap, and in fact coined the word "hiplife" in the mid-1990s by combining the words hip-hop and highlife. Rockstone was born in the UK in 1963 and spent most of his childhood between London and Accra. Because his stepmother is African American, Rockstone has also had constant access to American pop culture. At 18 he moved to New York, where he spent fifteen years in Brooklyn and Queens. During this time, he witnessed the emergence of the hip-hop of Grandmaster Flash and Lou Rodney C.

Rockstone began rapping in New York and then London, with his Sierra Leonean partner Freddie Funkstone. After some hits in London with his group PLZ ("Parables, Linguistics and Zlang"), Rockstone attended the 1992 PANAFEST (Ghana's biannual Pan-African festival) and decided to move back to Ghana. In Accra, he founded Kassa Records with DJ Rab, a rapper from Queens, and has put out three albums since his ground-breaking 1997 debut *Makaa maka!* ("I said it because I said it"). In addition to US influences, sources closer to home are evident in his 2002 hit "Keep Your Eyes on the Road", which was based on Alhaji K. Frempong's "Kyenkyen Bi Adi Ma'wu", while "Do the Do" uses a Cameroonian *makossa* rhythm.

Rockstone's videos have enjoyed exposure as far afield as South Africa and he has performed at the Kora awards. His face is familiar to all Ghanaians from the many billboards which have made him an advertising icon for Guinness.

Amekye went on to release an astonishing fifteen albums in the 1990s, and made enough money in the process to set up his own nightclub, the Abrantie Spot, one of the few venues in Accra where regular live music is guaranteed.

The Hiplife Boom

In the mid-1990s local versions of hip-hop, ragga and rap in the Twi and Ga languages became the rage with the youth, and the name "hiplife" (i.e. hip-hop highlife) was coined by Reggie Rockstone (see box above). Other hiplife artists, usually wearing the imported clothes and hairstyles of American rappers and using digital backing-tracks have proliferated since then. Prominent names include **Nana King**, **Daasebre**, **Lord Kenya**, **Akatakyie**, **Nana Quame** and the **Native Funk Lords**. Some songs have controversial lyrics, like Tic Tac's "Philomena Kpitenge" about genital rashes, and Ex Doe and Chicago, who have been criticized for introducing the sexually explicit and misogynist themes of US gangsta rap.

Many of the older generation complain that hiplife is too much oriented towards "casa-hare" (speaking fast) over imported American beat-box rhythms, and that hiplife artists prefer lip-synching (miming) onstage to performing live. However it is not fair to blame the youth for this, as during the late 1970s and 80s Ghana's live popular-music scene collapsed due to government mismanagement, political instability and a two-year night curfew, followed by excessive import duties on music instruments and the demotion of music in the school curriculum. Without the easy-to-produce electronic music of hiplife, the urban youth today would not even have an artistic voice.

Moreover, in the last few years some hiplifers have begun to use samples from old-time highlife masters such as K. Frempong, Blemabii, Pat Thomas and Blay Ambulley, famous for his song "Simigwado". Artists have also drawn from Fela's Afro-beat and indigenous Ghanaian rhythms such as the Ga *kpanlogo*. Those hiplifers who are less imitative of imported beats include the late **Terry Bonchaka**, **Buk-Bak**, **Castro**, **Adane Best**, **Omanhene Pozo** and **Akatakyie**. **Obour** and **Okonfo Kwade** have also begun to use traditional instruments, while **Sydney** and **VIP** have also begun to do some live as well as mimed shows.

Sankofa: Back to the Roots

Alongside the 1990s shift to hi-tech hiplife music, there has also been a resurgence of new forms of traditional Ghanaian music. This has been partly triggered by the boom in international World Music sales, a massive expansion of the Ghanaian tourist industry (650,000 visitors in 2004) and the increasing number of musicians and students who come to Ghana to study music and dance. Some come to Ghana's universities: hundreds of foreigners now come each year to the School of Performing Arts of the University of Ghana to learn old traditional drum dances and neotraditional ones that have emerged since the 1950s, such as the Ga *kpanlogo* and Ewe *borborbor*. Others come to the dozens of private drum centres, music archives

Jak Kilby

Atongo Zimba playing the lute-like molo

Kwese Asare's African Cultural Centre in Larteh. This foreign interest in local Ghanaian music has led to a blossoming of folkloric and neotraditional ensembles, some of which double up as teaching outfits, like the **Kakum Bamboo Orchestra**, Nii Tetteh's **Kusun Ensemble**, Richard Danquah's **Kusum Gboo**, **Suade** and **Sogo**.

Another aspect of the revival in Ghanaian "roots" music is the proliferation of bands and artists that fuse old and new, such as the **Afrikan Show Boys**, **Atongo Zimba**, **Aaron Bebe Sukura** and **King Ayi Soba**, all from northern Ghana. Then there are **Hewale Sounds**, the **Pan African Orchestra**, **Agorsor's Cultural Ensemble**, **Takashi**, the **Selorm Cultural Troupe**, the **Wassa Afrika Dance Ensemble** and the guitar and local lute combination of **Koo Nimo and Osei Korankye**. And the new-generation Wulomei, that under Nii Ashitey pioneered the rootsy Ga cultural music during the Seventies, and which is now being run by his son and daughter, **Nii Tei Ashitey Jr.** and **Naa Ashalay**.

and traditional-music schools that have proliferated since the late 1980s. These include Mustapha Tettey Addy's African Academy of Music and Arts (AAMA) at Kokrobite, the Dagbe Drum School in the Volta Region, the Kasapaa and Aklowa beach resort schools, the Gramophone Museum and the AGORO music NGO at Cape Coast, the BAPMAF Popular Music Archives at Ofankor, Ghanaba's African Heritage Library at Medie and

The revival of interest in the *kpanlogo* drumdance of the Ga people, created in Accra the early 1960s by Otoo Lincoln, Frank Lane and Okule Foes, is particularly notable. Together with the Malian *djembe*, Yoruba *bata* and the Hausa *dondo* drums, *Kpanlogo* drums are the most popular African drums played by international musicians and world music fans.

DISCOGRAPHY Ghana

⊙ **Akom: The Art of Spirit Possession**
Village Pulse, US
Beautiful field recordings of Akan religious drum music, made over seven years by musician Scott Kiehl. Incredibly powerful, especially on the long final track of *Tigare* drumming, designed to drive out evil spirits and encourage good ones.

⊙ **Bewaare – They Are Coming: Dagaare Songs and Dances from Nandom, Ghana**
⊙ **In the Time of My Fourth Great-Grandfather: Western Sisaala Music from Lambussie, Ghana**
Pan, UK
Music of northwestern Ghana recorded by musicologist

Trevor Wiggins in 1994 and presented with extensive sleevenotes. The first CD features harp and *gyil/dzil* xylophones playing recreational *bewaa* music and semi-secret *bagre* initiation music. The second consists of unaccompanied women's songs and men's songs with cane zithers, xylophones and whistles.

⊙ **Electric Highlife: Sessions from the Bokoor Studios**
Naxos, US/Hong Kong
A collection of mainly Ghanaian guitar-band music recorded by the Accra-based John Collins between 1984 and 1989. Artists include F. Kenya, the Happy Boys, Guyayo and the Beach Scorpions, with clarinet solos by Jimmy Beckley. Also

"Classical" Highlife Survives

In spite of the problems faced by the music industry there are still plenty of the old-time highlife bands and artists still operating, ranging from acoustic palm wine to electric guitar bands, such as **J.A. Adofo's City Boys**, the **African Heroes**, **Amekye Dede**, **Alex Konadu**, **Teacher and his Afrikana**, **Gyedu Blay-Ambulley**, **Nana Tuffour**, **Felix Owusu**, **Jewel Ackah's Butterfly Band**, **Kwabena Nyama**, **Desmond Ababio's Alpha Waves**, the **Megastar Band**, **Koo Nimo**'s **Adadam Agoromma** palm wine highlife group, **The Gold Coasters** and **The Western Diamonds**. The latter-Takoradi-based band was formed in the late 1980s and included **Papa Yankson** and **C.K. Mann** when it released *Diamonds are Forever* on Sterns, UK. In the mid-1990s C.K. Mann released *Timeless Highlife* in Canada and was later guest vocalist on the *Con Ghana Cuban* album.

Whereas some highlife artists have been operating abroad, others stuck it out in Ghana. One band set up in Accra in the late 1990s by three young musicians who wanted to create a contemporary brand of highlife was **NAKOREX**, an acronym for Nat "Amandzeba" Brew, Akosua Agyepong and Rex Omar. Omar later went solo and had a big hit with his risqué highlife song "Abiba Wadonkoto Ye Me Fe" (Abiba's Beautiful Movements Sweet Me). In 2004 he collected a Kora award. Brew also went solo and has had a number of successful releases based on indigenous Ga rhythms, like his *Kpanlogo* and *Demara* CDs. The highlife guitarist Ebo Taylor, who began his career with the **Stargazers**, **Broadway** and **Uhuru** bands has since 2002 been artist-in-residence at the Music Department of the University of Ghana at Legon, where he runs the **University Highlife Band** and has also teamed up with saxophonist Ray Allen in an Afro-jazz combo called **Unconditional Love**. Guitarist "Oscarmore" Ofori, once one of Ghana's most prolific highlife dance-band composers, has turned from highlife to folklore and is currently the chief *atenteben* flute and horn player of the traditional court orchestra of the chief of New Juaben. In 1988 big-band composer/arranger **Stan Plange** (ex-leader of the Uhuru, Black Star and Ghana Broadcasting Corporation bands) co-produced the highlife CD *Crabs in a Bucket* (Asante/Oyigbo), with percussionist **Okyerema Asante** (of Hedzolleh and Paul Simon's *Graceland* tour fame) and American vibes player Nick Robertson. The leader of the famous 1960s highlife band **The Ramblers** has been able to keep his band going in Ghana (even whilst living in Washington for a while) through a younger generation of musicians he had trained, led by Felix Amenuda and more recently Peter Marfo.

included is a dance-band highlife number by King Bruce's Black Beats and a Liberian folk tune recorded in 1978 by Collins' own Bokoor guitar band.

⭐ **Ghana – Popular Music 1931–1957**
Arion Dlsques, France

A musical treasure trove unearthed in 1998 by musicologist Serena Dankwa and historian Veit Arlt from the Basel archives of the Swiss Union Trading Company, which mass-recorded Ghanaian and Nigerian music for a quarter of a century. Includes acapella religious songs, palm wine guitar/accordion music, urban Ga street music and both guitar and dance-band highlifes. Also featured is a choral song by the Akropong Singing Band, composed and conducted by the famous Ghanaian art-music composer Dr Ephraim Amu. Extensive sleeve-notes.

⊙ **Ghana Soundz – Afro-Beat, Funk and Fusion in 70's Ghana, Vols 1 and 2**
Soundway, UK

Afro-fusion recordings compiled by Miles Cleret, who spent several years collecting material in Ghana. The two CDs include the James Brown-style Marijata, Afro-beat from Oscar Sully with the Uhuru Band, funky highlifes by Ebo Taylor and Bob Pinado, plus the Afro-funk of the Uppers International and Christy Azuma. There are also several tracks by K. Frimpong, who created an archetypal minor-key form of highlife that in some ways resembles Afro-beat – and like Fela Kuti's music, has endless potential for reworking.

⊙ **The Guitar and the Gun: Highlife Music from Ghana**
Earthworks, UK

Compilation of gospel, guitar-band, dance-band and cultural

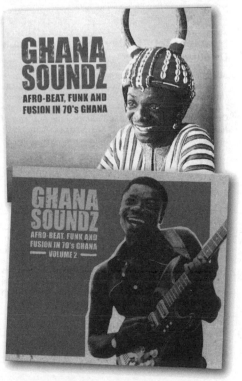

highlifes recorded between 1981 and 1984 at John Collins' Bakoor studios. Great tracks by F. Kenya's guitar band and Salaam's Cultural Imani Group, with a gospel highlife by the Genesis Gospel Singers.

⊙ The Highlife Allstars – Sankofa
Network, Germany

Nine top-class highlife tracks, mainly of the electric guitar-band type, with four by guitarist "One Man Thousand" Alex Konadu and two by Prince Osei Kofi (ex-African Brothers). In addition there are lovely acoustic palm wine guitar tracks by Kwadwo Tawiah, while Kwaku Abeka provides a rare example of brass-band highlife, the oldest and almost extinct form of the genre.

★ The Rough Guide to Highlife
World Music Network, UK

Fifteen tracks of Ghanaian and Nigerian highlife giants from the 1950s to the 1980s. Of the Ghanaian artists, E.T. Mensah represents big-band highlife, while King Onyina, Nana Ampadu (African Brothers) and T.O. Jazz (with singer Kojo Menu) provide examples of the more rootsy guitar-band style. For contrast there is George Darko's "Hilife Time", an early 1980s disco "burgher-highlife" crossover.

⊙ The Rough Guide to Nigeria & Ghana
World Music Network, UK

Subtitled *Juju, Afrobeat, Fuji – Living the Highlife*, the thirteen-tracks dip into the four main indigenous pop genres of the two countries. Highlife is well represented, with tracks from E.T. Mensah, E.K. Nyame, Eric Agyeman, The Sweet Talks, Osadebe and Sir Victor Uwaifo, alongside Nigerian fuji, juju and Afro-beat luminaries. There are also several excellent crossover numbers.

★ Vintage Palmwine
Otrabanda, Holland

Three legends of acoustic palm wine highlife, again recorded by John Collins – the late T.O. Jazz (Thomas Osei Ampoumah), the rougher and more earthy Kwaa Mensah and Koo Nimo, who contributes two breathtaking guitar instrumentals. One T.O. Jazz track is live.

Mustapha Tettey Addy & the Royal Obonu Drummers

Addy and his brothers learnt traditional music in the early 1960s from their father, a Ga priest, and helped to create the recreational *kpanlogo* drum-dance. After living, recording and touring in Europe, he returned home to form the Obonu Drummers and in 1988 founded the Academy of Music and Arts in the village of Kokribite near Accra, now a mecca for drummers and other musicians.

⊙ Smart Boys
Weltwunder, Germany

Songs based on Ga street music, such as *gome* and *kpanlogo*, with amusing lyrics in pidgin English.

Hewale Sounds

This twelve-piece neotraditional instrumental group consists of four *atenteben* bamboo flutes, the *seprewa* harp-lute, a one-stringed fiddle, two xylophones, the giant Ga *gome* frame drum and assorted other local drums. The group was formed in 1996 by Dela Botri, who had learnt to play the *atenteben* flute in Nana Danso's Pan African Orchestra. In 2004 they played alongside Stevie Wonder in Accra.

⊙ Trema
Peogal and Co., Ghana

If you can find it, this features eleven songs of traditional and Afro-fusion Ghanaian/African music.

Kakraba Lobi

Having been taught to play the pentatonic eighteen-key wooden *gyil* xylophone by his father, Lobi himself went on to teach at the University Institute of African Studies until 1987. He has performed all over the world, and passed on his skills to his son, S.K.

⊙ Song of Nhira'
Manadara Music, US

Beautiful songs from a master of his instrument, accompanied by percussion and Valerie Dee Naranjo on second *gyil*.

Koo Nimo

Nimo (Daniel Amponsah) is a folk guitarist who combines 1920s finger-picking Akan palm wine guitar techniques with those of the classical Spanish guitar, adding a touch of American jazz and Brazilian bossanova. He first recorded in the 1950s, and is currently running his Adadam Agoromman group, which includes acoustic "box" guitar, bass, giant *premprensua* hand-piano and Akan percussion.

★ Tete Wobi Ka
Human Songs Records, US

Recently recorded palm wine highlife from the master of the genre. Instruments include acoustic guitar, Akan drums, cow-bells, *premprensua* (which the player sits on) and the traditional Akan *seprewa* harp-lute.

Kwabena Nyama

Now in his eighties, Nyama is one of the last surviving Akan palm wine highlife acoustic guitarists who rose to popularity between the 1930s and 50s. With the renewed interest in "unplugged" music, Nyama and his group have made several tours of Europe in recent years.

⊙ Sunday, Monday
Buda, France

Thirteen lovely songs, accompanied by various singers and two musicians, one providing the bassline on a *premprensua*, the other a high-pitched timeline by tapping a beer bottle with a coin.

Reggie Rockstone

The hiplife pioneer, whose travels abroad have moulded his style and perspective and still give him an edge over local competitors.

🎦 Last Show
OM/Kassa Records, Ghana

Highlife-style tunes with raps in Twi and English, all based on digital disco-funk, minor-key highlife and R&B beats. Tracks like "Mobile Phone" illustrate Rockstone's flair for storytelling; his wry take on domestic strife has a universal resonance.

Aaron Bebe Sukura and The Local Dimension Palm Wine Band

Sukura taught xylophone at the University of Ghana, where he also worked with dance groups, a theatre company, the Pan African Orchestra and Hewale Sounds. Local Dimension is a university-based band led by Sukura (on *seprewa*, mbira and gyil) and John Collins (guitar and harmonica), backed by local percussion.

★ N'yong: Acoustic Ghanaian Highlife
Arion, France

Recorded in 2002, the fifteen tracks were composed by Sukura and are sung in Dagari and Twi by Sukura and

Kojo Menu. They range from acoustic palm wine highlifes to songs based on traditional Akan, Ewe and northern rhythms.

Cindy Thompson

Thompson is one of the top female gospel stars. Together with the Daughters of Glorious Jesus, she won the National Gospel Awards in 2003 and went on to represent Ghana at the Gospel and Roots Festival held in the Republic of Benin later that year.

📷 Messiah
CINANT, Ghana
Lively Pentecostal songs in a highlife and reggae vein, as well as two slow ballads and a song in traditional 6/8 polyrhythmic time.

Nana Tsiboe and the Supa Hi-Life Band

Tsiboe is a percussionist and singer who now lives in Britain, where he has played with Dade Krama and The Master Drummers of Africa.

⊙ Ahom Breath
Tuntumi, UK
A very relaxed album, mainly based on highlife with an acoustic rather than electric feel.

Guy Warren (Kofi Ghanaba)

Ghanaba began his musical career with the famous Tempos highlife dance band, and then moved to the United States in the 1950s, where he worked with Thelonius Monk, Miles Davis and Max Roach and released a sequence of seminal Afro-jazz albums (all out of print, alas).

⊙ The Divine Drummer/Odumankuma
Retroafric, UK
Afro-Jazz recordings made by Warren/Ghanaba in London in 1969-70, partly based on Ga songs from his native Accra, and using African percussion, flutes and xylophone, as well as occasional snare drums. The tracks range from high-energy to very minimalist material.

Captain Yaba

A Fra-Fra musician who played the two-stringed *koliko* or *molo* lute (an ancestor of the banjo), Yaba toured Europe in the mid-1990s with the Ninkribi band, but died in 2001 after returning to Ghana.

⊙ Yaba Funk
RetroAfric, UK
A reissue of the 1996 *Tinanure* album, with backing by Ninkribi. The music may be lacking in variety but not momentum.

Atongo Zimba

Zimba became a traditional minstrel in Accra and worked with the blind street musician Onipa Nua, before moving on to do opening acts at Fela's Afrika Shrine. He has also performed the *griot* role in Kwame Kwei-Arma's *Elmina's Kitchen* at the National Theatre in London.

⊙ Savannah Breeze
Hippo Records, Holland
Zimba plays the northern Ghanaian *molo* lute, with London-based session musician Alfred Bannerman (ex-Boombaya and Osibisa) on guitar. The songs are in English, and range from local-type northern Ghanaian tunes to Frafra raps and Afro-fusion numbers.

🎵 PLAYLIST
Ghana

1 HWEHWE MU NA YI WO MPENA
K. Frempong and his Cubano Fiesta from *Ghana Soundz Vol 1*
An archetypal minor-key highlife number by this guitarist/composer, with horn players George Amissah and Arthur Kennedy.

2 ASATOO Koo Nimo from *Tete Wobi Ka*
Palm wine highlife guitar music that has the rhythmic lilt of the graceful polyrhythmic Akan *adowa* dance

3 OH PAPA F. Kenya from *The Guitar and the Gun*
Outstanding electric guitar-band song by Francis "Powerhouse" Kenya, with the late great Paa Gyima on lead guitar.

4 BA WO NI AYA YE Kpagon Band from *Ghana Popular Music 1931–1957*
Lovely Accra street tune, recorded in 1939 but prefiguring current Ga "cultural groups" such as Wulomei and Bukom.

5 BONE BIARA SO WO AKATUA Nana Ampadu and the African Brothers from *The Rough Guide to Highlife*
Bouncy highlife tune recorded around 1970, including the great guitar licks of the late Senior Eddie Donkor.

6 BANGBALABO Atongo Zimba from *Savannah Breeze*
A high-energy song that perfectly blends Zimba's lute and gravelly voice with hi-tech backing, chorus and effects.

7 TIZAAR KUTUOR GMETA Aaron Bebe Sukura and the Local Dimension Palm Wine Band from *N'yong: Acoustic Ghanaian Highlife*
Slow, relaxed and interesting combination of the *seprewa* harp-lute, acoustic highlife guitar and *gome* bass drum.

8 ME MERE BEBA Kwadwo Tawia from *The Highlife All Stars – Sankofa*
Sung in 6/8, with intertwined acoustic and electric guitars and a *premprensua* bassline.

9 AH Reggie Rockstone from *Last Show*
Begins as a minor-key highlife song, then Rockstone takes over to rap in Twi about his best friend stealing his wife.

Guinea

move over mali

Mory Kanté on the road
Youri Lenquette

Compared to neighbouring Senegal and Mali, Guinea (aka Guinea-Conakry) has a rather low profile on the World Music scene. Even so, it is one of the greatest places for music in West Africa. Indeed, Guinea is like the elderly relative of West African music – frail, perhaps, but knowing all the best stories. Following independence from France in 1958, a confident new sound was born. Guinea's state-sponsored dance orchestras captured audiences with a popular new style rooted in Cuban salsa and the artistic heritage of the Mande *jelis*. A music that was fiercely modern yet solidly grounded, it soundtracked the 1970s and 80s – Guinean music's golden age – and is still echoed in Guinean pop to this day. Katharina Lobeck is all ears.

Conakry, Guinea's capital, is a sticky melting pot. Desperate it may be, but it's still the place that promises hope and work for many Guineans from the rural areas of the country's four regions, which are geographically and culturally distinct. In La Basse Côte, stretching from Conakry along the coast, the Sussu are the dominant ethnic group. The Futa Jallon mountains, in the heart of the country, are where the majority of Guinea's Fula population live. The savannah plains of Haute Guinée are the homelands of the Mande, and the rainforest of the southeastern corner (Guinée Forestière) is home to a variety of people, including the Toma, Guerze and Kpelle. Though these demarcations are by no means precise, and historical interchange between the areas has always been strong, there are clear differences in language and culture – including music.

The sound most commonly associated with Guinean music is that of the grand dance bands of the 1970s. That sound and the popular styles that have evolved from it are all firmly rooted in the traditions of the Mande *jelis* (West Africa's hereditary praise singers). Their repertoire and styles pervade Guinean pop, and most of the successful musicians still come from *jeli* families. (For an in-depth explanation of *jelis*, *griots* and Mande history, see the Mali chapter)

Yet artists from other backgrounds have increasingly impacted on the national scene. Fula singers have turned the carnivalesque percussion and flute rumble of the *nyamakala* (artisan) ensembles from the Futa Jallon into raucous pop. The cheerful rattle of *kirin* (calabash) and *gongoma* (gourd), the favourite percussion instruments of Conakry's Sussu "buskers", have launched acts like vocal/percussion group **Les Espoirs de Coronthie** to pop stardom. Artists such as **Seyni Malomou** and **Sia Tolno** are adapting the music from the rainforest region for a pop market, while numerous hip-hop groups underpin their raps with a patchwork of Guinean musics and American beats.

Some local contemporary productions may on the surface sound like throwaway soulless pop. Stars often have a shelf life that barely exceeds that of a ripe papaya, and releases that show true inspiration are rare. But under the cheap cloak of clanging synthesizers that marks most of Guinea's Abidjan-produced cassettes lie the musical riches of the stately empires of West Africa.

The Kings' Singers

The traditions of the **Mande** *jelis* have been the single most important influence on Guinean popular music (for a detailed description of Mande culture and music see the Mali chapter). Guinean *jelis* have a reputation for excelling in the sweet, romantic side of Mande music, rather than the weighty historical narrations that their Malian counterparts are particularly known for. The distinctive wail of *jeli* singing, the rolling melodies of the *balafon* and the cascading solos of Mande guitarists are the substance of most Guinean styles, from the lush dance sound of **Bembeya Jazz** to the *kora*-rock of the **Ba Cissoko** trio and the Mande-*zouk* of **Fode Baro**. *Jeli* families have settled all over the country. There is hardly a place in Guinea, where you wouldn't encounter a *jeli* ready to sing your praises and those of your ancestors in exchange for a gift of money. Yet their traditions are strongest where Mande culture is most prominent – in Haute Guinée.

Kankan is the capital of Haute Guinée. The blanket of red dust that covers roads and houses there lends it an almost ethereal quality. The blistering heat that grips the region has life either grinding to a halt, or ignites tempers with the fever of rebellion – the University of Kankan is famous for regularly voicing political dissent. It is also home to some of the most distinguished *jeli* families, which have spawned such influential musicians as the late **Facelli Kanté** (the famous guitarist and singer of **Les Ballets Africains**), **Manfila Kanté** (the guitarist featured on many of Salif Keita's recordings), **Oumou Dioubaté** (one of the most famous female singers of Guinea today) and the thunder-voiced **Mory Djeli Deen Kouyaté**, nicknamed the "Pavarotti of Mande music".

Niagasolla, a small huddle of huts in the high north of the country, is a place that won't divulge its historical secrets to just any visitor. This is the village where a branch of the Kouyaté clan, the most prestigious of all *jeli* families, guards the reputed ancestor of the *balafon* – the *soso-bala*. The *balafon* is the instrument most characteristic of Guinean music, being central to the history of the Mali Empire.

Today the *balafon* is the single most popular *jeli* instrument of Guinea, perhaps due to the fact that it links the history of the Mande with that of the Sussu, who are also experts on the instrument. The classic recordings of *balafon* maestro **El Hadj Djeli Sory**, who made his name as leader of Guinea's National Ensemble, demonstrate the beauty of this instrument. Guinean star **Mory Kanté**, who shook global dancefloors with his hit "Yeke Yeke" in the 1980s, started his career as a *balafon* player. The works of Guinean guitarists such as **Manfila Kanté** and **Sekouba Diabaté** show how the percussive bounce of the *balafon* has been adapted by guitar-

Old ways meet new: Sekou Bambino performing with El Hadj Deli Sory

ists to create the typically Guinean style of finger-picked guitar playing.

Both the *balafon* and the *djembe* – West Africa's most famous instrument – straddle the cultural worlds of the Mande and Sussu. *Djembe* playing is not a hereditary craft, but can be taken up by anyone. However, it is strongly associated with the *numuw* (blacksmiths), who fabricate household metal items, sacred objects and masks, carve the bodies of the *djembe* and also play the drums. The Sussu king Soumaoro Kanté was a blacksmith, and it is possible that the *djembe* originated with the Sussu. Today, it is deeply integrated in the traditions of many ethnic groups, albeit more particularly associated with the Mande.

Guinea is one of West Africa's most renowned centres of *djembe* playing, and the percussion camps of internationally acclaimed artists like **Mamady Keita** and **Famoudou Konaté** attract large numbers of "drumming tourists" to study the intricate polyrhythms of the country's celebrated percussion ensembles. Mamady Keita had a long spell as lead drummer and artistic director of the renowned **Ballet Djoliba**, while Famoudou Konaté played for many years with **Les Ballets Africains**. Since 1987, the fiery drum and dance ensemble **Les Percussions de la Guinée** has continued their work.

Though the *djembe* is played all across West Africa, rhythms differ from country to country, and even within the Mande world. In Guinea, the typical Mande patterns have been combined with rhythms of other peoples, including the Sussu, Baga and Guerze, resulting in a distinctive national *djembe* style. The most famous *djembe* rhythm is without doubt the *dundumba*, typically played by a group comprising two or more *djembe* drums, and a couple of double-headed bass *dundun* drums.

The Futa Jallon

"The Futa Jallon is a place of Islamic saints", explains a popular Fula folksong celebrating the plateau region, which spans approximately 80,000 square kilometres in the western interior of Guinea. It is one of the country's Islamic centres, due to the regional prominence of the Fula, one of West Africa's largest ethnic groups.

Culturally distinctive Fula communities live in almost every West African country, from Mauritania to Mali. While some of them still adhere to their traditional nomadic cattle-herding lifestyle, others settled down centuries ago and established powerful Islamic empires in various parts of West Africa, including the Futa Jallon. In 1725, the increasing efforts of Muslim Fula from Macina and Fuuta Tooro to convert the "animist" residents of Futa Jallon sparked off the first West African jihad under the leadership of Karamoko Alpha. Having defeated their adversaries, the victorious Fula clans formed a Muslim *Almamaate* (theocracy) in Futa Jallon, and established a hierarchical order that divided society into free-born, hereditary occupational groups and captives. This socio-political structure had a strong impact on music-making in the region.

The musicians of Fula Futa Jallon are called *nyamakala*. As musicianship was something that was frowned upon in this pious Muslim society, few *nyamakala* came from the class of the free-born. Some took to strumming the *keronna* (a small lute related to the Mande *ngoni*) yet the majority of *nyamakala* were found among the captive community. Their inferior social status and an alleged lack of shame or inhibition granted these artists a certain licence to indulge in behaviour the Muslim upper class despised. The captive *nyamakala* had at their disposal musical instruments that the Muslim leaders had tried to rid society of – *djembe* and *dundun* drums and other percussion instruments that were now socially unacceptable due to their associations with pre-Islamic religion, and the *seerdu* or *tambiru* (shepherd's flute), which had a reputation for stirring "dangerous" emotions in listeners. The *nyamakala* united these powerful outdoor instruments in high-energy shows that are still an integral part of baptisms, weddings and other community celebrations today. The *djembe*, *horde* (calabash) and *laalaa* (shakers) drum out a relentless triplet beat, the flute player threatens to keel over with the effort of playing high-pitched trills and singing at the same time, and dancers engage in acrobatic routines that could put skilled breakdancers to shame. *Nyamakala* acts are often side-splittingly funny, performing daring and often lewd clownery and dance routines in baggy *pantalons buffons*, and their performances provide a licence for people – and most significantly women – to drop their usual reserve and burst into furious dancing and loud laughter.

The *nyamakala* are not only renowned for their musical skill but also for their knowledge of sorcery and witchcraft, and while their shows are widely enjoyed, the musicians themselves are often regarded by the public with a mixture of fear, contempt and respect. The most highly skilled *nyamakala* are said to be able to cut off body parts, curse adversaries or stun them through the use of magic. *Nyamakalayaagal* – the art of the *nyamakala* – is still today regarded as an occupation only worthy of those of low social rank, and many artists are still strongly associated with their ancient captive descent. *Nyamakalayaagal* does not enjoy the same hereditary continuity as the art of the Mande jelis – the current generation of *nyamakala* is gradually disappearing and fewer people take up the craft, causing the tradition to transform rapidly. **El Hajj Moyyere**, the sharp-tongued and quick-witted doyen of Guinea's *nyamakala* community, has never achieved the public recognition he undoubtedly deserves and is not finding youngsters to follow in his footsteps.

However, elements of the *nyamakala* sound – trimmed, tailored and tamed for wide public consumption – have found their way into the works of an increasing number of Fula artists making an impact on the national music scene, including **Petit Yero**, **Binta Laly Sow**, **Fatou Linsan** and the rapidly rising star **Lama Sidibé**. The husky sound of the Fula flute *seerdu*, meanwhile, has not only become a staple of the cassettes of Guinea's Fula recording artists, but has found its way into a number of international releases. The flute of Abidjan-based **Baba Galle Kanté** has lent the requisite Fula flavour to numerous Guinean productions, while Paris-based star flautist **Ali Wagué** has contributed his stunning solos to a wealth of internationally available recordings, most notably to the classic album *Sarala* by **Cheikh Tidiané Seck**, **Hank Jones** and an ensemble of Mande musicians.

Modern Music Begins

Until independence and the advent of the grand dance orchestras – traditional music and slick urban styles developed in completely independent ways with virtually no impact on one another. While the ancient artistic expressions of Guinea's many ethnic groups had their place in life-cycle rituals, ceremonies and celebrations, the first urban orchestras appeared in Conakry and other cities during the years of colonization. These ballroom bands played a mixture of European and Latin American popular music, such as the *beguine*, the waltz, tango and *paso doble* to the French and the aspiring African elite. One of the earliest orchestras known in Guinea was **Philharmonie Jazz**, founded by **Sidiki Diabaté**, one of the first Guineans to play the guitar. Better known and more influential, however, were two Conakry-based ensembles – **La Douce Parisette** and **La Joviale Symphonie**. These two orchestras dominated Conakry's music scene throughout the 1950s, entertaining lucrative and fashionable audiences with Latin dance music and the occasional Guinean "folk" piece. La Joviale Symphonie was where Guinea's famous saxophonist, the late **Momo Wandel Soumah**, started his career. When he later developed his charming and unique brand of Afro-jazz in the 1990s, he put the lessons he had learnt in "ballroom school" to new and original use. He joined the orchestra in 1952, initially as a banjo player, before taking up the clarinet and later his trademark instrument, the saxophone. In 1955, he joined La Douce Parisette as a clarinet player and stayed with the orchestra until its dissolution with Guinea's independence in 1958.

Already influential in those years was **Keita Fodeba**, a poet and musician who was to play a central role in the development of Guinea's post-independence sound. A student of Dakar's famous Ecole William Ponty, which threw up a number of influential musicians of the time, he pursued a forward-thinking vision of music, and established **Les Ballets Africains** in the 1940s, anticipating some of the artistic developments that were to shape Guinean music after independence.

The early twentieth century was also when the guitar made its appearance on the Guinean music scene. It was probably introduced by army recruits returning from Europe after World War I, and was soon to become the ultimate symbol of modernity, replacing the banjo as the instrument of choice in Conakry's fashionable ballroom bands. Musicians such as **Sidiki Diabaté** and **Facelli Kanté** (who was musical director of Les Ballets Africains throughout the late 1940s and the 50s) were among the first to adapt the playing techniques of traditional instruments, such as *balafon* and *ngoni*, to the guitar. They paved the way for the generation of Mande guitarists that developed this sound to perfection in the post-independence dance orchestras.

The Independence Era

'For 60 years we only said "Yes". Well, this time may the sons of Guinea all say "No!" Again "No!" Have no fear, be without dread. The Lord, the Almighty will help you.' With these words **Jali Mamadou Kanté**, a well-known *jeli* of the 1950s, urged the Guinean population to vote for complete independence from France, rather than to remain a member of the French community, as France's president Charles de Gaulle had proposed. The Guinean nation did indeed say "no", and on October 2 1958, Guinea became the first French colony to gain independence. **Sékou Touré** became the first president, and the PDG became the ruling party. He set upon constructing his so-called Communocracy, a governmental system founded on a mixture of Africanist, Marxist-Leninist and Islamic principles that proclaimed equal rights and status for every citizen yet turned, over the twenty years of Touré's reign, into one of the most coercive dictatorships of post-independence Africa. Music lovers, however, tend to look at the Touré era less as a period of political oppression, than as the golden age of Guinean music. Despite the country's disastrous economic situation and lack of civil liberties, post-independence Guinea has produced some of the most celebrated West African bands, and created a flourishing music scene that influenced many neighbouring countries.

Graeme Ewens

Les Amazones de Guinée – 1970s girlpower

Bembeya Jazz

Jak Kilby

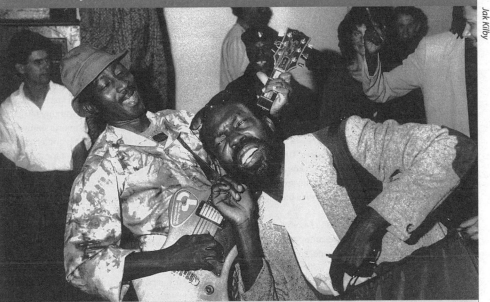

Sékou "Diamond Fingers" Diabaté on guitar

None of the dance bands prominent during the Sékou Touré era can rival **Bembeya Jazz** in terms of success and enduring popularity. Founded in 1961 by **Emile Condé**, a Guinean entrepreneur, the band was originally called Orchestre de Beyla, after the small town in Guinea's forest region in which they lived. In 1962 and 1964, they represented their region at the national artistic competition Biennale and won both times. Clearly too popular to remain in a remote province, they were called to Conakry in 1966, where they were crowned with the title Orchestre Nationale Bembeya Jazz.

Like most dance bands of the time, Bembeya Jazz performed mainly Latin-flavoured interpretations of Mande classics, yet they infused their versions with artistic imagination and a sweet swing that few of their contemporaries could rival. The group's original lead singer, **Aboubacar Demba Camara**, became Guinea's first true superstar. His sedate, honeyed voice set him apart from the *griot* singers that fronted other bands, and lent Bembeya Jazz a unique appeal. It also provided a beautiful contrast to the excited buzz of **Sékou Diabaté**'s guitar playing. At the FESTAC in Lagos in 1977, one of many pan-African festivals where Bembeya Jazz appeared as a main act, this supremely gifted guitarist was given the title "Diamond Fingers". The epithet stuck, and is still as appropriate as ever. "'Diamond Fingers' possessed a dexterity that no other instrumentalist had. We all remained standing, but he could leave our line and perform all sorts of stunts while playing those extraordinary solos', says Bembeya Jazz's trumpeter **Achken Kaba**. Nothing proves this better than his legendary piece "Petit Sekou", a celebration of his unique talent, that consists of an intricate jigsaw of dazzling guitar solos, punctuated by infectious laughter.

Bembeya Jazz recorded ten albums on the Syliphone label, among them the artistically daring *Regard Sur Le Passé* (1968), and their acclaimed live album *10 Ans De Success* (1971). In 1973, the band experienced a tragic shock. While on tour in Senegal, Demba Camara tragically died in a traffic accident. The Guinean nation went into mourning. Bembeya Jazz only began to recover from the loss when the young **Sekouba Bambino Diabaté** joined them in 1976.

Guinea's dance-band era ended with Sékou Touré's death in 1984, which sent Bembeya Jazz into a state of hibernation. Though the group never officially disbanded, they maintained a low profile both in and outside Guinea, and were gradually superseded by younger generations of artists. But in 2002, they set out to conquer the world once more. Several members of the original line-up, among them Sékou "Diamond Fingers" Diabaté, and a few select newcomers recorded the album *Bembeya* and presented it to audiences worldwide on their first international tour for years.

Syliphone Records

The Syliphone label was created by the government in the mid-1960s and featured Guinea's regional and national modern orchestras. The recordings are remarkable documents tracing the development of Guinean popular music from its early Cuban influences to that of soul, funk and, in the late 1970s, *soukous*. The label was very influential, and its groups toured widely throughout West Africa, with several orchestras appearing in Europe, Cuba, the USSR and the US. Many Syliphone LPs have become African classics, such as *Regard Sur Le Passé* by Bembeya Jazz. Recorded in 1968, the LP featured a single track spread over both sides (a first in Africa at the time) which took the form of a modern praise song to Almami Samori Touré, a nineteenth-century resistance fighter against French colonial rule. It also seeks to enshrine Sékou Touré's position as Samori's spiritual heir and actual descendant The orchestration included *balafon* and percussion alongside brass and electric guitars, with **Sékou "Diamond Fingers" Diabaté**, arguably Africa's greatest guitarist, on excellent form.

Maninka recording artists such as Sékou Diabaté dominated the Syliphone catalogue, and the influence of the *griots* is pervasive throughout. Many examples of traditional *griot* songs such as "Soundiata", "Duga" and "Keme Bourema" are found on Syliphone recordings, and their modern reinterpretations were a central focus of Guinea's cultural policy.

Nations such as Mali and Burkina Faso followed Guinea's example, though neither matched the output of Syliphone. As the label was state-controlled, many recordings were propagandist in tone. Some albums featured the President's poetry and speeches, whilst others were dedicated to the initiatives and policies of his government. Such praise was poorly directed when one considers the horrors to which the president subjected the population, but as documents which trace the development of African popular music the catalogue is an invaluable resource and a testament to an era when popular music in West Africa forged its own identity.

The Syliphone catalogue inspired a generation of musicians to test their creative boundaries, and it showed the world that African music and culture was alive and well after its long period of neglect under colonial rule.

Graeme Counsel

The 1960s and 70s were the time of the great Guinean dance orchestras, such as **Kélétigui et ses Tambourins, Balla et ses Balladins, Les Amazones de Guinée, Super Boiro, Horoya Jazz** and of course, **Bembeya Jazz**, the most famous orchestra of all. The development of a unique, modern Guinean music was an important part of Touré's political agenda. Describing culture as 'a better means of domination than the gun', he saw contemporary music as a perfect means of proudly reclaiming Guinea's African heritage, as well as a vehicle for state propaganda. Soon after gaining the presidency, Touré embarked on an unprecedented programme of state-sponsored arts development under the direction of the Ministry of Arts and Culture led by Keita Fodeba.

He paid the most important musicians a regular civil servant's salary, thus buying them the time to devote themselves fully to their art. A network of local, regional and national bands and dance troupes that participated regularly in competitions was also established. There were **dance orchestras** that played pieces inspired by folk music on Western instruments, there were *ensembles instrumentals*, made up entirely of traditional Guinean instruments, and there were **ballet troupes**, performing sophisticated choreography of African dances to the accompaniment of drums.

Between 1965 and 1984, the country's national record label **Syliphone** put out 81 LPs and 75 45rpm singles, that have since steadily been re-released on the Paris-based Bolibana and Syllart labels. The Conakry-based **Ensemble Instrumental de la Radiodiffusion Nationale** became a veritable school of music, where players of traditional instruments from all ethnic groups combined their distinctive styles in bombastic recitals of the classic *jeli* repertoire. The Ensemble brought forth many renowned artists, including *balafon* wizard **El Hadj Djeli Sory Kouyaté**, as well as the feted *jelis* **Mama Kanté** and **Kadé Diawara**, the latter nicknamed the "archangel of Mande music" for her heavenly voice.

The first orchestra to be established (in 1959) was the **Syli National Orchestra**, *syli* meaning "elephant" (the nickname given to Sékou Touré). The group's first guitarist was **"Grand" Papa Diabaté**, who continued the revolutionary work of **Facelli Kanté**, taking his *balafon*-inspired Guinean guitar style to new elaborate levels. With an uncompromising vision and a larger-than-life personality he taught many of the guitarists of the independence era (often for free), and is one of the great legends of modern Guinean music. Many other musicians of the Syli National Orchestra were drawn from the old colonial ballroom bands, among them saxophonist **Momo Wandel Soumah**. 'We were pushed to return to our source, our own folklore', he explained. 'So we would go to the villages, drill and dig deeply in the soil of our hometowns and we found gold – beautiful songs that we would arrange and introduce into our orchestras.' With Papa Diabaté's guitar at its centre, the Syli National Orchestra launched an original new style, the Guinean *rumba*. It was primarily based on traditional songs and rhythms that were combined with elements of Latin music. This sound was adopted by all the orchestras that soon mushroomed across the entire country. It was later developed beautifully by **Balla et ses Balladins** and **Kélétigui et ses Tambourins**, the two offshoots of the Syli National Orchestra (having grown unmanageably large, it had been split into the two groups in 1963.) One of the most outstanding examples of this vibrant new style is the stunning love song "Sara", a staple of Balla et ses Balladins. Its haunting guitar solo by **Sékou "Docteur" Diabaté** (brother of Papa Diabaté) is one of the most memorable moments of guitar magic ever created.

Alongside the Balladins' bass player **Famoro Kouyaté** and rhythm guitarist **Kemoko Kouyaté**, the "Docteur" also participated in another exciting venture, forming the core of the **Guinean Quintet**, which accompanied the South African singer **Miriam Makeba** during her performances and recordings. Makeba and her husband Stokey Carmichael, a central figure of America's Civil Rights Movement, had moved to Guinea when their outspokenness and political activism made their situation in the US too perilous. Makeba moved to the town of Labe in the Futa Jallon, where her humble abode can be visited to this day. She recorded two LPs for Syliphone, which show her emulating the Mande vocal style, and introducing it into a jazz/soul context.

Balla et ses Balladins and Kélétigui et ses Tambourins enjoyed enormous popularity, each with their dedicated group of fans and their fixed rehearsal spot. Balla could be heard practising at the Jardin de la Guinée – today an inconspicuous bar – while the wide outdoor arena of La Paillote served as base for Kélétigui and his band. Other groups, including **Camayenne Sofa**, the **Horoya Band** and the **Super Boiro Band** never quite attracted the same interest and were less prolific. But there was one group that challenged their reign, and which was soon to rise above all others – **Bembeya Jazz** (see box on p.141). This

mighty machine wrote some of the most memorable tunes of the time, including their signature song "Bembeya" and the hymn to the national army "Armée Guinée". Their star attraction was **Sékou "Diamond Fingers" Diabaté** (also known as "Bembeya" Diabaté), the most gifted guitarist of his generation. Today, their name has become synonymous with the Guinean dance band era.

While the orchestras brought the Guinean rumba into the concert hall, the **ballet troupes** celebrated the richness of the nation's many dance and drumming traditions. The two most famous Guinean dance companies are the **Ballet Djoliba**, established in 1965, and **Les Ballets Africains**, who are the better-known group abroad. Founded by Keita Fodeba in Paris several years before, the dance troupe was now invited to Conakry, where it became an emblem of the new Guinea. Introducing dances, masks, songs and costumes from every Guinean region into dazzling performances, it brought Sékou Touré's ideal of cultural unity of all ethnic groups, and his concept of a newly forged "authenticity", to a receptive public. On frequent tours abroad, Les Ballets Africains introduced the new traditions of the young nation to the world. It's a tragic irony, however, that some of the ancient roots they drew on were deliberately destroyed by governmental decree. Touré's desire to rid the country of all manifestations of beliefs in ancient traditions of magic and sorcery led him to order the eradication of masks and dances. The coastal **Baga** people, for instance, who practised a mixture of Christianity and animist religion, lost most of what remained of their traditional rites and relics in raids during the 1950s.

Sory Kandia Kouyaté, one of Guinea's most famous vocalists, started his career in Les Ballets Africains. Blessed with the sonorous voice of an opera tenor and the elegant timbre of a well-trained *griot,* he was not only able to move his listeners deeply, but made also a perfect ambassador for the proud, confident and independent Guinea that Touré aimed to show to the world. Sory Kandia Kouyaté recorded a three-part anthology for Syliphone, entitled *L'Epopée du Mandingue*, which remains one of the most beautiful examples of classic, acoustic Mande music.

If music was sweet in the early days of the young Guinean nation, it took on an increasingly bitter aftertaste as Touré's regime turned more dogmatic. From the late 1960s onwards, the initial creative fervour was channelled by the Cultural Revolution, which gave Touré's party, the PDG, complete control over the arts, and institutionalized the uncritical adulation of Sékou Touré. Praise and flattery of the influential or rich has of course always been a fundamental element of *jeliya* (the art of the *jelis*). But Touré's personality cult exceeded all that had come before. Many of the staggeringly beautiful songs released during that period have next to no lyrical content apart from the inflated exhortation of the leader of the nation. The most famous praise song of Guinea's first president is the striking "Mandjou", written by the Malian star **Salif Keita**. The piece was Keita's way of thanking Touré for awarding him a gold medal for his concert with the Rail Band in Conakry in 1976. Keita later reworked it in a slick, urbane arrangement for his 2001 album *Folon*. Asked later if he regretted having sung a praise song to the dictator, Keita was pragmatic: 'I don't have any regrets. It was a different time. From the moment I knew what dictatorship meant, I hated it.'

The wealth of outstanding recordings made during the Sékou Touré period remains perhaps its only positive legacy, yet the beautiful compositions are inseparably linked to the political conditions under which they were created. Nowhere is this more apparent than in the song "PDG Lannata Sine" by the **Ensemble Instrumental de Labe**. It's a cynical celebration of the chilling fate that met Keita Fodeba, the conceptualizer of the golden age. He had left the Ministry of Culture to become Minister of Justice, and he ordered the construction of the infamous Camp Boiro where thousands of Touré's adversaries perished. When he himself later fell from grace, he faced execution in the very prison he had helped create, a story the song relates with youthful voices and a shimmering backdrop of flutes, *balafons* and guitars: "Fodeba has been arrested, Sékou Touré, you are helping our Guinea. Fodeba has been arrested, the PDG will never let Guinea fall."

New Identities: the 1980s and 90s

By the early 1980s, Guinea's already dire economic situation had worsened further. The once vibrant music scene was also severely affected by this state of depression. The large orchestras gradually became too difficult to maintain, and financial support was reduced or completely discontinued. When Sékou Touré succumbed to a heart attack in 1984, his socialist-inspired regime died with him, and the last remnants of his elaborate system of state-sponsored arts crumbled to pieces. The new government under General Lansana Conté (installed by a military coup) embarked on a programme of privatization, and paved the way for a rampant capitalism which manifested itself in the spread of formal and informal business networks. Music was now to become a profit-generating enterprise whose development lay in the hand of private investors. The first to establish an independent record label was Diouldé Sall, a former Guinean expatriate who founded the still existing company **Superselection**. This is today one of several production houses that stand in fierce competition with each other. The formal business sector of the Guinean music industry is closely tied in with unofficial activities, including piracy and bootlegging, which are conducted by some of the production companies as well as by street vendors.

Only the most prestigious groups of the First Republic, such as the National Ensemble and Les Ballets Africains, remained partially funded by the new government. The others were either disbanded or continued a marginal existence, since private enterprises had little interest in devoting their finances to the maintenance of these unprofitable "dinosaurs". They preferred to focus their attention on individual artists who promised far greater financial returns. This change in emphasis resulted in the emergence of a Western-style pop star culture in which individual singers rather than whole ensembles became the focus of public interest. They were Guinea's new generation of *artistes modernes*.

This shift of focus became possible through a crucial technological advancement – the growth of the **cassette industry**. Domestic cassette players reached West Africa in the mid-1980s, and Guinea's local production and dissemination of tapes started shortly after. Before, records had only been released on vinyl, which had been available to only an affluent few. Cassettes were affordable by many, and recorded music began to be consumed in an unprecedented degree. This completely changed the face of musical creation, performance, appreciation and dissemination. The big orchestras of the previous decades suddenly became dispensable, and though the sound they had shaped formed the backbone of most new creations, studio production techniques altered it greatly. The standard format that evolved featured the voice of a star singer, a *vedette*, draped over a backdrop of synthesized strings, keyboard-generated horn sections, drum-machine beats, a female chorus and some live instrumentation. At the same time, the Antillean *zouk*-beat, popular in West Africa since a regional tour by the band **Kassav** in the mid-1980s, began to be mixed with local rhythms. The so-called Mande-*zouk* gradually attained an almost ubiquitous presence, with the smooth-voiced **Fodé Baro** as its chief exponent.

The first solo artists to achieve prominence were those singers that had already excelled in the orchestras. They included **Kerfala Kanté** (an extraordinarily gifted composer) and **Mory Djeli Deen Kouyaté**, whose moving version of the popular *jeli* song "Nanfulen" from his 2000 album *Könöninta* is a great example of Guinea's romantic approach to *jeliya*.

Among the women, **Kadé Diawara** made a spectacular return to music, after having disappeared from the scene in the 1970s, when she claimed jealous competitors had destroyed her vocal gifts by means of sorcery. She was in excellent company, with **Mama Kanté**, her former colleague from the National Ensemble, ex-Amazone **Sona Diabaté** and **Mama Diabaté**, a gifted singer, *balafon* and *kora* player from the **Horoya Band**, all making impressive solo debuts. **Oumou Dioubaté**, formerly a singer with the Ensemble de Kankan, soon eclipsed her competitors in international and local fame, winning the hearts of Guinea's female population with empowering lyrics, and the hearts of many men with her striking looks.

However, none could match the dazzling rise of **Sekouba Bambino Diabaté**, one of the greatest singers of the contemporary Mande scene, and Guinea's most revered *vedette*. A *jeli* from Siguiri in the far north of Guinea, he had already attracted wide attention while performing as lead vocalist with Bembeya Jazz, and he embarked on a hugely successful solo career. Ever since his solo debut *Sama*, each of his cassettes was eagerly awaited, and reaffirmed his status as a national icon. Though he has strong links to the World Music scene of Paris, he has never left his home country, which has enabled him to keep closely in tune with

changing trends, and has gained him much respect from the Guinean population.

In the 1980s, unfavourable recording and performing conditions drove many Guinean artists out of the country, initially to Abidjan and later to Paris. The singer, *kora* and *balafon* player **Mory Kanté** was among them. When the cassette industry took off properly in the mid-1990s, Abidjan became the single most important recording centre for Guinean music. A staggering 90% (if not more) of all Guinean releases were recorded in Abidjan's JBZ studio complex, and only the political upheaval in Côte d'Ivoire has prompted Guinean artists to look for other recording spaces, including studios in Dakar and Bamako (Guinea lacks proper recording facilities to this day). The vast majority of local Guinean artists thus relied on the same small pool of sound engineers and studio musicians, which inevitably resulted in a strong standardization of sound.

With the increasing focus on recorded, rather than live music, release parties (*dédicaces*) suddenly became the most important events in the artistic calendar. The first artist to celebrate a high-profile album launch was **Sekouba Bambino Diabaté**. The spectacular event was held in 1992, for the release of his second cassette *Le Destin*. The party, still widely remembered today, united a stunning selection of local and international greats at the glitzy Hotel Mariador. *Le Destin* went on to sell a staggering 15,000 copies in less than a week (unheard of at that time), and was later released internationally on the German label Popular African Music. The rising young star **Ibro Diabaté** recognized the power of a well-organized and well-advertised launch event, and celebrated his stunning debut *Allah Nana* (1993) in equally grand style. Produced in Paris by **Boncana Maiga**, the delicately arranged album established the honey-voiced vocalist as one of the hottest newcomers. Unfortunately, his four subsequent cassettes never quite matched the originality and confident stride of the first, and he remains virtually unknown outside West Africa.

Gradually, a new generation of artists emerged, whose fame began to rival or even exceed that of their (often literal) forebears. Two of Sory Kandia Kouyaté's sons carried on their father's torch: **Sekouba Kandia Kouyaté**, who had inherited his father's striking features and charismatic persona, and **Kabine Kouyaté**, whose voice has an uncanny resemblance to Sory Kandia's booming tenor. He made his name with *Kabi*, an album full of modern interpretations of his father's greatest hits. The

record moved Guineans to tears, and formed a solid bridge between great songwriting and contemporary production. The national popularity of **Djeli Fode Kouyaté**, son of Mama Kanté and a nephew of Mory Kanté, is only surpassed by Sekouba Bambino. Both feet steeped in classic *jeliya*, he also understood how to extend his appeal to the country's young audience, by spicing his 2002 release *Gnalemba* with cameos by Guinean rap star **Bil de Sam** and the much-loved Ivorian starlet **Monique Séka**. **Oumou Dioubaté**'s reign as the queen of fast-paced Mande-pop was rivalled by her younger sister **Missia Saran**, whose husky blues voice and progressive style, displayed beautifully on the fiery, Boncana Maiga-produced *Petit Piment* (1998), attracted a huge following. Boncana Maiga has also tried to propel his protégée and partner **Kamaldine** to global fame, by lending his producer's touch to her album *Gbilen* (2004). The cute, Bollywood-and-*zouk*-flavoured record won her a Kora award in 2004, yet has so far failed to make an impact outside Africa. She has yet to attain the status of more established singers, such as the hugely popular **Sayon Camara**, a young *jeli* who sings exclusively in Sussu, and is married to the gifted guitarist **Mammadou Lakras Cissoko**. Highly danceable Congolese-style rhythms and amusing lyrics full of tongue-in-cheek relationship advice have made her a favourite with Guinea's female population. The whole country can still sing along to the pieces on *Dinguiraye*, her debut album from 1998.

Guinea in the World

By the time many Guinean artists began to turn to the buzzing scene of Abidjan, Guinea's most famous musician of the 1980s, **Mory Kanté**, had already left the Ivorian capital (and the Rail Band- with whom he had been playing) for global success in Paris. With his first release *Mory Kanté à Paris* he began an unstoppable climb towards stardom. His second album *10 Kola Nuts* still had a strong Mande flavour, especially in songs like "Teriya", a version of the Rail Band's old number "Balakoninfi". Yet even on this album, Kanté's trademark mix of Mande sounds and a relentless disco beat was already well developed. In 1988, his version of the old favourite "Yeke Yeke" (a love song from Guinea) reached #1 in several European charts and, remixed, became a standard of the early acid house scene. Though he was never quite able to repeat the coup, it launched him to international stardom, and contributed significantly to the high profile African music enjoyed in the 1980s.

By the mid-1980s, the centre of the Mande pop world had shifted to Paris, home to a busy, progressive African music scene. **Oumou Dioubaté**, who relocated there in the late 1980s, had her big breakthrough in Paris, after the most influential producer of Guinean music abroad, **Ibrahima Sylla**, signed her for the recording of her first international album *Lancey* (1995). Sylla was also the man to launch the career of **Sekouba Bambino Diabaté** abroad. His 1997 album *Kassa*, which features the haunting, piano-accompanied ballad "Damansena", beautifully showcases his soaring, romantic tenor voice. Its successor *Sinikan* (2002), a slick, Parisian production, stands as one of the most brilliant works of contemporary African music.

In the early 1990s, the charged Parisian dance-floor productions gave way to a quieter brand of Mande music. *Kora* player **Jali Musa Diawara**, half brother of Mory Kanté, was one of the first and most memorable proponents of this retro-acoustic sound. His classic album *Yasimika* set the tone for many releases that followed later. The sought-after record features a subtle acoustic version of "Yeke Yeke" and "Haidara", one of the most beautiful African songs ever. Recorded in Abidjan in 1983, it became a cult classic when re-released by Hannibal Records in 1991.

Central to the new, rootsier sounds were the imaginative works by Guinea's great guitarists. **Kanté Manfila** had settled in Paris, where he continued working with Malian superstar Salif Keita. Both had already spent years together in the Malian Rail Band and Les Ambassadeurs. The *Lost Album*, which was "found" in 2005, beautifully documents their intimate musical understanding in a 1980 session. In 1994, Kanté Manfila's albums *Tradition* and *Kankan Blues*, the latter recorded in a portable studio in the heart of Haute Guinée, established him as a deeply original artist, but strangely failed to turn him into the global star he deserves to be. The roots of blues and jazz were also the foundations of the unique solo works of saxophonist **Momo Wandel Soumah**, an imaginative composer and singer endowed with a thundering Louis Armstrong-style bass. On his 1996 album *Matchowé* he took Coltrane's "Afro Blue" home to the motherland, greeting it with *djembe* rhythms, flowing *balafon* and the gently quivering Maninka flute of the late **Mamady Mansaré** – the former star flautist of Les Ballets Africains, a position then taken up by his son, also called Mamady Mansaré. His 1999 album *Afro Swing* became a cult classic abroad, turning the man, in his sixties, into one of the most unlikely innovators of Guinean music.

Mory Kanté

Jak Kilby

'We have a problem in modern African music with the use of contemporary Western instruments,' **Mory Kanté** complains. 'They've replaced the *kora* and the *balafon*. The electric bass has taken over from the *bolon*. The Western drum kit has knocked out the *congas* and the *djembe*.'

It is an odd complaint coming from the man who was responsible for putting techno beats and synthesized keyboards into African music with his disco-driven, electrified hi-tech 1987 dancefloor hit, "Yeke Yeke". Yet, like **Youssou N'Dour** and **Salif Keita**, Kanté has returned to a more tradition-based acoustic approach in the 21st century. 'It was time,' he says. 'I felt a mission to give the traditional instruments a place in the scheme of contemporary music, somewhere between the sound of the *griots* and international pop.'

He was born in 1950 into a celebrated family of *griots* in a remote country town in upper Guinea. Kante's father and grandfather were *balafon* players. He soon switched to the *kora* but initially made his mark as a guitarist and singer – first with the **Appollos** and then with Bamako's legendary **Rail Band**. 'We took Malian music and modernised it so you could dance to it,' Mory says. 'We added a Cuban influence and Western dances like the Jerk. We were interpreting James Brown, Marvin Gaye and Otis Redding songs. We were all young and we didn't care.'

By the mid-1980s he had moved to Paris and launched a solo career. The breakthrough came in 1987 with the album *Akwaaba Beach*, which included a re-recording of "Yeke Yeke", a song he'd previously covered in more traditional style. It became a huge international hit. Further albums followed in similar vein until he dramatically changed tack with 2004's acclaimed acoustic album, *Sabou*.

His renewed interest in tradition also extends to building a cultural centre in Conakry called Villa Nongo. 'There will be a couple of recording studios, a research centre for traditional instruments and a music school,' he says. 'And the first project is to record all the old *griots* before they are gone so their knowledge isn't lost forever. In our oral tradition, every *griot* that dies is like a library that burns.'

Nigel Williamson

Djessou Mory Kanté and the grandmaster **Papa Diabaté** both released stunning albums of unadorned guitar playing on the Popular African Music label that showcase the flowing, subtly percussive beauty of the Guinean finger-picked guitar. **Sékou Bembeya Diabaté**, too, picked up on the trend. His understated album *Samba Gaye* (1997) featured husky vocals by his wife **Djanka**

Diabaté, while *Guitar Fö* (2004) revisits many of his former glories. However, this back-to-the-roots movement remained focused on the international World Music market and had little impact back in Guinea.

The Music Scene Diversifies

The most established names of Guinean music are to this day artists from prestigious *jeli* families. Yet since the mid-1990s, this prevalence of Mande music has gradually been challenged by musicians from other backgrounds, who have taken up music as a matter of choice, not birthright. The first to mark their place on the "free music market" were artists of Fula background. A handful of Fula artists had already enjoyed some success in the late 1980s, notably **Bah Sadio**, whose tender guitar-and-voice album *Folklore Peuhl* (1988) is a tear-jerker of a record, haunted by the pain of the émigré. Sadio had recorded this intimate work while in exile during the Sékou Touré years, but it had only been released in Guinea afterwards.

The most common sound of 1990s Fula pop had, however, little in common with Bah Sadio's humble (and humbling) work. When **Amadou Barry** climbed to the top of the national charts in 1994 with the *zouk*-inspired beat, catchy accordion riff and cheeky lyrics of "Joma Galle", the music of the *nyamakala* had found its twentieth century articulation. Artists such as **Petit Yero**, **Fatou Linsan** and **Binta Laly Sow** left their local ceremonies and the shoddy *nyamakala* image behind and reinvented themselves as *artistes modernes*. Relentless dance beats, built from typical *nyamakala* triplets, suave Mande *zouk* and fluttering flute solos paved the way to the top of the charts. The typically raunchy lyrics of their songs stemmed directly from the *nyamakala* tradition, and contributed largely to their success. (*Mowlannan*, "Rub my body" was the title of Petit Yero's greatest hit, *Bulu Njuuri*, "the source of honey" by Binta Laly Sow a love ballad as daring lyrically as it was beautiful, while **Sekouba Fatako**'s releases are simply explicit – and sell *en masse*). The one Fula singer that has consistently produced the most imaginative, deeply rooted and forward-looking works is **Lama Sidibé**, whose debut *Falaama* (1999) sold out in a matter of weeks. His second album, *Séguéléré*, was one of the biggest sellers of 2005.

The intricate polyphonies and cross-rhythms that mark the traditional music of Guinea's forest region have still to make their impact on Guinean popular music, though ex-Amazone **Seyni Malomou**, the R&B-leaning **Sia Tolno** and **Nyanga Loramou** have won some acclaim.

The most unexpected chart-toppers of recent years were two Sussu groups. **Les Étoiles de Boulbinet**, named after their neighbourhood near Conakry's harbour, had the brilliant idea of combining the humble street-instrument *kirin* (a lamellaphone made from three iron keys attached to half a calabash), the *gongoma* drum, the *balafon* and various percussion instruments into an ensemble buzzing with the rugged ambience of inner-city Conakry. Their acoustic home production *Waa Mali* (1997), based entirely on the traditional rhythms and instruments of the Basse Côte, became an unexpected chart climber. It proved contagious. Soon after, a second band took the same format to even greater success: **Les Espoirs de Coronthie**. They made raw, acoustic music cool, and worthy of Conakry's dancefloors. Their numerous young, dreadlocked band members lived a stunning rise from street-roaming youngsters to nationally celebrated stars over 2004, when their second album *Duniya i guiri* was the only music that Guineans seemed to want to hear. It nestled for weeks at the top of the charts, even stealing the #1 spot from Sekouba Bambino Diabaté. Les Espoirs may call themselves the "hope of traditional music", yet their approach to production and arrangement is in fact very contemporary, and indicates new avenues for Guinean popular music.

In a similar vein, the Switzerland-based singer **Maciré Sylla** blends Mande music and Sussu vocals with smooth strands of jazz, while the quartet around *kora* player **Ba Cissoko** combines a rootsy base with the inspired outlook of a young generation searching for new routes. In 2004, the ensemble surprised the world with their debut *Sabolan*, an album that takes gracious *kora* melodies for a walk around the city and simmers with the mischievous funk only an urban *griot* could produce. They are one of few Guinean bands that have made a name for themselves outside Africa, and they have used their newfound success to nurture and support a new generation of Guinean instrumentalists. When they're not touring abroad, they are busy organizing concerts back home, sourcing new artists and spreading the message that had lately been lost among many upcoming artists: that patient practice, meticulous work and the study of an instrument can ultimately be more rewarding than the quick assembly of a short-lived pop production.

Guinea has also vibrant reggae and hip-hop scenes, though the true ground-breaking works in those genres have been rare, and little has trickled beyond Guinean borders. **Kill Point** are the godfathers of Guinean hip-hop. They have been around since the early 1990s, and have today almost the role of mentors, organizing hip-hop festivals and supporting newcomers. Most young rappers look closely to the well-developed hip-hop scene of neighbouring Senegal, and the most successful groups, such as the female trio **Ideal Black Girls**

and the R&B/ragga outfit **Degg J Force 3**, have often approached hip-hop savvy producers in Dakar to record their cassettes. The best-known name in Guinean hip-hop abroad is still **Bil de Sam**, whose clever rap-version of the *jeli* classic "Sunjata" received some unexpected airplay in the UK.

⭐ **40ème anniversaire Syliphone Vols 1 & 2**
Syllart, France
These quality selections of the best of the Syliphone years do justice to the breadth and beauty of the music created during the golden age of Guinean music – the 1970s and 80s.

⊙ **Guinée: Les Nyamakala du Fouta Djallon**
Musique du Monde/Buda, France
Classic document of the traditional music of Guinea's Fula community, with detailed liner notes. An eye-opener.

⭐ **Guinea: Music of the Mandinka**
Chant du Monde, France
No other compilation documents the roots and variety of Mande music as engagingly as this selection of 1950s field recordings by French ethnomusicologist Gilbert Rouget.

⊙ **Les Leaders de la Guinée**
Syllart, France
Features most of the leading male vocalists of Guinea today, including Ibro Diabaté, Fode Baro, Djely Fode Kouyaté, Sekouba Bambino and Sekouba Fatako. Every one of the tracks on this compilation became a major hit in Guinea.

Balla et ses Balladins

One of the greatest bands of the golden age.

⊙ **Objectif Perfection**
Popular African Music, Germany
This compilation of their popular classics features two stunning versions of "Sara", one of the finest Mande love songs ever written. 1970s Guinean rumba at its absolute best.

Les Ballets Africains

The famous national orchestra founded in the 1940s by Keita Fodeba was largely responsible for bringing the rhythms of the *djembe* to the world.

⊙ **Héritage**
Musique du Monde/Buda, France
Recorded in Conakry in 1995, this production ranges across Guinea's cultural heritage, including the musical narration of the mythical origin of the *balafon*. A richly woven sound tapestry.

Bembeya Jazz

The greatest orchestra of Guinea's independence era inspired countless groups across West Africa, and is still the group most widely associated with the Guinean sound.

⊙ **Live: 10 ans du Success**
Bolibana, France
An atmospheric session, recorded in Guinea. Some wild solos from Sékou "Diamond Fingers" Diabaté, the inimitable lead guitarist, and the unforgettable voice of Aboubacar Demba Camara.

⊙ Bembeya
Marabi, France
The album that announced the band's re-emergence to the world shows a more mature and calmly settled Bembeya Jazz. Nevertheless, a little lacking in inspiration.

★ The Syliphone Years
Stern's, UK
A well-presented double CD which unites all the big hits and a few rare gems from the band's best period, with good sleeve-notes to boot. Chock-full of spine-tingling moments and great grooves.

Ba Cissoko

This exciting Marseille-based quartet play a brand of *kora* funk-rock that is absolutely unique: forward-looking yet steeped in the traditions of the Mande *jelis*.

★ Sabolan

Marabi, France
The group's international debut gives centre stage to Sékou Kouyaté's rapid-fire, distorted *kora*. High-energy music that steers a courageous path past all clichés and preconceptions.

Mama Diabaté

This former member of the Horoya Band is a hugely respected all-rounder.

⊙ Koffi Cola Na Yo
PAM, Germany
Mama Diabaté's classic album beautifully showcases her husky vocals in a refined, semi-acoustic setting.

Sekouba Bambino Diabaté

There isn't a bigger star in Guinea than Sekouba Bambino Diabaté. He's Guinea's national icon, and proves with every album how much he deserves the love his people show him.

★ Kassa
Stern's, UK
This terrific album includes some hi-tech dance tracks as well as the stirring, contemplative ballad "Damansena", where Sekouba Bambino is accompanied on piano by Paulinho Vieira (of Cesaria Evora's band).

⊙ Sinikan
Syllart, France
This elegant production by Francois Bréant (producer of Salif Keita's acclaimed album *Soro*) sees Bambino gracefully lace classic Mande sounds with a multitude of other flavours from soul and R&B to hip-hop. Includes a stirring version of James Brown's "It's a Man's world". Contemporary African music at its best.

Jali Musa Diawara

Mory Kanté's brother enchanted the world in the early 1990s with his inspired *kora* compositions.

★ Yasimika
Hannibal, UK
Superbly ethereal, flowing music on guitars, *kora* and *balafon* with luscious choruses by Djanka Diabaté and Djenne Doumbia, plus soaring vocals from Jali Musa himself. Includes the eternally beautiful Mande love song "Haidara". A haunting, timeless classic of Mande music; nothing he has done since can match it.

Kadé Diawara

One of the great female voices of the post-independence years.

⊙ L'Archange du Manding
Bolibana, France
Rolling love songs with acoustic guitar accompaniment. A highly sought-after 1970s recording of one of Guinea's greatest female vocalists.

Oumou Dioubaté

Nicknamed "La Femme Chic-Choc" for her looks and confrontational attitude, Oumou Dioubaté has pioneered a successful Mande/dancefloor crossover.

⊙ Wambara
Stern's, UK
Stunning melody lines, irrepressible beats and nice guitar work mark a set of original songs by a great *jeli* from Kankan.

Les Espoirs de Coronthie

Who would have thought that the re-evaluation of acoustic sounds would be spearheaded by a band of streetwise Conakry boys? They are the old voice of a young generation.

⊙ Dununya Igiri
Sonia Store, Guinea
The songs of this album, rooted in the percussive traditions of the Basse Côte, were on everyone's lips in 2004 and 2005. Subtle rhythms, layered percussion and smooth choral song make this an outstanding work.

Mory Kanté

This pioneer of Mande disco pop was one of the first great stars of World Music.

⊙ Akwaaba Beach
Barclay, France
Kanté's breakthrough album, featuring his worldwide hit "Yeke Yeke" is hi-tech *kora* music for the dancefloor.

⊙ Sabou
World Music Network, UK
Having hit a dead end with his numerous dance productions, the techno *griot* unplugged and released this graceful acoustic album.

Mamady Keita

Guinea's most revered *djembe* soloist is a master of intricate *djembe* and *dundun* drumming.

⊙ Hamanah
Fonti Musicali, Belgium
It's hard to pick one album from Mamady Keita's prolific output – they are all spiced with Keita's solo wizardry. This record is devoted to the well-known *dundumba* rhythm, and features Famoudou Konaté.

Famoudou Konaté

One of Guinea's most brilliant *djembe* drummers, who started his career with Les Ballets Africains.

⊙ Guinea: Malinké Rhythms and Songs
Buda, France
Mature, stately renditions of classic Maninka rhythms by Famadou Konaté's tight ensemble of drummers and singers, with added balafon and kora tracks.

Mory Djeli Deen Kouyaté

Little known outside the Mande world, Mory Djeli Deen Kouyaté is one of the greatest vocalists of contemporary Guinean music.

⊙ Könöninta
Super Selection, Guinea-Conakry
Delightfully of-its-time Mande pop, featuring Mory Djeli's mighty bass voice over the trademark synths of Jean-Philippe Rykiel. Includes his beautifully worked version of the *jeli* classic "Nanfulen".

El Hadj Djeli Sory Kouyaté

The former leader of the National Ensemble remains to this day Guinea's most renowned *balafon* player.

⊙ Guinée: Anthologie du Balafon Mandingue / Vol. III Le Balafon en Liberté
Buda/Musique du Monde, France
Third of a four-volume set, recorded in 1991 at the Palais du Peuple in Conakry, this showcases El Hadj's luminous talent.

Sory Kandia Kouyaté

With his operatic voice, Sory Kandia Kouyaté was one of the most celebrated singers of the independence era.

★ L'Epopée du Manding Vols 1 and 2
Bolibana, France
This anthology of Mande music by Guinea's greatest singer of the independence era reigns among the most beautiful recordings of pieces from the classic *jeli* repertoire. Recorded in Guinea around 1969.

Kanté Manfila

After cutting his teeth as one of the guitar wizards of Les Ambassadeurs, this talented artist launched a solo career.

⊙ Tradition
Celluloid, France
Gorgeous rolling acoustic melodies with guitar and *balafon*, featuring his cousin Mory Kanté on *kora*.

⊙ Kankan Blues
Popular African Music, Germany
The first of a three-part series of acoustic Mande blues sessions, this was recorded via a portable studio in Kankan in 1987, several years before the term "desert blues" became fashionable.

Bah Sadio

Bah Sadio is one of the artists for whom the golden era was leaden – he emigrated during the Touré reign and never returned home. His only recording shows his original style of guitar playing, a technique based on Fula traditions rather than that of the Mande.

⊙ Folklore Peuhl
Sonafric, France
Hauntingly beautiful 1975 recording of solo guitar and voice by one of Guinea's neglected children of the independence era. Hard to get hold of, but worth every effort.

Lama Sidibé

Guinea's most outstanding Fula artist thoroughly researched the musical traditions of Futa Jallon and integrated them into bristling semi-acoustic productions.

⊙ Faalaama
Gris Gris Productions, Guinea
Lama Sidibé's 1999 debut turned him into a national star overnight. Packed with relentless beats, soaring Fula flute solos and Lama's throaty vocals, it's one of the most beautiful works of Fula music to be released in Guinea, only rivalled since by Lama's follow-up *Ségulére* (2005).

Les Soeurs Diabaté

Three of the leading women of Guinean music: multi-instrumentalist Mama Diabaté; Sona Diabaté from the Amazones de la Guinée; and her sister Sayon Diabaté.

⊙ **Donkili Diarabi**
Popular African Music, Germany
Smooth, semi-acoustic outing that truly does justice to the talents of these women.

Momo Wandel Soumah

A mercurial multi-instrumentalist, his career from the colonial era up to the new millennium both reflected and departed radically from Guinea's changing musical styles.

⊙ **Afro-Swing**
Fonti Musicali, Belgium
A storming showcase of the distinctive brand of Mande jazz that won him a cult following worldwide.

Maciré Sylla

Young Sussu singer currently based in Switzerland, who is one of the most original expat Guinean artists.

⊙ **Sarefi**
Ethnomad, Switzerland
A jazzy, soulful second album. Maninka flute by Cédric Asseo and a tight, cosmopolitan rhythm section provide a beautiful backdrop for Sylla's sultry voice.

Guinea-Bissau

backyard beats of gumbe

Gumbe master Manecas Costa
Jon Lusk/Redferns

Guinea-Bissau is a small patch of jungle, grassland and mangroves, wedged between Senegal and Guinea. It is one of Africa's poorest countries and has had its fair share of upheaval: first a long struggle for independence that finally came about in 1975, then a highly destructive civil war in 1998–99, followed by a failed coup and more political turmoil. But even though Guinea-Bissau may be in a pretty awful state, its infectious gumbe music provides a defiantly upbeat contrast and is one the most joyful sounds to be heard anywhere on the African continent. So say Guus de Klein and Bram Posthumus.

How many people know the music heroes of Guinea-Bissau – or any heroes from the country, come to mention it? Maybe some might remember the name of Amílcar Cabral, one of the great men of African decolonization, killed shortly before independence. Bands in Bissau, the capital, have always sung about him, but since most venues have been destroyed in the recent fighting, those few musicians left in Bissau nowadays sing along with the women cooking in the open air, about the waste of Cabral's revolutionary heritage by the ousted president Nino Vieira. In 2005, there were only two night clubs in the centre playing canned music and one called Lenox on the road to the airport where bands occasionally turn up. You need to keep your ear to the ground for news of such events, but things may improve.

People still cherish some of the symbols of the 1974 revolution but what preoccupies them now is survival. Yet the people of Guinea-Bissau *are* survivors and in the midst of hardship their music has taken on a vital role.

Guinea-Bissau's special music is **gumbe**, which the *African and Sierra Leone Advertiser* warned its readers against as early as 1858: "Gumbay dancing in all its forms is notoriously the cause of many vices." Today it combines a contemporary sound with the ten or more musical traditions that survive in the area. Some compare it to the samba, though it's much more polyrhythmic. Bissau has had a few electric bands for some years, but most are unplugged; indeed, at most music venues (and there are many) there is not a plug in sight. The lyrics of gumbe are in **Kriolu**, a creole synthesis of African languages and the colonial Portuguese; it is said to have sprouted on the Portuguese ships where local sailors worked. Kriolu is an integral part of gumbe music. And it has a lot to tell.

Backyard Beats

If you walk a little in Bissau, before the hot sun disappears behind the mango trees, and head off the sidewalks into the *bairros*, you are almost bound to stumble upon a small backyard where fifty or so people have gathered to hear music. A group of women will be sitting in a circle, boys and girls around them. In the centre stands a big bucket filled with water and in it a calabash turned upside down. A boy slides one palm over the surface of the calabash, the other hand slaps it; the sound given off is like an early disco rhythm box. Soon, other calabashes are being played with wooden objects, spoons and other instruments resembling cooking implements. At a certain point the tempo of spoons and wood is about eighty beats per minute, as if people are waiting for something. And they are. A girl jumps into the circle and all at once, in time with her dancing – hands low, knees high – the wood musicians double their speed and the spoon-players treble their pace.

And what do they sing about? They sing about cars they will never own. They make jokes about the owner of the newest Nissan Patrol ("The chef will have to wait like us when the station has run out of gas, both his Nissan and his Patrol!"). They sing about their hard life and about Amílcar Cabral and the Tuga, the former Portuguese rulers. They sing love stories their grandparents sang, and they sing about the *irão* – mysterious forces found in trees, water, stones and in certain individuals. They sing about their daily struggles, money problems and AIDS. They know all the songs by heart and have no need to rehearse. The rhythm will change while the beat keeps steady. Occasionally, a worn-out guitar will add some chords the player has heard outside a disco where he hangs around at night – without money to pay the *entrada*. And whatever they're singing about, there's always fun in gumbe music.

When they're in town, those few musicians who have a more or less professional status, will come and sit down at the outskirts of the circle and fit in with what is happening. Of course, when there's electricity, they plug in. And they'll add some lyrics about the thirty-five-storey buildings they have seen abroad.

Ethnic Traditions

Gumbe is a catch-all word for any kind of music in Guinea-Bissau. But technically, it is just one of several Kriolu mixtures of ethnic and modern culture. In Bissau city you will also find **tina** and **tinga** – more acoustic than gumbe, but very Kriolu, with lots of spoons and calabashes. And there are other more ethnic styles like **kussundé** and **broxa**, or **brosca**, from the Balanta people; **djambadon** from the Mandinga people; and **kundere** from the remote Bijagos islands. Like gumbe, all these musical styles are performed and shared around the Bissau cooking pots.

The ethnic styles are close – in their musical structure – to the traditional sounds that are bound up with **ceremonial activities**: funerals, the calling up of spirits, initiation rituals and the request for good harvests. These very traditional musical styles are precarious, and there have been some efforts (notably by the teacher João Neio Gomes at the Instituto das Artes) to record them before they're forgotten.

Music and Independence

Kriolu music played an important role in the Guinea-Bissau struggle for independence. It brought people together, perhaps more successfully than political rallying, and gumbe, as the common ingredient flavouring the country's many different dishes, could in some manner be called the voice of unification.

With the departure of the Portuguese in 1974, Guinea-Bissau was left with literally no musical heritage (beyond ceremonial music) after more than three hundred years of colonial domination. Even the fado, which influenced so many musicians in the lusophone areas of Angola, Mozambique and Cape Verde hadn't penetrated the local culture of Bissau. So it is possible to pinpoint exactly when the modern music of Guinea-Bissau started.

It began with the production of the first vinyl record by a Guinea-Bissau musician: a 45rpm single recorded in Portugal in 1973, just one year before independence. The two songs – gumbe style with acoustic accompaniment – were sung in Kriolu by **Djorçon (Ernesto Dabó)**, who had just left the Lisbon marine band. The A-side was "M'Ba Bolama" (I'm going to Bolama), its lyrics loaded with double meaning, speaking loud and clear to young Africans living in Portugal as well as in Bissau and the liberated zones, to declare that freedom was coming. One year later, the record was used as part of the celebrations of the country's liberation and independence.

The producer of this first record was the poet and composer **Zé Carlos** (José Carlos Schwartz). He was the charismatic leader of what is recognized as the mother of all contemporary Guinea-Bissau bands, **Cobiana Djazz**. The group was already very popular in 1972, inspiring a great many school-goers in Bissau to join the liberation forces in the forest. That year, Zé Carlos and other members of the band were expelled by the colonial police (the PIDE) and sent into internal exile on the tiny Ilha das Galinhas. Carlos remembered the happiness on the island in a song called "Djiu di Galinha" (Song of Galinha), which is also the title of the album he later recorded in the US at the invitation of Miriam Makeba, who had met him when she performed in Bissau after the liberation.

Cobiana Djazz were the first band to achieve recognition on a national level. With their Kriolu music they literally accompanied the Guinea-Bissau people on their way to freedom. In the euphoric post-revolutionary period that followed, the band was closely associated with the new government which promoted its music as the banner of a new national culture. In spite of this, Cobiana Djazz released just one LP, *Zé Carlos e Cobiana Djazz*, in 1977. It was produced in Portugal: there was still no local music production or distribution. The only copies available are on worn-out cassettes but just about every adult in the country knows all the songs by heart.

Cobiana Djazz did not remain art-of-the-state for long. Within a few years the socialist government, deprived of the charismatic leadership of Amílcar Cabral, slid into incompetence and nepotism. It was criticized by Carlos (then a member of government) in his poetic way, a criticism that led to his falling out of favour and even to a new term of imprisonment. He died in May 1977 in a suspicious plane crash in Havana, where he had travelled as a government representative. After Zé's death, Cobiana Djazz went downhill and by 1982 most of its members were abroad. The group was revived briefly in 1986 with new musicians.

There are remarkable political and musical parallels between Cobiana Djazz and **Bembeya Jazz** of neighbouring Guinea. Musically, both groups – Bembeya a decade earlier and doubtlessly inspiring Cobiana – used their ethnic background as ingredients for the Kriolu musical soup they created, adding a strong rhythmic basis in their *kabasgarundi* (great calabashes). Politically, too, both groups lost faith with their governments, after having been an integral part of the movement for independence.

The other early group to attain star status in Guinea-Bissau was **Super Mama Djombo**. Formed shortly after independence, they were the icon of the socialist party, even accompanying the president on visits abroad. Their first album, *Cambança*, recorded in Portugal and released in

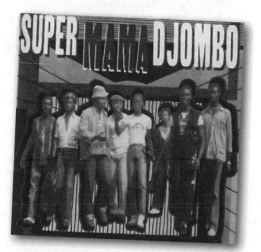

1980, was a big popular hit. The people knew all the songs by heart already but the more sophisticated arrangements on the record, and the electric guitar accompaniment, contributed greatly to the album's success.

The government, however, was unamused by the lyrics on some of the tracks – and even more so by the group's follow-up release, *Festival*. Songs which glorified the PAIGC party were juxtaposed with songs mocking corruption within the very same party, with titles like "Ramedi ki ka ta kura" (A Remedy that Does Not Cure). It was hardly surprising when the group began meeting with difficulties – like finding a stage to perform on, or even a rehearsal room.

Other bands in the first decade of Guinea-Bissaun music were less closely aligned to the regime. Among the most popular were **Africa Livre**, **Kapa Negra**, **Tiná-Koia** and **Chifre Preto**. None of these ever recorded on disc, although **Sabá Miniambá** – a group formed in 1978 with ex-members from almost all the aforementioned bands – did get a vinyl release. **Kapa Negra** recorded a CD in 1992 (*20 anos de Capa Negra*), which does not come anywhere near the melodic quality of the multi-layered, guitar-driven original.

The 1980s: On a Shoestring

There was a growing number of solo careers among this intermingling of groups. **Zé Carlos** was the first to have his own album, supported by Miriam Makeba. He was followed by **Kaba Mané**, who recorded an infectious *kussundé* style album entitled *Chefo Mae Mae*, sung in the Balanta language with *kora*-like electric guitar, and by **Sidónio Pais**, Kapa Negra's vocalist. **Ramiro Naka** switched between solo projects and playing African covers with his band **N'kassa Cobra**.

In the 1980s, revolutionary enthusiasm was no longer the only stuff of lyrics but social and political concerns seeped into even the hottest dance music. There was reason enough for it. The country was in dire financial straits, the shops virtually empty, with hardly enough food to go round. The musicians lived through what the people lived through and have often reflected their concerns. **Zé Manel**, Djombo's drummer, who recorded "Tustumunhus di Aonti" (Yesterday's Testimony) in 1983, was forbidden to perform in public because of the lyrics of his songs, written by the poet Huco Monteiro. The singer **Justino Delgado** was arrested for making President Nino Vieira the target of his sarcasm, and his records became very popular as a result. More seriously, Salvador "Tchando" Embalo, a singer from Bafata

in central Guinea-Bissau, spent two years in jail before moving to Europe. He now lives and works in Denmark.

In the 1980s – and even today – professional Bissau musicians probably number no more than a hundred, so working temporarily with members of other bands is the norm. Many performances are simply small projects, while most recordings can only be done abroad. So the 1980s saw Sidónio and Justino Delgado leaving for Lisbon, and Ramiro Naka and his band settling in Paris. The scene was – and is – one of musicians more or less commuting between Bissau and Portugal, where they had small contracts and sometimes a gig.

Even the few Bissau producers, notable among them the film-maker Flora Gomes Jr., are forced to record in Lisbon. In Bissau, there is just one small studio at Rádio Difusão Nacional, the state radio-station, which produces a few cassettes for local release. Instruments and equipment have to be bought outside the country, often with help from *cooperantes* (development workers) from Holland or Scandinavia.

The 1990s: Survival and War

In the first half of the 1990s, things did not improve much for Guinea-Bissau's economy, despite IMF loans and market liberalization. Sure,

Zé Manel

Cobiana Records

Bidinte

Jorge da Silva Bidinte was born in Bolama, the old capital of Guinea-Bissau. It is a port city in the Bijagos archipelago, just off the coast and a place where music is part of daily life much in the same way as is, say, traffic noise. Legend has it that his father was not entirely convinced of the wisdom of his son's career move when young Bidinte started playing gumbe on a mandolin he had found in an abandoned house. Fortunately dad never managed to put a stop to his son's musical adventures. Once he and his family had moved to the capital, Bissau, where he attended secondary school, Bidinte's drive to make music proved unstoppable. The family happened to live in the Ajada neighbourhood, a meeting point of musicians. He also met the poet **Maio Copé**, whose lyrics he began to set to music.

Forays further afield soon followed. In 1978, he was invited to go to an international youth festival in Havana, Cuba. He then moved to Lisbon, yet another meeting point of artists, including Bidinte's fellow islander **Justino Delgado**. Together they set up a band called **Docolma**, which recorded a few albums, now forgotten. But the real shocker came in 1992, when he was invited to perform in a Madrid nightclub. While in Spain he discovered flamenco and confesses that he was completely blown away. He immersed himself in the music and tried out all sorts of different combinations with his very own gumbe. The result is pure magic.

the stores became better stocked, but with goods most people were unable to buy. The music scene, however, benefited from a more open market, and had no shortage of inspiration.

Most visible was the opening of a cluster of private open-air clubs in Bissau, and a little more money invested in the discos – Cabana, Capital and Hollywood. These played a wider range of music than of old – a lot of *soukous* and other African dance music, a little Stevie Wonder and salsa. But the main dish here, and on Radio Pidjiguiti, a new private station, was still gumbe.

As the decade progressed, several of the country's top musicians became established in France – **Ramiro Naka** and **Kaba Mané** – and Portugal – **Sidónio Pais** and **Justino Delgado** – where they released albums. Others followed, like **Zé Manel** who moved to California. Their sound grew more sophisticated, still narrative, but attuned to the demand for a faster disco tempo. Back home, **Tabanka Djaz** became the first really commercial band, with a polished sound, while **Gumbezarte**, a nine-piece multicultural band led by **Maio**

Coopé, brought together different ethnic styles in a funny and exciting Kriolu style. Both toured abroad but recording and distribution remained major problems. Most releases were produced in Portugal, with very little money, or in Conakry (Guinea) with even less.

Luckily, it is not just old veterans who fill up Guinea-Bissau's soundscapes. New names and albums have made their appearance on the scene. Artists like **Bidinte** (see box above), **Guto Pires**, **Nino Galissa** and **Manecas Costa** (see box overleaf) have all emerged in the past few years with interesting work. None of this constitutes a complete overhaul of the rich musical heritage of the country: gumbe is still very much in evidence. Not all of it is equally successful (almost all of them can stray into lame and unconvincing attempts at reggae). But these are certainly artists with refreshing ideas.

In the chaos of the war during 1998–99, most local bands disintegrated and in some cases members lost touch with each other. Among the handful who chose, or were forced, to sit out the conflict

Manecas Costa and the Gumbe

Peter Culshaw pays a visit to Manecas Costa in Guinea-Bissau

Manecas Costa's superb record *Paraiso di Gumbe* highlights the infectious national rhythm, the gumbe, and features songs about his own Balanta people; the forest shrine he visits and other more personal subjects. But much of it is about the problems of the country: hunger, corruption, suffering, poverty – the familiar tragic African litany. Costa says he remembers the joy of independence when he was eight years old in 1974: 'There was a big fiesta, a continual party that went on for days; everybody drinking beer and dancing. There was a lot of hope. After that great moment, what did we achieve, how have we progressed? I would love to just write about love, women and happiness. Look around – it's a tropical paradise, but I see misery around me here.'

The Portuguese left the country with little infrastructure, and coups, civil war and border disputes made conditions worse. For musicians, life was always a struggle and often dangerous. As a boy, Costa remembers '…the sound of gunfire, troops in the street. I remember hiding under my bed.' He recalls how, when he was 14, 'I was in the audience when a friend sang an opposition song. I heard one of the army guys say, "Does he know he'll be in jail or dead tomorrow?" As I was his friend, I had to go into hiding. My father was terrified for my life.' Still, there were some perks under the Soviet-backed post-independence government – the Cubans came in numbers and one of them gave Costa guitar lessons.

Another problem for musicians, which explains the scarcity of Guinea-Bissau albums, is that there are no recording studios in the country. 'The only place you could record was at the radio station, and it was very poor quality,' Costa said.

Eventually, he went into exile in Lisbon and recorded some tracks which, via a compilation called *Palop Africa*, came to the attention of his album's producer, Lucy Duran.

Guests include the glamorous **Ira Tavares** and Venezuelan harpist **Carlos Orozco**. The end result – great, well-sung tunes, mainly in creole Portuguese – is the international debut of an African star who has begun to put Guinea-Bissau on the musical map.

The album is named after the top club in Bissau, where Costa spent a lot of time in the early 1980s when local band **Super Mama Djombo** were becoming known in West Africa, if not globally. 'It was a magical place, an outdoor club under the stars … It's a mosque now.'

The opening track of *Paraiso di Gumbe*, "Nha Mame", tells how Costa's late mother comes to him in dreams: 'I would like nothing more than for her to see the fruits of her efforts to educate me and encourage me in music. If only I could see her dance again.'

Jonathan Stewart

in Bissau were Miguelinho N'simba, Narciso Rosa and Sidia Baio. Gumbezarte's drummer, Ernesto da Silva, was last heard of in a refugee camp in Dakar. In Bissau, right now, there is currently no intact band, and the opportunities for any musicians left in the capital to perform for cash have competely dried up.

To Portugal's credit, most Bissauans who could afford the journey found a relatively welcoming reception in **Lisbon**. Here, the musicians in exile meet every day at the Praça de Figueira, many of them between shifts on construction sites or office-cleaning. And they manage to find gigs here and there, playing together quite frequently (at the Praça Sony, for example, on the former Expo site, which is quite popular at weekends).

Meanwhile, back home, the people in the countryside are somehow holding life together, receiving refugees from the fighting around the capital, and reinvoking old ties of family and kinship to avert total disaster.

DISCOGRAPHY Guinea-Bissau

There are few Guinea-Bissau CDs and cassettes, even in the best World Music shops. If you happen to be in Lisbon you may strike lucky at the gigantic FNAC in the centre of town or in a far more modest bookshop called Ler Desvagar in the Bairro Alto area. Also try the music stalls at the market on the Praça de Espanha. Cobiana Records (*www.cobianarecords.com*) is a US-based record label dedicated entirely to the music of Guinea-Bissau. You can order on-line there. Another fairly good on-line shop is *www.som-livre.pt* but delivery can be slow.

⊙ **Popular Music from Guinea Bissau**
Intermusic, South Africa
A decent compilation with songs from Tabanka Djaz, Justino Delgado, Rui Sangará, Néné Tuty and others. Most are interesting, though the liner notes are misleading.

⊙ **Guiné Lanta**
Atlantic Music, Netherlands
A collective record from the Guinean and Capeverdean community in Rotterdam (the title means "Guinea Stand Up"), with Tino Trimo, Dina Medina and others. It showcases various styles, including rap, and a children's song.

Aliu Bari

Aliu Bari was one of the founders of Cobiana Djazz, who, pre-war, had seemed a bright hope.

⊙ **Tributo ao Cobiana Djazz Nacional**
Sons d'Africa, Portugal
Bari delicately brings some of the group's older traditional sounds to the urban surface, avoiding electronic booby traps, with a lofty, nostalgic voice and occasional fine electric guitar solos by Manecas Costa. A worthy tribute to the first band of independent Guinea-Bissau, released in 1998.

Bidinte

Bidinte is a very distinct new voice out of Guinea-Bissau, who honed his talents at home before travelling to Cuba, Portugal and Spain. His latest work brings together two distinct musical styles – West African and Euro-Arabian – based on intimate knowledge. Which is why his music is so convincing.

 Kumura
Nubenegra, Spain
Subtle and distinctively coloured music reflecting a multiplicity of sources and influences, from David Byrne (who was present through most of the recording) to flamenco, with melting Kriolu lyrics delivered with tender skill. After this beautifully produced album, Bidinte ought easily be able to step into the long-vacant shoes of former international stars from Guinea-Bissau, Ramiro Naka and Kaba Mané.

⊙ **Iran di Fanka's**
Nubenegra, Spain
More in the same vein, but the tone of his lyrics often has an almost desperate edge. War has crept into songs like "Acampamentos" (Refugee camps) and the music, while still gentle and caressing, gets an occasional heavy rhythm thrown in. West Africa, Congo and of course the flamenco from his current home country Spain are all present – Andalucia's master guitarist Paco Cruz plays a major role – but this remains very distinctly a Bidinte production.

Zé Carlos

Poet, singer and leader of Cobiana Djazz, Zé Carlos died at the age of 27 in a mysterious plane accident, having made albums critical of the regime he had supported through the liberation struggle. He was a major talent, and was persuaded by Miriam Makeba to go to the US for a recording session.

⊙ Djiu di Galinha
Comissariado de Estado da
Guinea-Bissau, Guinea-Bissau

Poetic and narrative, with soft American blend – the album was arranged by William Salter. Though Carlos is occasionally out of tune, he is an inspired artist. Makeba provides the backing vocals.

Cobiana Djazz

Cobiana Djazz were literally "a revolutionary band" in the 1970s, though not a jazz one. They inspired all modern Guinea-Bissau bands, despite the fact that they only released one album, in 1978.

⊙ Zé Carlos and Cobiana Djazz
Cobiana Records, US

Recently remastered for its first appearance on CD. Virtually every adult in the country knows the songs on this much-loved album by heart.

Manecas Costa

Manecas Costa showed musical promise from a very early age and by his teens was a rising star, working local traditions (from his own Manjak tribe, but also from the Balanta, the Diola and others) into his compositions. When political intolerance and turbulence took over the country, Costa headed for Lisbon, where he worked with the likes of Waldemar Bastos and Paulinho Vieira and started recording.

★ Paraiso di Gumbe
Late Junction, UK

The international breakthrough. Eleven songs that are declarations of love to his country, its people, its gumbe and the place of his birth. Yes, the music is unobtrusive – gentle acoustic ripples (and some real ones, coming from a water drum) – but these songs will get under your skin and never leave.

Justino Delgado

Delgado was born on one of the small isles of the Bijagos archipelago. He is best known for the stories he weaves into his songs, which are often sarcastic. Unfortunately, the wit of his words is rarely matched by the musical arrangements, in which synthesizers and rhythm boxes abound.

⊙ Ley dy Byda
Sons d'Africa, Portugal

A continuation of the style developed on his earlier albums: more songs about life in Bissau and the human minefields one finds there. The opening track is an incredibly infectious tune that will have you on the floor in seconds. Most of the rest of the music does not match that level, however.

Mama Djombo

It was Mama Djombo (a.k.a. Super Mama Djomb.) who really put gumbe on the World Music map. They were a favourite of the first independent government, but like Cobiana Djazz, soon fell out with them. Because they were untouched by sophisticated producers, their 1980s recordings still sound remarkably fresh.

★ Super Mama Djombo
Cobiana Records, US

A fine retrospective of the music that made Guinea-Bissau

dance in the 1980s. Tightly woven around a bunch of ringing guitars, the band drives through fourteen songs, including soaring ballads ("Gardessi") and old-fashioned dance tunes, like "Pamparida". All tracks sound distinctly lo-fi and the resemblance with neighbouring Guinea's Bembeya Jazz is, at times, uncanny.

⊙ Os Olhos Azuis de Yonta
Cobiana Records, US

This is the soundtrack to a 1992 film by Guinea-Bissau's premier film-maker, Flora Gomes. The band has moved with the times, which in this case means that rather bland synthesizers underpin and punctuate the music. Nevertheless, the mournful vocals remain, and the title-track is a killer ballad.

Nino Galissa

Nino Galissa is originally from the Gabu area of Guinea-Bissau. Born into the Mandingue *griot* tradition, he picked up a *kora* at a very early age. But Galissa has now moved to cosmopolitan Barcelona, and it shows. His earlier albums were scarcely noticed but this looks set to change with his third offering, released in 2004.

⊙ Mindjer
Ventilador Music, Spain

A clean production and a pretty successful attempt at writing modern songs around *kora* and keyboards, with drums and electric guitars. Shows some influence from new Senegalese singer-songwriters like Pape and Cheikh, but Galissa is on the road to becoming very much his own man. "Barcelona", an ode to his adopted city, is the upbeat highlight.

Gumbezarte

Gumbezarte were the most interesting band to emerge from Bissau in the 1990s. Led by the witty and inventive Maio Coopé, this multicultural group included veterans from Cobiana Djazz and Mama Djombo (Miguelinho N'simba and Narciso Rosa), as well as young talents like Sanha N'Tamba on bass and Ernesto da Silva on drums.

★ Gumbezarte Camba Mar
Balkon Zuíd, Guinea-Bissau; Lusafrica, France

A 1998 release, with gumbe in the name and in several of the songs, but the album is really an electrifying tour of lesser-known music styles, including *kussundé* and *djambadon*. No synths or drum machines; the album was mixed as the group wanted it to be, with lovely shifting rhythms.

Juntos Pela Guiné-Bissau

An ad hoc group of musical refugees currently based in Lisbon, including nearly all the big names, as well as Portuguese and Capeverdean artists.

⊙ Mom na Mom
Vidisco, Portugal
Collective wail of grief ("Mom na mom" means "hand in hand") over the destruction of Bissau, including songs and poems – the latter both in Kriolu and Portuguese – and beautifully produced by Juca Delgado.

Kaba Mané

Born into the Beafada – a Mande people – Mané is master of a variety of ethnic styles. He learned the *kora* when young and plays electric guitar in *kora* style.

⊙ Best of Kaba Mané
Mélodie, France
This has good tracks from Mané's delightfully infectious *Chefo Mae Mae* album – in the *kussundé* rhythm of the Balanta people, this was the first to dent overseas charts – and its equally seductive follow-up, *Kunga Kungake*.

Zé Manel

Zé Manel is Mama Djombo's drummer. His first solo effort, *Tustumunhus di Aonti*, was filled with excellent political commentary and fine ballads. He has since moved to the US, where he continues to record albums, including his disappointing 2004 album *African Citizen*.

⊙ Maron di Mar
Cobiana Records, US
Recorded in California in 2001, this is an excellent mix of French, US and Caribbean ingredients, never straying too far from the original gumbe. A thrilling title track, though Manel's two forays into reggae are unconvincing.

Ramiro Naka

Naka is an exuberant talent who makes gumbe rock without destroying its uniqueness. Though living in Paris, he remains very popular in Bissau.

⊙ Salvador
Mango, UK
Showcase album with material ranging from upfront rock on the title-track to Kriolu/Capeverdean inflection on "Tchon Tchoma" and "Rabo de Padja" and an appealingly offbeat roots sound on "Nha Indimigo".

⊙ Po di Sangui
Naka Production, France
In part a soundtrack album – of the Flora Gomes movie about the relationship between culture and nature (co-starring Naka) – and part compositions inspired by traditional melodies recalled while Naka was on location in eastern Guinea-Bissau. Check out track 8, his version of "Canua Ca Na N'Cadja".

Netos de Gumbé

This Lisbon based eleven-piece band have kept their gumbe rootsy and acoustic.

⊙ Nô Cana Nega Nô Guiné Bissau
Sonovox, Portugal
Short but rather sweet, this 2003 album features rousing call-and-response vocals, *kora* and plenty of percussion. The closing "Canto Moço" is a dead ringer for an Afro-Peruvian *zancudito*.

GUINEA-BISSAU

1 **LEY DY BYDA Justino Delgado** from *Ley dy Byda*
The incredibly infectious title-track from Delgado's latest album.

2 **PAMPARIDA Mama Djombo** from *Super Mama Djombo*
The melody is based on a simple children's tune and then develops into something that made all of Bissau stop what they were doing – and dance.

3 **MARON DI MAR Zé Manel** from *Maron di mar*
This Afro-European mix (made in America) really does work – mostly because the gumbe is never far away.

4 **PAIXÃO CRIOLA Tabanka Djaz** from *Sintimento*
Tabanka's trademark rhythm, great vocals and an excellent horn section. Dance away!

5 **BALUR DE MINDJER Dulce Neves** from *Balur di Mindjer*
Both traditional and modern, this is a plea by the country's only famous female vocalist for better treatment of women.

6 **DINHERO TA KABA MAMA Rui Sangará** from *Pô di Buli*
Killer ballad, beautifully done with understated synths and percussion. Great vocals too.

7 **AMI CU AWINI Bidinte** from *Kumura*
Mournful vocals, a subtle flamenco rhythm, plus some beautiful interplay between guitar and percussion.

8 **DJUNDA DJUNDA Manecas Costa** from *Paraiso di Gumbe*
Costas' lament about social decline in his country is perhaps the best illustration of the insidious charm of his music.

Dulce Neves

As a teenager, Neves had a bewitching influence on Mama Djombo's music with her extremely high voice. She gets better and better as a solo artist.

⊙ N'ha Distino
Sonovox, Portugal
There have never been many female singers on Bissau stages and Dulce's voice can compete with the strongest male ones. This album was one of the hits in Bissau just before war broke out in 1998.

⊙ Balur di Mindjer
Maxi Music, Portugal
Neves wrote all the songs – on marriage, AIDS, women and love – while Manecas Costas produced, arranged and played

a lot of guitar. The sound is clear and includes a real brass section and occasional *kora* playing. Styles range from catchy modernized traditional stuff (the title-track) to smooth ballads ("N'Tchánha") with plenty of gumbe in between.

Janota Di Nha Sperança

Sperança was involved in an effort to re-establish Cobiana Djazz in 1986 and now makes his own records.

⊙ Senhorío
Atlantic Music, Netherlands

An autobiographical album. Being a construction worker in Portugal paid a lot better than being a top musician in Bissau but when money was stolen from him and he couldn't pay the rent, nor buy a ticket back home, he realized that he was no better off than a slave.

Tabanka Djaz

Bissau's bestselling band, the group started in the mid-1980s, in a Bissau restaurant called *Tabanka* (Village), and was an instant hit with its customers. Tabanka Djaz has since gone on to success as far afield as the US.

⊙ Sperança
Sonovox, Portugal

Commercially produced dancehall music, but gumbe none the less.

⊙ Sintimento
Sonovox, Portugal

The band continues to explore its successful formula on this album. Highly danceable, excellent brass riffs, clever use of synthesizers and of course Micas Cabral's compelling voice, the band's greatest asset.

Taffetas

In 1995 Swiss-born bass player Christophe Erard met a young *kora* player from Guinea-Bissau, Ibrahima Galissa. Guitar player and sound engineer Marc Liebeskind met the two in 1999 and Taffetas have been gradually evolving from and around their improvisations. BBC Radio 3's Charlie Gillett was suitably impressed and made their debut album possible.

⊙ Taffetas
Most Records, UK

Switzerland meets Guinea-Bissau and most of the time it works. Based loosely around traditional West African tunes ("Diarabi" is very much in evidence on two of the tracks) and Alpine harmonies, Taffetas spin a loose web of subtle improvisation. On the other hand, the inclusion of Hindi-like vocals by an Italian singer is rather odd.

Tino Trimo

Tino Trimo is an artist with the voice – and the ambition – to cross borders. To date, however, he's been less successful than his colleagues in Tabanka Djaz, whom he reproaches for stealing some of his songs.

⊙ Kambalacha
MB Records, US

An album for gumbe fans – traditional songs played live in the studio. Strong album, great voice.

⊙ Katoré
Vidisco, Portugal

A nicely produced, very danceable disc. There's a drum machine, of course, but it's unobtrusive.

Indian Ocean

a lightness of touch

René Lacaille – the séga sound of La Réunion
Philip Ryalls/Redferns

The music of tropical islands often seems to have a lightness of touch compared with mainland forms. Unselfconscious borrowings, sometimes dating back centuries, and disparate influences which have at one time or another been cast ashore create accessible creole blends, full of common musical denominators and no longer so firmly rooted in their original soil. Nowhere is this more the case than in the western Indian Ocean, as Graeme Ewens, Alain Courbis and Werner Graebner discover.

The Indian Ocean washes the coasts of three continents. In its western half, the monsoon winds once blew the sailing dhows in a back-and-forth pattern that took them from East African coastal waters to the Gulf, on to India and beyond, and then back again. The old trading routes have made connections between many varied cultures, and on the thinly dispersed islands descendants of African, Arabic, Indian, Polynesian, Far Eastern and European forebears have lived for centuries with differing degrees of cooperation and assimilation.

The Comoros

The tiny **Comoros Islands** lie between the north coast of Madagascar and the mainland. As with their dominant neighbour, the former colonial language is French, and one of the islands, Mayotte, remains an outpost of France. There is a huge Malagasy influence but the dominant cultural millieu, especially of the poorer people, is closer to the Swahili world of East Africa.

Twarab – similar to the *taarab* of Zanzibar – is the most popular music on the islands, and especially on Grand Comoro. It differs from the classic Swahili music in having more Western instrumentation in place of the Arabic flavours of *qanun* and violin, resulting in a funkier and very dance-driven sound. The leading groups on Grand Comoro are **Sambeco** and **Belle Lumière**, electric ensembles who use keyboards, guitar, drums and percussion. Like most of the local groups, they are run and backed by village youth associations, and play mainly at weddings, occasionally in a concert setting. **Mohamed Hassan** was a local star in the 1950s and 60s, and was, unusually, a professional musician. He sang and played *oud* – *twarab* at this stage was still based on *oud* and violin – with local *msondo* drum and tambourine at Comorian weddings as far away as Madagascar.

Twarab is also a strong force on the island of Anjouan, especially in Mutsamudu, its largest town. Saif el-Watwan, founded in the 1950s, is the most prominent orchestra. For a long time it was led by singer, *oud* and violin player **Said Omar Foidjou**, accompanied by accordion and percussion. More recently the group has introduced electric guitars, keyboards and drum machines. A special feature of *twarab* in Mutsamudu is the existence of a number of all-female orchestras. Best known is **Mahabouba el-Watwani**, which was founded in the 1960s and has similarly adjusted its instrumental line-up over the years, most recently using small Casio organs, bass guitar, drumkit and congas.

On **Anjouan** and **Moheli**, a favourite type of musical entertainment is topical songs accompanied on the *gabusi* (a lute related to the Yemenite *qanbus*). **Boina Riziki**, from the Mohelian town of Fomboni, is considered to be the best *gabusi* player on the islands. He performs with **Soubi**, who plays the *ndzendze*, a box-shaped instrument that he derived from the Malagasy *marovany*. Their music is situated somewhere between Zanzibar *taarab* and Malagasy, the latter most evident in the vocal harmonies. **Papa l'Amour** and **Bawurera** are Anjouan's favourite *gabusi*-based groups.

The main rhythm of *gabusi* derives from the *mgodro* (possession) dance. Domoni town is famous for adapting *mgodro*, and the female *wadaha* dance, into an electric band consisting of two or three guitars, bass guitar, drum set and percussion. **Asmine Bande** are the oldest of these groups, and **Super Band Ulanga** and **Mahabou** are more recent ones.

Two Comoros musicians who fuse local traditions and international styles are **Maalesh** and **Salim Ali Amir**. Salim Amir leans heavily on studio production, playing all instruments himself and creatively mixing local rhythms and melodies with those of reggae, *zouk* or *soukous*. Maalesh's is a more subtle synthesis: accompanied by just one or two acoustic guitars and quiet percussion, his songs evoke local *ngoma* melodies and *qasida* chanting, and incorporate musical influences picked up during his time working on the Kenya coast and in Saudi Arabia.

Over the past three decades, many Comorians have migrated to France, and there are large communities in Marseille, Lyon and the Paris area. The first Comorian artist based in France to leave a mark was the dreadlocked singer-guitarist **Abou Chihabi**, who composed the first Comoros national anthem in 1976, but had to flee two years later following a coup. He plays a style of music known as **variété** – an upbeat sound featuring horns, keyboards and electric bass – that is popular mainly among the Francophone middle class, at home and in France. **Chebli** is a younger singer who migrated to Marseille and then to Paris; his second CD, recorded with a top crop of musicians from Congo, Cameroon and the Antilles, reflects the metropolitan experience. The lyrics and song topics are still Comorian, but the music betrays a more Francophone consciousness. **Mikidache** and **Baco** provide more local cues on their releases by featuring the Comorian *gabus*, the Malagasy *valiha* and a number of local percussion instruments. But these references quickly dissolve into a more orthodox mainstream type of pop. A stronger roots sound is presented by **M'toro Chamou**, another young singer-guitarist from Mayotte now living in France.

Mauritius

Further out in the Indian Ocean, this former French and British colony of over one million inhabitants has yet to make much of a mark on the musical map.

Séga is the most popular musical form, common to both the major population groups – Indian (about two-thirds) and Creole (one-third), descended from slaves. The style evolved out of old European dances such as the polka or quadrille and uses 6/8 rhythms. It is performed by drums (commonly the *ravanne*) and voices. The master in this style was **Ti Frère**, who was popular in the 1950s and 60s.

At the end of the 1970s *séga* became a political medium, with artists like **Lélou Menwar**, **Bam Cuttayen**, **Nitish and Ram Joganah**, **Grup Latanié** and **Soley Ruz** singing on behalf of the poor. A lighter form of *séga* was, however, still being performed at local dance parties on electric instruments.

A blend of *séga* and reggae called *seggae* appeared in the late 1980s and early 90s with very popular groups including **Racinetatane** and **Ras Natty Baby and the Natty Rebels**, who sold up to 75,000 cassettes of their major albums. Racinetatane's lead singer Kaya died in police custody in 1999 – an event that sparked three days of rioting between the Creole and Indian populations.

Modern *séga* remains very popular; the best-selling band in recent years is **Cassiya**, formed in 1988 but still going strong. In the last few years, music from Bollywood films has also taken off and groups like **Bhojpuri Boys** have

become very successful. Ragga and a new style called **seggaemuffin** are also favourites among young people.

La Réunion

The smaller island of **La Réunion** (2512 square km, with 750,000 inhabitants), which lies between Madagascar and Mauritius, is a *département* of France (like Martinique and Guadeloupe) and a popular holiday destination for well-off French visitors. Regular international music festivals such as Sakifo, Artkenciel and Manapany celebrate *francophonie* as much as local culture. The population is a unique blend of people who have arrrived since the end of seventeenth century from Africa, India, China, Europe, Madagascar and the Comoros. All cultures and religions co-exist in relative harmony, and people prefer to call themselves "Creole" rather than any name indicating their origins.

The two main Creole musics are **séga** and **maloya**, a closely related form based on African roots, with percussion and vocals. *Maloya* was once in danger of disappearing along with other oral traditions, since it was for many years almost forbidden because of its association with the local communist party (PCR), who used it as a symbol in their fight for the island's autonomy. In 1981, when France was led by socialist president François Mitterrand, the PCR gave up that fight and joined the French government. Private radio stations were reintroduced and the Réunionese rediscovered *maloya* as it became free from political associations.

Today *maloya* and *séga* are no longer in danger, and there has been a real musical explosion since the end of the 1990s. Between 250 and 300 albums are produced on the island every year, more than half in these two styles. Sadly, during 2004 and 2005 some great figures of the elder generation died – the four great *maloya* luminaries **Lo Rwa Kaf**, **Granmoun Lélé** (see box overleaf), **Granmoun Bébé** and **Granmoun Baba**, as well as **Maxime Laope**, one of the greatest *séga* singers.

Firmin Viry is now the eldest living maloya singer and he is honoured every December 20 – the anniversary of the abolition of slavery – when many *kabars* (traditional outdoor parties with *maloya* players) are organized. He plays the symbolic instrument of *maloya*, the *kayamb*, a kind of shaker made of sugarcane flower stems filled with seeds. A big bass drum (*rouleur*), the musical bow or *bob* (like a Brazilian *berimbau*), triangle and female chorus singers complete the sound of this Réunionese blues with its roots in slavery. The other great master of

Pure Dynamite

At the age when most of us start planning for retirement, Julien Philéas (popularly known as **Granmoun Lélé**) became a professional musician. In 1990, after many years of manual labour in the sugar factory close to his hometown of Saint-Benoît on Réunion, he met French producer **Christian Mousset**. So began his new career as the leading ambassador or "dynamite father" of *maloya*. As director of the annual Musiques Métisses festival in Angoulême, France, Mousset arranged the first public appearance of Lélé and his family band outside Réunion. This led to many international tours, and recordings for the Label Bleu/Indigo and Marabi labels.

Lélé had been playing *maloya* in his family's band since he was 18, taking part in the *servis kabaré*, a popular religious and musical ritual unique to Réunion. As for his Creole stage name, "Granmoun" means "mature man" or "grandfather" and "lélé" is "le lait" – milk – which they say the young Philéas was always begging from his mother.

By 1977, Lélé had founded his own group, although their performances were generally conducted for neighbours, family and friends, more or less in secret because of the ban on *maloya*. He adapted traditional songs, but also wrote prolifically and introduced new instruments to the standard *maloya* ensemble. Lélé was also known for his fiery performances at the chapel where he prayed and preached every day, worshipping his "petit bon Dieu" in much the same way as followers of Haitian voodoo or Cuban santería.

'He was not only a musician, he was also a kind of priest, but a very cool priest. And a very funny priest,' recalls Mousset, who was involved in all four albums the "Great Witchdoctor" produced. These were *Namouniman* (1993), *Soleye* (1995), *Dan Ker Lélé* (1998) and *Zelvoula* (2003). *Zelvoula* featured a guest appearance by Madagascan band Jaojoby, and Lélé returned the favour by contributing guest vocals to their 2004 album *Malagasy*. He also collaborated with **Bob Brozman** and **René Lacaille** on their joint album *Digdig* (2002).

The group toured the islands of the Indian Ocean, India, Africa, New Caledonia, Canada, Scandinavia, Japan, Brazil and various parts of Europe, making a strong impression wherever they went. Despite suffering ill health in the last four years of his life, Lélé was active to the very end.

Jon Lusk

maloya is **Danyèl Waro**. A staunch advocate of Creole culture and language, his concerts are always very generous and impressive.

Since Granmoun Lélé's death, his family have tried to keep his spirit alive through **La Troupe Lélé**. And a new generation of traditional *maloya* groups including **Kiltir**, **Destyn**, **El Diablo**, **Kozman Ti Dalon** and **Lindigo** have been inspired by his colourful shows and powerful blend of percussion with African, Indian and Malagasy roots. Among younger groups more influenced by Firmin Viry, the most notable are **Melanz Nasyon** and **Ras Mêlé**. In the last few years some very strong female personalities have appeared on the *maloya* scene. The two most successful

are **Christine Salem** (from **Salem Tradition**) and **Nathalie Natiembé**.

Séga hasn't had much impact beyond local dance halls since the 1960s, when electric instruments were introduced. However, there are some artists – such as **Pat'Jaune** and **René Lacaille** – who have returned successfully to the traditional acoustic instrumentation.

The Seychelles

The Seychelles, a frail independent archipelago of 115 islands, is a former French and British colony situated a thousand miles off the East African coast. The 80,000 inhabitants live mostly

Danyèl Waro (right) from La Réunion

on the three main islands of Mahé, Praslin and La Digue. Their musical identity is quite endangered as most artists have to play international hits for tourists in big luxury resorts to make a living.

In their very short history – they were discovered just over two hundred years ago – the Seychelles have, like Mauritius and Réunion, received people from Africa, the Indian Ocean and Europe. This is naturally reflected in their music.

The *moutia* comes from the African heritage of former slaves and is close to Réunionese *maloya* or Mauritian *séga*, with only drums and voices. It used to be danced on the beach around a fire after a hard day's work. As in the neighbouring islands, the most popular music is *séga*, accompanied by a very festive and suggestive way of dancing. The most famous artists are currently **Patrick Victor**, **David Philoé** and **Jean-Marc Volcy**.

Jenny de Letourdie is one of the most beautiful voices currently performing *romances de l'ancienne France* – a kind of love song of European influence – as well as a traditional music and dance form called *kamtolé*, directly inspired by old *schottische*, *vals* and *contredanse*. A group called **Latroup Kiltirel Nasyonal Sesel** presents a very good show featuring all these traditional musics and dances. The musicologist **David André** and accordion player **John Vital** are some of the leading figures in these styles. Younger musicians have been mixing their cultural roots with more modern styles like reggae, rock, French songs and American country music. One of the most popular and professional is **Ralf**, a very expressive songwriter.

DISCOGRAPHY Indian Ocean

⊙ **The Rough Guide to the Music of the Indian Ocean**
World Music Network, UK
This rare overview of the region includes decent tracks from Réunion, the Comoros, Mauritius and the Seychelles, as well as a number of artists from Madagasca and Zanzibar. There's even an example of *séga-tambour* from the little-known island of Rodrigues. A good place to start before dipping into the albums listed overleaf.

Comoros

⊙ Linga 1: Musique de l'île d'Anjouan
CIS, Comoros

This compilation of *gabusi*-based *mgodro* sounds from Anjouan is the best presentation of the genre. Featuring Papa l'Amour and Bawurera, among others, the recordings are a mix of acoustic tracks on *gabusi*, percussion and voice, and more produced tracks incorporating synthesizer, bass guitar and drum backing.

★ M'chago: Wadaha and M'godro
Kachou Musique, Comoros

The best introduction to current music from Anjouan, featuring mostly guitar bands from Domoni, all specializing in electric adaptations of the traditional *wadaha* and *mgodro* dances. Irresistible dance rhythms, from the sensual female *wadaha* groove to the super-fast and *benga*-like *mgodro*.

⊙ Musiques traditionelles de l'île d'Anjouan
Inédit, France
⊙ Musiques traditionelles des Comores
Buda, France

These two CDs show the wealth and breadth of Comorian traditional music and its connections to the Swahili-Islamic world, mainland Africa and Madagascar. The music is varied, trance-like and compelling. The second CD includes some *gabusi* and *ndzendze* songs by Boina Riziki, Soubi (Moheli), and Mayotte's Langa and Kilimanjaro.

⊙ Sambe-Comores: Modern Traditions from Grande Comore
Dizim Records, Germany

Belle Lumière and Sambeco have been the most popular *twarab* groups on Grand Comoro since the 1990s. This release features some of their greatest hits as well as some older *twarab* favourites by 1950s musician Taanchik (covered by his sons) and Hiyari Nour, the leading 1970s group.

Salim Ali Amir

Multi-instrumentalist, composer and producer Salim Ali Amir is Grand Comoro's most active musician, who also fronts his own band Ngaya.

⊙ Ripvirwa
Studio 1, Comoros

Salim has released more than a dozen cassettes and CDs under his own name over the past two decades. These are his latest works, mixtures of local styles and rhythms with a wide array of influences and very polished arrangements.

M'toro Chamou

A young singer-songwriter from Mayotte.

⊙ M'lango
CDC, Mayotte

Though Chamou is indebted to his elders, this album exudes youthful exuberance and a more homely approach when it comes to the adoption of local rhythms like *mgodro*.

Chebli

Chebli Msaidie is a Comorian musician and producer who lives in France.

⊙ Promesses
Sono/Next Music, France

Chebli covers some of the traditional *twarab* and *ngoma* repertoire from Grand Comoro, but otherwise, like the releases by Baco and Mikidache, this is more cosmopolitan in outlook.

Abou Chihabi

This guitar-playing Comoran rastaman began with the Dragons, then moved on to the Angers Noirs, before forming his own more avant-garde group Folkomor Ocean, with which he scored a major success in France.

⊙ African Vibrations
Playasound, France

Abou fronts a fully functional five-piece group, which oozes sophistication – slightly experimental, perhaps, but nothing too extreme.

Mohamed Hassan

Oud player and singer Mohamed Hassan was one of Grand Comoro's biggest *twarab* stars in the 1950s and 60s.

⊙ Duniya – Twarab Legend from Grand Comore
Dizim Records, Germany

Most of Mohamed Hassan's past hits are assembled here in a new recording made in 1999. His voice has aged admirably and his strong, rhythmic *oud* playing is more reminiscent of the *gabusi* than conventional *oud* styles.

Houzaiyan

Houzaiyan are an all-female *twari* group from Anjouan island.

⊙ Owa
Kachou Musique, Comoros

Performances of *twari* at weddings are gorgeous spectacles with hundreds of women, all clad in colourful *chiromani* cloth, joining the chorus and dancing along with the main performers. The CD captures some of this spirit – beautiful vocals and chorus response, accompanied only by *twari* frame drums.

Maalesh

Maalesh is part of a new wave of Comoran musicians looking to fuse local melodies and rhythms with international styles.

⊙ Wassi Wassi
Mélodie, France

A fusion of Indian Ocean and more remote sounds, just acoustic guitars and light percussion in a softly floating style akin to Brazilian *canção*.

Mikidache

Mikidache is a singer-songwriter and bandleader, again based in France.

⊙ Mikidache
World Connection, Netherlands

Mikidache following in Maalesh's footsteps. This CD was recorded in France with a large crew of guest musicians from France, Madagascar and the African continent, which somehow blurs the Comorian identity of the songs.

Boina Riziki and Soubi

Boina Riziki (*gabusi*) and Soubi (*ndzendze*), both from Moheli island, are one of Comoros' most respected traditional ensembles.

★ Chamsi na Mwezi
Dizim Records, Germany

Boina Riziki and Soubi alternate in singing and playing their respective stringed instruments, producing a purely acoustic

Chamsi na Mwezi

Boina Riziki & Soubi

Gabusi and Ndzendze from Moheli, Comoros

dizim records

sound that is accompanied simply by *mkayamba* rattle. Their repertoire consists of traditional and modern topical songs.

Zainaba

Zainaba is Grand Comoro's most in-demand praise-singer at wedding celebrations.

⊙ **Comores: Chants de Femmes**
Buda, France
Traditional songs that highlight Zainaba's charming voice, with a sparse accompaniment of just chorus and percussion.

Mauritius

Cassiya

The bestselling group in Mauritius were formed in 1988 and took their name from Cassis, the suburb of Port-Louis which they come from. With their lead singer Désiré François they became popular in the early 1990s.

⊙ **Neuf**
Cassiya/Interport, Réunion
As the title indicates, this 1995 album was Cassiya's ninth, and includes nine examples of the most popular modern Mauritian *séga*. It's very festive music with a brass section, percussion and backing vocals, typical of what many Mauritians enjoy in the local dance halls and parties.

Kaya

Kaya (aka Joseph Reginald Topize) was born in 1960 and became a Bob Marley fan when reggae music arrived in Mauritius. With his group Racinetatane, he became popular by mixing reggae and *séga* rhythms to create the popular *seggae* style.

⊙ **Zistwar Revoltan**
Discorama, Réunion
One of the most representative *seggae* CDs. Backed by all the instruments of a reggae combo and traditional percussion, Kaya sings about peace, humanity and equality, and against racism and slavery.

Ti Frère

Ti Frère is the most symbolic figure of traditional séga in Mauritius. He did not know how to read or write but was able to improvise great songs.

⊙ **Hommage à Ti Frère**
Ocora/France
Ti Frère was 92 years old when he died in 1992 and Radio France's Ocora published this compilation of his songs, recorded live at home or at fairs. Some of these songs, such as "Papidou" and "Roseda", became real Mauritian standards.

La Réunion

Granmoun Lélé

The "sorcerer" of *maloya* music grew up on Réunion considering death as an occasion to celebrate. Customs were adapted to modern life, but his gruff, no-nonsense voice spanned worlds of understanding.

★ **Zelvoula**
Marabi/ France
The last album made by this master of traditional *maloya* before his death in 2004, recorded live in the studio with his family group (including his wife and eight of his children) providing the chorus and a drum sound deep in both tone and meaning.

Nathalie Natiembé

Very powerful on stage, Nathalie Natiembé emerged as a singer quite late after raising five children and working more as a poet on the island. She opens *maloya* to new horizons.

⊙ **Sanker**
Marabi, France
This 2005 album has a very authentic Réunionese feeling and integrates all her influences – from rock and World Music to electronica – into a local style.

Pat'Jaune

These white countrymen from the Réunionese mountains provide a nice taste of traditional *séga*, which shows many influences from old European dances like polka, mazurka, quadrille and valse.

⊙ **Larisé**
Discorama, Réunion
This 2005 album is their third, and features pleasant accordion and violin parts, sometimes reminiscent of cajun music.

Salem Tradition

This group is one of the leaders of the new generation of traditional *maloya* and is fronted by Christine Salem, who began singing very young.

⊙ **Fanm**
Cobalt, France
With a very strong voice, Salem sings her own language derived from her different origins: Creole, Comorian and Malagasy.

Firmin Viry

Firmin Viry was one of those who kept *maloya* alive when it was banned. He plays *kayamb* to accompany simple songs which refer to deeper themes, and is now the oldest keeper of this tradition in public concerts.

⊙ **Ti Mardé**
Label Bleu/Indigo, France
Reissued in 2005 by Discorama (Réunion), this album show-

cases most of the standards of traditional *maloya*. The most famous is "Valet, Valet" an adaptation of a very old French traditional song. Most of the lyrics are about the daily life of people in the sugarcane fields.

Danyèl Waro

Currently the most famous *maloya* singer on the island, Waro considers himself more a militant than an artist, and is devoted to saving and developing Creole culture and language. A real Creole poet, he makes his own traditional instruments and often plays for humanitarian causes.

⭐ **Bwarouz**
Cobalt, France
Beautifully recorded at his home in the hills of Réunion. Waro writes his own songs rather than adapting traditional repertoire, addressing subjects such as domestic violence.

The Seychelles

⊙ **Musiques populaires des îles Seychelles**
Buda Musique, France
This archival compilation brings together various styles of authentic Seychelles musics such as *séga*, *kamtolé*, romances and popular songs.

Patrick Victor

One of the most popular songwriters in the Seychelles.

⊙ **Redanmsyon**
Seychelles Artistic Productions, Seychelles
Original songs with a lot of emotion and poetry about daily life on Mahé, the main island of this archipelago.

Jean-Marc Volcy

This musicologist and artist is working hard to modernize traditional musics from the Seychelles.

⊙ **Gou Kreol**
Seychelles Artistic Productions, Seychelles
Especially noteworthy here are Volcy's lyrics about Creole culture and common heritage.

PLAYLIST
Indian Ocean

1 KANIZA Mahabou from *M'chago: Wadaha and M'godro*
A sensuous slow *wadaha* rhythm, a sweet guitar sound pointing to the African mainland and Malagasy-sounding chorus vocals: cultures meet on Anjouan island.

2 UZADE Maalesh from *Wassi Wassi*
Voice, acoustic guitars and light percussion: it's hard to pick out any distinctively Comorian ingredients besides the language, yet this has the floating quality of all Indian Ocean island music.

3 TSOZI Belle Lumière from *Sambe–Comores: Modern Traditions from Grande Comoro*
High-tech *taarab* from Grand Comoro: synths evoke the heritage of acoustic instruments from the Arab world, while Moussa Youssouf's voice soars on top.

4 KAMPANANI Soubi from *Chamsi na Mwezi*
A song accompanied only by the *marovany*-like *ndzendze*: Soubi's groove is just irresistible.

5 ANEIL Danyèl Waro from *Bwarouz*
Waro's impassioned, aching lament about domestic violence is backed by sparse percussion and "le bob".

6 L'ANNÉE L'ARRIVÉE Firmin Viry from *Ti Mardé*
Africa meets India – a traditional *maloya* about the Indian sacrifices that are always put off till the next day, as there is no hurry to prepare oneself for God.

7 CILAOS Nathalie Natiembé from *Sankèr*
A very fine melody between *séga* and *maloya* from a very sensitive female voice, magnificently supported by Regis Gizavo's accordion and a percussion groove.

8 MO TIZIL Kaya from *Zistwar Revoltan*
This *seggae* song became a hymn for Creole people dreaming about unity, recognition of their own culture and equality with other communities.

9 ROSEDA Ti Frère from *Hommage à Ti Frère*
A traditional Mauritian *séga* about the hard life of country people, with *ravanne*, *maravane* and triangle.

10 GOU KREOL Jean-Marc Volcy from *Les Seychelles: nouvelles tendances*
A typical Seychelles *séga* by one of the islands' most successful musicians, blending modern instruments with traditional roots.

Kenya

the life and times of kenyan pop

Chuka drummer
Getty

Kenya has always had one of the most diverse and intoxicating musical cultures in Africa. Yet the immense talent is rarely acknowledged internationally and seldom given the resources it needs to flourish. Doug Paterson, who has been observing and documenting the scene for more than thirty years, provides the low-down.

There is no single identifiable genre of popular Kenyan music, but rather a number of styles that borrow freely and cross-fertilize each other. Many Kenyan musicians direct their efforts towards their own linguistic groups and perform most of their songs in one of Kenya's indigenous languages, while others, aiming at national and urban audiences, sing in Swahili or the Congolese language Lingala.

Up to the mid-1990s, the common denominator among all these styles was the prominence of **guitars** – interweaving with each other, or delivering dazzling solos – and the **cavacha rhythm**: the Bo Diddley-esque beat popularized in the

Kenya's Tribal Music

Kenya has a rich network of tribal (a term used widely in the country) musical cultures, though not all have survived intact into the twenty-first century. Throughout the country, music has always been used to accompany rites of passage and other events, from celebrations at a baby's birth to songs of adolescence, warriorhood, marriage, harvest, solar and lunar cycles, festivities, religious rites and death. Nowadays, however, the majority of Kenyans are Christian, and **gospel** music reigns supreme – sadly not the uplifting version of the US or South Africa, but a tinny, synthesized and homogenous form.

Gospel has all but obliterated traditional music, and among the Kikuyu (Kenya's largest tribe) or the Kalenjin (who comprise much of the government), the old tribal music is almost extinct. Elsewhere, to hear anything live, you need a lot of time and patience, and often a local family's trust, though there's a certain amount of recorded music available. The following is a very brief tribe-by-tribe rundown of more easily encountered traditional music and instruments. Obviously, there's much more available if you know where to search and what to ask for: essential reading for this is George Senoga-Zake's *Folk Music of Kenya* (Uzima Press, Nairobi, 1986).

Akamba

The tradition of the Akamba, best known for their skill at drumming, is sadly now all but extinct. There's only one commercial cassette available, *Akamba Drums* (Tamasha); it covers many styles and can be ordered from the Zanzibar Curio Shop in Nairobi.

Bajuni

The Bajuni are a small ethnic group living in the **Lamu** archipelago and on the nearby mainland, and are known musically for an epic women's work song called "Mashindano Ni Matezo". One of only very few easily available recordings of women singing in Kenya, this is hypnotic counterpoint, the vocals punctuated by metallic rattles and supported by subdued drumming. You can find it in Lamu, Kilifi or Mombasa.

Borana

The Borana, who live between Marsabit and the Ethiopian border, have a rich musical tradition. The Arab influence is readily discernible, as are more typically Saharan rhythms. Most distinctive is their use of the **chamonge guitar**, a large cooking pot loosely strung with metal wires. On first hearing, you'd be forgiven for thinking that it is funky electric guitar, or some earthy precursor to the blues, depending on the context.

Chuka

Once again, sadly practically extinct, Chuka music from the east side of Mount Kenya – like that of the Akamba – is drumming genius. Your only hope is to catch the one remaining band, who currently play at the Mount Kenya Safari Club near Nanyuki.

Gusii

Gusii music is Kenya's oddest. The favoured instrument is the **obokano**, an enormous version of the Luo *nyatiti* lyre which is pitched at least an octave below the human voice and can sound like roaring thunder. They also use the ground bow, essentially a large hole in the ground covered in a tightly pegged animal skin with a small hole cut in the centre. A single-stringed bow is placed in the hole and plucked, and the sound defies description. Ask around in Kisii and you should be able to pick up recordings easily enough.

Luhya

Luhya music has a clear Bantu flavour, easily discernible in the pre-eminence of drums. Of these, the **sukuti** is

mid-1970s by Congolese groups such as Zaïko Langa Langa and Orchestra Shama Shama. This rapid-fire percussion, usually on the snare or hi-hat, quickly took hold in Kenya and continues to underlie a great sweep of Kenyan music, from **Kakai Kilonzo** to **Les Wanyika** and **Orchestre Virunga**.

However, the music scene in Kenya today is very different from that of only five or ten years ago. Sadly, this is at least in part down to veterans dying away – including a startling number of men in their forties or fifties. Though AIDS may be a factor in many of these cases, it is rarely confirmed; more often, we hear about deaths caused

best known, sometimes played in ensembles, and still used in rites of passage such as circumcision. Tapes are easily available in Kakamega and Kitale.

Luo

The Luo are best known as the originators of **benga** (for more on which see the main article). Their most distinctive musical instrument is the **nyatiti**, a double-necked eight-string lyre with a skin resonator which is also struck on one neck with a metal ring tied to the toe. It produces a tight, resonant sound and is used to generate complex, hypnotic rhythms. Originally employed in the fields to keep tired workers alert, the music typically begins at a moderate pace and quickens progressively; the player also sings, the lyrics covering all manner of subjects, from politics to moral fables.

Maasai

The nomadic lifestyle of the Maasai tends to preclude the carrying of instruments and as a result their music is one of the most distinctive in Kenya, characterized by astonishing **polyphonous multipart singing** – both call-and-response, sometimes with women included in the chorus, but most famously in the songs of the *morani* (warriors), in which each man sings part of a complex multi-layered rhythm, more often than not from his throat. The songs are usually competitive (expressed through the singers alternately leaping as high as they can) or bragging – about how the singer killed a lion, say, or rustled cattle from a neighbouring community.

The Maasai have retained much of their traditional culture, so singing is still in use in traditional ceremonies, most spectacularly in the *eunoto* circumcision ceremony in which boys are initiated into manhood to begin their ten- to fifteen-year stint as *morani*. Tourists staying in big coastal hotels or in game lodges in Amboseli and Maasai Mara often have a chance to sample Maasai music in the form of groups of *morani* playing at the behest of hotel management. Cassettes are difficult to find.

Mijikenda

The Mijikenda of the coast have a prolific musical tradition which has survived Christian conversion and is readily available on tape throughout the region. Performances can occasionally be seen in the larger hotels. Like the Akamba, the Mijikenda are superb drummers and athletic dancers. The music is generally light and overlaid with complex rhythms, impossible not to dance to.

Samburu

Like their Maasai cousins, whose singing is very similar, Samburu musicians make a point of not playing instruments – at least in theory. In fact, they do play small pipes, and also a kind of guitar with a box resonator and loose metal strings, though these are played just for pleasure, or to soothe a crying baby, and are thus not deemed "music". Listen out also for the sinuously erotic rain songs, peformed by women in times of drought. For cassettes, ask around at the lodges and campsites in Samburu/Buffalo Springs National Reserves, or – better still – in Maralal.

Turkana

Until the 1970s, the Turkana were one of Kenya's remotest tribes, and in large part are still untouched by Christian missionaries. Their traditional music is based loosely on a **call-and-response** pattern. The main instrument is a kudu antelope horn with or without finger holes, but most of their music is entirely vocal. A rarity to look out for are the women's rain songs, sung to the god Akuj during times of drought. Visitors are usually welcome to join performances in Loiyangalani, for a small fee.

by TB, malaria, diabetes or heart problems. Either way, the effects have been devastating – not only the direct loss of talent, but also the loss of musicians who anchored the Kenyan musical scene in its historical context.

A new generation of musicians and producers is beginning to make its mark, though it remains to be seen where this new direction will lead.

The Early Days

Even before 1900, guitars were being played among the freed slaves around Mombasa, and by the 1920s the instrument had a group of quite well-known exponents, including such names as **Lukas Tututu**, **Paul Mwachupa** and **Fundi Konde**. Their songs dealt with secular topics but were similar in form to church music, with several verses and a refrain.

In a separate development, from around the mid-1920s there were several dance clubs in the Mombasa area playing music for Christian Africans to do European dancing. The **Nyika Club Band** was one such house band, comprising guitars, bass, banjo, mandolin, violin and sax/clarinet. As for the rest of Kenya, there's little in the historical record of this period about what was happening musically, apart from singing and drumming – and a bit of accordion among the Kikuyu.

During World War II, many African soldiers were sent to fight in Ethiopia, India and Burma, and some of the coastal musicians were drafted into the Entertainment Unit of the King's African Rifles. With a couple of Ugandan recruits, the group comprised guitars, mandolin, accordion and drums, and after the war they continued as the **Rhino Band**. Based at first in Kampala, they soon worked their way down to Mombasa. After they split in 1948, some of the members formed the distinguished **Kiko Kids**, and other dance bands.

From the early 1950s, the spread of radio and a proliferation of recording studios pushed genuinely popular music across a wide spectrum of Kenyan society. Fundi Konde was a prominent broadcaster and also recorded on HMV's Blue Label series. His early songs, and especially his chord sequences, were closely allied to those of contemporary European dance bands, and it's a fair guess that if they had been in English rather than Swahili, much of his tight, melodic, very rhythmic output would have found favour with the pre-rock'n'roll tastes of Europe and America.

Finger-Pickin' Good

While Fundi Konde's urbane style was much in demand, the "second generation" of Kenyan guitarists were making their names, often with a dif-

Graeme Ewens Collection

Fadhili William (left) and Fundi Konde, Kenyan pop pioneers

ferent playing technique: the thumb and forefinger **picking style** first heard in the music of eastern Congolese players like **Jean Bosco Mwenda** and **Edouard Massengo**. Bosco's recordings were available in Kenya from 1952 and by the end of the decade he and Massengo had moved to Nairobi.

This "finger"-style music has a lively, fast-paced bounce, especially where a second guitar follows the lead guitar with syncopated bass lines. The Kenyan finger-pickers sometimes pursued solo careers, but more usually they formed small guitar-based groups, with two-part vocal harmony and simple percussion using maracas, tambourines, wood-blocks or even soda bottles. From the mid-1950s, this new sound gained a huge following and produced spectacular record sales. AGS, the African Gramophone Store, one of the bigger labels, claims to have sold 300,000 copies of **John Mwale**'s "Kuwaza Sera" 78rpm.

By the mid-1960s, however, finger-style acoustic guitar bands were losing ground to other electric guitar styles. The rhythms of the new urban Swahili music were also influenced by Congolese rumba and South African *kwela*, or what was locally called **twist**. Twist's underlying rhythm is the beat of "Mbube" (The Lion), a faster version of the internationally better known "Wimoweh".

The old styles were absorbed in part into the new music, and many ideas taken up by the electric bands were based on the finger-picking and soda-bottle percussion. One of the most important groups of the new electric era of the 1960s was the **Equator Sound Band**, first formed in 1959 as the Jambo Boys, a studio and performing combo for the East African Records company. Led by **Fadhili William**, they went on into the 1970s as African Eagles and Eagles Lupopo. Some of the most famous names of the period – Daudi Kabaka, Gabriel Omolo, Sylvester Odhiambo and the Zambian émigrés Nashil Pichen and Peter Tsotsi – distinguished the line-up. Typical Equator elements were the two-part vocal harmony, a steady, often "walking" bass and a bright, clean lead guitar. There's often a strikingly American feel in the guitar solos and chord patterns, suggesting pervasive rock and country influences.

Benga Wizards

The late 1960s and early 70s was a time of transition in Kenyan music. While the African Eagles and others continued to play their brands of Swahili music, many top Kenyan groups, such as the **Ashantis**, **Air Fiesta** and **The Hodi Boys**, were playing Congolese covers and international pop, especially soul music, in the Nairobi clubs. At the same time, a number of musicians were honing the **benga style**, which was soon to become Kenya's most characteristic pop music.

Although *benga* originated with the Luo people of western Kenya, its transition to a popular style has been so pervasive that today practically all the local bands play variants of it and most of the regional or ethnic pop groups refer generally to their music as *benga*. As a pop style, it dates back to the 1950s, when musicians began adapting traditional dance rhythms and the string sounds of the *nyatiti* and *orutu* to the acoustic guitar and later to electric instruments. During its heyday, in the 1970s and 80s, it dominated Kenya's recording industry and was exported to western and southern Africa, where it was very popular.

By any measure, the most famous *benga* group is **Shirati Jazz**, led by **D.O. (Daniel Owino) Misiani**. Born in Shirati, Tanzania, just south of the Kenyan border, Misiani has been playing *benga* since the mid-1960s. His style is characterized by soft, flowing and melodic two-part vocal harmonies, a very active, pulsating bass line that derives at least in part from traditional *nyatiti* and drum rhythms, and stacks of invigorating guitar work, the lead alternating with the vocal. Misiani, who is rightfully credited as one of the founding fathers of the genre, is still going strong, with a full performance schedule that included European and American tours in 2005.

Tragically, many of the other big names in *benga* music have passed away. Between 1997 and 2001, a whole raft of stars disappeared: **George Ramogi**, leader of the Continental Luo Sweet Band; pioneers **Collela Mazee** and **Ochieng Nelly**, who performed either together or separately in various incarnations of **Victoria Jazz** and the **Victoria Kings**; and crowd-pleasing bandleaders **Okatch Biggy** (Elly Otieno Okatch, of Heka Heka), and **Prince Jully** (Julius Okumu, of the Jolly Boys Band). All in all, a devastating loss of talent and knowledge of *benga* music and its history.

Promisingly, however, Heka Heka, various Heka Heka offshoots and the Jolly Boys have continued to flourish, moving into more risqué benga performance. With Jully's wife, Lillian Auma, assuming control of the group and fronting the Jolly Boys as Princess Jully, the response has been nothing short of phenomenal.

One Luo name which doesn't fit neatly under the *benga* banner is **Ochieng Kabaselleh** and his **Luna Kidi Band**. His songs were mostly in Luo, but sometimes with a liberal seasoning of Swahili and English. Likewise, his melodies and harmonies were from the Luo *benga* realm but the guitar, rhythm and horns suggest Congolese/Swahili influence. Kabaselleh, who languished in prison for several years for "subversion" in the 1980s, returned to the music world with a flood of new releases in the 1990s. In 1997, he toured the US with his group and recorded his first international CD release, *From Nairobi with Love*. In 1998, however, he too died – in this case from complications related to diabetes.

A related group that Kabaselleh started in the late 1970s with several of his brothers continues today as **Bana Kadori**. The name, meaning "children of Dori", refers to Kabaselleh's mother, Dorcas, a respected musician of her day. Originally brought together as a recording group, they are now an active performing band. Their music runs the range from Kabaselleh's hybrid *benga*-rumba style to mainstream benga.

Luhya Legends

Many of Kenya's famous guitarists and vocalists come from the Luhya highlands just to the north of Lake Victoria and Luo-land. In addition to the early finger-picking guitarists like John Mwale and George Mukabi, it was the ancestral home of Kenya's "**King of Twist**", **Daudi Kabaka** (who died in 2001) and still-active twist proponent **John Nzenze**. While these musicians fostered broad appeal through Swahili language, other Luhya musicians stayed closer to their home areas, musically and linguistically – such as **Sukuma bin Ongaro**, famous for his humorous *benga*-esque social commentaries in Luhya.

Another key Luhya artist is **Shem Tube**, the vocalist and guitarist leader of Abana ba Nasery (The Nursery Boys). The group are still active, but their **omutibo** style is best known in Europe via the 1989 GlobeStyle retrospective, *Abana ba Nasery*, focusing on their heydey in the 1960s and 70s. Back then, the band blazed a path, combining traditional Luhya rhythms and melody lines with a two-guitar line-up and three-part vocal harmonies in a way that foreshadowed today's Kenyan pop.

More recently, Abana ba Nasery have had a string of local hits as an electric band under the stage names **Mwilonje Jazz** and **Super**

Bunyore Band (listen, for example, to Super Bunyore's "Bibi Joys" on the *Nairobi Beat* compilation). And in 1990, they explored the compatibility of their music with strands of European folk in *Nursery Boys Go Ahead!*, with guests including members of the Oyster Band and Mustaphas as well as Ron Kavana and Tomás Lynch.

Kikuyu:
Prayers for the Country

As Kenya's largest ethnic group, the **Kikuyu-speaking people** of Central Province and Nairobi are a major market force in Kenya's music industry. Perhaps because of their built-in audience, few Kikuyu musicians have tried to cross over into the national Swahili or English-language markets.

Kikuyu **melodies** are quite distinct from those of the Luo and Luhya of western Kenya and their pop manifestations also differ significantly in harmonies and rhythm guitar parts. In contrast to Luo and Luhya pop, **women vocalists** play major roles as lead and backing singers, and many of the top

Denis Lewis/Globestyle

Abana ba Nasery – heavy on the Fanta

groups have women's auxiliaries – duos and trios invariably called the something-or-other sisters. Most often, Kikuyu pop takes the form of the *benga/cavacha* style, but popular alternatives are also based on country and western, reggae and Congolese *soukous*.

The king of Kikuyu pop is **Joseph Kamaru**, who has been making hit records since the release of "Celina" in 1967, performed, on one guitar and maracas, with his sister Catherine Muthoni. Since then he has carved out a small empire for himself – including his **Njung'wa Stars** band and the Kamarulets dancers, two music shops and a recording studio. He sees himself as a teacher, expressing the traditional values of his culture, as well as contemporary social commentary, in song. In the early 1990s, his recording "Mahoya ma Bururi" (Prayers for the Country) gently criticized the Kenya government, resulting in his shop being raided and his songs being banned from the airwaves. This, however, did little to harm Kamaru's popularity: his band was fully booked, playing regular "X-rated, Adults Only" shows to packed nightclub crowds. Thus his announcement in 1993 that he had been "born again" came as a bombshell for his fans. Much to their disappointment, Kamaru abandoned the pop scene to devote his efforts to evangelical activities and gospel music promotion.

The void created by Kamaru's departure from the pop market has at least partly been filled by one of the rare female headliners in Kikuyu pop, **Jane Nyambura**. Known these days simply as "Queen Jane", she's a staunch advocate for the inclusion of traditional folk forms and local languages within contemporary pop. Her use of tribal languages has limited her radio exposure (such music is deemed "tribal" in official circles) but Jane and four of her brothers and sisters now make their living from her band.

Another key figure is **Daniel 'DK' (Councillor) Kamau** – the hit-maker regarded as having brought Kikuyu music to the mainstream. DK released his first three records in 1967, while still at school, and continued with a highly successful career throughout the 1970s, after which he moved into politics. He returned to the stage in the 1990s, with a new group, the **Lulus Band**, but has continued to address political and human-rights issues, sometimes in partnership with singer-composer **Albert Gacheru**.

Kamba Calliope

East and southeast of Nairobi is a vast, semi-arid plateau, the home of the **Kamba** people, linguistically close relations of the Kikuyu. Kamba pop

music is firmly entrenched in the *benga/cavacha* camp, though with its own unique elements. One is the delicate, flowing rhythm guitar that underlies many arrangements. While the primary guitar plays chords in the lower range, the second guitar, often in a high register, plays fast patterns that mesh with the rest of the instrumentation to fill in the gaps. The result, which has the seamless flow of an old carousel calliope, is discernible in many of the recordings of the three most famous Kamba groups: the **Kalambya Boys & Kalambya Sisters**, **Peter Mwambi and his Kyanganga Boys** and **Les Kilimambogo Brothers Band**, led by the late **Kakai Kilonzo**.

These groups dominated Kamba music from the mid-1970s. Mwambi, although he can get into some great guitar solos, has a following that comes largely from within the Kamba community, his pound 'em-out musical style lacking the variation needed to keep non-Kamba speakers interested. The Kalambya Sisters are a different story. Backed by Onesmus Musyoki's Kalambya Boys Band, the Sisters were famous, even notorious, throughout Kenya and even had a minor hit in Europe with "Katelina", the comic tale of a young woman who drinks too much *uki* home-brew and gets pregnant with annual regularity. The soft, high-pitched, feline voices of the Sisters whine engagingly in unison over the sweet guitar work of Musyoki and the Boys. A phenomenon of the 1980s, the Kalambya Sisters are long gone as an active group. These days, the mantle of Kamba female pop star belongs to **Peris Mueni** and her **Kakongo Sisters** band, who have released a very successful string of cassettes from the late 1990s to present.

To reach a larger audience, a number of local-language artists have turned to Swahili, which is widely spoken throughout East and Central Africa. Kakai Kilonzo and Les Kilimambogo Brothers band were always identified as a Kamba band, but once Kakai started recording in Swahili, the group enjoyed widespread popularity in Kenya. With socially relevant lyrics, intricate guitar weaves and a solid dance-beat backing, Les Kilimambogo were national favourites until Kakai's death in 1987.

These days, another generation of musicians, relative newcomers to the Kamba hall of fame, is drawing most of the limelight away from the old guard. The **Katitu Boys Band** has come to dominate the Kamba cassette market. Leader David Kasyoki, a former guitarist with Mwambi's Kyanganga Boys, won the 1992 Singer of the Year award for "Cheza na Katitu" (Dance with Katitu). Other groups of the new generation include **Kimangu Boys Band**, **Kiteta Boys** and **Mutituni Boys Band**.

Congolese & Swahili: Big-Name Bands

The **big-name bands** in Kenya can usually muster sufficiently large audiences for shows in sprawling, ethnically diverse towns like Nairobi, Nakuru or Mombasa. Unlike the groups with a particular ethnic leaning, the national performers can appeal to a broad cross-section of the population with music that tends to be either a local variant of the **Congolese** sound or **Swahili music**, a Kenyan-Tanzanian hybrid sound, unique to Kenya.

In Congolese and Swahili popular music, songs typically open with a slow-to-medium **rumba**, the singer ambling through verses, backed by a light percussion of congas, snare and hi-hat. Then, three or four minutes in, the song shifts into high gear, with rumba and verse giving way to faster rhythms and prominent instrumental parts (especially solo guitar and brass). Swahili music, particularly, has remained fairly faithful to this two-part structure, though today both Swahili and Congolese musicians often dispense with the slow rumba portion altogether.

While Swahili pop is usually associated with Swahili lyrics, it isn't distinguished by the language. Indeed, one of the greatest Swahili hits of all time, the Maroon Commandos' "Charonyi Ni

Wasi" is sung in Taita (a related but distinct language). Today, Nairobi's Congolese music, almost exclusively sung in Lingala in the mid-1970s, is also linguistically diverse, with artists such as Samba Mapangala and Orchestra Virunga making a conscious effort to bring their music closer to the Kenyan audience through the use of Swahili.

There are some significant points of divergence in the Swahili and Congolese styles in Kenya. The tempo of Swahili music is generally slower, and while the Congolese musicians are famous for their vocals and intricate harmonies, Swahili groups are renowned for their guitar work: demon solos and crisp, clear guitar interplay.

Immigration Department

Congolese musicians have been making waves in Kenya since the late 1950s. It was the **Congolese OS Africa Band** that opened Nairobi's famous Starlight Club back in 1964. But it wasn't until the mid-1970s, after the passing of the American soul craze, that music from Congo began to dominate the city nightclubs. One of the first musicians to settle in Kenya during this period was **Baba Gaston**. The rotound Gaston had already been in the business for twenty years when he arrived in Nairobi with his group Baba National in 1975. A prolific musician and father (he had twelve children), he stole the scene until his retirement as a performer and recording artist in 1989.

While Gaston was getting settled in Nairobi, the Congolese group **Boma Liwanza** was already on the scene at the Starlight Club and the popular **Bana Ngenge** were about to leave Nairobi for a year in Tanzania. **Super Mazembe**, meanwhile, had just completed their migration from then Zaïre to Kenya (by way of Zambia and Tanzania), and soon to follow were **Samba Mapangala and Les Kinois**.

The latter were an early prototype of **Orchestre Virunga**, the supergroup that Samba Mapangala put together with Super Mazembe singer Kasongo wa Kanema. In 1984, the band ran into problems with work permits, and broke up, but guitarist Sammy Mansita soon put together a new all-star group, **Ibeba System**. When Ibeba first took over from Virunga at the Starlight, the group sounded almost exactly like its predecessor, but over several years performing at the JKA Resort Club they became an act in their own right, with a good mix of *soukous* and covers of African pop.

The ultimate Congolese crossover band in Nairobi, and darlings of Kenya's young elite, were **Vundumuna**. The group formed in 1984 – with guitarist **Tabu Frantal**, Ugandan vocalist Sammy

Vundumuna

Kasule and ex-Virunga bassist Nsilu wa Bansilu – and quickly gained institutional status, packing in the crowds with their performances at the Carnivore. With the best equipment in the city, they presented a clean, hi-tech sound fusing Congolese *soukous*, *benga* rhythms and elements of Western jazz. Their flawless horn arrangements blended beautifully with the keyboard playing of leader **Botango Bedjil** (BB Mo-Franck) and Frantal's guitar. After three LPs and a rising tide of popularity, the future was looking bright until, once again, the Immigration Department struck. The group played its farewell concert at the Carnivore in late 1986 and since then have worked abroad in places as far afield as Japan and Oman. Between jobs, they return to Kenya (several band members have Kenyan wives and children), where they've been allowed to play short stints as guest performers. BB Mo-Franck and sax player Tabu Ngongo have stayed on in Japan, playing African music in BB's groups – **Bitasika** and **MAMU** (Modern African Music) – and releasing a couple of nicely produced CDs.

The loss of Vundumuna set the stage for the return of Orchestre Virunga, and when they took up residence in Nairobi's Garden Square Club in 1988 they were greeted with the same abundant enthusiasm they had left behind three years earlier. With a captivating stage show, they played dazzling renditions of all their familiar hits and new compositions. Sadly, in 1993, Samba gave up on the local nightclub scene and disbanded the group,

though he still performs for special events in Kenya, tours abroad and makes records. Although the musicians continue to change, nothing has altered Samba Mapangala's formula: a catchy, not over-complex melody, faultless vocal harmonies, innovative, interlocking guitar lines and superbly crafted horns floating over light, high-tensile percussion.

Samba Mapangala was not the only one disillusioned by the business of music in Nairobi. By the early 1990s, Nairobi's status as an island of opportunity for Congolese musicians had fallen flat. With harder economic times, a declining record industry, fewer live venues and restrictive work rules, Nairobi had become a departure point for greener pastures rather than the promised land itself. Some musicians headed to Tanzania, while others signed up to play outside Africa – particularly Japan, in recent years, where a number of Nairobi's Congolese musicians have formed touring groups such as **Angusha Band**.

In the last decade, however, the Kenyan Congolese music scene has been on the upswing once again, with a host of new names and places to work. Congolese artists on the current scene include **Rhumba Japan International**, **Tindika Umba and Bouger-Musica International**, and **Bilenge Musica**, whose CD, *Rumba Is Rumba*, places them among the top *soukous* bands anywhere. There are also some new permutations on familiar names, such as **Orchestra Les Mangelepa** and **Orchestra Mazembe Academia**, while **Lessa**

179

Lassan and Orchestra Popolipo are comfortably installed in the Motherland Bar.

Wanyika Dynasty

Songs with **Swahili lyrics** are part of the common currency of East African musical culture. Kenya's own brand of Swahili popular music has its origin in the Tanzanian styles of the 1970s but has followed a separate evolutionary path since then. It retains some classic Congolese elements (light, hi-hat-and-conga percussion and delicate two/three-guitar interweave), but is instrumentally sparse, with the bass filling in gaps, often in syncopated rhythms. Trumpets and saxes are common in recorded arrangements but usually omitted in club performances because of the expense.

One of the first Tanzanian groups to migrate to Kenya was Arusha Jazz, which later became the legendary **Simba Wanyika Original** (Lion of the Savanna). Founded by Wilson Peter Kinyonga and his brothers George and William, the group began performing in Mombasa in 1971 and started recording singles for Phonogram the following year, quickly making a name for themselves. In 1975, with Tanzanian recruit Omar Shabani on rhythm and Kenyan Tom Malanga on bass, the band shifted their base to Nairobi and released their first album, *Jiburudisheni na Simba Wanyika* (Chill Out with Simba Wanyika). Over their twenty-year history in Nairobi, the group were favourites of the city's club scene and made scores of recordings. They broke up in 1995 after the deaths of first George (in 1992) and then Wilson Kinyonga.

Interestingly, Simba Wanyika's international releases present a rather different sound from their typical recordings for Polygram in Nairobi. In both *Simba Wanyika Original: Kenya Vol I* and *Pepea*, the group has taken a page from the *benga* handbook and quickened the pace considerably, albeit without giving up their great guitar work, creamy sax (on *Vol I*) and pleasing, listener-friendly vocal lines. For purists interested in their local, live sound, the albums *Haleluya* and *Mapenzi Ni Damu* are more representative.

The name "Wanyika" is also associated with various other related bands. In 1978, for example, the Kinyonga brothers' core supporting musicians left to form **Les Wanyika** – including rhythm guitarist "Professor" Omari Shabani, bassist Tom Malanga, drummer Rashid Juma and vocalist Issa Juma (who had only joined a month before). The new group signed up Tanzanian lead guitarist **John Ngereza**, who had been playing in Kenya with the Congolese group Bwambe Bwambe, and after six months' practice began performing at Garden Square. They soon found fame across Kenya with the massive hit "Sina Makosa" (It's Not My Fault), and went on to became one of Nairobi's top bands for two decades. Their Swahili-language rumba was distinguished by imaginative compositions and arrangements – a lean, clean sound and the delicious blend of rhythm, lead and bass guitars. In their studio tracks (many of them more than ten minutes long), the guitars don't really solo in the usual sense but playfully embellish, aided by a pair of trumpets or a saxophone. Their vocals are great, too, handled by Ngereza, with solid harmonies from Mohamed Tika and other Swahili session vocalists.

Ngereza's inclusion as a guest artist on Orchestre Virunga's 1997 US tour finally brought him some international exposure outside Africa – as well as his first international CD, *Amigo*, in 1998. Sadly, the same year saw the death of Professor Omari, who had composed many of the group's early hits, and Ngereza himself died in 2000.

Other incarnations of the Wanyika brand included the various groups – Super Wanyika, Super Wanyika Stars, Wanyika Stars, Waa-Nyika, L'Orchestra Waanyika and Wanyika Super Les Les – headed up in the 1980s by **Issa Juma**, who had established himself as a premier vocalist back in the early days of Les Wanyika. He is forever associated in Kenya with Sigalame, the eponymous character of his 1983 single. Sigalame (now part of Kenyan vocabulary) is a mysterious character who has disappeared from family and friends but is rumoured to be "doing business" in Bungoma. What kind of business? ("Biashara gani?") With so many illegal activities to choose from, it was up to the listener to choose an answer.

One of the most productive artists of the 1980s, Issa released many numbers in the Swahili-*benga* fusion style of "Sigalame". Yet, he has been more adventurous and creative than most of the Swahili artists in his willingness to take his music in different directions. With producer Babu Shah, some of his songs sound very much like the Conglese music of the time, while others are closer to the old rumba style of Simba Wanyika.

Although the Wanyika bands have been dominant in Swahili music, it is not their exclusive domain. Foremost among other Tanzanians and Kenyans performing in the Swahili style are the **Maroon Commandos**. Members of the Kenyan Army, the Commandos are one of the oldest performing groups in the country. They came together in 1970 and initially focused on covers of Congolese hits. But by 1977 they had come out as a strong force in the Swahili style, and had huge success with the Taita-language song "Charonyi Ni Wasi". Within their genre, the Commandos do not limit themselves to any sort of rigid formula – like many of the Swahili groups, they use trumpets and sax liberally, but at various times have added keyboard and innovative guitar effects. At their most creative, they mingle Swahili and *benga* styles.

In Kenya today, however, the Swahili rumba sounds of groups like the Wanyika bands and Maroon Commandos are nearly extinct. From time to time, new bands form but, currently, the only serious proponents of the genre (aside from Maroon Commandos) are **Abdul Muyonga and Everest Kings**. The style, however, remains widely available in recordings, including a recent release from the late Twahir Mohamed's **Golden Sounds Band**, appropriately titled *Swahili Rumba*.

Hakuna Matata...

International influences have always been a part of Kenyan music but where Kenyan pop meets the tourist industry, at the resorts to the north and south of earthy Mombasa, another distinct style can be heard. Here, a band can successfully make a living just playing covers at hotels. **Tourist pop bands** typically have highly competent musicians, relatively good equipment and, overall, a fairly polished sound. In live performances, the best of them play an eclectic selection of old Congolese rumba tunes, popular international covers, a few Congolese favourites of the day, greatest hits from Kenya's past and some original material that leans heavily towards the American/Euro-pop sound but with lyrics relating to local topics.

The most successful group in this field has been the oddly named **Them Mushrooms**, recently renamed **Uyoga** (Swahili for "mushroom"). At the time of their formation, in 1972, Them Mushrooms were a reggae band without an audience. However, as they gravitated towards the hotel circuit for work, they switched to a more commercial sound encompassing international covers, African pop standards, a little soca and reggae and some Kenyan variants of *benga* and the coastal *chakacha* rhythm.

Them Mushrooms graduated from the coastal hotel circuit when they moved to Nairobi in 1987, but their music lives on at the coast, most notably their crowning achievement: the perennial tourist anthem "Jambo Bwana", with its unintentionally ironic refrain "Hakuna matata" (No problems). However, while Uyoga are proud to take credit for this insidiously infectious bit of fluff, they also have more serious musical intentions.

Uyoga have been one of Kenya's most prolific bands. Over three and a half decades, they have produced a series of successful collaborations, highlighting artists ranging from the pioneering Fundi Konde, *taarab* star Malika and the Kikuyu singer **Queen Jane (Nyambura)**. They now own and operate one of the best studios in the country, and their recent work has taken them back to their first love – reggae – with the CD *Kazi Ni Kazi* (Work is Work), released on the Kelele label.

Uyoga's long-time counterpart in the hotel circuit, **Safari Sound**, has also joined the reggae brigade with another Kelele release called *Mambo Jambo*. This group already has the distinction of having Kenya's best-ever selling album in *The Best of African Songs*, a veritable greatest hits of hotel classics.

Kelele Records

Uyoga, the band formerly known as Them Mushrooms

Ndiyo Hiyo Video!

The twenty-first century has seen music videos taking Kenya by storm. Gyrating their hips to the *kapuka* beat, young Kenyan musicians mime the words to a funky new release, wearing either the baggy jeans, sunglasses and trainers of American hip-hoppers or – when they want to "authenticate" their performances – the red chequered cloth and white, red and blue beads of traditional Maasai dress.

Back in the 1980s, on the state-owned Kenya Broadcasting Corporation (KBC, formerly Voice of Kenya), the *Sing and Shine* programme pushed local gospel music into the mainstream and created star singers such as the Katangas and Mary Atieno, while the early 1990s saw the private TV channel KTN (Kenya Television Network) broadcasting American hip-hop and R&B, and Jamaican reggae and dancehall, as well as Congolese *soukous*. But there were hardly any Kenyan music videos until the late 1990s, when Hardstone and Shadz o' Blak collaborated on "Msichana Mwafrika" and Jabali Afrika produced "Aoko".

By the turn of the millennium, music videos had become a major feature on Kenyan TV, but they were still predominantly foreign. The tides turned in 2002, when the new EATV (East African TV) advertised for local musicians to submit videos, in the process kicking off a video-making frenzy. Before long, there were homegrown videos ranging from Eric Wainaina's satirical "Nchi Ya Kitu Kidogo" to Suzanna Owiyo's dramatic "Sandore", from Kayamba Afrika in traditional costumes to Nameless's sleek, high-budget affairs. So big is the craze that studios such as Ogopa DJs, Homeboyz and Bluzebra set up video-making divisions.

And it's not just Kenya: music videos are such a rapidly growing trend across the continent that MTV has recently set up a channel dedicated to the African music industry. Gone are the days when people gathered around a little transistor radio to hear the latest hits.

Njane Mugambi

New Directions

In the early 1990s, the Kenyan music business was at a low point. Diminishing sales and competition from music pirates meant that, in a business sense, recording music was hardly worth the effort. And much of what *was* released was hardly worth buying. By the middle of the decade, however, a number of factors came together to set the stage for something of a musical revolution. The take-off of commercial FM radio boosted the profile of foreign styles such as ragga, house, dancehall, hip-hop and R&B, while computers and other equipment became more affordable, enabling a new wave of artists to explore a new wave of production techniques.

Groups emerged combining local elements – language, subject matter and sometimes melody and instrumentation – with American and European styles. Some of the pioneering names of the mid-1990s include **Five Alive**, **Hart**, **Shadz o'Blak** and **Hardstone** (Harrison Ngunjiri), who had a smash hit with "Uhiki" – an ambitious but successful offering mixing parts of Marvin Gaye's "Sexual Healing" with Kikuyu folk music and rap.

Producer **Tedd Josiah** was one of the creative forces behind this explosion of new styles. Sensing the shifting tide in Kenyan music, he put together two compilation CDs – *Kenyan: The First Chapter* (1998) and *Kenyan: The Second Chapter* (1999)

– of emerging artists, such as the hip-hop outfits **Kalamashaka** and **Gidigidi Majimaji**. The latter had a hit with "Ting Badi Malo" (Throw Your Hands Up), which they followed up by a superb solo album, *Ismarwa*, blending hip-hop with traditional African instrumental sounds and melodic Luo verses. The latter, in 2002, became part of the cultural fabric of the nation with their hard-hitting rap "Who Can Bwogo Me?" (Who Can Scare Me?). Though not written as a political statement, the song was adopted as the theme of the successful opposition party in the country's election. The word "unbwogable" has since entered the Kenyan lexicon.

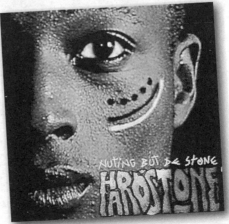

Josiah and other producers, such as **Bruce Odhiambo** and **Suzanne and Gido Kibukosya**, are working with a diverse set of artists. **Mercy Myra**, for example, has attained star status in the Kenyan R&B field, while **Eric Wainaina**'s 2001 album *Sawa Sawa* combined the social commentary of the Redykyulass TV comedy team with songs about life in Kenya performed in a rock-*soukous* style. Thanks to the album, Wainaina was co-winner of the East Africa prize at the Kora awards (an honour he shared with Kenyan gospel/R&B artist **Henrie Mutuku**).

More recently, other production companies have come on the scene. In much the same way that Josiah's *Chapters* CDs introduced a host of new artists to the public, **Ogopa Deejays** have put out various compilations with a focus on the style known as **kapuka** – a mixture of Kenyan hip-hop, ragga and house. The tracklists read like a who's who of the pop charts: the late **E-Sir**, **Redsan**, **Kleptomaniaks**, **Wahu**, **Big Pin** and **Mr. Lenny** to name just a few.

Kapuka gets plenty of radio play, but Kenyan hip-hop artists are keen to distance themselves from the genre, which they criticize for its shallowness and lack of meaningful social content. They point out that a great many *kapuka* practitioners come from relatively privileged backgrounds – such as rapper CMB Prezzo, the self-proclaimed "president" of the younger generation who once hired a helicopter to drop him at an award ceremony. In contrast, most of the "true" Kenyan hip-hop scene centres around the youth of urban housing estates and slums, and gets little exposure.

Another segment of Kenya's new music scene are the musicians looking to incorporate traditional instruments, rhythms and melody into contemporary pop music. **Yunasi**, **Kayamba Afrika** and US-based **Jabali Afrika** are groups that blend rich vocal harmonies with "traditional" African percussion and string instruments, plus varying levels of guitar, bass and keyboards. **Nairobi City Ensemble** takes a slightly different approach, incorporating what they term "authentic melodies" and touches of traditional instruments into

Suzanna Owiyo

a generally contemporary sound with modern instruments and guest rappers. Finally, singer-songwriter **Suzanna Owiyo** brings together contemporary sounds with traditional melodies and instruments of her Luo culture. Her first album generated a lot of excitement (and was picked up for international release under the title *Mama Africa* by the ARC label), and her second album, *Yamo Kudho*, released in Kenya in 2004, is even more polished, delivering sublime melodies in a bright acoustic sound.

This latter category of artists has received financial support from organizations such as Nairobi's Alliance Française, and generates a certain amount of interest on the international World Music scene, but is less popular among the Kenyan youth. As for the future, it's hard to say which of the new styles will dominate, or whether the hip-hop generation will one day return to the rumba and *benga* fold. The one thing that is certain is that we're in the midst of an interesting time, with lots of new players, many of them still learning the game. And it will be fun to hear the music evolve.

A number of tape compilations of traditional music are available in Kenya. CDs below are mostly available from African specialists worldwide.

⭐ Guitar Paradise of East Africa
Kenya Dance Mania
Earthworks/Stern's, UK

These two CDs provide an excellent introduction to Kenya's various styles, although not always the best or most representative material from the artists. Highlights on *Guitar Paradise* include Super Mazembe's classic "Shauri Yako" and Ochieng' Kabaselleh's "Achi Maria". On *Kenya Dance Mania* are some Kenyan classics of the 1970s and 80s, including Les Wanyika's "Sina Makosa" and Maroon Commandos' evergreen hit, "Charonyi Ni Wasi".

⊙ Kilio cha Haki
UpToYouToo, Netherlands

A treasure trove of innovative hip-hop talent from Nairobi's Eastlands slum area. The excellent notes transcribe and translate the poignant Swahili lyrics. Proceeds from the sale of the CD are donated to the development of a permanent, locally run studio in Eastlands.

⊙ Luo Roots: Musical Currents from Western Kenya
GlobeStyle, UK

The Kapere Jazz Band and others perform versions of the traditional music of the Luo people, originators of the *benga* style.

⊙ The Most Beautiful Songs of Africa
ARC Music, UK

Quite a good collection of (largely) 1970s Kenyan and Tanzanian music. The mix is eclectic, with the Congolese dance sounds of Super Mazembe and Bopol Mansiamina, *taarab* music of the coast, and Tanzanian dance music from Afro 70, not to mention one of Miriam Makeba's best versions of the Swahili song "Malaika" (the one that served as the model for Angelique Kidjo's rendition).

⊙ The Nairobi Beat: Kenyan Pop Music Today
Rounder, US

A collection of first-rate mid-1980s music compiled by the author of this article and showcasing a cross-section of musical varieties. It includes some of the best examples of regional *benga* styles – Luo, Kikuyu, Kamba and Luhya – plus a couple of Swahili and Congolese dance tunes for good measure.

⊙ The Rough Guide to the Music of Kenya and Tanzania
World Music Network, UK

A sampling of the many styles of popular music that co-exist in Kenya today, from guitar-centric *benga* and Swahili rumba styles to current day "traditional" sounds and the shifting sounds of the younger generation (including Gidigidi Majimaji's "Ting Badi Malo" and Suzanna Owiyo's "Kisumu 100").

⊙ The Secret Museum of Mankind, Music of East Africa, Ethnic Music Classics: 1925–48
Yazoo, US

With selections from across East Africa, this is a fascinating window onto traditional and popular sounds of the 1930s and 40s. Of the eleven selections from Kenya, most feature guitar accompanying traditional songs. On some tracks there's a sense of the *benga* that emerged two or three decades later.

Abana Ba Nasery

From western Kenya, this trio keeps alive a style of music they pioneered in the 1960s and early 70s.

⊙ Classic Acoustic Recordings from Western Kenya
GlobeStyle, UK

These original recordings from the 1960s and 70s. A charming collection of finger-picking acoustic guitar music from Bunyore, Kenya.

⊙ Nursery Boys Go Ahead
GlobeStyle, UK/Xenophile, US

Made on their 1991 tour to the UK, this CD captures the crisp ABN sound and places the trio in some interesting (and sometimes rockin') collaborations with European artists.

⊙ Rujina Kalando
Equator Heritage Sounds, US

A chance for squeeze-box fanatics to get some rare recordings of African accordion, with Oguta Bobo singing and playing. The songs mix traditional melodies and rhythm with 1960s lyrics that are filled with humour for those who understand Luo.

Sam Chege's Ultra-Benga

Raised by his grandmother in rural central Kenya, Chege received a solid grounding in Kikuyu music before going to study in Nairobi and the US. A former music journalist in Kenya, his own output fuses Kikuyu roots with other local styles and Congolese influence.

⭐ Kickin' Kikuyu-Style
Self-release, CDBaby.com, US

A great example of Kikuyu *benga* music, with its solid pulsing kick drum and interlocking guitars (with seriously delayed reverb). This lively, fun, well-recorded music makes a fascinating contrast to the Luo *benga* of D.O. Misiani, George Ramogi or Victoria Kings.

Gidigidi Majimaji

Perhaps the most innovative and successful of Kenya's new breed of music stars. The Gidigidi Majimaji duo (Joseph Ogidi and Julius Owino) burst on the scene with "Ting' Badi Malo". Even if you can't understand the clever lyrics, their mixture of African styles and contemporary hip-hop is fresh and catchy. Their song "Who Can Bwogo Me?" became the unofficial anthem of the political opposition in Kenya's 2002 elections.

⊙ Ismarwa
A'mish, US; CDBaby.com

The fusion of local African sounds with international hip-hop has been tried many times, but rarely does it work so well as this.

⊙ Many Faces
Gallo, South Africa

Recorded with a number of South African guests, this album offers a mix of Gidigidi Majimaji's Kenyan sounds with kwaito and other styles from South Africa.

Golden Sounds Band

Led by the late Twahir Mohamed (a brilliant saxophonist and arranger), Golden Sounds were among the last of

Kenya's great full-sized Swahili rumba bands. They played in the tradition of the Wanyika bands, Maroon Commandos and Nairobi Matata – though with a much denser vocal and instrumental sound.

⊙ Swahili Rumba
Naxos World, US
East African rumba with a little *soukous* guitar and a lot of reverb. It's one of the best recordings ever to come out of Nairobi, though you need to hear it a number of times to appreciate all that it offers.

Ochieng Kabaselleh & the Luna Kidi Band

From the area around Lake Victoria, Kabaselleh, who died in 1998, was one Kenyan bandleader whose music always stood apart – an interesting mix of Luo *benga*, Swahili rumba and Congolese *soukous*.

⊙ Sanduku ya Mapendo
⊙ Achi Maria
Equator Heritage Sounds, US
These two collections of Kabaselleh's double-sided singles from the 1980s provide an excellent showcase for his unique style.

Kakai Kilonzo

Kakai was at the top of Kamba-language music in Kenya from the mid-1970s until his death in 1987. But with catchy Swahili lyrics and a tight *benga* sound, he had fans all around the country and beyond.

⊙ Best of Kakai
Shava Musik, Germany
A fine compilation of 45rpm singles from the mid-1980s. Interestingly, most of Kakai's singles split a song into two parts for the A and B sides of the record. Here we get both parts of six tracks plus a one-side bonus.

Fundi Konde

One of Kenya's renowned early guitarists and the creator of many classics, Konde had his heyday in the 1950s but was rediscovered by Kenyans forty years later through his collaboration with Them Mushrooms. Recently, he has enjoyed another renaissance performing with the Tanzanian veterans Shikamoo Jazz.

⊙ Fundi Konde Retrospective Vol 1 (1947–56)
RetroAfric, UK
Enticing, historical Kenyan pop. Many of his tunes are rumbas, though a couple sound like reggae precursors. Imagine a vocal line like a mellow, two-part "Chattanooga Choo Choo"; add a smooth, jazzy electric guitar, bass and clarinet and you have the typical Konde recipe.

Les Wanyika

The last of the great Swahili rumba bands in the "Wanyika" lineage. Especially stunning are the eloquent, interlocking guitars of John Ngereza and "Professor" Omari Shabani.

★ Paulina: The Best of Prof. Omari Shabani and John Ngereza
Tamasha, Kenya
This local Kenyan release is an absolute gem, bringing together some of Les Wanyika's finest materials – "Paulina", "Pamela", "Ufukara Sio Kilema" and more. Should you come across it in Kenya or on the Internet, snap it up.

Samba Mapangala and Orchestre Virunga

From the mid-1970s to the early 90s, Orchestra Virunga were one of Kenya's most exciting groups and the Congolese vocalist, Samba Mapangala, was one of Kenya's most gifted talents. He has since relocated to the US but is still a favourite in East Africa.

Ian Anderson

★ Virunga Volcano
Earthworks/Stern's, UK
This first CD from Samba Mapangala and Orchestra Virunga is in a class all of its own. It's a perfect album, with each song developing like a story over a ten-minute period, exploring different combinations of rhythm, melody and harmony right through to the finish. As fresh and enticing today as it was when created, back in the early 1980s.

⊙ Feet On Fire
Stern's Africa, UK
Samba Mapangala on top form and in an East African groove, recorded on the 1991 UK tour.

⊙ Ujumbe
Earthworks/Stern's, UK
Samba's 2001 release picks up right where he left off: great melodies and harmonies, lush guitar, sublime sax and that eminently danceable East African rumba beat.

⊙ Virunga Roots Volume 1
Self-produced, US, CDBaby.com
A great mix of recordings made in 1989 in Nairobi and Paris. The Nairobi numbers have luscious horns and a great East Africa feel; the Paris tracks were done with some of the great Congolese session men and have a slicker European sound.

D.O. Misiani and Shirati Jazz

Daniel Owino Misiani has been doing what he does for so long (still playing after more than thirty years), that it's probably time to promote him from father of the genre to grandfather.

⊙ Benga Blast!
Earthworks/Stern's, UK
A fine collection of songs from the definitive name in Luo *benga*, this presents the rough, unpolished, mono sound of the old Pioneer House studios.

⊙ Piny Ose Mer/The World Upside Down
GlobeStyle, UK
An original GlobeStyle recording made in Nairobi – clean, polished and in stereo. While the musical content is pure Shirati, the mix is unusual for the group.

Ayub Ogada

Ayub Ogada has been bridging cultural boundaries over the last two decades – in his productions at Nairobi's French Cultural Centre in the 1970s, in the renowned African Heritage Band, which he co-founded in 1979, and in the London scene with the group Taxi Pata Pata in 1986. He is still at it today, giving solo performances on the *nyatiti*, the traditional Luo harp.

⊙ **En Mana Kuoyo**
Real World, UK
This quiet, largely acoustic CD, which starts with *nyatiti* and praise songs, is full of beautiful melodies and captivating rhythms. "Chiro" is a new rendering of the popular and lively Kenyan tune "Western Shilo".

Gabriel (Gabby) Omolo

One of the long-time members of the Equator Sound Band, Omolo later went on to found the Apollo Komesha Band. He had several major hits in the 1970s, including "Lunch Time" and "Tony Onyango", and recently emerged from retirement to rekindle his career with a new Apollo Komesha Band.

⊙ **Lunch Time (with Omondi Jassor)**
Equator Heritage Sounds, US
This compilation is a bit sketchy in terms of audio quality (some of the tracks sound as though they were taken from cassette) but the songs are first rate. There are 1970s rumba and *benga* gems, while the mid-1980s rap "Baba Otongolo" contains some stunning guitar licks (and is a hilarious dig on economic conditions in Kenya if you understand Swahili).

Suzanna Owiyo

The female singer-songwriter-guitarist is a rare breed in Kenya. Suzana Owiyo came to people's attention with "Kisumu 100", celebrating the centenary of the city on Lake Victoria. She's completely contemporary in her sound but enjoys blending in elements from her Luo roots.

⊙ **Mama Africa**
ARC Music, UK
Her first CD is delightful mix of traditional instruments, acoustic guitar and electric sounds – with a few rough edges.

⊙ **Yamo Kudho**
Blu Zebra, Kenya
Picking up where *Mama Africa* left off, this album is altogether tighter and more polished.

Simba Wanyika Original

Simba Wanyika Original were one of Kenya's favourite Swahili rumba bands from the early 1970s until the recent deaths of both the founding brothers, George and Wilson Peter Kinyonga.

⭐ **Pepea**
Kameleon Records, Holland; Stern's, UK
Their only solo CD, this is superbly produced, allowing the band to shine on some of their biggest hits of the previous twenty years. Highly recommended.

PLAYLIST
Kenya

1 **ACHI MARIA** Kabaselleh Ochieng and his Luna Kidi Band from *Guitar Paradise of East Africa*
Kabaselleh's hybrid blend of *benga* and Congolese and Swahili rumba at its finest.

2 **CHEREKO** Nyota Ndogo from *The Rough Guide to the Music of Kenya and Tanzania*
Taarab, the popular music of the East African coast, meets hip-hop culture.

3 **EAST AFRICA** Golden Sounds Band from *Swahili Rumba*
The Golden Sounds pay tribute to East African music in this upbeat rumba tune.

4 **NGOMA** Suzana Owiyo from *Mama Africa*
Ngoma means drum, or a celebration with drums, and this song captures the feel of them.

5 **SHAURI YAKO ORCHESTRA** Super Mazembe from *Giants of East Africa*
From the golden age of African pop, this is one of the best-known songs throughout the entire continent.

6 **SEFUE** Nairobi Yetu from *Kilio cha Haki*
Innovative hip-hop from the Nairobi Eastlands. Totally infectious.

7 **POLE POLE** Simba Wanyika from *Pepea*
One of the favourite songs of Simba Wanyika fans, with lovely interlocking guitars.

8 **COPOLO ONESI** Kalambya Sisters from *The Nairobi Beat: Kenyan Pop Music Today*
Kamba-language mid-1980s *benga*: the "feline" sounds of the Kalambya Sisters.

9 **AHMED SABIT** Samba Mapangala and Orchestra Virunga from *Virunga Volcano*
Be prepared to melt when the guitar solos kick in, just before the three-minute mark.

10 **OBIERO** Ayub Ogada from *En Mana Kuoyo*
A completely contemporary sound from Ogada's *nyatiti* lyre, and a rich, serene yet engaging voice.

Orchestra Super Mazembe

This Congolese group played the dance halls and bars of Kenya for nearly thirty years before their recent (perhaps temporary?) demise. With songs such as "Kasongo" and "Shauri Yako", theirs is the definitive sound of East African Congolese rumba.

Giants of East Africa
Earthworks/Stern's, UK
Mazembe's early-1980s LP, *Kaivaska*, kindled much of the mid-80s enthusiasm for Afro-pop in the UK and Europe. This collection has five of the best songs off that album, plus "Shauri Yako" and another five tracks previously unavailable outside Kenya.

Them Mushrooms/Uyoga

Them Mushrooms have sprouted in several forms over their thirty-year history, and have now rebranded themselves as Uyoga. Since 1993, they've returned to their reggae origins.

Them Mushrooms
Rags Music, UK
After the first two songs, "Jambo Bwana" and "Mushroom Soup", the remainder of the CD is the Mushrooms' remakes of classic Kenyan tunes from the 1950s and 60s.

Kazi Ni Kazi
Kelele Records, Germany
Them Mushrooms fully entered the reggae camp with this CD, and they sound perfectly at home.

Jambo Bwana
Kelele Records, Germany
Beach-hotels reggae at its best.

Victoria Kings

One of the great *benga* groups from Luo country, the Victoria Kings started in the 1970s with Ochieng Nelly as bandleader and were soon joined by Collela Mazee. The result was one of the top-selling recording groups of *benga*'s golden age – the late 1970s and early 80s.

The Mighty Kings of Benga
GlobeStyle, UK
A different perspective on *benga* (ie not Shirati Jazz) and a very good compilation at that.

Eric Wainaina

Part of the Five Alive singing group in the mid-90s, Wainaina then went off the US to study at the Berkelee College of Music. The resulting CD, made in the US, was warmly received in Kenya in 2001 and he is now one of the stars of Kenya's new generation. He brings together an innovative mix of Kenyan pop sounds with Euro/American Influences.

Sawa Sawa
Wainaina/Kaufmann Productions, US/Kenya
This superbly crafted debut spans a broad range of styles from uptempo African dance rhythms to ballads and "smooth jazz" sax. It contains hit "Nchi ya Kitu Kidogo", about corruption and bribery in Kenya, and (for Swahili speakers) interludes from the Kenyan comedy troupe Redykyulass.

Liberia

music from the ashes

African Gospel Acapella
AGA

For almost a decade and a half, Liberia was world news for all the wrong reasons – namely the two extremely violent civil wars that swept through this small West African nation between 1989 and 2003. One of the things these conflicts destroyed was a budding music industry. But local music is coming back and, what's more, it is getting *more* local. Liberia's interior, largely isolated for long periods, is proving a source of inspiration to music producers, and home-grown music is taking off – much of it recorded in peoples' living rooms. Frequent visitor Bram Posthumus provides the low-down.

Early in the nineteenth century, slave owners and idealistic African American missionaries in the United States created the American Colonization Company, with the aim of establishing a colony in West Africa. The slave owners simply wanted to send black Americans back to Africa, but the missionaries intended to "civilize" the African locals who, in their view, had sold their ancestors into slavery. The colony was set up in 1822 and became Liberia (literally 'free country') in 1847.

Unsurprisingly, the culture of the African American settlers clashed somewhat with that of the locals, and the **Americo-Liberians** (as the settlers came to be known) quickly established an elite. This group – which, ironically, for a time traded people from Liberia's interior as slaves – has produced every one of the country's presidents since the time of independence, with the exception of 1980–89, when a sergeant named Samuel Doe held power. Doe's downfall was followed by civil war and hundreds of thousands of Liberians fled the country. They are only now returning.

Liberia's music reflects this unique history, combining classic West African elements with influences of America and the Christian church, plus lyrics that – over the last two decades at least – have frequently referred to war and corruption.

Traditions and Choirs

Liberia is home to at least seventeen distinct ethnic groups. Each group has its own musical traditions, though they all share elements familiar from other West African musics – complex polyrhythms and call-and-response vocals – plus liberal use of the *sasa*, a bead-filled shaker hung by a string from one hand and played with the other. Liberia's traditional music can still be heard today at weddings, funerals and naming ceremonies, as well as political and religious festivals. They can also be heard on disc: Folkways and Rounder have issued a few recordings of the music of the Vai, who live on the coast near Monrovia, and the forest-based Kpelle and Dan. Furthermore, some contemporary musicians – including **Won Ldy-Paye**, **E. Kaikpai Paasewe** and **Princess Hawa Moore** – have incorporated elements of these old musics into their modern styles.

Another key Liberian style is choir music, introduced by settler ministers in the nineteenth century and soon popular around the country. Liberian choral music is largely a religious affair, though the secular equivalent also exists, spearheaded in the 1950s by **The Greenwood Singers**. The choral scene has been seriously damaged by the war, but Monrovia still reverberates with the sound of singing that emanates from its many churches, and the **African Gospel Acapella** is keeping that tradition alive outside the country.

Over the years, the tradition of the church choirs has also helped inspire a wide range of other religious styles in Liberia. Artists fully or partly dedicated to these various "gospel" musics include **Evangelist Zack Roberts**, **Ebenezer Kojo Samuels**, **Hawa Moore**, the **Musical Messiahs** (now in the US after two of its members were assaulted in the early stages of the war), **Evangelist Sarah Thomson** and **Twale Geply**.

Sweet Liberia: Pre-War Songs

The 1950s saw the first recordings of the Liberian singers who borrowed styles from neighbouring countries – including palm wine from Sierra Leone and highlife from Ghana. An important name from those days is **Howard Hayes**, a blind pianist who wrote and performed catchy tunes in any style he could lay his hands on: palm wine, calypso, even ragtime. As time went by, however, American styles – R&B and rock'n'roll – increasingly dominated the airwaves, and it was left to **Molly Dorley** and **Anthony Nagbe** to kick-start a real African music scene in Liberia. Dorley's band, the **Sunset Boys**, became popular with songs like "Grand Gedeh Oh! Oh!" (his 1969 birthday present to President Tubman), and Nagbe's **Tejajlu Musical Group** performed local songs in indigenous languages. Other popular outfits in those pre-war optimistic years were **Zack and Gebah**, responsible for a patriotic ballad called "Sweet Liberia" and the band **Liberian Dreams**, which recorded the famous song "OAU Welcome to Liberia".

In the 1970s and 80s, army musicians **Robert Toe** and **Jimmy Diggs** made names for themselves, recording cassettes featuring a combination of local and international material. Diggs sang in his native Gbandi language – quite unusual for Liberia in those days. Then there was keyboard player T. Kpan Nimely, who set up the **Monrovia Brothers** with guitarist Donald Cooper. Again, they played a mix of reggae and highlife, peppered with Afro-rock and something they called "discolypso", described by the Ghana-based music journalist John Collins as "a disco or funk version of Sierra Leone's popular *maringa* music from the mid-70s". Nimely died in 2005.

War and Exodus

The Organization for African Unity (OAU) visited Liberia in 1979, the last year the country knew any real peace. In April there were riots over the staple food, rice, which had become unaffordable. Exactly one year later, Samuel Doe crashed into power and at the end of the decade, on Christmas Eve 1989, Charles Taylor, a former civil servant in Doe's government, entered the country with a group of armed men, starting the first civil war.

The songs changed with the times. "Don't Play Foul", by a duo known as **Hayes and Harvey**, was a popular tune just before the war. On the surface it was about that ubiquitous Liberian theme – men and women cheating each other – but on another level the song reflected the growing exasperation of the Liberian public with their errant politicians. During the civil war, musicians composed numerous pleas for peace. **Zack Roberts** made an impression with "Stop the Fighting" in the mid-1990s, and the **Swa-Ray Band** sent out a clear message with "We Want Peace". The latter group also highlighted the plight of refugees in "Mass Exodus", while **Miatta Fahnbulleh** dedicated her 1997 album *A Song for Liberia* to her 200,000 compatriots who had not survived the war.

In 1997, Charles Taylor won the presidential elections, employing the surreal campaign slogan "He killed my pa, he killed my ma, I'll vote for him." Liberians understood its message very well: that if they did not vote for him, Taylor would go on killing, so they put up with him. Finally, the war was over, but few people were happy. "Suffering", a popular song from 2000 by a young artist called **Levi Jesse Zenawii**, summed up public sentiment with lyrics such as the following. The song's typically simple format – a straightforward fast beat, keyboards to fill in the harmony and a singalong melody – made the message all the more poignant.

The atrocious Taylor government and the second civil war (2000–03) pushed most of the prominent figures in Liberian music abroad. Some moved to the US, including the Swa-Ray Band, female singer **Naser Sokay** (who has since produced plenty of upbeat music with her Liberian husband Jake D), and drummer and singer-songwriter Joe Woyee, whose US-produced album *Brand New Antiques* is rather bland. **Peter Cole**, from central Liberia, moved to Senegal, where he recorded the equally bland *Stay Alive*. Other artists to leave included Miatta Fahnbulleh, **Princess Fatu Gayflor** and Stephen Worljoh (aka Big Steve), as well as female star Yatta Zoe, who recently returned home after prolonged stays in Guinea and the Netherlands.

The styles of most of these artists is pretty conventional, shifting between traditional rhythms and plenty of highlife and reggae. More modern styles – such as hip-hop – are popular, but local recordings are few and far between. There has been one important release, however, from a group called **The Boyz of Butuburam**. This 2002 production came about when young German-Liberian producer Alexander Dworak visited the Butuburam refugee camp in Ghana. He was impressed by the young rappers there and recorded them in a local studio. He took the tapes back to Germany and turned them into an excellent album.

Back on its Feet?

Liberia's music industry received many body blows during the wars. Artists left, and recording studios and radio stations were looted, destroyed and burned to the ground. And today, many problem remain. Piracy is rampant, the cost of importing equipment is prohibitive, and a lack of electricity forces producers and artists to rely on expensive generators. Furthermore, Liberia's musicians have to battle with competition from US artists, the ever-present reggae, mass-produced Congolese *ndombolo* and the latest craze, *zouglou* from neighbouring Côte d'Ivoire.

Where are the streets they promised?
Where are the roads they promised?
Where are the schools and good jobs?
I'm gonna shout
Beyond the walls of Jericho
For the whole world to hear my cry
I want to let you know
We are suffering

No job
No work
No food to eat
There is suffering in the world today

One Producer's Story

E. Tonieh Williams is an important Liberian record producer. He got involved in music in 1972 and played in various bands, such as Melody 8 with Titi K. Roberts (who would be killed in 1990). In the mid-1970s he moved to Nashville in the US, returning in 1978 to set up the band Liberian Dream with **Zack Roberts** and **Gebah Swaray**. 'We made what we called Afro-Disco Music,' Williams explains. The band recorded the single "OAU Welcome to Liberia", with "We Like It Like That" on the flipside. 'It was our way of saying how pleased we were with Liberia. It cost us $18,000 to produce and we hoped the president and our government would help us. What did the president, Tolbert ... do? He bought two copies!'

Before long, Wiliams was running the first Liberian-owned studio – a state-of-the-art set-up called Hotline. It cost $65,000 to equip, and Zack and Gebah, Hayes & Harvey and Robert Toe all recorded there. But nothing remains – a rebel leader called Prince Johnson carted it all off to his military base in 1990. So these days, Tonieh works from home, with a desktop computer attached to a keyboard and a mic. "I simply cannot live without a studio in my life. But given time and God willing, we will come back to the level where we were before the war." Rap from home (away from home).

Despite all this, Liberian artists and producers have soldiered, and the industry has slowly crawled back to its feet. By the time Liberia was choosing its new president, in October 2005, the market was flooded with cassettes containing stern warnings to vote wisely, delicious wisecracks about corrupt politicians and government and plenty of local musical colour. And local tracks by the likes of **Zack Roberts** or **King O'Bryant** were finding their way onto the airwaves thanks to pioneering radio DJs. Fittingly, even one of the main presidential candidates, football legend **George Oppong Weah**, is a musician of sorts. His album – produced with a Pan-African outfit featuring Manu Lima, Boncana Maiga and Coco Mbassi – is an ode to the Liberian national team.

With thanks to John Collins, Tonio Williams and DJ Rogers at Liberia's Radio DC 101

DISCOGRAPHY Liberia

Liberia is cassette country. In Monrovia, street hawkers on Broad Street and a few shops around the Randall/Carey Street junction stock a bunch of titles, usually pirated and of poor quality. Virtually all of the CDs listed below are produced and distributed in the US, though they remain hard to find. If your local music store cannot help, try the Internet. Pan African Allstars (*www.panafricanallstars.com/liberia*) supplies discs by Miatta Fahnbulleh, the Swa-Ray Band, Fatu Gayflor, C.C. Barnard and Meka Suz. Kinzo Music Works (*www.kinzomusicworks.com*) sells CDs by Naser Sokay and her husband Jake D.

⭐ Various Songs of the African Coast: Café Music of Liberia and Ghana
Guthrie Alberts, US

The bulk of the material on this compilation – recorded in 1954 by the US traveller Arthur Alberts – is Liberian, with main roles for the blind pianist Howard B. Hayes and The Greenwood Singers. Musically, you'd be forgiven for thinking you had just landed in Trinidad – there's calypso as well as ragtime-like work rumbas – but the parlance and humour is distinctly local. Everyday life is the subject matter: courtship, marriage and gossip.

African Gospel Acapella

The six members of African Gospel Acapella were enrolled at Liberia's only school for the blind in the 1980s. When the school was ransacked in the war, the six were scattered throughout the country, but they managed to regroup in 1992 and sang on Monrovia's streets. In 1998 they got political asylum in the US, where they continue to perform, sending money home to support their families and various projects for the disabled. For more information, see *www.africangospel.org*.

⊙ For Me to Live in Christ
African Gospel Acapella, US

Excellent close-harmony singing, steady rhythms – this gospel album has it all. American influences are discernible but the sequencing of chords is distinctly African, and various Liberian languages are used besides the English. Even if you don't care for the religious message, you'll love the singing.

The Boyz of Butuburam

The "boyz" are refugees who lived in the Butuburam camp in Ghana – and may still be there. A chance encounter with a German-Liberian arranger and producer resulted in one

PLAYLIST
Liberia

1 **DEI YA MONNUE Hawa Moore** from
  A Yam Yam Sae
  A traditional wedding song in a cool performance with lively percussion and call-and-response
  vocals.

2 **ALELOKPE Princess Fatu Gayflor** from *Awoya*
  Fast-moving forest beats set to modern synths
  and drums.

3 **MASS EXODUS The Swa-Ray Band** from
  Mass Exodus
  Seminal mid-1990s lament about refugees forced
  to leave their beloved homeland.

4 **AFRICAN LOCOMOTION Ebenezer Kojo
  Samuels** from *Peace*
  High-energy Afro-jazz funk, performed live.

5 **WE ARE ALL AFRICANS The Boyz of
  Butuburam** from *Pray for Liberia*
  The impressive opening track of an excellent rap
  album.

remarkable album. Hopefully this loose group will turn
into a real crew.

★ **Pray for Liberia**
  United Sound, Germany
There's a slightly jazzy atmosphere to this collection, perhaps,
as one reviewer suggested, because of Francophone influences. The opening track offers a darkly brooding soundscape; guitar licks, reggae, deft sampling and traditional
drumming all appear later on. The message could not be
clearer: politicians should stop messing with our lives. Highly
recommended.

Princess Fatu Gayflor

Born in 1966 in Kakata, central Liberia, Gayflor is a popular
female singer, nicknamed the "Golden Voice of Liberia". She
joined a cultural troupe at the age of 12, became their lead
vocalist a few years later
and in 1984 travelled with
them to the US, where she
is now based.

⊙ **Awoya**
  Samantha's, Liberia
One of the few Liberian
albums that is fairly widely
available, *Awoya* is a collection of infectious dance
tunes and interesting and
intricate traditional polyrhythms played on mod-
ern instruments – plus the

inevitable reggae tune. Gayflor's voice is slightly flat but
pleasant enough, the main drawback being the overuse
of echo-chamber synths and horns added in Pamphile de
Souza's Abidjan studio.

Princess Hawa Moore

Hawa Moore is of Vai royal lineage, hence the title Princess.
Her biggest musical influence was her father, a member of
The Greenwood Singers, and she made her name first as a
choir leader, then as a recording artist and backing vocalist
for Miriam Makeba. She has been living and working in the
USA since 1991.

⊙ **A Yam Yam Sae (I Have Nobody)**
  Institute for Cultural Partnerships, USA
Hawa Moore's only US release features her very pleasant
voice in traditional and highlife songs and some of her own
compositions. With crisp production and gentle, acoustic
instrumentation, it adds up to a highly likeable album.

Ebenezer Kojo Samuels

After taking theatre, music and dance courses in Germany
in the 1960s, Samuels returned to Liberia and founded the
Afro-jazz band Kapingdbi, which toured Africa, Europe
and the US. *Hey
Brother* is their
best-known
album but it's
a rare find. The
band stopped
in 1986 and
Samuels returned
to Germany three
years later, where
he works both as
a musician and
visual artist.

★ **Peace**
  One World Media, Germany
This must have been one helluva party. E.K.S. and his band, X
(short for "excellence"), romp through some high-energy jazz,
funk, Afro-beat and a bit of highlife and reggae. There's a very
credible cover of Fela's "Shakara" and the band's own compositions easily hold their own.

Gebah and Maudline Swaray
(The Swa-Ray Band)

Maudline started singing when she was 8, and guitarist, composer, arranger and producer Gebah was part
of the famous Zack and Gebah duo that scored hits in
Liberia with "Keep On Trying" and "No Peace No Love". The
husband-and-wife team are now based in the US, where
they set up a small production company called Swaray.
Maudline works at Columbia University.

★ **Mass Exodus**
  Swaray, US
The title-track is the centrepiece of this fantastic 2002 album.
With plaintive singing and a typically Liberian abundance of
biblical references, it's a seriously brooding track, reflecting
the plight of Liberians who, like the Swarays, felt they had
lost their country to the conflicts. The other tunes range from
the simple and catchy to the seriously danceable, mostly key-
board-driven with occasional highlife-style guitar.

Libya

a cultural crossroads

Zakar musicians with pipes and bendirs
Hulton Archive/Getty Images

Libya is a huge country with a small population and an even smaller musical reputation – even fans of Arab music tend to know little of its artists or musical traditions. There are long-standing political reasons for this neglect, but perhaps now that Colonel Gaddafi's regime is opening up to the wider world, the undoubted riches of its musical heritage will become better known. Robert Nurden investigates.

Midway between sub-Saharan Africa and Europe, and half-way along the Arab world's east–west axis, Libya has always been something of a crossroads. This has been to its advantage – it has inherited a rich mix of cultural traditions – but also to its disadvantage: the country was subject to incursions by Phoenicians, Greeks, Romans, Turks, Italians, French and English before gaining independence in 1951. No surprise, then, that its musical influences point in many directions.

As well as its distinct dialect (which derives from the Nile Valley) one major factor separating Libya from its Arab cousins is the bizarre and seemingly never-ending reign of its dictator, Colonel Gaddafi, and the ubiquitous committees of his Socialist People's Libyan Arab Jamahiriya. The regime has done much to meddle with musical life, despite the fact that the 1969 coup that brought Gaddafi to power was postponed to avoid a clash with a concert being given in Libya by legendary Egyptian singer Umm Kulthum. In the late 1970s, for example, a decree went out that homegrown music influenced by the West was "imperialist". Western instruments were collected from schools, homes, shops and recording studios, piled in Tripoli's Green Square and burned. This led to many young musicians fleeing the country; some went to Italy and other parts of Europe, but most to Cairo.

Musicians have also had to face long-term state promotion of a strictly limited notion of Libyan folkloric culture, as well as the travel and financial restrictions imposed on most Libyan citizens. For these and other reasons, the country's artists seldom attend international festivals – and in Libya itself, live music has tended to be a rather private affair.

Today, however, Tripoli's streets are teeming with music shops, and sounds pour out of countless poky stalls selling cut-price CDs and cassettes. It looks like pent-up creativity of many years is beginning to make itself heard at last.

From Folk to Progressives

Libyan folksongs – the words and sentiments of which have changed little over the years – are mostly heard at weddings. In some regions, men and women are segregated and perform different musical functions. In Tripoli, for instance, *zenzamat* (female professional singers) perform songs while women guests dance in a circle, clapping, singing and repeating the melody. The instruments used are *darbuka* (goblet drum) and *bendir* (frame drum). At a *zakar* ceremony, meanwhile, male professional singers play, sing and dance throughout long celebrations; the format varies from one

Exiled songwriter Nasser Mizdawi

region to another, though most groups use *zukra* (Libya's much-loved bagpipes) and *darbuka*.

In recent decades, this folk heritage has been drawn upon by popular-music artists. Singers regularly employ folk melodies in their songs with string-orchestra accompaniment or (in the case of younger artists) electric guitars, keyboards and drums. This so-called "progressive music" – a fusion of European pop, African music and Arab elements – was pioneered by exile **Nasser Mizdawi** (born 1950). His songs, which laid the foundations for a whole generation of urban Arab performers, have been heard around the world, both through his own live appearances and in cover versions by other artists such as Egyptian Amir Diab. The instruments Mizdawi employs are for the most part Western – piano, violin, keyboards, drums and guitar – though he also plays *oud* (lute). His band, **Annusur** (Eagles), released their first album, *Ughniyat an elghurba*, in 1976 and gained instant popularity.

'This kind of modern Arab music can still be tricky for Westerners to understand ... but it tells a strong human story,' explains percussionist Saleh Miller. 'Western music has an exact equivalent – it's called country and western.'

Somewhere between folk and the progressives are traditional singer-songwriters such as **Nouri Kamal**, whose spare, haunting songs, tightly bound together by *oud* and *zukra*, are powerful meditations on love and nature. In these desert songs, the words are all-important and there's a sense of formality that gives a distinctly Egyptian

Ma'luf

A special place is reserved in the Libyan soul for **ma'luf**, the country's own version of the classical Al-Andalus music brought over from Spain by Moors escaping the Christian *reconquista*. Performed by skilled musicians at specific ceremonies, the style is also known as **nuba** (literally, a group of musical pieces or a programme).

Despite its extreme formality, ma'luf forms a vital element in the lifeblood of Libyan music. This is ethereal music, dominated by the sound of the *ney* (flute), which symbolizes God. Praising Allah but also giving advice to mortals, the style is seen as cleansing, and many Libyan households hire ma'luf groups to clear their homes of evil spirits. Its repetitiveness is a key part of its effect and often induces trance-like states.

The genre has two distinct song forms: *muwashshahat* and *qasidah*. One is the setting of a verse chorus; the other the faithful rendition of a long ode. The *nuba ma'luf*, meanwhile, is a suite sung by a male choir in a predominantly homophonic texture with polyphonic passages provided by individual instruments. The singers repeat each song several times before they proceed to the next, gradually increasing the tempo towards a rousing conclusion.

Traditional ma'luf is performed by the Sufi brotherhoods who meet in the *zawya* (mosque communal room) and regard this music as a kind of prayer – and a way to attract young people to join Sufi lodges. Today, however, a modern version – as pioneered in 1964 by *oud* player and singer **Hassan Araibi** – is much more widespread, and broadcast daily on radio and television. A typical modern ma'luf ensemble includes Western instruments (violin, cello and double bass) as well as local ones (*ney, oud, qanun* (zither), *tar* (tambourine), *darbuka* and *bendir*). Traditionalists remain firmly of the view that ma'luf belongs in the zawya, but progressives claim that the old way can be safely embedded in the new.

feel. Kama's resolutely traditional approach has led to him being revered by the older generation. **Salam Kadry**, a singer in the same mould, commands almost as much veneration.

Politics and Pop Songs

The singer who perhaps best represents the complex nature of Libyan music – politically as well as stylistically – is **Mohammed Hassan**, whose natural, roughed-edged Bedouin-style voice has echoed down the airwaves for years. In the 1970s, Hassan was to all intents and purposes Gaddafi's court musician, and even penned a song drawing a parallel between the dictator and the Prophet Muhammad, using references such as "Messenger of the Arabian Desert". But aside from these unashamedly political tributes, Hassan has written hundreds of beautiful, highly rhythmic songs that tell of ordinary Libyan lives, with sparse *oud* accompaniment.

Another key singer is **Ibrahim Fahmi** (from the port of Benghazi), who invariably sets modern words to conventional folk rhythms. Like Hassan, he was wrote and sung patriotic songs for his Gaddafi, but in his later work there's an Algerian *rai* influence as well as the beginnings of a Libyan reggae sound that has since been taken up by the younger generation.

Modern European pop influence can be clearly heard in the work of **Ahmed Fakrun**, who intro-duced the single into the Arab world in 1975 with "Awedny" (Promise Me). He has collaborated with numerous international producers throughout his career and recorded for world-class labels. Flanking his electric bass with harmonica, guitar and piano, as well as various traditional stringed instruments, he developed a unique style drawing on wide influences – from the Libyan desert and Indian temples to the Scottish Highlands and streets of New York.

Leading the young talent is **Cheb Jilani**, born in 1976 into a family of musicians. Trained in *muwashshahat* singing (as well as *oud* playing and orchestration), he was able to replicate the vocal styles of legendary Arab singers such as Umm Kulthum and Mohamed Abd el-Wahab, and he rapidly became popular. Marrying classical singing to modern sounds, Jilani has combined nostalgia for the old with aspirations for the new, and also explored a pan-Arabic identity: his 2003 album *Oyouniy Sahara* featured dialects of Lebanon and Syria as well as Libya.

Another significant figure is **Hameed al-Sha'eri**, who went into exile as a young man and went on to become one of the most sought-after singer-songwriters and producers in the Arab world. Though based in Egypt, his music retains some of its Libyan character – that unique musical sensibility that unites all the artists discussed above. 'We have a special style of songs in Libya which are different from other Arab countries,' explains Dr Abdalla Sebai, professor of music at Tripoli University, 'a

Hameed al-Sha'eri

compound rhythm which differentiates it from other Arab rhythms. It is part of our identity, and this private style, in the Libyan dialect, is essential to how we express ourselves.'

Desert Blues

Wearing long, shimmering, green and golden dresses, twelve beautiful women ululate and clap while indigo-turbaned men brandishing camel canes dance and shuffle across the hot sand. The *zukra* wails, the *imzad* sings, the *oud* lilts, the *shakshaka* (castanets) shakes and the *ganga* and *tindé* drums keep up a pounding rhythm. Welcome to the Touareg music and dance festivals that take place each year in Ghat and Ghadames – Libya's answer to Mali's Festival in the Desert.

Based in the Fezzan (the Libyan part of the Sahara) the Libyan Touaregs are nomadic and semi-nomadic people descended from the Berbers who today number approximately 10,000. Their music 'is the nearest you'll get to desert blues', says Amelia Stewart of Simoon Travel, which organizes Sahara tours with a musical emphasis. 'It's not too fanciful to speculate that these songs are inspired by the clip-clop (*huda*) rhythms of the camel and miles of undulating sea sand. It is truly hypnotic.'

Women's songs include *tindé nomnas* (praise songs), *tindé n'guma* (songs of exorcism) and *ezele* (dance songs). They are all usually in responsorial form with rhythmic accompaniment and hand-clapping. *Tichiwé* (men's songs) are lyrical in nature and tell of the beauty of women. Accompaniment is provided by the *imzad* – a spiked-fiddle with a gourd and goatskin resonator – and the *tindé*, a mortar and goatskin drum. Other common instruments are *tazammarfft* (a sorghum-stem flute), *assakhalebo* (water drum), *tabl* (kettledrum) and *tahardent* (three-stringed lute).

Libya doesn't have any internationally celebrated Touareg bands comparable to Mali's **Tinariwen**. However, the country can claim to have facilitated those desert revolutionaries' first steps in music: the band-to-be were provided with a rehearsal room and guitars – along with intensive weapons training – after joining a Gaddafi military training camp.

DISCOGRAPHY Libya

Artists such as Mohammed Hassan, Nasser Mizdawi, Ahmed Fakrun, Ibrahim Fahmi, Nouri Kamal, Salam Kadry, and Cheb Jilani have recorded extensively but their music is rarely available internationally. Scour the Tripoli music shops and take pot luck. Cinephiles may also want to investigate Geeta Dayal's *Folk Music of the Sahara: Among the Tuareg of Libya* (2003), available via Amazon.

Al-Maqthtafat Min Funun al-Ma'luf wa l-Muwashshahat
Al-Alamiya, Libya
This series of fourteen cassettes, though hard to track down, provides a good sample of traditional *ma'luf* music.

⊙ Libye: Chants des Oasis
Al Sur, France
Released in 2000, this 3-CD set encompasses a wide range of stunning desert music by Touareg and other musicians from southwest Libya. On the first disc, a man performs improvised poetry (*srewa*) with flute accompaniment, singing of loyal camels, shining stars and formidable women. The second disc has vigorous rhythms and an altogether more sub-Saharan feel, while the third features haunting folksongs, backed by *oud* and drums, from a group called Weddey.

Hameed al-Sha'eri

Still based in Cairo, this popular Libyan singer-songwriter performs in an Egyptian style for an Egyptian audience. But his music retains a Libyan flavour and he does a few songs in his native dialect.

⊙ Ghazaly
EMI Arabia, Syria
A collection of contemporary love songs arranged with Western instruments.

Touareg de Fewet

A Touareg group from Libya's rocky southwest.

★ Libye: Musiques du Sahara
Buda Musique, France
Thunderous drums, tinkling *oud*, shrill female vocals and trance-like clapping act as the intro to an extraordinary solo performance from a male artist. This weaving and shaping of musical curves continues throughout eight tracks of desert rock.

Madagascar

a parallel universe

Squeezebox maestro Regis Gizavo
Ian Anderson

While European countries harness their architectural landmarks as symbols for instant recognition, the trademarks of Madagascar are furry lemurs, pop-eyed chameleons and the giant fossilized eggs of the extinct elephant bird. You'd be forgiven for thinking the place didn't have a human population at all. Yet the eighteen distinct ethnic groups of this relatively isolated giant island (it's two-and-a-half times the area of Britain and half as big again as California) not only exist, they have extraordinary cultures. Just as the awesome landscape can vary from rainforest to thorny cactus desert, from high, barren mountains to palm-fringed beaches, so the music is multifaceted. It sounds like it comes from a parallel universe, familiar yet oddly different. Ian Anderson has been trying to figure it out for a decade and a half, and he's still only scratching the surface.

Madagascar is an island of puzzles and surprises. Even around the capital, Antananarivo (popularly known as Tana), the varied landscape and architecture could convince you that you were in central Europe, or West Africa, or the high Andes, or maybe Asia with its terraced rice fields. You look at the people and they could possibly be Indonesian, Asian, African or South American. Then you hear the music, which contains few clues, passing sounds, harmonies, riffs, playing styles and instruments that all seem to be related to other parts of the world. But it is audibly unique.

The island's earliest inhabitants, the Vazimba, were of Malayo-Polynesian origin (as is the consonant-rich Malagasy language), arriving, from the third century AD, via Southeast Asia and East Africa as well as directly across the Indian Ocean. There are still some distant cultural connections with parts of Indonesia, and these racial origins explain the almost Polynesian harmonies that are found in the music of the Merina, the highland people. Undoubtedly more can be traced back to the slave trade, Arab sailors, Welsh missionaries and the long period of French colonization. The proximity of East Africa and its airwaves has had a strong influence, too, notably on the coastal styles of electric guitar dance music called **watcha watcha** (in the northwest) and **tsapika** (in the southwest) which are first cousins of **Kenyan benga** and **South African township music** respectively.

But that still doesn't explain why the musicians who accompany the travelling players called **hiragasy** – among currently popular troupes are those of **Ramilison**, **Razafindramanga** and **Rakoto Kavia** – so puzzlingly resemble Mexican street bands, or display a myriad of other connections to anywhere and everywhere. I had thought this was explained by the fact that Madagascar's main cash crop, vanilla, originated in Mexico and that the Mexicans who came over to teach the cultivation process might have included musicians. But in fact the vanilla orchid vine arrived via La Réunion (following failed attempts to grow it in Europe). So has all the music in the world bumped into Madagascar at some time in history? Or did it all start here and wander off somewhere else?

Highland Hitmakers

In the 1960s a Malagasy pop group called **Les Surfs** had a string of French chart hits with Francophone covers of Spector and Beatles songs. But they were a one-off, and the first major modern group in Madagascar was **Mahaleo**. Emerging at a time of student unrest in the early 1970s, they fused Western soft rock with typical Malagasy harmonies, rhythms and traditional instruments like the *kabosy*. Combined with complex, meaningful lyrics addressing many aspects of the lives of Malagasy people, their music became enormously popular and their songs known by everybody. Still in occasional action – they celebrated their thirtieth anniversary in 2002 with a major concert, subject of the documentary film *Mahaleo* – members of the group are now doctors, social workers and, in the case of leader **Dama**, have even served as parliamentary deputies.

Following Mahaleo's lead came multi-instrumentalist Paul Bert Rahasimanana, otherwise known as **Rossy**, who formed the group that bore his nickname. They became the most successful band of the 1980s, touring in Europe and evolving a dynamic, fairly hi-tech stage act that mixed roots styles from the island with the latest trends in the world's music. Rossy was skilled at tailoring things to the audience: European pop, Johnny Clegg and *zouk* influences for the home crowd, where they had a following from all echelons of society, and conversely a more Malagasy roots repertoire abroad. Rossy faded from the international scene in the 1990s. The political upheaval of 2002, which saw the final ousting of the unpopular dictator Ratsiraka, whom Rossy had publicly supported and received funding from, forced him to leave for exile in France, in fear of his life.

Formed in 1994, the biggest name in recent times – first on the international circuit and eventually with a series of hits at home, too – have been **Tarika** ("group"), who emerged in 1994 Fronted, unusually, by women – sisters **Hanitra Rasoanaivo**

Tarika

Ian Anderson

and **Noro Raharimala** – this younger band mixed the acoustic instruments and styles from other areas and tribes with the distinctive, melodic vocal harmonies of the Merina, incorporating the results into a live act high on energy and visual impact. Their five albums to date are notable for songs, particularly those written by leader Hanitra, which combine controversial and hard-hitting political subject matter with upbeat, danceable music. Tarika have been Madagascar's most successful musical export in recent years, but a traumatic and financially disastrous US tour caused them subsequently to cut back on touring abroad. Hanitra and Noro now also have a fully electric band, **Tarika B**, for local work.

Another important contemporary group are **Solo Miral**, who play a music they call *vakojazzana* – a fusion of *vakodrazana* traditional music and jazz. They are a quintet (mostly brothers) and their leader, **Haja**, is a staggering and totally original electric guitarist in *marovany* style. The hardworking members of Solo Miral are also often seen in other bands, in demand to accompany many of Madagascar's domestic superstars. International recognition, long overdue, has eluded them, although they showcased at the 1997 Womex (the annual World Music industry-fest) in France and became one of the first bands to gain release on CD in the local market.

With local newspaper headlines like "Rickymania!", **Ricky** (Randimbiarison) has been in the spotlight for years, though his uncompromising career approach always denied him international recognition and his first record deal came only in 1998. Malagasy singing is usually at its strongest in harmony but Ricky is one of the island's best-ever solo vocalists. Locally, he often works with an electric band

Ian Anderson

Kaiamba label, "half-green" singles

which includes the finest musicians in town, particularly **Tôty**, who pioneered an extraordinary bass guitar style based on the *marovany*, and some of the members of Solo Miral. Abroad, Ricky has toured with *marovany* player Matrimbala and acapella group Salala, but his more typical work was revealed in all its glory on the MELT 2000 album *Olombelona Ricky*.

Half-Green and Salegy

The electric dance band music called **watcha watcha**, similar to Kenyan *benga*, comes from the north-western coastal region (which receives clear mainland African radio signals) and is popular in places like Mahajanga. But the island has a number of other modern dance styles, including the lilting **séga** (also common in nearby Mauritius) and most characteristic and omnipresent of all, the driving 6/8 **salegy** rhythm. This is heard all over Madagascar, though the electric version is generally connected to the north, particularly the Sakalava people in Diego Suarez and Mahajanga.

Back in the 1970s, there was a thriving record industry in Madagascar, in the course of which hundreds of *salegy* and *watcha watcha* 7" singles of vibrant dance music were produced, some of which reputedly sold over 60,000 copies. But the last local singles were pressed by DiscoMad in the mid-1980s. The record plants closed in the deteriorating economic climate, and masters have been lost or destroyed. Now, even in the capital, you can barely find a few very scratchy, secondhand copies on market stalls. Yet singles by **Orchestre Liberty**, **Jaojoby**, **Jean Fredy** or **Abdallah** rivalled the recordings of famous bands from mainland Africa. Many have a distinct Malagasy style, a few directly

Traditional Instruments

Traditional instruments are a major feature of Malagasy roots bands – and they are stunning in their variety and imagination, both in look and sound.

The most famous instrument is the **valiha**, a tubular zither made from drainpipe-diameter bamboo with around 21 strings running lengthways all around the circumference, lifted and tuned by small, moveable pieces of calabash. Traditionally the strings were strands of bamboo skin lifted from the surface but nowadays they tend to be unbraided bicycle-brake cable, giving a sound similar to a harp or the West African *kora*. The leading player was the late **Sylvestre Randafison**, a virtuoso who was once a member of the celebrated traditional music ensemble **Ny Antsaly**, the first Malagasy group to tour extensively abroad in the 1950s. Other masters include **Zeze** (Zeze Ravelonandro, who died in 1992), **Tovo**, **Rajery**, Paris-based **Justin Vali** (Justin Rakotondra-soa) and the late **Mama Sana**, an incredible old singer from the west coast who wore coins braided into her hair and attacked her instrument with the ferocity of a Mississippi blues guitarist.

Madagascar's other zither is the **marovany**, a suitcase-like wooden box with two sets of strings on opposing sides. One of the best and most influential players was the late, legendary **Rakoto-zafy**, but once again it's a common traditional instrument, particularly in the south. Virtuosity abounds among traditional players, including Masikoro musician **Bekamby**, Tulear's **Madame Masy**, **Monja** from the Antandroy tribe, **Daniel Tombo** from the east coast and younger city players like Tarika's **Donné Randria-manantena**.

Ny Antsaly featuring master valiha player Sylvester Randafison (centre)

absorbing East African and South African sounds (particularly those produced by the influential **Charles Maurin Poty**).

There was a hiatus in the late 1980s and early 1990s when that whole genre of music – known colloquially as *tapany maintso* (half-green) because of the half-green labels of the long-defunct Kaiamba label which produced the wildest of these discs – was in danger of vanishing into undocumented history. But as production changed to cassettes, eventually a new generation of recordings came onto the market, and in 1992 Jaojoby was recorded in Madagascar for a Western-label CD, and **Tianjama** (ex-Orchestre Liberty) made the first successful new *salegy* cassettes in the classic style for Mars (DiscoMad's successor).

From the mid-1990s, there were more and more regular local cassette releases by names like **Mily Clement**, the heavily *soukous*-influenced **Dedesse**, the wildly raw **Lazan'i Maroantsetra** and the first female *salegy* star, **Ninie**. In the twenty-first century, the arrival of the latest technology in Madagascar has meant that CDs by local artists are now everywhere, often on their own independent labels. *Salegy* has made it through into the digital age, with names to watch out for including **Dr J.B. and The Jaguars**, **Lego**, **Toto Mwandjani** and the all-girl **Koezy**.

Sounds of the South

Although Madagascar is theoretically united by a national language, in practice tribal cultural differences are quite profound and have been maintained by vast distances and poor communications – a journey by road from the central capital to Tulear in the southwest takes several days, and

The traditional, end-blown flute is the **sodina**, whose undisputed master was **Rakoto Frah**. A charming old man with an impish twinkle in his eye, he has represented Madagascar all over the world and his picture appeared on the local 1000-franc banknote whilst he still lived in a tiny house in Isotry, the capital's poorest area.

The **kabosy** (also known as *mandoliny* in the southwest) is a small guitar with four to six strings and partial frets. It's a relatively easily made instrument – the body is often just a rectangular box and the strings fishing line or unbraided bicycle-brake cables – but it's played to a high standard. It's not uncommon to encounter small groups of boys on street corners or country roadsides playing with the drive of electric guitar bands, sometimes even including a larger, bass version. The best-known exponents are **Jean Emilien** – who, like many other players, also utilizes harmonica on a neck rack – and **Babata** from the west coast.

The **jejy voatavo**, mostly used by the Betsileo tribe, has a large calabash resonator, a neck with huge block frets and two courses of strings on ninety-degree opposed sides. Its sound can be reminiscent of the Appalachian dulcimer.

Finally, the **lokanga** is a three-string fiddle, once again often with a simply made box-style body, played mainly by the Bara and Antandroy tribes from the south. Among several notable players is **Surgi** of the group **Vilon'Androy**.

Madagascar also has a wide range of **indigenous percussion** – struck, scraped and shaken, ranging from condensed-milk-tin shakers to large drums – plus numerous other less common instruments including musical bows (*jejy lava*), leg xylophones (*katiboky*) and bamboo whistles (*kiloloka*).

Imported instruments have also been adapted for local use. The **accordion** is found all over, if less so these days because of difficulties in getting spare parts for repairs. The most famous younger player, **Regis Gizavo**, now resides in Europe. The **piano** has long been an upper-class favourite for accompanying choral singing, and **guitars** are found everywhere. Along with fiddle and accordion, it's **brass and woodwind** instruments that are the characteristic sounds for the *hiragasy*, the popular mixture of street theatre, oration, opera and dance. The same brass players make the joyful noise for Madagascar's extraordinary *famadihana*, or reburial ceremonies. And, as it has done worldwide, the West African **djembe drum** has also now firmly established itself on the island.

"Tourist" instruments, especially *valiha* and *jejy voatavo*, are offered for sale in the markets, hotels and on the street. But if you're visiting Madagascar and in the market for musical instruments, beware. They look pretty hanging on the wall but they are rarely very playable (and often harbour fearsome Malagasy woodworm). It's better to seek out and buy from a good musician or instrument-maker. There's a notable shop run by musician Rajery at Lot IVP3ter Ankadifotsy, Antananarivo 101, or you can contact the Malagasy cultural centre Antshow, Lot VK 67 Ter AC, Ambatolava, Morarano, Antananarivo 101, Tel 56547.

national radio transmissions cannot penetrate the mountains. In Tulear, as in many distant population centres, the only way to get a recording distributed is often to make it yourself and give it to the many street-market bootleggers to copy and copy again. The omnipresent sound is of **tsapika** (or *tsapiky* as it is also spelled).

Leading local artists and bands playing *tsapika* include **Orchestre Rivo-Doza**, **Teta**, **Tsy An-Jaza**, **Jean Noel** and **Rasoa Kininike**. Their unmistakable Malagasy groove is layered with blockbuster township drive, whilst lead guitarists scatter dazzling, fractured lines over the top of full-scream female voices. It took a relatively long time for the word on *tsapika* to spread abroad, but Stern's released the excellent *Tulear Never Sleeps* compilation on their Earthworks label in 2003 and the cat is now truly out of the bag.

Tulcar was also the place where **D'Gary** grew up – a stunning guitarist who has evolved a complex style based on the sound of the *marovany* and other local instruments like the *lokanga*. Many consider that he surpasses other African acoustic guitar greats such as Ali Farka Touré or Jean Bosco Mwenda. First recorded by Mars in the early 1990s, he has released a series of increasingly excellent albums onto the international market on French label Indigo.

Ian Anderson

D'Gary

Famadihana: Reburial Parties

Hiragasy dancer

The Malagasy people have enormous respect for their ancestors, who are thought to continue their existence on a spiritual level. This is reflected in the huge amount of money that an extended family will invest in their tomb – sometimes a far more substantial dwelling than the house for the living – based on the logic that the amount of time to be spent there will eventually be far greater than the insignificant period on earth. A man is traditionally entombed in his native village, whilst a woman will be buried with her in-laws.

Equally large amounts of money – sometimes stretching a family's resources to the limits – are spent on the traditional **famadihana**, or reburial parties. These are not held at fixed intervals: perhaps a person may have expressed a wish as to frequency before their death, or a living relative may receive a hint from the ancestor that the tomb is cold and they need new clothes. The event will last a whole day and involves much feasting, drinking, dancing and merry-making by the entire extended family and local village. Musicians, usually a *hiragasy* troupe playing instruments like trumpets, clarinets and drums that can be heard above a rowdy crowd outdoors, will be hired to play nonstop to drive the affair on. The party will process to the tomb, disinter the remains of the loved one, rewrap them in fresh cloth (traditionally known as *lamba mena* – red cloth – even though it is rarely red these days), carry them around the area on their shoulders to see the new local sights, provide them with food and drink and finally put them back to rest, resealing the tomb.

The whole affair is totally joyous, not the least bit macabre, and the music is wild and glorious. Outsiders – if officially invited – can be made very welcome. The best time of the year for maximum *famadihana* yield is September.

Njava are a family band from the Antemoro tribe in the southeast of Madagascar. Evolving from a fairly dull electric band, they relocated to Belgium, went acoustic and back to their traditional roots. They were one of the hits of the 1995 Brussels Womex, with a very professional showcase that won them many fans, a lot of subsequent festival work and the attention of legendary Japanese producer Makoto Kubota (whose credits include work for Shoukichi Kina, Sandii and Detty Kurnia) for their debut album.

Regis Gizavo is Madagascar's best accordion player. With a formidable reputation already in the bag before winning the RFI Découvertes and emigrating to France in 1990, he developed a sophisticated technique on the chromatic button accordion, working sessions with Manu Dibango, Ray Lema, Les Têtes Brûlées and Corsica's I Muvrini before finally launching his solo career.

Other recent and current artists to watch out for from the south include largely acapella groups

Malagasy Guitar: a Word with Bouboul

There is no single, uniform Malagasy guitar style. Between the almost mainland African lead guitars of the electric *salegy* and *watcha watcha* bands from the north, through courtly, classical highland plateau playing with echoes of nineteenth-century parlour music, Hawaiian slack key and ragtime, to the dauntingly dense flurries of the *marovany*-inclined players like D'Gary, N'Java's Dozzy, Solo Miral's Haja and the tsapika players from the southwest, there are major gulfs.

Etienne Ramboatiana, aka **'Bouboul'**, is a legend among Malagasy musicians. He was Madagascar's first electric guitarist in the early 1950s, and later toured the world with a circus. A captivating, sparkling-eyed gentleman in his sixties when interviewed, he was a mine of information that could fill a book about the history of the guitar in Madagascar and the origins of the high plateau style in Antananarivo. The following is a short extract from an interview with Ramboatiana on the subject of Malagasy guitar, first published in *fRoots* magazine, in April 1998:

'As we all know, the guitar is a foreign instrument but in the time of Ranavalona III [the last Queen of Madagascar], the guitar, viola, 'flûte traversière' and mandolin all arrived together. The vazaha played those instruments and people just watched. We realised that the guitar was only an accompaniment to the mandolin. So the Malagasy wanted the guitar to be independent. We wanted it to sing a song not to only accompany. The Malagasy sang in harmony a lot, with breathing technique and lots of melodies, so we wanted the guitar to do all these. The Malagasy guitar style was born!

'There was a competitive spirit because of the piano. The piano was brought here before the guitar by missionaries and its place was always in the royal court. In La Haute Ville, people had piano, while "les grand bourgeois", in Ambatovinaky and Faravohitra, had harmonium, saxophone and accordion, and in Ambodin'Isotry [the poor part of Antananarivo] they had the guitar wizards. If you went down still further, what you would find in people's homes were traditional instruments.

'When people down here heard that the piano made a really high sound, they put the capo on their guitars. When there was a very bassy sound they changed the bass strings by re-tuning it into C and G to get what we call today Malagasy style. I changed my bass string into D because it's just too much to change it to C. In Antananarivo, some people would even change that string into a piano wire to get that big bass note.

'Since the piano was used for theatrical pieces, that's what guitarists translated onto their guitars. In 1942, these guitarists would go out serenading. They wore caps, big clothes and scarves, and girls would come out. They had to stop around Faravohitra because if they continued upwards, they would get soaked because people from La Haute would throw dirty water on them. La Haute is a piano place. Faravohitra was the highest area a guitarist could go up to and then they had to go back to Ambodin'Isotry where they came from.

'If you really want to find out about the Malagasy guitar style, it came from the way the Malagasy played the piano, but the piano was only copying the valiha. So the valiha is the origin of it all, then on to the piano and then on to the guitar.

'Things changed around about the second world war. The Malagasy got some style out of Charlie Kunz's songs, a German who ran away to England. Then Randrianarivelo arrived. He brought another style of guitar. Then I arrived. One day, around 1951, Harry Hougassian, a Hawaiian guitar-player and Mounitz (a Jewish player) played here in Madagascar. I was really taken by their whole way of playing. Harry played one of those guitars you put on your lap and slide it across and Mounitz accompanied him. [Hougassian was a celebrated Armenian player of the Hawaiian guitar, still alive and at the time running a restaurant in Paris.] Every time a new guitarist arrived and brought a new style, others just took an inspiration from it.'

Where to Find Music in Antananarivo

It's no longer difficult to find **live music** in the capital. You may run into traditional music unexpectedly in the streets, as part of a ceremony or celebration or simply in someone's home. The different venues have programmes which try to work a month ahead, and then there are the local newspapers, which give details of what's on every day. Keep an eye open for concert posters, especially open-air ones (there's a new medium-sized open air-venue which was inaugurated by a music festival in March 2005). Check out clubs and restaurants aimed for the *vazaha* (foreigners) because they tend to put on traditional music.

A good bar venue for *salegy* bands is the funky *Hotel Glacier* in the Avenue de L'Indépendence, run by Charles Maurin Poty. More formal concerts take place at the Roxy Cinema, CCEsca Antanimena, the Centre Culturel Albert Camus in Analakely which has a regular programme and puts on World Music acts such as Tarika, Zap Mama, Ismael Lô, etc, and the Cercle Germano-Malagasy in the Analakely district, which has been renovated. The *Alliance Française* (Ampefiloha Andavamamba) has been enlarged and has a regular music programme which local people attend because the ticket price is so low.

The recently built Malagasy arts centre Antshow (Ambatolava, Mora-rano, Tel 56547) puts on authentic and excellent roots-based bands but only operates on a special project basis, since it is solely run by local artists – if you are travelling to Madagascar, make sure you know ahead of time what will be on there during your stay. Restaurants and hotels such as *La Residence* (Ank-erana) tend to do jazz, *Le Ravinala* (15km away from the centre and fairly new) accommodates all sorts of music styles whilst *CLT* (Antsaka-rivo) has cabaret. The newly built *Big Bang* restaurant also puts on some *salegy* bands, while *Le Grille du Rova* (near the palace) puts on some traditional music on Wednesdays. Big-

Young students of the Valiha High project housed in the Antshow Arts Centre in Antananarivo

Ian Anderson

ger places to see bigger acts are: *Antsonjombe, Antsahamanitra, El Dorado* and *Palais de Sport*.

Oddly enough, the best bets for a good selection of original (ie non-pirate) cassettes and increasingly now CDs of local music are the growing number of huge supermarkets that have opened up for the better-off. You can also find a good range at Super Music store (Andohan'Analakely), Jumbo Score, Conquette and Champion.

Thanks to Randriampanahy Mahery for help updating this section

---

Salala and **Senge**; Antandroy roots bands **Tsimi-hole**, **Vaovy** and **Vilon' Androy** with their wailing *lokanga*s, Fort Dauphin's **Dada De Fort Dauphin** and the wild *kabosy*-led **Hazolahy.**

Westernization and Back to Roots

What happened with music in Madagascar in the late 1980s and 1990s was a mirror on the whole culture. With the opening up of the economy, TV beamed Western styles into the wealthier homes, while the rich few, making their shopping pilgrimages to Paris, brought back synthe-sizers, drum machines and European fashion. "Vita Gasy" (Made in Madagascar) had become synonymous with "worthless'" and both the rural roots traditions and the more sophisticated high-land *kalon' ny fahiny* (old-time songs) still being performed by older groups like **Ny Sakelidalana** and **Voninavoko** were becoming ignored by the trendsetters.

A new breed emerged of rich-kid pop stars and artists with wealthy patrons. They included Euro-pop chanteuses with names like **Bodo**,

Justin Vali playing a *marovany*

Poopy, **Landy**, **Mbolatina** and **Tiana**; a style of bubble-gum *salegy* (all Mickey Mouse synths and drum machines); and embarrassing mainstream rock bands. All things European, and especially American, and the standard multinational hits soon found their way onto local radio. Judging by the piped music in hotel restaurants in the more remote parts of Madagascar, it sometimes seems as if this is where old rock albums go to die.

By the early 1990s, it looked like curtains for Malagasy roots and tradition-based music. However, outside influence has had a beneficial effect. The catalyst was GlobeStyle Records' 1985 recording trip which produced two classic compilations that set the stylistic and artistic agenda for other Western producers. Among these were the **Henry Kaiser** and **David Lindley** recording, *A World Out Of Time* (1992), on which the American guitarists played local material with many of the island's leading and emerging roots musicians.

In the wake of all this, the 1990s saw a considerable amount of international touring, recording by European and American labels, and festival appearances, spearheaded by Tarika, D'Gary, the **Justin Vali Trio**, Njava, Jaojoby, Rajery and Regis Gizavo. Back home, the message that the West liked all this music helped to reinvest pride in the culture. Traditionally rooted musicians could, suddenly, not only aim to make a living from music (something almost unheard of before) but travel abroad as well. So the musical climate changed again: at the end of the long national strike in early 1992, one local newspaper pointed out that while Madagascar was in desperate straits, at least Malagasy musicians were achieving something in the wider world.

Madagascar's musical individuality is certainly not at risk any more. As artists went out and enjoyed success around the world in the 1990s playing Malagasy roots music, even the snobby rich were forced to admit that Malagasy culture was something to be proud of after all. However, government, cultural and tourism organizations have singularly failed to realize what good these musicians have done as ambassadors for their country. Funding support, travel assistance and sponsorship have been virtually non-existent, other than to the chosen few who were happy to appease the old dictatorship before 2002. So far, since then, corruption has considerably decreased but official support for those working the hardest to promote Malagasy cultural traditions has improved little.

The Malagasy still haven't got their equivalent of a Youssou N'Dour – a national superstar making new music out of traditional styles that translates to the international market. But surely on a huge island where the most important people are your ancestors, it can't be impossible for people to preserve their roots.

205

Music Under Ravalomanana

In 2002, following six months of near civil war, the old regime of President Ratsiraka was finally removed, replaced by the democratically elected government of Marc Ravalomanana. Like many other areas of life, this has had a major impact on the music scene of the capital, Antananarivo.

New Youth Music

With the success of a reality TV programme – *Pazzapa* on independent TV station RTA – has come an explosion of teenage kids trying to copy the music of Mariah Carey and boy bands. The show recruits young singers from six different provinces to compete against each other in interpreting the songs of other older pop artists; the whole competition is televised over a month. The programme itself is a straightforward version of the French TV show *Star Academie*, with RTA producing an album for the winning artist. Names to emerge so far include **Aina**, **Tosy** and **Hentsoa**.

Rap, Ragga and Hip-Hop

The hip-hop and rap scene evolved a little while ago in Madagascar, where artists like **18,3** proved adept at melding the Malagasy tradition of spoken proverbs with this new and not unrelated musical form. But recently it has become much bigger and has really gained status in Antananarivo. Unlike the *Pazzapa* scene, these artists are much more crude, provocative, underground and often rebellious. The scene really took off when the award-winning French group Tragedie – which included a footballer-turned-rapper of Malagasy origin – came to Madagascar. Current artists in the rap scene include **Shao Boana** and **Krutambull**.

New Traditional Music

The new roots scene established in the 1990s continues to flourish. Groups such as **Hezbollah**, **Erimbity**, **Ravinala**, **Panako**, **Tambours Gasy**, **Dada de Fort-Dauphin** and **Hazolahy** are becoming more recognized. One of the most notable international releases of Malagasy music in 2004 was the **Vakoka** project, which brought together an all-star group from various regional cultures. World Music Network released the resulting album.

Vakoka recording session

New Independent Music Labels

For many years, privately owned label **Mars** (formerly DiscoMad), run by successive generations of the De Comarmond family, held a virtual stranglehold on the Malagasy recording industry, making it effectively the national label. However, the opening up and liberalization of the economy in recent years, coupled with the democratization of the recording process through new technology, has resulted in a growth in independent labels. Veteran producer **Charles Maurin Poty** has been producing roots artists like *marovany* master **Monja** and the group **Vilon' Androy** for both international release and his local Tolimana label. Foremost among the independents is **Dosol**, run by the former pop star **Bodo**. After singing at rallies during the presidential campaign in 2002, she gained a position at the Ministry of Arts and Culture and became the director of artists' promotion. Along with her husband, Naivo, she has built up her own label with a roster of Madagascan pop musicians which now outnumbers that of Mars.

The music industry boom

Because the pop scene in Madagascar has become so huge (with the stars playing to audiences of forty to fifty thousand) there's now more of a music business infrastructure. Promoters and management companies have grown up to professionalize the industry, to allow the new pop artists to be produced in a fairly professional way. The arrival of people prepared to finance music that addresses contemporary problems – like the environment and AIDS – has also contributed to the music industry's sudden growth.

Randriampanahy Mahery

The best bet for finding a good selection of original (i.e. non-pirate) cassettes and CDs of local music is one of the growing number of huge supermarkets. There's also a good range at Super Music store (Andohan'Analakely), Jumbo Score, Conquette and Champion. Amazingly, there have now been several hundred or more CDs released of Malagasy music, and since some of the choicest items from previous editions of this book are no longer available, the task of recommending a selection gets ever harder.

⊙ Madagascar: Generation 2004
Mars, Madagascar
The Mars label regularly releases overviews of currently popular music that are always high on keyboard cheese and programmed drum. This one includes Jaojoby, Teta, Koezy, Toto Mwandjani, Hazolahy and Dada de Fort Dauphin among its sixteen tracks.

⊙ Madagasikara One: Current Traditional Music
⊙ Madagasikara Two: Current Popular Music
GlobeStyle, UK
GlobeStyle's two anthologies, recorded by Ben Mandelson and Roger Armstrong in 1985, led the way for most other Western recordists' activities. Featured names included Rossy, Tarika Sammy, Mahaleo, Rakoto Frah, Zeze and *salegy* band Les Smokers. Both sets sound as fresh as ever, and have excellent notes.

⊙ Madagaskar 1: Music From Antananarivo
⊙ Madagaskar 2: Music Of The South
⊙ Madagaskar 3: Valiha: Sounding Bamboo
⊙ Madagaskar 4: Music Of The North
Feuer & Eis, Germany
Next to hit the field was the first of these four fine thematic acoustic sets from Birger Gesthuisen's label, now also available as a boxed set. *Vol 1* introduced the best of remarkable *kabosy* player Jean Emilien and featured more Rossy, Sammy, and Rakoto Frah and Zeze together as Kalaza. *Vol 2* went on to showcase the intriguing southern traditions which GlobeStyle hadn't been able to reach, while *Vol 3* collected together the very best players of the *valiha*, notably Sylvestre Randafison, the stunning Tovo and the last recordings of Zeze. *Vol 4* again fills previously undocumented areas with some exceptional recordings of Sakalava rapping and unique instrumentalists.

⊙ The Music Of Madagascar: Music Of The Coast And Tablelands 1929–31
Fremeaux, France
A double CD, well remastered from old 78s originally recorded in Madagascar, particularly featuring the golden age of *valiha* orchestras, sing-ing troupes and some local field recordings. Plus excellent notes, rare photos, recording memorabilia and discographical info.

⊙ Prophet 6: Madagascar
⊙ Prophet 25: Madagascar Côte Ouest
Philips/Kora Sons, France
Charles Duvelle field-recorded some excellent sets for the renowned Ocora label in the early 1960s, and these beautifully packaged compilations – with classy photos and good bilingual notes – consist of previously unreleased gems from the same sessions. First-rate *marovany*, *valiha*, *lokanga* and *jejy voatavo* players, plus some superb examples of *hiragasy* troupes in full flight on the first set, plus rarer music from the Masikoro tribe in particular on the west coast volume.

★ The Rough Guide to the Music of Madagascar
World Music Network, UK
The essential sampler of Malagasy sounds, featuring many of the artists and styles mentioned in this chapter. Released in 2005, it covers everything from solo *marovany* to *tsapika*, *salegy*, rare historic tracks and brand new favourites

⊙ Tulear Never Sleeps
Earthworks/Stern's, UK
The electric bands of the main city in Madagascar's southwest kick up fearsome, pumping, sun-dried energy. Recorded in Madagascar, this was the first album to bring the *tsapika* genre to the world's attention: a classic.

⊙ Tsapiky: Panorama d'une Jeune Musique de Tuléar
Arion, France
The electric bands and the acoustic roots of tsapiky, recorded in the field and including an extraordinary wild military brass band version of one of the big local hits!

Jaojoby

Solo Miral

D'Gary

The brilliant D'Gary is a guitarist with a dazzling technique based on the style of the *marovany* (box zither) and *lokanga* (local fiddle).

⊙ Akata Meso
Indigo/Label Bleu, France
D'Gary's fourth album displays his skills to the full on both electric and acoustic guitar. Apart from the local *katsa* shaker, the percussion accompaniment also features *tabla* and conga on some tracks.

Feogasy

Feogasy feature various veteran ex-members of Mahaleo and Lolo Sy Ny Tariny plus flute man Rakoto Frah.

⊙ Tsofy Rano
Les Nuits Atypiques/Mélodie, France
Showcases grand old-style highland harmonies and the guitar of Erick Manana.

Regis Gizavo

Regis Gizavo is the undisputed squeezebox boss of Madagascar, up there in the world rankings with the likes of Flaco Jimenez.

⊙ Samy Olombelo
Indigo/Label Bleu, France
Regis has evolved a massive sound during his solo career, here accompanied as usual by superb percussionist David Mirandon.

Jaojoby

Jaojoby is the king of kings of *salegy* and leads one of the world's great live bands, an unstoppable music machine featuring lots of his family.

★ Malagasy
Discorama/Harmonia Mundi, France
After years of trying to really capture the awesome drive of the band in action, this one comes as close as is ever likely.

Monja

Mahafy Gégé Monja comes from Ambovombe Androy in the deep southwest of Madagascar, but has travelled extensively around the island playing the traditional *marovany* box zither, on which he's a master.

⊙ Marovany
Cinq Planètes, France
Beautifully recorded by the king of Malagasy producers, Charles Maurin Poty, this is one of the best recent recordings of the instrument.

Rajery

One of the hardest-working and creative of younger players of the *valiha*, Madagascar's tubular bamboo zither.

⊙ Volontany
Indigo/Label Bleu, France
Following in the footsteps of Tarika, the new roots movement among young city-based musicians in Madagascar is producing high-quality gems like this.

Rakotozafy

Dubbed "the Robert Johnson of Madagascar", Rakotozafy was an equally legendary, mysterious and toweringly influential *marovany* player – one of the most important figures in the recent history of Malagasy music.

⭐ **Valiha Malaza – Famous Valiha**
GlobeStyle, UK
A lovingly prepared reissue, taken from surviving Malagasy master tapes, and enhanced by Ben Mandelson's excellent sleeve-notes.

Ricky Randimbiarison

One of Madagascar's most inspiring modern male singers, Ricky is backed by a first-rate team of players including influential bassist Tôty and members of Solo Miral.

⊙ **Olombelona Ricky**
MELT 2000, South Africa
Tracks on his long awaited international debut (produced by Alrto MoreIra) range from the out-and-out rootsy to some with a strong jazz-rock influence, but it's all uncompromisingly Ricky.

Solo Miral

The band Solo Miral includes some of Madagascar's finest modern musicians, including the stupendous *marovany*-style guitarist Haja.

⊙ **Gasikara**
Mars, Madagascar
The first album in twenty years by this renowned band features traditional instrumental sounds and local rhythms updated onto electric instruments with skill, taste and imagination.

Tarika

This multi-instrumental roots dance band is led by sisters Hanitra (Rasoanaivo) and Noro (Raharimalala). They have had huge success in Europe and the US with their albums and live shows, and since 1999 have topped the Malagasy charts on several occasions.

⭐ **10: Beasts, Ghosts & Dancing With History**
Triloka/Artemis, US
Culled from their four studio albums, hit singles, remixes and live recordings, this is a tenth-anniversary celebration of Madagascar's deservedly best-known musical ambassadors.

Tianjama

Alongside Jaojoby, Tianjama is another major veteran from the golden age of *salegy* 45s, and still leading a great current band.

⊙ **Best Of Tianjama**
Mars, Madagascar/France
Includes most of their biggest 1990s hits from cassettes made for the home market.

Daniel Tombo

A significant *marovany* player from the east coast, Tombo was first recorded on the famous GlobeStyle trip in the mid-1980s and now leads an excellent traditional ensemble.

⊙ **Toamasina Serenades**
Buda, France
Playing *marovany* in the style of the late great Rakotozafy,

PLAYLIST
Madagascar

1 INDOSIKO ANAO Jaojoby from *Malagasy*
It's only a love song, but defy yourself to stay seated as the primal force of the *salegy* machine from the north grabs you.

2 TSY KIVY Tarika from *10: Beasts, Ghosts & Dancing With History*
Accentuating the positive, this bright, upbeat song from their now sadly unavailable *Son Egal* album has become a political theme tune.

3 RAMANJAREO (NY ANY AMINAY) Rakotozafy from *Valiha Malaza*
Flights of metallic fantasy as the late legendary king of *marovany* players gets to work on his beaten-iron instrument.

4 MAROVAOY Bemiray from *The Rough Guide to the Music Of Madagascar*
The soaring vocals and crying brass of a highland *hiragasy* troupe, never better recorded.

5 ZAZA SOMONDRARA D'Gary from *Akata Meso*
World-class guitar and the sweet vocals of his usual singing partner Rataza.

6 FOKAFOKA Ny Antsaly from *The Rough Guide to the Music Of Madagascar*
An elegant, historic gem from the early 1960s: *valiha* master Sylvestre Randafison's group (all now deceased) with their classic Merina blend.

7 TARAKA Daniel Tombo from *Toamasina Serenade*
From Tamatave on the east coast, powerhouse *marovany* and frantic traditional *jijy* rapping.

8 NENI BABA Jean Noel from *Tulear Never Sleeps*
Tulear guitar hero leads the band in the music loved by saphire miners and bandits in the wild south west.

9 ZAZA MITOMANY Ricky Randimbiarison from *Olombelona Ricky*
A bit of *vakojazana* to quiet the crying baby, with the great voice of Ricky fronting some of Tana's leading musos.

10 ERA Vakoka from *Introducing Vakoka*
The all-stars at play from the special project album that united them in a frenzy of creation, featuring the guitar of Solo Miral's Haja and voice of Tarika's Hanitra.

Tombo's energetic ensemble feature some fine examples of *jijy*, Madagascar's traditional rapping style.

MADAGASCAR

209

Vakoka

Canadian producer Sean Whittaker asked Tarika's Hanitra Rasoanaivo and percussionist Pana to assemble an all-star cast from across the island, who then workshopped together for a month to write and arrange this wonderful project.

★ **Introducing Vakoka**
Introducing/ World Music Network, UK
Many of Madagascar's best roots artists mixing up regional styles from all over in an inspired collaboration, conclusive proof that the old Malagasy proverb "unity is power" has the ring of truth.

Justin Vali

Valiha virtuoso Justin Vali is based in Paris, from where he continues to regale the world with his gifts.

⊙ **The Sunshine Within**
Bush Telegraph, UK
Vali's most recent (1999) outing finds him on top form, exploring new styles as well as his usual energetic, almost classical approach to acoustic Malagasy roots music.

Vilon' Androy

Led by Surgi, a virtuoso of the Antandroy *lokanga* violin, this group follows in the footsteps of pioneers from the area like Vaovy and Tsimihole.

⊙ **Pelake**
Tolimana, Madagascar
Wailing *lokanga*, dense female harmonies and skittering percussion mark this typical group sound from the dry, thorny south, home of the cattle rustlers.

Malawi

sounds afroma!

Chief Chipoku Band
Pamtondo

Under the dictatorship of 'Life President' Hastings Banda, who gave the country its name, male visitors to Malawi were forbidden to have long hair, women had to wear skirts below the knee and flared trousers were illegal. When elections were held in 1994, however, Banda was promptly booted out, and Malawi is now a free and vibrant nation. Though it remains poor, music is everywhere, as John Lwanda reveals.

In 1859, 120 years before the first CDs, David Livingstone heard the xylophone music of southern Malawi and with typical Scottish enthusiasm, described it as "wild and not unpleasant" – one of the first World Music reviews. Although international exposure has so far eluded all but a handful of Malawi musicians, they have had a strong influence on their peers in southern and East Africa. And despite its many problems – cassette piracy, a lack of studios and a shortage of electric instruments – Malawi itself has strong musical traditions and some distinctive contemporary bands.

Banjos, Jazz and the Malawi Beat

Malawians are great travellers and have taken their music to every city from Nairobi to the Cape. Malawian soldiers served in Central and East African British battalions during World War II, and as well as spreading their music, a number brought back guitars and new musical ideas.

From the late 1940s to the early 1960s **banjo and guitar duos** were the dominant format in dance music, usually with the banjo leading and the guitar playing rhythm. Leading exponents of this style included the **Thailo and Kapiye Duet** and the **Paseli Brothers**. Other musicians, such as **Barry Paseli** and the **Chikuni Brothers**, used single or duelling guitars for backing, while polio victim **Ndiche Mwalale** was a noted slide-guitar player. Another form of music current during this period was *makwaya* (acapella choral singing). **The Zomba Evening Birds** and **De Ndirande Pitch Crooners** sang four-part barber shop harmonies influenced by South African groups such as the Manhattan Brothers. In the late 1960s, South African *kwela* music was popularized by migrant workers returning from South Africa, most notably by **Daniel Kachamba and his Kwela Band**.

The next craze was "**jazz bands**", a tradition that remains very active. Malawian jazz is not exactly jazz in the Western sense. The bands are made up of rural or semi-rural popular musicians using whatever acoustic instruments are to hand – imagine an acoustic Kanda Bongo Man or Shirati Jazz and you have an idea of the sound. Leading groups have included the **Jazz Giants** and **Alan Namoko and Chimvu Jazz**. Namoko, who died in 1995, was a great figure – a blind bluesman who turned out a stack of earthy roots music on banjo, acoustic guitar and percussion.

In the late 1960s and 1970s, as in Zimbabwe and Zambia, urban musicians began electrifying various traditional rhythms. This resulted in the **afroma** – the afro-rock-Malawi beat – whose best exponents were the band **New Scene**, led by **Morson Phuka**, who had been the leader of the Jazz Giants and was a father-figure for Malawian popular music until his death in 1991. A talented vocalist, composer and arranger, Phuka trained countless musicians, and other bands followed in New Scene's footsteps. Notable 1970s electric bands included **The Deaf Ears**, **Masaka** and the Lilongwe-based **Chitipi Sounds**, who specialized in East African and funk-influenced songs like "Anyamata Asiposi" ("Fashionable young dudes"). Another Lilongwe band, **The Roots** sang their Malawi soul music in English, while **Maurice Maulidi** and **Songani Swing Stars** preferred a trancy ska-tinged afroma, as did early **Saleta Phiri**.

Kalimba, led by the late guitarist **Griffen Mhango**, played everything from pop to jazz and was another training-school for a host of young musicians; **Makasu**, the most successful band of the period, was a Kalimba offshoot. Other more polished urban outfits of the time included **African Express Band**, the **MBC Band** (the house band of the Malawi broadcasting corporation) and **Muzipasi**, which briefly included lead guitar by **John Selolwane Longwe**, who worked with Manu Dibango and on Paul Simon's *Graceland* tour.

A remarkable feature of Malawi popular music is how some individuals and bands – often constrained by poverty and the cost of electric instruments – remained resolutely acoustic. Alan Namoko and Chimvu Jazz were a case in point. Another was the highly influential guitarist **Dr Daniel Kachamba**, who, together, with his flute-player brother **Donald Kachamba** and Moya Aliya cooperated in various musicological proj-

Ethnographer's Corner

Malawi is a small, landlocked country dominated by the beautiful Lake Malawi. Its eleven million inhabitants are packed into a largely rural 94,000 square kilometres – an area little larger than Scotland or Maine. Of the nine tribal and linguistic groups, the **Chewa** are the largest, making their language the national lingua franca.

This ethnic diversity means that there are numerous **traditional dances and rhythms**. These include the Chewa and Nyanja masked *gule wa mkulu* (the big dance); the Ngoni's *ingoma* war dance; the *likwata* and the *beni* "military" dance among the Yao; the highly stylized and chic *mganda* among the Tonga; *tchopa* among the Lomwe; the healing *vimbuza* of the Tumbuka and Henga; and the Nyanja's *likhuba* and *chitsukulumwe*.

Many local songs and dances were recorded in the 1940s and 50s by Alick Nkhata and **Hugh Tracey** (see Southern Africa Archives chapter), and can still be heard in the villages today. A common source of such songs is **women pounding maize** in a mortar, their thumping producing complex **pamtondo** rhythms that accompany their songs of lament, blues, gossip or celebration. Popular musicians are influenced by these long-standing traditions and although most performers are male, many of the songs sung by young bands are *pamtondo* or *kumpanda* songs – music traditionally sung by women as they work or tend their children.

During the Banda period, the most popular non-commercial music in Malawi was also female in origin, the **mbumba** (women) music – songs of celebration and praise with drum accompaniment, based on traditional dances and sung at ruling-party and state occasions. Mbumba was also played widely on the radio, but with Banda's demise it is now mostly heard on hawkers' cassettes. Mbumba music was repressive stuff in those days, but now the merits of the music, especially that by **Dowa Mbumba** can be appreciated. Their so-called **Dowa Symphony**, an hour of mesmerizing party sloganeering, included "Kokoliko ku Malawi" ("It is dawn in Malawi"), an elaborately arranged, highly melodic party propaganda song sung to thunderous drum accompaniment.

Since the end of the Banda dictatorship (1964–1994), new political parties have introduced their own music and appropriated previous mbumba styles and songs. Conversely, musicians have been keen to remain free of political constraints: in a largely oral culture like Malawi, music plays a large part in disseminating information. Some artists have thus resorted to the pre-colonial role of (self-appointed) *alangizi* – traditional counsellors. *Alangizi* deal with social and moral issues, and like court jesters, have some immunity from political harassment. Prominent *alangizi* include **Malume Bokosi**, **Dennis Phiri** and **Joseph Nkasa**, whose hit "Nkhope" harshly criticized Malawians for voting for politicians with no developmental ideals.

---

ects with Gerhard Kubik. **Joseph Nangalembe**, who was famous for his strummed guitar, acerbic social lyrics and yodelling, also eschewed electrification.

Several other bands remained acoustic. These included **Mikoko Band** – a banjo-led dance outfit whose music carried controversial socially and politically tinged lyrics – and the **Ndingo Brothers Band**, well known for their *nyau*-influenced pop. Many rural and semi-urban bands gained national popularity playing homemade instruments and singing folk-based material. When these young men sang grown-up material about family life, separation and survival, marriage, love, alcohol and witchcraft, they showed how they had appropriated lyrics, melodies and rhythms from women's *pamtondo* songs.

Two notable survivors from this 1970s generation are the **Lucky Stars Duet** (of "Chinafuna Mbale" fame), still performing their drinking songs to duelling guitar backing at the **Shire Highlands Hotel**, and **Stonard Lungu**. A familiar sight at festivals and music events around Blantyre, Lungu is a skilful acoustic guitarist and composer of memorable tunes.

From Kwasa Kwasa to Nyambo

In the 1980s and 90s Congolese *soukous*-style music took hold across Malawi in a local form called **kwassa kwassa**, whose rhythms and melodies blended particularly well with local time signatures. So too did **ska** and **reggae**, which also became a popular part of the mix. The prime exponents here were **Sapitwa**, who also featured gorgeous vocals.

Live in Malawi!

If you're visiting Malawi, check out some of the following venues and bands.

The **French Cultural Centre** in Blantyre is a premier venue for live entertainment, featuring popular and traditional music as well as theatre. Other regular live music venues in Blantyre include *Harry's Bar*, the *Lingadzi Inn* and the *Paradise Motel*; in Mzuzu, check out the *Mzuzu University Hall* and *Mzuzu* and *Chenda* hotels. The *Great Hall* at Chancellor College, Zomba, and *Club Makakola* and the *Sun and Sands Hotel* in Mangochi all have in-house bands and guests such as **Billy Kaunda** and **Lucius Banda**. The **Lake of Stars Malawi music festival** (see www.lakeofstarsfestival.co.uk), which began in 2004, has now grown into a major regional event, featuring both local and UK acts.

Most hotels have local village troupes that play traditional music and perform *beni, gule wamkulu, chinamwali* and other dances at weekends (tipping is recommended). The Department of Culture's Bernard Kwilimbe, TVM's Waliko Makhala and the MBC's Dyson Gonthi are useful contacts for village troupe performances. If they are on, be sure to see **Samban'goma** or **Dygo** at the French Cultural Centre. A number of African-owned entertainment venues also cater for tourists who like to get off the beaten track – check out **Tilipano** and **Tiyamike** in Lilongwe, for example. In the more vibrant urban and township areas, live bands play most weekends at the larger community halls or "bottle stores" (bars), while itinerant rural musicians play around most trading centres.

If you're looking for specific acts, the **Chief Chipoka Band** dishes out a mixture of pop, reggae and traditional folk at *Nkopola Lodge* against the delightful Nkopola beach, while **The Roots** and other bands perform at the *Lilongwe Hotel*. **Wyndham Chechamba**, a 70-year-old blues and jazz pianist plays regularly at the *Mount Soche* and *Ryalls* hotels. **Mulangeni Sounds** appear at the *Mulangeni Resort* in Mangochi, while **Gotani Sounds** can be found at *Gotani's* in Mzuzu. Finally, **Lucky Stars** play at the *Shire Highlands Hotel*.

The Zaïre sound was also incorporated into the big band sound of the Jazz Giants, **The Army Strings** and the **Police Strings Band**. In the 1970s and 1980s these state-sponsored bands had access to good instruments and attracted many aspiring musicians into their ranks. Of these, Pearson Milanzie, **Kenneth Ning'anga** and **Elias Kaliati** went on to front their own bands.

Many electric bands in the 1980s continued to follow the afroma format to varying extents, including **Mulangeni Sounds** and Ethel Kamwendo and The Ravers. In the 1990s a number of new bands like **Evison Matafale and the Black Missionaries**, Gotani Stars, **Love Aquarius** and Vipya Vibrations were successful for varying periods, though because of rising costs, a trend for a fluid core of musicians backing "star" or named musicians emerged.

The dominant music since independence has been **gospel** in all its forms – acapella, electric, employing traditional melodies and rhythms, or, more often than not, reggae-fied. The **Alleluya Band**, formed by the multi-instrumentalist **Paul Banda**, was the first electric gospel band to achieve major success, performing for the Pope when he visited Malawi in 1989. Their irresistible blend of

traditional rhythms and melodies with reggae, Western gospel, *soukous*, pop and jazz has proved perennially popular.

More recent rivals of the Alleluya Band include the **Millenium Sound Checks**, while gospel choirs, notably the **Mhango Salvation Choir** and **Mount Sinai Choir**, are also firm favourites. Soloists like **Allan Ngumuya** have broken through to individual fame from gospel bands, and **Wambali Mkandawire**, initially considered a gospel singer, has found international recognition. Although under-represented in Malawi music, notable female performers have included the MBC Band's Chichiri Queens, Mary Chidzanja Nkhoma (Mala-wi's answer to Miriam Makeba) and **Ethel Kam-wendo**, ex-lead singer of The Ravers.

A number of Malawi musicians have sought greener pastures abroad, including Masauko Chipembere (of **Blk Sunshine**), South African-based singer **Nankhoma Chidzanja**, and members of the younger generation such as Scottish-based **Nathan Chalamanda** and producer Qabaniso Malewezi. Both in and outside Malawi, meanwhile, younger musicians are fusing local rhythms and folktales with hip-hop. A good example of this is the **nyambo** music – a neologism coined from *nyimbo* (song) *mwambo* (culture) and *miyambi* (proverbs) – of the **Real Elements**.

DISCOGRAPHY Malawi

The availability of recorded local music in Malawi has increased greatly in recent years, though sadly most of it appears on pirate cassettes sold by street hawkers. While there are stalls selling cassettes and CDs in the markets of Mzuzu, Lilongwe, Zomba and Blantyre, vendors can also be found in most high streets, their music blaring out of clapped-out speakers. Always look for authentic tapes and CDs – these carry the characteristic *banderole* stickers of COSOMA, the Copyright Society of Malawi, which has led the way in Africa in combating music piracy. The Clifton Bazaar, Portuguese Trading Centre, Metro, Consumer Electronics and OG Issa stores in Blantyre and Mottani Brothers in Zomba are the largest shop outlets.

Overseas, the best source is Pamtondo, 5c Greystone Ave, Rutherglen, Glasgow G73 3SN, Scotland; fax 01698 851472; www.pamtondo.com. Run by the author of this chapter, Pamtondo releases Malawian music on its own label and also imports cassettes from time to time.

⊙ **Banjoes, Guitars and Fifties**
⊙ **The Sizzling Seventies**
⊙ **The Multi-Party Nineties**
Pamtondo, UK
Three CDs containing a wide variety of rural, urban, traditional and syncretic acoustic and electric music. Lo-fi but high-quality.

⊙ **From Lake Malawi to the Zambezi**
Popular African Music, Germany
Moya Aliya Malamusi continues where Hugh Tracey left off, recording the traditional music of different communities in the southern half of Malawi in the 1990s.

★ **Music from Malawi (Zonse Ndi Moyo)**
Pamtondo, UK
An excellent compilation offering an up-to-date survey of musicians and styles, including both Lucius and Paul Banda, Alan Namoko, Love Aquarius, Kalimba, Overton Chimombo and Ethel Kamwendo.

⊙ **Music Tradition of Malawi**
Auvidis/Unesco, France
Examples of music for the *gule wamkulu*, *ingoma*, *mganda*, *tchopa* and *vimbuza* dances, as well as the now rare *bangwe* (zither) and other traditional music. Excellent value and good introductory notes.

⊙ **Northern & Central Malawi: Nyasaland 1950 '57 '58**
⊙ **Southern & Central Malawi: Nyasaland 1950 '57 '58**
SWP Records/ILAM, Netherlands
These Hugh Tracey recordings give a flavour of traditional and popular music in the 1950s, including the *bangwe*, the one-string lute (*kaligo*), drum orchestras and xylophones, as well as vocal harmonizing and polyphonic singing. For musicologists and enthusiasts alike.

★ **The Original Pound: Pamtondo's Greatest Hits**
Pamtondo, UK
Just what it promises: many of Malawi's great 1970s and 1980s electric and acoustic bands, including Kalimba, Dr Kachamba, New Scene, Kathumba and Masaka.

⊙ **Popular Malawian Songs: 10th COSOMA Anniversary 1992–2002**
Copyright Society of Malawi, Malawi
A decade of great pop hits. For an updated picture, try *50th Anniversary of OG Issa* (OG, Malawi).

▦ **Rhem Singles Collection Vols 1 and 2**
Rhem, Malawi
The RHEM collective involved experienced producers and young instrumentalists, playing in styles from traditional and ballads to afroma, reggae and hip-hop. Uneven but essential listening.

Alleluya Band

Led by Paul Banda and his brother, Lucius, Malawi's leading band play mainly electric gospel.

▦ **Mtendere**
Sounds of Malawi, Malawi
Crisp, intelligent arrangements, tasty guitar and heavenly voices. Features the awesome "Mudzisankire njira" (Choose your destiny).

Lucius Banda

The Alleluya vocalist has a side-career as a reggae artist, with polemical songs much influenced by Lucky Dube and Bob Marley. He gets braver by the month.

🎵 Take Over
Zembani, Malawi
A danceable and highly political album castigating poor leadership. Features brother Paul producing and playing guitar.

Paul Banda

Malawi's answer to Stevie Wonder, Paul Banda is also a prolific solo artist.

🎵 The Best of Paul Banda
Sounds of Malawi, Malawi
Sweet voice, subtle production and a successful mix of electronics with local and foreign rhythms.

Nathan Chalamanda

This young musician, now based in Scotland, made his debut with the American Rick Deja.

⊙ Hometown Stranger
Deja, US
An enjoyable blend of new and reworked Malawi melodies with a jazz-rock combo.

Peter Chidzanja

Chidzanja has been a regular at the *Lilongwe Hotel* for two decades. His *chechule* (folk tales based on frog adventures) are in line with the *griot* tradition of West Africa.

🎵 Chechule
Oreta Enterprises, Malawi
A reminder of how important it is to have English translations sometimes. "I went to Malawi", Chidzanja sings on the anti-HIV title track, "and found Mr Chechule (Mr Frog) wearing a condom."

Overton Chimombo

A veteran of the Malawi music scene who achieved solo success in the early 1990s.

★ Zasintha
Scan Music UR2, Malawi
Chimombo hit the mark in 1994 with this brilliant production, bubbling with clever lyrics and jumpy Lomwe and Sena rhythms. Musicians like veteran bassist Lester Mwathunga and D. Nyirenda on keyboards make this one of the most accessible of the cassettes to foreign ears.

Richard Gadama

Ex-MBC engineer and music entrepreneur.

⊙ Fatsa
RG Studios, Malawi
If you wonder where the continuity music on Televison Malawi (TVM) comes from, wonder no more. Traditional music given electric keyboards arrangements.

Daniel Kachamba

Dr Daniel Kachamba (1947–87) was Malawi's premier folk musician from the 1960s until his death. A talented guitarist, he formed the roots-oriented New Scene band with Morso Phuka, fusing elements of rumba, South African kwela and *sinjonjo*.

🎵 Dr Daniel Kachamba's Memorial Tape
University of Malawi
Kachamba's spiritual side comes across strongly in the lyrics on this haunting recording.

Donald Kachamba

Daniel's brother is a *kwela* flute player who has toured all over Europe and Africa.

⊙ Malawi Concert Kwela
Le Chant du Monde, Germany
A delightful and individual adaptation of the kwela sound.

Elias Kaliati and Kenneth Ning'anga

Former Army Strings bandleaders let loose in the studio.

⊙ Typical Traditional Songs
Studio K, Malawi
Traditional songs backed by electric instruments. Very funny if you understand the lyrics!

Ethel Kamwendo

Ethel went from child star to fronting Ethel Kamwendo and The Ravers, then to born-again songbird.

⊙ Amen Yesu Wandimasula
Gospel Songs, Malawi
Sweet and infectious gospel: the title track insinuates itself into your mind like a Kylie song.

Billy Kaunda

This ex-Allelujah Band member has become a successful soloist.

🎵 Alibe Mau
Imbirani Yawe, Malawi
Smooth vocals and well-crafted reggae melodies do not hide the clever political satire. Now that Kaunda is a politician himself, it will be interesting to see what he does.

Evison Matafale and The Black Missionaries

Matafale was the leader of a small Rastafarian musicians' community. His death in police custody in 2001 was blamed on the then ruling UDF *achikulire* (godfathers).

⊙ Kuimba 1 and 2
Aktone, Malawi
Pure reggae with very Malawian barbed lyrics commenting on political and social inequalities.

The MBC Band

The MBC (Malawi Radio) Band was started soon after independence and has been a training ground for many musicians, playing everything from South African *mbaqanga* to afroma, cabaret Jazz and reggae.

⊙ Kokoliko ku Malawi
MBC Music, Malawi
This hard-to-find LP remains the only commercially available recording from the band. A ground-breaking mix of traditional and modern instruments with an Afro-jazzy groove.

MALAWI
Playlist

1 **CHE CHITEKWE MULIBWANJI? Alan Namoko and Chimvu Jazz** from *Ana Osiidwa*
The title translates as "Mr Chitekwe, how are you?". Atmospheric guitar intro, attacking guitar lead, lived-in Namoko blues vocals and an inspired band on form.

2 **NKHOPE (MASK) Joseph Nkasa** from *Tigwirane Manja*
Danceable, jerky, bottom-heavy Malawi ska, with humorous and intelligent lyrics.

3 **KWANU NKWANU Ned Mapira** from *Malawi Popular Songs: 10th COSOMA Anniversary 1992–2002*
"East or west, home is best." As country blues and longing as Malawi music gets – patriotism meets love song over an uptempo melodic arrangement.

4 **TINGASALE KWA NGOSWE Nathan Chalamanda and Rick Deja** from *Hometown Stranger*
Chalamanda updates the 1960s Barry Paseli banjo classic with a jazz-rock arrangement that works extremely well. The title means "I will tell our marriage guardian".

5 **MULUNGU ADZATEMBENUZA Dr Daniel Kachamba** from *The Original Pound*
Kachamba's guitar strumming, deceptively simple like some of Thomas Mapfumo's best work, has a spiritual trancy groove, with lyrics about personal and social justice.

6 **CHECHULE (MR FROG) Peter Chidzanja** from *Chechule*
Traditional folktale arranged for electric band in gritty fashion. Chidzanja brings it bang up to date, with Mr Frog now wearing a condom.

7 **MAU (GOSPEL) Mount Sinai Choir** from *Go Konko*
Pure acapella: "They hear the gospel, and yet to them it's only words, words."

8 **KUMIDIMA (BEYOND THE LIVING) Billy Kaunda** from *Alibe Mau*
Sweet melodic message reggae. Kaunda mourns friends lost to early deaths.

9 **DZIKO LINO NDI LATHU (THIS IS OUR COUNTRY) Thailo and Kapiye Duet** from *Banjoes, Guitars and Fifties*
Crisp banjo and vamping guitar. A classic three-minute single.

10 **ZANI MUWONE (COME AND SEE) Wambali Mkandawire** from *Zani Muwone*
For those who like African music à la Dibango or Salif Keita's *Soro*: Afro-jazz with organ, horns, swooping arrangements, melodies and chants.

Ben Michael

A university graduate turned popular musician, Michael sings some of his characteristically Malawian songs in English. An obvious and accessible first port of call for Anglophone tourists.

⊙ **Thawa Moto**
High Density, Zimbabwe
Funny, satirical, memorable and hummable tunes.

Millenium Sound Checks

Nine-piece combo who are doing what the Alleluya Band were doing a decade ago.

▦ **Gule wa Kwathu**
Studio K, Malawi
Traditional rhythms and melodies, electric instrumentation and entertaining but serious lyrics.

Wambali Mkandawire

A Kora award nominee, Mkandawire is a musicians' musician who hails from a musical family.

★ **Zani Muwone**
Instinct Africaine, South Africa
Songs that subtly mix traditional rhythms, melodies and chants with gospel, Afro-jazz and sophisticated arrangements, plus the best musicians South Africa can provide. Highly recommended.

Mount Sinai Choir

The in-house choir for the Presbyterian church in Ndirande – Blantyre's answer to Soweto.

▦ **Go Konko**
Clifton Bazaar, Malawi
Ladysmith Black Mambazo-style gospel from Malawi. Sheer sanctifying pleasure!

Stanley Mthenga

Mthenga specializes in Sena (Lower Shire ethnic group) beats and melodies.

▦ **Mtchona**
Malawian Sounds
As the Sena are cousins of the Zimbabwean Shona, the music is similar to Zimbabwean jit jive.

Alan Namoko and Chimvu Jazz

Blind bluesman Nakomo was a major figure of the 1970s and 80s with his acoustic "jazz band".

⊙ **Ana Osiidwa**
Pamtondo, UK
A classic Namoko recording of raw guitar and vocals with tea-chest percussion.

Allan Ngumuya

A gospel singer and preacher, Ngumuya is one of Malawi's most prolific artists.

▦ **Umkonde Yesu**
Malawi Gospel Sounds, Malawi
Superbly emotive singing, simply backed by guitars, drums and keyboards, plus occasional sax.

Phungu Joseph Nkasa

Self-styled prophet Nkasa became Malawi's best-selling artist ever in 2004.

 Tigwirane Manja
OG, Malawi

A *tour de force*, mixing Chewa proverbs, philosophy and social commentary, backed by a thunderous mixture of drum-and-bass-heavy ska and lyrics in a sing-song hip-hop style that is close to traditional *beni* and *manganje* chants. The lyrics appeal for unity ("Tigwirane Manja"), but elsewhere criticize both deceitful political promises and Malawians' political choices.

Dennis Phiri

A product of the Alleluya gospel school of music, Phiri is a self-styled social counsellor.

Ulangizi
Imbirani Yawe, Malawi

This well-produced cassette contains the sublime "Tikutha" ("We perish"), an HIV/AIDS awareness song sung in a slow *ingoma* style. Other tracks mix reggae with indigenous beats and melodies.

Saleta Phiri

Sadly, Saleta died following a brief bout of malaria in January 2005. Funny, versatile and innovative, he was Malawi's answer to John Chibadura.

Ndirande Blues
Pamtondo, UK

Neotraditional electric music with a country-blues feel and humorous lyrics on social issues.

Tikhu Vibrations

This award-winning group have travelled to Europe, thanks to their UK backer, Gill Hunter.

Tikhu
Tikhu, UK

An up-to-the-minute stew of gospel, hip-hop, pop and traditional styles.

Tiyamike Band

An electric gospel band produced by the Alleluya crew at their own studio.

Mudaona Kuwala
Sounds of Malawi, Malawi

Blistering, as-live electric gospel. The title-track alone is worth the price of this cassette.

Mali

gold dust by the river

Amadou & Mariam with Manu Chao
Pierre Rene-Worms

Mali has an ancient musical culture, which owes much of its extraordinary wealth to the legacy of the Mande empire, founded nearly 800 years ago. Passed down by generations of *jelis* (the lineage of traditional musicians) – though not exclusively these days – this is essentially Africa's classical music. Lucy Duran returns to the source once more.

⏩ **Touareg music** *Although some of its best-known practitioners, such as the Tartit Ensemble and Tinariwen, are based in Mali, the music of the Tamashek, or Touareg, tribes is covered in the Niger chapter.*

Bamako, capital of Mali, is justly famous for its music. This dusty, sprawling, low-rise city, built along the banks of the Niger River, in a landlocked country with few natural resources, has a surprisingly vibrant music scene. Local sounds blare out from radio stations, recording studios, market stalls and ORTM (Mali's national TV station). Live groups perform throughout the week at hotels, restaurants, nightclubs, concert halls and impromptu outdoor venues. And then there are Bamako's famous Sundays, where the entire city becomes a riot of colour and rhythm.

Few African countries have contributed so many important artists to the World Music market: **Salif Keita**, **Toumani Diabaté**, **Habib Koité**, **Kandia Kouyaté**, **Oumou Sangaré** and the late **Ali Farka Touré** being but a few. Despite the high levels of unemployment, the poverty, dirt and traffic, the crowded living and the rising costs, Bamako remains one of West Africa's most endearing, peaceful and musical cities.

Music for Sundays

On their highly acclaimed 2004 album *Dimanche à Bamako*, Mali's award-winning **Amadou & Mariam** paid tribute to the Sundays of their beloved home town – "the day of weddings, of drumming, of the *ngoni* (small lute), of the voices of griots". Sunday is indeed the day of *griots*, or *jelis* as they are called in Bamana, one of the **Mande** languages (see below) and the main language of Mali apart from that of the French colonisers from whom the country gained independence in 1960. The *jelis* are hereditary musicians, praise singers and historians, who for centuries have dominated professional music in the region and have their own repertoire and musical instruments. While quite a few *jelis* have become established internationally, most of them operate on a purely local circuit, making a living by performing at events such as weddings and child-naming parties. Mali has endured different political regimes, and venues, styles and dance bands have come and gone, but these life-cycle events remain the hub of musical life. Sunday is traditionally the day civil weddings take place, the last stage of a long cycle of traditional and Islamic marriage rites.

While the men of the family occupy themselves with official matters either in the mosque or the town hall, parties are organized by women for women. Take a stroll around Bamako on a Sunday, and you can see what Amadou & Mariam are singing about – the parties are impossible to miss. Held on the street just in front of the houses of newlyweds' families, they are a veritable feast for the ears and eyes. A tarpaulin awning gives shelter from the scorching sun (or rain during the summer months) and the musicians play through a giant sound system that turns a private affair into a concert for the entire neighbourhood.

More than anything else, weddings are a barometer of the current popular trends and fashions. With up to five hundred civil weddings on any given Sunday in Bamako, there may be as many as a thousand parties happening around the city (one for the bride's family and one for the groom's). The music of Bamako's weddings links the old *jeli* tradition with contemporary and global music in a highly creative way: no matter how "modern" it may sound, the music is regarded as "traditional" and is the bread and butter for many of Bamako's musicians.

Sumu and Sandiya

The demand for music at life-cycle events has been the lifeblood of local popular music. There are two types of ensemble. The **sumu** is the preferred ensemble for weddings. The **sandiya**, on the other hand, is more common at child-naming ceremonies; it does not require amplification, and is easier to organize at short notice. It creates a joyful atmosphere and in essence is more traditional than the *sumu*.

Many of the tunes in the standard traditional repertoire date back several hundred years, such as "Lamban" (a song in praise of the art of the *jeli*), "Sunjata" (telling the story of the heroic ruler **Sunjata Keita**), "Turamaghan" (in praise of one of Sunjata's generals) and "Bambougoudji" (about a nineteenth century prince of the Bamana kingdom in Segou, central Mali. These tunes have been played so often that they are more like blueprints for improvisation than fixed melodies – like jazz standards they are constantly updated with new interpretations, peppered with references to global rhythms and dazzling, virtuosic ornamentation. "Bajourou" is one of the most popular tunes at weddings. Its static harmonies and slow tempo provide a perfect framework for endless guitar improvisation. Another tune, "Diawoura" (also spelt "Jawura"), from Kita, with its uplifting dance rhythm and rolling melody, has been popular on the wedding circuit since the early 1980s. Some twentieth century love songs have become classics, however, such as "Jarabi" (also spelt "Diarabi"), which talks of the power of passionate love, and which advises youths to follow their hearts in their choice of marriage partner.

In Mande culture men traditionally play the musical instruments, while *jelimuso* (female *jelis*)

Kelly Price Publicity

Mali music: Afel Bocoum chilling out on the Niger River with Damon Albarn

are the chosen singers. This division of musical labour according to gender, as well as the preference for the female singing voice, holds true for almost all kinds of music in the region. Only the dance bands of the 1970s and 80s were all male, which is probably either a legacy of the Cubans in West Africa or perhaps because dance bands play at bars and nightclubs, considered inappropriate venues for women singers by Malian Islamic society.

During the 1980s, Mali's dance bands began to lose their public, broke up or resettled in Europe, while at home the focus shifted to female stars. Women were already popular as the lead singers of the **Ensemble Instrumental National** (**EIN**), Mali's national, state-sponsored orchestra founded shortly after independence, and in the 1980s many began solo careers. It is no accident that women have created some of the most popular tunes of the twentieth century *jeli* repertoire, such as "Jarabi". Though less known outside the country, they are the true stars of Bamako's local music scene, and are at the heart of its creativity.

Girl Power, Mali Style

If you watch television in Mali, you might almost think that music there was for women and by women only. The weekly music programme *Top*

Étoiles features the public's favourite artists, most of whom are women; the singers perform to backing tapes, so the male instrumentalists are nowhere to be seen, giving the impression that this is an all-female affair. An interesting consequence of the predominance of the female voice is that many of their songs have concerned issues that affect women adversely, such as polygamy and arranged marriages. A striking example is **Kandia Kouyaté**'s poignant "San Barana", a heartfelt plea for co-wives to respect each other, based on her own personal experiences. Songs about the problems women face in marriage are very popular at wedding parties. If the new bride is marrying a man who already has other wives, she may find solace in such songs.

Many famous and legendary female singers from the early days of independence onwards, such as **Kandia Kouyaté**, **Tata Bambo Kouyaté**, **Fanta Damba**, **Fanta Sacko**, **Ami Koïta**, **Naïny Diabaté** and **Bako Dagnon** became famous primarily at wedding parties. Kandia (see box overleaf) is firmly grounded in the Maninka tradition of her home town of Kita, one of the great centres of *jeli* music, and the birthplace of many of Mali's best musicians, including guitarist and bandleader **Djelimady Tounkara**, and balafonist **Kélétigui Diabaté**. Malian men will often say that the style of Malian women singers is supposed to be "traditional", but in practice, more and more are making

221

Kandia Kouyaté

The only *jelimuso* who has managed to convey something of the flavour and intensity of the more traditional kind of *sumu* in her recordings is **Kandia Kouyaté**, a true *ngara* (master *jeli*). She has a natural, effortless vibrato, impeccable rhythm and timing and such expressive powers that when she launches into serious praise mode, her voice seems to put connoisseur listeners (especially those who understand her words) into a trance, as if transported back in time to Mali's great past. While extolling the virtues of her patrons, she can also make very pointed and sharp criticisms of society, in true *ngara* style. For this reason, she is sometimes known in Mali as "la dangereuse".

Kandia was born in Kita in 1958, into a celebrated lineage of master musicians (*ngara*). She learnt the trade of her ancestors (*jeliya*) from her father (a *balafon* player), her mother (a singer) and later on, from an uncle in Bamako, with whom she began performing on the wedding circuit in a type of ensemble popular in Mali in the late 1960s–early 70s called **Apollo**.

The Apollos were an important but undersung musical phenomenon of Bamako's flourishing music scene during the 1970s. They were halfway between the acoustic *sumu* ensemble and the Cuban-style dance bands of the time, combining traditional instruments like *balafon* with electric guitars, Afro-Cuban percussion such as timbales and drumkit.

Kandia Kouyaté was one of the few women to sing with the Apollos, who introduced her to the popular repertoire of the time, the dance hits of Guinean bands like Bembeya Jazz. In 1984, Kandia recorded a ground-breaking LP *Hommage à Amary Daou*, which launched her career in West Africa as a solo artist and shifted public attention towards the new breed of female singers. It also highlighted her gifts as an arranger.

Kandia attached herself to specific patrons such as the celebrated Malian millionaire **Babani Sissoko**, whose lavish gifts famously included a small airplane, so that she could fly up to sing at his remote village in Dabia, northwest Mali. Master musicians are not supposed to court international fame, and so it was only in the late 1990s that Kandia's first international recordings appeared. After her brilliant guest appearance with Guinean singer Sekouba Bambino Diabaté on his album *Kassa*, the influential Paris-based Senegalese producer **Ibra-hima Sylla** signed her to his label. Sadly, poor health resulting from a stroke in 2004 has prevented her from doing any more recording.

Lucy Duran

daring inroads into popular and global styles, with varying degrees of success.

Ami Koïta is one of the great modernisers of the sumu or wedding music tradition. Born in Joliba, to the west of Bamako (as was Salif Keita), she was recruited into EIN. The group's members were recruited from around the country during Mali's Biennales festivals; they played for state occasions and festivals, and provided a showcase and training ground for many of Mali's great female singers.

Ami Koïta's first solo recording was *Wajan* (1971). The title song was the direct inspiration for "Mandjou", which propelled Salif Keita and Les Ambassadeurs to international fame in 1978. This is an example of how the dance bands drew on the art of women singers.

Ami Koïta released a series of LPs and cassettes in the 1980s and early 1990s, with many songs dedicated to her main patron – a Senegalese businessman by the name of "Concorde" Gaye (so-called because he took so many Concorde planes), and who famously provided her with a new car every two years. Her music became increasingly contemporary-sounding, adding trumpet, saxophone, violin, synthesizer and drum machine to the usual *jeli* instrumentation. While some of her songs were in the Mande tradition, others were (controversially) influenced by Congolese *soukous*, *zouk* and even salsa, earning her the epithets *jeli finesse* (the sophisticated *jeli*) and *jeli pachanga* (from the Cuban 1960s dance rhythm called pachanga, which is how salsa is often referred to in Mali).

Tata Bambo Kouyaté is another of Mali's most important and influential singers of the first post-independence generation. She rose to fame in the early 1960s with her song "Bambo" (hence her nickname), about the popular new law of 1962 protecting the rights of women in marriage. Her husband and musical partner **Modibo Kouyaté** was the first to introduce the electric guitar into the previously all-acoustic *sumu* ensemble in the late 1980s, along with pedal effects. This modernized and transformed the sound of wedding music, bringing it ever closer to popular contemporary dance styles and confirming the central role of women singers in Malian popular culture.

Less well known abroad is **Naïny Diabaté**. Born and raised in Bamako, she was one of the very few women to perform occasionally with the Rail Band back in the early 1980s while still in her late teens.

The current star of the *sumu* scene is **Babani Koné** (born 1968). A charismatic singer, she first came to attention when she won the prize for best solo vocalist in Mali's 1984 Biennale festival. Since 2000, her popularity has verged on cult celebrity status. No *jelimuso* has ever had such a huge following, making her one of the most wealthy of Mali's female singers. When performing for a *sumu*, her style is quite traditional, but she has also recorded four albums aimed at the dancefloor, tinged with non-Malian rhythms like *zouk*, salsa and Congolese dance music. While her dance tracks, cluttered with synthesizers, animate local nightclubs, they do not sell well abroad – the gulf between how Bamako's women sound at the *sumu*, and how

they are represented on CD, with a few notable exceptions, is considerable. As a consequence, the central importance of the *jelimuso* in contemporary Malian music, and the raw energy, beauty and passion of the *sumu* and *sandiya* parties, remain largely unknown by World Music fans.

Mande History

Why is it that one of Africa's poorest countries is so intensely musical? Much of this has to do with the fact that this part of Africa was the centre of several great empires dating back to the tenth century – a history that is preserved by Jelis. The Mande peoples are now spread across several West African countries, with substantial communities abroad as well, but their ancestral homeland is a relatively small region of savannah that straddles the border between upper Guinea and western Mali. It's an uneven triangle, each side of which is no more than 250km long, cutting through remote countryside, known as **Manden**. The people who trace their origins to this heartland call themselves *Mandenkalu* (or *Mandekalou*), that is, people of Manden. It's a name which has strong associations with history, music and the power of the word: the ability of master *jelis* to "make things happen" through their didactic and often esoteric lyrics.

This is the birthplace of the great emperor Sunjata Keita, who founded the Mali empire in around 1235. His personal *jeli*, **Bala Faseke Kouyaté**, who played the *balafon* (xylophone), was the ancestor of all the Kouyatés, who are regarded as the only true lineage of hereditary musicians. To this day, anyone by the name of Kouyaté is a *jeli*, whether or not they actually play an instrument or sing. Sunjata's rise to power is a story of love, betrayal, sorcery, battles and bravery, giving insight into the pre-colonial world of West Africa. Luckily, there are many recordings of "Sunjata", from the most traditional to swinging dance band versions. Two famous ones were recorded by the **Rail Band** in the early 1970s, featuring both **Mory Kanté** and Salif Keita as lead singers. The Kanté version in particular has been copied by many artists – which is somewhat ironic, since he belongs to the same lineage as that of Sunjata Keita's enemy, Sumaworo Kanté.

Mande's Hereditary Musicians

Traditionally, Mande society is stratified, and social rank is usually indicated by surname. First are the nobles or "freeborn" (*horon*), consisting of lineages such as Keita, Konaté and Traoré, descended from Sunjata Keita and his generals. In pre-colonial times, they were the patrons (*jatigi*) of the second social category: artisans called *nyamakala*, often described in the literature as a "caste". This relationship has survived into the twenty-first century, but the patrons are increasingly of different social backgrounds. In fact, some of the most famous are themselves artisans, such as the Jeli **Babani Sissoko**. The third level of Mande society, called *jon*, is composed of the descendants of former slaves or captives from wars. In the twentieth century this group has become largely integrated into other levels of society.

All the occupational professions have their own surnames. For example, the Kantés are blacksmiths (though many are also musicians), and the Kouyatés (variant spelling Koité, not to be confused with Koïta) are exclusively *jelis*. The surnames Diabaté (Jobarteh in English), Koné (a variant of Konté), Sissoko or Cissokho (with variants Suso in The Gambia, and Damba and Sakiliba for women), Kamissoko, Soumano, Dambélé, Tounkara and Sacko are also commonly though not exclusively found among *jelis*.

Until the end of the nineteenth century, when colonial rule put an end to traditional kingship, the *jelis* were attached to the courts of local kings (*Mansa*). They entertained and educated the nobility with their epic songs and stories. They guarded the knowledge of genealogies and the complex "praise names" attached to every surname. To a great extent they continue to perform these functions to this day. In the words of Toumani Diabaté, 'they are the needle that sews.'

The *jelis* guard their profession and knowledge with jealousy and some secrecy. Until recently it was difficult for a non-*jeli* to take up music as a profession, and in practice very few have done so. One of the best-known exceptions is Salif Keita.

"It's not easy to find a trustworthy person" is a constant refrain of Mande songs, reminding both *jeli* and patron of their duty of loyalty to each other. Those who consider themselves patrons rely heavily on the advice and diplomacy of their *jeli*. The presidents of Mali, Guinea, The Gambia and Senegal have had thousands of songs dedicated to them by *jelis*, who always find ways of criticizing and advising, as well as praising.

Jeli Languages and Instruments

There are several closely related Mande languages spoken in at least seven different West African countries. The major Mande languages are: **Maninka**, the language of the Manden heartland in western Mali and eastern Guinea; **Bamana**, spoken in central Mali, a legacy of the Bamana kingdom and Mali's second official language after French; and **Mandinka**, spoken in The Gambia, southern Senegal and Guinea-Bissau. Maninka and Bamana are quite close. Mandinka is the most different, being about as close to Bamana as Spanish is to Italian. The three terms are often used interchangeably by outsiders when talking about Mande music, but they have distinct musical styles and repertoires.

By far the best known of the traditional *jeli* instruments is the *kora*. As a type of instrument, it is unique to the Mandinka, although it shares some basic features with hunters' harps, such as the raised bridge and calabash resonator. Although some of the most famous *kora* players are from Mali, the *kora* itself is said to come originally from the Mandinka kingdom, which was based in present-day Guinea-Bissau and extended to Senegal and The Gambia. In Mali, there are two main families who play the *kora*: the Diabatés and the Sissokos, and they live side by side, having been given adjacent plots of land by Mali's first president, Modibo Keita. The two musicians who were given the land, **Sidiki Diabaté** and **Djelimady Sissoko**, were both in fact born in The Gambia, to parents who had settled there from Mali.

Sidiki Diabaté (c. 1922–96) was probably the most influential of all *kora* players in the twentieth century, in terms of developing a virtuoso solo style, and popularizing certain pieces in the repertoire such as "Kaira". His son Toumani Diabaté is probably the greatest living *kora* player, steeped in the *jeli* tradition but also at home in any number of other styles, from jazz to flamenco, without relying on any modifications such as pedals or extra strings, which other *kora* players such as the Senegalese musician Soriba Kouyaté exploit.

One of the oldest and most prestigious of the Mande *jeli* instruments is a lute with three to five strings, a resonator carved from a single piece of wood and a skin sound table. In Bamana and Maninka it is called *ngoni* (sometimes spelt *koni* or *n'koni*); in Mandinka, *kontingo*. West African slaves re-created it in the New World, as the banjo. The *ngoni* is the main instrument of the Bamana *jelis* of central Mali. Although it is not as popular and ubiquitous as the guitar, it remains a staple part of the *sumu* ensembles in Bamako, holding its own side by side with the electric guitar, thanks partly to amplification, and also to the influence of two brilliant players, **Moriba Koïta** and **Bassekou Kouyaté**.

From Mali to Mississippi ... and Back

When **Duke Ellington** was asked if he'd ever heard any African music, the great bandleader replied that he'd been making it all his life. At the time it was a controversial remark, for ethno-musicologists were still arguing heatedly over whether the roots of American jazz and blues could be traced back to Africa. Today it is widely accepted that the origins of the music developed by black sharecroppers in the Mississippi Delta in the early decades of the twentieth century can be traced back to Africa via the slave ships. The cultural trade routes connecting the blues and the music of West Africa have been mapped and explored in noted collaborations between the likes of **Toumani Diabaté** and **Taj Mahal** and **Ali Farka Touré** with both **Ry Cooder** and **Corey Harris**.

In recent decades, the cross-pollination has grown more complicated as the music has travelled back and forth across the Atlantic. African guitarists such as **Lobi Traoré**, known as the "Bambara bluesman", admit to listening to **John Lee Hooker** when growing up and so contemporary African musicians have been influenced by American blues practitioners whose music has its origins in a centuries-old folk memory of Africa.

When the late Ali Farka Touré was asked how he felt when he first heard Hooker he replied: 'I thought "he's taken our music"' That music comes from history. How did it get here? It was stolen from Africans.' Shortly before his death in 2001, Hooker was asked if he had heard Ali Farka Touré and received a remarkably similar answer. 'Yeah, I heard him and I said "he's stealing our music." Then people started telling me "no, we stole *his* music because it all comes from Africa"'.

Lobi Traoré also believes that just who influenced whom has become highly confused. 'When I was young, before I even knew I would become a musician, I listened to a lot of American blues,' he says. 'Maybe I was inspired by it. Maybe the blues was inspired by Africa. Maybe it's just a coincidence. But listen. The music I play comes from me and from my place.'

However, the white American blues-rock singer **Bonnie Raitt**, who has played with both Lobi Traoré and Ali Farka Touré, has no doubt about the link. She describes how she felt when she first heard Malian music: 'I absolutely could not believe that something as close to the Delta music existed in Africa. The kind of blues that most gets me is Robert Pete Williams, Fred McDowell, Skip James, Son House, John Lee Hooker, the really dark, stark music – and here it was, mirrored back to me.'

The African American bluesman Taj Mahal first visited Mali in 1979, 20 years before he recorded *Kulanjan* with Toumani Diabaté in 1999. He says of their collaboration: 'It's a real connection with my ancestors. I've always been searching for American music that still connects with the African tradition. It's been unbroken for 71 generations and the Mande people are responsible for the way guitars and banjos were played in the United States. They're the creators of that specific rhythmic style you hear when someone picks up a blues guitar and starts picking on it and that sad sound, the melancholy, that you hear in the blues and in the older African music.'

However, the American blues-man Corey Harris, who recorded much of his album *Mississippi to Mali* with Ali Farka Touré in Mali, is more circumspect. 'I'm not trying to say the blues all came from Mali. It's just one of the strains, the really strong strains that make up black music in America,' he says. 'The point is you can take that music that we have over here, and it can go over there and be conversant.'

Nigel Williamson

Ali Farka Touré (left) with US bluesman Taj Mahal

225

Basekou Kouyaté is considered to be the leading *ngoni* player among the younger generation and has drawn on Koïta's style, extending it to include references to jazz, blues and flamenco. The third melody instrument of the *jelis* is the *bala* (better known as *balafon*), a kind of xylophone. It usually has between 18 and 21 keys cut from rosewood, suspended on a bamboo frame over gourd resonators of graduating sizes. The heartland of *balafon* playing is Guinea, though Mali has many notable players nonetheless. The most influential of them is Kélétigui Diabaté, who was born in Kita and served in many of Mali's first bands after independence, such as **Orchestre Nationale A**, playing several instruments including guitar, trombone, and violin. During the 1990s, he was a regular member of Toumani Diabaté's Symmetric Orchestra and then Salif Keita's band, and he currently performs with Habib Koité. Kélétigui devised the strategy of playing two *balafons* together, tuned a semitone apart, so that this fixed-pitch instrument could play a fully chromatic scale in a modern dance or jazz band – now standard practice among the new generation of Malian balafon players such as **Lassana Diabaté**.

Finally, there are three Mande drums: the *tamani* (talking drum); the *djembe*, a single-headed goblet drum with a high-pitched tone, played with both hands; and the *dunun*, a large double-headed cylindrical drum slung over the shoulder and played with a crooked stick in one hand, while the other hand strikes an iron bell with a ring.

Regional Styles and Repertoires

There are three main regional styles of Mande *jeli* music, corresponding roughly to the three main Mande languages. **Maninka** *jeli* music is the most widespread and influential. It has seven-note scales, and long, florid and virtuoso melodies that adapt well to harmonic arrangements. Many of the top performers of both Guinea and Mali, such as Salif Keita, Kassé Mady Diabaté, Kandia Kouyaté, Toumani Diabaté, Habib Koité and Sekouba Bambino Diabaté specialize in the Maninka style. It has been a major inspiration for the Rail Band, **Les Ambassadeurs** and **Badema National**.

The **Bamana** style of central Mali tends to be more static, with mostly five-note (pentatonic) melodies, in slow tempo. The preferred instrument is the large *ngoni*, and it is closer to the music of the northern desert regions, and thus the blues. Bamana *jeli* music is considered classical and prestigious. Recordings of the late, blind Bamana *ngoni*

player and singer **Banzoumana Sissoko**, "the old lion" from Segou, are still broadcast on the radio on major holidays and important occasions.

One of the first to popularize the Bamana *jeli* style was the late **Fanta Damba**, a famous *jelimuso* star in the 1970s, originally from Segou. Babani Koné cites her as her biggest influence, and Senegalese superstar Youssou N'Dour, while still in his 20s, made a pilgrimage to Bamako to meet her after recording "Wareef", which was inspired by her song "Djadjiri". She was largely responsible for popularising the Bamana piece "Bajourou". **Mah Damba** and the late **Hawa Dramé** are other well-known female exponents of Bamana music.

Bamana folk music has strong, driving dance rhythms, so it's hardly surprising that it has been adapted for the dancefloor, for example in the music of the singer **Abdoulaye Diabaté**, from Koutiala in the southeast. Though not well known outside Mali, he is particularly admired for his outspoken lyrics criticizing aspects of modern society.

Another singer who performs mainly within a Bamana style is Mali's highly acclaimed young singer-songwriter **Rokia Traoré**, though she also brings in many non-traditional elements as

Benoit Peverelli

The iconic Rokia Traoré

well. She does not come from a traditional musical background, which gives her the freedom to experiment, and she has become an iconic performer on the World Music scene as well as at home. She points out that the Bamana tradition is extremely diverse, covering *jeli* and non-*jeli* traditions, including the highly rhythmic dance music of the *balani* (two large interlocking pentatonic *balafons*) and the expressive *bara* line dance performed by women.

Habib Koité goes way beyond the confines of his own native *jeli* tradition from Kayes in the northwest of the country, borrowing songs from many different ethnic traditions around Mali including the Bamana and the hunters of the south (as on "Maya"). He often asks, 'Why borrow from global styles, when we have a whole world of different kinds of music within our own country?'

Another musician who draws mainly on the non-*jeli* Bamana style, mixing it with a raw electric blues sound, is singer-guitarist **Lobi Traoré**, a regular performer on the bar circuit of Bamako's vibrant nightclub scene. The music of Amadou & Mariam, although venturing boldly into the world of French rock and pop, is nevertheless profoundly based in their own Bamana culture. Both musicians originally hail from Bougouni, on the border with the Wasulu region, and this is evident in their strong rhythms and pentatonic melodies. An excellent example is their track "Coulibaly", which honours the royal lineage of Segou.

Dance Bands and Cultural Authenticity

The modernization of music in Mali dates back to the 1950s with the creation of regional orchestras who played foxtrots, waltzes and tangos for colonial administrators and their families. Mali's first president, **Modibo Keita** (1960–68), followed the example of neighbouring Guinea, with its policy of "cultural authenticity", and initiated the annual "Semaines de la Jeunesse" youth festival, in which regional bands and artists competed with each other for national recognition. He founded the **Orchestre Nationale A**, Mali's first national electric dance band. Led by Kélétigui Diabaté on guitar and **Tidiané Koné** on sax, it had a standard Latin/jazz line-up, although the strong presence of guitar, drawing on Mande styles, gave this band a distinctive local flavour, which was to become the model for future dance bands.

President Keita also founded the **Ensemble Instrumental National** (EIN). In its hey-day, the EIN had up to forty members, and was a powerhouse of musical performance, playing an important role in keeping alive traditions.

In Bamako, an orchestra was founded for each section of the capital. The most popular of these district bands was **Pioneer Jazz of Missira**. **Djelimady Tounkara** (later to become the lead guitarist of the Rail Band) was a member of Pioneer Jazz in the early 1960s, and this was his first experience away from purely traditional Mande music. 'At that time our bands weren't using folklore, just Latin American music, some jazz and some rock,' he said. 'I especially liked Chuck Berry and I tried to imitate his style.'

Throughout the 1960s, the biggest outside influence on Malian popular music, as in the rest of Francophone Africa, was Cuban dance music. Even when dance bands performed Mande tunes they were almost invariably given Latin arrangements, and Latin music continues to have a following even today; every weekend, the group **Tarras** performs Cuban-style music at nightclubs in central Bamako. Salif Keita's biggest hit of the 1970s, "Mandjou", has a clear Latin tinge, though was actually based on a *jeli* praise song, originally composed by Ami Koïta. In an interview for BBC Television in 1989 Salif remarked: 'I consider it a duty for all Malians to love Cuban music, because it's through Cuban music that we were introduced to modern instruments.'

Mali's second president **Moussa Traoré**, who came to power following a military coup in 1968, further encouraged cultural authenticity. Following the example of neighbouring Guinea, Traoré initiated the influential Biennale Festival in 1970. Thus the search for a more traditional idiom began. Gone were the imitation Cuban costumes, now replaced by tunics of tie-dyed damask or bogolan, the patterned mud-dyed cloth of the Bamana.

Many of the country's most celebrated artists were first "discovered" at the Biennale festivals, such as singer Nahawa Doumbia and **Super Biton de Segou**, who won first prize at the first Biennale in 1970 and then again in 1972. Their Bamana rhythms translated powerfully onto guitars and horns, creating a new style.

The Rail Band vs Les Ambassadeurs

Tidiané Koné was another of the major figures in the campaign to return to folklore. His wizardry on the *ngoni* was legendary. In 1969, Koné set up the **Rail Band du Buffet Hôtel de la Gare**, which went on to launch Mory Kanté.s and Salif Keita's careers.

In 1971, a rival band was formed in Bamako, **Les Ambassadeurs du Motel**, the resident band of a small hotel in Bamako. While the Rail Band was known for its roots repertoire, with songs like "Sunjata", Les Ambassadeurs were more experimental and international in outlook; at least half numbers were foreign-style pop – rumbas, foxtrots, French ballads, Cuban and even Senegalese Wolof songs.

Two Guinean musicians now arrived on the scene: Mory Kanté, a singer and multi-instrumentalist from eastern Guinea; and his cousin **Kanté Manfila**, an innovative guitarist who had learnt to play in Côte d'Ivoire. Manfila became leader of the Ambassadeurs, while Mory became a second singer in the Rail Band.

In the Rail Band, Mory Kanté was immediately seen as a potential rival to Salif Keita. They both had powerful, inspirational voices and were adept at praise lyrics. During 1972, Salif made a brief trip out of the country, and on his return found Mory doing the lead singing. Salif's response was to defect to Les Ambassadeurs, which created an uproar among his fans and even greater rivalry between the two bands.

A third *charanga*-style band, originally called **Las Maravillas de Mali**, whose members had spent several years training as musicians in Havana Cuba, were renamed Badema National ("the national family") as part of the cultural authenticity drive, and like the EIN, were government-sponsored. They recruited the singer Kassé Mady Diabaté, bringing him to Bamako from his village, Kela, in order to introduce a more traditional repertoire.

By the late 1970s, both the Rail Band and Les Ambassadeurs had moved their base to Abidjan, where the recording studios were. The Rail Band returned to Mali to play at the Buffet de la Gare, the beer garden of Bamako's train station, but their audiences dwindled. Les Ambassadeurs had a massive hit with their song "Mandjou", recorded in 1978. And this group was to produce some of West Africa's most successful musicians, such as **Amadou Doumbia** (now of Amadou & Mariam and former guitarist with many of Mali's dance bands including Les Ambassadeurs).

Old Music, New Era

By the early 1980s, local audiences had begun to lose interest in the old-style dance bands. The Biennale Festival ceased altogether in 1988, the year of the Touareg rebellion in the north of Mali. New experiments in Mande music coming out of Abidjan and Paris – such as the 1984 album *Mory Kanté à Paris*, which included his first version of the electric *kora* dance track "Yeke Yeke" – made the Cuban-style arrangements of *jeli* tunes by Mali's dance bands seem outdated. Focus shifted from the collective identity of the dance bands to the individual singers who took up solo careers with their own groups. At home in Bamako, it was the women singers who were gradually becoming the true stars of the local music scene. Some new privately sponsored dance bands formed, such as **Zani Diabaté's Super Djata Band**, which cultivated a rocking Wasulu/Bamana sound, but by the early 1990s most of its members had emigrated to Europe.

Meanwhile, a new kind of music was coming up that would eventually challenge the monopoly of the *jelis*. **Wassoulou** expressed perfectly the mood of the country, which was ready for a change. In 1991, a series of student demonstrations protesting against the government's refusal to pay school bursaries resulted in a popular uprising and a clash with the army, in

Because

Mariam and Amadou

which over a thousand people lost their lives. A military coup followed, led by Colonel Amadou Toumani Touré, who then handed over power to a democratically elected government in 1992 under President Alpha Oumar Konaré.

All this had a profound effect on the music scene. Local culture once again began flourishing. With freedom of the press, many private radio stations opened, and new venues for music called "éspaces culturels" began to appear around Bamako. These were up-market restaurants and bars that featured small groups playing live music. Many important contemporary artists and musical trends have come out of this circuit. The Biennales were resumed in 2003, but it remains to be seen whether they will have the same impact on local music as before.

Djelimady Tounkara, with the Rail Band lead guitarist

Meanwhile, the original Rail Band still survives, despite losing their sponsorship and original venue. They perform occasionally at the Djembe club in the Lafiabougou neighbourhood, but their main audiences are now at festivals abroad. Their leader, guitarist extraordinaire **Djelimady Tounkara**, occasionally joins them, but has mostly taken up a solo career with his own semi-acoustic group. The closest thing to a dance band is **Toumani Diabaté's Symmetric Orchestra**, which combines elements from traditional *jeli* music and global styles, with a semi-acoustic line-up of twenty or more. However, unlike the bands of the 1970s, it has no horn section. Their regular Friday night gigs at the Hogon club in Bamako are now legendary. In addition, Toumani Diabaté has influenced a whole generation of young *kora* players in Mali.

Salif Keita – Mali's Superstar

The most famous of the musicians from the dance-band era is *Salif Keita*, who, more than any other individual, is responsible for fusing Mande music with world beats. On both his mother's and father's side he is a Keita and there was no precedent for someone of such noble lineage to take up singing as a profession, as if a *jeli*. Salif trained as a schoolteacher but poor eyesight prevented him from teaching as a profession.

In 1980, Salif Keita, Kanté Manfila and two other musicians from Les Ambassadeurs spent four months in the US making another of their classic records, *Prinprin*, with local session musicians. But in 1982 Salif left the band altogether and moved to Paris, eventually coming up with the fusion album *Soro* with French keyboardist **Jean-Philippe Rykiel** under the guidance of Senegalese producer **Ibrahima Sylla**.

Soro's phenomenal success marked the beginning of the World Music boom. Many of Salif Keita's original group of musicians – some of whom, like **Cheikh Tidiané Seck** and guitarist **Ousmané Kouyaté**, had remained with him since the days of Les Ambassadeurs – were encouraged to form their own groups, and a spate of *Soro* soundalike albums came and went, often featuring the same group of musicians, and produced in the same studio by Sylla. On *Soro,* Salif had finally abandoned all trace of Latin influence, instead working with contemporary sounds from the global world of rock and pop. Also, he was no longer primarily using the idioms of *jeli* praise song, but had begun to draw on other Malian styles, especially the melodies of Maninka hunters, which was his real heritage: his father Sina Keita was the head of the hunters' association in his village Joliba.

Salif Keita has always been torn between his deep love for Malian culture and music, and a desire to be part of the global world of pop and rock; his musical output veers between large-scale rock albums such as *Ko-Yan* and *Papa*, and the more recent acoustic albums such as *Moffou*. For

Salif Keita

the first time in many years Salif has chosen a band that is almost entirely Malian and Guinean. Furthermore, since Mali's new democracy, he has invested in a recording studio and nightclub (also called Moffou), is producing local artists, and now spends long periods living and working in Mali reconnecting with his roots.

Current Trends

In recent years, Mali, like other Francophone West African countries, has had its share of **hip-hop** groups. A rhythmical, poetic, dynamic and uptempo spoken lyric, providing social comment over music, is hardly a new idea in Malian music. It's one that's many centuries old, in fact: the elder male *griots* used a similar method to narrate events and epics, as do also the *fune*, a special group of Mande artisans dedicated exclusively to performance of the spoken word.

Two of the pioneering and most influential and successful Malian rap groups are **Les Escrocs** and **Tata Pound**. Les Escrocs are not a typical rap group in that they use a live band of *jeli* instruments and the music and choruses are clearly in the *jeli* style. Tata Pound are three youngsters from Bamako who rap in Bamana, and work in a more mainstream style using a backing of samples with hip-hop and reggae sounds, and are noted for their outspoken criticisms of the government. Their most recent album, *Cikan* (Le Message), includes a collaboration with Ivorian reggae superstar **Tiken Jah Fakoly** and a cover version of Salif Keita's *Prinprin*. Fakoly himself has similarly bold lyrics, and

his criticizing of corrupt politicians in his native Côte d'Ivoire forced him to flee the country. He is now settled in Bamako, where he has opened a studio. He is enormously popular among the youth and is single-handedly reviving interest in **reggae**.

The trend in Mali at present is towards smaller, semi-acoustic groups featuring mainly traditional instruments, such as those of singers Kassé Mady Diabaté and Habib Koité, *kora* players Toumani Diabaté and Ballake Sissoko, and Djelimady Tounkara. They all draw primarily on the celebratory *jeli* style, such as one might hear at a wedding party, although their experiences of collaborating with international artists bring a new, more contemporary perspective to the tradition. The cross-fertilization between "traditional" wedding music and modern music is inevitable, given that many of the musicians play in both domains.

Kassé Mady Diabaté is arguably as mighty a singer as Salif Keita, though more rooted in the *jeli* tradition. His 1988 album *Fode* was meant to be an answer to *Soro* but did not get much press attention. His second album for the Paris-based producer Ibrahim Sylla, *Kela Tradition* (1991), an all-acoustic recording of some of the classic *jeli* songs, showed this to be his true forte, as further demonstrated in his 2002 album *Kassi Kasse*, recorded on a mobile studio in his native village, Kela. He has since gone on to participate in Sylla's fine album *Mandekalou*.

Kassé Mady Diabaté

One other important trend in Mali since the mid-1990s has been a new interest amongst the urban youth in the *balafon* music of the Senufo people from the south of the country. The lead performer of *balani* is **Neba Solo**, a brilliant player and singer who has adapted and modernized the tradition by adding bass notes to the xylophones to fashion a more pronounced bass line.

Ali Farka Touré:
the Donkey that Nobody Climbed On

Ali Farka Touré invented "desert blues" three decades before the marketing men got there. Propelled by pulsing rhythms, his flowing guitar licks and drones were also unmistakably the work of a musician who had grown up beside the drifting waters of a great river.

His long graceful *boubous*, toothy grin and regal manner helped make him an unforgettable presence on stage. Whether toting an electric or acoustic guitar, his hands appeared hardly to move across the strings as he coaxed out a unique mix of influences from the rich traditions of northern Mali's sandy Sahel, spiced with elements of African American blues. He told his song-stories in a nasal but oddly compelling voice, and every now and then might treat his mesmerized but slightly perplexed audiences to a high wailing solo on his one-stringed fiddle, the *njarka*. If he seemed otherworldly, it wasn't without reason.

'I have all the spirits. I work the spirits and work with the spirits,' he once told Lucy Duran while explaining the source of his music's mysterious power. In his song "Cross Road Blues", American legend Robert Johnson told of going to a mythical crossroads where he sold his soul to the devil in exchange for being able to play the blues, and Ali's account of his own spiritual and musical awakening has uncanny echoes of this tale.

Born Ali Ibrahim, he was the only one of his parents' first ten children strong enough to survive. They gave him the absurd nickname of *Farka* ("donkey") so that the greedy spirits wouldn't want to steal him away, too. With no formal schooling, he spent a very harsh childhood in the town of Niafunké, on the banks of the Niger River, where he became fascinated by the music played at spirit ceremonies. At the age of 12, he took up the *djerkel* (one-stringed guitar). Shortly afterwards, he claims to have suffered something like a possession by one of the local *djinns* (spirits), which caused "attacks". In order to be cured, he was sent away to another village for a year to undergo a painful kind of exorcism, after which he began playing again and was 'very well received by the spirits'. He soon picked up the *ngoni* and *njarka*, eventually transposing their disparate styles onto guitar.

Unlike the majority of Mali's musicians, he was neither a *jeli* nor from the dominant Mande culture. Though both his parents were from the Songhai ethnic group – whose ancestors once overthrew the Mande and ruled Mali from 1460 to 1591 – Ali soaked up the music of all the peoples he was surrounded by in the north, singing his folklore-inspired songs in seven local languages, with a particularly bluesy influence apparent in his Tamachek (Touareg language) pieces. He was also a great believer in an integrated Mali, challenging the country's cultural and economic divide by dabbling in the music of the south as well.

As Ry Cooder observed shortly after Ali's death in February, 2006: 'Ali was a seeker. There was a powerful psychology there. He was not governed by anybody, he was free to move about in his mind.'

Unfortunately he was too ill to leave his beloved farm and travel abroad to collect the Grammy award he received for *In The Heart of the Moon*, his joint 2005 album with Toumani Diabaté, and didn't live to see the release of his final album *Savane*. But it's a fine epitaph for such a great artist, revisiting his love of the *ngoni* and once more exploring the links with other folks' blues, which had so much resonance with his own.

Jon Lusk

Wassoulou

Wassoulou, so-called because it came from the region of Wasulu in the south, was based on some of Mali's most ancient traditions, which had been imitated by the youth as a kind of acoustic village popular music. It had strong messages of social freedom and powerful dance rhythms, and young women singers were its main stars.

Wasulu is a remote corner of the country that straddles Mali, Guinea and northern Côte d'Ivoire. The roots styles that *wassoulou* draws from are found right across the region, but contemporary *wassoulou* music is specific to Mali. The region is populated by farmers, hunters and blacksmiths of mainly Fula descent, as shown by the four most common surnames (Sidibé, Sangaré, Diakité and Diallo).

What makes the music of Wasulu different is that here, even though there are *jelis*, anyone is free to sing or play an instrument. Since musicians play by choice, they call themselves *kono* – "song-birds". The explosive emergence of Wasulu "song-birds" challenged the monopoly of the *jelis*, and opened up possibilities for new styles and creativity, while attracting new, younger audiences who were tired of hearing praise songs in honour of the military government. In the words of *wassoulou*'s most famous star, Oumou Sangaré: 'At first, when women singers of *wassoulou* wanted to perform in public, the *jelis* gave us a hard time ... this has been a real struggle for us but in the end we're coming out on top because the public is tired of being extorted for money.'

A lot of *wassoulou* sounds quite traditional, but it dates from after independence and really only took off in the late 1980s. It combines two types of roots music, characterized by two instruments which have circulated far beyond their local habitat: the hunters' harp, recreated in a smaller, higher-pitched version called the *kamalengoni*, and the *djembe* drum. The original hunters' harp, the *donsongoni*, and the music (and culture) of hunter societies in general, is currently enjoying a wave of popular interest in Mali. As for the *djembe*, it has become Africa's most universal drum, played around the globe by hundreds of thousands of people. But few of them realize that it comes from Wasulu, where it's played for the *komo* (an all-male secret society of the blacksmiths) and *sogoninkun*, a masquerade for the end of harvest.

Hunters' Music

The music of Mali's hunter societies (*donsoton*) is considered to be among the oldest surviving forms of music in Africa, and is probably the ancestor of the music of the *jelis*. The hunter societies are inter-ethnic and egalitarian (only women and children are excluded) and may have up to 100,000 members. In the past, hunters served as guardians of the village, providers of meat and healers. Although there have been restrictions on hunting for many years now in Mali, hunters continue to play important roles as healers, diviners and musicians.

When they meet on festive occasions the hunters' musicians (sometimes called *sora*, or *jurufokono* – "string-playing songbird") play their six-string harps and sing vivid epic stories of legendary hunters. In recent years, this esoteric music has acquired something of a cult status, evoking a sense of pride in the country's great heritage. Major festivals organized in Bamako in 2001 and 2005 have celebrated their blues-like melodies, powerful rhythms and graceful dances.

Bamako's market resounds to the music of literally hundreds of cassettes featuring hunters' musicians who have become quite popular, such as **Seydou Traoré**, **Amadou Sangaré** and **Sibiri Samaké**. Many listeners are struck with the strong similarities between this music and that of *gnawa* (which allegedly was brought to Morocco by Bambara slaves from Mali) and the blues. **Yoro Sidibé**,

Issa Bagayogo

from Yanfolila, in deep Wasulu, is currently the local "star" of hunters' music.

Birth of the Kamalengoni

The story of how hunters' music was appropriated by the youth goes back to the 1950s. In Wasulu, boys and girls in the villages would organize dance parties when the moon was bright, playing a six-string instrument called *ndan*, consisting of several individual bows, each one with a single wire string, mounted on an upside-down calabash.

Most *wassoulou* musicians say that the first *kamalengoni* player was **Allata Brulaye Sidibé**, who had the idea of improving and adapting the *ndan*. First he turned the calabash around so it was facing upwards, then attached the strings to a single long neck, in effect creating a smaller and higher pitched version of the hunters' harp (*donsongoni*). Allata Brulaye's "invention" became extremely popular throughout the region, but also was strongly censored by parents and village leaders.

The appropriation of what had been a sacred instrument for the entertainment of unmarried youth was considered scandalous. The elders disparagingly called it *samakoro*, meaning "bedbug" or "flea", complaining that it made people dance as though they were itching uncontrollably from flea bites. Interestingly, with its funky rhythms and jerky dance steps, it has some similarities with the jitterbug dance of the 1950s, which also gets its name from a bug. Only much later when it gained some respectability, in the 1970s, was it renamed *kamalengoni* (male youth harp).

Allata Brulaye was the first to record on the *kamalengoni* in the late 1970s, but it was the singer **Coumba Sidibé** from Yanfolila who first brought the music to Bamako.

These days the *kamalengoni* thrives in the villages of Wasulu, alongside the music of hunters, and no longer meets with disapproval. In the city as well, the *kamalengoni* has become a favourite instrument of the youth, as it is portable and cheap to make, and not difficult to play at a basic level. Players such as **Benogo Diakité** (with Oumou Sangaré's band since 1990), Haruna Samake and, most recently, **Kokanko Sata** – the first woman to play the *kamalengoni* – are the best-known exponents.

Wassoulou Women

Despite the importance of the *kamalengoni*, the true stars of *wassoulou* music have always been female singers. **Coumba Sidibé**, who was recruited into EIN in the mid-1970s in order to introduce the sounds of her region, soon went solo, with a fully electric band. Her gritty voice and driving *jembe* rhythms, derived from her background as a *sogoninkun* singer, were appreciated as much as her lyrics.

Coumba paved the way for other artists such as **Kagbé Sidibé** (no relation), who cultivated an electric style based on *sogoninkun* rhythms. In the late 1980s, **Sali Sidibé** (also no relation) challenged Coumba's popularity with her hypnotic voice and a more rootsy sound, using traditional instruments like the one-string fiddle (*soku*), the Senufo xylophone, the *bolon* (four-string bass harp) and the *kamalengoni*. Ten years later, male singer and *kamalengoni* player **Issa Bagayogo** (better known as "Techno Issa"), developed the remix sound which made him a favourite with UK DJs. Meanwhile, the unique voice of **Nahawa Doumbia** was also remixed by French DJ Frederic Galliano on his *Frikyiwa Collection Vol 1* (2000).

Doumbia was one of the pioneers of the *wassoulou* sound, although she only began using the trademark *kamalengoni* many years after she became established. The orphaned daughter of a Mande blacksmith from a remote village in Wasulu, with a plaintive, child-like voice, she was famous in Mali for her participation in the Biennale festivals, and in 1980 was voted Best Singer for her song "Tinye De Be laban", later recorded on her album *Yankaw*. Doumbia's favourite style is the vigorous *didadi*, a harvest dance from Wasulu, which features *djembe* and *dunun* drums. In the late 1980s and early 90s she recorded three hi-tech electric albums in Paris for the Syllart label, and she was meant to be a kind of female answer to Salif Keita, but her more recent work is increasingly acoustic and back-to-roots. She draws directly on the sacred repertoires of the hunters.

Oumou Sangaré: the Songbird

No one has broken social taboos in Mali quite like Oumou Sangaré, with her outspoken criticism of polygamous marriage and her celebration of female sensuality. And no one has taken *wassoulou* music around the world as she has.

Born in Bamako to parents from Wasulu, her mother's unhappy experience as the first wife abandoned by her husband in favour of a new bride, was to have a lasting impact on Oumou, becoming the dominant theme of her songs. 'Polygamy is false, ultra-false, it's sheer hypocrisy,' she declares. Oumou began singing at an early age at wedding parties in Bamako with her mother (a *sogoninkun* singer). Her international career began with the group **Djoliba Percussions**, with whom she came to Europe for the first time in 1986, to great acclaim. Back in Mali she started her own semi-acoustic band and recorded her first album when she was just 21 years old and still unmarried. Aptly named *Moussolou* ("Women"), it was released in 1990 and was an instant hit, selling over 200,000 cassettes. It addressed a number of women's issues but none so radically or controversially as in the song "Diaraby Nene" (Love fever), an overtly sensual piece about the "shivers of passion" and female sexuality. *Moussolou*'s back-to-roots sound gave Oumou's version of *wassoulou* its real impetus.

'My style of *wassoulou* was radically different from that of other *wassoulou* singers. First of all I

John Milded

Oumou Sangaré

placed the *kamelengoni* at the centre of my sound … because it's the instrument in Wasulu that the young people love most. And my songs are directed at the youth. The elders are already set in their ways, they're already polygamous, you can't change them… "

Oumou's second and third international albums, *Ko Sira* and *Worotan*, explore the problems of polygamy and arranged marriage more explicitly.

Many of her songs are inspired directly by hunters' songs, such as "Sabou" and "Mogo Te Diya Bee Ye". Others like "Yala" push *wassoulou* closer to the world of dance music.

On stage Oumou Sangaré is formidable. Tall, beautiful, radiant, charismatic, a wonderful dancer, surrounded by some of Mali's best musicians, she is the ultimate songbird, a true ambassador for Malian women and music.

DISCOGRAPHY Mali

⊙ **An Be Kelen**
Panart, The Netherlands
These field recordings were made in Kela, one of Mali's most-celebrated *jeli* villages, and feature the famous Diabaté family, the late Kela Balaba, master of the word, reciting the Sunjata story with *ngoni* accompaniment. A real taste of the true *griot* tradition.

⊙ **The Festival in the Desert**
Triban Union, France
A memento of the legendary Festival in the Desert 2003 in the minuscule hamlet of Essakane, west of Timbuktu. It's a feast of international and Malian attractions including Ali Farka Touré, Oumou Sangaré, Tartit, Tinariwen, Robert Plant and Lo'Jo. But the real stars were the local traditional Tamashek troupes, some of whom featured on this technically and artistically excellent live recording.

★ **Mali lolo! Stars of Mali!**
Smithsonian Folkways, US
A journey from the heart of traditional Mande *griot* music (Kassé Mady Diabaté, Kandia Kouyaté, Toumani Diabaté) through hunters' traditions (Yoro Sidibé) and their urban offshoot, *wassoulou* music (Kokanko Sata Doumbia and Oumou Sangaré), followed by a trip to the northern desert with Tinariwen, Tartit and Ali Farka Touré, with singer-songwriters Habib Koité and Rokia Traoré, and hip-hop from Les Escrocs too. Excellent liner notes by Banning Eyre.

⊙ **Mandekalou**
Sterns, UK
Some of Mali and Guinea's greatest musicians come together for a unique all-star, all-acoustic recording that showcases the grand old Mande *jeli* tradition. Featuring Kandia Kouyaté, Sekouba Bambino Diabaté, and Kassé Mady Diabaté amongst others, it is beautiful listening.

⊙ **The Wassoulou Sound: Women of Mali**
Stern's, UK
A ground-breaking 1994 compilation which still sounds great, it features a range of styles and female voices from Wasulu before it became well known. Includes early pioneers of the "Wassoulou electric" sound, Kagbe Sidibé and Coumba Sidibé, plus the haunting semi-acoustic style of Sali Sidibé and Dienaba Diakité.

Amadou & Mariam

Mali's celebrated blues-rock duo have been working together since 1980, three years after they met at the Institute for the Young Blind in Bamako. They have slowly gained an audience outside West Africa since achieving major-label status in 1998.

★ **Dimanche à Bamako**
Radio Bemba, France
This 2004 breakthrough is very much enlivened by the omnipresence of world music superstar Manu Chao as a hands-on producer who brings some studio technicolor to their previously rather monochrome music. Et voilà! Amadou's noodling guitar grooves jump from the speakers as never before.

Issa Bagayogo

Singer and *kamelengoni* player "Techno Issa" has worked with producer Yves Wernert to bring out the full potential of *wassoulou* music for the dancefloor.

⊙ **Sya**
⊙ **Tassoumakan**
Six Degrees, US
Two fine albums out of Mali's influential Bogolan Studios. *Tassoumakan* is much more "techno" than Sya, but both have clear roots in southern rural Mali, where Issa comes from.

Afel Bocoum

An associate and protégé of Ali Farka Touré, Afel Bocoum (born 1955) worked with the river-blues guitarist since he was a young teenager. The magical song "Dofana", on Ali's *The Source*, is his composition.

⊙ **Alkibar**
World Circuit, UK
Recorded locally, at the same time as Ali's *Niafunké* album, this comes from a smaller, understated mould, though the inflections and swirling rhythms are similar and the deeply spiritual nature of the music is unmistakable.

Abdoulaye Diabaté

Much loved for his uncompromising lyrics that comment on life in Mali today, this *jeli* from Sikasso (in the southeast) has been a key singer on the local scene since the late 1960s.

⊙ **Bende**
Cobalt, France
The uptempo rhythms and pentatonic melodies of his region, such as *balani* (the pentatonic music of the Bamana *balafon*) and *gnoko* (a style of the Minianka people) are showcased, although the electric guitar is ever present.

Kassé Mady Diabaté

Owner of one of the most cherished voices of the Mande world, though not well known outside West Africa, his singing rivals Salif Keita for beauty and lyricism.

⊙ Kassi Kassé
Hemisphere, UK
Kassé Mady represents the classic *jeli* tradition from Kela in southwest Mali, where this all-acoustic Grammy-nominated album was recorded on a mobile studio with an all-star team including Fantamady Kouyaté (of the Symmetric Orchestra) on lead guitar.

Kélétigui Diabaté

This septegenarian left-handed *balafon* player and multi-instrumentalist has long been a well-known session player.

⊙ Sandiya
Contrejour, Belgium
Finally in 2004, he recorded his own album, featuring a host of guests such as Habib Koité, Djelimady Tounkara, Toumani Diabaté and the Ensemble Instrumental National, on mostly instrumental versions of Mande classics. Kélétigui's inimitable, warm and effortless *balafon* makes for superb listening.

Sidiki Diabaté, Batourou Kouyaté and Djelimad Sissoko

Mali's three greatest *kora* players of the older generation.

◉ Cordes Anciennes
Barenreiter Musicaphon, Germany
A classic 1970 recording, it features rippling instrumental duets by these legendary figures. A privileged view into the past.

Toumani Diabaté

Mali's most brilliant kora virtuoso, Toumani Diabaté is an ambitious and highly creative artist and has collaborated with a wide range of international musicians.

⊙ Kaira
Hannibal, UK
With exquisite melodies such as "Alla l'aa ke" and "Jarabi" and superb musicianship, this is instrumental solo *kora* in the classic style that could hardly be better within its genre.

WITH BALLAKE SISSOKO
★ **New Ancient Strings**
Hannibal, UK
These instrumental *kora* duets were recorded in Mali on state-of-the-art equipment, showing the extraordinary artistry of these two young cousins following in their legendary fathers' footsteps.

WITH TAJ MAHAL
⊙ Kulanjan
Hannibal, UK
The best interface so far between the blues and Malian music has excellent vocals from sultry *wassoulou* singer Ramata Diakité and Kassé Mady Diabaté. In both *wassoulou* and jeli styles, but the best chemistry is between *wassoulou* and the blues.

WITH ALI FARKA TOURÉ
⊙ In the Heart of the Moon
World Circuit, UK
A laid-back, graceful, and unique collaboration with the master blues guitarist from the north, revisiting old *jeli* songs popular around the time of Mali's independence. Winner of a Grammy award in 2006.

WITH THE SYMMETRIC ORCHESTRA
⊙ Boulevard de l'Independence
World Circuit, UK
As bandleader of a large and eclectic group of brilliant musicians, Toumani takes the art of the *kora* to new levels of virtuosity and expression. Combining different traditions from around the Mande cultural world, it reflects Toumani's own pan-African philosophy.

World Circuit

The Symmetric Orchestra

Kokanko Sata Doumbia

Although she first came to international attention through her contribution to Britpop musician Damon Albarn's *Mali Music* CD, this feisty woman with a powerful voice – born in a remote Wasulu village in 1968 – has been playing professionally for many years.

⊙ Kokanko Sata
Honest Jons, UK
This first international release by the only woman to play the *kamalengoni*. Recorded by a mobile studio under a mango tree on the outskirts of Bamako, this atmospheric, rootsy album takes you to the heart of the *wassoulou* tradition.

Nahawa Doumbia

A Bamana singer with a pure fresh voice, Nahawa Doumbia was one of the first *wassoulou* artists to gain international release.

Yankaw
Cobalt, France
Nahawa is here in acoustic mode, with superb solos on *balafon* and *djembe*, plus a moving acapella autobiographical song about growing up as an orphan in a remote village.

Salif Keita

Mali's golden voice, Salif Keita remains totally inimitable. Almost every one of his records is interesting and enjoyable, as he has traded production ideas with collaborators from Carlos Santana to Steve Hillage.

Soro
Stern's UK; Mango US
These hi-tech (and very 1980s) arrangements of Mande music have contributions from ex-Ambassadeurs guitarist Ousmané Kouyaté and French keyboard player Jean-Philippe Rykiel – the perfect backdrop to some extraordinary vocals.

⭐ Moffou
Universal, UK
The first of Salif Keita's semi-acoustic "back-to-roots" albums is a mixture of lyrical love songs in *jeli* style and *wassoulou* funk, provided by the brilliant *kamalengoni* player Harouna Samaké – plus a gorgeous opening duet with Cesaria Evora.

Ami Koïta

One of Mali's best known jelimuso divas, she pioneered the use of keyboards and electric guitars in women's praise song.

Songs of Praise
Stern's, UK
Some fine vocals and classic songs, compiled from albums recorded in the early 1990s.

Habib Koité

This *jeli* turned singer-songwriter has a populist, pan-Malian approach.

Foly
Contrejour, Belgium
Habib Koité can be a bit too restrained on his studio albums, but this double CD with live recordings of him and his group Bamada makes for great listening, and features most of his best songs.

Kandia Kouyaté

Kandia Kouyaté has been Mali's top *jelimuso* for the past quarter century. Her forceful voice and choral arrangements (in the 1980s she pioneered those dreamlike female choruses which are now the hallmark of Mande music) are in a similar vein to Salif Keita's, and her working of traditional social and court music has earned her a status unequalled by any other Malian female artist.

⭐ Biriko
Sterns, UK
This fine showcase for her heart-wrenching, powerful vocals and lyrics is matched by splendid, virtuoso and delicate acoustic guitar work by Djelimady Tounkara and Ousmané Kouyaté, amongst others.

Le (Super) Rail Band du Bamako

The Rail Band were the buffet band at Bamako train station, and have served as a school for many of Mali's finest singers and musicians since 1969, including Mory Kanté and Salif Keita.

⭐ New Dimensions in Rail Culture
GlobeStyle, UK
The legendary band are at a peak of mellowness in Abidjan in 1981, featuring the rich, warm voice of Lafia Diabaté and the rocking guitar of Djelimady Tounkara.

WITH MORY KANTE AND SALIF KEITA

Sunjata
Syllart, France
A legendary live recording from 1972, with two of West Africa's greatest singers performing an extended version of the great classic song. A glorious example of Mali's top dance band at the height of the cultural authenticity movement, albeit with a strong Latin tinge.

Sibiri Samaké

A virtuoso singer and *donsongoni* player, Samaké is one of the foremost exponents of hunter's music.

Djitoumou Kono
Buda Music, France
One of the few available international releases of hunters' music, this is Samaké's second album, recorded in Paris, and produced by French keyboard player and arranger Jean-Philippe Rykiel.

Oumou Sangaré

Charisma, outspoken views and a stunning voice have made Oumou Sangaré the biggest star of *Wassoulou* music, while a World Circuit contract has deservedly helped to propel her onto the World Music stage.

⭐ Oumou
World Circuit, UK
A compilation drawing from the superstar Wasulu songbird's first three highly acclaimed international albums, plus remixed versions of additional tracks from cassettes only released in Africa such as "Yalla". Wassoulou music at its best, with poignant lyrics about the problems that women face in marriage today, especially polygamy.

Allata Broulaye Sidibé

The man credited with creating the youth harp.

Allata Broulaye: initiateur du kamalen n'goni
Ousmane Haidara Productions, Mali
Broulaye was pulled out of retirement from deep in the remote Wasulu countryside by Ousmané Haidara (Oumou Sangaré's husband) and brought to a studio in Bamako to record some of the most sizzling and hypnotic *wassoulou* music ever. He died only a few months later, so this is a one-off.

Ballake Sissoko

A young *kora* player, he is best known for his *New Ancient Strings* collaboration with Toumani Diabaté.

PLAYLIST
Mali

1 MANDJOUES Ambassadeurs International from *The Mansa of Mali*

An epic, meandering praise song made on stolen studio time in 1978 – the most iconic of Salif Keita's early career. Never mind that it was in praise of a notorious dictator, Guinea's first president, Sékou Touré.

2 MALIYO Super Rail Band du Bamako from *New Dimensions in Rail Culture*

A wonderfully dreamy, meditative cut from their stunning 1982 album, featuring vocals by Lafia Diabaté and the inimitable guitar of Djelimady Tounkara.

3 MADAN Salif Keita from *Moffou*

A brilliant acoustic dance track that builds to an exhilarating rhythm, driven by funky *kamalengoni* playing from Harouna Samaké, powerful vocals from Salif and ethereal female chorus.

4 DIARABY NENE Oumou Sangaré from *Oumou*

The *kamalengoni* drives this song along with its punchy rhythm, blues-like riffs and ethereal harmonics. Oumou's soaring voice makes for a high goose-pimple rating.

5 SAN BARANA Kandia Kouyate from *Biriko*

Intricate interlocking acoustic guitars are the bedrock of this haunting minor-key ballad with heartfelt vocals from Kandia pleading with co-wives not to fight.

6 HAWA DOLO Ali Farka Touré from *The Source*

Mali's late sorcerer of the guitar at his most gentle, playing an acoustic instrument, accompanied only by sympathetic percussion and backing vocals. Like a very sparse and special lullaby.

7 SUPER 11 Takamba Super Onze from *Festival In The Desert 2003*

Don't even try counting the cross-rhythms on this passionate and utterly mesmerizing slice of desert blues!

8 LA RÉALITÉ Amadou & Mariam from *Dimanche à Bamako*

The blues-rocking duo from Bamako get a thorough turbo-charge courtesy of Manu Chao on this driving number from their hugely successful "crossover" collaboration.

9 KABA MANSA Kassé Mady Diabaté from *Kassi Kassé*

A rolling acoustic version of "Fode", an iconic song about a nineteenth-century king with an all-star acoustic team of *griots* including Fantamady Kouyaté on guitar and Lassana Diabaté on balafon.

10 KITA KAIRA Toumani Diabaté and Ballake Sissoko from *New Ancient Strings*

Sublime instrumental duet by two Malian *kora* maestros; timeless music of delicate and exquisite beauty.

Jon Lusk/Lucy Duran

⊙ Tomora
Indigo, France

Ballake comes out from under the shadow of his cousin Toumani on this superb solo album, with some wonderful *kora* solos and fine collaborations with other Malian musicians, including Rokia Traoré.

Djelimady Tounkara

The master guitarist and leader of the Rail Band, Djelimady has long been a musical force to be reckoned with in his own solo right.

⊙ Solon Kono
Marabi, France

This second solo album from 2005 combines techniques and songs from his days as leader of the Rail Band, and the wedding music he plays regularly around Bamako.

Ali Farka Touré

While Ali Farka Touré's spiritual life was the major inspiration of his music, his distinctive guitar style and rough nasal vocals led to him being dubbed the John Lee Hooker of Africa. He collaborated with some big names from the West, notably Ry Cooder, but always on his own terms.

⊙ Radio Mali
World Circuit, UK

A beautifully produced compilation of radio recordings in Ali's swinging, bluesy style, it was recorded between 1970 and 1978, a decade or more before he achieved international recognition, and at a time when, as he says, 'I was an absolute fool for the guitar.' The World Circuit team painstakingly trawled Bamako's radio archive and, considering the antiquity of the source material, the results here are little short of miraculous.

⊙ The Source
World Circuit, UK

Perhaps almost as essential, this sees Ali link up with Taj Mahal, Nana Tsiboe and British Asian Nitin Sawney on tabla. The best of another ten great tracks are "Hawa Dolo" and the upbeat loping river sound of "Mahini Me".

★ Savane
World Circuit, UK

Ali's farewell album gained a poignancy from its release, shortly after his death in 2006. But it would have been remarkable at any time: a magnum opus of defiant power and conviction and as pure an expression of the blues as any you will hear. It is a wonderful partnership of old – listen to the *ngonis* (plucked lute) and hear where the

Appalachian banjo had its roots – and modern, with top guest appearances from Pee Wee Ellis and Little George Suereff.

ALI FARKA TOURÉ AND RY COODER

⭐ **Talking Timbuktu**
World Circuit, UK

With Ali in seamless slide-blues collaboration with Ry Cooder, it hits with a rawness and conviction underlining the sense that here is simply a group of great musicians listening hard to one another and playing together in a room.

Boubacar Traoré

Boubacar Traoré is a veteran non-*jeli* singer and guitarist from the western city of Kayes.

⊙ **Mariama**
Sterns, UK

Solo voice and guitar convey haunting love ballads in a unique troubadour style. The first and still the best of all his albums.

Rokia Traoré

This young singer-songwriter with a highly distinctive voice is a charismatic rising star.

Ali Farka Toure with Ry Cooder — Talking Timbuktu

⊙ **Bowmboï**
Label Bleu/Indigo, France

Traoré's third and best album to date is still acoustic music based on the pentatonic Bamana tradition but fused with global elements including two tracks featuring the Kronos String Quartet.

Mauritania & Western Sahara

the modes of the moors

Daby Touré – Mauritania's new voice in Paris
Real World

The Islamic Republic of Mauritania – a huge, sparsely populated country stretching between Morocco and Senegal – is where West Africa meets the Maghreb. Contrary to stereotypical descriptions that portray this chunk of the Sahara as being "the same as it was centuries ago", Mauritania has undergone profound social, political and musical transformations over the last forty years. Most of the country is desert and a series of droughts (starting in the 1970s) has changed virtually all aspects of Mauritanian society. In 1950 about seventy percent of the population were nomads, but in 2005 only seven percent remains so, and over ninety percent lives in or around cities. Despite their recent urbanization, Mauritanians have remained deeply attached to elements of their rural cultures, as Matthew Lavoie explains. The disputed territory of Western Sahara, claimed and administered by Morocco, is also covered in this chapter as the music and culture of its Sahranis has close affinities with Mauritania.

Anne Hunt

Khalife Ould Eide Dimi mint Abba

Although Mauritania's population is small, it is not ethnically or culturally homogenous. The country's name comes from its dominant ethnic group, the **Moors** (Maures in French), who can be divided into "white" Bidans (who claim ancestry from north of the Sahara) and "black" Haratins (whose physical ancestry lies in sub-Saharan Africa). Both groups speak Hassaniya, an Arabic dialect, and more or less share the same culture. It is the nomadic culture of the Moors that give present-day Mauritania much of its unique character, but the country is also home to other ethnic groups including the **Pulaar**, **Soninke** and **Wolof** (collectively referred to as the Afro-Mauritanians), each of which has its own language, culture and musics.

The music of all these groups can be roughly divided into "folk" and "classical" styles. The first category consists of lullabies, work songs, game songs, courting songs and religious praise songs. The second category consists of the musics of the Moorish *griots*, the **iggawen**. Theirs is perhaps the most distinctly Mauritanian style, a synthesis of North African Berber, nomadic Touareg and sub-Saharan Wolof, Pulaar, Soninke and Bambara musics.

Moorish Music

In previous eras, the *iggawen* were attached to the "tents" of Bidan warrior chiefs. The Bidan consid-

ered an ear for music as a sign of nobility, and the *iggawen* were appreciated for the aesthetic refinement of their poetic and musical skills. The musicians would follow the chiefs on raids, extolling their bravery and encouraging them during battles. And they would entertain their patrons with praise songs about the great deeds of their ancestors, and the virtuous characteristics of their tribes.

Even today, the *iggawen* still perform primarily at private events. Aside from the occasional government rally, they rarely give public concerts, and neither do they release many recordings: the first professional studio in the country opened only in 2003.

Unlike *griots* in Mali, Senegal and elsewhere, the *iggawen* do not perform epic songs. The building blocks of their music are a set of five **bhor** (modes): *karr*, *vaghu*, *lekhal*, *lebyaal* and *lebteyt*. These are basically seven-note scales (they're not distinguishable by rhythm) and are played in a fixed order, with each subdivided into two parts: the so-called "black" (*lekhal*) and "white" (*lebyaal*). These two parts are different ways of playing the modes, emphasizing different degrees of the scale and varying from a legato-like style (in the black section) to a more staccato approach (in the white section).

There are different instruments for men and women. The traditional male instrument is the **tidinit**, a small hourglass-shaped lute with two melody strings and two or three shorter strings for embroidering the main tune. Today, however,

Sahrawi Sounds from the Refugee Camps

Although it was officially declared a Spanish colony in 1912, the Spanish were never able to subdue the **Bidan** tribes of the Western Sahara – a huge tract of desert between Morocco, Algeria and Mauritania. Bidan resistance increased as colonies throughout sub-Saharan Africa won their independence in the 1960s. In 1973, the resistance was organized under the political umbrella of the **Frente Popular Para la Liberacion de Sagui el-Hamra y de Rio de Oro** (the **Frente Polisario**). When the Spanish dictator Franco died in 1975, Spain lost no time in ridding itself of its colonies and the Western Sahara was hastily abandoned.

Spain's retreat did not, however, realize the Frente Polisario's dreams of an independent Western Sahara. Spurred by nationalist and economic motives (in the late 1950s immense phosphate reserves were discovered in the region), Morocco and Mauritania quickly stepped into the political vacuum, and laid claims to the area. In 1975, Morocco's King Hassan led a mass march of Moroccans to the Western Sahara, asserting their "ancestral" right to live there. That same year, approximately 200,000 **Sahrawis** (the Bidans who recognize the political authority of the Frente Polisario) left the region and settled in four camps across the border in southwest Algeria where they formed the **Sahrawi Democratic Arab Republic** (SADR), under the direction of the Frente Polisario. In 1979, after several Polisario guerrilla attacks against Nouakchott, Mauritania withdrew its claims to the Western Sahara and Morocco occupied the whole territory.

The Frente Polisario resisted Moroccan occupation as vigorously as they had the Spanish, and for sixteen years Morocco and the SADR were engaged in a bitter war. A stand off was finally reached in 1991 with a UN-brokered ceasefire. Today, the status of the Western Sahara remains unresolved. Morocco continues to populate the region with settlers from the north, and the SADR continues the struggle for an independent Western Sahara.

To the uninitiated ear, the music of the Sahrawis sounds identical to Mauritania's Moorish Bidan music – both groups play the *t'bel* (*tbal*) and the *tidinit*, for example. However, it is different in several substantial ways. First, the Sahrawi musicians do not adhere to the rules of Bidan classical music. Second, there are fundamental thematic differences in the song texts used: Sahrawi music is highly political, telling of the difficulties of life in the refugee camps, the pain of war, the need for solidarity and the longing for independence.

The fact that the music of the Sahrawis has travelled beyond the camps in the Algerian desert is thanks to the efforts of the Spanish record label **Nubenegra**. Over the past decade, starting with the release of the three-disc set *Sahrauis: Music of the Western Sahara*, Nubenegra's **Manuel Dominguez** has devoted considerable energy to spreading his passion for the music of the Sahrawis. The masterpiece among Nubenegra's half-dozen Sahrawi recordings is **Mariem Hassan**'s disc with the group **Leyoad**. Other Sahrawi musicians of note on Nubenegra include guitarist **Nayim Alal** and the late guitarist/composer **Baba Salama**.

MARIEM HASSAN-DESEOS

most male performers prefer the electric guitar. The female instrument is the **ardin**, which looks like a back-to-front *kora*. It has a body made from a large, skin-covered half gourd, through which a curved wooden pole is inserted. Between ten and fourteen strings are attached to this pole with leather thongs. Other instruments used by the *iggawen* are the **tbal** (or *t'bel*), a large kettle-drum traditionally played by women but now mostly played by gay men.

The Birth of Modern Music

The father of modern Moorish music is **Sidaty ould Abba**, born in 1924. Sidaty learned to play the *tidinit* while watching his father perform, and inherited his powerful voice from his mother. In 1958, when French radio engineers travelled to Mauritania, Sidaty reluctantly made his first recordings. Two years later, at the time of Mauritania's independence, he travelled to Senegal and recorded the new nation's national anthem. Radio made Sidaty a star, and he continued to record throughout the 1960s and early 70s, making his last recording in 1980 for the twentieth anniversary of Mauritanian independence.

Amongst *iggawen* and knowledgeable listeners, Sidaty's voice is still the benchmark against which all other singers are judged. In 1962, Sidaty brought an acoustic guitar to Mauritania and gave it to his brother **Cheikh ould Abba**, who was the first person to record traditional Moorish music on that instrument. Both brothers were part of a cohort of musicians – which also included **Sid Ahmed Bekaye ould Awa**, **Ahmed ould Dendenni**, **Isselmou ould Nevrou**, **Mennina mint Aliyen**, **Mahjouba mint Meyde** and **Ahmedou ould Meyde** – who gained national reputations through the recordings they made for Mauritanian national radio. They all performed traditional repertoire.

Born in 1958, Sidaty's daughter **Dimi mint Abba** inherited her father's powerful voice and natural talent. Ever since her 1976 debut on Mauritanian national radio, Dimi has been Mauritania's most loved singer. Well versed in the traditional repertoire, she was one of several musicians who introduced a new style of Moorish music. This small group consisted of Dimi's first and second husbands – **Seymali ould Hamed Vall** and **Khalife ould Eide** – as well as Khalife's brother **Seddoum**. The style they created, while still rooted in the inflexible rules and modes of Moorish music, was much slower than the traditional repertoire. Rhythmic diversity gave way to a languid, melodic style that highlighted rich poetic texts sung in classical Arabic (as opposed to Hassaniya).

The new style was developed over a series of duet recordings featuring Dimi with either Khalife or Seddoum, their melancholy voices accompanied only by Dimi's *ardin* and Khalife or Seddoum's guitar. Of the two brothers, Khalife (who died in 2001) was generally considered the better poet, and Seddoum the greater musician – his biting attack and slinky phrases on the guitar forming the perfect foil for his clear, soaring voice.

Dimi continues to be the most in-demand of Mauritania's *iggawen* and Seddoum is also still performing, though less frequently than in the 1980s and 90s.

Jakwar

The other great musical innovation of the 1970s was the creation of **Jheich ould Abba**, a blind virtuoso *tidinit* player from Atar, in the north. Jheich was a curious and restless musician with modern ideas. In 1976, he developed a new style and repertoire of dance music that he called **jakwar**, after the French fighter jets that often flew over northern Mauritania during the Saharan war. Like the jets, his new music was modern and fast, bringing together the rhythms of Haratine folk music and the melodic sophistication of Moorish classical music.

Jakwar was hugely popular at weddings, especially after Jheich started amplifying his *tidinit* (and replacing his female percussionists with

Malouma Mint Meidah and Mauritanian 'Pop'

Mauritania's most internationally successful artist, **Malouma mint Meidah** is the daughter of Moctar ould Meidah, one of the most respected *griots* of his generation. Although she is solidly grounded in the traditional Moorish repertoire, her music is an amalgam of Wolof, Pulaar and Moorish styles with Arabic popular music and American R&B. Malouma grew up listening to all of these musics, and has blended them into a cocktail that plays to the strengths of her limited voice. During the 1990s, she worked with her brother, keyboard-player **Arafate ould Meidah**, on a repertoire of songs that, as she says, would 'bring Mauritanian music out of its ghetto to be heard, accepted and loved throughout the world.'

In 1998 she released her first CD, *Desert of Eden*, recorded in Dakar with her brother and several Senegalese session musicians. Five years later came *Dunya*, a much stronger disc, and the first ever CD entirely recorded in Nouakchott. Produced by the Algerian jazz guitarist **Camel Zekri**, *Dunya* features Pulaar, Soninke and Wolof musicians as well as **Mohammed ould Deddah ould Choueikh**, one of the best young Moorish guitar players. Well received in Mauritania and critically acclaimed in Europe and the US, Malouma is on the brink of becoming the first Moorish artist to win a wide international audience.

men, who he found were able to fulfil their energetic role for longer). Many *iggawen* were taken with the new style – especially **Hammadi ould Nana**, who realized that the electric guitar, with its controlled distortion, was the ideal instrument for *jakwar* music, and created songs that sounded like a cross between Jimi Hendrix, Dick Dale and Ali Farka Touré.

The musical innovations of Jheich and Hammadi form the bedrock of the music performed at Moorish weddings today. Jheich died in the late 1980s, but his legacy is kept alive by his son **Idoumou ould Jheich** – and also by **Jheich ould Badou**, son of Jheich's best student, **Cheikh ould Badou**. Today, the young Idomou and Jheich perform at virtually every wedding in Nouakchott.

From 1989, much to the chagrin of her fans, Dimi moved to Morocco, where she lived until 1996. Her absence created a vacuum in the Moorish musical world that was quickly filled by a group of talented singers from Eastern Mauritania. Foremost among them was the brother and sister team of **Ooleya mint Amartichitt** and **Deye ould Amartichitt**. Their style was markedly different from Dimi's languid reveries: pushed by Deye's relentless, angular guitar playing, Ooleya's performances had the energy and power of a possession ceremony. Although Deye no longer regularly gives concerts, Ooleya remains one of the most popular performers in Mauritania.

Two other singers whose reputations were made in the early 1990s are the cousins **Mohammed ould Hambare** and **Baba ould Hambare**. The pair, who rarely perform together, are both extremely accomplished *tidinit* and guitar players. Baba is usually accompanied by his brother **Isselmou ould Hambare**, one of the best guitar players performing today.

Of all the singers who became popular in the late 1990s, none has more charisma than **Mohammed ould Chighaly**. His success was linked to that of his brother **Jheich ould Chighaly**, who often accompanied him.

When Dimi returned to Mauritania in 1996 she started performing in the energetic, rhythmic style that had become popular in her absence.

The Current Scene

Today, although Dimi, Ooleya and Mohammed ould Hambare remain the most in-demand singers, there is a new generation of musicians whose stars are rising. Two of the most promising are **Nora mint Seymali** and her younger brother **Sidi ould Seymali**, both of whom benefited greatly from the musical instruction of their father Seymali ould Hamed Vall, and from their time spent performing with Dimi. Sidi, who is without a doubt the best male singer of his generation, often performs with Idoumou well Abba – or with the 19-year-old guitar virtuoso **Sidi ould Ahmed Zeidane**, who plays a "customized" seven-string electric instrument.

Ooleya's daughter **Mneitou mint Nevrou** is destined to be one of the greatest female singers of the decades to come. Still in her early twenties, Mneitou performs with her husband **Luleide ould Dendenni**, who was Dimi's guitar player for six years. All of these young musicians perform the style of music that was popularized by Ooleya and the Hambares – rhythmic, driving music that favours the *karr*, *vaghu* and *lekhal* modes.

Special mention must also be made of **Sidaty ould Seddoum ould Abba**, an elusive and flawless singer who splits his time between Nouakchott and southern Morocco. Although largely unknown to Nouakchott's music-loving public, Sidaty is the "singers' singer", acknowledged by a majority of *iggawen* as one of the best.

Haratin Music

While the Haratins are avid fans of Moorish classical music, they also have their own folk musics. One of the most important is the religious praise song known as **medh**. In its most basic, amateur form, *medh* features a solo singer accompanied by a chorus, several percussionists and the handclapping of the audience. This is folk music, performed under the light of the moon in desert encampments. There are also several semi professional *medh* singers who accompany themselves on the *tidinit* or guitar. The most loved are **Bror**, **Aydat** and **Mohammed Guitar**.

The popular music most associated with the Haratins, however, is a unique, stripped-down version of the *jakwar* style invented by Jheich ould Abba. Gone are the five modes of the Moorish classical repertoire and the well-constructed melodies. All that's left is a trance-inducing riff, repeated until the dancers are exhausted. The two kings of this genre are **Busheme** and **Kabrou**.

Afro-Mauritanians

For centuries, the three Afro-Mauritanian ethnic groups have farmed the fertile floodplains on both side of the Senegal River valley. Aside from a few local *griots* (mostly percussionists) who perform at traditional ceremonies, the music of the Wolof, the smallest of the three communities, is best considered as the northern fringe of Senegalese **mbalax**. But the Pulaar and Soninke have their own unique styles.

Pulaar Music

In the stratified, hierarchical society of the Pulaar, there are separate musics for different occupational groups – fishermen, weavers, blacksmiths, etc. Aside from these amateur performers, there are a few *griots*, or *gawlo*. These professionals are the masters of two distinct genres: **lélé** (sung poetry extolling feminine beauty, cultural pride and love for the land) and **goumbala** (songs praising famous warriors). Both of these styles are sung to the accompaniment of the *hoddu* lute. Mauritanian masters of the genre include **Ali Hamadi Ali Sy**, **Amadou Koly**, **Amadou Tamba Diop** and **Samba Miriam Diallo**. Much of this traditional repertoire has also been transposed to the guitar by the likes of **Samba Demba Djadje Ba** and **Djombolo Ba**.

Over the course of the last few decades there as has been a folkloric revival movement. Singers, such as **Ousmane Hamady Diop** and **Samba Diye Sall** created new genres of neo-folk music, the wango and wala fendo. Inspired by the musics of Baaba Maal, there is a new generation of Pulaar artists whose traditional roots have produced modern fruits. The most popular are **Ousmane Gangue** and his group **Koode Pinal**. Less popular but far more interesting is the group **Yellitare Lenal**, which features the singer **Ousmane Guisse** and the guitar player **Seydou Sarr**. Lastly, there is **Moussa Watt**, one of the visionaries of the modern Pulaar music scene in Nouakchott.

Sounds of the Soninke

The heartland of the Soninke is the heart of the pre-colonial empire of Ghana: the lower Senegal River valley, where Senegal, Mali and Mauritania meet. On the Mauritanian side of the border the Soninke are concentrated in two regions, Gorgol and Guidimakha. As with the Pulaar, Soninke society – along with its amateur music – is divided into occupational groups. Soninke *griots*, called **gesere**, perform historical epics and praise songs; their ensembles usually consist of one musician playing the *ganbare*, a gourd lute, and one or two other musicians playing the guitar. Soninke music is built around pentatonic melodies rather than chord sequences. Its power comes from the tension created between the guitar and the *ganbare*, each weaving solos in and out of the main melodic riff.

Beside the traditional styles, Soninke musicians have also created a unique modern dance music. The popular artist **Hawa Djimera** performs with a group that includes *ganbare*, electric guitars, talking drum, bass, keyboards and backing vocals. In the last few years, the young singer **Demba Tandia** has become popular performing in a similar style.

Daby Touré is the Afro-Mauritanian musician with the most international visibility. He was born in Mauritania, but spent several formative years of his life in a small village near Kaedi (the capital city of the Gorgol region), where he was steeped in the traditional musics of the Soninke, Pulaar and Wolof. During his adolescent years in Nouakchott he discovered the musics of Dire Straits, Bob Marley and Stevie Wonder, all of which were powerful influences. In the late 1990s, he formed the group **Touré Touré** with his cousin Omar. Dissatisfied with this experience, Daby moved to Paris and spent several years working on a series of songs that expressed his diverse musical experiences. The result was his first CD, the terrific *Diam* – a disc that manages to be convincingly traditional and modern at the same time. He has, since, been recording at Real World in England, and has become highly succesful on the Paris live scene.

Daby Touré

All of Mauritania's musics are woefully under-represented on CD, but cassettes of all the musicians discussed in this chapter can be found relatively easily on the music stalls of Nouakchott. As for live music, every visit to Mauritania should include an evening spent enjoying the music of the *iggawen*. If you are planning a trip to the country and are interested in hearing some music, feel free to contact the author of this chapter at *lavoiematthew@hotmail.com*.

Moorish Music

⊙ **Le 'Medeh' par les Haratines de Mauritanie**
Club du Disque Arabe, France
The only album of Haratin folk music available. This release features field recordings of praise songs to the prophets as they are performed in desert encampments and small towns throughout the Mauritanian Sahara. This music features a solo singer, backed by a chorus of fellow villagers and several percussionists. A raw and beautiful disc featuring some of the more renowned singers of the *medh* repertoire.

⊙ **Mauritanie – Concert sous la tente**
⊙ **Griots de Mauritanie: Hodh occidental – Trarza**
⊙ **Musique Maure: Mauritanie – Ely ould Meiddah, Moktar ould Meiddah**
Prophet, France
These three discs are reissues of Charles Duvelle's field recordings from 1965 and 1969. The first is the most interesting, being the only available recording of one of the giants of the first generation of post-independence Moorish musicians: Sid Ahmed Bekaye ould Awa – the best available example of the traditional *tidinit* repertoire. The other two discs are for specialists only.

★ **Mauritanie – Musiques Traditionelles**
Club du Disque Arabe, France
An essential recording featuring some of the greatest living traditional *tidinit* players – Sid Ahmed ould Ahmed Zeidane, Youba Mokhtar ould Chighaly, Bouh ould Boba Jiddou and the late Seymali ould Hamed Vall. It's all here – solo *tidinit*, *tidinit* and *ardin*, male and female singing. The disc also features the wonderful Lalla mint Teneikmich.

⊙ **The Sounds of the Western Sahara, Mauritania – Field Recordings by Deben Bhattacharya, 1978**
Arc Music, UK
The liner notes are dreadful and the track sequencing terrible, with the modes out of sequence (imagine rearranging the movements of a Beethoven symphony). However, most of the music is fantastic. The recordings are warm, well balanced and intimate – the way Moorish music should be heard – and the singing and playing first-rate. The disc features the best available recording of a *tidinit* solo.

Dimi mint Abba

The most revered Moorish artist of the last thirty years, Dimi has a marvellous voice and remains the most in-demand artist on the Nouakchott wedding circuit. Although very enjoyable, her two CDs fail to capture the depth of her talent, so we've also listed a great solo cassette (hundreds more appear every year), plus a couple featuring Dimi with Khalife and Seddoum. Their collabora-

tions are the highpoints of the last thirty years of Moorish music.

⊙ **Moorish Music from Mauritania**
World Circuit, UK
A must-have, but also a missed opportunity. This is the best-quality recording of Dimi and Khalife together, but the material is atypical, performed in a style that the artists (or producers) presumably think will appeal to Western audiences. Dimi and Khalife's languid ornamental reveries are pushed aside and replaced with mid-tempo "songs" that do not allow the artists to stretch out.

⊙ **Musique & Chants de Mauritanie**
Auvidis, France
This intimate recording allows Dimi to showcase her expressive voice, and comes closer to the style that she is most comfortable singing – Moorish music meant for concentrated listening.

▦ **Nouadhibou**
Available on virtually all of Mauritania's music stalls, this wonderful cassette, recorded in the late 1970s, features Dimi's voice accompanied only by her *ardin* and an acoustic guitar. Moorish music does not get any better!

DIMI AND KHALIFE

▦ **El Kintawi**
The music that made both of their reputations. The pair sing their hearts out accompanied by *ardin* and electric guitar. This is a style of music that focuses almost exclusively on melodic improvisation and ornamentation. There is a steady rhythmic pulse but it's definitely for listening, not dancing.

DIMI AND SEDDOUM

▦ **Aid el Moloud**
It is very hard to choose one cassette from all the wonderful recordings these two have made together. This one is among the very best.

Ooleya mint Amartichitt

One of the best-loved Moorish singers, Ooleya popularized an intense, driving style of traditional Moorish music. A mainstay of the Nouakchott wedding circuit, she is an exciting performer who whips her audiences into a frenzy.

★ **Praise Songs**
Long
Distance, France
This is the best available recording of Moorish music. More than any other, this disc duplicates the sound of a Nouakchott wedding. All of the trademarks of Ooleya's style are captured – the dramatic melodic swoops, the rhythmic energy, the interplay between

Ooleya's voice and her sisters' backing vocals. The highest recommendation.

Nema mint Choueikh

One of the great singers of Moorish classical music, Nema has a raspy voice that frays beautifully as she pushes it to the limit.

⊙ **Ne'ma mint Choueikh: Hawl, Traditional Mauritanian music from the Trarza Region**
PAM, Germany
A long-overdue release by one of the most powerful voices in Moorish music.

Khalife ould Eide

This expressive singer with a warm and frayed voice is revered by aficionados of Moorish music. His cassettes are easy to find in Nouakchott.

Cabano 4
Khalife takes his time going through all of the modes, accompanying himself on the electric guitar. The essence of his talent distilled onto cassette.

Seddoum ould Eide

The best male singer of the 1970s and 1980s, Seddoum is well represented on Nouakchott's cassette stalls. A highlight of his many recordings is his guitar playing, which sounds vaguely like the electric mandolin playing of the south Indian musician U. Srinivas.

Savaar Sa'ida
Tabib
Two good-quality recordings that demonstrate why Seddoum is so beloved by fans of Moorish music. Be warned: the rubbery guitar playing and the yearning vocals can prove quite addictive.

Ensemble el-Moukhadrami

This ensemble brings together musicians from several of the great families of Moorish music – a rarity given that *iggawen* tend to perform only with musicians they are closely related to. The ensemble was brought to Paris to perform at the Institut du Monde Arabe.

⭐ **Chants de Griots**
Institut du Monde Arabe, France
The perfect introduction to Moorish music, this disc presents the five modes (and their sub-modes) played in their correct order. This is an example of what you can expect to hear if you invite *iggawen* to perform in your living room. Musical intimacy, a variety of tempos – it's all here.

Malouma mint Meidah

The first "crossover" star of the Moorish music world, Malouma has created a style of Moorish pop that highlights the strengths of her limited voice.

⊙ **Dunya**
Marabi, France
The first CD recorded entirely in Mauritania, this is much stronger than Malouma's debut. Despite a few tracks marred by schmaltzy rock guitars, it features well-constructed songs and tight arrangements that allow her voice to shine. The album displays Malouma's diverse musical passions, but remains identifiably Moorish. This is classical Mauritanian music with the rough edges bevelled off.

Nora mint Seymaly

The daughter of Seymali ould Hamed Vall, Nora is one of the best of the new generation of Moorish singers. She performs almost exclusively with her husband Jheich ould Chighaly.

⊙ **Tarabe**
Elzo Productions, Mauritania
This release does not represent Nora's typical sound. Indeed, it attempts to push the boundaries of Moorish classical music. Whereas Malouma's sound veers towards easy listening, this has hints of contemporary folk-rock. The results are hit-and-miss, but definitely worth checking out. Nora's voice sounds fantastic and Jheich's guitar is biting and exciting.

Afro-Mauritanian Music

Recordings of Pulaar music are most easily found at the specialist cassette stalls in Nouakchott's Cinquième and Sixième neighbourhoods. One of the best is Standard Brakna near the Marche Sixième. The best source for Soninke Music, meanwhile, is Camara Productions, who have three stores in Paris and one in Bamako, and offer recordings of many great artists. Unfortunately, recordings of Hawa Djimera, one of Mauritania's most-loved Soninke musicians, are very difficult to come by.

Mansour Seck

Mansour Seck, a talented Pulaar guitarist and singer, has become known throughout the world thanks to his long - standing partnership with Baaba Maal (whose best recordings were inspired by the Pulaar music).

⭐ **N'der Fouta Tooro Vol 1 & 2**
Stern's Africa, UK
These two fantastic releases from the masters of Pulaar neo-folk are the best available recordings of the music that drives fans crazy on both sides of the Senegal River valley. The ensemble features acoustic guitar, *kora*, *hoddu*, percussion and the voices of Mansour Seck, Ousmane Hamady Diop and Baaba Maal.

Daby Touré

A member of the family that gave the world the 1980s African supergroup Toure Kunda, Daby basked in Mauritania's multi-ethnic musical stew before moving to Paris with his father in 1989.

⭐ **Diam**
Real World, UK
One of the most refreshing Mauritanian discs in recent years. Most of the tracks are built around Daby's voice and guitar, with only sparse percussion accompaniment. His songs draw you in with their strong melodies, lilting rhythms and memorable choruses. Daby is a truly modern artist but his body of songs retain the depth of the traditional repertoire.

Sahrawi Music

⊙ **Sahrauis: Music of the Western Sahara**
Nubenegra, Spain
The 3-disc set that introduced the wider world to the music of the Sahrawis. The first disc features women singers (including the great Mariem Hassan) accompanied by the *tidinit*, *t'bel* and acoustic and electric guitars. The second and most interesting disc features a cross-section of contemporary Sahrawi music, with highlights in the tracks featuring Nayim Alal, and the third features political songs by the group Martir Luali.

PLAYLIST
Mauritania &
Western Sahara

1 **MEMA (MODE KARR) Ooleya mint Amartichitt** from *Praise Songs*
Featuring Ooleya's powerful voice, this number packs all of the intensity and melodic drama of Moorish music into six minutes of musical bliss.

2 **LEBLEIDA (MODE KARR) Malouma** from *Dunya*
A great version of one of the most famous Moorish dance melodies, featuring the electric guitar of Mohammed ould Ddah ould Choueikh.

3 **BEYT HARB (MODE VAGHU) Ensemble El-Moukhadrami** from *Chants des Griots*
The opening of the mode *vaghu* delivered by the wonderful voice of Fatma mint Siyyed. A beautiful example of a Moorish praise song.

4 **VAGHU (MODE VAGHU) Lalla mint Teneikmich** from *Mauritanie – Musiques Traditionelles*
The only available recording of one of the best living singers of Moorish roots music – a voice from another century.

5 **ZRAGUE EL BILLAWI Unknown Artist** from *The Sounds of the Western Sahara, Mauritania*
A beautiful, intimate recording of solo *tidinit*, probably performed by the late great Seymali ould Hamed Vall.

6 **SAWT ELFAN (ART'S PLUME) Dimi mint Abba** from *Moorish Music from Mauritania*
Dimi stretches her voice in a number that betrays her love for the music of Umm Kulthum. The mode is *lekhal*.

7 **LEYIN LEBYADH Unknown Artists** from *The Sounds of the Western Sahara, Mauritania*
An intimate recording in that captures all of the nostalgic power of the "minor" *liyyen* mode, probably featuring the *tidinit* and voice of Seymali ould Hamed Vall.

8 **LIBTEITE Sid Ahmed ould Ahmed Zeidane** from *Mauritanie – Musiques Traditionelles*
Melodic, meditative music in *lebteyt* mode that draws you in deeper with every listen; played on the *tidinit* by one of the instrument's living masters.

9 **SOUKABE LEYDAM Ousmane Hamady Diop** from *Mansour Seck, N'der Fouta Tooro Vol 1*
Even if you don't understand the lyrics you can feel the "weight" of this Pulaar acoustic roots music.

10 **IRIS Daby Touré** from *Diam*
A catchy melody and chorus, with sparse musical accompaniment. Daby's genius distilled in one perfect song.

★ **Medej: Cantos Antiguos Saharauis**
Nubenegra, Spain
A wonderful disc of religious praise songs featuring many of the singers introduced on the above box-set. The album features a half-dozen terrific singers (including Mariem Hassan) accompanied by fervent encouragement, handclapping, t'bel, tidinit and guitar.

Mariem Hassan

The most outstanding vocal talent to emerge from Nubenegra's Sahrawis recording project, Hassan has a wail that rises out of her diaphragm and knocks you between the eyes. Homesickness was never conveyed in music with such force.

★ **Mariem Hassan con Leyoad**
Nubenegra, Spain
An enthralling and beautiful disc featuring the core of the Nubenegra Sahraouis stable, guitarists Nayim Alal and Baba Salama.

⊙ **Deseos**
Nubenegra, Spain
As good as her previous recording with Leyoad, this 2005 disc features Mariem with two guitar players, a trap drummer and backing vocals. It strips the music of the Sahraoui down to the essentials: Mariem's powerful voice and nervous guitars.

MAURITANIA & WESTERN SAHARA

Morocco

a basic expression of life

Festival time: Berber musicians on the tourbus
Neil Van der Linden

Wherever you go in Morocco you're likely to hear music. It is the basic expression of the country's folk culture – indeed, to many of the illiterate country people it is the sole expression. Traditional music remains very much a part of life, evident at every celebration, and most spectacularly so in the mountains, where long and ancient pieces are performed by the entire communities of Berber villages, while in the cities there is a strong classical tradition handed down by the Arabs from the east and Andalusian Spain. Since the 1970s Morocco has also spawned a powerful indigenous strain of roots-fusion music, ranging from fierce protest songs to innocuous good-time dance music – sounds that you'll hear blaring out of taxi radios, bus station PA systems and ghetto-blasters in shops, cafés and restaurants. David Muddyman, Andy Morgan and Matthew Lavoie soak up each of the country's scenes.

Although the most ubiquitous musical phenomenon in Morocco is the amplified sound of a *muezzin* calling the faithful to prayer, most music in the country is performed for the sake of entertainment rather than religion. At every weekly *souk*, or market, you will find musicians playing in a patch of shade, or a stall blasting out the cassettes they have on sale. In the evenings, many cafés also feature musicians, particularly during the long nights of Ramadan. Television also plays its part, with two weekly programmes devoted to music, and the radio stations broadcast a variety of different styles. In fact, thanks to the huge penetration of satellite dishes and cybercafés in recent years, Morocco has opened its ears to many of the same sounds that hold sway in Europe and North America – rap in particular.

For all this, perhaps the most rewarding way of plunging into Moroccan's astoundingly rich traditional and folk music culture is via its festivals (see box overleaf) – including the often wild **moussems**, of which more below.

Berber Music

Spread throughout North Africa, the **Berber** are the first known inhabitants of its northwestern corner. Over the course of centuries, the Berber monopolized the Saharan trade in salt, gold and slaves, spreading their culture, language and politics throughout the region. The overwhelming majority of Moroccans have Berber "blood", and Berber culture forms the bedrock of Moroccan civilization. Of the various Berber cultures, the

Tachelhit speakers of the High Atlas (the Chleuh) and of the Souss valley, east of Agadir, have particularly rich musical traditions.

There are three main categories of Berber music: village music, ritual music and music performed by professionals. All are quite distinct from Arab-influenced forms in their rhythms, tunings, instruments and sounds.

Village music is essentially a collective performance. Men and women of the entire village will assemble on festive occasions to dance and sing together. The best-known dances are the **ahouache**, in the eastern High Atlas, and the **ahidus**, performed in the Middle Atlas. In each, drum (*bendir*) and flute (*nai*) are the only instruments used. The dance begins with a chanted prayer, to which the dancers respond in chorus, the men and women gathered in the open air, in a large ring around the musicians. The *ahouache* is normally performed at night in the patio of the kasbah; the dance is so complicated that the musicians meet to prepare for it in a special group called a *laamt*. A variation on the *ahouache* is the *bumzdi*, in which one or more soloists perform a series of poetic improvisations. Over the last twenty years, thanks to cassette recordings, several masters of the *bumzdi*, including **Raïs Ajmaa Lahcen** and **Raïs Ihya**, have become nationally known, while **Muha Hussein** and **Imin Tanoute** are the biggest names in *ahouache*.

Ritual music is rarely absent from any rites connected with the agricultural calendar – such as *moussems* – or major events in the life of individuals, such as marriage. It may also be called upon to help deal with *djnoun*, or evil spirits, or to encourage rainfall. Flutes and drums are usually

Neil Van der Linden

Ahouache master Muha Hussein

Festivals in Morocco

Given Morocco's rich and diverse musical culture, it can be frustratingly difficult for visitors to enjoy live music. Even in large cities such as Marrakech and Casablanca there are very few nightclubs that feature interesting live music – just plenty of pedestrian tourist-bait groups. The majority of musical performances in Morocco are still invitation-only events such as weddings, baptisms and private concerts. The best bet is to plan a trip around a **moussem** (regional festival) or a music festival. There are currently over a dozen worthwhile annual festivals that feature many different styles of music. For a list consult *www.minculture.gov.ma*.

The most-established and best-organized are the **Essaouira Gnawa Festival** and the **Fes Festival of Sacred Music**, which represent the two extremes of the spectrum. The former, held every June in the charming seaside town of Essaouira, has the festive atmosphere of a *moussem* and in recent years the three-day festival has drawn over 300,000 visitors. As the name suggests, the focus is Gnawa music and most of the concerts are free. Every year, the organizers invite a half-dozen World Music artists (ranging from Jaleo to Ali Farka Touré), a half-dozen Gnawa *ma'alem*s, a handful of jazz musicians, and several popular Moroccan groups. The festival always ends with a monster jam session featuring as many *ma'alem*s as can be coaxed on to the stage. Fans with a little extra cash can also enjoy intimate Gnawa performances held in the courtyards of several traditional Moroccan homes.

Sufi group at Fes Festival

If the Essaouira festival is increasingly becoming the Moroccan Woodstock, the Festival of Sacred Music in Fes remains a more exclusive affair. Held over a week in early June, it draws a large foreign crowd and the cream of Moroccan high society. Although every year there are several wonderful concerts of Moroccan music (usually *al-âla*, or explicitly religious music), the majority of the artists now programmed are proven commodities on the international festival circuit – think Ravi Shankar, Youssou N'Dour, Gilberto Gil et al. – and prices are on a par with festivals in Europe and the US.

Other festivals of interest include the annual **Milhûn festival** and the **Gharnati festival** held in Oujda. But the musical event of the year is perhaps **July 30**, the day on which Moroccans celebrate their allegiance to their king. This is the one day in the year where Moroccan music of all styles can be easily and bountifully enjoyed. In every city there are free concerts in concert halls, schools, parks and roadside tents.

Matthew Lavoie

Gnawa group at Essaouria Festival

the sole instruments, along with much rhythmic handclapping, although professional musicians are used for certain events.

The **professional musicians**, or *imdyazn*, of the Atlas mountains are itinerant, travelling during the summer, usually in groups of four. The leader of the group is called the *amydaz*, or poet. He presents his poems, which are usually improvised and give news of national or world affairs, in the village square. The poet may be accompanied by one or two members of the group on drums and *rabab* (a single-string fiddle) and by another known as the *bou oughanim*. The latter is a reed player, throwing out melodies on a double clarinet, and also acting as the group's clown. *Imdyazn* are found in many weekly *souks* in the Atlas.

A group of women Berber musicians from the Houara region near Taroudant have caused an international sensation over the last decade with their strident vocals and loping rhythms driven by metallic percussion. Originally known as **Bnet Houriyat**, "The women of the Houara", they have recently changed their name to **Bnet Marrakech**. They are the "stage" incarnation of a musical culture that still exists at a grass-roots level throughout Morocco.

Rwaïs

Groups of **Chleuh Berber** professional musicians, from the Souss valley, are known as **rwaïs**. A *rwaï* worthy of the name will not only know all the music for any particular celebration, but have its own repertoire of songs – again commenting on current events – and be able to improvise. A *rwaï* ensemble can be made up of a single-string *rabab*, one or two *lotars* (lutes) and sometimes *nakous* (cymbals), together with a number of singers. The leader of the group, the **raïs**, is in charge of the poetry, music and choreography of the performance. Fine clothes, jewels and elaborate gestures also have an important part to play in this ancient rural form of musical theatre. Female *rwaï* performers form their own ensembles of **raysat**, mainly comprising singers and *lotar* players.

A *rwaï* performance will start with the *astara*, an instrumental prelude played on *rabab*, giving the basic notes of the melodies that follow (this also makes it possible for the other instruments to tune to the *rabab*). The *astara* is not in any particular rhythm. Then comes the *amarg*, the sung poetry which forms the heart of the piece. This is followed by the *ammussu*, a sort of choreographed overture; the *tamssust*, a lively song; the *aberdag*, or dance; and finally the *tabbayt*, a finale characterized by an acceleration in rhythm and an abrupt end.

Apart from the *astara* and *tabbayt*, the elements of a performance may appear in a different order, the arrangement and duration of the various parts being decided upon freely by the *rwaïs*.

The first *rwaï* to make a professional studio recording, in the 1940s, was **Hadj Belaid**, a musician who travelled throughout North Africa and the Middle East and is still revered for his poetry. Other greats of the 1950s and 60s include **Raïs Lhoucine Achtouk** and **Raïs Brahim Chtouki**. The major talents of subsequent generations include **Hadj Mohammed Damciri**, **Raïs Ahmed Bazmaouen** and **Raïs M'Barek Aissar**. Current favourites include **Aarab Aatigui**, the magnificent female star **Raysa Fatima Taabamrant**, plus **Fatima Tahihit** and **Aicha Tachinouit**.

Andalous Music

Morocco's classical music comes from the **Arab-Andalusian tradition** and is to be found, with variations, throughout North Africa. It is thought to have evolved around a thousand years ago in Cordoba, Spain (then ruled by the Moors), and its invention is usually credited to an outstanding musician from Baghdad called **Ziryab**, aka "Le Merle" or "The Blackbird". One of his greatest innovations was the founding of the classical suite called **nuba**, which forms what is now known as andalous music, or **al-âla**. There are, in addition, two other classical traditions, **milhûn** and **gharnati**, each with a distinctive style and form.

Andalous music, far from being a scholastic relic, is very much alive. But it remains a rather elite music form, and its regular slots on national TV have recently started to give way to "lower-class" Berber musics.

The Nuba

Originally there were twenty-four *nuba* linked with the hours in the day, but only four full and seven fragmentary *nuba* have been preserved in the Moroccan tradition. Complete *nuba* last between six and seven hours (they're rarely performed in one sitting) and are usually chosen to fit the time of day or occasion. Each *nuba* is divided into five main parts, or *mizan*, of differing durations and rhythms – much like a Western classical suite. If a whole *nuba* were being performed then the five rhythms would be used in order: *basît* (6/4), *qaum wa nusf* (8/4), *darj* (4/4), *btâyhi* (8/4) and *quddâm* (3/4 or 6/8).

Traditionally, each *mizan* begins with instrumental preludes – *bughya*, *m'shaliya* and *tuashia* –

which are followed by a number of *sanaa* (songs). There can be as many as twenty *sanaa* within a given *mizan* although for shorter performances an orchestra may play only three or four before proceeding to the next rhythm. Some *sanaa* deal are religious, glorifying the Prophet and divine laws. Others, however, deal with subjects generally considered taboo in Islamic society, perhaps signifying pre-Islamic, nomadic roots. The fourteenth *sanaa* of the *basît mizan* in **Al-'Ushshâq**, for example, tells of the desire for clarity following a night given over to the pleasures of sex and wine:

> *Obscure night steals away*
> *Chased by the light*
> *that sweeps up shadows*
> *The candle wax runs*
> *as if weeping tears of farewell*
> *And then, suddenly and behold,*
> *the birds are singing*
> *and the flowers smile at us.*

When the Arabs were driven out of Spain, which they had known as Al-Andalus, the different musical schools were dispersed across Morocco. The school of Valencia was re-established in Fes, for example, and that of Granada in Toua and Chefchaouen. Centuries on, the most famous **andalous orchestras** are those of **Fes** (led by Mohammed Briouel), **Rabat** (led by Haj Mohamed Toud) and **Tetouan**.

Many fans of andalous music mourn the passing of the "golden age" in the 1970s and 80s, when a trio of masters – **Abdelkrim Raïs**, **Abdesadak Chekara** and **Moulay Ahmed Loukili** – led the Fes, Rabat and Tetouan orchestras. But it seems that this venerable style, although ancient, is also very resilient, and it lives on in the new century. Two singers, in particular, have done a great deal to encourage the devotees of *al-âla*: **Hadj Mohammed Bajdoub** and **Abderrahim Souiri**. Their many cassettes are continuing proof that the music is alive and well.

A typical andalous orchestra uses the following instruments: *rabab* (fiddle), *oud* (lute), *kamenjah* (violin-style instrument played vertically on the knee), *qanun* (zither), *darbuka* (metal or pottery goblet drums) and *taarija* (tambourine). Clarinets, flutes, banjos and pianos have all been used from time to time with varying degrees of success.

Milhûn

Milhûn – a semiclassical form of sung poetry – is much less dry than such a definition would suggest. Musically, it has many links with andalous music, having adopted the same modes as *al-âla* orchestras and, like them, uses string instruments and percussion. But the result can be quite wild and danceable – and, unlike andalous music, which has always been the province of an educated elite, *milhûn* was originally the poetic expression of artisans and traders. Indeed, many of the great *milhûn* singers of the twentieth century began their lives as cobblers, tanners, bakers or doughnut sellers.

The *milhûn* suite comprises two parts: the *taqsim* (overture) and the *qassida* (sung poems). The *taqsim* is played on the *oud* or violin in free rhythm and introduces the mode in which the piece is set. The *qassida* is divided into three parts: *al-aqsâm* (verses sung solo), *al-harba* (refrains sung by the chorus) and *al-drîdka* (a chorus where the rhythm gathers speed and eventually announces the end of the piece). The words of the *qassida* can be taken from anywhere – folk poetry, mystical poems or nonsense lines used for rhythm.

Al-Thami Lamdaghri, who died in 1856, was one of the greatest *milhûn* composers. He is credited with many well-known songs including "Al-Gnawi" (The Black Slave), "Aliq Al-Masrûh" (The Radiant Beauty) and "Al-'Arsa" (The Garden of Delight).

The **milhûn orchestra** generally consists of *oud*, *kamenjah*, *swisen* (a small, high-pitched folk lute), the *hadjouj* (a bass *swisen*), *taarija*, *darbuka* and *handqa* (small brass cymbals), plus a number of singers. The most renowned singer of recent times was **El Hadj Houcine Toulali**, who dominated the vibrant *milhûn* scene in Meknes until his death in 1999. Other singers of note are **Abdelkrim** and **Saïd Guennoun** of Fes, **Haj Husseïn** and **Abdallah Ramdani** of Meknes,

Inédit/Auvadis

The Gharnati Ensemble of Rabat

Moussem Madness

The place to hear the wildest Moroccan music is a **moussem** – a festival devoted to the memory of a holy man. Many are held during *mouloud*, the annual celebration of the Prophet's Birthday (the date of which changes according to the lunar calendar). One of the biggest *moussems* in the country is that of **Sheikh Al-Kamel**, which sees thousands of Aissawa Sufis flock to the shrine of the fifteenth-century saint Sidi Ben Aissa. One of the main Sufi brotherhoods of Morocco, the Aissawa have spectacular music with ceremonial trumpets, *ghaita*s (shawms) and barrel drums.

The event is half-pilgrimage, half-festival, with screaming wooden oboes and the thunder of drums, smoking kebabs, freak shows and a fun fair, and thousands of hooded *jalaba*s as far as the eye can see. Aissawa groups from the whole country process to the shrine, led by ceremonial flags. As bands reach the shrine they bow their flags in veneration. Devotees and dancers form a ring around the musicians. From time to time a woman will enter the ring and be drawn by a female member of the troupe into a sort of trance. Eyes roll, heads shake and limbs flail. Members of the Moroccan Red Crescent are on hand with roll-up stretchers and take several semi-conscious bodies away. 'Do you have events like this in England?' asks one local participant. Not really. 'Life is easy there,' he suggests, 'we have many problems and everyone has things they need to escape from for a while.'

Away from the processional area there's a crowd gathered in the shade of a mulberry tree where some serious trance business is under way. There's a flute player, frame drummers and a wizened woman with tattoos on her face collecting donations from the crowd. Suddenly a woman appears and lies right down in front of the band. It's an act of total submission as she pushes herself into the dusty ground. Then she kneels up and faces the musicians. Two companions hold her as she sways from side to side until she goes still with her mouth jibbering silently. They try different rhythms on her and by the end, she seems calmer – at least as she's led away.

There's a class-based snobbery that runs through Moroccan Sufism. These **Jilaliate musicians** are often dismissed by intellectuals for their commercialism, flamboyant music and popular appeal. But the power of the music and the obvious need for their services is overwhelming. This is popular spirituality and medicine at work, Moroccan style.

Simon Broughton

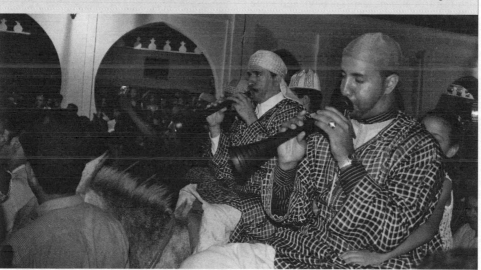

Muhammad Berrahal and **Muhammad Bensaïd** of Salé and the brothers **Mohammed** and **Ahmed Amenzou** from Marrakech.

Over the last ten years several women have started to sing *milhûn*. The first to break the gen-der barrier was **Touria Hadraoui**, who is also an accomplished novelist. Then came the highly talented **Majda Yahyaoui** (a student of Toulali's) and **Sanaa Marahati**, whom many consider the future of the genre.

Gharnati

Gharnati, the third music of Arab-Andalusian tradition, derives from the Arabic word for Granada, the great city of Arab Andalusia. It is mainly played in Algeria but there are two important centres in Morocco: Rabat and Oujda (near the Algerian border). As with *al-âla*, it is arranged in suites or *nuba*, of which there exist twelve complete and four unfinished.

The *gharnati* orchestra consists of plucked and bowed instruments together with percussion: the usual ouds and *kamenjah*s supplemented by banjo, mandolin and *kwîtra* (Algerian lute).

Sufi and Gnawa Music

The Islamic **Sufi brotherhoods**, or *tarika*s, see music as a means of getting closer to Allah. The aim is for those present to reach a state of mystical ecstasy. In a private nocturnal ceremony called the **hadra**, the Sufi brothers attain a trance by chanting the name of Allah or dancing in a ring holding hands. The songs and music are irregular in rhythm and quicken to an abrupt end. Sufi music also features at *moussem* (see box), and some brotherhoods play for alms in households that want to gain the favour of their patron saint.

The **Jilala Brotherhood** (whose name is known to many via the roots-fusion group **Jil Jilala**) are the devotees of Moulay Abdelkader Jilal. Their music is deeply hypnotic and mysterious, carried forward by the plaintive cycling of the *qsbah* flute and the mesmeric beats of *bendir* frame drums. Other brotherhoods still practising their own brand of "ethnopsychic" healing in various parts of Morocco are the **Hamadcha** – followers of Sidi Ben Ali Hamduj and Sidi Ahmed Dghughi – and the musically peerless **Aissawa** from Meknes, who venerate the sixteenth-century holy man Sidi Mohamed Ben Aïssa.

Gnawa

The **Gnawa** – or **Gnaoua** – brotherhood is a religious confraternity whose members are descendants of slaves, servants and prisoners brought from across the Sahara by the Arabs. They have devotees all over Morocco, though the strongest concentrations are in the south.

The brotherhood's members claim spiritual descent from **Sidi Bilal**, an Ethiopian who was the Prophet's first *muezzin*. Most Gnawa ceremonies, or *lilas* (so called because they usually last all night long, *lil* being Arabic for "night") are held to placate spirits who are inhabiting a person or place. These rites – which are often held to help people with mental disturbance or scorpion stings – have their origins in sub-Saharan Africa, and this can be detected in the music. The principal instrument, the *gimbri* or *sentir*, is a long-necked lute almost identical to instruments found in West Africa. The other characteristic sound of Gnawa music is the *garagab*, a pair of metal castanets, which beat out a trance-like rhythm.

Each Gnawa troupe is led by a *ma'alem* (master), who plays the *gimbri* and sings the main vocal parts. The most famous living examples are **Mustapha Baqbou** and **Mahmoud Guinea**, both of whom have recorded with Bill Laswell and many other international names. Both belong to great dynasties of Gnawa *ma'almin*, and indeed there are many who still assert that you can only be born a Gnawi, and never made into one.

The adaptability of Gnawa music is one of its most remarkable qualities, and in recent times it has been blended with many other forms including jazz, rock, funk, hip-hop, drum'n'bass.

Jak Kilby

Gimbri player Mustapha Baqbou

From Egypt to Morocco ... and Back

Ever since the introduction of phonographs to Morocco, music fans throughout the country have avidly listened to the latest sounds coming out of Cairo. Egyptian popular song in classical Arabic – by the likes of **Umm Kulthum** and **Mohamed Abdalwahab** – had a profound impact on many Moroccan musicians, prompting many to produce music in the same vein. It's hard to identify any distinctly local traits in the results, but Morocco can be proud of several wonderful singers in the style, some of whom have become appreciated throughout the region and the Middle East. The first great star was **Houcine Slaoui**, whose 1940s recordings were loved throughout North Africa. Then came **Ahmed Bidaoui** (in the 1950s) and the extremely successful **Abdelhadi Belkhayat** and **Abdelwahab Doukkali**, both of whom had thirty-year careers. Various female singers inspired by Umm Kulthum and Lebanese star Fairuz also made names for themselves, the most memorable being **Latifa Amel** and **Bahija Idriss** (both popular in the 1960s) and **Samira Said**, who has won popularity throughout the Middle East in the last two decades.

Chaabi and Fusion

A vague term, which means simply "popular", **chaabi** refers to a variety of musical styles, just as the term "pop music" does in the West.

Al'aïta

The oldest of the main *chaabi* styles is **al'aïta**, the music of the Arabic-speaking rural populations of Morocco's Atlantic coast. The music – performed during private and public celebrations as well as in concert – is usually sung in Darija (Moroccan colloquial Arabic) and tells of love, loss, lust and the realities of daily life. *Al'aïta* music consists of two parts. First comes the *lafrash*, which sets the mood with a slow instrumental prelude (usually played on the violin) and several verses sung in free rhythm. Then the music shifts gear and the band kicks into the *lahsab*, a highly syncopated dance segment that lasts as long as the crowd can take the jackhammer rhythm.

At its most basic, an *al'aïta* ensemble consists of a male or female vocalist, a violinist, several percussionists (on tiny hand-held *taarija* drums, *bendir* frame drums and clay *darbukas*) and female backing vocalists. Some groups also feature the *oud* or *lotar*. The best-loved *al'aïta* singers over the years have included **Bouchaïb el Bidaoui**, **Hajja Hamdaouia**, **Fatna bent Lhoucine**, **Khadija el Bidawia**, **Hajib** and **El Hadj Abdelmoghit**. None of these singers, however, can match the rhythmic intensity and precision of the six-fingered (literally) violinist **Abdelaziz Staati**.

Over the last few decades, as the rural populations of the Atlantic coast have settled in Rabat and Casablanca, a new style of "synthetic" *al'aïta* has become popular. This is the music that is most often heard blaring out of cassette stalls in the medinas of Casablanca and Rabat. It shares the same basic structure as the older style but features keyboards, electric guitars and drum machines alongside the traditional instruments. The best of these groups, cranking through a deafening sound system, can generate as much excitement as their roots counterparts. The heavy hitters include **Orchestre Jedouane**, **Orchestre Senhaji**, **Khalid Bennani** and **Moustapha Bourgogne**.

Roots-Fusion

During the 1970s, a more sophisticated version of Moroccan music began to emerge, with groups setting themselves up in competition with the commercial Egyptian and Lebanese music that dominated the scene at the time (see box above). These groups usually featured *hadjuj* (bass *gimbri*), lute and percussion (*bendirs*, *darbukas* and *tantans*) – plus bouzoukis, banjos, congas and electric guitars when the group in question could afford them. The work of these **roots-fusion** artists combined Berber music with elements of Arab *milhûn*, Sufi ritual, Gnawa rhythms, Western pop and rock, reggae, rap and occasionally political lyrics.

The new genre was a major revolution in taste and outlook whose influence can still very much be felt today. Indeed, if it were not for the fact the the movement's heyday was in 1970s – and thus predated the World Music explosion – then Moroccon music, rather than Algerian *rai*, might have become the international face of North African pop. The three leading lights of the scene were Nass el Ghiwane, Jil Jilala and Lemchaheb.

Nass el Ghiwane, the most politicized of all the roots-fusion groups, laid great emphasis on their lyrics, which lambasted lazy government officials

Jak Kilby

Jil Jalala

and bemoaned social injustices. The band was originally a five-piece (banjo, *hadjuj*, *bendir*, *tantan*, *darbuka*) fronted by the powerfully melodic voice of **Boujemaa Hagour**, but after Hagour died in the mid-1970s (at the hand of the Moroccan secret services according to some) **Omar Sayid** took the lead. In 1998 another key member, Larbi Batma, died, but the group is still touring and giving fiery energetic performances, albeit without any new recorded material.

Jil Jilala was formed in 1972 as a Sufi theatre group devoted to their leader, Jilali. Their music is based on the *milhûn* style, using poetry as starting point. More recently they have worked with Gnawa rhythms and occasionally included a *ghaita* in their line-up. The group's central figures are conga player and lyricist **Mohammed Darhem** and **Hassan Mista**, who plays an amplified fretless *buzuk*. The pair are accompanied by the *bendirs* of Moulai Tahar and Abdel Krim Al-Kasbaji, and have recorded with a variety of *hadjuj* players, including **Mustapha Baqbou**.

The third major roots-fusion group, **Lemchaheb** is probably the Moroccan band best known abroad, through its work with the German band **Dissidenten**. Featuring the virtuoso guitar and *buzuk* of Lamrani Moulay Cherif, they are also the most Westernized of the three big names.

Another important group is **Tagada**, formed in the 1970s by the Gnawa *maâlem* Chérif Regragui, from Essaouira. Their popularity among the cognoscenti almost rivalled that of Nass el Ghiwane at one time. Although they have never had a Euro-

pean record release, Tagada is still very active and well worth catching live.

Berber Power

The roots-fusion movement in turn inspired a new generation of Berber musicians, foremost among them the group **Izanzaren** from Agadir. Started in 1974, the group was the first of the "Berber Power" groups to sing, in Tachelhit, about the cultural discrimination suffered by Morocco's Berber populations. Musically, Izanzaren sound similar to Nass el Ghiwane, but rhythmically they have a bit more punch. Other artists performing in a similar style include **Archach**, **Oudaden** and **Inrzaf**.

One of the most creative of the new breed of Berber singers is **Ammouri M'barek**, who grew up listening to French popular music and American rock'n'roll. If Nass el Ghiwane are often called the Moroccan Rolling Stones, M'barek is the Moroccan Bob Dylan. His first musical experience was singing in a French-pop covers band, but in the late 1960s he switched to Arabic. Since the 1970s, he has created some of the most innovative Berber music – first with the group **Usman** and then as a solo artist.

In the 1980s, another generation of groups emerged, combining traditional and modern influences, this time based in Marrakech but concentrating on Gnawa rhythms. The most successful of these has been **Muluk El Hwa** (Demon of Love), a group of Berbers who used to play in the Djemaa El Fna in Marrakech. They have recorded their all-

Najat Aatabou

Najat Aatabou is a roots-fusion singer who has been something of sensation in Europe, though never achieved the same popularity at home. She is proud of her Berber heritage and uses traditional Berber rhythms, though she now sings in Arabic or French and her ensemble sometimes use electric instruments – which blend beautifully with more traditional *oud* and *bendir*. Her songs often address inequalities between men and women, though she is equally capable of writing love songs.

Aatabou's first release, the eye-opening *J'en ai marre* (I am Sick of It), sold 450,000 copies. Her second cassette, *Shouffi Rhirou* (Look for Another Lover), and every subsequent release have sold more than half a million copies, and she is now a huge star throughout the Maghreb and can fill large venues in Europe. A

wonderful compilation CD, *The Voice of the Atlas* (which includes "Shouffi Rhirou"), is available on the GlobeStyle label.

Najat is not the only Berber singer from the Middle Atlas plains to have "crossed over" to Darija (Moroccan Arabic) audiences. Born in Khenifra, **Mohammed Rouicha** is probably the most popular Berber musician from the Middle Atlas. Rouicha is a deeply moving player of the *outar*, an instrument similar to the Chleuh *lotar* but with a bigger body and thicker neck. Since he started performing in the 1970s, he has recorded over thirty cassettes. He sings, in both Darija and Tamazight, of the plight of Morocco's rural poor. Accompanied by two driving percussionists and strident background vocalists, Rouicha is about as "roots" as music gets.

acoustic line-up with the Spanish group **Al Tall**, creating an album that fused medieval Valencian music and Arabic poetry from Andalusia. One of their contemporaries, **Nass el Hal**, offer two shows – one with *buzuk* and violin, the other with drum-kit and electric guitar.

International Fusion

Morocco is an ideal starting point for all kinds of fusion experiments. From the 1960s on, such disparate figures as Brian Jones, Ornette Coleman, Jimi Hendrix and Pharaoh Sanders have been attracted by its rhythms, and the collaborations have come thick and fast since. One of the earliest attempts to combine Moroccan music with European electronic sounds was made by the German group **Dissidenten**. Beside their rocky collaboration with Lemchaheb, the band worked with star *nai* player **Mohammed Zain** and Gnawa *gimbri* players Abdellah el Gourd, Abderkader Zefzaf and Abdalla Haroch.

Since then, all manner of Moroccan sounds have been successfully blended with reggae, funk, hip-hop, house and drum bass by groups such as

Gnawa Diffusion and **Gnawa N'joum Experience** from France, **Gnawa Impulse** from Germany and **MoMo** from London. UK-based Moroccan-born producer **U-cef** has also been a pioneer in this field, while in Belgium the madcap Flemish globetrotters **Think Of One** have recorded enjoyable, accessible and authentic Moroccan sounds with various musicians.

Other names to look out for include **Yosefa Dahari**, who has worked with David Rosenthal and Gil Freeman on the Worldly Dance Music label; **Hassan Hakmoun**, a New York-based Gnawa musician who mixes it in the city with all manner of ideas and musicians; and **Bachir Attar**, leader of the Jajouka troupe, and again New York-based these days, who has recorded with jazz saxophonist Maceo Parker under the direction of avant-garde funk producer **Bill Laswell** and with the UK-Asian guru Talvin Singh.

Laswell has also been involved in production work with the group **Aisha Kandisha's Jarring Effects** (AKJE), who mix Moroccan trance sounds with rock, hip-hop and techno. They released an amazing debut CD, *Buya*, in 1991 on the Swiss Barbarity label, and followed up with the techno-

f Roots Archive

Aisha Kandisha's Jarring Effects

driven, Laswell-produced *Shabeesation*. They have an attitude as radical as their music – akin to, say, Cypress Hill or Ice Cube. Their name refers to a female spirit, whose very mention is taboo, and their lyrics question Moroccan social and religious norms. The **Barbarity** label has now released many titles by AKJE and other like-minded bands, such as **Amira Saqati**, **Ahlam** and **Argan**. Other Moroccan fusionistas of note are German-based long-haired rocker **Houssaine Kili**; blues fanatic **Majid Bekkas**; Gnawa-influenced **Nass Marrakech**; and the blind *oud* player **Hassan Erraji**, now living in Wales.

In Spain there have been a couple of notable collaborations between flamenco musicians and Andalusian orchestras, such as that of **José Heredia Maya** and **Enrique Morente** with the **Tetouan Orchestra**, and **Juan Peña Lebrijano** with the **Tangier Orchestra**.

Rai, Rap and Rock

Moroccans have taken easily to **rai** (see Algeria Rai chapter), especially in the northeastern part of the country around the towns of Oujda and Al Hoceima, which share cultural roots with *rai*'s birthplace – Oranie in Algeria. Algerian *rai* stars such as Cheb Khaled and Cheb Mami are widely

heard in *souks*, while home-grown stars in the genre include **Cheb Khader**, **Cheb Mimoun** and the superb **Cheb Djellal**, a pop-*rai* legend from Oujda whose cassettes are hard to find but are required listening. **Sawt El Atlas** have also made huge strides with their poppy, *rai*-flavoured sound and have sold handsome numbers of CDs in their adopted home of France. *Rai* influence can also be heard in the local folk sound of artists such as **Rachid Briha** and **Hamid M'Rabati**.

More recently, **hip-hop** has become immensely popular in Morocco and though the homegrown scene still largely underground, the most popular crews – **H-Kayne** from Meknes and **Fnaïre** from Marrakech – have attained some national visibility. The young urban hipsters of modern cities like Casablanca, Rabat and Agadir have also become fond of **house**, **R&B** and **funk**. This scene features Casablanca-based artists such as **Hoba Hoba Spirit** – who blend rock, funk, reggae and Gnawa music – and **Barry**, who combines bossa nova with reggae and Gnawa elements.

Heavy metal is another burgeoning fashion. However, in 2003 the Moroccan authorities showed the limits of their tolerance for the wayward antics of young rock fans when they (briefly) imprisoned members of the heavy metal bands **Nekros**, **Infected Brain** and **Reborn**, along with five of their fans, on charges of moral depravity

Despite a considerable increase in CD reissues in recent years, some of the best Moroccan music is still only available on cassette. In Morocco itself, cassettes of all kinds are readily available in any market – and you can also buy videos of many artists (bear in mind that these are French format and not playable on many UK/US machines), and even a few DVDs. This is a selection of artists who are still primarily only available on cassette, and who deserve a much wider international audience.

Archach

Featuring the Gnawa *guimbri*, the banjo and lots of terrific singing, the band's early cassettes are great – especially their eponymous debut.

Bnet el Ghiwane

An all-female troupe of modern troubadours, with a nice line in unison singing to bass, *bendir* and banjo backing.

Saïd Berrada and El Moqaddem Ben Hamou

Both of these masters have released terrific aïssawa cassettes.

Cheb Djallel

The *rai* prince from Oujda is an absolute must. His cassette *Le Prince de la Chanson Maghrébine* is the one to ask for.

Essiham

A fine roots-fusion outfit from the 1980s who never saw the light of day on CD.

Mahmoud Guinea and Mustapha Baqbou

Although they have both collaborated with countless musicians and producers at home and abroad, these two great Gnawa *ma'almin* still sound their best on their early cassettes.

Hajja Hamdaouia

One of the queens of al-aïta. Her four cassettes are all excellent – lots of percussion, violin, some funky keyboards and her very expressive voice.

Hamid El Kasri

Increasingly popular over the last several years, Hamid El Kasri is the best Gnao singer around.

Raïs Ajmaa Lahcen and Raïs Ihya

The reigning kings of ahouache have over a dozen cassettes on the market – all of them well worth purchasing. This is stark and powerful music.

Abdelaziz Staati

Wild violin playing and intense rhythms. All of his cassettes are winners, though start with *Staati Live in Paris*.

Fatima Taabamrant

The queen of Berber music from the Souss valley has various cassettes and keeps getting better. To many first-time listeners, her music almost sounds Malian.

and playing "anti-Islamic" music. Clearly not all of Morocco is ready just yet for full-on head-banging and satanic T-shirts.

Sephardic Music

Moroccan Jews, many of whom have now emigrated to Israel, left an important legacy in the north of the country, where their songs and ballads continued to be sung in the medieval Spanish spoken at the time of their expulsion from Spain five centuries ago. Apart from the narrative ballads, these were mainly songs of courtly love, as well as lullabies and biblical songs, usually accompanied on a *tar* lute. In 2000 Rounder Records released a two-CD set of Paul Bowles' rousing recordings of Moroccan Jewish liturgy, which transport you into the heart of what was once a vibrant subculture (but now, sadly, almost extinct).

Of all the great Moroccan Jewish singers the one who has left the most indelible mark on Moroccan music history is **Samy el Maghribi**. He was born in Safi in 1922, and moved with his family to Rabat in 1926. Inspired by the Algerian singer Samy el Hilali, he was one of the most appreciated classical Arabic singers of the 1950s. In 1960 he moved to Canada, and in subsequent years devoted himself to a liturgical repertoire.

Moroccan Sephardic traditions and music continue to thrive in Israel, the best-known names including **Albert Bouhadanna** and Rabat-born **Emil Zrihan**, whose music mixes Arab and Andalusian influences with the Hebrew liturgy.

There has been quite a boom in CDs of Moroccan music in the past decade or so. However, in Morocco itself, cassettes are still a very common musical medium (see previous page).

⊙ Anthologie de la Musique Marocaine
Ministère de la Culture, Morocco

A fairly comprehensive anthology that covers all the big genres of Moroccan folk and traditional music. There are 31 CDs, divided among four thematically organized boxed sets. The first covers the Middle Atlas, al-aïta and Saharan music, while the second includes women's groups from Meknes, Marrakech and elsewhere. The third covers Gnawa, Aïssawa, Jilala, Hmadcha and Daqqa, while the fourth and final set presents Jewish music, classical Arabic song, Rif mountains music and nationalist songs. All include liner notes in French and Arabic and can be purchased at the Ministry of Culture in Rabat.

⊙ Morocco: Crossroads of Time
Ellipsis Arts, US

An excellent introduction to Moroccan music that comes with a well-designed and informative book. The disc includes everything from ambient sounds in the Fes Medina, to powerful Jilala and Gnawa music, andalous, rwaï, Berber and some good contemporary pop from Nouamane Lahlou.

⊙ The Rough Guide to the Music of Morocco
World Music Network, UK

Contemporary Moroccan sounds from the likes of the Amenzou Ensemble, Nass el Ghiwane, Nass Marrakech, Jil Jilala, Mustapha Bourgogne, Bnet Marrakech and U-cef.

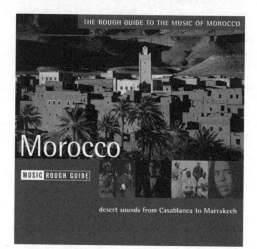

THE ROUGH GUIDE TO THE MUSIC OF MOROCCO

Morocco

MUSIC ROUGH GUIDE

desert sounds from Casablanca to Marrakech

⊙ The Secret Museum of Mankind: Music of North Africa 1925–48
Yazoo, US

This release features some rare 78s of Moroccan Jewish music, Berber music and some early al-aïta. The notes include some early pictures as well. This is a necessary listen for any serious fan of North African music.

Andalous/Classical

★ Maroc: Anthologie d'Al-Melhûn
Maison des Cultures du Monde, France

A 3-CD set containing performances from many of Morocco's finest milhûn singers. Among this set's wonderful selections is one of Haj Houcine Toulali's signature pieces. A good introduction.

Orchestre Moulay Ahmed Loukili de Rabat

Loukili was a pupil of the great Mohammed al-Brihi of Fes and for many years was a member of the city's andalous orchestra. He then moved to Tangier and later Rabat, where he led the orchestra until his death in 1988. He is still considered the greatest master of andalous music of the past half-century. Hadj Mohamed Toud, a former disciple of Loukili, currently leads the Orchestra.

⊙ Nuba Al-'Ushshâq
Inédit, France

This fairly daunting boxed set is not for the casual listener and is priced accordingly (£75/$120). But if you develop a serious interest, it's worth investigating. The set is one of eleven that were released by the Maison des Culture du Monde and the Moroccan Ministère de la Culture. The entire 73-disc project documents the eleven existing nubas in their entirety, performed by the five best al-âla orchestras in the land.

⊙ Escuela de Rabat
Pneuma, Spain

A well-documented and beautifully presented collection of al-âla nubas from the late 1950s and early 60s. The recordings were made for Moroccan radio and they sound wonderful. This is a rare recording from one of the most revered masters of the genre.

Ahmed Piro

Piro is an "enlightened amateur" from Rabat who has been decorated by the king of Morocco for his contributions to Moroccan cultural life.

WITH AMINA ALAOUI

⊙ Ahmed Piro et son Orchestre avec Amina Alaoui Gharnati
Auvidis, Paris

This collaboration resulted after Piro heard the France-based singer Alaoui at a festival of Arab-Andalusian music in Oudja, and offered to accompany her with his orchestra. There are not many recordings of Gharnati available and this is the best on the market. Piro and Alaoui are both very strong singers, and Piro has been at it longer than most.

Ihsan Rmiki

After ten years of study at several Moroccan conservatories, Ihsan Rmiki has – over the last five years – become one of the stars of the Moroccan classical music world, performing in France, Spain, Jordan and Yemen, and with heavyweights like Hadj Mohammed Bajdoub.

⭐ **Al-Samâa: Ecstatic spiritual audition**
Institut du Monde Arabe, Paris
This is an essential release – a studio recording made in Morocco featuring two long pieces that present the spiritual side of *al-âla*. Rmiki leads an intimate six-person ensemble that includes oud, violin, *rabab* and percussion. Her voice is superb and the music is more immediately moving than many recordings of Moroccan "classical" music.

Ustad Massano Tazi

Master rebab player and singer Ustad Massano Tazi practises traditional music therapy based on the idea that being healthy corresponds to a harmonious balancing of the humours. This practice includes the *himmara*, an ecstatic dance, and the playing of certain modes to help to heal certain disorders. To achieve this Tazi plays with instruments all but lost in the modern world.

⊙ **Musique Classique Andalouse de Fès**
Ocora, France
Beautifully recorded and presented, this CD includes Nuba Hijaz Al-Kabir and Nuba Istihilal.

MAROC
USTAD MASSANO TAZI
Musique classique andalouse de Fès

AIMP
Archives Internationales
de Musique Populaire
GENÈVE

Ocora

El Hadj Houcine Toulali

Born in 1924, Toulali developed a passion for *milhûn* as early as 1945. His first recording for Moroccan radio, made in 1959, immediately vaulted him into the elite of the genre's interpreters. Over the next forty years he recorded more than fifty cassettes and made many television and festival appearances. He died on December 17, 1998 leaving behind an unparalleled legacy. His oeuvre remains the foundation of modern *milhûn*.

⊙ **Le malhûn de Meknes**
Institut du Monde Arabe, France
A fine live recording of the great *milhûn* master on top form.

Berber Music

⊙ **Les Imazighen Chants du Moyen-Atlas**
Institut du Monde Arabe, France
A fantastic live recording of musicians from the Middle Atlas, full of power and extravagant emotion. This release is the only easily available international recording of Mohammed Rouicha, and it's worth it just for him.

⊙ **Maroc, Anthologie des Rwâyes; Chants et Musiques Berberes du Sous**
Maison des Cultures du Monde
If you are interested in Berber music you need this 4-disc feast of rwaïs music that includes the great Raqiya Demseriya, Aarab Aatigui and rare recordings of Ammouri Mbarek in a traditional setting. They were made in Casablanca and the notes have the translations to several of the poems, including several by Hajj Belaïd.

⭐ **The Call of the Oasis: Compagnies musicales du Tafilalet**
Institut du Monde Arabe, France
These sublime recordings from the edge of the Sahara showcase four groups that were recorded during a music festival in Erfoud. Featuring the *snitra* lute, the banjo, lots of percussion and some great singing, the disc is a delight from beginning to end. The latest in a series of recordings that is making the Institut du Monde Arabe the go-to label for Moroccan music.

Hmaoui Abd El-Hamid

Hmaoui is a superb Berber player of the traditional Moroccan flute, the *nai*.

⊙ **La Flûte de l'Atlas**
Arion, France
Hypnotic and haunting flute-like *nai*, backed by percussion, oud and zither.

Gnawa and Trance

⊙ **Les Aissawa de Fes Trance Ritual**
L'Institut du Monde Arabe, France
Some entrancing and intricate music from the Aissawa brotherhood of Fes.

⊙ **Confrérie des Jilala**
Ocora, France.
A no-frills deep-roots recording of a Jilala brotherhood in full ecstasy.

⭐ **Gnawa Night: Music of the Marrakesh Spirit Masters**
Axiom, UK
Gnawa music at its evocative best, recorded by Bill Laswell.

⊙ **The World of Gnawa**
Rounder Records, USA
The most complete and informative Gnawa release available, this 2-CD set features several *ma'alems* (including Moustapha Baqbou) and presents a broad range of rhythms and musical suites not found on the average "crossover Gnawa" release. For serious Gnawa fans, the extensive and well-researched liner notes are worth the price of entry alone.

The Master Musicians of Jajouka

A legendary group of pan-pipers and drummers from a village in northern Morocco, the Masters' music has been passed through the generations down for centuries. The current leader of the main group is Bachir Attar. There is also a rival, splinter group using the Jajouka name.

⊙ **Apocalypse Across the Sky**
Axiom, UK
Without the electronic trickery of Brian Jones's seminal album, the power and clarity of these remarkable performers stands out all the more on this Bill Laswell produciton.

Tayfa de Cheikh Sidi Mohammed

A group led by the ritual leader and singer Cheikh Sidi Mohammed, and based in Meknes, where all of the best Aissawa groups come from.

⊙ **The Aïssawa Confraternity**
Ocora, France
This is the best available recording of Aissawa ritual music: three long tracks recorded in Meknes in 1998. After the percussionists spend ten minutes building the rhythm, and rearranging your brainwaves, the *ghaitas* come in and spin you into orbit. The next best thing to being there.

Gnawa Fusion

Maleem Mahmoud Ghania with Pharoah Sanders

Gnawa meets with the great sax player from John Coltrane's band.

⊙ **The Trance of the Seven Colours**
Axiom/Island, US
Gnawa-jazz crossover, recorded mainly in Marrakech.

⊙ **Gnawa Impulse Living Remixes**
Socadisc, France
A successful blending of traditional Gnawa with drum'n'bass and other electro flavours.

Gnawa Njoum

This Gnawa group from Essouaria are joined by musicians from the Paris electronic scene.

⊙ **Gnawa Njoum Experience**
Night and Day, France
One the most successful fusions of trad Gnawa with modern-day electronica. Sounds especially majestic in a club setting.

Roots-Fusion

Najat Aatabou (Aâtabu)

Aatabou is a successful Berber singer, born into a conservative family in the small town of Khemisset but long resident in Casablanca.

★ **The Voice of the Atlas**
GlobeStyle, UK
A superb collection of some of Najat's best-loved songs, including "Shouffi Rhirou".

Bnet Marrakech

The feisty all-woman ensemble from Houara, who have become the international ambassadors of Moroccan roots-fusion.

⊙ **Chama'a**
L'empreinte Digitale, France
The group in their typical favoured unstoppable freight-train mode. Powerful, to say the least.

Jil Jilala

Formed in Marrakech in 1972, Jil Jilala's big breakthrough came several years later with their famous transformations of several poems by *milhûn* great Hadj Houcine Toulali.

They reached their peak in the late 1970s, but have continued to record since.

⊙ **Chama'a**
Blue Silver, France
A classic early recording of the seminal roots-fusion rockers, which was only available on cassette until very recently. The title track "Chama'a" (Candle) is an old *milhûn* song given a moody modern makeover.

Nass el Ghiwane

Roots-fusionists, Nass el Ghiwane, like Jil Jilala, combined Sufi and Gnawa influences with modern lyrics concerned with social justice. Their singer, Boujmia, was killed in a car crash in the early 1980s, but the band have remained active since.

⊙ **Maroc: Chants d'Espoir**
Créon Music, France
Many recordings by the "Rolling Stones of North Africa" are marred by atrocious sound quality. This set, however, captures them razor sharp and passionate – and it includes their moving nine-minute tribute to victims of the Sabra and Chatila massacres in Lebanon.

Contemporary

Houssaine Kili

Born into a Berber family of musicians, Houssaine grew up on a diet of Moroccan and international popular music. An encounter with a German hippie in the late 1970s eventually led to him moving to Germany and joining the group Dissidenten. Several years later he went solo, releasing his debut in 1999.

⊙ **Mountain to Mohammed**
Tropical Music, France
Kili's second release is a minor masterpiece of contemporary Maghrebi rock. How Morrocan music sounds when reworked by an inveterate Neil Young fan.

Nass Marrakech

This innovative group is based in Barcelona, though their name, which means "People of Marrakech", underlines their roots.

⊙ **Bouderbala**
World Village, US
A curious mix of styles on a vaguely Gnawi foundation, with some excellent songs and innovative arrangements.

Sawt El Atlas

One of the most popular contemporary Moroccan groups in France.

⊙ **Donia**
Small/Sony Music, France
Unapologetically pop and *rai*-flavoured tunes.

World Fusion

Aisha Kandisha's Jarring Effects

Roots-fusion meets techno (and rock and hip-hop) in the work of this radical 1990s group, who have collaborated with, among others, Bill Laswell.

El Buya
Barbarity, Switzerland

This debut 1991 album has not been bettered, with its intoxicating mix of Moroccan melodies and traditional string instruments with scratching reverb and rushes of industrial noise.

Juan Peña Lebrijano and the Orquesta Andalusi de Tanger

Juan Peña Lebrijano is a legend of deep flamenco and has performed around for the world for more than forty years. Tangiers remains one of the cradles of Andalusian classical music, and the small group featured on these discs includes some of the city's most talented musicians.

⊙ **Encuentros**
GlobeStyle, UK
⊙ **Casablanca**
Hemisphere, UK
A stunning cross-cultural blend that combines the passion of flamenco with the beauty and grace of andalous music.

MoMo

A London-based three-piece who fuse Gnawa roots with electronica.

⊙ **The Birth Of Dar**
Apartment 22, UK
Moroccan roots with a heavy dance beat. (Dar means "house" in Arabic.)

Muluk El Hwa

An all-acoustic Berber group who play only traditional instruments.

⊙ **Xara Al-Andalus**
Erde Records, Germany
A collaboration with the Spanish group Al Tall, fusing medieval Valencian music and Arabic poetry from Andalusia.

U-cef

A Moroccan producer based in London.

⊙ **Halalium**
Apartment 22, UK
This 2000 album, his only release so far, fuses the roughneck

PLAYLIST
Morocco

1 **EZZAH'RA DA KRABAL Raid Boudjemaa** from *The Secret Museum of Mankind; the Music of North Africa*
One of the only recordings easily available on CD of the one of the greats of southern Berber music. Hear the links between Berbers north of the Sahara and musical traditions to the south.

2 **JILALLA Moustapha Baqbou** from *Gnawa Night – Music of the Marrakech Spirit Masters*
The power and beauty of Gnawa ritual music distilled into four minutes by the great Moustapha Baqbou. You can't ignore the thump of his *guimbri* and the keen of his voice.

3 **DHIKR Tayfa de Cheikh Sidi Mohammed** from *The Aissawa Confraternity*
A great recording of ritual music as you would experience it at an Aissawa ceremony in Meknes. The percussion and vocals drag you in and ten minutes later the *ghaitas* send you into orbit.

4 **FIRST STAGE ALONG THE PATH Ihsan Rmiki** from *Al-Samaa*
Religious music performed according to the rules of Andalusian classical music. If you have been put off by the slow and plodding large Andalusian ensembles, this recording of Andalusian "chamber" music will make you reconsider.

5 **BAGHI NARJAH Najat Aatabou** from *The Voice of the Atlas*
The stuttering bass line, the jackhammer percussion and Najat's voice made this a huge hit throughout Morocco 20 years ago. Najat's music is where Arabic pop and Berber roots meet.

6 **AL KAOUINI Compagnie El Hashemi Nhass** from *Compagnies Musicales du Tafilalet*
Moroccan roots music at its best – the sound of the High Atlas Mountains. The violin and flute provide the melody and the five percussionists do the rest.

7 **MAHMOUNA Nass el Ghiwane** from *The Rough Guide to Moroccan Music*
More than a music group, Nass el Ghiwane have shaped the daydreams and politics of several generations of urban Moroccans. A great example of their trademark Gnawa and banjo sound.

8 **AL-HARRAZ Haj. Hussein Toulali** from *Anthology of Melhun*
Even if you don't understand the poetry, the melodies and languorous tempos will win you over. Take your time and the melodic and rhythmic nuances will soon have you addicted.

sounds of the English capital with traditional *chaabi* and Gnawi, often to wondrous effect.

263

Yosefa

An Israeli-resident Moroccan Jewish singer, mixing traditional songs and sounds with dance culture.

⊙ **Dahari Yosefa**
Worldly Dance, UK
Dancified English and Maghrebi songs. A bit of an exotica product but one that lives up to its promise.

Jewish Moroccan music

⊙ **Sacred Music of The Moroccan Jews**
Rounder Select, US
Haunting recordings made by Paul Bowles in 1959 of Jewish liturgies from Essaouira and Meknes.

Samy el Maghribi

A legendary Jewish musician whose pride of place in the annals of Moroccan music proves what a big influence Jews once had on urban music.

⊙ **Samy el Maghribi**
Club du Disque Arabe, France
A fine collection of old recordings.

Mozambique

a musica continua

Mabulu
World Music Network

A *luta continua* (Portuguese for "the struggle continues") was the slogan of the struggle for Mozambican independence, and in a country that went on to suffer seventeen years of civil war, a succession of devastating floods and droughts and an ongoing AIDS epidemic, it remains all too apt. Mozambican music, however, has thrived since independence, and ranges from giant timbila orchestras to the salsa-inflected groove of marrabenta, from oil-can guitars through hip-hop to the phenomenon of Maputo jazz-fusion. Celso Paco and Tom Bullough report.

Mozambique, lying on the east coast of southern Africa, was a **Portuguese colony** for five centuries from 1498 to 1975. Before this period, the area was divided between the matrilineal north – where indigenous **Bantu** speakers had mixed with **Arab** immigrants to create the **Swahili** language group – and the patrilineal south, where the **Tsonga**, **Bitonga**, **Chopi** and **Ndau** were dominant. Despite the Portuguese influence, the musical traditions of these groups survived colonialism – Chopi **timbila** orchestras, for example, were allowed to perform at official visits – although by the time of the war of independence, which began in earnest in 1964, Mozambican leaders were using Portuguese language, ideas, culture and religion in their struggle against Portuguese rule.

In 1975, Mozambique won its **independence**, and the ruling Frelimo (Frente de Libertação de Moçambique) party came to power. Independence brought to a new generation the discovery of a cultural heritage that had been ignored in the urban areas during the centuries of Portuguese colonization. Mozambican **bands**, which prior to independence had played European-style music, began to abandon it as they embraced the patriotic spirit sweeping the country. Bands reformed using improvised musical instruments and began to play roots-style music similar to that heard and performed in Tanzania, Zambia and other countries in the region.

In the centre of Mozambique, a musical style resembling that of Zimbabwe appeared, while southern Mozambique was strongly influenced by the music brought into the country by the returning workers who provided cheap labour in the South African mines. Throughout the country, revolutionary lyrics were fitted to these regional melodies along with the usual social commentaries and life stories.

In 1978, the Ministry of Education and Culture managed to organize a **National Dance Festival** involving half a million people from around the country. One result of this festival was the formation of a National Song and Dance Company and a Children's Dance School. Two years later, the Ministry organized a **festival of traditional music** in the capital, Maputo. The mere fact that the traditional musicians, with all their local instruments made of gourds, thongs, reeds, horns and skins, came out of the bush and the shanty towns to perform on public stages was an act of cultural recognition and national renaissance.

Meanwhile, the **war** between the Frelimo government and the South African-backed Renamo rebels, which had started before independence, led to the loss of at least a million lives (out of a population of fifteen million), with millions more orphaned, displaced or traumatized. The Mozambican people were more than ready for peace, and in 1994 the first multiparty elections were successfully held.

Through all of this, Mozambican musicians – like **Chico António**, **Salimo Mohammed** and the band **Ghorwane** – were writing and performing songs that echoed the frustrations of the Mozambican people while encouraging them to act together for a better future.

Centro de Formacão Fotogtafica, Mozambique

National Song and Dance Company of Mozambique, Celso Paco on drums

266

Coastal Music: Timbila

The range of traditional music and traditional musical instruments found in Mozambique is a reflection of its ethnic diversity and its geography. The best-known style is the **timbila** music of the Chopi people of Inhambane – a highly developed and sophisticated music played on the **mbila** (plural *timbila*), a type of xylophone. Found only in Inhambane, timbila range in size from the four-key bass *chinzumana* (or *chikulu*) to the eighteen- or nineteen-key high-pitched *sanje* (or *chilanzane*), with resonators made from *masaala* or pumpkin gourds. Their scale is not a familiar one to Western ears, and a unique buzzing sound is produced by a plastic (originally animal intestine) membrane placed over a hole in the gourd.

There is a theory, based on the pattern of trade routes and similarities in the musical scales, that the presence of the xylophone in Africa can be accounted for by traders introducing it from Indonesia (home of *gamelan* orchestras) through Madagascar and East Africa. Whatever the case, the quarter-million Chopi people on the Mozambican coast have developed a firm tradition of composing for voice and xylophone which now occupies a hugely important place in their lives.

The spellbinding music of **Venancio Mbande** and his timbila orchestra of around fifteen dancers and as many singers can be heard most Sunday afternoons at his house in Zavala, Inhambane Province – and yes, you really can just turn up to the sessions uninvited. So any trip to the paradisiacal beaches of Inhambane should be timed to enable you to meet this traditional musician who has played in London's Albert Hall. To find his house, take the main road to Inhambane out of Maputo and about 27km north of Quissico (just after the village of Guilundo) you will see a yellow sign reading *Centro de Musica Chopi Catini* – his house is on the right, about 100m from the road.

Another internationally known timbila player from Zavala, Eduardo Durão, shares the same love of this traditional musical form, adding to it a strong desire for experimentation. He has performed a number of concerts where timbila and Western instruments combine to produce a new and very exciting style, working with musicians such as bassist Nataniel Filiphino, Finnish saxophonist Eero Koivistoinen, English saxophonist Karen Boswell and drummer (and co-author of this article) Celso Paco. Eduardo is the head of the timbila school in Maputo and is also a composer with the National Song and Dance Company

Although timbila are the best-known internationally, Mozambique has a variety of **other** traditional instruments, including *xitende* and *xivokonvoko* (one-string gourd bows), *xizambe* and *xipendane* (mouth bows), *xitata* and *kalimba* (thumb pianos), *xigovia* (gourd flute), *nyanga* (pan-pipes), *mbala-pala* (antelope horn), *valimba* and *makwilo* (regional timbila), the six- or seven-string *pankwé* and the flute-like *tsudi, mutoriro* and *xirupe*. Many of these are accompanied by *gocha* and *masseve* (rattles), the percussive *xikitsi* and a range of *tambores* (drums), such as the *bendi* from Tête province and the distinctive *mlapa*, which is mounted on an earthenware resonator.

Several **field recordings** of timbila and other traditional music are now available on CD, and for those who can't make the trip, a video called *Mozambique Three* has footage of some of the groups featured on the GlobeStyle CDs.

Marrabenta Pulse

Marrabenta music, Mozambique's main urban dance rhythm, was born during the colonial period as a result of external musical influences and attempts to produce foreign musical instruments using locally available materials. To entertain themselves, people who couldn't afford to buy guitars, for example, would create their own versions using five-litre oil tins, pieces of wood and fishing line. The term derives from the fact that these guitars were played with great enthusiasm until the strings broke; in Portuguese, *rebentar* means "to break" and *arrabentar* is the pronunciation in the local languages. Marrabenta music shares certain similarities with Latin American calypso and salsa, and Angolan *merengue*.

During the early years of this music marrabenta composers used native languages and played simple, repetitive sequences. The key rarely varied from song to song and in general the words delivered messages of social criticism, praise or, more often, love. The "Kings of Marrabenta" of this era include the late great **Fany Pfumo**, **Dilon Djindji** (see box overleaf) and **Lisboa Matavel** (both of whom have seen their careers revived by their recent work with Mabulu), **Xidimingwana** (with his "talking" guitar) and **Maekwana**, who famously pledged not to 'leave beer until the day I die'. Each one of these has insisted that they are the greatest marrabenta performer.

Marrabenta was mistrusted by the Portuguese as a medium of revolution and a cultural form they were powerless to control. During the war of liberation, the colonial government closed down numerous marrabenta venues on the grounds that they were terrorist centres.

After independence, many young singers

Dilon Djindji: King of Marrabenta

Tom Bullough meets Dilon Djindji, the 78-year-old "King of Marrabenta", at his home in Marracuene, north of Maputo.

How did you first get started?

I started playing in '38, when I was young, like my grandchildren. Back then, I was playing traditional music on an oil can guitar with only three strings, and I also used to listen to music on a gramophone – traditional Shangaan music – a long time ago when hardly anybody had a gramophone. I just learnt from watching and listening and I made my own guitars in my spare time, but my father didn't like it so I used to have to go off to practise in the bush.

I didn't hold a proper guitar until around '47, but even then I always used the marrabenta tuning, *afina cãomatola*, and I always used finger-picking, not a plectrum like other players. That's why nobody else can play marrabenta like Dilon!

When did you first hear the word marrabenta?

In '46. When I was young, I was strong and powerful, and I was always being invited to play at parties. The word marrabenta comes from *rebentar*, which means "to break" in Portuguese, but in slang it also means "to party", so I was given the nickname "Marrabenta" because I was the guy who could always party, the guy who was never tired. When I played back then I had a very sexy style, and by the end of the night I would always have one or two women… So, *rebentar* means something like that as well!

When did you start to play in clubs?

I started to play the bars up in Lourenço Marques [colonial Maputo] in '67, so then I had to learn to behave myself! I played solo for about five years, then, in '72, I formed the Strelas de Marracuene [Marracuene Stars], although when I made my first recordings in December 1975, at Radio Mozambique, I was recording alone. My first single was "In Marracuene, There Is a King of Marrabenta" and it was a hit around the country.

You wrote all your own material?

Yes – I don't take anything from anyone.

Were your lyrics affected by the civil war of the 1970s and 1980s?

I never wrote about these issues. The songs I write are simple songs about simple things that happen every day in people's lives. Anyway, by April '84, when the war came here to Marracuene, I had given up playing and was working as head of the local farmers' association. I didn't even pick up the guitar for eighteen years.

Djinji shows his Marrabenta steps

World Music Network

Why was that?

Because I could earn no money from it, and I just wasn't enjoying it any more. Also, my music was not respected here. Only foreigners respected me. In '83, Sam Mangwana from Zaïre came to Marracuene to find me, and… [He produces a study by an Austrian ethnomusicologist, showing the seven pivotal developments of twentieth century African music.] You see? "1952: Dilon Djindji invents Marrabenta." You see? The Austrians understood, even if the Mozambicans didn't.

How did Mabulu come about?

Well, Roland [Hohberg – Mabulu's manager] approached me in 2000, and I liked the idea of Mabulu because they were already famous, and I wanted to be able to play around the world, so that the world could know my material through their music. The people still need those songs, they need them to be rerecorded and remastered, but often it is hard for the younger guys in Mabulu to catch my sound. That's why, in 2000, I recorded my solo album, *Dilon*, with only old musicians. You see, Mabulu need me for that marrabenta juice! Even at this age, I'm still Marrabenta!

emerged to write marrabenta songs that focused on their hopes and feelings, and the style took a lift in the late 1970s when **1001 Music Productions** recorded and promoted a great number of local artists at large concert venues. *Amanhecer* (Sunrise), an LP compilation of Radio Mozambique recordings was released, including some of the artists promoted by 1001, and following its success other compilations were produced under the generic title *Ngoma* (Drum).

In the immediate post-independence period a number of Mozambican artists living outside the country returned, bringing with them new influences to add to the existing, somewhat insular, mix. One such was Fany Pfumo, who used jazz elements in his compositions to create a unique sound. Born into a poor family in 1929, Pfumo was forced to abandon Mozambique for the better working and living conditions of South Africa. Contact with recording companies in Johannesburg saved him from the mines and launched him as a successful singer, with hits such as "Loko ni kumbuka Jorgina" (When I Remember Jorgina). Most of his singles were recorded by HMV in South Africa, often in collaboration with fellow-Mozambican **Alexander Jafete**, and many of them combined marrabenta with South African kwela.

The creation of the **Grupo Radio Moçambique** (the national broadcasting company house band) was the beginning of a new era for Mozambican popular music. Radio Mozambique continues to facilitate the dissemination of Mozambican music by releasing recorded material by local artists.

Jazz-Fusion

The past fifteen years have seen the development of a distinctive form of Mozambican jazz-fusion, often involving traditional instruments. Jazz itself has been popular in Maputo since shortly after independence, when British saxophonist John Marney led a series of jam sessions. These inspired musicians such as **João Cabaço**, who sang jazz interpretations of marrabenta classics, **Hortêncio Langa**, the current head of the musicians' union, and saxophonist **Orlando da Conceição**, who played with the seminal **Maputo Jazz** and taught saxophone to the likes of **Ivan Mazuze**, **Moreira Chonguiça** and composer **Orlando Venhereque**.

It was not, however, until 1992 that **da Conceição** and **Celso Paco** (both then teachers at the National School of Music) began to experiment with a fusion of sax, timbila and traditional Chopi rhythms, which resulted in **Kinamatamikuluty**, a group whose sound lies somewhere between Venancio Mbande and John Coltrane. The success of this project led to further collaborations, including **Malhangalene Jazz Quartet** and, notably, **Pazedi Jazz Band**, formed by Paco ("Pa"), saxophonist **Zé Maria** ("ze") and bassist **Dino** ("di"). The latter group, since Paco's relocation to Norway, has expanded to include a range of traditional instruments.

The recent jazz-fusion boom is the result of a number of factors, but particularly the upsurge in public jam sessions during the late 1990s, when clubs such as Gil Vicente and Tchova Xita Duma brought together musicians from radically different backgrounds. This experimental climate helped to create some of the country's most important young groups – such as the ten-piece **Timbila Muzimba**, who combine traditional sounds with jazz and even hip-hop.

The diversity of Mozambican culture (with strong Arab, Brazilian, Portuguese and West African influences, together with influences from neighbouring countries) makes fusion a natural form of expression, and its exponents include some of the country's most established musicians. **Chico António**, former trumpeter with Orchestra Marrabenta Star de Moçambique, now plays an idiosyncratic mixture of traditional rhythms with jazz, heavy metal and echoes of Frank Zappa. Similarly, the popular group **Xitende**, originally an offshoot of **Salimo Mohammed**'s **Xigutsa-Vuma**, blend traditional sounds with reggae, funk, jazz and Afro-beat to electrifying effect, while Carlos Gove's **Nondje** project underpins experimental jazz with the timbila of his own Chopi background.

Sounds Today

Traditional rhythms played on traditional instruments can still be heard in the rural areas of Mozambique. And they're kept alive in the cities by new migrants as well as cultural groups such as the **Companhia Nacional de Canto e Dança** (National Song and Dance Ensemble), created at the end of the 1970s as a symbol of national unity.

Orchestra Marrabenta Star de Moçambique, formed in 1979, was the first group to play top-quality marrabenta music and take it on tour to Europe, and, though the group is no longer together, it played an important role in nurturing many of the country's current stars. Its leader, **Wazimbo**, enjoy considerable popularity as a solo artist, while percussionist **Stewart Sukuma** (Luis Perera) has developed into one of Mozambique's top male vocalists. **Mingas**, the leading female singer in the country, also began singing with the orchestra, and has since accompanied Miriam Makeba on a world tour and performed with Nondje. The orchestra's two outstanding trumpeters, **Chico António** and **José Mucavel**, also became successful solo artists: Antonio performs fusion, while Mucavel produces his own mixture of traditional rhythms from across the country.

One of Mozambique's best-known and longest surviving bands is **Ghorwane**, which continues to play despite a series of departures and untimely deaths. Lead guitarist with Salimo Mohammed in the early 1980s, **Pedro Langa**, who was tragically murdered in 2001, formed Ghorwane with the late **Jose Alage** (**Zeca**), and they first found international success when they were invited by Peter Gabriel to WOMAD in 1990, and subsequently recorded their first and so-far finest album, *Majurugenta*, on Gabriel's Real World label. Ghorwane's music is based on Mozambican traditional songs and rhythms, with some South African influences mixed in. As well as lead, rhythm and bass guitars, the band features two trumpets, sax, keyboard and percussion line-up plus vocals from **David Macucua** (who was leader until 1997) and **Roberto Chitsondzo** (a fine composer, guitarist and singer who took over as leader in 1999).

Another important artist is **Paulo Miambo**, a veteran solo performer with a voice similar to that of the late Fany Pfumo, and one of the greatest marrabenta composers. Paulo recorded songs through the 1980s, released an album in 1996 and is currently gaining a reputation as a producer of various local artists – whom he encourages to record and release discs in South Africa.

Most Mozambican bands who have had CDs released come from the south of the country. One important exception is **Eyuphuro**, a band devoted specifically to the promotion of the music of the Macua ethnic group from Nampula province in northeastern Mozambique. They were actually the first group in the country to release a CD: their *Mama Mosambiki* was one of Real World's earliest offerings, and embraces the lightly textured *tufo* rhythm. The band toured Europe for a long period, split at the end of the 1980s and reformed in 1999 thanks to persuasion from German producer **Roland Hohberg**. They have since resumed touring and recorded a new but disappointing CD, *Yellela*.

Hohberg has raised the profile of Mozambican music significantly on the world stage over the past decade, especially since 1998, when he established the first independent studio in the country, Studio Mozambique. Perhaps his greatest success has been **Mabulu**, who were nominated in the Newcomer category of the 2002 BBC World Music awards. Bringing together old and young musicians in one group, Mabulu ("dialogue") includes rappers such as **Chiquito** as well as veteran marrabenta performers such as **Dilon Djindji**, **Antonio Marcos** and the late **Lisboa Matavel**. The project has sparked controversy among purists, but with two CDs and successful tours in Europe, America and Australia, Mabulu – together with the young marrabenta revivalists, **Moz Pipa** – are very much the modern face of marrabenta.

Of the younger bands playing in Maputo, one of the best is **Kapa Dêch** (**K10**) – a versatile pop outfit which fuses aspects of East and West African music with rock and reggae influences. Younger still, **Banda Azul** performs both as a group and a deeply funky backing band for some of the finest young singers and rappers in the capital.

The rise of hip-hop has been one of the most exciting recent developments in Mozambican music, although the likes of Alberto Machavele, Armando Mazwai and Raúl Baza were pioneering the art of spoken lyrics as long ago as the 1970s. Since 2001, the Mozambican-run **Studio Kandonga** ("under-

Frank Drake/Womad

Abdul Remane Gino and Zena Bakar of Eyuphuro

ground" in Shangaan) has produced most of the country's hip-hop, fostering the talents of promising rappers such as **Gina Pepa** and **Mr Arssen** (who, in the spirit of music in Maputo, are as likely to be seen performing with timbila or jazz musicians as they are with a hip-hop backing track).

Outside Maputo, the same trends do not always hold sway and while Beira, Mozambique's second city, has produced groundbreaking hip-hop act **Djovana**, its leading bands, **Djaaka** and **Mussodji**, play a style of music closer to Zimbabwean chimurenga than to marrabenta. Built around timbila patterns, with a strong, rootsy horn section, Djaaka has been particularly successful, touring regionally as well as in Holland and the UK.

The Musical Diaspora

The pressures of survival in Mozambique have led many important musicians to move abroad, and especially to the thriving jazz scene in South Africa. Some of the country's best jazz musicians are now based in Johannesburg – such as guitarist **Jimmy Dludlu** and drummer **Frank Paco** – while the prominent Cape Town fusion group **Tucan Tucan** features Mozambicans Tony Paco, Ivan Mazuze and Helder Gonzaga, and combines elements of African music with Latin rhythms and Spanish, Portuguese and English lyrics.

Other expatriates include **André Cabaço** and **Costa Neto**, both of whom live in Portugal, and bassist **Childo Tomas**, who is based in Spain and plays with Cuban pianist and composer Omar Sosa. Until his murder in 2004, one of the most significant Mozambican musicians living abroad was bassist and composer **Gito Baloi**, who became popular after performing and releasing albums with the South African trio **Tananas**. Although she stayed in Mozambique, the other great loss that year was **Zaida Chongo**, who – partnered by her husband, the guitarist and composer Carlos Chongo – became one of the country's best-loved singers. Her funeral in Maputo was second in scale only to that of President Samora Machel.

DISCOGRAPHY   Mozambique

⊙ Anumadutchi – Drums of the World
Koch Records, US
Named after a composition by Venancio Mbande, "Anumadutchi" – meaning "For you, Dutchmen" – brought together lecturers and students from the Royal Dutch Conservatory who have studied timbila under Mbande and drums under the likes of Aly N´Diay Rose (son of the Senegalese percussion master Doudu N´Diay Rose).

⊙ Arcos, Cordas, Flautas
C.I Crocevi/Sud Nord Records, Italy
Musicians from all over Mozambique play all kinds of handmade friction, wind and string instruments. Rubbing sounds produced by a bow interact with a rattle stick and with overtones from the mouth, which is used as a resonator, while traditional flutes made of hard-shelled wild fruits produce fascinating interlocking sounds and rhythms.

⊙ Atenção: Desminagem!
Kandonga, Mozambique
A collection from Studio Kandonga, kings of the fast-moving Maputo rap scene. Angry and innovative, hip-hop moçambicano starts here.

⊙ Forgotten Guitars from Mozambique
SWP Records, Netherlands
Fantastic acoustic marrabenta from the 1950s. Artists include Aurelio Kuwano, Feliciano Gomes, Andrea Sithole, Inacio Macanda and the duo Laberto Wamusi and Gabirel Bila.

⊙ Ilha de Moçambique
C.I. Crocevia/Sud Nord Records, Italy
A collection of distinct and charming Swahili songs and chants by acclaimed groups from the north of Mozambique

highlights the importance of women in this matrilineal society. The album also includes a song by fishermen at work.

★ Kerestina – Guitar Songs from Southern Mozambique 1955–57
Original Music, US
Recorded by ethnomusicologist Hugh Tracey, this is the best available compilation of guitar songs from southern Mozambique. The musicians are from the countryside and the music is characterized by the powerful sounds of acoustic guitars and male vocals, with occasional high-pitched female backing harmonies. The musicians complain and joke about life and changing times in a rap form.

⊙ Mozambique One
GlobeStyle, UK
Mainly acoustic field recordings, some of regional folk bands singing and playing self-made traditional instruments such as the *kanakari* (a four-string banjo with an antelope-skin head) and the *pankwe* (a five-string board zither with two large resonators).

⊙ Mozambique Two
GlobeStyle, UK
Consisting partly of sessions with regional folk bands, partly of field recordings, this second set includes songs about social issues and daily life: in "My Bed and my Wife", for example, a husband speaks lovingly of sharing a small blanket with his spouse.

⊙ Mozambique Relief
Naxos, UK
Produced in aid of the victims of the floods in 2000, this includes Stewart Sukuma, Jose Mucavel, Gito Baloi and Ghorwane.

★ Music from Mozambique
Caprice, Sweden
Everything from traditional drums and intricate handclapping to experimental blends of timbila and heavy metal guitar.

⊙ Rough Guide to Marrabenta Music
World Music Network, UK
With artists such as Dilon Djindji, Zé Guimarães (of Marrabenta Star de Moçambique), Pedro Langa (Ghorwane), Neyma and Lisboa Matavel (Mabulu), this features some of the greatest Mozambican singers.

⊙ ¡Saba Saba!
GlobeStyle, UK
Acoustic dance music from Nyampula in the northeast interior, an exuberant kind of Afro-skiffle with multi-layered vocals.

⊙ Sounds Eastern & Southern
Original Music, US
Full of wonderful acoustic guitar music from the 1940s and 50s, most of it recorded by the legendary ethnomusicologist Hugh Tracey.

★ Southern Mozambique
SWP Records, Netherlands
Extending into the 1960s, this is another Tracey-recorded collection, this time of *xigovia* gourd flutes, vocal songs, frenetic timbila and rhythms to accompany *zore* belly dancing.

Gito Baloi

A superb South African-based composer and virtuoso bass player, Baloi won the Best Contemporary Jazz Band award at the 1996 FNB awards for his work with Tananas and collaborated with – among many others – Chude Mondlane, Mzwaki Mbuli and Mali's Askia Modibo. Tragically, he was shot dead in Johannesburg in 2004.

⊙ Remembering: The Best of Gito Baloi
Sheer Sounds, South Africa
Including tracks from his solo albums *Ekaya*, *Na Ku Randza* and *Herbs & Roots*, his hits with Tananas and a duet with Nibs Van Der Spuy (which Baloi was promoting on the night of his death), this is an excellent retrospective collection.

Zaida & Carlos Chongo

A husband-and-wife team, with Carlos as bandleader, composer and lead guitarist and Zaida initially as a dancer, then as one of the most famous voices in Mozambique. Carlos started playing an oil-can guitar and had his first big hit, "Timpondo", in the early 1980s. Zaida was born in 1970 and performed with Carlos for thirteen years. Her death in 2004 was mourned nationwide.

★ Homenagem à Zaida
Vidisco, Mozambique
Another posthumous retrospective, drawn from Zaida and Carlos Chongo's eight albums between 1993 and 2004. With Carlos's mesmerizing guitar licks and tracks as enchanting as "Toma que Ti Dou" and "Alfândega", this is an absolute must-buy.

Djaaka

A group of musicians and dancers from Beira who became well known after their success at the Music Crossroads Competition. They mix traditional music from central Mozambique with contemporary grooves.

⊙ Mbole Mbole na Yona
Zammo, Mozambique
Zimbabwean chimurenga sounds coupled with timbila and saxophone.

Dilon Djindji

Born in 1927 in Marracuene, a district capital in the south of Mozambique, Dilon Djindji built his first, three-string guitar from an oil can at the age of 12. He began performing at parties and ceremonies, where he was given the name "Marrabenta".

★ Dilon
Riverboat
Extraordinarily, his first album. And extraordinarily good it is too.

Eduardo Durão

Composer for Mozambique's National Song and Dance Company, Durão has received criticism from conservative timbila players for his experimental approach.

⊙ Eduardo Durão Timbila Ensemble
Naxos World
A fine fusion of timbila with Western musical instruments.

Eyuphuro

A line-up of roots musicians singing in the Macua language from the north of Mozambique. The group went on a long tour of Europe, playing at festivals and on recording sessions organized by WOMAD.

⊙ Mama Mosambiki
Real World, UK
Highly melodic acoustic-guitar music, with delicious bass-guitar lines and a number of carefully pitched traditional hand-drums providing excellent backing to the powerful voice of Zena Bakar. Best when her vocal chords are at full stretch, as on her beautiful composition "Kihiyeny".

Ghorwane

The masters of Mozambican urban dance music, grafting contemporary beats onto traditional roots.

★ Majurugenta
Real World, UK
Still their finest hour, and a party album par excellence, its big sound demands big speakers. Coloured by the breezy sax of the late Zeca Alage, this one always gets people moving.

⊙ Kudumba
Piranha, Germany
Ten tracks of magically seductive, light and breezy dance music to make you jump and jive – the result of more than ten years of work.

K10 (Kapa Dêch)

A group of young musicians who gained national and international recognition after winning the Music Crossroads Southern Africa competition in 1997.

⊙ Katchume
Lusafrica/BMG, France
A range of dance music played on Western instruments, but based on traditional rhythms and melodies, and incorporating influences from East and West Africa. As they sing on "Sumbi", "Success is like a coal train that starts slowly but finally gets to its destination."

Mabulu

A joint venture between musicians of the older and younger generations.

⊙ Karimbo
World Music Network, UK
The band's struggle to complete their first album during the heavy rains, flooding and power cuts of 2000 gives a sense of triumph to the result.

⊙ Soul Marrabenta
World Music Network, UK
Swinging marrabenta and rap.

Antonio Marcos

The Mabulu mainstay is also a sublime solo performer, combining his ethereal, high-pitched voice with reggae and marrabenta.

⊙ Vusiwana
Vidisco, Mozambique
A great find for fans of Mabulu – Marcos gives himself a free rein.

Massukos

Vibrant music from the Niassa province of northern Mozambique.

Massukos

⊙ Kuimba Kwa Massuko
Sons d'Africa, Mozambique
A treasure trove of traditional songs, electric guitars and harmonized voices.

PLAYLIST
Mozambique

1 WUKATI LAKUKAWA HINENGUE
Feliciano Gomes from *Forgotten Guitars from Mozambique*
Like José Feliciano, Gomes is a singer and acoustic guitarist, but this also features a non-American style of rap.

2 RATANANG Tucan Tucan from *Xiluva*
Fine lead/harmony vocals over jazzy chord progressions, a groovy bass and vibraphone, and fast "one drop" drumming.

3 NGOMA MACANDJO Mabulu from *Karimbo*
A ragga-style vocal intro ushers in guitar chords, timbila and rap.

4 M'TSITSO Venancio Mbande from *Timbila ta venancio*
Just listen to the interplay between the timbila lead and the rest of the orchestra.

5 TIPANGUENE NDGIRA Utci Acena from *Music from Mozambique*
Call-and-response vocals from a traditional female choral group, with interlocking handclapping and powerful drumming.

6 NHIMBA YA DOTA Wazimbo from *Nwahulwana*
Great singing and percussion sounds, with a metal guitar solo and rounding off with a traditional "Tsonga" choir.

7 MFUMO SAMBA Gito Baloi from *Remembering: The Best of Gito Baloi*
With the bass playing the main melody, this features piano chords and a Latin percussion solo.

8 A FÚRIA DAS ÁGUAS Face Oculta from *Atenção: Desminagem!*
A laidback Kandonga production. Chilled beats and floating voices, but the fury is never far beneath the surface.

9 MARIA TERESA Dilon Djindji from *Dilon (also on The Rough Guide to Marrabenta Music)*
A 1950s classic about a man caught between two women – the voices are accompanied by handdrums and acoustic guitar.

10 TOMA QUE TI DOU Zaida & Carlos Chongo from *Homenagem à Zaida*
Irresistible pop music, with Zaida on vocals and keyboards. Best served with lots of sunshine.

Venancio Mbande

Venancio Mbande, a much-respected traditional music master, is the leader and the composer for a full-strength timbila ensemble. He makes his own instruments and has toured with the group in Europe and the US.

⊙ Timbila ta Venancio
Naxos World, UK
The living tradition of timbila, the xylophone of the Chopi people. This gloriously ancient, vibrating music survived colonialism thanks to its role in official occasions.

Chude Mondlane

The first female jazz singer in Mozambique, Mondlane has influenced many young female vocalists on the local urban music scene.

⊙ Especiarias do Corao
Vidisc, Mozambique
An album that brings together a variety of international styles, from heavy Afro-beat to hip-hop, chachacha and jazz. "Obrigada Madame Chude" uses a mix of Portuguese and English over a strong African beat, combined with a loose-limbed melodic line.

José Mucavel

An acoustic guitarist who has developed a solo career since leaving the Grupo Radio Moçambique.

⊙ Compassos 1
Musicrea, Denmark
Guitar music that retains much of its traditional rhythmic identity. Yodelling vocals, hand-drums and backing harmonies by a wild, high-pitched female vocalist, set off by smooth soprano sax.

Orchestra Marrabenta Star de Moçambique

After setting the local pace in the 1980s, the Orchestra toured Europe several times, representing the contemporary sound of Mozambique. Many of the country's top musicians are Orchestra Marrabenta alumni.

⊙ IndepenDance
Piranha, Germany
Runs the whole spectrum from loping dance grooves to brooding songs like the closing track, "Nwahulwana".

⊙ Marrabenta Piquenique
Piranha, Germany
Popular tunes from southern Mozambique, splendidly rearranged by the orchestra using electric guitars, percussion and horns.

Stewart Sukuma

One of the hardest-working musicians on the urban scene, Stewart Sukuma (Luis Pereira) began his career around 1980 in a school band.

⊙ Afrikiti
CCP Record Company, South Africa
Recordings made with South African musicians, incorporating musical influences from neighbouring countries.

Tucan Tucan

Featuring brothers Frank, Celso and Tony Paco on percussion, and arrangements from the Argentinian keyboard player Muriel Marco, Tucan Tucan includes both Mozambican and South African musicians.

⊙ Xiluva
Xiluva Music, South Africa
A powerful mixture of music inspired by Afro-fusion, samba and Latin jazz.

Wazimbo

One of the most popular singers in the country, and founder of the Orchestra Marrabenta Star de Moçambique, Wazimbo was previously the lead singer with Grupo Radio Moçambique, the Radio Mozambique house band.

⊙ Nwahulwana
Piranha, Germany
A "best of" compilation from Wazimbo's time with the Orchestra Marrabenta Star de Moçambique. Lots of great guitar work, with wandering bass lines and grooving percussion. The title track featured on the soundtrack to the film The Pledge, starring Jack Nicholson.

Namibia

little brother struggle

Herero musicians, c.1910
Collection of Werner Pieper

Visiting tourists often have difficulty finding "real" Namibian music. Not much is available in stores, clubs and theatres, and even though "traditional" music is still commonly practised, strangers are not always welcome. The music industry, still in its infancy, is struggling to get off the ground. Without the financial support of foreign agencies and wealthy relatives, Namibian recordings probably wouldn't stand a chance. So how did this situation come about? Can it all be blamed on colonial history and the pressure of big brother South Africa? Minette Mans speculates; with thanks to Werner Pieper.

Namibia has been dominated by foreign nations for nearly two centuries. The South African occupation and apartheid system resulted in resistance and a protracted armed liberation struggle, of which many traces can still be found in the music. When South African troops departed before independence in 1990, musical dependency remained. With its small population, the country has only one city – the capital, Windhoek. This is where all the contemporary musicians hang out, waiting for the chance to break into the big time. Apart from several medium-sized towns, the population is settled in villages and agricultural land, with little access to television and other modern conveniences.

'Patches' of Practice

Bordered on three sides by other nations, Namibians have adopted many aspects of the musical styles of their neighbours. Understandably, people trade and communicate across borders with people in Angola, Botswana, Zambia and South Africa. It's not surprising, therefore, to find that the country's music tends to be organized into large **patches** that share similar musical practices internally, but sound different from other patches. These are roughly the northern, central, and southern patches, with a few smaller eastern patches.

In the north – the least arid area – the musical traditions resemble what visitors have come to expect in Africa – drums, song and energetic dance. The **Valozi** of the eastern Caprivi region and **Kavango** (the collective term for the Sambyu, Kwangali, Hambukushu and Gciriku people) use sets of drums in ritual and entertainment events. The driving rhythms and dance that emphasizes hip and skirt swings (**mashamba**) and shoulder vibrations give this music energy and excitement. Women sing, men drum and everybody dances. In the central north the liberation war is still fresh in everybody's minds, and the numerically and politically dominant **Owambo** people's songs – of young and old – recall the liberation struggle, so that **omaimbilo emanguluko** (freedom songs) form a core part of the musical identity of this region. Here drums are played mainly by girls nowadays, in the **oudano** songs, also danced and sung. Unlike the northeastern music which weaves different drumming tones and patterns into one another, these drums replicate the clapping and stamping patterns of the feet in *oudano*. In the past, large **efundula drums** played by men, sometimes in groups of up to forty, accompanied the feminine "traditional marriage" ceremony. With rapid Christianization in the twentieth century, this practice has all but disappeared, since missionaries objected to the drums and dance. Yet the church had a notable influence on the style and structure of music. In **uukorasa** songs, sung by the youth at church gatherings, the dance movements are in chorus formation, the songs remind one of *makwaya* songs of Kenya and South Africa, and the texts may combine religious and liberation messages. Younger musicians tend to favour *shambo*, a local fusion that looks to traditional forms such as *eenghama* but with modern instruments and rhythms. This is evident in the music of **Set-son and the Mighty Dreads**, as well as **Ngatu** and **Steve Hanana**.

Even up and coming musicians like **Eelu** (as yet unpublished), are playing around with old songs learnt from grandparents and others. By contrast, the northwestern **Ovahimba**, culturally and linguistically **Herero**, celebrate their identity mainly in **praise incantations**. The Herero being cattle people in heart and soul, these hypnotic chants praise ancestors and heroes as well as the cattle of ancestors and the places where grazing is good. In

Minette Mans

Owambo women performing *oudano*

ondjongo, the most important dance-game of the Ovahimba, their arms are held up high to signify cattle horns and ownership of cattle.

In southern Namibia, where **Nama** people predominate, songs are an interesting blend of **Afrikaner**, **German** and their own musical influences. Choral performances are popular, and the language clicks give these songs an unmistakeable edgy rhythm. When dancing the **langarm** and **namastap** (both couple dances, the latter performed in a long line), the accompaniment is played on guitars and accordion or keyboard. A characteristic sound effect is the wailing slides of notes on the keyboard. In this *langarm* style, the swinging, souped-up waltz rhythm make it eminently danceable. In modern-day recordings of different song styles, but especially the popular **Damara punch**, these influences are still clearly evident. **Dube and the Peace Soldiers** with their album *Better Dayz* is an example. This Damara-Afro-fusion and Khoe-jive, as it is described by Dube, is popular for its danceability.

Bilo bile heri

Towards the eastern border, the unique singing traditions of **San** (Bushman) people (**Ju/'hoansi**, **!Kung** and **Kxoe**), have found their way into recordings and performances. These polyphonic songs with characteristic "yodel" sounds and intricate clapping patterns are difficult to replicate, but dance groups and bands bring in some instrumental riffs that imitate musical bows and traditional vocal techniques to add flavour to their music. The Ocora compilation *Ju/'hoansi Bushman Instrumental Music* is a spell-binding blend of voice and instruments, featuring their lamellophones, bows, and **pluriarcs** – multi-bowed instruments, usually five bows with strings attached to a boat-shaped resonator. Of course, the music of the different

San groups shares many characteristics across the eastern border with Botswana. **Kuela Kiema**, originally from Botswana but resident in Namibia, digs deep into his musical heritage to sing songs of healing and trance, using his mouthbow and *dingo* (lamellophone) to accompany his evocative songs. Unfortunately his album *Bili, bilo heri* is currently unavailable; a pity, because this music is moody and intense and conveys the essence of this tradition convincingly. One of the few contemporary female singers from eastern regions is **Lydia Tsâtagos** who is experimenting with Afro-fusion, using her eastern Damara musical background to great effect. Her pre-release song *Ma oa te* holds promise of good things to come. The singer **Patricia** has been around longer and is better known for her blend of urban and traditional sounds.

Imported Sounds

The central area around Windhoek is a cultural salad-bowl. All kinds of sounds and rhythms are tossed into this experimental mix, and people are often more concerned about what the music "says" than how it sounds. Foreign always seems to be better in local minds, so clubs and theatres showcase bands playing Angolan kizomba (**Impactus 4**), *zouk* and *soukous* (**Papa Fransua and Tropical Tune**, **Boetie & Janice**, **Kondombolos**, **Omidi d'Afrique**). By far the most popular urban youth groove is **kwaito**, imported from South Africa and the best-selling local music around. **Gazza**'s songs with irresistible, driving kwaito beat regularly make the local hit parade, and sell surprisingly well. **The Dogg** does kwaito as well as hip-hop. **Shikololo**, newcomer **Shiku** and others are following the same trend, unfortunately with little to distinguish one from another. The main thing, however, is to create danceable music. Several young hip-hop artists have made an appearance – The Dogg, **Don Gabrio**, **Pablo D'ablo**, **Boli Mootseng** and others – usually producing one album only. Bolli's album *Out on Bail*, however, does contain some ballads, like "Lickle While".

Few of the older musicians have managed good cross-ethnic songs, but **Jackson Kaujeua** must be the exception. Although he isn't as active on the music scene these days, few will forget his songs during the time of the struggle about freedom, nationalism, patriotism and love in almost all the local languages. Happily, his best-known compositions, like "!Nubu !guwus", still remain on radio playlists.

Reggae-based sounds have found a firm hold in the central region, but seem mostly to come from the northern part amongst Oshiwambo-speaking people. **Ras Sheehama**, one of Namibia's most experienced and popular musicians, favours traditional reggae, and his song "City Young Girl" remains a firm favourite. He started off with his band more than a decade ago, and has of late developed smoother singing, with a South African recording studio seeing to slick backing. His most recent release *Pure Love*, takes a new direction into Oshiwambo ballads and soft jazz sounds. *Ngatu* also composes his own *shambo* songs on the album *Biggest Gift*, and he brings his own mixed musical traditions into his work.

Looking for a Revolution

Given the above, it sounds as though the recording business is booming. Sadly, this is not so. One of the effects of colonialism in Namibia is **big-brother syndrome**, otherwise known as living in the shadow of South Africa. Namibians tend to believe that other African musicians are better than locals. For many years there have been hardly any facilities in Namibia, and musicians are encouraged to do their recordings in South Africa, using their backing musicians and singers. Apart from the high cost, those albums are distributed in South Africa but are really hard to find in Namibia – except by contacting the artist him/herself. At the same time local record stores, most of which are South African franchises, do not distribute Namibian recordings. Luckily someone like Ras Sheehama is popular enough to ensure that his records can usually be found in stores. A few small stores in the city centre have a fairly good local selection, distributed in most cases by musicians themselves. Here you might be lucky enough to find albums by **Eric** (Mahua), **Backos**, **Pulakena**, **Elemotho**, **Steve Hanana**, **Richo** and others. In 2004, Backos' song "/Ûbagu" from his album *Backos-JB's* proved very popular on radio playlists. This song, despite being sung in the Khoekhoe language, was enjoyed by people across the different language barriers. Interestingly, this album was financed by a construction company, hence the "JB's". Though lately unavailable, Backos insists that it will be "back on the shelves soon".

None of the internationally known labels exist in Namibia. Recently Welwitschia (!Narusib) Music Studios took the initiative of taking several groups on the road for a series of shows to raise awareness and, hopefully, some funds. Producers like **Narusib** prefer to specialize in one musical style, his being Damara punch. As one musician says, 'He (the producer) makes the music. The singers just sing.'

The fact that almost every album in Namibia emerges on a "new" label is a concern. Many of these are under-financed or poorly managed, and start up and rapidly close down. In addition, session or studio musicians are not readily available or affordable for most bands, so producers use PC-based home studios, resulting in often tinny and poorly balanced sound quality. A musician like **Kakazona Kavari** (Konganda) has an interesting voice and brings in appealing musical effects from his Herero heritage, but his songs would be greatly enhanced by better backing. The same applies to people like **Pablo D'ablo O'outlaw** (Alles Mumwe), **Patricia** and others. 'But we like that sound. It is traditional,' says Lydia Tsâtagos.

One positive development is that local radio stations are picking up the call from the artists' union Oruuano to give far more airtime to local artists. Stations like Radio Energy and Radio Kosmos have done this and really made a difference to artists' public image. So, despite the current lack of enterprise, the sudden surge of available CDs made possible by the cheap home-based studios, might encourage a stable music industry in the near future.

Festivals

Since independence in 1990, cultural troupes, festivals and competitions have suddenly taken off. The Directorate of Culture and Heritage at the Ministry of Basic Education, Culture and Sport started a **National Cultural Festival**, through a regional process of elimination, with the best entrants ending up at the national festival. The purpose of the festival is mainly to celebrate cultural diversity and encourage people to become familiar with the cultures of the entire region. Because such events didn't happen in the past, the early entrants had some difficulties in adapting their traditional performances for a removed audience. But the lure of a substantial cash prize and a possible government-funded tour has had a motivating effect. But unfortunately, no recordings of these groups have yet seen the light.

The promulgation of the Policy on Arts and Culture of the Republic of Namibia (2001) confirmed the government's view on the importance of heritage preservation and the festival continues on an annual basis. Unfortunately, all the arts have taken a back seat on the government's priority list, and remain ridiculously under-funded. Namibia's musicians really need to get up and take control of their own industry before it runs aground completely.

⊙ **Namibia. Songs of the Ju/'hoansi Bushmen**
⊙ **Namibia. Ju/'hoansi Bushmen Instrumental Music**
Ocora-Radio France, France

Though the first is currently out of print, these two rare albums give a wonderful overview of the most important Ju/'hoan songs and instrumental music, including games, hunting and trance songs. Recorded in the 1990s by ethnomusicologist Emmanuelle Olivier in the Nyae Nyae area during her doctoral field research.

⊙ **A Hand-full of Namibians & Papa Wemba**
FNCC/Hothouse Productions, Namibia

A compilation of Namibia's best-known contemporary musicians, along with Papa Wemba. As a cross-section, this is a good introduction to local sounds and musicians.

Ras Sheehama

Born in 1966, Namibia's most famous reggae star Ras hails from a well-known family in the far north. Ras started his musical career in the 1980s, won the Sanlam music award 2003 and has performed in many countries.

⭐ **Pure Love**
African Cream Music, South Africa

This album showcases Ras' voice against a slick backing. Ranging from straight reggae to more jazzy fusion ("Midnight") and the lovely ballad in Oshiwambo, Inotila, with its simple guitar accompaniment.

Backos

With his band, Amako, Backos sings in the much-loved southern style of Damara punch. He works in Windhoek at a local education college, but collaborates closely with friend and producer Naruseb at the coast to create their distinctive sound.

⊙ **Backos-JB'S**
Amako Productions, Namibia

With music composed by Andrew !Aibeb, and vocals by Backos, this album brings typical music of southern Namibia, but managed to transcend ethnic barriers in its popular appeal.

Set-son and the Mighty Dreads

Set-son Wahengo and the band The Mighty Dreads, consisting of his brothers, Tulonga and Jackson, on rhythm and lead guitars, Erik Hamutenya on bass, and Steven Naruseb on keyboard. All are from the north, except Naruseb, and have been performing together for several years.

⊙ **Kula-Umone**
Self-produced, Namibia

A cool fusion of traditional Owambo songs and original compositions. The title-track, with the sound of *okabulumbumbwa* (bow) recreated in the intro, manages to invoke a real Namibian sound and makes a welcome entrance on the Namibian music scene.

PLAYLIST
Namibia

1 **INOTILA Ras Sheehama** from *Pure Love*
An Oshiwambo ballad expressing hope and support in facing problems of the modern world.

2 **KULA-UMONE Set-son and The Mighty Dreads** from *Kula-Umone*
The opening recalls traditional resonated bow sounds, while the clapping and vocals suggest images of *omupembe* – the leaping dance of young men.

3 **!NUBU !GUWUS Jackson Kaujeua** from *A Hand-full of Namibians & Papa Wemba*
A classic Namibian song in Khoekhoe celebrating the beautiful roundness of a young woman.

4 **UBAGU Backos** from *Backos-JB's*
This track is not only danceable, but its catchy hook made it a popular local hit.

5 **PYTHON Various artists** from *Namibia. Ju/'hoansi Bushmen Instrumental Music*
This recreational women's song is accompanied by the four-string *pluriarc* (with a metal can as resonator). Three voices blend in characteristically gentle singing.

Niger & Touareg

sounds of the sahel

Tinariwen
Éric Mulet

Niger is a huge, landlocked nation, merging with the Sahara to the north, and it has tended to be in the shadow of the great musical cultures of West Africa. The Sahel drought of 1973 left an enduring legacy of economic hardship, halting the country's small output of recordings. Again, in 2005, the country was more concerned with keeping famine at bay than with promoting music and the arts. Yet although Niger may command a very small space in the CD racks, François Bensignor contends that there's a store of good sounds here – from traditional music to hip-hop. And in recent years the music of the nomadic Touareg, who span Niger, Mali and Algeria, has become positively hip thanks to the Festival in the Desert and the phenomenal Tinariwen.

Niger's diverse culture embraces the largely nomadic Touareg in the north, the Hausa in the centre and south, the Beriberi in the east, the Djerma and Songhai in the west and the Dendi in the south. All these groups have their own distinctive traditional musics.

A Map of Niger

The **Touareg** comprise only around three percent of Niger's population, but their culture is remarkable. They live in the northern regions of the Ténéré desert and Aïr mountains and still travel throughout the Sahel. They have kept up a tradition for vivid and refined **courtly love poetry**, praising women's qualities in the blooming Tamashek language. Music can be played by anyone, both men and women – there is no professional caste – and, as with most nomadic cultures, there are few instruments. On the periphery of the desert, around the town of Tahoua, Hausa influences have crept in, characterized by the art of folk fiddle and calabash percussion.

The **Hausa** people, who make up just over half the country's population, live in central southern Niger, around the town of Maradi. Their music can be recognized by the beautiful melodies of their chordophones, especially the little two-stringed *molo* lute; by the *duma* percussion, played by a seated drummer pressing the skin of the drum with his foot to vary the sound; and by the *kalangu*, a talking drum often found in modern orchestras.

Music in Zinder in the southeast is characterized by the big double-skinned *ganga* drum with resonator, the *alghaïta* shawm and the long *kakati* trumpet.

Further east, the **Beriberi** people, who live near Lake Chad, also play the *alghaïta* but are best known for their beautiful polyphonic singing, comparable to the polyphony of the **Wodaabe Fulani**, whose famous, face-painted dancing ceremony for young men, the *gerewol*, is such an important annual date on Niger's calendar.

In the western part of the country along the Niger River, where the capital Niamey is located, live the smaller groupings of **Djerma** and **Songhai**. Musically, the region is notable for a wide variety of instruments from other parts of the country and across the borders, including lutes, fiddles, flutes, and various percussion instruments. They are usually played solo in their respective home regions but musicians in western Niger play them together in orchestras.

In the far southwest along the Benin and Nigeria frontiers is the land of the **Dendi**, who use techniques and instruments from both of the neighbouring countries. They are known for performing some of the finest music in Niger.

Cultural Policy

In strongly Muslim Niger, music as entertainment is not readily accepted, and for many years after independence there was little cultural policy, unlike in Mali or Guinea. However, after the death of the military dictator Seyni Kounché in 1987 the new government looked to music as a means of bringing the cultures together. Previously, with each community playing their own traditional music in a non-professional environment, the different groups in Niger were largely ignorant of one other's music.

A competitive music festival was launched, the **Prix Dan Gourmou**, with a cash prize and a national tour of the youth club circuit for the winner. It was set up by, among others, **Alassane Dante**, formerly director of the National Ballet and co-director of the Centre Culturel Franco-Nigerien (CCFN). The contest prompted the formation of music and dance ensembles throughout the country. Some wanted to add modern instruments to the traditional ones, and this in turn led to the establishment of the **CFPM** (Centre for Musical Training and Promotion), as a place where musicians could be trained in modern techniques and instruments. This materialized in 1990, thanks to a six-year grant from the European Fund for Development.

Over the years, the centre has been progressively stripped of its equipment, such as microphones and instruments, but it remains a useful workspace with rehearsal rooms, a small studio and a performance hall. In 2005, the French overseas development agency funded the purchase of new instruments, but compared to neighbouring countries Niger is still under-resourced. The capital Niamey has only two small studios, one of them the CFPM studio, and the country has only two tape-duplicating companies. Generally musicians produce their own cassettes and then pass them on to small distributors; if they can sell two thousand tapes they're doing well, considering all the cheap copies put out by pirates.

Formed with the best musicians working at CFPM and five singers — **Moussa Poussy**, **Yacouba Moumouni**, **Adam's Junior**, **Fati Mariko** and **John Sofakolé** — the group Takeda played at MASA 1995 in Abidjan, which helped some of the musicians move forward. Following Boncana Maïga's advice, international producer Ibrahima Sylla signed singers Moussa Poussy and **Saadou**

Touareg Rockers and Desert Blues

No one quite knows for sure where the nomadic **Touareg**, or **Kel Tamashek** as they call themselves, came from originally. Sometime between the eighth and twelfth centuries AD, they migrated south and populated the vast plains and remote mountain ranges of the southern Sahara desert. They brought their **Berber**, or Amazigh, culture with them and today it is clearly evident in their language, **Tamashek**, and their matriarchal society. These roots also explain the Tamashek people's profound attachment to music and poetry.

The two instruments that form the bedrock of traditional Tamashek music are the *tindé* drum, and a one-stringed fiddle called an *imzad*. Both are the strict preserve of women. Men content themselves with the *teherdent* lute, the shepherd's flute, singing and handclaps. They also express themselves with sword dances and camel parades. Traditional *tindé* troupes and *imzad* virtuosi are legion, but the group that has most successfully brought these traditional sounds to a worldwide audience are the **Tartit Ensemble** from the Timbuktu region, led by the charismatic and determined **Fadimata Walet Oumar**, aka "Disco". Tartit, which means "Union", was formed in the Mauritanian refugee camps which gave the people of northern Mali sanctuary during the bitterest years of the Touareg rebellion in the early 1990s. Their music is a traditional response to modern hardships.

In contrast, **Tinariwen**, who come from an area called the Adrar des Iforas in the far northeastern corner of Mali, swapped their traditional instruments for guitars in the late 1970s and early 80s. Their founder and leader, **Ibrahim Ag Alhabib**, is credited with inventing the modern rock-generation style of Tamashek music, which has become known simply as "guitar".

The band formed in Tamanrasset in 1979, and they developed their music in military camps set up in Libya by Colonel Ghaddafi to train young Tamashek men how to fight. During the rebellion Tinariwen became the pied pipers of the rebel movement, and their songs galvanized the young dispossessed Tamashek youth, who were living the *clandestino* life in Algeria or Libya, into concerted revolt. Since the first **Festival in the Desert** in 2001, Tinariwen have become global musical nomads, taking their message of desert pride to the four corners of the earth.

Further east in the desert of northern Niger, a singer and guitarist called Abdallah Ag Oumbadougou, a.k.a. **Abdallah du Niger**, is a skilful exponent of that same desert guitar style. His collaboration with the French composer and musical visionary **Philippe Eidel** on the score of the 1997 film *Imuhar, une légende* remains a crucial signpost to potential future styles of Tamashek music. The score was enhanced by the participation of the wonderful **Groupe Oyiwane**, a musical collective of long standing from northern Niger. Abdallah du Niger is re-emerging onto an international stage as part of a new Franco-Nigerien project called **Desert Rebelle**, which involves notable France-based artists like Tryo, Gnawa Diffusion, Mano Negra, Sally Nyolo and IAM and friends from northern Niger. Other Tamashek groups from Mali and Niger that deserve notice, and a recording deal, are **Tarbiat**, **Telouat** and **Tidawt**.

Moving north, Tamanrasset, the oasis in the southern Algerian desert which is the closest thing the Tamashek people have to a capital city, has a surprisingly prolific music scene. But there's one musical clan that dominates this part of the world: the **Othmani family** from Djanet in the Tassilli 'n' Ajjer region. **Baly Othmani**, an *oud* player and vocalist of renown, almost single-handedly lifted Tamashek music out of obscurity in the 1990s, with the help of the roving American musician and composer **Steve Shehan**. The clan matriarch **Khadija Othmani** is a poet and singer of rare qualities, and she reigns over a family which boasts generations of accomplished singers and musicians. Many of them perform on an extraordinary CD entitled *Ikewan,* or "Touareg Memories". All lovers of Tamashek music were shocked by news of the death of Baly Othmani in June 2005. He was swept away by a flash flood brought on by one of the torrential downpours that curse and bless this most arid of landscapes during the brief annual rainy season.

Andy Morgan

Mamar Kassey back home

Bori. Both their albums were produced in Abidjan's JBZ studio by Boncana Maïga and arranged by Abdoulaye "Abdallah" Alassane, the guitar player and leader of Takeda. (Most of the tracks from these albums subsequently appeared together on the CD *Niamey Twice* on the Stern's label.)

In 1997, Abdallah went to Bamako to produce **Adam's Junior**'s reggae album on Salif Keita's label. Abdallah also worked with Yacouba Moumouni's group **Mamar Kassey**, playing on both their albums, *Denké-Denké* (1998) and *Alatoumi* (2000), and touring internationally with the group before moving to the United States.

Mamar Kassey was the first group to bring the very particular flavour of Nigerien music to a worldwide audience, and this international recognition found an echo with audiences back home. In a country where musicians generally receive little support, the group showed that it was possible to create modern Nigerien music based on rich local traditions. Their example inspired young groups such as **Super Bonkaney** in Niamey and **Dangana** in Zinder. Formed in 2001, the latter is showing great potential, according to Philippe Conrath, director of the French festival Africolor and the Cobalt label: 'In order to get away from the local popular dance music and find their own sound, these musicians decided to replace the drum set with two large terracotta jars struck with the hand or with sticks, a high hat, a cymbal and a snare drum. They make a fabulous sound … They alternate bass, guitar and kalangu solos with rock'n'roll-style efficiency – in a way that might surprise an international audience.'

Hopping Youth Clubs

'Niger has something that none of the neighbouring countries has: an active network of youth clubs with viable equipment in each one,' declares Alassane Dante. And hip-hop has come along and made the most of it. Nigerien rap has followed in the footsteps of **Tod One**, a pioneering group formed by young Nigeriens living in exile in Belgium. Tod One played at the very first rap concert given in Niamey at the CCFN in 1996. There were two other groups there, too – **Massacreur** and **Wassika**. Wassika was the first group to write its lyrics in the national languages, Hausa and Djerma. In 1999, it merged with another group, **Wongary**, to form **WassWong**. A number of competitions broadcast on the radio and television boosted rap's popularity over the next few years, and Radio Ténéré's support for the group **Lakal Kaney** helped spread the hip-hop craze to the country's remotest regions. In 2001, Niamey had about a hundred rap groups; two years later, the newspaper *Le Sahel* counted 250 groups in five of Niger's seven départements. In 2001, four groups, **Black Daps**, **Djoro G**, WassWong and **Kaïdan Gaskia**, all of whom had already cut an album, got together to form a collective, **Lilwal**. Kaïdan Gaskia took part in the benefit concert Music Against Hunger organized by Niger's first lady, Madame Laraba Tandja, a month after the Live 8 concert in 2005. Co-organized by Initiative Jeune, Unicef and the CCFN, the "Scène ouverte rap" competition was held in 2004. The prize for the three winners, **Sah Fonda** (from Tillabery), **MTS Matassa** (from Zinder) and **Metaphore** Crew (from Niamey), was a tour of some of the country's youth clubs. Comprising around ten concerts and a circuit of about 3000km, it took them as far as the town of Arlit, in the middle of the desert. There's nothing like being thrown in at the deep end.

DISCOGRAPHY Niger & Touareg

NIGER & TOUAREG

★ The Festival in the Desert
IRL, UK

This recording from the 2003 Festival in the Desert has become a classic – and rightly so. You can almost feel the sand between your toes, with performances from Tinariwen and Tartit, as well as Ali Farka Touré, Oumou Sangare, LoJo and Robert Plant.

⊙ Anthologie de la musique du Niger
Ocora, France

Wonderful historical recordings made in situ back in 1963 by composer and ethnomusicologist Tolia Nikiprowetsky with Songhai, Djerma, Hausa, Beriberi, Touareg and Fulani traditional musicians. A must.

⊙ Niger – Music of the Touaregs Vol 1: Azawagh
⊙ Niger – Music of the Touaregs Vol 2 : In Gall
VDE-Gallo, Switzerland

Recorded between 1973 and 1998 by two Swiss researchers, François Borel and Ernst Lichtenhahn, these two albums feature less-well-known aspects of Touareg music such as the *belluwel* and *akhaguwwen* singing techniques of the peoples of the Azawagh region in northwest Niger. Some fine examples of their music can be heard on vol 1. On vol 2, devoted to the peoples living around the small town of In Gall, you can hear the *alghasbah* flute backed by voices humming a drone, as well as the mystical chant known as *dhikr*.

⊙ Wodaabe Fulani: Worso Songs
Inédit, France

This record captures the strange singing and handclapping that accompanies the *worso* ceremonies of the Wodaabe section of the Fulani. *Worso* is a ritual in which young men compete with their clothes, jewels, painted faces and dancing, over several nights, to be elected the most handsome by the assembled young women.

Abdallah du Niger

In terms of physical beauty and cultural wealth, the northern Nigerien city of Agadez and the Aïr desert that surrounds it take some beating. Abdallah Ag Oumbadougou, a.k.a. Abdallah du Niger, has been the leading musical light of this area for years. His skilful desert blues renditions on the guitar and his powerful vocal style have made him extremely popular.

WITH PHILIPPE EIDEL

⊙ Imuhar (St George)
Sony, France

The iconoclastic French producer Philippe Eidel obviously took a lot of pleasure from his one-off encounter with Tamashek music. Abdallah du Niger provides the basis of his experiments, but other Nigerien musicians including Salar

Abnou and Ajo also contributed raw material, which Eidel then enhanced with the help of a whole host of Parisian instrumentalists, and a touch of slide guitar from the prolific Bob Brozman. The results are patchy, but in places very, very good, and moreover, some of Eidel's ideas offer templates for future Tamashek styles.

Saadou Bori and Moussa Poussy

Two singer-songwriters who worked together in the national music school's house band, Takeda, and went on to bigger things in Abidjan. Both have spiritual backgrounds: Djerma performer Moussa Poussy as the grandson of a traditional healer and Hausa-speaker Saadou Bori as a practitioner of *dango* (Hausa spirit music) and trance-dancing.

⊙ Niamey Twice
Stern's, UK

A double helping of modern Niger, recorded in Abidjan under the direction of Ibrahima Sylla and previously released in West Africa on two separate cassettes. Six original compositions from each singer swing along happily, Poussy's mostly in Mande style, though with a nod to Alpha Blondy's reggae. The music of Saadou Bori is more interesting for its rare presentation of Hausa influences, and on the more offbeat numbers – "Dango" and "Bori" – the spirit-loving polyrhythms bubble through frenetically.

Etran Finatawa

Etran Finaawa are in the Tinariwen mould, producing powerful trance-like music, with rock guitars and driving percussion and chanting. The group consists of four

Tartit Ensemble – heartbeat of traditional Touareg music

Touareg and six Wodaabe (distinctive in their striking face paints). Despite different heritages and languages, they are both nomads of the Sahelian savannah and were brought together by the interest in desert sounds created around the annual Festival In The Desert.

⭐ Introducing Etran Finatawa
World Music Network, UK

Although the Touareg and Wodaabe cultures are allegedly very different this debut album suggests that, musically at least, there's far more that unites them than divides them. This set of songs concerns healing, herding cattle and even camel racing. Some are disarmingly simple, consisting of little more than hypnotic patterns beaten out on calabashes underpinning call-and-response vocals. Others are more developed with snaking, bluesy guitar lines, such as 'Surbajo', a cracking pop tune that is basically a desert chat-up song.

Harouna Goge

Harouna, just like his father, though against his wishes, has become a virtuoso of the small one-stringed *goge* fiddle, whose soundbox is made of iguana skin and from which Harouna takes his surname.

⊙ Niger: musique Dendi
Ocora, France

Harouna sings here the music of the Dendi country which extends across southern Niger and northern Benin. His songs, mostly spirit invocations, are accompanied by the *goge*, occasionally joined by a flute, a one-stringed lute called a *kountiji* and gourds.

Mamar Kassey

Mostly inspired by Fulani, Hausa, Songhai and Djerma traditional music, Mamar Kassey is the first group from Niger to take its music to an international audience, and it can now compete with the best from Mali.

⊙ Denké-Denké
Daqui, France

Fula flute, *molo* lute and *kalangu* talking drum drive thirteen

beautiful songs on historic, social and more personal themes. One of them, "Yacouba", tells the lead singer's story from his youth in the bush to his adult life as a musician.

⭐ Alatoumi
Daqui, France

Sharp as the Harmattan wind cutting through the desert, Mamar Kassey's style deepens with this second album. Their worldwide tours have taught the band how to shape a song for any listener, but always in their luminous idiom. Traditional instruments and chanting take you on a fascinating journey through the Sahel.

Othmani Family

Based in the Algerian oasis of Djanet, the Othmani family is one of the most important preserving the traditions of Touareg music.

⊙ Ikewan: Touareg Memories
Long Distance, France

An atmospheric recording that takes you to the heart of Touareg Sahara, featuring the veteran Khadija Othmani on vocals and her sons Othman and the late lamented Baly. One track features the *imzad*, the emblematic Touareg fiddle.

Tartit Ensemble

In the 1980s and early 90s a devastating combination of drought and rebellion almost obliterated the old nomadic ways and drove many Tamashek people into exile. Founded by members of the powerful and progressive Kel Antessar tribe, Tartit's music preserves the *tindé* drum heartbeat of traditional Touareg music, but their lyrics are resolutely focused on the trials and tribulations of modernity.

⭐ Ichichila
Network, Germany

Still probably the best recording of traditional Tamashek music available on CD, there's a certain discipline and creative focus brought to bear on the raw and unselfconscious grooves of traditional campsite music.

Tinariwen

More than any other, this group of rebel poet guitarists embody the Kel Tamashek's struggle with oppression and exile.

⊙ **The Radio Tisdas Sessions**
IRL, UK
A raw and rugged snapshot of Tinariwen recorded in their native town of Kidal. With its slicing guitar riffs, loping *takamba* beats, call-and-response vocals and cracking handclaps this music is both unique and resolutely modern.

★ **Amassakoul**
IRL, UK
This 2004 album, coming on top of the *Festival in the Desert* CD, really put Tinariwen on the map and helped them capture a BBC World Music Award. Its production is a little more sophisticated but the same bluesy guitar riffs and camel-lope rhythms come through loud and clear.

PLAYLIST
Niger & Touareg

Niger

1 **MAÏGA ET TOURÉ Mamar Kassey** from *Alatoumi*
A praise song to the major royal families: the Touré who rule Gao and the Maïga of Tinfirma.

2 **ZATAW Harouna Goge** from *Niger: musique Dendi*
Reki Tamtalla sings the praises of the spirit Zataw in Songhai, accompanied by the goge, flute and gourds.

3 **BELLUWEL** from *Niger – Music of the Touaregs Vol 1: Azawagh*
A young girl imitates a simple clarinet, cupping one hand to her mouth and tapping her throat with the other hand.

4 **BODJO Amo Goda** from *Anthologie de la musique du Niger*
Accompanied by a kalangu and a kurutu drum, a woman's solo voice and four backing vocalists sing in praise of young male drivers.

5 **GEREOL Wodaabe Fulani** from *Worso Songs*
The well-known dance of the last phase of the Worso ritual, this superb cycle alternates chant and song.

Touareg

1 **AMASSAKOUL 'N'TÉNÉRÉ Tinariwen** from *Amassakoul*
The deep strum of electric guitar and bluesy vocals puntuate this song –"Traveller in the Desert"– from the celebrated Touareg rockers.

2 **TAMALLET N'AYOR Othman Othmani** from *Ikewan*
A slow nostalgic song accompanied by Tarzagh Benomar on the bowed *imzad*, the quintessential Touareg instrument, evoking the desert.

3 **HOLIYANE HOLIYANA Tartit** from *Ichichila*
A circular pattern on the guitar and handclaps accompany the female vocals in this captivating song of seduction.

4 **HEEME Etran Finatawa** from *Introducing Etran Finatawa*
Just voices, percussion, ululation and handclaps, on a song in praise of racing camels.

5 **ARIYALAN Tidawt** from *The Festival in the Desert*
From the town of Agadez in northern Niger, this Touareg band with their swathes of turban and electric guitars did a great set at the 2003 Festival.

Nigeria

africa's stumbling giant

The great Fela Kuti
Ian Dickson/Redferns

With over 140 million people, 250 distinct languages and hundreds of ethnic and sub-ethnic groups, Nigeria is a nation of unique complexity in Africa. Made up of huge, densely populated cities, small villages and rural landscapes, it encompasses the commercial capitals of Lagos and Onitsha, the great seaports of Calabar and Port Harcourt and the ancient city-states of Kano, Sokoto, Oyo, Maidugari and Benin. Its best-known cultural exports – juju, Afro-beat and fuji music – barely scratch the surface of the vast and vibrant cultural topography of the nation. Andrew Frankel begs the reader's indulgence for the short shrift he gives so many of the worthy styles and genres.

I n terms of cultural output Nigeria is unrivalled in Africa, with hundreds of studios, thousands of performance venues of all sizes and countless artists and performing groups throughout the country. Yet, excepting its few internationally known African pop icons (**Fela Kuti**, **Sunny Ade** and **Femi Kuti**), the country's artistry remains a mystery to all but the most ardent adventurers into Nigerian music – those who go to the country, or ply Nigeria's expatriate market shops in Hackney, Brooklyn, Frankfurt, Milan, Dubai, Singapore and other foreign cities where communities of Nigerians have landed and swelled in the four decades since independence.

Nigerian Uniqueness

What makes Nigerian music so vast yet so insular? First, with 140 million citizens and growing, Nigeria's internal population is audience enough to sustain most artistic endeavours, and most artists tailor their music to a domestic audience. Another factor is its relative wealth. Although the trend since the 1980s has been towards eliminating the once enormous middle class in favour of super-rich and super-poor, Nigeria is still an economic giant in Africa, with oil, industrial and trade revenues in multiples of billions. Still another factor is what you might call cultural myopia. Nigeria's rich cultural heritage is a great source of pride, and Nigerians also have a great sense of the intrinsic worth of their nation, at least in the abstract sense. While any Nigerian will share a grousing session with you about what is wrong with the country (it is a long list), their passion for Nigeria shines through. All this is to say that most Nigerian music is made for the unique tastes of Nigerians.

One principle is consistent throughout all of Nigeria's forms of musical expression – the power and primacy of words as the formative element of expression. In fact, in many of Nigeria's cultures, there is no word for music, but rather a variety of highly evolved categories for speech, poetry and metaphor as well as terms for drumming, dance and song. Thus Nigerian music is primarily shaped by the power of words and verbal expression, in both indigenous languages and English, with such concerns as harmony and tuning relegated to a secondary status.

Nigerian Peoples

Nigeria is broadly conceived of in four major regions in alignment with the major ethnic groups. In the north are the **Hausa**, **Fulani** and **Kanuri**, who make up some 29 percent of the population.

The Kanuri, descendants of the Kanem Bornu empire (AD 800–1800), and the Hausa, founders of seven great city-states, including Kano (AD 993), Zaria (AD 1000) and Katsina (AD 1100), were until the beginning of the nineteenth century the dominant political powers in what was to become northern Nigeria. But between 1804 and 1808 the previously pastoral and often oppressed Fulani rose under the leadership of Usman Dan Fodio to conquer all of the north of Nigeria and beyond, incorporating it into his vast Sokoto Caliphate, the biggest empire in Africa since the fall of Songhai in the sixteenth century.

In the southwest, the **Yoruba** and their numerous subgroups make up around 21 percent of the population, traditionally residing in regional city kingdoms such as Ife, Oyo and Ijebu. As with the Hausa and Kanuri, the political geography of the Yoruba was profoundly shaped by Usman Dan Fodio's campaign, which saw the sacking of numerous kingdoms. The Fulani raids also led to the establishment of the city of Abeokuta ("under a rock") as a safe refuge for the Egba subgroup, and of a vast refugee settlement called Ibadan, which remains Nigeria's second-biggest city today. The Egba are famed for their political and artistic achievements – both President Obasanjo and the Kuti family are Egba.

The southeast is home to the **Igbo** people who make up some 18 percent of the nation. Igbos dominate much of Nigeria's trade, import and export business, as well as a thriving manufacturing industry specializing in copies of almost anything one might like to buy from car parts to clothing. The major Igbo cities are the trading centres of Onitsha, Aba and Owerri.

The Niger Delta area is increasingly being recognized as a fourth distinct region, both for its importance as the oil-producing centre of the country and for its increasingly prominent civil strife. The region is wildly diverse and includes the **Kalabari**, **Ikwerre**, **Okrika**, **Ibani** (Bonny and Opobo), **Ekpeye**, **Ogba**, **Etche**, **Khana**, **Gokana**, **Eleme**, **Ndoni** and **Abua** peoples, to name a few.

The remaining 35 per cent of Nigeria's population are found in several diverse but autonomous regions. The **Benin** people, though related to the Yoruba, are centered on the kingdom and modern city of that name. The Riverine region on the far southeastern edge of Nigeria around the city of Calabar is populated by the **Efik**, **Ejagham** and **Bekwara** peoples. The city of Jos in the Plateau region in the centre of the country was established as a mineral trading camp in the early twentieth century, and has a consequentially diverse regional population. In the Sahelian region north of the

Yoruba are the **Nupe** and a variety of related ethnic groups.

Each of these hundreds of ethnic groups has distinct musical and cultural traditions which it is beyond the scope of this article to describe, so we will limit ourselves to a few of the major trends.

Instruments

The Yoruba people are well known for their elaborate drumming traditions, some of which – along with Yoruba religion – have taken root in Brazil, Cuba, Surinam, the US and elsewhere, where they continue to thrive as living traditions. The heart of Yoruba music is the **spoken language**. Elaborate language, formulaic speech (metaphors, proverbs and poetry) and a rich tradition of oral history are central to traditional Yoruba cultural identity. Because Yoruba itself is a tone language, the sound contours of formulaic speech (the tonal and rhythmic patterns of commonly used phrases) can be replicated by multiple-pitched instruments in a way that is easily recognizable by any Yoruba speaker. Much, if not all, Yoruba traditional music is built around the spoken language as replicated on instruments.

While Yoruba percussion comes in endless varieties, two common percussion ensembles found widely today are the *dundun* and the *bata*. *Dundun* are hourglass shaped, variable-pitched instruments with leather tensioning thongs connecting the membranes which cover each end of the hourglass. They come in a wide range of sizes and are played by anything from a solo artist to large sonorous orchestras of over fifty drummers. An *iya ilu* (mother drum) will establish the rhythm and tempo and all the accompanying drums will pick up complex interlocking rhythms to support the mother drum's speechifying.

Bata are conical-shaped drums with fixed-pitch skins stretched across both heads. The *iya ilu bata* is worn horizontally across the player's front. The low-pitched end is played with a hand while the high-pitched end is beaten with a leather strap (*bilala*). *Bata* are typically played in ensembles of three or four players, with an *iya ilu*, a slightly smaller support drum called *omele abo* and a much smaller set of *bata* called *omele ako* and *kudi* which are bound together in sets of two or three. *Bata* are traditionally associated with Sango – the Yoruba god of thunder – and are still the drums of choice for many traditional religious practices. Because of this association they have come under fire from Christian and Muslim leaders in Nigeria and have noticeably diminished, though they remain a vibrant tradition. Other Yoruba percussion instruments include *bembe*, *koso*, *abinti*, *agogo*, *shekere* and *sakara*. The musical principles which organize them – interlocking polyrhythmic background with a lead drum speaking – hold true for each of these ensembles, and still define both traditional and pop Yoruba music today.

Hulton Archive/Getty images

Tiv flautists

The Igbo perform in a great array of musical styles, but one commonly found instrument is the *ikoro*, or slit gong. A log of wood is hollowed out through a narrow slit leaving lips on either end of the slit which can be beaten with a mallet or stick to produce a woody-keyed sound much like a marimba. The ikoro can have many pitches depending on the thickness of the wood in different places along its surface. Because Igbo, like Yoruba, is a tonal language, the ikoro can be used as a "speaking" instrument.

Another common and influential Igbo instrument is the *udu* pot drum. Like the southern Indian

289

ghatam, it is a resonant ceramic vessel which has a bright staccato pitch when tapped on the side, and a deep resonant boom when the player strikes the open mouth of the vessel.

In the north of Nigeria one finds the string instruments common to the whole West African Sahel, such as the three-stringed lute called *molo*, and the boat-shaped lute called *kontigi* by the Hausa (related to the *xalam* in Senegal and *gimbri* in Morocco). These are usually played solo as an accompaniment to vocal music, and one of northern Nigeria's greatest praise singers, **Dan Maraya**, performs primarily on a *kontigi*.

Form and function are guided by environment, so in contrast to southern Nigeria, where dense populations and complex social order are expressed musically in large complex musical ensembles, in the rural parts of northern Nigeria where nomadic herders still wander the plains, one finds a variety of portable solo instruments ranging from Jew's harps to flutes and reed instruments.

In the north's city-states where emirs still reign, royal arrivals are still announced by the *kakaki*, a brass trumpet over ten feet long – one of the iconic symbols of the nation. The Hausa and Kanuri also have an hour-glass-shaped talking drum (*kananngo*), of slightly different construction from its southern counterpart, which is played in small ensembles to support courtly praise song.

In Nigeria's diverse middle states, home to the **Ayu**, **Bada**, **Cori**, **Duguri**, **Eggon**, **Tiv** and many others, there are rich traditions of *balafon* or xylophone worn around the neck and played polyphonically in ensembles of four or more with the support of gourd rattles.

In the delta region, peoples such as the **Isoko** and **Sekiri** have lush-sounding vocal music in which they sing in parallel fourths and fifths (harmonies which sound quite exotic to the Western ear) to the accompaniment of large and deeply resonant drums made from the hollowed stumps of palm trees.

Juju

In Nigeria, even the most contemporary pop music is deeply rooted in tradition, and the most traditional music draws constantly from the popular and contemporary. Yet as coastal trade increased

around the turn of the twentieth century and people began to live in multi-ethnic communities, unique urban cultures began to emerge. In Lagos – destined to become Nigeria's commercial and for a time its political capital – by the 1920s, one could find Nigerians of every ethnicity, as well as a variety of Europeans, Latin Americans and foreign Africans.

In Lagos's earliest urban neighbourhoods such as Isale Eko, Ebute Meta and Obalende, one could find local and imported alcohol in small social halls such as the palm wine parlours. In these places and at gatherings, city-dwellers would sing contemporary songs derived from folk music styles which reflected their urban experience, accompanied by makeshift rhythm instruments such as a palm wine gourd, a shaker or a glass bottle. Popular stringed instruments such as mandolin and guitar were added, and by the late 1920s **juju music** had emerged as a Yoruba popular genre. Early pioneers such as **Tunde King** and **Irewolede Denge** became some of Nigeria's first musical stars. By the 1950s popular music was flourishing in a wide range of styles, with **Tunde Nightingale**, **J.O. Araba** and **C.A. Balogun** being the most prominent juju artists.

In the 1950s Nigeria's (and Africa's) first broadcast radio station began further to popularize the sounds of Nigerian musicians. Later in the decade, a young carpenter named **I.K. Dairo** began his rise to stardom, becoming Nigeria's first international musical star, and the only African musician to receive an MBE. Dairo dominated the social scene of western Nigeria until the 1970s, paving the way for hundreds of other juju bands including **Prince Adekunle**, **Lady Balogun** and **Moses Olaiya**.

In the 1970s, younger upstarts **Ebenezer Obey** and then **Sunny Ade** began to achieve popularity, and by 1975 they had finally eclipsed Dairo's achievements. Throughout the 1970s, 80s and early 90s they battled for dominance of juju music. In 1992, **Shina Peters**, formerly of the group **Shina Adewale** (with partner **Segun Adewale**), rose to prominence on a wave of "Shinamania" as the voice of a new generation with his "Afrojuju" style. For a time Shina was the most popular juju musician, and in the mid-1990s Obey retired from music to pursue a calling as a pastor. However, after a two-

Nigeria's Record Industry

The record industry first emerged in Nigeria in the early 1920s when British entrepreneurs first began to market phonograms and recordings to the emerging middle and upper classes in Nigeria. By the mid-1920s the earliest recordings of local Nigerian musicians were being made and pressed as shellacs for sale in Nigeria.

It was in the 1950s, however, that the industry began to mature. Several factors conspired to make this so. Radio had opened up a whole new awareness and interest in local and international sounds. The postwar global economy was humming along, and even pre-oil Nigeria was booming. And the record industry was maturing internationally. The commercial capital of Lagos in particular looked like a ripe opportunity, and Decca, EMI and Philips Records all set up small recording studios.

By the end of the decade the trade was booming, Nigeria's first stars had emerged, and alongside them African music entrepreneurs. Among these pioneers were **Chief Olajoyegbe (Jofabro Records)** and **Chief Abioro (African Songs)** who were active in setting up local labels such as Nigerphone, Ibukun Orisun Iye, Mut Moksun and Niger Songs. Following the model of the international companies, these Nigerian labels recorded locally, had their discs manufactured through Decca, EMI or brokers for other manufacturers, and then had the finished goods shipped back to Nigeria.

In the mid-1960s, **I.K. Dairo** and **Haruna Ishola** jointly founded Africa's first artist-owned record company. **STAR Records** followed the Decca model. In fact, both artists would go to Decca studios and record one record for Decca and one or more for STAR in the same session. The manufacturing was still done abroad by Decca, but they controlled distribution and marketing themselves. By the early 1970s, every successful artist began to follow this model, with **Obey Records**, **Sunny Alade Records** and so on emerging. In the late 1970s, Phonodisc Nigeria became the first and largest domestic record pressing plant.

In the early 1980s, as profit margins on LPs became thin, cassettes created new opportunities. It was also at this time that piracy first reared its head. A new cottage industry of **duplicators** sprung up which were ironically called "recording studios". In almost every small town and all over Nigeria's vast urban centres, entrepreneurs with a stereo system, a turntable and a cassette player set up shop. Customers could come in and listen to whatever they liked and leave with a freshly recorded cassette. **Piracy** had arrived in the most innocent way, but its impact was felt far and wide. With the bottom falling out of the market, many of the international companies began to reduce their investment or close up shop altogether. The once mighty, world-class studios of the 1970s (**Afrodesia**, **EMI**, **Shanuolu** and even Ginger Baker's **Axe Studios**, where Wings recorded *Band on the Run*) began to coast on their existing equipment.

By the mid-1980s, the growing numbers of musicians were keeping every available studio in Nigeria working round the clock. However, lack of new tape or spare parts was beginning to take its toll. While the grand records of the 1970s and early 80s sounded big, lush and pristine, many records of the late 1980s and 90s exhibited buzzes, hums and reduced fidelity. Few musicians could afford new tape, so it became standard practice to wipe old multi-tracks and masters to track new ones.

By the early 1990s, most artists were releasing music on their own labels, or on small pioneer labels from local entrepreneurs, but there was no centralized distribution, an ill-defined market and runaway piracy of anything remotely successful. As the pirates became more successful, moving their manufacturing to Asia and importing by the container load, they drove prices down, forcing the artists to compete for their own sales. The introduction of the **CD** and **digital media** in the 1990s further exacerbated the situation. Today, it is estimated that pirate copies outsell authentic works ten to one.

In spite of these staggering challenges, new studios continue to open, new record labels and producers continue to appear, and Nigeria's unstoppable artists continue to record and perform. A milestone for 2005 was the independent marketing and sale of over one million CDs by singer **Tony Tetuila** and rapper **2Face**, giving hope to Nigeria's other independent artists. The war between artists, record companies and pirates rages on and it is difficult to know where it will go, but it is clear that for now it has taken a heavy toll.

year break from 1990 to 1992, King Sunny Ade re-emerged as a major force and has dominated juju music ever since. A new generation of juju musicians, including **Dele Taiwo** and **Paul Dairo** (son of I.K. Dairo), cut their teeth in the economically difficult 1990s but failed to gain the international prominence of their predecessors. By 2000, juju music had ceased to be Nigeria's favourite pop

Richard Trillo

Sunny Ade

genre and for the youth of today it is considered more of a historical sound. Fortunately for Nigeria's few remaining juju icons, the political and business leaders of the nation were raised on their music, so they remain popular and heavily patronized by Nigeria's modern elites, with little competition. After a recording hiatus of almost ten years, King Sunny Ade released *Divine Shield* (his 113th record) in Nigeria in December 2004.

Highlife Nigeria Style

Widely credited as having evolved in Ghana, **highlife** was the dancehall music of Africa's emerging elites, whose new, modern "high" style of living inspired the name. Though Ghana took the lead, Nigeria was never far behind in embracing the genre as its own. Many early highlife bands emerged from military and police marching bands, where musicians could get access to hard-to-find and expensive instruments, but the broad popularity of highlife, combined with a growing middle class, quickly gave rise to a class of professional highlife musicians.

By the 1950s, stars such as **Bobby Benson**, **Cardinal Rex Lawson**, **Roy Chicago**, **Victor Uwaifo** (now Minister of Culture of Benin), **Ambrose Campbell** and **Dr Victor Olaiya** (the "evil genius of highlife") were in constant demand, and their records were enjoyed widely alongside those by Ghanaian highlife icons like **E.T. Mensah**. Highlife was performed and enjoyed across ethnic lines, by Igbo, Hausa and Yoruba alike. Fifties highlife, taking its inspiration from the Ghanaian style and from American jazz, was fuelled largely by brass and wind instruments, with a percussive rhythm section driving the dance rhythms. This was goodtime music in an era of growing prosperity.

In eastern Nigeria, Igbo and Efik bandleaders expanded the role of guitars and blended a new brand of guitar highlife uniquely their own. Early bandleaders like **Stephen Amechi**, **Zeal Onyiya**, **Celestine Ukwu** and the **Peacocks International** inspired a generation of youths in the 1960s to

Collection Graeme Ewens

Danceband highlife with Bobby Benson

make guitar-style highlife – with its twangy interlocking guitar lines and punchy horn refrains – their own, transforming it from music of the elites to that of the people. Stars such as **Stephen Osita Osadebe**, **Inyang Nta Henshaw**, **Peter Effiom** and **Mike Ejeagha** arose in this era.

Sadly, the upward trajectory of highlife in Nigeria was badly hampered by the Nigerian civil war which devastated eastern Nigeria from 1967 to 1970. Ethnic tensions during and following the war undermined the national potential of Igbo music as Igbos were vilified in western and northern Nigeria. More devastating still, the Biafran economy and most of its frail infrastructure collapsed.

Healing came quickly, and by the mid-1970s a whole new crop of highlife musicians emerged. **Stephen Osita Osadebe**, who had started his career in the 1960s, re-emerged and remains the leader in Igbo highlife today. Bands and singers such as **Oriental Brothers**, **Oliver deCoque** and **Ali Chukwuma** rose to prominence as they re-engineered Igbo highlife to be more guitar-based, with longer, evolving arrangements, and dug deeper into the indigenous culture, making it more Igbo cultural music than modern urban social music. Other popular bands included **The Nkengas**, actually the defecting band of Chief Stephen Osadebe, whose seminal *Live In London* is still considered one of the great recordings of Nigerian highlife.

Today, highlife in Nigeria primarily enjoys the status of classic pop music, yet several prominent highlife artists remain on the scene. In addition to Osadebe and Oliver deCoque and his **Ogene Super Band**, there is **Onyeka Onwenu**, one of Nigeria's leading female artists. In recent years her music has taken on a gospel tinge. Of the younger generation, **Sunny Neji** is probably the leader of the pack. Starting his career as a backing singer in Onyeka's band, he writes and performs highlife-influenced pop music which also weaves in elements of Congolese music, funk, pop, juju and more. His 1997 album *Mr Fantastik* propelled him into the limelight, and his 2003 album *Unchained* also enjoyed wide success, particularly the hit love song "Oruka".

Traditional Pop and Apala

A wide range of music is performed, recorded and released in Nigeria each year in the realm of what can only be called "traditional pop" – music based directly on a traditional music style but performed in a popular format or by a musician seeking to achieve notoriety. Examples include the Egedeege cultural ensemble from eastern Nigeria and Show Promoter and his band from Imo state. By far the most dramatic kind is Yoruba **apala**, a traditional form of social music from the Ijebu region of Yorubaland in what is today Ogun state. The ensemble for apala music is led by a set of hourglass-shaped talking drums called *gangan* or *adama,* accompanied by *agogo* bells, *shekere* (gourd rattle), *acuba* or *ogido* (a local relative of the conga drum), maracas, wood block or claves, and call-and-response backing vocalists. The resulting rich and surprisingly melodic web of sound grooves and pulses like nothing else.

Collection Graeme Ewens

Dr (Sir) Warrior & Oriental Brothers

In the 1960s, two apala singers performing traditional music at traditional events and recording traditional songs, **Haruna Ishola** and to a lesser degree **Ayinla Omowura**, became major pop figures in Nigeria. Their respective record companies positioned them as competitors for the same market, fuelling their rising popularity and the interest of the Nigerian paparazzi.

Sadly, both singers died in the early 1970s, Ishola of natural causes and Omowura from injuries sustained in a bar-room brawl. For almost thirty years no other apala singer achieved their level of notoriety, as the genre made way for fuji and other forms of percussion-based music. Then suddenly, in 2003, **Museliu Ishola**, one of Haruna's sons, burst onto the national music scene with an updated apala music which remarkably retained all the richness and intensity of the original, while adding occasional drum machines and rappers to bring it into the twenty-first century. Since then, fans young and old have rallied to the apala sound once again.

Fuji Fever

Despite some similarities, **fuji** music does not have its roots in apala music, but rather is based in the Islamic communities of Nigeria's Yoruba people.

Queen Salawa Abeni

Islam predates Christianity in Nigeria by some centuries, but until Usman Dan Fodio's military campaign in the nineteenth century it was found primarily in the great city-states of the north. So the religion is a relative newcomer to the Yoruba, and as with Christianity the primarily *orisha*-worshipping Yoruba have taken and "Yorubanized" it. The celebration of Ramadhan was, by the mid-twentieth century, a major event in Lagos. A tradition evolved in which groups of young men would traverse the Muslim neighbourhoods singing improvised music to the accompaniment of pots, pans, drums, bells and whatever else was available, to wake the believers by 5am for morning prayer. This tradition came to be called *ajisaari*, or *wéré*, and by the 1970s was so widespread that individual *ajisaari* singers began to achieve notoriety.

In 1966, I.K. Dairo and Haruna Ishola sponsored a competition among Lagos's *ajisaari* singers. A young man name **Sikiru Ayinde Barrister** emerged victorious with a recording opportunity. It was Barrister who, by his second recording, gave the music the name fuji, attributed by various urban legends to Fuji tinned mackerel, the elaborate and classical structure of the music (as in fugue) or Japan's Mount Fuji. A competitor quickly arose to galvanize fuji fans into two camps: **Kollington Ayinla** crowned himself "Baba Alatika", father of the common man. Whereas Barrister delved into broad social commentary with a comical bent, Kollington focused more on spiritual issues, enemies and other more traditional themes. Barrister evolved his makeshift band to include a range of talking drums, shakers, bells and a chorus. Kollington added *bata* drums to his music, calling it *bata fuji*.

By 1985, there were dozens of fuji artists. Fuji is often contrasted with juju, and in general this is apt. Juju is guitar-based, fuji percussion-based. Juju is predominantly Christian-oriented music, and fuji primarily Islam-oriented. Juju patrons are the educated upwardly mobile, whereas fuji patrons are the poor. However, both are strongly rooted in the Yoruba traditions of patronage and praise singing, and both wax philosophical about social issues, politics and more.

By the late 1990s, *fuji* was beginning to overtake juju as Nigeria's number-one popular music. Because of its Islamic bent, it found a wider audience in the non-Yoruba north, and had a bigger potential audience as economic pressures created fewer haves and more have-nots. Most importantly, all that was required to start a fuji band was a singer and some local percussion. By the 1990s, every city, town and village was brimming with aspiring local fuji players, while the capital required to acquire a guitar and other Western instruments had caused juju and highlife to diminish measurably.

While Kollington and Barrister have remained the titans of fuji, another singer has emerged to become the clear leader and innovator. **Wasiu Ayinde Barrister** was a backing singer in Barrister's band before going solo. With an innate sense of popular trends and a magnetic personality, Wasiu stormed the fuji world in 1984 with his innovative *Talazo Disco*. Over the past two decades Wasiu, now known as **KWAM** (King Wasiu Ayinde Marshall), has outstripped all competitors. Other popular figures include **Adewale Ayuba**, who rose to fame, then moved to the US to spend a decade in Brooklyn, only to return eventually to Nigeria to rebuild his fan base. **Abass Akande Obesere** was fuji's answer to the youth's desire for a bawdy, urban icon, and remains a popular force.

As fuji musicians have sought to evolve they have moved in some surprising directions. With the addition of horns, keyboards and even guitars at times, their music has come to sound juju-like. Obesere distinguished himself by using drum machines in a land where brilliant percussionists are abundant. Simultaneously juju, in response to fuji's popularity, has become more percussive and fuji-like. However they evolve, the two styles remain distinctly Nigerian, appealing broadly to Nigerians at home and abroad, while being almost completely overlooked by the rest of the world.

Waka

Concurrent with fuji's rise was the ascendance of **waka** music. Similar to fuji, waka is vocally ori-ented music backed by a percussion orchestra of Yoruba talking drums and hand percussion. The major distinction between the two is that waka's stars are women. Like fuji, waka's artists tend to be Muslims, and its audience largely the Muslim middle and lower classes; the title *Alhaja* borne by so many waka divas shows they have participated in the Hajj, the religious pilgrimage to Mecca. Notable among scores of waka singers are **Alhaja Asanat Ejire Omo Aje** and **Alhaja Chief Batile Alake**. However, the undisputed queen of waka (and an under-appreciated ambassador of Nigerian music in general) is **Queen Salawa Abeni**, whose career spans almost three decades. For a time in the 1980s, she was inseparable from fuji innovator Kollington Ayinla, even sharing a backing band with him, though by the 1990s the two had gone their separate ways. Nigeria's leading woman of song, Salawa has done much to secure a respected role for women as singers of popular and praise music. She boasts dozens of records and a broad international following, which she fosters with regular tours to Europe and the US.

Fela Kuti and Afro-beat

Probably the best-known icon and the largest musical personality from Nigeria was **Fela Anikulapo Kuti**. Born in the city of Abeoku-ta, Fela was the child of a Western-educated minister father and a social activist mother. When he was sent off to London to study at Trinity College, he shifted his studies from medicine to music. On a visit to Los Angeles in 1966, he was deeply influenced by the Black Power movement. Returning to Nigeria, he formed his first group, the **Koola Lobitos**, who played a hybrid of jazz and high-life with modest success in Lagos.

In the late 1960s, Lagos was a focus of musical experimentation, with

Fela Anikulapo Kuti

From Kalakuta to Kakadu: Shanties, Shrines and Nite-spots

Early musicians in Nigeria were subject to the whims of wealthy patrons who owned the means of their livelihood: instruments and a regular place to play. In the 1950s, **Bobby Benson** built his own **Hotel Bobby**, and inside it the famous Caban Bamboo club to perform in. This became a model for every successful musician, for in a music industry where no royalties were paid and most performance opportunities set the musicians as background to a celebration, this was the most certain path to a regular audience and financial stability. Even today it is considered the mark of success for a musician in Nigeria to have his own place.

In the 1960s, **I.K. Dairo** opened the **Kakadu** night club in Lagos's booming Sabo district, and **Victor Olaiya** built first his nightclub and later the *Stadium Hotel*, where he still performs.

In the 1970s, **King Sunny Ade** opened his **Ariya Niteclub** in Jibowu, while Ebenezer Obey opened his **Miliki** spot in Ikeja. Jazz icon **Art Alade** had the sublime and classy **Art's Place** in Suuru Lere. Most notable of the era, **Fela Kuti** took the compound of his mother's house at Jibowu and turned it into a nightclub, then a scene and eventually the **Kalakuta Republic**, declaring it independent from the Federal Republic of Nigeria.

In the 1980s, **Sikiru Ayinde Barrister** had his **Fuji Chambers**, and Fela Kuti regrouped after the loss of Kalakuta by building his **African Shrine** in Ikeja. However, by the mid-1980s it became very difficult for musicians to afford their own spot, and performing at the discretion of a club or hotel owner put a lot of pressure on them to play certain styles and attract certain crowds.

By the mid-1990s several new venues had opened up, including **Maison Française**, the **British Cultural Centre**, the **Muson Centre** and a few small galleries that began to feature a wider variety of Nigerian music than was generally available elsewhere. Still, those wishing to be innovative and control their scene needed a venue, and today two of Nigeria's most progressive artists have one. Lágbájá's **Motherlan** is an open-air 1000-capacity amphitheatre built in the late 1990s on a hill overlooking a lovely ravine in Ikeja. Lágbájá performs there on the last Friday of each month (not by accident also the monthly payday for most wage earners). Femi Kuti's **New African Shrine**, an open-air covered venue in the Alausa section of Ikeja, is in some ways a homage to Fela's African Shrine. When he is in the country, Femi performs more frequently than Lágbájá, following a pattern set by Fela. He also hosts opening bands on occasion.

Jak Kilby

Femi Kuti

jazz, funk and African music vying to dominate a booming social scene which included **I.K. Dairo**'s juju, **Orlando Julius**'s Super Afro Soul, **Geraldo Pino**'s James Brown renditions (see Sierra Leone chapter), **Bobby Benson**'s highlife and more. It was in this cauldron that Fela began to evolve his music, combining a love of jazz, funk, traditional music and ritual with his social activism, black consciousness and outrageous showmanship to produce a unique style which he dubbed **Afrobeat**.

Fela declared his compound an independent republic, and was continually pushing the bounds of social and political rebellion in what is generally a socially and politically conservative country. He antagonized the police, the army and the federal government, and it was no surprise when he was jailed from 1983 to 1986. Once he emerged his audience had largely moved on, and the combined forces of a crumbling economy and an oppressive government undermined the impact of his powerful social message. Though he remained an important figure until his death in 1997, he was never able to regain the intensity of his pre-prison days.

During his life, no musician other than his eldest son Femi dared try to compete with Fela in the style of Afro-beat. But like an African Johnny Appleseed, after his death a veritable sea of Afro-beat and Afro-beat-influenced artists rose up to fill the void. Nigeria now boasts dozens of Afro-beat outfits, with straight Afro-beat, Afro-beat-rap, Afro-jazz, Afro soul and more.

In the realm of pure Afro-beat, **Femi** leads the pack, both at home and abroad, performing at his New African Shrine as often as three nights a week to a growing crowd of regular fans. However, many Nigerians feel that younger brother **Seun Kuti**, who is backed by much of Fela's original **Egypt 80** band, is the real heir to Fela's look, style and sound. Fela's longtime friend and collaborator **Dede Mabiaku** also performs a remarkably Fela-like brand of Afro-beat and has a steady following. And there are many lesser-known artists, such as **Baba 2010**, **Alariwo of Africa**, **Korikima** and **Amala**. Outside of Femi's New African Shrine, there are no specific Afro-beat venues in Lagos, but the wide range of hotels, nightspots, cultural centres and festivals feature live music.

Even more impressive is the impact Afro-beat has had on a global scale (see box overleaf), from the horn-driven sounds of New York favourites **Antibalas** to the Afro-beat hip-hop of London's **Weird MC**. Fela's life's work has transcended that of a mere man. As aptly described by the artist **Lágbájá** in his song "Abami", Fela has entered the realm of the divine and become an *orisha*, a deity, and the ripples of his legacy continue to spread.

Praise Singing the Big Boss

In the past two decades, as the Nigerian economy has gone from bad to worse, the attendance at formal religious ceremonies has swelled dramatically. Houses of worship have sprung up in homes, in fields and in the decaying hulks of abandoned industrial complexes; they are literally everywhere. On the last Friday of each month, two million Nigerians convene in a field between the commercial capital of Lagos and the second-largest city of Ibadan to hold – under the title of the Redeemed Christian Church of God, commonly called Redeem Camp – the largest church service on the planet. Religion has become a major force in the social, cultural and economic life of the nation. This in turn has had a major impact on the music industry.

Churches in Nigeria have always boasted music, and by the 1970s musicians had begun to emerge from the church movement. Popular groups such as the **CAC (Christ Apostolic Church) Good Women's Choir** made a strong regional impact as recording and performing ensembles. Over the 1970s, 80s and 90s, icons such as **I.K. Dairo**, **Sunny Okosun** and **Ebenezer Obey** traded in their guitars for sceptres and became leaders in their own church movements. By the 1980s, when **Timi Osukoya** had his hit record *Divine Assurance*, religious music had begun to emerge as popular music. As piracy, security issues and economic problems have eroded opportunities in the music business over the past two decades, new opportunities for a career as a gospel musician – with a growing audience, paid work as a sideman and access to instruments and studios – have increasingly opened up.

Jak Kilby

Chief Ebenezer Obey

Nigerian gospel sounds little like its American namesake, encompassing a wide range of musical expression. In many church movements, particularly the smaller ones, the music has much in common with local folk styles, adapting widely available traditional instruments and local vocal

Nigeria Abroad

There is hardly any country on the planet where you will not find a community of Nigerians living and working, and likewise Nigerian artists. Of course the best known and most successful of these are in the major entertainment capitals, and Nigerians tend to gravitate towards the English-speaking world.

In London, although performers regularly come over from Nigeria, homegrown artists are making more and more of an impact. While there are many juju, gospel and fuji artists, it is hip-hop which has spawned innovation and gained most popularity. Female rapper and pioneer **Weird MC** (Shola Idowu) has long been offering her Afro-beat-infused raps, while more recently **JJC** (aka Skillz) **and the 419 Squad** have risen to international prominence with their debut album *Atide*. The fabulous **Wunmi** (granddaughter of Victor Olaiya) has had a huge impact with her Afro-beat/highlife-infused dub music, working with the Bugz in the Attic collective in London and the noted **Kunle Adeniyi** (King Sunny Ade's son) in New York. The UK also boasts Nigeria's only two crossover superstars, the sultry **Sade Adu** and the power crooner **Seal**.

Philip Ryalls/Redferns

Wunmi

The US has even more Nigerian musicians, of every generation and level. The enigmatic **Lijadu Sisters**, who rose to fame on Decca Records in the 1970s, are now residents of New Jersey and perform widely. **Obiajulu Osadebe**, son of Chief Stephen Osita Osadebe, and **Eugene deCoque**, brother of Oliver deCoque, dominate the east- and west-coast Igbo highlife circuits respectively. In the 1990s, Nigerian highlife singer **Mike Okri** and reggae singer **Jheri Jhetto** relocated to Los Angeles, where they both work and perform prolifically.

Oakland, California, has become the major hub of Nigerian music in America, beginning with the presence of **Orlando Julius Ekemode**, whose various band members have spawned a generation of Nigerian creativity. The city is now home to **Tunde Williams**, responsible for the sublime trumpet work on the best of Fela's records, talking drum virtuosi **Rasaki Aladokun** (of King Sunny Ade fame) and **Sikiru Adepoju** (Ebenezer Obey, Mickey Hart), and dozens of others. Probably the most successful of Nigeria's expatriate bandleaders is **Kenneth Okulolo**. Once King Sunny Ade's bass player, and a noted producer, Kenneth is an outstanding bass player, and leads **Kotoja**, as well as the **West African Highlife Band** (WAHB), a veritable supergroup of Bay Area Nigerian musicians.

The US also boasts some part-time residents who are major figures in Nigeria. **Sikiru Ayinde Barrister** has built his Shubuola ("stumble over wealth") Palace on Staten Island. Afro-beat saxophonist **Adeniji "Heavy Wind"**, a part-time resident of Florida, is building a growing following for his Afro-beat-jazz in both Nigeria and the US.

As for Europe, after leaving the **Africa 70**, legendary drummer **Tony Allen** settled in France, and now has an international profile. Another veteran of Fela's band, respected percussionist **Segun Damisa**, is beginning to make inroads in France with his own brand of Afro-beat. And in Germany, **Ade Bantu Odukoya** is making a splash as a producer, singer and rapper, performing with **Brothers Keepers** and the **Schal Sick Brass Band**.

Of course, not all the giants who've emigrated have received the recognition they deserve and three artists deserve special mention in this regard. In the Afro Funky 1970s, the group **Mona Mona** reigned supreme in Nigeria, and when bandleader **Joni Haastrup** departed to the US, everyone expected great things. Unable to land a big record deal, he eventually settled in the Bay Area, where he lives today, playing and recording with a variety of musicians. Afro-beat star **Orlando Julius Ekemode** moved his entire group to Oakland in the mid-1980s, but never achieved the national notoriety one might have expected. He currently lives in Ghana where he is a vibrant part of the Afro-beat and highlife resurgence. Finally, **Ambrose Campbell** was one of Nigerian pop's great 1960s icons before moving to London, where he operated a nightclub. By the early 1970s Ambrose had moved to Hollywood, where he struck up a friendship and songwriting partnership with Willy Nelson and Leon Russell, which resulted in a Grammy, and many hit records. His work is compiled on *London Is The Place For Me 3* (Honest Jon's).

traditions. In the larger and more affluent churches, one finds guitars, drums, organs, choirs and more.

Popular Lagos musicians have been heard to complain that the best backing musicians have been gobbled up by the churches. Nigeria's most successful gospel stars have absorbed many of the influences of Western soul and gospel music, and cross-pollinated them with indigenous rhythms and grooves.

Both Sunny Okosun and Onyeka Onwenu had successful careers in highlife before succeeding as gospel singers. **Buchi Atuwonuwu**, **Kunle Ajayi**, **Chuks Ofojebe**, **Faladey**, **Folake Umosen** and **Ben Okafor** are among the many highly successful gospel artists. Then there are the hybrid sounds such as gospel-reggae (**Christafari**), gospel-jazz (**Soji Enigbokan**) and gospel-hip-hop (**Lex** and **Lekanskills**).

With their direct access to a vast market, the backing of powerful churches and the widely sought positive messages they are putting forward, gospel artists are currently enjoying support and opportunities that other artists can only dream of.

Reggae, Hip-Hop, Rap and Beyond

Reggae has been an important genre in Nigeria ever since Bob Marley conquered the world in the 1970s. Among Nigeria's top artists are **Ras Kimono**, **Blakky**, **Evi-Edna Ogholi** and **Orits Williki**, though none have achieved the heights of popularity and the brief flicker of international acclaim of **Majek Fashek**. His 1990 album *Prisoner Of Conscience* and 1991's *Spirit Of Love* received rave reviews at home and abroad. Many thought Majek's success would open the door for other Nigerian artists, but that was not to be, and personal difficulties on the road, on stage and in the studio scuttled his great trajectory. Though he remains popular and active in both the US and Nigeria, neither he nor any other Nigerian reggae artist has been able to match the international notoriety he brushed up against in the 1990s.

Hip-hop began to gain popularity in Nigeria in the mid-1990s, though it was not until the end of that decade that any domestic rappers began to be taken seriously. The initial success of **The Remedies** was probably the catalyst. Formed in 1997, the group released two songs, "Judile" and "Sakomo", which became overnight hits in Nigeria. Though The Remedies lasted only three years, its three founders showed the way for the serious exploration of hip-hop and rap in Nigeria. **Tony Tetuila** reshaped his career as a pop/soul singer and is still enjoying wide popularity. **Eddy Remedy** continued with rap, and – probably the most popular and certainly the most controversial – **Idris Abdulkareem** wears the self-proclaimed title of "Nigeria's greatest rapper".

Much of the early Nigerian rap was ragga-style with a heavy Jamaican influence, but by 2001 every kind of indigenous Nigerian music had begun to cross-pollinate with rap and hip-hop styles. By 2004, groups like the **Trybesman**, **Plantashun Boyz**, **B.A.N.T.U.** and **Ruggedman** had broadened the field and its popularity.

The strong relationship between Nigeria and the UK has made Nigerian rap into an international genre. Rappers based in London enjoy success as Nigerian homeys, while those based in Nigeria have strong followings among British-Nigerian youth. This was demonstrated when the UK-based **JJC and the 419 Squad** won the 2004 Kora award for Best African Group in Johannesburg. To further underscore the ascendancy of African rap, when MTV recently launched its hundredth channel, MTV Africa, broadcasting to 48 countries, they did so with simultaneous concerts in Abuja (Nigeria) and South Africa. The Nigerian concert was headlined by Ludacris, supported by JJC and the 419 Squad and rising star **2Face Idibia**, who became the first Nigerian rapper to have his video broadcast on MTV.

While contemporary Nigerian rap is obviously aimed at an international audience, it is also clearly rooted in Nigerian culture. With song titles and vernacular that regularly delve into pidgin English and local languages, the tinny production which is the hallmark of most contemporary Nigerian studios, and themes which clearly speak to a global Nigerian audience, these artists have a foot in two worlds. For once, it appears that the world may be poised to reach out and embrace them as they are. Only time will tell.

Some of Nigeria's best talents have forged new styles and genres which don't fit any category or norm. A classic example of this is **Prince Nico Mbarga** whose "Sweet Mother" (1976) is one of the biggest hits in African music history. Combining the influences of Cameroonian *makossa* with Igbo highlife and a little bit of rock 'n' roll, Prince Nico and his band Rocafil Jazz defined a new style and sound which remain unique to this day.

Today, new artists are evolving their own individual sounds in urban Nigeria. **Daddy Showkey** is an outstanding example. Born and raised in Lagos's infamously rough Ajegunle quarter, Showkey naturally absorbed a wide range of culture and lots of street smarts. In Ajegunle and many of

In a Suburb Near You...

Despite the fact that they enjoy relatively little mainstream market appeal outside their own country, scores of Nigerian artists tour the world each year. The largest Nigerian expatriate communities are probably in **London**, **New York**, **Washington DC**, **Houston** and **Chicago**. They have their own networks or promoters, agents, producers and even established venues and events to which Nigerian artists come on tour each year, keeping the expats connected with their homeland and allowing the artists international bragging rights. These concert tours take place completely under the radar of non-Nigerians, with artists playing to all-Nigerian crowds.

A typical scenario involves a promoter bringing a group to one country, renting an inexpensive house for the group to use as home base and then selling shows to local promoters throughout the country or region. Travel, wherever possible, is by crowded passenger van. The shows tend to follow the format of ones back home, with the artist spending a good deal of the show praise-singing local patrons and being sprayed (having money, a gesture of thanks for the praise, pasted on their sweating foreheads). The **spray money** goes a long way towards shoring up shoestring budgets for artists, and is often shared with agents and promoters. It's a tough business.

Of course, though the events are by and for Nigerians, others are always welcome to experience late shows, good food and dancing until daylight to non-stop grooves. To locate such events, try checking in your local Nigerian grocery store, video store or restaurant. They will surely be able to put you in the loop for upcoming shows in your local school gym, banquet hall or back alley, and you won't regret the experience.

Lagos's rougher neighbourhoods the streets are run by "area-boys" – tough street thugs who control business by extorting protection money, run petty street scams, provide or revoke security and generally terrorize the residents.

Daddy Showkey evolved a stage persona which is simultaneously homage to and caricature of the area-boys, adorning his stage line-up with dancing muscle-bound area-boys as well as the more typical female backing singers. His music draws equally from reggae, soca, highlife and a wide range of Nigerian influences. Other musicians such as the popular **Baba Fryo** have followed in this direction.

Another remarkable artist is the man known simply as **Lágbájá**, which in Yoruba means the equivalent of "somebody, anybody or everybody". Lágbájá, who wears a mask to conceal his true identity, is the faceless voice of the masses, the social conscience of the so-called "common man". Lágbájá emerged during the tyrannical rule of despot Sanni Abacha, at first to a mixed response. However, by 1995, when he released his first cassette, his unique musical blend, socially incisive and sometimes satirical lyrics and upbeat stage shows had propelled him to broad popularity, and by the late 1990s he had become one of Nigeria's top artists. Lágbájá combines influences of juju, Afro-beat and highlife with R&B, pop, funk, soul and hip-hop. His influence in Africa extends far beyond the borders of Nigeria and this is an artist to watch.

Future Grooves

What lies in the future for Nigeria's music scene? The lack of a music industry poses a real challenge for some of the nation's budding talents, and such gifted singers as **Sammy Needle Odeh** and **Yinka Daves** struggle to build business opportunities which match their skills. There is no lack of talent in any Nigerian genre, only a drought of opportunity and reward. If, one day, Nigeria truly begins the long and challenging resurrection so many hope for, and can sustain a business environment where intellectual property is respected, where the general public feels safe to go out at night, where spendable income makes it possible for the common man to patronize the arts and where industry makes those arts accessible to its citizens, then Nigeria will once again be among the giants of the world in musical and overall artistic achievement.

Lágbájá, the man in the mask

Most Nigerian music imports can be found through online retailers, and in Nigerian grocery stores in cities throughout the world. Alternatively, many Nigerian artists now have websites with musical samples and even CD sales, as noted below in the discography.

⊙ **Lagos Chop Up**
⊙ **Lagos All Routes**
Honest Jon's Records, UK
Between the 1950s and 70s the Lagos music scene was booming, with world-class studios, dozens of record companies and countless venues featuring a wide variety of talent. These two samplers capture a nice, if random, cross-section of that era, from juju to jazz, apala to highlife. The sound quality isn't always great, but these may prove your best bet for finding classic tracks by Rex Lawson, Bobby Benson, Sir Victor Uwaifo, Mike Ejeagha and other icons of yesteryear.

★ **Nigeria 70: The Definitive Story of 1970s Funky Lagos**
Strut, UK
As "boxed" sets go, this is one of the best. It is comprehensive and cohesive in its approach to one incredible era in Lagos. Clearly a labour of love, this compilation will take you back to one of Nigeria's most fertile musical eras, through music and interviews.

Traditional

Nigeria's greatest wealth is traditional music, and yet there is very little available on record outside the country.

⊙ **AyanAgalu: Sacred Yoruba Bata Music for 12 Orishas**
Rakumi Arts, US
Yoruba *bata* music may be Africa's most influential export, having morphed into Cuban *bata* and influenced everything from Ricky and Lucy to Carlos Santana and Gloria Estefan. This CD features twelve tracks of traditional bata music in praise of several Yoruba deities (*orishas*).

Juju

King Sunny Ade

He began his career playing highlife in the early 1960s, but as a result of three albums he made for Island in the early to mid-1980s, King Sunny Ade briefly became one of the world's best-known African artists. His profile is lower these days, though there have been sporadic comebacks.

★ **Juju Music**
Island Records, UK
The album which opened the door for African music internationally back in 1982, and still a classic. With percolating talking drums, playful call-and-response vocals and slinky, understated guitar work, it defined the international sound of juju music.

⊙ **Synchro Series**
IndigeDisc Music, US
A compilation of Ade's music from immediately before and after the release of *Juju Music*. Moving from open, extended compositions to short, punchy produced tracks, it under-

scores a big step in Africa's embracing an international musical aesthetic.

I.K. Dairo

The godfather of juju music, who led its evolution from a local social music to a popular genre, I.K. Dairo is said to have built Decca Records West Africa with his sales.

⊙ **Definitive Dairo**
Xenophile, US
Dairo's early peak years are best captured on this recording made at Decca studios in London for his own STAR Records label.

Ebenezer Obey

When Ebenezer Obey retired from performing to dedicate his time to being a full-time pastor in the late 1990s, he was kind enough to reissue all of his classic music on CD, some of which is available outside Nigeria.

⊙ **Juju Jubilation**
Hemisphere, UK
This largely mid-1970s mix of politics, philosophy and great grooves is classic Obey.

Shina Peters

In the last decade of juju's dominance, Shina Peters started a craze called Shinamania among his youthful fans, propelling him from regional popularity to national stardom. For almost a decade, he battled King Sunny Ade for the crown of juju king.

⊙ **ACE: Afrojuju Series 1**
CBS Records, Nigeria
In the first instalment of his Afrojuju, singer and lead guitarist Shina Peters sets the tone for the new musical evolution to come. Using the basic structure of juju, he ups the pace to a youthful frenzy, adds a heavy dose of fuji-influenced drumming, and uses a much more direct vocal style than the heavily proverbial approach of King Sunny Ade or Ebenezer Obey. Shina also puts on a wilder and more dramatic stage show.

Apala

Alaji Haruna Ishola

Ishola was considered the master of apala, which, though a traditional genre, became as popular as any Nigerian pop genre in the 1960s and 70s.

⊙ **Apala Messenger**
IndigeDisc, USA
This is one of the few collections of Ishola's lush musical landscapes, incredibly melodic, trance-inducing percussion and profound Yoruba lyrics.

Museliu Ishola

Haruna's eldest son, who filled the void left by the death of his father three decades on. In any Yoruba town or market, you will be sure to hear Ishola's music blaring from half the stereos you pass.

⭐ Soyoyo
STAR Records, Nigeria
The title-track of this 2003 breakthrough album is a cover of one of his father's hits, but superb production, rap vignettes and drum machines give it a twenty-first-century update. The accompanying DVD is a real slice of Nigerian pop culture.

Fuji

Sikiru Ayinde Barrister

One-time rival of Kollington but now peacefully co-existing with him in a market big enough for both, Barrister started life as a *wéré* musician before poverty drove him into the army. Availability of any of his eighty-plus recordings released in Nigeria and the three released abroad is random at best but Barrister is consistently satisfying.

⊙ Questionnaire and Reality
Barry Black Music, Nigeria
This is a worthy if late career sample of Barrister's trademark sounds.

Kollington Ayinla

Kollington's approach to fuji has always seemed more melodic (if one can describe all-drum music as such) than the work of other fuji bandleaders.

⊙ Warning!
Babs Music and Video, Nigeria
With his trademark voice, and lyrics which often focus on political problems and the supernatural, this album offers a good sample of Kollington's current style. The Honest Jon's compilations have some recordings of Kollington's earlier years when he was playing his *bata fuji*.

Wasiu Ayinde Marshall

The leading contemporary fuji innovator, who has carved out a career between London and Lagos, Wasiu has always pushed the boundaries of the genre with such hybrids as fuji disco, fuji reggae and fuji funky, to name a few.

⭐ Big Deal!
Baba Laje Records, Nigeria
This 2003 release is an ample example of Wasiu's boundary-crossing approach, alternating between straight fuji, jazz fusion fuji, pop fuji and even a fujified highlife track. A worthy listen throughout.

Highlife

Sunny Neji

A beloved fixture on the Nigerian scene, Neji started his career as a background singer and studio voice. His first solo foray in the early 1990s garnered him modest national acclaim, and subsequent popular videos and live performances have cemented his reputation as a major singer, composer, producer and performer.

⭐ Unchained
O'Jez Music, Nigeria
This album showcases not only Neji's work, but typical Nigerian production. It's a mix of his usual highlife, makossa,

pop and more, the highpoint being the hit "Oruka" – classic contemporary Nigerian pop.

Chief Stephen Osita Osadebe

Chief Stephen Osita Osadebe's highlife is sublime, philosophical and impossible to resist, but sadly almost none of it is available outside Nigeria.

⊙ Sound Time
IndigeDisc Music, US
A compilation of some classic tracks from the early 1980s when the chief was at the top of his game. The slow but irrepressible dance groove of "Nri Sports Club", the swinging quick-step beat of "Gwam Owku" and the entrancing, jazzy "Ana Masi Uwa Masi" show just three of the dozens of facets of this remarkable artist.

Afro-beat and Other Styles

Tony Allen

In the 1970s heyday of Fela Kuti's great band Africa 70, Tony Allen was always credited as drummer and leader. More than that, he constructed the basic ingredient of Afro-beat with his own four limbs, 'given to be used', as he used to say.

⊙ Black Voices
Comet, UK
This was Allen's return from the wilderness, a spacey dubstyle CD in which the groove rules, almost subliminally at times. Featuring tenor guitars, stabs of keyboard, juju-type vocals and touches of Manu Dibango, Sunny Ade and P-Funk, this is adventurous stuff on the active side of minimal from an acknowledged master.

Fela Kuti

With a gigantic chunk of the Fela catalogue available on CD these days, it is hard to choose which of his incredible works is most representative. *International Thief Thief* and *Zombie* are probably the greatest. However, the lesser-known albums below may offer more typically classic Fela.

⊙ Kalakuta Show
Kalakuta Records, Nigeria
This details the sacking and burning of Fela's Kalakuta Republic by the military, set to a smoking slow groove which would make anyone dance.

⊙ Confusion
EMI Records
Confusion, a live recording of Fela's Africa 70 band, uses one particular hectic crossroads in Lagos (Oju Elegba) as a metaphor to explore the problems of an entire corrupt nation. The frenetic groove underscores the message perfectly.

Femi Kuti

It can't be easy to follow in the musical footsteps of a father like Fela, but Femi has done so with grace for many years. After flirting with highlife and jazz influences with his band Positive Force, he eventually found his way back to straight Afro-beat.

⊙ Shoki Shoki
Barclay, France
Shoki Shoki is at once cutting-edge and classic Afro-beat, reaching back to the tight arrangements of Fela's golden

PLAYLIST
Nigeria

1 ESHU Various from *Ayan Agalu*
Eshu is the trickster or deity of the crossroads; Yoruba know you must always placate him before embarking on any serious venture.

2 OPERATION FEED THE NATION Ebenezer Obey from *Juju Jubilation*
This leisurely twenty-minute epic preaches on the need for Nigeria to achieve agricultural self-sufficiency against a backdrop at once lush and percussive.

3 SYNCHRO SYSTEM King Sunny Ade from *Juju Music*
The record that opened the ears of much of the world to African music. It holds up just as well today.

4 LATE MATTHEW TOYE Alaji Haruna Ishola from *Apala Messenger*
Entrancing drums and rich vocals pay homage to Matthew Toye, a friend and patron of the artist who had recently passed away.

5 SOYOYO Museliu Ishola from *Soyoyo*
The kola nut does not fall far from the tree. After everyone thought apala was dead, the son returned, sounding like the father in the modern age.

6 OJU ENI MALA/AMERICA OTEYI 1 Wasiu Ayinde Marshall from *Big Deal!*
Tales of his musical conquest of America, where he enjoys the international pleasures of egusi stew (very traditional) with lobster (very American).

7 YOU ARE MY AFRICAN QUEEN 2Face Idibia from *Face 2 Face*
Nigeria's rising star of rap is from one of Africa's worst ghettos, but he sings about love and respect.

8 ZOMBIE Fela Kuti from *Zombie*
In arguably his most profound work, Fela lambasts soldiers mindlessly following orders. Better bone up on your pidgin English – it's worth the effort.

9 MAMONNEY HORNS/MAMONNEY Lágbájá from *Africano*
Holy smoke this band can rock, and yes that is the Gangbe Brass Band jamming that wild horn line while Lágbájá runs down the world's most worshipped idol, money.

10 ANA MASI IFE UWA Chief Stephen Osita Osadebe from *Sound Time*
This genius of highlife can rock, throw down a groove, get jazzy and wax philosophical, as this masterwork ("This is my life story") shows.

years but combining them with Femi's own fresh approach. Never a dull moment.

Hip-Hop

JJC and the 419 Squad

JJC (a.k.a. Skillz from Big Brovaz) has become one of London's up-and-coming African producers and JJC and the 419 Squad are becoming a household name among Nigerian youth worldwide.

⊙ **Atide**
Big Ballerz, UK
This confident debut brings together sounds and influences as diverse as US R&B, UK garage, Latin music, hip-hop and the Nigerian passion for comedy in the form of audio skits.

2Face Idibia

With a growing reputation, and videos on the new MTV Africa, 2Face Idibia is fast becoming the international face of Nigerian rap. He won the first Best African Act award at the 2005 MTV Europe Music awards in Lisbon.

★ **Face 2 Face**
Face 2 Face, Nigeria
This is 2Face's debut album, part of the emerging sound and culture of Africa's youth.

Miscellaneous

Lágbájá

Arguably Nigeria's most profound, and probably its most mysterious, artist. Speaking out about political and social ills, or sometimes just entertaining, Lágbájá is constantly pushing the boundaries of Nigerian popular music.

★ **Africano: The Mother of Groove**
Motherlan' Music, Nigeria/US
Probably the best-produced record ever to emerge from Nigeria, this is a deliberate attempt to underline the African roots of Western pop music, with catchy pop and African music set to the rootsiest African drum grooves you may ever have heard. Pop, soul, rap, funk and Afro-beat, this album has a little of everything, and it ends with nine drum groove samples which will have DJs and producers salivating. You can also sample some at www.lagbaja.com.

Daddy Showkey

His music combines reggae, rap, highlife and gospel, but there is much more to Daddy Showkey than what you can hear on a record: he is an icon, a character, a caricature and an innovator in Nigerian pop culture.

⊙ **Ghetto Soldier**
Felin Records, Nigeria
This album may be hard to find, but you can preview both music and video for this unique artist on his website www.daddy-showkey.com.

Pygmy Music

forest songs from the congo basin

Orchestra Baka Gbine
Sue Hart/Baka Beyond

The Pygmy peoples of Central Africa produce some of the word's most extraordinary vocal music – rich polyphony that's at once completely beguiling and bafflingly complex. But the forest-based hunter-gatherer communities that gave rise to this music are at risk. Aside from the terrible civil wars that have ravaged the region in recent decades, the Pygmies have witnessed their traditional hunting areas converted into logging concessions and wildlife reserves. Their remarkably music may prove an effective tool in the struggle to make their voices heard and to save their homelands, as Dave Abram and Jerome Lewis explain.

One hour before dawn, shreds of mist still hang below the canopy of the Cameroonian rainforest. A myriad invisible insects announce their presence with a layered wall of noise, punctuated by an occasional bird call or the blood-curdling cry of a tree hyrax. At first, the strange new notes that echo through the darkness could be part of this ever-changing non-human soundscape. But the *yelli*, descending in yodelled steps that swell and merge to form haunting chords, are the songs of the Baka, the indigenous hunter-gatherers who inhabit this remote tract of tropical forest. Reverberating between the giant tree trunks, their polyphonic pre-dawn chorus is a bid to mesmerize the animals so that they will succumb more easily to the hunters' spears and nets later that day.

The **Baka** are one of dozens of indigenous hunter-gatherer groups living in the equatorial forests of the Congo Basin; others include their neighbours the **Gyeli** and **Kola** in Cameroon, the **Aka**, **Bongo** and **Mikaya** in Congo-Brazzaville, and the **Mbuti**, **Sua**, **Efé** and **Twa** in the Democratic Republic of Congo. Scattered throughout the forest in over ten countries stretching from the Cameroon coast to the hilly borders of Rwanda and Burundi, these forest-dwelling peoples have beguiled outsiders for millennia. Featured in ancient Egyptian and later Greek and Roman murals, they have been referred to since the era of European explorers as **Pygmies** because of their small stature.

Despite speaking different languages and living in a variety of situations today – from nomadic hunter-gatherers to sedentarized farmers and land less urban beggars – Pygmy peoples recognize their shared history as hunter-gatherers and as the first peoples of the Central African forests. And, despite their differences, all Pygmy peoples make distinctively rich polyphonic music to celebrate the forest in their ritual life; they have very egalitarian societies that use demand-sharing and other levelling mechanisms such as mockery to even out inequalities. All groups experience discrimination from their non-Pygmy neighbours. They are frequently stereotyped by outsiders as dirty, animal-like, primitive and inferior.

The Pygmies' aptitude for music is striking to the visitor. Whether butchering a duiker antelope, bathing in the river or simply sharing a spliff around the fire, music is ever-present. In camp sessions, voices usually carry the tunes. But the Baka also make instruments from materials found in the forest and will spend hours each day playing them. Their songs range from simple melodic phrases without words, or clapping and rhyme games for children, to longer, more complex "story-tales" – **likanos** – relating traditional origin myths.

The **tunes**, most of which are rooted in five- or seven-note scales, tend to be divided into syncopated parts for different voices, embellished with overlapping harmonies and accompanied by various kinds of percussion – none of which will tell

Su Hart & Martin Cradick

Baka children clapping

Pygmy Polyphony

Pygmies are renowned not just for their skills as singers, dancers and hunters, but also for their rejection of authority. In a Pygmy forest camp no one has power over another: people do as they choose, ideally with consideration for others, and announce their intentions at dawn and dusk meetings. When people strongly disagree with each other, each person simply does what they want; and if the disagreement continues they move camp to avoid each other. Despite this seemingly casual arrangement, camp members sensitively coordinate their activities according to implicit values to ensure that all participate in hunting and gathering enough food to satisfy everybody.

An appreciation of this social structure enables a better understanding of the Pygmies' music, which is similarly based on the relative autonomy of each participant within implicit rules. There are no signs of hierarchy during music-making. One individual may assume the function of beginning the song, inspiring participants when it starts fading, and perhaps starting the next song, but their voice is soon lost in the mass of others. At some stage, a new song initiator will replace the previous one without fuss. This is accepted by all so long as the newcomer can equal or better the preceding song. If they don't, people immediately mock them, singing out "moyibi" (thief), and someone else will take their place. Equally, there is no observable hierarchy in the distribution of parts within a piece: everyone is free to join whichever part of the polyphony they wish. And, unless there are ritual reasons, all camp members – children, women and men – participate equally.

Pygmies' use of instruments is limited by their nomadic movement. Most of their instruments are easily made from forest materials or utilitarian objects: they tap iron blades against each other, beat cut-down tree trunks, branches, bamboo or buttress roots with sticks, or turn papaya branches into flutes and raffia leaves into harps. Drums are normally only kept at permanent campsites or in farmers' villages.

Ethnomusicologist Simha Arom has dedicated his life to understanding Central African polyphony, especially that of the Pygmies. He explains how the music achieves a sense of continuous development by the repetition of overlapping phrases. Generally, the vocal pattern lasts a total number of beats divisible by both two and three, and the percussion will exploit both these ratios. For example, for a sung "period" of 24 beats, a drum ostinato may last for eight beats, while tapped iron blades might add a twelve-beat pattern. These parts are themselves usually structured so as to avoid symmetries: so the twelve-beat pattern of the iron blades may be subdivided into groups of five and seven beats. These overlapping rhythmic phases explains the music's sense of incessant dynamism and tension.

Melodically, the singers draw on a wide stock of modules suitable for each piece of music and usable at precise moments in the overall pattern. These fit together in such a way that there are consonant intervals (usually fifths and octaves) at key points; between these points, dissonances are possible. If, by coincidence, too many singers find themselves singing in unison they immediately diverge by choosing different formulas.

Making sense of all this on paper is one thing; trying to work out how all the singers and players fit together when listening to a dense Pygmy polyphony is another matter.

Martin Cradick & Su Hart

Baka earth bow

you what gives Pygmy music its unique defining quality. For when these elements flow together the result is something magical: rhythmic, melodic music alive with unexpected dissonances.

Music in Forest Life

In his famous ethnography of the Mbuti of Congo, American anthropologist Colin M. Turnbull – whose best-selling book *The Forest People* brought the first detailed, accessible description of Pygmy life to Western readers – explores the relation between the forest and the Mbuti's music. According to Turnbull, his Pygmy informants regarded the forest as a kind of benevolent, all-powerful "parent", able to provide sustenance and affection for its "children" as long as they were able to communicate with it. The principal way the Mbuti did this was through singing. 'Song', wrote Turnbull in 1965, 'is used to communicate with the forest, and it is significant that the emphasis is on the actual sound, not on the words … The sound "awakens" the forest … thus attracting the forest's attention to the immediate needs of its children.'

In common with many hunter-gatherer societies, Pygmies such as the Mbuti or Baka do not maintain the hard and fast distinctions between formal and informal work and play as do Western societies. A tune that crops up in a full-moon fireside session could well be the same one deployed in a spirit possession ritual or pre-hunt *yelli*, and even during what seem to be important ceremonies, laughing and joking are the norm.

Nevertheless, different styles of music tend to accompany different activities. To amuse themselves while bathing in the river, for example, Baka women and children will plunge, slap and beat their hands in the water to create polyrhythmic sounds and rhythms known as **liquindi** (water drumming). And when the group is lazing around in camp after a good meal, someone is sure to strike up a tune on a **limbindi** (a thin string bow, whose pitch is changed with the chin), the **ieta** (bow harp) or **ngombi** (harp zither), which everyone else will add to with a harmony or percussion line, tapping on pots and hollow logs and shaking seed pods. This kind of spontaneous, pure entertainment music forms a constant backdrop to life in camp, and has an important social function: by drawing the group together in time and in tune, it eases the stresses and strains of close communal life. Some of the most enjoyable sessions are those which are instigated after an argument.

Among the Baka and other Pygmy populations, music is also used as a medium for moral and spiritual instruction. *Likanos* advise people on how to behave by giving guidance on key matters such as sharing (essential in hunter-gatherer economies), marriage arrangements and hunting techniques. Some also explain the origins of the animals, plants and natural forces in the forest (one well-loved Baka *likano* concerns a man who danced too slowly and was turned by Kumba, the Creator Being, into a millipede).

Lastly, music has a specific role in **rituals**: rites of passage, spirit visitations and divination ceremonies conducted to establish the source of witchcraft, to heal a sick person or to help find animals in the forest. The words "song" and "dance" (*bé*) are the same in Baka, and it is through "singing the dance" that the spirits of the forest are invoked. In fact, spirits are believed to have handed down the Baka's music in the first place: the songs and dances flow through them into the world.

Perhaps this explains why the Baka, in keeping with their egalitarian way of living, make little or no distinction between performer and audience. Even in *jengi* or *boona* ceremonies, where a spirit actually enters the camp (in the form of an initiated man dressed in a special ritual costume), most of those present will participate equally in the music and drama. That said, certain individuals may lead the singing or dance if they know the words and movements better than anyone else. It is the leader's job to keep the tune going when it flags, to prompt, initiate or bring a song to an end. This role is not formally conferred, and implies no special privileges. As with hunting and gathering, or the hundreds of other skilled tasks the Baka perform in the run of their lives, an individual takes a key role in a group activity if he or she has marked talent for it, for the greater good of the group rather than their own prestige.

Listening to the Forest

Ethnographers, musicologists and anyone who has lived in the forest with Pygmy people are bound to have asked themselves where this extraordinary musicality comes from. The answer, like so much else in the Pygmies' life, stems from the forest, or more particularly, its rich soundscape. Moving around the rainforest paths, where dense vegetation prevents you from seeing very far, hearing becomes the primary sense. In the absence of visual pointers, the Pygmies find their way by tuning into auditory landmarks: to the sound of particular trees, to the flow of a river or to noises from different encampments, and by calling to one another, often over long distances.

It's not surprising, therefore, that forest-dwellers become skilled listeners at a very early age. More-

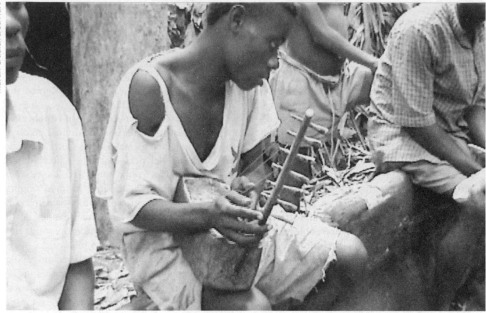

Martin Cradick & Su Hart

Baka musician playing the *ieta*

over, they do not have to contend with the backdrop of irrelevant noise that assails us in modern cities. In Western countries, people learn "not to listen"; Pygmy children, on the other hand, are encouraged to develop sensitivity to the sounds around them, not least of all by listening to, and becoming involved in, the music that constantly surrounds them in camp. Older children help keep their younger brothers and sisters amused by teaching them tunes, dances and clapping games, and these help integrate skills essential for life in the forest.

The Pygmies' keen sense of hearing can lead to incidents that bewilder their less sound-aware visitors. When, for example, an elephant is killed by hunters many miles away in the forest, the women back at camp may know of the kill hours before the hunters return. The death of such a large animal sparks off bird calls in the vicinity, which will in turn send sound ripples through the forest. And when these reach the women, they start to sing celebrations.

This uncanny sensitivity to sound, combined with an early start and plenty of opportunity for practice, perhaps explains the Pygmies' highly developed musical ability. Good group musicship is, after all, ninety percent listening.

Beyond the Forest

Early travellers tended to describe hunter-gatherer peoples of Central Africa as if they existed in isolation. But semi-nomadic groups like the Baka, Efé, Aka, Babenzélé and Mbuti no longer (and probably never did) live entirely cut off from the rest of the world. Although they may spend many months hunting and gathering in the forest, economic or social ties eventually pull them back to more permanent settlements, to visit relatives and trade with their Bantu neighbours.

Inevitably, the music of the African villages and towns on the edge of the forest has influenced the Pygmies, and some of the instruments most commonly found in their camps – log-and-skin drums, or the **ieta** (bow harp) for example – may have been originally copied from the Bantu.

The recent advent of portable radios and tape cassettes has had an even more dramatic impact. These days, young guitar-playing Baka lads can skillfully imitate the *zouk* and *soukous* sounds they hear tinkling over on the airwaves from Congo – riffs that are rudimentary compared with their own traditional sounds. What's more, performing them in market towns can earn new respect from the Bantu.

Pygmy Fusion

In the late 1950s, when he was conducting the anthropological fieldwork that would later form the basis for *The Forest People*, **Colin Turnbull** made many hours of recordings of Mbuti music, selections of which were subsequently released on vinyl. These quickly became classics of their type, revealing for the first time the essential complexity

The Baka Music House

PYGMY MUSIC

Eka Morgan, producer of BBC World Service feature *The Pygmy Music House*, explains how this innovative collaboration is helping to promote Pygmy culture.

Since 1992, **Martin Cradick** and **Su Hart** have travelled nine times to visit the Baka Pygmies living in southeast Cameroon. Su Hart explains why she thinks the Baka have such a sensitive and creative musical culture: 'You can't see very far in a rainforest. Colours aren't important, they only have three names for colours. But you can hear a long, long way. If you are walking along a pathway with the Baka, suddenly they'll stop, they'll be like statues, and they'll be listening for the way. They'll hear the wind in the tall trees, or a river far away and they'll know exactly where they are. They navigate by the sounds. And good listening makes you a good musician.'

Martin Cradick adds: 'All the Baka sing, from the youngest to the oldest and there is no sense of performer and audience. The music helps to create a strong community in the forest. Often there is a big argument and then later people will play music together and completely heal any rifts through the togetherness achieved in their music making.'

On their first visit to the Baka, Cradick and Hart brought a guitar and mandolin with them. 'The Baka were very keen to hear us play,' says Cradick, 'Then we found that about two or three of the young men could play guitar and so it was easy to join in on mandolin. Their traditional music, such as *yelli*, was much harder to join in with as the rhythms and melodies were strange to our ears.'

After that first trip to the Baka, Cradick and Hart formed a band, **Baka Beyond**, which is now made up of musicians from six countries in Africa and Europe. The first two CDs that the band released were *Spirit of the Forest*, a mixture of their music with that of the Baka, and *Heart of the Forest*, which is pure Baka music.

For twelve years, Cradick and Hart have been trying to find the ideal way to pay the Baka royalties from the band's recordings. They created the charity Global Music Exchange, which distributes essentials such as medicine, cooking pots, machetes, soap and salt. Then the Baka came up with the idea of a Music House, to showcase their musical talent and improve their status in the community.

Cradick and Hart brought a French-speaking timber-frame builder to the forest. The Baka are still semi-nomadic and live between camps near logging roads and settlements in the heart of the forest. The Music House was built in one of the camps in the middle of a rainforest clearing, surrounded by the Baka's small leaf huts, known as *mongulu*. The Baka worked together with the local Bantu people in the construction project, and the Music House is now the only two-storey building in a 200km radius.

The Baka plan to make recordings there and to perform to paying audiences from the local town. Dundelo, the leader of this group of Baka Pygmies, says: 'I am very happy with the new Music House. I want the Baka and Bantu to work together with music and to earn money, so the village can develop far into the future.'

of Pygmy polyphony and an equally extraordinary instrumental tradition.

Turnbull's tapes also inspired a second generation of ethnomusicologists, among them the French-Israeli **Simha Arom**, who lived among the Babenzélé of the Central African Republic in the 1960s. It was a track on one of Arom's releases, featuring *hindewhu* (a technique in which a single-pitch reed whistle alternates with sung notes to produce a melody line) that was later picked up by African American jazz pianist Herbie Hancock's drummer, Bill Summers, and turned, with the help of an empty beer bottle, into the famous remake of "Watermelon Man" featured on Hancock's ground-breaking album *Headhunters*.

In retrospect, Summer's bottle-blowing antics were a seminal moment in World Music history, marking as they did the first fusion of an African Pygmy idiom with a Western tradition. Since then, Pygmy-inspired sounds have found their way into an array of different recording projects, from Brian Eno and John Hassel soundtracks to **Zap Mama** acapella numbers.

By far the best-known deployment of Pygmy music, though, came with the 1993 release of the multi-million selling *Deep Forest* CD. French europopsters **Eric Mouquet** and **Michel Sanchez** came up with a formula combining soft techno, samples of a spread of indigenous (mainly African) traditions and a rather cloying nostalgia for the "ancestral wisdom" of indigenous peoples. The opening track begins with the line: "Somewhere deep in the jungle are living some little men and women. They are your past; maybe they are your future." Described by one critic as the 'Benetton of music-marketing concepts', Deep Forest proved phenomenally successful. Two and a half million copies were sold in its first three years, and it remains the best-selling World Music fusion album ever made.

However, Deep Forest has not managed to resolve considerable controversy over their claims to return money to the original performers. At best, only a tiny fragment of the money the *Deep Forest* earned has made its way back to some forest people – and not even the main performers. Although this is a common ethical dilemma when traditional music is "sourced", or sampled, others have made considerable efforts to address it. One example of how different things can be is that of **Baka Beyond**, the UK's Pygmy-Celtic fusion band (see box on previous page).

Survival

Fair-trade and other ethical issues aside, record royalties ought to find their way back to the forest because they provide a means of supporting the survival of traditional Pygmy society, whose existence has come increasingly under threat in the past two or three decades from logging companies, road builders and the temptations of wage labour.

Whether or not Pygmy groups and their music will survive these changes depends on how successfully they are able to negotiate rights over their forest homelands. For without the forest, the Pygmies soon lose their economic independence. No longer able to provide for themselves by hunting and gathering, they are forced to drift into roadside settlements and to lead an impoverished life on the margins of a society that, at best, treats them as second-class citizens.

Traditional music has already shown signs of succumbing to the strain. In recent years, the nocturnal *yelli* songs that have for hundreds, possibly thousands, of years echoed through the Cameroonian rainforest, have become a rarity. Some Baka groups have reportedly gone several seasons without singing *yelli* before a hunt, complaining that there have been too many disturbances in the surrounding forest for them to be successful. And every year that passes without a *yelli* being performed increases the chances of this unique musical form being lost forever.

DISCOGRAPHY Pygmy Music

⊙ **Anthologie de la musique Congolaise Vol 2:**
Songs of the Okapi Forest – Mbuti, Nande & Pakombe
Tervuren Museum with Fonti Musicali, Belgium
The early tracks on this album provide some beautiful examples of Mbuti polyphony, which is less overlaid than Babenzélé or Aka polyphony and thus more accessible to the uninitiated.

⊙ **Anthology of World Music – Africa:**
The Ba-Benzélé Pygmies
Rounder, US
One of the best of a recently released group of ethnomusicological recordings. Worth getting for the astonishing virtuosity of the *hindewhu* whistle solo alone – a simultaneous song and whistle tune, which has to be be heard to be believed.

⊙ The Baka Forest People: Heart of the Forest
Hannibal, UK; Ryko, US

Martin Cradick's field recordings, made in 1992, showcase the Baka's extraordinary polyphonic singing and their various instruments, interspersed with evocative eavesdroppings on camp life. Seamlessly stringing together trancy instrumental grooves, sploshing water drums, kids' campfire rhymes and, best of all, *yelli* songs that draw you deep into the forest, the selection gives a generous overview of Baka music without descending into dry ethnomusicology. And everyone on it (except the omnipresent cicadas) gets a cut of the royalties.

⊙ Bayaka: The Extraordinary Music of the Babenzélé Pygmies
Ellipsis Arts, US

American Louis Sarno has lived with the Babenzélé people for over a decade, recording their music and writing about their life in the forest. This CD features the pick of his tape collection, remastered by wildlife and natural sound supremo Bernie Krause, with a lavishly illustrated book to accompany the recorded material. Best choice for the anthropologically inclined.

★ Centrafrique: Anthologie de la Musique des Pygmées Aka
Harmonia Mundi, France

This double-CD set features digitally remastered versions of Simha Arom's prize-winning 1978 recordings, which first put Pygmy music on the world map. The quality doesn't compare with the albums listed above, but the 32 tracks cover the gamut of the Akas' musical output, from large-scale divination rituals involving dozens of participants to intimate contrapuntal duets.

⊙ Centrafrique – Pygmées Aka, Chants de Chasse, d'Amour et de Moquerie
Ocora, France

A lovely compilation of Aka instrumental music. The recordings of stringed instruments and flutes are accompanied by ethnomusicologist Susanne Fürniss's notes.

⊙ Echoes of the Forest: Music of the Central African Pygmies
Ellipsis Arts, US

A selection of Colin Turnbull, Jean-Pierre Hallet and Louis Sarno's best recordings, packaged with sixty pages of photographs and text describing Pygmy life. Credit is due to the Ellipsis label for putting this product together for the price of a regular CD.

★ Mbuti Pygmies of the Ituri Rainforest
Smithsonian Folkways, US

Colin Turnbull's massively influential original recordings among the Mbuti in the late 1950s are here digitally remastered and accompanied by Turnbull's original notes and a new introduction by Michelle Kisliuk.

⊙ Pygmées
Editions Dapper, France

A 1991 collection of samples from the Musée Dapper's archives that sets out to challenge the concept that Pygmies are an isolatable ethnic or racial group. The accompanying book is packed with engaging background info, and the original tapes have been digitally remastered.

Jeremy Avis

Musicologist, singer and xylophone player Jeremy Avis spent two years studying Baka music in Cameroon, and was Martin Cradick's collaborator on *Heart of the Forest*.

⊙ Junglebean: Moving With Intent
Camwood Productions, UK

Avis's debut album features a couple of tracks based on Baka grooves, with techno trance, drum'n'bass patterns, medieval *cantigas* and oriental *maquams* thrown in for good measure.

Baka Beyond

UK-based Baka Beyond started after ex-Outback guitarist Martin Cradick and his wife, Su Hart, spent six weeks with the Baka in Cameroon. From this early hands-on stab at Afro-Celtic fusion has evolved an increasingly sophisticated sound, blending Baka riffs with Scottish island ballads and the Hendrix-Romanian-Gypsy fiddling of Paddy Lemercier.

★ Spirit of the Forest
Hannibal, UK; Ryko, US

The title-track of this first album is Baka Beyond's musical mission statement. Field samples of forest *yelli* yield seamlessly to studio recordings of Martin Cradick's rich mandolin and guitar, while meticulously produced African percussion lays down an infectious groove.

⊙ Meeting Pool
Hannibal, UK; Ryko, US

The highpoints of this more ambitious, elaborately produced second offering are as much Gaelic (the spine-tingling ballad "Ohureo") and Turkish (Lemercier's soaring eastern-influenced violin playing) as Cameroonian, but the forest roots are retained through sensitive sampling of Baka music and, once again, some powerful percussion. A truly inspired cultural mix that defies categorization.

Orchestre Baka Gbine

Baka Gbine are long-time collaborators with Baka Beyond – an acoustic band, from the Cameroon rainforest, near the Congo border, who have been honing their skills on guitar, and giving a fresh treatment to their traditional vocals and percussion.

★ Gati Bongo
March Hare Music, UK

Gati Bongo is a very special field recording: a collection of simple acoustic guitar, mandolin and light percussion-backed songs. Each features one solo vocal, mostly sung by group leader Pelembir Dieudonné, responded to by a predominantly female chorus. The hunters' call singing style, known as *yelli*, runs through Baka Gbine's music and this album features the interwoven yodelling for which Baka song is best known. The guitar work also reflects the influence of Congolese acoustic

Su Hart/Baka Beyond

rumba; the guitar runs combined with the yodels are slightly reminiscent of some of the early recordings of Congo music's father-figure, Wendo Kolosoy.

Deep Forest

French duo Michel Sanchez and Eric Mouquet set out in the early 1990s to create lyrical electronic music "imprinted with the ancestral wisdom of African chants". The result was one of the most successful (and controversial) discs of the whole World Music phenomenon.

⊙ Deep Forest
Epic, France

Synths and sequenced bass and percussion spice up samples of music from various "primitive societies" (*sic*), including Central African Pygmies, on this first and best Deep Forest album. Critics would maintain that it is essentially a rehash of the Noble Savage cliché in amorphous eurotechno.

Zap Mama

Zap Mama is a Belgium-based, all-women acapella group whose members are of mixed African and European descent. Their leader, Marie Daulne, was born to a Belgian father and Congolese mother in Africa, where, as a young child, she lived with the Pygmies in the forest.

★ Zap Mama
Cramworld, Belgium

Zap Mama's acclaimed debut album, which occupied the number one spot in Billboard's World Music chart for four months, includes a wonderful cover of a piece from Arom and Taurelle's 1966 ethnographic LP, entitled "Babanzélé". Using eight voices and *hindewhu* whistle, it is the most complete, authentic reproduction of Pygmy polyphony by a Western group to date.

⊙ Sabsylma
Crammed Discs, Belgium

On this 1994 album, Marie Daulne uses Zap Mama to explore the potential for synergies between their vocally dominant acapella style and mainstream Western pop genres such as drum'n'bass, rap and funk, plus other major World Music traditions from India and the Arab world. The results are playful and sometimes funny, but always groovy and often beautiful.

PLAYLIST
Pygmy Music

1 MBOLA (TWO VERSIONS) from *Centrafrique: Anthologie de la Musique des Pygmées Aka*
Although both tracks are of the same song, the differences are remarkable and demonstrate the inspired and endless possibility for variation that Pygmy polyphony permits.

2 ELEPHANT HUNT SONG from *Mbuti Pygmies of the Ituri Rainforest*
A beautiful example of male polyphonic singing. An elephant hunter recounts a kill, accompanied by other men.

3 WOMEN GATHERING IN THE FOREST from *Bayaka: The Extraordinary Music of the Babenzélé Pygmies*
This track exquisitely captures the resonance of women's singing. The music is intended to warn animals of the women's approach, as they look for food under the lush forest canopy.

4 YELLI 1 from *The Baka Forest People: Heart of the Forest*
This beautiful elephant-hunting polyphony is used by the women to "tie up" the spirits of elephants so that men can go and kill them safely.

5 EMBEMA from *Centrafrique: Pygmées Aka, Chants de Chasse, d'Amour et de Moquerie*
A relaxed men-only thumb-piano piece that captures the atmosphere of a quiet evening at the men's seating area in camp.

Rwanda & Burundi

echoes from the hills

Ballet Inganzo of Rwanda
Inshuti

Rwanda and Burundi share one of Africa's most distinct musical cultures, with their dramatic troupes of drummers, based on royal tradition. But there is a modern sound, too, which has developed in part through the region's diaspora, after the devastating genocide of 1994. Dorian Hayes and Karengera Eric Soul document the region's musical rebirth.

During the pre-colonial era, when the entire Great Lakes Region (including Rwanda, Burundi, eastern Congo, western Tanzania and what is now southern Uganda) resembled a vast patchwork of fiefdoms and chieftancies, the role of the court musicians was crucial to the prestige of the Tutsi royal family. At that time, the principal socio-ethnic groups – Hutu and Tutsi (together with the indigenous Twa Pygmies who account for roughly one percent of the population) – lived in relative harmony.

Intermarriage and social mobility between the agrarian Hutu majority and the Tutsi cattle owners were common in these years. Both peoples had similar origin stories that suggested migration from other regions, with the Tutsis claiming that their lineage stretched back to the kingdoms of Ethiopia and Egypt. The parallel evolution of the Kinyarwanda and Kirundi languages of Rwanda and Burundi – both part of the Bantu family – reveals close kinship, and the two countries share many cultural and demographic similarities.

Sadly, German and later Belgian colonial rule ossified existing social divisions, and planted the seeds of future conflict in Rwanda and Burundi. The Europeans sought to exploit the *de facto* class structure they discovered along rigidly ethnic lines. In practice this meant installing the Tutsi nobility in positions of power that sanctioned widespread abuse of the Hutu majority, and establishing an apartheid system, complete with passbooks, identity cards and fixed tribal identities.

As a result of the growth of a radical movement known as "Hutu Power" and the sudden switch of allegiance by the Belgians after independence, the 1980s and 90s saw both countries convulsed by civil war between Hutus and Tutsis. Recent estimates suggest that over 900,000 Rwandan Tutsis and moderate Hutus were murdered by militias and government troops in a hundred days of carnage between April and June 1994. A further 300,000 have died in ongoing conflict in Burundi.

Traditional Music

The cultural upshot of these horrific events is that traditional music in both Rwanda and Burundi has remained – with a few notable exceptions – a largely unknown quantity in the outside world. This fascinating, centuries-old culture has so far failed to find a significant audience on the international music scene. Another, more positive consequence is that these traditions remain remarkably unchanged. The performance practices of groups like the **Drum-**mers of Burundi** in Bujumbura, the **National Ballet of Rwanda** in Butare and **Ballet Inganzo** in Ruhengeri (see box opposite) have changed little since their forebears paid tribute to the king and his noble clans centuries ago. Such performances, whether in Kigali's grand Amahoro Stadium or in dusty school fields across the region, undoubtedly offer some of the purest, most potent and visually stunning musical experiences in sub-Saharan Africa.

The traditions of Rwanda are rooted in a ritualized dance known as **ikinimba** or **inhore** ("the dance of heroes"), which relates the history of the region and recalls the feats of mythical heroes, kings and warriors. Over the years, this dance has been used to dramatize the many tales and legends, indeed the entire oral tradition of the region. Other songs and dances commemorate important social occasions (e.g. birth, marriage, hunting, seasonal change, invocation of the spirits) or evoke the area's natural beauty and the value of the local cattle, which have been vital to the well-being of the population for generations. During the era of European rule, these ceremonial songs and dances were described as an African form of "ballet", a term that continues to be widely used. Nowadays, the ballet can be seen immortalized as a symbol of national pride on Rwandan banknotes and on national TV, as well as on stages across the country.

In addition to the songs and dances, this music is usually accompanied by a number of distinctive instruments. At the heart of every ballet troupe are the mighty **ingoma**, double-headed drums made from hollowed-out tree trunks of varying sizes, up to 4ft tall, and covered with taut cowhide. The *ingoma* have long been used as a kind of bush telegraph to transmit messages across the region's hilly terrain. As well as the drums, many groups feature the **inanga** (similar to a lyre or zither); the **iningiri** (or *wuturi*, a violin-like instrument with a calabash attached); the **umuduri** (or *munahi*, a musical bow); the **makondera** (or *umwirongi*, a vertical flute); and the **ikembe** (a small thumb-piano which originated among the Twa Pygmies).

Many of the same performing styles and instruments can be found in both Rwanda and Burundi. There are, however, numerous regional variations. In Burundi, for example, the *ingoma* is often the sole accompaniment (see box opposite), while on the islands of Inkombo and Ijwi in Lake Kivu, Rwandan music has mingled with the music of the Shi people from South Kivu in DRC. Performance practice in the northwestern Rwandan provinces of Gisenyi and Ruhengeri has similarly incorporated

The Drummers of Burundi and Ballet Inganzo

Ten drums hewn from huge African logs stood in a semi-circle around a larger drum painted the red, green and white of the Burundian flag. Nearby, the Drummers of Burundi, tired from their long journey, munched on sandwiches. Half an hour later, clad in red and green togas, the drummers stood, fresh-faced and expectant behind their drums. Their leader let out a cry, which they all took up before slamming their sticks onto the drum-heads in a rhythmic onslaught of such power and volume that the assembled journalists and photographers were practically blasted back through the door. One by one, the drummers played the painted drum at the centre, leaping around it with a lithe elegance, drawing their sticks around their necks in gestures at once ferocious and humorous. The Drummers of Burundi are the ultimate African drum experience, a catharsis of energy, grace and athleticism so intense it can only be sustained in bursts of forty minutes at a time. It was seeing the drummers that inspired Thomas Brooman to organize the first WOMAD festival in 1982, the event that effectively sparked off the whole World Music boom.

Graeme Ewens

The Drummers of Burundi

Burundi shares Rwanda's legacy of inter-ethnic hatred and violence. Since the dark days of the mid-1990s, retaliatory massacres have claimed the lives of some 300,000 people, and it remains to be seen whether recent elections will represent a decisive step back from ethnic conflict. The Drummers of Burundi are Hutu, though traditionally they played only for the Tutsi king, or mwami, and accompanied him everywhere (in Kirundi, the words for "drum" and "king" are the same). But the last mwami was assassinated in 1972. The Drummers – whose skills are passed down through particular families now play for the president and other dignitaries.

'The drum is a respected instrument in Burundi', said Gabriel, the spokesman. 'Even these drummers cannot play the drums when they feel like it. The drums are only beaten for special ceremonies. And not everyone can dance to the drums. You cannot just go into a shop and buy a drum. The people who make the drums, the people who play the drums and dance to them, are the same people.'

If the Drummers of Burundi are among the most successful and visible musical exports from Central Africa, then Ballet Inganzo are the grass-roots ambassadors for regional reconciliation. Like many similar troupes in Rwanda, Ballet Inganzo is made up of members from each of the three main ethnic groups. For founder François Nkinzehwiki, the Ballet originally offered an opportunity to 'collect the three groups under the umbrella of a national culture'. After many years of traumatic and dehumanizing experiences, François believes that singing and playing in the Ballet allowed the members 'to feel that they are again human and accepted'. And he should know: before moving back to Ruhengeri in northwest Rwanda, François worked as a teacher in the hellish refugee camps of Goma, DRC, where the group was formed.

Like the Burundian drummers, and their fellow musicians across the country, the teenaged members of Ballet Inganzo all have other occupations: mechanics, clerks, and principally farmers. In Rwanda, as in Burundi, the role of the musician is a highly prized honour. Ensemble-leader Alfred Sibomana explains: 'Music helps me enjoy and to "carry life" with a different perspective.' Alfred's formative role in the Ballet is a source of deep personal pride, giving him recognition, control over his own life and influence in the community.

In comparison with the forceful attack of Burundian drumming troupes, the Rwandan Ballet offers a more modulated spectacle. As London audiences witnessed in some of the capital's most prestigious music venues in 2002 and 2004, their performances combine fluid, stylized dance moves, aching close-harmony singing and percussive pyrotechnics. At a time when much of the Western media seemed fixated on stories of horror and bloodshed, the Rwandan Ballet gave an alternative message of hope.

With thanks to Mark Hudson

Cécile Kayirebwa and the Rwandan Diaspora

Dorian Hayes

The contours of culture in the Great Lakes Region stretch back centuries into the pre-colonial past. The musicians of today, from the globally famous likes of Cécile Kayirebwa and the Master Drummers of Burundi to the grassroots troupes found all over the country, can trace their heritage directly to the Abiru, or court "ritualists", of the sixteenth and seventeenth centuries. Through these artists, ancestral stories are preserved and modernized, connecting a people – many of them in exile miles from the "Land of a Thousand Hills" – to their living history. As Cécile Kayirebwa told us in Brussels in March 2005, 'The music carries an education, the culture, the history, the memory and even the geography of the country. The important elements of what we are about, as human beings and as Rwandan nationals, is documented in the music.'

Unfortunately, this rich oral tradition is once again in danger. From the days of colonial oppression, and more recent purges of the nation's culture, Rwandan traditional music and dance now face a more insidious threat. Due to the country's horrific recent past, Cécile explained, many people have forgotten the language [Kinyarwanda]: 'They are therefore completely cut off from the culture, separated from their roots … They are like a people without culture.' Listening to Cécile's lament, it became clear that one of the more subtly devastating effects of the recent upheavals in Central Africa is that a whole generation might be severed from their history. Worse still, the living, oral nature of these traditions is such that, without regular performance and training, they might simply disappear from the cultural map.

It is for this reason that Cécile and a small band of supporters and enthusiasts in Europe and Rwanda are currently working to raise the profile of this endangered culture. This is the purpose of Cécile's Ceka-I-Rwanda project, which – alongside her own recording career – seeks to revive and preserve the traditions of Rwandan music and dance for the generations now living outside the region. In the former colonial capital of Brussels, Cécile has watched the sad waves of political refugees wash up and increase to a deluge in recent years. As she explained, 'Every time I have hope that things might be getting better, I see all these new people coming in [to Europe], and that there's obviously still lots of trouble. This has been especially true since '94. There are so many refugees, there is no longer a network, people don't know each other … it's all too mixed and disordered.'

While it is certainly heartening and exciting to see confident, talented young Rwandans like Corneille and Soul-ID achieving great success telling their stories in the new context of modern beats and cutting-edge technology, Cécile's more rooted, traditionalist approach is no less vital. As she puts it, with a wry smile, 'What young people need is…a venue where they can go and see and play the instruments and take part in workshops. In this way, the culture will once again become organic, lively, and interactive, not filed away in a cupboard.' With another album of characteristically soulful traditional Rwandan music in the pipeline, and a song specially written for the movie *Shooting Dogs*, it is to be hoped that Cécile will indeed be able to raise the profile of her beloved culture in the years to come.

characteristic features from Congolese culture.

Traditional music has produced numerous notable musicians over the years, many of them players of the *inanga* – they include **Maître de Rujindiri**, **Hervé Twahirwa**, **Victor Kabarira**, **Abakobwa B'Iwaku**, **Kirusu**, **Sebatunzi and Sentore**, **Muyango** and **Cécile Kayirebwa** (see box). Singer-composer and cultural educator **Massamba** from Bujumbura played a key role in nurturing the development of a Burundian version of the Rwandan Ballet throughout the 1980s and 90s; his group Indashyikirwa was largely made up of Rwandan refugees in exile south of the border. Since 1998, Massamba has lived in Brussels, working to promote the traditions of the Great Lakes Region.

Tragically, musicians were often specifically targeted by death squads during the 1994 genocide; many were murdered, while many more fled into exile. This is particularly sad, since musical performance had traditionally been one of the few areas of Rwanda's cultural life where Hutu, Tutsi and Twa worked together, and because musicians and performers generally tend to scorn the significance of ethnic distinctions. On a more chilling note, at the time of writing, **Simon Bikindi**, formerly the Director of Rwanda's National Ballet and one of the country's leading cultural figures prior to 1994, was awaiting trial at the International Criminal Tribunal for Rwanda (ICTR) in Tanzania, for the crime of inciting and participating in acts of genocide. In a country where word-of-mouth and the radio are the principal means of communication, long-standing musical traditions have occasionally been hijacked as a conduit for propaganda and ethnic hatred.

Contemporary Music in Rwanda

The decade since the genocide has witnessed a gradual flowering of innovation and creativity. This rebirth has been fuelled in part by the return from exile of a generation of performers and artists, and by the growing strength and unity of the Rwandan diaspora community. Unfortunately, there are only two recording studios in the whole country, and musical performance is still dominated by a small elite of promoters.

During the early 1990s, bands such as **Imena**, **Impala**, **Ingeli** and **Nyampinga** would enliven the towns and villages of Rwanda. These groups generally sang in the Kinyarwanda language, but played music that reflected the influence of Congolese rumba and *soukous*, reggae and *zouk*.

Now, prospects for several of these orchestras have brightened considerably. Ingeli recently reformed under the grand name of **Ingeli Pan-African Band**, featuring members from Rwanda, Burundi, DRC, Uganda and Kenya; they now perform at major regional events such as the 2004 Awesome Africa Music Festival, in Durban. **Imena**, too, have recently begun touring again, appearing at the 2005 Zanzibar Swahili Music Festival.

Many exciting solo talents have emerged from these ensembles, including singers like Jean-Paul **Samputo** and Boni Ntage (both ex-Nyampinga; virtuoso guitarists Soso Mado (ex-Impala) and Mahuku Gilbert (a.k.a. "Belos"); drummers Kana Jean Claude, Karim and Ileri Mukasa; and bassists Thierry Gallard, Youssouf and **Marco Polo**. Like musicians all over the continent, these artists – many of whom remain unknown in the outside world – tend to produce cassettes for the local market which are pirated and circulated among the country's youth, along with imported hip-hop and R&B, which is popular everywhere in the region. Perhaps the most talented of all is guitarist **Aimé Murefu**, a young musician and brother of Jean Mutsari (see below) whose fingering technique – clearly influenced by the likes of Jimi Hendrix and Carlos Santana – is world-class. Some exiled artists exiled have recently begun to return to Rwanda to help in the country's reconstruction. One such figure is **Albert Byron** who now lives and works in Kigali.

Many talented Rwandan musicians still live in exile, particularly in Brussels. Inspired by the example of Cécile Kayirebwa, the most prominent is bassist and guitarist **Jean Mutsari**, who has established the band **Kirochi Sound** and continues to pursue a career as a session musician with Vaya con Dios and Aura Msimang, among others. Other musicians on the Brussels scene include guitarist François "Chouchou" Mihigo (ex-Ingeli and Ingenzi); Ben Ngabo Kipetit, who pursues parallel careers as a contemporary and traditional performer, sometimes blending the two in various bands; neotraditional singer-guitarist Jean-Baptiste Byumvuhore; and the singer **Muyango**, who performs with the women's ballet **Imitari**.

Among the current crop of contemporary performers putting Rwanda on the map is Montréal-based singer and rapper **Corneille**, who projects stirring depictions of his early life in Rwanda over the backdrop of modern R&B. Hugely popular in Belgium and France, and with a recent Grammy nomination for his album *Parce qu'on vient de loin*, it is to be hoped that Corneille will find a true crossover audience outside the French-speaking

The Mighty Popo

world in the years to come. Other members of the Great Lakes diaspora working at the cutting edge of contemporary music include the Brussels-based nu-soul group Soul-ID and Afrogroov ambassador **DJ Eric Soul**.

New Music in Burundi

Modern music in Burundi is concentrated in the capital, Bujumbura, and as in Rwanda, the bands tend towards hybrid formulas influenced by reggae, *zouk* and of course the rumba and *soukous* of neighbouring DRC. Many of the most popular songs are in Swahili, the *lingua franca* of the entire region. (Burundi also has a long-established ethnic Swahili community in the southwest of the country, on the shores of Lake Tanganyika.)

In Brussels, a number of musicians of Burundian origin, such as **Ciza Muhirwa**, have joined Rwandan or Congolese groups, or have taken up funk, like **Eric Baranyanka**, with his band **The Nile**. The most striking figure on the scene, however, is probably **Khadja Nin**. Having grown up in Burundi and DRC, Nin later moved to Brussels, where she has worked with the Belgian musician Nicholas Fiszman on a series of CDs since the early 1990s. Her multilingual talents and remarkable looks are now slickly produced and packaged, somewhat in the international fusion style of Angelique Kidjo; her 1999 album, *Ya*, signalled the arrival of a huge star. Another rising star from Bujumbura is **The Mighty Popo** (a.k.a. Popo Murigande), now based in Canada. Popo has pioneered a fluid, funky mix of traditional Central African music, Afro-beat, juju, reggae and politicized pan-African lyrics, all of which come together to powerful effect on his most recent CD, *Ngara* (2003).

DISCOGRAPHY Rwanda & Burundi

Rwanda

★ **Anthology of World Music: Africa: Music from Rwanda**
Rounder, US
A comprehensive survey of Rwandan traditional music, divided into performances by Tutsi, Hutu and Twa. While the cascading opening track recalls the Drummers of Burundi, there's also great variety, from wailing lone voices to solo instruments, choruses and even a dangerous ritual song.

Detailed liner notes by Denyse Hiernaux-L'Hoest, who made these recordings.

⊙ **Musiques du Rwanda**
Fonti Musicali, Belgium
A valuable CD compilation taken from a much larger collection of field recordings by Jos Gansemans, the pre-eminent Belgian expert on the region's musical and ethnographic traditions.

⊙ Rwanda: Polyphonie des Twa
Fonti Musicali, Belgium
Another Gansemans collection, this features polyphonic music of the Twa Pygmies of Rwanda, revealing interesting musical links with the Baka and other Pygmy peoples of west Central Africa.

Ballet Inganzo

Indicative of the re-emergence of community ballet troupes across the country, Inganzo represent the triumph of youth and creativity over adversity.

⊙ Ballet Inganzo
Inshuti, UK

An inspiring modern rendering of traditional musical styles from northwest Rwanda. Recorded in London, during their successful UK tour in 2002. Order from Inshuti-UK: info@inshuti-uk.org.uk

Corneille

Strongly influenced by US funk and soul, Corneille was beginning to make a name for himself in Rwanda when the war forced him to flee to Germany. Now based in Canada and performing solo after years of working with various groups, he is finally receiving the attention he deserves.

★ Parce qu'on vient de loin
Wagram Music, France
Sharp R&B grooves, great singing and stark, often harrowing lyrics about Corneille's traumatic journey to his current position as one of the world's leading Francophone vocal artistes.

Cécile Kayirebwa

The most striking voice in Rwandan song, Cécile has been based in Brussels since 1973, where she was a long-time member of the multicultural band Bula Sangoma before setting up her own groups, Inyange and Céka-I-Rwanda. On solo albums, she is often accompanied by Belgian jazz players. She is a passionate educator and ambassador for Rwandan culture worldwide.

★ Rwanda
GlobeStyle, UK

Delicate, haunting songs and a voice that lingers in the memory. Released in 1994, Rwanda was a giant step forward for Cécile. Making use of traditional Rwandan instruments and polyphonic vocal harmonies, the subtle arrangements also feature sparse keyboards and violin. The resulting blend is hard to categorize, reminiscent at times of Celtic folk music and Middle Eastern rai. Magical.

⊙ Amahoro (Peace)
Etna Records, Belgium
A beautiful, mesmerizing blend of ancient and modern. Cécile's most recent album combines the distinctive influences of gospel and South African jazz.

Samputo

After beginning his career as a church singer, Samputo was influenced by Bob Marley, Stevie Wonder and Jimmy Cliff. Having lost his parents and several siblings during the genocide, he has been strongly committed to helping the new regime achieve reconciliation and progress.

⊙ Testimony from Rwanda
Rootstock, US
Samputo's heartfelt and moving tribute to the millions killed and displaced in the Rwandan genocide. A gentle, sometimes elegiac mix of traditional and modern, with tight accompaniment from a typically multicultural support band.

Eric Soul

Son of Rwandan legend Cécile Kayirebwa and co-author of this chapter, Belgian-educated Eric Karengera is a successful DJ and promoter with residencies in some of London's funkiest venues.

⊙ Afrogroov
Respect At Work, UK
A showcase for Eric's blazing fusion of traditional and contemporary African sounds with modern "mixology". Includes dazzling mixes of a new generation of Afro-beat artists including Keziah Jones, TY, plus "Inzozi" from his mother's Amahoro album. Available from eric_soul@hotmail.com.

PLAYLIST
Rwanda & Burundi

1 **MAMA NDARE Ballet Inganzo** from *Ballet Inganzo*
A beautiful wedding song featuring emotive harmonies and an intricate melody line.

2 **IKIMANURA Nyanza** from *Music from Rwanda*
Six sacred drums played by one drummer, in a stirring song in praise of the "royal drums" and the king.

3 **UMUNEZERO (HAPPINESS)**
Cécile Kayirebwa from *Rwanda*
A stunning blend of *makondera, inanga, ingoma* and fretless bass.

4 **NGARAMBE Samputo** from *Testimony from Rwanda*
A stately, mysterious groove, with guitar, traditional percussion and choral singing.

5 **MA'AFRIKA The Mighty Popo** from *Ngara*
Featuring a beautiful *kora*-like guitar intro and bluesy solos, a striking Fela-inspired groove and Popo's trademarked vocal declamations.

6 **PARCE QU'ON VIENT DE LOIN Corneille** from *Parce qu'on vient de loin*
"Because we come from far away." A deceptively relaxed, guitar-led slice of modern R&B, overlaid with Corneille's soul-searching story of fear and triumph over adversity.

Burundi

⊙ **Burundi: Musiques Traditionelles**
Ocora, France
An ethnomusicological collection.

The Drummers of Burundi

Originally court drummers for the king of Burundi, the Drummers rose to international prominence through the impact of their dramatic live performances. Performed at WOMAD 2004 to huge acclaim.

★ **The Drummers of Burundi – Live at Real World**
Real World, UK
Probably the region's most celebrated recording, "Les Tambourinaires du Burundi" is a thirty-minute improvisation whose surging rhythmic power offers an intense, almost physical experience.

The Mighty Popo

A star on the large Burundian diaspora scene in Montréal, Popo has been nominated for many awards for his albums, from the earthy *Tamba* (1997) to the more varied *Dunia Yote* (2000). He now takes his funky reggae-inflected Afrobeat and fiery singing on frequent tours of Africa and Europe.

★ **Ngara**
Global Village/CBC Records, Canada
Popo's rich fusion of styles really comes together on this album, released in 2003.

Khadja Nin

Nin initially made a name for herself with songs in Swahili, sung over Western-styled rhythms. These early crossover attempts have gradually given way to more rooted songs in various languages.

⊙ **Ya**
BMG, France
A beautiful, liquid blend of sensuous vocals and Swahili lyrics with the band's tight phrasing.

São Tomé & Príncipe

island music of central africa

The Brazilian-style dança-congo
Collection of Caroline Shaw

Situated in the Gulf of Guinea, 270km off the coast of Gabon, the twin islands of São Tomé and Príncipe (population 150,000) are cultural crossroads, absorbing influences from Portugal, West Africa, Brazil and beyond. Conceicão Lima, Caroline Shaw and Emile Chabal explore a remarkable musical melting-pot.

Some years ago, an influential figure on São Tomé questioned the future of **Forro**, the most important creole language of the islands. Would Forro be able to survive the ever-increasing influence of Portuguese – the official language, taught in schools and used by the media? 'Don't worry', replied an old hand, 'as long as the popular theatre exists and, above all, the music, our language shall not die.'

And so it has proved throughout the history of São Tomé and Príncipe (STP) since 1471, when Portuguese navigators first landed on the then uninhabited archipelago. From the start, the immigrants, adventurers and deportees from Portugal mixed and intermarried with the slaves from the African mainland who had been brought to work on the sugar plantations. Thus evolved the special creoles of the islands – **Forro** and **Lunguié** – each sustained by a rich musical tradition that has always been open to new influences.

Since the beginning, STP's history has been one of a mixing of peoples. Whether as a slave-trading depot or as a producer and exporter of sugar, and later of coffee and cocoa (long the principal crop), the islands have been a crucible for a unique fusion of cultures. West Africa, Mozambique, Angola, Cape Verde, Brazil, the Caribbean, Portugal – all have left their mark on the archipelago's cultural traditions. So, too, has island politics. The plantations were nationalized when STP achieved independence from Portugal in 1975, although the Marxist ruling party lost power after one of sub-Saharan Africa's first multiparty elections in 1991.

Rhythms and Dance

The defining rhythms of the music of STP are **ússua** and **socopé** on the island of São Tomé – the biggest island where the majority of the population lives – and **dêxa** on Príncipe, some 140km away.

Both *ússua* and *socopé* are binary rhythms, with cadences marked by **drums** and **cattle bells**, and were probably brought in with the influx of slaves from the sixteenth century onwards. However, European influences are also present. For example, the traditional dance which accompanies *ússua* has its origins in Portuguese ballroom dancing. This (and other local dances) are extremely formal, reflected both in the dancers' costumes and in the steps and gestures, which are full of bows and other forms of courtly finesse. The *dêxa* has a three-beat rhythm also based on drums and cattle bells and is believed to have the same origins.

Music and **popular theatre** long formed part of the same sphere of artistic expression, and some

of the subjects can be traced far back to the influences which shaped the islands' culture. **Tchiloli**, for example, is a drama brought to the islands by the Portuguese in the sixteenth century that features a mesmerizing foot dance, accompanied by a flute and drum. Another important combination of music, dance and theatre in the repertoire of STP is the **danço-congo**, which assembles more than twenty performers, dressed in extravagantly colourful outfits, "crowned" with exuberant ornaments of silk paper. Masters, servants, devils, angels and the jester, or "Bobo", confront each other in a masquerade symbolizing the primordial struggle between the forces of good and evil.

Traditional performance from the Tchiloli soundtrack

Whilst the *danço-congo* is essentially perceived as a spectacle to be watched, the **puíta** is a ceremony for public participation. This national rhythm is deliriously powerful and it is probably the most African São Toméan sound, characterized by the sounds of a drum-like instrument open at the end, with a stick attached to the centre of the drum-skin. When rubbed, it produces a grunting noise. Couples dance in the middle of a large circle formed by the assistants and gradually come closer to one another until the moment of climax when bodies clash, generating hysteria among the watching crowds. This rhythm – which was probably brought by Angolan slaves and maintained by contract labourers – is so contagious that it has been endowed in popular belief with supernatural powers to summon the spirits of the dead, to exorcise bad spirits and to heal. These beliefs are deeply rooted in the popular imagination, though sceptics put them down to the crowds' consumption of large quantities of alcohol until sunrise.

Modern Music

Music has played an important role in the recent political history of São Tomé and Príncipe. During the era of the one-party state (1975–1991), song was used as a vehicle for political criticism that could not be overtly expressed, and since the multiparty elections, any rally that doesn't include a musical band or a folkloric group is condemned to failure.

The content of song lyrics tends to focus on the age-old themes of love, jealousy and betrayal, but they always contain a measure of social and political comment delivered by metaphor. One of the early protagonists of this tradition was the legendary group **Leoninos**, whose influence throughout São Tomé has been crucial. Founded in 1959 by Quintero Aguiar, their achievement derived from three factors: the effort to modernize traditional folklore; their belief in the value of creole as a medium; and a strong sense of cultural and national identity. The group marked a significant development in the instrumental development of *tunas*, the everyday bands of STP – usually a couple of guitarists, a violin player or two and sometimes a flautist. The introduction by Leoninos of drum and mandolin to the ensemble brought a new status to such sounds.

One of the group's most celebrated songs, written by Olívio Tiny, was "Ngandu" (Shark). The lyrics tell of a shark that seized control of the ocean and brutally expelled all the other fish. This anti-colonial metaphor was too much for the authorities, who promptly banned the group's songs from the Portuguese-controlled radio station. Leoninos disbanded in 1966, but the following year another group, **Os Úntués**, emerged to continue their fusion of traditional and modern influences. Led by Leonel Aguiar, these middle-class musicians weaved an eclectic mix of musical references that ranged from Bob Dylan through Astor Piazolla, Aretha Franklin, BB King, The Beatles and James Brown, to the Latin dance rythms of chachacha, mambo and bolero.

The Úntués's greatest influences, however, came from Congolese rumba, and in particular Kassanda Nico, Franco and Rochereau. Rooted in these various influences, the Úntués were able to move from the local to the international and back again, modernizing and re-styling São Toméan folklore along the way. Gradually, the **electric guitar** became dominant, and the overall sound became "Africanized" with cattle bell, *reco reco* (a bamboo or wooden instrument with notches cut into it, over which a rod is rubbed) and drums.

The mid-1960s to mid-1970s was a golden age of São Toméan popular music. During this period, another famous group, **Mindelo**, became a major rival to Os Úntués. Assembling a number of different local rhythms plus the Angolan *rebita*, they created a high-energy fusion they called *puxa*. The two groups attracted audiences from opposite ends of the social spectrum – the Úntués were middle-class experimentalists, while Mindelo had working-class fans.

Also popular were Sangazuza, Quibanzas and the Leonenses, whose main vocalist – **Pepe Lima** – has had a successful solo career interpreting *soukous*. **África Negra** are the most enduring band of this period. Under their leader **João Séria**, they have continued playing their exciting blend of Congolese, West African and Caribbean rhythms into the twenty-first century. Príncipe is home to groups such as Repteis, África Verde and Os Diablos do Ritmo. The latter was founded in 1967 by **Gilberto Gil Umbelina**, who is perhaps Príncipe's best-known musician. After stints in Paris and Lisbon he was awarded the Prix Découverte de Radio France International in 1987.

The two decades following independence were years of economic crisis and musical stagnation. Ageing sound systems and the difficulty of importing new equipment led to a decline in the quality of music production. There was also a scarcity of good new songwriters in a country that had in the past produced such respected names as Zarco, Gette Rita, Zé Nbruete and Manjelegua.

The islands still suffer from a severe shortage of resources, but there have been some opportunities to increase the exposure of São Tomense music. The **Cena Lusófona**, which promotes communication between Lusophone countries across the world held its annual festival in São Tomé in 2002. Numerous musicians, both young and old, appeared alongside other visual and performing artists. Similarly, the ethnomusicological interest in Tchiloli folk theatre – which resulted in a recording of Tchiloli music for Lisbon's Expo '98 – has brought the performing art of the island to a wider audience.

However, many of the archipelago's most famous musicians live abroad – mostly in France and Portugal. The Lisbon-based **Juka**, whose songs are often to be heard at African parties in Portugal, is a representative of this westward-looking trend, though his music has more in common with the Caribbean than with his own island home. A less

well-known performer, **Açoreano**, also living in Lisbon, is notable for the very opposite reasons: his attachment to the old traditions of *ússua* and *socopé*, despite having absorbed some international influences.

Other exiles include the Paris resident **Felício Mendes**, born in Príncipe, who is remembered at home for having organized a youth band, Os Canucos das Ilhas Verdes, from which emerged several key artists: Tonecas, Vizinho and Felicio's nephews Zezito and **Kalú Mendes**. Kalú has gradually come to be recognised as one of the archipelago's best arrangers and has produced a number of works with Felicio, including a CD of old island hits.

Sadly, São Tomé and Príncipe remain on Africa's musical periphery. Recording facilities are poor and distribution outside Portugal is extremely limited. The singular lack of economic development bodes ill for the future. The importance of the performing arts should, however, ensure that the islands continue to absorb traditions from the four corners of the globe – most recently Antillean *zouk* and the growing spectre of American R&B. As the older generation give way to the younger, traditional local rhythms will be remoulded to speak to a new generation. Superstars like Manecas Costa and Cesaria Evora have proved the enduring appeal of Lusophone African music. It should only be a matter of time before the island crossroads of São Tomé and Príncipe gain their rightful place at the heart of Africa's musical world.

DISCOGRAPHY   São Tomé & Príncipe

The poor distribution of music from São Tomé means your first port of call should be some of the more widely available Lusophone African compilation albums, which have the advantage of setting the music in its regional context. Also check the Natari: Music of Africa website (*www.natari.com*), which carries a wealth of African music available via mail order from the friendly Nick Dean, who often provides personal commentaries on the items he stocks.

★ 1975–1995 Independencia
Tinder Productions/Lusáfrica, US/France

A great collection of Lusophone African music, worth getting simply for Gilberto Gil Umbelina's inspirational "Vôa, Papagaio, Vôa". Also features good tracks from África Negra and Sum Alvarinho.

⊙ The Journey of Sounds: São Tomé: Tchiloli
Tradisom, Portugal

The "Journey of Sounds" series of CDs was produced for Expo '98 and covers every Lusophone nation. This disc is devoted to the music of traditional Tchiloli dramas – foot dances

accompanied by drums, rattles and flutes. It's by no means pop music, but the rhythms are impressive and varied.

⊙ PALOP Africa
Stern's Music, UK

Collects artists from across Lusophone Africa, including a cut from the most recent África Negra album, alongside a number of exciting tunes from the musicians of Lisbon's African diaspora.

★ São Tomé e Príncipe: Musiques de l'Ile du Milieu
Buda Records/Universal, France

Perhaps more accessible than the above CD, this showcases local drums, voices and instruments, including the *viola bimba*, which sounds remarkably like the *berimbau* used in Brazilian *capoeira*.

Açoreano

Born in São Tomé in 1960, Açoreano has lived in Lisbon since 1990. What is so wonderful about his music is that while he has made some concessions to the market, he never ignores his island roots.

⊙ Que Maravilha
Sonovox, Portugal

A celebration of the rhythms of São Toméan music, covering *socopé*, *ússua*, and *xtléva*, all distinctively marked by the use of drums and bass, plus the guitars and trademark cowbell.

⊙ 86–Xuxa
Disconorte, Portugal

A clear shift from his first work, Açoreano goes for a more commercial approach here, with *zouk* and hyper-energetic Angolan *kizomba* and *cuduro*, interspersed with gentler São Toméan rhythms.

África Negra

Formed in the late 1970s, África Negra are one of Lusophone Africa's most popular bands, mixing *soukous*, off-centre reggae and Nigerian highlife to produce a stimulating fusion. After being inactive for a while, their leader João Sería returned with a new line-up and a new album in 1999.

🎛 Ginga Pó
Own label

Classic África Negra: frontman Sería treats us to strong vocals and the band move easily between Congolese rumba and mid-Atlantic reggae. Sadly, the recording is not up to the same quality.

Juka

Based in Portugal since the age of 14, Juka is currently the best-known São Toméan singer, popular throughout the Lusophone world. He's a fine performer, wowing his audiences with *zouk*-style arrangements and fancy dance moves, having been a member of a dance troupe before achieving fame.

⊙ Solitário
Sons d'África, Portugal

An energetic and colourful selection of Juka's latest songs. He moves from hyped-up *soukous* to contemplative "ballads", including a guest appearance from local rapper Drop Jy. This impeccably produced album points towards a more international future for the music of São Tomé.

Pepe Lima

The lead singer of the Leonenses in the 1970s, Pepe Lima has had a relatively successful solo career. He mostly reinterprets Congolese music, singing *soukous* in French or the local Creole.

⊙ Ê Exigóla
Own label

A selection of charming, self-penned *soukous*, accompanied by suitably angular guitar solos and French one-liners. Derivative perhaps, but enormous fun nonetheless.

Felício Mendes

Mendes is a conservatoire-trained musician from Príncipe who played with Os Úntues in São Tomé and is now based in Lisbon. His lyrics are often socially committed, even when the theme is love.

⊙ A Roda dos Sete
Exitos Estúdios, Portugal

Epitomized by the song "Tolerance", Felício urges São Toméans to get together and move towards a better future: nobody but they themselves can build it. Guitars, percussion and organ define the sound, influenced by Congolese rumba and a smattering of Caribbean rhythms.

Kalú Mendes

Felício Mendes's nephew Kalú is a hugely talented multi-instrumentalist and a prolific songwriter, who seems to get involved in almost every serious musical project on the islands.

★ Tio e Sobrinho
Movieplay, Portugal

The title means "uncle and nephew": Felício and Kalú journey through the musical heritage of the two islands, blending *socopé* and *dêxa* with *zouk* and rumba.

PLAYLIST
São Tomé & Príncipe

1 DOBRAS África Negra from *Ginga Pó*
Beg, borrow or steal this delicious reggae-inflected tune, complete with ominous backing vocals, ghostly keyboards and a luscious bassline.

2 MARY LUIZI Pepe Lima from *È Exigóla*
A delightful Franco-style *soukous* that sounds like it escaped straight from the Congo.

3 VÔA, PAPAGAIO, VÔA Gilberto Gil Umbelina from *Independencia*
An infectious, Brazilian-influenced, guitar-driven dancefloor number.

4 ALLO CHERRY Juka from *Solitário*
A plaintive, bouncy ballad which Juka uses to pull all the right heartstrings in the hope that his darling will listen to him once again.

5 ALICE África Negra from *Independencia*
A skilfully executed *soukous* done with the band's usual flair and hard edge.

6 ROSA VIOLA KA MOLE KU SÊBÊ DÊ Anonymous from *Musiques de l'Ile du Milieu*
The haunting and elegiac sound of the *berimbau*-like *viola bimba*, played by the only surviving exponent of the instrument in São Tomé.

Senegal & The Gambia

a tale of two countries

Orchestra Baobab
Jon Lusk/Redferns

In Senegal, international capitalism meets traditional African commerce head on. In the centre of the capital, Dakar, just yards from the offices of the multinationals, lies the teeming warren of the Marché Sandaga, the vast market where every Senegalese cassette is for sale. Everyone, from the ragged beggars to the sleek-suited executives and the turbanned women in billowing robes and stiletto heels, seems to radiate poise and self-possession – the same nonchalant swagger that underpins *mbalax*, the rhythm that has come to define Senegalese music. Mark Hudson, who can't stay away, describes the development of one of Africa's most dynamic music scenes, both in Senegal and neighbouring Gambia, with help from Doudou Sarr and Paul Hayward in downtown Dakar and Lucy Duran on Mande music.

An arid slab of the Sahel, **Senegal** signified little in the Anglo-American consciousness until the emergence of its musical superstars – **Youssou N'Dour** and **Baaba Maal** – in the 1980s. They have had an impact on the World Music scene out of all proportion to the country's population, and the daring with which they have mixed indigenous and modern forms is a reflection both of the richness of Senegalese traditions, and of the focus Dakar and its studios have provided for experiment and cultural exchange.

The Gambia, a former British colonial enclave virtually surrounded by Senegal, was little developed in the colonial era, and was long regarded as a backwater state. Comprising three hundred miles of desolate riverbank and a small strip of coast, it shares Senegal's ethnic mix and range of traditional music. Its artists have played a role in modern Senegambian music, particularly in the 1970s, when the **Super Eagles** (later renamed Ifang Bondi) were in the ascendant with their "Afro-Manding blues", and the country was a meeting place for exiled African musicians. But an attempted coup in 1981 led to a long period of stagnation. While a number of interesting new artists emerged towards the end of the 1990s, it remains to be seen what prospects there are for future musical development.

Mande Senegambia

Even in Dakar's most Westernized circles, the air resonates with the traditional courtesies – the praise names of the feudal world. Senegal and Gambia share the same **jali** or **griot** tradition as Mali and Guinea, in which music is in the hands of a class of hereditary praise singers known as *gewel* in Wolof and *gawlo* in Pulaar. This is a legacy of the Malian Mande (or Manding) empire of the fourteenth to sixteenth centuries, which stretched into Senegambia and was reinforced in the early nineteenth century by an influx of *griots* from Mali following the break up of the Bamana empires. Many of the Senegambian griots trace their ancestry to Mande. The *xalam*, the characteristic Wolof lute, is an adaptation of the Mande *ngoni*, and both its repertoire and much Wolof, Fula and Tukulor music is derived from Mande music.

But Senegambian **griot** music is far more than a watered-down blend of Mande influences. The very different character of the so-called West Atlantic languages – **Wolof**, **Pulaar** and **Serer**

– together with the influence of **Serer polyphony** and the liturgical singing of Senegal's **Islamic brotherhoods** have combined to give the *griot* music of these groups a distinctive flavour.

Senegambia also has its own Mande population, the **Mandinka**, who form the largest ethnic group in the Gambia. Interacting with surrounding groups, the Mandinka *jalis* have created their own sophisticated musical culture in which the typical Mande instruments – *kora* and *balafon* (xylophone) – are played in a manner considered "hot" (uptempo) and funky compared to the cooler and more classical Malian style. Indeed, Senegambia's musical traditions are essentially rhythmic, and the region contains several particularly vigorous, complex and distinctive percussive styles. Despite competition from more modern entertainment, these traditions continue to thrive, borrowing and adapting from each other in the urban world.

Wolof Traditions and Negritude

Yet Senegal was oddly late, not only in exploiting these traditional riches in a modern musical context, but in developing its own distinctive popular style. The reason was mainly the country's colonial history. Senegal's links with Europe run long and deep. The Portuguese were here in the fifteenth century, and the first French settlements were established in 1659. In the late nineteenth century, Senegal became the administrative base of France's vast West African empire, and the inhabitants of the four main towns were given **French citizenship** and voting rights to the National Assembly in Paris. Whole generations of schoolchildren grew up believing themselves to be French and desiring no other identity.

Initially a source of pride, this policy of assimilation ultimately led to disillusionment and alienation, giving rise to **negritude**, a philosophy of cultural rediscovery that was hugely influential in the postwar period, and of which Senegal's first president, the poet Léopold Sédar Senghor, was a prime exponent. Senghor's commitment to his country's culture ensured that Senegal became a leader in African literature, cinema and the visual arts. The music of the *griots* was promoted as an African classical tradition, too, through the creation of traditional troupes and ensembles.

Popular music, however, was ignored by the state, and grew of its own accord amid Dakar's explosive urbanization and the emergence there

Gambian Traditions and Developments

One of Africa's smallest, but most densely populated countries, The Gambia gives an impression of particular musical vitality. Indeed, while Gambia is best known as one of the great centres of the Mandinka *kora*, almost all of the region's other traditions are to be found, writ large, in this tiny riverbank country – from the flutes and fiddles of the nomadic Fula and the giant *balafons* of the forest Balanta people to intriguing pockets of influence from Guinea-Bissau and other Creole enclaves along the West African coast. And although the country is 95 percent Muslim, Christmas is a particularly good time to sample its heady musical diversity, when the streets of the coastal connurbations, Banjul and Serekunda, reverberate to the rhythms of competing and sometimes terrifying masquerades – the Mandinka *kankurang*, Jola *kumpo*, Wolof lantern boats and many more. And you don't have to go far from the towns to encounter an even more **elemental musical world**, where life is ordered by the seasons, where music is inextricably bound up with the cycles and rites of work, initiation, marriage and birth, and where every activity, even the cooking of a meal, is the occasion for song, improvisation and rhythm.

But for all this teeming musicality, the story of The Gambia's organized music scene is by and large a sad one – a legacy of four decades of neglect, economic deprivation and sometimes outright official hostility. Yet The Gambia has had its moments of glory. Indeed, for a period in the 1960s and 70s Gambian musicians were actually ahead of their rivals in Dakar.

Kitted out in locally run-up Sgt Pepper suits, Gambia's **Super Eagles** were one of the top West African bands of the late 1960s. Their vigorous blend of rumba, soul and Swinging London pop, with touches of Congolese guitar, highlife and Wolof *ndagga* rhythm, easily rivalled anything produced in Senegal at the time. Their arch-rivals **Guelewar** featured Layé Ngom's bluesy organ and brother Moussa's grainily textured *griot* voice, and they closed their sets with a barnstorming psychedelic version of "Hey Jude".

But in 1970, after a visit to London, the Super Eagles changed their approach radically. "We were shocked to discover that people in Britain found our traditional music more exciting than copied Western music", says founder Badou Jobé. 'So when we returned to The

Collection Graeme Ewens

of **Wolof**, the language of the kingdoms of Dakar's hinterland, as a new lingua franca and the focus of a genuinely national culture. The city now teems with second, third and even fourth-generation Dakarois of every ethnic background who consider themselves to be Wolof and speak no other African language: Youssou N'Dour, the most famous proponent of Wolof culture, is in fact a Serer on his father's side and a Tukulor on his mother's.

A further influence on these migrants from the Sahel is popular Islam and in particular the Sufi brotherhoods, whose mystical philosophies and quintessentially African approach to religion pervade even the poppiest Senegalese music to a quite extraordinary degree.

Dance Music: the 1960s and Star Band

In 1960, few Senegalese had access to recorded music of any kind. The country's handful of dance bands were loose ensembles based on particular nightclubs serving a small bourgeois elite who wanted "sophisticated" Western sounds. Traditional music was considered embarrassingly primitive, and with the caste associations of the *griot* tradition, actually shameful.

The country's best-known combo, **Star Band**, was formed by Ibra Kasse of the *Miami* nightclub to play at Senegal's independence celebrations. They played Cuban and Latin covers by the likes

Gambia, we spent two years travelling round the country researching traditional music, talking to old musicians and learning the *kora* and *xalam*.'

Drawing on a broad range of traditional sounds, they called their new music "Afro-Manding blues", and changed their name to **Ifang Bondi**, a Mandinka phrase meaning "be yourself", which refers to a fearsome masked figure that appears during male initiation – a powerful local image if ever there was one. While they found themselves virtually turfed offstage at Dakar's annual Nuit de Port gala by well-heeled punters wanting tango and rumba, up-and-coming younger musicians like Thione Seck and Youssou N'Dour were deeply impressed. Ifang Bondi's pioneering approach was an undoubted influence on Senegalese *mbalax*, but their development was stymied by the collapse of the Gambian music scene after an attempted coup in 1981. Moving to Holland, they were almost alone in flying the flag for Gambian music through the 1980s. But the next significant development in Gambian music was to come from a very different source.

Mandinka revival

Mandinka *kora* culture traditionally centred on the courts of the small kingdoms along the upper reaches of the Gambia river. But today's Mandinka *griot* – or *jali* – capital is Brikama, a dusty market town in the southwest of the country. Great Gambian master musicians have included the late **Alhaji Bai Konteh**, **Jali Nyama Suso** and **Amadou Bansang Jobarteh**. But younger members of the three great *kora* families have latterly taken diverse paths, with **Foday Musa Suso** going to New York in the 1970s and founding the **Mandingo Griot Society**, an early attempt at *kora* fusion. He has since become a fixture on New York's avant-garde scene, collaborating with Philip Glass, Bill Laswell and the Kronos Quartet. His contemporary **Dembo Konté** took a more traditional route with his Casamancais cousin **Kausu Kouyaté**, touring and recording their typically uptempo "coastal" *kora* sounds to considerable international acclaim in the late 1980s.

Back home in the 1990s, other younger members of Gambia's *jali* families – notably former schoolteacher **Jaliba Kuyateh** – spearheaded a revival of Mandinka music, setting up semi-acoustic ensembles with amplified *koras*, hyperactive percussion and whatever electric instruments were available. With other bandleaders including **Tata Dindin** and **Pa Bobo Jobarteh**, these combos travel the suburbs and villages plying the weddings and baptisms with their relentless, tumbling dance music.

In their wake came a crop of interesting new talents: charismatic Wolof traditional singer **Mam Tamsir Njie**, slinky-voiced young *griotte* **Sambou Susso**, and **Mass Lowe**, who provided a pleasing N'Dour-influenced Gambian variant on *mbalax*. Guelewar veteran Laye Ngom, meanwhile, revived his career as **Abdoul Kabir & the Goumbe Goumbe Band**.

While rap and Jamaican ragga are massively popular, they have yet to produce any interesting local variants. And all the signs are that with hyperinflation and a tense political situation, the Gambian music scene is once again in the doldrums.

of Pacheco and Orquesta Aragon, without understanding a word of the lyrics. During the 1960s and 70s, however, the group became the focus for a gradual process of Africanization. Cuban songs were adapted into Wolof, and traditional (principally Wolof and Mandinka) songs and rhythms were introduced along with the **tama**, a high-pitched talking drum. At certain points in the evening, audiences would break off from couple-dancing and form circles for displays of loin-thrusting traditional dances like the *ventilateur* (referring to the explicit gyrating of the dancer's buttocks), spurred on by the frenetic drumming of the *tama*.

As players continually left and rejoined, Star Band gave birth to a whole dynasty of bands, through whose family tree many of the crucial developments in Senegalese music can be taced. When the group decamped to the Sahel Nightclub, it was replaced by one of its offspring, **Number One du Senegal**, featuring gravel-voiced Pape Seck, while in 1970, another bunch of alumni formed **Orchestra Baobab** to play at the swanky new club of the same name. All these bands, however, were soon to be eclipsed by a group whose brief career completely changed the face of Senegalese music.

Orchestra Baobab – Still Growing

Youri Lenquette/World Circuit

'When I arrived in Senegal in 1968, there was only Cuban music', says Togolese guitarist **Barthelemy Attisso**. 'Back home, we were listening to Nigerian highlife and Congolese guitar music, but if you walked past a club in Dakar, you would swear there were Cubans playing inside. Yet they were all Senegalese!'

In 1970, when **Orchestra Baobab** were formed, Dakar was still in many ways a French city, a tropical Marseille of gleaming art deco apartment blocks and pavement cafes. But in 1970, a new club opened in the heart of the Plateau, the European quarter, whose house band radically altered the city's cultural complexion.

Created by a group of young businessmen and politicians, the **Baobab Club** quickly established itself as Dakar's most exclusive nightspot, decorated by Senegal's top artists, with a bar in the form of a baobab trunk. Veteran **Star Band** saxman **Baro Ndiaye** was brought in to provide the music, and he quickly recruited a number of younger players, including two students – guitarist **Barthelemy Attisso** and singer **Rudy Gomis** – and a policeman, percussionist **Balla Sidibe**.

While Senegal's elite danced till dawn, Orchestra Baobab began leavening the strictly Afro-Cuban diet with a rich array of African elements. Attisso brought his florid, idiosyncratic version of Congolese guitar; Gomis the lilting ballads of the Casamance, Senegal's forested southern region. Nigerian saxophonist **Peter Udo** introduced a touch of honking highlife, while **Laye Mboup**, a charismatic Wolof *griot*, brought the neo-Islamic sounds of Dakar's hinterland. They were soon Dakar's top band, packing out the Baobab Club seven nights a week. And while they weren't the first to introduce **local elements** into Senegal's Latin-dominated music scene, they did it more coherently and with more originality than any of their rivals. 'Every member of the group comes from a different place and a different tradition", says Gomis. "We keep them all in balance and that's always been the essence of the group.'

But while Baobab remained Senegal's leading group up to the late 1970s, the balance of society was changing. The band barely noticed it, but out in the *quartiers populaires*, the sprawling, largely impoverished suburbs, where nobody cared about suits, ties or the cha-cha-cha, a pop revolution was underway, centred round a young singer called Youssou N'Dour and a raw new music called **mbalax**.

'Ordinary people had been desperate for a form of music they felt was theirs', says Gomis. 'Musicians like **Youssou N'Dour** provided that by making music which was much more obviously Senegalese. But it was based only on the Wolof traditions of Dakar, and that is only part of what we do.'

Finding themselves without gigs, and unwilling to adapt to the new trends, Baobab split in 1985, and might have ended up a mere footnote in Senegal's musical history were it not for the belief of a small number of Western enthusiasts, notably **Nick Gold** of World Circuit Records. Indeed, it's ironic that while Africa's new stars were hitting their first wave of popularity in the West – signing with majors and releasing over-produced fusion albums – Western connoisseurs were starting to look back towards the earthy, organic feel that had attracted them in the first place.

Repackaged as *Pirates' Choice*, Baobab's 1982 album *Werente Serigne* was a hit for World Circuit in 1989. But it was only the success of Buena Vista Social Club that enabled Gold to realize his dream of bringing Orchestra Baobab back together. He found Gomis running an African language school for foreign aid workers, while Sidibé and other band members were eking out a precarious living playing in hotel foyers. Attisso was eventually traced to a commercial law practice in his native Togo, though he hadn't picked up a guitar in 15 years.

A reunion concert at London's Barbican Centre in 2001 provoked ecstatic responses. Far from crassly modernizing their music, as many had feared, the group looked and sounded as though they had stepped through a 70s timewarp. After a year of euphoric touring, they made a triumphant return to their native Senegal, coinciding with the release of a new album, *Specialist in All Styles*, their first in nearly 20 years, and co-produced by their old "nemesis" Youssou N'Dour – who had been, it turns out, a huge fan all along.

"We're like the baobab tree", says Gomis. "Even when it's chopped down it just can't help growing."

Dakar Superstar: the Rise of Youssou N'Dour

In 1977, the younger members of Star Band, including the entire rhythm section, left to form **Étoile de Dakar**, which immediately became the top group in Senegal. Their music was a wonderful mix of full-blooded *griot* singing, blaring horns and throbbing, undulating rhythms. Not, in retrospect, such a departure from the efforts of Baobab and Number One. But it wasn't just Étoile's music that was important, it was their attitude. They were young and defiantly proud of their Senegalese identity. They sang almost entirely in Wolof, flaunting the traditional *griot* origins of their music and their own image as lads on the corner. The two main singers, **El Hadji Faye** and 18-year-old **Youssou N'Dour**, became Senegal's first real pop stars, addressing not the elite but the youth of the whole rapidly urbanizing, demographically exploding country.

Rivalry broke the group apart after only two years, with El Hadji Faye and guitarist Badou Ndiaye forming **Étoile 2000**. Their first offering, "Boubou N'Gary", was a compelling collision between Faye's brooding *griot* voice, screaming fuzzbox guitar, a talking drum and an echo chamber, but after two repetitive efforts they disappeared from view.

N'Dour, meanwhile, formed **Super Étoile de Dakar**, taking full control not only of the music, but the group's business affairs. From having been relatively anonymous nightclub entertainers, musicians would now present themselves not only as cultural heroes, but as entrepreneurs too. N'Dour was still only 21, but with his dashing personality and extraordinary wail, he soon rose to become the country's number one star, a position he has held ever since. He sang about the people's joys: their traditional festivals, the excitement of the city, the importance of respecting one's parents and remembering one's roots. Above all, he sang for women: he used words and phrases traditionally associated with women, praised rich and famous women, praised his own mother, and, by implication, all mothers and all women.

Meeting the challenge of a new generation of more politically conscious musicians such as Super Diamono in the early 1980s, N'Dour began tackling social themes like economic migration, the importance of African identity and apartheid – expanding the role of the griot from simple icon of cultural identity to social critic and political commentator.

N'Dour embarked on a series of numbered cassettes, producing one for each of the most important religious festivals, and pushing the concept of the Senegalized Cuban orchestra to its limits. He and his musicians drew on the complex cross-rhythms of the *sabar* drum ensemble – in which pitched drums pursue a succession of dialogues with sudden changes in tempo and rhythm – to create exhilarating new structures. The interplay of voices and indigenous vocal techniques such as **tassou** (a visceral traditional rap) and **bakou** (the trilling that accompanies Wolof wrestling), added to the drama. 'In my group,' N'Dour has said, 'I gave some of the traditional sabar parts to the guitar, some to the keyboards, while the rhythm guitar took on the role of the *mbung mbung* drum.'

It was the rhythm of the *mbung mbung* – known as *mbalax* – that gave its name to this idea of transposing traditional rhythms to electric instruments, and regardless of precisely who came up with the idea, it has provided the dominant strain in Senegalese music to date.

Jazz, Funk and the Faye Brothers

Since the 1960s, a whole school of Senegalese musicians have looked to jazz, funk and fusion for inspiration, and align themselves as much with an international jazz ethos as they do with Senegalese cultural pride.

Xalam, named after the traditional Wolof lute, were founded in 1970 by drummer **Prosper Niang**. When their "new thing" jazz tastes and provocative lyrics proved too radical for home audiences, they decamped to Paris, over a decade before that move became the norm for African artists. Still revered by Senegalese musicians, Xalam collaborated with Westerners as diverse as Dizzie Gillespie and the Rolling Stones, though by the time of their 1988 hit album *Xarit*, their music was basically supercompetent jazz-funk distinguished by Senegalese percussion and Souleymane Faye's gritty *griot*-style vocals. Prosper Niang died in 1989, but Xalam's legacy is continued by **Missal**, who appeal strongly to that small section of Senegalese society for whom *mbalax* will always be "mere noise".

A more distinctive fusion approach, and one highly influential on the development of *mbalax*, has been that created by the band **Super Diamono** and the **Faye** brothers: **Adama** – Weather Report enthusiast, keyboard player and arranger with Super Diamono, Youssou N'Dour and Thione Seck; **Laminé** – rock-loving guitarist with Super Diamono and his own Lemzo Diamono; **Habib**

The Ups and Downs of Youssou N'Dour

'I was the eldest child, and my father was very against me singing', says Youssou N'Dour. 'No one in our family had been educated, and he wanted me to be a doctor or a lawyer. But eventually he agreed to let me sing with the **Star Band**, and from that moment I knew I was going to do a lot of things.' And he certainly has. Born in 1959, in the Medina, Dakar's original "native quarter", Youssou started singing at circumcision celebrations before his voice had even broken. And he was inducted into the Star Band, then Senegal's top group, at the age of 16.

Hailed in the 1980s as the man who would give African music a Bob Marley-style commercial breakthrough, he survived the collapse of that expectation despite being twice dropped by Western majors. He has made a vast amount of music, from the sublime to the atrocious, and is now not only probably the most famous and influential man in Senegal, but also Africa's most famous musician and the single most significant figure to emerge from the whole World Music phenomenon. Indeed, he's become a figurehead for Africa as a whole, tirelessly promoting the idea that there's more to this vast continent than corruption, AIDS and genocide, and establishing a reputation as wise, humane and, above all, sensible.

Yet the real Youssou – the factors that have allowed him to rise so far from relatively humble origins – has remained elusive. 'I believe in God," he says matter-of-factly. "God has his friends. He helps people who make an effort. And [he adds with a touch of weary grimness] I've really made a lot of effort.' Yet despite this almost mystical sense of destiny, you can still occasionally detect a trace of the insecurity of the person from the wrong side of the tracks – the boy from the Medina looking out on the world of the *toubab*, the white man, to which he can never accede.

'When I was growing up, most people around me felt very far from the people who were governing the country. And when I started playing music, it was only in the Medina and the other *quartiers populaires* that people appreciated it. For a long time the top people didn't regard what I do as music at all. It was only when people abroad started talking about my music that it was accepted by the elite at home.'

Descended on his mother's side from a long line of **Tukulor griots**, N'Dour made his name giving traditional culture back to the youth of this demographically exploding country, filtering it through influences from Latin music, funk, soul and jazz, and saying: 'This is you!' Having achieved an unassailable position at home, he began looking further afield. But while many of his West African rivals – notably Salif Keita – sought new careers on Paris's immigrant scene, N'Dour took a very different route.

'I respect French culture, but I never felt Paris was the place for me to develop. There's been too much between us in the past. When I first played in Paris, it was mostly Senegalese who came to see me, but in London the crowd was 80 percent British, and people were coming to talk to me in a way I hadn't experienced before – people like **Peter Gabriel**.'

With Gabriel's support, N'Dour was soon an important figure in the nascent World Music scene, signing to Virgin in 1988 amid a tremendous fanfare of publicity and expectation. He was dropped after two poor-selling albums, but re-signed to Sony, and just as hopes of that vital crossover hit had all but evaporated, he released

– funkateering bass guitarist, since the age of 16, of Youssou N'Dour's Super Étoile; and latterly **Tapha** – whose "marimbalax" keyboard sound has become de rigueur in 21st-century Senegalese dance music.

Super Diamono's new sound combined spooky organ with plaintive horn riffs and crunching, hypnotic *sabar* rhythms – heard to revolutionary effect on their 1982 cassette *Jigeenu Ndakaru* (Women of Dakar). Fronted by husky-voiced street guru **Omar Pené** and youthful singer-songwriter **Ismael Lô**, *Diamono* were a Dakar "people's band", eschewing griotry in favour of a conscious attitude, combining reggae-inspired militancy, jazz cool and Senegalese Sufi mysticism in a way that

made Youssou N'Dour seem almost tame and homely. Singing about unemployment, corruption and the pitfalls of polygamy, they articulated the discontents of an ever-expanding population of disaffected, largely male youth.

By the mid-1980s, with Lô replaced by the neo-*griot* voice of **Mamadou Maiga** and the dreadlocked zaniness of **Moussa Ngom**, Super Diamono were probably the most influential band in Senegal. Fans engaged in running street battles with supporters of Youssou N'Dour's Super Étoile. But with musicians continually coming and going, Diamono's star waned. In 1991, they were completely reformed by Omar Pené with a bunch of top session musicians whose slick funki-

"7 Seconds", a duet with British soulstress **Neneh Cherry** that became one of the biggest selling records of the 1990s. The day he stepped off the plane in Dakar with that gold disc was a pivotal moment in Senegalese history. N'Dour was now untouchable, his status beyond what could be achieved by anyone else. He set about developing Senegal's music industry, building studios and cassette plants that doubled the industry's capacity, while increasing his own financial stake. Meanwhile, he was again dropped by his record label, when his next album *Joko* – an all too blatant attempt to appeal to the people who bought "7 Seconds" – flopped in 2000.

The Western media should by any normal yardstick have lost interest in N'Dour long ago, yet he had stored up an amazing backlog of goodwill, and his next album, the semi-traditional *Nothing's in Vain*, was accorded a rapturous critical welcome simply because it represented something close to a return to form. Yet while he can't now be ignored by the West and is rich even by Western standards, he must still understand how most of his countrymen feel faced by the fact that it is the West – the white man – that not only has everything, but seems to own this world.

'It is very hard to accept. When we see the prosperity of the West, we think, "Look at that, man! They've got everything!" But our elders say: "Why did God create the *toubab*? To make things a little easier." Because the *toubabs* bring a lot of things in terms of infrastructure. They can give a lot. And we believe that in the next world, maybe, the situation is going to be reversed.'

Yet beyond such fatalistic acceptance, he must sometimes wish he could have done it all without having to rely, to some extent at least, on Western magnanimity.

'If you come from Africa with your economic poverty and your cultural riches, and you meet someone like Peter Gabriel or a person from a big record company, and they tell you that what you are doing is marvellous, that makes you feel powerful. Even if you don't know who they are, if they tell you that you think you are *down here*, but really you are *up here*, that gives you more confidence than if someone from Africa said that. Maybe that's not right – but it's the reality!'

Mick Hutson/Redferns

"7 Seconds" at Live 8: Youssou duets with Dido

ness well complemented his earthy melancholy. While his musical incarnations have moved in and out of public favour, Pené still speaks to the Senegalese people with an authority rivalled only by Youssou N'Dour.

Seck and Lô

As the 1990s progressed, two major names were added to those of Youssou N'Dour and Baaba Maal in the panoply of Senegalese superstars: **Thioné Seck** (ex-Orchestre Baobab) and **Ismael Lô** (ex-Super Diamono).

Thione Seck was descended from the *griots* of Lat Dior, king of Kayor and leader of the last Wolof resistance against the French. His boyish, yearning voice, skills as a philosophical improviser and his penchant for fine tailoring have made him a favourite of the *diriyanké* – the magnificently robed matrons of Dakar. While serving his apprenticeship with Baobab, he also ran a traditional ensemble with members of his family: the plaintive riffing of the *xalam* and cracking *sabar* rhythms backing his luminous voice.

On forming his own band **Raam Daan** (meaning "crawl slowly towards your goal"), Seck transposed this type of music to electric instruments, with guitar lines interweaving in a way that at times sounds almost Californian. As his music has grown ever more busy and frenetic, the

Thioné Seck

The Man from the North: Baaba Maal

Baaba Maal's flamboyant showmanship and dark, intense voice, combined with astute promotion, have given him a profile in the West to rival that of Youssou N'Dour or Mali's Salif Keita. Charismatic and highly articulate in many languages, the only thing impeding his total dominance at home is the fact that he sings not in Wolof, but in **Pulaar**, the language of the nomadic Fulani people who are found across the Sahel from Guinea to Sudan.

Settled along the Senegal river in northern Senegal, the Tukulor sub-group of the Fulani to which Maal belongs have practised a puritanical Islam since the twelfth century, and are seen as the people most keen to preserve their ethnic and linguistic identity in the melting-pot of modern Senegal. Maal called his band **Daande Lenol**, the Voice of the Race.

Born into a noble family in Podor on the Mauritanian border, Maal studied at the Dakar conservatoire before winning a scholarship to study music in Paris. On his return, he went on a journey through West Africa with his family *griot*, the blind guitarist **Mansour Seck**, researching traditional music and paying his dues as a musician in the time-honoured way. After dabbling in acoustic music and Afro-reggae, he formed Daande Lenol, immediately creating a stir with a rabble-rousing Tukulor variant on *mbalax*.

Djam Leelii, an acoustic album recorded in 1984, was released in Britain in 1989, where Maal and Seck's raw nasal voices and serenely rhythmic guitar picking were considered a revelation. 'Like hearing Muddy Waters for the first time', declared DJ John Peel. Since then, Maal has alternated acoustic and increasingly hi-tech electric albums and performances, just as he has mixed designer knitwear from Joseph with sumptuous traditional robes.

Maal's major album of the 1990s, *Firin' in Fouta*, was a daring slab of Afro-modernism, including everything from break beats to Breton harps, ragga, salsa and New Age drones. It launched Senegalese rappers **Positive Black Soul** on the world stage, and gave birth to the **Afro-Celt Sound System**. While *Nomad Soul* (1998), which involved no fewer than seven sets of producers – including Brian Eno – was for many the nadir of the hi-tech approach to African music, the semi-acoustic *Mi Yeewnii (Missing You)* from 2001 was seen as a return to core values. Maal's relative silence over the following four years – due largely to the travails of his British label Palm Pictures – is indicative

magnificent serenity of his delivery has remained remarkably constant, tackling themes sacred (the manifold greatness of God) and profane (music piracy, skin lightening and dangerous driving). He celebrated his affinity with Eastern sounds on *Orientation* (2005), a striking collaboration with Indian and Arab musicians.

Ismael Lô's cool-voiced balladeer persona and taste for Antillean rhythms and French *chanson* suggest a cosmopolitan sophistication that sets itself apart from the Senegalese mainstream. But *mbalax* anthems like "Jele bi" and "Ceddo" and such quintessentially Senegalese subjects as the social importance of tea drinking ("Attaya") and the enterprise of street traders ("Baol Baol") speak directly to the Dakar masses.

Lô moved to Paris in the mid-1980s, and four albums recorded there with **Ibrahima Sylla** typify the glossy, aspirational feel of much African music of the time – the sheer modernity of their sound disconcerting Western listeners even more than they did African ones. But the highly crafted *Iso* (1994) did not make the anticipated breakthrough with the European public, and Lô's profile has been much reduced in recent years.

Baaba Maal

Peter Culshaw encounters Baaba Maal on home ground.

Had disco been invented in the time of the Old Testament, it would have been something like this. We are on the edge of the desert in northeastern Senegal and the locals have been assembling for days, having walked or travelled here by camel, horse or lorry from their village mud huts. I've arrived after a 12-hour drive from Dakar in a battered Mercedes. A PA system has been set up on the sand, and at three in the morning, Baaba Maal's band kicks into one of the most danceable grooves I've ever heard.

Jak Kilby

Baaba Maal himself makes a grand entrance, dressed in flowing white robes, looking more like a prophet than a pop star, both shaman and showman – although a trio of gyrating dancers in bikini tops and skirts add a contrary profane element. An impossibly elegant Senegalese woman in a spangly turquoise dress and gold sandals shimmies along the sand to give Baaba Maal some money, as nearly all the crowd do during the course of the night. Baaba Maal begins to dance like a pixie, and at nearly 50 he has the energy of a man half his age. Above in the clear desert night there are countless stars which make the sky seem very low, like a billion-dollar light show.

Baaba Maal sings love songs, updated versions of traditional African songs, songs to the local holy men – called *marabouts* in this part of the world – and verses from the Koran. There's a strong social message too: songs about the environment, how Africa should be united, songs raising consciousness about AIDS, criticizing the caste system.

More than anything, there's a message of hope for the local **Fulani** people. They know he could be singing in a sold-out venue in London, Paris or New York, but he's playing for them, in their language, near where he was born, the proceeds from these concerts raising money for local literacy projects, for health centres, for local schools.

Several of the audience come up to me and tell me in broken French that Baaba Maal is himself a *marabout* with magical powers who is able to bring rain, cure illness and even predict the future. At the end, the *griots* tell him how important he is for the Fulanis not just in Senegal but throughout Central Africa. And then he gets in his car and is driven off at speed into the wilderness, disappearing in a cloud of sand.

I left with a quite different impression of Baaba Maal from the one I had got after a brief meeting in London, where he seemed the image of a chic intellectual. Fluent in English, French and several African languages, he was happy to talk about African politics or French philosophy, and was dressed in Parisian designer gear. This was the utterly contemporary Afro-modern Baaba Maal of *Firin' In Fouta* and *Nomad Soul*.

Audience for one

I meet Baaba Maal the day after the show in the desert, at a whitewashed hotel in the nearest small town of Ouro Sogui. The temperature is well into the hundreds and he is relaxing, wearing a designer shirt and leafing through a copy of the ultra-glossy magazine *World of Interiors*. People keep giving him houses, he says, one in Guinea recently and one south of Dakar.

When I shake his hand, I get quite a powerful electric shock and jump back. Perhaps it was the static on the new rugs, but Hilaire, his keyboard player, tells me later: 'It was because he has such spiritual energy – his *baraka*. It is overflowing.'

I ask Baaba Maal if he can really change the weather. 'Well, one time I went to a village and there had been drought and I prayed for rain, and although there wasn't a cloud in the sky, half an hour later it began to rain.'

Baaba Maal's father was a fisherman who would sing to the spirits of the river, but also a *muezzin* who called the faithful to prayer. The singer's musical roots are similarly mixed. As well as traditional music, he was brought up on Cuban music and soul. 'I didn't know this music wasn't Senegalese until later', he declares.

Baaba Maal is an unusual being, totally at home in different cultures, utterly modern and a visionary futurist, yet inspired and sustained by the spiritual core of centuries of tradition. And, prophet or not, there are still small miracles – in the village they perform that night, the kids are singing his song warning of AIDS, and there is a row of saplings where last year there was desert.

of how reliant even the most high-profile African musicians can be on one Western outlet.

A World Apart: Casamance Hothouse

Separated from arid northern Senegal by The Gambia, the verdant southern region of **Casamance** is a world apart, culturally and musically. The Jola *bougarabou*, four large pitched drums played by one man to the accompaniment of palm-leaf clappers, and the Balanta *balo*, a gourd xylophone played by two men, are instruments of a semi-forest world of villages hidden among palm groves and silk cotton trees, where animist traditions strongly persist.

There is also a strong **Mandinka** presence, and the region has produced many great *kora* players, notably **Lalo Keba Dramé** and **Soundioulou Cissoko**. The first group to use the kora in a modern band context were the local **UCAS** (Union Culturelle et Artistique de Sédhiou) **Jazz Band**, formed in 1959 and still going strong.

But the Casamance's most famous musical product, **Touré Kunda**, were a band before their time, playing to audiences of 20,000 French fans before the term World Music had even been thought of. The brothers Ismael, Sixu and Amadou Touré went to Paris as students in the late 1970s. By 1979, they were combining their own Soninke and Mandinka melodies with *mbalax*, highlife, soul, salsa and a reggae beat they called *djambaadong* (leaf dance) to create a fresh and tuneful pan-Senegalese sound.

After Amadou's tragic death on stage, a younger brother, Ousmané, joined the group, proving a fine singer and adding greatly to their stage presence. Touré Kunda notched up a gold disc with sales of over 100,000 for *Paris Ziguinchor Live*, recorded on their triumphant return to the Casamance. But while their 1985 album *Natalia*, produced by Bill Laswell, was an interesting early foray into hi-tech, the perceived lightness of their approach found little favour in Britain. Their chequered career perhaps demonstrates the very different expectations of French and British audiences.

Female Performers

In contrast to Mali's *jelimusow* and the Congolese *vedettes*, Senegalese women were slow to make an impact. The first international release by a Senegalese woman, the snappy, Sylla-produced *Cheikh Anta Mbacke*, was recorded in 1989 by *griotte* **Kiné**

Lam at a time when Midi equipment was making the recording process much more accessible.

Women artists, the proverbial "neglected resource", were suddenly flavour of the moment. Traditional divas such as **Daro Mbaye**, **Madiodio Gning** and the great **Khar Mbaye Madiaga** were whisked into studios by a new breed of producer-entrepreneurs, notably **Laminé Faye**, ex-Xalam guitarist **Cheikh Tidiane Tall** and latterly sometime Super Diamono keyboardman **Papis Konaté**. With arrangements ranging from full band with brass section to the cheapest drum machines and synthesizers, the results can be hard on Western sensibilities – though they always sound fantastic blaring from Dakar taxis with all levels pushed to the max.

Kiné Lam's 1993 album, *Sunu Thiossane* (Our Tradition), created a new trend: the traditional lute and percussion ensemble discreetly modernized with bass and synthesizer. Every *griot* of any worth, male or female, has since recorded a cassette, if not several, in this style, usually paeans to great holy men, arranged in a "by the yard" fashion by Tall.

The booming Wolof soul singer **Aminata Fall**, who made a big impression on Duke Ellington during the First Festival of Negro Arts, held in Dakar in 1966, is earthy in a different way. While her collaboration with rappers **Positive Black Soul** caught influential Western ears, and she has guested with **Harmattan**, an experimental jazz group with Habib Faye and Cheikh Lô's guitarist Omar Sowé, ill-health and personal problems have thwarted her considerable potential.

Another woman born into the *griot* tradition, but educated, highly articulate and projecting a glamorous, modern image is **Coumba Gawlo**. Her rather shrill voice has received several Paris productions from Ibrahima Sylla, making sharp comment on social issues and turning traditional songs like "Miniyamba" and "Yomale" into stunning ballads.

Rap and New Directions

For decades a relatively small number of pioneering performers fought for the central spot in Senegalese music. But in the mid-2000s the scene is characterised by radical diversification. At one extreme is one of Africa's biggest and most dynamic rap scenes. At the other, there is a whole range of neo-traditional music, among which the most notable current figure, **Fatou Laobé**, is a specialist in **tassou**, a staccato traditional rap originally performed the morning after marriages by women of the Laobe woodworking caste, and accompanied by graphic explanatory dancing. Backing her abrasive voice with flailing percussion and "marimba" keyboards, she is a fascinating example of tradition reinventing itself in the modern world.

In between, the proliferation of new studios and a vastly increased cassette-production capacity has given rise to a new generation of *mbalax* artists, for whom the likes of Youssou N'Dour and Thione Seck are, if not exactly has-beens, certainly parental figures. First out from the older generation's shadow were **Alioune Kassé**, son of Star Band founder Ibra Kassé, who saw himself as a Senegalese Michael Jackson, and his more macho rival **Alioune Mbaye Nder**. The latter's mid-90s performances at the *Thiossane* nightclub, which drew bigger audiences than those of its owner, Youssou N'Dour, signified the arrival of the *Génération Boul Falé* (Don't Care Generation) – named for their blasé attitude towards authority and conventional politics. Young girls flaunted their midriffs, while dashing young men performed the *bakhou* wrestlers' strut around the dancefloor.

Recording on threadbare budgets, the offerings of **Assané Ndiaye**, **Assané Mboup** and **Ousmané Seck**, and female singers **Marie Ngoné Ndioné** and **Maty Thiam Dogo**, constitute a kind of "**garage mbalax**" – though they've often been backed by well-established outfits like Thioné Seck's Raam Daan or Laminé Faye's hyperactive "hard *mbalax*" combo, **Lemzo Diamono**. Currently defunct, Lemzo effectively created the prevailing *mbalax* sound. While classic mid-1980s *mbalax* looked simultaneously towards tradition and outwards to a range of external influences, hard *mbalax* turns inward, churning the original formula into an ever denser rhythmic brew – the horns long since dropped in favour of battling synthesizers, great phalanxes of *sabar* drummers and the essential rumbling "marimba synth".

While the exquisite-voiced **Fallou Dieng**, another graduate of the Lemzo stable, has established a distinctive, more mellow style, an even younger, punkier generation is emerging, exemplified by **Papé Diouf**, **Abdou Guité Seck** and the already deceased **Ndongo Lô**. Hailing from Pikine, Dakar's biggest and poorest suburb, Lô spoke to the most desperate section of Senegalese youth – the children of illiterate rural migrants, who find it all too easy to fall into a life of crime yet are often among the most devoted supporters of the country's great holy men.

Among new women performers, the glamorous **Viviane N'Dour** – Youssou's sister-in-law – has moved in a very popular R&B crossover direction, duetting with rappers but retaining the *mbalax* base. The younger and cheekier **Ndeye Kassé** and **Titi** see themselves as Dakar Britneys, but still record paeans to holy men, such as the Wolof sage Ahmadou Bamba.

While none of this chauvinistically local, youthful clamour has much of a following outside the country, there are now whole dimensions of Senegalese music that find their principal audience abroad. Indeed, although Dakar has a small, but growing salsa scene centred around diehard rumbero **Papé Fall**, Senegal's most famous salsa band is undoubtedly the Paris-based **Africando**. Created by producer Ibrahima Sylla as a one-off tribute to the Latin-dominated sounds of the immediate post-independence era, Africando teamed the earthy voices of three Senegalese veterans – **Papé Seck** (from Number One du Sénégal), **Medouné Diallo** (of Baobab) and sometime Super Étoile vocalist **Nicolas Menheim** – with top salsa session men in New York. After Seck's untimely death, he was replaced by Puerto Rican **Ronnie Baro** and the late **Gnonnas Pedro** from Benin, with cameos from an extraordinary range of star vocalists now stretching over six consistently entertaining albums.

Dreadlocked Sufi mystic **Cheikh Lô**, sometime drummer with Xalam and one of the Baye Fall – a grassroots offshoot of the influental Mouride brotherhood – also has roots in the Afro-Cuban period. But he has spun his eclectic tastes into a highly distinctive sound that has found favour both at home and abroad. Backing his freewheel-

Sufi mystic and singer-songwriter Cheikh Lô

"Hip Hop Dou Mëssa Dé – Hip Hop will never die" shouts the editorial of *Starrap*, Dakar's first hip-hop glossy. It's not the message that's interesting, but the fact that there is a local hip-hop magazine that shifts enough copies to keep going. Senegalese hip-hop also has its own dedicated TV shows, countless radio programmes, annual awards and festivals, studios, clothing lines, dancers and graffiti artists. And it's found its new global ambassadors – **Daara J**, one of Senegal's most widely touring bands in recent years. In 2006, hip-hop in Dakar, one of the great capitals of African rap, is alive and well, and utterly integral to the city's bustling ambiance.

A persistent urban music myth has it that Dakar alone is home to about 3000 hip-hop crews – a figure as vastly inflated as a rap star's ego, but one that still underlines the genre's popularity. There are probably many more Dakar kids that dream of becoming rap stars, but the city's vibrant hip-hop community is actually quite small and close-knit. The circle of successful performers still revolves largely around the big names that have moulded the movement from day one. Right at the centre is Sene-rap's holy trinity: **Positive Black Soul** (PBS), **Daara J** and **Pee Froiss**. **Didier Awadi** (one half of PBS) now sits big business-style behind a desk at his impressive Sankara studio complex. His ex-partner **Duggy-Tee** released one of the biggest hip-hop sellers in 2005. Pee Froiss's leader **Xuman** is still the serene centre of gravity he has always been, and Daara J promote Dakar's street sounds worldwide.

Rewind 20 years, and you find the same names among the pupils of Dakar's more privileged colleges, emulating Bronx-cool and mimicking the American rap twangs of the LPs their parents brought back from the US. The first touch of uniqueness, such as Wolof lyrics, was added when two of the fiercest rivals of the scene, Didier Awadi's **King MCs** and Duggy-Tee's **Syndicate**, joined forces to found Positive Black Soul. In the early 1990s they emerged as the leaders of the pack with the anthem "Boul Falé" (Don't Worry), which became the motto of an entire generation. Signed to Island Records in 1995 and championed by French rapper MC Solaar, they achieved some international renown and became huge stars at home. They used their status well, pumping finance into the Dakar scene, purchasing sound systems, organizing concerts, and producing bands – among them the trio Pee Froiss, one of the more politically charged outfits of the time, whose committed stance has contributed strongly to Sene-rap's reputation for "conscious" hip-hop. It was also PBS that gave an initial push to Daara J, whose girl-giddying formula of rap-ragga-soul came to characterise Sene-rap for many years and cemented the nation's ongoing marriage of reggae and hip-hop.

By the mid-1990s, home-grown hip-hop was threatening to outshine even *mbalax* – but the glamour soon wore off. Money ran dry, international interest waned, and a few violent incidents during concerts discouraged promoters from staging hip-hop events. Until in true, rivalry-fuelled hip-hop style, a new school emerged. **Rapadio** and **BMG44** are two names associated with the second hip-hop generation. They clad themselves in an aggressive street-soldier image, less attracted to the bling side of hip-hop, than its potential for giving a voice to the voiceless. Their success (as well as the wider availability of American hip-hop) helped spread the music beyond the tidier neighbourhoods to rough suburbs like Pikine and Thiaroye, where kids had little means but much to rap about. During the 2000 elections numerous MCs, notably Xuman, chose to use their art to encourage youngsters to get on the register and vote – not for any particular party, but to have a say. The youth turnout was staggering, and the newly sworn-in president, Abdoulaye Wade, was no doubt grateful for the unsolicited support.

ing balladry with semi-acoustic *mbalax* rhythms, glances towards flamenco, Capeverdean *morna*, Congolese rumba and heavy doses of Sufi philosophy, his *Ne la Thiass* was one of the most attractive African debuts of the late 1990s. Though the 1999 follow-up *Bambay Gueej* was less memorable, his third album *Lamp Fall*, belatedly released in 2005, proved to be something of a comeback, enlivened by the participation of Brazilian guest musicians.

Concurrently, a whole Senegalese "folk" scene has emerged, which draws as much on Western balladry and protest singing as it does on local acoustic traditions. The messages of the movement's precursor, the maverick 1970s singer-songwriter **Seydina Insa Wadé**, proved politically sensitive and he was forced into exile in Paris – though his career recently revived through the interest of younger artists such as **Les Frères Guisses** and **Pape & Cheikh**. The latter consciously modelled themselves on the likes of Simon and Garfunkel and the Everly Brothers, combining Western pop structures with a strong folklore element, whereas Fulani guitarist **Laye Sow** and Soninke balladeer **Daby Touré** both employ a sparser, more groove-based approach, rooted in the hypnotic lute riffing of Senegal's northern desert fringes.

Aiding regime change was the last big act of Sene-rap before it fell into an uneasy slumber. *Mbalax* reclaimed the airwaves, few new artists appeared on the scene, and the movement was declared incurably ill. Enter the third era. While hip-hop's star was fading at home, the international market began to take a renewed interest, culminating in an international deal for **Daara J**.

The belated hype helped kick-start the latest chapter in Senegalese hip-hop history. Let's call it the age of professionalism. Gone are the days of dodgy four-track recordings and cheap beats – today's rap artists produce works of international standard in their home studios, always aspiring to the business example of Awadi. Chart-toppers by **Xuman**, **Baay Sooley**, **Dakar All Stars**, young upstart **Fou Maladé** and soul-crooner **Carlou D** sit smoothly between Jay-Z and 50 Cent in a nightclub mix. Dancefloor-oriented, these tracks don't really care if you can barely perceive their message above the grinding of hips.

Today's Sene-rap stars integrate more than ever into the global hip-hop as well as World Music market (the latest album by **MC Fata**, for instance, was produced by members of the US Ruff Ryders posse) and benefit from the interest of international hip-hop greats such as Akon and Disiz La Peste, as well as from increased media opportunities. And tomorrow's stars are discovered in Senegal's very own pop-idol show *Hip Hop Feeling*. "Hip Hop Dou Mëssa Dé" may be rap hyperbole, but the music looks certainly set to retain a comfortable presence until the next youth movement storms the scene.

Katharina Lobeck

Daara J Productions

Daara J waiting for the call in Dakar

While the revival of the venerable **Orchestra Baobab** has been almost entirely European-inspired, the album that has most divided Western and Senegalese listeners is undoubtedly Youssou N'Dour's *Egypt*. Originally conceived of as personal spiritual music for his family's private use, *Egypt* backed Wolof praise songs for Senegalese religious leaders with an Egyptian orchestra of the sort that backed great Arab singers such as Umm Kulthum, whose music N'Dour had grown to love in childhood. Bringing together two great, yet massively divergent Islamic musical forms, N'Dour sought to celebrate both the breadth of Islamic culture and the tolerence and magnanimity of the Senegalese approach to religion.

Yet while Western audiences swooned at this ambitious and often astonishingly beautiful work, the Senegalese response was one of bemusement. What was the point of it all? Where was the *mbalax* rhythm? Still, when N'Dour returned to Dakar with the 2004 Grammy Award for Best Contemporary World Music Album, that reaction quickly changed. Far from losing his way, as had been feared, Senegal's favourite son had triumphed once again.

Senegal

⭐ **Double Concentré 100% Pure**
Dakar Sound, Netherlands
Vol 5 in an ongoing and fascinating "Anthology of Modern Senegalese Music", this is an eclectic, excellent compilation of vintage and more recent material, from prime Star Band to *griot* N'Diaga M'Baye on magnificent acoustic numbers. Includes all of Thione Seck's *Chauffeur Bi* on a bonus CD.

⊙ **A Land of Drummers**
Village Pulse, US
A sampler giving an overview of a six-volume series of excellently recorded, beautifully packaged volumes of Senegalese drumming, each devoted to a master in a particular style.

⊙ **Rough Guide to the Music of Senegal and the Gambia**
World Music Network, UK
Worthwhile mid-priced introduction to the region with generally good selections from most of the significant names – though sadly no women artists!

⭐ **Streets of Dakar – Génération Boul Falé**
Stern's, UK
Gutsy, invigorating overview of the late 1990s scene, showcasing a wealth of emerging artists, from the earthy neo-traditional sounds of Fatou Guewel and Gambian *kora* duo Tata and Salaam to rap and super-charged *nouveau mbalax* from Assané Ndiaye and Lemzo Diamono. With Alioune Kassé and Fallou Diena providing more reflective moments, this is a rich and entertaining collection.

Africando

Three veteran Senegalese vocalists of the Afro-Cuban period teamed up with top salsa session men in New York. After Vol 2, stalwart Papé Seck was replaced by Ronnie Baro and Gnonnas Pedro, with guest appearances from stars like Rochereau and Sekouba Bambino.

⊙ **Africando**
Stern's, UK
If the basic recipe appeals, you'll no doubt love all four volumes to date. The first volume sets the tone in fine style and is probably the best.

⊙ **Mandali**
Stern's, UK
Relaunched as Africando All Stars and featuring Salif Keita, Koffi Olomidé, Thioné Seck and Lokua Kanza as star guests, this fifth volume is rip-roaring, super-polished entertainment all the way.

Daara J

The name means "School of Life", and Daara J are among Senegal's most "conscious" rappers.

⭐ **Boomrang**
Wrasse, UK
The group's third album returned Sene-rap to international glory, bagging them a BBC World Music award. It's a stylish mix of hip-hop, Latin and reggae beats that makes you feel the Dakar heat.

Fallou Dieng

Long Youssou N'Dour's stand-in at the legendary Thiossané Club, husky-voiced Dieng has established himself as the most melodic of the younger generation of *mbalax* artists.

⊙ **Medina**
Sterns, UK
Vibrant contemporary *mbalax* – not hugely original, but distinguished by Dieng's exquisite voice.

Wasis Diop

Category-defying Paris-based experimentalist whose sultry mumble delights some and bemuses others. About as far from the Dakar street-vibe as Senegalese music gets.

⊙ **Everything is Never Quite Enough**
Wrasse, UK
Good compilation, full of clever touches and including tuneful duets with Liana Fiagbé and an arresting Wolof cover of Talking Heads' "Once in a Lifetime" with David Byrne and Amadou & Mariam.

Étoile de Dakar

The Star of Dakar were Senegal's first pop stars and probably the country's most influential band ever, launching Youssou N'Dour onto the world stage.

⊙ **Étoile de Dakar: Vols 1–4**
Stern's, UK
Not just historically important, but wonderful music in its own right. All the essential material is here (except the first hit "Xalis"), rendered oddly more tinny and raucous than the original cassettes. Vols 1 and 3 are essential masterpieces. Most would say the same for Vol 2, while Vol 4 is less significant, but still worthwhile.

Étoile 2000

After Étoile de Dakar's split, Hendrix-loving guitarist Badou Ndiayé and *muezzin*-like singer El Hadji Fayé formed their own band.

⊙ **Étoile 2000**
Dakar Sound, Netherlands
A selection from their first three cassettes. Wild, amazingly raw music taking an almost punk direction never heard before or since.

Coumba Gawlo

Coumba Gawlo is a new star in Senegal – the *griotte* as glamorous independent modern woman.

⊙ **Aldiana**
Syllart, France
A compilation featuring sassy modern *mbalax* and the wonderful traditional song "Miniyamba".

Fatou Gewel

Fatou Gewel is a gutsy diva of neo-traditional song.

Fatou
Stern's, UK
Earthy anthems to great religious leaders and moral homilies backed by *xalam*, percussion and occasionally kitsch keyboard interventions.

Jalikunda Cissokho
Vibrant, multiple *kora*-led family ensemble from Casamance that spawned the Ellika and Solo duo.

Lindiane
Jalikunda, Senegal
Despite the promise of a "multi-cultural" direction and European guests on electric instruments, it's the strongly traditional base that makes this lively set so enjoyable.

Dexter Johnson & Star Band
Settling in Dakar in the 1950s, Nigerian saxman Johnson became a legendary figure in Senegal's emergent music scene.

Series Sangomar, Vol 2
Dakar Sound, Netherlands
Johnson's playing may be a touch smooth and international, but these super-rare 1970s recordings give privileged glimpses of a vital moment of Africanization.

Lemzo Diamono
The band of ex-Super Diamono guitarist "Lemzo" Faye takes *mbalax* in a hardcore rhythmic direction.

Marimbalax
Stern's, UK
If you can get your head and feet round the relentless activity, you'll be partaking of an integral Senegalese experience.

Cheikh Lô
A maverick talent mingling semi-acoustic influences with Sufi mysticism and an irresistible voice.

⭐ Ne la Thiass
World Circuit, UK
Strong songs and a warm organic feel make for grown-up pop with real international appeal. His international debut from 1996 is still the best of his three releases so far.

Ismael Lô
One of Senegal's top singers, Lô made his name with Super Diamono in the 1980s. He has become a cool-voiced balladeer combining international sophistication with crowd-pleasing local grooves.

Diawar
Stern's, UK
Containing the irresistably breezy "Jele bi", this is probably the best of Lô's Syllart albums. The CD reissue contains an extra album's worth of material from previous outings.

Los Afro-Salseros de Senegal
Members of four vintage Senegalese bands gather in Havana's Egrem studios under the direction of Orchestra Baobab saxman Issa Cissokho.

En la Habana
PAM, Germany
Featuring a whole squad of legendary figures, including singers Laba Sosseh and Papé Fall and guitarist Yahya Fall, this was clearly a truly inspired occasion.

Baaba Maal
The Fulani superstar's dark, intense voice and flamboyant live shows have given him an international profile second only to Youssou N'Dour,

⭐ Djam Leelii
Palm Pictures, UK
Maal and his mentor and childhood friend Mansour Seck recreate the tunes of their native region, with buoyant acoustic guitar rhythms and nasal singing at once gentle and intense. Music to be transported by, and, commercially, extremely successful. The new CD version contains extra tracks.

Firin' in Fouta
Mango, UK
An exciting and surprisingly coherent slab of Afro-modernism. UK producer Simon Emmerson finds Celtic resonances and enlists salsa hornmen and Wolof ragga merchants. A highpoint of its kind.

⭐ Missing You (Mi Yeewnii)
Palm Pictures, UK
After the dreadful *Nomad Soul*, Maal returned to form with this superb semi-acoustic set. Featuring knee-trembling massed percussion, the late Kaouding Cissoko's exquisite *kora* and contributions from dance experimentalists De Lata and Sidestepper, it may yet prove Maal's most satisfying album.

Alioune Mbaye Nder et le Setsima
Rough-hewn heartthrob Mbaye Nder is the first superstar of the post-N'Dour generation.

Jak Kilby

Nder et...
World Connection, Netherlands
Mbaye Nder has a nasal, keening and very traditional voice, while his band rock enjoyably in mainstream *mbalax* fashion – though without adding to the music's essential formula.

Nicolas Menheim & le Super Sabadaor
Sharp-voiced Dakar rumbero and sometime Super Étoile vocalist who found fame with Africando before returning to his original Afro-Cuban ensemble.

Commandante Che Guevara
PAM, Germany
Smoothly arranged and briskly played Wolof *son-montuno*. Menheim's braying voice stands out.

Youssou N'Dour
From his time with Étoile de Dakar, through to collaborations with Peter Gabriel and Neneh Cherry, N'Dour has produced a body of work that is erratic, extraordinarily varied and completely fascinating. Continually reworking old material, his

attempts to cater to both home and international markets have been a touch over-calculating at times, but his later work shows a more personal and holistic approach.

WITH SUPER ÉTOILE DE DAKAR

 Youssou N'Dour et Super Étoile de Dakar:
Vols 1–16 and subsequent numberless releases
Local cassettes
N'Dour and his trusted cohorts take Dakar street grooves with strong Latin retentions to the portals of international superstar collaboration, via some wild, wacky and continually surprising routes. Vols 6, 7, 9 and 10 are particularly strong. Vol 8, heavily remixed, became *Immigrés*, but the music works best as one extraordinary stream of consciousness. Most of these are impossible to find, but a multi-CD compilation, planned for 2006, could become one of the great albums.

YOUSSOU N'DOUR

⭐ **Immigrés**
Earthworks, UK
A homage to Senegalese migrant workers, full of rich, simmering open-ended grooves, this much-loved, mid-period classic has been lovingly remastered, and at mid-price is indispensable.

⊙ **Inédits 84–85**
Celluloid, France
Selections from one of N'Dour's most fertile periods. Complex arrangements, sudden tempo changes and a strong jazz influence make for ambitious, challenging and highly rewarding music.

⊙ **The Guide: Wommat**
Sony/Columbia, US
His most successful attempt at giving *mbalax* the big-budget, international treatment. Containing many moods, it seems uncertain in places, but "7 Seconds" (with Neneh Cherry) was a huge hit.

⭐ **Egypt**
Nonesuch, UK
This album of praise songs to local Islamic sages, backed by an Egyptian orchestra, was N'Dour's most surprising move yet, but with his transcendental singing, it fully deserved its Grammy award.

YOUSSOU N'DOUR AND YANDÉ CODOU SENE

⭐ **Gainde: Voices from the Heart of Africa**
World Network, Germany
Yandé Codou Sene is the *grande dame* of Serer song and with her daughters creates an elemental polyphony. N'Dour directs and joins them on several tracks. A unique and extraordinary work.

Orchestra Baobab

Baobab were the seminal Senegalese dance band of the 1970s, introducing many great singers in a variety of languages as their Afro-Cuban rhythms became rawer and earthier.

⭐ **Pirates' Choice**
World Circuit, UK
Full of lilting rhythms, extraordinary guitar playing and the atmosphere of a simpler place and time, this beautiful 1982 album is one of those albums everybody loves. Digitally remastered from the original tapes and

including a whole album of recently "rediscovered" vintage material.

⊙ **Specialist in All Styles**
World Circuit, UK
Their greatest hits revisited after their 2001 reunion, proving they had lost none of their original spark. Features an epic reworking of the classic "Utru Horas" with Ibrahim Ferrer and Youssou N'Dour.

Pape & Cheikh

Senegal's Simon and Garfunkel model themselves on Western acoustic duos, but are deeply rooted in their Serer region of central Senegal.

⊙ **Mariama**
Real World, UK
Packed with hooks and big anthemic choruses, but dotted with traditional motifs and graced by Pape's dramatic growl, this artfully arranged set makes highly satisfying listening.

Omar Pené & Super Diamono

The "people's band" of Dakar's proletarian suburbs in the 1980s/early 1990s, Diamono mixed reggae militancy, jazz cool and hardcore traditional grooves.

⊙ **Fari**
Stern's, UK
Combines two cassettes from the early 1990s, when main man Pené had reformed the band with top Dakar session men. A bit smooth for some tastes, but the overall feel is deeply Senegalese.

Positive Black Soul

The first Senegalese hip-hop act to make an international splash are still soldiering away.

⊙ **Run Cool**
Warner, US
Senegal's original rap band enlisted the help of such hip-hop heavyweights as Salaam Remi for this 2001 set. Worth it for the furious "Xoyma" alone, though it strangely failed to make an impact.

Royal Band Thies & Dieuf Dieul

Legendary proto-*mbalax* combo from Senegal's railway city.

⊙ **Meanwhile in Thies**
Dakar Sound, Netherlands
Bursting with energy and strong on talking drums, jangling guitars and rabble-rousing neo-*griot* vocals, this presents a convincing and highly enjoyable variant on the Étoile de Dakar sound. Excellent compilation, also featuring tracks from the even more obscure Dieuf Dieul.

Mansour Seck

Lifelong *griot* Mansour Seck was (and is) a mentor of Baaba Maal. He plays masterful acoustic guitar and sings with a gently rasping deftness.

⊙ **Yelayo**
Stern's, UK
Never less than one hundred percent grounded in its Fula soil, this is Seck's third solo album and probably his most attractive – the first to feature a female chorus.

Thioné Seck

Former Orchestra Baobab singer Thioné Seck, like many Senegalese artists, isn't revealed at his best on any one album. But Dakar's gentleman crooner is an essential voice in the nation's music.

⊙ **Chauffeur Bi**
Dakar Sound, Netherlands
Beautiful acoustic album, also included as a bonus CD on *Double Concentré*.

⊙ **Orientation**
Cantos, France
Revisiting some of his most enduring songs with traditional musicians from Egypt and India, this explores Seck's affinity with oriental music in a serene and often strikingly beautiful manner.

Laye Sow

Northern Senegalese singer and guitarist in the Fulani "folk" style popularized by Baaba Maal.

⊙ **Djamano**
Orange World, Poland
Gentle, sparsely arranged guitar sounds, elements of overt bluesiness and understated yet passionate singing and songwriting make for a very satisfying debut.

Super Cayor de Dakar

Veteran salsa band who have made a comeback in the wake of Africando and Orchestra Baobab.

⊙ **Embouteillage**
PAM, Germany
Spirited mixture of Cuban rhythm and talking drum that evokes the glory days of Baobab and Étoile.

Suuf

One-off meeting of Senegalese and British musicians including Les Frères Guissses and Robert Plant guitarist Justin Adams.

⊙ **Debbo Hande**
Late Junction, UK
A world away from the usual fusion banalities, this creates a warm synergy, with classical piano, Pink Floyd-style guitar and African folk instrumentation interacting in a very fruitful way.

Touré Kunda

A band of Casamançais brothers whose tasteful fusion made a big but brief impact in the mid-1980s.

⊙ **The Best of Touré Kunda**
Charly, Germany
Solid collection from their heyday on the Celluloid label, featuring most of the hits from a career that could be ripe for reappraisal.

Seydina Insa Wadé

Eccentric and politically controversial precursor of the current Senegalese folk new wave.

⊙ **Xalima**
Stargazer Records, Ireland
Comeback album, featuring some strong melodies and an odd variety of arrangements from tasteful cello and accordeon to Jean-Phillipe Rykiel's 1980s-style synths.

Xalam

The late Prosper Niang's pioneering band pursued a Wolof jazz direction way back in 1970.

⊙ **Apartheid**
Mélodie/Encore, France
Jazz funk à la Sénégalaise, well recorded, and their only album currently available.

The Gambia

⊙ **Griots of West Africa and Beyond**
Ellipsis Arts, US
New York-based *kora* player Foday Musa Suso takes left-field producer Bill Laswell to meet musician relatives in far-flung Casamance villages. Superbly vivid recordings, interspersed with pieces by Suso, Philip Glass and Laswell. A fascinating project, accompanied by a lavishly illustrated book.

⊙ **Sounds of the Gambia**
Arch, UK
From Gambian-style *mbalax* to hard-driving *kora* fusion from Jaliba Kuyateh and Tata Dindin, this is a good overview of recent trends, though it is two women, Fatou Ngum and the entrancing Sambou Susso, who steal the show.

Tata Dindin

Tata Dindin, son of the esteemed Malamini Jobarteh, is a Young Turk of the *kora*.

⊙ **Salam: New Kora Music**
World Network, Germany
Tata leaves behind his dance band for this gently emotive and highly accomplished set.

Ifang Bondi (Super Eagles)

Ifang Bondi (formed as Super Eagles) have been standard-bearers for Gambian music since the 1960s. They have been based in Holland since 1984.

⊙ **Gis Gis**
MW Records, Netherlands
Features Fula and Mandinka sounds from young traditional musicians in a very modern context.

Amadou Bansang Jobarteh

Amadou Jobarteh is The Gambia's senior exponent of the crisp up-river (*tilibo*) style.

⊙ **Tabara**
Music of the World, US
An intimate atmosphere creates a strong sense of music from bygone days.

Pa Bobo Jobarteh & Kaira Trio

A young member of the esteemed *griot* family, specializing in wild live performances.

⊙ **Kaira Naata**
Womad Select, UK
A pleasing and relatively meditative set, recorded on location and with rousing rhythmic support.

Alhaji Bai Konteh

Late great exponent of the Casamance *kora* style, with bluesy tuning and lightning-fast variations.

⊙ Alhaji Bai Konteh
Rounder, US
Atmospheric 1972 recordings made at Konteh's home in Brikama.

Dembo Konteh & Kausu Kouyaté

Alhaji Bai's son and his brother-in-law have become well-known from extensive touring.

★ Kairabi Jabi
Weekend Beatnik, UK
The cream of the duo's late 1980s recordings: joyous, intricate, uplifting music, with Mawdo Suso guesting on *balafon*. Revelatory in its time and still inspiring.

⊙ Jali Roll +1
Rogue, UK
The duo go electric with members of 3 Mustaphas 3. Energetic and enjoyable, though not the best collaboration of its kind.

Jaliba Kuyateh

An innovator in semi-electric *kora* dance music who has surrounded himself with a madcap posse.

🎦 Tissoli
Jololi, Senegal
A tumbling barrage of *kora*, *balafon*, bass, drums, percussion and a lonesome trumpet, all hitting deep traditional grooves. Crazy and wonderful.

Super Eagles

Pioneering band whose blend of Latin, Afro-American and African sounds helped pave the way for Senegalese *mbalax*.

⊙ Senegambian Sensation
RetroAfric, UK
Delightful set, with a vintage, swinging pan-African feel, and highly different from anything produced in musically dominant neighbour Senegal.

Jali Nyama Suso

Suso was a revered elder statesman of the *kora*, sadly departed.

⊙ Gambie: l'Art de la Kora
Ocora, France
Tuneful, accessible playing and singing in both up-river and coastal styles. Recorded in 1972.

Papa Susso

Distinguished US-based singer and *kora* player who remains faithful to the up-river tradition.

⊙ Sotuma-Sere
Traditional Crossroads, US
No-frills recording that exudes conviction, eschewing instrumental fireworks in favour of languid passion and a beautiful outdoor acoustic. A must for the aficionado.

PLAYLIST
Senegal & The Gambia

1 IMMIGRÉS Youssou N'Dour from *Immigrés*
Forget "7 Seconds", this is the Dakar superstar's definitive signature groove – insistent and gloriously loose, but with everything falling perfectly into place.

2 MACINA TORO Baaba Maal & Mansour Seck from *Djamm Leelii*
Something of the feel of the old US sharecropper South blends with a touch of mystical African Islam in the incantatory singing and hypnotic guitar grooves.

3 ÉTOILE 2000 Boubou N'Gary from *Étoile 2000*
Howling fuzzbox guitar, talking drums and an echo chamber collide with some of the hardest, darkest *griot* singing ever on this still unmatched punk-*mbalax* masterpiece.

4 NONGUI NONGUI Number One du Sénégal from *Double Concentré*
Rambunctious, gutsy talking-drum pop, with a remorselessly jumping groove and Papé Seck's fabulous, gravelly lead vocal.

5 MARIAMA Papé & Cheikh from *Mariama*
A plaintive Mandinka traditional song given a rabble-rousing modern folk-pop treatment, with spine-tingling contributions from teenage *griot* diva Cissé Diamba Kanouté.

6 NE LA THIASS Cheikh Lô from *Ne la Thiass*
Mellow, earthy *mbalax*-folk with a flamenco flavour from the Sufi balladeer.

7 UTRU HORAS Orchestra Baobab from *Pirates' Choice*
Majestically melancholy ballad, blending the Afro-Cuban and the inimitably Senegalese in one of the veteran band's best-loved moments.

8 BOOMRANG Daara J from *Boomrang*
Catchy title track featuring a cameo vocal by Malian singer Rokia Traoré.

9 GAMBIA/ZAMBIA Super Eagles from *Senegambian Sensation*
Gorgeously dulcet pan-African anthem from the pioneering Gambian band, showing that, in musical terms, the tiny riverbank country is far more than a mere adjunct to Senegal.

10 JELE BI Ismael Lô from *Diawar*
Sparkling 1980s *mbalax* with the silky voiced *chansonnier* getting just the right balance of Dakar guts and Parisian gloss.

Sierra Leone

from palm wine to protest

Abdul Tee-Jay
Philip Ryalls/Redferns

It is hard to feel anything but sympathy as Sierra Leone attempts to recover from decades of decline and a bloody civil war. The local recording industry died in the 1970s, and for a long time, the country that gave us palmwine music has been unable to field any homegrown acts to play on the world stage. Now, however, a few revival bands and singers are attempting to recreate the golden years, while younger artists are blazing their own trails. Bram Posthumus, Ed Ashcroft and Richard Trillo chart the country's mixed musical times.

S.E. Rogie

Sierra Leone gained independence from Britain in 1961. Since then, however, gross mismanagement, a string of coups d'état, various forms of neo-colonialism and eleven years of war (from 1991 to 2002) have all taken their toll on a country whose six million people should be able to enjoy a very decent standard of living. The soil is fertile, and there are diamonds, gold, bauxite and other minerals, and abundant rumours of offshore oil. A venal and unaccountable elite, however, remains firmly entrenched.

This is not a promising environment for cultural life, of which there is very little evidence. A truly music-mad nation, whose people have an enormous capacity for all manner of merry-making, Sierra Leone relies largely on outsiders – including its very own exiles – for entertainment. Even though this sorry state of affairs is now changing slowly, this is still sadly true: what you are supposed to see and hear in Freetown is more frequently found in Washington, DC or London, homes to a large diaspora.

Palm wine and Milo

Palm wine is the naturally fermented sap-juice of the oil palm and a very popular West African drink. In Sierra Leone, the music that traditionally accompanies it is known as palmwine music or **maringa**, first made famous by **Ebenezer Calendar and his Maringar Band**. Calendar (1912–1985) played a soft, breezy, calypsonian verse-and-chorus style of music, which came in part from the Caribbean freed slave immigrants who gave the country's capital Freetown its name and an enduring creole (or *krio*) culture.

Another source of the Freetown maringa may well be found among the Kru-speaking people of Liberia. The Kru were great sailors, who hired themselves out to the foreign ships coming in from Europe. The Portuguese were among the first to arrive, bringing the guitars that the Kru took up with great success. These and other multinational trading expeditions along the West African coast spread the Kru guitar style far and wide.

Calendar himself was the son of a soldier from Barbados. While

Ebenezer Calendar

he made a name for himself as a coffin maker, his music soon took over and in the early years of independence he was a mainstay of the Sierra Leone Broadcasting Service. His popular song "Double Decker Bus" captures the good times of those first post-independence years: a heady, slightly tipsy, afternoon sound – like the party on wheels that reportedly ensued when the bus in question first hit the streets of Freetown.

Welcome to Sierra Leone double-decker bus.
The manager is Mr Stobbart,
His assistant is Mr Garmon.
They are trying to do their level best
By sending the double decker.
Welcome to Sierra Leone double-decker bus,
Alleluia. Welcome to Sierra Leone double-decker bus.
Mr Stobart, Mr Garmon and the citizens
Had a party in east to west.
My grandfather and my grandmother
Refused to go to the top stairs.
Welcome to Sierra Leone double-decker bus,
Alleluia. Welcome to Sierra Leone double-decker bus.

Calendar had previously played a kind of music known as *goom-bay* (or *gumbe* – see Guinea-Bissau), a style that led to an interesting offshoot in the form of **milo-jazz**, popularized by **Olofemi ('Doctor Oloh') Israel Cole and his Milo-jazz band**. Milo-jazz was a percussive street music requiring no amplification, whose signature instrument was the shaker, made with a Milo (chocolate powder) can filled with pebbles. As recently as the 1990s, milo-jazz remained popular in Freetown, but war and economic hardship have all but obliterated it.

A Brief Golden Era

Sierra Leone's musical heyday was the 1970s. A new generation of bands that had grown up in the years following independence began to develop their own styles and sang about sweet Salone (*krio* for Sierra Leone), swinging Freetown and of course love and sex. Their explicit lyrics brought some of them into conflict with the new authorities. Musically, they still drew largely from the calypso and maringa but they did away with some of the traditional instrumentation, adding electric guitars and horns, and borrowing from other African countries (most notably Congo and Ghana), Western R&B and pop tunes. Leading groups included the wonderful **Afro-Nationals** (Sierra Leone's answer to TPOK Jazz), **Orchestra Muyah** and **Super Combo**. These groups developed what became known as "soca-beat", which is still very much part of community life. While artists like **Bunny Mack** and **Abu Whyte** began to make waves, a special place must be reserved for **Geraldo Pino**, an almost forgotten bandleader who had a lasting influence on none other than **Fela Kuti**. Pino and his band (The Heartbeats) brought **James Brown**'s heavy funky big-band sound to the whole of West Africa, and when Fela heard it, it set him on the path that would eventually lead to Afro-beat (see Nigeria chapter). Things would never be the same again.

Exile and Revival

One of the few artists to break through on the international scene was **S.E. Rogie** (1926–1994), who built on the palmwine tradition by applying electric guitar to the style. After having his own band in the 1960s, he left Sierra Leone for the US in 1973 and finally moved to Britain in the late 1980s, where he proved a great cultural ambassador. His greatest successes were "My Lovely Elisabeth" and "Go Easy With Me", a song with lyrics as irresistibly suggestive as the music. Rogie only returned to Freetown in the early 1990s, playing benefit concerts for war refugees. He died shortly after the release of his last CD, ironically titled *Dead Men Don't Smoke Marijuana*.

Rogie's story is really that of post-golden-era Sierra Leone. In the 1980s and 90s, the rare success stories have been those of exiles. The veteran

London-based multi-instrumentalist **Abdul Tee-Jay** has spent a long time slowly but surely building up his reputation and now has an audience on both sides of the Atlantic. There are many others like Tee-Jay, most of whom have not had the same success: **Ansumana Bangura**, a one-time member of Miriam Makeba's band, has forged a career in Germany, while **Seydou** records interesting and beautiful fusion material in his adopted Spain. **King Masco** knocked out a lot of palmwine-based ribaldry in the US during the 1990s (*African Love* being his best-known album), while his fellow US-based countryman **Daddy Ramanu** uses a combination of traditional and calypso/highlife influences for the dancefloor beats on his albums *De-Culture* and *Attitude*. A few hold out in their home country. **Great Steady Bongo** has had big hits with "Kormot Bi En Me" and more recently with "Wake Up", and an album called *Ar De Make*. **Ngoh Gbetuwai**, a Mende from the town of Moyamba, produced a CD (*Biza Body*) in the 1990s and another titled *Ngoyeah* (Unity) in 2000. Most of the homegrown productions suffer from the usual 1990s musical contamination of drum machines and tinny keyboards.

Great Steady Bongo

Lately, however, there has been something of a small revolution going on in the music scene, mainly due to the return of yet another exile, James Bangura, better known under his artist name **Jimmy B**. He spent long spells in the US and especially South Africa, where he came into contact with *kwaito*. In the late 1990s, he returned to Sierra Leone and set up a recording studio called Paradise. This became the launch pad for a whole raft of young artists, whose musical reference points were radically different from that of their parents: R&B, hip-hop, reggae, ragga and *kwaito* (Brenda Fassie's "Vuli Ndlela" was a huge hit all over West Africa). Apart from Jimmy B himself, the cream of the crop are **Sisters With Attitude**, **Ahmed Janka Nabay** (who also works as a jingle producer) and, best known of all, **Daddy Saj**. Radio did a lot to popularize this new wave of artists and the Freetown clubs started playing their music. There has even been something of a revival of the **Afro-Nationals** and another leading 1970s band, **Sabannoh 75**, which resurfaced as **Sabannoh International**. And finally, like everywhere else in Anglophone Africa, there is a massive industry around gospel, with singers like **Vicky Formah** and **Johnny Wisdom** catering to a following that is far more interested in the message than the music.

But it is the younger generation that is making the waves, against huge odds, not least the fact that you will be hard pressed to find a fully functioning music venue anywhere in Freetown. One reason is electricity: the city's power grid has largely broken down. And unfortunately, the young music scene suffers from the same problems as the rest of society. Jealousy and backbiting begin as soon as someone has a modicum of success: thus Jimmy B was accused of siphoning off royalties, and while this has never been proved, it has put a damper on his career.

The overarching national concern is reflected in the title of by far the biggest recent hit in Sierra Leone, **Daddy Saj**'s "Corruption 'E Do So'" (Corruption, 'Enough is Enough'), a bouncy rap track

on a ragga beat. A track that fills up the Freetown dancefloors in no time, it is the rallying cry of the young, who watch their politicians lead the country back into the same moral morass that preceded the civil war. A song by **Wan Pot Sojas** sums up their feelings – "Ar Vex" (I'm pissed off) – a call for education, jobs and a decent life. Sierra Leone's elites have been singularly deaf to such pleas, so the singers will have to just crank up the volume a bit more – until the next power cut.

DISCOGRAPHY Sierra Leone

⊙ **African Elegant: Sierra Leone's Kru/Krio Calypso Connection**
Original Music, US
A fascinating ethnomusicological document, although elegant isn't the word that immediately springs to mind in describing these ragged old Decca takes. Still, there's redemption in most of Ebenezer Calendar's numbers.

★ **Sierra Leone Music**
Zensor, Germany
Wolfgang Bender's lovingly packaged compilation of Freetown, *krio* and up-country tracks is a real collector's item. The tracks were recorded for radio in the late 1950s/early 60s and include Calendar's famous "Double Decker Bus", a celebration of independence and a lot of traditional material from local communities

all over the country. Excellent accompanying booklet, including some of the lyrics.

Afro-Nationals

The band was created in the 1970s by the legendary Sulay Abubakar and raw, husky singer Patricia Koroma. Dubbed the TPOK Jazz Band of Sierra Leone and not without reason, featuring the sweet lead guitar, trademark brass and percussion that epitomized the era.

⊙ **Classics 1 & 2**
H&R Enterprises, US
Classics 1 is a collection of remastered original hits, including "Money Palava" and "Mother-In-Law", while Classics 2 gives us the band after it re-formed in 1998, re-recording some of its old songs and adding a few brand-new tracks.

1 **DOUBLE DECKER BUS Ebenezer Calendar and his Maringar Band** from *Sierra Leone Music*
Delightful and slightly tipsy palmwine welcome to a short-lived addition to Freetown's transport system.

2 **MONEY PALAVA Afro-Nationals** from *Classics 1*
Their biggest hit, with all the right ingredients: sweet guitar, rumba rhythms, great vocals.

3 **KPINDIGBEE (MORNING, NOON AND NIGHT) S.E. Rogie** from *Dead Men Don't Smoke Marijuana*
A Rogie classic. Laidback vocals, laidback guitars, slow rhythms – now where's that hammock?

4 **AFRICANS MUST UNITE Geraldo Pino & The Heartbeats** from *Heavy Heavy Heavy*
The funk bass underpins a distinctly 6/8 African beat that carries a strong message.

5 **THE WELL Seydu** from *Diamond Tears*
Beautifully performed acoustic nostalgia for the motherland.

6 **RO-MAKE Abdul Tee-Jay** from *Kanka Kuru*
The unstoppable dance tune that propelled him onto the British stage

7 **A BUY YOU EVERYTHING Abdul Tee-Jay** from *Palm Wine A Go-Go*
His other, palmwine side. Irresistibly funny song about a boy who buys her everything only to be told that he is being a nuisance.

8 **CORRUPTION "E DO SO" Daddy Saj** from *Corruption "E Do So"*
The anthem of postwar Sierra Leone, the stomping hip-hop/raggamuffin tune telling the country's corrupt leaders to "pack and go".

Jimmy B

Rapper and producer who returned from exile to rescue the music scene and got quite a bit of flak for his efforts. He is still one of Sierra Leone's most popular artists, but apart from a "Best Of" album in 2000, nothing new appears to have been released.

⊙ **Make 'em Bounce**
EMI, South Africa
Hip-hop, rumba and even South African *mbaqanga* (the title track is a fantastic remix of Mahlatini's "Gazette") all come together on this, his most recent release.

Ansumana Bangura

A drum maker and player in his younger years, Ansumana was accidentally left behind by Miriam Makeba's band

while on tour in Germany in 1980. He then came to the attention of the small independent label Shave Musik, which released his first and so far only album.

⊙ **Sierra Leone People**
Shave Musik, Germany
There's a bit of everything here: highlife, palmwine, traditional society music, milo-jazz… A pretty uptempo and (unsurprisingly) percussive album, in his own *fankadama* ("mix with everything") style.

Daddy Saj

Daddy Saj (real name Joseph Cole) shot to fame with the title-track of this CD, striking a real chord nationwide. Initially inspired by Western rappers, he stayed close to his roots for his debut, but the follow-up, *Densay Densay* (Rumours) suffered from Western influences. A third album, *Faiya 4 Faiya*, was released in late 2005.

⊙ **Corruption "E Do So"**
Own label, Sierra Leone
Hip-hop, a whiff of old-fashioned *goom-bay* and more than a dollop of ragga. The main attraction, though, is the urgent message to Sierra Leone's government and politicians: get things right or else… This is the authentic voice of Sierra Leone's youth.

King Masco

A favourite for Sierra Leoneans, both at home and overseas, catering as he does to their taste for saucy lyrics and deadpan innuendo. He churns out albums regularly, his latest (though not his best) being *Firestone*.

⊙ **African Love Record**
H&R Enterprises, US
His best and most popular album includes the very rude but hysterically funny "Run Away". Pity about the keyboards and drum machines.

Geraldo Pino

Originally a singer and guitarist with a covers band, The Heartbeats, Gerald Pino got hooked on James Brown in the 1960s. Rechristening himself Geraldo Pino, he changed his sound radically and went everywhere, including Lagos, where a young Fela Kuti – then playing highlife – was awestruck. Pino himself made a few albums in the 1970s and then lapsed into undeserved obscurity.

⊙ **Geraldo Pino and The Heartbeats: Heavy Heavy Heavy**
RetroAfric, UK
The funk basics: bass, drums and fuzzy guitars – are all present and correct. The singing and shouting could have come straight out of the US and there are the ubiquitous set-pieces

for keyboards. When the music takes a holiday from funk, however, the message comes through even louder and clearer: here's an Africa that shouts freedom and is asserting itself. No wonder Fela was so impressed.

S.E. Rogie

Sooliman Ernest Rogie (1926–1994) developed an effortlessly laidback guitar style: think of a mug of palm wine under a tree in the shade. *Palm Wine Guitar Music: The 60's Sound (Cooking Vinyl)* has his earlier hits "My Lovely Elizabeth" and "Please Go Easy With Me".

★ Dead Men Don't Smoke Marijuana
Real World, UK

The beauty of palmwine music lies in its simplicity, and Rogie's last album has the same quiet thoughtfulness as its predecessors. Highly enjoyable, as long as you don't mind the variations on what is basically the same theme.

Seydou

The Freetown-born Seydou was strongly influenced by the chanting of his Fulani-Mandinka mother and his grandfather's drums. Before settling in Spain, this talented multi-instrumentalist lived for a while in Fela's commune in Lagos and in London.

⊙ Freetown
NubeNegra, Spain

Fuses many different styles, from Afro-beat and highlife to funk, soul and flamenco influences. Seydou seems equally at home on the reflective "Palm Wine Talk" as on the more electric and upbeat "Chica Boom Boom". Polyrhythmic, beautifully played and produced.

⊙ Diamond Tears
NubeNegra, Spain

"Gentle" is the word for this mainly acoustic album, with guitars and percussion leading the way through a garden of sounds and songs. Too gentle for some perhaps, but there is beauty in the title-track and a romantic nostalgia in songs like "The Well" and "Suffer".

Abdul Tee-Jay

Hard-working singer, songwriter and multi-instrumentalist, Abdul Tee-Jay has long been the most prominent Sierra Leonean musician in the UK, working the club circuit with his particular take on soca beat. He made three albums in this highly danceable vein (*Kanka Kuru*, *Fire Dombolo* and *E' Go Lef Pan You*) before slowing down considerably and reliving that good old palmwine/highlife music of old.

★ E'Go Lef Pan You
Tee-Jay Disque/Stern's, UK

This is Tee-Jay's most exuberant collection of dance tunes, but with more traditional material than its two high-energy predecessors. The palmwine style on "Jorlay Baby" and the highlife medley "Guitar Boy" are simply delightful.

★ Palm Wine A Go-Go
Far Side/Stern's, UK

When Abdul puts his electric guitar down and goes acoustic, his music goes into another world. This is a return to the very roots of palmwine, with a bunch of highly catchy, classic tunes. As Nigel Williamson wrote in *Songlines*: "It's unashamedly retro … with breezy verse-and-chorus songs and rudimentary instrumentation of guitars, shakers, penny whistle and bottle."

South Africa |
popular music

nation of the voice

New SA diva Thandiswa Mazwai
Gallo

South Africa is home to a remarkable diversity of musical styles, which have multiplied bountifully (and not a little confusingly) since the end of apartheid. Despite the wide regional and stylistic variations, a powerful vocal focus and a strong emphasis on dance are the underlying strengths of much of the best South African pop. To the despair of many purists, digitized and programmed beats are increasingly widespread, but creativity and talent remain alive and well, as Rob Allingham and Gregory Mthembu-Salter explain.

South Africa has a diversity of pop music styles that is unparalleled in the rest of Africa, a diversity that reflects its complex class structures and population mix. The strongest indigenous influences are probably *mbaqanga*, a black township style with vocal harmonies and deep "groaning" male vocals, and Zulu acapella, both of which have won considerable international recognition. African American music has historically been a huge influence on South African pop too, from vaudeville, jazz and funk to soul and disco, and out of the mix have come styles such as *marabi*, township jive and bubblegum. Today, the dominant pop sound is *kwaito*, which draws heavily on house and hip hop, with local variants on R&B also finding an appreciative audience.

Deep Roots

South Africa is one of the world's oldest inhabited areas, and it has perhaps the earliest-charted musical history, dating back to the Stone Age, around 4000 years ago. At this time, it seems, groups of hunter-gatherers known as **San**, or Bushmen, sang in a uniquely African click language (the "!" and other clicks in modern Bantu languages are an inheritance), fashioned rattles, drums and simple flutes, and exploited the musical properties of their hunting bows. Present-day San music still sounds quite otherworldly.

Then, some 2000 years ago, another group called the **Khoi** are believed to have filtered down from the north with their herds and pushed out the San. Known pejoratively as Hottentots, the Khoi are now extinct as a group, though their mixed race, or "coloured", descendants are an important part of South African society. Khoi music seems to have been more complex than San: Vasco da Gama noted in 1497 that his Khoi hosts greeted his arrival with a five-man ensemble of reed flutes.

Later, in around 200 AD, the first **Bantu-speaking** peoples arrived in the region, and by the beginning of the seventeenth century Bantu linguistic groups – **Sotho**, **Xhosa**, **Zulu** and others – had completely occupied what is now South Africa. Their musical glory was their vocal tradition, with songs to accompany every routine, ritual and rite of passage. Each tribe had distinct and characteristic songs, tonalities and harmonies, but the underly-

Henry Scurfield/Natal Newspapers

Zulu-traditional musicians

ing musical structure was the same – two or more linked melodic phrases, not sung in unison, but staggered to produce a simultaneous polyphony. This arrangement may well have been a Bantu invention – it was certainly an African one – and it underlies the basic "call-and-response" structure of many African-American styles including gospel and its later derivatives, doo-wop and soul.

The West, Urbanization, Marabi and Jive

In the hinterland, the first contact with **Western music** usually coincided with the arrival of Christian missionaries, who made their first visits in the early nineteenth century. Once the **mission school system** was established, it provided most of the few educational opportunities available to Africans, and always included a musical training. Out of this system came **Enoch Sontonga** – who composed the national anthem, "Nkosi Sikelel' i Africa", at the turn of the century – and later, nearly every prominent black composer and performer right up until the 1960s.

But the most important catalyst for musical evolution was **urbanization**. Cape Town was big enough to attract American musicians in the 1840s, while Johannesburg grew rapidly in the 1880s after the discovery of gold. Among the many professional musicians who travelled to South Africa before World War I were African-American minstrels, vaudevillians and ragtime piano players. A remarkable series of tours was undertaken in the 1890s by **Orpheus McAdoo's Jubilee Singers** who introduced black spiritual singing to great acclaim from the South African public – black and white alike.

By the 1920s, Africans had established a secure foothold in the cities despite increasing government restrictions. Out of the necessity of coping with the nightly curfew that applied to all Africans, an entertainment institution, the "**Concert and Dance**", developed in Johannesburg – by now the largest African city south of the Sahara. Vocal groups and comedians held the stage from the beginning of curfew at 8pm until 11pm. Then, after midnight, dance bands with names like the Merry Blackbirds and the Jazz Maniacs played until 4am, when it was once again legal to go on the streets. The **Jazz Maniacs** were a rough-and-tumble outfit, and while they played dance music for black middle-class audiences, they also incorporated elements of a style from Johannesburg's black slumyards called *marabi*.

Originally, **marabi** was banged out on battered **pianos** to the percussive accompaniment of pebble-filled cans in countless township shebeens – illicit drinking centres (the sale of alcohol was illegal to Africans until 1962 except in government beer halls). Structurally, *marabi* consisted of a single phrase built around a three-chord progression repeated endlessly in the indigenous fashion, while melodically it was a highly syncretic form, providing enough space for improvisation to incorporate snatches of anything from traditional melodies to hymns or current popular fare from Tin Pan Alley.

Some time later, perhaps by the mid-1930s, *marabi* was being played on **guitars**, **banjos**, and **concertinas** but the underlying structure remained the same. By the postwar years and into the 1950s, a number of related popular urban styles based on three-chord *marabi* patterns were being played and sung in different languages and on a variety of instruments in townships throughout southern Africa. By this time, the music was often referred to as **jive** (as in 'violin jive' or 'Ndebele jive'.) Meanwhile, in Johannesburg and other South African cities, *marabi* and American swing were combining to create **African Jazz**.

A Music Industry

By the late 1940s, southern Africa boasted a remarkable collection of black music styles. These included the distinctive African-Western crossovers of the cities and a variety of tribally differentiated styles. The latter varied in their make-up from the almost purely Indigenous to the Westernized. Most of these styles existed outside any commercial infrastructure, and thus constituted a genuine folk music in the broadest sense of the term.

The occasional local **recordings** tended to document the music passively, without affecting its style or substance. The UK-based **Gramophone Company Ltd**, producer of the HMV and Zonophone labels, initiated the first commercial recording sessions in Africa by dispatching a portable field unit to Cape Town and Johannesburg in 1912. Later sessions in the company's London studio produced the first recorded version of "Nkosi Sikelel' i Africa" by ANC co-founder **Sol Plaatjie** in 1923, and 150 landmark recordings by composer Reuben Caluza's Double Quartet in 1930.

Eric Gallo's Brunswick Gramophone House sent a few Afrikaner and African musicians to London in 1930 and 1931 to record for their new Singer label. And **Gallo** went on to build a local studio – the first in sub-Saharan Africa – which produced

The Producers

The most powerful producers ran virtual fiefdoms within the leading record companies; five in particular loom large.

Strike Vilakazi (Trutone)

Strike Vilakazi ran Trutone's black division from 1952 to 1970. A vocalist, trumpeter, drummer and composer, he directly influenced the course of popular black music by recording pennywhistler Spokes Mashiyane in 1954, touching off the kwela craze. Four years later, in an even shrewder move, he persuaded Mashiyane that his pennywhistle music would be even more popular when played on a saxophone. The earliest mbaqanga style, or sax jive, resulted – a sound that would dominate South African black popular music for many years.

Cuthbert Matumba (Troubadour Records)

Cuthbert Matumba singlehandedly developed Troubadour Records into a giant that at times controlled much of the African market. In addition to a multitude of hits, his catalogue included practically every urban and urban-rural crossover style from the Cape up through Central Africa. He had a gift for composing simple, catchy melodies and wrote especially topical lyrics.

Matumba permanently employed a large contingent of studio singers and musicians who spent eight hours a day recording (under a variety of names). Despite this assembly-line approach, the innovative spirit remained strong, thanks to a policy encouraging moonlighting by musicians from other companies. Matumba kept his ear to the ground by playing test pressings on the Troubadour-mobile and gauging public reaction. Any promising record was available in the shops 24 hours after it had been recorded. Troubadour's decline was abrupt: within four years of Matumba's death in 1965, the label's few remaining assets had been swallowed up by Gallo.

Rupert Bopape (EMI/Mavuthela)

Rupert Bopape joined EMI as a producer in 1952 and quickly built up the industry's most successful African jazz catalogue by employing key figures like Zacks Nkosi, Elijah Nkwanyane and Ellison Temba on a permanent basis. But his real talents lay in developing vocal groups. In the early 1960s, his most successful pennywhistle band, with their all-male vocal style, were the Black Mambazo. Their all-female counterparts were the Dark City Sisters, probably the single most popular vocal group in South Africa in the first half of the 1960s.

In 1964, Bopape moved to Gallo to run a new African operation (later called Mavuthela). Within two years, the label dominated the market with a mbaqanga vocal style called mqashiyo, the most famous exponent of which was Mahlathini and the Mahotella Queens, backed by the Makgona Tsohle Band.

David Thekwane (Teal)

The last of the old-style producers to carve out a significant niche in the music industry, David Thekwane began producing for Teal in 1972 after a fairly successful career as a saxophone jive artist under Strike Vilakazi. Thekwane had a violent personality and often intimidated his musicians physically. Nonetheless, throughout the 1970s, his Teal artists – especially The Movers, consistent hit-makers who evolved a winning mixture of marabi and local 'soul' – accounted for a substantial percentage of all African record sales. His mbaqanga stars included sax jivers Thomas Phale and Lulu Masilela, accordionist Johnson Mkhalali, and vocal group The Boyoyo Boys.

Hamilton Nzimande (Gramophone Record Co.)

Hamilton Nzimande was the last of the "big five" to remain active in the music business. In a thirty-year producing career he oversaw a remarkably broad cross-section of African music, from the last sessions of African Jazz great Zacks Nkosi to the earliest bubblegum pop of some of the biggest names of the 1980s and early 90s.

Nzimande got his break as a producer in 1966, when he went to help run the Gallo subsidiary Gramophone Records. By the mid-1970s, his mbaqanga catalogue almost rivalled Mavuthela's under Rupert Bopape. He was the first producer to take local soul music seriously and made it massively successful, with bands like the Inn-Lawes and the Beaters, who spawned solo star Sipho "Hotstix" Mabuse. It was at Nzimande's suggestion that the hugely successful Soul Brothers copied their vocal harmony style from Zimbabwean Shona township music.

Nzimande also set trends in gospel recordings by popularizing the Zulu acapella style, cothoza mfana, that anticipated the sound which would make Ladysmith Black Mambazo so famous, and he was the first to successfully promote large apostolic choirs such as Izikhova Ezimnqini.

its first masters in 1933, effectively marking the inauguration of the South African music industry. By the mid-1950s, a number of other operations had been established: **Trutone**, a local branch of EMI; **Teal**, another EMI subsidiary which later separated and grew into a formidable presence; and **Troubadour Records**.

Meanwhile, Gallo Africa and its subsidiary, Gramophone Record Company, were producing over a million discs a year in the early 1950s. This was becoming big business, and as the decade progressed the record companies put in place a system of African **talent scouts and producers** (see box) which was to shape the new music for the next three decades.

Radio began to play a crucial role quite late, from 1962, after a "development programme" for **Bantu Radio** was implemented by the white government – in reality a cynical exercise in apartheid wish-fulfilment. Broadcasting was to be a propaganda tool to foster "separate development". In the cities, monolingual programming would encourage ethnic identity while in the rural Bantustans radio would provide the voice of incipient nationhood. It was intended that the rural stations would feature exclusively the traditional music of their regions, in order to encourage ethnic separatism. In practice, the Bantustan stations had to play a mixture of styles just to gain a listenership. The failure of the traditionalism policy reflected the government's ignorance of rural people. Music and culture in the rural areas hadn't remained suspended in a traditional timewarp, and economic development had diluted the indigenous character of the hinterland.

Nontheless, Bantu Radio handed the record companies a powerful marketing tool and enabled them to reach a mass market immediately. Radio also opened up new rural markets for record companies, encouraging them to focus more attention on areas outside the cities where individual rural traditions were being combined with modern, urban-based influences.

After the advent of radio, however, the lyrical content of African recordings became more conservative. In the 1950s and before, black musicians often recorded material that commented openly on the social and political issues of the day – "Sobadubula Ngembayimbayi" by the Alexandra Swing Liners, released in 1955, contained the chorus "We will shoot the whites with bazookas". The new African radio services instituted a draconian censorship code and mobiles were banned as a "public hazard". Purely commercial considerations inevitably led to a great deal of self-censorship on the part of labels and their artists.

Pennywhistle Jive: the Kwela Boom

Pennywhistle jive, which was focused as usual on Johannesburg, was one of the first musical styles to become a commercial phenomenon and the first to win a measure of international renown. The indigenous predecessor to the pennywhistle was the reed flute of cattle-herders, with three finger-holes. When the herd boys came to the cities, they bought similar tin whistles with six finger-holes, made in Germany.

Willard Cele, a disabled teenage musician living in Alexandra Township, Johannesburg, is credited with the discovery that by placing the flute's mouthpiece at an angle between the teeth to one side of the mouth with the soundhole slanting outwards, its tone was not only thickened but it was possible to vary the pitch of each note and vastly extend the instrument's melodic capabilities. Although Cele himself was to die young, his new style quickly inspired a legion of imitators, especially following his appearance in a 1951 movie, *The Magic Garden*. Groups of three and four **pennywhistlers** were soon working out elaborate arrangements where a lead flute would extemporize a melodic line over chords provided by backing flutes.

After years, indeed decades, as an exclusive township phenomenon, pennywhistlers moved into the suburbs and city centres in the early 1950s where they were part of the urban environment for another decade. In the white areas, the potential financial rewards were greater but so were the dangers. Flute musicians, some of them not even into their teens, would travel out of the townships to perform on street corners and in parks, playing a cat-and-mouse game with the police who would arrest them for creating a "public disturbance". Eventually this musical presence attracted a white following, particularly from rebellious suburban teenagers referred to as "ducktails" (the equivalent of teddy boys in the UK or "juvenile delinquents" in the US). It was the ducktails that renamed pennywhistle jive **kwela** (meaning "climb up", the command barked out to Africans being arrested and ordered into the police van). The term eventually became generic and it was as kwela that the music spread elsewhere in southern Africa, notably to Malawi, through migrant workers.

It took several years for the record companies to wake up to the commercial potential of the pennywhistle. Little flute material was released until 1954, when **Spokes Mashiyane**'s "Ace Blues" backed with the "Kwela Spokes" became the biggest African hit of the year. Record producers began to take flute jive seriously and in the following decade around a thousand 78rpm pennywhistle discs were issued.

After his initial success, Spokes Mashiyane remained the most famous pennywhistler, although another flute star, **Abia Temba**, was also very popular throughout the 1950s. Troubadour's two biggest pennywhistle artists were **Sparks Nyembe** and **Jerry Mlotshwa**, whose material was released using an endless number of pseudonyms. The **Black Mambazo** from Alexandra Township recorded for EMI; they too appeared under different names. In 1957, they recorded a popular local hit called "Tom Hark", which featured on British TV and promptly caught the public's fancy, perhaps because of its slight similarity to the skiffle music that was popular at the time. It was issued as a UK single and promptly rose to number two in the charts.

Gallo's pennywhistle catalogue eventually cornered the largest share of the market and featured the greatest number of top-notch players, especially after the company lured Spokes Mashiyane away from Trutone in 1958 (he became the first African musician to receive royalties rather than the standard flat studio fee). The label's pennywhistle productions often featured quite elaborate arrangements by Gallo musical director **Dan Hill**, a fine clarinettist and bandleader.

Among the company's principal pennywhistle artists were the **Solven Whistlers** from Jabavu-Soweto, instantly recognizable by their jazz-influenced harmonies and sophisticated compositions, largely the work of **Peter Mokonotela**. The Solvens' lead flute, **Ben Nkosi**, was probably the single greatest pennywhistle soloist, his best work exhibiting a level of technique and improvisational dexterity that belied its execution on such a simple instrument.

The beginning of the end of the pennywhistle craze can be precisely pinpointed with the song "Big Joe Special", Spokes Mashiyane's first recording on **saxophone**. Much as his "Ace Blues" had created a sales sensation and inspired a legion of imitators four years before, "Big Joe Special" proved to be the trendsetting hit of 1958. In its wake, every black producer now wanted material by similar-style sax players, and most pennywhistlers, providing they could obtain a saxophone, were happy to deliver it.

From Sax Jive to Vocal Mbaqanga

The sax is obviously a more versatile instrument than the pennywhistle and from the standpoint of both the players and their audience connoted an urbane, pan-tribal sophistication satisfyingly contrary to the apartheid image of the heathen tribalist. Only the white kwela fans were disaffected: it proved impossible for African street musicians to perform with a saxophone at their former city and suburban haunts. Now they were limited to playing in the townships, a world beyond the ken of even the most rebellious white teenager.

After the success of "Big Joe Special", sax jives became the dominant black musical genre, a development which didn't meet with universal approval. One jazz saxophonist, Michael Xaba, disdainfully referred to the new style as **mbaqanga** – a "dumpling" in Zulu but in this instance connoting "homemade" – since most of its practitioners were musically illiterate. Ironically, the name soon gained a common currency as a term of endearment and indeed, the craze for instrumental *mbaqanga* went on to last for almost another two decades.

Sax jives were usually built around very simple repeated melodic fragments, so much of their appeal and interest depended on their instrumental accompaniment. Initially, the sax was backed with the same *marabi*-derived acoustic 2/4 rhythm of most flute jives. Then, beginning in the early 1960s, the rhythms became discernibly heavier, more elastic and more African. The **electric bass**, in particular, with its higher volume, sustaining and attack capabilities, provided the foundation for the new style. The pioneer African bass player whose innovations played such a major role in shaping this evolution was **Joseph Makwela**. His bass guitar, the first one imported into South Africa, was purchased from a local white session musician who had seen an example of the newly developed instrument when Cliff Richard and The Shadows played Johannesburg in 1960.

Makwela and **Marks Mankwane**, another influential figure who was the first African musician to exploit the electric guitar fully, formed the nucleus of the famous **Makhona Tsohle Band**, which backed the Gallo studio's *mbaqanga* saxophonists like West Nkosi but also accompanied their vocal groups. The band's electric sound became an integral part of a new vocal genre developing in the mid-1960s which also went under the name of *mbaqanga* and then later *mqashiyo*.

The **vocal component** of *mbaqanga* developed directly from the 1950s township vocal styles made famous by groups such as the Manhattan Brothers and The Skylarks. These styles had at first been copied directly from African-American models but local musicians increasingly Africanised their sound. One of the crucial developments leading towards *mbaqanga*'s characteristic harmonies was the use of **five vocal parts** rather than the four-part harmonies common in African-American styles. Female studio vocalists at Troubadour discovered that if the single tenor line was divided into a high and low tenor part, the resulting harmonies took on a breadth that was reminiscent of traditional vocal styles.

A group of session vocalists at EMI, the **Dark City Sisters**, usually featuring the sweet-voiced lead of Joyce Mogatusi, became the best-known African vocal group of the early 1960s using this technique which rapidly became a distinctively South African sound. Their style was still described as vocal jive but the formative harmonies of *mbaqanga* were already evident.

Another element which defined much of the classic vocal *mbaqanga* output was **groaning**: bellowing, ultra-bass male vocals that contrasted dramatically with softer, all-female harmonizing. At first this was a commercial gimmick invented by **Aaron Jack Lerole** of EMI's **Black Mambazo** in the early 1960s. Lerole subsequently gained a measure of groaning fame as Big Voice Jack, and in the process managed to shred his vocal chords permanently. His efforts were soon overtaken by

Simon "Mahlathini" Nkabinde. As a teenager, Mahlathini secured a considerable reputation as a singer of traditional wedding songs in Alexandra Township, where he led a large female group in a typically African, polyphonic fashion. His magnificant bass voice was naturally suited to the groaning style and Rupert Bopape began to utilize it in conjunction with varying combinations of EMI session vocalists. Meantime, Nkabinde developed an aggressive and dramatic stage persona as Mahlathini The Bull, greatly enhancing his growing reputation.

When Rupert Bopape left EMI for Gallo in 1964 he took Mahlathini along with him. All the essential *mbaqanga* elements now coalesced at the new Gallo-Mavuthela production facility: the male groaner roaring in counterpoint to intricately arranged five-part female harmonies, underpinned – thanks to the Makhona Tsohle Band – with the new-style, totally electric instrumental back-up. After several years of growing popularity, vocal *mbaqanga* began to be referred to as **mqashiyo**, from the Zulu word meaning "bounce" – though *mqashiyo* was actually the name of a popular dance style; no musical characteristic distinguished it from vocal *mbaqanga* in general.

As was the case at EMI, Bopape's regular roster of female session singers was nominally divided into several distinct groups. These line-ups maintained a degree of regularity for live performances, but in the studio vocalists were fairly interchangeable, and in any event the output of each group was simultaneously released using a number of differ-

Trevor Herman/Earthworks

Mahlathini rehearses with the Mahotella Queens

ent names. For example, the vocalists who performed live as the **Mahotella Queens** were also the Dima Sisters, the Soweto Stars and Izintombi Zo Mqashiyo on two different Gallo record labels.

Rival producers attempted to emulate Mavuthela's success with *mqashiyo*. Only one, however, Hamilton Nzimande at GRC, managed to build a strong roster. His two best-known groups were **Amatshitshi** and **Izintombi Zezi Manje Manje** (The Modern Girls), but Nzimande's crew also included two wonderful groaners, the brothers **Saul** and **Bhekitshe Tshabalala**, as well as a great instrumental backing band, **Abafana Bentutuko**. These provided stiff competition for Bopape's Mahlathini/Mahotella Queens/Makhona Tsohle steamroller.

In the 1970s, the female chorus-plus-groaner formula retained its popularity when practised by old favourites like the Mahotella Queens, but almost every successful new *mbaqanga* group had an exclusively male line-up. At the forefront were Gallo's **Abafana Baseqhudeni** ("Cockerel Boys", so named after the company's rooster trademark), an extremely popular five-man line-up featuring the bass leads of Potatoes Zuma and Elphas "Ray" Mkize as well as groaner Robert "Mbazo" Mkhize. Their main rivals during the decade were the David Thekwane-produced **Boyoyo Boys**, a male vocal group led by principal composer Petrus Maneli. Their half-chanted harmonies and loping rhythms gave them a unique sound and one of their biggest successes, "Puleng", later caught the ear of British producer **Malcolm McClaren** who subsequently transformed it into the 1981 British number one hit "Double Dutch".

Zulu Acapella: Mbube and Iscathamiya

In the 1920s, as an industrial economy began to develop in Natal, **acapella vocal styles** became closely identified with the area's emerging **Zulu working class**, newly forged as rural migrants found employment in mines and factories. Forced in most cases to leave their families behind and live in all-male hostels, they developed a weekend social life based on vocal and dance group competitions, staged within and between hostels, and judged by elaborate rules and standards. By the late 1930s, acapella competitions were a characteristic of Zulu hostels throughout industrialized Natal and had also spread to Zulus working in Johannesburg.

In 1939, **Solomon Linda's Original Evening Birds** – a group from Pomeroy in northwestern Natal – began recording for Gallo's Singer label. Their evocative rendering of Linda's song "Mbube" (The Lion) proved to be a commercial milestone. "Mbube" was probably the first African recording to sell 100,000 copies and it later provided the basis for two American number one hit records, "Wimoweh" by The Weavers in 1951 and "The Lion Sleeps Tonight" by The Tokens in 1961.

The Original Evening Birds exerted a vast stylistic influence as dozens of imitators sprang up in the wake of their success, thus setting the scene for the next stage in the long history of Western-influenced Zulu music. **Mbube** became the generic term for a new vocal style that incorporated Linda's main innovations: uniforms for the group, highly polished but softly executed dance routines and – most importantly – the use of a high-voiced lead set against four-part harmony where the ratio of the bass voices to the other parts was increased to two or three. These characteristics were at the heart of the music through the late 1940s as *mbube* evolved into the **isikhwela jo** or "bombing" style – so named because of its strident, almost shouted harmonies – and into the 1960s, when a far smoother approach became popular.

Gallo

"Mbube' composer Solomon Linda (far left) with his Evening Birds

Ladysmith Black Mambazo

Ladysmith Black Mambazo, led by the unbelievably nice **Joseph Shabalala**, is without any doubt South Africa's most popular group internationally. Confirming this status, the group won a Grammy in 2005 for their album *Raise Your Spirit Higher* in the "Traditional World Music" category, to sit alongside the one they won in 1988 in the same category for *Shaka Zulu*. In addition to the Grammys, Ladysmith Black Mambazo have performed with a lengthy roster of rock'n'roll celebs, and lent their sweet vocals to countless otherwise dreary commercials. Their collaborations have often been musically dissatisfying, and sometimes downright awful, but whatever else they might do, Ladysmith Black Mambazo have also always been careful to release new material preserving their status as the best group there is at Zulu acapella, or *iscathamiya*.

They owe their initial popularity within South Africa to the beauty of Shabalala's poetry, and the group soon became part of the staple fare on **Radio Zulu**. In 1973, the group released their first album, *Amabutho*, which was a huge success, being the first African LP to achieve official Gold Record status (sales of 25,000 plus). Ladysmith Black Mambazo retained their popularity during the 1970s, but by the mid-1980s the boom was over, with many urban black South Africans dismissing their sound as "hick".

Warner Brothers

Then, just in time, **Paul Simon** heard the group's music, and fell in love with it. Travelling to South Africa, he recorded two tracks co-composed with Shabalala, "Homeless" and "Diamonds On The Soles Of Her Shoes", which subsequently became hits on the album *Graceland*. Simon then brought Ladysmith Black Mambazo with him on his world tour. To the anger of many activists, Simon failed to consult the anti-apartheid movement about this apparent violation of the cultural boycott, then a crucial component of sanctions against South Africa. However, he was subsequently exonerated by the UN anti-apartheid Committee.

Joseph Shabalala with Paul Simon, during the Graceland tour

Though Simon was politically naïve, at least – unlike many – he properly credited his collaborators. In addition, he used his rock icon status to promote Ladysmith Black Mambazo in the international arena, laying the foundation for the group's massive subsequent success.

Ladysmith Black Mambazo have since shown they have the discipline and sheer musical talent to sustain this success, despite having been at times severely tested. Shabalala in particular has suffered many tragedies in recent years, including the brutal murders of close family members, but retains a positive and poetic outlook on life, which apparently precludes any form of bitterness. As well as the music, it is this Mandela-like approach to life that continues to endear Ladysmith Black Mambazo to the world. Despite their advancing age, LBM appear to have years of performance left in them.

SOLTH AFRICA | Popular Music

By the mid-1950s, the pan-tribal audience that had once purchased substantial quantities of *mbube* and *isikhwela jo* recordings by groups such as the Morning Stars and the Natal Champions had fallen away, and interest in Zulu acapella reverted to the hostels. Then, in the 1960s, the audience broadened once again following the establishment of **Radio Zulu**, which gave extensive exposure to Zulu acapella and could be heard throughout Natal, as well as in large areas of the Transvaal and Orange Free State. One Radio Zulu programme was par-

ticularly influential: *Cothoza Mfana*, hosted by Alexius Buthelezi, featured acapella vocal material exclusively. Indeed for a time, the newer, smoother style which superseded bombing was known generically as *cothoza mfana*.

The architects of the Bantu Radio system, and especially its administrative director, Evonne Huskinson, were keen to promote *cothoza mfana* because the style incorporated the secular lyrics that had characterized most Zulu acapella since at least World War I. With a judicious application of influence and suggestion, *cothoza mfana* lyrics could easily be tailored to promote the twin pillars of apartheid: tribal identity and ruralism. A typical example was a radio recording by the New Hanover Brothers subtitled "Hurrying of People In Durban So Disturbed Him, He Caught Train Back Home".

When the record industry at first showed only a minimal interest in *cothoza mfana*, Bantu Radio bridged the gap by recording their own transcription discs, and for many groups these provided a first step before graduating to commercially issued recordings. This was the case with Enock Masina's **King Star Brothers**, the most influential acapella group of the late 1960s and early 70s, who had featured on Radio Zulu for at least four years before they finally landed a contract with Hamilton Nzimande at GRC in 1967. By this time the King Stars' style was called **iscathamiya**, a term derived from the Zulu word meaning "to stalk or step softly", which described the dance routines that the group invented to match their swelling, polished harmonies.

But it was Gallo-Mavuthela producer West Nkosi's signing of another group of Radio Zulu veterans, Joseph Shabalala's **Ladysmith Black Mambazo**, ('Black Mambazo' signifying the 'Black Axe' that would defeat all opponents in group competitions), that transformed the status of Zulu acapella.

Neo-Traditional Styles

While most South African styles evolved against a backdrop of migration to the towns and – with the exception of *mbube-iscathamiya* – have assumed a pan-tribal character, the **traditionally based music** of the **Sotho**, **Zulu**, **Pedi** and **Shangaan** rural areas, adapted to imported instruments, is an important element in South Africa's musical range. Interestingly, too, these neo-traditional music styles – which are usually labelled "Sotho Traditional", "Zulu Traditional" and so on – don't always use the Western seven-note scale. **Sotho** melodies and harmonizations, for instance, are based on a six-note scale where the lead vocal – characteristically a combination of half-sung, half-shouted praise lyrics – is delivered in a rapid, staccato fashion. The actual melody is often most strongly suggested by the response from the chorus voices or instruments.

Sotho Sounds are one such contemporary group. They use homemade instruments based on shepherd's guitars, and have recorded a CD for Real World. They perform regularly at Malelea Londge in Lesotho and have toured internationally with the WOMAD organization.

Sotho and Pedi Traditional

Neo-traditional music has quite a long history. Zulu, Sotho and Xhosa **vocal/concertina records** were produced by several companies as early as the 1930s. They consisted of a basic call-and-response structure with a concertina counterpoint to the lead vocal instead of the former group voices. The concertina became popular after World War I following the large-scale import of cheap foreign models known as *bastari* after a popular Italian brand.

Tshwatla Makala was the first neo-traditional musician of any commercial significance. A Sotho, he used deftly fingered runs on a concertina to counterpoint his vocals and became a mentor to numerous other concertina artists. The next Sotho-Traditional development was a pure acapella style called **mohabelo**; frenetically intoned lead vocals and chanted response choruses, first popularized by the group **Basotho Dihoba**, led by Latsema Matsela, who was born in Lesotho, the source for his music.

A later evolutionary stage of Sotho-Traditional saw the concertina replaced by an accordion leading an electric backing band. Propelled by pounding bass lines and often including multivoice response choruses, these combinations produce a powerful sound. The first LPs appeared in the late 1970s, and **Tau Oa Matsheha** were the first famous group of this type.

The European influence on the principal neo-tradional style of the **Pedi** (related to the Sotho) is suggested by its name, **harepa** (derived from harp). In the nineteenth century, Lutheran missionaries began to proselytize among the Pedi, bringing with them the German **autoharp**. Local musicians soon adapted the instrument to indigenous musical forms, plucking its strings in a single-note fashion to accompany their vocal music. The African call-and-response structure has remained, as have the Sotho-style harmonies – but the characteristic descending melodic lines of *harepa* strike most uninitiated listeners as alien and astringent. The most prolific and successful artist from the 1970s, when there was a little Pedi Traditional harp boom, is probably the Gallo label's **Johannes Mohlala**.

Zulu Traditional

Zulu Traditional followed a unique course by embracing the **guitar**, which had first been introduced by the Portuguese in the sixteenth century. It was compatible with Zulu harmonic practice and became popular after cheap locally made instruments became available in the 1930s. For several decades – though sadly less so today – the sight of a Zulu man with a guitar, picking out a melody while walking along a rural road, was familiar. Among all the different southern African cultures, only Zulus, the related Ndebeles of Zimbabwe and the Shangaan took up the instrument.

The father figure of Zulu Traditional performance and recording is **John Bhengu**, born in central Zululand in 1930. As a street musician in Durban in the early 1950s, he earned a formidable reputation through his skill in adapting indigenous melodies to the guitar, and particularly for his unique fingerpicking style, called *ukupika* (before Bhengu, the guitar was always strummed). His records on the Troubadour label helped establish a standard Zulu Traditional structure that became the model for several generations of performers, each song beginning with the *izihlabo* – an instrumental flourish – followed by the main melody, then interrupted once by the *ukubonga*, a spoken declamation of praise for clan, family, chief or even the singer himself.

In the late 1960s, Bhengu switched from acoustic to electric guitar and adopted a new persona as the sensationally successful **Phuzushukela** (Sugar Drinker). Backed with a full *mbaqanga* production package that included an electrified rhythm section and backing vocals, this led to a golden era for Zulu Trad music in the 1970s. Hundreds of recordings were produced by dozens of bands, constituting some of the most easily assimilable performances in any neo-traditional style.

In the last couple of decades, Zulu traditional music, which is usually referred to as **maskanda**, a Zulu derivation from the Afrikaans word *musikant* (musician), has undergone a further change. The concertina has mounted a surprising comeback and as a foil to the guitar is now a mandatory part of any group, while urban pop has had an influence through increasing electronic instrumentation in the studio, and the usual bass-and-drum rhythms modified to disco patterns. The result is a loss of the roughness that generated much of the style's appeal, though some of the newer stars are awesome. Chief among them are **Phuzekhemisi**, **Ihash' Elimhlophe** and **Mfaz' Omnyama**, whose shows are dynamic affirmations of *maskanda* power with line-ups that include up to a dozen vocalists, instrumentalists and dancers.

Maskanda is seen primarily as the music of rural and migrant worker Zulus, though some artists have made an effort to court the attention of urban black youth. Apparently following pressure from his children to modernize his sound, **Ihash' Elimhlophe** has recorded several albums that successfully incorporate elements of kwaito, including 2003's excellent *Mkhulu*, which features the crossover hit *2010*. However, *maskanda* artists know they have to tread carefully with innovation, since their core audience continues to display no great enthusiasm for change.

Gallo

Maskanda star Phuzekhemisi

Shangaan/Tsonga Traditional

The first **neo-traditional** recordings of the **Shangaan** (a language group of the region bordering Mozambique) were made by **Francisco Baloyi** in the early 1950s for Gallo. These contained call-and-response vocals and a circular structure, descending melodic lines and harmonies which sound more African than European, together with a distinctly Latin rhythm section made up of a guitar and several percussion instruments.

In the 1950s and 60s, **Alexander Jafete** and **Fani Pfumo**, two versatile Mozambicans who played guitar and mandolin with equal facility, made hundreds of recordings for every studio in Johannesburg. Their work included contributions to many jive/*mbaqanga* sessions but they also recorded a large number of "**Portuguese Shangaan**" items that mixed those two elements. After 1975, with Mozambique's independence and revolution, and the opening of a Shangaan station by Radio Bantu, Shangaan Traditional style was largely stripped of its Portuguese components.

The typical line-up of a **modern Tsonga band** ("Tsonga" has replaced "Shangaan" as the favoured designation since the 1994 elections) features a male vocalist leading a female response chorus, an upfront lead guitar and an electric keyboard or synth, with a bass-and-drums rhythm section pounding out a disco beat. The first prominent group with this new sound was **General MD Shirinda & the Gaza Sisters** in the mid-1970s (one of their songs later became "I Know What I Know" on Paul Simon's *Graceland*). Today, the hottest group playing Tsonga Disco (as it is now labelled) is Tusk Records' **Thomas Chauke & the Shinyori Sisters** who have spent around two decades at the top, and are still probably the best-selling group in any neo-traditional genre.

The most successful Tsonga artist of all was the late **Peta Teanet** (who died in 1996, allegedly in a car crash). His style was in fact a combination of urban bubblegum-pop and Tsonga lyrics. As in the case of Shirinda and Chauke, he largely owed his popularity to the relentless promotion of Radio Tsonga which, unlike most other former homelands stations, has continued to champion own-language artists.

Local Soul

In the late 1960s, **American soul music** gained an enthusiastic following among black and coloured township teenagers – Wilson Pickett, Booker T and the MGs, and Percy Sledge were especially popular. The local record industry eventually issued hundreds of 45rpm "seven singles" by local soul outfits sporting names like The Question Marks and The Hurricanes.

Most of this music – typically featuring a Farfisa organ, a spare melodic outline on an electric guitar and a dance rhythm from bass and drums – does not make for inspiring listening. Instrumental performances predominated and where there were vocals, English lyrics were generally preferred to African languages, though they sounded awkward.

In the mid-1970s, when imported US disco music became popular, local soul was easily transformed into local **disco**. Recording techniques, and in some instances the level of musicianship, had improved and more sophisticated keyboards came in. The characteristic disco bass lines and drum beat were grafted onto the bottom end but otherwise the other elements of the soul formula remained much the same. All these developments heralded a revolution in taste which profoundly affected every subsequent township music style.

There was also a generation cleavage (the older township residents disliked soul) which the political events of 1976 widened into an abyss. The spontaneous **uprising** of school children against government authority that marked the beginning of the end of apartheid was soon also directed at township parents and grandparents who were accused of selling out to the system. This political judgement was extended to matters of style and taste, including music. Virtually every pre-soul genre was now regarded by the young with suspicion, not merely for being old-fashioned but indicted as a government-sponsored, tribal opiate. The local audience for *marabi*, sax jives and *mqashiyo*-style *mbaqanga* vanished overnight, never to return. Even an internationally renowned band like the late, great Mahlathini and the Mahotella Queens are now virtually forgotten in their own country, although the latter made a comeback in 2000 with their *Sebai Bai* album on the French label Marabi, and have since maintained a lowish international profile through guest appearances on the *One Giant Leap* project, and most recently on Ernest Ranglin's CD *Alextown*.

The few soul and disco bands that achieved more than ephemeral popularity did so by tampering with the standard musical formulae in some trademark fashion. The most commercially successful were **The Movers**. Discovered and first recorded by Hamilton Nzimande, and then under the tutelage of David Thekwane, their secret was to temper soul with a healthy dose of *marabi*. The organ remained a prominent part of the foundation, but in addition to the usual chord patterns keyboardist Sankie Chounyane played intelligent, jazzy solos. More importantly, The Movers' sound featured prominent saxes, either grouped as a section or playing extended solo lines. And the band had writing ability: their hundreds of recordings included many strong, original compositions, as well as covers.

The second Important Soul band was the **Soul Brothers**, also discovered by Nzimande, in 1975. The Brothers' most distinguishing characteristic was their two-part, almost quavering vocal harmonies, inspired by certain Shona vocal groups popular in Zimbabwe in the early 1970s. Otherwise, the band's saxophones and their rhythm section were more reminiscent of the later type of electric bass *mbaqanga* than of archetypal soul.

The Movers' complicated style defied easy imitation and in any event David Thekwane's reputation was enough to make any would-be close imitators somewhat wary. In contrast, the Soul Brothers spawned literally dozens of ephemeral clones, most of whom contented themselves with attempting their vocal style and organ accompaniment. Today the Soul Brothers are regarded as one of the country's oldest groups (although only two remain from the original line-up) and they remain active both in the studio and on tour. Despite a high level of synthesizer saturation, their style is now referred to as *mbaqanga*, proof positive of the

White South African Music

The major influences on modern **Afrikaner music** – as with Black South African music – have been American. While Afrikaner musical roots lie with Dutch and French sources, **hillbilly string bands** added the final ingredients to a concertina-led brand of dance music which began to be recorded in the early 1930s. Within the Afrikaner community there was also a decided predilection for imitating the most mawkish and maudlin elements of American **country music**. In the 1930s, a legion of melancholic duos and trios specialised in **trane trekkers** (tear jerkers) and the same sentimental tendency was still very much in evidence among a later generation of artists influenced by the American Jim Reeves (massively popular amongst Afrikaners). There are, of course, clear parallels between the experiences of Afrikaners and whites in the American south.

The growing nationalist fervour of Afrikanerdom after World War I revealed a class-based musical fault line. The audience that preferred concertina dances and trane trekkers was agrarian or urban working class. In contrast, most Afrikaner nationalists came from a more educated, middle-class background, with musical prejudices fashioned by European culture. Traditional melodies were championed as the true voice of the "volk" but were acceptable only if rendered in "serious" performance.

The musician who dominated the postwar years was accordionist **Nico Carstens** with his lightly swinging dance music. The trend thereafter was to incorporate MOR sounds, then later in the 1970s, Eurobeat. Afrikaner music lost much of its distinctiveness in the process, as well as most of its young audience, who – like the English-speaking whites – increasingly preferred European pop and rock.

For most of the 1980s and early 90s, the general state of the music was exemplified by the most – indeed almost the only – commercially successful Afrikaans entertainer of the day, **Bles Bridges**, a Wayne Newton imitator whose trademark was throwing plastic roses at his predominantly middle-aged female audiences. An exception to this blandness was offered by a small, subversive "alternative" movement led by journalist **Johannes Kerkorrel**, who with musicians **Koos Kombuis** and **Anton Goosen** formed the Gereformeerde Blues Band. Kerkorrel has been called the Bob Dylan of white South Africa and his satirical songs, which mocked the stolid Afrikaner mind-set, were regularly banned by the authorities.

Since the 1994 elections, Afrikaner music has undergone something of a revival. The shock of losing political power has led to a grave concern that the language and culture of the Afrikaner is going to wither away and die unless concerted efforts are made to preserve them. A new crop of young Afrikaner artists is currently enjoying commercial support from their community for the first time in many years. They include **traditional boeremusiek** revivalists, closely associated with Afrikaner right-wing politics, and all-acoustic, traditional Afrikaner **orkes** such as **Oudag Boereorkes** who have recorded several albums and occasionally appear at overseas festivals. For the most part, though, Afrikaans music is stylistically conservative and continues to be based on MOR, pop, or modern country models from overseas.

One very different Africaner strand is represented by **Johnny Clegg**, who began performing Zulu-Traditional material with **Sipho Mchunu** in the early 1970s, then later expanded into a full electric band format as **Juluka**. The increasingly Westernized sound eventually led to Mchunu's departure and the band dissolved to be replaced by a new line-up called **Savuka**. Clegg has enjoyed major success in France as 'Le Zoulou Blanc', and a more limited popularity in the UK and America. While much of his music sounds predominantly Western, and his group's image remains highly dependent on their energetic Zulu dance routines, there's no denying Clegg's commitment to freedom during the darkest days of apartheid, when his open embrace of African culture was an audacious statement.

Plenty of other interesting performers have emerged in recent years, but most are working in genres whose local variant has little that is distinctive or unique about them. These include popular rockers **Springbok Nudegirls**, punk band **Fokkofpolisiekar**, weird indie band **Boo!** and loud punk poet **Karen Zoid**.

Ralph Resnik/Safari Records

Sipho Mchunu and Johnny Clegg

all-encompassing elasticity of that label.

The Cannibals, starring the young guitarist **Ray Phiri** (now famous through recording and performing with Paul Simon), achieved recognition playing instrumentals under their own name and backing various Gallo *mqashiyo* artists such as Irene Mawela and the Mahotella Queens. In 1975, the band was paired with Jacob "Mpharanyana" Radebe, probably the single finest male vocalist of the soul-disco era. Four years of recordings followed (until Radebe's death in 1979) under the name **Mpharanyana and the Cannibals**, and the best of these, featuring Radebe's impassioned vocals and monologues together with a sharply produced backing of hot guitar, saxes and female choruses, invite favourable comparisons with Otis Redding's similar-sounding Stax material. The Cannibals eventually evolved into **Stimela** in the 1980s, updating their style with more contemporary Afro-jazz soul and funk influences.

Sipho "Hotstix" Mabuse \tarted out with the Afro-rock band **Harari**, which managed to develop a big multiracial following, and subsequently reached local superstar status in the later 1980s with huge hits like "Burnout" and "Jive Soweto" (the latter featuring West Nkosi on sax) which finally achieved a seamless, totally South African, synthesis of *mbaqanga*, pop and soul.

Bubblegum

The development of township music from the mid-1980s to the mid-1990s saw the ascendency of a slickly produced brand of African pop referred to by its fans and detractors alike as **bubblegum**. In certain respects, bubblegum was basically an indigenous style – more vocal than instrumental, with the vocals arranged as overlapping call-and-response patterns where one short melodic phrase is repeated in traditional fashion. In others, it reflected the culmination of more contemporary tendencies. The modern love affair with electronic keyboards now triumphed completely; bubblegum was awash with synthesizers and even the modified disco beat which propelled the music was usually produced by an electronic drum box. Saxophones were rarely heard, while the guitar fell completely out of favour.

The longest-running success story in the genre has been vocalist **Dan Tshanda**. Beginning with his first group, **Splash**, Tshanda assumed total creative control as a composer-producer and then went on to develop a number of equally popular spin-offs including the Dalom Kids, Patricia Majalisa and Matshikos, whose recordings still sell in quantities. Another long-running star is **Sello 'Chicco'**

Twala, who like Tshanda is an all-round vocalist, instrumentalist, arranger, composer and producer, most notably of Brenda Fassie. One of his biggest hits, "We Miss You Manelo", was a coded tribute to the then-imprisoned Nelson Mandela. A later piece of political commentary which also became a hit, "Papa Stop The War", resulted from a collaboration with **Mzwakhe Mbuli**, where the almost hypnotic spoken cadences of the "people's poet" were set against Chicco's collage of synth textures and backing vocals.

Chicco contributed in the late 1980s to the success of "The Princess Of Africa", **Yvonne Chaka Chaka**. "I'm In Love With A DJ", her first single in 1984, was one of the first big bubblegum hits and launched a career that produced a string of gold and platinum discs. Chaka Chaka's belting alto voice with its distinctive timbre accounts for much of her popularity, but her success is also due to her unusually well-crafted and arranged material and her willingness to perform throughout the continent, which has won her many fans, particularly in Francophone Africa. In 1997, she recorded her finest album to date, *Bombani*, and, significantly, sales in the UK and Europe outstripped those in South Africa, pointing to the increasing gulf between the tastes of younger township music fans and African music consumers overseas.

Apartheid straitjacketed South African music, as it did the whole society, and when the strait-

Jak Kilby

Bubblegum belter Yvonne Chaka Chaka

Brenda Fassie – Africa's Pop Goddess

Brenda Fassie, South Africa's very own pop goddess, was born in Langa township, Cape Town, in 1964, and died in Sunninghill Hospital, Johannesburg forty years later. The death of Brenda, or Ma Brrrrrr as South Africa affectionately nicknamed her, came at the end of a two-week coma following a drug overdose. The event became a national prayer vigil and visitors to her hospital bedside included Nelson Mandela, his ex-wife Winnie, current president Thabo Mbeki, and countless other celebrities and friends. People prayed in churches, radio phone-ins, bars, shebeens and clubs, but to no avail. Brenda, it seemed, had partied and performed too hard for just too long.

Jak Kilby

Judgemental religion is big in South Africa, and there are not many people who approve of crack-addicted lesbians. Yet she was truly loved – a measure both of how profoundly South Africans appreciate music that touches their hearts, and how truly brilliant she was.

Although Brenda was easily South Africa's biggest pop star, she still had her critics. The sticking points seem to be the often tinny drum machine rhythms, the lack of virtuosity from her musicians, and the rather cheesy feel. Yet this is a feature of nearly all South African township pop since the 1980s, when disco took off and Casio synthesizer keyboards became affordable by the black community. The sound caught on, and even today many black South Africans prefer their music tinny.

So while drum machine programming on most of Brenda's songs is poor, her music has several great strengths. Foremost of these is her voice, which though not particularly sweet, has exceptional range and immense emotional power, enabling her to express both the pain and defiance of township South Africa. While her lyrics could be banal, at their best they were sharply observed, laced with outrageous asides, delivered in the latest, most inventive and bizarre township slang (often dreamed up by Brenda herself).

During her "**bubblegum**" years in the 1980s, Brenda scored some huge hits, including the classic anthem "Weekend Special", about the life of a woman waiting in mid-week to be the weekend girlfriend of a married man. Undoubtedly, however, her best music came during the late 1990s and early 2000s when her producer, **Sello "Chicco" Twala**, crafted exactly the right sound for her. Together, often in the midst of Brenda drug binges, they produced a string of classic recordings, drawing creatively on a range of homegrown musical styles, including *mbaqanga*, gospel (complete with full-throated backing singers) and housey *kwaito*. Hits included the massive "Vul' Ndlela", as well as "Nomakanjani", "Thola Amadlozi", and (just before her death) "Ntsware Ndibambe".

Live, Brenda was a gamble. She adored crowds, especially ones that adored her, and could deliver astonishing performances that drove them wild. Sometimes however – particularly towards the end – the adulation mixed badly with what was happening backstage, and Brenda would become unstable and petulant, repeatedly demanding to know from the crowd whether it really loved her.

Such histrionics were largely reserved for South African audiences. When Brenda performed elsewhere in Africa, she played it straight, winning for herself an enormous new fan base across the continent. Interestingly, Brenda had a particular liking for Congolese music, perhaps because she spent so much time in the Johannesburg suburb of Hillbrow, where many Congolese lived, and cut a tune with **Papa Wemba** on her 1996 album *Now Is The Time*.

Brenda's funeral was a national event. Ten thousand people gathered on a sports field for the ceremony, where a stage was packed with every South African singer worth their salt, plus Mbeki and much of his cabinet, while in front of it was displayed Brenda's fabulously over-the-top gold coffin. At one point, the crowd surged through the barriers and a fatal crush seemed inevitable until the barriers were removed. The crowd poured into the gap and Mbeki took the microphone and cajoled them all into sitting down. The show went on, no-one was hurt, and in the end everyone had a chance to say how much they loved her – Ma Brrrrr could not have wished for better.

jacket started loosening in the 1990s, remarkable diversity bloomed. In contrast to most African countries, where record companies have to market only a handful of music categories – imported, local pop, traditional and gospel would be a typical combo – in South Africa music executives have had to dream up dozens of genres to try to capture and sell the mix, and even then there are problems, particularly since artists are ever keener to work in a variety of styles. There's not space for everything here, and so inevitably, there are many omissions both in terms of artists and genres. Instead, what follows is an in-depth look at contemporary styles that set South Africa apart in the musical world, starting with the most important one – **kwaito**.

Kwaito Kulture

Although what it means gets less and less clear, **kwaito** is one of the most important contemporary genres. It started off when local DJs at township street bashes began slowing the tempo of **US Chicago House** recordings by artists such as Robert Owen, The Fingers and Tony Humphries, and found that young black people – unlike the mostly white rave and trance crowd – responded positively to the new beat.

Early kwaito (in the early and mid-1990s) was mostly a pretty sparse affair, with much of the sound borrowed from the bubblegum music it gradually displaced, though with less emphasis on the keyboards and more attention given to the drum and bass. There was plenty of dross, but much of the kwaito of this era was excellent and can still cut it today. Killer tunes include Chicco's "Ubaba uyajola", "Jakalas" by **Tsitsibana** and "Ding Dong" by **Joe Nina**.

Defying predictions from its detractors that it was too shallow and insubstantial to last, kwaito not only survived but matured in the late 1990s and early 2000s, when a number of artists emerged capable of whole albums' worth of good material. One of the best of these groups was **TKZee** featuring **Zwai** and **Kabelo**, who combined some excellent tunes with a fine sense of style, picking up on the increasingly open and opulent materialism of the emerging black middle class. **Bongo Maffin** was another of the better kwaito outfits, blending the stirring female vocals of **Thandiswa Mazwai** with the raw Jamaican-style ragga male vocals of Zimbabwean ex-pat **Appleseed**. In the grand tradition of British 1970s pomp rockers, Bongo Maffin released *The Concerto* in 1998, dividing the tracks into three "movements". As a whole, the album does not live up to its portentous billing, but contains gems nonetheless including "Thath'isigubhu"

("Take The Drum"), which quickly established itself as one of the great South African dance tunes.

Looking good has always been an important part of kwaito, and two groups who took that further than most were **Aba Shante** and **Boom Shaka**. Both were sexy female trios, happy to strut their stuff on stage and video. Boom Shaka's most famous song must be their controversial 1998 rendition of the national anthem *Nkosi Sikelela* (which Mandela disapproved of). Otherwise, Boom Shaka's music was unexceptional, but their outfits and dance routines were always superb. Much the same could be said of Aba Shante, who nonetheless scored a deserved hit in 1999 with "Vuk'unzenzele" ("Wake Up And Do Your Own Thing"). Aba Shante were one of the many groups produced by **Arthur**, the self-styled "king of kwaito", who also released

Thandiswa Mazwai – Africa's Lauryn Hill?

Gallo

The Divas

Apartheid reserved its worst for black women, pressing upon them highly constrained and exploitative economic relations, which for most meant either being dumped in homelands to provide free family support for migrant workers, or being prevented in townships from doing anything much except teaching and nursing black people and doing domestic work for whites. When the apartheid shackles came off, black women were quick to take creative advantage of the new possibilities, and have been steadily making their mark in nearly every once white-male-dominated field.

In the music industry, a crop of stylish and talented young black female singers has emerged since 1994, some of whom have already notched up considerable experience in the business. Former Bongo Maffin female vocalist **Thandiswa Mazwai** is perhaps the most prominent of these divas, her high profile aided by the lavish promotion and attention accorded her first solo album *Zabalaza* (2004). Pre-release publicity made much of the two weeks that Thandiswa spent in an Eastern Cape village with Xhosa roots music *grande dame* **Madosini**, and several of the tracks on *Zabalaza* draw superbly on traditional Xhosa music.

Less culturally aware, but just as feisty, have been **Thembi** and **Lebo Mathosa**, who both came out of Boom Shaka to release solo albums. Lebo hit platinum in 2001 with *Dream*, and after some delay, in 2005 released the follow-up *Drama Queen*. Thembi released *S'Matsatsa* in 2001, which sold reasonably well, though she has achieved more prominence by acting a lead role in the TV drama *Gaz Lam*, as an up-and-coming young singer in big, bad Johannesburg.

Another young diva in the kwaito/R&B mould is **Mshoza**, who released the superb debut album *BullDawgz First Lady* in 2001, featuring the killer track "Kortes". Since then, unfortunately, Mshoza seems to have gone off the boil, and her follow-up album *Bhoza* was a disappointment. **Simphiwe Dana**, on the other hand, is going from strength to strength. This diminutive young Xhosa singer burst onto the scene in 2004 with *Zandisile*, a haunting and stylish mix of traditional sounds and contemporary jazz. Simphiwe is excellent live and was a particular crowd favourite at Cape Town's annual international jazz festival in 2005.

Mezzo-soprano and composer **Sibongile Khumalo** represents a very different kind of diva. Best known as an award-winning opera singer – and as the voice behind the national anthems at the 1995 Rugby World Cup finals – there are many sides to her musical character. Like Oumou Sangaré and Tarika's Hanitra, Sibongile's mission is to develop an authentic, indigenous canon of recital songs. She draws her music from diverse sources, working with choral composers like **Motsumi Makhene**, jazz composers such as **Themba Mkhize** (who is often her arranger) and the late **Moses Molelekwa**, and others active in popular and traditional music and gospel. She has also been active in introducing the original songs of the late **Princess Constance Magogo DInIzulu** to contemporary audiences. On one memorable occasion at the Market Theatre, she even covered pop diva Brenda Fassie's first hit "Weekend Special".

Sibongile Khumalo

with thanks to Gwen Ansell

a number of popular tunes of his own, including the provocative "Don't Call Me Kaffir" in 1995 and the mindless but fun "Oyi Oyi" in 1997. Arthur's brother **Makhendlas** was also a fine kwaito star, until his tragic death at a concert.

White South Africans have never really warmed to kwaito, but have made an exception for **Mandoza**, who achieved a massive crossover hit in 2000 with "Nkalakatha", which still receives extensive airplay on predominantly white as well as black radio stations. Mandoza, a former jailbird who used to perform with popular kwaito stars **Chiskop**, has a gruff, macho shouting vocal, to which his astute producer **Gabi Le Roux** adds a kind of hard-rock stomp backing capable of being grasped by even the most clod-footed dancer. Another successful shouter is **Zola**, who shot to fame when he played the gangster Papa Action in the hip TV drama *Yizo Yizo*, and currently hosts his own popular TV show. Although the tunes are often not up to much on their own, Zola's lyrics are more thoughtful than most, and he is not afraid to experiment either, even including Zionist gospel music on some albums.

Since 2000, kwaito has moved on, with perhaps the most popular trend being towards more conventional house music and trance. In too many instances, unfortunately, the results of this quest for an "international" product are bland, but there are a few exceptions. **Brothers of Peace** are one of the better kwaito/house groups, and, if you can handle the metronomic doof-doof beat, their most recent effort *Life 'Iskorokoro* makes for compelling listening. The other premier group in this category is **Alaska**, whose last album *The Return* contains some fine tracks. Also deserving mention are two Durbanites calling themselves **Revolution**, whose 2004 album *Another Level*, featuring contributions from jazzers like **Jimmy Dludlu**, **Pops Mohammed** and **McCoy Mrubata** was one of the best releases of 2004. Meanwhile, much of the best South African trance comes courtesy of the **MELT Music** label, and particularly *Sanscapes Volumes 1&2*, which feature Kalahari Bushmen vocals and instrumentation, intriguingly mixed and blended by top trance DJs.

The other main kwaito trend since 2000 has been to go **retro**. Here, the prime exponents are the hugely successful trio **Mafikizolo**, most of whose biggest hits, such as "Ndihamba Nawe" ("I'm Going With You"), draw on old-style *kwela* or *mbaqanga* beats, and who complete the effect on stage and video by wearing stylish retro clothing. Tragically, one of the trio, Tebogo Madingoane, was shot dead during a late night altercation at a traffic light in Soweto in 2004, and Mafikizolo's subsequent release *Van Toeka af* showed the group to be sorely missing his creative input. **Malaika** have also adopted the retro formula to considerable commercial, though debatable artistic effect, while another retro-man of note is **MXO**, whose mellow, loved-up 2004 album *Peace Of Mind* is heavily influenced by 1970s funk and soul. Since leaving TKZee, **Kabelo** has also explored the funk-*kwaito* connection, with at times irresistibly dance-inducing results, though his latest offering *And the Beat Goes On* – while pleasant enough – was rather short on ideas.

Urban Roots

Sitting alongside South Africa's neo-traditional music is another related genre, best described, perhaps, as urban roots. Like their neo-traditional counterparts, urban roots musicians draw heavily on South Africa's indigenous cultures for

Conscious ballads – Vusi Mahlasela

their inspiration, but unlike the neo-traditionalists, infuse a sophisticated urban sensibility to their sound, giving it a smoother feel and more appeal for city and international audiences. One veteran musician in this mould is **Jabu Khanyile**, who released the superb *Mmalo-we* in 1994, and *Umkhaya-lo* the following year with his group Bayete. The two albums feature strong production, beautiful melodies, his trademark floating vocals and great lyrics. He has been pretty prolific since but never quite seems to match the quality of his mid-1990s output.

Ringo is another urban roots star who peaked in the mid-1990s. Originally from Cape Town, he won the slightly tacky national "Shell Road to Fame" talent competition back in 1986 with the group Peto, but later moved to Johannesburg, releasing his first solo album *Vukani* in 1996. His second album, *Sondelani*, went double platinum, with the title-track, the slow-moving love anthem "Sondela", becoming a big, big hit and confirming Ringo's heart-throb status for thousands of adoring female fans. Ringo seemed to lose focus after this, and subsequent releases have lacked bite, though *Baleka*, released in 2004, showed signs of a return to form.

One urban roots singer who just seems to get better and better is **Busi Mhlongo**. A Zulu with a strong sense of her roots, Busi has been around for quite a while, recording in London in the 1970s with exiled South African jazzers like **Dudu Puk-wana** and **Julian Bahula** before moving to Holland for much of the 1980s. Her first solo album *Babemu* was released on a Dutch label in 1993, and showed potential, though the production was often perverse, smothering Busi's fat *maskanda* basslines with dollops of stodgy keyboard. Busi's switch to MELT Music shortly afterwards proved an inspired choice, and she delivered the excellent and well-titled *Urbanzulu* in 1999. Here at last, the production was immaculate and entirely appropriate, perfectly showcasing her powerful roots talents. **Indiza**, released in 2002, mostly consisted of fairly forgettable dance remixes of Busi's earlier work, but *Freedom*, which came out a year later, was a phenomenal album, beautifully conceived and stylishly executed.

Another stalwart of the music scene is **Vusi Mahlasela** who began performing in the late 1970s. Vusi, who is from Pretoria's Mamelodi township, joined a poets', musicians' and actors' co-op in 1981 called 'Ancestors of Africa' which soon ran into trouble with the security forces. This sharpened his political consciousness and led to him joining the openly pro-ANC Congress of South African Writers in 1988. As a result, Vusi began playing at rallies, where his beautifully sung ballads formed a poignant counterpoint to the angry tirades of political activists. His first solo album, *When You Come Back* (1992), is a true classic, and his second *The Wisdom Of Forgiveness*, released in the key election year of 1994, provided strong artistic support to the dominant theme of Mandela's theme of forgiveness and reconciliation.

Roots guitarist **Madala Kunene** began his career busking on Durban's beachfront, before going professional in the 1970s. In 1993, he released his first solo album, *Freedom Countdown*, produced by legendary jazzman **Sipho Gumede**, following it up with the excellent *K'onko Man* in 1995. Over the years, and thanks to his many and eclectic collaborations, Kunene has grown hugely as a musician, retaining his Durban Zulu roots, but branching out in some intriguing and inspiring directions. His 2002 collaboration with the late **Baba Mokoena Serakoeng**, entitled *First Double*, was one of his best – inventive, soulful and entrancingly beautiful. Small wonder Mandela once told him: "I wish you could play for me everywhere I go".

Though hardly urban roots bands, **Moodphase 5ive** and **Freshlyground** also combine old and new school sounds to innovative and at times impressive effect. Both are from mellow Cape Town, and their line-ups are a rainbow mix of young, black, Coloured and white hipsters. Fronted by the talented singer **Zolani Mahola**, Freshlyground are the more influenced by World Music of the two: making liberal use of feel-good *mbaqanga* riffs, mbira and fiddle folk melodies. Moodphase 5ive take a lot of their inspiration from drum'n'bass, and use turntables as well as instruments in their live sets, but also draw sufficiently from homegrown musical traditions to have a distinctively and refreshingly South African feel.

Cape Hop

Hip-hop is a global phenomenon in which South Africa, which has always looked to the US for cultural inspiration, is a keen participant. As seems true almost everywhere else, local hip-hop has been an ideal vehicle for frustrated ghetto youth to get things off their chest, usually formulaically but occasionally with originality and wit. Since much of it is largely copied from the US, it is fair to ask why anyone from the outside should be interested in South African hip-hop. Aficionados would give two reasons: first, that the music and its lyrics provide unique insight into what is going on in the country's many forgotten ghetto regions, and second, that amongst all the dross there is some genuine innovation. One of the most interesting developments is the increasing tendency for Coloured hip-hop artists from Cape Town to rap in Afrikaans, the first language of not just Afrikaners but also most Coloured people in South Africa's Western Cape.

A sharp distinction is drawn by the local hip-hop community between **commercial** and **underground** artists, though which groups fit into which category is hotly contested. The difference seems to be that commercial artists have record contracts with established companies and therefore allegedly water down their lyrics to suit corporate sensibilities, while underground artists jealously guard their integrity, preferring to control the production and distribution of their music themselves.

Hip-hop's South African standard-bearers are undoubtedly Cape Town's **Prophets of Da City**, who released their first album *Phunk Phlow* in 1994. Although they have a recording contract with a major and an international touring track record, even hardcore underground fans seem to have time for the Prophets, who have remained lyrically innovative and mostly steered clear of tedious hip-hop clichés. Another commercial outfit that has retained underground credentials is the well-named female trio **Godessa**, while the commercially successful **Skwatta Kamp** get shorter thrift from underground purists. **Brasse Vannie Kaap** are another well-known, engaging and successful outfit who are often dissed by hip-hop fans, for allegedly parading outdated clichés of Cape Coloured life. Those

369

Reggae

Reggae also took root in Africa, following Bob Marley's famous concert celebrating the independence of Zimbabwe in 1980. **Lucky Dube** dominated the local reggae scene for years, following the enormous success of his 1990 album *Slave*, which sold over 500,000 copies. Dube started out playing *mbaqanga* in the 1970s, switching to reggae in 1984, and has since remained firmly in this pre-ragga mode, with lilting beats and a vocal delivery modelled closely on that of Peter Tosh. Dube's most recent releases show him to have lost touch with his original constituency, singing his heart out about such matters as the high taxes he has to pay these days. The local scene has moved on, and among the new prime movers are the excellent Cape Town label **African Dope Records**, founded by drum'n'bass maestros **Krushed and Sorted**, who have discovered and released an impressive array of reggae, drum'n'bass and other artists, including Godessa, Moodphase 5ive, and, most recently **The Real Estate Agents**.

most rated by underground purists include Cape Town's **Parliament**, **Wildlife Society**, **Fifth Floor**, and **Lions of Zion**, who as their name suggests blend hip-hop and reggae, along with **Basement Platform** from Johannesburg.

DISCOGRAPHY   South Africa | Popular Music

Many of these releases are Gallo recordings issued in South Africa either by Gallo Record Company itself or by Polygram South Africa's Teal subsidiary. However, some are also available on the labels of overseas licensees – usually BMG (UK), Celluloid (France) or Shanachie (US).

⊙ **African Dope Soundsystem**
African Dope Records, South Africa
Compilation from the Cape Flats of mostly ragga beats, with slices of acid jazz and jungle thrown into the mix for good measure. Featured artists chant out in an intriguing mix of Jamaican patois and English, Xhosa and Afrikaans slang on Babylonian oppression, South African style.

⊙ **All the Hits (Vols 1–5)**
EMI, South Africa
Pretty comprehensive selection of hits from EMI's CCP label's considerable stable of local pop artists. Includes Brenda Fassie, Mandoza, Ringo, Doc Shebeleza and many, many more.

⊙ **Amandla!: A Revolution in Four-Part Harmony**
BMG, South Africa
Soundtrack to the movie of the same name, tracing the role of music through the years in the struggle against apartheid. Many of the featured artists are established stars, such as Abdullah Ibrahim, Vusi Mahlasela, Miriam Makeba, Hugh Masekela and Sibongile Khumalo, and there are also fine contributions from lesser-known luminaries such as the Pretoria Central Prison choir.

⊙ **Expressions: Words Unlimited**
Outrageous Records, South Africa
Fine compilation of hard-hitting contemporary SA hip-hop, featuring partly commercial artists and partly their underground counterparts. "It Is Wonderful" by H20, featuring a hookline from an old Ella Fitzgerald song is precisely that… wonderful.

★ **From Marabi to Disco**
Gallo, South Africa
A one-stop compendium of the history of urban township music as it developed in South Africa from the late 1930s to the early 80s. Every major genre is illustrated with original, long-unavailable recordings of the most famous artists (as well as a few who have dropped off into an undeserved obscurity). Twenty-eight tracks and every one a classic!

⊙ **The Indestructible Beat of Soweto Vol 6: South African Rhythm Riot**
Earthworks, UK
This collection features *mbaqanga*-jive, maskanda and kwaito, with Brenda Fassie's huge 1999 hit "Vuli Ndlela", hardcore trad Zulu maskanda from Ihashi Elimhlophe; kwaito king Arthur Mafokate's biggest hit "Oyi Oyi"; plus gospel songs, *mbaqanga*-jive stars Chicco, Mahlathini and the Mahotella Queens, the Soul Brothers and more.

⊙ **!Ingubi Tietie**
MELT Music, South Africa
Beautifully recorded original songs of the Kalahari Bushmen, produced by jazz legend Pops Mohammed. For once, label blurb about this being the "very roots of trance" is not wrong. Enchanting stuff.

Jackpot 15,000
Jackpot 16,000
Gallo, South Africa
Two cassette compilations of classic 1960s and 70s hit singles from producer Hamilton Nzimande's roster of sax and accordion jive.

⊙ **The Kings and Queens of Township Jive**
Earthworks, UK
A showcase of some of the big names in township music from the 1970s.

⊙ **Mbube Roots**
Rounder, US
A wonderful survey covering the history of *mbube* and early iSulu acapella or *iscathamiya*.

⊙ **The Rough Guide to The Music of South Africa**
World Music Network, UK
An essential collection ranging from Ladysmith Black Mambazo to West Nkosi; from the Boyoyo Boys to Bheki Mseleku; from Noise Khanyile to Yvonne Chaka Chaka and back to the Elite Swingsters. Miriam Makeba is here, as is Lucky Dube and half a dozen other bands and artists. There's even a track by Solomon Linda's Original Evening Birds singing "Mbube".

⊙ **Sanscapes: Future Visions of the Bushmen Vols 1–2**
MELT Music, South Africa
Trippy stuff from the ever-innovative **MELT Music** label, giving the music of the Xo San Bushmen (and women) the full trance treatment, courtesy of a range of DJs and mixers.

⊙ **Singing in an Open Space**
Rounder, US
The only neo-traditional historical survey, charting two decades of development of Zulu-Trad from simple acoustic guitar accompaniment to a full band format.

⊙ **Siya Hamba! 1950s South African Country & Small Town Sounds**
Original Music, US
A mix of neo-traditional (even a Pedi autoharp!) and early township jive, recorded by musicologist Hugh Tracey (see Southern Africa Archives chapter).

⊙ **Street Bash Vols 1–3**
Teal, South Africa
Excellent compilations of classic kwaito from the mid 1990s, but they are getting hard to find. Grab one if you see one!

⊙ **A Taste of The Indestructible Beat of Soweto**
Earthworks, UK
This is a sampler compiled from the first five volumes of the *Indestructible Beat of Soweto* series, which highlights over fifty great tracks from the 1980s, mixing later-phase mbaqanga, some soul and even the more urbanised of the neo-traditional genres.

⊙ **Yizo Yizo 1–3**
Ghetto Ruff, South Africa
Useful samplers of the indie side of the contemporary kwaito music scene. The tracks, which feature groups like Skeem, O'Da Meesta and Ghetto Luv, come out of the controversial *Yizo Yizo* TV series, the first in South Africa to realistically portray contemporary township life from a youth perspective.

Alaska

One of the best housey kwaito outfits around, though their drum-programming skills could use an upgrade.

⊙ **Most Wanted**
Sony, South Africa
Three killer tracks on this 2000 release, which seems to be as much as one can ask, from these smooth-dressing amaGents.

⊙ **The Return**
Sony, South Africa
The follow-up to *Most Wanted*, released in 2002. The compositions are weaker than previously, but the production is stronger, giving it a fuller sound on the dancefloor.

Amampondo

This impressive "back to the roots" group draws its inspiration from a multitude of indigenous styles, both instrumental and vocal, from all over southern Africa.

⊙ **Drums For Tomorrow**
MELT Music, South Africa
At last, a magnificently produced showcase of Amampondo's diverse musicality that manages to overcome the inadequate recording technique that plagued the group's earlier albums.

Bongo Maffin

One of the best *kwaito* groups to have emerged in the late 1990s, blending the potent female vocals of Thandiswa Mazwai with the ragga-style roughness of Appleseed.

★ **Bongolution**
Sony, South Africa
Released in 2001 as the follow-up to *The Concerto*, and the last before Bongo Maffin's constituent parts went their separate ways, this is a much stronger album, and gave the band a massive hit with the perky, uptempo "The Way Kungahkona".

Brothers of Peace

Perhaps the best house/*kwaito* outfit in South Africa, working a fine range of indigenous sounds and melodies into the basic thudding format.

⊙ **The D Project: Life 'Iskorokoro**
Sony, South Africa
Some great tunes in this, the Brothers' fourth album, not least the title-track. A *skorokoro* is a car that's in such dodgy shape that it cannot be driven outside the township, while the notion that life in general can be like this is inspired indeed.

Reuben Caluza's Double Quartet

Reuben Caluza was one of the first South Africans to meld local and American vocal styles into a new secular composite called "ragtime" (absolutely no relation to the American piano-based style) that anticipated the later development of *mbube* and Zulu acapella or *iscathamiya*.

⊙ **1930s – African Ragtime**
Heritage, UK
This album provides a good cross-section of Caluza's landmark 1930 London recordings and comes with translations and excellent notes by Veit Erlmann.

Yvonne Chaka Chaka

Chaka Chaka, the self-styled "Princess Of Africa", is one of the finest and most popular vocalists to come out of the bubblegum genre. Her songs are built around melodies and arrangements which are usually far more interesting and compelling, at least to a Western ear, than those found in most bubblegum material.

The Best of Yvonne Chaka Chaka
Teal-Polygram, South Africa
This album features all of Yvonne's biggest hits, including "I'm In Love With A DJ", "Umqombothi" and "Motherland".

Bombani
Teal-Polygram, South Africa
Chaka Chaka's latest offering laces local township pop with Afro-Pop influences to wonderful effect (a sensible decision given her popularity in Central and East Africa).

Chicco

Sello "Chicco" Twala, has been one of the biggest names in bubblegum through the 1990s, and a talent equally adept at singing, composing or producing.

The Best of Chicco
Teal-Polygram, South Africa
A compendium of Chicco's most popular recordings including, "We Miss You Manelo", his paean to the then-imprisoned Nelson Mandela.

Simphiwe Dana

A very promising young Xhosa singer with a strong sense of her cultural heritage and good taste in smooth jazz too.

Zandisile
Gallo, South Africa
Dana's first solo album has been well received by the critics and public alike, and is certainly executed with composure and panache. It sometimes feels a little ponderous, but maybe success will loosen Dana up in future recordings.

Lucky Dube

Lucky Dube won African and global attention as a reggae star with his early 1990s albums, *Slave* and *Prisoner*, which were South Africa's topselling discs of the decade.

Prisoner
Shanachie, US
This 1991 album – still Dube's best – is a kind of homage to Peter Tosh in its vocal style and Wailers-era arrangements. But the rasta message of liberation and suffering gained new currency in a South African context.

Ihash' Elimhlophe

Ihash' Elimhlophe has made more effort than his *maskanda* peers to update his sound and keep the youth listening, while remaining true to his musical roots.

Mkhulu
DCC, South Africa
Much of the album is fairly standard maskanda fayre, but in a number of tracks Ihash' Elimhlophe has made a real effort to modernize his sound, and some of the results are remarkably good.

Brenda Fassie

The country's greatest pop star, who died a tragic death in 2004. Nearly every album is worth getting, though what follows is arguably the cream of the crop.

★ Memeza
EMI, South Africa
One of South Africa's greatest pop albums, featuring Brenda's biggest ever hit, "Vul' Ndlela". There are some other great

tracks too, including haunting gospel melodies like the beautiful "Sum' Bulala".

Amadlozi
EMI, South Africa
One of Brenda's most innovative albums, combining her trademark *mbaqanga/kwaito* dancefloor killers, soaring gospel, and Congolese-style *kwassa kwassa*.

Mali
EMI, South Africa
The last album Brenda recorded before she died, it has a more subdued, subtler groove than most of her work. A stunning cover too, showing that Brenda was a fashion queen to the end.

Kabelo

This former TKZee star has stayed in the limelight since leaving the band, both for his music and his high-rolling habits. His favoured persona is a Snoop Dogg-style "ghetto fabulous" pimp, but that aside, he has been responsible for some of the best *kwaito* around over the last few years.

Everybody Watching
Primedia, South Africa
Released in 2000, this is probably the best of Kabelo's solo albums, and includes the funky township rude boy anthem "Pantsula 4 life".

Jabu Khanyile and Bayete

Jabu Khanyile and his group Bayete found fame in 1994 with his attractive lisping growl on the glorious hit "Mmalo-we". The drummer and singer presents himself as the face of World Music from South Africa – whacking out a powerful, confident mix of urban roots and other African sounds.

Mmalo-we
Mango, UK
A strong selection of dance hits and ballads from the gentle Jabu, with Bayete on cracking form, effortlessly exploring a fine selection of Afro-Jazz riffs. It kicks off with the hit title-track.

Africa Unite
Mango, UK
Mellow backing singers and an innovative instrumental line-up – including *kora*, harp, violin and Cuban *tres* (a small guitar with three pairs of strings).

Madala Kunene

Former busker from Durban who has blossomed at the MELT Music label, taking Zulu roots music in wonderful new directions.

WITH BABA MOKOENA SERAKOENG
First Double
MELT Music, South Africa
A particularly fine Kunene album, released in 2002, low key, but combining beautifully executed *maskanda*, old-style *mbaqanga*, ballads, jazz and more.

Ladysmith Black Mambazo

The soaring acapella harmonies of this dozen-strong Zulu male choir were propelled by Paul Simon's *Gracelands* album into the international limelight, putting their *iscathamiya* style on the World Music map. They have recorded dozens of albums of their own: the two below serve nicely as ports of entry to a recording career as it has evolved over almost three decades.

⊙ The Very Best Of Ladysmith Black Mambazo
Nascente, UK
Excellent and informed compilation of LBM from the early days to the late 1990s.

★ Raise your Spirit Higher
Wrasse, UK
Astonishing 2003 comeback album after some dodgy collaborations. This extra-length UK version actually includes material from two albums. After a shaky rap by leader Joseph Shabalala's grandsons, Ladysmith get down to what they do best; unadorned *iscathamiya*. Hypnotic and compelling, it's a magnificent testament to the healing power of music

Sipho Mabuse

Soul artist Sipho 'Hotstix' Mabuse – a vocalist, composer and multi-instrumentalist – first tasted fame as a member of The Beaters and Harari before becoming a local solo superstar in the 1980s.

⊙ The Best of Sipho Mabuse
Gallo, South Africa
Mabuse's two essential hits "Jive Soweto" and "Burnout" are nicely packaged on this ten-track compilation.

Madosini

Madosini Manquina, known as "The Veteran" in the area of Mpondoland-Transkei from which she hails and more recently as the "Queen Of Xhosa Music", is an entrancing vocalist who accompanies herself on several indigenous instruments.

⊙ Power To The Women
MELT Music, South Africa
Robert Trunz of Melt Music showcases Madosini's artistry with sympathetic and imaginative production techniques – the result is a wonderful exposition of tradition enhanced by technology.

Mafikizolo

One of the most popular bands of recent years, and deservedly so, mixing *mbaqanga*, *kwela* and *kwaito* to great effect, spiced with some excellent lyrics.

★ Sibongile
Sony, South Africa
Classic album, including the hit kwela tune "Marabi" and the *mbaqanga* dancefloor giant "Ndihamba Nawe". Highly recommended.

⊙ Kwela
Sony, South Africa
Follow-up to *Sibongile*, employing much the same formula but with some nice new touches added. "Kwela Kwela", featuring Hugh Masekela, is particularly good. Alongside all the dance tunes there is also a great ballad, "Emlangeni".

Vusi Mahlasela

Sweet-voiced urban roots man Vusi Mahlasela mixes jazz, folk and *mbaqanga* to create an Afro-pop style that's easy on the ear, and has proved especially popular with European audiences.

⊙ The Wisdom of Forgiveness
BMG, South Africa
Released in 1994, this is one of Vusi's earlier recordings, but also one of his best, celebrating the advent of democracy with gentle, uplifting ballads.

Mahlathini and the Mahotella Queens

The combination of Simon "Mahlathini" Nkabinde's groaning bass and the exquisite female harmonies of the Mahotella Queens, backed by the all-electric Makhona Tsohle Band, forged the template for vocal *mbaqanga*, one of the characteristic styles of the townships for almost two decades.

⊙ Young Mahlathini: Classic Recordings With The Mahotella Queens 1964–71
Gallo, South Africa
All the greatest hits of the band which was the contemporary equivalent to The Beatles in a South African township context.

⊙ The Best Of Mahlathini And The Mahotella Queens
Gallo, South Africa; BMG, UK
A fine selection of highlights culled from later albums recorded after the band reformed in the late 1980s and began touring the world.

Makhendlas

Kwaito star Oupa "Makhendlas" Mafokate was born in Diepkloof, Soweto, and released his first solo album in 1996. *Jammer*, his third album, was his first big hit but he died in tragic circumstances in November 1998, first shooting an aggressive fan backstage at a concert, and then turning the gun on himself.

⊙ Jammer
EMI, South Africa
A disc that features the massive hit "Ayeye Aho", which catapulted the natty-dressing Makhendlas to a spell in the kwaito limelight in 1998.

Mandoza

This rough-voiced *kwaito* shouter has enjoyed huge crossover success with rock fans, largely thanks, it seems, to his astute producer Gabi Le Roux.

⊙ Nkalakatha
EMI, South Africa
Most of the album is unremarkable, but the title-track, which still receives heavy airplay on SA radio stations, is a stomping winner.

⊙ Godoba
EMI, South Africa
The album uses much the same formula as Nkalakatha, but also branches out, quite successfully, into gospel. The title track is good, but "50/50" is even better, and has proved a perennial dancefloor success.

Spokes Mashiyane

Spokes Mashiyane was the first and probably the most famous pennywhistle jive star.

⊙ King Kwela
Gallo, South Africa
This is a reissue of a classic 1958 Trutone LP originally produced for the white teenage market, featuring Spokes' most popular early recordings (including his first hit, "Ace Blues") as first issued on 78s for the African trade.

Thandiswa Mazwai

Ex-lead vocalist of Bongo Maffin, Thandiswa has since gone solo and risen to prominence as one of the country's foremost young rootical musical divas.

⊙ **Zabalaza**
Gallo, 2004
Innovative, well-hyped though somewhat underwhelming debut album, featuring lilting Xhosa melodies and contemporary urban sounds.

Mzwakhe Mbuli

Mbuli emerged on the ANC scene in 1981, with poetry recitals at activists' funerals. Performing at President Mandela's inauguration was the highlight of his career, but he subsequently served a jail term, controversially convicted of armed robbery – and was released in 2004.

⊙ **Resistance Is Defence**
Earthworks, UK
⊙ **UMzwakhe Ubonga UJehovah**
EMI, South Africa
A pair of albums tracing Mzwakhe's musical development, from the fiery political commentary of *Resistance Is Defence* to the gospel music of his latest album. The poetry is all set to stirring, if sometimes over-formulaic, *mbaqanga* beats.

Busi Mhlongo

One of the main urban roots singers active in South Africa today, whose recorded output has really benefited from the care and attention given her by the MELT Music label.

⊙ **Urbanzulu**
MELT Music, South Africa
The musical centre of this album is the (near) exclusively all-male *maskanda* genre. Here Mhlongo returns to her Zulu roots and stakes out the territory for her gender with an awesome display of intense vocal pyrotechnics, aided and abetted by MELT's usual superlative production values.

★ **Freedom**
MELT Music, South Africa
Arguably even better than *Urbanzulu*, this is a great album, full of powerful roots material, beautifully performed and produced.

The Movers

The Movers played a combination of local soul and African Jazz and sold more records in the process than any other South African band of the 1970s.

⊙ **The Best of the Best Vol 1 and Vol 2**
Teal-Polygram, South Africa
All the Movers' biggest hits on a couple of strong compilations. Vol 2 is worth getting just for the wonderful track "Soweto Inn" with vocalist Sophie Thapedi.

Mpharanyana

Jacob "Mpharanyana" Radebe was the finest township soul singer of the 1970s, and became a legend, dying young at the height of his career.

▦ **Burning Soul**
Teal-Polygram, South Africa
A nice introduction to some of the many great Mpharanyana recordings. The vocalist was usually backed by one of two fine bands, The Peddlars and The Cannibals (the latter with a young Ray Phiri on guitar), and many tracks feature cracking production work by West Nkosi.

MXO

Up-and-coming singer who has already carved out a successful niche as a mellow, loved-up funky groover.

⊙ **Peace of Mind**
Sony, South Africa
MXO's debut album, and a pretty good one at that, mixing soulful and sometimes passionate lyrics with laidback funky beats, all spiced with distinctive South African flavours.

Shiyani Ngcobo

All the big *maskanda* stars are from northern KwaZulu Natal, but Ngcobo is from the south coast, bringing a mellower, subtropical sensibility to the genre.

⊙ **Introducing Shiyani Ngcobo**
Sheer Sound, South Africa
A beautifully recorded contemporary roots album, and because it's all acoustic, Ngcobo's wonderful guitar-picking sound can be heard properly, undrowned by thumping bass and drum beats.

West Nkosi

West Nkosi, who died in 1998, is remembered today as an ace producer but he began his career in the l960s and 70s as one of the most successful sax jive artists.

⊙ **Rhythm of Healing: Supreme Sax and Pennywhistle Jive**
Earthworks, UK
This collection of West Nkosi's biggest hits will not only serve as a great introduction to sax jives, the single most popular African genre of the 1960s and 70s, but is also guaranteed to get any dancefloor hopping.

Mfaz' Omnyama

Along with Phuzekhemisi and Ihash' Elimhlophe, Mfaz' Omnyama is one of the great maskanda stars.

⊙ **Ngizebenzile Mama**
Gallo, SA
"I've been working Mum" promises Mfaz' Omnyama in the

PLAYLIST
South Africa |
Popular Music

1 VUL' NDLELA Brenda Fassie from *Memeza*
Brenda's biggest-ever hit, with a great lyric about two gossips at a wedding, set to a classic rousing *mbaqanga* beat.

2 THATH' ISIGUBHU Bongo Maffin from *The Concerto*
Great feel-good *kwaito* number, perfect for line-dancing, township style.

3 KHULA TSHITSHI LAMI Busi Mhlongo from *Freedom*
Haunting Zulu ballad, beautifully arranged and produced, from a true maestro of urban roots.

4 NDIHAMBA NAWE Mafikizolo from *Sibongile*
Surely one of the all-time great South African dance tunes, from one of the most potent groups on the kwaito scene today.

5 NKALAKATHA Mandoza from *Nkalakatha*
Definitive stomp rock/kwaito combo that was a huge and deserved crossover hit for Mandoza on release in 2000, and is still very popular.

6 LELILUNGELO ELAKHO Ladysmith Black Mambazo from *The Very Best of*
Characteristically exquisite vocal delivery from Joseph Shabalala and crew, with a subtle and poetic lyric too.

7 MBUBE Solomon Linda's Original Evening Birds from *From Marabi to Disco*
Recorded in 1939, and unquestionably one of the great South African tunes, frequently plagiarised but never bettered. Linda never received any money from the covers – most famously that in Disney's musical, *The Lion King* – in his own lifetime, but a South African law case finally won rights and payments for his family in 2006.

8 IT IS WONDERFUL H20 from *Expressions: Words Unlimited*
Contemporary South Africa shows it still deliverys with this lovely tune that re-works an old Ella Fitzgerald line, adding mellow, well-paced hip-hop lyrics.

9 KUKE KWAGIJIM' IVENI Mfaz' Omnyama from *Ngisebenzile Mama*
A superb example of the Zulu *maskanda* style, ultra-masculine, yet graceful and melodic.

10 SONDELA Ringo from *Sondelani*
One of the finest South African love songs of the modern era, beautifully rendered by Xhosa heart-throb Ringo.

title track, and so he has, cooking up a storm in this, as in all his many other releases.

Phuzekhemisi

Phuzekhemisi is one of the most successful of the current crop of artists in the *maskanda* field.

⊙ **Amakhansela**
Gallo, South Africa
Any Phuzekhemisi album you find is worth a listen, and this is a particularly good one, featuring his trademark fingerpicking *maskanda*, wonderful lyrics, hearty backing vocals and thumping beats.

Revolution

Durban house/*kwaito* duo increasingly rising to prominence on the basis of their first album, and with plenty more up their sleeves for the future.

⊙ **Another Level**
Universal, South Africa
Revolution's first album, and a good one too, working from a house base complete with metronomic doof-doof beats, but building jazz and traditional sounds into the mix.

Ringo

Ringo Madlingozi possesses a great tenor voice with a timbre and phrasing that recall the jazz singer, Victor Ndlazilwane. He's also a fine composer and his records are surprisingly popular with the younger kwaito crowd.

⊙ **Sondelani**
CCP, South Africa
This very successful album actually begins to run out of steam at about the halfway mark but it's still worth getting just for the first six songs which are both melodic and memorable, especially the third track, "Sondela".

Skeleton

Skeleton are a real roots *maskanda* group from Durban. Their lead singer, Themba Ngubane, lives in one room in a hostel with his wife and nine children, has a job in a fast-food restaurant and puts up with a violent environment which brings him few opportunities to play.

⊙ **Skeleton**
MELT Music, South Africa
One of this energetic label's most accessible new releases. Pumping tracks of *maskanda* – the hard, dance beat sound of modern-traditional Zulu – surge with power and added animation from MELT labelmates Busi Mhlongo and Mabi Thobejane.

Soul Brothers

The Soul Brothers are both the longest-surviving and most influential band to come out of the South African soul genre although as time went on their style was increasingly lashed with generous dollops of straight *mbaqanga*.

⊙ **Jive Explosion**
Earthworks, UK
A great survey of the band's recordings from the early 1990s, full of swirling organs, sax riffs and sweet vocal harmonies.

TKZee

One of the *kwaito* supergroups of the mid-to-late 1990s, combining the portly Kabelo's pimp hustler style and Zwai's clean-cut image to some effect.

★ Halloween
BMG, South Africa

By far the best TKZee album, released in 1998 and featuring the superb kwaito anthem "Dlala Mapantsula", and many other hits besides, including the mellow and melodic Johannesburg anthem "We Love This Place".

Zola

Zola hit the TV screens as a bad, bad gangsta in the drama series *Yizo Yizo* but has since transformed himself into the people's friend, helping make chosen viewers' dreams come true. His *kwaito* is mostly average, but he is capable of real inspiration and innovation.

⊙ Mdlwembe
Ghetto Ruff, SA

A number of strong tracks on this album from 2001, including the anthemic "Ghetto Scandalous" and the superb gospel tune "Mzioni".

⊙ Bhambatha
Ghetto Ruff, South Africa

Zola's latest and best-produced release, which has being selling strongly since it came out in 2004.

South Africa | Jazz

hip kings, hip queens

Miriam Makeba
Jon Lusk/Redferns

The decade between World War II and the late 1950s produced a classic era of jazz in South Africa, establishing a base unique in Africa that has continued to produce great singers and players. Rob Allingham and Gwen Ansell chart the connections, talk to the major figures and listen to the current state of play.

The postwar era was a time of tremendous growth and innovation for Africans in all the arts, and it corresponded to a substantial increase of population in the townships as migrants poured in from the rural areas to take jobs in a rapidly expanding industrial economy. Living conditions remained sub-standard or desperate for many, but before the draconian structures of the new apartheid system were fully implemented, township residents indulged themselves with a certain reckless optimism and even an illusion of permanency and belonging.

Some black South Africans had long looked to what they called "Africans in America" for aspirational models against the tribalism, traditionalism and ruralism idealized by colonialism and, after 1948, enforced by apartheid. Jazz crystallized sophisticated urban and political aspirations – but there was more. Trumpeter **Johnny Mekoa** expresses it well: 'This was our music and these were our black heroes … but also, it sounded a bit like our own music.' Middle-class urban Africans before apartheid were developing a strong social and economic base: many had benefited from a broad mission education and some were freeholders, owning their own property. They enjoyed the cinema and classical and choral music, homegrown vaudeville (called Concert and Dance), ballroom dancing and jazz. Residential segregation placed them cheek-by-jowl with their much poorer neighbours. Out of this mix came the jazz society of the 1940s and 1950s, associated with suburbs like Cape Town's **District Six** and Johannesburg's **Sophiatown** and immortalised on the pages of black illustrated magazines like **Drum**.

Swing

In the cities and ports, US jazz on record was available, and avidly collected by black fans and players. They kept up to date with US trends, but clung on to swing long after it was being displaced in the US by R&B and bebop. Unlike earlier African American music, which had been transmitted directly by visiting performers, no early American jazz or swing player, black or white, toured South Africa (the first, Tony Scott, arrived much later, in 1956). Printed orchestrations, films and recordings provided the sole source of inspiration. South Africa's awareness of swing, however, had come through Allied soldiers during World War II, who brought with them records of the latest swing band hits from Britain and the US.

By 1950, most South African towns supported at least a couple of local jazz bands. The cities of

Cape Province – East London, Port Elizabeth and Cape Town – were particularly jazz-oriented, perhaps because of their predominently Xhosa populations: the complex harmonies and structures of traditional Xhosa music may have helped to foster an intuitive understanding of jazz harmony and improvisation.

But, as usual, it was in **Johannesburg** that the cutting edge of innovation was keenest, and where musicians found the greatest number of bands and the biggest audience. The city's "Concert and Dance" circuit had earlier spawned Solomon "Zulu Boy" Cele's **Jazz Maniacs**, the archetypal African jazz band of the late 1930s. After World War II, the equally influential **Harlem Swingsters** were active for several years. Alumni from both bands went on to create other groups, some of which remained popular for another two decades.

Alto saxophonist-composer **Isaac "Zacks" Nkosi** from the Jazz Maniacs, together with tenor man **Ellison Temba** and trumpeter **Elijah Nkwanyane**, helped make up the front line of the **African Swingsters**; the same group of musicians also recorded under many other names such as the Country Jazz Band and the City Jazz Nine. Another ex-Maniac, tenor saxophonist **Wilson "King Force" Silgee**, led the **Jazz Forces**. **Ntemi Piliso** left the Harlem Swingsters to form the **Alexandra All Stars**, thus initiating an important career as a tenor soloist, composer and bandleader.

Players had long applied an indigenous approach to their swing music: weaving in licks from traditional and popular tunes and composing their own swing-style standards. A main source was **marabi**, the earliest syncretic urban style of the 1930s, based on a I-IV-V chord progression and basic instruments. **Cele** is credited with applying the swing band line-up, and voicings alternating the call and response of brass and reeds to this format. By the late 1940s, as apartheid became the law, nationalist players revisited those African roots, deliberately developing a more original, adventurous style they dubbed **African jazz**, or **mbaqanga**.

Frequently this included extended solos, ranging from restatements of the melody (sometimes simple, sometimes highly ornamented) to imaginative, technically advanced and challenging excursions. By the late 1950s, urban players say they were struck "like a thunderbolt" by the first bebop discs they heard. In settings like the Odin Cinema and the arts centre at Dorkay House in Johannesburg, players experimented and improvised – most famously, clarinettist/altoist **Kippie Moeketsi**.

The Jazz Singers

The 1940s and 50s was also the great era of **female African jazz vocalists**, many of whom modelled their style on the likes of Ella Fitzgerald or Sarah Vaughan, but like their instrumentalist counterparts, sang what were essentially *marabi*-structured melodies.

The late **Dolly Rathebe** was the first to come to prominence as the leading actress-singer in the first African feature film, *Jim Comes To Jo'burg* (1948). She also starred in the superb *Magic Garden* in 1951, and as "The Queen Of The Blues" retained her fame and popularity for another decade. Next in the spotlight was Zimbabwean **Dorothy Masuka**, who began her sensational career as a vocalist and recording artist in Johannesburg in 1951. Like Dolly Rathebe, Masuka was also a famous cover girl in the black picture press.

Male jazz singers were a far less common breed, but there were a number of male vocal quartets. The best known of these was the **Manhattan Brothers** led by Nathan "Dambuza" Mdledle, whose celebrity matched Rathebe and Masuka. Although regarded as part of the local jazz firmament, the Manhattans' roots lay in a slightly different African-American tradition: the secular-pop branch of close-harmony singing that antedated jazz and later developed alongside it in a parallel fashion, eventually producing groups like the Mills Brothers and the Inkspots and then later still, doo-wop. Philemon Mokgotsi's **African Inkspots** offered the Manhattans some stiff competition until the mid-1950s, when the **Woody Woodpeckers** led by **Victor Ndlazilwane** eclipsed both groups with their striking mixture of Xhosa-traditional and American jazz-influenced melodies and harmonies.

Miriam Makeba was the last singing star to come out of this classic jazz era, and the most significant. She first came to public attention as a featured vocalist with the Manhattan Brothers in 1954, then left to record with her own all-female **Skylarks** vocal group while touring the country with impressario Alf Herberts' **African Jazz & Variety**, a talent vehicle which launched the careers of many black artists. In 1959, Makeba took on the female lead in *King Kong*, the South African-Broadway musical crossover billed as a 'jazz opera' with a fine score by pianist-composer Todd Matshikiza. Sharing the top billing was Nathan Mdledle of The Manhattans. To circumvent apartheid regulations, which rigidly segregated public entertainment, it was often staged at universities. where this slice of township life electrified its audiences, black and white alike.

Miriam Makeba with the Manhattan Brothers

At the very apogee of this success, Makeba left the country for the United States. There she quickly re-established her career with "The Click Song" and "Phatha Phatha" and transferred her celebrity status to the international stage, the first South African to do so. She also fired an opening salvo in the external battle against apartheid with her impassioned testimonial before the United Nations in 1963. The South African government, irritated by the glare of adverse publicity, responded by revoking her citizenship and right of return. After her marriage to Stokely Carmichael, one of the leaders of the Black Panthers, she was also harassed by the American authorities and, despite support from Marlon Brando, Nina Simone and others, fled to exile in Guinea.

Makeba was only the first exile of many. In 1961, *King Kong* was staged in London where it enjoyed a successful run. And after the show closed, many of the cast – including the four Manhattan Brothers – chose not to return. The outward rush of South Africa's artistic talent had begun.

Progressive Jazz: the 1960s

In the 1960s, South African jazz divided into two distinct strains, similar to the dichotomy affecting American jazz in the immediate postwar years. On the one hand, the *marabi*-style dance bands still commanded a large following and a new African Jazz band, the **Elite Swingsters**, began a long and distinguished career by recording "Phalafala", probably South Africa's biggest selling jazz disc ever. On the other, a new type of jazz was evolving that emulated the American avant-garde led

Mama Africa – Miriam Makeba

Over more than half a century as the continent's best-loved diva, **Miriam Makeba** has earned the nickname "Mama Africa". It's an accolade that reflects not merely the emotional warmth of her singing but her indomitable spirit, for during the darkest years of apartheid nobody better epitomized township music's unique ability to offer hope and joy in the face of the deepest tragedy and adversity.

She began her singing career with the **Manhattan Brothers** in 1954 before leaving to record with the all-female group **The Skylarks** and to tour with the review African Jazz and Variety alongside singers such as **Dolly Rathebe** and **Dorothy Masuka**. It led to her being cast as the female lead in the township-based jazz opera *King Kong* and when the show was booked to tour England in 1959, she signed on – a decision that led to her not being able to return to the land of her birth for more than 30 years.

Under the patronage of **Harry Belafonte** she relocated to America, achieving international recognition both for her singing and for a stirring address to the United Nations on the evils of apartheid, which resulted in the South African government revoking her citizenship and right of return.

Her private life was at times troubled and her husbands included **Hugh Masekela** and the Black Panther activist, **Stokely Carmichael**. In exile she moved restlessly between America, Europe and Africa, making her home for a while in Guinea and singing as the new, post-colonial continent took shape, criss-crossing Africa but never able to return home. She sang in Nairobi at Kenyan independence, in Luanda at Angolan independence, in Addis Ababa at the inauguration of the Organisation of African Unity and in Mozambique for Samora Machel. Finally she returned to South Africa in 1990 at the personal invitation of Nelson Mandela after his release from prison.

There's a joyous purity and innocence about her early recordings and songs such as "Pata Pata" and the "Click Song". But in truth, her musical output has been patchy. Few of her two dozen-plus albums are consistently great and most have mixed knockout tracks with sentimental ballads. Yet it hardly matters. Her voice, her dignity and her strength have combined to make her an iconic figure who has inspired every other female singer on the continent. She is Mama Africa – a name not invented as part of some cynical marketing campaign but conferred by the masses, although the tag has since been given an official air after President Thabo Mbeki named her South Africa's Goodwill Ambassador to the rest of the continent. We shall not see her like again.

Nigel Williamson

by Thelonious Monk, Sonny Rollins and John Coltrane, and which strove for a more self-conscious artistry. It also incorporated an overtly political dimension as protest music, a wordless assault on apartheid and all that it symbolized.

Despite the fact that it was essentially elitist and indeed less "African" than its *marabi*-based counterpart, this jazz on the American model became, indeed remains, inexorably identified with the people's struggle. Trumpeter **Hugh Masekela**, trombonist **Jonas Gwangwa**, pianist **Dollar Brand** (aka **Abdullah Ibrahim**) and that most forward-thinking of the older generation of jazzmen, **Kippie Moeketsi**, constituted the core of the progressive first wave. Masekela and Gwangwa had played together as teenagers in the **Father Huddleston Band** (named after their mentor, the famed English anti-apartheid Anglican priest) before graduating to the **Jazz Dazzlers**, a small band that included Moeketsi and provided the instrumental accompaniment to *King Kong*.

In 1959, **John Mehegan**, a visiting American pianist, organized a famous *Jazz In Africa* recording session, featuring Masekela, Gwangwa and Moeketsi. This produced the first two LPs by African jazzmen and the first opportunity to overcome the time restraints imposed by the three minute-a-side 78rpm format. After Mehegan's departure, Capetonian Dollar Brand arrived to take over the piano. The resulting formation, now called the **Jazz Epistles**, recorded another album and garnered a great deal of critical acclaim for its performance at the first **Cold Castle National Jazz Festival** in 1960. But not long afterwards, both Masekela and Gwangwa left for the United States – where they would remain in exile for another three decades – while Brand eventually made his way to Switzerland and international jazz renown, in 1962.

The departure of three of the principal Epistles left a large gap in the local jazz scene, but the 1962 *Cold Castle Jazz Festival* demonstrated that a new generation had been inspired by their example. Pianist-composer **Chris McGregor** and tenor saxophonist **Dudu Pukwana** were probably the most famous and influential musicians in this new wave. Kippie Moeketsi remained an inspiration and **Gideon Nxumalo**, an older pianist-composer who like Moeketsi had grown up in

the Harlem Swingsters, blossomed into a particularly original talent.

The best players from several different bands which had performed at the 1963 Cold Castle Festival were gathered together under the direction of Chris McGregor, and produced a classic LP,

Still Grazin': Hugh Masekela

After a tempestuous and volatile career, the once volcanically angry Hugh Masekela has emerged in the post-apartheid era as the benign and avuncular elder statesman of South African music. After cutting the first album by a black South African jazz band in the late 1950s, Masekela fled with his trumpet into exile – like so many of his generation – where he remained for 30 years. Upon his return to South Africa in 1990 he was, by his own admission, impatient and bitter.

Yet as he approaches the twilight of his long career, he has mellowed, dedicating much of his time and energy to fostering the emergence of new South African talent and writing a reflective, revealing and life-affirming autobiography (*Still Grazing: The Musical Journey of Hugh Masekela*, 2004). 'The book was an opportunity to try to apologize to the people whose heads I stepped on during my way up and through my madness,' he said following its publication. '…the best thing I can do now is to encourage a new generation of talented people to come through.'

True to his word, his 2005 album *Revival* found him giving the spotlight to an array of young kwaito-influenced singers and producers such as **Zwai Bala**, **Corlea** and **Malaika**, while on his last tour of Britain he talked animatedly of an ambitious plan to put together an international touring showcase for emerging pan-African talent.

Columbia

Few are better placed to bring it off, for after his ex-wife Miriam Makeba, the veteran trumpeter remains the Rainbow Nation's best-known cultural ambassador on the international stage. During his time in exile he flirted with pop success in the 1960s, appearing at the Monterey festival with Jimi Hendrix and Janis Joplin, playing on the Byrds' number one hit *So You Want To Be a Rock'n'Roll Star* and scoring an American number one under his own name when his *Grazin' In The Grass* knocked the Rolling Stones' *Jumpin' Jack Flash* off the top spot. Into the 1980s he appeared on Paul Simon's groundbreaking *Graceland* album and was even afforded the accolade of an hour-long "in concert" broadcast on BBC station Radio One, when African music was briefly considered fashionable around the time of the Nelson Mandela 70th birthday tribute at Wembley.

Now approaching 70 himself, he has in recent years reduced his international touring with the result that his infrequent appearances have assumed the status of events rather than mere concerts.

Nigel Williamson

Hugh Masakela

Jak Kilby

Dudu Pukwana blowing for freedom

Jazz: The African Sound, perhaps the finest single product of a brilliant era. Sadly, it also proved to be a swansong. A general wave of oppression had followed the Sharpville massacre of 1960 and, as the government dug in with its new order, many of South Africa's best talents fled into exile.

The progressive jazzers were badly affected as apartheid regulations designed to separate mixed-race bands and audiences became increasingly onerous. In the face of this dispiriting onslaught, McGregor, Pukwana and their entire band, **The Blue Notes**, including **Louis Moholo**, left the country for good in 1964. The Blue Notes, and their later manifestation the **Brotherhood of Breath**, added a distinctive touch to a rather stale UK jazz scene but, as was the case with other exiles, their influence on musical development in South Africa ceased at that point.

Meanwhile, Back Home

Repression and censorship scarred the jazz scene the exiles had left. With broadcasting fragmented

after 1960 into tight, ethnically-exclusive boxes (Radio Zulu, Radio Xhosa etc collectively dubbed Radio Bantu) record companies colluded with the authorities to eliminate syncretic, politically suspect musics. White censors ruled on what could be played.

Yet the music continued. Open-air jazz festivals were sponsored by liquor companies when prohibition for blacks was lifted; these extended the public visibility of the music. A festival hero was guitarist **Phillip Tabane**, who, working with percussion and reed players, created a sound blending indigenous Venda and Pedi spirit music with jazz chords and improvisation.

Both old-style *marabi*-based bands and modern progressive jazz outfits continued to seek what space they could. The former, determined not to be displaced by the rise of small, cheap, guitar-based pop groups, introduced electric rhythm sections and continued to score hits with extended dance tracks that often took up a whole LP side, such as the Elite Swingsters' "Now Or Never".

The latter felt more pressure. Bands such as **Tete Mbambisa's Soul Jazzmen**, **Shakes Mgudlwa's Soul Giants** and various outfits featuring saxophonists **Winston Mankunku Ngozi** or **Duke Makasi**, and trumpeter **Dennis Mpale** played intense, improvised modern jazz with a message. Coltrane disciple Mankunku's "Yakhal'Inkomo" ("for the black man's pain," he says) sold an estimated 100,000 units in 1968.

The soulful, funky mood of US hard bop found its equivalent in bands like **Henry Sithole's Heshoo Beshoo Band**, inspired by its wheelchair-bound guitarist **Cyril Magubane**. These players were also responding to the new vibe of the townships, where Soweto Soul – funky pop music accompanied by assertive styles of dress (dashikis, Afros) and Black Power salutes – was on the rise, in bands like **Sipho "Hotstix" Mabuse's Harari**.

By the 1970s, sophisticated but unlicensed township music clubs – most famously The Pelican in Johannesburg's Soweto, and Club Galaxy in Cape Town's Rylands – were giving space to this new music, and independent record labels like **Rashid Vally's Kohinoor** (later The Sun/As Shams) were releasing it. Kohinoor was the label on which Dollar Brand (on a brief return to African soil) recorded "Underground in Africa" and his major hit "Mannenberg: a Tribute to a Cape Township". This had started life as a *marabi* classic, was given the big-band treatment by bandleader Zacks Nkosi, and was reborn again in this slower, passionate version which gave its reed soloist, **Basil Coetzee**, his enduring soubriquet.

These musics were primarily urban. Traditional sounds and *marabi*-based African jazz still ruled the rural areas. But jazz players could cross the divide, as pianist **Lionel Pillay** did with his hit "Plum and Cherry" and Heshoo Beshoo – now **The Drive** – with "Way Back Fifties".

An avant-garde was developing too, in bands like **Gilbert Matthews' Spirits Rejoice**: "a bit of free jazz, a bit of jazz-rock and our own music too," said one of its players, saxophonist Kaya Mahlangu. But after the Soweto Uprising of 1976, censorship tightened and spaces for performance closed up further: not only mixed audiences but any large gathering became suspect. Jazzmen did session work, or backed pop artists. Times were tough, jobs were few; those who kept jazz alive did so at immense personal cost.

The world's response to apartheid repression was the consolidation of the cultural boycott. Jazz players disliked the isolation, but concede that it once more forced them to look inside themselves, at indigenous sources of inspiration. Despite limited performance and broadcasting opportunities, bands like The Drive (until it was decimated by a road accident) and the much younger **Sakhile** maintained the project of drawing on both African roots and developments (in this case, fusion) in the international jazz world.

Formed in 1981 by graduates of Spirits Rejoice, Harari and Malombo, Sakhile (We Have Built) was probably the most musically sophisticated of the groups trying to craft a modern indigenous sound, but there were many others, including **Sankomota**, **Bayete** and the racially mixed **Tananas** as well as avant garde outfits like **Carlo Mombelli's Abstractions** (which featured Makasi and magnificent guitarist **John Fourie**) and Cape saxophonist **Robbie Jansen's Estudio**. Independent record labels – Kohinoor had now been joined by Lloyd Ross' **Shifty** in Johannesburg and Paddy Lee Thorpe's Mountain in Cape Town – released their sounds; the majors were still obediently doing what apartheid playlisting demanded. While jazz fought for space with the burgeoning pop music industry, there was a high degree of audience crossover: in the townships, people were likely to groove to both **Brenda Fassie** and Bayete. **Music schools** (Funda and FUBA in Johannesburg and MAPP in Cape Town) taught jazz skills alongside black culture and history. And when the United Democratic Front was formed to unify political resistance in 1982, the band that played at its launch was the *marabi* revivalist **African Jazz Pioneers**, seen as embodying the cultural spirit of the nation.

New South Africa

The transition to democracy removed the segregation and censorship that had bedevilled jazz. It also opened South Africa to a tsunami of international pop music which the industry was ill equipped to deal with. Jazz's record of resistance won it great esteem – but not many resources.

Nevertheless, several developments have helped indigenous jazz survive. While the majors were slow to respond to the new environment, a fresh crop of indy labels, most notably **Sheer Sound** and **MELT**, were quick to record music reflecting the new mood. The two pioneering albums were piano-led: *Finding Oneself* by **Moses Taiwa Molelekwa** and *Trains to Taung* by **Paul Hanmer**. Molelekwa, a brilliant young pianist who took his own life tragically young, fused strains of *marabi* and the complex polyrhythms of Pedi indigenous music with phrasing and improvisation inspired by, among others, Herbie Hancock. Capetonian Hanmer drew in a pan-African groove, with guitar and drums from Zimbabweans **Louis Mhlanga** and **Jethro Shasha**.

With the airwaves freed, independent **radio stations** like Kaya-FM, P4 and FMR offer general and specialist listeners generous jazz and well-informed DJs, and state radio stations all have their (now liberated and diverse) jazz slots – usually on Sunday mornings. Specialist jazz magazines have found it harder to survive. **Jazz clubs** such as the **Bassline** in Joburg's Newtown and **Club Mannenberg** in Cape Town follow the model of the pioneering **Kippie's**, closed after more than a decade in 2004 when its foundations collapsed. **Jazz schools**, such as Johnny Mekoa's Gauteng Jazz Academy and the National Arts Festival's summer school, the **National Youth Jazz Festival**, in Grahamstown, as well as university music departments (Durban was the pioneer) teach the skills. And jazz festivals, such as the national Joy of Jazz circuit and the Cape Town International Jazz Festival (founded as the sister event of the Netherlands' North Sea Jazz Festival) provide platforms.

But as in the rest of the world, jazz is now an elastic definition, and most of these events and institutions need to stretch it wide, into smooth, hip-hop and even pop, to ensure revenue.

The new jazz itself embraces many voices: the country's top-selling jazz artists stretch from guitarist **Jimmy Dludlu**, whose George Benson-inspired vocalizing over the strings is spiced with Mozambican marrabenta rhythms, and saxophonist **Zim Ngqawana**, who uses traditional Xhosa sounds alongside ferocious free

Zim Ngqawana

On stage, reedman Zim Ngqawana is a big presence: tall, broad and with a fondness for flowing African robes. The first South African jazz player to score with music that is often fearlessly avant-garde, his music outsells many popular, dance-oriented jazz players.

Yet however adventurous his approach – performances can involve a motor-horn, a harmonica, vocalization in the deep Xhosa tradition and poetry as well as sax, piano and the rest of a jazz quartet – his music is always grounded in the experience of his audience. 'Music isn't just notes. Every note has a social meaning. I'm singing my mother's knowledge of the plants that grew around her, and my father's religion.'

Born in 1959 in the Eastern Cape, Ngqawana began his career playing flute for a reggae cover band. Drawn to jazz, he played in a late version of Pacific Express in Cape Town before going to university, finally studying under Darius Brubeck (son of Dave) at Durban. A performance at the 1988 Detroit IAJE Conference opened up scholarship opportunities, and Ngqawana studied further with Archie Shepp, Yusuf Lateef and Max Roach and played in the Amherst Graduate Band.

Heads Up

'When I was leaving, my master Max Roach, embraced me at JFK and reminded me our responsibility is to preserve our cultures. My goodness! I realised I didn't know anything about his culture – or about so-called African culture either!'

Back home, Ngqawana worked regularly in Abdullah Ibrahim's South African band, and immersed himself in more study. A collaboration in Norway produced his first album, *San Song*. Four others have followed: *Zimology*, *Ingoma*, *Zimphonic Suites* and most recently *Vadzimu*.

In 2004, he brought together a 42-piece classical orchestra with hip-hop artists and scratch DJs for an event that presented walls of noise, haunting, Webern-like string arrangements, layered African percussion and big, lush saxophone ballads – enough ideas to fuel South African jazz for a year.

Over the years, Ngqawana's music has alluded to everything from the lives of migrant miners to globalization. His audiences know the repertoire and will sometimes even sing along with a dauntingly complex flute line. 'It's the music of the ocean and the mountain and how we are connected to them,' he says. He may, eventually, run out of ways to pun on the word Zim in his album titles – but he's unlikely to run out of captivating, challenging ideas for a long time.

improvisation. Hanmer continues to craft an original sound; he stretches his composing, these days, to string quartets as well as jazz ensembles. Saxophonist **McCoy Mrubata** fronts a big group that picks up the tradition of bandleaders like Tete Mbambisa, in music that echoes Cape tradition while never sacrificing infectious dancing rhythms. **Carlo Mombelli's Prisoners of Strange** in Johannesburg and **Mark Fransman's Tribe** in Cape Town explore the music's more imaginative outer reaches, while **Voice** revisits the bebop and hard-bop spirit of the 1950s and 60s with a distinctive modern edge. Singers range from Maggie Nicholls-style improvisers such as **Siya Makuzeni** and **Octavia Rachabane**, through cabaret and club vocalists like multi-award-winners

Gloria Bosman and **Judith Sephuma** to World Music practitioners like **Jabu Khanyile**, **Ringo Madlingozi** and **Shaluza Max Mntambo**. While a decade ago the fear was that South African jazz might lose its national character, it's clear today that engagement with international developments is running parallel with a fresh interest in the possibilities of roots. One example is the very fruitful collaboration between the polyrhythms of Cape Town ensemble **Amampondo** – formed in the 80s – and British saxophonist **Alan Skidmore**. He was the first British jazzman to visit South Africa after the end of apartheid, and his work with Amampondo has resulted in a European festival tour and two albums, *The Call* and *Ubizo*.

Yet jazz in South Africa – as worldwide – is now a niche music. It's genuinely popular, with a big (but not monogamously faithful) fan-base. Yet many of those fans have too little disposable income to buy CDs or attend clubs and festivals; in commercial terms, they don't count. (Some compensate by forming savings clubs – *stokvels* – to buy CDs and host township listening sessions.)

The country's biggest-selling genre by far is gospel; youth pop genres – including imported sounds – come second. The real renaissance in the music has not yet been matched by a solid financial base. Which, sadly, puts South African jazz artists on much the same footing as their counterparts elsewhere in the world.

DISCOGRAPHY South Africa | Jazz

As in the South Africa pop music discography, many of the following items released on South African labels are available overseas through licensees.

⊙ Africa Straight Ahead
Heads Up, US
One of many Sheer compilations – released by their US partner label Heads Up – this is a good selection of current artists and styles, from the "straight ahead" of the title to lyrical and easy listening.

⊙ King Kong: Original Cast
Gallo, South Africa
The soundtrack of the seminal 1959 "Jazz opera" starring Miriam Makeba and the Manhattan Brothers with Kippie Moeketsi and Hugh Masekela among others.

⊙ From Marabi to Disco
Gallo, South Africa
This starts with vaudeville and swinging *marabi* influenced jazz, but as the title suggests, also demonstrates how jazz traded influences with more popular music styles over the decades.

⊙ Outernational Meltdown: Jazzin Universally
MELT, South Africa
If you want to sample the melting-pot of jazz ideas that were around in the early 1990s, just after liberation, this key disc of a sprawling 3-CD set of rough, sometimes self-indulgent, sometimes magical collaborations conveys the mood of the times perfectly. Almost everybody who's anybody now was in those studios then.

⊙ Soweto Blues
Sheer Sound, South Africa
Companion volume to a history of South African jazz, this highlights tracks that reflect political debates and struggles from the 1950s to date.

The Blue Notes

One of South Africa's legendary progressive jazz bands, The Blue Notes were led by pianist Chris McGregor with Dudu Pukwana (alto sax), Nick Moyake (tenor sax), Mongezi Feza (trumpet), Johnny Dyani (bass) and Louis Moholo (drums). The nucleus of the band would eventually reform as the Brotherhood Of Breath.

⊙ Live In South Africa 1964
Ogun, UK
The Blue Notes captured live on the eve of their departure into exile in the UK.

John Fourie

Probably the country's finest jazz guitarist, Fourie was named Talent Deserving Wider recognition by Downbeat, worked at Ronnie Scott's Club in London, with Ray Ellington on the *Goon Show* and with Lee Morgan in the US in the early 70s, before returning home.

⊙ Solo, Duet and Trio
Sheer Sound, South Africa
Jazz in its "international" definition; a collection of standards so superbly interpreted it'll take you a while to forget these versions

Hotep Idris Galeta

In exile, Galeta played piano for Jackie McLean and taught at Hartford. Back home, he's a university teacher once more; his live appearances are rare and treasured.

⊙ Malay Tone Poem
Sheer Sound, South Africa
A collection of Galeta's own compositions, interpreted in the company of many of the significant young names on the scene. Joyous and compelling music, masterful piano.

Paul Hanmer

Cape Town-born pianist Hanmer plays, composes, teaches and explores recital music as well as jazz. He's just finished a string quartet.

⊙ Trains to Taung
Sheer Sound, South Africa
The first post-liberation, crossover modern jazz album. Went gold two years after its release and still sells steadily: a gorgeous series of slow, compelling quintet grooves.

Abdullah Ibrahim

Called Dollar Brand before his conversion to Islam, Ibrahim has made enough records to fill a book, expressing his unique blend of tricky Cape rhythms (called *goema*), solid hymn-like chords and sweeping lyrical ballads. Much of his catalogue is, however, out of print, including essentials like "Mannenberg".

★ African Sun
BMG, UK
Just one of a series of BMG South African jazz releases featuring Dollar Brand, aka Abdullah Ibrahim. Here he plays together with a raft of other luminaries.

Abdullah Ibrahim aka Dollar Brand

WITH THE NDR BIG BAND

⊙ **Ekapa Lodumo**
Enja, Germany
Ibrahim with a big-band – a chance to savour his compositions and arrangements.

Jazz Epistles

The Epistles were the late 1950s South African version of the US school of progressive jazz featuring the best local technicians of the period, pianist Dollar Brand (aka Abdullah Ibrahim), reedman Kippie Moeketsi, trumpeter Hugh Masekela and trombonist Jonas Gwangwa.

⊙ **Verse One**
Gallo, South Africa
The band's one and only recording, made before most of its members went into exile overseas, is now considered to be a South African classic.

Miriam Makeba

"Mama Africa" is an awesome tag but one that Makeba wears with ease. Over 50 years, she, more than anyone, has been the voice of African music. Exiled from South Africa from 1959, she returned in 1990 at the invitation of Nelson Mandela on his release from prison. The albums she has recorded are patchy, but the voice is always there, always stirring, and – now settled back home – she is still singing wonderfully.

⊙ **An Evening with Makeba and Belafonte**
WEA, US
South African folk and liberation songs in duet. It's still the voice of a naïve, young singer fresh from home – so clearly bursting with talent she set New York afire.

⊙ **The Guinea Years**
Sterns Africa, UK
Makeba has learnt from wherever she found herself. Here, she takes on the role of *djelimuso* in company with support from the likes of Sékou Diabaté and imports a sharply urban sensibility that influenced a whole generation of African female vocalists.

★ **Welela**
Phillips, US/UK
Makeba's last great album – every track a gem, superbly backed, arranged and produced, and with Miriam singing at her magnificent best

Manhattan Brothers

More Sophiatown veterans; a close-harmony quartet on the model of the Mills Brothers, but with plenty of Xhosa roots music woven in amidst the boogie-woogie and smooth swing.

⊙ **The Very Best of**
Sterns, UK
Exactly what the title says it is: a greatest hits selection from South Africa's most popular male singing group of the 1950s.

Hugh Masekela

Trumpeter/vocalist Masekela, along with Makeba and Ibrahim, was and remains South Africa's most successful jazz export, and the most prolific recording artist.

⊙ **Still Grazin'**
Universal, US
This companion to his recently-published autobiography provides a retrospective on his career, including some little-known treasures.

⊙ **Revival**
Sony, South Africa
This latter-day release sees Hugh playing and singing better than ever: less funkily frenetic, more considered and happy to let a good tune breathe.

Dorothy Masuka

Although born in Rhodesia (Zimbabwe), Masuka made her name in South Africa in the 1950s, where she had a highly successful career as a singer and composer, playing with Miriam Makeba and Hugh Masekela. So she deserves a place in both this and the Zimbabwe chapter.

⊙ **Mzilikazi**
Gallo, South Africa
Blues, acapella gospel songs, and more swing than a suspension bridge. Auntie Dot (as she's called) demonstrates that while she may be less well-known than some others, she may be the best of the crop.

Chris McGregor and The Castle Lager Big Band

The winners of the 1963 Castle Lager Jazz Festival were brought together under this name for this one-off, all-star studio recording directed by pianist McGregor.

★ **Jazz: The African Sound**
Teal Polygram, South Africa
This album constitutes some of the most glorious moments in the history of South African jazz and is especially noteworthy for the solo contributions of Kippie Moeketsi who, in the opinion of many, was the country's single greatest jazz talent.

Louis Mhlanga

He's worked in Zimbabwe, Mozambique and London, and at King Sunny Ade's studio in Lagos. Mhlanga is a dazzling guitarist in a range of contexts, with fast fingers and an even faster brain.

⊙ **Shamwari**
Sheer Sound, South Africa
As close as you'll get to Mhlanga live; modern African jazz to dance to.

Moses Taiwa Molelekwa

Raised by a serious jazz fan father, Molelekwa got his early music education at the FUBA Academy before working with Hugh Masekela, with Brice Wassy and Joanna McGregor in London.

⊙ **Finding Oneself**
MELT, South Africa
This was the CD that announced his unique piano voice to the world: simple tunes laid on often complex rhythmic bases; moving ballads and clear homage to the *marabi* heritage.

⊙ **Live at the Nantes Jazz Festival**
MELT, South Africa
The piano voice has matured in this posthumous release, which demonstrates a monster improvising talent in the company of Sakhile saxophonist Kaya Mahlangu.

Carlo Mombelli

Fretless bass player Mombelli played with sax hero Duker Makasi and John Fourie in the band Abstractions, and worked with Lee Konitz and others. Now back home, he's picking up fans across the social divides for quirky, abstract sounds with a touch of electronica.

⊙ **When Serious Babies Dance**
Instinct Africain, South Africa
An eclectic mix of improvised sounds and ideas that's never less than compelling. Great solos from saxophonist Sydney Mnisi and John Fourie.

McCoy Mrubata

Sax player and composer Mrubata has grown from an inventive young player with an infectious attack into a

Heads Up US

PLAYLIST
South Africa | Jazz

1 **PROP HAT** Paul Hanmer and Jethro Shasha from *Taung*
Superb duet from a pianist and a sadly now deceased drummer, off the album that kick-started the jazz renaissance of the 1990s.

2 **STIMELA** Hugh Masekela from *Still Grazin'*
The ultimate Masekela track on his classic album. Bluesy trumpet and a gravel-throated narrative about the evils of apartheid and migrant labour.

3 **MFAN'OMNCANE** Dorothy Masuka from *Mzilikazi*
Sophiatown jive at its best from the smoky-voiced Ms Masuka, who also wrote the song.

4 **I REMEMBER BILLY** Chris McGregor and the Castle Lager Big Band from *Jazz: The African Sound*
Heartbreaking clarinet on his own composition from Kippie Moeketsi, backed by the best musicians of the early 1960s.

5 **ME, THE MANGO PICKER** Carlo Mombelli from *When Serious Babies Dance*
Mombelli's song of longing for home, recorded while he was in Germany and voiced by the delicious Siya Makuzeni.

6 **NTATE MOHOLO** Moses Molelekwa from *Finding Oneself*
Marabi, the oldest jazz style, interpreted by one of the youngest players of the early 1990s; a tribute to Molelekwa's piano-playing grandfather.

7 **YAKHAL'INKOMO** Winston Mankunku Ngozi from *Yakhal'Inkomo*
The saxophone master, from the top-selling jazz album of 1968 and possibly several other years – the label lost the sales records!

8 **QULA KWEDINI** Zim Ngqawana from *Zimology*
A traditional Xhosa song reconfigured by a challenging modern jazzman.

9 **SEVEN** Tananas from *Unamunacua*
Fast, rhythmically tricky and intricately imagined. Is it jazz? Who cares!

10 **IDA** Voice from *Quintet Legacy Volume II: Songs for Our Grandchildren*
Written by reedman Sydney Mnisi for his mother, this may be the most beautiful South African jazz ballad of the 2000s.

unique voice, applying that attack to far more challenging, roots-inflected material.

★ Icamagu Livumile
Sheer Sound, South Africa

On this award-winning album the band (including Hanmer) giving total commitment to absorbing music.

Bheki Mseleku

The grandson of a revered vaudevillian, pianist Mseleku played pop and jazz in South Africa before moving to the UK and building a stellar career that involved solo recitals and collaborations with Pharoah Sanders among others.

⊙ Celebration
World Circuit, UK

His first UK album, with Courtney Pine, Steve Williamson and others; as joyous as the title suggests, with the spirit of Coltrane hovering benignly.

Zacks Nkosi

Zacks Nkosi, a bandleader, composer and saxophonist of the first order, was one of the most important figures during the golden age of African jazz in the 1950s and 60s.

⊡ Our Kind Of Jazz
EMI, South Africa

This is a reissue of a mid-1960s LP which in turn had been compiled from recordings that originally appeared as 78s. It remains the only contemporary testimony to the existence of what was once the largest and greatest body of African Jazz recordings of the 1950s and 60s, featuring not only Zacks himself but also the talents of Ellison Themba, Elijah Nkwanyane, and Michael Xaba.

Winston Mankunku Ngozi

Without doubt the country's finest saxophonist – you hold your breath when this veteran plays.

⊙ Yakhal' Inkomo
Teal, South Africa

This double CD includes his most famous album plus another late 60s outing, *Spring*. Intense, clearly Coltrane-influenced playing, but still a unique voice.

Zim Ngqawana

The country's most inventive and interesting saxophonist, his output has stretched from work with Abdullah Ibrahim to jazz with a 42-piece symphony orchestra plus hip-hop artists.

★ Zimology
Sheer Sound South Africa

His second album, and first as leader, crystallized his sound and established his voice as a composer. Essential.

Gideon Nxumalo

Pianist and composer Nxumalo was another outstanding South African jazz talent whose career stretched from the early 1950s through to the mid-70s.

⊙ Jazz Fantasia
Teal-Polygram, South Africa

This recording taken from a 1962 concert – featuring material that Nxumalo wrote for the occasion – is the only surviving example of sax maestros Kippie Moeketsi and Dudu Pukwana playing together.

Tananas

This combination of three improvisers – Steve Newman, a white guitarist; Ian Herman, a Coloured drummer; and Gito Baloi, a black Mozambican bassist – cocked a snook at apartheid in the 1980s. Sadly, Baloi was murdered by thugs in 2004.

⊙ Unamunacua
Gallo, South Africa

The same imaginative vision applied to a much bigger ensemble that includes the talents of fearless Cape saxophonist Robbie Jansen and brilliant Zulu fiddler Noise Khanyile.

Tribe

Cape Town Jazz tends to be influenced by a flourishing club and dance culture that can drive it towards easy listening. Not so Tribe, an improvising quartet driven by the intense conversations between pianist Mark Fransman and driving drummer Kessivan Naidoo.

⊙ Our Language
Ready Rolled South Africa

Abandon your expectations and be prepare to be absorbed by the music.

Voice

Voice brings together some of the hottest young jazz players around, including leaders in their own right pianist Andile Yenana and trumpeter Marcus Wyatt. Wearing other hats, piano bass and drums are also the country's most in-demand jazz rhythm section.

⊙ Quintet Legacy Vol II: Songs for our Grandchildren
Sheer Sound, South Africa

Modern jazz: updated bebop and hard bop but with an unmistakably South African twist. If Kippie Moeketsi were alive today, he'd approve – and probably sit in.

South Africa | Gospel

I've got the power

Ladysmith Black Mambazo
Leon Morris/Redferns

Gospel music is one of South Africa's best loved sounds. Gospel discs sell more than any other genre, and, in the townships at least, there's a great choir on every corner. South Africans love the way gospel celebrates the voice – the country's finest and most abundant musical asset. And they love the gospel story of oppression and redemption that seems so closely to mirror their own. Gregory Mthembu-Salter stands up.

With gospel music the **voice** is all-important; it soars to the heavens and descends to the deepest miseries of the human condition. South Africa's gospel music draws on a variety of traditions. In particular, American music influences much of the output. Pentecostal churches from the US have made a big impact in South Africa and have large followings. In addition, American gospel music is a staple in the media, just like its secular musical counterparts.

However, it's the African influences which render South Africa's gospel music unique. This is particularly the case with the **Zionist churches**, which have been fiercely independent since the beginning of the twentieth century and have consciously incorporated African traditions into their rituals and music. The most successful Zionist recording artist must be Sotho singer **Solly Moholo**, blessed with a hoarse but wonderful voice, charged with emotion and exultation, and great backing singers. So popular is Moholo is that South African president Thabo Mbeki used him to draw vast crowds at ANC rallies in the 1999 election campaign, where Moholo gave unflaggingly rousing performances to his adoring fans.

Another inspirational, if odd, roots gospel artist is **Sam Zondi**, who heads up **Imvuselelo Yase Natali**. Before he found religion, Zondi used to be a pop singer known for outrageous stunts on stage, but gospel has proved the perfect outlet for his charismatic personality. Imvuselelo are a large outfit – as many as 60 can appear live – who provide an awesome wall of sound, all set to a pulsating beat, with Zondi and his inner circle of lead vocalists fronting them in ecstatic fashion.

Star Voices

Among the astonishing number of artists with a talent for gospel music in South Africa, the reigning queen remains **Rebecca Malope**. Her releases routinely go platinum, each one filled with instant anthems craftily conceived by producer **Sizwe Zako** and belted out by the diminutive star. For many, Malope's finest effort was *Shwele Baba* in 1995 which featured the usual strong songs but real musicians too, who have been somewhat absent from her later recordings.

Another great female gospel artist, and Rebecca's closest rival, is **Deborah**, who has enjoyed enormous success since 2000 with a string of powerful recordings, including the recent *Ngikuxolele*.

Rebecca Malope

Also hugely popular over the last few years have been the **IPCC**, a Pentecostal choir – mostly appealing to the middle-aged and older gospel fans – who have enjoyed considerable success since their 1996 debut release, *Uthembekile*. And then there is **Amadodana Ase Wesile**, a choir of Methodist stalwarts, always dressed in dark suits and red waistcoats, who keep time by thumping a Bible as they intone their hymns of righteousness. Recordings sadly lack the mischievous humour with which they leaven their message in the flesh.

While Malope is Sizwe Zako's biggest star, others in his stable have also made lasting names for themselves. **Vuyo Mokoena** got his big break with Rebecca Malope and has featured on most of her recent albums, but really came to prominence in 1997 with a vintage Zako-style stirring anthem entitled "Njalo!".

Mokoena has also been involved, along with **Jabu Hlongwane, Mthunzi Namba** and **Lindelani Mkhize** in the most successful gospel project in South Africa in recent years, **Joyous Celebration**. The idea behind Joyous Celebration is a simple one: recruit the best in young gospel talent, compose new material and rearrange old classics for them, showcase it all with a touring show that mixes solo and choral artists in a slick but nonetheless emotionally charged presentation, and record the results. The response from audiences has been consistently ecstatic, and at the time of writing, the project is still touring and we are up to Joyous Celebration 9, with no end in sight.

Much of the best output of **Ladysmith Black Mambazo** (see South Africa Popular Music) is gospel, invariably beautifully crafted odes of praise with characteristic additions of aptly chosen Zulu proverbs. There is usually at least one of these in the increasing number of South African gospel music compilations aimed at the overseas market, like the excellent 1998 release *Gospel Spirit of Africa*.

The version of "Nkosi Sikelele" performed by the **Imilonji Kantu Choral Society** (also on *Gospel Spirit of Africa*) is a good example of the more classical choral style popular among an older generation of gospel fans, many of whom are themselves in similar choirs. Such choirs perform a mixture of self-composed and European classical works accompanied by a large orchestra.

At the other end of the spectrum, it has become almost obligatory now for even the coarsest of pop stars to include at least one rousing gospel tune in their repertoires. This is partly just recognition by the record companies of the strong selling power of gospel music, but it also shows how steeped in gospel South African musicians really are – whatever genre they specialize in.

Live Witness

Despite the enormous number of gospel recordings of every style, most gospel still goes unrecorded for lack of opportunity. Yet every township and rural area has countless choirs, groups and soloists, many of whom are extremely powerful and moving. **Live performances**, whether in a church, a night vigil, or simply in someone's back yard, are a rich and unforgettable part of South African cultural life, providing important clues about the sources of its people's justly legendary resilience, forbearance and powers of reconciliation.

DISCOGRAPHY   South Africa | Gospel

For artists such as Ladysmith Black Mambazo, see also the South African pop music discography.

⊙ Gospel Grooves
EMI, South Africa
A fine compilation of both gospel artists and secular ones trying their hand at the medium, including Mandoza, Brenda Fassie, Arthur and Ringo. Excellent.

★ Gospel Spirit of Africa
Gallo, South Africa
This excellent gospel compilation ranges from Ladysmith Black Mambazo to a variety of lesser-known artists, many with a strong Zionist influence, including the Leeukop Prison Choir and their wonderful rendition of Rebecca Malope's "Moya Wami".

⊙ Joyous Celebration Vols 1–9
Sony, South Africa
Most of the set are live recordings of the lively Joyous Celebration road show. A number of the contributions are heavily influenced by American gospel, but there are still plenty of uniquely South African offerings here to keep you praising.

Imvuselelo Yase Natali

Led by the irrepressible Sam Zondi, this massive and remarkable choir is one of the most charismatic and interesting singing in the country today.

⊙ Izigi
BMG, South Africa
Dating from 1999, and perhaps the choir's best recording to date, this features the hit single "Laze Laduma". If ever there was music for jumping up and down to, this is surely it.

IPCC

The International Pentecostal Church Choir found instant success with their 1989 debut album, and have grown in popularity ever since, partly as a result of the immense membership of their church which is the fastest growing in Southern Africa.

★ Uthembekile
Tusk, South Africa
This was the album that made the IPCC so popular among South African gospel lovers. Stirring, rootsy gospel sounds from a stunningly strong-voiced choir.

Rebecca Malope

Malope, South Africa's biggest gospel star, is from the township of Lekazi near Nelspruit in Mpumalanga, and launched her career by winning a nationwide talent contest in 1987. These days, most of her releases go platinum within weeks and she is branching out in new directions, promoting new talent and trying her hand as a producer.

★ Free at Last: South African Gospel
EMI/Hemisphere, UK

An excellent anthology of Malope's fabulous music, inflected with a township pop sensitivity, and powered by impassioned petitions to God that build inexorably to anthemic odes to His goodness and mercy.

Solly Moholo

Zionist gospel's first major recording star, the likeable Solly Moholo is proving pretty prolific, producing some great music. His music videos feature the secret weapon of the trademark South African Zionist Church mass choral leap.

⊙ Motlhang Ke Kolobetswang
EMI, South Africa

Hardly a snappy title, and the backing is a bit tinny, but this is a great gospel album nonetheless. Moholo and his choir sing magnificently and the melodies are plain wonderful.

Vuyo Mokoena and Pure Magic

Vuyo made his name singing with Rebecca Malope but has gone on to pursue a highly successful solo career. Rebecca's talented producer Zako produces him and is a key component of Vuyo's anthemic, sing-along style.

⊙ Njalo
EMI, South Africa

A perfect example of producer Sizwe Zako's craft, with Vuyo's lusty vocals bursting through the stirring keyboards-driven accompaniment to great effect.

PLAYLIST
South Africa | Gospel

1 MOYA WAM Rebecca Malope from *Free At Last: South African Gospel*
Superbly rousing gospel anthem, featuring Rebecca on cracking form as she belts out heartfelt lyrics about her and the Holy Spirit.

2 AVULEKILE AMASANGO Ishmael from *Gospel Grooves*
Usually a pop star with more earthly concerns, here Ishmael has death and the afterlife in mind for this gospel dance classic.

3 IZIGI IMVUSELELO Yase Natali from *Izigi*
Jumping handclapped beats and wave after wave of unstoppable choral sound – if this is what heaven sounds like, why didn't they tell us earlier?

4 DIPHALA DI RAPEDISA MOPORESIDENTE THABO MBEKI Solly Moholo from *Motlhang Ke Kolobetswang*
With the backing choir on particularly fine form, Solly Moholo wishes President Thabo Mbeki the Lord's blessing and inspiration.

5 UMMALI UTHEMBEKILE IPCC from *Uthembekile*
A song from the IPCC's great first album, with all their trademark gospel beats (the kind Nelson Mandela jives to), righteous lyrics and gently stirring choral vocals.

Southern Africa |
Archives

hugh tracey: pioneer archivist

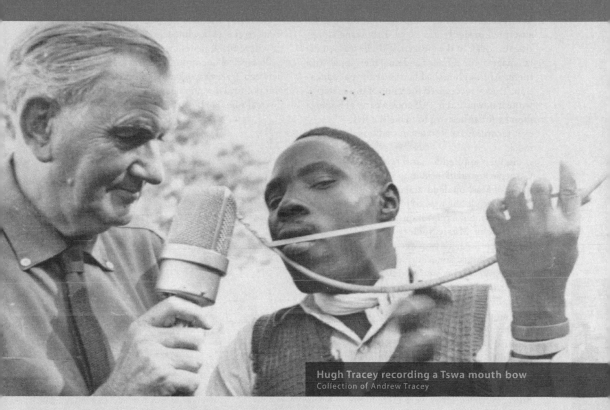

Hugh Tracey recording a Tswa mouth bow
Collection of Andrew Tracey

For anyone who was interested in African music in the dark days before World Music, Hugh Tracey (1903–1977) was a pioneering, even a paternal, figure. During the 1950s and 60s, his "Music of Africa" series of 10-inch LPs on Decca – superb recordings of traditional music from central, eastern and southern Africa, graced with his inimitable commentaries – were one of the very few ways the Western listener might encounter African music. Mark Hudson takes up the story.

Hugh Tracey (1903–1977) was the father of African ethnomusicology. He set up the first organization devoted to the study and preservation of traditional African music, the first library and the first magazine of African music – at a time when the very concept of "African music" barely existed. His archive, the **International Library of African Music**, remains probably the greatest repository of African music in the world.

One of eleven children of a doctor in Devon, England, Tracey left for **Southern Rhodesia** (Zimbabwe) at seventeen to work with his brother who had received land as compensation for injuries sustained in the World War I. Labouring alongside the locals in the tobacco fields, he learned the language of the Karanga and sang their songs with them. Although he had had little formal education, Tracey recognized the value of this material, wrote it down, and in 1929 took a party of Karanga men to Johannesberg to make the first ever recordings of Rhodesian traditional music.

He then applied for, and received, a Carnegie Foundation grant to survey the music of **Mashonaland**, and over the following decades he worked in broadcasting and created a mini-industry around his **African Music Society** at Roodeport, South Africa (work continued by his musicologist son Andrew at Rhodes University). He became established not only as *the* expert on African music but virtually embodied white interest in African music.

Tracey's great testament was the **"Sound of Africa" series** of 210 LPs: the fruits of annual field trips throughout southern, central and eastern Africa between 1948 and 1963, of which *The Music of Africa* series were mere highlights. The composers Ralph Vaughan Williams and Gustav Holst, whom he met in London in 1931, advised him to eschew analysis in favour of recording as much as possible. He set out to record every aspect of a musical world that was disappearing before his eyes.

Looking Back

Despite the huge growth of Western interest in African music, and the development of the whole World Music phenomenon, little was heard of Tracey's

recordings over the last three decades, apart from a few items on compilations.

This was partly because, with advances in Africa's recording industries, and the perceived desire of Western audiences to engage with Africa's own view of itself, the old ethnomusicological approach, in which musicians were presented as anonymous representatives of an ethnic group, was seen as obsolete. But more than that, Tracey himself became tarnished, written off by a new generation of musicologists as a tool of the apartheid system and even a creator of its educational policies.

Certainly the idea of Tracey singing African songs to classes of white schoolchildren in an Africa where black people were practically invisible makes us feel uncomfortable. But the relationship between Tracey's work and South Africa's cultural and political development is a complex and paradoxical one. He blotted his historical copybook

Collection of Andrew Tracey

Hugh Tracey trying out a chisanzhi *mbira*, Angola, 1956

by working for the South African Broadcasting Corporation at a time when "Bantu" radio stations were being set up to bolster "separate development". Yet this had the side-effect of nurturing a whole rich stratum of neo-traditional music.

Tracey espoused theories of cultural development that were archaic even in the 1950s, believing, according to musicologist Veit Erlmann, that there was "something innate in the African that would prevent him playing the piano in a satisfactory way." While he was obsessed with gaining acceptance for African music as a subject for academic study, Tracey was an instinctive populist. He encouraged musicians to cut their pieces into two- or three-minute nuggets suitable for 78rpm records and would count musicians in one after the other to make the rhythmic structures apparent to even the laziest of listeners.

Yet it is a mistake to try to judge Tracey by today's standards. As a teenager growing up in apartheid South Africa, and as a keen collector of township jive records, **Trevor Herman**, creator of the *Indestructible Beat of Soweto* series, could not help but be aware of Tracey. "You just knew of him as a guy who had made this incredible collection of music and instruments. To equate him with the creators of apartheid is bullshit. For those people African music was just rubbish!"

Indeed, Tracey may have believed that certain musical tunings were "innate to the African" – having recorded and analysed several thousand of them himself – but before him it had been believed by whites that there were no tunings in African music, that Africans were incapable of systematic tuning.

Tracey fulminated against the "proletarian grey" of urban sounds, but he recorded a great deal of popular music, championing the marvellous guitar music of East Africa and helping many semi-urban musicians on the road to success – notably the great Congolese guitarist **Jean-Bosco Mwenda**. Despite his baleful warnings about commercialization and "degradation", Tracey predicted that the values and structures of traditional African music would assert themselves through popular music – very much as has happened in the African pop renaissance of the last thirty years.

Tracey died in 1977, nurturing the hope that African composers would one day turn to his recordings for inspiration. Ten years ago, that idea would have seemed risible, but with a growing acceptance that a wide range of forms – from Western classical to traditional – are all part of South Africa's heritage, that day may not be far off. As **Sibongile Khumalo**, one of the country's leading singers and herself a musicologist puts it, 'What matters is the music Tracey left behind. And that is of the greatest importance to every African person.'

DISCOGRAPHY Southern Africa | Archives

Thanks to a superb 32-volume retrospective on the Utrecht-based Sharp Wood (SWP) label, Hugh Tracey's legacy is now accessible to all. Beautifully remastered from original tapes and complete with archive photos and full notes, each CD in the series presents a picture of a particular musical world – an aspect of a civilization which has in many cases otherwise completely disappeared. Distributed internationaly by Stern's, the following filed recording CDs are particularly recommended.

Others in the series, devoted to popular and dance music, are recommended in the Zambia discography, and elsewhere in this book.

⊙ At the Court of the Mwami – Rwanda 1952
SWP Records, Netherlands
Powerful drum rhythms (more complex and varied than the famous Drummers of Burundi), heart-rending love and praise songs, bow and horn music. In the light of the events of the 1990s, the names of the drums – "The Dominators", "The Terrifiers" – and the clear distinction between Tutsi and Hutu music gives these sounds a poignant and ominous ring.

⊙ Kalimba and Kalumbu Songs – Northern Rhodesia 1952 & 1957
SWP Records, Netherlands
Lyrical and reflective sounds with the *mbira*-related *kalimba* and the *kalumbu*, a musical bow – instruments whose role has largely been usurped by the guitar.

⊙ Origins of Guitar Music in Southern Congo & Northern Zambia 1950, 51, 52, 57 & 58
SWP Records, Netherlands
With influences ranging from traditional *likembe* music to Country & Western, the guitar music of the copper-mining towns was a vibrant example of the emergent urban culture of the 1950s. This evocative volume features now legendary names Jean Bosco Mwenda and George Sibanda, alongside more rumba-influenced sounds from northeastern Congo.

⊙ Southern Mozambique – Portuguese East Africa
Sharp Wood, Netherlands
Southern Mozambique is the area below the Zambezi River, where Tracey recorded many times between 1943 and 1963.

The fabulously complex orchestral xylophone *timbila* music of the Chopi people was his particular passion. Three legendary masters are featured here, alongside exquisite Sena and Ndau *mbira* music and extraordinary Gitonga "singing horns".

⊙ Tanzania Vocals – Tanganyika 1950
Sharp Wood, Netherlands

Rich and majestically multi-layered, the voices of the different sexes rising in great waves, these recordings of vocal gatherings beneath vast savannah skies are imbued both with a profound dignity and all the "Out of Africa" romanticism you could possibly want.

PLAYLIST
Southern Africa | Archives

1 **HINGANYENGISA MASINGITA Ten xylophones led by Katinyana** from *Southern Mozambique*
Chopi orchestral xylophones in full pummelling overdrive, while a male chorus gives a stirring rendition of "Listen to the Mysteries", a key Chopi song.

2 **MANYANGA Six Hundred Chagga Men and Women** from *Tanzania Vocals*
A rousing lone voice orchestrates surging crowds of exultant young women and grunting and sighing men. Inspirational stuff.

3 **NIMUZE TUGWERAGWERE A Father, Son and One Other Man** from *At the Court of the Mwami*
Recorded a decade before the kingdom of Rwanda turned into a Republic, this praise song is redolent of a forgotten, historic world.

4 **SITIMA SENDA NA MOTO Josiasi Yemba Mate** from *Kalimba and Kalumbu Songs*
A fabulous *mbira*-powered paean to the joys of rail travel – the metallic sound and vocal impersonation evoking the days of steam in a dreamy fashion.

5 **MASENGA Ilenga Patrice & Misomba Victor** from *Origins of Guitar Music*
The roots of Congolese rumba are just discernible in this copper miners' recreational song with two guitars, bottle-jangling percussion and a feel that is at once joyous and slightly despairing.

Sudan

still yearning to dance

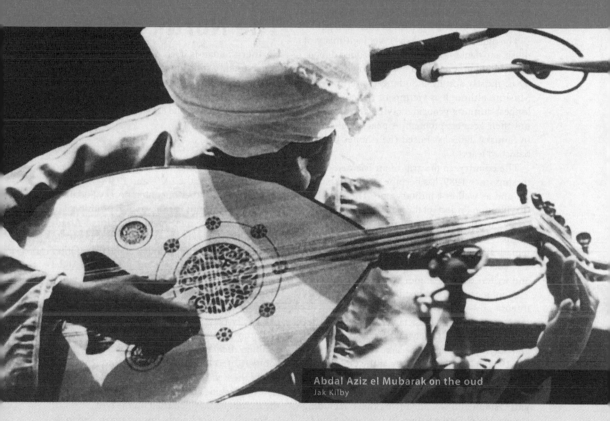

Abdal Aziz el Mubarak on the oud
Jak Kilby

Home of the "whirling" dervish and the pogo-ing Dinka, Sudan has been an exciting meeting-ground of African and Arab musics, but for the past two decades, civil war and religious dogma have combined to create a singularly hostile cultural environment. Peter Verney, a long-time former resident of a country that leaves an indelible impression on all who visit it, surveys the scene at home and abroad, with the help of extra information from Helen Jerome and Moawia Yassin.

Sudan is Africa's largest country and its people – three hundred ethnic groups – embody such a collision of Arab and African cultures that it's often impossible to tell where one culture ends and the other begins. Arab tribes arrived in the fourteenth century from across the Red Sea and the northern fringe of Africa; in the sixteenth century, West Africans began journeying through northern Sudan on the pilgrimage to Mecca. Both settled and intermarried with the indigenous people. Southern Sudan, largely cut off until the mid-nineteenth century by the vast swamps of the White Nile, was treated as a source of slaves, ivory, ostrich feathers and gold.

The age-old argument over the legitimacy of music and dance under Islam has an added dimension in Sudan. One third of the people affected by it, mostly southern Sudanese, are not even Muslim, although as victims of the continent's longest-running genocidal **civil war**, music was not their greatest problem. A peace deal signed in January 2005 has raised their hopes but not banished fears.

The country, in the grip of an Islamist dictatorship since 1989, has become a cultural battleground as well as a military one. The so-called "Civilization Project" of the National Islamic Front (NIF) extended in the 1990s from Orwellian "peace camps" – where war-displaced women were systematically raped – to the destruction of cultural artefacts and the imprisonment of popular artists and writers deemed immoral or anti-Islamic.

A unique tradition of popular music came under intense pressure and became a life or death matter. Many celebrated musicians were forced to flee Sudan; music was largely taken off the airwaves and public performances became risky. In November 1994, in a stabbing frenzy at the Omdurman Musicians' Club during a propaganda campaign against secular music, a teacher killed singer **Khogali Osman** and wounded two others, including singer **Abdel Gadir Salim**. In the face of public resistance, and keen to cast itself as "not the Taliban" after 9/11, the regime eventually changed its approach.

Tuning in to the local TV and radio stations in 21st century Khartoum, it would be easy to get the impression that the grim days of the 1990s are over. Music is everywhere in the Sudanese media, the **National Music Festivals** have been relaunched, and tens of thousands – including political leaders with their families – attended performances by the veteran **Mohammed Wardi** when he returned to Sudan after years of exile.

But this is a smokescreen, a subtler form of the same repression: many songs still cannot be aired in public, and many musicians are still harassed or living in exile. Music cannot be performed after 11pm, and the diversity of folk music and dance of Sudan is still at risk. Outright terror has been replaced by inconsistency: one branch of government may approve and even fund a cultural event, while another wing, usually security police, moves in on the night and bans it. Fear and uncertainty helps keep art unadventurous, and much of today's music consists of retreads of old songs, playing safe.

The North

Northern Sudan is itself divided – to the point of personality splitting, sometimes. Few people wholeheartedly support the government's obsessive division of the sexes, and many older folk look back nostalgically to the era before sharia law.

Early Days and Jazz

Modern urban music in northern Sudan began taking shape between the 1920s and 1940s. Regarded by some as the father of contemporary Sudanese music, singer **Khalil Farah** was also prominent in the independence movement. **Ibrahim al-Abadi** (1894–1980) found new ways of wedding poetry to music, regarded as unorthodox at the time. Other early singer-songwriters included Abdallah Abdel Karim, better known as **Karoma**, who wrote over four hundred songs.

These **lyric songs** of northern Sudan were originally played on the **tambour** (lyre) using pentatonic scales, and are quite distinct from the Arabian *maqam* structures. When the far more sophisticated **oud** or lute was introduced from across the Red Sea, Sudanese players developed a style of plucking and striking the *oud* strings from the technique they had used on the lyre.

Song lyrics are hugely important in Sudanese music – indeed the lyricists and poets are as celebrated as the singers. The Sudanese Graduates' Congress used a song entitled "Sahi ya Kanaru" (Wake Up, Canary) to spread resistance to British rule. And since then, many others have used the image of a beautiful creature, woman or lover to refer obliquely to their country, and have sometimes stirred feelings sufficiently powerful to get the author jailed. Translations, of course, rarely capture these allusions.

Urban musicians introduced violins, accordions and horns – and the odd flute and mandolin – after World War II, electric guitars in the 1960s and electronic keyboards in the 1980s. These were used by Sudanese to beef up their traditional styles. Those from the traditions of northern, western and central Sudan took styles such as **haqiiba** – a chant with chorus and minimal percussion – infused them with Egyptian-Arab or European elements, and developed **al-aghani' al-hadith** (modern songs). As early as the 1920s, Egyptian producers brought Sudanese singers to record in Cairo, and orchestral instruments began to replace the call-and-response of the chorus.

Southerners, Nuba and other non-Arab communities were well represented in the armed forces across the country. For impoverished young conscripts in post-independence Sudan, the **police and army "jazz-bands"** offered the best access to equipment, and what started out as British military brass-band styles often metamorphosed in the 1960s and 70s to become "jazz" in the East African sense, imitating the intersecting guitars of Kenya's Shirati Jazz and the Luo-language bands around Lake Victoria. Franco-style Congolese *soukous* was influential too, known in its Sudanese variant as **Je-luo**.

Odd and tantalizing styles of **horn playing** were adopted and adapted from traditional music, as well as from these foreign imports, which, from the 1960s on, included further-flung stars such as Ray Charles and Harry Belafonte, who made a big impression on urban Sudanese musicians such as **Osman Alamu** and **Ibrahim Awad**, the first Sudanese singer to dance on stage. In the 1970s it was the turn of James Brown and Jimmy Cliff. The ebullient **Kamal Kayla** modelled his funk-shout style on the hugely popular JB, although he is now in retirement, breeding exotic pigeons. The 1980s made Bob Marley and Michael Jackson household names in the most unexpected places. Marley was recognised by some as the spiritual kinsman of Sudan's own Sufi dervishes, and was an inspiration to thousands of ghetto kids.

Inspiration from Hendrix and Santana has been woven into the mix by guitarists such as the Zande Jazz bandleader **Sebit Fantaz**, and is displayed on Mohammed Wardi's 1994 *Live in Addis Ababa* set.

Players and Poets

Many of the best musicians appear in different backing groups. For example, **Abdel Gadir Salim's Merdoum Kings** and the **Abdel Aziz el Mubarak Orchestra** – the two best-known groups abroad – have shared the virtuoso violinist Mohammed Abdallah Mohammediya, bass player Nasir Gad Karim, accordionist Abdel Bagi Hamoda and sax player Hamid Osman, who died in 2004.

While the lush big-band arrangements (as well as the musicians) of Abdel Gadir Salim and Abdel Aziz

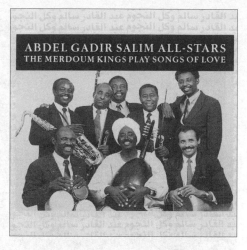

ABDEL GADIR SALIM ALL-STARS
THE MERDOUM KINGS PLAY SONGS OF LOVE

el Mubarak's bands are similar, their lyrics are very different. Whereas Abdel Gadir sings of a farm girl tired of waiting for her man to come so that she can wipe the sweat off his face, Abdel Aziz is more likely to proclaim his admiration for a woman's high heels.

Abdel Gadir Salim was born in Dilling, in the Nuba mountains, in the same village as his sax player Hamid Osman. After studying European and Arabic music at the Institute of Music and Drama, he shifted in 1971 from composing "Khartoum city songs" to folksongs, and had a hit with "Umri Ma Bansa" (I'll Never Forget You), which is still part of his repertoire. His home area of Kordofan and Darfur has its own unique rhythms and songs, with which he has flavoured his music.

From Darfur itself comes singer **Omar Ihsas**. His band get close to a "Sahel blues" sound for his song "Sorairoun", and there is a juicy sax break in "Hamra", a hymn to a red ox. His tender appeal for tribal harmony on "Darfur Salaam", a homegrown "Give Peace a Chance", is heartbreakingly catchy, as audiences in Chad, the Arab world and Europe discovered in 2005.

In 1988 **Abdel Aziz el Mubarak**, from Wad Medani, was the first Sudanese artist to play WOMAD, accompanied by a dozen musicians romantically resplendent in long white *jellabiya*. Next day they appeared at London's Jubilee Gardens wearing tuxedos. His love songs are songs of the city:

Every pleasure in the absence of your eyes
Is incomplete and does not touch me.
Every road that does not take me to you
Is a dark road that doesn't deserve the walk.
Darling, all through my life
I have been longing for your smile.

Mohammed Wardi, Mustafa Sidahmed and Yusuf al-Mousli

Peter Verney

Less well known abroad, but as famous in Sudan as Mubarak or Salim, are **Abdel Karim el Kabli**, **Mohammed el Amin** and **Mohammed Wardi**. Kabli is a walking cultural memory-bank, a folk-lorist who can talk in depth about the background of any number of Sudanese songs, and who plays *oud* in a variety of styles with deceptive ease. From the same generation, Amin is revered for his majestic voice and superb *oud* playing, as well as his brilliant compositions and arrangements. Born in Wad Medani, central Sudan, in 1943, he began learning the *oud* at the age of eleven. He wrote his first songs aged 20, and has frequently been in trouble with the military rulers. He was jailed by Nimeiri's regime in the 1970s and moved to Cairo in 1989 to avoid similar run-ins with the NIF. However, he returned to Khartoum in 1994, where he has kept a low profile.

Kamal Tarbas is now referred to by admirers as the King of Sudanese Folk Music, though (perhaps because of his earthy populism) he is dismissed as a vulgarian by those who like their lyrics more elevated in tone. His immediately recognizable laidback voice is set against revolving tom-tom rhythms and swaying accordion, derived from the *hibaaq* style and fleshed out with strings in later recordings such as *Ya Rait*.

Mohammed Wardi's soaring "golden throat" has won him acclaim right across the African Sahel and the Arab world. This singer from Nubia spent the 1990s in exile. His music always stirs emotion for many Sudanese, sometimes with directly political allusion and sometimes more obliquely. He was born in 1932 near old Wadi Halfa and schooled across the border in Egypt, beginning his music career in Khartoum in 1959. Four decades and three hundred songs later, he can stand on a stage, hand in pocket, the epitome of relaxation, leaving the audience to complete the lines of a song – and make the hairs stand up on the back of your neck. The effect of his voice at a human rights demonstration outside a Sudanese embassy abroad is even more intense.

Wardi has often set to music poems by **Mahjoub Sharif**, who writes in colloquial Arabic, mixing observations on everyday life and politics with love songs and poems for children. He has also been detained for long periods under Sudan's military dictators, but even in a remote western desert prison he continued writing lyrics that became songs of resistance.

Poem by Mahjoub Sharif

Hey, buffoon!
Cling tightly!
Beware falling apart!
Beware and be alert!
Bend your ears to every sign of movement
Keep watch on your own shadow
and, when the leaves rustle,
Shut yourself off and keep still!

Life is so dangerous, buffoon.

Open fire!
Bullets aimed at everything
every word uttered
every breeze passing
without your permission
My lord buffoon.

Instruct the sparrows,
the village lanterns,
the towns' windows,
every whispering blade of grass
to report to you.

As police, let the ants infiltrate
and build the security state
Ask the raindrops
to write their reports,
Buffoon…

The songs of **Abu Araki al-Bakheit**, like Wardi's, were banned from the airwaves by the NIF. In the early 1990s, he was arrested and told by the authorities not to sing his political songs at public gatherings. He responded by saying he would prefer silence, and would no longer play. The public outcry at this news eventually prompted him to sing again, but at the cost of repeated harassment and threats. His friends say he is walking a tightrope, and his popularity is his only protection.

The multi-vocalist band **Igd el Djilad**, formed in the 1980s by a dozen young music students, are in a similar position. Their music strives to be both forward-looking and reflective of the country's roots, using rhythms and chants from right across the country. To an outsider this seems innocuous enough, but it's an approach that takes guts: members of the group have been arrested and threatened on several occasions. Rather than being stopped from playing altogether, they were forced to give written assurances that they would not provoke the authorities with songs about poverty and famine.

Women Singers

Half a century ago, urban women singers such as **Mihera bint Abboud** and **Um el Hassan el Shaygiya** began creating individual styles from the rich oral heritage of traditional women's songs. The most famous woman from this era was the accomplished **Aisha el Fellatiya**, who made her name as a singer during World War II, when she toured the camps of the Sudan Defence Force across North Africa to boost the troops' morale.

Demurely echoing the rise of the 1960s girl groups in the West, a few female duos rose to local popularity, including **Sunai Kordofani**, **Sunai el Nagam** and **Sunai el Samar**. In the early 1980s, three gifted teenage Nubian sisters with a supportive father formed the group **Balabil**. Trained by *oud* player and songwriter Bashir Abbas, who also found lyricists and musicians for them, they attracted an avid following around the Horn of Africa, though even then their yearning undertones were sometimes considered sufficiently "over-sensuous" to get them banned from TV. The group reunited for the first time in ten years to play in Eritrea in 1997, and recorded for Rags Music. **Hadia Talsam**, the most talented sister, has also recorded solo in Cairo.

The fortunes of women singers mirror the social trends of recent years. Consider the extreme case of **Hanan Bulu-bulu**, the poutingly provocative Madonna of 1980s Sudanese pop. After the popular uprising that overthrew President Nimeiri and ended his repressive version of Islamic sharia law, Hanan reflected a new mood as she warbled and wiggled her way to fame at the 1986 Khartoum International Fair. Her notoriety arose from her stage act, which borrowed the sensuous bridal "dove-dance" of Sudanese weddings and orchestrated the often saucy songs of the urban women's *daloka*, or tom-tom tradition, also known as *al-Sabata*

But the backlash came soon after, as Islamist hardliners banned her concerts and beat her up for immoral behaviour. They insulted her "half-Ethiopian" background, which for them was a euphemism for sexual licence. She was by no means the best singer – her mewing little girl's voice and coarse repertoire never rivalled the poetic and emotional impact of other, more soulful female artists – but her naughtiness was a welcome antidote to the hollow pieties of the fundamentalists. Apparently, she's still performing, somehow, somewhere.

Further credit should go to women such as **Gisma** and **Nasra**, from whom Hanan Bulu-bulu stole much of her act. In the 1970s and 80s they pioneered a performance version of the erotic *kashif* wedding display, coupled with torrential drumming and worldly-wise lyrics. They were popular at private gatherings and were frequently arrested for the irreverence of their songs. Despised by the political elites of Left and Right, they were regarded as a much-needed source of dirty realism by the lower classes. Lyrics such as "Hey Commissioner, we know your Toyota's the pick-up for the groceries, and your Mercedes is the pick-up for the girls" and "This sharia is driving us to drink" were never likely to endear them to the authorities. Most Sudanese women can drum and sing, and less genteel urbanites delighted in reproducing Gisma and Nasra's salty treatment of the traditional *daloka* style.

The closest you can get to this on disc are the recordings by **Salma Al Assal** and **Setona**. The latter is a renowned henna artist from Kordofan, western Sudan. Currently resident in Cairo, and playing well-received gigs in Europe and America, Setona gives lusty voice to a generous handful of well-known women's songs, fleshed out by a largely male band. The artist formerly known as Prince is reported to have sought out Setona for a henna tattoo job. It's a pity he didn't publicize her music.

A 2005 CD by Salma Al Assal and a group of women singers stays closest to the original *daloka* or *Al Sabata* sound, complete with stirring references to "Ya Bashir" – one of the Zar spirits, not the military dictator. A more sobering reminder of the roots of women's songs in ancient *hakamat*

§ęţŋ̇ə
[TARIQ SUDAN]
african crossroads

or war songs surfaced in the 21st century when the womenfolk of the notorious Janjaweed militia sang to urge their menfolk on to more killing in Darfur.

At the more polite end of the market is the blind singer **Hanan an-Nil**, who in 1992 released *al-Farah al-Muhajir* in Cairo. She accompanies her delicate, wistful songs on an electronic keyboard. Finally, the most promising contemporary artist in international terms is **Rasha**, a young woman of seemingly impeccable taste and assured talent, loyal to her roots and possessing a breadth of repertoire to rival any of the men. Her second album, *Let Me Be*, includes the laceratingly powerful "Your Bloody Kingdom".

Southern Sudan

In 1992, the controllers of Radio Juba wiped its unique tapes of the celebrated southern Sudanese singer **Yousif Fataki**. It's an apt demonstration of the government's attitude to the largely Christian south – erasing a cultural artefact to make way for its own propaganda. And although south Sudan, like the Nuba Mountains, creates plenty of music, opportunities to hear it have been limited.

This is beginning to change, with the emergence of Southern Sudanese women singers such as the rising Shilluk star **Nyachan**, who has played in both Khartoum and London, **Nancy Ajaj** (resident in the Netherlands) and **Nyankol Mathiang Dut** (Canada), who combines Ngok Dinka lyrics and ululation with northern-style synthesizer beats.

Add this to the success in Nairobi of the multilingual African hip-hop of ex-child-soldier **Emmanuel Jal**, and it's clear that a resurgence is possible. A musical collaboration between Emmanuel and

Abdel Gadir Salim in 2005 marked Sudan's most optimistic cultural milestone for a long time, and Emmanuel Jal joined the Live8 African line-up.

Southern Survivals

In the 1970s and 80s, while there was peace, the southern capital Juba had nightlife: groups like **The Skylarks** and **Rejaf Jazz**, and venues like **DeeDee's Disco**, taking their inspiration from Kampala and Nairobi. All are long gone, dispersed by war, although a couple of Skylarks were sighted gigging in Uganda in 1998. Nowadays the best chance to hear southern Sudanese music may be in church, possibly in the refugee camps in northern Uganda, or among the rebel soldiers. Sometimes the participants are the same: in eastern Equatoria I met a priest, a dead ringer for Spike Lee, training a chapel choir consisting of both SPLA fighters and seminarians.

The **Dinka** tribe used to hymn their fabulous long-horned cattle, leaping around like the born basketball players they are. **Zande** folk music is as playful as their folk tales, which feature a trickster like the Jamaicans' Anansie or Brer Rabbit of the US Deep South. These days the peoples of south Sudan have an ever-growing repertoire of new songs about war and liberation, some of which were captured on a 1997 recording, *New Sudan Sings,* that sounds worlds away from the sleek orchestras of Khartoum. Atmospheric glimpses of peacetime roots music are found in 1970s and 80s field recordings by David Fanshawe, Robert Gottlieb and Artur Simon, made when landmines and Kalashnikovs were less of a hazard to ethnomusicologists.

The Nuba

The **Nuba** of southwest Sudan are not to be confused with the Nubians – including artists such as Wardi and Hamza al-Din – from Nubia in the far north of the country. Both groups are indigenous Sudanese, rather than of "Arab" origin, but any link is ancient history.

Caught on the dividing line between the warring cultures of north and south Sudan, the Nuba are fighting back against a government programme of ethnocide. Under the squeeze of the crude Islamization campaigns, the diverse, multi-religious Nuba communities are defending their culture as much as their land. The Kambala, or harvest festival, is still celebrated across the region, and there is a proliferation of new songs and artists.

When journalists were flown in to the Nuba mountains for an anniversary celebration in 1998

Dance & Trance: Sufi Dervishes

Given the current regime's restrictions on cultural expression, it is ironic that it was Sufi dervishes (*darawiish*), who brought the first wave of Islam to Sudan. In the religious tradition of *zikr* (remembrance), the dervishes use music and dance to work themselves into a mystical trance. Undulating lines of male dancers dance their way to ecstasy with a physical grace that confounds age. Their tolerant spirit profoundly influenced the easygoing approach that characterized Sudan until relatively recently.

The most spirited rhythms are mainly for women, in the psychotherapeutic *zar* cult. *Zar* sessions combine mesmeric drumming with incense, massage and a licence to release deep frustration. Under the guidance of the *sheikha az-zar*, gatherings last either four or seven days, with dawn-to-dusk drumming to draw out different spirits that plague people and have to be pacified.

These are occasions outside the bounds of life's ordinary rules, when women can smoke and drink and act out rebellious fantasies without having their religious piety or social respectability called into question. The *zar* cult is older than Islam and works around and through it rather than competing against it. But like everything else that challenges the ruling National Islamic Front's social programme, *zar* has suffered a government clampdown, being viewed as pagan and anti-Islamic.

Peter Verney (with thanks to Neil van der Linden)

---

by the charismatic Nuba SPLA leader Yousif Kuwa, they were treated to a concert in the remote mountain retreat, amplified thanks to solar power. The band playing were the vibrant **Black Stars** – part of a special "cultural advocacy and performance" unit of the SPLA in the Nuba mountains. Their most famous vocalist is **Ismael Koinyi**, an accomplished guitar player who sings in Arabic and several Nuba languages. Other vocalists include **Tahir Jezar**, **Jelle** and **Jamus**.

Electricity is a rare luxury, however, so Nuba bands usually play their form of **Je-luo** – a catch-all term here for Kenyan or Congolese guitar styles – unplugged, with stringed *rababas* (clay-pot bass drum), tin bongos and shakers. While the lyrics dwell on the battles, military and psychological, that the Nuba have to go through, the dancing often goes on till daybreak.

Where Next?

Sudan entered a new phase in January 2005 with the signing of a "Comprehensive Peace Agreement" between the largely southern SPLA rebels and the government. They're not dancing yet in the streets of Juba, the southern capital, but there are grounds for hope despite the difficulties ahead.

In 2005, South Sudan's "ex-child-soldier rapper" **Emmanuel Jal** went from playing Nairobi church halls to inclusion on the *Rough Guide to the Music of Sudan* compilation, securing a last-minute opportunity at "Live8 – Africa Calling" at the Eden Project in Cornwall, and joining in a CD

for the War Child charity. His producers on tracks such as "Gua", "Aiwa" and "Elengen" gave him a hefty "African-Arab dancefloor remix" sound on the *Ceasefire* album which he recorded together with "Northerner" Abdel Gadir Salim.

Darfur is a different matter, with warfare still affecting millions. Its music lives on, however, ably represented by **Omar Ihsas**, the ex-nurse turned soul singer from Nyala who deserves every bit of the acclaim that has grown with his European visits. His band has conjured up some engaging, Sahel-bluesy backings and a CD is eagerly anticipated. Omar Ihsas's evident depth and integrity bring to mind **Sherhabeel Ahmed**, one of the pioneers of modern Sudanese music and now one of its wise old men, who also continues to explore the boundaries but lacks a Western outlet.

Video has become so commonplace that it is worth recalling how little (if any) footage exists of stars from a few decades ago. The late **Khidir Bashir**, long celebrated for his stage performances, for example, doesn't seem to be in anyone's video catalogue, and decent cassettes are a rarity. The same applies to **Hawa Tagtaaga** and other pioneer performers. It is therefore encouraging to hear that the Institute for Traditional Music Archives (TRAMA) plans to publish recordings from its archives at the University of Khartoum. On video, TRAMA has music and dance from Darfur recorded in the 1980s and 90s, showing a very different side of Sudan from the recent images of war.

In northern Sudan, religious dogma continues to distort debate. **Hanan an-Nil**, the blind solo

Emmanuel Jal

female performer who was once a tasteful inter-preter of traditional songs, has reportedly decided that singing is *haram* (forbidden under Islam) and has given it up. Barcelona-based **Rasha**, on the other hand, who has the makings of an interna-tional star, has taken Sudanese women's music to new areas of outspokenness. Meanwhile the Sufi

Tijani brotherhood, who trace their origins to Fes, Morocco, still perform *zikr* in Omdurman, safe in the knowledge that their ancient, mesmerizing rhythms and chants of praise won't offend the authorities, because they're not – from a religious point of view – classed as music.

SUDAN

DISCOGRAPHY Sudan

A growing number of Sudanese CDs have been released on the international market, but few people in Sudan have CD players and many classic performances are still only on tape – if you can find them. A good selection of cassettes is available from Natari in the UK and Africassette in the US.

⊙ **Music of the Nile**
ARC, UK
These 1970s field recordings by David Fanshawe (the basis of his composition "African Sanctus") capture atmospheric aspects of rural life on the journey through Egypt, Sudan and Uganda.

⊙ **Musiques et Chants du Soudan: l'Ile de Touti**
Institut du Monde Arabe/Blue Silver, France
From Tuti Island, where the Blue Nile meets the White Nile at Khartoum, comes this tremendously evocative recording by some of Sudan's best musicians, featuring flute and violins. Further Institut du Monde Arabe CDs include music from the Beja of eastern Sudan, the Berta of Blue Nile province, the Nuba mountains and Nubia, plus artists Abdel Karim el Kabli and Mohammed Ali Gubara.

⊙ **Waza – Music of the Berta Blue Nile**
Wergo, Germany
A rare chance to hear the traditional music of the Ingessana and Berta people of the Blue Nile. It's sheer fun, traditional and avant-garde at the same time, with a wonderful atmo-sphere, and splendidly recorded. Sonorous, sinuous horns and flutes of all shapes and sizes start off simply, but build beautiful Moondog-like meshing patterns over sizzling per-cussion, as men and women chant and ululate gleefully in the background.

⊙ **Rain in the Hills: Beja Ballads of Port Sudan**
Original Music, US
Staking out the distinctive identity of the people of the Red Sea hills with vigour and wit, these 1995 field recordings by John Low feature gritty *oud* players and a lusty fishermen's band.

★ **The Rough Guide to the Music of Sudan**
World Music Network, UK
The rough and the smooth, the love-lorn and the worldly-wise, are side by side in this selection of stars and unknowns

from the land of the two Niles. Includes fascinating tracks unavailable elsewhere by Joseph Modi and the women of Omdurman and Chukudum, alongside stunning acoustic and electric sets by Rasha, Mohammed el Amin and Mohamed Wardi. A million square miles in 63 minutes?

⊙ The Rough Guide to the Music of North Africa
World Music Network, UK
As well as two characteristic tracks from Abdel Aziz el Mubarak and Abdel Karim el Kabli's albums, this useful sampler also includes the Nubian Hamza el Din's delicate "Ashranda".

⊙ Sounds of Sudan
World Circuit, UK
Solo acoustic recordings of Abdel Gadir Salim and Abdel Aziz el Mubarak playing *oud*, and the Shaygi tambour player Mohamed Gubara. Highly informative background notes by Moawia Yassin.

Tariq Abubakar and The Afro-Nubians

Sudanese saxophonist-singer Abubakar settled in Toronto in the 1990s, becoming one of Canada's best-known African musicians. Dissolving Sudan's north–south cultural divide by setting Arabic lyrics to *soukous* melodies, he sang earnestly of peace and unity until his death at 32 in 1998.

⊙ Tour to Africa
Stern's, UK
⊙ Great Africans
Festival, Canada
⊙ Hobey Laik
Festival, Canada
Abubakar's albums venture much further into African musical territory than other Sudanese artists. Often bold, sunny and bouncing with energy, he also appeals wistfully for tolerance and diversity. Once you get used to his growly voice, his fusions have a special charm. He is sorely missed.

Mohammed el Amin

The sonorous Amin, now in his mid-50s, has long been one of Sudan's best-loved singers and composers, and his legendary 1980s concerts in London, Manchester and Moscow spawned thousands of bootleg cassettes. But when will someone put his best group recordings onto the world market?

⊙ The Voice of Sudan
Haus der Kulturen der Welt, Germany
An intimate solo acoustic set recorded in Berlin in 1991. It captures his smokily majestic voice and nimble *oud* playing in glorious epics such as "Habibi" – an altogether subtler treatment than the roller-coaster riffing of the 1980s electric version.

Salma Al Assal

One of the best young exponents of traditional women's songs in Sudan. See also next entry.

⊙ Songs of al-Sabata
ARC, UK
A genuine attempt to capture the vigorous *daloka* drums and often raucous spirit of women's songs.

Azza/Hassouna Bangaladish

Led by percussionist Bangaladish, this quasi-"traditional" ensemble specializes in early twentieth-century secular love songs, with vocals by Salma al Assal and Mohamed al Semary.

⊙ Hossam Ramzy presents "Azza"
Arc Music, UK
The first in a series of productions by Cairo-based Hossam Ramzy. A delicious, swirling mini-orchestral stew of accordions, mandolin, *oud*, violin and percussion, this is an upbeat version of the folk-derived style pioneered by Kamal Terbas, with a couple of passably earthy lead singers.

Awlad al-Bura'i

Sheikh Abdel Rahim al-Bura'i (d. 2005) was the best known of Sudan's Sufi sheikhs, or spiritual teachers, and was reputed to have mystical powers. He wrote a great number of songs which used the traditional style, but which also dealt with contemporary topics such as the Iraq war.

⊙ Sacred Songs from Nubia & Kordofan
Institut du Monde Arabe, France
Not al-Bura'i himself, but his followers, the Awlad al-Bura'i (Sons of al-Bura'i), who produce devotional chanting and drumming to uplifting and hypnotic effect.

Hamza el Din

A Nubian ethnomusicologist, composer and virtuoso *oud* player, Din has spent most of his life outside his birthplace. US-based and now in his 80s, he still performs at least two concerts every year. With his Zen-like complexity-in-simplicity, the echoes of home remain strong.

★ A Wish
Sounds True, US
Excellent 1999 album featuring Din's gently meditative vocals in a variety of simple acoustic settings, sometimes accompanied only by his own *oud*, sometimes by percussion, *ney* and even cello. Beautiful music, beautifully presented, with explanatory liner notes written by the man himself.

Virtuoso *oud* player Hamza el Din

☉ Lily of the Nile
Water Lily Acoustics, US

Like a night journey under a starry desert sky. After the hypnotic melancholy of four epic *oud* songs comes a compelling tour de force on the deceptively simple *tar*, a *bodhran*-like hand-drum.

Dinka Malual

A US-based group of south Sudanese refugees led by singer and composer Mayen Deng Akoon.

☉ Wunda, Wunda!
Rakumi, US

The result of a multicultural arts project, this CD recreates a range of traditional Dinka songs and styles fairly successfully, with the occasional modern twist in the lyrics.

Igd el Djilad

This young vocal group – half a dozen harmonizing voices and half a dozen players – are revolutionary (for Sudan) in their readiness to use material from the whole country – north and south, African and Arab. Their best moments, oddly enough, recall early Steeleye Span.

☉ Madaris
Pam Jaf, Germany

So perky that you might mistake some of the songs for TV jingles. Sometimes too earnest, as in the songs to make children behave well, but the delicate covers of Nuba and southern Sudanese songs still bring a tear to the eye, probably for the same reason they get the band into trouble.

Abdel Karim el Kabli

The avuncular poet, composer and folklorist Abdel Karim el Kabli, now in his 70s, has become a walking encyclopedia of the musical heritage of north, east and central Sudan. He embraces both colloquial and classical styles, and is equally beloved by academics and ordinary Sudanese.

☉ Limaza
Rags, UK

An album full of musical sparkle and his best recording to date, with some stunning interplay between Kabli's *oud* and the violins, flute and bongos. He wrote "Sukkar, Sukkar" (Sugar, Sugar) in 1962, a gently lilting take on the twist, which he claimed could be traced back to the *zar* ritual.

Abdel Aziz el Mubarak

One of Sudan's great international stars, Abdel Aziz has been a top bandleader since the mid-1970s. With his fondness for spangled jackets and polished love songs for the ladies, he could sometimes be taken for the Bryan Ferry of Sudanese music, albeit with a better voice.

★ Straight from the Heart
World Circuit, UK

Mr Tuxedo does his Arab nightclub stuff to great effect on this live album, showcasing the lush and ornamented sound of his Khartoum big band. Features the crowd-pleasing "Na-Nu Na-Nu".

Rasha

A gentle-voiced northern Sudanese singer, Rasha has an accomplished and thoughtful grasp of traditional and contemporary styles, which she carefully varies. She lives in exile in Spain.

☉ Sudaniyat
NubeNegra, Spain

Her first album convincingly shows off her range, from Sufi meditations to big-band wedding songs, and is eminently listenable, warm, sophisticated and sensual. Backed by a variety of Spanish and Sudanese musicians who innovate but don't intrude, she sings with a soulful sensitivity.

☉ Let Me Be
Intuition, Spain

Stretching out to impressive effect, Rasha makes bluesy, jazzy music with a purpose and a poignant soul. The moody and compelling "Your Bloody Kingdom" is bloody marvellous. Elsewhere the horns have echoes of stuttering Ethiopian funk and powerful lyrics – in English – about women's rights.

Abdel Gadir Salim

Salim's rich, powerful voice and dynamic arrangements produce music which is less fussy and more hard-driving than many of his urban counterparts. His songs strive to be closer to countryside directness, while the arrangements reflect his studies of both Sudanese and Western music.

★ The Merdoum Kings Play Songs of Love
World Circuit, UK

An enduring favourite: *merdoum* is one of the vocal and drum styles of Kordofan, Salim's homeland in western Sudan. An all-star band helps give this recording fire and precision, polish and funk.

☉ Nujum al-Lail/Stars of the Night
GlobeStyle, UK

Recorded live in London in 1989, and refreshingly faithful to his big-band sound.

WITH EMMANUEL JAL

☉ Ceasefire
Riverboat, UK

The combination of Salim, the mature singer and instrumentalist, 26-year-old Nuer rapper Jal and 21st-century production techniques produces music as optimistic as the title. "Aiwa" (Yes), the opening track is irresistibly danceable and affirmative, and Salim's attempt at rap honourable.

Setona

When Setona, the Princess of Henna, let rip on her 1998 tour of Europe and North America, Western audiences

1 **AL-AJIKO Salma al Assal** from *Songs of al-Sabata*
Sultry women's drumming, deep and resonant, drives a song in praise of the Kordofan region and the beauty and intelligence of its people.

2 **AKWANI (MY BROTHERS) Tariq Abubakar and The Afro-Nubians** from *Tour to Africa*
Based on a wistful, woody, Zande xylophone melody, and uplifting in its call for Sudan's wildly diverse peoples to see each other as equals – "all my brothers".

3 **YA IZZANA Abdel Aziz el Mubarak Orchestra** from *Straight from the Heart*
Deliciously languid and yearning love song with dreamy interplay between Hamid Osman's saxophone and Mohamediya's violin, caught live at Hackney Empire.

4 **AIWA (YES) Emmanuel Jal and Abdel Gadir Salim** from *Ceasefire*
Inspired production work, sampled accordion, violins and ululation, and a slamming beat make this a dancefloor favourite. South meets north in celebratory mood.

5 **KOMSSOU Setona** from *Tariq Sudan*
Upbeat, saucy, full-tilt and best played loud – excellent for jostling and swaying after a glass or two of *marissa* – the local beer.

6 **KADUGLI Joseph Modi** from *The Rough Guide to the Music of Sudan*
The breathy female chorus and *balafon* riff of this song – about meeting again in Kaduqli after the war – highlight the gruff voice of this former child soldier.

7 **YOUR BLOODY KINGDOM Rasha** from *Let Me Be*
Musically a crossover into jazz-blues territory, the English lyrics, haunting and defiant, give this song real potency.

8 **SOLO ANTHEM Dinka Malual** from *Wunda, Wunda!*
The stirring, clear voice of an unaccompanied Dinka singer, Mary Athou Acouch, expressing her personal faith.

9 **TRUMPET ENSEMBLES NO. 1 Waza** from *Music of the Berta Blue Nile*
Massed single-note horn players produce a gloriously wacky Moondog-like syncopation.

10 **UMRI MA BANSA Abdel Gadir Salim** from *Sounds of Sudan*
The powerful, elegant simplicity of this acoustic *oud* performance makes this one of the best versions of Salim's most famous song. The title means "I'll Never forget".

got their first proper taste of the earthier side of Sudanese women's culture.

⊙ **Tariq Sudan – African Crossroads**
Blue Flame, Germany
This is urban women's *daloka* music, tarted up a bit but still authentic. Setona's voice is swampy, hoarse and gritty, and only a little inhibited by the studio. Inevitably, the recording doesn't match the headlong intensity of the live drum-only versions of these songs.

Mustafa al Sunni

Based in London since the 1990s, singer and *oud* player Sunni performs to the diaspora in the UK and Europe. He has a diverse repertoire from the *hagiba* classical tradition and *turath* folksongs.

⊙ **Songs of the Sudan**
Nimbus, UK
Accompanied by Abd al Hafiz Karar on percussion, Sunni plays an acoustic blend of traditional and contemporary songs in the popular urban style of late 20th-century Sudan. The contemporary lyrics, written in collaboration with poets and translated in the notes, deal with love, loss and longing.

Mohammed Wardi

Wardi's first hit was in 1960, and he still has the most extraordinary effect on a Sudanese audience, having come to embody the collective memories and aspirations of an entire nation. He sings not only in Arabic but also in his native Nubian, drawing on 7000 years of culture.

⭐ **Live in Addis Ababa 1994**
Rags Music, UK
The wrinkled old Nubian effortlessly enraptures an entire stadium, with his band sailing along like a felucca on the Nile; swaying strings, tumbling tom-toms, musing saxophones and choppy guitars create a majestic waltz, over which he unfurls his impassioned, weary choirboy voice.

Tanzania & Kenya |
taarab

the swahili coastal sound

Zuhuru Swal and Mombasa party
Werner Graebner

Taarab is the popular music of the Islamic Swahili people of the East African coast – encompassing Tanzania and Kenya, and in particular the islands of Zanzibar and Lamu. Originally a wedding music, it spread widely via cassettes and radio to beome a general feature of the aural landscape along the coast. Werner Graebner looks into a unique East African style.

At first hearing, **taarab** sounds distinctly Arabic, especially the Zanzibar variety with its Egyptian film-orchestra-style line-up, or if you're down in Mombasa, you may be struck equally by its links with Indian film music. Yet taarab lyrics are invariably Swahili and in its voice and local *ngoma* (drum-based dance music) rhythms it's equally and essentially African. In fact, the combination of Africa, Arabia and India in this Indian Ocean musical culture expresses the complex identity of the Swahili people well.

Taarab is **sung poetry**, so the lyrics and vocals are especially important. The voice is identifiably Islamic, yet it's as far from the sounds of Cairo as Baaba Maal. Vocals that cut through the instrumentation are popular among the Swahili and there's a distinct preference for high, clear female voices.

Rhythm is crucial, too, and no band features fewer than three percussion players, most often on *dumbak* and *tabla* (small drums) and *rika* (tambourine). Taarab is generally based on the rhythms of local *ngoma*, the *kumbwaya* being the most prominent on the coast. Latin American rhythms are part of the mix, too, through the influence of Cuban records in the 1940s.

While some instruments used in taarab are oriental in origin, like the Arabian **oud** (lute) and **qanun** (zither) or Japanese **taishokoto** (a kind of typewriter banjo), most used in today's ensembles are of Western provenance. **Organs** and **electric keyboards** often substitute for the accordions and harmoniums used in the earlier part of the twentieth century, while **guitar** and **bass guitar** are found in almost every band. European **stringed instruments** – violin, cello and double bass – are features of the large Zanzibar-type orchestras. A big change has taken place in "taarab" over the past few years, with so-called modern taarab and its backbiting *mipasho* songs becoming most popular with the audience.

Taarab Roots

After a time when African elements were stressed, current cultural values on the coast now favour a stronger link to **Islamic roots**. For example, recent writing from Zanzibar attributes the origin of the taarab to Arabic or, more specifically, Egyptian roots. The word "taarab" in fact derives from the Arabic *tariba* – to be moved or agitated – and, although it gained currency only in the 1950s, has broadened to cover the whole music and its context.

The Egyptian attribution derives from the chronicles of the **Ikhwani Safaa Musical Club**, founded in 1905, which is viewed in some circles as the source of taarab (see box overleaf). Yet this view does not account for the phenomenon of **Siti bint Saad**, the most famous of all Swahili singers. The Zanzibar-based Siti and her musicians were the first East Africans to make commercial records, recording hundreds of songs between 1928 and 1931. Members of the **Culture Musical Club**, the largest club in Zanzibar, highlight her career as an example of the African roots of taarab – and the influence of African music on the music of the Arabian Peninsula. Instruments, music styles and musical groups from East and northeast Africa are common in Yemen, and as far afield as Kuwait and Iraq.

Collection of Werner Graebner

Siti bint Saad and her group in the 1930s

Ikhwani Safaa Musical Club

"First we called ourselves **Ayal Mama**, and we played local dances like *kinanda cha marwas*, *tari la diriji*, or Arabic ones like the *ras-ha*. Then we started to play inside: **Abdalla Saleh Buesh** used the *kinanda* [qanbus] and **Moh'd Ali Elyas** played an *oud* made in India. Then Buesh started to teach himself the violin. It was at this time, in around 1902–3, that *Sayid Ahmed Bin Sumeyt*, the then chief kadhi of Zanzibar, gave us the name of **Ikhwani Safaa**. The club was officially registered in 1905, and we got a club house in Kokoni [a quarter of Stone Town]. In 1907 we decided to order musical instruments from Egypt: These were an 'ûd, qânûn, duff and ney. Now we really started to rehearse."

These are excerpts from a club history sketched by **Shaib Abeid Ba-Rajab**, one of the club's founders. At the time, Zanzibar was a cosmopolitan place: since the mid-nineteenth century the sultans had excelled in getting fashionable entertainment from around the Indian Ocean and beyond. There were Turkish brass bands, a Goan band playing Western classical and dance music, and Sultan Bargash even introduced an Egyptian *takht*. Intellectual developments at the turn of the century favoured all things Egyptian, from the importation of books and Islamic journals (the Ikhwani club also started its own library), to Egyptian gramophone records and musical instruments.

The club really came into its own in the 1940s and 1950s, sporting a big orchestra in the Egyptian *firqa* fashion, made popular by films and records by the likes of **Mohamed Abd-el-Wahhab** and **Umm Kulthum**. These big orchestras were all the rage in the whole Swahili sphere, and Ikhwani became one of the leading trendsetters. With the advent of these orchestras, taarab became much more formal in terms of its composition and presentation. The music was presented on a decorated stage, with musicians wearing frocks. Improvisation gave way to stylized development of songs, and the lyrical structure became regular and rhymed, following the traditions of classical Swahili poetry, but taarab still remained more of a social than a professional or commercially motivated activity.

In July 2005 Ikhwani Safaa celebrated their centenary in style, with a week of concerts, lectures, exhibitions and a new recording featuring some of the club's most important songs.

Werner Graebner

Musicians and local historians from Lamu and Mombasa favour the African hypothesis, referring to the older **Lamu traditions** of Swahili poetry. This poetry was always meant to be sung, and there are descriptions dating back to the nineteenth century of performances called *gungu* and *kinanda* showcasing this poetry, accompanied by gongs, small drums and the *kibangala*, a stringed instrument.

Other interesting pointers in this web of opinions are provided by the social occasions on which taarab is played. Like the *gungu* and *kinanda*, which it has supplanted, taarab is well integrated with the festive life of the Swahili, and **weddings** are the main ceremonies where it is performed.

The taarab **recording industry** is an interesting story in itself. From 1928 to 1931 all the major record companies active in Africa, including HMV and Columbia, recorded taarab, though in the postwar years it was left to local, mostly Asian-owned music stores. The most prominent of these was the Mombasa-based **Mzuri label** which made and released hundreds of taarab records from the 1950s to the mid-1970s.

Lamu and Mombasa

On **Lamu** island, the old centre of Swahili culture and literature on the northern Kenya coast, most weddings are served by a few amateur groups. One of these is a small group led by **Famau Mohamed**, who accompanies himself on the Indian harmonium. As most areas in the Lamu archipelago are still without electricity, acoustic instruments have to be used and the harmonium is loud enough to cut through the din of percussion and merrymaking. But it's a tough job for the singer. For the weddings of more well-to-do townspeople, professional groups from Mombasa or Malindi are bussed in.

The **Zein Musical Party**, now based in Mombasa, is the heir of Lamu's taarab tradition. Its leader, **Zein l'Abdin**, was born in Lamu and hails from a

family in which the Swahili arts were highly valued. Together with the Swahili poet Sheikh Nabhany, he has unearthed a number of old poems, dating back to the nineteenth century, which he has included in his repertoire. Zein is not just a fabulous singer and composer but ranks as the finest *oud* player in East Africa and is well known throughout the Islamic world.

Other long-established Mombasa favourites include **Maulidi Musical Party**, named after singer Maulidi Juma, who play both traditional Swahili wedding songs and the Hindi-style songs characteristic of Mombasa taarab, in which Swahili words are set to tunes from the latest Bombay movie. The group is a typical Mombasan ensemble, with a sound based on keyboards (with a strong harmonium flavour) and accordion, guitar, bass guitar and percussion fills.

Zuhura Swaleh became the leading female taarab singer in the 1970s. She first hit the Mombasa scene with the Zein Musical Party and then formed her own group. Zuhura was responsible for the popularization of the *chakacha*-style taarab, very much loved by the female audiences and a precursor to today's *mipasho* lyrics. Performed for women exclusively as a part of the wedding celebrations, *chakacha* is a fast dance rhythm and usually features very ribald lyrics. Zuhura introduced both the rhythm and cutting-edge lyrics into taarab, with great success. Another feature of Swaleh's group was its use of the *taishokoto*, a very distinctive sound in Mombasa taarab.

A second female singer, and for a while the undisputed queen among taarab singers, was **Malika** (Asha Abdo Suleiman). In the 1970s, she occasionally sang with Zein, but then got married in Somalia. She performed and recorded in Mombasa in the 1980s, backed by Maulidi Musical Party, but when civil war erupted in Somalia she settled in Mombasa and started her own group. In the early 1990s Malika had one of the biggest hits in taarab history, "Vidonge", a song that was widely covered, even by dance bands from Nairobi, like Samba Mapangala and Virunga.

All the Mombasa singers mentioned are now in their late 50s or early 60s. Zein and Maulidi continue in a low-key fashion, Zuhura performs occasionally as an invited guest singer, and Malika has migrated to the US as a Somali refugee. Meanwhile a new generation of stars has emerged, **Yusuf Mohamed "Tenge"**, originally from Malindi, is the up-and-coming male singer, following in the footsteps of Maulidi and **Juma Bhalo**, who used to be the hero of Indian-style taarab.

Currently the most promising female singer is **Amina**. Early in her career Amina used to perform with the top Mombasa pop bands like Mombasa Roots and Safari Sound. After a family break, she is now back as a taarab singer with the most interesting sounds to come out of Mombasa in a long time. Amina and group go back to their Bajuni traditions, incorporating elements of Lamu archipelago *ngoma* dances, with an interesting mix of acoustic and electric instruments, featuring *taishokoto* and harmonium, as well as electric guitar, organ and bass. Another plus on Amina's side is that Mombasa's most famous female poet, Khuleita Muhashamy – composer of "Vidonge" and many more of Malika's biggest hits – is her aunt and now writes exclusively for her. One of their songs, "Dawa Yangu", has already achieved cult status, having been played on Mombasa radio stations daily for the past three years.

Zanzibar Culture Club

Club life was one of the main features of taarab in the first half of the twentieth century. In Kenya most clubs have faded away, but in Zanzibar club life is still intact.

At the **Culture Musical Club** (CMC), the largest such establishment in Zanzibar, members meet every night to socialize but chiefly to rehearse new songs for upcoming première shows held on important Islamic holidays. Under the leadership of violinist Kesi Juma, the CMC sports the hottest string section in taarab – up to eight violins in unison with accordion and keyboard; *qanun* virtuoso Rajab Suleiman, whose clear ripples grace the top of the orchestra's arrangements; and a four-strong rhythm team. They draw on a large pool of singers and composers, among whom the current singing stars are **Makame Faki** and **Fatma Issa**.

Like other CMC members, Makame Faki leads his own **kidumbak ensemble**. Kidumbak takes its name from the two small drums (*ki-dumbak* means small dumbak) that form the basis of these groups. A kidumbak also features sheets of sound from a violin, and a tea-chest bass rumbling beneath, giving cues to the dancers, *mkwasa* (claves) and *cherewa* (maracas). Vocals are sung in turn by all members of the group, in a cycle of generally rather nasty lyrics. To contemporary ears kidumbak sounds like a mix between *ngoma* and taarab, but it may well represent the roots of taarab, from a time before the Arab-styled orchestras came into vogue in Zanzibar town in the first decades of the twentieth century.

Kidumbak is played in the streets for any kind of festivity or just as an evening entertainment. The better-off in the classier **Stone Town** area of Zanzibar despise it as a kind of poor-folks' taarab. To them it is *ng'ambo* – "on the other side" – belonging to the poor quarters of town, with their palm-thatched huts.

The Stone Town side of the musical spectrum is represented by **Ikhwani Safaa** – the oldest musical club on the island (and most probably in all of Africa), which celebrated its centenary in 2005. The change in fashion towards modern taarab has hit both Ikhwani Safaa and Culture Musical Club, pulling away many of the best singers and musicians. Fast money can be earned in the modern taarab business, while club life and performances are more of an evening pastime for no financial gain. As a consequence of the fashion changes the Club rarely performs these days and attendance at rehearsals has been dwindling. However, they have done very well in their anniversary year, and it is to be hoped that the impetus can be maintained.

Kidumbak ensemble

The "Little Granny" of Zanzibar

'I started smoking when I was eight, and I also like to drink. Even today I don't need a microphone to sing.' Ninetysomething Bi Kidude (Fatma Baraka) is not your typical Zanzibari character, and especially so for being a woman. She is outspoken, though not lacking in values: 'In the past, taarab was a respectful thing. When we sang in public we used to wear a veil, and the vocalist used to stand still, concentrating on the actual singing. There was also none of the abusive language that is used in today's *mipasho* songs.'

Kidude's uncle, Buda Swedi, used to play in Siti bint Saad's group, and as a girl she used to hang around Saad's house, pretending to sleep as she soaked up the songs that were played there at the all-night sessions. In her youth, the November to May period was a busy and entertaining time of the year for the townspeople, as the town was flooded with sailors from across the Indian Ocean, waiting for the monsoon to turn for their return journeys. The nights were filled with *ngoma* dances from the Gulf and Red Sea areas, like the *sumsumiyya*.

Werner Graebner

Kidude learned how to play the drums from visiting sailors, and in the 1940s she went to Dar es Salaam, living at and performing with the Egyptian Music Club. Over the following decades, and back in Zanzibar, Kidude became known as a practitioner of *msondo* or *unyago*, songs and music for the female initiation rituals that she inherited from her family, originally from the Ngindo region of mainland Tanzania. Kidude also performed with the small women's taarab clubs, most notably Sahib el-Ary. She came into the Zanzibari audience's consciousness in the 1980s as an interpreter of songs from Siti bint Saad's time.

In the 1990s she toured the globe with the Zanzibar Taarab All Stars, Twinkling Stars and Culture Musical Club, and impressed audiences with her robust character and gorgeous *ya-leil* vocal improvisations. While her deep and powerful voice is not actually one of the preferred voice colours in Swahili taarab, this international recognition has led to more appreciation at home. In 2005, Kidude was honoured with a Womex award, and despite her advanced age, she shows no signs of slowing down. As she says: 'Whenever I sing, I feel like a 15-year-old girl again.'

These days, both Culture and Ikhwani Safaa rarely perform in public. With changes in fashion and the general economic climate, wedding performances have come to a standstill, and even the previously important shows on Islamic holidays now only attract small audiences. Members of the two orchestras have found a new source of income though, performing acoustic taarab in smaller settings in various tourist hotels around town. One of the first groups to work the hotel circuit were the **Twinkling Stars**, formed by Ikhwani Safaa renegades, violinist and singer **Seif Salim Saleh**, *qanun* player **Aliy Salum Basalama** and singer and violinist **Mohamed Ilyas**. Both Seif and Aliy died recently, leaving Ilyas with a small group of shifting personnel. Occasionally the group would present **Bi Kidude** (see box above), the doyenne of Zanzibar taarab, a robust lady in her 90s with a gorgeous voice.

Modern Taarab

Among the modern taarab groups, **East African Melody** is the most prominent act, with a sound dominated by a pair of keyboards, solo guitar and a tiny drum machine. A breakaway group, **Zanzibar Stars Modern Taarab** with lead singer **Mwanahawa Ali**, are Melody's main rivals on the scene. Both of these groups often perform in Dar es Salaam. A number of less prestigious (and therefore less expensive) groups cater for the wedding market; they include **Diamond Star**, **Magereza** and

413

Sanaa Taarab. Compared to the differentiated string arrangements of Culture and Ikhwani Safaa, they can sound bland to Western ears, but to the local fashion-conscious Zanzibari audience they are contemporary and give them music to dance to. They are also champions of *mipasho*, the backbiting songs so popular among the female audience.

Though not strictly taarab, another recent development needs mentioning: **Cool Para**, a young DJ has coined a new style and term, **taa-rap**, hoping to bring Zanzibar and taarab into the twenty-first century. Cool Para has taken elements of taarab songs by Ikhwani Safaa and Siti bint Saad and turned them into modern love songs for the youth, with elements of rap and hip-hop.

Tanga: Black Star

In the early 1960s the **Black Star Musical Club** of Tanga, a small town on the northern Tanzanian coast, transformed the whole taarab scene. Up until then, taarab was the near-exclusive province of Islamic Swahili – people who claimed long Swahili ancestry and often overseas origins. Then Black Star introduced a new modern style, with guitar and bass and a more danceable base. Taarab was revolutionized and began crossing national boundaries to audiences as far away as Burundi and Congo/Zaïre. Today, most taarab groups active in Tanzania, Burundi and Kenya are modelled on the style and instrumentation of the Black Star Musical Club, its offspring **Lucky Star** and their star female singer **Shakila**.

Tanga itself went a bit quiet from the mid-1970s, but recently new voices have emerged. Chief among them is **Mwanahela**, whose clear, powerful tones are close to Shakila's. With her group **Golden Star**, Mwanahela has become one of the favourites on the music market up and down the coast. In the 1990s, however, much of the music business shifted to Dar es Salaam, and so many musicians have moved there, including Shakila, members of Lucky Star and Golden Star. One of the Tanga bands that has left a mark on the modern scene is **Babloom**, which is now also based in Dar es Salaam.

Dar es Salaam

As with Tanzania's dance band scene, so the taarab scene focuses increasingly on **Dar es Salaam**. Dar has had taarab clubs since the early twentieth century and in the 1930s two important clubs were founded, the **Egyptian** and **Al-Watan Musical Clubs**.

In the 1980s, both clubs were outshone by various state-run or private taarab orchestras, orga-

nized along commercial lines. The first to become prominent was **JKT Taarab** – *Jeshi la Kujenga Taifa*, the "Army for the Construction of the Nation", the national youth service. JKT's line-up – for a time East Africa's largest taarab orchestra – was similar to the Zanzibar orchestras, featuring a violin section, *qanun* and *oud*. In contrast to the more restrained Zanzibar style, however, JKT created a lot of rhythmic excitement, and performances usually wound up in dancing. Led by violinist and singer **Issa Matona**, the band featured many fine female vocalists, among them Shakila (of Black Star fame).

The political and economic liberalization of the early 1990s led to new developments on Dar es Salaam's taarab scene. Two large (and rival) orchestras were at the forefront of this evolution: **Muungano Taarab**, owned by a businessman, and **TOT** (Tanzania One Theatre), which is closely related to the ruling CCM party. Both groups offered a variety of styles – a kind of integrated family entertainment including stage versions of ethnic *ngoma*, *kwaya*, theatrical plays and taarab. Shows were performed on Saturday and Sunday afternoons at social halls all over the city. Yet the culminating climax of their performances was the taarab: TOT and Muungano presented the flashiest taarab ever heard in East Africa, adding synthesizer and a dance band-style rhythm section to regular taarab instruments like violin, accordion and local percussion.

With the advent of **East African Melody**, the music became standardized, the line-up being reduced to two keyboard players, solo and bass guitar, plus drum machine. This process was mainly driven by cut-throat competition between the bands, focused on getting the most famous female star singers and having the hottest *mipasho* lyrics bashing the other bands' singer(s).

So what is **mipasho** and what creates all the excitement? *Mipasho* song lyrics are deliberately offensive and celebrate the institutionalized rivalry between groups. *Mipasho* shows are boisterous affairs: hundreds of women in the audience take part, dancing up to the lead singers at appropriate sections of the song, to give *tuzo* money and to show their affiliation to one group or another, or to direct attention to a member of the audience against whom they may have a grudge. Once or twice a year the groups have a face-off to find out who can muster the more boisterous following.

The latest development on the Dar es Salaam scene is a crossover between taarab and **Zaramo ngoma**, sometimes called **Segere** after the genre's first big hit. The earliest proponents of this style were **Young Stars Modern Taarab**, also called

mwanaSegere. *Segere* is an electrified mix of Zaramo *mchiriku*, Swahili *chakacha*, and taarab. The songs are really extended medleys stringing together various lyrics, choruses and melodic lines.

Young Stars have now split up, but all its members continue under the Segere flag. **Tandale Modern Taarab** is another group playing a similar style.

⭐ Zanzibar: Soul and Rhythm
Virgin Music, France
Lavishly documented 2-CD longbox, which features the island's major taarab clubs on one CD and different kinds of festive musics, like *beni*, kidumbak, Bi Kidude's *msondo*, *qasida* and *sumsumia* on the other. Highlights include Makame Faki's covers of hits by Bakari Abeid, Bi Kidude's "Kijiti" and Issa Matona singing an extended version of "Hongera", the Swahili wedding song par excellence.

⭐ Zanzibara 2: Golden Years of Mombasa Taarab 1965–75
Buda Musique, France
Recorded in the 1960s and 70s, this includes some of the earliest recordings of later masters like Zein l'Abdin, Maulidi Juma and Zuhura Swaleh, plus 1960s favourites Yasseen, Ali Mkali and Matano Juma. The *taishokoto* is a prominent sound on many songs. Highly recommended.

Amina

Mombasa's new taarab star combines the legacy of Malika and her songwriter Khuleita with Bajuni roots music in an interesting mix of acoustic and electric instruments.

⊙ Dawa Yangu
Mbwana Radio Service, Kenya
Apart from the hit title-track, this includes a Bajun *kishuri* song, along with some of Khuleita's favourites from the past. A remix of these songs is in preparation for international release.

Black Star & Lucky Star Musical Clubs

Black Star Musical Club and its offspring Lucky Star were the groups that put Tanga – a small town on the coast of northern Tanzania – on the musical map in the 1960s. Their innovations, such as the introduction of electric and bass guitars, as well as a more dance-oriented approach, led to a revolution in taarab that was imitated throughout Tanzania and beyond.

⭐ Nyota: Classic Taarab from Tanga
Globestyle, UK
Essential recordings, originally on early 1970s singles. You can't help but fall in love with the voices of Sharmila, Shakila and Asmahan, the guitar work and that wonderful Tanga bass.

Culture Musical Club

Culture Musical Club (CMC), Zanzibar's largest orchestra, today combines the best of sounds in the world of taarab. Typical large string section along with a mixture of Arab and African instruments, and soaring vocals over infectious local rhythms.

⊙ Taarab 4: The Music of Zanzibar
GlobeStyle, UK
Recorded during Globestyle's 1988 trip to the island, this features some classical tracks from Zanzibar's taarab repertoire, including Bakari Abeid's "Sabalkheri Mpenzi".

⊙ Spices of Zanzibar
Network, Germany
⊙ Waridi
Virgin, France
Their latest recordings. Both releases feature CMC's current crop of singers – Fatma Issa, Makame Faki and former member Rukia Ramadhani as a guest – along with some instrumentals.

⭐ Kidumbak Kalcha: Ng'ambo – The Other Side of Zanzibar
Dizim, Germany
Members of CMC, led by singer/composer Makame Faki, playing kidumbak, Zanzibari roots taarab. A different perspective on Zanzibari music, in that kidumbak is basically a dance music. Includes kidumbak versions of some of Makame's best-loved songs, Fatma Issa's "Mpewa Hapokonyeki" and the definitive Indian Ocean-style version of "La Paloma".

DJ Cool Para

A young rapper who has created a blend of taarab and rap that he calls taa-rap.

⊙ Taarap Style
Alakeifak Y2K, Tanzania
Turns the conventional Ikhwani Safaa taarab song "Raha ya Moyo Wangu" into a modern love story, with a rap update on the lyrics and a musical combination of modern taarab and bongo flava hip-hop. An interesting experiment.

East African Melody

East African Melody was formed in Abu Dhabi (UAE) to play at weddings of the resident Swahili population. In 1995, the band went on a tour of East Africa and never looked back. Their style, based on electric instruments and drum machine, became the model for modern taarab in general.

⊙ Viumbe Wazito
⊙ Paka Mapepe
FKW, Tanzania
The first CD features "Nikumbatie", one of the most enduring modern taarab songs of recent years, sung by star singer Rukia Ramadhani. The second is EAM's 2005 release: the title song, which translates as "Stray Cat", is a good example of the current state of *mipasho* backbiting lyrics.

Golden Star Taarab

Mwanahela Salim is the lead singer of this club from Tanga, which became popular in the 1990s.

⊙ Chonge
⊙ Ngarawa
GMC, Tanzania
Both CDs are recent re-recordings of early 1990s hits by Golden Star, otherwise recorded by Mbwana Radio Service in Mombasa. Mwanahela's clear and beautiful voice floats above the rather standard fare of modern taarab accompaniment.

Ikhwani Safaa Musical Club

Ikhwani Safaa is Zanzibar's oldest and most revered musical club, founded in 1905, and must boast getting on for a thousand years' worth of collective experience.

★ Taarab 2: The Music of Zanzibar
GlobeStyle, UK
Recorded in 1988, this shows Ikhwani Safaa in its prime, with the typically lush string arrangements and sweet melodies over laidback Latin rhythms. Enjoy the voices of Rukia Ramadhani, Mohamed Ilyas and Seif Salim. The latter's "Nipepee" is a highlight.

⊙ Zanzibara 1: 1905–2005: A Hundred Years of Taarab
Buda Musique, France
A recent recording, giving a historical perspective on the club and some of its major songs. Highlights include "Cheo Chako", sung by Rukia Ramadhani and exemplifying the club's intricate and varied style of composition, and the instrumental "Zinduna", a composition dating from the 1950s. All the splendour of a Zanzibar-style acoustic taarab orchestra.

Bi Kidude

Kidude is an institution on Zanzibar island, being famous for her contemporary remakes of songs from the Siti bint Saad repertoire.

⊙ Zanzibara 4: The Memory of Zanzibari Music
Buda Musique, France
An overview of Kidude's recordings from 1988 onwards. Includes recordings with Sahib el-Arry, Zanzibar Taarab All Stars, the Culture Musical Club and AfroArab Groove.

Kilimani Muslim School

Kilimani Muslim School are the masters of *qasida*, religious songs centred on the life of the Prophet, with an intricate rhythmic accompaniment from a set of tuned frame drums.

⊙ Music from Tanzania and Zanzibar, vol.3
Caprice, Sweden
This recording is hampered by less than satisfactory acoustics, which tend to muddy the rhythmic finesse of the tuned percussion. Recommended nonetheless for the beauty of the voices.

Malika

Malika was the undisputed queen of Mombasa taarab in the 1980s and into the 1990s.

⊙ Tarabu: Music from the Swahili of Kenya
Shanachie, US
Recorded during a concert tour in Germany in the 1990s. By this point, unfortunately, Malika's voice had deteriorated as a result of a throat operation, but her musical and performing skills still shine through. When in Mombasa try to get hold of one of her early cassette recordings.

Issa Matona

Born in rural Zanzibar in 1930, singer and violinist Issa Matona led the Dar es Salaam-based JKT Orchestra from the late 1970s. He also worked solo and is most popular as an interpreter of the Swahili wedding song par excellence, "Hongera" or "Kimasomaso". He died in a car accident in 2005.

⊙ Kimasomaso
FKW, Tanzania
A recording of some of Matona's favourite songs, in modern taarab style with keyboards and drum machines. Many of his recordings go under the name of "Kimasomaso", but cassette copies of the original early 1980s Tanzania Film Co (TFC) recording can still be found.

Famau Mohamed

Famau Mohamed is one of the few taarab musicians still active in the Lamu area.

⊙ Tarabu: Chants d'amour
Colophon, Belgium
A window on the past, featuring harmonium, tablas and local percussion as an accompaniment. The plaintive singing style is close to Indian *ghazal*, but also typical of the northern Swahili coast.

TOT Taarab

Dar es Salaam's leading modern taarab group in the 1990s – a rhythmically infectious hi-tech outfit, mixing electric with acoustic instruments and percussion.

⊙ Cassette No. 10
Mamu Stores, Tanzania
Fashionable mid-1990s taarab. Includes tough lyrics and Ali Star's smash hit "Natanga na Njia".

PLAYLIST
Taarab

1 **BASHRAF SALAMA Culture Musical Club** from *Spices of Zanzibar*
The typical sound of an acoustic Zanzibari taarab orchestra. A relaxed and slowly building groove, with master violinist Khamis Shehe at his best.

2 **DADA Matano Juma** from *Zanzibara 2: Golden Years of Mombasa Taarab 1965–1975*
One of taarab's most original voices, and always adventurous with his line-up, featuring fat organ sounds and a drumkit instead of the usual light percussion.

3 **MACHO YANACHEKA Black Star Musical Club** from *Nyota*
Tanga taarab may rightly be termed the first modern taarab. It had lots of crossover success back in the 1970s, and this song makes quite clear why.

4 **KIJITI Bi Kidude** from *Zanzibar: Soul and Rhythm*
Nonagenarian vocal prowess: Bi Kidude evokes the times of Zanzibar's first singing star, Siti bint Saad, in this famous episode from the 1930s.

5 **SEGERE Young Stars Musical Club** from *Segere*
The song that started a new style, combining coastal *ngoma* rhythms with electric taarab instruments, and the incisive song lyrics of modern taarab/*mipasho*.

6 **NIPEPEE Ikhwani Safaa Musical Club** from *Taarab 2: The Music of Zanzibar*
A sweet old song by Zanzibar's oldest orchestra. Singer Seif Salim at his best.

7 **MUSIWE NA MSHANGAO Zein Musical Party** from *Zanzibara 2: Golden Years of Mombasa Taarab 1965–1975*
An early recording by *oud* master Zein l'Abdin, with a nice arrangement including *taishokoto* and *nai*.

8 **HONGERA Issa Matona** from *Zanzibar: Soul and Rhythm*
The Swahili wedding song par excellence: Issa Matona was its master interpreter, with a never-ending string of words. Lively interaction with the audience too.

9 **PARARE Zuhura** from *Jino la Pembe*
Zuhura Swaleh's trademark is the fast chakacha rhythm adopted from the infectious female *ngoma* dance, and including the genre's incisive lyrics.

10 **NIKUMBATIE East African Melody** from *Viumbe Wazito*
Modern taarab in a more reflective mood, highlighting the sweet voice of Rukia Ramadhani, one of taarab's most celebrated singers.

Young Stars Musical Club

Originators of the heavy Zaramo crossover-style taarab, featuring singer Siza Abdalla.

⊙ **Segere**
⊙ **Segere 2**
FKW, Tanzania
The original recordings that gave the label "Segere" to the whole style. Heavy percussion and bass, rap-like vocals, and chorus sections and melodies taken from popular *ngoma* songs.

Zein Musical Party

Oud master Zein l'Abdin hails from Lamu island on the north Kenyan coast, but now lives in Mombasa. He is also known for his research into old Swahili poetry.

⊙ **The Swahili Song Book**
Dizim, Germany
All acoustic versions of timeless Swahili classics, like "Loho ya Kihindi", "Maneno Tisiya" and "Mnazi Wangu", along with some of Zein's own recent compositions.

Zuhura & Party

Zuhura Swaleh, one of Mombasa's outstanding female singers, has an energetic style firmly based in chachaka *ngoma* rhythms.

⊙ **Jino la Pembe**
Globestyle, UK
A fine introduction to taarab music, this is a compendium of Zuhura's most popular chakacha songs, notably "Parare" and the title tune, recorded on a European tour with the Maulidi Musical Party.

Tanzania |
Popular Music

the land of use-your-brain

Jagwa Music
Thomas Petroc

Tanzania has strong traditions of popular music, from the Cuban-styled dance bands originating back in the 1940s, through the Swahili Islamic style of *taarab* (an East African coastal style, covered in the previous section), to a current generation of local hip-hop and rappers. Werner Graebner looks at a scene that is currently in major transition.

Back in the early 1980s the Zaïre-born but long-time Tanzania-resident Remmy Ongala wrote a song called "The Doctor": "A bicycle has no say in front of a motorbike / A motorbike has no say in front of a car / A motorcar has no say in front of a train." He couldn't have better described the shock of economic and political liberalization in the 1990s, which saw the majority of Tanzanians locked in a tight fight for survival. For musicians, the effects were disastrous: a rash of private TV and radio stations began playing international pop round the clock, state organizations cut off support for their roster of dance bands and social halls, and everyone from hotels to corner grocery stores installed a TV to play music videos. Audiences for live music – a decade ago Dar es Salaam had a scene unequalled in Africa – fell off dramatically, and most bands were down to scraping a living.

Still, even with these inroads, many facets of Tanzanian musical culture – the importance of lyrics, dance and competition – remain intact, and often have meaningful roles where you would least expect to find them. Thus the disco phenomenon focuses on dance championships, which include local speciality genres. And words retain their impact in the new youth musics *bongo flava* (hip-hop) and *mchiriku* (neotraditional street dance/rap) scenes. Taarab, too – or *mipasho*, as people call it these days – entered a new era of popularity as a kind of competitive sport. There is now a flourishing new scene: night clubs and dance halls are alive and blazing again; a new copyright law is slowly taking hold; and the music industry has entered a boom period, with Dar es Salaam replacing Nairobi as the trendsetting new centre of East African music production

Muziki Wa Dansi

The craze for dance music – **muziki wa dansi** – began in Tanzania back in the early 1930s. Cuban

Collection of Werner Graebner

The Morogoro Jazz Band

Formed in 1944, Morogoro was one of the first jazz bands in what was then Tanganyika. A break-away group from the Cuban Marimba Band, led by Salum Abdallah, it became one of East Africa's most popular bands in the 1950s and early 60s. At the time this photo was taken, the young Mbaraka Mwinshehe had recently joined. He became one of the region's outstanding guitarists, singers and composers and his songs ruled the airwaves until his death in a car crash in 1979. His last song, "Shida" (Trouble), was the biggest-ever-selling record in East Africa.

The picture shows the band in 1968, with (from right to left) Kulwa Salum (sax, vocals, bandleader), Choka Mzee (drums), Mbaraka Mwinshehe (lead guitar, vocals), Peter (bass), Issa Khalfani (rhythm and lead guitars), Shaban Nyamwela (vocals, bass), Rajab Bilali (bongos) and Abdallah Hassani (maracas).

rumba records were all the rage and the urban youth organized itself into "dance clubs", like the **Dar es Salaam Jazz Band**, founded in 1932. Early instrumentation added brass instruments to a layer of local drums, with strings following – violins, banjos, mandolins and guitars. Bands sprung up all over the country: **Morogoro Jazz** (see box on previous page) and **Cuban Marimba** in Morogoro town, **Tabora Jazz** and **Kiko Kids** in Tabora, and so on. There were connections between groups all over the country, and competitions – a legacy of the colonial *beni* (brass band) and *ngoma* (song, drum and dance event) societies. By the 1950s, popular bands and musicians included **Salum Abdallah**'s **Cuban Marimba**; **Atomic** and **Jamhuri Jazz** (both from the coastal town of Tanga), and in the capital, the **Kilwa**, **Western** and **Dar es Salaam Jazz Bands**.

Yet the privately run music and dance clubs that dominated the postwar scene became obsolete within a few years of independence in 1961, when most Tanzanian bands began to operate under the patronage of state organizations, a system that lasted until the end of the 1980s. These organizations owned the instruments and employed the musicians, who drew more or less regular wages, plus a percentage of the gate collection. In 1964, the first group founded under this new regime was the **Nuta Jazz Band** (associated with the National Union of Tanzania, hence the acronym), and other bands formed under the umbrellas of the police, army, national service, party youth wing, Dar es Salaam city council or bus service.

Given this framework, it is perhaps hardly surprising that Tanzanian bands have displayed a remarkable collective strength. Musicians come and go (and a band can employ different "squad members" from night to night), yet a band's musical character remained (and often remains) recognizably the same. The **Ottu Jazz Band**, the current incarnation of Nuta Jazz Band, is a classic example. A number of prominent original members – among them Muhiddin Maalim and Hassani Bitchuka – left to form Dar International and later Mlimani Park Orchestra – but in the early 1990s Bitchuka and Maalim were back, effortlessly picking up the group's mainstream style, with its brassy Cuban-style horns. Bitchuka has now moved back to Mlimani, but in their fifth decade, the band – still led by Muhiddin Maalim and with the help of longtime singer and composer Moshi William – is stronger than ever.

A similar pattern applies to **Vijana Jazz Band**, the band of the youth organization of CCM (Chama cha Mapinduzi), the ruling party, and for years one of the country's best and most consistent bands. They were responsible for changing styles in *dansi*, having added synthesizer and electronic drums to the usual guitar, trumpet and sax line-up in 1987. The new instrumentation helped to attract a new, youthful following: however, they fell off after "privatization" in the mid-1990s, when the CCM handed the instruments over to the musicians, and stopped paying regular wages.

The group who, more than any others, had taken hold in the 1980s was **DDC Mlimani Park Orchestra**. Formed in 1978, Mlimani cooed their way into the hearts of Tanzanians with an endless string of hits sung and composed by Hassani Bitchuka, Cosmas Tobias Chidumule, Shaaban Dede and others. Mlimani is famous for the themes and intricate poetry of its lyrics: as in taarab, good, topical lyrics are an essential feature of Tanzanian music. However Mlimani's instrumental sounds – the interplay of the guitars and finely honed horn arrangements – are their trademark, making them one of Africa's outstanding bands. Composition and arrangement are usually group processes in Tanzanian dance music, but the force behind Mlimani is clearly **"King" Michael Enoch**, a hugely experienced player and arranger who first joined the Dar es Salaam Jazz Band in 1960 as a solo guitarist, soon adding bandleader duties.

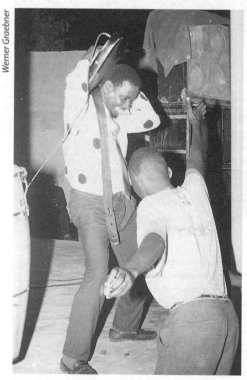

Werner Graebner

Ottu Jazz Band doing a Hendrix

DDC Mlimani Park Orchestra

Mlimani's live (and recorded) sound is typical of classic Tanzanian *dansi*. The opening of a song is usually slow, giving the audience the chance to savour the lyrics. The heat then builds with a faster second section known as the *chemko*, featuring tight interplay of three or four guitars and call-and-response games by the horns. Most of the dancing is based on popular street *ngoma* rhythms such as the *mdundiko*, or the *gwaride*, a line dance.

Like many bands, Mlimani have a team of between twenty and thirty musicians for live events, of whom maybe fifteen might be on stage at any one time. The basic line-up is three guitars, bass guitar, drumkit, *tumba* (congas), two or three trumpets, two or three saxophones and three to five singers.

While it is often the collective image and entertainment that count most, all the bands feature fine individual musicians who have their own followings. Conflicts arising from the need for personal expression are rife in a musical culture where the average outfit has twenty or more members. Musicians are forever moving between bands in search of greener pastures.

These moves occasionally generate quite chaotic conditions. A classic example occurred in 1985 when businessman Hugo Kisima disbanded **Orchestra Safari Sound** (OSS) and lured away six of Orchestra Mlimani Park's leading musicians to form the new **International Orchestra Safari Sound** (IOSS). The reshuffle left the former OSS leader, twelve-string stylist Ndala Kasheba, without a band to lead, and Mlimani in serious trouble. For a time IOSS, led by former Mlimani singer Muhiddin Maalim and guitarist Abel Balthazar, were contenders for their old band's position of supremacy.

Safari Sound itself reformed and entered a golden period when **Nguza Viking**, solo guitarist extraordinaire and former leader of Maquis, took over the leadership at the end of 1991. The band came back to high acclaim with a new *mtindo* called "Rashikanda Wasaa", and Nguza landed an instant hit with "Mageuzi" (Changes), a song about the political reforms under way in Tanzania – the transition to a multiparty system. Inexplicably, however, in spring 1992, the owner disbanded the orchestra yet again.

After leaving OSS, **Ndala Kasheba** joined Orchestre Maquis for some time before going out as a solo performer. From the late 1980s he led **Zaita Musica**, which plays a style much indebted to *zouk*, and had a smash hit with "Monica" in the early 1990s. Recently, Kasheba was headed for a comeback with a new recording and international release featuring his acoustic twelve-string sound, but sadly he died shortly after its release in October 2004.

Apart from the old-time *muziki wa dansi* orchestras, a number of new bands have come up over the past ten years. Catering mainly for a younger audience, they are modelled on Congolese youth bands like Wenge Musica, stripping away the horn sections, basing their sound on guitars and synthesizer fills. Like their Congolese counterparts, they play fast and energetic dance music, but for the most part their songs lack memorable words and melodies, so they are best savoured as live acts. Most popular among these bands are **African Stars Band "Twanga Pepeta"**, **Extra Bongo**, **Double M Sound** and **African Revolutions Band**.

No Sweat from Congo: Maquis and Matimila

In the late 1970s a more laidback Congolese sound became popular in Tanzania through bands like **Orchestra Maquis Original** and **Orchestra Safari Sound** (OSS). A rather genteel affair compared to Mlimani or Ottu, they adopted the motto *Kamanyola bila jasho* (Dance Kamanyola without sweating).

Originally from the Lubumbashi area of southeastern Congo (then Zaïre), Orchestra Maquis settled in Dar in the early 1970s. It is quite common for musicians from that area to tour East Africa, and Nairobi's recording studios have always attracted numerous musicians from the Congo. Yet in Tanzania foreign musicians are a lot more integrated into the local scene and they usually sing their songs in Swahili. For an outsider, the Maquis style (especially their vocal harmonies) may sound close to Kinshasa *soukous*, but it's really the other way round: the eastern parts of the Congo have always had closer cultural and economic ties to East Africa than to the Congo basin.

Orchestra Maquis caused a stir with each new dance style (*mtindo*) they invented. *Zembwela* for example, introduced through their 1985 hit "Karubandika", was so pervasive that the name is still commonly used as a synonym for dancing per se. But in the 1990s, they went through hard times. Many of the original founder members left or died (rumours of sorcery went around Dar), and debtors took what remained of their assets, including their instruments. Individual musicians tried to get support from local investors and for a time three splinter groups played around Dar, all carrying the Orchestra Maquis imprint in their name.

Werner Graebner

The strongest and only one surviving at this point is **Bana Maquis**, led by Tshimanga Assosa.

Another Congolese fixture in Tanzania's music scene is **Remmy Ongala**. Born in the Kivu region of eastern Congo, he came to Dar in 1978 to join **Orchestra Makassy** – his uncle Makassy's band. When Makassy wound up the band and moved to Nairobi in the early 1980s (see Kenya chapter), Remmy joined **Orchestra Matimila** (later Super Matimila), becoming the bandleader.

Remmy's personality and outspoken lyrics created a magnetic appeal and the band became established on the WOMAD festival circuit. Unfortunately, their local reputation suffered, and while the tours and recordings helped to buy much-needed equipment, and to make Remmy independent of a band-owner, the demands of touring, with only a few and less prominent musicians, destroyed the original line-up. Playing dances around Dar es Salaam did not generate enough income to support more than one star in a band.

Nevertheless, Remmy was always good for a hit, and his comments on the ills of Dar city life or politics always came with his own typical slant or language. Over the past few years Remmy has had to continue on a much reduced scale due to his ill-health. He suffers from the effects of a stroke plus diabetes and is no longer able to play the guitar, singing from a wheelchair if his health allows him to perform at all.

Remmy became a born-again Christian recently and gave up singing in dance halls. Now a gospel singer, he is one of several dance music vocalists to have taken this direction. Among the first was former Mlimani Park singer and composer Cosmas Tobias Chidumule, who left secular music in the early 1990s to perform and record exclusively in religious contexts. Ongala's uncle Makassy was another big name who "converted" several years ago. As in many other African countries with proliferating churches, *kwaya* (choir) and other forms of Christian music have become a substantial part of the music business. There are estimates that as much as thirty percent of the Tanzanian market may be in religious music.

Hotel Pop

Although separate from the *dansi* scene, "**hotel bands**" are linked to it by their personnel. Many a young musician trained in dance music has taken up the new work opportunities created by hotels hiring a resident band. Hotel bands, however, are smaller groups and their sound is normally dominated by the keyboard. There is one guitar player instead of two to three, and they may feature just one saxophone or trumpet instead of a horn section. The rhythm is usually more rock-based and the lyrics less elaborate.

Probably the most interesting among these is **Kilimanjaro**, a band which has existed since the 1970s and was originally named The Revolutions. Most band members hail from the Tanga region on the northern Tanzanian coast, where the band also started to play. They later moved to Dar es Salaam, and become famous as *mwanaNjenje*, named after their first album and hit song from the 1980s. "Njenje" was the adaptation of a coastal *chakacha* song into a cooking new electric arrangement, and to this day Kilimanjaro is famous for its modern adaptations of *ngoma* songs. Led by Mzee Njenje and Waziri Ally, Kilimanjaro has often played extensive engagements oversees, especially in the Gulf area, and it is now the resident band at the Ambassador Plaza, where it has played every weekend for the past few years.

Other bands on Dar's hotel circuit, past and present, include **M.K. Group**, **Tanza Musica**, **Bantu Group** (led by ex-Vijana Jazz guitarist Hamza Kalala), Nguza Viking's **Achigo Stars**, **Ndala Kasheba** and King Kiki's **Zaita Musica**.

Bongo Flava

Around the streets of Dar there are many sign-writer kiosks sporting larger-than-life portraits of US rappers and hip-hop artists like Tupac Shakur and Ice Cube. Young sign-painters use these images to advertise their trade and talents, identifying the new role models of Tanzanian youth. These point beyond Tanzania or Africa, as does one of the anthems of the new generation, "Ni Wapi Tunakwenda" (Where are we Heading) by Swahili rap star **2-Proud**:

I want to know where I will go
I know where I come from,
Where I'll go, I don't know
Let me tell you:
I'm looking for a passport now
I am going to stow away on a boat
Where ever I'll arrive,

I will forget this African condition
I'm tired of home
I continue to be harassed.

Swahili rap had been in the offing for quite some time, with Dar's **Kwanza Unit** taking the palm of being Tanzania's first rap group back in the 1980s. But a lack of production facilities held back local creativity and forced the rappers to rely on readily available backing tracks. As a result the Tanzanian style was initially highly derivative. The situation has changed fast over the past few years, though, with many new studios opening and catering for the rising demands of a booming market.

Kwanza Unit was a kind of supergroup with about ten rappers under the leadership of Rhymson. The first star in terms of popularity and sales was solo-rapper **2-Proud**. His first cassette "Ni Mimi" (It's Me) was a big hit in 1995 and helped set up the market for Swahili-language rap. In 1998, he hit the market with the first state-of-the-art local production made in the studio of Master J. Other groups of the day included **Da De-Plow-MaTZ**, and **GWM**. (Gangsters with Matatizo) who scored a big rap hit with "Cheza Mbali na Kasheshe" (Stay Away from Problems).

Swahili rap or **bongo flava** – as youth musics are now called collectively – has come of age within the past few years. It has become the dominant music on the market and in the media. *Bongo* means "brain" in Swahili: in Dar es Salaam, or Tanzania as a whole, it has come to stand for "the town/country where you have to use your brains in order to survive". Hip-hop has established itself as a voice of the marginalized urban youth, topicalizing the problems of survival with high rates of unemployment, diseases like AIDS, common societal ills like corruption and so on. This holds especially true for the **TMK** "ghetto" faction of *bongo flava*, so named after the poor neighborhood of Temeke, one of Dar's suburban areas. Temeke is the origin of some of the more radical and critical artists and groups, like **Gangwe Mobb**, **GWM** (Gangsters with Matatizo) or the leading current star **Juma Nature**.

Nature is a local hero. He is a great lyrical composer and his creative wordplay and original style has something that most hip-hop artists fail even to come close to. Running a close second is **Ferooz**, a founder member of the legendary **Daz Nundaz** crew, famed for creativity, vocal prowess and bringing out timely and pertinent tunes that reach deep into the hearts of thousands of admirers. His song "Starehe", in which he plays the role of an AIDS patient in hospital, became an overnight regional anthem and helped him embrace a

fan base of people of all ages across borders. Other artists treading a fine line between pleasing their fans whilst upsetting the authorities are **Professor Jay**, **Inspecta Haroun** and **Wagosi wa Kaya**.

East Coast stands in opposition to the critical group just described: "East Coast" is mainly the posh urban neighbourhood of Upanga, origin of a number of middle- and upper-class artists like **TID (Top In Dar)**, **Crazy GK** and **Mwanafalsafa**. Theirs is a smooth vibes and R&B orientation within **bongo flava**, with love songs and partying being the most common lyrical topics. The softer voices of **Mr Paul**, **Mr Nice** and the female voices of **Lady JD** and **Ray C** also belong to this latter group. To outside listeners their music sounds rather derivative and modelled on African American pop, with the sole difference being substitution of Swahili lyrics for English ones.

While much of Tanzanian youth music, especially in the Dar es Salaam area, was and still is dominated by outside models, a number of artists from the more rural areas and smaller towns have started to integrate local musical culture with contemporary production and styles. Thus the Arusha-based Maasai collective **X-Plastaz** has very successfully integrated into their beats the traditional breathy and rhythmic Maasai singing style and typical jumpy dancing. Similarly Tanga-based **Mr Ebbo**, of "Mimi Mmasai" (I am a Maasai) fame has sung a number of songs from the Maasai vantage point. Even earlier on, artists from Zanzibar had begun to integrate rhythms and elements of taarab music into their act: thus the **Struggling Islanders** have recorded with the East African Melody Modern Taarab group, and **DJ Cool Para** is seeking to create a new style that he calls **taa-rap**. An up-and-coming group from Zanzibar with a strong political message is **Wazenj Kijiwe**.

Tradition & Innovation

Experimentation with local music forms is not just a rapper's domain. **Saida Karoli** is a young singer from the Bukoba region of northwestern Tanzania, who has almost single-handedly created a buzz for the integration of local rhythms, melodies and regional languages with modern instruments and production. Singing in her Haya mother tongue, and turning folk melodies into infectious new music, she hit the pop charts almost immediately after the release of her first recording in the fall of 2001. **Maua Chenkula** is another young female singer – again from the Bukoba region – following in Karoli's footsteps.

Under the erstwhile Ujamaa cultural policy, all regional musical traditions had been subordinated to the creation of a national culture based on Swahili. Recording in a local language was rarely allowed on the national radio station, which for a long time had been the sole recording facility in the country. In terms of music, founder president Julius Nyerere had asked his cultural bureaucracy to take the "best of all tribes" and create a new "national" folklore. The result was usually a combination of regional musical forms with song lyrics in praise of government, party and their leaders. Otherwise, the bureaucracy also fought and actually banned non-licensed developments like the street *ngoma* developing in Dar es Salaam (see below). Over the years Tanzanians developed a strong aversion to anything that sounded like "traditional music".

Thus, the beautiful music of the likes of **Hukwe Zawose** and the **Master Musicians of Tanzania** was rarely heard or appreciated within the country. Actually the group was an outcome of the aforementioned cultural policy. The members were instructors at the Bagamoyo College of Arts (a teachers' training college), and for decades the group was Tanzania's figurehead ensemble when it came to representing the country's musical culture abroad. Due to Hukwe Zawose's talent, and his bringing in of many family members, the ensemble had a strong slant towards music from the Gogo ethnic group of Tanzania. Foreign audiences thus got to hear Gogo vocal techniques, giant hand marimbas and specially invented neotraditional instruments like the *iseze* fiddle (which was magnified from the original instrument and had resonating strings added).

As stunning as it all sounds, for Tanzanians it was hardly digestible, as almost all of the ensemble's songs were in praise of government or party, their leaders and programmes. In more recent years Zawose had taken new steps and formed

Jagwa Jive

Mchiriku is a Dar es Salaam street music, popular mainly with the poorer sections of society. Despite lack of radio airplay and general media attention, *mchiriku* has become one of the city's major youth musics, along with *bongo flava*.

Jagwa Music was founded in 1972 as a *chakacha* group. *Chakacha* was immensely popular at the time, coming down the coast from Mombasa along with the taarab of the likes of Zuhura Swaleh. Originally a Swahili wedding dance, performed exclusively for women, *chakacha* was transformed and modernized in Dar es Salaam into the multi-faceted *mchiriku* – street-dance entertainment catering for both sexes and most occasions. Thus Jagwa and other groups now use a set of Zaramo drums, along with items of bricolage: a stool heavily beaten with rhythm sticks and small hand-held Casio toy organs, amplified along with the lead vocal by car-battery powered megaphones, have become the omnipresent signifiers of modernity. Song lyrics are embellished on a day-to-day basis with spontaneous commentary, depending on what is in the news or who is in the audience. And there are usually witty observations about the daily struggles for survival in a world of poverty and injustice.

Jagwa Music is Dar es Salaam's most prominent *mchiriku* group and have released ten cassette albums so far. In their home town, Jagwa still perform regularly at weddings and traditional ceremonies, but of late they have made it into clubs and onto the world stage. They have moulded *mchiriku* – customarily based on a lot of audience interaction and participation – into a powerhouse performance with a choreographed non-stop gymnastic workout, combining theatrics, acrobatic prowess and a lot of humour.

a new group **Chibite**. Sadly, he and his nephew Charles died in 2003 and 2004 respectively. Yet, as the examples of Maasai rappers or Saida Karoli's adaptation of Haya musical culture show, the traditions are alive and well. Even stronger things are going on in the streets of Dar es Salaam.

Mchiriku Madness

They call themselves **Night Star Musical Club**, **Atomic Advantage**, **Tokyo Ngoma**, **Msusu wa Chuma** (Sanding-paper), **Gari Kubwa** (Big Car) **Buti Kubwa** (Big Boot) and **Jagwa Music**, and they play a street entertainment called **mchiriku**. With an instrumentation stripped down to bare essentials – just a small Casio keyboard, four drums and vocals – the sound relates to what Swedé Swedé have been doing in Kinshasa.

Walking around any of Dar's poorer suburbs on a weekend night, one is bound to run into a *mchiriku*. From afar it is usually the high din of the Casio that cuts through the night. Closer up you make out the deep throb of drums and the amplified solo voice. Amplification is a distinguishing feature, setting *mchiriku* apart from other urban *ngoma* forms popular in Dar es Salaam. The bands often work with battery-powered systems seemingly used decades back to make public announcements, but feedback and distortion are part of the desired effect, as the singers bellow out songs for hours on end, joined by a chorus of fellow club

members and the audience. Intermittent keyboard melodies offer the singers the chance to catch breath, and four differently tuned drums are part of the line-up, the lowest being placed over a hole dug into the street or ground to give a booming sound.

Mchiriku derives from a wedding *ngoma* of the Zaramo people, who make their home in the area surrounding Dar es Salaam. The official occasion for the urban *mchiriku* can range from anything like a wedding celebration, naming or circumcision ceremonies, and habitually involves the whole neighbourhood. Later in the night, *mchiriku* usually takes in the city's low-life, attracting drunkards and dope fiends, pickpockets and the queens of the night. Because of illegally brewed liquor, drugs, unruly lyrics and licentious dancing, the public performance of *mchiriku* was officially banned for some time in the mid-1990s.

Mchiriku groups record prolifically, with dozens of new cassettes on the market all the time. The songs are not unlike those of Remmy Ongala or the young rappers, talking about the plight of the youth trying to make a decent living, or commenting on larger political or social issues. More recently there has been some extension of the traditional line-up to include bass guitar or guitars, aiming for a cross between dance music and *ngoma*.

Reggae and Ragga

Like most other African countries, Tanzania has a small but dedicated **reggae** subculture. Bands first popped up in the 1970s, inspired by Bob Marley, but many soon faltered due to lack of instruments and infrastructure.

Jah Kimbuteh and his band **Roots and Kulture**, who started up in 1985, put reggae on the Tanzanian music map. Together with **Justin Kalikawe's Urithi Band** and **Innocent Galinoma** (now based in the US), Kimbuteh represents the mainstream of Tanzanian reggae, with lyrics in both Swahili and English, in the style of Marley and Peter Tosh.

Among the younger reggae musicians, **Ras Innocent Nyanyagwa** performs an interesting mix of traditional roots-rock reggae with folk beats from Tanzania's southern highlands, occasionally adding songs in his Hehe mother tongue to the common Swahili lyrics. Other new artists, like the **Jam Brothers** or **Stybar's Reggamuffin**, add elements of dub and rap.

Special thanks to Yusuf Mahmoud for his help with this article

---

DISCOGRAPHY Tanzania | Popular Music

⊙ **Bongo Flava: Swahili Rap from Tanzania**
Outhere Records, Germany
A good selection of *bongo flava*'s greatest stars and recent hits, including Juma Nature, Afande Sele, Prof. Jay, Gangwe Mob, Daz Nundaz, X-Plastaz and Mr Ebbo.

⊙ **Music from Tanzania and Zanzibar 1 & 2**
Caprice, Sweden
Recorded by the Swedish Concert Institute in Dar es Salaam, Dodoma and Zanzibar in 1996, these recordings present performances by (mostly) government-sponsored cultural and dance troupes, plus some pieces by graduates from the Bagamoyo College of Arts.

★ **Muziki wa Dansi: Afropop Hits from Tanzania**
Africassette, US
Recorded by Radio Tanzania in the 1980s when Tanzanian dance bands were at their most sophisticated, this features some of the best songs from that era. It includes highlights from the Orchestra Maquis repertoire, Juwata Jazz's brassy sound and selections from International Orchestra Safari Sound, featuring the voices of old masters Muhiddin Maalim and Hassani Bitchuka. A later track has Bitchuka and Maalim reunited with their former colleagues from Juwata.

⊙ **The Rough Guide to the Music of Tanzania**
World Music Network, UK
A collection of recent recordings from Dar es Salaam and Zanzibar studios, exploring the diversity of Tanzania's popular musics, from the typical guitar-driven and horn-embellished sound of dance bands like Mlimani Park, Vijana and Ottu Jazz, to Saida Karoli's Haya vocal colours, hip-hop with a Maasai tinge, *kibati* – neotraditional rap from Zanzibar – and much more.

Gangwe Mobb

The duo of Inspekta Harun and Luten Karam, from the Temeke section of Dar es Salaam, started out together in 1995 and are one of Tanzania's strongest and most consistent rap groups.

⊙ **Simulizi ya Mapenzi**
GMC, Tanzania
Rooted in the Temeke "ghetto", with lots of street slang, strong narration and witty lyrics.

Imani Ngoma Group

Imani Ngoma is a Zanzibar-based ensemble specializing in *ngoma* dance traditions.

⊙ **Bape: Songs and Dances from Zanzibar**
Dunya Records, Italy
A selection of *ngoma* dances from the islands as well as mainland Tanzania, including *msoma*, *sindimba*, *gonga* and *ngoma*.

Jagwa Music

Jagwa is the most prolific among the many *mchiriku* groups active around Dar es Salaam.

▦ **Volume 9: Mtoto Wacha Kupiga Mayoee**
FKW, Tanzania
Jagwa's recordings hardly convey what *mchiriku* is like as a live performance, and the recording quality of their cassettes thus far leaves much to be desired. While we wait for their first CD (and maybe DVD) release, this one gives a glimpse of *mchiriku*'s raw power.

Saida Karoli

Born in the Kagera region in the northwestern corner of the country, Karoli is one of the rising stars on the Tanzanian music scene.

⊙ **Kanichambua Kama Karanga**
⊙ **Mapenzi Kizunguzungu**
FM Productions, Tanzania
Even though most of her songs are in a regional language, Karoli hit the Tanzanian charts immediately after the release of her first album in the autumn of 2001. Hers is a music with a strong ethnic flavour, based on local Haya rhythms and melodies. The first CD contains initial hit "Maria Salome", while the second offers more variety and is generally better produced.

Ndala Kasheba

Moving to Tanzania in the late 1960s, the late Ndala Kasheba played with Fauvette, Safari Nkoi and Orchestre Maquis, and led Orchestre Safari Sound, one of the hottest bands on the Dar scene in the late 1970s/early 80s. Together with former Safari Sound bandmate King Kiki, he formed Zaita Musica in the early 1990s. The acoustic twelve-string guitar was Kasheba's trademark sound.

⊙ **Yellow Card**
Limitless Sky, US
Kasheba's last recording contains new songs, like "Yellow Card", alongside some of his old hits like "Marashi ya Pemba" and "Mpaka Manga".

Kilimanjaro

Many members of Kilimanjaro hail from the Tanga region on the northern Tanzanian coast. The band excels in modern adaptations of traditional *ngoma* rhythms and songs from that area. They are currently the resident band at Dar's *Ambassador Plaza Hotel*.

⊙ **Kinyau-Nyau**
⊙ **Gere**
Kilimanjaro, Tanzania
Modern arrangements of traditional songs are the highlights here, with *Kinyau-Nyau* featuring the hit "Tupendane", sung by female singer Nyota Waziri – a beautiful song with a taarab flavour.

Kwanza Unit

Kwanza are considered to have been Tanzania's first rap group.

📷 **Kwanzanians**
FM Music, Tanzania (distributed by Rahh, Holland)
This well-produced 1998 release presents a hip-hop reworking of King Kiki's and Orchestre Safari Sound's 1979 dance band hit "Msafiri".

Mlimani Park Orchestra

The essence of the Tanzanian dance music experience: great songs, voices and vocal harmonies, racy guitar interplay and sumptuous horn arrangements inspired by traditional melodies.

⭐ **Sikinde**
Africassette, US
A selection of Mlimani's greatest hits c. 1980–87. "Neema" features the expressive voice of Cosmas Chidumule and was twice voted Song of the Year by listeners of Radio Tanzania.

⊙ **Onyo**
⊙ **Maneno Maneno**
GMC, Tanzania
More recent recordings featuring the voices of Hassani Bitchuka and bandleader Shaban Dede.

Mr Ebbo

Abel Roshila Motikaa, a.k.a. Mr. Ebbo, is a young Maasai rapper who works out of Tanga province.

⊙ **Fahari Yako**
GMC, Dar es Salaam
Even the life experience of the nomadic Maasai is becoming urbanized and globalized in today's Tanzania. Mr Ebbo sings with his own Maasai-Swahili slant on living in Tanzania today

and about upholding Maasai cultural values. Includes the smash hit "Mimi Mmasai" (I am a Maasai).

Mr Nice

"Mr Nice" (Lucas Mkenda) is one of the biggest sellers on Dar's *bongo flava* scene. More of a crooner than a rapper, he calls his style "takeu" (from the initials of Tanzania, Kenya, Uganda).

⊙ **Rafiki**
⊙ **Bahati**
FKW, Tanzania
Some of these songs sound like Kenyan Swahili songs of a several decades ago, updated with synth and drum machine. Not really convincing, but very much liked by local audiences.

Mbaraka Mwinshehe Mwaruka

With Morogoro Jazz and Super Volcanoes, the late singer/guitarist Mbaraka Mwinshehe ruled the East African music scene in the 1970s with a string of hits released by the Nairobi-based Polygram.

📷 **Ukumbusho Vol 1**
📷 **Ukumbusho Vol 3**
📷 **Pesa No.1**
Tamasha, Kenya
Vol. 1 has Mwinshehe's voice at its best on the 1979 hit "Shida" (Trouble), posthumously released and the biggest-ever seller on the East African market. *Vol. 3* and *Pesa No.1* feature some nice early 1970s recordings with the typical Morogoro Jazz horn sound.

Nia Safi & Imani Group

Nia Safi is an interesting experiment combining elements of various *ngoma*, with acoustic taarab and electric instruments.

⊙ **Kibati: Zanzibar 2003**
Heartbeat Records, Tanzania
Zanzibar traditional *ngoma* like *bomu*, *msewe*, kidumbak, *lelemama* in new clothes. "Kibati", in a modernized traditional rap-like form, is the outstanding track.

Orchestre Makassy

Makassy's band, featuring Mose Fan Fan and Remmy Ongala, was one of the major forces on the Dar es Salaam scene in the late 1970s. Part of the band moved to Nairobi in the early 80s.

⭐ **Legends of East Africa**
ARC Music, UK
Originally on Virgin, this was one of the best releases of African music in the early 1980s. Recorded in Nairobi, it featured a scaled-down version of the original Dar es Salaam band, minus Remmy Ongala. The CD edition is a great reminder of these golden times, with the bonus tracks made up of equally fine recordings by Remmy Ongala and Super Matimila.

Orchestre Maquis Original/ Bana Maquis

Maquis was the principal representative of the Shaba (eastern Congolese) sound among Dar Es Salaam based-bands in the 1970s and 80s.

📼 Karubandika
Ahadi, Kenya

Typically lavish horn arrangements, the voices of Kasaloo Kyanga and Kyanga Songa, and Nguza Viking's outstanding solo guitar work make these classics of the Tanzanian dance repertoire. The LP is out of print but cassette copies of this and other releases are still available.

⊙ Leila
DakarSound, Netherlands

Issued under the name of Bana Maquis, but most of the tracks are from a 1993 cassette by Maquis Original. All the songs highlight the voice and compositional skills of Tshimanga Assosa.

Nuta Jazz Band

Established in 1964, Nuta was the first new jazz band of the national phase. The band is still active under the name of Ottu Jazz Band.

📼 Old is Gold
Tamasha, Kenya

Features songs from the beginning of the 1970s, with early samples of Muhiddin Maalim's voice and the typical brassy horn sound.

⊙ Kilio cha Mtu Mzima
Ujamaa Planet, UK
⊙ Piga Ua Talaka Utatoa
FKW, Tanzania

These recent recordings mainly feature prolific composer and singer Moshi William.

Remmy Ongala & Super Matimila

One of Tanzania's most respected singer-composers, especially well known for the pungent social criticism of his songs. Ill health has greatly curtailed his activity in recent years.

★ Songs for the Poor Man
Real World, UK

His best international release. Features the hard drive of "Kipenda Roho" and Remmy's own all-time favourite "Mariamu Wangu", which is based on the popular *mdundiko ngoma* from Dar es Salaam.

⊙ The Kershaw Sessions
Strange Roots, UK

Some of Remmy's later songs, recorded at different BBC sessions over the years. This one comes closest to Matimila's live sound and gves a good taste of the band's fantastic three-guitar work.

Werner Graebner

Juma Nature

Juma Kassim Ally, a.k.a. Juma Nature is the leading *bongo flava* artist and also head of the Temeke-based Wanaume Family rap collective.

★ Ubin-Adam Kazi
GMC, Tanzania

A stylistically varied album combining great lyrics, vocals and choruses with lots of local flavour, including hints of *ngoma*. Highly recommended.

PLAYLIST
Tanzania | Popular

1 **MTOTO AKILILIA WEMBE Mlimani Park Orchestra** from *Sikinde*
Great voice, excellent lyrics, Zaramo *ngoma* rhythm and Mlimani's famous lush horn arrangements: Tanzanian dance music at its peak!

2 **SHEREHE Jume Nature** from *Ubin-Adam Kazi*
The current state of *bongo flava*: varied instrumental colours, vocals and chorus lines with lots of local spice. Almost Zawose-like.

3 **TAMBIKO Vijana Jazz Band** from *Shingo Feni*
Sweet-sounding guitar interplay, saxes and voices on top. Refers to an old *ngoma* spirit dance from Tanga region.

4 **KIBATI Nia Safi & Imani Group** from *Kibati: Zanzibar 2003*
Kibati, traditional rap in a cooking contemporary environment.

5 **MARYAM WANGU Remmy Ongala & Super Matimila** from *Songs for the Poor Man*
With Ongala's voice in a loving mood, it all ends in Dar's famed *mdundiko* groove.

6 **BAMIZA X-Plastaz** from *Maasai Hip Hop*
Lots of Maasai colours in the voices.

7 **WACHA KUPIGA MAYOWE Jagwa Music** from *Volume 9: Mtoto Wacha Kupiga Mayoee*
Tinny Casio organ, big rhythm, lots of energy.

8 **OMUKHAILE KILINJWE Saida Karoli** from *Mapenzi Kizunguzungu*
A unusually quiet song, Saida's voice with acoustic guitar and a little percussion.

9 **VIDONGE Gangwe Mobb** from *Simulizi ya Mapenzi*
Bongo flava rappers pay tribute to one of the most famous taarab songs, featuring *mipasho* queen Nasma Khamis.

10 **MPENZI LUTA Orchestra Maquis Original** from *Karubandika*
A 1980s hit featuring Nguza Viking's fat guitar and the sweet vocals that Maquis were famous for.

Afande Sele

Afande Sele (Selemani Msindi) is one of the most outspoken young Tanzanian artists. He belongs to the "ghetto" faction of rappers.

⊙ Darubini Kali: Mfalme wa Rhymes
GMC, Tanzania
The title song explains the artist's role of talking about the ills and problems of society. At another level, it also criticizes Upanga rappers for just singing about love and the good life.

Shikamoo Jazz Band

Shikamoo is a respectful greeting addressed to older people. This reunion of musicians originally active from the 1950s–70s was enabled by instruments donated by the UK-based Helpage organization.

⊙ Chela Chela Vol 1
RetroAfric, UK
Recorded shortly after the band's formation. A later live recording of the band on their UK tour in 1995 will soon be available on the same label.

2-Proud (Mr II)

Mr II is one of the pioneers of Tanzanian rap, becoming the music's first star in the 1990s. Mr II keeps a low profile these days and has all but retired from live performance.

⊙ Millenia
Kwetu Entertainment, Tanzania
Recorded only a few years ago, this is already rather dated musically in its dependence on US models, indirectly showing how *bongo flava* has progressed since then. Interesting lyrics, though.

Vijana Jazz Band

Vijana Jazz was formed in the early 1970s under CCM's Umoja wa Vijana (the ruling party's youth wing) and became one of the strongest and longest-lasting bands on the Tanzanian scene.

⊙ Shingo Feni
GMC, Tanzania
Great new recording of some of Vijana's favourites from the 1980s. All the songs feature great guitar work and the classic horn arrangements that are one of the band's trademarks.

X-Plastaz

X-Plastaz hail from Arusha in the country's northeast and incorporate elements of Maasai musical and dance forms into their act.

⊙ Maasai Hip Hop
Outhere Records, Germany
Unlike many Tanzanian hip-hop productions, which are still overly in thrall to US models, X-Plastaz offer a much more adventurous approach, digging up their local roots in an incredible amalgam of Maasai acapella chants and body language, exciting Swahili rhymes and modern production values. A well-produced debut.

Hukwe Zawose & The Master Musicians of Tanzania

Hukwe Zawose was for a long time the leader and spiritual force behind Tanzania's National Music Ensemble, based at the Bagamoyo College of the Arts.

⊙ Tanzania Yetu and Mateso
Triple Earth, UK
⊙ The Art of Hukwe Zawose
JVC, Japan
⊙ Chibite
Real World, UK
Though these recordings combine music and instruments of the various Tanzanian ethnic groups, this is hardly traditional music. The heritage of Ujamaa-style Swahili political lyrics makes it a kind of a consciously created "national folklore". Recommended nonetheless for the giant thumb-piano sound of Hukwe Zawose and the inimitable Gogo voice style.

Uganda

strong roots and new shoots

Geoffrey Oryema
Exil Musik

After years of turmoil under Idi Amin and then Milton Obote, Uganda has had a period of relative stability since Yoweri Museveni was elected president in 1986 – notwithstanding the incursions of the Lord's Resistance Army in the north. The capital city of Kampala has grown at a tremendous rate, and brought the country's popular music along with it. So far, few artists have enjoyed success in the World Music scene – the best known are those living permanently abroad, such as Geoffrey Oryema and Samite Mulondo. Yet back home, as Andy Cooke and Sten Sandahl discovered, Kampala's music is bubbling, and a new generation of artists is experimenting with rap and ragga, as well as re-discovering the country's strong traditional roots.

The Kampala Scene

Back in the 1960s and 70s, Kampala's bands would perform around the hotels and nightclubs, playing covers of popular Western music, as well as Afro-jazz, *soukous* and other material from neighbouring Kenya and Congo. Many of the early bands included refugee musicians from Democratic Republic of the Congo, who sang in Lingala. Life for a musician in Kampala became increasingly difficult – there was no money, as Idi Amin had ruined the economy, and no audiences, for it wasn't safe to go out at night. Many of the best musicians fled the country.

In the 1980s, a confident home-grown Ugandan sound began emerging, sung in Luganda, the language of the capital. A pioneer of this sound was the late **Philly Lutaaya**, who in Sweden put together a band that reads like a *Who's Who* of Ugandan popular music from the 1970s, including percussionist **Gerald Nnaddibanga**, singer **Sammy Kasule**, **Hope Mukasa**, **Frank Mbalire** and others. Philly's 1987 album, *Born in Africa*, was hugely successful back home, and became standard repertoire for Kampala's bands.

President Yoweri Museveni finally brought a degree of peace to Uganda in 1986, and since then it has been the **Afrigo Band**, led by **Moses Matovu**, which has largely dominated the Kampala scene. A typical "jazz band", it includes a brass section, keyboards and guitars, singers and dancers. Several band members, including **Rachel Magoola**, have spun off into successful solo careers.

By the late 1990s, with a generation fascinated by the reggae and rap styles aired on the numerous private TV and radio stations, a new style of music had emerged. This came from artists such as **Ragga Dee**, **Chameleon** and **Emperor Orlando**. Their winning formula mixed Ugandan styles with rap and ragga, and their Luganda songs have become big hits.

Kadongo Kamu

An important style of popular music, enjoyed especially by the older generation, is Uganda's "country music", *kadongo kamu*. Meaning "just a small guitar", the style has its origins in the troubadour musicians that would travel around selling songs. Their songs, rooted in tradition, can focus on any subject – from mocking the paying audience to giving advice about love, or to relating the downfall of Idi Amin. The late **Bernard Kabanda** was a master of this delightful style. He used to busk around Kampala's bars with his homemade guitar, and happened one night to charm Swedish producer Sten Sandahl with his mesmerizing guitar technique – a lucky break, as Bernard then went on to tour in Europe and record for Peter Gabriel's Real World Records.

Back in the 1950s, **Christopher Sebbaduka** (known as the grandfather of *kadongo kamu*) and others began arranging the music for a full band line-up, and today's stars, such as **Paulo Kafeero** and **Fred Sebatta**, are accompanied by groups. Their story songs, resonating with people's daily struggles, are enjoyed throughout the country. They tour throughout Uganda, acting out their often hilarious songs in theatres, and can even sell out stadiums.

Traditional Music

Outside of the big city, there is a great wealth of music and dance traditions – as Uganda is made up of over thirty different ethnic groups – and their wonderfully varied and rich musical traditions still thrive, despite the decades of civil war.

After the country gained independence in 1962, the Ministry of Culture brought together the best traditional artists from all regions into the national troupe, **Heart Beat of Africa**, as a symbol of unity. The group went on to perform around the world. Since then, there have been a few other pan-Uganda groups, notably the **Ndere Troupe.** This group has a refreshingly creative approach to dance, and it performs in Uganda and abroad.

Royal Court Music

Uganda encompasses four ancient kingdoms, and their kings were great patrons of music. In the palace of the most powerful king, the **Kabaka of Buganda,** there were six different ensembles that lived in the palace and performed each day. These included two xylophone ensembles: three musicians playing a 12-key *amadinda*, accompanied by drummers; and six musicians playing the much larger 22-key *akadinda*. A favourite instrument of many Kabakas was the *entenga* drum chime – a row of 12 carefully tuned drums played by four musicians who, like the xylophonists, interlocked their parts at speed to sound out the melodies of royal songs. Two other groups included singers. The *abalere ba kabaka* (the king's flautists) played a consort of six different-sized notched flutes. The *abadongo*, a more varied ensemble, featured several *endongo* lyres with bowl-shaped resonators,

a similar number of different-sized *endingidi* tube-fiddles, plus drummers and flute players.

Each of the courts maintained a band of trumpeters. The instruments were made from sections of gourd or of wood, and each played only one or two notes, with which the ensembles sounded the traditional praise songs. The Kabaka's *amakondere* trumpeters were conspicuous at important public events such as coronation anniversaries. On these occasions, a huge battery of royal drums (many with individual names and histories) sounded powerful tattoos. Finally, the Kabaka had his own personal harpist, who was the source of much of the ancient palace repertoire. The shape of this slender, low-toned instrument called *ennanga*, so like those featured on the walls of ancient Egyptian temples, suggests that this may have been a tradition that stretches back for millennia.

These traditions came to an abrupt halt, however, when in 1966 Prime Minister Milton Obote sent the army to storm the Kabaka's palace, and shortly after abolished the kingdoms. Many royal musicians refused to play again until their kings returned from exile. They had a long wait: it wasn't until 1993 that three of the kingdoms were restored, by which time only a handful of musicians in Buganda were still actively performing royal music, including the late **Albert Ssempeke** and the late **Evalisto Muyinda**, two very versatile musicians. Since then, the palaces have tried to revive royal music. The palace in Bunyoro has a new generation of royal trumpet players; in Buganda, royal instruments have been rebuilt, and musicians are again invited to the palace to entertain guests.

Village Music

In many parts of Uganda no wedding, graduation party, political meeting or presidential visit would be complete without music and dance. Traditional singers often regard themselves as educators and leaders: just like the *kadongo kamu* guitar singers in Kampala, village singers choose topical themes and convey these through witty, humorous stories. The government often commissions groups to compose plays and present these in villages, often for educational purposes – to teach people about AIDS prevention, for example.

In western Uganda, some of the most graceful traditional dancing can be found. Cattle ownership features strongly in the life of the Banyankore people, and to the accompaniment of flute and drums they dance with their arms stretched out to symbolize the long horns of their beloved livestock.

In Buganda, fast hip-shaking *embaga* dancing can be seen at weddings. Based in Kampala, **Tebifanana Abifuna**, with their large ensemble of drums, must be the busiest traditional group in Uganda, often splitting up to serve several weddings and parties in one night. Some traditional singers, such as **Annet Nandujja**, have become popular in the capital. Her group, **The Planets**, is one of several theatre groups that perform to crowded venues in Kampala, and they have even performed in soap operas for Ugandan TV.

Across the river Nile from Buganda is the district of Basoga, where some of the most wonderfully varied ensemble playing in East Africa can be heard. **Siragi Kirimungu**, whose songs are sold in large numbers on locally produced cassettes, has a typical line-up: his *embaire* xylophone, played by two men, is accompanied by three drums, a couple of tube-fiddles, four *enkwanzi* pan-pipe players, a flute and a shaker to produce a mesmerizing kaleidoscope of sound. In addition, recordings by the **Nakibembe Xylophone Group** are helping to popularize another sound from the villages – that of a huge 21-key xylophone played by six musicians, who work through complex arrangements, often at breakneck speed. **Nile Beat Artists** take **Soga** music to Kampala and beyond. They organize a festival each year, have performed several times in Kenya and once even accompanied their paramount chief to London.

North of Busoga and Buganda are the regions of Teso and Lango, where the dominant sound heard at festivals and gatherings is that of the **lamellaphone** (thumb-piano), called *akogo* in Teso and *okeme* in Lango. This instrument is thought to have arrived early in the twentieth century, with porters from the Congo. Nowadays thumb-piano groups can be large, with fifteen or more musicians playing instruments of different sizes from treble down to bass. The scene is competitive, and good groups work up tight vocal and instrumental arrangements for their performances. In villages where electricity is scarce, they provide music for youth to dance all night to, even covering current pop songs.

Further north still are the Acholi people, who, like the Lango, have close historic and language links to Sudan. The Acholi are admired in Uganda for their traditional dancing, thumb-piano bands and beautiful *nanga* trough-zither playing (all of which forms the musical background of **Geoffrey Oryema**). Yet these days, there are few opportunities for village groups to practise and perform, as since the 1980s, the whole region has been disrupted by rebel forces of the so-called **Lord's Resistance Army**. Perhaps the strongest music-making in Acholi today is in the churches, whose choirs are often accompanied by harps of different sizes.

Their closely related neighbours living on the west bank of the Nile, the Alur, are well known for their very large village trumpet bands, seen occasionally at national celebrations in Kampala. Recently, women's clubs have picked up trumpets and are increasingly taking part. The *adungu* harp is another Alur instrument, one traditionally tuned to a five-note scale. These days it is more often given a Western seven-note tuning, which better suits church singing, with its Congolese-style harmonies. It is rapidly becoming a national instrument, used in schools throughout Uganda, and even reaching Kampala's recording studios. Wherever it is played it sounds a happy blend of old and new traditions, representing what is best about the music and people of this friendly country.

With thanks to Paul Mwandha, Eben Haase, Sam Kasule and Peter Cooke

DISCOGRAPHY Uganda

⊙ **Abayudaya: Music from the Jewish People of Uganda**
Smithsonian Folkways, US
Beautiful singing from a Jewish community based deep in the heart of Uganda – adapting traditional Jewish rituals and prayer, they sing in a mix of Hebrew, Luganda and Lusoga to the accompaniment of *adungu* harp and drum.

★ **Kampala Sound: 1960s Ugandan Dance Music**
Original Music, US
Recorded in Nairobi between 1964 and 1968, this collection of Ugandan musicians (mostly with local Kenyan musicians backing them) is a vital part of the history of African pop. And who is the fantastic sax player, "Charles", who appears on "Hamadi"? Not even Original Music can say.

⊙ **The King's Musicians: Royalist Music of Buganda – Uganda**
Topic Records, UK
A great starting point, painting a picture of a royal music tradition in crisis. We hear spirited performances on the Kabaka's birthday, just months before the army destroyed the palace in 1966. By the 1980s, royal music lay solely in the hands of a few experts, like Albert Ssempeke and Evalisto Muyinda.

⊙ **Music from Uganda Vol 1: Traditional**
⊙ **Music from Uganda Vol 2: Modern Traditional**
⊙ **Music from Uganda Vol 3: Echoes of Kampala**
Caprice, Sweden
This valuable series of discs was produced in Uganda in 1996 by SIDA (Swedish International Development Agency). *Vol 1* includes an extraordinary xylophone piece (from Baganda royal musicians), and features the unearthly sound of the *ennanga*. *Vol 2* can hardly fail to get under your skin – just listen to the Holy Rosary Church Choir's adaptations of European hymns for massed harps and Acholi singers. It also features several tracks from troubador Bernard Kabanda, playing guitar and beating out the rhythm with his elbow. *Vol 3* was put together by Edel "Eko" Akongu Ekodelele with musicians from his own and other contemporary Kampala bands, including vocalist Juliet Ssessanga and Dede Majoro. Eko uses the rhythms and language of his native Teso culture on some tracks, and on others collaborates with traditional Baganda musicians to produce interesting new fusions.

★ **Royal Court Music from Uganda**
Sharpwood Productions, Netherlands
This album collects the best of the recordings that music collector Hugh Tracey made when he visited three of the royal courts in 1950 and 1952. With the rulers' encouragement, he captured some great performances, particularly in the Kabaka's palace, when royal music seemed to be flourishing.

⊙ **Tipu pa Acholi**
PAN, Uganda
A well-recorded album of traditional music from Acholi territory. All are local musicians and singers performing their normal, everyday music.

★ **Uganda: Village Ensembles of Basoga**
VDE-Gallo/AIMP, Switzerland
Recorded on location in villages in the Basoga district of southeastern Uganda, these amateur and semi-professional traditional groups showcase a wide variety of musical forms, instruments and ensembles. The music is marvellous, and the recording quality excellent.

Afrigo Band

Led by saxophonist Moses Matovu, Afrigo is the oldest and best-known band working in Kampala. The core of the band started off in the late 1960s in an earlier version of the band called The Cranes.

⊙ **Tugenda mu Afrigo**
African Culture Promotions, UK
So wonderful live, Afrigo has yet to produce a convincing album. The song "Bakulimba", however, inspired by Basoga music from eastern Uganda, was an impressive new direction for them.

Chameleone

Jose "Chameleone" Mayanja is one of a new generation of Ugandan artists that are successfully experimenting with rap and ragga. He travelled throughout East Africa as a DJ, before recording his first hits in Nairobi. He sings in Luganda, Swahili and sometimes even Rwandese.

⊙ **Mambo Baado**
Kasiwukira Studios, Uganda
The backing instruments are fairly minimal, and typical of Ugandan pop – just drumkit and keyboard sounds – yet the melodies and their arrangement have that catchy quality that ensure they are enjoyed as much by young children as their parents.

Bernard Kabanda

Kadongo kamu singer Bernard Kabanda used to busk around Kampala's bars, before his tours in Europe led to a recording session in Peter Gabriel's Real World studios. He died tragically young, at 40.

★ **Olugendo**
Womad Select, UK
This informal recording captured Bernard at his best. He sings sweetly whilst he manages to mimic a whole band with his guitar, complete with bass beats and bursts of percussion. The songs include funny stories about women and alcohol, as well as more serious tales of murder, AIDS and the liberation struggle against Milton Obote's dictatorship.

Rachel Magoola

In the 1990s, Rachel emerged as one of the most popular of Afrigo Band's singers, composing a number of their hits. In 2001, she left the band to launch her solo career, and has since moved to London, making waves in the World Music scene.

⊙ **Songs from the Source of the Nile**
ARC Music, US
Featuring many of Rachel's Ugandan hits – originals and adaptations of traditional songs from around the country – it's a pleasant, varied listen. Whilst its over-reliance on keyboard sounds is typical of Ugandan pop, her relaxed voice shines through.

Evalisto Muyinda

Evalisto Muyinda (1914–94) was a former royal xylophone player of the Kabaka who had a deep knowledge of the royal repertoire.

⊙ **Evalisto Muyinda**
Pan, Netherlands
A truly great record, with excellent liner notes, displays a profound mastery of an ancient and now near-extinct tradition.

Ndere Troupe

Led by Stephen Rwangyezi, the Ndere Troupe is a performance group of twenty or so students and graduates from Makarere University – resident players of the National Theatre in Kampala.

⊙ **Kikwabanga**
PAN, Uganda
Ndere Troupe are more appreciated for their creative dance choreographies than their music. Yet this album captures their spirit well, and is boosted by sweet solo performances by professionals from Busoga, Kigezi and West Nile.

PLAYLIST
Uganda

1 OKWAGALA OMULUNGI KWESENGEREZA Temutewo Mukasa from *Royal Court Music from Uganda*
Mukasa shows off the astonishing playing and singing skills that made him the last great royal *ennanga* harpist of the Kabaka's court.

2 SSEMATIMBA NE KIKWABANGA Abalere ba Kabaka from *The King's Musicians*
One of the last public performances of the royal flute band, playing their highly ornate music with spirited drumming in 1965.

3 AKASOZI BAMUNANIKA Albert Ssempeke from *The King's Musicians*
Albert plays lyre and sings, accompanied by solo xylophone and fiddle, whilst the drummers work through tight variations for the dancers. Captures the thrill of a traditional wedding party.

4 OLUMBE LW'AMAANI John Kasata's Group from *Uganda: Village Ensembles of Busoga*
A beautiful example of *soga* music, with skilled and sensitive *enkwaansi* pan-pipe playing.

5 KALAHUDIYA Ndere Troupe from *Kikwabanga*
Herbert Bagesigaki from Kigezi, southwest Uganda, praises his lover's beauty whilst accompanying himself exquisitely with a *nanga* trough-zither.

6 POYO WIC IKOM MEROK Dim Abilo from *Music from Uganda Vol 2: Modern Traditional*
Dim Abilo from Lango region sing long texts tightly as a group whilst playing a funky groove on fifteen *okeme* thumb-pianos of different sizes. In this song they warn their community about thieves.

7 ETTAALA YA BBULU Bernard Kabanda from *Olugendo*
Bernard blames the blue light and drink for mistaking old Josephina for a beautiful young woman. Solo *kadongo kamu* guitar playing at its best.

8 KAGUTEMA The Big Five from *Music from Uganda vol 3: Echoes of Kampala*
One of the first-ever mixes of Kampala pop with traditional instruments that helped to break the mould in Kampala in the late 1990s.

9 EXILE Geoffrey Oryema from *Exile*
Geoffrey cries out for peace in Uganda, accompanied by beautiful soft guitar playing recorded in Peter Gabriel's studio.

10 JAMILA Chameleone from *Mambo Baado*
A great example of Uganda's new style of rap-influenced pop music, one raising awareness about domestic violence.

Geoffrey Oryema

Geoffrey Oryema had to flee Uganda (in the boot of a car) during the Amin era. Settling in Paris, he has almost singlehandedly put his country on the World Music map through festival appearances and some stylish discs recorded for Real World.

⊙ Exile
Real World, UK

An elegant album of songs with characteristically sweet Acholi roots. Oryema sings beautifully and plays local varieties of harp and thumb-piano, beside acoustic guitar, while production is handled sympathetically by Brian Eno.

Ragga Dee

Ragga Dee (Daniel Kasibwe) is a pioneer of Uganda's new style of pop, having recorded the first Ugandan rap song in the 1990s. He blends Swahili and English into his Luganda songs, which are popular as much for their message as for their beat.

⊙ Nuggu
Kasiwukira Studios, Uganda

Nuggu ("Envy") has ten songs in a variety of styles, from *soukous* to ragga. It's mostly drumkit and keyboards, with guitar added on some tracks, and female vocals on others. Ragga Dee's rapping is distinctive throughout, with hints of a Jamaican accent at times.

Samite

Samite Mulondo lives in exile in the US where his music has developed from days at home playing covers of rock and pop with the band Mixed Talents. He has become Uganda's unofficial cultural ambassador to the US along the way.

⊙ Silina Musango
Xenophile, US

Tighter than *Pearl of Africa Reborn*, this album still draws on a lot of traditional material, as well as input from Europe and the West Indies. Better produced and distilled, Samite is clearly on the move.

Zambia

evolution and expression

Amayenge
Mondo Music

In comparison with its neighbours, Zambia has a low profile on the world's musical map. Although it produced the distinctive African pop sounds of Zam-rock and *kalindula* in the 1970s and 80s, the severe economic downturn of the 1990s had a devastating effect on the local music industry, which has only recently shown signs of recovery. Ronnie Graham, Simon Kandela Tunkanya and Kennedy Gondwe report.

Collection of Graeme Ewens

Alick Nkhata (left) recording in the countryside in the 1960s

After a relatively short struggle for self-determination, Zambia inherited a significant copper-based economy at independence in 1964. A new African elite of administrators and technocrats tended to adopt the culture of their former British colonial rulers. In the capital, Lusaka, and the towns of the Copperbelt, however, urban migrants held onto rural musical traditions as they adopted Western instruments and adapted foreign styles.

From Independence to Zam-rock

In the early 1960s, the main provider of – and outlet for – music in Zambia was the Zambia Broadcasting Service, which made pioneering field recordings of traditional music across the whole of southern central Africa. The ZBS director was musician **Alick Nkhata**, who often worked with the archivist Hugh Tracey (see Southern Africa Archives chapter), and also formed the **Lusaka Radio Band**, Zambia's first indigenous group. With the mandate to promote Zambian music, the band thrived on translating these rural recordings into the scored musical language of the West. Now known as the **Big Gold Six Band**, the group – which still has two of its original members – keeps the memories of this era alive in sessions at Lusaka's *Inter-Continental Hotel*.

The Radio Band was a one-off, however, and Zambian radio played mostly **Congolese rumba**. This was also the dominant style in Lusaka's handful of upmarket hotel ballrooms, frequented by the new elite and remaining colonials, who relaxed to bands like the Broadway Quintet, Crooners and De Black Evening Follies, playing "copyright" (cover) versions of foreign hits.

Seeing an opportunity to produce and market local music and with the help of former ZBS employee **Peter Msungilo**, a British immigrant called **Graham Skinner** established DB Studios in Lusaka's Cha Cha Cha road. He was soon followed by the **Teal Record Company**, a subsidiary of South Africa's Gallo and the Zambia Music Parlour (ZMP), which did not record but managed artists and marketed their music. Both Teal and ZMP set up in Zambia's second city, the Copperbelt town of Ndola. A music scene was emerging in the multicultural mining camps of the north Zambian Copperbelt: at first, a kind of folk music, with singer-guitarists like **Stephen Tsotsi Kasumali**, **William Mapulanga** and **John Lushi**, then a more rock-style sound.

In the early years, **Zam-rock** used Western-style guitars and drums. The songs were in English and sometimes local languages, and they were rebellious, protesting, for example, against tribal taboos on sex and relationships. The pioneers included **Musi-o-tunya**, a short-lived combo named after the Victoria Falls, who released Zambia's first commercial LP, and the unsettlingly named army group, **The Machine-Gunners**. These early bands were heavily influenced by **Osibisa** (the London-based Ghanaian combo), who visited Zambia in 1972. Their influence was mainly in spirit, in that bands like Musi-o-tunya interpreted traditional rhythms using a mixture of Western and traditional instruments such as marimba and drums. The rock influence was still there and so the music came to be known as Zam-rock.

ZAMBIA

437

Emmanuel Jaggari Chanda

Emmanuel Chanda is one of Zambia's few surviving musical greats of yesteryear. Known to his fans as "Jaggari" – a name derived from his idol Mick Jagger of the Rolling Stones – Chanda was born in northern Zambia in 1951 and grew up in a Copperbelt town. 'My getting into music was rather accidental,' he recalls. 'At that time, our economy was strong and jobs were readily available in the mines upon completing secondary school. I could have perhaps ended up as a miner.'

Jaggari was introduced to music by classmates who jammed with a local band called Black Souls. Hungry for success, Jaggari later went on to play with the Black Souls and other bands. He was associated with many Zambian musicians like the late Paul Ngozi, Ackim Simukonda and Zimbabwean legend Oliver Mtukudzi. Nevertheless, he admits that Zambian music has always been heavily influenced by Western styles.

'In our time, music was very competitive, but just like now, we had not found music we could call Zambian,' he notes. 'And unfortunately, up to now, we tend to think that *kalindula* represents Zambian music. To me, every ethnic group in Zambia has its own music and *kalindula* is just one of those types of music from Luapula Province.'

In the 1970s, Jaggari played for the Great WITCH, a band many consider to be Zambia's greatest to date. These days he has given up performing live and now spends most of his time at church, but he has fond memories of his musical past. 'In our time, we had songs for different occasions. For example, we had songs for initiation ceremonies, songs to celebrate a newly born baby. There were also songs for a hunting or expedition, healing music, lullabies and so on. But now, it's all love songs.'

He is critical of the effects of the digital revolution. 'Much as the computer is here to stay, … it discourages creativity,' he argues. 'Computer music lacks the human element and it is that element that sets out the mood and feeling a listener enjoys. Little wonder most of our musicians fail to perform live music except play-backs.'

Despite the death of many friends and three of his six children, Jaggari refuses to be called lonely: 'Musically, I am lonely, but spiritually I am not.'

Kennedy Gondwe

The crowning glory of Zam-rock was **Great WITCH** (standing for "We Intend To Cause Havoc"), a band that achieved a huge following. They expressed the concerns and preoccupations of the younger generation, satisfying the curiosity created by the worldwide popularity of rock through the wholesale adoption of influences from The Beatles, The Rolling Stones, and later Jethro Tull. Fronted by lead singer Jaggari Chanda, their popularity has never been surpassed. In this era many other bands and artists such as **Keith Mlevu**, **Rikki Illilonga**, **Rikki Banda**, the **Peace Band** and **The Tinkles** tried to sound as Western as they could.

Another significant group of the time was **Emmanuel Mulemena**'s **Sound Inspectors**. The late Mulemena was one of the most influential of Zambia's folk balladeers. Not a Zam-rocker, his more subtle messages were urban-based social commentaries that dealt with life on the less affluent side of town. He appealed to a wide audience, as he sang in the main Zambian languages. After his untimely death during the *kalindula* era (see below), his band, renamed the **Mulemena Boys**, kept the spirit of his music alive for a while with a series of hit singles and a *Tribute to Emmanuel Mulemena* album, a phenomenally successful reworking of his compositions. The Mulemena Boys succeeded in outselling their late bandleader, probably due, at least in part, to adhering more to the danceable *manchancha* beat of Northwestern Province, which in structure and rhythm is very close to *kalindula*.

Kalindula Arrives

The Zambian state was an isolated regime in the late 1970s, ploughing its own furrow on the wrong side of the Cold War divide, fearful of the appeasement of apartheid by Reagan and Thatcher, and of Ian Smith's dangerous regime in white-ruled Rhodesia across its closed southern border. Against this backdrop, and in the cause of solidarity and national identity, President **Kenneth Kaunda**, himself an enthusiastic amateur guitarist, issued a decree that no less than 95 percent of music on the radio was to be of Zambian origin – nineteen songs for every Top 20. The president argued for Zambianization – the creation of a unique Zambian musical identity, something akin to Mobutu's call for *authenticité* in Zaïre.

The result was not quite the cultural roots revival Kaunda had intended. Instead, every Zambian

Kenneth Kaunda unplugged with this chapter's co-author, Simon Kandela Tunkanya

teenager with a box guitar and a singing voice tried their hand at being a pop star. Hundreds of bands were established, often by opportunistic entrepeneurs with a truckload of instruments, to play note-perfect renditions of other African styles.

Meantime, the established musical community responded to Kaunda in its own way. **Paul Ngozi**, one of Musi-o-Tunya's most talented former members, created a new style of music by retaining rock-guitar solos and putting his lyrics into local languages, giving Zambian music a new dimension. An associate of the Great WITCH, Ngozi gradually transformed his music by changing the beat and bass lines to closely resemble the *chitelela* beat of Eastern Province. At the same time the Great WITCH were including more ethnically based songs in their later albums. This dabbling with ethnic beats ceased with the departure of Emmanuel Jaggari Chanda, after which they tried to sound disco but faded into obscurity.

The ethnically based songs of the Great WITCH inspired some musicians to explore their own roots, among them **Kris Chali** of **Amayenge** and **John Mwansa** of the **Five Revolutions**. Mwansa released a song called "Mukanfwilwa", which sold over 50,000 and even made an impact in neighbouring countries. This inspired a plethora of artists and by the mid-1980s, **kalindula** – named after a one-string bass instrument found in all parts of Zambia – had developed into a full-fledged Zambian urban dance style. Brasher and funkier than *soukous*, *kalindula* was characterized by rhythmic

guitars and a solid, rapid-fire bass line, often with a melodic lead guitar accompanying the vocal.

The first wave of *kalindula* and other similar styles such as *manchancha* was spearheaded by **Junior Mulemena Boys**, **PK Chishala & The Great Pekachi Band**, the **Masasu Band**, **Serenje Kalindula Band**, **Shalawambe** and the **Oliya Band**, and stimulated sufficient interest for British tours, while Paul Ngozi established a following in South Africa. By the late 1980s, there were half a dozen LPs out on Western labels. Other groups soon followed as *kalindula* moved away from its origins and became a generic Zambian style.

At the turn of the decade, Lusaka's city-centre hotels still preferred Zaïrean bands covering the latest Kinshasa styles, but for the majority of Zambians a good night out revolved around copious quantities of Mosi beer and *kalindula* action on the dancefloor. Not that the two styles were completely separate. **Nashil Pichen Kazembe** was a kind of bridge between the Congolese influence and both Zam-rock and *kalindula*, and he inspired others such as **Peter Tsotsi Juma** and **MB Papa Kado**, who continued to explore a middle line somewhere between rumba Zam-rock and *kalindula*.

Another significant, if short-lived, group of this period was **Maoma Band**, which played reggae with a Zambian flavour. They broke up after releasing only one single while on tour in Germany, where co-founder **Spuki Mulemwa** remained to pursue a successful solo career on a string of albums, most recently *Songs for Mama Zambia*.

ZAMBIA

Tribal Music, Dance and Instruments

Zambia has 72 distinct ethnic groups and seven main languages, all of which have converged in the mining and other towns. They are basically of Bantu origin, and two centuries before came largely from the Kola region in the ancient Luba-Lunda kingdom. Each group once had its own music and culture, but even under colonial rule, urban development grew rapidly and the ethnic groups interacted with each other to create tribal cultural and musical crossbreeds. Still, it is possible to identify five distinct, geographically defined, tribal musical currents that continue to some degree, and have fed into modern Zambian music.

Eastern Province: Cewa, Nyau and Ngoni

High pitched *vimbuza* (talking drums) are characteristic of the Cewa people and their *Nyau* dance. The Ngoni are distinguished exponents of the *Ingoma* dance, their powerful voices shaped by years of battlefield war-cries, accompanied by vigorous foot-stomping as they brandish their shields, urged on by the women with rhythmic clapping.

Northern Province: Bemba

Low pitched *kalela* drums, beaten with sticks, are prevalent among the Bemba of the north, who also developed a string instrument – the *babatone* – made from animal skin, with the string drawn over a drum by a wooden handle, and fashioned rather like a double bass. This style formed the basis of *kalindula*.

Western Province: Lozi and Nkoya

The xylophone is the outstanding instrument among the Lozi and Nkoya, and depending on the occasion and the size of the instrument, it can be played by one or up to four people. It is constructed of slats of wood placed over a long platform, with reverberators made from gourds arranged in descending order of size.

Northwestern Province: Luvale and Kaonde

The *kachacha* beat is the typical sound of northwest Zambia, particularly among the Luvale people. It is created from combinations of up to six drums, with dancers rhythmically stamping their feet. The Kaonde people's version is the *manchancha* with three drums complemented by dancing women. This is mainly an initiation dance for girls who are coming of age.

Southern Province

The renowned talking drum – known here as *tonga* – is played by squeezing on the stick inside the drum with wet fingers. It is used as an accompaniment by a solo praise singer or village poet, expressing joy or lamentation depending on the occasion.

Amidst this ethicization of Zambian music a young artist named **Ballad Zulu** produced a major hit single, "Cook On", which, although keeping to ethnic roots, was a fusion number with a Western R&B structure and sung in English. The effect on some of the artists of the future was similar to that of Musi-o-tunya on the Great WITCH.

Zambian Music in the 1990s

If the 1976 presidential decree created *kalindula*, a new phase in Zambian music emerged under the more liberal MMD government of the **1990s**. Economic crisis led to the complete collapse of the faltering Zambian music industry, while the cultural barricades that Kaunda had used to protect indigenous music were torn down and the sounds of the world flooded in.

Musicians had to contend with the harsh reality of a devasted economy and competition from imported music. Few were up to the challenge, and most of the *kalindula* bands broke up. Sadly, too, a number of the old veteran artists died during the decade, among them Nashil Pichen Kazembe, PK Chishala and **Joyce Nyirongo** – probably the finest Zambian woman vocalist of the previous two decades.

Economic collapse was exacerbated by reliance on copper mining as the sole driver of Zambia's economy. As copper prices went down, inflation spiralled and foreign exchange became scarce. Teal, who owned the only record-manufacturing plant in Zambia, found it increasingly difficult to operate. The 1980s also witnessed a shift in format from vinyl to cassettes, which paved the way for piracy. Zambia did not enact a copyright protection law until 1994, by which time the market for legitimate audiotapes and CDs had been almost destroyed. Major companies like Teal and Music Parlour closed.

When copyright laws were finally passed, artists like Ballad Zulu made a comeback. The **Sakala Brothers**, the late **Robert Omart Mapara**, **Victor Kachaka** and others emerged, though most still had no record companies behind them.

Another blow to the music industry was AIDS, with many popular musicians succumbing to HIV. A generation of musical knowledge was lost, leaving younger musicians without mentors. Having peaked in the mid-1980s, Zambian music went into a cycle of decline, mainly as a result of deaths among its pioneers. Nevertheless, a small group of musicians survived and persevered.

Jordan Katembula – J.K. to his fans

Mondo and the Re-Emerging Music Industry

At the turn of the millennium, the only reputable record company was **Digital Networks International** (DNI), which focused on reissuing songs by the late *kalindula* greats such as PK Chishala. This, however, did not deter new artists like the late Anthony Kafunya, a.k.a. **Daddy Zemus**, who arrived on the scene with instant hit songs like "Salaula" and "Juju Lover" in the mid 1990s. His "Zamragga" style was a fusion of *kalindula* and rap, and his success inspired artists such as Davies Ngoma (**Nasty D**), Mukusha Chembe (**MC Wabwino**), Cullen Chisha (**2wice**), **Black Muntu** and the **Muvi Posse**.

In 1999, a new record company, **Mondo Music**, was founded. Although it has now closed its recording studio to concentrate on distribution, Mondo Music has dominated the local charts in recent years, with some of its artists participating in the prestigious Kora African Music awards, and visiting South Africa, the UK and Japan. Among the leading musicians Mondo has produced is Jordan Katembula. Known to his fans simply as **J.K.**,

he has thus far recorded three albums. Mondo's success led to many other recording studios being set up, along with CD and cassette production companies. Some enterprising musicians have even opened their own studios. And as in the 1970s, audiences brought up on a diet of Western music are now demanding Zambian pop music with a local flavour.

The Twenty-First Century

In Zambia today, the media – both private and government-owned – have adopted a deliberate policy of promoting local music. This includes both newspapers and radio stations such as Hone FM, which has a policy of playing 75 percent Zambian music. Leading stations such as Radio Four, Radio Phoenix and Q-FM all run charts for top local songs as selected by listeners. The same applies to television, where a sales-based chart, the Sounds Top 20, runs on a weekly basis.

Yet despite attempts by artists to market their individual styles with labels that suggest a local flavour, it is often argued that Zambia no longer has a distinct type of music. Nasty D calls his music "Zambezi", the defunct Black Muntu referred to their music as "Kalifunku", the Sakala Brothers call theirs "Makewane", Ballad Zulu does "Zambeat" and so on.

Some Zambians like their music traditional, and without Western influences. Then there are those who prefer a Zambian version of the R&B, ragga, and pop sounds on MTV, MCM, Channel O and elsewhere. Others stick with *kalindula* oldies that have been reissued on various compilations such as Mondo's *Sounds of Zambia* series, which pays tribute to the musicians of the 1970s and 80s. There have also been reissues of music by the likes of PK Chishala, Paul Ngozi and Nashil Pitchen Kazembe.

Nevertheless, there are still audiences for new acts like the **Glorious Band**, Mashombe Blue Jeans, **Mutende Cultural Ensemble** and even veteran **Phillipo Chimbini**. The gospel scene is also highly active with artists like **Matthew Ngosa**, Mr. Fortune, **Adonai Pentecostal Singers**, Jojo Mwangaza and the **Original Brothers**. With veteran female artists like Joyce Nyirongo and Violet Kafula either dead or retired, the torch has been passed on to the new generation by the likes of **Jane Osborne** and **Maureen Lupo Lilanda**. Other significant newcomers include **Angela Nyirenda**, Lilly T, **Namakau**, Nalu, **Kanji**, the Rare Roses, **Sista D** and Marsha Moyo.

DISCOGRAPHY Zambia

⊙ Batonga Across the Waters
Sharp Wood, Netherlands
This unique collection presents exciting dance rhythms, woeful elegies and relaxed ballads, all recorded in Tonga villages in Zimbabwe and Zambia. The arrangements feature drums, *kankobela* (a type of simple thumb-piano), *kalumbu* (musical bow), plus guitar and bottle percussion.

⊙ Kalimba and Kalumbu Songs
Sharp Wood, Netherlands
These 1950s field recordings have been meticulously remastered, and the sound is wonderful, a testament to archivist Hugh Tracey.

⊙ Origins of Guitar Music
Sharp Wood, Netherlands
More Hugh Tracey recordings from the 1950s. This material deserves the widest possible audience. The guitarists are not all virtuosos, but they have an easy command of complex dance rhythms that would confuse most players anywhere else. Any serious guitarist simply has to hear this music.

⊙ Sounds Of Zambia – Vols 1 & 2
Mondo Music, Zambia
The first in a series featuring some of Zambia's greatest musicians and their *kalindula* and Zam-rock hits from the 1970s to 90s. Uneven sound quality but nonetheless engaging.

⊙ Zambia Roadside – Music from Southern Province
Sharp Wood, Netherlands
This compilation of contemporary pop recordings begins with some absolutely addictive acoustic guitar music, followed by glorious women's choirs and continuing with a beautiful mix of styles.

★ Zambush Vol 1: Zambian Hits from the 80s
Sharp Wood, Netherlands
Kalindula is one of Africa's most memorable styles and still sounds bold and thrilling today. The beat is drawn from the traditional rhythms of the Bemba-speaking people of Zambia's central, northern and Luapula provinces. This collection features greats such as the Serenje Kalindula band, Five Revolutions and Amayenge.

★ Zambush Vol 2. Zambian Hits from the 60s & 70s
Sharp Wood, Netherlands
Another superb example of the art of reissuing lost music in an appealing and highly informative way. Includes Nashil Pitchen Kazembe, Emmanuel Mulemena and the Big Gold Six.

Ballad Zulu

This ground-breaking artist was the first to release a version of "Cook On", a fusion of *kalindula* and R&B that launched his career in 1990. His reclusive nature has been his Achilles heel.

⊙ Chusi
Nilasu Records, Zambia
This 2005 release is Ballad Zulu's third album and arguably Zambia's most polished pop effort to date. With its *chitelela* and *chingande* rhythms, kalindula and Zam-rock stylings and influences that include samba, soul and Zam-folk, it has both a contemporary and identifiably Zambian feel.

Kris Chali & Amayenge

Amayenge are probably Zambia's best-known band on the international scene, having toured extensively since their founding in 1978. Chali was their leader until his death in May 2003.

⊙ **Dailesi**
Mondo Music, Zambia
Recorded just before Chali's death, this became a fitting and hugely popular tribute, showing why this band has been the leading force in *kalindula* for the past two decades.

Jordan Katembula (J.K.)

A Kora award-nominated artist whose background is in gospel and rap.

⊙ **Helena**
Mondo Music, Zambia
This 2003 release is the second album from "Zambia's Singing Sensation" and shows a rapidly developing musical maturity. A mix of R&B and *soukous* sung in Zambian languages, this album features a guest appearance by Zimbabwean music legend Oliver Mtukudzi on the song "Dzokera".

Alick Nkhata

A former director of the Zambian radio station, founder of the radio band and a talented singer-songwriter, Nkhata was killed by Rhodesian soldiers during a cross-border raid in 1974.

⊙ **Shalapo**
RetroAfric, UK
A selection from Nkhata's large output of guitar songs – perhaps a hundred compositions all told.

Serenje Kalindula Band

The first Zambian band to play the authentic sounds of *kalindula*, the popular and respected traditional dance style from Luapula Province in the north of Zambia.

★ **Zambian Legends**
Mondo Music, Zambia
Apart from their *kalindula* tunes, this "best of" features "Fwanda fwanda-ing'oma yabalala" – the dance of the Lala-speaking people of Serenje and Mkushi districts in Central Province.

Danny Siulapwa

One of the new kids on the block, known to his fans as Danny "Masiku Onse" after his debut hit. Following an early association with Amayenge, he now has his own live band.

⊙ **Kaya**
Mondo Music, Zambia
Mixing humour with social commentary, and delivered in a ragga style every bit the equal of its Jamaican models, *Kaya* is a great collection of thoughtful, funny and sentimental tracks.

Zimbabwe

mbira, sungura and chimurenga: play it loud!

Oliver Mtukudzi
Philip Ryalls/Redferns

Zimbabweans play the good-time music of suffering. A plummeting economy has brought Harare's nightlife to its knees, and many musicians have succumbed to AIDS, but for those who remain, music is more important than ever. Despite everything, the hotels, nightclubs and beerhalls continue to thump and groove – their PA systems greatly improved in recent years – and punters still throng the dancefloors, shaking their bodies and easing their troubles. Banning Eyre and Tom Bullough talk to Harare's musicians through the din.

Zesa! Zesa! Put more Zesa! Harare's nightclubs reverberate with this cry at the end of the month when payday brings out the crowds. Zesa is the national electricity board, struggling, as everywhere in Africa, to meet the needs of its consumers. On payday they want to forget their troubles and go out dancing to the gospel-tinged rumba anthems of **Leonard Zhakata** at Club M5, **Oliver Mtukudzi**'s soulful stomp and swing at Gwanzura Stadium or the good-time *sungura* of **Alick Macheso** at Helenics Sports Club.

Harare, the capital of Zimbabwe, means "don't stop" – a good name for a city where the bands go on forever, in several senses. Many of them are dependent on their venues for equipment and practice time, and sometimes they have to play until dawn in all-night *pungwe* style. Before independence, the *pungwe* was a dedication to the liberation struggle. Now these Herculean performances are dedicated more to beerhall profits – more hours means more drinking time and more bucks. The music reflects the *pungwe* set-up and its demands. Songs are often long and complex, with phrases and tunes repeated to familiarize the audience with a song, before the band begins to play around with the intricate rhythms that have been set up by the guitars and the voices.

It is a tough life playing the local circuit, and those musicians lucky enough to make it "outside" (overseas) are often reluctant to return to the gruelling way of life back home. As **Dorothy Masuka**, the veteran jazz singer from Bulawayo, explains: 'If I want money I must go out – a concert here will give you about enough to buy a bag of mealie meal [staple of ground corn]. I wouldn't do what the youngsters are doing these days – Kambuzuma today, Highfield tomorrow – it's too much hard work. You play in the bar and people come to drink. They don't appreciate your music. I'd rather play one big concert a year and not work the rest of the time!'

Tough Times

Two and a half decades after winning its independence, Zimbabwe is in deep trouble. The once cherished revolutionary government is now widely regarded as corrupt and mismanaged, its failure plain to see in the 75 percent unemployment rate, 300 percent inflation and mass emigration seen recently. Worryingly, such instability threatens to reignite dormant hostilities between Zimbabwe's dominant **Shona** population and the large **Ndebele** population in the south.

In recent years, the music industry has been in a constant state of crisis. Public belt-tightening has steadily reduced the crowds in Harare's famous nightclubs, while many of the best – such as *Sandros* – have closed altogether. The 100 percent local music policy imposed on state radio by the government has generated extra work for some musicians, but much of the music now produced consists of ersatz homegrown hip-hop and ragga, and the independent media have been all but destroyed. The strategy of Minister for Information and Publicity, Jonathan Moyo – fortunately sidelined in early 2005 – has been as effective as it has been egomaniacal. Power FM (the national "youth" radio station) has been swamped by his own compositions, extolling government policy, while other songs have been banned and musicians have increasingly been forced to play at giant state "galas" in order to make a living.

In the midst of this crisis, one of the few indications of the true feelings of the embattled Zimbabwean people has been the collapse of support for pop fusion star **Andy Brown** and rumba legend **Simon "Chopper" Chimbetu** since they accepted commissions to make records in favour of the government.

Worse still, Zimbabwe's pop music pantheon continues to be devastated by an alarming series of untimely deaths, many of them attributable to AIDS. Since 1990, Zimbabwe has lost the major singers James Chimombe, John Chibadura, Robson Banda and Leonard Dembo, as well as gospel superstar Brian Sibalo, *mbira* maestro Ephat Mujuru, three founding members of the Bhundu Boys (including Biggie Tembo), at least ten members of Thomas Mapfumo's Blacks Unlimited (including *mbira* guitar legends Jonah Sithole and Joshua Dube), eight members of Oliver Mtukudzi's Black Spirits, three members of the Four Brothers and core musicians from the Lubumbashi Stars, the Hohodza Band, the Zig Zag Band and many others.

Not all of these tragedies stem from AIDS, but most do. Get to know anyone in Harare well and you'll invariably hear about the deaths of friends, and on the TV and radio there are constant features on the disease, countering a prevailing culture of denial. That said, Zimbabwe's people and its musicians are nothing if not resilient, and in the face of all adversity, payday still finds Harareans flocking to beerhalls to hear their favourite bands. It takes more than inflation, AIDS and a propaganda fog to keep these people down.

Beerhalls and Biras

"It's you who make Castle great!" announces the most popular beer advertisement in Zimbabwe. The essential in the manic mix of Harare night-life is beer: people are fiercely loyal to their brand, whether it be imported Castle or Lion, locally brewed Zambezi or Bollingers, or the cheaper African *chibuku*, sold in brown plastic jugs called scuds (after Sadaam Hussein's famous missiles). Booze flows liberally during and between sets, and there's a real art to negotiating the intricate weave of Zimbabwean rhythms, keeping the upper body steady while loose legs and busy feet work the floor and tightly wrapped fingers clench the neck of a dangling beer bottle. Dancing is a communal affair and nobody needs to feel left out. If the band is good, people of all ages come on the floor – men with men, women with women, children with adults, groups and loners.

The public tends to be as fanatically devoted to their chosen band and its set as they are to their favourite beer – a loyalty of taste that new or experimental groups frequently bewail. People like to know the songs. Even Thomas Mapfumo is obliged to churn out the old favourites in his shows, and a new band needs to have a very big hit to persuade people to come out to a live show.

As electrification and development have spread through Zimbabwe's rural areas, **beerhalls** similar to those in the capital have sprung up in many small towns and "growth points" (developing commercial centres in the rural areas), and bands once confined to the cities can now nurture their audiences town by town. This fanning out of electric music might be seen as an urban infraction on the pastoral way of life, but for people to gather and dance with music and beer is nothing new in this country. Home-brewed "seven-days" beer has long played an essential role in the **bira**, an all-night ceremony of traditional music, chanting and dancing that brings Zimbabweans into contact with the spirits of their ancestors. This village ritual can be seen as the prototype for the modern beerhall.

Ancestor spirits continue to play an important role as counsellors in many Shona communities, especially in the rural areas, but also in Harare's poor, high-density suburbs. Spirits are seen as intermediaries between people and God; the older the spirit, the nearer to God. At a *bira* ceremony, the iron-keyed *mbira* is believed to summon ancestor spirits to come and possess a spirit medium who then offers advice on the matter in hand.

The Mbira

Foreign observers often call the **mbira** a "thumb piano", though most players reject the term as denying the essential African quality of the instrument. At a *bira* ceremony, three or more *mbiras* play complex, interlocking parts as they render songs from an ancient repertoire, going back a thousand years or more.

When played, the *mbira* is housed in a large, halved calabash which both amplifies the instrument's sound and also obscures it with the buzzing of shells or bottle caps attached to the edges of the gourd. The effect is mysterious and powerful, and when animated by the insistent, broken-triplet rhythm of the *hosho* (shaker) and the tricky offbeats of the *ngoma* (hand-drum), *mbiras* can keep people dancing all night. The singing that accompanies *mbira* music is otherworldly, rising from a soothing murmur to gut-wrenching cries.

In the 1930s, music archivist Hugh Tracey found the mbira almost extinct, but it has had a major revival in the last thirty years. The independence war played a part, with *mbira* music becoming associated with a national sound. And in the 1980s and 1990s, the *mbira* has had success among World Music fans. Its accessibility to Western ears is perhaps due to the innate harmony of the music. Unlike most traditional African forms, which are subservient to tonal language, metric and rhythmic form, *mbira* music is built on a unique harmonic patterning, based on cyclical patterns of two-note chords. The soundscape which a *mbira* creates also contains many melodies,

Judy Kendall

Getting on down at Queens Garden

or "inherent patterns", once you're able to tune your ear to them.

The list of great *mbira* players in Zimbabwe is long, and some of the best ones may be known only to those in their surrounding villages. A few veteran players like **Stella Chiweshe**, **Ephat Mujuru**, **Dumisani Maraire**, **Sekuru Gora** and **Tute Chigamba** have gained reputations on the international festival circuit, and they have been joined in recent years by innovative, younger players like the phenomenal **Forward Kwenda** and **Garikari Tirikoti**. *Mbira* music calls for improvisation, so there's always room for a young lion to break new ground with the instrument, particularly in non-ceremonial settings.

For many players, however, the *mbira* is a sacred thing – rather than a source of musical display. **Amai Muchena**, who played *mbira* with the group **Muri ko Muchena** (Muchena Family), explained, 'I don't play in beerhalls, because the spirit is like a God to go to if there are problems.' She sees the instrument primarily as a means of healing. 'To get a message to the spirits you make an appointment and then speak to the spirit. If you have a problem, you must buy some clothes and beads and cook beer and then have a party and play *mbira* then everything will be okay. If someone is suffering and sick from a spirit I will play *mbira* until the spirit comes up and then talk to it. It might say "buy a gun or spear to keep in your house".'

Stella Chiweshe, probably the best-known player on the international circuit, has provoked some criticism for mixing sacred and commercial music, a controversial issue in a country where music is so close to the spiritual centre of life. She certainly uses the mystique of the instrument in her shows, sometimes going into a trance on stage. With her penetrating eyes, habitual snuff-taking, ankle charms and dreadlocks falling in front of her face, she has a powerful presence. She is partly based in Germany, these days, and more often performs overseas than in Zimbabwe. She still tours solo or with the **Earthquake Band**, with whom she pioneered the translation of *mbira* styles to marimba. Her daugher **Virginia Mukwesha** (in Zimbabwe, women take their father's surnames) has carved out a similar niche, sometimes mixing *mbira* and *jiti* styles

Within the past few years, the *mbira* scene has been dominated by **Mbira dze Nharira**: a defiantly traditional six-piece group whose extraordinary debut album, *Rinemanyanga Hariputirwe*, was the result of eleven years' research and development. Other intriguing players include **Chiwoniso Maraire** – daughter of Dumisani Maraire – whose 1998 release, *Ancient Voices*, provided a fresh, pop

Philip Ryalls/Redferns

Stella Chiweshe on the *mbira*

take on the *mbira* sound, and **Albert Chimedza**, an *mbira* maker, poet and composer who has devoted himself to "liberating" the *mbira* from the restrictions of its history, using it to play a range of different types of music in his collaborations with Japanese, Malagasy and Italian jazz musicians. As an instrument and sound pattern, *mbira* also plays a role in electric groups, notably that of **Ephat Mujuru's Spirit of The People**, and in the thoroughly electric style of Zimbabwe's best-known musician, **Thomas Mapfumo**.

Mapfumo: Chimurenga Man for All Seasons

Thomas Mapfumo – known to Zimbabweans as Mukanya (the monkey, his totem) – has been the country's most famous musician for the past quarter-century. The proverbial Lion of Zimbabwe fathered electric *mbira* music and developed the **chimurenga** music style, named after the struggle that brought the country its independence in 1980. He rose as a warrior troubadour and champion of the liberation fight, but survives as the government's most fearless and prominent musical critic. In Mapfumo's worldview, there is no contradic-

Thomas Mapfumo, still a rebel

his line-up, making the band into a kind of folk orchestra in which the three *mbira* players functioned as a rhythm section, even as he created songs that incorporated Afro-jazz, West African flavours, reggae and otherworldly R&B.

Mapfumo's hypnotic music has always drawn on Zimbabwe's wealth of traditional songs and chants, as well as his own far-flung modern influences, ranging from Elvis and Otis Redding to Chicago Transit Authority and the African jazz that flourished in this region during the 1950s and 60s. Singing in Shona was a brave and crucial step for a generation that had been taught to look down on their cultural traditions as backward. Initially, Mapfumo's experiments were viewed with bemusement, but he was soon followed by other musicians, who openly acknowledge his influence – notably **Oliver Mtukudzi** (of whom more later), and **Comrade Chinx**, a choirmaster for the liberation troops who now makes pro-governnment recordings.

Just as the *mbira* had a firm place in the strong spiritual world, so electric *mbira* music became a tool of the liberation war in the 1970s. Like the political songs that animated all-night village *pungwes* led by the guerrillas, Mapfumo's *chimurenga* songs engaged those in towns and cities, awakening solidarity with the fighters. The irresistible beat provided an opportunity for community song and dance, an affirmation that was vitally necessary for a society split by secrecy, repression, guerrilla warfare and counter-terrorist activities. Shona and Ndebele lyrics could not be understood by the majority of the white population and so were a valuable means of communication for the liberation movement. Some of the lyrics of Mapfumo's songs were overtly political, while others made use of the Shona tradition of "deep proverbs" to conceal messages of resistance: "Oh grandmothers / Oh mothers, oh boys / There's a snake in the forest / Mothers take hoes / Grandmothers take hoes / Boys take axes." Before the liberation war was over, Mapfumo had been briefly jailed by the white authorities, a clear sign of his effectiveness.

tion there. Although he was often portrayed as a champion of black ascendance, his real mission was for the poor and oppressed, and more deeply still, for the recovery of vanishing African culture. Today's Zimbabwean leaders may be Africans, but their capacity for oppression and their disregard for ancient ways rivals that of the Rhodesians, as Mapfumo sees it. Hence, the *chimurenga* continues.

Like most Zimbabwean musicians who started out in the 1960s, Mapfumo began his career playing "copyright" music – cover versions of Western hits – the early 1970s, with the Hallelujah Chicken Run Band, he started writing and playing his own songs. By the time he founded Blacks Unlimited in 1978, he was singing in Shona and experimenting with traditional sounds and beats. His guitarists and bass player adapted *mbira* melodies to rock instrumentation, the drummer played the tripping rhythms of the *hosho* on his hi-hat, while the singers and brass section layered on melodies. From the start, the sound was original and very popular, and evolved year by year. The late 1980s found Mapfumo adding actual *mbiras* to

Mapfumo remains a legend in Harare. He continued to perform at a frantic pace up until the summer of 2000, when he moved his family to the US and effectively went into self-imposed exile. Mapfumo's 1989 song "Corruption" had signalled a change in his politics, with its frank attack on the graft and greed that was beginning to rot Robert Mugabe's regime. A decade later, songs like "Disaster" and "Mamvemve" (Tatters) openly decried the regime as a failure. These songs were unofficially banned, but subsequent albums like *Chimurenga Rebel* (2001) and *Toi Toi* (2003) saw most of their songs explicitly denied airplay by a government no longer shy to censor independent voices. Exile has not been healthy for Mapfumo's career, because it has substantially separated him from his audience. Up until 2003, he always dared to return and play massive, year-end concerts, but these could hardly make up for the hundreds of six- to nine-hour shows he typically played each year when he lived back home, and in 2004, he declined to make even his traditional year-end gesture.

Still a tireless and prolific composer, Mapfumo has nevertheless continued to record excellent and uncompromising albums, using a stripped-down band he has maintained in the United States. Just as during the 1970s war years, Zimbabweans mostly have to resort to illegal, shortwave radio broadcasts in order to hear those songs, but those who do understand that Mukanya has not abandoned the fight, and that he remains one of the most engaged and creative bandleaders and unique, beautiful singers in the history of African popular music.

A number of Blacks Unlimited musicians have also pursued careers on their own, including guitarists **Jonah Sithole (Deep Horizon)**, **Joshua Dube (Shangara Jive)** and **Ashton "Sugar" Chiweshe (Batonga Crew)**, *mbira* player **Chartwell Dutiro**, now based in the UK, and singer **Patience Mudeka**. None of these has proven particularly successful with the Zimbabwean public, but all have musical merit.

Tuku Music

For most of the past quarter-century, **Oliver "Tuku" Mtukudzi** was the second giant of Zimbabwean music, although today, his record and concert sales exceed those of Mapfumo, both at home and abroad. Also forged during the liberation war years, Tuku's art has generally danced at the fringes of the country's turbulent politics, sometimes arousing controversy, but never crossing the line into brazen condemnation of the government. This survivor's strategy, combined with a rich, soul-tinged voice, splendidly matured songcraft and perhaps the best management of

any band in Zimbabwe, has brought Tuku to the top. He is now popular enough to tour successfully throughout much of southern Africa, in Europe and in the US. He has produced dozens of albums and appeared in films, including the socially aware *Jit* (1990), and *Shanda* (2002), an evocation of his career beginning with the liberation war years.

The oldest of seven children, Mutukudzi scored his first hit in 1977 with a group called **The Wagon Wheels.** Soon, he was fronting his own band, **The Black Spirits**, with whom he has recorded and performed ever since. His music is an innovative blend of Shona *mbira* pop (he acknowledges Mapfumo as an influence), South African township jive, rumba and soul. Always keen to experiment, Tuku is known for switching from *mbaqanga* and jazz fusion in one album to "ancient deep traditional beats" in the next. Despite that openness, he remains a strong traditionalist. For example, his album *Kuvaira* is typical Shona: 'It's not fused to any other kind of music. I did it for the older people of Zimbabwe, for those who want pure pure Zimbabwe music, straight straight deep deep deep deep traditional sounds.' The title-track remains a staple of Mtukudzi's live show.

Tuku's swinging renditions of the rootsiest beats, accompanied by his soulful voice and husky laugh, are irresistible. Tall, slim and handsome, with a big stage presence, an easy manner and a slick line in dance moves, his performances with The Black Spirits are captivating. He is also a highly socially conscious and moral artist, intensely aware of the importance of his lyrics (which are important to all Zimbabwean music). He sang the first AIDS song in Zimbabwe, and his lyrics place an emphasis on discipline: 'If one is disciplined then one is less likely to be corrupt. I believe in who we are, so my songs – though some might be in a different beat or a fusion of Western beats – don't run away from our tradition. I use proverbs and idioms that we use from long back when I sing in Shona. In English my lyrics change, but I'm an African so I record my English as I speak it.'

"Tuku Music" – as the Mtukudzi blend is sometimes called – has at last achieved international success as one of the most accessible and delightful forms of African pop around. Tuku's songwriting even won the ear of American singer Bonnie Raitt. She adapted his song "What's Going On" as "One Belief Away" in 1999, and covered his jive-gospel number "Hear Me Lord" in 2002. Tuku stirred controversy when his 2000 song "Wasakara" (You're Worn Out) was read as a cue to Mugabe to step down. But the singer weathered the storm, steadfastly rejecting the political spin observers put on

Oliver Mtukudzi

Tom Bullough meets Oliver Mtukudzi in his home town of Norton (September 2004).

What music were you listening to as a child?

I heard only *mbira* music, choir music and Korekore drumming rhythms until I was something like 6 or 7, when radio arrived in Zimbabwe. One of our local businessmen bought a small radio and the whole community used to go to his shop, just to sit and listen to this little speaker. Me, I would go there whenever I got the chance! I started hearing soul music, I suppose, in the early, mid 1960s: James Brown, Otis Redding, Wilson Pickett. I was amazed by the instrumentation, because the only instrument I knew was a three-string guitar. And that's when I began to wonder whether it was possible to play those instruments whilst singing Zimbabwean music.

When did you start to write songs of your own?

I started creating my own songs at secondary school. The first few ones were love songs, but they didn't do very well. Then, after I left school, for three years I couldn't get a job. So I started to write about that, about my experiences, and the first song I wrote, "Dzandimomotera", spent eleven weeks at Number One! It was big! That was '76, with Wagon Wheels. Wagon Wheels, featuring Oliver Mtukudzi!

Your music was also important to the war of independence.

My music of the 1970s was all to do with the struggle. It was like, I wasn't a politician, and I'm not a politician. But I started to write music, trying to send messages from the urban areas to the boys in the bush. I'd use clever lyrics, to sort of cut ourselves from the then-regime, so that they didn't understand what we were talking about. So, yes, our music had an effect on the way that the war went, because it gave whoever was fighting in the bush a reason to keep fighting.

How did your music change with independence?

During the struggle, I was really a messenger. I was singing about the people and it's the same thing now, but the issues are different. Now, too, there are lots of issues that need to be addressed. The AIDS epidemic, for example, is something that you can't keep quiet about.

You must be disappointed about the way that Zimbabwe has developed?

Well, in a way, yes. Because, at independence, all we expected was glory. When I can't get a loaf of bread for me and my kids, when I can't get fuel, you do have to think, where did we go wrong? The prices change every two days, every hour, and there is so much corruption. All that is disappointing.

But you never confront the authorities in your music?

My music is not for the government, my music is for the people. It's about where the problem starts, about lack of discipline. If we don't respect the next person, then we're killing ourselves.

You've been amazingly successful internationally.

Since *Tuku Music*, in '98, I have had a lot of work outside Zimbabwe, but it wasn't sudden! This was after two decades, twenty years! It was down to my experience, really. I never thought that I would ever have such a big international market, but I always knew that what I was doing was going to pay off some day. I just didn't know how.

You've even been on the David Letterman Show.

I didn't know who David Letterman was! If I had, I'd have been nervous. But he was nice. He'd chosen a couple of tracks he wanted me to perform…

So he knew who you were?

Yeah! He knew who I was!

his song. He continues to live and perform large concerts in Zimbabwe, despite near-insurmountable logistical challenges.

In the late 1990s, Tuku also began to work with a southern African supergroup called **Mahube**. Founded by South African **Steve Dyer** (of **South-**

Oliver "Tuku" Mtukudzi

ern Freeway), the original idea was to develop a style of music representative of the whole of southern Africa, to be presented at a 1998 festival in Germany. But the show received such acclaim that the Mahube line-up now incorporates twelve musicians, including members of Southern Freeway and The Black Spirits, renowned female vocalists Phinda Mtya and Dieketseng Mnisi, and Malawian guitarist George Phiri, plus a range of guest artists, many of whom appear on their second album *Qhubeka!* (2004).

Jit Hits the Fans

The term **jit** originally applied to a kind of recreational drumming and singing performed in Shona villages, but it has become a catch-all term for Zimbabwe's guitar-driven electric pop, which incorporates elements of Central and East African rumba, South African jive and local traditional music. You could try to sub-classify jit bands as rumba, sungura, *tsava-tsava*, *mbira* pop or whatever, but many of the most successful acts in Zimbabwe's pop history don't fit neatly into categories. The goal of appeasing a beerhall crowd can't be confined to any single genre.

The original hybrids were, perhaps, **Zexie Manatsa and The Green Arrows** – the first band in the country ever to record an LP. Formed in 1968, by 1974 they had been "discovered" by South African producer West Nkosi, who gave guitarist

Stanley Manatsa his distinctive wah-wah pedal and helped to mould their kwela-influenced sound. The Green Arrows were as bizarre as they were brilliant ("Chechule wavale boton" is about a frog wearing bell-bottoms), and their single "Musango Mune Hanjaiwa" still holds the record for the most weeks at number one (17, no less!). In 2005, the band reunited in Harare.

Robson Banda and The New Black Eagles are another shining example. Though Banda traced his roots back to Zambia, and Shona was actually his third language, he emerged in the 1980s as one of the most compelling voices in Shona pop and continued to record and fill the beerhalls up until his death in 1998.

More strictly jit, the **Four Brothers** have been a leading band over the past couple of decades, their sweet vocals soaring over rippling guitar riffs and sure-fire dance rhythms. Marshall Munhumumwe, the group's leader for twenty years, was Thomas Mapfumo's uncle and learnt drums and singing from him. Their first hit, "Makoro" (Congratulations), was dedicated to the freedom fighters at independence, and they became one of the top Zimbabwean bands of the 1980s. They called themselves the Four Brothers in order to remain equal, so that no brother would become "big" – a fate that has shattered too many Zimbabwean bands in the past. Although popular in the West, they stick firmly to their roots, choosing to record in Harare. They play frequently at home and abroad, though sadly without their songwriter, who suffered a devastating stroke in 1997 and died in 2001.

One beerhall jit veteran still on the scene is **Paul Matavire**, the blind singer, songwriter and front man for the **Jairos Jiri Sunshine Band**. The group grew out of a welfare organization founded to assist the reintegration of disabled Zimbabweans into society, and their songs often incorporate acute social observations. Ironically, Matavire himself was sentenced to a one-year prison sentence for rape in the early 1990s, though he has since, amazingly, reclaimed his career and a good measure of his popularity.

Overseas, the best known jit band of the 1980s was **The Bhundu Boys**, whose flowing and energetic dance music – with its "popcorn" style of guitar-playing and rousing vocal harmonies – earned them a name in the UK, where they became semi-resident. They were never as popular at home, and their music moved too close to Western pop (as on the disastrous *True Jit* album) in the late 1980s. Their frontman, the charismatic Biggie Tembo, later left to join the Ocean City Band, and had a brief career as a gospel singer before his tragic suicide in 1995. After he left, the group lost two bass

Simon "Chopper" Chimbetu and dancers

genre", but it has a strong Congolese flavour, and his voice shimmers like those of South Africa's Soul Brothers. Zhakata's fans always cite his lyrics as his strongest hook. They say he has an uncanny knack for probing the psychic and spiritual crisis of Zimbabwe. One Harare music journalist wrote that Zhakata's latest songs have "the substance of a classic novel and the elegance of great poetry". Nobody ever said that about the songs of *kwassa-kwassa* kings or *soukous sapeurs*.

Another rumba survivor is the guitarist and songwriter **Jonah Moyo**, who formed the **Devera Ngwena Jazz Band** just before independence. Their music is a highly infectious form of rumba, achieving great success in Zimbabwe in the 1980s, and while their popularity has waned, they continue to perform in South Africa, where Moyo now lives, and released a new album, *Devera Ngwena 30*, in 2004.

Rumba with a message has long been a successful formula in Zimbabwe. Until his premature death in 1997, **Leonard Dembo** consistently played Zimbabwean heartstrings with his homespun songs. Born in Masvingo, Dembo stumbled into a career in music with the Bulawayo group **Barura Express** before moving in 1980 to Harare, where he worked as a session musician. His early efforts made overnight stars of a group called The Outsiders, and once at the helm of his own band, Dembo polished his folksy rumba epics, which included the song "Chitikete," one of the best-selling singles ever in Zimbabwe.

John Chibadura, with his band the **Tembo Brothers**, was one of Zimbabwe's biggest-selling rumba artists in the 1980s and the early 90s. A one-time goat-herder and truck driver, he appeared a shy, introverted "anti-star", but once on stage exploded in bare-chested bravado, combining rumba with full-throttle dance music. To non-speakers of Shona, the songs sound happy and upbeat, but the lyrics often describe grim social conditions and deep-rooted fears, which, with typical Zimbabwean stoicism, were always sung over a defiantly good-time beat.

With the new millennium, the good-time beat has become more important than ever. The rise of **sungura** – a development of rumba, influenced by *mbaqanga* and East African *kanindo* – has been embodied in the success of **Alick Macheso**, the "King of Sungura". A former member of the **Khiama Boys**, Macheso – or "Borrowdale", as he is known to his fans – rose to prominence in 2000 with his third album, *Simbaradzo*, which is

players and their keyboardist to AIDS. A version of the band soldiers on, with little hope of recapturing their old glory.

Rumba-Sungura

In Zimbabwe, song lyrics and dance idioms are the keys to popularity, and many of the biggest sellers these days are local **rumba** artists, notably Simon Chimbetu and Leonard Zhakata. While the dominant influence in Zimbabwean rumba is from Congo (ex-Zaïre), it has a fast triplet feel that is unique, and comes from *mbira* music.

Simon "Chopper" Chimbetu was a veteran of the Zimbabwe rumba scene from his 1980s band, the Marxist Brothers. With his group, the **Dendera Kings**, he was loved for his infectious pop hooks and clever, humorous lyrics, but after recording *Hoko* in support of the government in 2002 he saw his fan base evaporate and he mainly performed at government-organized events until his death in 2005.

Still relatively popular, **Leonard Karikoga Zhakata** graduated from the early 1990s rumba group, Maungwe Brothers. As a solo artist, Zhakata was named "Best Musician" in numerous 1990s polls, and had a huge success with his 1996 release *Nzombe Huru*. He calls his music "a sound above

currently the most successful release in Zimbabwean history, having sold over 400,000 copies. Continuing in the style pioneered by **John Chibadura**, **Leonard Dembo** and **System Tazvida**, he plays powerful dance music with his **Orchestra Mberikwazvo**, and is known for his trademark bass-strumming technique, his socially conscious — though decidedly apolitical — lyrics and his famous "gallop" dance.

In spite of the loss of Macheso and other members in 1997, the Khiama Boys continue to perform with "Senior Lecturer" **Nicholas Zakaria**, who is number two in the fiercely competitive world of *sungura*. Zakaria has been the group's main composer and lead guitarist since 1986, and both his clear, melodic guitar and his "Borrowdale" dance are reminiscent of Macheso, although his lyrics are closer to gospel. With other major artists including **Tongai Moyo and Utakataka Band**, the *sungura* scene now provides the backbone of the Zimbabwean music industry, and rules in the rural areas, where most Zimbabweans still live.

Over the years, Harare has also hosted a number of rumba bands and musicians from Congo. They include the **Real Sounds**, adoptive Zimbabweans who were formative in mixing the Zaïrean beat with the Zimbabwean *mbira* to produce a sound that they christened *rumbira*. This eleven-piece band combines a rolling, *soukous*-style rumba beat, the frenetic performance of a steaming cohort of brass and an exuberant drummer. It makes for compulsive dancing and an unmissable live show. They have an enthusiastic following both at home and overseas.

Another transplanted Congolese rumba outfit, **The Lubumbashi Stars**, play rumba in the classic 1970s style, complete with five singers harmonizing lusciously and dancing in tight formations. For many years, they were a staple of Harare's club scene, but they have since relocated to Botswana.

Praise the Lord and Pass the Sadza

It's not surprising that Zimbabwe's recent travails should inspire a surge in sales of **gospel music**, and indeed, gospel may be the fastest-growing sector of the local music market these days. Powerful gospel vocalists from South Africa dominate the scene, but Zimbabwe is producing more and more successful gospel artists every year.

Zimbabwe's first real gospel star was **Jonathan Wutawunashe**, who had a series of hits with his group the **Family Singers** in the early 1980s before he moved to Washington DC and then to Brussels. The Family Singers still play in Harare, with Wutawunashe when opportunity arises.

Perhaps the biggest star of the following decades was **Brian Sibalo**, who formed his group **Golden Gospel Sounds** at 19 and went solo in the late 1980s, scoring many hits before his tragic death in 1997. Sibalo was a member of the **Apostolic Church**, a distinctly Zimbabwean Christian sect whose enormous ranks are evident on Saturdays, when they can be seen in their white garments, gathering under trees for services. Apostolics eschew both churches and the Bible, preferring to get their religious truths through direct experiences with the divinity. Following Sibalo's death, the major gospel artist was probably **Machanic Manyeruke**, leader of **The Puritans**, although he has since been eclipsed by **Charles Charamba** and **Fishers of Men** whose smooth, *sungura*-flavoured anthems are second in popularity only to Alick Macheso. Attractive and accessible, Charamba and his wife and former backing singer, **Mai Charamba** are the uncontested leaders of a form that makes up around 50 percent of the music played on state radio: an astonishing achievement, given the dominance of South African gospel as recently as the late 1990s.

Of the numerous other gospel performers making an impression, **Fungisai Zvakavapano** is unquestionably the rising star, her sales competing with Charamba and her tearful performances reflecting a wider swing towards the drama of the Pentecostal church. Also falling beneath the gospel banner are acts as diverse as the **Mahendere Brothers**, with their high-energy fusion of gospel and rumba, and **Culture T**, a ragga MC, now based in the UK, who has recently turned his talents to the service of the Lord.

Ndebele Pop: The Bulawayo Sound

Compared with Harare, **Bulawayo** – in the southwest province of Matabeleland, on the South African border, where the majority speak the Zulu-related language Ndebele – is a sleepy one-horse town, with rather low-key music venues. Bulawayan musicians feel acutely that the dominant positions in Zimbabwe are occupied by Harare

Dorothy Masuka, Zimbabwe's voice in jazz

Africa in her early days, later fleeing to London to escape from the white minority-ruled Rhodesia, and campaigning for a free Zimbabwe all over southern Africa. Like many Bulawayan musicians, Masuka draws a lot on South African influences, playing a mixture of swing and local melodies in a style known as *marabi*. 'The Ndebele-speaking people who live in Matabeleland and Bulawayo are Zulus. They came into this country and settled in Matabeleland. My grandfather, for example, comes from a village in South Africa in Natal. This is why the traditional kind of music down south is South African.' A big, glamorous personality, Dorothy Masuka is still one of Zimbabwe's strongest female performers.

The torchbearer of **Ndebele pop** through the 1980s was **Lovemore Majaivana**, a flamboyant if uneven, performer with a rich powerful voice and a penchant for brilliantly coloured, skin-tight lurex suits. He was one of the few Bulawayo names to have made it big in Harare after independence, and the Zulu influence was very strong in some of his music, though he also used *mbira* melodies in his songs. He released his first album for five years in 2000, but has since retired to the US.

Black Umfolosi are an acapella group of singers and dancers from Bulawayo – an amazing live experience with their precise and acrobatic singing and dancing to a strong Zulu beat – and clearly reminiscent in style and content to **Ladysmith Black Mambazo.** They are regular fixtures on the international World Music festival circuit, where, since 1991, they have been joined by **Imbizo** (meaning a mass gathering in Zulu) – a nine-man Bulawayan group in a similar style, who have performed in the UK several times and appeared at the WOMAD Festival in 2001.

The leading Ndebele musician to buck the pro-Shona trend and win a national audience is poet, storyteller and bandleader **Albert Nyathi.** An independence war veteran and acclaimed

and the culture of the peoples of Manicaland and Mashonaland.

But this has not always been the case. Back in the 1950s, Ndebele artists like guitarist **George Sibanda** were the big stars in this part of Africa. Sibanda is even credited with influencing guitar legend John Bosco Mwenda, one of the seminal figures of Congolese music. 'Before the 1980s', the Bulawayo-born singer Dorothy Masuka recalled, 'blacks and whites played together in Bulawayo and there was a good music scene – but somehow after independence there was a split between Shona and Ndebele – things got moved to Harare and Bulawayo has never recovered. If there are musicians from Matabeland in Harare then they play Harare music. They [the Shona] are actually the owners of this country.'

Dorothy Masuka, one of the key musicians of African Jazz (see South Africa Jazz chapter), has had a career that spans nearly fifty years. She sang with Miriam Makeba and Hugh Masekela in South

poet, Nyathi fronts the band Imbongi, which plays everything from Shona traditional music to Afro-jazz, rumba and jive in the manner of South Africa's Soul Brothers. Nyathi has recently been seen performing more frequently in the UK than he has in Zimbabwe, but Bulawayo remains ably represented in Harare by the township jazz of Dumi Ngulube and the sweat-soaked performances of Lwazi Tshabangu – a former backing singer of Lovemore Majaivana, who follows his style closely.

In Bulawayo itself, the **Cool Crooners** have received a great deal of attention over the past few years since their "discovery" by a French documentary maker, Patrick Meunier, and a string of tours across southern Africa, Europe and America. Formed by members of two 1950s groups, the Cool Four and the Golden Rhythm Crooners, the Cool Crooners have their roots in 1920s Johannesburg *marabi* and are proudly the oldest township jazz band in Zimbabwe. They are one of several groups to have been supported by the astonishingly vibrant Amakhosi, the only independent arts centre in the country, which, in spite of the economic climate, has been nurturing a talented new generation of pop, soul, jazz, *kwaito* and *sholosho* (Ndebele *mbaqanga*) musicians, releasing their work on their own Ziyakhupha label.

New Directions

As previously noted, new bands make their mark with difficulty in Zimbabwe. Venue owners are reluctant to take them without a hit record, and with no contracts, will drop them at a moment's notice if they can book someone better known. To find a venue, a new band usually needs to work its way, playing in the outlying "growth points" – a tough graft.

With the political and economic crisis, several promising bands of the 1990s have failed to meet their potential, with members either succumbing to illness, the struggle to survive or the lure of government funding. In the latter case, the obvious example is **Andy Brown**, a guitarist and songwriter who mixed Zimbabwe sounds with rumba, jive, reggae, ragga and rap to great success in the 1990s, and was widely seen as the future of Zimbabwean pop. Having recorded *Tongogara* and *More Fire* in support of the government, however, he was abandoned by his fans and now performs only rarely. The **Hodhodza Band**, on the other hand, have survived three deaths, several line-up changes and relocation to the UK, to tour internationally and record ten albums to date.

One result of all these pressures tends to be a reluctance to experiment among young musicians. Many of the up-and-coming bands in Harare play *sungura* in direct imitation of Alick Macheso, while the "urban grooves" scene is typified by straight Shona versions of American or Jamaican artists, complete with MTV dance routines. Nevertheless, local ragga is particularly popular in Harare and the surrounding townships, and the likes of **Major E and Booker T**, **Decibel** and **Kooligan and Kalabash** are all regular features of the live music scene (albeit with the help of backing tracks), while the immense success of **M'Afriq** in 2004 demonstrates that there is ample scope for a more Zimbabwean take on the "urban" sound.

Among the younger guitar-led bands, the exuberant **Afrika Revenge**, led by childhood friends Willis Wataffi and Taz Moyo, have been especially successful, their "Afro-soul-jazz" strongly influenced by Oliver Mtukudzi. Over the past five years, there has been something of a resurgence of jazz in Harare, and groups such as **Dudu Manhenga and Color Blu** and **Jazz Invitation** – who blend hip-hop and Dorothy Masuka-style jazz – are among the best around.

Afrika Revenge

Lastly, if you get the opportunity to see, or buy anything, by an extraordinary Tonga group from the Zambezi valley, the thirty-strong **Simonga**, take it without hesitation. The Tonga are Zimbabwe's third largest ethnic group and the *ngoma buntibe* performed by Simonga is at once pure Tonga tradition and a radical departure from anything you are likely to have heard before. They play the traditional – and entirely undespondent – funeral music of the Tonga: a call-and-reponse-based frenzy of horns, drums, rattles, wailing voices and stamping feet. They have collaborated with a number of progressive composers from Zimbabwe, South Africa and Austria, and have recently performed with Maliko, a Zambian *ngoma buntibe* group with 110 members.

⊙ **The Rough Guide to the Music of Zimbabwe**
World Music Network, UK
A fine introduction, ranging from Stella Chiweshe to the Real Sounds' great thirteen-minute soccer song "Tornados vs. Dynamos (3-3)".

⊙ **The Soul of Mbira: Traditions of the Shona People**
Nonesuch Explorer, US
These classic recordings of traditional *mbira* music were made by Paul Berliner during the early stages of the liberation war.

★ **Zimbabwe Frontline Vol 2: Spirit of the Eagle**
Earthworks, UK
If any one record sums up what's special about Zimbabwe pop, this is it. With emphasis on the roots sounds of Thomas Mapfumo and Robson Banda, this compilation puts the focus squarely on Zimbabwe's richest musical sources. Start here and you won't go wrong.

⊙ **Zimbabwe Frontline Vol 3: Roots Rock Guitar Party**
Earthworks, UK
Old favourites John Chibadura and the Four Brothers each contribute a handful of tracks to this volume, delivering their trademark clean-cut guitars and upbeat rhythms. Less familiar names including *mbira*-modulated Max Mapfumo and the brilliantly kicking Zimbabwe Cha Cha Cha Kings. All combines to evoke an open-air Harare beer garden.

Robson Banda & The New Black Eagles

Banda is best known for his lean, guitar-driven take on the *mbira* pop sound. Call it *chimurenga redux*, but none of the depth is lost.

⊙ **Greatest Hits Vol 1**
Zimbob-5, Zimbabwe
The only international release from one of Zimbabwe's best electric roots pop bands, this is a must for fans of that genre.

The Bhundu Boys

The Bhundu Boys championed pan-Zimbabwean music in the 1980s, becoming one of the most popular and widely travelled Zimbabwean bands before calamities laid them low in the 1990s.

⊙ **The Shed Sessions**
Sadza, UK
An irresistible double CD, comprising almost all of the classic *Shabini* and *Tsvimbodzemoto* albums, plus more…

Black Umfolosi

This Ndebele group is Zimbabwe's answer to Ladysmith Black Mambazo, making up in style for what they may lack in originality.

⊙ **Festival Umdlalo**
World Circuit, UK
Showcase for the group's mellow acapella talents.

John Chibadura & The Tembo Brothers

The veteran Chibadura remained the top performer of high-energy rumba until his death in 1999.

⊙ **More of the Essential**
CSA, UK
Essential indeed if you want to know what revved up Zimbabwe's rumba machine in the 1980s and early 90s. Congolese fans take note; an expert demonstrates how to do tight dance numbers Zim style.

Stella Chiweshe

As a woman playing *mbira*, Stella Chiweshe has never worried much about conformity. But though willing and eager to experiment, her fidelity to tradition is undeniable. She goes deep every time.

⊙ **Kumusha: Pure Mbira Music from Zimbabwe**
Piranha, Germany
No complaints here: if you like *mbira* you'll soon be in a trance.

⊙ **Ambuya?/Ndizvozvo**
Piranha, Germany
Ambuya?, her first international album is a magnificent experiment, only troubling purists with its lively 3 Mustaphas 3 participation on bass and drums. The *Ndizvozvo* EP, recorded for John Peel's radio show, has a wonderfully rich *mbira* tone.

The Green Arrows

The biggest stars of the 1970s, all wah-wah and innovation. Produced by West Nkosi, The Green Arrows were the link between *chimurenga* and South African *kwela*, and, happily, they have now reformed.

★ **Four-Track Recording Session**
Analog Africa, US
20 crucial tracks from their peak – 1974-79. The session includes such fuzztone spectaculars as "The Towering Inferno" (inspired by the Steve McQueen movie), as well as more delicate numbers like "Musango Mune Hanjaiwa".

Hallelujah Chicken Run Band

The original *chimurenga* outfit, featuring both Thomas Mapfumo and Joshua Dube. HCR were formed to entertain workers at Mangura Copper Mine, but wound up revolutionising Zimbabwean music.

⊙ **Take One**
Analog Africa, US
An imperative collection of HCR's singles from 1974–79. This is the moment that *mbira* music met electric instruments, and you don't get more rootsy than that!

ZIMBABWE

PLAYLIST
Zimbabwe

1 **CHITIMA NDITAKURE Thomas Mapfumo** from *Chamunorwa*
"Train, take me away". Hypnotic and heavy on the *mbira*, this is as rootsy as it gets.

2 **NDIMA NDAPEDZA Oliver Mtukudzi** from *Tuku Music*
About the most beautiful moment on a beautiful album – the perfect Tuku blend of soul and groove.

3 **KUROJA CHETE The Bhundu Boys** from *Shed Sessions*
Even the struggle to pay the rent sounds like a cause for celebration!

4 **MISORODZI Dumisani Maraire** from *The African Mbira*
All the sorrow of Africa.

5 **AMAI VARUBHI Alick Macheso** from *Simbaradzo*
Macheso urges dialogue between wives and husbands – over an unstoppable *sungura* beat.

6 **MAPIYEMANA Stella Chiweshe** from *Kumusha*
Pure trance-inducing tradition – *mbira*, voice, clapping, drums and *hosho*.

7 **TORNADOS VS DYNAMOS (3–3) Real Sounds** from *Vende Zoko*
An epic piece of rumba: the greatest football clash in Zimbabwean music history!

8 **KANA NDAGUTA Jonah Sithole** from *Sabhuku*
All the skill of the maestro, with none of those slightly iffy keyboards…

9 **NDIVUMBAMIREIWO Four Brothers** from *Zimbabwe Frontline Vol 3: Roots Rock Guitar Party*
Awesome, no messing Shona guitar pop.

10 **KUMAKORODZI Mbira dze Nharira** from *Rinemanyanga Hariputirwe*
Weaving, ethereal voices. *Mbira* music at its best.

Alick Macheso

The biggest Zimbabwean star to emerge in the new millennium. His nickname, "Borrowdale", refers to Harare's Borrowdale horse-racing track and his much-loved "gallop" dance.

⊙ **Simbaradzo**
Gramma, Zimbabwe
An upbeat soundtrack for troubled times: 400,000 copies sold and counting!

Lovemore Majaivana

The king of Ndebele pop music, with at least half an eye on South African *mbaqanga*.

⊙ **The Best of Lovemore Majaivana**
ZMC, Zimbabwe
A fine selection of tracks from his 1980s heyday. The keyboards might have dated, but there's no disguising the power of his voice.

Thomas Mapfumo

Zimbabwe's most influential musician of the 1980s, Mapfumo is known as the guru of *mbira* pop, but his music encompasses everything from African jazz to jit, *tsava tsava*, rumba, reggae and rock. Just call it *chimurenga* music – Zimbabwe's proudest export!

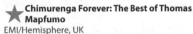 **Chimurenga Forever: The Best of Thomas Mapfumo**
EMI/Hemisphere, UK
A fine sampler, offering more than a taste of his range from 1978 to 1993, and with good notes, too.

⊙ **The Chimurenga Singles: 1976–80**
Shanachie, US
A re-release of a wonderful Earthworks collection of Mapfumo's war-years hits.

⊙ **Toi Toi**
Anonym, US
Probably the best of Mapfumo's recent releases, containing some fine, horn-driven funkiness and an intriguing Malian influence.

Dumisani Maraire

A superb *mbira* player, Dumisani Maraire was Visiting Artist at Washington State University in the early 1970s and pivotal in spreading awareness of traditional Shona music to America during the 1970s and 80s.

⊙ **The African Mbira: Music of the Shona People**
Nonesuch Explorer, US
Originally released in 1971, this is a sublime selection of traditional material, accompanied by voice and *hosho*.

Dorothy Masuka

One of the big singing stars of the African jazz swing sound, Masuka's career goes back to the 1950s. Though no longer a trendsetter, the grand lady of Zimbabwean song still performs her classic music.

⊙ **The Definitive Collection**
Wrasse, UK
Fairly well-named compilation covering early hits and later material from more recent albums *Pata Pata* and *Mzilikazi*.

Mbira dze Nharira

Perhaps the finest group to emerge from Zimbabwe in recent years, Mbira dze Nharira play pure, uncompromising *mbira* music.

⊙ **Rinemanyanga Hariputirwe**
ZMC, Zimbabwe
Mbira, *hosho* and mesmerizing vocals, this is their glorious first CD – eleven years in the conception!

Oliver "Tuku" Mtukudzi

A giant of an artist in Zimbabwe, Tuku hasn't received the international recognition he deserves. The locals love him for his wise, conscious lyrics and *hunhu* (moral values), but Mtukudzi's soulful tenor and languid *chimurenga*-style guitar transcends all language.

⊙ Shoko
Piranha, Germany
An irresistable selection of Tuku hits, re-recorded in Germany. Apparently, the session sounds almost too slick to the man himself, but few listeners will complain.

⊙ Ziwere MuKøbenhavn
Shava, Germany
Mbaqanga meets *mbira*-beat with hard-driving results. And what a persuasive liner booklet!

★ Tuku Music
Earthsong, UK
This 1998 release is near flawless – a CD that you can put on repeat and enjoy for hours on end, delighting in the tunes, the Shona *mbira* patterns, the voices (wonderful harmony singing from Mwendi Chibindi and Mary Bell), the lilting guitar (Tuku himself plays acoustic throughout the disc). The lyr-ics are impressive, too – socially conscious as ever and neatly summarized in the notes.

Real Sounds

The band's founders originated in Congo (ex-Zaïre), but came to sing in Shona, paving the way for homegrown Zimbabwe rumba.

⊙ Vende Zoko
Cooking Vinyl, UK
Close your eyes and you could be in Congo. But listen harder for that characteristic nippy Zim guitar style.

Jonah Sithole

The late king of *mbira* guitar was, off and on, a singer, songwriter and bandleader in his own right. Over two decades on the music scene, Sithole established himself as a pioneer of the country's roots pop sound.

⊙ Sabhuku
Zimbob-4, UK
A sublime sampling of Sithole's work during the years he left Blacks Unlimited to head his own band, Deep Horizon.

Part 2

Middle East

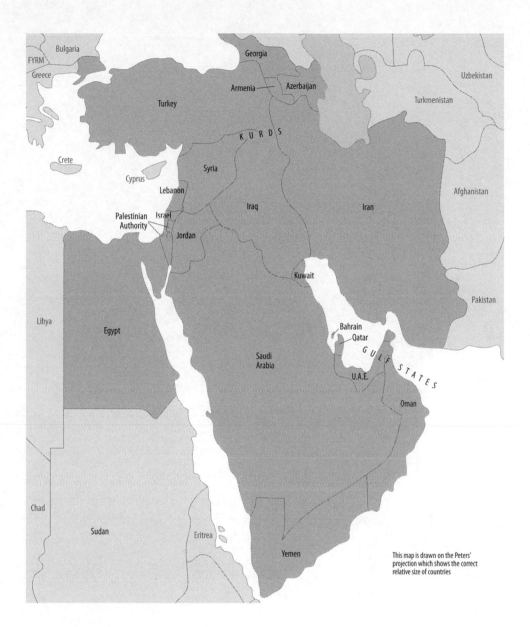

This map is drawn on the Peters'
projection which shows the correct
relative size of countries

Middle East

Arab World/Egypt | Classical 463
Arabesque 475
Armenia 481
Azerbaijan 489
Egypt | Popular/Street Music 495
Georgia 505

The Gulf 510
Iran 519
Iraq 533
Israel 539
Jewish Music | Sephardic 551
Jordan & Bedouin Music 559

Kurdish Music 563
Lebanon 572
Palestinian Music 580
Syria 589
Turkey 595

Arab World/Egypt |
Classical

music, partner of poetry

The iconic Umm Kulthum

From the twentieth century onwards, Egypt – and, specifically, Cairo – has dominated the Arab musical world. For an Arab singer (and it is singers who are accorded overriding respect) to make it, she or he had to do so in the Egyptian capital. And so it has been since the 1920s, when the gramophone and radio meant that the Arab world, with its shared language, religion and culture, was for a long while listening to the same music. It makes sense, therefore, to place a part of the history of Arab music as a whole in this chapter on Egypt. Below, David Lodge, Bill Badley and Neil van der Linden look at the traditions of Classical Arab song and profile its superstars.

Because of the elevated place given to the word in Arab culture, where poetry is the highest of all art forms, the role of the singer has always been to take the word to the people. Arab song and musical expression reached its first golden age between the eighth and twelfth centuries, followed by a long period of stagnation and Turkish influence under Ottoman rule. It was reborn during the twentieth century against a background of nationalist fervour and political instability, and developed amid a modern age of radio, films, the gramophone record and later cheap cassettes.

The Arab world's singers and writers, through the language and emotional power of popular song, have been influential in determining the identity of nations, expressing the hopes of their people and on occasions threatening their states. Music has retained a unique power in the Arab world, and it offers listeners a window to its personality. The survey that follows looks at the region's shared classical music, and its former superstars.

Classical Arab Music

Classical Arab music is enjoyed throughout Arab society and transcends all ages and social barriers. It is a musical arena that, ever since the first recordings, has been dominated by a small number of Egyptian or Egypt-based **pan-Arab superstars**, adored by the masses. Their popularity has given these giants of the stage enormous cultural significance. They have been, in their time, more influential than presidents and a stronger binding factor – swaying the moods of society at large by touching the lives of many individuals with their poignant lyrics and sultry melodies. From humiliation in military defeat to the personal wounds of love, their music has provided sustenance during long periods of pain and introspection.

Typically, Classical Arab singers will perform pieces up to an hour in length, in highly charged melancholy tones, dwelling on the themes of tragic fate, or love – forbidden or unrequited – beckoning the listener to wallow in metaphor and listen as the lyrics unfold to the story of his or her own life. As the greatest of Arab singers of the twentieth century, **Umm Kulthum**, sang in "Enta Umri" (You Are My Life):

> Your eyes brought me back to my lost days.
> They have taught me how
> to regret the past and its wounds.
> What I experienced before my eyes
> saw you is wasted time.

> How could they count it as my age?
> You are my life, whose morning
> started with your light.
> You are, you are, you are my life.

> Lyrics by Ahmed Shafik Kamel, music by
> Mohammed Abdel Wahab, 1965

Shared Roots

> Love, wine, gambling, hunting, the pleasures of song and romance, the brief pointed elegant expression of wit and wisdom. These things he knew to be good. Beyond them he saw only the grave.

> Anonymous, translated from Arabic

From a thousand years or more before Islam, the **nomadic Arab tribes** had firmly established the hedonistic character of their music. In those days, music was primarily a job for women. Female **singing slaves** were brought to the cities to entertain the noble houses and caravanserais, both as geisha-like entertainment women and as artists.

The singers would accompany warriors onto the battlefield, banging *daf* and *tabla* and singing war songs of **rajaz poetry** (*rajaz* is the metre of a camel's feet on sand) while the combat ensued, and en route would be always at the ready to stir the spirits of the soldiers. At tribal nuptials the women singers and musicians led the celebrations, and they were there too on the Hajj to Mecca – which was in those pre-Islamic days a pagan pilgrimage – where they would sing and dance around the Kaabah, the sacred stone.

The principal male performers of the time were **mukhanathin** – young, transvestite slaves – from whose ranks came the majority of male musicians. With the arrival of **Islam** in the seventh century, all these entertainers experienced the wrath of the more orthodox Muslims, while the transvestites suffered ridicule from society at large; however, their skills were nurtured in the protective courts of certain less pious caliphs who appreciated their antics at feasts and banquets.

In more orthodox Islam circles both singing and the playing of musical instruments were considered sins, and swiftly banned. Yazid III, a noted Umayyad caliph, warned in 740 AD: "Beware of singing for it will steal your modesty, fill you with lust and ruin your virtue." Unlawful instruments were destroyed, singers were considered unworthy witnesses in court, and female slaves who turned out to have a vocal inclination could be taken back to market and exchanged. The **call to prayer** by the **muezzin** and the recitation of the full **Koran**,

Koranic Recitation: the Basis of Islamic Music

In Egypt, a **Koran reciter** (*moqri*) will first have to be judged worthy by a committee of religious scholars. He is tested on the complexity and subtlety of his mastering of the *maqams*, and in his agility in dispensing, through them, the words of God. By protecting the Arabic "scales" throughout the ages in this way, a religion that shuns music has in effect kept the music alive. Today the classical Koranic recitation still plays this role by continuing to demand only the most perfect rendition of ancient Arabic modes from the most able voices – a sure defence against encroaching Western influence. The full resonance of the call to prayer from some of the finest and most accomplished singers in the world is sheer delight.

The **tajwid**, the musically elaborate style of Koranic recitation, was brought to its peak in Egypt. It involves intricate melodic and cadential formulae and ornaments, and, importantly, pauses between the phrases. The Koranic chant unfolds slowly. Notes are held for a long time and vocalizations on a vowel or a consonant make it possible for the *moqri* to pass from one region of a mode to another and change register with an interval of one octave or more. Here, there is room enough for individual styles. The *maqam bayati* is a favourite mode with Egyptian chanters. Many popular reciters have crossed over to pursue very profitable careers in the secular field – most notably Sayed Darwish, and Umm Kulthum.

Some of the most adored voices are those of **Mohammed Rifaat** and **Sheikh Abdelbasset Abdessamad**, whose CD series *Le Saint Coran* (Clube du Disque Arabe) is highly recommended. In Cairo's *souks* the cassettes by **Sheikh Muhammad Mahmoud at-Tablawi** are tremendously popular. You can access recordings at *kitabullah.com/qaris/tablawi*.

Islam's holiest city, Mecca, is in Saudi Arabia, a country dominated by Wahabi Islam – a very strict and conservative interpretation, which has been much exported in recent years. Nowadays we hear the Wahabi style of recitation in many parts of the Arabic world. It is much simpler and unadorned, consisting of a limited range of six tones at most, and dismisses the rich microtones of classical Egyptian and Syrian reading. In fact throughout the Islamic world there is a surprising variety of interpretations, which merge other vocal traditions in the recitation. For instance, in Sudan a pentatonic "African" style can be found while in Turkey the singing styles of classical Turkish music are incorporated.

which in their best-represented forms are supreme examples of the complex *maqams* (the scales on which Arab music is based), are not by themselves considered as music.

The emotional input of a sheikh in the recitation is guarded by strict rules about pitch and tempo. A celebrated Cairo court case in 1977 ruled: "The Holy Koran contains the words of God, who recited it in a manner we do not comprehend. Koran recitation is an act of compliance and does not involve innovation." To induce *tarab* – enchantment – through delivery of the Koran is a complex matter, indicative of the fear in Islam of the influence of music on human nature. **Sufism**, the mystical version of Islam, turns this enchantment into a principle, and tends to unite religious and musical expression, although not through the words of the Koran.

Thanks to her image as a pious woman, Umm Kulthum was able to bridge classes and created some great twentieth-century spiritual anthems based on religious themes, like "Naj al Burda" (The Cloak of the Prophet), "Salou Qalbi" and her rendering of texts by the eighth-century Baghdad female mystic poet Rabiah al-Adawiyyah.

Largely denied figurative expression in Islamic art, Arab culture reserves special importance for the language. The important place of poetry in society has partly to do with the tradition of **narrative** among the nomadic tribes, as a means of killing time and staying awake in tiring landscapes and giving the impression of control over an unpredictable environment. In pre-Islamic times, the poet was magnificent; a spokesman on policy, a judge in dispute and a voice to praise heroes and scorn enemies. With the arrival of Islam, the Koran's rich language, rhythm and rhyme became the textbook of artistic creation. Poets wrested the limelight from the splendid cultural centres of Damascus and Baghdad. Today the special place of poetry in Arab music is still proudly guarded. Songs are judged primarily on their words, and music without them is considered a "religion without a scripture".

Soon after the advent of Islam, Arab music gained a suitor from an unexpected quarter. The Arab musical world was under the protection of the caliph's court in Baghdad, where away from the jurisdiction of the Islamic purists, enjoyment and creativity reigned. This was the hedonistic world

Theory, Scales & Rhythm in Classical Arab Music

The musical knowledge and theories of the Ancient Greeks have come to us largely through the surviving works of early Islamic writers. Chief among them was **Abu Nasr al-Farabi** – one of the greatest philosophers and scholars in Islamic history. Born in Transoxiana (now Uzbekistan) around the year 872, he studied and taught in the three cities that are the exalted triumvirate of classical Arab music: Baghdad, Cairo and Damascus. He wrote on numerous subjects. His main writing on music was the *Kitab al-Musiqa al-Kabir* (Grand Book of Music), a work which sets out tonal systems (*maqams*), metrics (*iqat*), different kinds of melodies (*alhan*), instruments (*al-alat al-mashhura*) and their tunings (*taswiya*).

Much of what he wrote is still relevant. **Melody** is organized into a series of **maqams** (melodic modes), any given one of which (*maqam*) has a distinctive scale which is based around 24 quarter-notes – as opposed to the twelve semitones of Western music. Each mode then has its own ethos and is often associated with a particular mood, season or body humour: Safi al-Din, in the ninth century, devised one for every hour of the day. Today there are estimated to be about forty in use in Egypt, while Baghad boasts over seventy; however, many of these scales are closely related and can be grouped into families. This wide range of modes means an Arab musician has a highly complex job and it is this wide spectrum of musical colours that makes Arab music so infinitely fascinating.

Rhythm theory is complicated as well. Centuries of music have produced a sophisticated range of rhythms. Rhythm patterns vary greatly in length, from two beats to up to 88. Of the over one hundred rhythms, or *iqaat*, in the Middle East, there is a distinct regional distribution, and in each region only a certain number are regularly used.

of Harun al-Rashid (786–809) and the *Thousand and One Nights* (see chapter on Iraq).

This was an age of great advances for Arabic culture, an era of intellectual order and discovery, which pushed Arabic culture to the forefront of medieval art and science. At a time when Europe was in the so-called "Dark" Ages, Arab culture was having a golden age, with Arab scientists and rulers pondering the power of imagination, and about the effects of music on the human soul.

Emerging Traditions in the Twentieth Century

The first Egytian leader in almost two thousand years – roughly since Cleopatra – to ignite the idea of an Egyptian identity and nation was an Albanian, **Mohammed Ali**, the first Ottoman governor in Cairo after Napoleon left. Although Napoleon's campaign in Egypt was a failure in military terms, Mohammed Ali was impressed by European modernity and he started to modernize Egypt after the European model, leading Egypt to practical independence from the Ottoman empire. His successors continued in his footsteps. Intellectual and artistic life ignited as this sudden clash with modernity shook the Arab world out of a deep-rooted complacency.

Egypt, fired by nationalism after two millennia of foreign rule, emerged to lead the quest for an **Arab renaissance**, and soon was recognized as the Arab cultural heartland, with Cairo as the *Umm-al-Dunya*, the Mother of the World. It was also the focus of musical innovation. Adopting what was left of the fading Turkish musical culture and – here and there – borrowing from Western influences, a new defiant Arab music emerged in the coffeehouses and theatres. In attending this rebirth of music and song, and attempting to bring Arab music into the modern age, the **Cairo music scene** struck a dynamic balance between tradition and the seductive promise of Western advances.

Arab culture proved quite vulnerable to the sophistication and technical know-how of Europe. Despite having designed several musical notation systems as early as the ninth century (purely intended, however, as a means for clarifying theory, not for composing), Arab music was rarely written down, and by the late 1800s musicians had moved a long way from ancient theory.

At the end of the nineteenth and start of the twentieth centuries a range of innovators were to lay the foundation for a golden era of Arabic music in Egypt. Major names included singers like Salama Higazi, Yusuf Manyalawi, Abdelhay Hilmi and Saleh Abdalhay, and the next generation, which initiated the real breakthrough to modernity: Sayed Darwish, Munira Al-Mehdiya, Naima al-Misriya, Fathya Ahmad and Umm Kulthum. The most notable composers for the latter, were **Mohammed al-Qasabgi** and **Zakaria Ahmad**.

In 1932, at an extraordinary pan-Arab conference in Cairo, the first (attended by the European composers Béla Bartók and Paul Hindemith), musicians from the Arab world gathered to take stock of their musical output. They found a wide diversity from one end of the Arab world to the other. Thus began a campaign to rekindle an interest in tradition, and to search its roots for guidance.

The West was seen as a possible source of inspiration. Composers were keen to make the most of Western advances, many of whose root ideas had passed from Arab hands during the previous twelve hundred years, or the concept of harmony, which gradually got adopted into Arab composition. **New instruments** from Europe such as the cello were greeted with enthusiasm. As the century progressed, the double bass and Western reed instruments, even the electric guitar, bass and organ were added to the Arabic ensemble, which soon became a full-blown orchestra. Studios were re-equipped with the latest technology, and composers plagiarized or parodied melodies from Mozart and Beethoven to Bartók, giving them

Mohammed Abdel Wahab

form with a jazz back-beat or Hollywood rumba. In many songs of the 1960s there is a strong hint – a kind of proto-sampling – of Western classical melodies, for instance in the music of **Mohammed Abdel Wahab**. Yet this was no imitation. Foreign themes were woven into dense layers of drones, unisons and parallel octaves of the Arab orchestra, and the Eastern feel was maintained.

Despite these modernizing trends, many traditional themes remain in Arab music from its distant heritage. Arabic music still centres on **the singer**, whose vocal ornamentation and improvisational skills enrich the song from "merely a chicken, without the nice fat which gives it taste", as one local saying puts it. The live *hafla* (party) atmosphere, with repeated shouts of praise and demands for encore from the audience, is still vital to the performance. Music continues to be the partner of poetry, while vibrant rhythm, fine melody and ancient instruments remain pivotal to the sound.

Along with technical advance came the **media**, which have played a dominant role in the music of the Arab world. Some of the biggest Western music companies moved in on Cairo early in the twentieth century, and before long entrepreneurs were touting village café-goers with the new phonograph, which they would operate for a fee. The piercing voices that emerged from the whirling contraptions at their feet seemed to pronounce that life was never going to be the same again. Yet the three-minute phonograph was hardly suited to the tradition of the long Arab song, and music had to wait for radio in the late 1920s before it discovered the new opportunities offered by technology. Film, and later television, provided a stage for popular song, which found an expanding record-buying public.

By the 1920s more or less the whole Arab world, wherever there were radios and phonographs, was listening to the same Arab music for the first time. With its mass appeal, a **superstar industry** developed fast. Through these publicly adored giants of song arose the cult-hero poet-lyricists like **Ahmed Ramy**, **Bayram al-Tunsi** and the "prince of poets" **Ahmed Shawki** – all of whom wrote for Umm Kulthum. As well as classical poetry about lost and unfulfilled love, they expounded revolutionary new messages that implied the right to personal fulfilment and expectations alongside the duties of family and religion. In the case of Umm Kulthum's "Al-Atlal", lost love became a metaphor for political disillusion. The longer songs could reach the listeners through the live concerts on radio and later the television, as well as through the advent of the LP, which actually encouraged singers to make longer songs.

But what proved the most revolutionary of media innovations was the least spectacular. The **tape cassette** appeared in the early 1970s and put the music industry into the hands of the public, turning its control from businessmen to the streets (though the men in suits have been staging something of a comeback lately). Suddenly everyone could copy if not produce music, and it sometimes seemed nearly everyone did make music. Coinciding with a period of dramatic social change – the 1980s arrival of Arab youth culture and pure pop music – the cassette offered a format for a new wave of popular aspirations and opened the floodgates to songs moving away from acceptable musical standards. It allowed the working classes to voice their discontent for the first time, and with a contemporary breed of urban folk music they have successfully embarrassed traditional Egyptian good taste (for more on which, see the chapter on popular and sheet music). In many parts of the Arab world the audiocassette is still more important than the CD. In fact in recent times the **DVD** rather than the audio-CD is taking over, usually filled with copies of music stars' TV shows.

Superstars of Cairo

The Arab Classical musical arena – and Cairo as its fulcrum – has always been dominated by a clutch of iconic singers, enjoying huge popularity and influence across the Arab world.

Profiled below are eight of the finest: **Sayed Darwîsh** (1891–1923), **Umm Kulthum** (1900–75), **Mohammed Abdel Wahab** (1910–91), **Farid el-Atrache** (1914-74), **Asmahan** (1917–44), **Leyla Murad** (1918–95), **Abdalhalim Hafez** (1922–77) and **Warda al-Jaza'iriya** (born 1940).

The only other Arabic singers of roughly the same period who could match them are **Nathem al-Ghazaly** from Iraq (see Iraq chapter), the still-active **Fairuz** (see Lebanon chapter) and, to a somewhat lesser extent, contemporary performers **Sabah Fakhry** from Syria and **Wodya as-Safi** from Lebanon.

Sayed Darwîsh

At the age of 25, **Sayed Darwîsh** (1891–1923) was a travelling actor fallen on hard times. However by the time he was 30 he was hailed as the father of the new Egyptian Arab music and hero of the cultural renaissance. He rose to fame with his controver-

sial **"innovation" musical movement** of the 1910s and 20s, in which he blended Western instruments and harmony with forgotten Arab musical forms and Egyptian folklore. More importantly, he wrote words for the Egyptian people: dedications for the tradesmen, operettas for the hashish dealers and daring anti-British nationalism for the masses, like "Bilaadi Bilaadi" (My Country, My Country), which became the national anthem.

> My country my country,
> my love and heart is for you.
> Egypt, the mother of countries,
> You are my wants and desire,
> And your Nile has given
> so many gifts to your people.

Countless songs made him famous, many of them still in the Arab repertoire. His talent for elaborate melodies and for eloquent socio-political commentary made him the most popular songsmith of his time. "Zourouni", as still performed by Fairuz is probably his best known. However, after a composing career of just seven years, Darwîsh died of a cocaine overdose, aged 32. Mourned by thousands, he now lies in the Garden of the Immortals in Alexandria.

Farid el-Atrache and Asmahan

Farid el-Atrache (1914–74) and his sister **Asmahan** (born Amal el-Atrache in 1917, died 1944) were born to noble Druze parents in the Syrian/Lebanese border area of Jebel al-Druz. Due to political upheavals in the region, their early years were spent travelling around the major cities of the Levant, but after their father's death their mother finally settled in Cairo. She knew how to sing and

Farid el-Atrache on set, 1930s

play the *oud* (not as uncommon then as now) and performed at private parties.

The musical talent of the youngsters was quickly recognized and soon they too were making a living playing in Cairo's numerous clubs and radio orchestras. However, it was the birth of the **Egyptian film industry** in the 1930s that launched them as household names throughout the Arab world: *Intisar al-Shabab* (The Triumph of Youth) was the first of many films in which they starred, with Farid also writing part of the music, along with other venerated composers like Mohammed al-Qasabgi, Riyadh as-Sunbati and **Mohammed Abdel Wahab**. Their rise was tragically terminated when Asmahan drowned in a car accident, just as she was about to finish the film *Gharam wa Intiqam* (Love and Revenge). Rumours still circulate that the brakes of her car were cut, or that her driver deliberately created the accident. And in the great tradition of rumour machines of the Middle East, there are numerous conspiracy theories, laying the blame at the feet of a jealous Umm Kulthum, or Asmahan's conservative family back in Syria – not only because she was a singer, but also because she had married five times. Other candidates are the British (she was rumoured to be spying for the Germans) or the Germans (maybe she was a spy for the British!). In the great tradition of music however, this untimely demise has done nothing to dim her fame, and Asmahan is still fondly remembered as the tragic *femme fatale* cut down in her prime.

Farid's enforced solo career continued with a string of films with his lover, the dancer **Samia Gamal**, and he performed to great acclaim right up to the end of his life. His later films, when he often appears as an oily old smoothie who ought to know better, belittle the remarkable legacy of his earlier work, but in fact somewhat reflected his later walk of life as a gambler, heavy drinker and womanizer. Nevertheless, in his prime he was a virtuoso *oud* player with an alluringly rich voice, and one of the Arab world's most inventive composers.

Umm Kulthum

Umm Kulthum (1900–75) was the modern Arab world's greatest singer. Stern and tragic but rigidly in control, this was a woman who, in her heyday, truly had the Arab world in the palm of her hand. With melancholy operettas that seemed to drift on for hours, she encapsulated the love lives of a nation. Her stage presence was charged by a theatrical rapport with her audience: a slight nod of the head or a shake of her shoulders and her fans were in uproar.

She learned to sing by reciting Koranic verse dressed as a boy in the village where her father was the sheikh, and had her first artistic success at wedding parties (still cross-dressed). She owed her stunning vocal agility and masterful command of the complex *maqams* to her training in religious chanting. She was educated in the secular field by the poet Ahmed Ramy, and of her total output of 286 songs, 132  were his poems. Her voice was the epitome of the Arab ideal – saturated with *shaggan*, or emotional yearning, and powerful enough, on occasion, to shatter a glass (so legend has it). She was once encouraged by the audience to sing a line 52 times over, which she did while developing the melody each time.

Apart from Allah, Umm Kulthum seems to be the only subject about which all Arabs agree, a fact that has always given her special political significance. Although originally affiliated with the Egyptian royal family (and almost engaged to one of its members), after the revolution of 1952 she embraced Nasser's pan-Arab ideals, and drew Arabs together by extending a pride to them during some of the most difficult periods of their history. Nasser used her nationalist songs to keep the masses behind him and timed his major political speeches carefully around her broadcasts.

Officially, she remained a great campaigner for the traditional Arab song, but each of her new recordings contributed to a step-by-step evolution, and sometimes revolution – for example by using electric guitars or organs in the songs written for her by Mohammed Abdel Wahab in the last decade of her career. Her golden period was the early 1940s, when Zakaria Ahmad wrote some of his best songs for her and Riyad as-Sunbati his first. She also made films around this time, but stopped when she was 45, considering it pathetic to keep on playing young girl roles.

Umm Kulthum virtually monopolized the Egyptian music industry, and was a shrewd business woman aside from the career propulsion afforded by her tremendous musical talents.

Umm Kulthum's Composers

Umm Kulthum's initially fruitful co-operation with her mentor-composer **Mohammed al-Qasabgi** ended when he, allegedly, persuaded another composer, **Riyad as-Sunbati**, to offer one of his new songs to a rival singer, Asmahan. However, he remained as her *oud* player, and when he died a chair was always left in the orchestra on which his instrument was placed.

Then, at the end of the golden period in the 1940s, she fell out with **Zakaria Ahmad**. This time it was about the royalties – or rather lack of royalties – for the songs he wrote. Umm Kulthum considered it suffient to pay the composer a one-off amount, no matter how often she sang a song or whatever she did with it. Typically, she considered herself as the co- if not main creator, often extending a song into one of the long pieces for which she became famous.

After this second dispute, her main composer was **Riyad as-Sunbati**, who penned many great classics of the later period. His most renowned composition for her was "Al-Atlal" (The Ruins), which marked a return to a "Classical" format, and was actually written in 1966, when Umm Kulthum was already working with **Mohammed Abdel Wahab**'s newer style. The lyrics of "Al-Atlal" consist of two combined poems by Ibrahim Naji, which seem to have conveyed the prevailing mood of disillusionment with the Nasser government. With the humiliating defeat by Israel in the Six Day War of the following year, the song soon came to symbolize a general feeling of disenchantment in the Arab world.

These two composers had the honour of providing the music for Umm Kulthum's only concert appearence outside the Middle East. At the Paris Olympia in 1968 she sang just three songs – Abdalwahab's "Enta Umri" and "Fakarouny" and Sunbati's "Al-Atlal" – in a concert that lasted from 10pm until 4am.

Neil van der Linden

At Umm Kulthum's funeral in February 1975, attended by many Arab heads of state, reportedly four million people followed her body through the streets of Cairo. At 10pm on the first Thursday of every month, all radio stations still play Umm Kulthum in memory of her momentous live radio concerts of the 1950s and 60s.

Mohammed Abdel Wahab

Mohammed Abdel Wahab (1910–91) was dubbed the "artist of generations", as the last remaining figure from the old guard, of which he was in fact a controversial member. His achievements spanned a long career from the 1920s as a singer, film star and eventually composer – a talent crowned when Umm Kulthum agreed to sing his "Enta Umri", (which featured an electric guitar for the first time in her career) and a small series of other songs.

As a composer, Abdel Wahab is remembered as the modernizer of Arabic music, liberating it, as his supporters see it, from the limitations of the traditional *takht* ensemble and allowing it to embrace Western-style tangos, waltzes and instrumentation. Others criticize his music for its eclecticism, if not overt plagiarism. He stood by his vision for modernization of the music all his life, demanding that 'the artist is the creator and has the full right to introduce new elements into

his music as he sees fit. We must always be open to new ideas and not resist change. Change is inevitable in everything'.

Ironically, in his later years Abdel Wahab became so contemptuous of other modernizers that he took his initiative a step further. In 1990 he released a Classical song into a market awash with the bleeping synths of the new youth pop. It was the first occasion in about two decades that he had sung his own composition, and the song, "Minrear Ley" (Without Why), was a blatant test of popular loyalty. It was viewed by many as the final gasp of a wounded musical genre but its immediate success went some way to prove that his vision for Arab music lived on.

Leyla Murad

Leyla Murad (1918–95) was a younger rival of Umm Kulthum, and it is rumoured that President Nasser hesitated between giving Umm Kulthum or Leyla Murad his highest honours. A movie star as much as a singer, her films – like the ones with Mohammed Abdel Wahab – always produced a string of hits.

She remained extremely popular until rumours began – probably spread by jealous factions – that she was spying for Israel: an idea that was fuelled by the fact that she was of Jewish origin. At a certain point Nasser intervened, but it was too late, and she abandoned her career. Nevertheless, her films are still regularly screened on Egyptian TV.

Abdalhalim Hafez

Abdalhalim Hafez (1927–77) was nicknamed the "Nightingale of the Nile" or just "Halim". In a society that generally reserves true respect for the old, he took over the musical arena in his early twenties to become the golden boy of the nationalist revolution of 1952. He came at the right time with short patriotic songs with a distinct melodic style that pleased both President Nasser as well as the young generation of the day, who embraced him as their spokesperson. Like Umm Kulthum and Mohammed Abdel Wahab, Abdalhalim Hafez was of humble origin, which added to his credibility.

By the 1960s his shorter light songs gave way to a partnership with Mohammed Abdel Wahab and a return to longer Classical forms. Almost all his life he was ill with bilharzia – a water-borne disease prevalent among those who work among the swamps and in the rice fields of the Nile. He faced his ongoing struggle for good health with a vulnerability that involved the nation and charmed the whole Arab world. For men, he offered a rather camp alternative role in an oppressively macho society. And his little-boy-lost image had women crooning to mother him. He died in 1977, perhaps the last superstar of the great artists' era.

Warda al-Jaza'iriya

Although definitely viewed as one of the Cairo superstars, **Warda al-Jaza'iriya**'s more pan-Mediterranean roots set her apart. Born near Paris in 1940 to a Lebanese mother and Algerian father (al-Jaza'iriya means "the Algerian"), she learned to sing from her mother and took her first steps

Warda – on computer desktop 'wallpaper'

Wardaonline.com

to stardom in her father's prestigious Paris night spot. This club was the meeting place both for the top names in Arab music whilst passing through the city and for supporters of the FLN (Front de Libération National, a group dedicated to Algerian independence from France). Both of these were to shape her musical identity: it was in this club that she was first heard by the Godfather of Arab music, Mohammed Abdel Wahab, and she has always been associated with her Algerian roots.

When her family was deported from France to Lebanon, Warda continued to sing in clubs, but her real break came with a move to Cairo at the beginning of the 1960s. Here, through the considerable influence of Mohammed Abdel Wahab and Riyad as-Sunbati her "Parisian" style quickly became popular.

Aside from a ten-year break from singing, Warda has remained at the forefront of Arab music. She has wisely shunned the "new Umm Kulthum" tag – partly out of respect for the undisputed diva, but also because the comparison is inaccurate; whereas Umm Kulthum's singing has an aching intensity that can be quite startling to the uninitiated, Warda's style is altogether more cosmopolitan and optimistic.

Festival of Arabic Music

For those who love the music of this golden era, the **Festival of Arabic Music** held at the Cairo Opera House in the autumn each year is worth a visit, led by **Ratibah al-Hefny**, daughter of Mahmoud al-Hefny, the man who set up the festival in 1932. Young singers give excellent renditions of the by-now classical repertoire. One artistic problem is avoiding imitation in a repertoire that is much more dependent on the original interpreter than Western classical repertoire. However, the Syrian Assalah al-Nasri and the Palestinian Kamylia Jubran have in recent years given excellent innovative concerts at this festival.

With the notable exception of Warda – who is still working – most of the Cairene superstars recorded their best work in the relatively early days of audio technology up to the late 1960s. Though the sound quality may not be that good, there is often a gripping intensity to these live or one-take studio performances. The longer-playing CD is a more suitable format than cassette for the extended Arab songs at which these singers excelled, and reissued and remastered collections have begun to appear. There have also been a number of good recent compilations of Classical Arab music on various Western labels. However, in Egypt you will find very little "old" (adim) music on the market – that is music before 1940.

See also the Syria and Lebanon chapters.

⊙ Arabian Masters – Les Plus Grandes Classiques de la Musique Arabe
Virgin, France
A double CD set featuring many of the legends: Warda, Mohammed Abdel Wahab, Abdalhalim Hafez and Umm Kulthum from Egypt, Fairuz from Lebanon, Saudi's Mohammed Abdu and a very long piece by the Iraqi Kazim al-Saher. The collection is limited by what EMI had access to (Umm Kulthum before her absolute peak years) and the liner notes are a bit skimpy.

⊙ Cafés Chantant du Caire Vols 1 & 2
Club du Disque Arabe, France
A collection of gems drawn from Les Archives de la Musique Arabe – mostly by the established artists or one hit wonders in the first decades of the twentieth century. Vol I has two early male stars, Saleh Abdalhay and Zaki Murad. Vol II features Munira al-Mehdiya, one of Umm Kulthum's main rivals. Songs by Qasabgi and Zakaria Ahmad predominate in both volumes.

⊙ Egypt: La Châdhiliya – Sufi Chants from Cairo
Institut du Monde Arabe, France
Sufi music sung by members of the al-Hamidiyah al-Shadhiliyah Brotherhood – a modern offshoot of the ancient Shadhiliyah order – conducted by their director Cheikh Mohammed al-Helbawy. Sufi music was also recorded in 1932 by Béla Bartók and Paul Hindemith at the Cairo Conference on Arab Music. However, recording techniques have improved and there is a real sense of being among the brotherhood on this disc.

★ Les grands noms de la musique du monde arabe
NFB, France
An excellent 2-CD set, highlighting the great Arab singers. Classical Egyptian traditions are represented by tracks from Abdalhalim Hafez, Farid el-Atrache, Asmahan, Mohammed Abdel Wahab, Umm Kulthum and Warda. And there are equally strong showings from the rest of the Arab world.

Mohammed Abdel Wahab

Mohammed Abdel Wahab was another mainstay of Egyptian music from the late 1920s until his death in 1991. Born from a humble family, he worked himself up as a "classical Egyptian" singer first and as an actor, and later as music innovator, criticized often for adopting Western novelties into his materials. But his best songs always had much to say, and as an innovator he was serious, despite some incidental gimmickry.

★ Treasures
EMI Arabia, Dubai
The best introduction to Abdel Wahab, this is a double CD with a selection of pieces from the master's better periods. Most notable is the astonishing forty-minute "Al Dooa' al Akhir" (The Last Blessing).

⊙ Volumes I–X
Club du Disque Arabe, France
Abdel Wahab's huge early output is slowly being released in its entirety on CD; volume X only takes us up to 1939, and as not much has been heard recently from Club du Disque Arabe, presumably this wonderful effort has come to an untimely end. The CDs are only modestly documented, but that is still better than anything released in the Middle East.

Farid el-Atrache and Asmahan

The late Farid el-Atrache and Asmahan – a brother-and-sister team – are from the Jebel el-Druz in Syria, on the Lebanese border, and as such are claimed by both countries, but they are Egyptian by adoption. Asmahan died tragically young. Farid had a longer career and is still honoured as "al-Malek al-Oud" (the King of the Oud).

FARID EL-ATRACHE

★ Farid el-Atrache: Les Années '30
Club du Disque Arabe, France
This selection of remastered songs from the 1930s show Farid as a young, potent performer – as opposed to the smoochy crooner he became in later life. Although many of the featured songs (with their then-fashionable strains of tango and lush European strings) might now sound quaint, they were right at the cutting edge in their day. On the basis of this CD it is easy to see how the melancholy Druze with matinée idol looks took the Arab world by storm.

⊙ Best of Farid el-Atrache Live
Voice of Lebanon, Lebanon
Farid was obviously a phenomenal live performer, and his often professed love of playing the oud is well to the fore on this collection: the dazzling taqsim (improvisation) at the beginning of his most famous work, "El Rabaïi" (The Spring) is the standard by which all others are now judged.

ASMAHAN

⊙ Asmahan
Baidaphone, Lebanon
Few recordings survive from Asmahan's short career but this includes many of her best-loved songs. The waltz "Layalil uns fi Vienna" (Delightful Nights in Vienna) was a hit in the late 1930s and is guaranteed to get old Cairo hands misty eyed. Similar compilations have appeared on French label Club du Disque Arabe and some less well-known labels, as well as on pirated CDs in Lebanon and Syria.

★ Hal Tayyama Al Banu/Hadith Ainean
EMI/Virgin, UK
These recently "discovered" longer recordings were published in a luxury cover, with the lyrics, but without any reference to the composers, the poet or the source of the recording, which EMI claim they are not sure of. Still a very worthwhile release. The two songs – the first by Mohammed al-Qasabgi,

the second by Riyad as-Sunbati – are performed with complete mastery by the 22-year-old singer.

Laure Daccache

Another great singer and prolific composer, whom history has unjustly overlooked. From a Lebanese Christian family, she rose to acclaim in Egypt, recording her first hit records (self-penned songs) when she was 8, in 1926. She now lives in Tunis.

⊙ **Laure Daccache L'Age d'Or du Chant Arabe**
Blue Silver, France
This collection includes five songs including the classic "El Ward" (The Roses) and her great anthem "Aminti Billah" (I Believe in God).

Sayed Darwîsh

Sayed Darwîsh lived fast and died young – the hero and founding father of the Arab music renaissance. His patriotic "Bilaadi, Bilaadi" (My Country, My Country) is the closest thing to a national anthem for Arab brotherhood and is played by marching bands all over the Middle East.

⊙ **Cheikh Sayed Darwiche – L'Immortel**
Baidaphon, France
Because he died in the early 1920s, there are only a handful of Sayed Darwîsh's recordings in existence. This short disc shows his passion rising above the crackly recording, with three songs full of thrilling vocal improvisation, throwing in snatches of European flavour that at the time was completely revolutionary. If you can track it down, there is also a 5-CD set issued by the Cultnat organization in Cairo, together with the Bibliotheka in Alexandria.

Abdalhalim Hafez

The "Nightingale of the Nile", Abdalhalim Hafez rose to fame on the wave of Egyptian nationalistic self-confidence during the 1950s and 60s. He was aided by a successful career in the emergent movie business, but struggled against the effects of bilharzia that killed him prematurely. After Umm Kulthum, his is the voice most often heard on the cassette players of Cairo taxis.

★ **Abdalhalim Hafez – Twentieth Anniversary Memorial Editon**
EMI Arabia, Dubai
This double CD includes a disc of early and late material. The former has seven film-score songs from the early 1930s, with classic Egyptian movie orchestration. The latter includes his best-known song, "Karia Al-Fingan" (The Fortune Teller). The variety in the arrangements, from "Classical" and folkloric to 1960s experimental, reflects the self-confidence and boldness of Egyptian culture during the 1950s and 60s.

Umm Kulthum (Oum Khalsoum)

No one has yet come close to Umm Kulthum, who is still considered the Arab world's primary diva. Her dramatic, angst-drenched performances may not be to everyone's taste, but to ignore her is to disregard one of the world's twentieth-century icons. Beware of the fact that many of her longer radio recordings were edited for LP, and the "missing" material is not always reinstated on subsequent CD reissues.

★ **Al Awla fil Gharam**
Sono Cairo/Sawt Al-Qahira, Egypt
A typical Zakaria Ahmad song of the "golden period", from 1944. Umm Kulthum's voice is at its best and her personality has matured. Other songs like "Ana fi intizarak", "Ahl Al-Hawa", "Al-Ahat", "Helm Al-Amal", "Ya Ayni Ya Ayni", all from the same period, are fantastic too.

★ **Salu Qalbi and Wulid Al-Huda**
Sono Cairo/Sawt Al-Qahira, Egypt
Both CDs are nationalistic as well as religious *qasidas* (high poetry) with lyrics by Ahmed Shawqi and music by Sunbati. "Salu Qalbi" includes two lines that became an incentive for Egyptian nationalist aspirations. As it appeared at a time of increasing nationalist agitation and dissatisfaction with the

---

PLAYLIST
Arab World/Egypt | Classical

1 AL AWLA FIL GHARAM Umm Kulthum from *Al Awla fil Gharam*
A typical Zakaria Ahmad song, this is a great lamenting piece from Egypt's First Lady of song, at her peak.

2 WE DARET AL-AYYAM Umm Kulthum from *We Daret Al-Ayyam*
One of the last recordings on which Umm Kulthum still had her full powers, it's also a kind of obituary for President Nasser, who died the year before. Try getting the 90-minute version on cassette in Egypt.

3 ERKHI S-SETARA Abdallatif Al-Banna from *Café Chantants du Caire Vol 1*
Raunchy song from 1925, composed by Zakaria Ahmad. Al-Banna, nicknamed the "Egyptian nightingale", impersonated women on stage and sang with a high voice.

4 KHAFIF KHAFIF Saleh Abdalhay from *Café Chantants du Caire Vol 1*
Supposedly the complaint of a deceived lover, this 1927 piece by Zakaria Ahmad is full of saucy double-entendres – a light note in the repertoire of this great singer.

5 HAL TAYYAMA AL BANU Asmahan from *Hal Tayyama Al Banu / Hadith Ainean*
The song that allowed the 22-year-old singer to break free from the shadow of Umm Kulthum.

6 QARIAT AL-FINJAN Abdalhalim Hafez from *Twentieth Anniversary Memorial Edition*
This very popular song includes experimental organ in an Arab orchestra, showing how confident Egyptian culture was then, contrasting sharply with mundane and inane contemporary pop.

continuing British presence and the abuses of King Farouq, audiences were quick to respond to the line "Demands are not met by wishing; the world can only be taken by struggle". "Wulid Al-Huda" declares: "You Mohammed are the leader of the Socialists" and "You Mohammed gave justice to the poor in front of the rich". Not very popular with the regime under royal rule, of course.

⊙ Awedt Aini (DVD/CD)
Sono Cairo/Sawt Al-Qahira, Egypt
In this 1958 song which can be translated as 'My eyes have got used to seeing you', Ahmed Rami, who was said to have an unrequited infatuation for Umm Kulthum, describes his depressed emotional state and how a glance from the beloved would be sufficient to revive his heart.

★ Al-Atlal (DVD/CD)
Sono Cairo/Sawt Al-Qahira, Egypt
One of her all-time bestsellers, full of melodrama and suspense. In 1955 the poet Ibrahim Nagui presented Umm Kulthum with his book of selected poems for her to choose one poem to sing. She liked "Al Atlal" very much but did not perform it until 1966, after his death. The words describe a lover reminiscing about his lost love and represented a new phase in her choice of lyrics. It also became a protest song against the political decline in the Arab world, notably after the defeat by Israel in 1967. Elaborate use of scales by composer Riyd as-Sunbati.

⊙ Enta Umri
Sono Cairo/Sawt Al-Qahira, Egypt
Umm Kulthum was greatly criticized at the time of "Enta Umri" (You are my Life) – composed by Mohammed Abdel Wahab – because of its electric instruments. As any buyer of her music will sooner or later have *Enta Umri*, it is perhaps more rewarding to search out "Hazihi Laylati" or "We Daret Al-Ayyam", which appeared at the end of the 1960s. If possible, get the live recordings of both, lasting about 90 minutes each, on cassettes available from Sawt Al-Qahira (Sound of Cairo).

Warda

Warda ("The Rose") is a true child of the Mediterranean; born in France of Algerian/Lebanese parents, she found fame in Cairo. After some years of ailing health she is now back on stage. There are many comparable CDs, but beware her "disco" period in the 1980s, when she was apparently in an artistic crisis.

⊙ Ya habibi la takol li/ Ale Eih Beyess Alouni
Voice of Lebanon, Lebanon/Greece
"Ya habibi la takol li" is by Riyad as-Sunbati, while "Ale Eih Beyess Alouni" is by Sayed Mekkaoui. Both composers also wrote for Umm Kulthum, whose mantle Warda has only partly succeeded in inheriting. This CD is very much "old school" Warda and reveals just why she is considered the last of the Egyptian classical superstars.

⊙ Warda
EMI Hemisphere, UK
This mid-priced compilation is an excellent introduction to Warda's more recent work. It is hard not to be seduced by the diva's creamy, mature voice.

Arabesque

oriental fusion

Egyptian-British-Belgian singer Natacha Atlas
Beggars Banquet

The dictionary definition of "arabesque" refers to a heavily stylized type of Arabic decoration, or something that is "strangely mixed" or "fantastic". That sums up dance music's new-found love affair with Arabic music perfectly. Just as Asian music lent itself to the complex tabla-style time signatures of drum & bass, Arabic percussive rhythms provide a perfect counterfoil to the repetitive beats of Western house and techno. Phil Meadley traces the roots of the new genre and maps its creative oases.

Huge international pop hits, such as **Holly Valance's** version of **Tarkan's** Turkish smash "Simarik", and the **Chemical Brothers'** single "Galvanize" (which sampled Moroccan singer **Najat Aatabu**'s ("Just Tell Me The Truth"), have gone some way to instil Arab influences into Western popular music. But the most intriguing developments in recent fusion music have been from Middle Eastern producers keen to meld their musical roots with the hottest club tunes.

The West Looks East

The West has long been fascinated by the Middle East and its rich and vibrant culture. In the twentieth century it was the hippy generation that tuned in, and North Africa became a Mecca for rock acts such as Led Zeppelin, The Beatles, Jimi Hendrix, and The Rolling Stones. Prog-rockers like **The Third Ear Band** and **Gong** incorporated intricate Arabic scales into their rock music. Two tracks that drew directly from the great Egyptian diva **Umm Kulthum** were "Master Builder", which appeared on Gong's *You* album, and **Steve Hillage**'s "Earthrise" whose opening phrasing was a direct cover of "El Alb Yeshak Kol Gamil".

The post-punk generation quickly followed suit. **David Byrne** and **Brian Eno** sampled Lebanese and Egyptian singers on their 1981 opus *My Life In The Bush Of Ghosts*, and the album was heralded as a benchmark not only of ambient electronic music, but also of multicultural popular art. However there was a hiccup when the track "Qu'ran" had to be excluded after complaints from Islamic groups who took exception to sacred Koran texts being sampled. In fact Byrne and Eno found the sample in *The Music in the World of Islam* series released by Topic Records in 1976.

Although acts such as **Public Image Ltd** and **The Clash** drew some influence from Arabic music, the next significant contribution to this area was made by German collective **Dissidenten** who collaborated with celebrated Moroccan band **Lem Chaheb** on their second album "Sahara Electrik". It became a surprise hit across Europe in 1983, although it failed to make a significant impact in the UK.

The late Israeli singer **Ofra Haza**'s seminal 1985 album *Yemenite Songs* drew inspiration from the sixteenth-century poetry of **Shalom Shabazi**, but it was the 1988 album *Shaday* which saw her move into the dance arena, and which spawned a UK Top 20 hit "Im Nin'alu". Her vocals were sampled by Coldcut on their remix of Eric B and Rakim's hip-hop classic "Paid In Full", and later M.A.R.R.S.' early house anthem "Pump Up The Volume".

Towards the end of the 1980s **Peter Gabriel** scored the soundtrack to the Martin Scorsese film *The Last Temptation of Christ* with music that travelled the world in terms of interest but with strong Turkish and Egyptian leanings. Re-titled *Passion*, the album inspired many Western producers to look deeper into North African traditions.

During the 1980s Killing Joke's **Jaz Coleman** became the first Western student to enrol at the Cairo Conservatoire. After studying the likes of celebrated composer **Ammar el-Sherie**, he collaborated with fellow classical music trainee and Art of Noise member **Anne Dudley** on the album *Songs from the Victorious City*, travelling to Cairo to record with violinist **Aboud Abdul Al**, string arranger **Tarek Aakef**, and percussionist **Hossam Ramzy**. This 1990 album still sounds remarkably fresh today.

The French Connection

No matter where you look, there is nearly always a strong French connection within Arabic music. Even **Mohammed Abdal Wahab**, the great Egyptian composer and *oud* player, had studied Western classical composition in Paris before he created a new style of Arabic film musical afterwards. Had it not been for his love of East/West fusion, one of Umm Kulthum's greatest songs, "Enta Umri", would never have been composed.

In 1989 *rai* superstar **Cheb Khaled**'s electro-funk album *Kutche* (with **Safy Boutella**) was co-produced by acclaimed French producer **Martin Meissonnier**, and paved the way for a succession of North African artists such as Cheb Mami, Faudel and Sawt El Atlas.

Two contemporaries of Khaled also made notable contributions during this era. **Rachid Taha** carved out a successful career in partnership with English producer Steve Hillage, whose techno leanings began with his own band System 7 in the early 90s. The Tunisian-born singer **Amina Annabi**, meanwhile, represented France in the 1991 Eurovision Song Contest before working with a succession of ground-breaking artists and collaborating with UK dance production team **Renegade Soundwave** on her classic self-titled 1999 album. More

recently, she has worked with UK-based Moroccan producer **U-Cef**.

There have also been several recent Franco-Arab projects of varying quality – not all of them conforming to the latest dancefloor trends – from the likes of British-born actress (and ex-partner of Serge Gainsbourg) **Jane Birkin**, Algerian comedienne **Biyouma** and Martin Meissonnier, whose Jamaican/Arabic album *Big Men* was a hit and miss affair.

Back to Morocco

The Master Musicians of Jajouka have played with The Rolling Stones, Ornette Coleman and beat poet William Burroughs. Their newest leader **Bachir Attar** hooked up with dub bassist and electronic pioneer **Bill Laswell** to produce the 1992 album *The Next Dream* – an album that saw the cacophonous trance-like rhythms of the large Jajouka ensemble pared down to *ghaita*

Jajouka

Bachir Attar

(double reed flute), *gimbri* (three-stringed lute), *lira* and percussion. Attar later worked with tabla player **Talvin Singh** to produce *Master Musicians of Jajouka featuring Bachir Attar* in 2000.

Another Moroccan obsessive was Swiss producer **Pat Jabbar**, who set up the North African dance imprint **Barraka El Farnatshi** in his hometown of Basel. After working with Moroccan bands in the mid-80s he formed the band **Aisha Kandisha's Jarring Effects** – named after a particularly terrifying Moroccan she-devil who had the power to freeze the blood in your veins. Jabbar set about creating a new kind of Moroccan dance scene, away from the popular Algerian *rai*, Egyptian pop and African-influenced music that could be heard on Morocco's famous **Radio Rabat**. For Aisha Kandisha's 1993 album *Shabeesation* Jabber joined forces with Bill Laswell, The Last Poets' Omar Ben Hassan and Funkadelic's Bernie Worrell, to help create one of the seminal Arabic techno albums of that era. The band went on to release a succession of groundbreaking records until leader **El Habib El Malak** left to become a politician in Marrakech. There is talk of Jabbar releasing a new Aisha Kandisha album in the near future, but in the interim he has continued to release inspired North African fusions from the likes of **Hamid Baroudi**, **Amíra Saqati**, Turkish hip-hoppers **Makale** and **Azzdine**.

The London Equation

In 1992, **Jah Wobble's Invaders of the Heart** released *Rising Above Bedlam* – a unique amalgam of booming basslines, multilingual vocals, and multicultural rhythms featuring the talents of **Ali Slimani**, Justin Adams, Sinead O'Connor and **Natacha Atlas**. The album was shortlisted for a Mercury Music Award and his next album *Take Me to God* upped the ante with guest vocals from the likes of Baaba Maal, Dolores O'Riordan and Najma Akhtar.

Created primarily in the early 1990s to make multi-ethnic dance music, **Aki Nawaz**'s **Nation Records** quickly became the prime mover of the new global beats movement. **Transglobal Underground** were at the forefront of this dance revolution and featured Natacha Atlas on their debut album *Dream of 100 Nations*. She then released what many considered to be the first Arabic/dance crossover single "Yalla Chant" in 1993.

TGU co-wrote her debut album *Diaspora* in 1995, and collaborated on 1997's *Halim* – her first attempt to get serious recognition from Arabic audiences. By 1999, her commitment to TGU had waned, although they produced her biggest hit single in France "Mon Amie La Rose". Her *Something Dangerous* album (2003) was a less successful foray into Jamaican dancehall and R&B.

Over the past ten years, TGU have become a prominent production team in the Middle East, and latterly have remixed some of Arabia's most famous pop stars such as Lebanese diva **Dania**, pop heart-throb **Yuri Mrakadi** and *shaabi* super star **Hakim**.

Arabesque Moderne

The late 1990s saw the Arabesque sound embraced by rich and famous socialites. Tunisian-born entrepreneur **Claude Challe** was a key figure on Paris's chic club circuit during the 1980s and 90s, helping rebuild the old punk hotspot **Le Bains Bouche**, and subsequently the **Buddha Bar**. His 1998 compilation, *Flying Carpet*, was the first real attempt to merge European dance culture with some of the best names in popular Arabic and Asian music. The likes of Khaled, Hossam Ramzy and **L'Orchestre National de Barbés**, made unlikely bedfellows for America's Tranquility Bass, Nitin Sawhney and Indian composer A.R. Rahman, but it worked, and the idea of a fashionable oriental dance scene was born.

Following a similar (but more specific) path was Algerian-born restaurateur **Mourad Mazouz**, who released the acclaimed *Arabesque* compilation to convey some of the ambience of his successful *Momo* restaurant in London. The compilation showcased the talents of acts such as **Gnawa Diffusion**, **MC Sultan** and **Omar Faruk Tekbilek** to a younger, club-savvy fan base. Both of these compilations became the blueprint for a plethora of subsequent Arabic beat compilations.

Away from the party circuit, the independent label **Apartment 22** released several groundbreaking releases from Moroccan drum & bass pioneer **U-Cef**, and Moroccan ex-pats **MOMO** (Music Of Moroccan Origin). Alongside bands such as Turkish breakbeat specialists **Oojami**, **Zohar** and Paris-based acts **Digital Bled** and **Smadj**, the late 1990s was a healthy time for Arabic fusion. The new millennium also saw notable contributions from **DuOud** (a partnership between Smadj and ex-**Ekova** *oud* player **Mehdi Haddab**), drum & bass producer **Naab**, oriental hip-hopper **Clotaire K** (see Lebanon chapter) and electronic freestylers **Aïwa**, not to mention the incredible turntable skills of America's **DJ Rupture**.

Apartment22

London-Moroccan U-Cef

The Istanbul Express

Recently, Arabic dance producers have started reclaiming their heritage. In Lebanon, house producers such as **REG Project** and **Said Mrad** have become clubbing icons, and in Morocco the dub heavy sounds of **Gnawa Njoum Experience** have made an impact. Turkey has also become a hotspot of Arabesque creativity. In particular, progressive jazz/dance label **Doublemoon**, have developed acts such as **Mercan Dede** (and his hard-trance alter ego **Arkin Allen**), **Orient Expressions**, Turkish female rapper **Aziza-A** and **Baba Zula**, who have all provided an exhilarating take on Turkish dance/roots fusion.

Other notable additions are percussion collective **Harem**, trance producers **M. Celaleddin Yüksel Project** and hip-hop artist **Sultan Tunç**, whilst exciting new label **Elec-Trip** have added hip dance sounds from **Selim Demirdelen**, **Techno Roman Project** and **Rebel Moves**, amongst others. Also, San Francisco label Embarka recently released an album by exciting new Tunisian talent **MC Raï**, who mixes up club beats and hip-hop with heavy rock and classic soul-searching *rai* vocals.

With a burgeoning club scene in Istanbul, as well as Beirut and Cairo, Arab dance music has never been stronger – and it's the Arab producers rather than the Western ones who are now leading the way.

DISCOGRAPHY Arabesque

Some of the early releases featured here are relatively hard to get hold of, but it's always worth searching amazon to see if there are any second-hand sellers, should you get stuck. Some of the newer Arabic fusion releases are only available on import in the UK, but there are several great on-line Arabic music stores that sell a wide selection of Middle Eastern dance albums. However you may have to look separately for the Turkish releases, and it might be

worth looking up the individual label websites for more details.

⦿ **Arabesque**
Gut Records, UK
From an original idea by Algerian-born restaurant owner Mourad Mazouz, this is the best of the Arabesque series (there were two more), and tracks such as Steve Hillage's

oriental mix of Stereo MC's "Fever", and the Bi Polar remix of Dahmane El Harrachi's "Ya Rayah" are still used by many global beat DJs today.

⊙ Flying Carpet by Claude Challe
Chall'Omusic, France
Apart from the luxuriously packaged *Buddha Bar* series, socialite DJ Claude Challe created probably the first Westernized Arabic dance mix CD, featuring great tracks from the likes of Hossam Ramzy, Lili Boniche, Gnawa Diffusion, and Mozart L'Egyptien.

⊙ Marrakesh Mission
Ocho, UK
Although not sticking strictly to the remit of modern Moroccan beats, this is a great round-up of various Westernized Arabic dance styles. Producers include Berlin's Eastenders, London-based Terry Hall & Mushtaq, Beirut's Soap Kills, Parisians DuOud and Istanbul's Sultana.

Aisha Kandisha's Jarring Effects

The pioneers of Arabic techno, Aisha Kandisha were formed in the early 1990s and revelled in mixing dance beats with *shaabi*, *rai* and *gnawa*.

★ Shabeesation
Barrakka, Switzerland/Morocco
Also featuring the talents of Bill Laswell, Bernie Worrell and The Last Poets' Omar Ben Hassan, this is Aisha Kandisha's most cohesive and funky album, featuring the classic Arabic techno anthem "A Muey A Muey".

Aïwa

Although based in the unlikely setting of Rennes, France, Aïwa (meaning "yes") is the brainchild of two Iraqi brothers Naufalle and Wamid with poetess Séverine, who make a heady concoction of oriental drum & bass, rock and jazz-funk.

⊙ Aïwa
Wikkid, Canada
A completely unique blend of oriental hip-hop, drum & bass, and techno, featuring the sensuous mumblings of bluesy lead singer Séverine.

Amina Annabi

The most progressive of Arabic female singers, Annabi redefined the boundaries of pop in France, whilst challenging outmoded stereotypes in various film roles.

⊙ Annabi
Mercury, France
Teaming up with UK dance outfit Renegade Soundwave alongside regular sidekick Martin Meissonier, this wonderful album showcased Amina's passion for jazz, dance and the Arab tradition.

Natacha Atlas

Former singer with Jah Wobble's Invaders of the Heart and Transglobal Underground, Atlas is one of the few European-born Arabic singers to have made an impact in the Middle Eastern music scene.

⊙ Ayeshteni
Mantra, UK
This album spawned Atlas's biggest hit "Ne Me Quitte Pas" (a fine Arabic cover of the Jacquels Brel classic) and shows her at the peak of her powers.

Dissidenten

This German collective were one of the earliest pioneers of global beat in the 1980s.

WITH LEM CHAHEB

⊙ Sahara Elektrik
Exil Musik, Germany
Their second album was recorded in Morocco with Lem Chaheb, and must count amongst the very first specifically Arabic/Western fusion albums. A little dated now, but singles such as "Fata Morgana" sound more Moroccan than European, and whip along at a fair old pace.

Anne Dudley & Jaz Coleman

This one-off project from Art of Noise cohort Anne Dudley and Killing Joke singer Jaz Coleman heralded a new era for fusion music.

★ Songs from the Victorious City
China Records, UK
Dudley and Colman hooked up in 1990 to produce one of the best examples of Egyptian/Western fusion. The album still stands up today due to its sympathetic use of technology and a fine array of guest Egyptian musicians.

Oojami

Turkish-born Necmi Calvi moved to London to become a teacher and hone his dance-music production skills. His Hubble Bubble club nights in London have brought over the best Arabic fusion bands and DJs.

⊙ Bellydancing Breakbeats
Ark 21, UK
Having landed a deal with Miles Copeland's Ark 21 records, Oojami set about re-defining Turkish breakbeat. The stomping track "Chicky" even made it onto the soundtrack of the film *Dirty Pretty Things*.

Orchestre National de Barbés

The Orchestre National de Barbès (ONB) – named after a largely immigrant suburb of Paris – is a group of up to twenty musicians, most of them French-based North Africans. At their core are *rai* musician Youcef Boukella, jazz player Safy Boutella and Arabic vocalist Larbi Dida.

⊙ In Concert
Virgin, France

Barbès are really best encountered live, as this fine, frenetic concert CD suggests. But this is a good second-best – a crisp, clean recording of their addictive crowd-pleasers.

Smadj

This highly original producer was born to Jewish parents in Tunisia. He moved to Paris and studied jazz composition, recorded a couple of ground-breaking albums for MELT 2000 and made a "duelling ouds" album with Ekova's Mehdi Haddab before signing with Mourad Mazouz's Most Records.

⊙ Take It And Drive
Most Records, UK

Although Smadj's music can be difficult, complex and dark, it's ultimately worthwhile persevering with, as this emphatically proves. Featuring the international talents of Rokia Traoré and Talvin Singh, this presents the cutting edge of Arabic fusion.

U-Cef

This enterprising Moroccan drum & bass producer spent time in New York and London learning his trade. Lately he's been moving in a more garage/hip-hop direction, but what he produces is always worth checking out.

⊙ Halalium
Apartment 22, UK

A unique album of oriental drum & bass – tracks such as "Gazel Fatma" and "The Moorish Matador" joined the dots between rock, funk and Moroccan drum & bass.

▣ PLAYLIST
Arabesque

1 EYE OF THE DUCK Natacha Atlas from *Marrakesh Mission*
An insistently funky mix of Jamaican dancehall and Egyptian bellydance, featuring the ragga toasting of Princess Juliana.

2 KALZOOM U-Cef feat Amina Annabi from *Marrakesh Mission*
Amina covers the great Umm Kulthum, and U-Cef adds a powerful, string-laden drum & bass backdrop.

3 ALAOUI (DIGITAL BLED DANCE MIX) L'Orchestre National de Barbés from *Flying Carpet*
An epic remix from Paris-based DJ Pedro, which manages to encapsulate all the best elements of Westernized Arabic dance music.

4 CHICKY Oojami from *Bellydancing Breakbeats*
A supremely funky slice of Turkish break-beat featuring the breakneck rapping of Samir Bouchakara.

5 SOUTANBI Gnawa Njoum feat Aïwa from *Aïwa*
The gutsiest slice of Gnawa this side of the Rif Mountains, this hypnotic track sees the Iraqi brothers hooking up with hot new French/Moroccan collective Gnawa Njoum Experience.

Armenia

the singing apricot tree

Ara Dinkijan (left) and his group Night Ark
Dina Guna

Carved out of apricot wood, the *duduk* has a plangent, reedy sound that is one of the most evocative on earth. And it virtually defines Armenia musically – giving it a haunting and melancholy air. As the Armenians tell it, when God was allocating land to the various peoples of the world, the Armenians turned up late and God said, "Sorry but all that's left is this pile of stones." It's an apt description of this rugged, landlocked Christian country sandwiched between its Muslim neighbours, Turkey and Azerbaijan. The country has suffered massacres, earthquakes and, from 1988 to 1994, war with Azerbaijan over the enclave of Nagorno-Karabakh. Djivan Gasparyan, Armenia's most famous traditional musician, says that the sorrowful sound of the *duduk* is a reflection of the fate of the people. Simon Broughton outlines the story.

Actually, the most famous Armenian musician is probably **Cher** (born Cherilyn Sarkisian), although there's nothing noticeably Armenian about what she sings. Born in California, she does reflect the fact that Armenians are scattered across the globe with significant communities in Iran, Lebanon, New York, Boston and especially Fresno – the grape-growing valley of central California where many refugees fled after the Turkish massacres of 1915. Armenian music flourishes in exile but, more than that of other diaspora communities perhaps, it is predominantly nostalgic in mood with a longing for the homeland.

The rhythms and melodic turns of Armenia are distinctive and easily heard in the music of the composer **Aram Khatchaturian** (1903–78), who spent most of his life in Moscow, but made the lively dance rhythms and descending phrases of Armenian melody his stock in trade. His ballet *Gayaneh* is full of typical Armenian motifs dressed in vivid orchestral colours.

Religious Music

What is a defining national feature for many Armenians is their Orthodox Christian faith. St Gregory the Illuminator converted the Armenian king to Christianity in 301 AD and Armenia became the world's **first Christian state**, a fact of which Armenians are inordinately proud. In the territory around the base of Mount Ararat, where the Armenians had lived since the eighth century BC, they developed a beautiful and distinctive style of church architecture and a rich tradition of liturgical music.

Melismatic **chants**, each composed in one of eight modes, made up the largest body of sacred chants, or *sharakans*. Medieval Armenian musical notation, known as **khaz**, allowed singers to improvise ornate embellishments around established melody types. Some of the oldest of these melodies can be traced back to pagan times, while new Christian chants were composed as early as 405 AD by **St Mesrop Mashtots**, the Armenian priest who brought literacy to Armenia by inventing the country's unique alphabet, still used today. Other notable priests whose music has survived include Movses Korenatsi (fifth century), Grigor Narekatsi (tenth century) and Neses Shnorhali (twelfth century).

One of the most renowned interpreters of the *sharakan* was soprano **Lucine Zakarian**, who served as soloist at the **Holy Cathedral of Etchmiadzin**, the seat of the Armenian Church. If you visit Armenia, it's certainly worth the trip to Etchmiadzin (20km outside the Armenian capital, Yerevan) to hear the Divine Liturgy sung by a choir made up of Armenia's best vocalists. There's also an ancient carving of the Virgin and Child, flanked by two angels and two *duduk* players. Those willing to venture further should head out to the monastery of **Geghard**, a fourth-century structure carved into the side of a mountain. Acoustics within produce a reverberation of up to a minute. If you are lucky you can catch the local choir but even in their absence it's a glorious experience.

All Armenian liturgical music remained monophonic until the latter part of the nineteenth century, when the renowned Armenian priest and composer **Komitas Vartabet** (1869–1935), who was schooled in Europe, introduced polyphony and Western-style composition into Armenian music. His arrangement of the Divine Liturgy in four-part harmony is still considered a master work, maintaining the Armenian spirit within the context of Western musical practice. Besides composing sacred music, Komitas travelled throughout the Armenian countryside from 1899 to 1910, collecting and notating more than three thousand folk tunes, some of which he arranged for performance with Western instruments such as the piano.

Old-time Armenian ensemble

The Massacres and the Diaspora

It is fortuitous that Komitas researched and collected that folk music when he did, since a few years later the Armenian population of historic Armenia (now part of eastern Turkey) was violently uprooted. The towns of Erzerum, Kars, Diyarbakir, Van and Harpoot were home to more than two million

Armenians before the **1915 Massacres** by the Young Turk regime – an act of brutal "ethnic cleansing" preceding the formation of the modern Turkish state by Mustafa Kemal Ataturk. After the massacre, most of the surviving Armenian population went into exile. Today scarcely any Armenians remain in the region.

As a result, Armenian folk music from this area has been more difficult to document than the music of the foothills of the Caucasus to the east, the region of present-day Armenia. Though the American-born children of those who fled the massacres preserved some of the Anatolian dance tunes and wedding songs of their parents and grandparents, hardly a native recording exists of Armenian traditional music. It is instead second- and third-generation Armenian Americans who have actively struggled to preserve this musical heritage. In particular, the *oud* player **Richard Hagopian**, born in central California's large diaspora community in 1937, has endeavored to document and pass on the music of Anatolian Armenians.

Preservation and performance of this music has been complicated by the fact that many Armenians from Anatolia spoke, and sang, not only in Armenian (an ancient language which is its own branch of the Indo-European language group), but Turkish as well. This has led to disagreements within the Armenian community itself over what precisely constitutes its musical heritage.

Folk Music

All Armenian folk music shares fundamental features with its Middle Eastern neighbours, including modal scales, the use of quarter-tones and the importance of improvisation within the traditionally established modes. The melodies are monophonic and played against a continuous drone, rather than chordal harmonies. The attempt to determine the ultimate origin of a particular Armenian melody may be impossible, however, since Kurdish, Turkish, Persian, Armenian and Gypsy musicians of Anatolia all intermingled under the Ottoman Empire for several hundred years.

What can be identified as Armenian are the styles of playing **instruments** such as the *oud*, (lute), *tar* (short-necked lute), *kanun* (dulcimer), *kamancha* (spike fiddle), *zurna* (shawm) and *dhol* (double-headed drum), especially the ways in which they have been played in modern times within the former Soviet Republic of Armenia.

Shoghaken Ensemble

Soviet-style **conservatoires** taught these instruments with the same rigour as the violin and piano, producing a number of renowned musicians whose performances are virtuoso, if controlled, versions of the folk repertoire.

The conservatoires also ironed out the microtones to make the music more "European" and one of the less-publicized effects of independence has been the revival of Armenia's traditional Middle Eastern modes and *makam*.

In Armenia today it is possible to hear traditional music at weddings and celebrations, but it's rare. Much more common are professional ensembles. Ironically Armenians in the US are more likely to dance the traditional dances such as *shalako* (solo dance in 6/8) or the *kochare* (men's line dance) at family celebrations.

There are several good folk ensembles based in Armenia like **Shoghaken**, the **Master Musicians of Armenia** and the **Mihr Armenian-Iranian Traditional Music Ensemble**. Since 1995 the group **Knar**, made up of Armenian and Turkish musicians in Istanbul, has been researching and performing Armenian repertoire from Anatolia.

While most of the instruments played in these bands come largely from traditions of Persian music, there's one, the double-reed **duduk** which is indigenous to Armenia and its plaintive sound has become something of a symbol of the country. *Duduk* music was listed by UNESCO as a Masterpiece of Intangible Heritage in 2005. Many duduk melodies that seem mournful to Western ears, however, just don't sound that way to Armenians. *Duduks* are often played at weddings and parties, but also associated with funerals. Carved from apricot wood, the *duduk* has a beautifully melancholy timbre which has found its way from the Armenian countryside to Hollywood soundtracks like *Gladiator* and *The Last Temptation of Christ*.

The best-known and probably the greatest contemporary *duduk* player is **Djivan Gasparyan** (see box opposite), although there are other fine players like **Gevorg Dabaghyan** and **Varazdat Hovhannissyan**. The *duduk*'s modern repertoire tends to be made up either of rhythmic songs and dances or slow, suite-like fantasies, perhaps including improvisation, exploiting the emotive nature of the instrument. Yo Yo Ma's Silk Road Project commissioned a piece for *duduk* and string quartet from the composer **Vache Sharafyan** who has written a number of chamber pieces combining Western instruments with *duduk*, *tar* and *kamancha*.

Ashoughs

Like the medieval French troubadours and the Turkish *aşiks*, Armenian **ashoughs** travelled the countryside in the seventeenth and eighteenth centuries carrying news and messages from afar through song. The most prolific and celebrated of them, **Sayat Nova** (1717–95), served as court singer and musician to the Persian Nadir Shah and later to the Georgian ruler Iraklii II. His favourite instrument was the **kamancha** and one of his most famous songs is dedicated to this instrument which he said could "console the broken-hearted, cure the sick and be fully appreciated only by a true artist."

Ashough songs are traditionally accompanied by the *kamancha*, *tar*, *kanun* and *duduk*, and Sayat Nova's songs are still regularly performed today. Modern singers of the ashough are highly respected artists who specialize in the genre and hardly an Armenian citizen exists who does not know the voices of legendary **Rouben Matevosian** and **Hovhaness Badalian**. They sing songs of love and tragedy, usually accompanied by large folk orchestras such as Tatoul Altounian's Ensemble – one of the most famous in the country.

Classical Music, Cabaret and Pop

Istanbul was the intellectual and cultural centre for Armenians in the Ottoman Empire, and, before the nationalist ethnic purification, the work of a number of Armenian composers and musicians was absorbed into the standard repertoire of late Ottoman music. The most notable was **Kemani Tatyos**

Ekserciyan (1863–1913), one of the finest composers of Ottoman classical music.

Armenians (and other ethnic minorities) were also prevalent in Istanbul's burgeoning nightclub and cabaret scene in the 1920s and 30s – one of the greatest being the blind *oud* master **Udi Hrant Kenkulian** (1901–78). Armenian women, joined by other minorities as well as the least intimidated Turkish Muslim women, also became popular nightclub singers in this period – **Suzan Yakar** was one of the best known.

With many Armenians in exile after 1915 a lively nightclub scene grew up in the US, where the Istanbul cabaret tradition were perpetuated in New York by Greek and Armenian musicians. By the 1950s there were dozens of clubs lining Eighth Avenue with names like *Port Said*, *Istanbul*, *Ali Baba* and *Seventh Veil*. Musicians who played there included singer and *kanun* player **Garbis Bakirgian** (who had performed for the sultan in Istanbul) and *oud* player **Marko Melkon**.

Today the meeting of Armenian and American styles continues with groups like Ara Dinkjian's group **Night Ark** which has linked Armenian folk music and instruments with jazz and New Age styles. He's also kept up the link with Greek musicians, composing for and performing with the singer Eleftheria Arvanitaki. Recently, it's been the **Armenian Navy Band**, founded by Night Ark's percussionist, Arto Tunçboyaciyan, that's been making waves. Tunçboyaciyan is based in the US, but the group includes many musicians based in Armenia. 'Avant-garde folk' is how Tunçboyaciyan describes his music which features Armenian instruments like *kamancha*, *duduk* and *zurna* with saxophones, piano, brass and drums.

There are also various strands of Armenian pop and rock music, particularly amongst the migrant

The Armenian Navy Band at their command centre

Djivan Gasparyan and the Duduk

Djivan Gasparyan is a national hero in Armenia and probably the only musician in this book to have a vodka named after him. He fully understands the reasons why the **duduk** has come to express the soul of the country: 'Every century a new misfortune falls on the heads of the Armenians. That's why our music is different from any other music. We dance wholeheartedly, we enjoy ourselves wholeheartedly, and we are sad wholeheartedly. It comes from our rocks, from our mountainous land, from our lives, from our history.'

Djivan Gasparyan was born in 1928 in Solag, a village close to the Armenian capital, Yerevan: 'My father was a fine *duduk* player,' Gasparyan remembers. 'I was his apprentice and I taught myself at his side.' But Gasparyan's initial inspiration came from the cinema. 'I was fascinated by the *duduk* players accompanying the film. Their ability to play a suitable melody for a sad or romantic scene and also to burst in with vivacious folk dances when the film demanded more dynamism. The film didn't interest me much. I was riveted by the music and its extraordinary ability to express the right feelings through the *duduk*.'

As a young boy he returned to the cinema day after day, getting in without paying and befriending the old musicians who explained the process of circular breathing necessary to play the accompanying drone part, or *dam*. He collected empty bottles and sold them in order to buy himself an instrument and join the musicians at the cinema as a *damkash* (drone player). He played for Stalin at the Kremlin when he was 18, and then joined the **Tatoul Altounian National Song and Dance Ensemble**. After completing his studies at the Conservatoire, he became a soloist and began touring internationally in the late 1950s.

Made of apricot wood and with a cane reed, the *duduk* has eight holes plus a thumb hole, rather like a Western recorder. Its range is no more than an octave, but it is capable – as Gasparyan learnt at the cinema – of the most powerful expression. It goes back at least as far as the fifth century AD, although some Armenian scholars believe it existed more than 1500 years before that. *Duduks* always come in pairs, or larger groups, with the soloist playing over a held drone which traditionally stays fixed. The repertoire is made up of instrumental versions of Armenian folksongs or *ashough* songs, special *duduk* melodies, folk dances – usually accompanied by a two-headed drum (*dhol*) – or improvisations.

The art of making the instrument is a highly skilled one. Gasparyan's preferred craftsman is Karlen Matevossian. 'He finds the right apricot tree, but I choose the particular piece of wood according to its size. The wood must be left for two years to dry before the master puts it on the lathe. The final positioning of the holes and tuning must be done by the musician himself. A good instrument can last three hundred years. Of course, lots of melodies are dedicated to the apricot tree. In my concerts I like to include "Tsirani Tsar" (The Apricot Tree)' – a famous folksong collected by Komitas.

Having taught at the conservatoire in Yerevan for over thirty years, Gasparyan is one of those responsible for elevating the *duduk* into an instrument with a classical status. He developed a *duduk* quartet with instruments of different sizes, including a large "bass *duduk*". Since the break-up of the Soviet Union, Gasparyan has worked hard to reconnect his music with the *makam* (Middle Eastern mode) that are part of Armenian music. 'I don't find it a sad-sounding instrument. It is a romantic and a classical instrument. Just as one would go to a concert to hear a violin, one can go to hear the duduk.' Gasparyan is also a fine singer and often sings ashough

minstrel songs during his concerts. 'I have to sing when I play. If I don't sing, I can't play as I do.' One of the things that distinguishes a good player is the ornamentation of the notes and the modal colouring of the Middle Eastern *makam* which gives the music an extra expressive power. It's something that's done by half, or fractionally, covering the finger holes. He has recorded and played with Turkey's great *saz* player **Erkan Oğur** and performed with Iranian musicians like **Hossein Alizadeh** in Tehran. 'There's lots in common in our music and dialogue and collaboration are the only way forward,' he says.

Maybe after his cinematic introduction to the *duduk* it was inevitable Gasparyan would end up playing on film soundtracks – including *Russia House*, *The Crow*, *The Siege*, *Onegin* and the Oscar-winning *Gladiator*. Proof enough that this ancient instrument still has its emotive power.

community in California. They include a fairly cheesy style of Armenian pop with a hint of folk melodies and a more Arabic-influenced style typified by **Adiss Harmandian**, favoured by Armenian immigrants from Lebanon. A younger Armenian singer-songwriter is **Gor Mkhitarian**, although despite singing in Armenian, his musical style is pretty American.

Since independence in 1991, a pop and rock culture has appeared in Armenia itself with the band **Vostan Hayots** singing songs commemorating the Armenian genocide which they even took to Stepanakert in Nagorno-Karabakh. Yerevan had its first rock festival in 2005, biz-

zarely held on a square surrounded by government buildings in the centre of the capital. The current Armenian pop diva is **Nune Yesayan**, who has released a great number of albums, including *Sayat Nova* which features contemporary versions of famous composer Sayat Nova's classic songs. Yesayan performed with Djivan Gasparyan to mark the 85th anniversary of the Armenian Genocide and then played with him on an extensive tour in the US. Her 2006 album *Deleh Yaman* marks the 90th anniversary of the massacres and the title-track includes Gasparyan and 24 young *duduk* players. In Armenia there's no escaping the *duduk*.

DISCOGRAPHY Armenia

The most comprehensive survey of Armenian music is the six-volume, 7-CD set Music of Armenia from Celestial Harmonies (US). Vol 1 includes choral and church music, ancient and modern; Vol 2 *sharakan* chants in beautiful arrangements by Komitas and others; Vol 3 focuses on the *duduk*; Vol 4 is an album of kanon music; Vol 5 is folk music played by the Shoghaken and Sasun folk groups; and Vol 6 features music from the Armenian-inhabited region of Nagorno-Karabakh within Azerbaijan. The discs are well recorded by David Parsons and come with very informative liner notes. As they are available separately, as well as in a set, some also feature in the individual recommendations below.

Folk Music

⊙ **Armenians on 8th Avenue**
Traditional Crossroads, US
New York's 8th Avenue was the centre of the city's Armenian and Greek communities and a taverna culture thrived there, reaching a peak in the 1950s. This CD, reissuing recordings from the 1940s and 50s, reveals a little-known world of classical and popular musicians like *kanun* player Garbis Bakirgian, *oud* player Marko Melkon and singer "Sugar Mary". A musical curiosity, but a fascinating one.

⊙ **Arménie 2: Musique de tradition populaire et des Achough**
Ocora, France
Various folksongs and ashough pieces by Sayat Nova and more recent troubadours accompanied by small instrumental groups and a couple of dubious, Soviet-style big ensembles.

⊙ **Haut-Karabagh: Musiques du Front**
Auvidis/Silex, France
An imaginative musical postcard from the war-stricken region of Nagorno Karabakh. Includes laments in a cemetery, songs about the struggle and military leaders and wonderful instrumental groups of clarinets, *duduks*, accordion and drums. Folk music that deals with contemporary realities.

⊙ **Kalaschjan: Rural and Urban Traditional Music from Armenia**
Schott Wergo/Weltmusik, Germany
A good cross-section of folk and ashough music from a concert at the House of World Cultures in Berlin. There's an outdoor ensemble of *zurnas* and *dhol* and a more refined ensemble of *oud, kanun, kamancha, duduk* and *dhol*.

Benik Abovian & Zaven Azibekian

A noted ashough, Abovian (born 1932) plays *duduk* and *zurna*, while Azibekian (born 1952) is an oboe and *duduk* player. They are both from the Tavush region on the border with Azerbaijan.

⊙ **Armenia: Traditional Musicians from Tavush**
Inédit, France
The appeal of this disc is the more folksy style of *duduk* playing plus two *zurna* and *dhol* tracks recorded at an open-air picnic. Also includes some atmospheric wooden flutes.

Armenian Navy Band

Arto Tunçboyaciyan's twelve-piece band playing "avant garde folk". Tunçboyaciyan was born in Turkey but emigrated to the US in 1981. He worked with Ara Dinkjian in Night Ark (see below) and started the Armenian Navy Band with up to a dozen musicians from Armenia in 1998.

⊙ **Natural Seeds**
Heaven & Earth, Germany
An impressionistic suite of pieces featuring *kanun, kamancha* and *duduk* as well as honking sax, Gil Evans-style piano from Vahagn Hayrapetyan and soaring strings. An Armenian equivalent of Miles Davis's *Sketches of Spain*.

Gevorg Dabaghyan

One of Armenia's best *duduk* (and *zurna*) players, born in Yerevan in 1965. He studied at the Komitas State Conservatoire, has made numerous recordings and plays on several film soundtracks.

⊙ Miniatures – Masterworks for Armenian Duduk
Traditional Crossroads, US
A very good solo *duduk* CD, with some deep, plaintive repertoire, but also religious chants and wild folk dances with Kamo Khachaturian on *dhol*.

⊙ Music of Armenia: Vol 3 Duduk
Celestial Harmonies, US
A rich variety of *duduk* music, some of it with moving and harmonic drones. Very fine playing which repays careful listening. Includes a couple of pieces appropriately about the apricot tree.

Djivan Gasparyan

Gasparyan is Armenia's most famous *duduk* player. Following conservatoire fashion, he developed various sizes of *duduk* that can be played in classical-style trios and quartets. He came to Western attention through a 1983 Melodiya recording that was released in the West as *I Will Not Be Sad in this World* (the title of a Sayat Nova song) in aid of victims of the Armenian earthquake in 1989. Gasparyan has gone on to do film soundtracks and musical collaborations with guitarist/producer Michael Brook. He has established a *duduk* school in Yerevan and acted as a musical ambassador for his country.

★ Armenian Fantasies
Network, Germany
A marvellous disc that features Gasparyan with an ensemble of *kamancha*, *tar*, *oud*, *kanun* and *dhol* drums. Various songs and dances are made into longer instrumental suites.

★ Heavenly Duduk
World Network, Germany
A great introduction to Gasparyan's art. The opening numbers have all the melancholic longing that typi-

fies the instrument, with some seductive microtones. But there are also some lively dance numbers with *dhol* accompaniment, songs (Gasparyan has a moving voice) and more classical arrangements of Komitas tunes for a *duduk* trio.

⊙ Fuad
Kalan, Turkey
An interesting collaboration with Turkish *saz* virtuoso Erkan Oğur. The combination of plucked *saz* and reedy *duduk* works well. Gasparyan's song "Mayrig" (Mother) is one of his emotional showstoppers and very haunting.

Richard Hagopian

Born in 1937 in the grape-growing area of Fresno, California where many Armenians settled, Hagopian learned the *oud* from Garbis Bakirgian and has extensively studied and played Armenian folk and classical music.

⊙ Kef Time
Traditional Crossroads, US
With *oud*, clarinet, *kanun*, guitar and percussion, Richard Hagopian's Kef Time group is a tribute to the cabaret-style music of Istanbul performed in Turkish and Armenian. Hot Armenian bellydance.

Night Ark

Founded by *saz* and *oud* player Ara Dinkjian in 1985, Night Ark is a quartet of American-born Armenian musi-

cians, including percussionist Arto Tunçboyaciyan. They have played frequently at international festivals and made four albums to date.

⊙ In Wonderland
Emarcy/Polygram
A 1998 release that has stood the test of time, colourfully merging Armenian melodies, rhythms and instruments with jazz and Western instrumentation.

Nune

Nune Yesayan was born in Yerevan in 1969 and became interested in singing folk music and performing jazz while a student. She came to nationwide attention by winning a "Pop Idol" show. She worked for several years performing in hotels in the Arabian Gulf, but since 1997 has returned to Armenia. She has made several albums and done many international tours.

⊙ Sayat Nova
Prime Entertainment, Armenia
Nune is essentially a pop musician, but one that makes gestures to traditional Armenian sounds and in this case to the songs of Sayat Nova. The famous "Kamancha", a song about the instrument, is one of the highlights.

Shoghaken Ensemble

Founded in 1991 by *duduk* player Gevorg Dabaghyan, Shoghaken is probably Armenia's best folk ensemble, dedicated to traditional-style performances.

⊙ Armenia Anthology
Traditional Crossroads, US
A good introduction to various forms of Armenian music including duduk, songs by Sayat Nova and vocals by Hasmik and Aleksan Harutyunyan.

⊙ Music of Armenia: Vol 5. Folk Music
Celestial Harmonies, US
A 2-CD set maintaining the standards of the Celestial Harmonies series. Alongside the rather refined Shoghaken Ensemble are tracks from Sasun, a more vernacular duduk, dhol and voices group. Slightly dour performances, but good sleeve notes.

★ Traditional Folk Dances of Armenia
Traditional Crossroads, US
A lively collection of traditional dances which breaks the notion that Armenian music has to be melancholy.

SHOGHAKEN ENSEMBLE   TRADITIONAL DANCES OF ARMENIA

Church Music

⊙ Arménie 1: Chants Liturgiques du Moyen Age et Musique Instrumental
Ocora, France

The first half of this disc concentrates on church music including *sharakan* by Mesrop Mashtots. Most of it is solo chant, some performed by Lucine Zakarian. The instrumental folk music features small ensembles of *kamancha*, *duduks*, *zurnas* and so on, including *duduk* player Vatche Hovsepian.

⊙ Music of Armenia: Vol 1 Sacred Choral Music
Celestial Harmonies, US

A beautiful introduction to Armenian church music recorded by the Haissmavourk Choir (with men and women's voices) in Geghard Monastery and Etchmiadzin Cathedral. Some of the tracks have fantastic clashing drones and harmonies.

Komitas

Komitas (1869–1935) was born Soghoman Sogomanian in Ottoman Turkey and adopted his pseudonym from a seventh-century Armenian poet and musician. Orphaned at an early age, he studied liturgical music and became a *vartabet* (priest). He was responsible for the most important collection of Armenian folksongs and melodies, made arrangements of them and worked on his Divine Liturgy for over twenty years. In 1915, during the Ottoman genocide against the Armenians, he was deported and imprisoned. He escaped with his life, but much of his work was destroyed and, after a mental breakdown, he spent most of the rest of his life in asylums in France.

⊙ The Voice of Komitas Vardapet
Traditional Crossroads, US

Of rather specialized interest perhaps, but these solo recordings of Komitas singing were made in 1912 in Paris. He has a strong baritone voice that is very moving through the crackles, particularly in one of the most beautiful and touching Armenian harvest songs, "Kali Yerg". At the piano, Komitas also accompanies one of his pupils, the rather operatic tenor Armenak Shahmuradian in some of his song arrangements.

⊙ Komitas: Divine Liturgy
New Albion, US

A full-blooded performance of Komitas's *Divine Liturgy* from the (all-male) choir of St Gayané Cathedral. A major work of Armenian liturgical music.

PLAYLIST
Armenia

1 SIRO HUSHER Djivan Gasparyan from *Heavenly Duduk*
A beautiful song performed with a *duduk* trio.

2 SHUSTAR Gevorg Dabaghyan from *Miniatures*
A lovely *duduk* meditation in *makam Shustar*.

3 APARANI PAR Shoghaken Ensemble from *Traditional Dances of Armenia*
A lively 5/8 dance from central Armenia and a typical Armenian melody.

4 AYSOR DZAINEN Haissmavourk Choir from *Music of Armenia: Vol 1 Sacred Choral Music*
A thirteenth century hymn, arranged by Komitas, with wonderfully weird bending notes. Recorded in Geghard Monastery.

5 OCEAN Armenian Navy Band from *Natural Seeds*
Wild breakneck dance music revealing how even landlocked peoples dream of sailing to a new world.

6 DELEH YAMAN Nune from *Deleh Yaman*
Lament for the genocide with Gasparyan and massed *duduks*.

Azerbaijan

in the mugham

Alim and Fershana Qasimov
Network Mediew

Alongside Georgia and Armenia, Azerbaijan is one of the three Transcaucasian republics that became independent in 1991 with the break-up of the Soviet Union. Each has a distinctive musical tradition that has been recognized (with careful even-handedness) as a Masterpiece of the Oral and Intangible Heritage of Humanity by UNESCO. In the case of Azerbaijan, it is *mugham*. Razia Sultanova and Simon Broughton describe this form and explore the country's wider musical heritage.

Bordered by Russia, Georgia, Armenia, Iran and the Caspian Sea, Azerbaijan has a population of eight million. (In addition, there are twelve million Azeris in the northern region of Iran, who make a significant contribution to Iranian music.) Since independence, Azerbaijan has fared better economically than Georgia and Armenia, thanks to its oil reserves in the Caspian Sea. There is still tension with Armenia over the region of Nagorno-Karabakh, which is ethnically predominantly Armenian and declared itself independent from Azerbaijan in 1991, and from which one million Azeri refugees have been displaced.

Azerbaijan was part of the Persian Empire until it was conquered by Russia in 1801, and the traditional instruments are the same as those found in Persian music: the *tar* (long-necked lute with a skin-covered belly), *kemençe* (spike fiddle) and *daf* (frame drum). But the Azeris speak a Turkic language, close to Turkish, and share the tradition of *aşiq* troubadours (*aşik* in Turkish). While the Turks are predominantly Sunni Muslims, the Azeris are mainly Shia, like the Persians. In Azerbaijan, therefore, three cultures meet – Turkish, Persian and Russian. Now, thanks to the oil, American-style capitalism has also moved in.

Meyxana – Wedding Rap

As anywhere in the world, the liveliest Azeri music is heard at weddings. There is a specific Azeri style called *meyxana* (wine-singing), performed by wedding singers known as *meyxanaçi*. The music is sharp and satirical – a four- or five-minute improvised commentary on characters and events. Although it's never been taken seriously by musicologists, *meyxana* has now become the most significant musical genre in Azerbaijan. Accompanied by keyboards, bass guitar and some traditional instruments like *balaban* (*duduk*) and *daf*, it can be seen as a continuation of the old *aşiq* tradition (see below).

In Soviet times *meyxana* was an unofficial "underground" music, sung in either Azeri or Russian, and described by the authorities as "hooligan poetry". One of the most notorious songs of the 1980s was "Zhiguli" (the name of the Soviet Fiat), by the singer Agasalim Salimov. The singer talks about his high-living thanks to his work for the KGB and his girlfriend's "messy situation" because her father is Russian and her mother is Azeri.

Nowadays, *meyxana* is appealing to a cross-section of Azeri society, despite its sometimes instructive and moralistic messages. It also makes political points, reflecting contemporary issues at a local level. A big hit in 2005 was "Dostum" by **Vüqar**, a singer from the Azeri capital, Baku. It flatters the city's mayor and the way he has mended the roads and criticizes those begging in the streets at traffic lights! Vüqar has been co-opted to sing campaign songs for the mayor and is also known for his praise songs for the late President Haydar Aliyev. Beyond the political arena, from wedding to wedding, *meyxana* embraces both a timeless tradition and a contemporary relevance which is what accounts for its popularity.

Aside from the *meyxana*, traditional weddings have other obligatory musical ingredients. The instrumental tune "Vaqzali" (from the Russian word for train station, *vokzal*) accompanies the entrance of the bride, and the bridegroom's melody "Bey Tarifi" is performed at the end of the wedding. Wedding dances originating in the rural western parts of the country, such as the women's *xalay* and men's *yallı*, have also found their way into the urban repertoire.

Weddings are an important source of income for singers and musicians. Traditionally, they were also the occasions for performances by musicians playing in Azerbaijan's two most significant musical traditions – the *aşiq* bards, whose music is rooted in popular culture, and the *mugham* singers, with their more refined, classical repertoire.

The Aşiq Bard Tradition

The word *aşiq* derives from Arabic or Persian and means "lover". Similar words are used in Turkish (*aşik*) and Armenian (*ashough*), and in the eighteenth century bards like the Armenian Sayat Nova in the cosmopolitan Georgian capital Tiflis (Tbilisi) commonly sang in Armenian, Turkish and Persian. The word comes from Sufism and refers to the *aşiq*'s love of God, which is often expressed through metaphors of human love or drunkenness. The *aşiqs* performed religious and love poems, moralistic tales and long lyric or epic ballads. All these would be modified and adapted to suit the audience in a wedding party or a teahouse. Great Azeri bards include **Dede Korkut** (or Gorgud, eleventh century), **Shah Ismail** (who founded the Persian Safavid dynasty in the sixteenth century), **Aşiq Qurbani** (sixteenth century) and **Aşiq Alaskar** (nineteenth century).

The *aşiq* tradition survives amongst the Azeris in both Iran and Azerbaijan, with singers accompanying themselves on the long-necked *saz*, or *çoğur*. Other instruments associated with the *aşiqs* are the *balaban* and *daf*. Top *aşiq* performers include **Alim Qasimov** – who is also the best-known *mugham* singer – and **Edalat Nasibov**, who

Asiq Emran Heydari

renders epic *aşiq* pieces in instrumental form on the *saz*, accompanied by dramatic body movements. **Emran Heydari**, from Iran, is another significant name.

Mugham

While the *aşiq's* music is rooted in popular culture, **mugham** is urban art music, the Azeri equivalent of the Turkish classical *makam* or Persian *dastgah*. The term *mugham* refers both to the modes in which the music is played (which are similar to those in Persian music) and to the genre itself. There are twelve main mugham *modes*, including *rast*, *shur*, *segah* and *chargah*, each with its own flavour and different tonal centres of gravity. Simplistically, *rast* can be seen as happy, while *shur* is perceived as sad. The *mugham* performance will, like a classical symphony, begin and end in one mode, but may modulate to others during the course of the piece. The suite usually begins with an improvisatory instrumental prelude and then alternates sung poetry and instrumental passages. It often builds to a climax of both emotion and pitch. Within the tonal constraints, it is up to the

Alim Qasimov

Alim Qasimov is one of the world's great singers and he has won the UNESCO award previously conferred on such musical heavyweights as Ravi Shankar and Nusrat Fateh Ali Khan.

When I visited the farm where Qasimov grew up, about 100km from Baku, a sheep was slaughtered in my honour before being disembowelled in front of me and turned into kebabs, which we washed down with vodka. Alim's father, Hamza, worked on one of the Soviet-style collective farms. They were never hungry, but the roof leaked and they couldn't afford enough clothes, let alone musical instruments. His father killed one of his goats to make him a frame drum, and a *tar* was fashioned out of an aluminium pan, with telephone wires as strings.

Alim's talent was evident early on, and while still a teenager he would sing at weddings. He eloped with his girlfriend Tamila – now his wife – after her relatively rich parents objected to their relationship, and took a series of jobs in oil plants and as a chauffeur. But at 21, Qasimov decided he was wasting his talent, so he enrolled with not one but three *mugham* teachers, who kept him busy from eight in the morning until late at night.

More conservative *mugham* singers, who stick to the written notes, feel that Qasimov is breaking too many rules of the genre. His justification for straying from the straight and narrow of *mugham* is that he is responding to and reinventing the spirit rather than the letter of the genre. At his modest flat in downtown Baku, he dug out a tape of a *mugham* singer, Mashadi Fazzaliyev, recorded nearly a century ago. The sheer passion of the music broke through the veils of time and poor recording quality. Now Qasimov is passing his knowledge to his daughter **Ferghana**, who often performs with him.

The most unforgettable moment of my visit was still to come. We drove out to the Yanar Dar, a natural Azeri wonder – a fire that has burnt for thousands of years through natural gas. Qasimov moved around the flames and began to sing: songs of love gone wrong, songs to nature and the divine, in a voice at once masculine and feminine, disturbing and inspiring with its intensity.

Peter Culshaw

singer to choose the poems and instrumental passages that make up the *mugham*.

The instrumental ensemble is usually a trio of *daf*, *tar* and *kemençe*. The *daf* is usually played by the singer, with the *tar* and *kemençe* often echoing or anticipating the vocal line. The instrumentation is Persian, although the *santur* and *ney* common in Iranian ensembles are not generally used by the Azeris, giving the music a leaner sound.

During the eighteenth and nineteenth centuries the city of Şuşa in Karabakh was a centre of Azeri musical life and known as the "Conservatoire of the Caucasus". An outdoor *mugham* festival was held here until 1988, when the conflict with Armenia began. In 1994, the *mugham* festival was re-started in Şakı, a historic town in the north of the country.

Without doubt the king of *mugham* singers is **Alim Qasimov** (see box on previous page). He's become the international face of Azeri music, celebrated for the emotional power of his voice and his expressive vocal ornamentation – an important part of *mugham*. He's also a master of the *tahrir* technique in which he adopts a high head voice, almost like yodelling. These esoteric vocal styles can seem exaggerated to those unfamiliar with them, but Qasimov's success in concerts at home and abroad, as well as his numerous recordings, are testament to the transcendental power of his performance. The way he caresses the *daf* drum (with its little jangling rings inside the frame) and then tosses it into the air with ecstasy as he sings is a sight to behold. He has performed for many years with the brothers Malik and Elsham Mansurov on *tar* and *kemençe*.

Other notable *mugham* performers include **Zahid Guliyev**, **Djanali Akberov** and the female singers **Sakine Ismaïlova**, **Sevintch Sariyeva** and **Aygun Bayler**, who also performs folk and jazz *mugham*. The number of women performing *mugham* here (as opposed to in Iran) is one of the more positive results of Soviet Russian influence.

Mugham on the Move

Russian musical influence in Azerbaijan goes back to the nineteenth century and can be seen in the work of **Uzeyir Hajibeyov** (1885–1948). He composed *Leyli & Majnun*, a mugham opera described as the first opera of the Muslim East. Its *Romeo and Juliet*-like story comes from a tale popular across the Persian world and fre-

quently referred to in *mugham* poetry. His opera *Koroglu* is based on a famous *aşiq* epic. *Azerbaijan Mugham*, a large orchestral work by **Fikrat Amirov** (1918–82), was recorded by the eminent conductor Leopold Stokowski, while **Haji Khanmammadov** (1918–2005) wrote five concertos for *tar* and orchestra.

Mugham music also influenced Azeri jazz, and the Baku Jazz Festival has a growing reputation. The pianist **Vagif Mustafa-Zadeh** began playing what he called "Mugham Jazz" in the 1960s, improvising in piano versions of Azeri modes and rhythms. Mustafa-Zadeh died tragically young in 1979, aged just 39, but his daughter **Aziza Mustafa-Zadeh** has followed in his footsteps. A singer and pianist, she brings a distinctly Azeri feel to her solo playing and it's not hard to hear the influence of *mugham* and folk dances in her compositions and ornamented scat singing. She left Azerbaijan in 1989 to pursue an international career.

Since independence, pop music in Azerbaijan has been very open to outside influences, with plenty of rap singers emulating Eminem and 50 Cent. Some bands, however, have retained a local

Remi Boisseau

Azeri singer Aygun Bayler at the Fes Festival

Aziza Mustafa-Zadeh

flavour by combining Western keyboards, guitars and drums with local instruments like the *tar*, *balaban* and *garmon* (accordion). These include **Bakustik**, **Bery Bax** and **Rast**. Predictably, there are strong influences on Azeri popular music from Russian *estrada* and Turkish pop and *arabesk*. Singers like **Aygün Kazimova** and **Brilliant Dadasova** could be compared to Turkey's Sezen Aksu in the way they combine Azeri traditional music with modern sounds.

The war over Nagorno-Karabakh has led to a rise in the popularity of patriotic songs, but more encouraging is the increasing popularity of *mugham*. In Baku there are now over thirty state-supported schools where, as part of the curriculum, students are taught to sing and play *mugham*. This is impressive since *mugham* is, after all, a difficult and sophisticated genre.

DISCOGRAPHY Azerbaijan

⊙ The Music of Azerbaijan
Rounder, US
A CD reissue of an old Bärenreiter LP made from material recorded by Radio Baku. It's a good introduction to traditional Azeri styles – *mugham*, *aşiq* music, instrumental solos and dances.

★ Azerbaidjan: Music and Songs of the Ashiq
VDE-Gallo/AIMP, Switzerland
A fine survey of the Azeri *aşiq* tradition with Emran Heydari accompanying himself on *saz*, Ashiq Hasan accompanied by *saz*, *balaban* and *daf*, and the ubiquitous Alim Qasimov with his *mugham* line up of *tar*, *kemençe* and *daf*.

Dede Korkut Ensemble

Named after the celebrated medieval *aşiq*, this trio of musicians is based in the autonomous region of Naxçivan, separate from the rest of Azerbaijan, between Armenia and Iran.

⊙ Heyya Gülü: Dances and Ashug Melodies from Nakhichevan
Pan, Netherlands
Lively music, often with an Armenian flavour. It features some of the distinctive instruments of the region, including *balaban*, flute, *zurna* and a bagpipe-*zurna* which does away with the need for circular breathing.

Sakine Ismaïlova

From the same generation as Alim Qasimov, Ismaïlova trained in Baku and is the leading woman singer in the *mugham* tradition.

⊙ Sakine Ismaïlova
Inédit, France
It is only since the twentieth century that women have been singing *mugham*. Ismaïlova has a typically elegant, mid-range voice with emotional drama where necessary. There are three

mugham on this disc, mainly with texts by the fourteenth-century poet Nizami. One of eight CDs in Inédit's *Mugam d'Azerbaïdjan* series.

Jabbar Kardyagdioglu Ensemble

Named after a prominent *mugham* singer, this trio ("The Sons of Jabbar Karyagdy") consists of Fahraddin Dadashov (*kemençe*), Mehlet Muslimov (*tar*) and Elchin Jalilev (vocals and *daf*). They teach at the conservatoire in Baku.

⊙ Uzundärä: Ancient Wedding Dance Music of Azerbaijan
Pan, Netherlands
A good collection of instrumental dances and songs. Although this is essentially folk repertoire, the tunes do get incorporated into the instrumental parts of classical *mugham* suites.

Edalat Nasibov

Born in 1939 in Armenia, but brought up in Azerbaijan where he learnt *saz* and singing at an early age, Nasibov started to win *aşiq* competitions and learnt with some of the great masters. He toured widely and was named an "Artist of the People of Azerbaijan".

⊙ The Art of the Saz
Ocora, France
The most impressive Azeri *saz* playing on disc, this is a collection of dramatic instrumental versions of many of the classic *aşiq* pieces, such as "Koroglu". Nasibov says he chooses not to sing in order to to enhance his instrumental technique.

Alim Qasimov

Qasimov was born in 1957 in the small town of Shamakha about 100km from Baku. He is now the undisputed king of *mugham* – and in 1999 won an IMC-UNESCO prize for "outstanding contributions to the environment and devel-

PLAYLIST
Azerbaijan

1 EY ENCALER Alim Qasimov from *Love's Deep Ocean*
A song of love and longing by Nizami sung by Qasimov and his daughter Ferghana.

2 KOROGLU Ashiq Hasan from *Azerbaidjan: Music and Songs of the Ashiq*
A poem from the Koroglu epic, with *saz*, *balaban* and drum.

3 KOROGLU MISRISI Edalat Nasibov from *The Art of the Saz*
Spectacular *saz* playing on a heroic melody from the Koroglu epic.

4 MAHUR AND RAST Yanar Dar from *Mugam from Azerbaijan*
A *mugham* sequence of instrumentals and songs with singer Sevintch Sariyeva.

5 VAGIF Aziz Mustafa-Zadeh from *Always*
Soft piano solo with contours and flavours of *mugham*, dedicated to her father.

opment of music". He performs and tours often, with the brothers Malik and Elshan Mansurov on *tar* and *kemençe* respectively.

★ Love's Deep Ocean
Network, Germany
The art of *mugham* singing is an acquired taste but this stunning disc is the perfect introduction, highlighting Qasimov's lighter repertoire based on *ghazals* and *aşıq* songs. He sings with his daughter Ferghana – a male/female duet quite unusual in the strict *mugham* tradition – accompanied by an expanded ensemble including *balaban*, clarinet and *nagara* drum alongside the usual *tar* and *kemençe*.

⊙ The Legendary Art of Mugam
Network, Germany
More serious repertoire than *Love's Deep Ocean*: a performance of *mugham Shur* is the main item here, although the disc also includes some popular folksongs with Ferghana.

⊙ Azerbaijan: Alim Qasimov
Ocora, France
Alim Qasimov's singing on this disc is full of passion, love and admiration, despair and miserable longing to see his beloved. The depth of emotion and sense of drama in his singing is worthy of a Greek or Shakespearean tragedy.

Yanar Dar

Formed by French *oud* player Marc Loopuyt, Yanar Dar is a good *mugham* group named after the eternal fire altar near Baku.

⊙ Mugam from Azerbaijan
Buda, France
Opening with a ripping dance prelude, the disc gets going with a swing. Vocalist Sevintch Sariyeva has a strong, but not too strident voice, even in the most emotive moments. Elshan Mansurov on *kemençe* and Eltchin Nagiyev on *tar* provide lovely rich instrumental textures. The CD is let down by the applause between sections which takes you back to a formal concert in France.

Aziza Mustafa-Zadeh

Aziza is a jazz singer and pianist who has created a distinctive synthesis of Azeri melody, classical (Bachian) piano, and jazz singing and improvisation.

★ Always
Sony, Germany
This 1993 album has the strongest Azeri character, with lively piano playing and skat singing. Features John Patitucci on bass and Dave Weckl on percussion.

⊙ Shamans
Decca, US
Aziza's brilliant performance on vocals, piano and percussion of songs which evoke the ambience of the steppes and its shamanic spiritual dimensions.

Egypt | Popular/ Street Music

satellites of love

Mulid folk band
Jak Kilby

Egyptian – and Arab – music has moved on apace with the new millennium. The illustrious tradition of classical song has given way to a revolution led by the music business giants and satellite TV. What hasn't changed, however, is the dominance of Egypt, and especially Cairo, in the Arab musical world. Not all the stars are Egyptian – there are top Cairene singers from Syria, Lebanon, Algeria and Moroccan – but they work with Egyptian composers and musicians, and sing in Egyptian Arabic (the lingua franca of Arab culture). Team Cairo – Reda el Mawi, Sam Farah, David Lodge and Bill Badley – take the pulse of the contemporary city, and look at popular Egyptian roots and rural folk traditions.

The size and confidence of the Arab market is partly responsible for Egyptians' emphatic rejection of music from other countries. The rejection of things foreign extends somewhat to Arab neighbours, too; cassettes or CDs from the Middle East (and even Algerian *rai*) are not common in the kiosks of Cairo. But the city is a supreme gathering point for **Egyptian roots**, a musical playground of cross-cutting influences and inspiration. The brassy jazz of Nubia from the hot African south plays alongside the haunting clarinet of the desert Bedouin; comic rap monologues of the Nilotic Saiyidis mix with the heart-rending tones of Classical song.

Neil van der Linden/Amr Diab

Sufi singer at a Cairo *mulid*

In this unique auditory environment – at venues ranging from the giant Sufi *zikr* street festivals to football stadium extravaganzas, from the raw theatre of a working-class wedding to a bellydance nightclub down Pyramids Road – Cairo offers Arab composers an extraordinary atmosphere for their inspiration. A word of warning, however, to anyone approaching Egyptian music for the first time. The scene is so diverse and moves so fast that almost everything changes by the time you've heard about it! If you can imagine coming to British or American music – in its entirety – as a total novice, you'll have some idea of the vista laid out before you.

Sufi Music and Trance

When the heart throbs with exhilaration and rapture becomes intense and the agitation of ecstasy is manifested and conventional forms are gone, that agitation is neither dancing nor bodily indulgence, but a dissolution of the soul.

Ibn Taymiya, writer and theologian (1263–1328)

While the religiously orthodox have long worked to keep music out of Islam, the Islamic mystics, the **Sufis**, instead sought to harness its power and turn it to the service of God. According to the ninth-century Baghdad philosopher Abu Suliman al-Darani, Sufis believe that "music and singing do not produce in the heart that which is not in it", and music "reminds the spirit of the realm for which it constantly longs". They assert that if you have moral discipline, you need have no fear of it. The Sufis thus helped to nurture Arab music through the ages when all around were doing their best to suppress it.

This "heretical" alliance of music and Islam is most intensely displayed at the giant **mulids** – festivals to celebrate the saint of a mosque – when upwards of a million worshippers and hangers-on gather together in defiance of fundamentalists and authorities alike. The union of body and music is encapsulated in the **zikr**, a dramatic ritual which uses song and dance to open a path to divine ecstasy. Sufis explain the alarming spectacle of entrancement with characteristic spiritual logic: "Music is the food of the spirit; when the spirit receives food, it turns aside from the government of the body."

To a binding hypnotic rhythm, heaving movements and respiratory groans, the leader conducts the congregation, reciting Sufi poetry, guiding them from one *maqam* mode to another. Bodies sway, heads roll upward on every stroke as they chant religious devotions with spiralling intensity. The *ney* (flute), played in a style depicted in the pharaonic tombs, alternates short, two-beat pulses on a simple melody line. Lifeless arms dangle, saliva slaps from open mouths, and eyes stare without seeing. Men collapse, convulsing, on the floor, while others run to lift them up, reciting to them verses from the Koran. The beat slows, and rows of sweating heads drop their gaze to the floor. Slowly, exhausted, the ecstatics return to the fray.

For the practising Sufi clans who have marched behind their flags and banners all the way from their village, the event is a display of clan loyalty, piety and pride. For the musicians who roam from one mulid to another throughout the year, turning popular village songs about secular love into an adoration of Mohammed the Prophet, it can also be a good living. In adaptation, these songs lose little of their earthly sexual passion: "It is he, it is only he who lives in my heart,

Rural Folk Music:
the Nile, the Desert and the Copts

Egypt is a land of many environments. The archetypal image is that of the crowded towns, villages and farmland of the Nile valley, but mountain wilderness and arid desert cover 96 percent of the country. The diversity also ranges from the European colour of the northern, Mediterranean coast to the African resonances of the south. From each geographically distinct area comes a distinct music.

Folk music in Egypt still performs a vital role in recording a popular version of history. With its own characteristic rhythms, instruments and voices, there is music to accompany almost every event, from the harvest to circumcisions. There is social criticism in the monologues about village goings-on, worship in the festival songs for Ramadhan, and mayhem in activities at weddings and mulids.

Saiyidi is the folk music of the **upper Nile valley**. Saiyidis (the name applies to the musicians as well as their music) are famous for their clever use of words and for their playful monologues set to music. The music features two instruments in particular – the *nahrasan*, a two-sided drum hung across the chest and played with sticks, and the *mismar saiyidi* trumpet. The characteristic rhythm of saiyidi, to which horses are traditionally trained to dance, is one of the most successful styles used in modern al-jil pop.

Among the best-known *saiyidi* stars are **Les Musiciens du Nil**. The 'Musicians of the Nile', a name given to them for overseas promotional purposes, are led by the singer **Met'al Gnawi**, the charismatic head of a Luxor-based Gypsy family. The group was unexpectedly chosen by the Egyptian government to act as Egypt's official folk group abroad. In Egypt he is best known for the saucy hit "Ya faraula" (My strawberry); Egyptians are fond of using fruit in sexual allegory. Another *saiyidi* star is Omar Gharzawi, known for his monologues defending *saiyidis* and their culture – they are traditionally the butt of Egyptian humour. Other names worth listening out for include **Sohar Magdy**, **Ahmed Mougahid**, **Shoukoukou** and **Ahmed Ismail**.

The folk music known as **sawahili** comes from the Mediterranean coastal area, and is characterized by the use of a guitar-like stringed instrument, the *simsimaya*, though the style found in Alexandria features the accordion. Famous sawahili singers include **Aid el-Gannirni** from Suez and **Abdou el-Iskandrani** from Alexandria.

As well as the various kinds of folk music, Egypt has two important ethnic musics – Bedouin and Nubian (see box overleaf). Bedouin music comes from the Western, Libyan desert, and the eastern arid zones of

Jak Kilby

Les Musiciens du Nil

Sinai and the Eastern desert. The main instrument is the Bedouin *mismar*, a twin-pipe clarinet which enables the player to produce a melody line and a drone simultaneously. Perhaps the best-known Bedouin singer is Awad al-Malki ("The Nightingale of the Desert.")

There is also an ancient liturgical music belonging to Egypt's **Coptic Christians** – sung in the ancient Coptic language. Its melodies and rhythm are closely linked to that of the *felahin*, the farmers of the Nile delta who have been working the soil for millennia, and it has been suggested that the extrapolated syllables of Coptic song recall the hymns of the ancient Egyptian priests. If this is so, then the melodies passed on by oral tradition, and the use by the Coptic Church of triangles and small cymbals, are the closest thing to the music of the pharaohs.

only he to whom I give my love, our beautiful Prophet, Mohammed, whose eyes are made up with kohl."

Long confined to centenary circles of religious congregations, Sufi songs gained a new status from the late 1990s, attracting a whole different legion of

followers. Young, educated, middle-class audiences now enjoy this genre in venues such as cultural centres or state theatres. Whether mere curious hanger-ons or genuine seekers of spiritual enlightenment, most of them owe their conversion to the emblematic **Yassin al-Tuhami**.

New Nubian, Old Nubian

Nubian music has its origins in the African south of Egypt, among the now displaced Nubian people. The construction of the second Aswan dam in the early 1960s – which created Lake Nasser, the largest artificial lake in the world – effectively drowned their civilization, as over 100,000 people were forcibly removed. In the wake of the flooding, the communities were transplanted south into Sudan and north into Egypt, including a significant community which moved to Cairo.

Nubian village music remains traditional, with ritual songs supported by a *daf* and hand clapping. In Cairo, it developed in new directions, forged by two opposing voices – the late **Ali Hassan Kuban** and **Mohamed Mounir** – who mirror the diverging paths of the city's Nubian migrants.

The original urban sound of Nubia came about through the music of Ali Hassan Kuban – who told of overhearing a jazz band in a Cairo nightclub, and deciding at once to add brass to his then folk-based music. Although unknown in Cairo outside the Nubian community, Kuban's unique music took him on many European tours and resulted in four internationally released albums. In Egypt, he campaigned tirelessly for the Nubian language, insisting that members of his musicians' cooperative sing in one of the two Nubian dialects. He died in June 2001 in Cairo aged 68, just after the release of *Real Nubian* on Piranha Records. His brash, urgent musical style inspired many others in Cairo, most notably **Bahr Abu Greisha** and **Hussein Bashier**.

Ali Hassan Kuban

They specialize in wild, wailing brass which lends a New Orleans feel to their sound.

Mohamed Mounir is a modern Nubian, who has produced some of the most sophisticated modern pop music in Egypt. He came to study in Cairo in the 1970s, already speaking Arabic as his first language, and considers himself an Arab Egyptian. Indeed, he is highly critical of the popular Nubian movement for a return to the homeland. His songs look for solutions to the problems of the wider Arab world – of which he feels Nubia is a part – such as the future of the Palestinians and the dilemma of Jerusalem. His home audience is dominated by students who appreciate his lyrics.

Mohamed Mounir

In the wider World Music market, **Hamza el-Din** is synonymous with Nubian music – in no small part due to the fact that he was resident in the West for thirty years until his death in 2006. Like those of Ali Hassan Kuban, his songs are deeply affected by the sense of alienation that many Nubians feel. He has collaborated with a number of Western musicians, notably the Kronos Quartet whose arrangement of his "The Water Wheel" is one of the highlights of their delightful *Pieces of Africa* album.

A younger Nubian fusionist is **Mahmoud Fadl** – an incredibly accomplished percussionist. He has worked with musicians from varying backgrounds and draws on South American influences as well as his own Arab/African roots – an alluring brew that has been particularly well received in Europe.

The elaborate poetry of Sheikh Omar Ibn al-Faridh, recited in the unique, informal style of al-Tohami, was drawing crowds from poor country villages and university campuses alike. And al-Tohami was soon to become the voice of Egyptian Sufism, performing in Europe and Latin America. Thanks to him, the once-forgotten mulid of Ibn al-Faridh, in the foothills of al-Mokattam in Cairo, became the gathering place of a new breed of Sufi enthusiasts – many of them Westerners – mingling with the usual crowd of dervishes and *zikr* dancers.

Bride and Home

A working-class (*baladi*) **wedding** in a cramped alley in central Cairo is possibly the finest exhibition of spontaneous musical theatre you can witness anywhere. On Friday and Saturday nights, the city becomes a patchwork of pulsing coloured light and searing noise, as the elaborate ritual of the marriage party gets under way.

First comes the *Hassabala* troupe, bugles and trumpets blaring (a style inspired by imperial British marching bands), who form a circle of up to

25 thundering wooden drums. Into this vortex of chanting and deafening rhythm go the whirling dancers and a stick-cracking folklore troupe from Upper Egypt. Once the bride and groom have been escorted away in a cacophony of noise, the music stops abruptly and the group dashes hurriedly into a waiting van which takes them hooting across town to their next appointment, possibly their fourth or fifth of the night.

Then the real party begins. A riotously made-up dancer laden with glittering sequins takes to the small stage, cavorting with the master of ceremonies, lifting her dress a little, pushing out her leg, lying on the floor and gyrating, rubbing up against him, playfully controlling the arena. This is **raks sharki – belly-dancing**. The dancer sings with flaying alto vocals – pop songs, classical songs, traditional songs, all made raw and raunchy. The makeshift stage becomes a platform too for the guests who wave banknotes in their bids to stay in the limelight, to dance, sing or play the fool, with unselfconscious bravado and humour. More than just honouring the bride and her father, this stream of musical cameos is all part of the drama that provides an outlet for the tensions that build up in the tight-knit community.

It is on these occasions that men may choose to settle lingering disputes, dedicating their advice, threats and guarded insults via the stage to their rivals in a furiously fast interchange. Up leaps a boy with a fistful of banknotes held high: he makes his greeting, echoed by the MC in a rapid, musical rap. "Greetings to the police, especially the police of Saiyida Zeynab who are our friends, greetings to the youth of Kal'aa, greetings to the people of Hussein. We want this wedding to be nice with no trouble." After a stream of appeals to family and friends, and a short break of music from the five-piece band lining the back of the stage, another singer, dressed in evening suit and tie, takes over, slowly wailing "Ya leil ya ein" (Oh! the night, Oh! my eyes!), a wild improvisation that pierces the dark from a deafening, distorted PA.

Music of the Youth

In Cairo, until as recently as the late 1980s, from every taxi radio-cassette deck and every street corner kiosk, day and night, emerged the haunting voice of Umm Kulthum or other Classical Arab superstars. While this music has far from disappeared, it is not as ubiquitous as it once was (though Umm Kulthum is still listened to constantly by expat Egyptians in the Gulf). Today, cassette and CD shops and fast cars are stocked up with other types of music, and commercial competition is intense among the hundreds of artists. The new sounds of Egyptian youth – **shaabi** (a kind of blues-folk) and **shababi** (Arab pop) – are the music of two social revolutions shaping the nation's modern outlook.

Pressure for change in the musical world of Cairo had been building up for some time, and the established music order could do little more than look on as an entirely new Egypt unfurled before them. Since the mid-1970s its Sadat's "open door policy" had welcomed Western business, which gave birth to a new enterprise culture in the big cites. In addition, the Gulf states and Iraq provided new work for millions of Egyptian labourers, craftsmen and technicians who sent back their pay cheques to create, in effect, a new urban middle class.

With their new-found spending power, this rapidly expanding social group has reinvented Cairo in their own image, complete with take-out food stalls, ear-splitting in-car hi-fi and, of course, street-corner kiosks crammed with their music. And their music, while taking inspiration from Arab Classical song, is essentially a reassertion of folk traditions, reaffirming Egyptian identity at a time of momentous and rapid change.

Shaabi – Art from the Workers

The humiliating defeat by Israel in 1967 shattered the pan-Arab dream of President Nasser, forcing Egyptians to face stark reality. From this abject poverty and humiliation they escaped into a new 'light song', which drew on folkloric themes to reassert a proud Egyptian identity. It was a movement away from the serious classical hue of tradition and towards a more humorous, even salacious spirit. At first this was a middle-class initiative, with singers like **Layla Nasmy** and **Aida al-Sha'er** popularizing these forms for the respectable community. But soon it gave way to working-class singers – and words from the present-day. This was **shaabi** (people's) music, and it found its heart in the working-class areas of Cairo – some of the most overcrowded communities in the world.

Shaabi singers specialise in the **mawal**, a freely improvised vocal in which the singer impresses on the listener the depth of his or her sorrowful complaint. It's a form which is found widely in Classical Arab music, although in a more refined style, and bears comparison with other 'folk-blues' like *fado* or *rebétika*. But *shaabi* songs aren't all sorrow: the traditional progression has a fast rhythmic beat emerging from the improvisation, to take the song through chorus after chorus to climax in a rousing dance tempo. These make the form perfect for both wedding celebrations and nightclubs.

The first *shaabi* singer to break into the mass market, in 1971, was the charismatic **Ahmed Adaweyah**. His lyrical irreverence, using the rough dialect of the streets, was the essence of his revolution. This kind of language had never been heard in song before and it came over, essentially, as a weapon of the working class, affirming their own values while mocking respectable society. Adaweyah's song "Setu" (composed by Farouk Salama with lyrics by Hassan abu-Atma), is a good example, poking fun at a middle-class lifestyle:

> Fast asleep he's fasting,
> He doesn't want to bother.
> And his granny and mummy are mothering him
> With honey and butter.
> Finally, but not that final,
> He's a weapon without a bullet,
> A failure at school and no good at work.

Full of metaphor and comical twists, Adaweyah's songs stamped *shaabi* character with the release of every cassette. His lifestyle and personality matched them; coming from a poor and uneducated background, he was a true working-class hero.

Adaweyah's provocative social commentaries served to hang Egypt's dirty linen in public, which didn't go down well with the government and ruling class, fearful that it would reinforce the popular Gulf Arab image of Egypt as an uncultured society. When, in 1991, Adaweyah received a surprise invitation to appear on TV (for the first time), his remarks were bleeped out, while songs with suggestive lyrics, or those that implied an immoral lifestyle, were banned.

One 1992 *shaabi* song, with the lines – "Her waist is like the neck of a violin, I used to enjoy apricots but now I would die for mangoes!" – caused an outcry among the middle class, raised on the sung poetry of Umm Kulthum. The song was banned, but the cassette was nevertheless available everywhere, sold upwards of half a million, and, with its euphemistic fruitiness, became a favourite of the gay community.

Equally unpopular with the censors is the emergence of the lyrical theme of political assertiveness. In his album *Ana Bakrah Israeel* (I hate Israel, released in the height of the second Palestinian Intifada), **Shaaban Abdel-Reheem** claimed that he was reflecting "the pulse of the street". This is an example of the lyrics that have launched his nationwide celebrity:

> I hate Israel, and am saying it out loud
> Even if I have to die, or be incarcerated
> It hates peace and loves destruction
> They are holding guns, while the others are holding lemons
> What have the heroes who are killed every day done wrong?
> The Egyptian people are sad, and their tears are flowing.

The word on the street is that because he praised the former minister of foreign affairs, Amr Mussa, in this song before President Mubarak, Mussa was vindictively dismissed from his position.

In the late 1980s, as Japanese VCRs and American films became established in back-alley society, so the younger generation was seduced into a world of foreign, modernizing values. Younger singers developed a fascination with the musical gadgetry of the West, and synthetic sounds began challenging the claim that shaabi was the only authentic Egyptian music. In the 1980s, on top of the traditional violins, tabla and squeeze-box were added drumkit, organ, synthesizer, saxophone and electric guitar. In the 1990s, beat boxes and samplers became more commonplace than traditional Arab instruments.

As the shaabi stars attempt to reach a wider public with their increasingly slick product, production values are more and more critically assessed. The shaabi form has also been "air-brushed" for radio and video consumption by artists like **Amr Diab** and **Hakim** – the new mainstream Egyptian popular artists.

Shababi

In the 1970s, fed up with listening to The Beatles, Abba and Boney M in a language they couldn't understand, the youth of Egypt decided they could do better. With the aid of samplers and quarter-tone programmes, Egyptian pop music – *shababi* (youthful) music – was born. It was a revolutionary development. The dance music that they produced bore the hallmarks of the Arab sound – trained, controlled voices sliding through infectious happy melodies, and distinctive, clear-as-a-bell backing chorus – but it was performed to a punchy techno-Arab beat.

Central to the movement was a young Libyan, **Hamid el-Shaeri**. Fleeing one of Gaddafi's anti-Western purges, Hamid came to Egypt in 1974 and started working with Egyptians on a new sound. He finally hit gold dust in 1988 with the song "Lolaiki" (If it wasn't for you), recorded in a back room, which sold in millions. It was sung

Shaabi Superstars

Shaabi stars tend to break through at local weddings and festivals, then, as they become famous, move on to engagements at nightclubs and big private weddings in Egypt and the Gulf. Below is a round-up of the main figures and some ideas on recordings to seek out. Note that although there are many shaabi cassettes and CDs available in Cairo, they tend to be transitory compilations, and you usually need to ask for a particular song rather than an album title.

Ahmed Adaweyah

Shaabi's first superstar was **Ahmed Adaweyah**, who remains the finest exponent of the thick, soulful tones of *mawal*. There are also numerous tapes of his with the title *Mawal Adaweyah*, each featuring a lengthy, heart-rending vocal improvisation. *Al-Tarik* (The Route) is one of his finest cassettes. Another pioneer of shaabi was **Kat Kut el-Amir**, who is remembered chiefly for the song "Ya Gazelle el-Darb il Ahmar" (You Gazelle of Darb il-Ahmar – an old quarter of Cairo), composed for a big private wedding.

The working-class hero **Shaaban Abdel-Reheem**, is outrageous, raw, repetitive, shocking, yet almost vulnerably unsophisticated. He is decidedly shunned by the establishment and looked down upon by almost everyone outside his immediate, if huge, following. But he seems to shrug it off, accepting that he's not "an artist", but a simple man of the people. Shaaban is famous for rapping wisdoms about life, as he celebrates his rise from ironing man to superstar. He speaks and sings his mind, which simply echoes what goes in the minds of millions around Egypt. Despite selling hundreds of thousands of copies of each release, wearing gold chains and two gold watches (one on each wrist "because he can afford it"), has yet truly to change him. Still singing at weddings and private functions, he lives in his "village" on the outskirts of Cairo, where he maintains a traditional lifestyle and keeps chickens and goats on his roof.

As two of the leading stars of **shababi music**, the multi-million-selling phenomena that are **Amr Diab** and **Hakim** are still going strong, thanks to their clever choice of catchy tunes, their good looks and the marketing machine humming along, almost audibly (yet very efficiently), behind them. **Ehab Tawfik**, one of the protégés of earlier icon **Hamid el-Shaeri**, has now eclipsed his mentor and is considered a front-line star in his own right. **Mostafa Amar**, also liberated from his early emulation of **Mohammed Munir**, portrays the eternal heart throb singer on stage and on screen.

Shaaban Abdel-Reheem

by a friend, **Ali Hamaida**, who, to the great relief of many, turned out to be a one-hit wonder (the song was okay once or twice, but all over town for a year...):

If It wasn't for you I'd never sing,
If it wasn't for you I'd never fall in love.
I have nobody without you.
You are my light and my sight,
My song Is only for you,
Lolaiki lo lo lo lo lo lo lo lo lo.

Lyrical themes of "boy flirts with girl, girl leaves boy, boy is miserable/finds new girl" did little to win over the older generation, but the popularity of the new feel-good scene couldn't fail to impress upon the established cultural guardians the strength of this new youth movement. The rags-to-riches story of "Lolaiki" also impressed the back-street entrepreneurs, and the new industry exploded overnight.

To the older generation, the new music-makers were little more than businessmen selling cheap

New Media, New Values

While the state was losing its monopoly on information to the newly launched satellite channels such as **al-Jazeera**, the music scene witnessed a burgeoning of numerous free-to-air Arabic satellite music channels. **Mazzica**, **Dream** and **Melody**'s hunger for fresh talents and video clips boosted the industry on an unprecedented scale. **Rotana**, the Saudi-owned music conglomerate, fuelled its own channels with in-house productions, contracting mostly Egyptian and Lebanese singers.

Radio waves, the hitherto exclusive playground of the state, witnessed the birth of newcomers that soon made obsolete the state radio format. **Nujoom FM** (Stars FM) and **Nile One**, which broadcast respectively Arabic and Western pop, adopted an upbeat, fast-paced rhythm, unknown to existing government-run stations.

They started soon after the launching of **Radio Sawa**, the brainchild of the US Broadcasting Board of Governors, with the self-confessed objective of promoting the American value-system after 9/11. Endowed with a budget of thirty million dollars, it broadcasts Western and shababi songs to most of the Middle East, with short segments of news analysis. The degree of success of its mission has yet to be assessed.

With the expansion of the musical scene across satellite channels, there is a veritable army of Arab stars competing with Egyptians for air time. Some of them are based in Cairo, such as the Moroccan **Samira Saeed** and **Latifa al-Arfawi** from Tunisia. But the invaders are arguably led by **Lebanese stars**, such as **Ragheb Alama**, **Diana Haddad**, **Elissa**, **Nancy Ajram** and **Haifa Wahbe**. Their Trojan horse, understandably, is that they, too, sing in the Egyptian dialect.

But surveying this changing landscape of popular music, you can't help but notice that this is the age of the **diva**. Arabic pop is certainly being dominated, thus far in the twenty-first century, by women. This explosion of satellite channels has focused the eyes, rather than ears, of the Egyptian music industry on introducing its own female sex symbols. The result is the emergence of stars like **Shereen** and **Ruby**. Like Diab, their music is polished (although Ruby's is arguably rawer and more shaabi), but far more sexual. Shereen was the revelation of 2002 with her hit song "Ah Ya Leil", which introduced her as an alternative *shaabi* singer. She soon moved towards the pop scene, adopting a more air-brushed image.

Such diva's song lyrics are no longer about begging the cruel, deserting and thoroughly undeserving, beloved man to come back and have pity. A lot of contemporary love-song lyrics are dismissive of the need for a man or his influence over his girlfriend or wife.

Samira Saeed

---

produce in the market. Gone were the intricate melodies, beautiful poetry, sympathetic use of *maqams* and natural sounds, and in came the rasping synthesizer and the three-minute pop-song format.

The shababi scene has also impacted on the European dance scene, in a number of crossover projects. Chief among them is the work that has been done by Tim Whelan and Hamid Mantu of London-based **Transglobal Underground**, who have immersed themselves in the Cairo music scene to great effect, as shown by their production contributions to **Natacha Atlas**'s CDs and a remix album of Hakim's best-known songs. Atlas (whose father is Egyptian) herself spent many years based in Cairo, soaking up the city's music. Her recent albums have developed this West-East synthesis.

Never one to miss out on a marketing opportunity, Amr Diab also put out a dance-remix album based on his ubiquitous hit, "Habibi". Hakim followed suit a few years later, and recorded the hit "Lela" with James Brown, which alternates between the respective styles of the two singers.

Finally, one ex-patriot Egyptian musician worthy of note is percussionist **Hossam Ramzy**. Born in Cairo, he lived in Saudi Arabia in the early years of his career before moving to England, where he worked for many years as a session musician and collaborator in Latin, jazz and pop styles with the likes of Peter Gabriel, Chick Corea and Robert Plant and Jimmy Page. He has recorded prolifically, and his most recent work has found him returning increasingly to his roots, as on the 2001 album *Rahhal* with the Gypsies of the Nile.

To get contemporary Egyptian releases, you'll need to check Arab-owned stores in major cities, or, of course, buy in Cairo. Even so, it's hard to make recommendations as they tend to be ephemeral compilations.

⊙ Egypt: La Châdhiliya – Sufi Chants from Cairo
Institut du Monde Arabe, France
A 1999 recording of members of the al-Hamidiyah al-Shadhiliyah Brotherhood, a relatively recent offshoot (founded 1906) of the thirteenth-century Shadhiliyah order.

★ Egypt – Music of the Nile from the Desert to the Sea
Virgin, France
A tall-format box-booklet with two CDs, that sets out to cover Egyptian music in all its forms, historic and present. It does a pretty good job, featuring singers from Umm Kulthum to Hamed, and a good range of instrumentalists, including Ali Hassan Kuban and Les Musiciens du Nile.

⊙ Mozart l'Egyptien
EMI/Virgin Classics, UK
Mozart's fascination with oriental mysticism is translated here by a blend of extracts from some of his greatest works (*The Magic Flute*, *The Abduction from the Seraglio*, etc) with rural arrangements from the north of Egypt (by Les Musiciens du Nile), or *dhikr* and Coptic hymns.

★ The Rough Guide to the Music of Egypt
World Music Network, UK
This compilation does justice to most of the prevailing genres produced by Cairo's music industry. The tracks range from Angham's ballads to Amr Diab's slick, flamenco-tinged disco and the New Age atmospherics of Mohamed Mounir.

Natacha Atlas

The success of her work, both in the Middle East and in the West, is a tribute to her efforts in bridging the divide between Arabic and Western music.

⊙ The Best of Natacha Atlas
Mantra Recordings, UK
A decent 2005 round-up of her work including "Eye Of the Duck", plus distinctive covers of "You Only Live Twice" and "I Put A Spell On You" as well as a possibly excessive three versions of "Leysh Nat'Arak".

Amr Diab

Like him or not, Amr Diab is the quintessential shaabi superstar of the Arab world and a role model for an emerging youth culture.

⊙ Kammel Kalamak
Rotana, Saudi Arabia
On this 2005 album, Amr introduces himself as a composer for the first time ("Kol sana wenta tayeb", "Agheeb Agheeb").

El Tanbura

Port Said isn't one of Egypt's most beautiful cities, but it has a great musical attraction in this local band who've been in existence since 1994. Assembled by Zakaria Ibrahim, who runs the El Mastaba Centre for Egyptian Folk Music in Cairo, what makes El Tanbura distinctive is the ancient *simsimiyya*

harp which looks like something out of a Pharaonic tomb painting and makes a funky backing to their songs.

★ The Simsimiyya of Port Said
Institut du Monde Arabe, France
Debut recording from 1999 of El Tanbura's traditional and Sufi repertoire with powerful vocals over lively percussion and plucked *simsimiyya* grooves.

⊙ Between the Desert and the Sea
World Village, US
A fresh album from 2006 that's getting the band noticed internationally, including "Zayy El Nhardah (The Canal Song)" written for the 50th anniversary of the nationalisation of the Suez Canal and quotes Nasser's cry 'Get up and take your freedom' which precipitated the 1956 Suez Crisis.

Hakim

Hakim is another million-selling teen heart-throb, with rather rougher edges than Amr Diab. Still going strong in Egypt, he has in recent years looked further afield in one-off collaborations with the likes of James Brown and Stevie Wonder.

⊙ Lela
EMI Arabia, Egypt
The title-track is the collaboration with James Brown, but Hakim doesn't depart from his trademark shaabi style.

Les Musiciens du Nil

Les Musiciens du Nil, drawn mainly from a Luxor Gypsy family, have been stars of the rural *saiyidi* style since the 1970s. They are still regulars on the international World Music festival circuit and have managed to preserve their authenticity.

⊙ Charcoal Gypsies
Real World, UK
This 1997 album features the group's standard instruments like *argul* and *rebab* with African and Middle Eastern percussion. It's clearly cousin to the music of more northerly Gypsies, and it's easy to see why they starred in the film *Latcho Drom*, about the roots of Gypsy music.

Ruby

After sending out shockwaves with her sensational videos, Ruby has begun to get recognition for her singing talents.

⊙ Fein Habibi
MSM, Egypt
The defiant lyrics on this 2004 album mark her out as a leader amongst the new breed of Egyptian female singers.

Mokhtar al-Said and El Ferka el-Masaya

Mokhtar al-Said is a top Cairene arranger; El Ferka el-Masaya (Orchestra of Diamonds) have accommpanied many of the great classical singers.

⊙ Amar 14: Jalilah's Raks Sharki 2
Piranha, Germany
Raks sharki is belly-dance music, and this is the classic orchestral "oriental" sound, by turns portentous and playful.

Nubian music

Hamza el-Din

A Europe-based fusionist for the last thirty years, Hamza el-Din's performances were much more sparse than many of his fellow Nubians. He has collaborated with the Kronos Quartet and others.

⊙ **Escalay – The Water Wheel**
Nonesuch, US
A fine example of Hamza el-Din's poised *oud* playing and rich voice.

Mahmoud Fadl

A master drummer who was born in Old Nubia. He founded the group Salamat and his numerous collaborators include Ahmed Adaweyah and the late Ali Hassan Kuban, plus of course his group The Drummers of the Nile.

J. Listen Man/Piranha

⊙ **The Drummers of the Nile in Town**
Piranha Records, Germany
This 2003 album is the third in a series of albums with The Drummers of the Nile and finds them back in Cairo, where they teamed up with accordionist Mohsen Allam and the *mizmar* ensemble The Khalil Family, among others. It's also a rare chance to hear the near-extinct traditions of the Hasaballah Brass Band.

Ali Hassan Kuban

Ali Hassan Kuban was a pioneer of urban Nubian music, introducing brass and other jazz elements. He became quite a star on the World Music circuit before his untimely death in 2001.

⊙ **Real Nubian**
Piranha Records, Germany
On this last album by the Godfather of Nubian Soul, he is supported by singer Salwa Abou Greisha, well known from her Piranha albums with Salamat and Mahmoud Fadl.

Mohamed Mounir

Mounir is a kind of singer-songwriter, with political pan-Arab lyrics. He sings in Arabic rather than Nubian.

★ **Ahmar Shafayef**
Mondo Melodia, US
On this 2002 album, Mounir still alternates between his Nubian roots and the more mainstream Egyptian love ballads. His style also carries a sharp political edge reflected in the words.

1 **KAMMEL KALAMAK Amr Diab** from *Kammel Kalamak*
Voted "Best Song of the Year 2005" by the listeners of Nogoom FM, a leading radio station.

2 **HALO ALEINA Mahmoud Fadl** from *The Drummers of the Nile in Town*
This rhythm is used at weddings to welcome the guests, and here features the sinuous clarinet, trumpet, sax and snare drum of the Hasaballah Brass Band.

3 **YOU ONLY LIVE TWICE Natacha Atlas** from *The Best of Natacha Atlas*
A rendition of the famous James Bond theme by John Barry and Leslie Bricusse, produced and arranged here by David Arnold.

4 **LEIH BIDARI KEDAH Ruby** from *Fein Habibi*
Addictive stuff from she who offends the older generation while thrilling the youth.

5 **AH MEN HALWTU Hakim** from *Lela*
Produced by Narada Michael, this song features Stevie Wonder on harmonica.

6 **SUQ AL-MANADI Les Musiciens du Nil** from *Charcoal Gypsies*
A traditional theme evoking a local rural market. Showcases the virtuosity of the group with the *rababa*, the horsehair-stringed instrument.

7 **GAMMAL (CAMEL DRIVER) Ali Hassan Kuban** from *Real Nubian*
This traditional Bedouin song immitates the gait of a camel and features accordion, *ney* and *oud* backing Ali Hassan Kuban's rather weary-sounding vocal.

8 **EKRAR Mohamed Mounir** from *Ahmar Shafayef*
A love declaration in Munir's own lyrical style.

Salamat

A Nubian group featuring Mahmoud Fadl and others, some of whom also appeared with Ali Hassan Kuban. With lyrics in Arabic, this is a less politicized, more good-time sound than Kuban's.

⊙ **Mambo El Soudani – Nubian Al Jeel Music from Cairo and Ezzayakoum**
Piranha, Germany
Strong whiffs of Sudan drift through these thumping songs, dense with hysterical alto-sax, tenor sax and trumpet.

Georgia

a musical toast

Duduk players on a Tbilisi mural
Simon Broughton

Transcaucasia is a region that has somehow got caught in the cracks between bigger geopolitical forces. When they were part of the USSR, Georgia, Armenia and Azerbaijan at least had some stability, but with independence that has broken down. With its lucrative oil reserves, Azerbaijan has fared well, but Georgia and Armenia, two Christian countries perched in a sort of no man's land between Europe and the Middle East, have suffered economic and political problems, on occasion warfare. Were it not for internal conflict, a history of corruption and proximity to the war in Chechnya, Georgia has everything it needs to be a tourist paradise: spectacular mountains, historic monuments, great food, and wine and a simply glorious traditional music. Simon Broughton raises a toast, which in Georgia has to be accompanied by music.

Georgia became the second Christian state in the world in 337 AD when Queen Nana and then her husband King Mirian III were converted to Christianity by St Nino of Cappadocia. King Trdates of Armenia, to the south, had adopted Christianity thirty years earlier. For both countries, the Christian faith is integral to their national identity, and Georgians have a sumptuous polyphonic choral tradition, unlike anything else in the region, in which they celebrate it. Georgian polyphony was proclaimed a Masterpiece of the Oral and Intangible Heritage of Humanity by UNESCO when they introduced the designation in 2001. The "intangible" equivalent of the World Heritage Sites, this designation is supposed to recognize traditional and popular expressions of 'exceptional value from an artistic, historical and anthropological point of view'.

Table Songs

As the Georgians tell it, when God was distributing land amongst the peoples of the earth, the Georgians were too busy drinking and feasting to turn up on time. When they arrived there was nothing left. "But Lord", they protested, "we were only late because we were toasting You." God was so touched by this that he gave them the land he was keeping for Himself – warm, fertile and fringed by the spectacularly beautiful Caucasus mountains. With feasting celebrated in a national myth, it's not surprising that it's the principal occasion for music making.

The traditional Georgian feast is led by a toastmaster (*tamada*) who proposes toasts according to certain accepted rules and customs. The first toast is always to God (not surprising given the national myth) and if there's music the first song will be in praise of God. The second toast is to long life and goes hand in hand with the ubiquitous "Mravaljamieri", a hymn of praise to life. The alternation of toasts and songs continues and the *tamada* embroiders each toast with philosophical statements or snippets of wisdom.

Toasts and music are often poetically linked. For instance, a toast to ancestors and elders might be followed by "Zamtari", a song about winter, the notion being that it's a celebration of people in the "winter" of their life.

As well as religious songs and specific table songs, **work songs** that were originally for harvesting or ploughing are now sung around the table. There's a beautiful type of ploughing song, *orovela*, that is found only in eastern Georgia. It's not polyphonic and sounds distinctly Armenian in character, with a narrow-range, melancholic solo line over a drone bass.

Polyphony

Georgian **polyphony** is usually in three parts and is generally sung by men, although women's groups do exist. Mixed groups are unusual since Georgian music tends to end on a unison note and the octaves produced with mixed voices are usually avoided. Often the main "melody" of the polyphony is sung by the middle voice, with the upper and lower voices either supporting it or weaving complex counter-melodies around it. In a mountainous country where contact is often difficult, styles vary from region to region, but the clearest differences can be heard between the east and the west.

The richest, most sonorous style is in the eastern region of **Kakhetia**. The area is famous for its wine, so it's not surprising that the best table and drinking songs originate here. Kakhetian singing has two solo voices intertwining with each other over a slowly moving drone bass sung by the rest of the singers. There are shimmering clashes and dissonances, tensions and releases, as the harmonies collide like tectonic plates. "Chakrulo", one of the most beautiful of Kakhetian drinking songs, was one of the pieces of earthly music chosen to go into space on the *Voyager* spacecraft in 1977 – almost a re-run of that national myth.

In the western regions of **Guria** and **Mengrelia** the bass lines are much more athletic and the whole style more virtuosic. Here the dissonances that sound so strange to Western ears but are so beloved in Georgian music seem even more acute. The men sing in a higher "head-voice" and a soloist indulges in a spectacular yodelling called *krimanchuli* with striking leaps and rhythmic patterns. The ancient Greek historian Xenophon wrote in the fourth century BC that the Georgians prepared themselves for battle by singing, and maybe this

Simon Broughton

Svanetian singers with *changi*

is the sort of thing he had in mind. These songs, which may include four independent voice parts, have become favourite showpieces for the professional choirs that perform Georgian songs on the concert platform. There are many historical songs and epics in this western style.

In the remote northern region of **Svanetia** the oldest traditions have survived. High in the Caucasus and cut off by snow for seven or eight months of the year, Svan culture escaped many of the invasions that affected the rest of Georgia throughout the centuries. The villages of Upper Svanetia still have spectacular medieval-style towers, as well as customs and rituals that have their origin in pre-Christian times. At wedding feasts here, toasts are drunk from a ram's horn – as depicted in the canvases of Georgia's celebrated artist Pirosmani – a practice that tends to be purely nostalgic elsewhere in the country. The music sounds distinctly archaic and severe. The harmony – angular and unpredictable – is in three parts with the middle voice leading. The range of each voice is narrow and all three parts move together syllable by syllable. Ritual songs to the sun and to St George are hugely popular in Svanetia and the Svans are famous for both their rhythmic round dances and, in a completely different character, their moving funeral laments. There's also an ancient Svanetian harp (*changi*) and a bowed viol (*chuniri*) which are sometimes used to accompany the voices.

Professional Choirs

Other old instruments like the three-string lute (*panduri*) of eastern Georgia and the four-string lute (*chonguri*) of western Georgia that are rarely used in practice are often used by **professional choirs** in Georgia who have taken up this repertoire. The most celebrated and prolific is the **Rustavi Choir**, created in 1968 by **Anzor Erkomaishvili**, who is descended from a long line of Georgian singers.

Booking a Band Georgian-Style

On an old winding street above the Metekhi church in old Tbilisi there's a place that looks like a cross between a tea-house and a taxi firm. You can't miss it because above the entrance are vivid paintings in the naive style of Georgia's most famous painter, Pirosmani. The pictures show musicians with pink and bulging cheeks blowing into *duduks* and striking drums. A notice declares it to be the "Centre for Players of Oriental Instruments".

Going in, it's much quieter than you expect. No puffing cheeks or wild drumming. Not an oriental instrument to be seen. Just a few guys drinking tea, reading the paper or playing dominoes. A man at a desk by the door is on the phone and jotting down notes in a ledger. But when the call comes to say, "We're having a little get-together to celebrate my son's engagement. Could you send some of your lads over to get things going?" these musicians will be round faster than a kiss-o-gram. For Georgians, music is an essential ingredient of any celebration. You can see them at the weekend dining al fresco in local beauty spots and, if they're not bursting out with their own homemade polyphonic singing, there'll be an instrumental trio wandering from group to group. This office in Tbilisi is here to provide music for weddings, birthdays – in fact, any sort of celebration.

The "oriental" instruments are *duduks*, clarinets and drums – instruments the Georgians have picked up from their Transcaucasian neighbours, the Armenians and Azeris. The tunes range from wild dances on clarinet and accordion with an insistent rhythm beaten out on a drum, to soft, reflective songs played by a couple of *duduks*. The instruments themselves are kept in the wooden lockers that line the walls, so they can be grabbed quickly when the musicians are needed in a hurry.

Simon Broughton

The Bureau: Dial-A-Duduk

Erkomaishvili is careful to gather members from all the regions of the country to keep the singing styles as authentic as possible. Of course, the performances are rather polished, but to hear them in concert (or on disc) is a surprisingly impressive experience. The group **Georgian Voices** are also strongly recommended. **Erisioni**, led by Djemal Chkuaseli, is more of a national song and dance troupe who've recently been touring a *River Dance*-type show called *Georgian Legend* in Western Europe and the US. Most interesting is **Mtiebi**, a collection of amateur singers led by Edisher Garakanidze who sing in a much more spontaneous way – not like a professional ensemble on stage and more like a group of family and friends. They also do a good line in romantic urban songs accompanied by guitar.

Suliko

I was looking for the grave of my beloved.
It was difficult to find.
With sorrow in my heart I cried:
Where are you, my Suliko?

The nightingale pining away
Concealed herself in the leaves of a tree.
I asked her in a sweet voice:
Is it you, Suliko?

The poetess shook her wings
And lightly touched a blossom with her beak
Sighing and chirping
As if she wanted to tell me: Yes, it is!

Words by Akaki Tsereteli

Urban Songs

Although polyphonic songs can be heard round the table of a high-rise flat in Tbilisi as well as at a village wedding in Svanetia, there's a very different style of "**urban music**" to be heard on every car radio-cassette player in Georgia or in the bars of downtown Tbilisi. Replacing the idiosyncratic harmonies of Georgian polyphony are sentimental songs – with infectiously hummable melodies, simple Western harmony and guitar accompaniment. The most famous song of the genre is "**Suliko**", a sad ballad of lost love immortalized as Stalin's favourite song (Stalin was a Georgian and is not unadmired, even now). The greatest of these urban groups was the **Tsisperi Trio**, sadly no longer active, although there are recordings of them still around.

A rougher and livelier sort of music is played (and sung) by instrumental groups around Georgia. They often feature a clarinet or a pair of *duduks* (*duduki*, soft reedy oboes of Armenian origin) accompanied by an accordion and a double-headed drum (*doli*). The music is wild, raucous and very compelling. Similar groups can be found throughout the Transcaucasian region.

DISCOGRAPHY Georgia

⊙ **Drinking Horns and Gramophones 1902–1914**
Traditional Crossroads, US
A remarkable collection of recordings of nine different choirs made by the Gramophone Company of Great Britain, who set up shop in Tbilisi in 1901 and sold 78rpm record players and recordings until 1914. Gigo Erkomaishvili (1840–1907), great-grandfather of Anzor Erkomaishvili (director of the Rustavi Choir), directs the Makvaneti Choir in seven songs.

⊙ **Georgia: Polyphony of Svanetia**
Chant du Monde, France
Quite a specialized – but fascinating – collection of field recordings made in 1991 by Sylvie Bolle-Zemp. The best survey of genuine Svanetian music on disc, with comprehensive notes.

⊙ **Georgie: chants de travail – chants religieux**
Ocora, France
Work songs and religious music recorded in 1977. Not easy listening, but the real thing. Rarely heard intensely rhythmic

naduri work songs, hymns and ritual songs from various districts and Svanetian hymns to the sun and St George as well as a funeral lament. The notes verge on the unintelligible.

⊙ **The Golden Fleece: Songs from Abkhazia and Adzharia**
Pan, Netherlands
Rare recordings of music from two distinct regions of western Georgia. The Abkhazian recordings were made in 1987 and 1991 with various folklore ensembles and feature instruments and repertoire different from other regions of Georqia. This is the land of plenty where, according to legend, Jason went in search of the Golden Fleece. The Adzharian repertoire, recorded in 1971, is closer to the Georgian style. Good notes.

★ **Soinari: Folk Music from Georgia Today**
Welt Musik/Schott Wergo, Germany
The best collection of "urban music" available in the West, featuring three ensembles. Soinari play *duduks*, accordion and *doli* drum; Mzetamze is a group of women who perform

"Suliko" and other songs; and Mtiebi perform urban songs as well as traditional polyphonic songs in a less professional, more authentic style.

Riho Ensemble

An ensemble of about a dozen singers from the Mestia region, led by Islam Pilpani and dedicated to singing the distinctive folk music of Svanetia.

⊙ Vocal Polyphonies from Svanetia
Inédit, France

Svanetian harmonies and vocal style take some getting used to, but this is a great selection of this ancient rugged music. "Lile" is an hymn to the sun and "Lazhghvazh" is a ritual song, performed here with bowed *chuniri* and *changi* harp.

Rustavi Choir

Georgia's most famous choir (about twelve strong), the Rustavi is renowned for its professional performances of polyphonic songs from all over the country. It was founded in 1986 by Anzor Erkomaishvili who still leads the ensemble. They have recorded more than a dozen CDs on various labels.

⊙ Georgia
Network, Germany

Eighteen folk and religious songs from various parts of the country, a couple with *changi* or *chonguri* accompaniment. As an added bonus there are six tracks from the Duduki Trio featuring mainly urban repertoire. A good combination.

★ Georgian Voices
Nonesuch Explorer, US

Fourteen tracks giving the best introduction to the various styles of Georgian singing. A couple of beautiful church chorales, Kakhetia's best drinking song, "Chakrulo", an *orovela*, Svanetia's strange "Lashgvash" march and spectacular vocal acrobatics from the Guria region. All songs acapella.

PLAYLIST
Georgia

1 **TSMINDAO CHMERTO** Rustavi Choir from *Georgian Voices*
With its shifting and clashing harmonies, this religious chorale transports you into the world of Georgian polyphony and religious architecture.

2 **CHAKRULO** Tsinandali Choir from *Table Songs of Georgia*
If it's good enough for the *Voyager* spacecraft then it's good enough for this playlist! The essential Kakhetian drinking song.

3 **LAZHGVAZH** Riho Ensemble from *Vocal Polyphonies from Svanetia*
The quintessential Svanetian song, with strange craggy harmonies and ancient instrumental accompaniment.

4 **ZAMTARIA** Mtiebi from *Soinari: Folk Music from Georgia Today*
A lovely melancholy song about winter, with guitar accompaniment.

5 **SULIKO** Tsisperi Trio from *Georgian Urban Songs*
Georgia's catchiest tune, as rendered by Tbilisi's greatest crooners.

⊙ Mirangula: Georgian Folk Songs
St Petersburg Classics/Sony, UK

This collection of eighteen songs takes its name from a sad Svanetian song accompanied here by *chuniri* and *changi*. Other songs from western Georgia are accompanied by *chonguri*. Another good introduction to the different styles of Georgian singing.

Tsinandali Choir

A professional ensemble based in Kakhetia, the wine-growing area of eastern Georgia. Tsinandali is one of the region's best white wines.

⊙ Table Songs of Georgia
Real World, UK

An excellent programme of songs that you might hear in the course of a slap-up feast in Kakhetia, from the opening "Mravaljamieri" to the closing spectacular "Chakrulo". Actually recorded by Melodiya in 1988, this is a great disc of Georgia's richest music. Crack open the wine, settle down and enjoy.

The Gulf

khaleeji comeback

Saudi star Mohammed Abdu
Corbis

Set against the great cultural nexuses of Cairo, Baghdad and Damascus, the Gulf countries have long thought of themselves as musical poor cousins. However, the vast economic wealth that has poured into the region since the discovery of oil in the late 1930s has heralded extraordinary social change. In the last decade, a new-found pride in *khaleeji* (Gulf) traditions has contributed to a burgeoning of homegrown talent that is starting to challenge the established reign of Egyptian musicians. For the younger generation in particular, the Cairo superstars of yesteryear that dazzled their parents have little relevance. Bill Badley surveys the six countries of the region.

Life in the Arabian Peninsula has traditionally centred on trade with neighbouring countries, either by sea or by camel caravan, which means that the musical culture has been anything but isolated. Influences from Africa, Persia and India can be heard in the region's different musical styles and, with thousands of expatriate workers from all over the world now living around the Gulf, the fusion continues.

Obviously, with a land mass of 2,250,000 square kilometres (albeit with a population of less than 30 million), there is considerable musical diversity to be heard across the Arabian Peninsula. The different styles are rooted in traditional ways of life that had, until recently, remained unchanged for centuries. The rhythms are often reminiscent of a camel's loping tread or the pull of an oar, while song lyrics are frequently influenced by Bedouin poetry.

Saudi Arabia

Secular music occupies an uneasy position in Saudi Arabia, as it is officially considered *haraam* (forbidden) by the Wahabi rulers (a strict and conservative branch of Sunni Islam). The passages of the Koran and Hadith (sayings of Mohammed, collected after his death) that deal with music are hotly debated by Islamic scholars: *tarteel* (literally "slow measured recitation", the music of Koranic chant) is deemed appropriate but anything that might be classed as *lahwal hadith* – which can include singing and listening to songs, paying for male and female singers or buying musical instruments for pleasure – is considered, at the very least, suspect. One of the most revered books of Hadith equates the playing of musical instruments with fornication and wine-drinking.

As Saudi Arabia is governed by traditional Islamic Sharia law, this puts musicians in a potentially awkward position: recording studios are few and far between, so musicians tend to travel to either Cairo or Dubai to cut tracks, and formal concerts are officially banned in many provinces, though this is erratically enforced. Despite such strictures, however, there is actually a fine musical tradition within parts of the kingdom, of which many Saudis are justly proud. The western and central provinces of Hejaz and Najd have always been particularly noted for their music and poetry, especially in the cities.

Although the religious authorities have now imposed strict measures to control any such artistic carry-on, it's interesting to note that the Hejaz cities of Mecca and Medina – containing Islam's two most holy shrines – were considered the most stylish and musical cities in the Arabian Peninsula until the end of the nineteenth century. Hejaz has long been exposed to a wide diversity of cultural influences from the millions of pilgrims visiting on Hajj, its links with East Africa and the trade caravans that carried spices and frankincense up from Yemen and Oman. The *hejazi* style is characterized by the intricate, improvised vocal preludes that begin a song, its refined percussion accompaniments and its modal system. In fact, one of the most immediately recognizable Arab scales, *maqam hejaz* (effectively D-Eb-F#-G-A-Bb-C#-D), is named after the region.

In marked contrast to the austere voice-and-percussion style that predominates in most parts of the kingdom, Hejaz has had its own distinctive ensemble (often misleadingly called the Hejaz orchestra) for accompanying singers. Traditionally this comprises *qanun*, violin, *oud* (normally played by the singer) and at least two percussionists, playing a variety of hand-drums. Songs using this chamber group are called *jilsat* (literally "seated music") and would have been played informally within the private homes of refined intellectuals. Even today, some of the big Saudi stars, like **Mohammed Abdu** and **Abadi al-Johar**, regularly release *jilsat* albums that are distinct from their more commercial "pop" output. Put simply, it's Saudi unplugged.

The founding father of modern music in Saudi Arabia is generally accepted to be **Tariq Abdul Haqim** – a distinguished multi-instrumentalist who has devoted his retirement years to curating his own museum about music in the region. Another venerable name is **Ibrahim Khafaji**, who wrote the music for some deliciously sensual verse ("your taste is the essence of sugar and my passion – in revealing itself to you – is now dried out"), as well as the Saudi national anthem. Without doubt, the most respected star of Saudi music is **Mohammed Abdu** who, with his many recordings, has done more than anyone to bridge the gap between traditional Gulf sounds and more contemporary, Egyptian-style music. For religious reasons he took a five-year sabbatical during the 1990s, and there is a feeling that he has never quite returned to his old form since then.

Of the younger generation, **Abdul Majeed Abdullah** outsells all others and is probably the only musician in the kingdom that can genuinely be called a pop star. However, with the rise of the Rotana media empire, more singers from Saudi Arabia are being launched onto the wider Arab market – though their creative shelf life can generally be counted in months. A scan of the Rotana website will always give an overview of who's currently hot.

Bahrain

The tiny island of Bahrain has been at the cross-roads of important trade routes for thousands of years and, in marked contrast to the nomadic life-style of the inhabitants of neighbouring countries, there has been urban settlement on the island since Mesopotamian times. Its strategic importance has meant a procession of occupiers over the centuries, each leaving their mark on the culture. Even the British, who have been taking a protective interest in the island since the late eighteenth century, have had an influence on local music: Bahrain is home to the Gulf's unique progressive rock band, **Osiris**. Although the group's performances are now rela-tively rare, they were probably the only Arab band to blend Eastern musical ideas with the mellotron-laden sounds of bands like Genesis and Camel.

In common with all the countries along the east-ern coast of the Arabian Peninsula, Bahrain has a long-standing heritage of pearl fishing. Tradition-ally, the divers' boats would go out to the oyster banks for up to two months at a time and it was common for the captain to employ a musician to entertain and lead communal songs. Pearl fishing was customarily done by poor Shiite men and, in recent years, the revival of their songs has been linked to their political struggle for recognition.

Art music, as found in nearby Iran and Iraq, is rare in Bahrain; however, it is here that the tradition of *sawt* – an urban dance-song – is strongest. Scholars argue over its origins but it is the particular blend of local and broader Arab musical and poetic styles that makes it so distinctive. *Sawt* is performed amongst men at social gatherings: a singer is accompanied on the *oud* and *mirwas* (small, double-headed drum) and by a chorus who interject the verses with exciting bursts of poly-rhythmic clapping. The tradition was refined and popularized during the first half of the twentieth century by **Mohammed bin Fâris**, a musician of noble origins who laid down quite rigid rules about how *sawt* should be performed. (The rules included absolute silence from the audience – which will raise a wry smile from anyone who has played in the Gulf recent-ly.) His legacy lives on in the ensemble that bears his name, and their concerts and recordings are probably the best formal performances of *sawt* to be heard today.

Sultan Hamid was memorably captured on field recordings by the ethnomusicologists Jean Jenkins and Poul Rovsing Olsenon in the early 1970s. However, Bahrain's most popular singer for many years has been the charismatic **Khalid al-Shaikh**, who is probably better known outside his homeland as a composer of successful songs for other performers.

United Arab Emirates

The UAE shares its neighbours' traditions of Bedouin and fisherman's dance songs, most notably the *ayalat al-harbia* (war dance) and the *alayat al-bahria* (sailors' dance). These can, frankly, sound rather meaningless and repetitive on recordings but, witnessed live, they are a revela-tion: stirring, muscular, drum-driven spectacles. Bedouin musicians traditionally played the *sim-simya* (a small, five-stringed lyre that originated in northeast Africa) and *rabab* (a simple fiddle), but the introduction of "foreign" musical instru-ments such as the *oud*, *qanun* and violin is now commonplace.

The most famous singer within the Emirates is – or more exactly, was – **Ali Burroghr**, a singing *oud* player whose witty and often scurrilous songs made him a firm favourite at any jolly gathering. However, for the last ten years he has been *matowr* (living a strict Islamic lifestyle) and, at his request, his cassettes and CDs were withdrawn from sale. Even so, there's still a thriving bootleg trade in his recordings. Burroghr's popularity did much to encourage other local musicians to start writing songs that drew on their own local traditions and to shun the heavily orchestrated Egyptian style. The best known of these is **Mehad Hamid**, from Sharjah, who writes cheery and anecdotal songs that are thought to be well suited to family enter-tainment.

The UAE is also notable for **Ahlam**, the Gulf's first female singer to move out of the "ladies only" wedding party circuit and onto the international stage. Many found this shocking and, even though

Ahlam

she is well established, it is quite common to meet Emiratis who claim that she is actually from Bahrain!

Given that Dubai is such an extraordinary hub of international commerce, drawing workers from all over the world, it is a little surprising that its music scene has yet to reach its full potential. A decade ago, people were predicting that it would become a production centre to rival Cairo; however, it is still more notable as a hungry consumer of music. All those expatriate workers – who make up 88 percent of the population – need entertaining, and stars from around the globe fly in for legendarily high fees. The bars and hotels of Dubai are also spiritual home to that very particular Gulf phenomenon, the Filipino cover band. Legions of these hard-working ensembles churn out note-perfect renditions of Western pop favourites; it would be quite possible to pub-crawl your way around the city and hear "Hotel California" a dozen times.

Qatar

There is still research to be done that will distinguish Qatar's musical heritage from that of its larger neighbours. The capital city of Doha was founded on pearl fishing and the work songs of the fisherman and the martial *ardha* dances (accompanied by percussion) can sometimes be heard and seen in the city on Friday afternoons.

Qatar's main musical export is the singer **Ali Abdul Sattar** who has released four albums on Rotana.

Kuwait

One of the less-reported tragedies of the First Gulf War was the loss of Kuwait's national sound archive, which held a treasure trove of music recordings from the whole region.

Kuwait shares with Bahrain a strong tradition of the urban *sawt* dance song (sometimes described as "Gulf Blues" but literally "the voice"), which mixes local dialect poetry and song forms with the more formal musical genres from Iraq, Persia and Muslim India. As in Bahrain, the singing *oud* player is accompanied by a small ensemble of percussionists and chorus singers. There was a flowering of *sawt* composing and performing during the 1970s, led by Abdul Aziz al-Muzuraj – better known as **Shadi al-Khaleej** (Bird Song of the Gulf) – which is now continued by the admirable **Ensemble Al-Umayri**.

Kuwait has produced more than its fair share of musicians who have had success across the wider

Arab world. Both the statuesque **Nabil Shuail** and **Abdullah al-Rowaishid** have had enduring careers and al-Rowaishid is one of the few musicians to have credibly combined successful CDs of pop music with the more serious *jilsat*. There was a brief flurry of excitement when the unlikely prospect of the Gulf's first boy band, **Miami**, burst onto the scene. Starting as a carbon-copy of their Western role models, they are now quite well established, releasing regular albums on the omnipresent Rotana label.

Yemen

Yemen is quite different from the rest of the Arabian Peninsula, not least because its oil revenues are a fraction of its neighbours'. However, though it is certainly the trickiest country in the region for Westerners to visit, it also has the most vibrant musical tradition. An indigenous Yemeni music industry as such does not really exist but the huge influence that the country's music and performers have on the rest of the Gulf makes it uniquely important.

Yemen is a country of immense contrasts and its music reflects this variety. However, one thing that unites all Yemeni music is the pre-eminence of the sung word. Yemenis delight in telling the story of a visiting Iraqi *oud* virtuoso who played a dazzling, improvised solo for a select gathering: after an hour he finished, expecting rapturous applause, but was instead greeted by polite silence; his audience assumed he was just warming up before he started singing.

Over the years, Zaydite (a branch of Shiite Islam) rulers in the north have often discouraged or even banned musical instruments and so there are many fine traditions of unaccompanied *nashshad* (hymn) singing to be heard. In rural areas, songs may be accompanied by a variety of drums and the northern Yemeni highlands are noted for the fluid way in which the drum rhythms reflect and follow the metre of the poetry.

The capital city of Sana'a is home to an exalted *homayni* form of sung poetry which combines local dialect verse with the more widespread Andalus *muwashshah* style. Traditionally, the singer accompanied himself on the small, plucked four-stringed *qanbus* or even the enchanting *sahn mimiyeh* – a copper tray that is balanced on the thumbs and rhythmically tapped by the other fingers. It is now much more common to hear the *oud* instead, though the compensation for this is that modern *oud* players from Sana'a have a distinctive and fiery playing style that is immediately recognizable.

Collection Christopher Wagner

Aden   Arab Dançe

Early twentieth century Yemeni trio

to dazzling heights. Qhat chews take place after lunch and it can seem as though everyone – including lorry drivers and the traffic policemen trying to direct them around major roundabouts – is indulging.

To participate, you'll need to be invited to a home session, where men or women (seldom the two together) meet together in the *mafraj* – a window-lined room at the top of the house. Seated on cushions around the room, the assembled company pick off the small leaves and chomp them into a ball that is kept in the side of the mouth. Initially the effect of chewing is enlivening: conversation is animated and the *oud* playing can be furious. However, as afternoon gives way to evening a mellowness falls upon the room and the pace slows until a sublime moment of blue evening light as the sun falls beneath the mountains around Sana'a, and the gathering breaks up for the call to prayer.

It would be hard to imagine Yemeni music (or life) without qhat and, until recently, daily life has gently moved around it – with little productive work being done after lunch and few of the rigours of a Western-style working day to worry about. However, qhat's effects can include insomnia, and the – illegal – introduction of alcohol into the equation has started to have a very negative effect, as people use vodka to help them sleep at the end of the day. Musicians – normally on the front line of anything to do with qhat – have been particularly affected by this damaging cycle and there are now moves from some quarters to discourage regular qhat chewing.

The Yemeni Jewish community, which numbered over 50,000 until Operation Magic Carpet airlifted the vast majority of them to Israel in the late 1940s, had its own rich and distinctive musical culture. It would be all but impossible to hear much of this inside Yemen today; however, the songs and dances have been kept alive by communities in Israel and America and came to international prominence through the singing of the late **Ofra Haza** (see Israel chapter). Just as many Yemenis have to leave their homeland to find work (rough estimates put the number working in other Gulf countries at over 750,000), many of the best musicians seek their fortunes elsewhere. One of the country's finest *oud* players, **Ahmed Fathey**,

By contrast, the music scene around the southern coastal city of Aden is much more cosmopolitan. This wonderfully raffish place was once the fourth-busiest port in the world, though it now feels extremely down at heel. However, its culture is very much more diverse than in landlocked Sana'a and this is reflected in the music. During the 1940s, the Aden Club grew up to encourage performances by local musicians and many of their compositions were strongly influenced by the renaissance in Arab music that was sweeping out of Egypt. A leading light of the Aden Club was **Khalil Mohammed Khalil**, whose song "Al-ward al-hamra" (The Red Rose) was shocking to conservative Yemenis and an unofficial national anthem for liberals and modernizers. Khalil is typical of many revered Yemeni musicians in that he was never a professional – he had a long and distinguished career with the British protectorate's prison service.

A concert, as it is known in the West, is rare in Yemen and you are most likely to hear semi-professional musicians playing at a wedding or amongst friends at a qhat chew. This mildly narcotic leaf is something of a national obsession amongst Yemenis and the effect of it inspires performers

and the highly regarded singer **Osama al-Attar** are now both living and recording in the UAE.

Until very recently, recordings of Yemeni music were hard to find outside the country. However, largely due to the evangelizing work of the **Institut du Monde Arabe** in Paris, this has changed and there are now probably more Yemeni CDs available in the West than from any other Gulf country. These tend to focus on the urban centres of Sana'a and, to a lesser extent, Aden.

Oman

Like Yemen, Oman's music is a legacy of its desert, mountain and seafaring past, which has brought influences from all over the Arabian Peninsula and the lands that lie along the eastern coast of the Gulf. Historically, Oman has also had strong ties with the East African island of Zanzibar, and the cross-fertilization of musical ideas between the two can still be traced. One of the Sultanate's oldest instruments, the five-stringed harp-like *tanbura*, arrived from Nubia millennia ago and the songs that are traditionally sung to it, the *fann al-tanbura* or *nuban*, are in Swahili and wistfully hark back to the days when the Omani court ruled over the island. None of Oman's settled communities, like Muscat or Salalah, has developed the same sophisticated, urban art-song tradition that is found in Sana'a, and much of the secular music is inextricably linked to dance that is itself bound up with work, warfare or celebrating the milestones of life (birth, circumcision, marriage and death).

Present-day Oman has a very particular and structured system of royal patronage for music which stems directly from Sultan Qaboos's personal interests and musical enthusiasms. Young musicians who show promise are awarded scholarships to the Sultan's School in Muscat, where they are taught about Western music by British teachers. From there they may be drafted into the Royal Oman Symphony Orchestra, a Royal Band for Music and Folklore or one of the numerous military bands. But although music is well supported in the sultanate, no musician has managed to become widely known outside the country and foreign stars still account for the majority of CD sales. There was excitement in 2003 when the singer **Salem al-Araimi** was signed to the influential Rotana records. He moved to Dubai in readiness for his big break but as yet nothing by him has been released and he supports himself by playing at private parties.

Oman's rich traditional musical heritage has been well documented and preserved by the forward-looking Oman Centre for Traditional Music. Through this, ethnomusicologists have recorded widely, and the centre's archives are some of the most extensive in the Middle East. None of its collection has been released on CD; however, its excellent website (*www.octm-folk.gov.om*) offers clear and detailed information about the sultanate's different musical genres, with downloadable examples.

DISCOGRAPHY The Gulf

Considering the number of recordings of local artists that flood the market in the Gulf, there are surprisingly few available elsewhere. Though this does seem to be changing, the majority of the CDs released by European companies are of the "ethnomusicology" type.

The packaging of pop musicians' CDs has become considerably more sophisticated in recent years and the former prevalence of cassettes has almost entirely given way to CDs. Arab artists in general are notoriously prolific, and Gulf musicians are no exception: many still release at least one CD a year and they are often just given a date. Despite attempts to impose some sort of copyright control, there is still a thriving bootleg trade and the packaging may not always reflect the exact contents inside (the listings are almost exclusively in Arabic): so, if you buy something from a market stall, be prepared for a surprise. Also note that the transliteration of artists' names from Arabic to English can vary enormously.

Saudi Arabia

⊙ **Musique de Unayzah: ancienne cité du Najd**
Inédit, France
An ethnomusicological recording but not inaccessible – with some fine Bedouin singing and drumming from central Saudi Arabia. Its clear explanatory notes, and translations of the all-important poetry, will be useful to anyone wanting to tackle this underrated genre.

Mohammed Abdu

Saudi musician Mohammed Abdu has done more than anyone to raise the profile and confidence of Gulf music.

⊙ **Ayouh**
MACD, Saudi Arabia
It's not easy to choose between the great man's hundred-plus releases. However, this live recording is considered by

many to be one of his seminal performances. In light of the way Saudi music has developed in the last decade, it does seem very Egyptian in style (the opening bars could have been lifted straight off an Umm Kulthum recording) but it is, nonetheless, one of the kingdom's musical landmarks.

Abdul Majeed Abdullah

Abdul Majeed Abdullah is extraordinarily successful and much admired by young Gulf women for his sensitive, smooth renditions.

⊙ Ghali
EMI Arabia, Dubai
This heavily produced and lavishly orchestrated offering from 2000 secured Abdul Majeed Abdullah's place as a superstar all over the Gulf. It is also just about the only Saudi pop record that is readily available in Europe.

Mohammed Amân

A leading exponent of the traditional *hejazi* style, Amân is unusual in that he has worked in both religious and secular music. Early in his career, he held the post of *muezzin* (religious cantor) at Islam's holiest shrine, al-Harâm al-Sharîf (The Noble Sanctuary of the Black Stone).

⊙ The Tradition of Hejaz
Ocora, France
Though nothing like as polished as Abadi al-Johar's performances, Amân's singing is a perfect example of the region's famed melismatic style.

Simon Broughton

Abadi al-Johar

Abadi al-Johar

Known to his fans as "The Octopus" on account of his prodigious *oud*-playing technique and manual dexterity. Al-Johar's star has waned a little of late but he is still worth hearing; his performances of *jilsat* (traditional "chamber" music) are among the most captivating and polished.

★ Abadi al-Johar '99
Music Box, Saudi Arabia
Traditional *jilsat* with some imaginative contemporary touches and beautifully poised ensemble playing. If you can track this down, it makes an ideal first stop on the Gulf music trail.

Bahrain

★ Music in the World of Islam: Lutes
Topic Records, UK
This excellent compilation includes only one track from Bahrain – a *sawt* performed by Sultan Hamid. However, even if the rest of the CD wasn't utterly splendid, that alone would justify the purchase!

Ensemble Muhammad bin Fâris

Bearing the name of the man who did more than anyone to revive interest in Bahraini *sawt* (Gulf urban music) during the middle of the last century, this group counts some of the finest traditional musicians on the island amongst its members.

⊙ The Sawt of Bahrain
Institut du Monde Arabe, France
A live recording that shows off the ensemble's rather refined style to great effect. Although a modern release, it is a glimpse of what music in the region was like before the cataclysmic changes that occurred after oil was discovered.

Khalid al-Shaikh

Khalid is Bahrain's most popular singer and his songs are covered by many of the region's other singers. He is never afraid to branch out in new directions, whilst keeping one eye firmly on his island roots.

⊙ Esmie wa Miladie
Rotana, Saudi Arabia
Khaled has always been one of the most creative songwriters in the Gulf, and his latest release shows a deft ability to marry Western and oriental pop conventions.

United Arab Emirates

Ahlam

Ahlam is the Gulf's first lady of song – quite literally, since when she started there were no others.

⊙ Ahlam
Funoon Emiraat, UAE
Many Emiratis voice the opinion that Ahlam is a good singer who could choose better material, but this is pretty good.

Mehad Hamid

Mehad Hamid is a very popular, homespun artist, whose songs are engaging stories of local life.

⊙ **Wail Qalbee**
Funoon Emiraat, UAE
Gulf family favourites.

Qatar

⊙ **Music of the Arabian Peninsula: Doha, Qatar**
Celestial Harmonies, US
You could be forgiven for thinking that this is a CD of music from Qatar… In fact, it is a beautifully recorded album of classical instrumental music from Iraq, well played by two expatriate musicians from Baghdad who now work in Qatar.

Kuwait

Miami

When the group first came together in the mid-1990s, they were the nearest thing to a boy band that the Gulf could offer. They're a bit long in the tooth now to be classed as such and have very successfully reinvented themselves as a catchy party band who blend a *rai* edge with Gulf rhythms and Arab pop. Don't be fooled by their rather syrupy image; they're well worth a listen.

⊙ **2004**
EMI Arabia, Dubai
The group release an album every year and this is held by many to be the perfect combination of their talents.

Abdullah al-Rowaishid

Kuwait's best-known singer who has, in recent years, moved away from his acoustic, traditional roots towards a more produced and generic Arab pop style. He is also a noted collaborator with other musicians and poets, an extremely fine *oud* player and a patron of up-and-coming talent.

⊙ **Weenak**
Rotana, Saudi Arabia
In marked contrast to his later CDs, this fairly roots-style recording from the 1990s allows us to appreciate just what a good singer and player Abdullah al-Rowaishid really is.

Nabil Shuail

A distinctive performer with a big, soaring voice and a big physique, Nabil is one of Kuwait's most enduring singers. His mainstay is the lush and smoochy ballad – particularly popular with the ladies…

⊙ **Shuail 2004**
Rotana, Saudi Arabia
Shuail's 2004 vintage is his most satisfying album to date. The opportunity to see the video for rousing hit "Min Qal" should not be missed as it offers a telling glimpse of everyday Kuwaiti folk: women in the home, showing off their latest designer outfits; men dancing together at a big outdoor knees-up.

Ensemble Al-Umayri

One of the few traditional Kuwaiti groups to have received any recognition outside their own country. Their rugged style is typical of the Kuwaiti *sawt*, with particularly virtuosic *kaffafa* (handclappers).

⊙ **The Sawt in Kuwait**
Institut du Monde Arabe, France
A live recording that is sometimes almost too raw: when everyone is up dancing and singing, it all becomes a bit of an audio bun-fight!

Yemen

⊙ **Aden Singing**
Institut du Monde Arabe, France
Solo tracks by Mohammed Naji and the veteran Khalil Mohammed Khalil provide an interesting contrast to the better-known music from Sana'a.

⊙ **Sacred Songs from Sana'a**
Institut du Monde Arabe, France
Sparse, monophonic *nashshad* singing that is at times austere and dignified, at others rousing and uplifting.

★ **Sanaan Singing**
Institut du Monde Arabe, France
A really delightful glimpse of old Sana'a, with Hasam al-Ajami playing the local *qanbus* and the late Ahmed Ushaysh accompanying himself with the shimmering sound of the *sahn mimiyeh* (copper tray).

⊙ **The Yemen Tihama**
Topic Records, UK

A marvellous collection of field recordings made by Duke Bakewell in the Red Sea province of Tihama during the 1980s, though it may be a little unrelenting for the uninitiated.

Ahmed Fathey

A national hero in Yemen but now living and working in the UAE, Fathey (sometimes spelt "Fathi") is widely regarded as one of the finest *oud* players in the Gulf, even though he has chosen to sell himself more as a singer.

⊙ **Habibi Ta'al**
Rotana, Saudi Arabia

Though frequently swamped by the heavy production, it's a treat when the master's *oud* playing shines through.

Hamud al-Junayd

The singer Hamud al-Junayd was born in the mountain region of 'Udayn in 1956 but has lived in the capital, Sana'a, for the last twenty years. He has slightly updated the traditional sound but keeps rigorously to its forms.

★ **Hamud al Junayd: Traditional Yemeni Songs**
Nimbus, UK

In Europe and the US, this is the most widely available and accessible CD of music from Yemen and, even without a mouthful of qhat, it makes entertaining listening.

Iran

the art of ornament

Ghazal crossover duo, Kayhan Kalhor (left) and Shujaat Khan ECM

Iranian music presents ancient and modern faces. The Persian classical tradition with its mystical and contemplative melodies is an intimate part of the culture, performed with an almost blues-like intensity. It is currently in revival at home, while outside Iran there is an equally vibrant Iranian pop scene, highly distinct with its pulsating dance rhythms; a homegrown pop scene has also recently started to develop. As you'd expect from a huge and predominantly rural region, ranging from the mountains of Iranian Azerbaijan, through desert expanses to the Caspian Sea, there are also numerous folk traditions. Laudan Nooshin reports on the revival of classical music since 1979 and Simon Broughton takes the pulse of the folk and pop scenes.

Iranians often say that their music is imbued with a sense of the vast desert, the mountain landscapes and the ancient and turbulent history of the country. The 1979 Iranian Revolution, which created the Islamic Republic, was cultural as well as religious, and was accompanied by a strong "return to roots", and a reawakening of interest in Iranian traditions. In the backlash against Western culture, directly after the revolution, pop music was banned until 1998 – some of Iran's own pop musicians eventually found a new home base abroad. But Iran's classical music has experienced an extraordinary renaissance – as have many of the arts – bringing new life and ideas to a musical tradition that goes back centuries.

Classical Music

Musiqi-e assil (classical music), which in Persian means "pure" or "noble" music, was originally a royal or aristocratic entertainment. Some people date this music back several thousand years, and although there isn't much evidence to show how the various melodies and instruments have changed over time, we can be sure that this is a music whose roots go back a long way. For Iranians, it is an important symbol of their culture – an intense, private expression, refined, contemplative, historically rooted, and with a close relationship to poetry.

Classical Iranian Instruments

Although related to others in the Middle East, the **classical instruments** of Iran are quite specific to Iranian music. They are also found in countries under the influence of Persian musical culutre, like Azerbaijan, Armenia, Uzbekistan and Tajikistan.

Tar and Setar

The *tar* and *setar* are both long-necked lutes whose strings are plucked and strummed. The *tar* is larger, with a relatively loud, more resonant and tangy sound, partly because the belly of the instrument on which the bridge rests is made of skin (rather than wood) and the strings are plucked with a metal plectrum. The sound of the *setar*, on the other hand, is soft and refined. It is often said to embody the spirit of Iranian music and is difficult to hear in a large concert hall without amplification.

Santur

The *santur* is a dulcimer, usually positioned on a small table in front of the musician who strikes the strings with two felted hammers. This instrument has grown in popularity since the mid-twentieth century, partly because it enables musicians to display their virtuosity to a greater extent than other classical instruments. This kind of technical display is fairly new to a music whose aesthetic ideals lie more in its spirit and "soul" rather than musical "fireworks".

Ney

The *ney* is an end-blown reed flute with a very soulful and breathy sound, said originally to have been a shepherd's instrument.

The sound of the *ney* was said by Mowlana (Rumi) to be a lament for its separation from the reed bed from which it was cut, and this image is used as a Sufi metaphor for the pain of separation from God or a loved one.

Kamancheh and violin

The *kamancheh* is a bowed spike fiddle played in front of the musician. It has a distinctive taut nasal sound, with a touch of sandy grit. It is the forerunner of the European violin.

Tombak (zarb)

The tombak, or *zarb*, is a goblet drum played with the fingers and palms of both hands and held diagonally across the player's lap. It rarely plays as a solo instrument and in classical performances is usually heard accompanying sections of the music with a regular pulse.

Classical pieces range through slow, quiet, contemplative passages – usually in the lower part of the singer's range – to melismatic displays of virtuosity known as **tahrir**. These are fast and ornamented passages, usually high in the vocal range and often compared with the singing of the nightingale. Their typical sound is soulful and intense, and the result is a mesmerizing arabesque, as voice and instrument speak to each other in turn.

Poetry and music go hand in hand in Iran, and much of the classical music is set to the words of medieval Persian mystic poets such as **Mowlana** (**Jalal Edin Rumi**, 1207–73) and **Hafez** (1325–89). Music is an important medium through which people experience this ancient poetry, whose messages are often seen to have contemporary significance. Poetry in turn gives music a respectability, since the written word has a higher status within Islam; in fact, much of the Islamic proscription of music is directed towards instrumental music. Today, it's still unusual to hear a performance of Iranian classical music without a vocalist, although there have been moves in recent years to emancipate music from words and to give instrumental music a validity in its own right.

From Courts to Cassettes

Until the beginning of the twentieth century, classical music was heard mainly at the royal courts and in the homes of wealthy amateurs. Most of the significant classical musicians of the nineteenth century were based at the courts of the Qajar monarchs (who ruled Iran between 1794 and 1925). This intimate music, with its close relationship to mystical Sufi poetry and philosophy, was well-suited to such gatherings, and it remained sheltered there until the 1900s.

The decline in the influence of the royal courts in the early twentieth century coincided with the opening up of classical music to a wider audience, through recordings and Western-style public concerts, and eventually through the important medium of radio. A further boost came with the arrival of cassettes, from the 1960s, which meant that music could be carried around discreetly – an important consideration in an Islamic society. The rapid pace of Westernization, however, meant that by the 1970s classical music was still a minority taste. There was a feeling that it belonged to a past age and was out of step with the modernizing nation state.

Prominent classical musicians of pre-revolutionary Iran include the singer **Gholam Hossein Banan**, probably the most-recorded voice in the country prior to 1979, and instrumentalists **Ahmad Ebadi** (*setar*), **Faramarz Payvar** (*santur*) and **Abol Hassan Saba** (violin, *setar*, *santur*).

Post-Revolutionary Revival

Culturally, the immediate post-revolutionary period was an extraordinary time, and for classical Iranian music, it was nothing short of a renaissance. The movement was led by a number of (mainly) younger musicians, many of whom are still active performers and composers. These musicians were not willing to follow tradition for its own sake and wanted to make classical music relevant to a contemporary audience. They breathed new life into the traditional repertoire. These musicians included the male singers **Mohammad Reza Shajarian** and **Shahram Nazeri**, female vocalist **Parisa** and the instrumentalists **Mohammad Reza Lotfi** (*tar*, *setar*), **Hossein Alizadeh** (*tar*, *setar*), **Parviz Meshkatian** (*santur*), **Jamshid Andalibi** (*ney*), **Kayhan Kalhor** (*kamancheh*), and the (Kurdish) **Kamkar family**, who have toured widely.

Persian masters, Mohammad Reza Shajarian, Hossein Alizadeh, Kayhan Kalhor and Homayoun Shajarian

The situation for musicians became particularly difficult during the Iran–Iraq war (1980–88) when it was felt that live musical performance, and the associated expression of joy, was inappropriate. Since the early 1990s, however, there

Mohammad Reza Shajarian

Mohammad Reza Shajarian is the nightingale supreme of Iranian music, a living legend whose superb technical skill, warm vocal style and vast knowledge of classical Iranian poetry have made him the most successful classical singer in the country.

Born in Masshad (in northeastern Iran) in 1940, Shajarian comes from a family with a long musical tradition. He began his singing career at the age of 18 with the local radio station in Masshad and moved to Tehran eight years later where he performed regularly on Iranian Radio until 1986 (many of these broadcast programmes were subsequently released as commercial recordings).

Following his appearances on national television in the early 1970s, Shajarian become a household name. But it was the musical renaissance which followed the 1979 Revolution, and his close creative work with other musicians at this time, which consolidated his position as the foremost musician of Iranian classical music.

Shajarian has given concerts around the world and worked closely with the most prominent contemporary classical musicians such as Mohammad Reza Lotfi and Parviz Meshkatian. As well as his busy performing and recording career, he devotes a considerable amount of time and energy to teaching and to research into the music of his native region of Khorasan. In 2005, his CD *Faryad* received a Grammy nomination.

World Network

Mohammad Reza Shajarian (left)

has been a renewal, with the emergence of many young musicians and an even wider audience for classical music than before.

While there was a spirit of optimism surrounding this revival, and opportunities for recording and live performance, it all happened largely in spite of the official policy. Whilst more moderate politicians cautiously welcomed the return to traditional culture, the conservative elements viewed even classical music as a potentially corrupting influence. New laws also limited women's public musical roles. Female singers were (and still are) only allowed to perform to all-female audiences, although there are no such restrictions on female instrumentalists. In recent years, some singers, such as **Parisa** and **Sima Bina**, have been given permission to tour and record outside Iran. Other women work as singing groups (which are allowed to perform). A good example of female vocal can be heard on the CD *Saz-é No* on which **Afsaneh Rasai** sings with **Hossein Alizadeh**.

Although there have been important female classical singers in the past, the instrumental tradition was almost exclusively a male one. But this is changing and it's no longer unusual to see a woman instrumentalist. The female singers **Parvin Javdan** and **Zohreh Bayat** have performed and recorded with a group of all-female instrumentalists.

Another development in the late 1990s was a government satellite television channel, *Jaam-e-Jam*, broadcasting from Iran to Iranians abroad. Its programming schedule includes classical music performances.

Modes and Improvisation

Iranian classical music is largely improvised, and this improvisation is based on a series of modal scales and tunes which musicians spend many years memorizing as part of their long training. Traditionally, there was a very close relationship between pupil and master, or *ostad* (a word which, along with other Persian words, was also taken up by musicians in North India) and teaching would usually take place in the *ostad*'s home. During the course of the twentieth century most teaching was taken over by conservatoires and universities.

The music is largely an oral tradition and the emphasis is still on strict rote memorization. Musicians never perform from notation, since each performance is a spontaneous expression by the musician – but one firmly rooted in the memorized repertoire; in other words, a unique "re-creation" of the tradition at each performance. A metaphor for this is the nightingale, a bird regularly encountered in the visual arts and poetry of Iran. According to popular belief, the nightingale (*bolbol*) has the most beautiful voice on earth as it sings of its unrequited love for the rose (*gol*). Moreover, it is believed that the nightingale never repeats itself in its song. In practice, of course, both nightingales and Iranian musicians do repeat themselves, but the metaphor is important for its ideal.

The repertoire is a collection of some two hundred pieces collectively known as *radif* (series), and the training of a classical musician essentially involves memorizing these pieces precisely. The individual pieces of the *radif* are known as *gusheh* (corner) – a short piece or melody, lasting from as little as fifteen seconds to as long as two minutes, with its own modal identity and often particular turns of phrase. It is these individual *gusheh*s that are memorized strictly by musicians and after many years of training form the starting point for creative improvisation in performance. The *gusheh*s are in turn arranged into twelve *dastgah*s (systems). These are ordered collections of modally related *gusheh*s (rather like a Baroque suite), and a performance of Iranian classical music will usually be in one of the twelve *dastgah*s.

Each of the two hundred or so *gusheh*s and the twelve *dastgah*s of the complete *radif* repertoire are individually named. Some of the names indicate a particular sentiment or emotion while others are names of towns or regions of the country. Some of these names are also found in the *maqam*s or *makam*s of Arabic and Turkish music, the two other important classical traditions of the Middle East. Historical contact between these cultures has resulted in cross-influences in the modes and their names, as well as in instrument types.

At the same time, there are significant differences between Iranian classical music and its neighbouring traditions. There are no rhythmic cycles in Iranian music as there are in Arabic and Turkish musics (and the even more distantly related Indian). Rhythmically, much of Iranian classical music is based on the metrical structure of the

poetry that is being sung (or implied in the case of the instrumental accompaniment).

Listening to Classical Music

When listening to this music, bear in mind that it is the **intricate beauty** and **ornamentation** of the solo melody line (usually with no regular pulse) that is of the utmost importance, inviting more of a philosophical than physical response. The musical interest is almost totally linear – there is no harmony and only a light drone serves to ground the music from time to time. People often draw parallels between the highly detailed melodic lines and the intricate designs of Iranian carpets. As in the carpets, the movement is meandering, as the musician exhaustively explores the melodic potential of a defined area before moving on to the next.

The length of a *dastgah* performance is largely up to the musician, taking into consideration the particular context of performance. Each individual *gusheh*, which in the studied repertoire might last thirty seconds, will be expanded in performance to last for several minutes, and often longer. A complete *dastgah* performance can last for several hours in informal settings, although nowadays something between thirty minutes and an hour is more usual.

Until the 1960s, a typical performance would have comprised a voice and a solo instrument, the latter supporting the vocal sections and playing short **instrumental interludes**, with the addition of a *tombak* for the metered sections. In the last thirty years or so, it has become common for performances to be given by an ensemble of musicians, usually including one of each of the main classical instruments, each musician taking it in turn to accompany the voice and to play solo interludes between the vocal phrases. It has also become common for performances to begin and end with a pre-composed ensemble piece. These pieces provide a frame for the main part of the performance, which is usually unmetered and improvised.

Simplifying somewhat, a typical classical performance begins with the opening (*daramad*) section of the chosen *dastgah*, followed by a progressive development of the material of each individual *gusheh*. As the performance continues, there is a gradual increase in pitch and tension – each *gusheh* is based around a slightly higher pitch range than the preceding one – until the music reaches the climax, or *owj*, of the *dastgah*. At this point there is usually a descent and return to the opening pitch area and "home" mode of the *dastgah* (as heard at the beginning) to conclude the performance. There may also be a concluding ensemble piece to round the performance off.

The important things to listen out for are the rising pitch level and the resulting overall arch shape of the performance, the alternating (or answering) of instruments and voice, and the explorations of the musicians reinterpreting the underlying tradition each time they perform.

Folk Music

Within Iran's seventy million people there are numerous ethnic minorities, each with their own language, culture and music. For example, an estimated 24 percent of the population is **Azeri**, living in the northwest of the country in the area adjoining the Caspian Sea, and about 8 percent of the population is **Kurdish**, mainly in the west of the country bordering Iraq and Turkey. Both groups have a strong influence on the country's music. Even among the Persian-speaking population there are many regional variations in dialect, lifestyle culture and music, one example being the nomadic **Bakhtiari** people. Regional folk music is widely performed in Iran, but less known abroad, where fewer recordings are available.

The Bakshi of Khorasan

Iranians often consider Khorasan, the large province in the northeast, the heartland of their bardic culture. The celebrated musicians here are the *bakshi*, epic bards (often Turkmen) who sing and accompany themselves on the long-necked *dotar*. The most famous of these is **Haj Ghorban Soleimani**, a veteran singer and *dotar* player from a long line of *bakshi*. The poems, texts and music he performs have been handed down orally for centuries. The colours and textures of his playing on the two-string *dotar* evoke the ancestral heritage of the region. Although the tradition is inevitably a dwindling one, there are younger musicians like the impressive **Rowshan Golafruz**, the ninth generation in a prestigious line of Khorasan bards. One of the best-known professional singers is **Sima Bina**, who has collected and recorded songs from her native Khorasan, many about the nomadic horse people of the region.

Kurdish Tanbur Players

In **Kurdistan** it is the *tanbur*, also a long-necked lute like the *dotar*, with two or three strings, that is central to the music. There are two centres of **Kurdish tanbur** playing and making: one around Guran where the belly is carved from a single piece of mulberry wood, the other around Sahneh where the belly is constructed from strips of wood. The *tanbur* is heard constantly in Kurdish folk music, but most remarkably at religious gatherings. It is considered a sacred instrument. There is a widespread, Sufi-like faith in Kurdistan whose adherents are called Yarsin, or **Ahl-e Haqq** (People of the Truth). It is a belief that is thought to predate

Simon Broughton

Haj Ghorban Soleimani playing the long-necked *dotar*

Islam and includes songs to the sun, as well as to Islamic figures like Ali, the Prophet's son-in-law, who is revered throughout Iran by the Shias. The *tanbur* is played at regular religious gatherings, as with the Alevis in Turkey.

One well-respected singer and *tanbur* player is **Ostad Elahi** (1895–1974), who widely recorded this repertoire, although his style is hard going for the uninitiated. More approachable is the music of **Ali Akbar Moradi**, currently the best player in the region. There is a substantial repertoire of sacred music that was only permitted to be heard by Ahl-e Haqq initiates. Worried that the tradition might be lost, Moradi sought permission from the spiritual leaders to record these ritual *maqam* for the first time and they've been released on the French Inédit label. The most famous group performing Kurdish folk music is **The Kamkars**, members of one family who are also talented players of classical Persian music.

Harold Hagopian

Ardavan Kamkar playing *santur*

Other Regional Highlights

In the hot and inhospitable territory of Makran in **Baluchistan**, split between Iran and Pakistan, there's a strong musical tradition associated with religious Sufi music, trance and healing. The music is played by the **Luri** caste who were linked by the eleventh-century Persian poet Firdausi to the Indian (Gypsy) musicians invited in the fifth century to play for the Persian Shah. The Luri musicians of Baluchistan play the extraordinary *sorud* fiddle, carved out of a single piece of wood and shaped strangely like a skull. It has a shimmering spooky sound, with resonant sympathetic strings. Other local instruments include the *damburag* (long-necked lute), *donali* (double *ney*) and the *benjo* (keyed zither).

In the mountains of central Iran, the raucous *sorna* (shawm) is played amongst the Bakhtiari and in **Lorestan**, which is also famous for its folk *kamancheh* players. Down on the **Persian Gulf** in Bandar-e Abbas and Qeshm Island, there are many "black" Iranians, descended from Arabs and African slaves. They have their own distinctive music with African percussion or Arabic *oud*. If you're in the region, search out the **Jahlé** band (Bandar-e Abbas) and *oud* player **Mohammad Sedigh Kamali** (Qeshm).

Iranian Pop

In the early twentieth century, there were various types of traditional urban music styles in Iran, but from the 1950s musicians began adopting Western musical styles and instruments. By the 1970s a strong **pop industry** had emerged – along with a core repertoire of nostalgic love songs – and this was the music that most people listened to at a time when classical music was increasingly regarded as out of touch with a modernizing country.

Iranian pop music drew – and draws – on elements from folk and classical traditions but using Western instruments such as electric guitar, keyboards, bass and drums. Its stars are exclusively **singers**, and their repertoire largely comprises love songs and nostalgic ballads.

With the banning of all pop music (both Iranian and Western) after the 1979 Revolution, many Iranian musicians left the country and settled in Europe or North America. The biggest influx was to **Los Angeles** – Tehrangeles to the million-strong immigrant Iranian population – where a thriving music scene has developed.

Since 1998 (following the election of reformist President Khatami in May 1997), restrictions on pop music in Iran have eased considerably. There are now a large number of local pop singers and bands whose music is available on commercial recordings as well as through the broadcast media and occasional public concerts (although obtaining government permission for the latter can prove problematic). With Iran's growing youth culture – and bearing in mind that an estimated 70 percent of the population is under the age of 30 – this "new pop" music has gained a considerable following. There is also a growing **grass-roots rock music scene**, although only a small number of bands have managed to gain government permission to record and perform in public (note that any public performance or commercial recording has to be authorized by Vezarat-e Ershad, the Ministry of Culture and Islamic Guidance). However,

Kayhan Kalhor

Iranian music has developed a much higher profile in recent years. That is partly because of some loosening up of the cultural policy of the regime, but also thanks to **Kayhan Kalhor** and his role as cultural ambassador. His powerful and poetic performances on the *kamancheh* bring the classical music of Iran to life. Kalhor was born in Tehran into a **Kurdish** family and learnt the violin as a child, but then he saw veteran *kamancheh* player **Asghar Ali Bahari** on television one day, got hooked and decided to take up this ancient ancestor of the violin himself. By the time he was 15 or 16 he was playing eighteen hours a day. The *kamancheh* has a penetrating, sinewy tone with a touch of deserty sandpaper to it. Kalhor kneels and spins the instrument from side to side to simplify the movement of the bow. 'It's like riding a wild horse', he says, 'but it has a deepness and warmth that I'm crazy about. It seems to come from a far distance and a far time and reach into parts of the soul that you haven't encountered before'.

In the late 1990s, Kalhor spent several years in the US and his brilliant debut CD *Scattering Stars Like Dust* came out on New York's Traditional Crossroads label in 1998. In America he built up useful contacts which have led to several high-profile tours and recordings with the singer **Mohammad Reza Shajarian** and the **Masters of Persian Music**. But despite his deep love for Persian classical music, Kalhor has also pushed out in new directions. He composed the music for an extended piece called *Night, Silence, Desert*, based on his research into the folk music of Khorasan and an excellent duo recording with his childhood friend in Kurdistan, *tanbur* player **Ali Akbar Moradi**. But the biggest impact was made by his revelatory explorations into the shared culture of Persian and Indian music in the duo **Ghazal**, with Indian sitar player **Shujaat Khan**. They made three recordings for Shanachie and then a brilliant live recording of intricate tracery, *Rain*, for ECM. The plucked, resonant sound of the sitar is brilliantly complemented by the long, sustained bowing of the *kamancheh*, the two instruments sometimes contrasting with, sometimes imitating each other. Kalhor has a particular ability to build musical bridges.

Simon Broughton

much of this music is available on band websites (see below). In 2002, the website tehranavenue. com hosted the first on-line rock music competition ("UMC", followed by another in 2004) which played a significant role in promoting and disseminating local rock music.

Pop Artists

The most popular pre-Revolution pop singer was **Googoosh** – who chose to stay in Iran even though she was unable to perform there. In 2000, Googoosh left Iran and (after more than twenty years of silence) toured North America and Europe, performing to ecstatic audiences in packed stadiums and concert halls. She now lives in Toronto. Other important singers, who moved to Los Angeles and have kept the old ballad tradition alive in performance and on cassette, include the female singers **Homeirah**, **Hayedeh** and **Mahasti** and the male **Shahram**, **Morteza** and **Hodi**.

Alongside them, a **new generation of LA-based musicians** (many of whom have never been to Iran) have created more uptempo songs with driving rhythms, or experimented mixing Iranian styles with rap and dance music. Their instruments are all Western, except for occasional use of an Iranian drum, but the rhythms are often based on folk and popular Iranian rhythms, and it is this, as well as the melodies and lyrics, which gives the music its particularly "Iranian" feel. This is music to dance to, and forms an essential ingredient at any Iranian social gathering.

Googoosh

American-based singers and groups to listen out for include **Siavash**, whose production is always good, although he tends to overdo the synthesized sounds; **Moeen**, always a favourite with his warm vocal sound; and **Andy**, strongly influenced by Western pop, as are **The Black Cabs** and **The Boys**.

Post-1998 pop singers in Iran include **Mohammad Esfahani**, **Ali Reza Assar** and **Shadmehr Aqili** (who moved to Canada in 2000). The first pop band – the highly successful **Arian** – was formed in 1999 and has released three albums to date, as well as touring extensively both in Iran and abroad. Many others have followed in their footsteps and there are now a number of local pop bands. As for other kinds of popular music, the first rocks bands to gain authorization for commercial releases were **Barad** (in 2003) and **Meera** (2004).

There is even one officially approved rapper, **Shahkar Binesh-Pajouh**, dubbed the "dapper rapper" who rather makes fun of the form, dressing in a suit and bow-tie to rap about Tehran's elite. "Underground" there are plenty more rappers and rock groups, like **O-Hum** who use the fourteenth-century lyrics of Hafez for their rock songs. O-Hum hasn't been granted a licence, not because of risqué words, but because rock'n'roll Hafez isn't considered proper. Much of this music circulates on the Internet (and young Iranians are avid browsers and bloggers) through sites like *www.zirzamin.se/*, *www.tehranavenue.com/* and *tehran360.com/main.php*. Since **Mahmoud Ahmadinejad** became president in 2005, it's not become clear what the attitude to local music is, although he has complained about Westernization. But if they clamp down on rock and pop, it certainly won't disappear, more will just go underground.

Arian Band

DISCOGRAPHY Iran

In the UK, specialist music shops in London include Shahram Video (561 Finchley Rd, London NW3 7BJ, 020 7435 2227) and Farhangsara (1261 Finchley Rd, London NW11 0AD, 020 8455 5550, <farhangSara@aol.com>). There are also many Iranian grocery shops in Kensington and on the Finchley Road that have a good stock of recordings. You can also buy on-line from companies such as Kereshmeh (*www.kereshmeh.com*), Caltex (*www.caltexrecords.com*) and Mahour (*www.mahour.com*) and can even order directly from Iran through websites such as the Tehran-based *www.hermes.com* and the Beethoven Music Centre (*www.beethovenmc.com*). In addition, sites such as tehranavenue and beethovenmc (*www.beethovenmc.com/htmls/link_artists.htm*) continue to provide information on, and reviews of, current events as well as links to the sites of bands whose music is not available commercially (see also *www.iranrockmusic.com*).

Classical Music

⊙ **Classical Music of Iran: The Dastagh Systems**
Smithsonian Folkways, US
Short performances recorded in Iran in the mid-1960s by some of the principal classical performers of the time (including Ahmad Ebadi), featuring a range of modes and musical instruments. This was the first recording of all the twelve *dastgahs*, intended to illustrate the tradition to non-Iranians, although the extracts are just too short to convey the feeling of the music in performance.

⊙ **Iran: Persian Classical Music**
Nonesuch Explorer, US
A select group of musicians, including female vocalist Khatereh Parvaneh, plus *tar* and *kamancheh*, and led by one

of the most important *santur* players, Faramarz Payvar. A disc made in 1973, aimed at demonstrating a range of modes and instruments to a non-Iranian audience, but with more continuity than the Smithsonian recording.

⭐ **The Rough Guide to the Music of Iran**
World Music Network, UK
A pioneering introduction to the country's classical, folk and pop traditions, including the underground band O-Hum. It includes everything from big-name musicians like Shajarian, Haj Ghorban and Arian to little-known trance musicians in Baluchistan and Jahlé, the band of African ancestry Andy Kershaw uncovered on the Persian Gulf.

Hossein Alizadeh

Born in Tehran in 1951, Alizadeh began his professional career at only 15 years old. He is considered one of the most important figures in contemporary Iranian music. As well as performing classical Persian music, he has also composed orchestral works for Persian instruments and many film scores.

⭐ **Iranian Music: Saz-é No**
Buda/Musique du Monde, France
An excellent single disc with stunning instrumental playing from Alizadeh on *tar*, *tanbur* and *setar* plus a couple of *ghazals* to words by Mowlana sung by one of the finest female vocalists, Afsaneh Rassa'i. Music full of exciting instrumental textures and a pure, meditative vocal quality.

⊙ **Improvisations**
Buda/Musique du Monde, France
A double CD recording of a concert given in Paris in 1994. Alizadeh plays *tar* and *setar* in the *dastgahs nava*, *bayat-e Tork* and *Homayun* with Majid Khaladj on *tombak*.

⊙ **Endless Vision**
Hermes Records, Iran
A wonderful encounter between Iranian and Armenian music featuring compositions by Hossein Alizadeh and Djivan Gasparyan, the latter well known to World Music audiences for his stunning performances on *duduk*. A live recording of a concert held in Tehran in 2003, which brought together Iranian and Armenian musicians in a historic collaboration.

Dastan Ensemble

Formed in 1991, Dastan Ensemble is one of the most innovative Iranian classical groups. The three core members are Hamid Motebassem (*tar* and *setar*), Hossein Behroozi-Nia (*barbat*) and Pejman Hadadi (*tombak* and *daf*). Their musicality, virtuosity and vision give Dastan's music a freshness and vitality almost unmatched in the contemporary Iranian music scene.

journey to persia

⭐ **Through Eternity: Homage to Molavi (Rumi) – Persian Devotional Music**
Sounds True, US
Featuring Dastan's original line-up (including Kayhan Kalhor on *kamancheh* and *setar*), this is a stunning performance of spiritual music inspired by Rumi, with the singer Shahram Nazeri.

⊙ **Journey to Persia**
ARC, UK
This more recent album (2003) continues in the vein of Dastan's earlier recordings with original compositions by the group for instrumental performance without a singer.

Kayhan Kalhor

Kalhor was born in Tehran in 1963 into a musical family and studied Iranian classical music with some of the great masters, as well as Kurdish folk music in Kermanshah. He has performed with top classical musicians such as Alizadeh, Shajarian and Nazeri, as well as folk musicians like Ali Akbar Moradi. He was also half of the innovative Ghazal duo with Shujaat Khan.

⊙ **Scattering Stars Like Dust**
Traditional Crossroads, US
Kalhor's innovative approach to the *kamancheh* – this recording starts with novel pizzicatos – gives his debut disc a freshness and verve. A whole disc of solo *kamancheh* (and *tombak*) can be daunting, but the intensity and drama here is captivating.

GHAZAL

⭐ **The Rain**
ECM, Germany
Before this live CD (2003) Kalhor and Shujaat Khan had recorded three Ghazal CDs exploring the connections between the Persian and Hindustani traditions. There's a thrill about two expert musicians improvising together while the plucked sound of the sitar and bowed sound of the *kamancheh* weaving their delicate traceries, complement each other perfectly. Shujaat sings too.

WITH ALI AKBAR MORADI

⊙ **In the Mirror of the Sky**
World Village, US
Another ground-breaking fusion, this time between Iranian and Kurdish music. This 2004 album features Kayhan Kalhor on *kamancheh* and Ali Akbar Moradi on *tanbur* and vocals.

MOHAMMAD REZA SHAJARIAN

⊙ **Night, Silence, Desert**
Traditional Crossroads, US
One of the first albums to interweave classical and folk by bringing together musicians from both traditions. Drawing on folk and mystic poetry from Khorasan set to the exquisite music of Kayhan Kalhor, the performance features Shajarian and classical folk troubadour Haj Ghorban Soleimani (from Khorasan). This recording has proved immensely popular in Iran.

Mohammad Reza Lotfi

Born in 1947 in Gorgan, northern Iran, Lotfi studied at the National Conservatoire in Tehran. Regarded as one of the greatest contemporary masters of the *tar* and *setar*, he has taught many of Iran's leading young musicians.

⊙ **Mystery of Love, Live in Copenhagen**
Kereshmeh Records, US
One of Lotfi's finest performances accompanied by *tombak* and *daf*. In his notes to the recording, Robert Bly writes: "Lotfi is a great musician. He pours his intense, astonishing music into the spiritual ear."

Parviz Meshkatian

Born in 1955 in Neyshabour, northeastern Iran, Meshkatian is the best *santur* player of the post-Revolutionary period. His unrivalled technique is simply extraordinary – he moves the hammers with such speed and subtlety that they can hardly be seen. What's more he looks like a prophet. He was a founding member of the celebrated Aref Ensemble with whom he has performed extensively throughout the world.

⊙ **Pegah (Dawn)**
Kereshmeh Records, US
Dazzling performances in *dastgahs segah* and *homayun* with *tombak* players Nasser Farhangfar and Jamshid Mohebi.

Shahram Nazeri and Ensemble Alizadeh

Shahram Nazeri, born in Kermanshah in 1949, is one of Iran's top classical singers, famed for his warm vocal style and technical mastery. He is second to none at Sufi repertoire.

⊙ **Nowruz: Traditional and Classical Music**
Network, Germany
Most of the music here is Persian classical music along with a few Kurdish tunes andl folksongs from Nazeri's native region.

Nour Ensemble

A French-Iranian collaboration directed by Christophe Rezai and comprising nine musicians.

⊙ **Alba**
Hermes, Iran
This debut CD presents a beautiful exploration of the common threads which connect Persian and Kurdish music with that of medieval Europe. A truly unique musical experience.

Hossein Omoumi

Born in 1944 in Isfahan, Omoumi started studying the *ney* at the age of 14. He taught at the National Conservatoire and at the University of Tehran. Since 1984 he has worked in France as a performer and teacher.

⊙ **Persian Classical Music**
Nimbus, UK
Stunning performances recorded in France in 1993. Omoumi performs in *dastgahs homayun*, *dashti* and *chahargah* accompanied by Majid Khaladj on *tombak*.

Paris-Tehran Project

A collaboration between the Paris-based Alain Brunet Didgeridoo Orchestra and the Tehran-based Shargh Music Ensemble.

⊙ **Paris-Tehran Project**
Hermes, Iran
A live recording of a concert given in Tehran in the spring of 2003, this CD is a vibrant mix of jazz and Iranian classical and folk traditions.

Mohammad Reza Shajarian

Born in 1940 in Mashhad, Khorasan Province, Shajarian (see box) is the undisputed master of Persian traditional singing – technically flawless. powerful and emotional. A major source of inspiration in Iranian music.

WITH ENSEMBLE AREF

⊙ **Iran: Mohammad Reza Shadjarian and Ensemble Aref**
Network, Germany
A live recording of a concert in Germany in 1987 with some of the finest Iranian musicians: Parviz Meshkatian (*santur*), Dariush Pirniakan (*tar*), Ardeshir Kamkar (*kamancheh*) and Jamshid Andalibi (*ney*) in *dastgah chahargah*. Strong folk influences in the lively ensemble sections framing the central section where the solo voice is accompanied in turn by each of the main instrumentalists.

WITH HOSSEIN ALIZADEH & KAYHAN KALHOR

⭐ **Faryad: Masters of Persian Music**
World Village, US
This double CD is already well on the way to becoming a classic. It brings together some of the great names of contemporary Iranian classical music: Mohammad Reza Shajarian, Hossein Alizadeh and Kayhan Kalhor, joined by Shajarian's son Homayoun (on vocals and *tombak*).

WITH MOHAMMAD REZA LOTFI & SHEYDA ENSEMBLE

⊙ **Sepideh ("Dawn")**
Soroush Multimedia Corporation
This album is a historic recording of one of the first concerts permitted after the Revolution in December 1979, after which the title piece "Sepideh" attained unprecedented popularity, effectively becoming an unofficial national anthem.

Dariush Talai

Born in 1952, Talai is a *tar* and *setar* player. Now based in Iran, Talai spent much of the post-revolutionary period in France where he was active in promoting Iranian classical music.

⊙ **Iran: Les maitres de la musique traditionelle Vol 1**
Ocora, France
This Ocora series is one of the best of Iranian music released on a Western label. Talai, on *tar*, performs with Mohammad Musavi (*ney*) and Majid Kiani (*santur*) – three leading virtuoso musicians.

Trio Chemirani

Three *tombak* virtuosos in one family – father Djamshid Chemirani and his two sons Keyvan and Bijane – comprise the Trio Chemirani. These musicians have lived in France for many years and have collaborated with a number of non-Iranian musicians, including Ross Daly and many singers on *The Rhythm of Speech* CDs (Accords Croisés).

⊙ **Tchechmeh**
Emouvance, France
Released back in 2004, this Persian percussion spectacular features Djamshid and Keyvan on *tombak* and Bijane on *tombak* and *daf*.

Folk Music

⊙ **Balouchistan: Music of Ecstasy and Healing**
Ocora, France
A double CD featuring great performances of trance, Sufi and healing music from the Iranian Makran. *Baluchistan: The instrumental tradition* (Ocora) is an excellent companion disc (recorded in Pakistan, as the Baluchis are found both sides of the border) and other excellent recordings of Baluchi music such as *Bardes du Makran* (Buda) and *Music of Makran* (Topic).

⭐ **Iran: Bards of Khorasan**
Ocora, France
Khorasan is the heartland of the Iranian bardic tradition. This disc features some of the best bakshi: veteran Haj Ghorban Soleimani, the dramatic Roshan Golafruz, Golnabat Ata'i (one of the very few female *bakshi*), and others.

⊙ **Iran: The Music of Lorestan**
Nimbus, UK
Rousing dance music from the southwestern province of Lorestan, featuring the loud outdoor instruments: *sorna*, like the *zurna* and *dohol* drum common throughout the Middle East. Played by Shahmirza Moradi and his son Reza.

Faradj Alipour

From the region of Lorestan, where the *kamancheh* is king, a celebrated folk performer on the instrument.

⊙ Tal: Kemancheh Duos
Art House, Iran

A dynamic 1996 recording of folk *kamancheh* with the classical *kamancheh* of Ardeshir Kamkar. A powerful meeting of two related but distinct voices.

Sima Bina

Born in Birjand in 1944, Sima Bina is the daughter of a leading classical musician. She collects and performs folksongs from Khorasan in the northeast, but also sings classical repertoire. In 1994 she was the first Iranian woman singer to tour Europe and the US since the revolution.

⊙ Hanaie – Flowers of the Desert
sima-bina.com

A magical collaboration between Sima Bina and the Dastan Ensemble, with whom she has also toured outside Iran. On this recording, Sima Bina performs folksongs from her native Khorasan in Shusutari and Esfahan modes, as well as one of the best-known compositions, the rousing "Midnight Sun", by Dastan member and *barbat* player, Hossein Behroozinia.

Shir-Mohammad Espandar

Born in 1927 in Bampur, Espandar is considered the great *donali* (double flute) player of Baluchistan.

⊙ Music of Baluchistan
Mahoor Institute, Iran

Some Sufi songs and beautiful instrumentals with the haunting sound of the double flute with *tabla*-like percussion. The *donali* is unusual in having two separate tubes which you put in your mouth; one is considered male the other female. The main melody is played on the female flute while the male mostly provides a drone. It's played with continuous breathing without pausing for breath.

The Kamkars

The Kamkars are a Kurdish family of seven brothers and a sister from Sanandaj in western Iran. They were taught by their father, the late Ustad Hassan Kamkar, one of the master musicians of the region. They play both Kurdish folk and Iranian classical music and have brought some of the folk modes and instruments into the classical tradition.

★ Nightingale with a Broken Wing
Real World, UK

The album takes its title from a melancholy and beautiful song, one of four songs about nightingales in this collection. Reflective love songs and energetic dance pieces giving a good sample of Kurdish folk music, well performed.

Hamid Khezri

Khezri is a *dotar* player, born in 1969 near Guchan in northern Khorasan although he can play in both the northern and southern styles. He has had a long collaboration with singer Sima Bina. He currently lives in Germany.

⊙ The Dotar of Khorasan
VDE-Gallo/AIMP, Switzerland

A CD focusing just on the instrumental side of the *bakshi*'s art. It reveals the range of colours and textures available on the instrument in hands as skilled as these.

Ali Akbar Moradi

Born in 1957 in Guran, near Kermanshah, Moradi is a master of the Kurdish *tanbur* (long-necked lute). He has also become versed in the spiritual music of the Ahl-e Haqq, the People of the Truth, who use the *tanbur* in their ceremonies. Moradi has toured several times in Europe and the US.

⊙ Mystical Odes and Secular Music
Inédit, France

While his four CDs of the ritual *maqam* are specialized listening, this is an excellent album of some of the spiritual songs of the Ahl-e Haqq and the best Kurdish *tanbur* playing.

Amrollah Shahebrahimi

Shahebrahimi, born in 1923, comes from the other Kurdish centre of *tanbur* playing in Sahneh. One of the veteran masters of the tradition.

⊙ Sama: Mystic Dance Ritual
Mahoor Institute, Iran

A fascinating and intimate recording of the spiritual music and songs of the region. He plays the *tanbur* with a delicate and percussive touch, full of tonal variety.

Haj Ghorban Soleimani

Born in 1920 in the village of Aliabad in northern Khorasan, Haj Ghorban is one of the world's great bards or *bakshi*. He plays his long-necked *dotar* and sings love songs, epic stories and moralistic tales in Persian, Turkish and Kurdish. He knows thousands by heart, but has written them down in huge handwritten volumes kept in his small Aliabad home. Although the demand for bards at weddings has all but disappeared, he has performed at concerts all over Europe.

⊙ Music of the Bards from Iran
Kereshmeh, US

Fifteen instrumental pieces and songs from the master, with his son Alireza Soleimani on second *dotar*.

Pop Music

Arian

Iran's first post-revolutionary pop band released their debut album in 1999 and have since released two more. Arian is unusual in including a female instrumentalist and composer/lyricist, Shahrareh Farnejad. Success and commercial promotion have led to suggestions that they have lost touch with their grass-roots origins, but Arian still has a committed following in Iran. They are the only Iranian pop band to have toured abroad.

★ Ta Binahayat (To Infinity)
Tarane Sharghee, Iran

Arian's third and most recent album (2004) continues in the vein of their earlier two albums. This is pop music with a message, including one track ("White Pigeons") appealing for global peace sung in English, Arabic and Farsi.

Ali Reza Assar

One of the first crop of post-1998 'new pop' musicians, Ali Reza Assar now has an immense fan base. He has created his own brand of "mystic pop" which draws on Sufi imagery and instruments (such as daf). Assar works in close collaboration with composer and saxophonist Fouad Hejazi.

PLAYLIST
Iran

1 DEL MIRAVAD ZE DASTAM Shahram Nazeri & Dastan Ensemble from *Through Eternity: Homage to Molavi*
A great example of Dastan and Shahram Nazeri in full swing with all the electricity of a live performance. Poetry by Hafez, music by Nazeri.

2 GHODSIAN-E ASEMAN Ali Reza Assar from *Kooch-e Asheghaneh*
Perhaps the best-loved song by this popular singer. The lyrics are by Mowlana (Rumi) and the song is full of Sufi imagery.

3 FARYAD Mohammad Reza Shajarian, Hossein Alizadeh, Kayhan Kalhor & Homayoun Shajarian from *Faryad: Masters of Persian Music*
Much of the intense nature of this track is due to the lyrics of contemporary poet Mehdi Akhavan Saless. Listen out for the interesting 7-time metre.

4 QQ BANG BANG Googoosh from *QQ Bang Bang*
Googoosh's best-selling post-2000 album comprises this one song in a CD/DVD package. Her commentary on the diaspora experience resonates deeply with many Iranians living outside Iran.

5 ZAKHM Meera from *Meera*
A luscious track which features funky bass and chord riffs under the beautiful strains of *ghelchack* which alternates with the sung verses.

6 FIRE Ghazal from *The Rain*
Elegant improvisations on sitar and *kamancheh* from Shujaat Khan and Kayhan Kalhor. Magical.

7 HEART'S LAMENT & SEMA OF THE BUTTERFLY Ali Akbar Moradi from *Mystical Odes and Secular Music*
Mystical odes on *tanbur*, vocals and *tombaks* from the People of the Truth.

8 SHAHPARAK Arian from *Ta Binahayat*
In what has become a recognizable trademark of Arian's style, the band sings allegorically of a butterfly trying to fly up from behind a wall and reach for the sky and eternity.

9 LARZAN The Kamkars from *Nightingale With a Broken Wing*
Rousing dance music from Iranian Kurdistan by this family of musicians.

10 SARI GALIN Hossein Alizadeh & Djivan Gasparyan from *Endless Vision*
An old favourite in Iran, this version of "Sari Galin" includes Azeri (Turkish), Armenian and Persian lyrics.

⭐ **Kooch-e Asheghaneh**
Avay-e Barq Records, Iran
Assar's first commercial CD (whose title means "loving migration") was released in 1999. It includes what is perhaps his most popular song, "Ghodsian-e Aseman", which is strongly suffused with Sufi symbolism and set to words by Mowlana.

Googoosh

The all-time diva of Iranian pop, Googoosh holds a very special place in the hearts of Iranians. She was Iran's most popular singer of the pre-revolutionary period but, living in Iran, recorded nothing after 1979. Since moving to Canada in 2000, Googoosh has released three albums, *Zartosht* (2000), *Q Q Bang Bang* (2003, CD/DVD) and *Last News* (2004).

⭐ **Q Q Bang Bang**
Taraneh Records, US
A remarkable music DVD which draws on the collective experience of a people whose recent history has included revolution and war, upheaval, separation and loss. Weaving together memories of home and the stark realities of life in diaspora, Googoosh expresses – in her own unique way – the contemporary experience of families scattered by the rupture of 1979.

⊙ **Pol (Bridge)**
Taraneh Records, US
Googoosh has a lyrical, breathy voice accompanied by soft strings and an easy-listening beat. The title-track here is one of her most celebrated love songs in a good collection of hits.

Meera

One of the many grass-roots rock bands currently active in Iran, Meera was the first to secure government authorization for an album release. Several members have previously played in other groups, including the now disbanded

Iranian-jazz fusion band Avizheh. Like many young people in Iran, these musicians are cosmopolitan and internationalist in outlook: through their music they seek to reconcile modernity and tradition and to reach out to a global audience whilst also expressing local concerns.

⊙ Meera
Gienne Records, Iran
Meera's first album (2004) creates a rich melange of sounds out of many different musical influences including progressive rock, jazz and traditional Iranian sounds. It features three guest musicians, including Reza Abaee whose spike fiddle, with its deeply soulful sound, adds wonderful colouring to the ensemble.

Moeen

Moeen is a 50-something singer with a modernized acoustic backing, including traditional instruments like violin, *tar* and *tombak*.

⊙ Panjereh (Window)
Taraneh Records, US
1997 album representative of his popular, but distinctively Iranian, style.

Siavash

A singer popular among teenage Tehrangeles. The music is Westernized Iranian pop.

⊙ Hamsayeha (Neighbours)
Caltex, US
One of his best CDs with cheerful uptempo songs, plus the more ballad like "Dokhtar Irani" (Iranian Girl).

Iraq

mesopotamia forever

Kazim al-Saher, Iraqi superstar
demgt.com

Iraq covers a large part of what used to be called Mesopotamia, one of the "cradles of civilization". This fertile area has always been attractive to settlers and invaders, and many of the key developments of Judaism, Christianity and Islam took place here. The area was controlled by the Ottomans from the 1500s until World War I, when the British took over. Soon after came the discovery of massive oil deposits – a mixed blessing at best. Winston Churchill, who helped draw the borders, claimed to have put three peoples together above two oil wells, and the legacy of this lives on, with the country ravaged by conflict in the aftermath of the US-led invasion of 2003. Since the invasion, musical life in Baghdad has all but ceased. Neil van der Linden describes the musical riches that hopefully will re-emerge.

raqi music has a long history. Some of the world's most ancient musical instruments are from the region, including a golden harp bearing the bull's head of Ur dating from around 2750 BC. Assyrian bas-reliefs also depict musical instruments. Around 800 AD, under the great caliph Harun al-Rashid, Baghdad's court rose to new heights, housing many renowned musicians. **Ziryab**, a young man of perhaps Persian or Gypsy origin, rose to fame at this court before settling in the Arab outpost of Cordoba, where he founded the first known music conservatory in Europe. He thus introduced Mesopotamian-Arabic music to the West, which had a far-reaching influence on European musical development.

The legacy of this long history is a rich and diverse musical scene, enthusiastically embraced by the Iraqi people who, as any concert by Kazim al-Saher, Ilham al-Madfai or Farida Mohammed Ali will show, simply want to enjoy themselves. Indeed, in peaceful times at least, Iraq can seem more joyful than any other Arab nation. That, more than anything, holds a promise for the future of Iraqi music, and for Iraq.

Maqam

Iraq has known a certain degree of wealth and urbanization for millennia, so it has a long-established urban middle-class music as well as more rural styles. The classical urban middle-class music is the **maqam**. In the Arab world, a *maqam* is a microtonal mode – a scale with intervals different from the tones and semitones of Western music. In Iraq, however, the term can also refer to a suite of instrumental and vocal music based on a fixed combination of scales. In this respect, the Iraqi *maqam* is fully comparable to the *makam* of Turkey, the *mugham* of Azerbaijan, the *shashmaqam* of Uzbekistan and Tajikistan and the *dastgah* of Iran – reflecting the fact that the music of Iraq is closer to that of its northeastern neighbours than to the Arab world. This is reflected in the prominence of the *santur* – a cimbalom widely used in Iran.

The traditional *maqam* line-up, or **tchalgi Baghdadi**, consists of a *djose* (spike fiddle), *santur*, *darbuka* drum and *riqq* (tambourine). At times *qanun* (zither) and *ney* (flute) are added, and all the instrumentalists contribute vocals in the *pesteh*, the lighter song which ends the *maqam*. Interestingly, despite Iraq's rich tradition of *oud* playing (see box), the lute is rarely used in *maqam* music, which further highlights the remoteness of Iraqi *maqam* from most Arab music.

Originally, *maqam* sessions were all-night affairs, conducted in bourgeois houses, fashionable

middle-class cafés and *zurkaneh*s – Sufi gathering places for ritual physical exercises, which still exist in Iran as well. The skills required for classical *maqam* singing are comparable to those needed for proper recitation of the Koran, and many contemporary *maqam* singers – such as **Hussein al-Athamy** and even the late Jewish singer **Filfel Gourgy** – perform both roles.

A landmark for Iraqi *maqam* on the international stage was the big Cairo meeting on Arabic music in 1932 (see Arab World/Egypt Classical chapter). There, the legendary singer **Mohammed al-Qubanchy** (1900–89) and his ensemble performed Iraqi *maqam* for a wide, knowledgeable audience (interestingly, six of his seven accompanying musicians were Jewish). Qubanchy is famed for having "modernized" *maqam*, emphasizing the expression and pronunciation of sung text. This was a departure from the traditional school of embellishment practised by the likes of **Rachid al-Qundarchi** (1887–1945).

Maqam is not the most immediately accessible of musics, but the Iraqi government has long promoted the style, and Qubanchy and his pupil **Yusuf Omar** (1918–87) were household names in the country until very recently, even among the working classes. Overseas, both artists are much less widely known, though at least they are represented on European labels, unlike other stars of the past such as **Ahmad Zaydan** (1820–1912), **Youssouf Huraish** (1889–1975), **Najim al-Sheikhli** (1893–1938), **Hassan Chewke** (1912–68) and **Sadiqa al-Mulayya** (1901–68). Iraqi radio archives and some private record companies are known to have had recordings of these artists, so let's hope that not everything has been lost in the current situation. The *maqam* group **Angam al-Rafidain** (Rivers of Mesopotamia) used to perform at the National Museum in Baghdad, but now their living has disappeared with many of the national treasures. They've recently had to rely on a few international tours.

Farida Mohammed Ali is a more recent *maqam* performer, and one of the few female musicians in the genre. Having fled Iraq, this young student of *oud* maestro Munir Bashir settled in Holland, recorded a series of fine albums and launched an international touring career. Another contemporary voice to be heard in Europe is **Hamid as-Saadi**, a one-time student of Yusuf Omar. Hamid's concerts give a good indication of what Yusuf himself sounded like. Unfortunately, for legal reasons he isn't able to perform outside the UK.

Hopefully, an improvement in the situation in Iraq will allow new resident singers and groups to break through. International recognition of the

Jewish Musicians in Iraq

Jews have been living in Iraq since the defeat of the ten northern Jewish tribes by the Assyrians and the conquest of Jerusalem by the Babylonians, and have participated considerably in cultural life. A renowned Iraqi *qanun* player **Salem Hussein** has said, 'The greatest times in Iraqi music were when the Jews were with us, and they were among the greatest musicians.'

Prominent Jewish names in the story of Iraqi music include **Salem Daoud**, **Filfel Gourgy**, **Yusuf Huraish**, **Salman Moshe**, **Selima Murad**, **Salim Shibbeth**, **Yusuf Zarur**, the prolific songwriting brothers **Saleh** and **Daud al-Kuwaiti** (who wrote a string of hits for Selima Murad and many others before emigrating to Israel) and their relative, the renowned Israeli *oud* player **Yair Dalal** (see Israel chapter). Nowadays there is an expat community in Israel actively keeping their Iraqi traditions alive, centred on the **Babylonian Heritage Centre** in Or Yehuda.

Until 1982, **Naim Twenna** – said to be an acquaintance of Saddam Hussein – lived in Iraq. He hosted Mohammed al-Qubanchy, Nathem al-Ghazaly and Selima Murad in his house in Baghdad, and was the head of the Iraqi music department of Israel Radio. **Naim Razjwan** of Ramat Ghan, who left Iraq as an adolescent, still organizes Iraqi music meetings for the Israeli radio and television. Filfel Gourgy (c. 1930–89) emigrated to Israel at a young age and became a skilled Iraqi *maqam* singer there.

genre came in 2003 when UNESCO designated the Iraqi *maqam* tradition a Masterpiece of the Oral and Intangible Heritage of Humanity.

Baghdad's Roaring Fifties

The 1950s brought Baghdad a first peak in prosperity, and a vibrant urban life. It was in this period that Mohammed al-Qubanchy's foremost student, **Nathem al-Ghazaly** (1910–63), put his mark on Iraqi music, turning *maqam* into a much lighter affair, mainly singing *pestehs*. His songs are widely known throughout the country to this day, and are performed by many contemporary artists. Ghazaly died quite young, but his wife, **Selima Murad** (1902–74), lived for another decade and remains the most popular female singer of the past, though she never achieved as much popularity in the rest of the Arab world as did her husband.

Afifa Iskander, an Assyrian who fled to Iraq during the genocide in Turkey, was perhaps the greatest female vocalist in Iraq in the 1950s. After Saddam Hussein came to power, however, she cut short her career, not wanting to sing for him, and refusing to be celebrated by the regime as the "grand old lady" of Iraqi music. According to recent information, she is still alive. Other notable female vocalists from the era include **Ensaph Munir**, originally from Lebanon, who was thrown out of Iraq because of an espionage affair, **Zuhur Hussein**, a rural singer from the south, **Narzjes Shawqi**, **Zakiya George**, **Lamiya Tawfiq** and **Wahida Khalil**.

In terms of political stability, the decade ended badly, with a 1958 coup abolishing royal rule. The royal family were butchered, as was Prime Minister Nuri as-Said, who had been viewed by many as the personification of the democratic promise of the last decade. Among those active in the coup was a young officer named Saddam Hussein.

The Assyrians

The Christian, Aramaic-speaking **Assyrian** people – assumed to be the descendants of the famous Assyrians of ancient times – are scattered through Iran, Syria, Lebanon, Jordan, Israel/Palestine and Turkey. Partly as the result of Turkish oppression in the early twentieth century, there's a strong Assyrian diaspora in Europe and North America. In Iraq, the Assyrians are based in the area around the northern city of Mosul, which was once promised to them by the British as the capital of a separate Assyrian nation.

The best-known Assyrian musicians within Iraq are *oud* legend **Munir Bashir** (1930–97) and his family, and singer Afifa Iskander. Bashir believed that Iraqi and other Arabic *maqam* music originated from the Assyrian church modes in the villages around Mosul.

As for the diaspora, there's Baghdad-born, California-based **Linda George** – a pop star who has recorded more than a dozen albums. In Lebanon, the priest and musicologist **Elie Kesouani** leads an ensemble which preserves the religious music of the Syrian Orthodox church, and in Aleppo, there's the ensemble of composer and conductor **Nouri Iskander**, who have released a CD titled *Syrian Orthodox Church Antioch Liturgy* (Inédit).

The Great Iraqi Oud Tradition

Iraq has a reputation for its *oud* players, among whom the brothers **Munir and Jamil Bashir** stand out. Born into an Assyrian Syrian Orthodox family in Mosul, they became nationalist musical icons and dominated Iraq's musical life from the end of the 1960s onwards. Jamil died in 1977, but left a strong musical legacy. Munir became the founder of the **Babylon Festival** and the head of the music department of the Ministry of Culture and Information under Saddam. However, in 1994 he suddenly left the country, thereafter dividing his time between Amman, Budapest (where his wife lived) and Paris, which had always welcomed him warmly. In the last decade of his life, Munir's music became very delicate and even somewhat esoteric, but he drew large audiences in Europe until his death in 1997.

Among today's *oud* players are Munir's student **Naseer Shamma** and his son, **Omar Bashir**. Naseer, from Kut in eastern Iraq, has made a name for himself across the Arab world. He left Iraq in the late 1990s when, he says, Saddam Hussein's courting of him became too threatening, and now lives in Cairo. Omar's music leans towards crossover. This is the curse of much current *oud* playing: many players think Western audiences would rather hear them imitating Spanish guitars than playing original Arabic music.

Munir Bashir

Rural Sounds

Besides the urban *maqam* tradition of Baghdad, Mosul and Kirkuk, Iraq has a palette of **rural musics**, representing the full spectrum of the country's ethnic groups and denominations. Recently, however, with huge numbers moving from the countryside to the cities, the boundaries between rural and urban music are starting to blur in places.

Rural music traditions have always been particularly strong in the Shiite towns and villages of mid- and southern Iraq, though recordings of past heroes such as **Massaoud Omoratly** (1930s–40s) and **Zuhur Hussein** and **Dakhil Hassan** (1950s–70s) are yet to be released internationally.

Bedouin songs – similar to those of the Arabian Peninsula and the Syrian desert – are found across much of the countryside, usually performed with accompaniment on bowed *rabbah*. Particularly popular is the *chobi* folkloric dance, comparable to the *dabke* of Syria, Jordan and Palestine. Current pop music stars such as Kazim al-Saher and Ilham al-Madfai always include a *chobi* session in their concerts.

Near the Persian Gulf, **khaleeji** music shows connections with the musical cultures of the Gulf states and the Iranian coast, home to many relatives of Iraq's southern tribes. The complex **iqat** rhythms of much Iraqi music (especially that of the rural south) suggest even more distant influences: those of sub-Saharan Africa.

Popular Music

There's no shortage of popular music in Iraq, despite the iron rule of Saddam Hussein during the 1980s and 90s. Without question, the biggest star is **Kazim al-Saher**, a household name in the

Ilham al-Madafi (centre) and his group

whole of the Arab world who is now crossing over to a wider international audience. Another big name is 60-something **Ilham al-Madfai**, known for feel-good renditions of Iraqi standards (including *maqam pestehs*). With his limited vocal capacities, Ilham is not the "voice of Iraq" that his record company claims he is, but a performance by him to an Iraqi audience guarantees enough fun to defy many misconceptions about the country. Familiar melodies of the past will be heard, often with the audience participating to such an

extent that Madfai hardly has to produce a sound. Other good middle-generation singers – such as **Sadoun Jabr**, **Mahmud Anwar**, **Fouad Salem** and **Hatem al-Iraqi** – have attracted less international attention, but remain very popular at home. Then there's **Majid al-Muhandis**, an upcoming performer who sings in the vein of Kazim al-Saher. Still only represented on recordings inside the Arabic world, his performances are frequently aired on Lebanese and Gulf TV, and he seem destined for big things.

DISCOGRAPHY Iraq

Radio and TV were well funded under Saddam, and documented Iraqi music-making as well. If things stabilize in the country, opportunities may arise to start exploring the stations' archives – as well as those of record companies like the great Tchakmakchi, which has recorded and supported all the great Iraqi singers. In the meantime, there are still a decent number of discs available internationally.

⊙ **Baghdad Blues**
Virgin/EMI, UK
This collection is uneven but wide-ranging, including two Transglobal Underground remixes of Kazim al-Saher's "Baghdad", some originals by Sadoun Jaber, classical *tchalgi*, rural music and a hymn to Baghdad by Lebanese singer Fairuz.

⊙ **Mesopotamix**
Virgin/EMI UK
Uptempo remixes of Iraqi singers and instrumentalists ranging from Nathem al-Ghazaly and Omar Bashir to younger, little-known names. Though not particularly authentic, as generic Arabic dance with an Iraqi flavour it's well worth hearing.

Maqam

Nathem al-Ghazaly

Some of Ghazaly's most beautiful material is still in the vaults of Iraqi Radio, if it survived the recent war. Nothing by his wife, Selima Murad, has yet appeared on CD.

★ **Nazem Alghazali vols 1 and 2**
Buzaidphone, Kuwait/Greece
Bad audio reproduction quality, but still essential. Vol 2 includes his beautiful *mawal* (unmetred improvisation) "Samra min Kawmi Issa" on the hopeless love between a girl from a Christian tribe and a boy from a Muslim tribe.

Filfel Gourgy

A fine Jewish Iraqi singer, who was renowned for recitations of the Koran in Baghdad. He later left for Israel, where he wrote many songs about his longing for Baghdad.

⊙ **The World Is Happy**
Magda Records, Israel
Filfel Gourgy composed most of his own *maqams*, *pestehs* and other songs. This was the first collection of his music to be issued by a Western commercial company, after his recordings had been widely but illegally circulating in Iraq.

Saleh & Daoud al-Kuwaity

Jewish brothers Saleh & Daoud al-Kuwaity achieved great success as composers and performers during the 1930s (they were said to be the ill-fated King Faisal's favourite entertainers). They never found the same success in their newly adopted home of Israel, but their recordings continued to be popular throughout the Arab world up until the 1960s (albeit with their names and new nationality omitted).

⊙ **Their Star Shall Never Fade**
Magda, Israel
Surviving relatives oversaw this double-CD remastering of some of the brothers' most popular songs. It's admittedly a connoisseur's choice, with a few scratches and crackles, but it's clear what accomplished musicians the brothers were, ranking alongside legends like Mohammed Abd el-Wahab.

Farida Mohammed Ali and the Iraqi Maqam Ensemble

One of the very few female *maqam* singers, in a fine ensemble with her husband, Mohammed Gomar, her brother and son. All now live in the Netherlands.

★ **Classical Music of Iraq**
Samarkand, Netherlands
This was the first CD of Farida's music to be issued in the West, recorded before her departure from Baghdad in August 1997. The sound quality is satisfying and the intensity of the performances is captivating.

⊙ **La voix de la Mésopotamie**
Long Distance/Harmonia Mundi, France
Another excellent album, with the advantage of a live atmosphere (it was recorded at the Festival les Orientales). At the end is a track of improvisations on Iraqi *iqat* rhythms.

Mohammed al-Qubanchy

Although he died in 1989, Qubanchy is still the best-known *maqam* singer in Iraq. For a singer of such stature he is sadly underrepresented in the international market, with only the two CDs listed below. There are some pieces by him on the website *www.iraq4u.com*. In Iraq there are endless recordings on cassette and vinyl.

★ **Congres du Caire 1 and 2**
Edition Bibliotheque Nationale, France
Two CDs of historical recordings made by the BBC at the Cairo

Arabic Music Congress in 1932. The audio quality is poor and, according to some, somebody has been messing with the editing, but this is still essential listening. Interestingly, six out of the seven musicians recorded here were Iraqi-Jewish.

Rachid al-Qundarchi

Senior to Qubanchy, Qundarchi laid more emphasis on vocal embellishment, and thus was of the "old school" of pure bel canto, which died out soon after him.

⊙ Musique savante d'Irak
Al-Sur, France
This is a very old recording, so there is a lot of hiss, etc. Due to the recording capacities of the time the *maqam*s are only short sections. The bel canto is not for the uninitiated, but it is beautiful.

Oud Players

Munir Bashir

Perhaps the most influential *oud* player in the Middle East. Together with his brother Jamil, he was a student of Sharif Muhieddin Haydar, who had studied in Turkey where he was known as Serif Muhiddin Targan. Together with their master, they were responsible for emancipating the *oud* as a solo instrument throughout the Arab world.

★ Maqamat
Inédit, France
A 1993 studio recording made in Budapest. The music is amazing, the virtuosity not so much in the notes (which are impeccable) as in the silences that grab the listener. The name *maqam* here refers not to the Iraqi *maqam* genre, but to the Arabic scales, of which some rare varieties exist in Iraq.

⊙ En concert
Inédit France
A magnificent live recording from 1988, the time of his main international breakthrough.

Khaled Mohammed Ali

Khaled Mohammed Ali is a good composer for the *oud*, and an excellent player, now living in the Emirates.

WITH HASAM FALEH

▦ Escaped Eyes
Funoun al-Emarat, UAE
For this recording he teams up with Hasan Faleh, the excellent *qanun* player of Kazim al-Saher's orchestra, finding new modulations and harmonies that fit in well.

Naseer Shamma

A student of Munir Bashir, Shamma is now the leading Iraqi *oud* player on Western stages. Though his emulations of Spanish guitar are best avoided, he is amazing when playing more Iraqi styles.

⊙ The Baghdad Lute
Institut du Monde Arabe, France
This live recording takes us on "a journey from Baghdad to Grenada". The "Spanish" pieces are less interesting, but the album closes with a dramatic fifteen-minute testament to the four hundred people killed when a bomb destroyed a shelter at al-Amiriyya on February 13, 1991 during the infamous Desert Storm operation. The mediocre sound engineering does not serve the *oud* well.

1 YAM AL OYOUN AL SOOD Nathem al-Ghazaly from *Mesopotamix*
Although a remix, with only recurring snippets of Ghazaly's beautiful voice and nothing characteristic of the usual accompaniment, this is very haunting.

2 SAMRA MIN KAWMI ISSA Nathem al-Ghazaly from *Nazem Alghazali Vol 2*
"The brown-haired girl from the Christian tribe": many Iraqis know this by heart, as it is in the repertoire of Ilham al-Madfai and Farida Mohammed Ali.

3 MAQAM SABAH Farida Mohammed Ali and the Iraqi Maqam Ensemble from *Classical Music of Iraq*
The *maqam sabah* (here with a text in the Baghdad dialect and classical Arabic), is the *maqam* with the largest number of microtones and nine notes in a scale instead of eight, giving it a very sad effect.

4 ZEIDINI ISHQAN Kazim al-Saher from *Fi Madrasat al-Hob*
Based on a poem by the famous Syrian poet Nizar Qabbani, and deservedly popular from Morocco to Muscat. A beautiful combination of catchy pop and innovative arrangements.

5 MAQAM MUKHALIF, AWSHAR, SIGAH, SABA Munir Bashir from *Maqamat*
It's easy to imagine this dramatic slow piece as a farewell to Baghdad, which Munir Bashir would not see again.

Pop

Ilham al-Madfai

The former pop guitarist turned light classical Iraqi music crooner.

⊙ The Voice of Iraq
Virgin/EMI, UK
A 2005 compilation of his regular repertoire, a series of covers of well-known Iraqi songs. As his Western promoters don't know the originals, however, Madfai gets the credits.

Kazim al-Saher

Iraq's "weapon of mass seduction", the handsome Kazim is the biggest name in Iraqi pop.

★ Barefooted
EMI, UK
The first of two albums released in 2004, this features a duet with Sarah Brightman. Apart from this superfluous track, it's a well-balanced album, with some good mainstream Arabic hits and some excellent work based on Iraqi tradition. Don't be put off by the synthetic-sounding synthesizer brass that opens the first track of the album.

IRAQ

Israel

narrow bridge/global village

Yair Dalal (right) with his group Asmar
Yair Dalal

'The whole world is a narrow bridge and the most important thing is not to be afraid,' said the eighteenth-century Polish rabbi Nahman. The whole world is also a global village and in the small state of Israel you can find Jewish immigrants from 127 countries all round the world. They started to return in 1882 after two thousand years of exile in the diaspora, and they brought with them their traditions, languages and, of course, their very different traditions of music. Israel, asserts Dubi Lenz, is the natural home of global fusion.

The **Altneuland** in Israel was the dream and Zionist vision of Theodor Herzl, fulfilling the long yearning for a "promised land". From 1882, the waves of immigration started, mainly from Eastern Europe, but also from Yemen, North Africa and Asia. With the declaration of the State of Israel in 1948 the influx escalated, and there were countries – Yemen, Libya, Iraq, Bulgaria – from where the whole Jewish community (or what remained after the Holocaust) came as one to their old-new homeland. In the years since then, Jews have continued to make *aliya* (from the Hebrew word "to go up"), particularly when circumstances grew difficult in their old homeland. Most recently, thousands have come from the former Soviet Union and Ethiopia.

Songs of the Good Old Land

An Israeli born in Israel is called a *sabra* (literally, the fruit of the prickly pear cactus – prickly on the outside and sweet inside) and conventional wisdom has it that if, on a Friday evening, you put a guitar in a sabra's hand, a harmonica in their mouth and add an accordion, song will fill the air. Those songs are known in Hebrew as *Shirei Eretz Israel Hay'shana Ve Hatova* – **Songs of the Good Old Land of Israel**. The words "old" and "good" are synonymous here – it is nostalgia which fills the throat (not that old times were much better – but that's the nature of nostalgia). These are songs born of the youth and kibbutz movements, songs thick with the dust of the road, redolent of suffering and, of course, love.

Many of these Hebrew songs are set to **Slavic and Russian melodies** adopted by the earliest Israeli songwriters from Eastern Europe. Most of the songs of the youth movement date from that time, and the best of them are known to everyone: for example, the Hebrew version of the famous Russian song "Katyusha".

For political reasons, those new Israeli songs were written in Hebrew – the language of the new country. Yet Hebrew was also the holy tongue, sacred and honourable and for many it was unthinkable that songs about mundane human affairs should be sung in the language in which men and women communicated with their God. Nonetheless, from 1948 there was a deliberate policy to encourage Hebrew at the expense of the languages of exile that the immigrants brought with them – principally **Yiddish** and **Ladino**, from the Ashkenazi and Sephardic communities respectively.

Until quite recently it was hard to find an Israeli musician dedicating him- or herself to **Yiddish** or **Ladino** songs, although some of Israel's best singers have released occasional albums in Yiddish (**Chava Alberstein**, **Mike Burstein**) or Ladino (**Yehoram Gaon**, **Lolik**, **Esther Ofarim**). However, in the last few years – perhaps because of the evolving success of **Klezmer** music and Ladino singers outside Israel – more and more Israeli musicians have gone back to their parents', or even grandparents', heritage and language, and recorded the "old" music with a new approach. Such artists include **Yasmin Levy**, **Suzy**, **Hadass Pal-Yarden**, **Kol Oud Tof Trio**, **Israeli Andalusian Orchestra**, **Udi Spielman**, **Eyal Sela** and **Shani Ben Canar**.

In the early years of the state of Israel, attempts were made to forge a specifically national style as well as a language of expression. It was said that Israeli music should be a bridge between the many musical cultures that had arrived on these shores, and it was felt that a new music should emerge free from the smack of exile. Deliberate attempts were made to **integrate Eastern and Western music**, but the results were somewhat forced – oriental (Middle Eastern and North African) rhythms and motifs not lending themselves easily to orchestration in a classical Western style.

The more successful composers in this "orientalist" style were **Mordechai Ze'ira**, **Moshe Wilensky** and **Sasha Argov** – all of whom were immigrants from Russia.

Yemenite Songs

From the 1930s to the 50s, oriental singers (from other Middle Eastern or North African countries) began to play an important part in Israeli music. These were mostly **Yemenites** such as **Bracha Zefira**, **Esther Gamlielit** and **Shoshana Damari**.

Yemenite singers have been hugely important in the development of Israeli music – the Jewish community in Yemen kept its tradition and way of living longer than any other community in the diaspora (from the first century AD until the end of the nineteenth century). Immigration from Yemen began in 1882 and concluded between 1948 and 1950. The Jews in Yemen had a very rich musical tradition. They sang on every occasion – in moments of sorrow and joy, songs of everyday life and prayer. Families used to gather and sing the old traditional songs with beautiful clear voices, mostly unaccompanied, as musical instruments were banned by the Muslims of the Arabian Peninsula.

In contemporary Israel, Yemenite Jews are amongst the leading popular artists. Current stars

Chava Alberstein: Shadow of Israel

On **Chava Alberstein**'s 2004 album *Motzai Khag* (End of the Holiday), there's a haunting song called "Shadow" about everybody having a shadow that walks alongside them and reflects their different aspects, good and bad. Alberstein could well be seen as that sort of uncomfortable shadow of her country. She's the same age as Israel itself and, having released over fifty recordings since the late 1960s, her development as an artist mirrors Israel's development as a country. Her first album, *Hine Lanu Nigun* (Here We Have a Song), was released in the same year as the Six Day War whose consequences still dominate the politics of Israel and Palestine. Her growing pains were Israel's growing pains, particularly the state's wish to create a national Hebrew culture, with its resulting marginalization of Yiddish.

Alberstein was born in Szczecin, Poland where her parents spoke Polish and Yiddish, and arrived in Israel as a baby. 'We came in 1950 to Haifa and were brought to a camp – it was a very poor camp with tents and it reminded many people of the concentration camps they'd been in during the war. It was very frightening for them because this was supposed to be a new country and a new beginning, but the beginning was very sad and hard. One of the first songs I wrote was "Sha'ar Haalia" [Gate of Immigration]. My story is the story of many new immigrants – combining the vision of both outsider and insider: part of my subject in music is the fact that I'm a mixture of diaspora and Israel. I've been described as the 'most Jewish of Israeli singers'. Israel is a new nation in the world, but in my music it is always the past and future together.'

Even in the early years when it was discouraged, Alberstein performed and recorded **Yiddish songs**. But her best-known project internationally is probably *The Well*, a ground-breaking 1998 collaboration with New York klezmer group **The Klezmatics** featuring new settings of Yiddish poetry. 'People always think of Yiddish as a language for humour and making jokes, but they don't realize there is a wonderful world of literature and poetry. The language itself has a sound, a softness, a warmth that Hebrew doesn't have. When I sing in Hebrew, it's basically for people in Israel. When I sing in Yiddish [as on her latest album *Lemele*, recorded in the Czech Republic], it's a universal message.' On the other side of Israeli culture, Alberstein also sings old Hebrew *niqunim* (religious songs), which brings her into conflict with the Orthodox community. But, as she says, 'For me Hassidic and religious songs are not a ritual thing, but part of my heritage and collective memory. I need them like I need Beethoven, Mozart and Shakespeare. It is very beautiful poetry and I get sad when Orthodox people want to restrict it to their own religious use. Judaism doesn't only belong to the Orthodox people, it belongs to me also.'

Alberstein has frequently been described as Israel's Joan Baez and admits American songwriters Baez and Pete Seeger were formative influences as musicians and icons. 'It was part of my growing up as a human being,' she admits. 'From a distance, I was involved with all kinds of rights movements in America. In my soul I was there. In the eternal argument about whether an artist should actively take part or sit in their room and write about lofty things, I've always believed in taking part.'

Alberstein started to get involved in politics at home when President Sadat of Egypt first visited Israel in 1977 to begin peace talks, and she became a vocal part of the Peace Now movement, a tendency which takes her beyond the arts pages of the Israeli newspapers. During the years of the Palestinian intifada she wrote "Chad Gadya" (One Goat), a song the authorities tried to ban from the radio: 'I based it on a traditional song we sing at Passover when we sit down to eat together. It is something like "The Woman Who Swallowed a Fly". In this version a dog bites a cat, a stick beats the dog, fire burns the stick, water puts out the fire, an ox drinks the water, a butcher kills the ox and then the Angel of Death comes, and so on. It is a circle of violence, and I wanted to make a modern song about this, and how you can get drawn into violence. Israeli soldiers in the occupied territories were behaving very brutally towards Palestinian women and children which was something new and shocking in Israel. This wasn't necessarily the soldiers' fault – it was the fault of the situation. To stop these people behaving like animals the occupation needed to be stopped.'

End of the Holiday didn't get airplay in Israel, and Alberstein has become increasingly disillusioned by Israeli politics over the last decade. 'Everything is politicized', she says. 'For example, the concept of suffering. Of course we suffer, but there are other people who also suffer. But everything here is compared to our own suffering. It is such a banal standard of measurement and a lot of people can't stand it any more'.

Simon Broughton (with thanks to Anastasia Tsioulcas)

include **Noa** (Achinoam Nini), **Gali Atari**, **Boaz Shar'abi**, **Zohar Argov** and the late **Ofra Haza** – the best-known singer outside Israel, through the success of her traditional *Yemenite Songs* album (1985) and her soundtrack for Spielberg's *Prince of Egypt* animation (1998). Haza's recordings drew on the **Diwan repertoire** – devotional songs that cover both religious and secular subjects and are performed at weddings and other celebrations.

Noa's music has an interesting take on the Yemenite tradition, combining elements of jazz with a marvellous voice and musicality; she has worked with Sting, Zucchero, Pat Metheny and Sardinia's Andrea Parodi. For Boaz Shar'abi, influences include Western music and Songs of the Good Old Land of Israel, as well as the Yemenite musical tradition.

The most recent addition to the Yemenite musical heritage is **Zafa**.

Roots and Fusions

Yemenite roots were not the only ones to resurface in the 1980s and 90s, as a new sabra generation looked to air their inherited music beyond the synagogues or family celebrations. Many musicians started to record "hard core" **Middle Eastern-style music**, often cheaply produced on small independent labels, as an alternative to mainstream Israeli rock and pop. A semi-underground cassette culture developed for their music, along with a few dedicated pirate stations.

Many major Israeli artists started their careers on the indie labels, being taken up by the mainstream labels once they'd made it. Their number include **Zehava Ben**, **Chaim Moshe**, **Margalith Zan'ani**, the late **Zohar Argov**, **Eli Luzon**, **Avner**

Gedassi, **Sarit Hadad** and the Israeli-Arab violinist and singer **Samir Shukri**.

For many of these and other contemporary Israeli artists, a fusion of Eastern and Western elements is a natural part of their creative processes and family history. **Ehud Banai** and his cousin **Me'ir Banai** offer rhythms and melodies from their Iranian heritage. **Yehuda Poliker** – one of the most popular rock artists in Israel – adds his Greek roots to his music, while **Miki Gavrielov**, who has written some of the best-known Hebrew songs, incorporates his Turkish ancestry. For **Shem Tov Levy**, one of Israel's most melodic pop composers, the key was when he was asked to write a soundtrack for Beni Torati's film *Desperado Square*. He brought to the score his Balkan roots mixed with Arab music, winning an Israeli Oscar for his work.

There is a particularly rich strain of musicians proclaiming their Moroccan heritage, among them **Sfatayim**, **Tanara**, **Sahara**, **Marakesh**, **Shimon Bouskila** and the biggest name of them all – **Amir Benayun** – a young, very talented *oud* player and singer-songwriter.

Other notable fusionists include the violinist and *oud* player **Yair Dalal** and his group **Al Ol** (see box opposite), who have forged a successful mix of Jewish, Arabic and other traditions; the **Ziryab Trio** (comprising *oud*, violin and Arabic percussion), who explore the traditions of Arabic and Turkish classical music; and **Tea Packs**, who with leader Kobi Oz, create an "oriental" pop akin to groups like Les Negresses Vertes. Then there is the cantor **Emil Zrihan** who combines the Arab-Andalusian tradition with the Hebrew liturgy; **Ilana Eliya** singing the Kurdish songs of her father; and the **Alayev Family**, blending the music of Tajikistan with Israeli songs. **Nash Didan** perform ethno-ambient music sung in the biblical Aramaic language that Jesus spoke (preserved for two thousand years by the Nash Didan Jewish tribe on the borders of Azerbaijan, Iran, Turkey and Russia). **Shlomo Gronich** sings Israeli-Ethiopian songs with the Sheba Choir, while **Atraf** even have a Hebrew take on Latin salsa.

Brazilian influence can be found in the music of **Tucan Trio**, the guitarist **Hagai Rehavia**, the percussionist **Joca Perpignan** and **Gadi Seri**, who mixes oriental music with bossa nova and calls the result "Arabossa". **Black Velvet**, **Evergreen** and **Kahol** are just three ensembles playing Celtic music – the last one mixing it with Middle Eastern music and Balkan beats.

The most significant fusion group, however, active for the past thirty or so years, are **Habrera Hativeet** (The Natural Gathering). They shook

Yair Dalal: Israeli Oud

Composer, violin and *oud* player, **Yair Dalal** frequently gets boycotted by festivals that actually support his desire for peace. He has played and recorded with Bedouin in Sinai, many Arabic and Palestinian musicians, and his song "Zaman el Salaam" (Time for Peace), was performed by Palestinian, Israeli and Norwegian children to celebrate the tentative steps towards peace by Shimon Perez and Yassar Arafat in 1994.

Dalal's parents came from Baghdad and he was born into the strongly musical Mizrachi (oriental Jewish) community. 'I was born in Israel,' he explains. 'But we spoke Arabic at home and it was the language of the "enemy". We listened to Arabic music and it was the music of the "enemy". So in the beginning I felt different, that there was something wrong. They are Ashkenazi and we're Mizrachi. When I went to WOMAD I played with an Iraqi *oud* player. It was fabulous. We share the same roots. We speak the same language, we eat the same food. He's an Arab, I'm a Jew. Many years ago it was like that. Why not now? Maybe it's a little bit naive, but I consider the Iraqi people as brothers. We've been living together for more than two thousand years.'

Sadly, the increasingly polarized situation in Israel and Palestine has meant that even the collaborative projects Dalal used to do have now become impossible. There are two similar festivals, the Palestinian-run Jerusalem Festival and the Israeli-run Jerusalem International *Oud* Festival, and, although they might share ideals, they can't share artists. 'My good friend Driss el Maloumi is an *oud* player from Morocco. I asked him to come to Jerusalem. He said "No way, if I come to Jerusalem I might lose my audience in other Arab countries. And then I can't go to other festivals because someone will say 'if he's coming from Israel, then I'm not coming from Syria or Lebanon'". This means that we artists are caught in the political situation even though we're trying to affect the opposite. Of course, a peace concert will not create a peace agreement between Palestine and Israel, but it will at least cheer people and heal people and help make a movement towards this peace.'

Simon Broughton (with thanks to Nathaniel Handy)

up Israeli music in the 1970s by forging a mix of Moroccan, Yemenite and Hassidic songs, and over the years have added influences from Africa, blues and classical music. They had to struggle for acceptance (the majority of Israel's media people were raised on Western music), but they have become one of the most influential forces in Israeli culture. **Shlomo Bar**, the group's prime mover, is

Nada Records

Bustan Abraham

eclectic in his tastes. He sings texts from the Old Testament and contemporary protest songs about the government's attitude towards new immigrants from North Africa.

A similar musical line was drawn by **Bustan Abraham** (Garden of Abraham), which was founded in 1991 by **Avshalom Farjum**, and existed for more than ten years. The group combined seven distinguished Israeli musicians – both Jews and Israeli-Arabs – who drew on Middle Eastern, Indian, classical, jazz, flamenco and American folk music in an original and compelling way, building musical and personal bridges between Arabs and Jews.

One of Israel's most successful ensembles is **Sheva** ('Seven') – who create and perform mostly original music, incorporating instruments from around the world and motifs from the roots of Hebrew and Arabic cultures as well as tribal cultures. These "flower-children of the new millennium" still believe in the strength of music to bring peace to the world, combining biblical texts, Sufi *zikrs* and updated prayers for peace and tolerance. Shortly after Sheva was founded (1997) in the mountains of Galilee they became a phenomenon in the Israeli World Music market, attracting thousands of people to their performances, creating a musical journey through meditation, prayer and celebration. Sheva's main singer – **Mosh Ben Ari** – started his successful solo career with the same musical elements of the ensemble.

The natural beauty of the northern part of Israel – the mountains of Galilee looking over the calm Sea of Galilee – inspires many Israeli musicians, among them **Essev Bar**. Tzfat (or Safed) – the capital city of the Galilee – is one of the four holy Jewish cities in Israel and a historic centre of the **Kabalah religion**, where many *tzadikim* (righteous holy people) are buried. It hosts an annual Klezmer Festival and at least two ensembles are connected with the area – one of them that of the marvellous violin player **Ben Canar**, who has gathered around him the best musicians from the Russian immigration to Israel. They play a mixture of East European Gypsy music and Klezmer with Middle Eastern influences. The other is **Eyal Sela**, whose latest big project is the music of the many cultures, traditions and religions that have influenced the area for hundreds of years.

Israel Borochov's East-West Ensemble has embraced pretty much everything from Western classical, rock and jazz to Far Eastern music, dedicating itself lately to "Hidden Spirituals" – sacred songs from Jewish mystic sources from all diasporas, the music of the Kabalah.

Israeli jazz, pop and rock are also imbued with an eclectic, multicultural approach. The enormously popular **Fools of Prophecy** are doing it very successfully with a fusion of reggae dub, alongside hip-hop and dance – all spiced with an eastern Mediterranean flavour. But the two best-selling albums of the last few years have been by the innovative **Idan Reichel's Project**. These combine beautiful Israeli love songs with Ethiopian elements plus rhythms from Jamaica, South Africa and even Surinam.

Abatte is a well-known Ethiopian musician who has performed throughout Europe. He is an expert on traditional Ethiopian music and Jewish religious music that is sung in the synagogues in Ethiopia by the *Kesim* (similar to *Cohanim* priests).

Many hip-hop bands and soloists (like **Subliminal and the Shadow**, **Hadag Nachash** or **Muki**) pair their Middle Eastern grooves with biting commentary in Hebrew, French, English or Arabic about the misdemeanors of politicians, the war, the occupation, suicide bombers, the economic situation and so on. The Israeli-Arab rappers (like **Tamer Nafar**) feel that as Israeli Arabs, they get it from all sides: to Arabs outside Israel, they are traitors and to many Israeli Jews, they are dangerous Arabs.

What's going on underlines the musical riches that Israel has within its borders as a result of over a century of immigration. Unlike Paul Simon, David Byrne or Hector Zazou, Israeli musicians have no need to travel very far to find their inspiration – so much is already close to hand. What's more, the fire under the melting pot is getting stronger and stronger.

DISCOGRAPHY Israel

⊙ Nada World Music Compilation
Nada records, Israel
This 2-CD set of Israel features bands that combine cultures and artists from East and West, Indian, Arabic, Persian, Turkish, Bulgarian, Irish, Balkan and Brazilian music, with a touch of jazz and classical western airs.

★ The Rough Guide to the Music of Israel
World Music Network, UK
Dan Rosenberg compiled this wonderful album with the biggest names and the best examples of Israeli music – from beloved icons like Chava Alberstein and Arik Einstein through World Music artists like Shlomo Bar, Yair Dalal and Yasmin Levy, to the "hottest" names of recent years like Idan Reichel and Hadag Nahash.

⊙ Songs from Lev Ha'Olam
Globalev/NMC, Israel
A unique compilation from Israel's Globalev label featuring tracks from the label's leading artists such as Sheva, Mosh Ben Ari, Avishay Bar Natan and many others.

Abatte

When saxophonist Abatte Barihun emigrated from Ethiopia to Israel he had to work as a labourer in a factory where he used chemicals that damaged his fingers. When his hands healed, he was able to return to his beloved saxophones and his unique music.

★ Ras Deshen
MCI, Israel
Named after the highest mountain in Ethiopia, near the most ancient settlement of Beta Israel (the Jews of Ethiopia), a region known for the modes on which the music of this album is based. Written by Abatte and pianist Yitchak Yadit, the music originates directly from Yom Kippur prayers of the Ethiopian Jews and mixes some contemporary classical music with Mediterranean flavours and a touch of blues and gospel.

Chava Alberstein

The "First Lady of Israeli Song" was born in Poland and came as a baby to Israel. Strongly influenced by American folk singers like Joan Baez, she has been a dramatic force on the Israeli music scene for over thirty years, and a political one, too, as a vociferous champion of the peace process.

⊙ Chava Alberstein – The Early Years
NMC, Israel
Chava Alberstein's albums from early in her career that started in the 1960s and went through to the 70s. Previously unavailable on CD, all the albums have been digitally remastered and come as a box set of eight CDs.

★ Chava Alberstein – End of the Holiday
NMC, Israel
Featuring songs written as little stories about people and situations in the backyard of Tel Aviv. The lyrics were written by Chava's husband, Nadav Levitan, while Chava is responsible for all the music, together with Ovad Efrat who produced the album.

WITH THE KLEZMATICS

⊙ The Well
Green Linnet/Xenophile, US
Chava has been back to her roots in five albums of Yiddish song. On this one she teams up with the cutting-edge New York Klezmer band, The Klezmatics, in brand-new musical settings of classic Yiddish poetry.

Gilad Atzmon

Raised as a secular Israeli Jew in Jerusalem, saxophonist Gilad Atzmon (he also plays the clarinet, *sol*, *zurna* and flutes) witnessed and empathized with the daily sufferings of Palestinians and spent twenty years trying to resolve for himself the tensions of his background. Finally disillusioned, he moved to England to study philosophy. Yet when he met Asaf Sirkis, a drummer from his homeland, Atzmon recovered an interest in playing the music of the Middle East, North Africa and Eastern Europe. He founded the Orient House Ensemble in London and started redefining his own roots in the light of political reality. Atzmon now regards himself as a dedicated political artist.

⊙ Exile
Enja Records, Germany
Gilad and the Orient House Ensemble try to remove the barriers between Jewish and Arabic cultures, emphasizing the similarity between the two peoples. The album features the great Palestinian singer Reem Kelani and renowned vocalist/ *oud* player Dhafer Youssef.

Balkan Beat Box

An anarchistic, international World Music band with two very talented Israeli musicians as leaders (Tamir Muskat on drums and Ori Kaplan on alto sax) that is conquering the clubs around the world with their live show.

⊙ Balkan Beat Box
Essay Recordings, Germany
A cabaret-circus-dancefloor, ethno party with Hebrew rapping and traditional Bulgarian singing. It's hot and crazy!

Balkan Beat Box

Zehava Ben

Zehava Ben is an Israeli vocalist of Moroccan heritage, born in 1970 and brought up in a poor neighbourhood in the southern city of Beersheba. She started her career recording many low budget "indie" albums ignored by the media. Blessed with a mesmerizing voice, she has become one of Israel's biggest stars.

⊙ Zehava Ben sings Umm Kulthum
Helicon, Israel
Accompanied by the Haifa Arab Music Orchestra conducted by Suheil Raduan, Zehava Ben's artistry should win over even the most fanatical fans of the legendary Arab diva Umm Kulthum.

Mosh Ben Ari

As a child of immigrants from Iraq, the main singer of Sheva, Mosh Ben Ari still believes that the language of music and art is much more powerful than that of the politicians.

⊙ Path (Derech)
Globalev/NMC, Israel
Mosh's second album is Israeli rock with scents of tropical reggae, Cuban rhythms, African beats and a touch of hiphop. Every song was written and composed by Mosh and produced by Mark Smullian.

Amir Benayun

A drug addict from a very young age, after his rehabilitation Amir started to work as a handyman, using the money to finance his first CD in 1999. He was raised on North African music, and as a child his father taught him to play the *oud*. His songs are accompanied mostly by acoustic Arabic instruments and lie somewhere between classical Arab music and *rai*.

⊙ Amir Benayun – Shalechet (Falling Leaves)
Helicon, Israel
Amir's third album, from 2002. Among his own touching love songs there is a beautiful Hebrew version of Jeff Lynn's "Now You're Gone".

Shani Ben Canar

Ben Canar was born in Russia into a family of musicians and composers. Having mastered the violin and guitar at an early age, he turned to percussion. He has played in many ensembles all over Europe and Israel and his journeys are reflected in his music, which takes in traditional elements from all corners of the world.

⊙ Nedudai (My Wandering)
Orange World Records, Poland
A journey through time and through the rich diversity of Jewish music from Poland, via the Balkans and on to Central Asia. Beautiful sounds of traditional stringed instruments (*saz*, *oud*) plus accordion, violin, clarinet and percussion mingle with joyful singing and cantor's wailing.

Bustan Abraham

Bustan Abraham's cross-cultural membership combine elements of both Eastern and Western traditions, including classical Arabic and European music, jazz, Indian, Turkish and flamenco. Their powerful stage performances have been greeted with standing ovations all over the world.

⊙ Ashra
Nada Records, Israel
This collection includes over seventy minutes of music gathered from the first five albums, focusing mainly on their more lively and upbeat repertoire.

Yair Dalal

Composer and violin and *oud* player, Yair Dalal's musical skills range from European classical music to jazz, blues and Arab music. He is a strong advocate for peace and has been involved in a number of Palestinian music projects. He works with his own Al Ol Ensemble, SheshBesh (four classically trained musicians exploring Middle Eastern music) and with a wide range of musicians from around the world.

⭐ **Silan**
Najema Music, Israel; Amiata, Italy
The Al Ol Ensemble (violin/*oud*, flute/clarinet, guitar and percussion) kicks off with the very catchy "Acco Malca" (Queen of Acco). Other treats include a wonderful Turkish-style Klezmer fantasy and an equally inventive treatment of a tune by *qawwali* master, Nusrat Fateh Ali Khan.

⊙ **Asmar**
Magda, Israel
With this album, Yair Dalal returns to his Iraqi musical roots. Guests include veteran Iraqi musicians such as *oud* player and singer Yossef Yaakub Shem Tov, the Israeli poet Ronny Someck, the Persian singer Maureen Nehedar and the Druze poet Salman Masalha.

⊙ **The Perfume Road**
Magda, Israel
The perfume road was the ancient route from the Red Sea to the Mediterranean used by merchants to deliver expensive spices and perfumes from the east to the west. Yair Dalal was inspired by this border-free society that existed two thousand years ago. He tries to show us, in musical terms, how different such a reality could be.

The East-West Ensemble

A really multi-ethnic group – which changes personnel from album to album – combining all sorts of musical styles. The driving force is Yisrael Borochov who plays synth, bass guitar, *tabla* and various percussion.

⊙ **Zurna**
IIM, Israel
Named after the Central Asian oboe that is found from China to the Balkans, this recording includes the Alayev family (from Tajikistan) playing the *doira* frame drum and accordion. A tasty blend of classical, oriental, jazz and Jewish styles.

Essev Bar

Essev Bar was founded in 1994 in the Galilee region of Israel. This area is well known for its wide cultural diversity and the band create a fascinating musical link between ethnic, electronic and World Music atmospheres.

⊙ **The Light Years (1994–2003)**
Adama Records, Israel
A compilation of the best tracks from the first decade of the band.

Esta

Esta, a four-piece world-beat/jazz-fusion group, combine Middle-Eastern and Mediterranean modal styles with elements of jazz, Celtic music, rock, and funk.

⊙ **Mediterranean Crossroads**
NMC, Israel
A remarkably successful music from such a radical mix. "Go-Go" combines Scottish music and funk, while "Deror Yikra" is a Yemenite song with Celtic touches.

Yehoram Gaon

Born in Jerusalem to a Sephardic family of Turkish origin, Yehoram Gaon was a member of the two most famous vocal groups of the 1960s – The Roosters and the Yarkon-Bridge Trio. He has recorded many romantic love songs and songs about Israel, as well as making occasional forays into Ladino ballads. One of Israel's most loved singers.

⊙ **Sung in Ladino**
NMC, Israel
Judeo-Spanish ballads from the last five hundred years, love songs for Zion, the Promised Land and Jerusalem – all accompanied by a symphony orchestra. These have had such a strong impact in Israel that many have become part of the religious heritage and are sung in prayer.

Sarit Hadad

Born in 1978 as the youngest of eight brothers and sisters – all of whom are musicians – she began performing at an early age and is now a pop superstar, having conquered the charts with dozens of songs.

⊙ **Miss Music**
Avi Gueta, Israel
Her thirteenth and latest album shows influences of Arabic *shaabi*, Greek *laïkó* and even *bhangra*, in a very professional ethno-sound production aimed at dancers as well as lovers.

Habrera Hativeet

One of the country's most consistently inspiring bands, Habrera Hativeet have been at the forefront of Israel's melting-pot music for over twenty years. They have been through several incarnations, but their leader Shlomo Bar has always imprinted his open-minded personality on the music.

⊙ **Faithful Waters**
Hed Arzi, Israel
The ultimate collection of Habrera Hativeet, and a retrospective demonstration of the talents of Shlomo Bar as a composer, singer and interpreter. New poetry alongside traditional prayers and Israeli "classical" songs awakened to a new life.

Ofra Haza

Ofra Haza was born in 1957 in Israel (her parents emigrated from Yemen) and as a teenage pop singer represented Israel in the Eurovision Song Contest. Her incisive voice and slightly ornamented singing style project her Yemenite songs with great power, but her success in Israel was built on poppy love songs, and that is how she is still best known. She died in 2000.

⭐ **Yemenite Songs**
Hed Arzi, Israel; Shanachie, US
A classic Israeli roots/fusion album, featuring songs from the Yemenite Diwan repertoire – most of them with lyrics by sixteenth-century Sephardic rabbi Shalom Shabazi expressing love for God, love for the Promised Land and just love. "Galbi" and "Im Nin'alu" were the most successful tracks that got remixed for the dance clubs.

Israeli Andalusian Orchestra

Arab-Andalusian music developed in the ninth century, – when the land of al-Andalus covered most of the Iberian peninsula – which draws its inspiration from both East and West. Directed by Dr Avi Eilam Amzallag, the orchestra is dedicated to preserving this ancient tradition.

⊙ Maghreb I and II
Magda, Israel

Maghreb I is selection of music that has been popular among Moroccan Jews for the last few centuries, from old Andalusia-style songs of the Middle Ages up to twentieth-century popular music. *Maghreb II* features Andalusian Arab classical music as well the more popular aspects of the Maghrebi repertoire, composed for a variety of family and community events.

Kol Oud Tof Trio

The Voice *Oud* Drum Trio is three musicians (Esti Kenan-Ofri, Armand Sabach, Oren Fried) from three lands (Italy, Morocco, Jerusalem) playing three instruments (voice, *oud*, drum). All are gathered in Jerusalem to play the music of Morocco, which recalls Spain, which in its turn yearns for Jerusalem.

⊙ Gazelle
Magda, Israel

A fascinating album that brings together Spanish women's songs from northern Morocco, sung in their original language, Haketia; songs in the Jewish Moroccan Arabic dialect; Moroccan Jewish liturgical music; and classical Andalusian songs in Hebrew.

Shem Tov Levy

Shem Tov Levy was born in 1950. As a child, he studied flute with the Israel Philharmonic Orchestra and composition and orchestration at the Tel Aviv Academy of Music. Levy works as a writer and arranger with the cream of Israel's contemporary singers and has written the scores for several TV and feature films.

⊙ Circle of Dreams
Magda, Israel

The soundtrack of the Israeli film *Desperado Square*. Shem Tov Levy returns to the sounds of his childhood, to the Balkan roots of his home, to the Yemenite She'arim neighbourhood.

Sameer Makhoul

This composer, singer and musician (*oud* and violin player) was born in Peki'in in Galilee into a family of musicians and poets whose roots in the village reach back for generations. A graduate of the Jerusalem Academy of Music, he teaches *oud*, violin and Arab music theory at the school of Ethnic Music at Bar Ilan University.

⊙ Athar
Magda, Israel

A blend of traditional Arab music, ancient poetry and Turkish and Andalusian music. An example of collaboration between Israel's very best Jewish and Arab musicians.

Amal Murkus

"Amal" means hope in Arabic, and 29-year-old Israeli-Arab singer Amal Murkus is full of it. She's already performed and recorded with Israel has best artists and appeared on TV and in films.

⊙ Amal
Highlights, Israel

"A white dove, a flower in its beak, in its eyes an unbreakable oath – never to let blood be shed between people" – lyrics from one of Amal's songs in her marvellous first album collaborating with the best Israeli musicians (Jews and Arabs). Warmly recommended.

The Nazareth Orchestra

Formed in 1990 by Suheil Radwan, who has been its director ever since, the aim of the orchestra is to spread appreciation for Arab art music, encourage local original talents and promote concerts. It features the best Arab and Jewish players who specialize in the performance of classical Arab music.

⊙ Oum Kolthoum – The Anniversary Tribute
Magda, Israel

A special tribute to the legendary singer Umm Kulthum, the diva of Arab classical music. Lubna Salame gives familiar songs like "Enta Umri" and "Al-Atlal" fresh and interesting new life.

Nash Didan

In 1929, immigration began from various villages on the borders of Azerbaijan, Persia, Turkey and Russia where the ancient Aramaic language was still spoken. Nash Didan (which means "our people") is a band of musicians, founded by Arik Mordechai, dedicated to preserving the language of this community.

⊙ Nash Didan Idaylu
Phonokol, Israel

If you want to dance to the old language spoken in the Bible – well, here it is. Mysterious voices, sounds mixed with operatic voices and instruments reaching back two thousand years.

Idan Reichel

At the age of 23, this young pianist and musician started to play with a simple music-recording program on his computer, inviting people over to record Hebrew and Amharic songs, instrumentals, love letters and even portions of the Bible. Two years later (2003) his first CD became the biggest hit in Israel and a second album followed in 2005.

Idan Reichel

Idan Reichel's Project
Helicon, Israel

Exciting music of the Ethiopian fusion that is taking Israeli popular culture by storm and bringing African idioms into the mainstream. In raw and moving bursts of music energy, Idan Reichel Project's debut album mixes Ethiopian folk music with Israel's multicultural sounds on hymns and intimate love songs. An ambient World Music crossover masterpiece..

Eyal Sela & Ensemble Darma

Though classically trained, Eyal Sela broadened his horizons when he discovered World Music. The Israeli clarinet and saxophone player and his ensemble are known for improvisation and combining contemporary ethnic styles and instruments from the Balkans and the Middle East.

Call of the Mountain
Nada Records, Israel

Mount Meron in the Galilee is a holy place – many religious people are buried there, among them Rabbi Shimon Bar Yochai who may have written the *Sefer Hazohar* (Book of Splendour), the basis of Kabalah. This CD brings the story of the creation of a unique Klezmer music in the Galilee, combining acoustic and electronic instruments with Sufi sounds and Mediterranean rhythms.

Sfatayim

Sfatayim ("lips" in Hebrew) come from the southern immigrants' village of Sderoth. They play traditional music from Morocco and original songs in Moroccan style.

⊙ Moroccan Party
Phonokol, Israel

The very danceable greatest hits of Sfatayim. A real Moroccan *hafla* with traditional and Western instruments. Sung mostly in Moroccan Arabic.

Sheva

A World Music ensemble, founded in 1997 in the Galilee, which employs instruments from around the world and motifs from the roots of Hebrew, Arab and tribal cultures. A phenomenon in Israel, Sheva attract thousands of people to their spectacular performances, which create a musical journey through meditation, prayer and celebration.

⊙ Live in Australia
Globalev/NMC, Israel

To get the true impact of Sheva you have to witness one of their live concerts, which are big celebratory affairs for both group and audience. This CD brings us as close as possible to such a feast of peace and music.

Tea Packs

Another group from Sderoth whose joyous lyrics – about love, life and politics – are driven along by Mediterranean-North African rhythms. Kobi Oz, the group's leader (of Tunisian origin) is one of the most colourful Israeli artists.

⊙ Your Life in Laffa
Hed Arzi, Israel

Laffa is a kind of pitta bread – and you can put your whole life with your troubles, with your happy moments, into it, to taste it and to see if you like it. This album from 1995 is the band's best.

Yosefa

Yosefa Dahari was born in 1971 of a Yemenite mother and Moroccan father. She began singing, like many Israeli musicians, while in the army. Most of her songs are in Hebrew, and she adds 1990s dance rhythms and production techniques to her dual inheritance.

PLAYLIST
Israel

1 EZLEINU BI'KFAR TUDRA Habrera Hativeet from *Faithful Waters*
Recorded in the 1970s, the song describes the life of Jewish people in the village of Tudra in the Atlas Mountains of Morocco.

2 IM NIN'ALU Ofra Haza from *Yemenite Songs*
The song that made the late Ofra Haza world famous, featuring the beautiful lyrics of the Jewish Yemenite poet Rabi Shalom Shabazi.

3 ZAMAN EL SALLAM Yair Dalal from *Al Ol*
Performed to celebrate the first anniversary of the Peace Accords, with a group that included fifty Palestinian and fifty Israeli children.

4 SALAAM Sheva from *Live in Australia*
"Peace on us and on the whole world" – this prayer of the "tribal" Sheva group really takes off in this live recording.

5 HINACH YAFFA Idan Reichel from *Idan Reichel's Project*
Based on words from the Biblical Song of Songs and with Ethiopian musical elements, this is one of the most beautiful of recent Israeli love songs.

6 MAYN SHVESTER KHAYE Chava Alberstein & The Klezmatics from *The Well*
Heartbreaking Yiddish song about a Jewish girl killed by the Nazis, composed and performed by one of Israel's greatest singers and the hottest New York Klezmer band.

7 BEHATITO KADUS KADUS Abatte from *Ras Deshen*
A prayer sung by the priests of the Ethiopian Jews in the ancient prayer language Geez. The chant seems to hint at the source of the blues.

8 YOCHANAN HA'SANDLAR Eyal Sela & Darma from *Call of the Mountains Ensemble*
The *nigunim* (tunes) of Yochanan Ha'Sandlar were meant to accompany wedding processions, and were also used for processions with the Torah scrolls.

9 AS YOU WILL Heeyam from *Heeyam*
A love song to God, combining Judaism and Islam. The lyrics are in Hebrew (Shye Ben-Tzur) accompanied by the meditative ecstatic singing of the Ajmeri Qawwals from Rajasthan.

⊙ The Desert Speaks
EMI Hemisphere, UK

An undemanding blend of Arabic and Western styles including music by Alon Oleartchik and Shlomo Gronich, with the evocative title-track describing the end of a relationship. Unfortunately, the traditional instruments are rather swamped by synthesizers and electronics.

Zafa

Zafa is an ensemble playing original Yemenite music with funky arrangements. This project is a joint venture of the Israeli singer Sharon Ben-Zadok, with Eyal Faran on sitar and strings, and Marc Smullian on bass and electronics.

⊙ Funky Grooves of Yemen
Globalev/NMC, Israel

This album integrates traditional Yemenite women's songs (that Sharon learned from her mother), with Indian songs she studied in Varanassi, India. The arrangements give the whole thing a modern feel.

Ziryab Trio

A spin-off from Bustan Abraham – a trio of first-class musicians from Arabic and Turkish backgrounds. *Oud* player Taiseer Elias leads the ensemble, with violinist Nassim Dakwar and the brilliant percussionist Zihar Fresco.

⊙ Oriental Art Music
Nada Productions, Israel; Crammed World, Belgium

Clear textures and sensitive playing of music by Tanburi Jemil Bey and twentieth-century Egyptian composers in a live concert. The trio are joined by Avraham Salman on *qanun* and Emmanuel Mann on bass for one of the most compelling recitals of classical Arabic and Turkish music around.

Emil Zrihan

Born in Rabat, Morocco, in 1954, Zrihan moved to Israel as a child where he has become a successful cantor and performer of sacred and secular music in the Moroccan tradition.

⊙ Ashkelon
Piranha, Germany

The album is named after the city in Israel where Zrihan lives, and includes both Moroccan folk repertoire and Judeo-Moroccan religious *mawaal*. Zrihan has a voice that cuts and soars and the ensemble of *oud*, violin, flamenco guitar, accordion, percussion and backing vocals drives this music in an unstoppable frenzy.

See also the chapters on Sephardic Music and Palestinian Music. The revival of Klezmer is covered in The Rough Guide to World Music Volume 3.

Jewish Music |
Sephardic

ladino romance

Ladino and flamenco singer Yasmin Levy
Philip Ryalis/Redferns

There are two great diaspora traditions of Jewish music: *klezmer*, born in Eastern Europe and developed in the US (see Volume 3 of this book), and Sephardic music, born in Spain and developed around the Mediterranean. Sephardic music, which is currently undergoing a boost in popularity on the World Music scene, is often described as the songs composed by the Spanish Jews, prior to their expulsion in the late fifteenth century. But the story is more complex than that. As Judith Cohen and Hilary Pomeroy explain, various cultures and layers of history have left their mark on the music.

The Key of Spain

Where is the key that was in the drawer?
My forefathers brought it with great pain
From their house in Spain
Dreams of Spain

Where is the key that was in the drawer?
My forefathers brought it with great love.
They told their children, this is the heart of our
home in Spain.
Dreams of Spain

Where is the key that was in the drawer?
My forefathers brought it with great love.
They gave it to their grandchildren for them to
keep in the drawer.
Dreams of Spain

Flory Jagoda (1984)

The year 1492 marked the final Christian *reconquista* of what is now Spain, when the troops of Ferdinand and Isabella took Granada, the last Moorish stronghold. In the same year, they proclaimed the expulsion of the Jews who had lived in the Iberian peninsula for over a millennium. Jews were given three months to arrange their affairs, sell off their homes and goods, and leave – or convert to Catholicism and stay on as **conversos** or "New Christians", in danger of being denounced as secret Judaizers by the Inquisition and tortured, imprisoned or burned at the stake. No one knows exactly how many of them left, but historians estimate the Jewish population in Spain just before the expulsion as 100,000–200,000. Five years later the process was repeated in Portugal, where a number of the Spanish Jews had moved.

Most of the exiled Sephardim made their way to establish communities in northern **Morocco** or the **Ottoman cities** of Constantinople, Thessaloniki and Jerusalem. There they continued to speak their language, now known as **Judeo-Spanish** or **Ladino**. The language and the name given to it differ from one place to another, but it generally includes archaic forms going back to medieval Spanish languages, mixed in with bits and pieces of Hebrew, Greek, Turkish, Arabic and, later on, Italian, French and modern Spanish.

These days "Sephardic" is often used to refer to almost any Jewish group that is not Ashkenazi (basically, of Eastern European origin), but this chapter concentrates on the original meaning, and songs in Judeo-Spanish/Ladino.

Origins and Evolution

Sephardic music grew from a domestic tradition maintained primarily by women. Central to this tradition were **romansas** (ballads), which told stories centred on basic human passions such as love, jealousy, hatred and revenge. Many of ballad lyrics were composed against the backdrop of Spain's wars between Muslims and Christians, and a recurring theme is the housebound wife left alone while her husband goes off to the wars.

Traditionally, these early songs were unaccompanied – women's hands were busy with various domestic tasks – though for **wedding songs**, women accompanied themselves on percussion (usually tambourine).

The Sephardic music we know today has come a long way from its Spanish roots. Even where the song texts can be traced back to pre-expulsion times, the **tunes** are mainly newer. Some Sephardic melodies share traits with the *cancioneros* (Spanish courtly songs) but, as a group, they are exuberantly eclectic, reflecting five centuries of exile. Indeed, the Sephardic repertoire includes elements adapted from classical Ottoman *maqams*, Moroccan rhythms, tango, Istanbul Gypsy and *gazino* songs, Greek operettas, the Charleston and popular nineteenth-century Spanish melodies. (One of the best-known songs in the Ladino repertoire is "Adio Querida", the tune for which appears to have come from the last act of Verdi's *La Traviata*.)

Most of the Sephardic songs featured in today's concerts and recordings are *kantigas*, which were mainly written in the eastern Mediterranean in the second half of the nineteenth century. These are shorter than the ballads and tell of love, bar mitzvahs, henna parties and weddings (including some examples in which the mother-in-law criticises the bride's dowry). While ballads have a formal structure of sixteen-syllable lines with a pause in the middle and repeated vowel sound, *kantigas* are mainly in simple four-line stanzas. Several popular *kantigas* imitate a common Turkish song form, the *sharkí*, where the verses are often completely unrelated to each other.

Another, lesser-known Judeo-Spanish song is the **kopla**. These usually had religious or moralizing themes and were sung by men.

Key Figures

Ironically, many of the most popular singers of Sephardic music are not themselves Sephardic, but a number of important performers are. **Gloria Levy** in New York exerted considerable influence over later performers. She learned her songs from

The Levy Legacy

One of the most influential figures in recent stroty of Sephardic music was **Isaac Levy** (1919–77). The books of songs that he collected from Sephardic immigrants to Israel is the basic textbook for most performers. He built up a vast collection of songs from Ladino singers from the Balkans, Turkey and Morocco, publishing ten volumes of cantorial songs and four of romansas and kantigas.

Turkish-born Levy emigrated with his family to Jerusalem at the age of three. He was a trained musician and synagogue cantor, and became the first director of Ladino broadcasts on **Kol Yisrael**, the national broadcasting company. Israel's National-al Authority for Ladino has released a double CD of some of the most popular songs as a tribute to Levy.

Levy's youngest child, **Yasmin Levy**, is at the fore-front of the Sephardic scene. Her remarkable voice and passionate performances won her a BBC World Music Award nomination in 2005. Whilst she also sings flamenco, and songs she has written herself, Yasmin remains devoted to the Ladino tradition so dear to her father, creating her own arrangements of the melodies Isaac collected. She has returned these songs to their Eastern roots, using breathtaking orna-mentation and traditional instruments such as the *oud*, rather than the guitar and piano that frequently feature in Western arrangements.

Yasmin's mother Kohava Levy has also released an album, *Estrella*, on the Adama label.

her mother, Emilie Levy, who grew up in Alexan-dria, and continued, well into her 80s, to sing in a choir and coach aspiring performers of Judeo-Spanish song. Her songs are mainly lyric songs, in a modern, *à la Franca* (European, as opposed to Turkish) style, performed with guitar and mando-lin accompaniment.

Another major influence and teacher has been **Flory Jagoda**. Known as "La Nona", Flory performs with her three grown children, and her record-ing *La Nona Kanta* (The Grandmother Sings) is an affectionate disc aimed at children. In Turkey, the best-known group is the **Pasharos Sefardíes** (Sephardic Songbirds). Karen Gerson and Izzet Bana infuse the quartet's lively performances with characteristic expressions and gestures, and are accompanied by traditional string instruments. Their repertoire consists largely of late nineteenth-century lyric and topical songs, often learned from

older members of the Istanbul community. **Jak and Janet Esim** also perform similar repertoire.

Israel considers Judeo-Spanish song as part of its heritage and for a long time most perform-ers learned their repertoire principally from the anthology collected by **Isaac Levy** (see box above). Among the best-known Israeli performers is **Yeho-ram Gaon**, a singing star from a Jerusalem family. Gaon's records have played a central role in dis-seminating songs from the eastern lyric and light religious repertoires, usually backed up by a small Western orchestra.

Many of the early performers recorded on 78rpm, such as **Yitzhak Algazi**, also sang in **Hebrew**. These pieces are usually prayers, *piyyu-tim* (songs of praise) or other religious texts. The tradition has continued with Moroccans like **Jo Amar**, **Haim Louk** and recently **Emil Zrihan** who function as cantors for their own congregations.

Paul Hensels

Emil Zrihan

In the right hands, the music has that heightened devotional intensity. Zrihan's backing includes *oud*, violin, accordion and *darabouka* (goblet drum) giving the music a real Moroccan sound and, like many cantors, he has successfully taken it into the concert hall.

A particularly convincing Israeli performer from outside the tradition is **Ruth Yaakov**, who specializes in Balkan and Turkish Sephardic songs. She is one of the rare singers who combine Western concert training with a traditional style, in her case a clear, low-to-middle range timbre with a strong edge. She performs with a trio of Middle Eastern musicians based in Israel.

Spaniards and Fusions

The first Spanish artists to record Judeo-Spanish songs were both women trained in Western concert music: **Sofía Noel** and the renowned **Victoria de los Angeles**. Folklorist **Joaquín Díaz** was the first to record the repertoire in a non-classical style, in

the 1970s. His vocal technique wouldn't be mistaken for Moroccan or Turkish, but his warm voice and extensive background in regional Spanish folk traditions have influenced many other singers.

Folklorist **Angel Carril** and the groups **Raices** and **La Bazanca** (led by Paco Díez) experimented with Spanish traditional singing styles and a mixture of Spanish and Middle Eastern instruments. **Rosa Zaragoza** has recorded combinations of songs from the "three cultures" of Spain (Jewish, Muslim and Christian). Also worth noting are two recordings (*Arbolera I* and *II*) by Spanish singers **José-Manuel Fraile** and **Eliseo Parra**. These are directed by Israeli ethnomusicologist **Shoshana Weich-Shahak**, who plays *qanun*, coached the singers in authentic performance style, and brought an intriguing selection of songs from her own field recordings.

Some Sephardic groups featuring classical early music specialists have ignored the living tradition and have chosen to reinvent a "historical" one. **Alia Musica** in Spain, **Accentus** in Vienna and

Altramar in the US the most obvious examples. They are good musicians, though their work is based on romantic misconceptions about a body of music going back to Medieval Spain, and they're often short on warmth and spontaneity.

At the other end of the scale are groups that aim to mix Sephardic song with all kinds of modern styles. For example, the band of New York-based Ladino singer **Sarah Aoreste**, whose family comes from Thessaloniki, fuses medieval *romansas* and *kantigas* with heavy rock and blues. Other outfits in North American include **Voice of the Turtle**, directed by Judith Wachs and featuring an eclectic assortment of medieval, Renaissance, early music and Middle Eastern instruments. Then there's **Alhambra**, led by Isabelle Ganz, and David Harrison's **Voices of Sepharad**, both of whom bring classical and cantorial training to the mix. The singer **Judy Frankel** has also recorded Sephardic songs.

Back in Europe, the Sephardic flag has been carried by singers in France (**Jacinta**, **Héléne Engel**, **Françoise Atlan**, **Sandra Bessis** and **Esther Lamandier**), Italy (**Liliana Treves Alcalay**), the Czech Republic (**Jana Lewitová**) and Greece (**Savina Yannatou**).

Song Preservation

In an attempt to stop the lesser-known Sephardic songs from disappearing completely, various ethnomusicologists have been making recordings of

Greek singer Savina Yannatou

the last authentic singers – mainly elderly people who grew up when the tradition still flourished in Jewish homes. Hundreds of songs have been collected in Israel by **Shoshana Weich-Shahak** (the *qanun* player with Arboleras, whose authentic-style performances span medieval Sephardic ballads and Ladino songs composed by recent immigrants to Israel). Likewise, Canadian academic **Judith Cohen** has collected Moroccan Sephardic songs and is now researching what has survived of the Sephardic tradition of Portugal's crypto-Jewish communities (she also plays with Montréal based Moroccan-Sephardic group Gerineldo).

DISCOGRAPHY Jewish Music | Sephardic

⊙ **Cantares y romances tradicionales sefardíes de Marruecos**
⊙ **Cantares y romances tradicionales de Oriente**
Tecnosaga, Spain
The Moroccan CD includes wedding songs (with exuberant drum and tambourine accompaniment) and ballads. Alicia Bendayan has a particularly fine voice. The Oriente disc has a similar collection of life-cycle songs and ballads.

⊙ **Kantes djudeo-espanyoles del Proyekto Folklor de Kol Israel**
Kol Israel, Israel
Israeli ethnomusicologist Shoshana Weich-Shahak has spent the last thirty years collecting authentic performances of Sephardic song from immigrants to Israel. The real thing!

⊙ **Romancero sefardí**
Tecnosaga, Spain
These parallel Eastern and Mediterranean versions of the same seven ballads bring out the difference in the two styles.

The oriental style is much more ornamental and free, the Moroccan more Spanish.

⊙ **Selección de romances sefardíes de Marruecos**
Tecnosaga, Spain
Twenty-two mainly medieval ballads from Morocco.

Berta Aguado

Berta Aguado has had enormous influence on today's generation of Ladino singers (Ruth Yaakov, Hadass Pal-Yarden, Yasmin Levy, etc). Born in Chanakele in the Dardanelles, Turkey, in 1929, Aguado emigrated to Israel in 1979. Berta's enormous repertoire and great voice have attracted the attention of researchers and performers alike.

⊙ **Cancionero sefardí de Turquía**
Tecnosaga, Spain
There are thirty-two tracks with an eclectic mixture of ballads, lyrical songs, *koplas*, nursery and modern songs.

Rabbi Isaac (Yitzhak) Algazi

Yitzhak Algazi was a Turkish Sephardic singer, revered for his virtuoso performances of synagogue singing, Judeo-Spanish songs and Turkish classical music. He died in Uruguay in the 1960s.

▦ Cantorial Compositions, Piyyutim and Judeo-Spanish Songs
Renanot, Jerusalem
Reissued 78s, on two cassettes, accompanying Edwin Seroussi's 1989 book, *The Life and Music of Rabbi Isaac Algazi from Turkey.*

Arboleras

An impressive group featuring Shoshana Weich-Shahak (*qanun*), José Manuel Fraile (voice) and Eliseo Parra (*oud*). Their first two CDs include traditional Sephardic repertoire performed in a traditional style. *Arboleras 1* contains a mixture of *kantigas* and *koplas*; *Arboleras 2*, featuring singer Carmen Terrón, focuses on Eastern and Moroccan ballads.

⊙ Arboleras 3
Tecnosaga, Spain
A collection of twentieth-century Sephardic songs with Charleston, foxtrot and tango. They describe the impact of modernization and secularization on the Sephardic way of life. Whilst the opening songs poke fun at the social habits of the time, others reflect social and economic problems. The last three songs describe the experiences of Sephardim adapting to life in their new homeland, Israel.

Sarah Aroeste

This young, New York-based artist has shaken up the world of Sephardic music with her funky blend of traditional Ladino song, rock, jazz and blues.

⊙ A la una
Sarah Aroeste, US
With a top band of four Israeli musicians, Sarah bridges Eastern and Western influences and shines a new light on these mainly nineteenth-century songs.

Françoise Atlan

With her Berber roots and classical training, French singer Françoise Atlan's repertoire encompasses early music, Sephardic song and, particularly successfully, Andalusian music. Her collaboration with Moroccan Muslim singer Zoubeïda Idrissi in *Chants de Traverse* (Atoll Music, France), Palestinian *oud* player Moneim Oudwan in *Nawah* (Buda Musique, France) and *L'Orchestre Arabo-Andalou de Fès* (Buda Musique, France) reveals the warmth of her voice.

⊙ Andalussyat
Buda Musique, France
Atlan's beautiful, clear voice shines out in this mixture of *romansas*, *kantigas*, and *koplas*. Whilst her style is classical rather than oriental (you can distinguish the separate notes in the melismata, whereas they should blend into each other) Atlan's conviction and intelligent interpretation stand out.

Albert Hemsi

Turkish-born Hemsi (1897–1975) studied music at thhe Milan Conservatoire. Having served in the Italian army during World War I, he returned home to be greeted by his grandmother joyfully singing old Sephardic ballads. Inspired by this to preserve his musical heritage, Hemsi began the systematic collection of songs in various eastern Mediterranean communities.

⊙ Coplas sefardíes
Buda Musique, France
Hemsi's settings for piano and voice of sixty traditional songs, collected in the Ottoman Empire in the 20s and 30s, have had a strong influence on classical musicians and singers. Pedro Aledo (voice) and Ludovic Amadeus Selmi (piano) perform this selection with charm and restraint.

Flory Jagoda

One of the most influential figures in the renaissance of Judeo-Spanish song, Jagoda was born in Sarajevo, Bosnia, and is now resident in the US. Her repertoire is from the eastern Mediterranean tradition; her own compositions have entered the folk tradition.

⊙ La Nona Kanta (The Grandmother Sings)
Global Village, US
Flory Jagoda is joined by her adult family. Few of the old ballads or life-cycle songs, but a musical window on pre-war Jewish Sarajevo.

Isaac Levy

A singer and composer, Levy switched career to become head of the Judeo-Spanish programme on Kol Israel (the state broadcasting authority) in 1954. This brought him into direct contact with Israel's large Sephardic community, enabling him to collect and publish many songs.

★ El Kante de una Vida – The Song of a Life
Hataklit, Israel
This double CD is a welcome tribute, revealing Levy's hitherto unknown warm, clear voice. The first disc features thirty popular Ladino songs with either guitar or orchestral accompaniment. In the last track, "Yo en la prizión", Isaac duets with his daughter Kohava. The second CD is a mixture of liturgical and Ladino songs (performed in Hebrew).

Yasmin Levy

Given her family background, it is not suprising that this young singer is passionately committed to preserving the Sephardic heritage. She is not only succeeding in that goal but has introduced Sephardic song to audiences in such diverse places as Moscow and Singapore.

1 MÁS ARIVA I MÁS ARIVA Berta Aguado
from *Kantes Djudeo-espanyoles del Proyecto Folklor de Kol Israel*
Berta's soaring melismatic phrases are a moving record of a vocal style that has almost entirely disappeared among the Sephardim.

2 PUNCHA, PUNCHA Isaac Levy from *El Kante de una Vida*
One of the most popular songs, often sung at speed. Here Levy's lilting, restrained voice emphasizes the intensity of the underlying passion.

3 NOCHES, NOCHES Yasmin Levy from *Romance y Yasmin*
Levy's opening sighs set the tone for this passionate ballad about a Spanish princess's overwhelming desire for her lover. A wonderful, haunting arrangement.

4 MUESTRO SENYOR Yasmin Levy from *Romance y Yasmin*
Levy has rearranged this Moroccan biblical ballad, performing it in oriental style with full use of melismatic phrasing and pulsing *oud*.

5 LA ROMANSA DE RIKA KURYEL Los Pasharos Sefaradis from *Kantikas para syempre*
Guitarist Selim Hubes' arrangement of Avner Perez's poem recalling a young girl who perished, "a piece of burnt coal", in a Holocaust crematorium.

6 SI VERÍAS AL RATÓN Mudéjar from *Al-Son*
A lively version of a popular Sephardic song from Bulgaria, complete with sweeping, infectious rhythms.

7 AY DICIME UN SI Ruth Yaakov Ensemble from *Ziara*
Tight playing and the powerful voice of Yaakov combine to make this an exciting track. Hard to believe that Yaakov is an outsider to the tradition.

8 UNA IHA TYENE EL REY Françoise Atlan from *Romances sefardíes: Entre la rose y le jasmin*
Atlan's crystal voice is subtly nuanced in this unaccompanied version of the medieval ballad, "The Beauty Who Will Not Sing".

★ **Romance y Yasmin**
Connecting Cultures, Netherlands
This CD reveals Yasmin's technical skill and the range of her incredibly beautiful voice. There are hauntingly intense performances of the *romansas* "Noches, noches" and "Muestro senyor". Particularly moving, too, are the love songs, "Kondja mia'" and the lullaby, "Nani, nani".

Los Pasharos Sefardíes

This Istanbul-based group consists of Karen Gershon (voice), Izzet Bana (voice), Selim Hubes (guitar) and Yavuz Hubes.

★ **Kantigas para siempre**
Gözlem, Turkey
Some of the most popular Ladino songs, mainly from the nineteenth century, performed with the Pasharos' characteristic gusto and charm.

⊙ **Zemirot**
Gözlem, Turkey
A new direction for the group: synagogue liturgy reproduced in authentic style.

Mudéjar

Mainly Spanish, but featuring Begoña Olavide on voice and psaltery, Mudéjar specialize in the music of Islamic Spain.

⊙ **Al-Son**
Nuba Records, Spain
A wonderfully atmospheric collection of Muslim, Christian and Jewish music from al-Andalus. It features three different versions of the well-known ballad "Noches, noches" – one vocal and two instrumental.

David Saltiel

Saltiel learnt many songs from his mother as a child in Thessaloniki. The family escaped the Holocaust deportations and Saltiel is now the last remaining performer of pre-war Judeo-Spanish songs.

★ **Canciones judeo-españoles de Tesalonica**
Oriente Musik, Germany
Accompanied by *oud*, *qanun*, violin and lyre, Saltiel recalls Jewish life in Salonika in the late nineteenth and early twentieth centuries – the 1917 fire that destroyed many homes, the young *cigarreras* working in oppressive conditions in the Regie tobacco factory, and the musicians wandering from tavern to tavern. A restrained, authentic performance of little-known songs.

SuZy

Born and raised in Turkey, SuZy has a wonderful voice, but never really intended to become a professional singer. She just wanted to pass on the legacy of the Ladino language and songs (which she learnt from her grandmother and aunt) to her sons. Her first recording garnered enthusiastic reactions from friends, family and professional musicians, and she started a new career in 1998.

⊙ **Aromas y Memorias**
Primary Music, Israel
Her previous albums, *Herencia* and *Estos Y Munchos*, focused on the "classical" repertoire of Sephardic Ladino songs, but this new double CD adds original music to the beautiful poems of Margalit Matitiahu.

Voice of the Turtle

A Boston-based quartet directed by Judith Wachs with Lisle Kulbach, Derek Burroughs and Jay Rosenberg. On the scene since the early 1980s, they have released a well-planned *Paths of Exile* series including music from Turkey, Morocco, the Balkans and Jerusalem, all with lyrics, translations and good notes.

⊙ Balkan Vistas: Spanish Dreams
Titanic Records, US

Repertoire from Yugoslavia and Bulgaria based largely on collections by Shoshana Weich-Shahak, plus the Flory Jagoda song "La yave de Espanya" (Dreams of Spain).

⊙ Full Circle: Music of the Spanish Jews of Jerusalem
Titanic Records, US

Includes songs from different parts of the Sephardic diaspora, mixing old favourites ("Adio kerida") with lesser-known songs ("Yo era un leoniko") and a rare romance ("Delgadina").

Ruth Yaakov

An Israeli singer with a powerful voice, Ruth Yaakov combines classical training with an authentic sense of interpretation. She had an instant hit with her debut CD, *Shaatnez*, and has gone from strength to strength since.

★ Ziara
Oriente Musik, Germany

An outstanding disc, introducing various little-known gems. As in *Shaatnez*, there are good accompanying notes and translations, and an excellent band of musicians.

Savina Yannatou

Though more commonly associated with contemporary Greek music, Yannatou and her band, Primavera en Salonico, brought an authentic local flavour to a disc of Sephardic songs.

★ Spring in Salonico
Lyra Records, Greece

Medieval ballads and more recent songs that reflect life in Salonica – once the largest Jewish community in the Ottoman Empire. There's "El encalador", with its risqué double entendres, and "Jaco" and "Primavera en Salonico", set in busy taverns where entertainment was provided by the Jewish musicians. In places, Yannatou's crystalline voice sounds almost too ethereal for these robust songs, but it's a great disc nonetheless.

Jordan & Bedouin Music

camel steps and epics of the sheikhs

Bedouin playing a *rabab*
Corbis

Jordan does not yet have the liveliest of music scenes, and only a handful of musicians from the kingdom have made a significant impact in other parts of the Arab world. However, considerable efforts are being made to encourage young musicians and the support given by the Noor al-Hussein Foundation to various music education projects, including a National Conservatory which teaches both Arab and Western styles, should give music in Jordan a higher profile in coming years, Bill Badley predicts.

ittle Jordanian music gets beyond the border, and few Arabs outside the country could name many Jordanian musicians. One reason for this is that the music "profession" is viewed with suspicion by many families. In some traditional communities, public performance is considered deeply unrespectable; on the other hand, while more progressive parents might consider the ability to play an instrument or sing to be a desirable social accomplishment, they would actively discourage their children from pursuing such an unreliable career path.

However, there are some very good musicians to be heard in Jordan. One of the finest – and most underrated – *oud* players in the Arab world, **Sakher Hattar**, performs music in the classical Arab style and can be seen regularly on local television with his group **Al-Fuhais**. The best-known popular singer is **Omar Abdullat**, who first came to prominence in the mid-1990s with his nationalist hit "Hashemi", which showed rural influences that are unusual in Arab pop music. The female singer **Qamar Badwan** is emerging as one of Jordan's current bright hopes and is beginning to gain some recognition at festivals and competitions abroad. Jordan's capital, Amman, has always been a refuge for exiled Iraqi musicians and is currently home to the well-known balladeer, **Ilham al-Madfai** (see Iraq chapter).

Among young educated Jordanians, the most successful musician to emerge in recent years is undoubtedly **Tareq al-Nasser.** This pianist/composer, schooled in both Eastern and Western music, writes heavily orchestrated pieces that owe much to the work of the Lebanese Rahbani family. With his twenty-strong group of musicians and singers, **Rum** (named after the stunning valley in the southwest of Jordan), al-Nasser explores ways of combining jazz, Western and Arab classical and Middle Eastern traditional sounds. Although the end result may sound a little overblown to European ears, the group's dramatically staged concerts in some of Jordan's stunning archaeological sites are extremely popular.

Indeed, visitors to Jordan may be pleasantly surprised by the opportunities to hear music being performed. The Jerash Festival, which takes place in various venues around the ruined Greco-Roman city during late July/early August, has grown since 1981 to become one of the most prestigious places to play in the Arab world. It offers the chance to hear both Jordanian and other Arab musicians of all styles in a pleasantly relaxed setting. Travellers in the desert areas like Wadi Rum are also likely to encounter Bedouin guides, who have been characteristically adept at harnessing the potential of their harsh environment. Bedouin tribes have traditionally journeyed all over the Arabian Peninsula, Levant and North Africa, but outsiders are probably most likely to encounter them – and hear their music – in Jordan.

Music of Movement

The music of the Bedouin is rooted in their nomadic traditions. While the songs and dances may seem rather repetitive at first, this reflects the desert landscape from which the music springs. Many Arabs and Westerners have a rather romantic view of the Bedouin, believing that they enshrine all that is noble about Arab culture. However, in practice, successive administrations in the Middle East have found the wandering Bedouin life-style rather inconvenient, as their traditional grazing grounds showed little respect for sensitive national borders. The Bedouin way of life has been rapidly changing over the last fifty years and many are now settled, but music still plays a central role in celebrating their traditional virtues of honour, generosity and chivalry.

Bedouin music is the music of movement and it is possible to hear the repetitive lope of camels' steps in many songs. However, it is the poetry of these songs that is most highly regarded by the Bedouin, and their roots date back to pre-Islamic times. Songs are used for every aspect of daily desert life: to mark births, marriages and death; to pass the tribe's oral history down the generations and to entertain around the camp fire at night. It's even said that, in times past, the *haadi* (leader of the caravan) would encourage his camels with particular songs during long journeys.

rum.com

Tareq Al Nasser

The most common Bedouin song forms are the *qasidah* (epic accounts of the tribe's heroic deeds) and *'ataaba* (yearning love poems). In marked contrast to the everyday culture of self-denial, the emotions expressed in love songs can be touchingly sensitive, as though poetry allows Bedouin men an opportunity to share a more tender side to their nature that would normally be frowned upon. Both *qasidah* and *'ataaba* are types of *zajal* – improvised sung poetry that is performed in public. However, the extent to which the words are completely extemporized is sometimes overstated, as the poet generally relies on a string of well-known phrases and ideas that are adapted to fit the occasion: "As the moon was rising, the birds flew to tell us that our friend Ahmed/Bill/Nadia has arrived from Amman/England/New York" (delete as applicable). These songs are sometimes introduced by the singer with a spoken prelude.

Bedouin Instruments

The instruments played by Bedouin musicians are, by necessity, simple, portable and crafted from readily available materials. The instrument that is most closely associated with them is the *rabab* (a single-stringed fiddle of which both the string and the bow are made of horse hair) that is used by singers to play simple accompaniments. Traditionally, any new visitor to a Bedouin tribe should be able to introduce themselves by singing their lineage to the *rabab*, though this custom has now all but died out. The other most popular melody instruments are more commonly used to play for dancing: the *shabbaba* is a simple cane flute, while the *mijwiz* is a reed instrument with two parallel pipes, one of which plays the tune while the other holds a drone, rather like a small bagpipe but using the player's cheeks as the bag. Dancing is nearly always accompanied by a more common array of percussion instruments, like the tambourine amd darbuka, and handclapping. Perhaps the most unusual and distinctive of all Bedouin percussion instruments is the *mihbaj* (a large, decorated wooden pestle and mortar that is used for coffee grinding). The deep thud of the pestle pounding the coffee beans is punctuated by the higher knocking sound as it is hit against the side of the mortar to create incessant rhythms, which can either imitate the slow pace of a camel or the more hurried gallop of a horse. These sounds are also laden with symbolism: they announce to all around that coffee will soon be shared in a communal ceremony of hospitality in the *madafah* (a sheikh's guest house) that will include singing as well as storytelling and the sharing of news.

There has always been a cross-fertilization of musical ideas between Bedouin and their urban neighbours, and this became more pronounced during the 1960s and 70s as many swapped their nomadic existence for something more settled. Urban musicians started to draw on Bedouin music and adapt it for their more sophisticated instruments like the *oud*, *qanun*, *ney* flute and violin. This, in turn, has fed back into Bedouin music, and tourists attending a "Bedouin entertainment" are as likely to find one of them playing the *oud* (which is not, strictly speaking, a traditional Bedouin instrument). More recently, Omar Abdullat used these **balaadi** (rustic) songs as a template for his own music when he first launched his career.

DISCOGRAPHY Jordan & Bedouin Music

Sadly, few recordings by Jordanian musicians are available internationally. This is a small selection to get started with.

⊙ Bedouin Songs, Wedding Songs, Fisherman's Songs from Aqaba
Inédit, France
This ethnological disc is not exactly easy listening, but it has fine examples of the intriguing textures of traditional music from the Aqaba area, where the desert meets the Red Sea. An interesting introduction to some of the origins of Arab song.

⊙ Bedouins of the Middle East
ARC, UK
Recordings made in Jordan and Syria by the noted ethnomusicologist Deben Bhattacharya during the 1950s. Much of this is music for dancing and some of the tracks can seem rather repetitive when heard out of context. However, there are some fine examples of Bedouin ballad singing and their distinctive, topical songs ("There's no one in the world like King Hussein, he's the only one for us!"). The very clear and informative booklet notes are a useful plus.

Sakher Hattar

Now promoting Jordanian and classical Arab music from his post at the National Music Conservatory in Amman, Hattar delighted his fellow countrymen when, at the age of just 20, he came from left-field to win the coveted International *'Ud* (oud) competition in Cairo in 1993. He is still very highly regarded by *oud* cognoscenti and tours internationally.

⊙ The Passionate Voice of the Oud
Crossing Borders, US

A mixture of Hattar's own pieces, Jordanian "folkloric" tunes and works by some of the last century's greatest composers for the *oud*, including Farid el-Atrache and Mohammed el-Qasabji. A fine showcase for Hattar's understated and intensely musical playing.

Omar Abdullat

Jordan's best-known singer, also known as Abdul Elat and sometimes just called Omar. After a slow start to his career in the late 1980s, he is now signed to the hugely influential Saudi Arabian label Rotana, with the result that his music has become less distinctively Jordanian and is now pretty standard pan-Arab fare.

⊙ 2005
Rotana, Saudi Arabia

In the absence of his fine first album, *Haan Waqt al-Safar*, Omar's latest offering on Rotana is a reasonable second best. The slick Egyptian production has smoothed out his interesting rougher edges, making him sound rather more ordinary. However, his is still a fine, world-class voice.

Rum and Tareq al-Nasser

Darlings of the Amman elite, Rum have carved out a niche for themselves playing al-Nasser's original compositions and arrangements of Arab songs in a style that cannily draws on everything from Leonard Bernstein to Ziad Rahbani, via bossa nova and occasional forays into 1970s progressive rock.

⊙ Ya Rouh
www.rummusic.com

This 1998 CD is a perfect introduction to Rum's intricate and stylized approach to contemporary Arab music. Future releases will draw more heavily on Jordan's folk-music traditions.

Kurdish Music

songs of the stateless

The Kamkars
Eva Skalla/Global Heritage

An ethnic and historical entity since the seventh century BC, and a territory as large as France, Kurdistan was in 1923 divided up amongst its neighbours – Turkey, Iran, Iraq, Syria and the Soviet Republic of Armenia. Ever since, the Kurds have become all too familiar with the techniques states can deploy to suppress language and culture to make a people disappear. Now, at least in one part of the Kurdish nation, the Kurdistan of Iraq, a new hope is emerging, with the end of the Saddam era allowing a powerful flowering of Kurdish culture. Eva Skalla and Parwez Zabihi listen to the sounds that give a voice to the Kurdish people.

usic is integral to Kurdish identity – and there are few places on earth where it has more meaning, as an assertion and expression of a culture. Historically, too, music has a central role in Kurdish society. In this land of mountains and high plateaux, lying between the Black Sea, the Iranian Plateau and the steppes of Mesopotamia, music has for centuries been the means of oral transmission of chronicles, epics and lyrical poetry. In a non-country, whose language and literature are suppressed, everything is sung and put to music to be committed to memory, and so passed down.

The music sings of the joy and sorrow of everyday life, gives rhythm to the labour of the field, magnifies mystic and erotic rapture, and helps the listener to relive the wars and insurrections that still punctuate the life of the Kurds. The Kurdish prince Salahaddin – the Saladin of the Crusades – is one of the principal heroes whose exploits feature in **epic songs**, though other sung events date back to the time of Alexander the Great, and seem scarcely less current than those describing the Gulf War. The epic song is a constant call to battle and a glorified, nostalgic reminder of the past, arming its listeners against the harsh realities of modern life, and defending their beliefs and identity. Even today when a *peshmerga* (Kurdish freedom fighter) dies in the hills, his comrades sing and dance, long into the night, to express their grief and say their farewells.

Bards, Minstrels and Songs

Traditionally Kurdish folklore is transmitted by **dengbej** (bards), **stranbej** (minstrels) and **chirokbej** (storytellers), usually from families of musicians. The feudal structure of society, however, in which every feudal lord would have his *dengbej* and would compete with fellow lords for the best, has changed greatly in the past century. The systematic destruction of Kurdish villages by the Turkish, Iranian, Iraqi and Syrian governments has resulted in a considerable movement to the towns and cities where a different kind of music scene has evolved. Nonetheless, the majority of Kurds are still rural people, and some are still nomads.

In Kurdistan there is a strong tradition of singing about unhappy, unrequited love, and unusually it is the women who compose and sing these **songs of love**, at least within their own village or valley, before the wandering minstrels – men – take them up and perform them on their travels. The repertoire of these roaming *stranbej* also includes **erotic poetry**, which is passionate and direct despite the Islamic culture. These singers are judged by their creativity, the beauty of their poetry and their ability to stir emotions.

There is also a strong body of **work songs**, used to accompany wool spinning and rug weaving, the threshing, winnowing and herding that are part of agricultural life, or the shearing of sheep and the birth of lambs that punctuate nomadic life. In addition, music is central to **weddings**, **births**, **funerals and feasts**. At all such events, young and old dance for hours – men and women together in long lines, arms linked. There are hundreds of different **dances** and they vary from region to region. The music is provided by village musicians who sing traditional or newly created songs, accompanied on the *zurna* (wooden shawm), *dhol* (drum) and *bloor* (flute).

A celebration of great importance to the Kurds is **Nawroz**, the New Year, held on March 21. Bonfires are lit in every village, picnics are eaten and everyone dances till dawn. The lighting of fires harks back to the pre-Islamic times and the Zoroastrian religion which, together with its forerunner, the ancient Yazidi religion, still survives amongst the Kurds. Yazidis are found both in Iraqi Kurdistan – around their sacred shrine of **Shekan Baazra** – and in Armenia, where there is relative freedom for Kurds. Their religious music, mostly sacred chants, survives, although few recordings are currently available. The Zoroastrian **chatta** (religious songs) are chants that were performed in the fire-temples of the Magi in praise of Zoroaster, and come from their holy book, the Avesta – thought by some to have been written originally in Orami, a dialect of Kurdish. They can still be recognized in the Houra, ancient and sacred songs from the Oraman area of Iranian Kurdistan.

There is religious music, too, among the various **dervish and Sufi cults** that proliferate amongst the mountain valleys; hypnotic and trance-inducing, its origins are ancient and pre-date Islam. As elsewhere, the **daf** (frame drum) and **shimshal** (*ney*, a long flute) are used by Kurdish Sufis as part of their ceremonies in order to induce trance.

Instruments and Rhythm

The **voice** takes the leading role in Kurdish music, with instruments secondary. Most Kurdish instruments are also found in the neighbouring musical traditions of Turkey and Armenia to the north, and Iran and Iraq to the south. The **balaban** (known as *duduk* in Armenia) and **bloor** are more common in the north and in the mountains, as are the **doozela** (double reed flute) and the **shimshal** – both very much folk instruments. Amongst the stringed instruments the **tanbur** (*saz*) is more common in the north, whilst the **kamancheh** (spike fiddle), which is thought to originate from Kurdistan, is more of a southern instrument. The **oud** also features in the south as do the **santur** (zither) and **tar** (lute) in more urban sophisticated contexts.

While the content of Kurdish music and songs is very varied, the words are usually set to one of five different **rhythmic patterns**. One is based on a Zoroastrian *chatta* with either eight or ten syllables in each line. The other four styles are simply three verses with lines of eight syllables, or two verses with lines of seven, ten or twelve syllables. The form consisting of two verses with lines of ten syllables is the most frequently used. Songs which are based on these five rhythmic patterns are considered to constitute the most ancient and traditional part of the repertoire. The **melodic line** is simple, its range consisting of only three or four notes, which are repeated as the different verses are sung. The form of the songs is strophic – one identical line of poem and music recurs at the end of each stanza like a refrain.

Kurdish music is **modal**, with the mode, or *maqam*, known as *kurdi* throughout the Arab world being, as you might imagine, predominant. However, all the different types of modal schemes which are found in Persian traditional, classical and folk music also exist in Kurdish music in Iran; in fact, it has been suggested that Kurdish music is one of the foundations on which Persian classical music has been built. As so much has been made of the influence of surrounding nations on the culture of the Kurds, it is important to consider how much the influence has been the other way. Kurdish musicians, especially within the diaspora, emphasize the independence of Kurdish music from Persian or Arab music, whilst national authorities prefer to marginalize Kurdish music as being a local species of another nation's music.

Partition States

Since partition in the 1920s the culture of the Kurds has been seriously disrupted. Travel between the various Kurdish regions has been – and is – severely restricted, while mass media have helped to impose dominant national languages even in the farthest-flung villages. Music has undergone different changes in the different countries, though it has remained in clandestine circulation between them through smuggled and copied cassettes. The arrival of satellite television and the Internet has radically improved the ability of Kurds to access their own music. In the autonomous region of Kurdistan of Iraq, three television stations and the satellite station Kurdsat (which is available worldwide) have made many music programmes featuring pop, traditional and classical music. Kurdish musicians from all over the world go as often as they can to perform in Howleer or Sulemaniyah. Even **İbrahim Tatlıses** from Turkey is planning to come to Iraqi Kurdistan to give his first Kurdish language concert.

Kurdistan of Turkey

Until recently, in **Turkey**, all songs in Kurdish were banned on pain of imprisonment, torture or death, both for musicians and listeners, though Kurdish musicians can now admit to being Kurdish. Throughout the last seventy years the Turks have been the most ruthless in their attempts to destroy all Kurdish culture. Many musicians have been imprisoned or killed or have fled into exile; others – such as the popular Arabesk singer **İbrahim Tatlıses** – have taken the easier path of singing in Turkish.

Despite the risks, Kurdish pirate radio stations have flourished, mostly run by partisans in the mountains, and a huge underground market for tapes of forbidden singers, passing from hand to hand and smuggled from one part of Kurdistan to another, has grown up. These days the music is increasingly likely to be downloaded from the Internet and listened to on an MP3 player. It is in this atmosphere of persecution that **Şivan Perwer**, the most famous and popular Kurdish singer today, came to the fore. Born in Urfa in Turkish Kurdistan, into a family of musicians, his earliest memories are of songs of loss and longing, always filled with the desire to live in a land free from persecution. From an early age his wish was to be the best *dengbej* and already as a child, composing his own songs, he was singled out for his remarkable voice.

Şivan rose to fame rapidly in 1972 at Ankara University, at the time of the Kurdish uprising in Iraqi Kurdistan. Cassette tapes made on the simplest equipment were smuggled into Iraq and Iran at great risk. Thousands were inspired by listening to his songs, thousands came to hear this charismatic and controversial figure with a breathtakingly beautiful voice sing live, always illegally and often at gatherings of *peshmerga* before they went into battle. In 1976 he had to escape Turkey and fled to Germany, where he continued recording.

Şivan Perwer

Turkey or Iran. Urban Kurdish musicians were able to study music in Baghdad and perform on Baghdad or Kirkuk radio, and they were permitted to take a limited part in the cultural life of Iraq as long as there was no hint of anything political.

One of the great names of the century was the legendary **Ali Mardan** (1914–80) from Kirkuk, an urban musician, singer and composer whose music sometimes showed Arab influences (he played with Arab orchestras), but was much appreciated and played by his fellow Kurdish musicians. Other important musicians include the first two female Kurdish singers to be recorded and to work on Baghdad radio, **Ayse San** and **Miryem Xan**, and **Mohammed Arif Jesrawi**, another influential figure, whose music was taken up by Kurds not only in Iraq but also in Iran.

In time, simple recording facilities became available, although a government licence was necessary to make any recording. Getting this licence could take several months as the poetry was heavily scrutinized by the censors for any political references, and so a highly symbolic language evolved: a flower or a beautiful girl would symbolize Kurdistan, the partridge the struggle for freedom. Many cassettes were recorded illegally on portable equipment and distributed clandestinely, with the result that numbers of musicians and poets were imprisoned or put to death for their defiance. **Karim Kaban** from Sulemaniyah was hanged, **Tasin Taha** was blown up, and **Tahir Tafiq** "vanished".

In 1974, after a popular uprising that cost many thousands of lives, the Kurds managed to win a degree of autonomy. They were allowed to publish in their own language; the radio stations in Erbil, Sulemaniyah and Kirkuk played Kurdish music; schools, universities and music schools, teaching in Kurdish, were established; and there was a prolific output of cassettes. However, within just a few years the situation deteriorated. Kurds would not abandon the idea of independence, and when

Şivan came to world notice when he took part in the Simple Truth concert at London's Wembley Stadium in 1991, an event he organized with Peter Gabriel and the Red Cross to raise funds for the Kurds in the aftermath of the Gulf War.

It is remarkable that Şivan should have such great popularity in all parts of Kurdistan and among the Kurdish diaspora as well as Azeris, Turks and Persians, given he is still banned from radio and television across the whole region, except in Iraq. Possession of one of his political cassettes can lead to a long prison sentence in Iran, and still only a few, of his cassettes (of traditional songs) are permitted for sale in Turkey.

Federal Kurdistan of Iraq

Before the emergence of Saddam Hussein, Iraqi Kurdish musicians fared better than those in

one of the Kurdish political parties sided with the Iranians in the Iran–Iraq War, wooed by hopes of independence, the Kurds experienced the horror of chemical bombing. Thousands of villages were destroyed and their menfolk were "disappeared" by Saddam's secret police.

With the establishment of the so-called 'safe haven', after the First Gulf War, the Kurds had more freedom, but in a climate of full economic sanctions and constant internal struggle and turmoil there were few funds for developing an infrastructure for recording. Since the overthrow of Saddam much has changed. The regional government has a confident new policy for the arts. The Ministry of Culture is building music institutes in Howleer and Sulemaniyah, and music festivals (including an international one) are being planned to take place as soon as things are calmer. In Sulemaniyah, there is a subsidized national orchestra and choir, led by conductor and composer **Karadahari**. The orchestra combines Western classical and Kurdish folk instruments.

Several music schools are flourishing, such as the Arts and Music college in Sulemaniyah, and at least two good-sized record companies are busy recording new work, attracting Kurdish artists from the diaspora such as **Naser Razazi** and even **The Kamkars** from Iran (see box).

Kurdistan of Iran

In Iran successive regimes have dealt harshly with any Kurdish attempts at politics, whilst allowing Kurdish-language newspapers and radio stations. Musicians have at times been imprisoned, as elsewhere, but there is a rich tradition in this region and some of the most sophisticated musicians have come from this part of Kurdistan.

A leading figure of recent decades has been **Hassan Kamkar**, who collected and arranged over four hundred songs from the villages, founded a school of Kurdish music in Sanandaj and trained many of the musicians, including his eight children, who have been in the forefront of the urban musical tradition. The Kamkars are unique. Keeping well clear of any political involvement, they have made a considerable name for themselves in the mainstream of Iranian music, playing and composing within both Iranian and Kurdish traditions. As a result of their influence it has become fashionable amongst Iranian musicians to discover long-lost Kurdish ancestors and to play Kurdish music as part of Persian music concerts.

The exceptional singer of Iranian classical music **Sharam Nazeri** is also Kurdish and frequently includes Kurdish material in his performances.

Other important figures include the singer-composer **Said Asghar Kurdistani**, who contributed much to Iranian classical music; the singer and poet **Abbas Kamandi**; and **Hassan Zirak**, an illiterate genius who composed over a thousand songs. Famous for his often erotic and sensual lyrics, straight out of the village tradition, Zirak travelled all over Kurdistan in the 1960s and 70s, and rare recordings of his, from various radio stations, have survived. **Hama Mamlê** and **Aziz Shahrokh** are also renowned for their remarkable voices. Mamlê died in 2004, but Aziz Shahrokh is still singing and is considered a living legend, performing his own music and also some of the songs of an earlier generation, in particular the music of Jesrawi. Other instrumentalists that are making a name for themselves are **Ali Akbar Moradi**, a virtuoso *tanbur* player, and **Kayhan Kalhor**, equally brilliant on the *kamancheh* (see Iran chapter).

Syrian and Armenian Kurdistan

Only in **Armenia** have the Kurds been free of the fear and restriction that pervades elsewhere, although their numbers are small. In Yerevan, there is a Kurdish faculty at the university where research has been done into Kurdish music, and there is a flourishing Kurdish radio station with a rich archive of recordings.

In **Syria**, the Kurds are an isolated and suppressed minority. However, musicians can now travel to Iraqi Kurdistan, where they find eager audiences.

The Diaspora

Faced with repression, war and destruction, over half a million Kurds were forced to flee their homelands in 1974 and 1991, and on a continuing basis. With the overthrow of Saddam, some Kurds from all regions are returning to a newly confident Kurdistan (of Iraq), from where the diaspora is now drawing new inspiration.

Large concentrations of course still remain in Germany, followed by Sweden, Britain, France, the US and Australia. Among the exiles there is a considerable musical community. At every major gathering of Kurds, whether for Nawroz, weddings or political events, musicians play and people dance their traditional dances. Audiences are eager to hear singers from all regions of Kurdistan.

In Paris, the **Kurdish Institute**, set up with the help of the Mitterands, does much to promote Kurdish culture. It has an archive of old record-

The Kamkars

The Kamkars are a family of seven brothers, a sister and now several sons and daughters, born in Sanandaj in Iranian Kurdistan and now living in Tehran. They are a formidable influence not only on Kurdish music but also on the music of Iran and the wider Kurdish community in Turkey and the Kurdistan of Iraq.

In 2004, they were the first group to be allowed to perform Kurdish music in full Kurdish costume in Istanbul and then in the city of Dyarbakar, where they played to rapturous audiences of many thousands, despite the ominous presence of tanks and Turkish soldiers in the background. Several of the brothers are talented composers. Hooshang, the eldest, is well known for his orchestral compositions, always drawing on Kurdish themes. Arsalan has written for film, for orchestra and for The Kamkars themselves, as have Ardeshir, Bijan and Pashang. Ardavan is probably the best *santur* player in Iran today, and is also a composer. His powerful, lyrical music breaks new ground technically and his *santur* can sound like a piano one moment, a percussion instrument the next. The Kamkars run a music school in Tehran which has 500 students.

In a recent interview, Hooshang was asked:

What is the situation of Kurdish music today and what has The Kamkars' influence been?

Before The Kamkars came onto the scene, Kurdish music was hardly known, even to the Kurdish people. There were no special groups and everything was very local, regional and amateur or semi-professional. There was the simple rural music and there was urban music, but little went outside of its community. Although very important to the Kurdish people, inseparable from their blood, it was undocumented, being passed on orally and so very susceptible to being marginalized or forgotten.

What The Kamkars have done is little by little make Kurdish music familiar to musicians, Kurds, even Iranians and foreigners. We have written it down and continue to do so. The Kamkars' music has developed in style and in influence to the point where now our style is dominant even in Persian music, and many classical Persian groups play Kurdish music as part of their repertoire and use the *daf*, which Bijan was responsible for introducing to Persian music.

Even in Iraqi Kurdistan several groups follow our style. An important feature we have introduced is teaching people to sit and listen to a concert. Before us, music was only played as a background to partying, eating, drinking and most importantly dancing. Now, even on TV programmes people are seen sitting on chairs and listening to music; music is taken seriously.

At last, the synthesizer, which has often been used to accompany a singer when musicians are not affordable, is being replaced by people learning to use original instruments again.

In Kurdistan [Iraq] institutes are being created, a new generation is beginning to be trained, music books are being translated into Kurdish and the situation is getting better all the time. We have been invited to found an institute in Howleer or Sulemaniyah, and when it is safe we hope to do that, as it will be well funded. There is a lot to do.

In Kurdistan [Iraq] we are attempting to influence musicians not to use Arabic melodies and not to be so influenced by Arabic music. Even in pop music I tell them to use Kurdish rhythms and atmospheres and melodies. Why use Spanish music or Madonna? Find Kurdish words and draw on your huge heritage.

Where are The Kamkars going now with their own music?

We continue to compose. Arsalan has two CDs out using Western techniques of composition with Kurdish rhythms and tunes played by an orchestra. Ardavan has a new CD, not yet released, based again on Kurdish themes.

Myself, I want to introduce some new techniques, developing Kurdish music into new realms. For instance, playing with words, rather like in Renaissance madrigals, dividing phrases up between different voices. Each voice singing in very different combinations. No longer just playing a song in the traditional way, repeating verses to one melody. The music is now getting complex. The techniques do not damage the underlying quality of the music, but they are new, they have not been heard in Iran either. The percussion instruments are used melodically. On our new CD *Hawra* (Chanting), initially released [by] Charchera, in Howleer, there is a piece "Halale Taniar" based on five different repeating phrases coming through, one by one. At one point, all five play with each other but do not disturb one another. Even the drum and all the voices originate from these five phrases. This is very new.

ings and has reissued many of these, as well as some new recordings. In **Sweden**, where several musicians have settled, there is a thriving musical community. It is here that young musicians have started to experiment, adding elements from Western pop, Western classical, jazz and Indian music to traditional Kurdish music.

Şivan's later records reflect these influences, as does the music of **Naser Razazi** and his wife **Marzia**, exiles from Iran who had a big following at Nawroz parties and gatherings. They recently returned to Iraqi Kurdistan, where Nazir is able to perform and to record with more musicians at his disposal than was ever possible in Sweden (Marzia died in 2005). **Najmeddin Ghulami** is another urban singer who has settled in Scandinavia. He has produced several recordings using traditional instruments, but also experiments with other formations and has recently introduced a synthesizer to his line-up.

Ciwan Haco, originally from Turkish Kurdistan, is now living in Norway, and playing with Norwegian musicians. He sings in Kurdish and, with some reference to Western rock music (such as Bruce Springsteen), draws his inspiration from the traditional music of northern Kurdistan (part of Turkey).

The relaxation of strictures in exile has led to the emergence of a generation of female singers, who in traditional Kurdish society would have been unable to make music a profession. **Gulestan**, Şivan's ex-wife, recorded and performed with him but is now making her own records of traditional and new songs accompanied on the *saz*. **Nilüfar Akbal**'s operatic training has influenced the way she performs, while Denmark-based **Nazé** mixes traditional instruments with synthesizer and guitar more successfully than most. **Aynur**, despite making it onto the cover of *fRoots* magazine, still suffers from a preoccupation with heavy reverb, any acoustic instruments on her recordings being lost in waves of processed percussion.

Other groups playing more traditional music include **The Razbar Ensemble** who play the trance music of the Ahl-e Haqq, and the **Living Fire Ensemble**, made up of musicians from all parts of the Kurdish diaspora. They play folk tunes and melodies from the different areas, in whose arrangements can be seen the influence of The Kamkars.

Many thanks to Hooshang Kamkar, Arsalan Kamkar, Parwez Zabihi, Şivan Perwer, Kendal Nizam, Ahmed Nejad, Newroz and Sheri Laiser for their help in preparing this piece.

DISCOGRAPHY Kurdish Music

A few recordings of Kurdish music (Şivan, The Kamkars, Moradi and the French anthologies) are now available from the megastores, but the majority can be found only at specialist outlets and from Kurdish organizations. Bahar Video in London (343 Green Lanes, N4 1BZ) is useful, while in Turkey SES Plak (WMÇ Blok No. 6410, Unkapani, Istanbul, Turkey; tel (90) 212 527 5261, fax (90) 212 513 5087) has an extensive selection of Kurdish pop music.

Kurdish music websites have proliferated in recent years and are an easy source of recordings as well as being an increasingly important access point for many Kurds. Most useful are *www.kurdonline.com/music*, which has links to many other Kurdish music sites offering downloads; *www.kurdland.com/main/music*, which allows you to listen to tracks by fifty popular artists; and *www.beznez.com/kurdishmusic*, which has links to many Kurdish artists' own websites.

⊙ **De Soran a Hawraman: Songs from Kurdistan**
Al-Sur, France
Mostly traditional and folk music recorded in France by musicians from both Iran and Iraq, featuring the *kamancheh*, *tanbur*, *daf*, *ney* and *duduk*. Good notes in French and English.

⊙ **Kurdish Music**
Auvidis/UNESCO, France
Field recordings made in Kurdish villages in Syria with instruments that include the *tanbur* (*saz*), *zorna* (*shawm*), *zil* (copper cymbals used by Kurdish nomads) and *tabalak* (clay kettledrums). Interesting notes in English.

⊙ **Muzîka Gelêrî ya Hekariyê/Traditional Music of Hakkari**
Kalan, Turkey
This astonishing and emotionally powerful collection of music from Kurdish highlanders is a milestone in ethnographic recording in the region. It focuses on the indigenous vocal music of Hakkari, relatively untouched by urban instrumental styles. Sung by well-known local *dengbej* as well as anonymous tribesmen and women, this is the music of Kurdish everyday and social life, including weddings and religious celebrations. Accompanied by book-length liner notes in Turkish, Kurdish and English.

Nizamettin Ariç

Filmmaker, composer, painter and singer Ariç is an accomplished *saz* player, now resident in Germany. He has made several solo CDs, singing both traditional and original songs in the style of the *dengbej*, the storytelling bard.

☉Zine
SES Plak, Turkey

Ariç's powerful and emotional voice is a perfect match for the longing expressed in these haunting, beautiful songs, mostly accompanied on the *saz*. Includes music from the film *A Song for Beko*.

Ciwan Haco

A refugee from Turkey, Ciwan has settled in Norway and is one of the bright stars of contemporary Kurdish pop.

☉ Dûrî-Carcira
SES Plak, Turkey

Ciwan's debut, featuring Kurdish and Norwegian musicians, was a big hit with the younger Kurdish audience.

☉ Gula Sor
SES Plak, Turkey

A more recent recording – Ciwan plays *saz* with a return to roots music.

Kayhan Kalhor

Kurdish Iranian Kayhan Kalhor is the undisputed star of the *kamancheh*, an ancient Middle Eastern bowed lute, sometimes called the spike fiddle.

WITH ALI AKBAR MORADI

☉ In the Mirror of the Sky
World Village, France

Beautifully balancing discipline and energy, love and anguish, this CD is a tasteful fusion of *kamancheh* and *tanbur*. Kalhor and Moradi tap into the pulse of their people, who long for a homeland to unify their many diverse cultural threads. At times, both players fire up, and a mesmerizing improvisation follows, intermingling spontaneity with the heavier messages of the *djamm* gatherings, devotional Kurdish Sufi ceremonies.

The Kamkars

The Kamkar family are certainly the most polished of Kurdish musicians. They are considered to be amongst the very best musicians in Iran today for both their classical Persian and Kurdish repertoires. Many of the group members play several instruments, as well as being gifted soloists and prolific composers. They are responsible for bringing Kurdish music into the mainstream in Iran.

★ Living Fire
Long Distance, France

This live recording, recorded in Paris, has a darker feel and perhaps more atmosphere and intensity than the well-known *Nightingale with a Broken Wing* (see Iran chapter).

Ardavan Kamkar

The youngest of the Kamkar brothers, Ardavan is considered the best *santur* player in Iran today. A prolific composer, he has taken the *santur* into new realms of expression and technical skill.

★ Over the Wind
Traditional Crossroads, US

All original compositions influenced by his Kurdish roots, this powerfully charged, lyrical and expressive CD released in 2001 is a fine example of his innovative playing and consummate talent.

Adnan Karim

Karim is one of a generation of musicians who developed their style in Iraqi Kurdistan but fled the oppression of the Iraqi government. He has settled in Sweden, but now returns to play and record in Iraqi Kurdistan.

☉ The Longest Night
Stran Music, Sweden

Adnan is the singer and composer of most of the songs on this recording in the traditional style. It was made in Sulemaniyah (Iraqi Kurdistan) by the music group of the Kurdish Fine Arts Society and remixed in Sweden.

Hama Mamlê

From a traditional family of musicians in Iranian Kurdistan, Mamlê was renowned for his beautiful voice. He was deported by the Shah's regime and lived in Sweden until his death in 2004.

☉ Zemane
Stran Music, Sweden

A collection of classic recordings on which he is accompanied by violin, flute, *santur*, tar, *oud* and *zarb* (*tombak* drum).

Ali Akbar Moradi

Steeped in the history, culture and religion of his native Kermanshah region, Moradi is a virtuoso of the *tanbur* (a long-necked, two-stringed plucked lute). A member of the Sufi Ahl-e Haqq (People of Truth), he plays at their *djamm*, ceremonies at which Sufis dance to music played on the *tanbur* (which they consider sacred) in order to enter a trance, a state of ecstasy, and achieve mystical revelation.

★ Iranian Kurdistan: The Ritual Maqam of the Yarsan
Naïve, France

Moradi is probably the only person alive who knows and has mastered all 72 *maqams* (modal patterns) of the Kurdish *tanbur*. Although austere and unrelenting, this remarkable and beautiful 4-CD box set is full of musical depth and intensity, and provides a rare insight into the real music of Sufi mystics, rather than the various concert adaptations.

Simon Broughton

Kayhan Kalhor and Ali Akbar Moradi (right, with *tanbur*)

Nazé and Newroz

Young musicians Nazé and her husband Newroz are refugees living in Denmark. She has a rich, dramatic voice and their music is a good example of the new Kurdish music with Western influences that is popular at parties.

WITH ORIENTAL MOOD

⊙ **Ax Kurdistan**
Own label, Denmark
Nazé and Newroz head up Oriental Mood, the group of Kurdish and Danish musicians featured on this recording playing a collection of traditional music and new songs composed by the couple.

Şivan Perwer

The inspiration of a whole generation of young musicians, Şivan was exiled by the Turkish government as the voice of a people demanding their independence. At least half of his Turkish CDs on SES Plak, the label with the best collection of Kurdish pop, are banned in Turkey. While most of Şivan's discs are traditional in style, on some he experiments with synthesizers and electric guitars.

⊙ **Chants du Kurdistan**
Auvidis/Ethnic, France
This collection of mostly traditional songs is a good introduction to Şivan's earlier music, in which he accompanies himself on *saz*.

★ **Kirive Vols 1 and 2**
SES Plak, Turkey
Şivan has eighteen CDs on SES Plak; these volumes are "best of" collections and a good place to start. They include many of his most famous political songs and some folksongs. Şivan accompanies himself on the saz, and other instruments featured include *duduk*, *bloor*, *oud* and *qanun*.

⊙ **Şivan Perwer**
Caprice, Sweden
A welcome change from his many commercial releases. Largely traditional love songs, with nothing overtly political, although in his own song "Tembura Min" (My Tembur), Şivan speaks of a country longing for freedom, and urges his instrument to spread love and understanding. This album is stronger for not being a manifesto, but a collection of fine and stirring music by a great performer.

The Razbar Ensemble

Based in Germany, the Razbar Ensemble are members of the Ahl-e Haqq who have dedicated themselves to upholding the spiritual music of their order.

⊙ **A Feast of the Divine**
⊙ **Leyli**
Arion, France
On these excellent recordings *tanbur*, *kamancheh* and *daf* accompany voices that slowly build with increasing tempo and gripping intensity into the ecstatic dance of the mystic.

Temo

Temo is a Syrian Kurd, resident in France since 1975.

⊙ **Derew**
Playasound, France
Derew (Falsehood) is an intimate recording of Kurdish bard repertoire, on which Temo accompanies himself on the *tanbur*. Some of the instrumental playing is exceptional.

PLAYLIST
Kurdish Music

1 DANCE OF WIND Ardavan Kamkar from *Over the Wind*
Exquisite improvisation that reveals all of Ardavan's skill and power.

2 KHOSHA HAWRAMAN The Kamkars from *Nightingale with a Broken Wing*
A powerful, lively dance tune that demonstrates the verve and skill that The Kamkars bring to traditional songs.

3 OURAD KHANI The Kamkars from *Live in Concert*
This exciting piece, composed by Hooshang Kamkar, is based on traditional chanting. (Currently download only.)

4 MAQAM-E GOL WA KHUK Ali Akbar Moradi and Kayhan Kalhor from *In the Mirror of the Sky*
Moradi is at his soulful best in this "Flower and Earth" *maqam*; perhaps this will tempt you to get his 4-CD box set.

5 HELABÇE Şivan Perwer from *Kirive Vol 1*
The story of the chemical bombings at Halabja – one of the songs that made Şivan a legend amongst the Kurds.

6 SEBRA MALA Şivan Perwer from *Şivan Perwer*
With a faster tempo, this is a favourite dance number which questions the lack of freedom for Kurdish women.

7 ZINE Nizamettin Ariç from *Zine*
Haunting and powerful, Ariç's voice soars through this song of longing.

8 GULA SOR Ciwan Haco from *Gula Sor*
A good example of Ciwan's pop appeal.

9 HEY VAYYAR Razbar Ensemble from *A Feast of the Divine*
Highly charged sacred music of the Ahl-e Haqq, featuring men's and women's voices with *daf* accompaniment.

Lebanon

the rising star in the middle east

The inestimable Fairuz

In its heyday after World War II, Beirut was known as the 'Paris of the Middle East': a chic, Eurocentric home to artists and intellectuals escaping despotism elsewhere in the Arab world. This cosmopolitan centre produced an intense and glamorous music scene that was shattered by the outbreak in 1975 of a brutal civil war which raged for seventeen years. However, as Lebanon rebuilt itself (before Israel's renewed attacks in 2006) the wealth of music being made there once again expressed the spirit and cultural vitality of this remarkable country. Bill Badley does the *dabke* once more.

Those living in Beirut during the hostilities tell extraordinary tales about the musical life during the conflict: the day when a group of armed guerrillas broke into the Conservatoire and tipped all the pianos out of top-floor windows; of elegant ladies in furs and Ferragamo shoes, tip-toeing through mortar craters and braving sniper fire to attend concerts in bombed-out churches. Through terrible times, the music played on.

Diverse Cultures, Diverse Styles

A number of factors contribute to Lebanon's unique musical identity. First, it is a country of extraordinary geographical variety: when it was a popular holiday spot for the *beau monde* of the 1950s and 60s, it was said that you could ski in the mountains during the morning and sunbathe on the Mediterranean beaches in the afternoon. The population is also a rich social, ethnic and religious mix that includes Sunni and Shiite Muslims; Orthodox, Maronite and Catholic Christians and Druze living side by side in shifting states of peace and harmony. This same polyglot blend that has contributed to hideously bloody and complex civil war, also gives the country an extraordinary wealth of musical genres. Since the days of the Phoenicians, Lebanese traders have travelled widely, bringing cultural influences back from all over the Mediterranean. Significantly, during the twentieth century the ruling elite in the cities was generally Christian, and had a much more indulgent view of music than Islamic rulers. This, along with the academic and cultural legacy of the French protectorate, gives Lebanon a unique ability to blend Arab and Continental styles and many in the Middle East consider the Lebanese to be the arbiters of taste.

Quite apart from the quality of its musicians, Lebanon's place at the centre of the Arab musical world would be secure through the prestige of its biggest summer festival, at Baalbek. Ever since 1955 some of the region's biggest names have performed in the magnificent setting of the Roman Heliopolis. Though the festival closed during the war – the area saw heavy fighting – its revival in 1992 was seen as a symbol of the country's regeneration. Today, it is one of the few places on earth where you can see Phil Collins playing next to Warda al-Jazairia.

In modern Beirut, no one sums up the multicultural nature of the city like the charismatic producer, director, entrepreneur and self-conscious nonconformist **Michel Elefteriades**. Through his innovative work with Elef Records he offers a platform for some of the most experimental artists working in the region and his Oriental Roots Orchestra collaborates tirelessly with a dazzling array of musicians from different cultures. Memorably, he brought the veteran maestro of Lebanese song, **Wadi al-Safi**, together with young Flamenco singer José Fernandez, and his part in reviving the career of Greek singing legend Demis Roussos will secure him a place of affection in many hearts; his engineering of an Arab-Latin fusion through **Hanine y Son Cubano** will possibly be remembered less fondly.

For decades, Lebanese song was presided over by an undisputed king and queen, **Wadi al-Safi** and **Fairuz**. Wadi al-Safi was born in 1921 and his enduring career has included work in film (most notably *Nar el Showk* – Fire of Passion), theatre *Ardouna ila el Abad* – Forever our Land) and a concert touring schedule that took him all over the world. His interpretation of classical song is revered throughout the Arab world, particularly his *mawaal* (sung improvisations). During the 1950s he was a guiding force in the preservation and rearrangement of Lebanese folk music using modern Arab instruments. Traditionally, these songs and dances would have been played on simple instruments like the *rabab* (single-string fiddle – see Bedouin music) and *mijwiz* (reed pipe); but this folk-music revival did much to preserve a culture that might otherwise have been lost as people moved from the countryside into the cities or emigrated. The broad reach of the Lebanese diaspora from this time is one reason why both al-Safi and Fairuz have an international profile that is the envy of many Arab singers.

Mawaal king, Wadi al-Safi (left)

Doing the Dabke

Lebanese traditional music is based around the communal dance form of *dabke*, which started as a popular village entertainment but is now found throughout the country. Originally these muscular dance-songs would have been performed in single-sex groupings but amongst young people today it is common for men and women to dance together. In the 1950s and 60s – when cities were rapidly expanding – urban Lebanese were drawn to the notion of the Arcadian, rustic idyll and a number of singers and composers exploited this. Early in her career, Fairuz was presented as a simple girl from the mountains and the elaborately staged *dabke* spectacles by the **Rahbani brothers**, featuring her and the full-throated **Sabah**,

became something of a national institution. Next to the immaculately presented and chic stars of the twenty-first century and the ethereally demure Fairuz, Sabah stands apart as something very different. Known as *as-saout al-jebel* (the voice of the mountains), she has a plangent roar that seems to summon up all the pain and suffering of her native land; her life has been filled with a litany of well-publicized romantic intrigues and she sports a wig at which Dolly Parton might cast wistful glances. Now in her 90s – and still making headlines – she is one of the most endearingly individual characters in the Levant.

In recent years it has been the Lebanon's pop music output that has started to create a real stir across the Arab world. Beirut has become a well-respected production centre and, though it can not

Fairuz and the Rahbanis

The Arab world superstar **Fairuz** (Nuhad Haddad) was born in 1934 to a Christian Maronite family in Beirut. While a teenager, the tender quality of her voice brought her to the attention of the newly founded Lebanese Radio Beirut, which she joined as a chorus singer. There, she soon became a leading solo singer, known for her interpretations of Classical Arab song. There, too, she met the bothers, **Asi** and **Mansour Rahbani**, struggling composers who at the time were earning their living as policemen. Fairuz and the two brothers (Fairuz and Asi married in 1954) worked together for the next thirty years. Asi composed the music; Mansour wrote the words – which in the early part of her career were largely nostalgic and romantic; Fairuz sang, sweeping all before her.

The Fairuz/Rahbani team was incredibly prolific and diverse. They reinterpreted Classical Arab song, bringing in Western and Eastern European styles (and keys) to the orchestration, combining the piano, guitar, violin and accordion with the *ney* and Arab percussive instruments. They even created hybrids with tango and rumba, and produced an Arabized version of Mozart's 40th Symphony, which at the time was considered extraordinarily innovative.

No Arab composer before or since has been quite so innovative. But the trio's most remarkable achievements were the huge musical plays that they mounted together at the Baalbek festivals – elaborate, operatic spectacles that drew heavily on the folk culture of rural Lebanon. Certainly the region has seen nothing on such a scale before or since, and these productions became a recognized showcase for other emerging Lebanese talent.

During the civil war, Fairuz's refusal to leave Beirut even during the worst of the conflict became a symbol of hope, and her first peacetime performance in the city was hailed as a landmark. She remains hugely popular with Lebanese diaspora communities all over the world, and she can fill any concert hall in Europe or the US, where there are Lebanese or Arab communities.

Fairuz and Asi parted in the early 1980s (Asi died in 1986), but she has continued to work with Ziad, the son from their marriage, as her musical director. Their 1990s collaborations have brought a new, more adventurous direction to her career. **Ziad Rahbani** (born 1957) has pioneered his own particular brand of Arab jazz and is considered by some to be one of the most individual musical forces working in Lebanon today. Whilst he is household name for the music he has written for his mother, his solo work has not been afforded the same recognition. He has continued the illustrious family tradition for music and drama, scoring for several plays and films.

yet challenge Cairo for sheer commercial weight and the number of studios, it has developed a reputation for quality and musical invention.

Female Stars

Despite considerable liberalization in recent years, there are few parts of the Middle East where it is possible for a female singer to be regarded with genuine respect – the whiff of the bordello still lingers. However, in Lebanon some women have risen above this. The tone was set in the 1950s by the young **Fairuz** who created a modern image distinct from the melodramatic agony of Umm Kulthum or the dolly simpering expected of pop stars. More recently, **Carole Samaha** has made the transition from serious classical actress to chanson diva whilst keeping her reputation intact. Part of her success may also lie in the fact that she has worked extensively with **Mansour** and **Marwan Rahbani**.

However, it would be wrong to suppose that Lebanon cannot field its own regiment of less serious stars, though they tend to have developed more colourful images than their anodyne Egyptian counterparts. First amongst these is **Nancy Ajram** who, with a combination of skilful marketing and slick production, has become the most notorious star of her generation. Her racy image has been enhanced by groundbreaking videos to songs which, as well as showing Nancy in less than modest dress, have featured transvestites and strong allusions to homosexuality – subjects generally considered taboo in the Arab world. Whilst her fans revel in these challenges to conservative values, her stance has caused scandal and even civil unrest when she tours: riots broke out when she performed in Bahrain and her concerts in Kuwait were banned. Inevitably, all this has only served to further her career. Also very popular, if rather less in-your-face, is pop princess **Elissa**.

Male Pop Singers

In much the same way, male Lebanese pop singers are generally marketed differently to the unashamed glitz of their Egyptian neighbours. Lyrics tend to be more thoughtful, production is a little less synthetic and images now incline more towards Paris and Milan than Cairo or Damascus. For many years, the undisputed King of Lebanese pop was the veteran **Walid Tawfiq** who, perhaps because he modelled himself so closely on Egyptian stars, is now looking and sounding a little tired. Almost as enduring is **Ragheb Alamah**, who sells himself as the ultimate romantic singer.

Much like a Levantine George Michael, he successfully made the tricky transition from teen heartthrob to mature artiste, leaving the field open for an apparently bottomless pit of younger models fashioned in his image. **Wael Jassar** has forged a similar career except – having first won the hearts of a thousand Lebanese grannies with TV appearances at the age of 8 – he had to reinvent himself from child star to adult performer. One of the most interesting of the younger singers is **Wael Kfoury** who – as well as looking like he has stepped off the pages of *Vogue* – has won competitions for his singing of folk music. He is now signed to the huge Saudi label Rotana and is tipped to be one of the most successful male singers of his generation.

It is significant that Kfoury's best-selling live album was recorded in Paris. He and many others are starting to look beyond the limits of the Arab world and see markets opening up for them across Europe. Similarly, the more musically ambitious singers in Lebanon are exploring an expanding range of musical genres. While flamenco and Latin sounds have been huge in Arab pop music for some time, there is something delightfully ironic about the way in which Lebanese producers have re-embraced their own folk instruments. For years it was possible to imagine that real, wooden instruments had been barred from Cairo recording studios; however, you'll now hear the same drum loops that European musicians like Natacha Atlas originally borrowed from Arab folk music turning up on Carole Samaha or Wael Jassar tracks!

Wael Kfoury

Sacred Sounds

With such religious diversity, Lebanon boasts an extraordinary array of sacred music. Given the enmity that can exist between the different faiths, it is interesting to note how musically similar many of their chants sound; and the same scales and inflections that eventually found their way into Gregorian chant can also readily be heard in Shiite recitations. For outsiders it is impossible to witness the vast majority of Druze worship as only initiates can attend the ceremonies. Funerals are the one exception to this and these offer an intriguing glimpse into an otherwise closed world. In contrast to mainstream Islamic music, women join in with the singing which moves between simple communal chant and delightfully ornate, melismatic orations by the priests, which can sound more like Arab art song.

In line with established Islamic doctrine, both Sunni and Shiite music is unaccompanied and monophonic. To the uninformed, it might be hard to hear many differences between the stark invocations of these two traditions; however, the distinctions – like added references to the Prophet Muhammad's cousin, Ali in the Shia chants – are highly significant. Some Maronite (Eastern Catholic) chants date back to the early years of Christianity and are sung in either Syriac (a dialect of Aramaic, the language spoken by Jesus) or classical Arabic.

The best-known interpreter of Christian music from the region is Lebanon's very own singing nun, **Sister Marie Keyrouz**; whose haunting performances have brought the music of the different sects to a much wider public. Her work with **L'Ensemble de la Paix** – dedicated to tolerance and universalism – has created a devoted following and her distinctive style appeals to fans of both early and New Age music. Her rather less mystical recordings of Western classical lollipops like Schubert's *Ave Maria* have not been so well received.

The Diaspora

The ravages of war inevitably created a musical diaspora as musicians left Lebanon for Europe, Australia and the US. In many cases, Lebanon's loss has been the world's gain; as these musicians have gone on to create some extraordinary fusions based on the sounds of their old and new homes. Best known amongst these is the poet and composer **Marcel Khalifa**, who chronicled the suffering of his country through the worst of times. Although he has been living in Paris since a controversial blasphemy trial in 1999, his brave, beautiful and defiant poetry – which arches between the radical polemic born out of the 1960s and the tender imagery of classical Arab verse – has been embraced by Arabs all over the world.

The intriguing and maverick *oud* player **Rabih Abou-Khalil** left Beirut in 1978 and has lived in Germany ever since. Although he plays the most Arab of instruments, his music is much more rooted in the conventions of European contemporary jazz and he has released recordings that range from full-throttle big band to solo *oud*. Ever one to defy expectations, he has turned his hand to composing a piece for *oud* and orchestra with the BBC Concert Orchestra.

Equally innovative, yet belonging to wholly different genre is the young Lebanese/Egyptian rapper **Clotaire K** who grew up in southern France but has returned to his parents' musical roots as a starting point for tracks that blend old Arabia with the grittier sounds of urban America. His multi-ethnic band has proved an exciting live draw, helping him win two nominations and one award in the BBC Radio 3 Awards for World Music in 2005.

Zad Moultaka and **Mahmoud Turkmani** have separately explored the Arab classic musical tradi-

Rabih Abou-Khalil

Pakzad/Enja

tion from their new European perspectives, negotiating the very different demands of two scale systems. Moultaka is now resident in Paris and his compositions show strong Gallic influences, particularly those of Debussy. Turkmani settled in Switzerland after studying classical guitar for several years in Russia. His most ambitious project yet is a major piece for Arab-European orchestra, choir and soloists based on the works of the celebrated Lebanese mystical poet and author of *The Prophet*, Khalil Jubran.

⊙ Anthology of World Music – Lebanon
Rounder Select, US
Though the presentation of this CD has all the allure of a 1950s school textbook, only the most stony hearted atheist could fail to be touched by these "conversations with God": devotions from three of the main branches of Islam found in Lebanon – Druze, Shiite and Sunni. Recorded in 1972 and released as part of a massive UNESCO series.

⊙ Folk Songs & Dances from Lebanon – Dabke Vol 1
★ Folk Songs & Dances from Lebanon – Dabke Vol 2
Voix de Liban, Lebanon
Recordings from the elaborate stage-shows (based around dabke folk dance) that were staged by the Rahbani brothers in the 1970s, with an illustrious line up that includes Fairuz, Wadi al-Safi & Sabah. Even though the traditional tunes are a little too cleaned up and orchestrated for some tastes, this is what many would consider golden era Lebanese folk music.

Rabih Abou-Khalil

After nearly 30 years living and working in Europe, Abou-Khalil's music is a highly individual blend of cutting-edge jazz with an oriental twist. Each CD he releases – be it with a 14-piece big band or in an intimate *oud* and piano duet – shows a new side to his mercurial musical personality.

⊙ Morton's Foot
Enja, Germany
Abou-Khalil's recordings are so different that it's hard to pick a single one. However, this 2002 release – accompanied by a quintet comprising drums, tuba, accordion, clarinet and the otherworldly voice of Sardinian bass singer, Gabriele Mirabassi – shows him at his most focused and approachable.

Ragheb Alamah

Alamah has come a long way since he arrived at the Beirut Conservatoire at the age of 15 with an *oud* under his arm. Initially, he was presented as being approachable, soulful and puppy-eyed (his website described him as "kind, generous and loving"); he is now an odd amalgam of cosy dad and leather-jacketed, suburban sex god.

⊙ Greatest Hits 1996–2005
EMI Arabia, Dubai
Although a blink of the eye for serious singers like Fairuz, nine years is a long career for an Arab pop star. Listening to this catalogue of hits, it is plain to hear how Alamah has moved away from the synthetic production favoured by Egyptians towards a more organic sound.

Nancy Ajram

Currently one of Lebanon's biggest exports and the face of Coca-Cola in the Arab world: whether or not you think Nancy Ajram's music lives up to the extraordinary hype is immaterial – she is an unstoppable force.

⊙ Ah Wa Nos
EMI Arabia, Dubai
The gnawingly catchy title track swept all before it across the Arab world. Contrary to rumours about Ajram being a mere producer's marionette, she is actually a perfectionist in the studio, and this album is about as well-crafted Middle Eastern pop music as it is possible to find.

Clotaire K

In bringing together the music he grew up with in his Lebanese-Egyptian family home with the defiant rap he heard coming from East and West Coast America, Clotaire has created something that seems to embody the mixed emotions of French-Arab youth in his native Montpellier.

★ Lebanese
Nocturne, France

Umm Khulthum samples collide with street beats and rapping in Arabic, French and English: scintillating and life affirming. And, as a nice little challenge to rapper stereotypes, he's also a very neat and tasteful *oud* player.

Fairuz

It's hard to stress just how central Fairuz is to the identity of many Lebanese – she is, without doubt, the most popular musician the country has ever produced.

★ The Lady and the Legend
Manteca, UK

Despite Fairuz's phenomenal popularity with Arabs all over the world, it was puzzling that her countless discs were so hard to find in the West. At last, this admirable sampler, released in 2005, offers a broad selection of songs that span her career.

★ Kifak Inta
EMI Arabia, Dubai

This recording was a milestone for Fairuz, as it marked the start of collaborations with her son, Ziad Rahbani. His background in jazz brought a whole new palette of colours to her sound and resulted in some of her most wistful and elegiac songs.

⊙ Yes'ed Sabahak
EMI Arabia, Dubai

Utterly charming recordings of early songs by Asi and Mansour Rahbani that summon up images of a cosmopolitan and carefree Beirut before the civil war. The naïve swing of the title track cannot fail but bring a smile to your face.

Sister Marie Keyrouz

Sister Marie's emotional performances of eastern Mediterranean Christian music undoubtedly have an unearthly quality to them: her recordings have opened up this magical repertoire to new audiences throughout the world.

⊙ Chant Traditionnel Maronite
Harmonia Mundi, France

This 1989 recording of songs and benedictions from the Maronite tradition is quite austere compared with the more elaborate arrangements found on Sister Keyrouz's later CDs, though this simplicity only serves to emphasize the antiquity and mystery of the music.

Wael Kfoury

Even with his glamorous image, everything about Kfoury's music screams "serious artist!" His style is rooted in the Levantine tradition of big ballad singers and he is considered by many to be the name to watch for the future.

⊙ Live in Paris
EMI Arabia, Dubai

The use of acoustic instruments and Kfoury's virtuosic *mawaal* (semi-improvised sung introductions) on this live recording are a definite nod to stars of yesteryear like Wadi al-Safi: a musical statement that sets him apart from transient pop singers.

Marcel Khalifa

The softly spoken poet who sang of his country's strife has become the mouthpiece for the modern ideals of Arab brotherhood and the Palestinian cause. His powerful verse is much loved by intellectuals and less admired by Muslim clerics: he has been living in Paris since a blasphemy trial in 1999.

⊙ Concerto al Andalus
Nagam, Lebanon

Many of Khalifa's most expressive songs and *oud* concerto performed with a large orchestra (which sometimes tips the balance from lush to slush). His gentle singing style and tender *oud* playing contrast alarmingly with the uncompromising passion and fiery imagery of his lyrics.

Zad Moultaka

A graduate of the National School of Music in Beirut, Moultaka gave up a promising career as a pianist in order to devote his energies to composing. He is undoubtedly one of the few people to have worked with both the Arab and Western scale systems and found an equal point of balance.

★ Zarani – Muwashahs with Piano
L'Empreinte Digitale, France

The very title of this album would raise eyebrows amongst Arab music purists, as *muwashahat* are classical sung poems based on the *maqams* (Eastern modes) and the piano cannot play the quarter tones that are intrinsic to them. However, Moultaka fearlessly blends Arab and European musical traditions and, remarkably, it works.

Wadi al-Safi

The grandfather of Lebanese song has toured and recorded tirelessly to bring his national music to a wider audience. He's in his 80s and still performing.

⊙ The Best of Wadi al-Safi, Vol. 1
Voix de Liban, Lebanon

Wadi al-Safi is the last of a generation of Middle Eastern singers whose music provided the soundtrack to the Arab struggle for self-rule in the years following World War II. This CD, with songs written by him and other veterans like Farid el-Atrache, is an evocative memento of Lebanon's past.

PLAYLIST
Lebanon

1 **KIFAK INTA Fairuz** from *Kifak Inta*
Although she originally made her name with Mansour and Asi Rahbani, this song – written by her son, Ziad Rahbani – encapsulates the cautious optimism of modern Beirut.

2 **AH WA NOS Nancy Ajram** from *A Wa Nus*
An unashamed dance-ditty that is about as far away as it's possible to get from the intellectual poetry of singers like al-Safi. This is the face of the new Lebanon.

3 **FISTANI Sabah** from *Folk Songs & Dances from Lebanon – Dabke Vol 2*
This call-and-response dance song is typical of mountain *dabke* and, with her raunchy delivery, no one leads it better than Sabah.

4 **ZIKRAYAT Sheikh Yussef Ali Abul Hosn** from *Anthology of World Music – Lebanon*
A Druze prayer for the dead which offers a very rare glimpse into the sacred rituals of this notoriously secret – but, in Lebanon, politically pivotal – religious group.

5 **HALLELUIA Sister Marie Kairouz** from *Chant Traditionnel Maronite*
A haunting, monophonic chant from the Levantine Catholic sect: music from the dawn of Christianity.

6 **BISSAHA Wadi al-Safi** from *The Best of Wadi al Safi, Vol 1*
Written for al Safi by Afif Radwan, this is a classic ballad of its time, with masterful interplay between singer and his orchestra.

7 **QALBI INKAWAH Wael Jassar** from *Allah Yikhallihum*
A swaggeringly confident dancefloor favourite.

8 **A'TEYTOUHOU MA SAALA Zad Moultaka** from *Zarani – Muwashahs with Piano*
Moultaka's take on a classical *muwashahat* juxtaposes Eastern and Western scales should leave our ears screaming; intriguingly, it sounds like the two in conversation.

Carole Samaha

Having started her career as a highly regarded stage and screen actress, Samaha now enjoys equal success as a pop singer with a mature and thoughtful approach. Partly due to her association with the Rahbani clan, she is often touted as the new Fairuz, though nothing she has yet recorded shows the same timeless quality.

⊙ **Ana Horra**
EMI Arabia, Dubai
Deliciously neat production – some might say so neat that some of her individuality is lost in the mix. However, it's hard not to be seduced by the infectious shimmy of her hit "Ghali Alayi".

Walid Tawfiq

Once considered the epitome of Lebanese pop, Tawfiq has now lost some of his following to younger, less overtly Egyptian-style singers.

⊙ **Ihtimal**
EMI Arabia, Dubai
The production and arrangements may sound dated but the confidence with which Tawfiq delivers his songs is a reminder to the young pretenders as to why he was held in such esteem for so long.

Mahmoud Turkmani

Since leaving Lebanon in 1984, Turkmani has lived and studied in Moscow and Switzerland. He has been hailed as an exceptional classical guitarist but it is as composer that he really stands out.

⊙ **Zâkira**
Enja, Germany
Turkmani's subtle and inventive arrangements of *muwashahat*. In contrast to Zad Moultaka, he writes for traditional Arab instruments using the composing techniques he learned in Russia and Europe; and, even though the musicians were perplexed by the very different musical language, the final result is mesmerizing.

Palestinian Music

sounds for a new state

Jerusalem duo, The Chehade Brothers
Elef Records

Despite the precariousnous of the peace that exists in the region, the last ten years have seen music in Palestine rise from being the sound of struggle to a celebration of emerging statehood. And, as Palestinian music reaches a wider audience internationally, it is still as much a statement of national identity as ever. Andy Morgan, Mu'tasem Adileh and Bill Badley chart the background and explore the current state of the Palestinian music scene.

Before the creation of the state of Israel in 1948, **Palestine** comprised a multifaceted collection of creeds, religions and races, all of whom had co-existed in relative peace for hundreds of years – at least until the turn of this century. Christians from Nazareth and Galilee, Druze people from the Lebanon and the Golan Heights, indigenous Jews, nomadic tribes who roamed the great deserts between the Mediterranean and the Gulf, Arab farmers and townspeople, Egyptians, Turks, Cypriots and Greeks – all were part of the cultural crossroads of the Holy Land.

Rural Songs: Dabke and Qawaali

Although the great city ports of Jaffa and Haifa were already sizeable commercial centres in the first half of the twentieth century, most Palestinians were rural people who had either settled to become **felahin** (farmers), or who still pursued a nomadic, Bedouin lifestyle. The music of the *felahin* comprised mainly functional songs for harvesting, tending the flocks, fishing, grinding coffee or making olive oil. There were also epic songs about old heroes and legends sung by itinerant storytellers or improvisers – **zajaleen** – who travelled from village to village with their box of tricks and retinue of players.

The most important occasions for music and merrymaking were **weddings** and their associated feasts. After the immense platters of meat and rice had been cleared away the party-goers would sing and dance. The dances were collectively known as **dabke**, which literally means "foot-tapping". They consisted of precise steps and jumps performed by linked chains of dancers. The music was provided by village musicians who sang traditional airs, accompanied by traditional instruments such as the *shababi* and *ney* (short flute and long flute), the *mijwiz* and *yarghoul* (shawms), the *tabla* and *duff* (drums), *rebab* (fiddle) and *oud* (lute).

Certain songs became so ingrained and widespread that they mutated into distinct song-forms with fixed melodies and verse structures over which new lyrics could be improvised. In terms of their rooted structure and versatility, these song-forms are comparable to the twelve-bar blues or even, lyrically speaking, to the limerick. The most common types of song-form, then as now, were the **dalauna** and the **meyjana**. Singers were judged as much by their word-play skills as by their vocal prowess. The ability to juggle words and phrases to fit the form brought local fame.

Nowhere are these skills more pronounced than in the art of the **qawaali** or **zajal**. The singers who practise this art engage in a kind of musical debate, each participant often representing one of the families at a wedding where they would discourse on the virtues and qualities of their patron families, or argue over the relative merits of dark- or light-skinned women. These punning, rapping, word-tussling sessions were always sung rather than merely recited.

In recent times certain *qawaali* and *zajal*, most notably **Abu Leil**, **Haddaji Rajih el-Salfiti** and **Abu Sultan**, have achieved fame across the Palestinian communities.

Songs of Partition

The tumultuous events of the late 1940s which led to the partition of Palestine and the creation of Israel in 1948 did not destroy the culture of the *felahin*. The many thousands of Palestinians who fled to the refugee camps of the West Bank and Gaza Strip took their musical traditions with them and kept them alive in their hostile new surroundings. The Arabs who stayed behind and continued to live in the new state of Israel, collectively known as "the Arabs of the 48", also clung tenaciously to their heritage.

Around the period of partition, the songs and dances of the felahin did not form part of the commercially exploited and recorded body of Arabic popular music. This area was dominated by the great Egyptian and Lebanese singers and songwriters of the day such as Umm Kulthum, Mohamed Abd el-Wahaab and Sayed Darwish (see 'Arab World/Egypt' chapter). The *felah* music was a hidden heritage, a common cultural bond among the Palestinian people completely unknown outside their own sphere of existence.

Nevertheless Palestine did have a musical scene of sorts based in the northern Israeli towns of Haifa and Nazareth, the only active, cosmopolitan centres for Palestinian music-making until the early 1970s. In these towns, songs were composed, performed and recorded. This urban genre of music was performed by small groups consisting of a singer and a few instrumentalists and was far removed in its complexity and sophistication from the country "folk" style of the *felahin*. Instead, these city musicians were attuned to the sounds coming from Damascus and Cairo, where the intricate art of classical Arab music was still revered and practised as it had been for centuries.

It was the versatility of the song-form that allowed the roots music of the *felahin* to survive the political upheavals of the late 1940s and to develop a stage further. In the new climate of fear, anger and alienation, the gist of the **improvised lyrics** that accompanied the *dalauna* and the *meyjana* began to reveal a harder edge. Instead of songs about the slender stalk of wheat swaying in the wind like the lithe body of the dancing woman, the newly dispossessed sang about the power of the gun and the dream of nationhood. Heroes and martyrs of the struggle such as the great Arab leader Cheikh L'Hezedin el-Kassam – who vowed to be the first to shoot the God of the British colonialists – were lauded in popular song. Even non-Arab figures like Che Guevara became part of the new folklore. Every significant event in the life of post-partition Palestine – the Six Day War, the Yom Kippur offensive, Arafat's speech to the UN in 1974, the belligerence of Saddam Hussein and the intifada – has at one time or another been celebrated or mourned in song.

The first singer to score a hit with a collection of essentially Palestinian songs was **Mustafa al-Kurd**, whose cassette release *Kullee Amal* (Full of Hope) enjoyed fervent popularity all over Palestine in the early 1970s. He sang of the daily suffering of Palestinians living under occupation and his radical concoction of local folk music, pan-Arab pop and Western rock found an eager audience outside the Middle East; not least amongst *kafeeya*-wearing students in Germany and Scandinavia, where he had a dwindling following even into the 1990s.

The dearth of recording studios and commercial infrastructure accessible to Palestinians in Israel and the Occupied Territories meant that the growth of modern Palestinian pop was slow and arduous: singers found their recordings and concerts subject to censorship until, eventually, the Israelis gave up trying to control the clandestine Arab cassette industry, and recordings became readily available – even if they had to be sold under the counter. In the late 1970s and early 80s a new movement of political theatre began to make its mark. Playwrights were often forced to use highly symbolic language to convey their defiant message, and theatrical performances were subject to much closer scrutiny than the playing of music, which continued more or less unheeded in the privacy of Palestinian homes. These theatre companies made much use of music and foremost among them was the group **El-Funoun**, founded in 1979.

After Al-Kurd's success at the start of 1970s, Palestinians had to wait until the end of the decade before other groups made a similar impact at home and abroad. One of the most successful pop acts was **Al-Ashiqeen** (The Lovers), who achieved fame all over the Arab world, a rare thing for a Palestinian artist. The theme of their most famous

Jak Kilby

Mustafa al-Kurd

cassette release, *Sirit Izz Deen El Kassam*, was the colourful life of holy man and freedom fighter el-Kassam. This period also saw the creation of **Sabreen**, which has become the most internationally successful Palestinian group. Founded by Said Murad in 1980, Sabreen means "People who are Patient" – a precondition for Palestinians.

The Intifada

The energy devoted to music-making intensified in the mid-1980s, especially among the youth of the occupied territories. The **intifada uprising**, a youth-led, stone-throwing revolt initiated in the Gaza Strip in December 1987, fuelled the desire to express political woes in song, and groups like El-Funoun and Sabreen carried the hard-edged sentiments of revolt to a receptive audience. Sabreen's album *Mawt a'nabi* (Death of a Prophet) is one of the lasting musical products of that time. 'The intifada started while we were in the studio making this album', remembers Said Murad. 'We saw young men throwing stones – and people got killed for that. We felt these people were the prophets of our new history and we named this album after them.' Musically, this album is very strong, with urgent, mournful vocals and a rich, plangent plucked accompaniment on instruments of the classic Arabic tradition: *qanun* (plucked zither), *oud*, *buzuk* (a strummed instrument related to the Greek bouzouki) and guitar.

Much intifada music was simple, disposable and worked like a newspaper, but it was effective. One of the most important figures was the songwriter **Suhail Khoury**. 'It was a very powerful time, a very revolutionary time,' he explains. 'People were in the streets every day. Ordinary people were fighting the occupation. And music was a part of this. I did a tape called *Sharrar* (Spark). The lyrics were very powerful, talking about things that had happened just a few days before. How they'd kicked the Israelis out of Nablus and so on. It was describing the daily life of the intifada and it was a very powerful tool.' After making the tape Khoury was stopped at a checkpoint in his car and arrested. The car and the tapes were confiscated. 'Somehow one tape leaked out to the community and it was copied in tens of thousands, one to another. We estimated that at least 100,000 were made. A big number in a small state. And the Israelis did quite a good marketing service for me because they announced on the radio and TV that I was arrested for making music and could be imprisoned for ten years. So everybody wanted to know what kind of tape that was. Of course, I'm laughing now, but I was tortured for twelve days. They wanted to know who composed, who sang, who played. I didn't tell them anything and I was sentenced to six months' imprisonment.'

Most of the intifada music was unsophisticated – usually based on well-known folksongs – but it carried great power in spreading the feeling of opposition amongst the people. One of the most important tapes was *Doleh* (Statehood), produced in 1988 during the first year of the intifada. The key figure behind it was **Thaer Barghouti** (himself a *zajal* improviser), and it was a collection of songs by various singers recounting deeds of the Israeli soldiers and everyday events of the rebellion. The title-track became very popular because it coincided with the announcement that the intifada would not stop until there was a state.

Beginnings of a State

In 1993, a Declaration of Principles was signed by Israel and the PLO, and in May 1994 the **Palestinian National Authority** was set up in the Gaza Strip and parts of the West Bank with the late Yasser Arafat as its president. As the turmoil of the intifada subsided and the situation stabilized, it became easier for musicians to work. For instance, **wedding bands** reappeared, having been put out of business during the fighting. Using *shababi* and *mijwiz* alongside modern instruments, they perform wonderfully rough and raw versions of the latest pop songs to come out of Egypt and Lebanon.

The Doves are Coming

Your food is a locust
Dipped in a drop of honey
Your dress, burlap and camel hair
Your shoes are thorns,
Your path is thorns, its flowers few.
O moon on the outer edge
O prophet exiled
Calling in the wilderness:
Widen the roads
For the deer of love and peace
Widen the roads,
The doves are coming from the mountain,
The doves are coming.

Lyrics by Hussein Barghouthi of Sabreen

The post-intifada music scene expressed the optimism felt by many Palestinians at the time and, even though Hussein Barghouthi's words seem premature in light of more recent political events, there are now very much better organized institutions in place to develop the future music scene. Along with the returning members of the PLO were musicians like the soprano **Tania Nasser** who had been in exile in Jordan for 19 years. Her powerful collaborative compositions with the feminist and political activist **Rima Tarazi** express the Palestinian struggle for freedom in songs that are stylistically similar to German *lieder*. The genteel appearance of these two women belies the powerful imagery of their songs that hit as hard as any protest song.

Continuing the political theatre tradition that grew up during the intifada, **El-Funoun Palestinian Popular Dance Troupe** synthesizes traditional music and dance with more contemporary ideas to create a spectacle that embodies modern Palestine. They started out with folk dances, but their choreography now includes non-traditional mixed (male and female) dances. Their theatrical production *Haifa, Beirut wama ba'ad* (Haifa, Beirut and Beyond) – based on the music of Lebanese poet and composer Marcel Khalifa – was an interpretation of the Palestinian experience whilst the later *Zaghareed* was aimed towards a younger audience.

Having established itself during the 1980s as the most influential and widely known Palestinian group, **Sabreen** has more recently transformed itself from touring protest band into a multifaceted cultural organisation that encompasses media production, event organization and music education. During the intifada, Sabreen was the loudest musical Palestinian voice to be heard in the wider world, and their experimental blend of traditional Arab song, jazz, Western and Indian classical music found a ready audience within their own land and beyond. As young Palestinians they were

El Funoun – Palestinian Art-Music

El Funoun

The road to success is never easy for folkloric ensembles anywhere in the world. They won't see their videos on MTV, and young musicians in most countries are generally more interested in trying to be the next Madonna, Robbie Williams or Green Day than learning the music of their grandparents. In Palestine, these obstacles seem trivial. Since their inception in 1979, **El-Funoun** (The Arts) has faced the arrest of many of its members, bans on public performances and increasingly disruptive travel restrictions both at home and abroad. Why risk arrest simply to sing and dance? For El-Funoun, the answer was easy. They realized that half a century on the losing side of history has left many Palestinian folk arts facing extinction.

The group of fifty singers, dancers and musicians began with a mission to revive regional folklore as a form of Palestinian identity. El-Funoun's early works were the result of extensive research in Palestinian villages, preserving centuries-old songs and dances, including the *dabke*, using traditional Arab instruments (*oud*, *ney*, and *qanun*). 'This was very controversial,' explains El-Funoun's Omar Barhgouti. 'According to the Israelis, we were supposed to be a people without a culture. Over the years, we have faced numerous attempts to suppress it.'

'During the intifada, our rehearsals were clandestine,' Barghouti remembers. 'We would rehearse underground. We had to play the music quietly. Imagine, trying to play music as quietly as possible. Everyone would whisper. At the time, these activities were banned, and we all knew that we faced being arrested every time an Israeli patrol passed by.' Over the past two decades, numerous members of the ensemble have been arrested. El-Funoun's co-founder Muhammad Atta has been jailed four times 'for posing a security risk and inciting violence', says Barghouti. 'Still, life continues, and we adapt. Not just us, Palestinians in general. Local concert organisers know that they are taking a risk when they arrange one of our concerts."

Border closings have become a fact of life in the Palestinian territories. After scores of accolades and awards, the group has still never played in Gaza or to many Palestinian communities within Israel. As Barghouti says: 'We've played in the United States, Spain, Sweden, throughout the Middle-East, and even Expo '98 in Portugal, but I think we'll get to perform on Mars before we ever get permits to go to Gaza. Even dancing itself is controversial to some – you see, traditionally, in our culture, dancing is for fun, for happiness. People used to say, "we are working so hard to defend ourselves against the occupation. Two people died yesterday, and you are dancing?" But we dance because we want to express ourselves.'

In addition to the Israeli occupation, El-Funoun faces countless obstacles in age-old local traditions. 'The purpose of El-Funoun is to challenge traditions, not just to preserve them,' says Barghouti. Their 1997 project, *Zaghareed* (Ululations), tells the story of a modern Palestinian wedding, where a young woman confronts her father as he discovers that she has a lover. The argument gets heated as she wants to break with tradition and defy her parents' wishes for an arranged marriage. 'Everyone is entitled to the right to choose, (a marriage partner),' explains Barghouti. 'This was very controversial when we first performed it, but we are used to defying traditions.'

Zaghareed is the cry of joy that Arab women make during weddings, and each region in Palestine has its own particular style. For their production El-Funoun collected ululations from Acre, Safad, Ramallah, Jerusalem and Bir Al Sabe. The ululations, they say, represent the unity of Palestinian culture, despite the disunity in Palestinian geography – the PNA administered areas, Israel, and the refugee camps in Lebanon, Syria and the rest of the diaspora.

Daniel Rosenberg

keenly aware of the need to build a bridge between East and West. In the words of their mentor, Said Murad, 'In the East you have to be in the music – it's not on paper outside you. When you play the *oud* or the *mijwiz* you improvise, you make your own music yourself. This is the philosophy of Eastern music. In Western music you have to be organized and the score is outside you. They are two different ways of thinking. What we are trying to do is find a common language between both. Our message from the beginning was how to make people live together.'

Since the departure of charismatic lead singer, **Kamilya Jubran**, the group has scaled down its live commitments and concentrates more on producing other artists and developing music education within Palestinian schools. Kamilya Jubran has been based in Paris since 2002 and, although the music she now performs is very much more experimental than anything attempted by Sabreen, she continues to push Arab song into new areas. She collaborates with European musicians and multimedia artists in a variety of projects, most notably **Wameedd** – a duo with electro-acoustic sound wizard, Werner Hasler.

Adel Salameh

Kamilya Jubran and Werner Hasler

Conversations with Palestinian musicians often come round to the enduring problems they face in travelling to perform. Until the opening of a national conservatory, the options open to Palestinians wishing to study the Arab musical tradition were very limited, even within the Arab world. This is particularly true for Arabs from Galilee who have no option but to hold Israeli passports. One remarkably gifted *oud* player from Nazareth, **Samir Joubran**, succeeded in attending the renowned Abdel Wahab Institute in Cairo. Now resident in Ramallah, he has a busy concert schedule both around the Arab world and in Europe. The son of one of the finest *oud* makers in the Levant, Samir has now been joined by his two younger brothers, Wissam and Adnan in **Trio Joubran**. Although ouds are rarely heard playing together, the trio have pioneered their own sound that shows off the instruments' richness and colour to great effect.

The ongoing difficulties of daily life for Palestinians have, inevitably, caused some musicians to leave and seek their fortunes abroad. Like many of the country's finest musicians, **Simon Shaheen** grew up in the Galilee and learned the *oud* and violin from his father. Since leaving his homeland he has forged a successful career in America, where he divides his time between teaching at some of the most prestigious universities – including Harvard and Yale – and leading his two groups, the **Near Eastern Music Ensemble**, which specializes in performances of classical Arab music and **Qantara**, a very New York blend that fuses Arab music with jazz, Western classical music and Latin American sounds. The virtuoso *oud* player, **Adel Salameh** was raised in Nablus and studied in Baghdad before moving to England and, more recently, France. The singer **Reem Kelani** has done much to popularize Palestinian traditional music in Britain through her concerts and work in schools.

New Opportunities

Since the establishment of the Palestinian National Authority in 1994, the music scene has developed rapidly, and what was once a clandestine expression of defiance became resolutely official and overground. This is best exemplified by the extraordinary success of the **Edward Said National**

Conservatory of Music which started modestly in Ramallah during 1993 but has grown into a flourishing organization with branches in Jerusalem and Bethlehem. In the past, it was necessary for promising young musicians to travel abroad to further their studies but the Conservatory now brings high-quality music education to over 500 students. Tuition on both Western classical and oriental music is offered and the Palestine Youth Orchestra was born in 2004. The Conservatory's director, appropriately enough, is former intifada singer and Israeli-jail bird, **Suhail Khoury**. As well as steering the organization, he also plays a pivotal role in the **Oriental Music Ensemble**, a group dedicated to re-establishing the Palestinian contribution to Arab art music after 50 years of isolation.

Believing the Conservatory to be based too closely on Western models, the Ensemble's former *oud* and *buzuk* player, **Khaled Jubran**, founded his own teaching institution, the Al-Urmawi Center, in the autumn of 2001. Jubran – brother of Kamilya and one-time member of Sabreen – is one of the most individual minds working in Palestinian music: he has collaborated with the renowned classical guitarist John Williams, and was chosen by the Birmingham Contemporary Music Group to play solo *oud* in the Jordanian composer Sa'ed Haddad's innovative *Toward the Unattainable Truth*.

Within the Western world music scene, there has been considerable support for collaborations between Palestinian and Israeli musicians; symbolically showing that music can bring people together where politicians and the gun have failed. From within the West Bank and Gaza, such projects are often viewed with considerable suspicion, and the reality is that it is very rare indeed for Arabs living in PNA administered land to work with Israeli musicians. This is partly because the sheer logistics of trying to rehearse together are a nightmare – there are roadblocks to negotiate and apparently simple things like driving around in a car with the wrong number plates can have dire consequences – and partly because the atmosphere is so discouraging for anyone with such an idea. Those collaborations that do take place (and there are some successful ones like **Bustan Avraham** and **Joseph & One**) are based in Israel and would find it very hard to perform in the Palestinian territories.

When compared to neighbouring countries like Lebanon, which pours teen idols out by the barrel-load, Palestine is notable for its lack of pop stars and a number of circumstances conspire against any young Palestinian hoping to match the success of Lebanese pop sensation Nancy Ajram. The first is a lack of recording facilities (Sabreen's studio in East Jerusalem is the only well-equipped one in the region) and any media or marketing infrastructure to take young talent to a wider audience. The aforementioned problems in travelling – not just outside the country but also between towns in the West Bank – make it difficult for anyone to gain more than minor cult status in their local area. Another more subtle factor is that Palestinian musicians' international image becomes indivisibly linked with their country's struggle for independence and that doesn't fit very comfortably with happy-people-having-a-good-time image universally favoured by Arab record companies. Eyebrows were raised when **Ammar Hassan** – whose father originally came from Nablus – was runner-up in the Lebanese *Super Star* TV programme (the Levantine equivalent of *Pop Idol*): even though Ammar was born and educated in Kuwait, he feels honour-bound to make frequent references to the injustices facing his father's country of birth. It will be interesting to see whether this helps or hinders his future career.

DISCOGRAPHY Palestinian Music

⊙ **Traditional Music and Song from Palestine**
Popular Art Centre, Palestine
The best introduction to Palestinian folk music: thirteen tracks from recordings made by the Popular Art Centre in El-Bireh on the West Bank. The disc includes five tracks featuring the powerful voice of Mousa Hafez, the leading Palestinian poet-singer, who lives in the refugee camp in Jineen. Available from www.popularartcentre.org.

The Chehade Brothers

This talented, multi-instrumentalist pair from Jerusalem play an eclectic mix of Mediterranean sounds and genres. Currently enjoying considerable success in Europe, they were nominated for a BBC award for World Music.

⊙ A Bridge over the Mediterranean
Elef, Lebanon

An intriguing album that shows off the brothers' prodigious talents: the hand of Michel Elefteriades – Beirut's cross-cultural collaboration Svengali – sits rather heavily on the production.

El-Funoun

El-Funoun literally means "the arts" and the group was founded in 1979 to present Palestinian song, music and dance. They are one of the country's leading theatrical and musical ensembles.

⊙ Zaghareed
Sounds True, US

The title means "ululations", the traditional cry of celebration, and the music and lyrics describe the various stages of a wedding ceremony. It all feels a little rehearsed and formal, but the musicianship on acoustic instruments like *oud*, *buzuq*, *mijwiz* and others is excellent and it adds up to one of the better examples of traditional Palestinian music.

Samir Joubran

As an Arab with an Israeli passport, Samir negotiated Kafka-esque bureaucracy to study in Egypt. Now based in Ramallah, he is one of the most charismatic young *oud* players performing today.

★ Tamaas
Daqui, France

There is a richness and vitality about Jubran's playing which is completely gripping. His compositions are an intriguing set of contrasts: wholly modern, yet firmly rooted in the taqasim (improvisation) tradition, fiery and virtuosic, but tempered by a broad sense of space and understatement.

Le Trio Joubran

Oud ensembles are rare, but these three sons of one of the region's finest instrument makers have created their own sound, blending classical Arab music with broader musical ideas.

⊙ Randana
Fair Play, France

Though some said that it didn't quite live up to their ravishing concert performances, the interplay between the three brothers in this 2005 studio recording is still extraordinary.

Kamilya Jubran

Once the voice of Sabreen, and now following her own path in Paris, Kamilya continues to be an experimental force, fusing traditional Arab song forms with jazz and electro-acoustic idioms.

⊙ Wameedd
Unitrecords, Switzerland

An atmospheric and ethereal collaboration between Kamilya Jubran and the Swiss sound-sculptor Werner Hasler, drawing on their shared backgrounds of improvisation and exploration.

Steve Sabella

Le Trio Joubran

Oriental Music Ensemble

Four of the finest musicians from the staff of the Edward Said National Conservatory of Music – on *ney*, *qanun*, *oud* and percussion – come together to play a variety of classical and traditional music from the region. After years of enforced isolation from their Arab neighbours, this group has more than just musical significance to Palestinians.

⊙ Emm el Khilkhal
Palestine National Conservatory of Music

Delightfully refined playing in the old style from real masters of the art: an important reminder that there is much more to life in Palestine than roadblocks and politics.

Sabreen

Undoubtedly one of the most influential music forces to have come out of Palestine. Although live performances are now rare and Kamilya Jubran has moved on to new things, their musical legacy lives on in their recordings and broader musical projects.

★ Death of the Prophet
Sabreen, Palestine

Although this is from 1987, it is still regarded as their finest CD, with wild *oud* playing from Said Murad and a hauntingly tragic tone to Joubran's vocals. Very musical and deeply expressive. Available from www.sabreen.org

Adel Salameh

A typical product of the Palestinian musical diaspora, Salameh has established himself as one of the most refined players working in Europe and collaborates with a variety of musicians from other musical cultures, including the flamenco guitarist Eduardo Niebla and the *sarod* player Krishnamurtri Sridhar.

⭐ **Hafla**
Enja, Germany
Salameh's recordings can be rather serious but on *Hafla* he lets his hair down with some like-minded musicians. His *oud* sound is wonderfully assured and is well complemented by the dark tones of Algerian singer Naziha Azzouz and Bruno Sansalone's chocolate-smooth bass clarinet playing.

Simon Shaheen

A stunningly virtuosic *oud* player and violinist, Shaheen grew up in a musical household in the Galilee and has since moved to New York, where he works tirelessly to promote knowledge about Arab music.

⭐ **Turath – Masterworks of the Middle East**
Times Square, US
The title means "heritage" – a word that is often used amongst Palestinians to express their sense of alienation. This is excellent classical Arab ensemble playing and is a perfect introduction to the whole genre.

PLAYLIST
Palestinian Music

1 **ZAFFAH Hajjeh Badriyeh Younes** from *Traditional Music and Song from Palestine*
Raw, simple and infectious: the sound of rural Palestine. Younes' guttural chanting bounces over the rock-solid percussion accompaniment.

2 **DOUCE BRISE Adel Salameh** from *Hafleh*
Salameh's delicate *oud* playing shimmers around the lotus-gorged stupor of Naziha Azzouz's yearning voice and Bruno Sansalone's luscious bass clarinet.

3 **A SONG FOR CHILDHOOD Sabreen** from *Death of the Prophet*
This recording from early in Sabreen's history shows them at their most passionate and articulate.

4 **SAMA'I NAHAWAND Simon Saheen** from *Turath – Masterworks of the Middle East*
Classical Arab ensemble playing doesn't get much more refined or perfectly turned than this.

5 **KIF EL HAL The Chehade Brothers** from *A Bridge Over the Mediterranean*
Just to prove that life in Palestine can also be light-hearted! All the eastern Mediterranean influences that the Brothers grew up around roll together in this merry piece.

6 **SAFAR Le Trio Joubran** from *Randana*
Based around a simple and yet aching *ostinato*; three ouds set out to explore a vast landscape of mood and colour.

Syria

sufis and superstars

Sheikh Hamza Chakour
Jak Kilby

Branded by US Republicans as a "rogue state", ruled for forty years by a Baath party regime described as harsh and repressive, yet possessing one of the world's oldest and richest cultures, Syria is little understood as a nation. But behind the closed doors of its ancient cities, traditional music flourishes, and Syria still produces some of the Arab world's top talents, as Roger Short discovered.

When Rouwayda Attieh reached the finals of the Beirut-based *Superstar* competition, the Arab world's version of *Pop Idol*, it was claimed that 97 percent of the Syrian population had voted for her. This figure is probably explained by multiple voting – one Syrian admitted to me that he had voted for her twenty times. National pride is big in Syria, brought into sharper focus by a political regime that has increasingly isolated itself from the West. But partly because of this isolation, traditional music is better preserved than in other Arab countries, and its popular music is less globalized and generally more sophisticated too.

Silk Roots

Damascus and Aleppo vie with each other, and various other places around the globe, for the title of the world's oldest city. Syria's traditions have been shaped by its strategic position on important trade routes, and by a history spent mostly as part of someone else's empire. Damascus was briefly the capital of the Muslim world under the seventh-century Umayyads, with a domain that stretched from Spain and North Africa to Persia. Five hundred years later, Syria was the political centre for Salah-ad-Din (Saladin) in his wars against the Crusaders, then for four centuries until 1918 it was ruled by the Ottoman Turks. A period under French mandate followed, until modern Syria was created in 1946.

Syria's most celebrated classical form is the *muwashahat*, songs based on a poetic metre that emerged in Moorish Spain, though its music probably owes more to Ottoman style. The solo/chorus form is sung with a mixed ensemble, normally including *oud* (the Arabic lute) the *qanun* (Arabic plucked zither) and often the *ney* (end-blown flute), with percussion from the *riqq* (tambourine) or *daf* (frame drum). This kind of ensemble, the *takht*, was vividly described in an eighteenth-century account by the Russell brothers, two British physicians who visited informal gatherings in homes and coffee-houses. One of the great tenor voices of the Arab world, **Sabah Fakhri** has popularized the *muwashahat* among several new generations of listeners, though he uses a band modelled more on the Egyptian-style string orchestra.

The tradition of informal *muwashshah* is kept alive by **Julien Weiss**, a Frenchman whose travels with his guitar as a 60s hippy brought him into contact with Syrian culture, inspiring him to take up the *qanun*, study the *maqams* (the Arabic modes), convert to Islam, rename himself Julien Jalal Eddine Weiss after the great Sufi master and poet Jalal Edin Rumi, and finally move to Aleppo, where he holds regular musical evenings in his fourteenth-century Mamluk mini-palace. With his Ensemble Al-Kindi (named after the ninth-century Islamic philosopher), he has taken his uncompromising approach to Syrian classical music to an international audience, through worldwide concert tours and a series of magnificently presented CDs.

Syria also has a rich tradition of solo instrumental virtuosity, nurtured by the music academies in Aleppo and Damascus. *Oud* player **Muhammed Qadri Dalal** explores the repertory of *maqams* that are unique to Syria, his style combining the traditions of the Turkish and Baghdad schools. **Abdullah Chhadeh** (see box) first learned the *oud* in a camp for refugees in the Golan, then was drawn to the *qanun*. After studying at the Conservatoire of Damascus he moved to the UK, and now records and tours internationally with his band Nara.

The Sultan of Tarab

In the frenetic world of Arab pop music, Syria is something of a quiet backwater. Damascus is better known as a centre of music piracy rather than music production, though the authorities are making efforts to change this with recently introduced copyright laws. But one of the Arab world's biggest stars was born in Syria. **George Wassouf** left the country at the age of 15 to make a career in the musical centres of Beirut and Cairo, but he still has a base in Damascus, and still sees himself as a son of Syria. And, typical of his compatriots, he has a respect for musical tradition that goes far beyond the lip-service paid to it by much of the industry. To his fans he is the Sultan of Tarab, the musical ecstasy that all Arab classical singers strive to achieve. Tarab doesn't come quickly, and Wassouf doesn't compromise with three-minute songs for the video-clip market – his songs are all five minutes or more, and his 2004 album *Etakhart ktir* ended with one lasting more than nineteen minutes. His website proclaims with pride that his 2005 single *Mariam* is based on the *qasida*, one of the oldest and most revered of Ara-

Abdullah Chhadeh, the Qanun and the Hookah

Roger Short

When **Abdullah Chhadeh** applied to the Damascus Conservatory, one of the world centres for Arab music, in the hope of studying the **qanun** or Arab zither, he was told that there was nobody to teach the instrument, but that he could join if he was prepared to learn the double bass. He agreed, only to find himself compelled to study Beethoven and Brahms into the bargain. He practised the *qanun* in his own time, though, and later amazed his tutors with a virtuoso rendition of Vivaldi's *Four Seasons* arranged for *qanun* and symphony orchestra.

Chhadeh was born in 1968, in a camp for refugees from the Golan Heights, the area of Syria that had been occupied by the Israelis the year before. His father bought him an *oud*, and Abdullah soon showed his potential for a career in music. Then, as a student, he was invited to perform in a *takht* (Arab orchestra), whose principal instrument is a *qanun* – and he decided that the heart and soul of Arab music lay in this instrument. But the *qanun* was not only a complex but also an expensive option. "My family was poor at that time", says Abdullah, "and I just explained to my Mum how I felt about the *qanun*. The next day she brought me her wedding jewellery and told me to sell it and go and buy a *qanun*. What she did then has affected how I play the instrument even now."

Qanun literally means "law", the same root as the English word "'canon'" – perhaps, suggests Abdullah, because the other instruments have to tune to it. In 1999, following an invitation to give a concert in London, he was offered a scholarship to study composition at the Guildhall School of Music. He has since made London his base, and In 2001 formed his band **Nara** – named, he explains, after the small piece of charcoal that fires up the *narghile* or hookah. The band combines *qanun* with jazz bass and drums, *ney* flute, and Arab-style accordion and percussion.

"In the past few years there's been a real misunderstanding about the culture of the Middle East", says Abdullah. "But through my music I'm trying to show people the beauty of Syria, the beauty of the people. So I combine the sound of the *qanun* with instruments that people in the West will find familiar. Maybe this way they can get something of the whole picture."

bic poetic forms. Rumour and controversy, often of his own making, have followed him throughout his career: many concert appearances have been cancelled owing to ill health, he was reported to have died of an overdose in 2001, and in 2003 he performed in Baghdad for the birthday of Saddam Hussein.

Superdivas

Rouwayda Attieh has managed to avoid sinking back into obscurity after reaching the 2004 *Superstar* finals. She was runner-up, but her decision to perform a classic by the Egyptian diva Umm Kulthum in the competition won her wide respect, and reminded the Arab world that, for Syria, old is not irrelevant. Her subsequent hits have never quite lost this connection, her full, deep voice recalling Kulthum's powerful tones. Like many divas before her, she has also embarked on a career in films.

In common with most Syrian stars, **Assala Nasri** lives abroad, having moved to the new capital of the Arabic music industry, Dubai. The gossip columns endlessly report her tempestuous personal life – her marriage problems, her plastic surgery, her disputes with other singers. Many of her songs are excessively orchestrated sentimental ballads, but she can also stretch to some impressive old-style classical virtuosity, as in the song "A'tazzibak" from her 2003 album *Ad El Hourouf*.

Having ignored Nasri's advice that she should retire because she was too old-fashioned, **Mayada el-Henawy** has secured her place as one of Syria's best-loved singers. Her career began in Cairo in 1977 when she was taken under the tutelage of the legendary composer Mohammed Abdel Wahab, and her early recordings were of Egyptian classical-style songs lasting thirty minutes or more. In the 1990s, declaring that her aim was to "modernize with style", she began recording shorter songs with lively rhythm tracks. She is now settled in Damascus, but still tours the Arab world, and can still attract thousands to her concerts, her appeal lying in her warmth and sincerity rather than virtuosity or glamour.

Sufi Nights

Every Wednesday evening, fifty to a hundred devotees of the prayer meetings of **Sheikh Ahmed Habboush** find their way to his *zawiya* – the building in which a Sufi sheikh receives his brotherhood – in the old city of Aleppo. The women sit at the back, and even visiting Western women are obliged to cover themselves in black. The men, led by Sheikh Habboush, sing the praises of Allah to the accompaniment of drums, with words that mix the poems of Rumi with modern lyrics. The singing grows more intense, the drums more pounding, and after an hour or so, in a moment of pure theatre, the room is plunged into darkness and everyone stands and sways to the rhythms, first gently, then with increasing intensity. The music and the movement induces a communal ecstasy as the name of God is chanted, and the believers experience an ethereal closeness to their maker. At the end, tea is served, and a visiting cleric preaches on the evils of the West, and the need for a spiritual *jihad*. A similar scene is played out in some four hundred regular Sufi prayer meetings in the city, but the meeting held at the home of Sheikh Habboush is probably the only one led by an internationally renowned singer.

Sufism thrives throughout Syria, and devotees don't experience the marginalization that Sufis suffer in most of the Arab world. The former Grand Mufti of Syria (the country's top religious lawmaker) was himself a Sufi sheikh, and Damascus offered a refuge for Mevlevis, the whirling dervishes, who fled Turkey after Sufi rituals were banned by the republic in 1925. Dervishes still whirl in Damascus, though visitors are most likely to encounter Mevlevis (*mawlawiyya* in Arabic) as

Sheikh Hamza Shakkur (centre)

part of a state tourist attraction. The guardian of the *mawlawiyya* musical legacy is **Sheikh Hamza Shakkur**, whose resonant bass voice can be heard in the Great Umayyad Mosque of Damascus, and on recordings with the Ensemble Al-Kindi.

Country Music, Syrian-style

Outside the cities, Syria's many minority communities maintain distinct folk music traditions: the Kurds in the north, the Druze in the west, the Bedouin in the Eastern desert. There's even an enclave in the village of Maaloula where the almost-extinct ancient Aramaic language is spoken – and sung. Throughout the villages of Syria, celebrations are marked by groups of men dancing the energetic *dabke*, accompanied by the strident sound of the shawm-like *mizmar*.

Ali Aldik has taken the raw vitality of the *dabke* and transformed it into a dancefloor success. A former wedding singer from the coastal town of Lattakia, he sings mini-epics about bringing in the harvest, village girls and simple country life.

His "Samra Wana al-Hasoudi" was a pan-Arab hit, despite being sung in the Syrian dialect. He says of his approach: 'When I first met the people in the music business, they told me it can't be done, you can't make this old village style attractive for the sophisticated city people. But I've promised my fans I'm going to make the music of our Syrian villages shine.'

DISCOGRAPHY Syria

Ali Aldik

His fans acclaim his style as "nu-dabke", deliberately raw and unsophisticated, but with energetic singing, sparking *oud*, spitting flute and a mizmar sound that doesn't lose too much from being synthesized. Avoid his widely-available US-produced *Beirut Live* album, which has poor sound quality and scrappy performances.

Aaloush
Super Star/Future, Syria
Evokes the atmosphere of the Syrian equivalent of a barn dance, with lively folk rhythms and the shouts of village girls adding to the excitement. No notes in English, sadly.

Asmahan

The stage name of Amal el-Atrache (1917–44), the young er sister of Farid el-Atrache (see below and Arab World/ Egypt chapter).

⊙ **Le Coeur a ses Raisons**
Buda Musique, France
A collection of her best songs that shows what Umm Kulthum might have been jealous about: traditional Arabic lyrics sung in a sexy, Western-nightclub style.

Farid el-Atrache

To the cognoscenti, Farid el-Atrache (1914–74) was perhaps the finest *oud* player of his generation; to his film fans, he was the sad troubadour of Egyptian cinema. He starred in more than forty films, and led the archetypal filmstar life, with a string of affairs including one with the wife of the exiled King Farouk of Egypt.

⊙ **King of Oud**
EMI Arabia, Dubai
Two full-length improvisations, recorded live with plenty of audience participation.

⊙ **Forever**
EMI Arabia, Dubai
A double album of greatest hits, both live and from film soundtracks, and including "Hebbina", later covered by Algerian rocker Rachid Taha.

Rouwayda Attieh

A product of *Superstar*, the Arab world's *Pop Idol*, who seems to be achieving lasting success.

⊙ **Min Nazra**
Music Box International, UAE
A strong debut, her deep-toned traditional voice given a powerful setting by driving Arab dancefloor beats.

Abdullah Chhadeh

His music is the product of his training in both Western and Arab classical styles, together with his love for jazz: his band Nara includes accordion, bass and Western percussion.

Seven Gates
ABYC Records, UK
An evocation of the gates of the old city of Damascus, from traffic jams to the quiet, winding pathways leading to the Bab-Al Salam (Gate of Peace).

Muhammed Qadri Dalal

Syria's finest *oud* player, uncompromising in his adherence to classical traditions.

Maqamat insolites
Inédit, France
Over an hour of spellbinding unaccompanied improvisations, beautifully recorded.

Ensemble Al-Kindi

Julien Jalal Eddine Weiss has led his Ensemble Al-Kindi in a series of superb albums which explore Syria's heritage of sacred and secular music, working with some of the country's leading traditional singers.

⊙ **The Aleppian Music Room – the Art of Classical Arab Singing**
Le Chant du Monde, France
The mystical yet sophisticated and refined atmosphere of Aleppo is nowhere better captured than on this double CD featuring the voices of Sabri Moudallal and Omar Sarmini. The album would grace any coffee table with its spectacular photos of the old city.

Sabah Fakhri

Syria's best-known musical ambassador in the Arab world. He has researched and revived many of the songs he sings, and transformed them into popular hits – his concert audiences sing along with every word and every twist and turn of the melody. He also has a place in *The Guinness Book of Records* for a ten-hour non-stop singing marathon in Caracas in 1968.

⊙ **Two Tenors and Qantara: Historic Live Recording of Arabic Masters**
Ark 21, US/UK
This internationally available release is shared between Fakhri and veteran Lebanese singer Wadi Al-Safi.

Sheikh Ahmed Habboush

The passionate intensity of his tenor voice has become internationally known through his recordings and tours with the Ensemble Al-Kindi.

⭐ **Aleppian Sufi Trance**
Le Chant du Monde, France
Not exactly an authentic evocation of a Sufi prayer night, as this recording includes forbidden instruments such as the *ney* and the *qanun*. But the singing is glorious, the playing immaculate, and the accompanying photos stunning.

Mayada el-Henawy

El-Henawy emerged as a pan-Arab star in the 1980s. One of her tracks features on the widely available compilation *Camelspotting* (EMI Hemisphere).

⊙ **Matgarabnish**
EMI Arabia, Dubai
This album ("Don't try me") ranges from the sublime to the (almost) ridiculously commercial, but is a rare Arab-world release with full lyrics in English.

Zein al-Jundi

A child star in Syria who then gave it all up to study architecture and design in Austin, Texas. She decided to return to music in the late 1990s. Her voice lacks technical brilliance, but makes up for it with her warm, sensitive approach.

⊙ **Traditional Songs from Syria**
ARC Music, UK
Recorded in Egypt under the direction of percussionist Hossam Ramzy, with a tightly organized acoustic ensemble.

Kulna Sawa

Syria's own World Music band, whose name means "all of us together", is a collective of Muslim and Christian musicians who set Arabic melody lines against an infectious blend of Western pop, funk and easy-listening jazz.

⊙ **Musaïque**
EMI Arabia, Dubai
Unlike most musicians in the Arab world, Kulna Sawa don't avoid political issues: in 2004 they went on a Concert for Peace Tour of the US, and their song "Umm al-Shaheed" is a tribute to the mothers of Palestinian suicide bombers.

Assala Nasri

Syria's very own diva, as celebrated for her private life as her vocal fireworks, has recently started singing in the *khaleeji* (Gulf) dialect. Critics say she is trying to cash in on the current vogue for Gulf music, but she insists it is because she admires the Gulf poets. Her recent work has been lightweight and commercial, but her older material shows more imagination.

⊙ **Ad el Hourouf**
EMI Arabia, Dubai
The colourful orchestrations, using the traditional sounds of *ney* and *qanun*, with only occasional touches of cheesiness, set off her deep, emotional vocal style perfectly.

⊙ **A Night at the Opera**
EMI Arabia, Dubai
A well-recorded live performance at the Cairo Opera, showing Nasri at her traditional best.

PLAYLIST
Syria

1 SEHERT EL LEYEL George Wassouf from *Etakhat Ktir*
This nineteen-minute track justifies his "Sultan of Tarab" title, an almost-symphonic exploration of musical ecstasy.

2 MAQÂM NAKRIZ Muhammed Qadri Dalal from *Maqâmat Insolites*
Some of the most intimate and focused music-making you could wish to hear.

3 MA'AWID A'AL DHEI'A Ali Aldik from *Aaloush*
This song, about a man, disillusioned with city life, who returns to his family and friends in his home village, reputedly made Syrian star George Wassouf weep.

4 FASL AS SAWI Sheikh Habboush from *Aleppian Sufi Trance*
If you are wanting to experience a true Sufi trance, look no further.

5 KEIF Abdullah Chhadeh from *Seven Gates*
A track which more than lives up to Chhadeh's definition of "Keif" as "an enchanting blissful feeling that begins to melt the mind like the sweet smoke of a narghile".

6 A'TAZZIBAK Assala Nasri from *Ad El Hourouf*
A curious melange of styles and colours, held together by a dazzling display of vocal pyrotechnics.

Sheikh Hamza Shakkur

His style is calm and restrained – though as it's music to accompany whirling dervishes, maybe the movement is exciting enough in itself.

⊙ **Takasim and Sufi Chants from Damascus**
Network, Germany
A sequence of songs and instrumental improvisations, graced by flawless playing from the Ensemble Al-Kindi.

George Wassouf

One of the Arab world's biggest stars, with a string of hit albums, Wassouf began his career with an angelic high voice, then reinvented himself with his current rough growl.

⭐ **Etakhat Ktir**
EMI Arabia, Dubai
Despite dance beats and hi-tech production – he owns a nightclub in Beirut – Wassouf is always firmly rooted in Arabic classical tradition.

Turkey

sounds of anatolia

Sufi musicians, early 20th century
Collection Christoph Wagner

Outside the country, Turkish music used to be mostly associated with belly-dancing, while recently the Mevlevi ("whirling") dervishes have gained wide popularity on the World Music circuit. Yet there's much more to Turkish music than that, as demonstrated by its great influence across the eastern Mediterranean and Balkans, and its growing following amongst the Turkish and Kurdish diaspora in northern Europe. Martin Stokes and Francesco Martinelli (with additional guidance from Tuna Pase) show the way beyond the stereotypes into an enticing variety, from refined classical forms to commercial Arabesk by way of rural bards and fiery Gypsy ensembles.

What we call Turkish music today is a multi-layered and multifaceted object, at its best a tradition representing the heritage of the many civilizations that flourished in the Anatolian area for thousands of years, at its worst a globally marketed pop music with a little bit of local colour thrown in. Not surprisingly, it was the latter approach that finally won the hearts of the Eurovision juries in 2003, with the conservatoire-trained soprano Sertab Erener wiggling seductively in a concubine costume.

After the foundation of the Turkish Republic in 1923, the country went through an enviable period of stability and development, even more impressive if compared to its neighbours in the Balkans, Caucasus and Middle East. **Kemal Atatürk**, having fought victoriously against the Western troops in Gallipoli and repelled the Greek invasion, pointedly discarded his military garb and said that the country would from then on fight its battles at home, for progress and civilization, rather than the conquest of territories.

The subsequent thrust towards the West in language and culture – exemplified by the adoption of the Latin alphabet instead of Arabic script – was reflected in Turkish music, as the oral tradition was transformed into a written repertoire following Western models. 'The capacity of a country to change is demonstrated by its ability to change its music', said Atatürk. But while he felt Turkish music was intellectually inferior to Western music, he famously loved folksongs and dances from his native Salonika, as well as light classical music. To this day collections of the songs he loved the most are sold on CD, and singers in concert will announce that they are going to sing one of them – implying support for his republican beliefs and a criticism of whatever form of religious integralism is currently prevalent. Atatürk's government financed the first ethnomusicological campaigns to collect folk music from the Anatolian countryside, and a generation of musicians was trained to propagate it, through the Turkish Radio and Television Station (TRT) and elsewhere.

Religious organizations expressed their opposition to the secular basis of the new Turkish democracy, to the point of exciting bloody uprisings in eastern Anatolia, and in 1925 the government forcibly closed by law all the Sufi *tekke* (lodges). The most important were those of the **Mevlevi order**, whose houses had been for centuries one of the most important places for the development of Turkish spiritual and classical music. For many years now, **Mevlevi music** has been performed in public only as a kind of tourist attraction in Istanbul and at the home of the order, Konya, in central Anatolia. But Mevlevi and other Sufi music has existed to some extent underground.

The foundation of the State Conservatoire in Istanbul in 1976 gave Turkish classical musicians a chance to get the same quality of training as the TRT musicians, and they gained an increasing share of radio and television airtime. Then, in the 1980s, the liberal president Turgut Özal deregulated the media. Pop, rock and Arabesk (a supposedly Arab-inspired popular genre) began to fill the private FM radio stations. The TRT made efforts to update its large orchestral formats, too.

Turkish Folk

Folk music is currently one of the most popular genres in Turkey. It is performed in daily life in its traditional, orally transmitted form but it has also become a commercial phenomenon, with a new wave of young singers performing the traditional songs in new orchestrations on TV and on disc.

Turkish folk music is dominated by the sound of the **saz**, a long-necked lute which comes in various sizes and with a varying number of strings. The most popular version is the **bağlama**, which is of medium size and has a shorter neck and more bulbous body.

Saz Music and the TRT Sound

Large ensembles of *saz*, heavily miked to boost the body of their sound, dominate the **TRT folk music** style. CDs and cassettes of such music can be found in their hundreds in music shops and at mobile street stalls. All bear the mark of **Belkis Akkale**'s tremendously successful style from the mid-1980s: large, buzzing, busy *saz* orchestras, driving rhythms, and a deep, soulful voice singing a *türkü* (folksong). Current exponents include **Gülay**, **Kubat** and **Sabahat Akkiraz**, who is steeped in the Alevi culture and performs the traditional repertoire but also takes part in contemporary projects.

Played as a solo instrument accompanying the singing voice, the *saz* has an intricate, silvery tone, providing not just notes and rhythmic patterns, but an ambience; it's a partner in a complex dialogue with the singer. Listen to TRT musician **Ali Ekber Çiçek**'s "Haydar Haydar", a complex and dramatic creation largely of his own inspiration but anchored in the expressive techniques of the aşık and Alevi mystics: it's hard to say whether

the instrument is accompanying the voice, or vice versa. In contrast, **Talip Özkan**'s intricate and idiosyncratic solo style embraces a variety of Anatolian tunings and plectrum techniques, but with each musical phrase embellished and nuanced to the utmost degree.

There are those who favour playing *saz* with a plectrum (*tezene* style) and those who play without (*şelpe*), plus many regional styles of playing and tuning. Though a simple instrument, the *saz* is capable of enormous variety. The leading players in Turkey today are **Arif Sağ**, **Erkan Oğur**, **Erol Parlak**, **Okan Murat Öztürk** and **Erdal Erzincan**. Öztürk also leads the best *saz* ensemble, the **Bengi Trio**. All have released excellent recordings.

Regional Folk

Despite the heavy colonization of *saz*-based music by the TRT, many other varieties of folk music exist in Turkey today, recognizable largely by the instruments and dances associated with them.

The quintessential rural **Turkish ceremonial music** combination is the **zurna and davul** (the shawm and drum duo that can be found from Turkey and the Balkans to Central Asia and China). Outside the large cities in the west of Turkey, or in their squatter suburbs (*gecekondu*), these instruments can be heard at almost any wedding or circumcision celebration, their enormous, unamplified volume indicating to all and sundry that something important is taking place. If you hear them, follow the sound, and you will almost certainly find yourself the object of warm hospitality (language no barrier) and be treated to a display of regional dance styles in somebody's home, or at a wedding salon (*düğünsalonu*) rented for the occasion.

In eastern areas of the country the dance will most usually be the stately chain dance known as the **halay** (arms linked or on shoulders); on the Aegean coast the **zeybek** is most common; elsewhere, and more or less everywhere, the **çifte telli** and **karşılama**, both dances for couples, predominate.

You will know you are among **Black Sea Turks** (**Laz**) if you hear a small upright fiddle (*kemençe*), a bagpipe (*tulum*), or a smaller and shriller version of the *zurna* and *davul*. They will be dancing the **horon**, the quick movements of which are said to imitate the wriggling of the *hamsi* – the anchovies that are such a conspicuous feature of their diet.

Most of Turkey's rural population (approximately half of the total) know, at least passively, these regional dances, and the music that goes with them. *Saz* has become an amplified instrument modelled on the electric guitar, and electronic keyboards and other technological developments have taken their place both in daily music-making in the home or for ceremonial occasions and on stage in the ensembles accompanying all the different varieties of Turkish music. Regional genres and instruments are well represented in the local cassette culture: look out for the music of the *sipsi* (a plaintive double reed instrument) in the southwest; the *mey* (similar to the Armenian *duduk*) in the southeast; accordion music played by Circassian migrants in the northeast; and Gypsy music to the sound of *darbuka*, metal clarinet, violin and *cümbüş* (a metal-bodied banjo) in Thrace and Istanbul.

All around the country contemporary musicians are updating and reinventing the local styles. For example, **Birol Topaloğlu**, a Laz *kemençe* player from the Black Sea coast, has collected local songs and arranged them into a series of striking albums. From the same area, popular singer-songwriters **Fuat Saka** and **Volkan Konak** offer their personal, updated version of folksongs.

The current popularity of folk music is supported by the *türkü* bars which have sprung up around İstiklal Caddesi in Istanbul and Kızılay in Ankara, where groups of young musicians play traditional songs with pop instrumentation. **Grup Çığ** is an exciting band performing *türkü* with electric guitars.

Aşık Music

There are said to be 20 million **Alevis** in Turkey today (out of a total Turkish population of 70 million), so it is little surprise that the best-known regional music is associated with the **aşık**, folk bards from these heterodox Muslim communities, originally from the central northeastern provinces of Sivas, Tunceli, Çorum and Erzincan.

Aşık sing a repertoire of songs of mystical quest, interspersed with invocations to the Alevi saints, and to Mohammed's brother-in-law, Ali, whom they regard as the rightful heir to the Prophet's spiritual tradition. (This is the belief of the Shia Muslims, although they have different practices from the Arab or Iranian Shiites.)

Traditionally *aşık* favour the three-string *saz* for its symbolism of the trinity of Allah, Mohammed and Ali and they sing to the solo saz, which is virtually a sacred object to the Alevi, rich in spiritual significance. Many of the *aşık*'s songs have words by or about **Pir Sultan Abdal**, an *aşık* martyr of the sixteenth century executed for his involvement with a rebellion against the Ottoman authorities. His birthplace, the village of Banaz near Sivas, is a place of pilgrimage.

Today's flourishing *aşık* revival was encouraged in the early 1970s by opera singer **Ruhi Su**, a fine *saz* player. He was not an Alevi, but was forcefully left-wing and lost his job at the opera as a result. His albums sold in large numbers, and still do. Folk music's top names – **Arif Sağ**, **Yavuz Top**, **Musa Eroğlu** and **Muhlis Akarsu** – have made excellent recordings both as a group, **Muhabbet**, and individually. A fire in Sivas, started by orthodox Sunni extremists during an Alevi festival in 1993, killed several distinguished musicians, including Akarsu.

Aşık music has always had a political edge. **Ali İzzet** and **Mahsuni Şerif** brought out its latent political protest in songs which ranged from passionate denunciations of social and political injustice to gentle satires on Turkish football. They were lionized by the urban Turkish left in the late 1960s. **Feyzullah Çınar** is another major representative of this tradition.

Aşık Veysel, a blind troubadour from Sivrialan in the province of Sivas, is a household name in Turkey. In comparison to Şerif and İzzet, he sang a gentler poetry expressing humanistic sentiments. Like many Alevi, he endorsed the secularist politics of the Turkish state, and was a keen teacher of Anatolian music. His most famous songs, such as "Dostlar Beni Hatırlasın" (May My Friends Remember Me) and "Uzun İnce Bir Yoldayım" (I'm on a Long and Difficult Journey), circulated widely around the country in both written and recorded form, and are still well known.

Although *Aşık* is a genre for *saz* and voice, there are a small number of experimental **orchestral versions**, notably by Yavuz Top and Arif Sağ. The special tuning of the *saz* used by them results in a particularly sombre and intense sound, with complex chord patterns emerging from the shifting drones.

A notable exception to standard *aşık* music is **bozlak**, a form of free-rhythm, semi-improvised declamation of scorching emotional intensity, somewhat akin to flamenco, which is associated with Alevi communities in western Anatolia. The singer sings at the top of his voice, and the saz is tuned in the "open fifths" manner, which allows for dramatic melodic flourishes and produces a sparse, astringent sound. Perhaps the greatest living exponent is **Neşet Ertaş**, from Kırşehir, a cult icon amongst folk-music enthusiasts in Turkey and the son of **Muharrem Ertaş**, another bozlak singer of mythic reputation. **Ekrem Çelebi** is perhaps the best known of a younger generation of bozlak musicians, and is an extraordinary virtuoso.

The aşık tradition takes on a second distinct form in the far northeast of the country, in the city of **Kars**. Here, the singers are considered to have fallen into a trance in which they receive gifts of musical and spiritual knowledge, and henceforth wander the countryside in search of their lovers, revealed to them by the prophet Elias. They make their living as entertainers and storytellers in the cafés of the cities of the northeast.

Aşıks still have a role in the regular **Alevi religious ceremony** (*cem*) which includes prayers, recitations and singing, and culminates in a circular dance, the *semah*. Alevi music (and the whole orientation of the sect) is far more rural and folklike than the more classical, high-art Mevlevi. It's possible to attend cem services at the Şahkulu Sultan (Merdivenköy) and Karacaahmet Sultan (Üsküdar) mosques in Istanbul on Sundays and Alevi holidays. Recently several cafés featuring singers with saz or a small band have appeared in Istanbul, off İstiklal Caddesi in Beyoğlu.

Classical Traditions

Urban Turkish musics divide into three genres: **religious** (*sema*), **art music** (*klasik* or *sanat*) and **nightclub** (*fasıl*). Definitions are, of course, not watertight, and they have overlapping repertoires and instruments (urban and Middle Eastern instruments quite different from those found in the countryside), and share the musical system based on *makam*.

The **makam** are musical modes or scales (with associated rules governing melodic flow and prominent notes) in which the musicians compose their songs and instrumental pieces, and, more importantly, weave their **taksim** (improvisations), which are essential to classical music performance. The makam currently practised in Turkey have a lot in common with those of the Arab world; the Iranian *dastgah* are more distantly related.

Classical Fasil and Later Developments

The *taksim* improvisation usually precedes, and also punctuates, the classical *fasil* – long suites of music which begin with an instrumental prelude (*peşrev*), end with a postlude (*saz semaisi*), and include vocal pieces known as **şarkı**. The tradition dates back to at least the fourteenth century, and composers include Ottoman sultans like **Selim III**, who was a Mevlevi Sufi and *tanbur* player. Among the later composers, **Buhurizade Mustafa Itri** (1640–1712) and **Hammamizade Ismail 'Dede' Efendi** (1778–1846) have to be mentioned. Their works are still a crucial part of the classic repertoire. Most *şarkı* sung today date from the late nineteenth century, the time of one of the great songwriters, **Hacı Arif Bey**.

These classical genres are, essentially, chamber genres, in which the instruments play as a loose collection of soloists, each taking turns at improvising *taksim*, and each elaborating the melodic and rhythmic line as they see fit. Songs and instrumental numbers thus differ greatly from performance to performance.

Typical **instruments** are the *ud* (lute), *ney* (end-blown flute), *tunbur* (long-necked lute, with frets), *kanun* (a zither, played on the knees) and classical *kemençe* (a spike fiddle as used in Persian music and different from the folk instrument of the Black Sea region). *Usul* (rhythm) is provided by the *kudüm* (a couple of small kettle-shaped drums), *bendir* (frame drum) and *def* (tambourine). There are many famous virtuosi associated with particular instruments, and recordings of them can easily be found: look out for **Tanburi Cemil Bey** (1871–1916) and **Necdet Yaşar** (born 1930) on the tanbur; **Yorgo Bacanos** (1900–77) and **Udi Hrant** (1901–78) on the *ud*; **Şükrü Tunar** (1907–62) on the clarinet; and **Ahmet Meter** (aka Halil Karaduman, born 1959) on the *kanun*.

Many instrumentalists and composers inhabit the world of professional **secular music-making**, whose association with the profanities of drink and dance led to its becoming the preserve of Istanbul's **Armenian, Jewish and Orthodox Christian communities**, and others, notably **Gypsies**, who could operate comfortably outside bourgeois Muslim respectability. A list of Armenian, Greek and Jewish musicians would include a very large proportion of all significant names in the Turkish musical world of the nineteenth and early twentieth century, and it would be hard to imagine the contemporary classical repertoire without the work of **Tatyos Efendi**, **Lavtaci Andon**, **Udi Hrant** or **Şükrü Tunar**.

Central to today's scene are some top-quality instrumentalists who are keeping the classical tradition alive as well as producing their own compositions. *Kemençe* player and conservatoire teacher **Ihsan Özgen** led his own ensemble **Anatolia** for a series of brilliant recordings and bred a new generation of musicians including his daughters Neva and Yelda. *Kanun* players **Göksel Baktagir** and **Ruhi Ayangil**, *ney* players **Kudsi and Süleyman Erguner** and **Sadrettin Özçimi**, and *ud* player

Kudsi Erguner Ensemble

Yurdal **Tokcan** are some of the most important contemporary soloists, while **İnce Saz** unites good soloists into an acoustic group playing an updated version of Istanbul and Balkan styles.

Gazel, or the art of vocal improvisation, has a place in both classical and religious styles, and was popularized by singers like **Hafız Burhan Sesiyılmaz**, **Abdullah Yüce** and **Kani Karaca**, who displayed in their singing a fascinating variety of voice colours. Their style later influenced female singers like **Safiye Ayla**, **Hamiyet Yüceses** and **Müzeyyen Senar**, considered to be the most important soloists in the field of classical song. The brilliant singer **Umut Akyürek** is *gazel*'s brightest new star, having released a highly successful debut album, *O Dudaklar Bülbüllesiyor*, in 2004.

Classical Stars

The theory and history of classical Turkish music is taught in local music schools, of which perhaps the most highly esteemed is the **Üsküdar Musîki Cemiyeti** in Istanbul. There are others in most major cities, and musicians gather at them to socialize or give regular public concerts. Many, if not all, of the top echelon of recording artists are conservatoire-trained, and singers, too, tend to have at least a passing connection with the conservatoires.

The voice lies at the heart of all classical genres. Since the time of **Münir Nurettin Selçuk** (1900–81), singers have assumed most of the trappings of the Western star system. Selçuk was the first solo artist to stand up at the front of the stage, with the other instrumentalists reduced to a backing role. He is now undergoing a major nostalgic reappropriation by the Turkish intelligentsia, after being somewhat forgotten. A dashing figure, his exquisite bel canto style was the perfect complement to his dandified Western dress sense.

Zeki Müren, perhaps the highest-rated vocalist in the latter half of the twentieth century, studied with Refik Fersan and Şerif Içli, and worked extensively with the composer **Müzaffer Özpınar**. After graduating from the Arts Academy, he started his career in the 1950s with perfect and passionate performances of classical vocal pieces

accompanied by TRT musicians. He became an icon on the Turkish music scene, performing his own compositions as well as specially composed pieces, and revolutionizing dress style through his own designs. Although his cross-dressing made it abundantly clear that he was gay, the Muslim-dominated Turkish audience refused to acknowledge, and to this day his pronounciation of the language is considered of the utmost elite quality. He flirted with Arabesk with "Kahır Mektubu" in the early 1980s, but throughout his career turned out austerely classical recordings.

Bülent Ersoy, Turkey's most famous transsexual, studied with **Müzeyyen Senar** and started her career while still a man as a singer of Turkish classical music. After gender reassignment surgery in 1981 she was banned for some years from TV, and lived in exile in Germany. Returning to Turkey, she reinterpreted the turn-of-the-century repertoire in a striking recording, *Alaturka* (1995). But the inclusion of a real call to prayer sung by Bülent herself on the opening track caused fury among devout Muslims, who were offended by the association of religion with this outrageous figure. Now, however, her artistry is widely celebrated, and TV shows feature her with orchestras and special guests.

Recordings of classical songs often add lavish accompaniments, usually heavily harmonized, and with the metallic ticking of drum machines replacing the lively rattle of the *darbuka*. **Adnan Şenses** pioneered this style in the 1980s; more recent exponents include **Mustafa Keser**, whose crooning, silky style also takes in songs from the Arabesk and folk repertoire.

Corazon/Intervista

Müzeyyen Senar

Peter Culshaw

The Whirling Dervishes and Sufi Music

Because of the Mevlevi connections to the Ottoman court and the Sufis' potential political strength, Atatürk banned the Sufi orders in 1926 and they remain banned to this day. However, in the mid-1950s, the **Mevlevi sema**, the whirling dervish ceremony, was revived in Konya where **Jalal Edin Rumi (Mevlana)**, the thirteenth-century founder of the order, is buried. The revival occurred partly because the Republicans had to share power with the Democratic party but also, according to musician Kudsi Erguner, thanks to the wife of an American diplomat who, when visiting Konya, enquired about the dervishes. A *sema* ceremony was hastily organized and it became a regular feature of the celebrations of the anniversary of Rumi's death which were performed each year in a Konya basketball court until a vast tent-like arts centre was opened for the purpose in 2004. In Istanbul, the beautiful eighteenth-century custom-built Galata *tekke* and other less conspicuous *tekkes* have been able to hold *sema* ceremonies by calling themselves museums rather than Sufi lodges. It's ironic that while tourist videos of Turkey promote Rumi and the whirling dervishes, Sufism as a religious practice must remain underground.

Even though the sema at the Galata tekke is performed largely for tourists, the Sufi Sheikh Nail Kesova and his musicians and devotees take it very seriously. It's a four-part, highly formalized ritual

that is supposed to lead to a form of ecstasy. Poetry by Rumi is chanted and a classical ensemble of *ney*, *ud*, *tanbur*, *kanun* and *kudüm* drums accompanies the ceremony. The reed flute, or *ney*, features strongly in Rumi's poetry and its yearning lament of separation from the reed bed is supposed to symbolize man's separation from God.

The growing interest in the mystical music of Islam is clear from the quantity of CDs available in Turkey. The most notable *ney* player in the Sufi tradition is **Kudsi Erguner** (born 1952), whose father and grandfather were also important figures in the Mevlevi musical tradition. Although he has lived in Paris since 1975, he frequently returns to Istanbul and has played an important part in the growing acceptance of the music. Reconnecting a younger generation with Sufi tradition is **Mercan Dede** (see box overleaf) who, taking Rumi as his inspiration, fuses the *ney* with electronic beats and whirling. He enjoys a cult following in Turkey and at festivals worldwide.

A more religious experience of Sufi music can be heard at the lodge of the Halveti-Cerahi sect, which places a heavier emphasis on the practice of *zikr*, a trance-inducing repetition of the names of God, and the collective singing of *ilahi* (hymns). This practice has been freed from the censorship of earlier years, but is still somewhat clandestine. One of the greatest Halveti-Cerahi sheikhs, **Müzaffer Özak**, did, however, make a superb recording of the Mevlevi ritual with Kudsi Erguner in the late 1970s.

Dede's Dervish

Mercan Dede (born Arkın Ilıcalı) is a unique figure on the club scene and festival circuit in Turkey with his combination of Sufi music and electronic beats. For him, the combination goes right back to the teachings of the founder of the **whirling dervishes** in the thirteenth century: 'Rumi says we are all like cross-eyed people and see everything separate. But when we look correctly, nothing is really separate, everything is one. The essence of Sufism is unifying everything. In my first gig I had this beautiful sound of a *ney* with underground techno beats and the whole energy on the dancefloor changed. In that moment I realized electronic music and Sufi music are just two different things telling the same story, but using different languages.'

Mercan's recordings are beautifully made and trance-like, but it's when he's on stage that his music really comes alive. At a concert in Konya celebrating the anniversary of Rumi's death, Mercan played *ney*, controlled the decks and had live instrumentalists on clarinet, *kanun* and Turkish percussion plus Mira Burke, a female whirler in a bright red robe. It was funky, intense, but also undeniably spiritual. 'When you look out at the dance floor you see people who are black, white, Jewish, Muslim, gay, straight… and it doesn't matter', said Mercan. 'In that one single space you realize that in essence we are all the same. That idea is the essence of Sufism, unifying the people and not worrying about who we think we are.'

Mercan was raised in Istanbul, but now divides his time between Turkey and Canada. At an early age he became fascinated with the *ney* – the reed flute associated with Turkish mystic music – and (not being able to afford a real *ney*) learned to play on a length of plastic pipe. He took the name Mercan Dede from an eccentric old character in a Turkish novel and recorded his first album *Sufi Dreams* in 1997 for the American-Turkish label Golden Horn Records. Since then he's recorded for the excellent Istanbul-based label Doublemoon. Mercan uses some of the classical *makam* of Turkish music (like Hicaz and Segah), but composes his own pieces.

'Rumi says a story about yesterday should be left behind. Today we have to tell a new story. I want to tell the story in today's language so I can speak to a new generation. I consider myself a whirling dervish. One of my feet is in the centre, but the other foot keeps turning.'

Simon Broughton

Alongside the Mevlevi, there is another important group of Sufis in Turkey, the **Alevi-Bektasi**. Their saint, **Haci Bektas Veli**, was also born in the thirteenth century and taught a humanist philosophy. While Mevlevi music is rather elitist and classical in style, Bektasi music is hugely popular and *saz* playing is an integral part of their religious gatherings. Haci Bektas insisted on the equality of women, and Alevi men and women dance together in their rituals, which is very unusual in the Islamic world. Bektasi songs frequently protest against injustice, which means many musicians have become popular "protest" singers and there has been repression from the authorities. There is an annual festival (August 16–18) at the saint's shrine in Hacibektas in Cappadocia.

Gypsies and Fasıl Music

Gypsies (known as **Çingene**) are an important presence on the Turkish music scene, and they are responsible for some of Turkey's most thrilling sounds – music often referred to as **nightclub fasıl**.

The music has sleazy associations with nightclubs (**gazino**) and **bellydancing** but it is also performed in more respectable restaurants. Down-market *gazinos* can be found anywhere, particularly around Laleli or Aksaray in Istanbul. Their seedy reputation has changed in recent years as a result of the Islamist municipality's efforts to "tidy up" Istanbul but it is still best to stick to the restaurants around İstiklal Caddesi. The renovated Çicek Pasajı is well worth a visit. Here, the music incorporates recent songs, and makes less effort to stick to classical formulas. This is, after all, music to drink and dance to.

Though many areas of nightclub repertoire overlap with what you might hear in a radio concert, or in the conservatoire, this is a very different kind of music. The classical values of precision and dutiful respect to past times are replaced by a demonstrative, present-tense music. The clarinet and *darbuka* dominate, and many, if not all, of the most noted instrumentalists are Gypsies. They play with great skill and passion. Tunes are tossed around with breathless ease; long notes are held on the clarinet for extended yet exquisitely poised moments during improvisation; *kanun* and violin decorate and interrupt; a torrent of noise and gestural energy flows across the musical event, carrying all before it. Violinists spice the music up with lightning-fast glissandos that swoop and squeak, and clarinettists favour the low-G clarinet whose throaty sound gives this music its special character. The best place to hear Gypsy musicians around İstiklal Caddesi is the **Badehane bar** in Tünel.

Perhaps the most famous of all *fasıl* musicians is the clarinettist **Mustafa Kandıralı**. Born in 1930, he worked for the TRT and has recorded widely. Other celebrated Gypsy musicians include the **Erköse brothers** (clarinettist Barbarosos Erköse is still performing) and the wonderful clarinettist **Selim Sesler**.

Selim Sesler

Burhan Öcal, from Kırklareli in Thrace, is a virtuosic *darbuka* player who graduated from the Istanbul conservatoire. Although he is not from a Gypsy family, he is familiar with the music of his native town and created a combination of classical Turkish and Gypsy musics with his Oriental Ensemble; more recently he has developed a different form of it in a fusion with ethno-jazz (with Jamaladeen Tacuma) and even drum'n'bass. The band **Laço Tayfa** draw on the Gypsy music of Bergama; their leader is clarinet player **Hüsnü Şenlendirici**, who played in the early ethno-jazz experiments by **Okay Temiz** and is now attracting huge audiences by giving his music a popular twist.

Western-Style Art Music

The Turkish Republic gave impulse to the creation of a national school of Western-style art music,

stressing the introduction of polyphony and counterpoint. The most important figures were **Cemal Reşit Rey** (1904–85), **Ulvi Cemal Erkin** (1906–72) and **Hasan Ferit Alnar** (1906–78). Schooled in Paris, Germany or Austria, these musicians variously tried to combine the colours, themes and rhythms of Turkish music with European orchestration, inspired by Bartók, Hindemith and the Russian Five. Their music has only recently gained some popularity thanks to a new generation of soloists. Violinist **Cihat Aşkın** in particular released a series of successful CDs focusing on the small-format chamber music repertoire, interspersed with arrangements of traditional tunes, while pianists **Seher Tanrıyar** and **Vedat Kosal** recorded Cemal Reşit Rey's transcriptions of folksongs.

Minority Musics

It is only relatively recently that music in Turkey can be said to have become a true reflection of the country itself, rather than what its politicians hoped it could be. Most important has been the acknowledgement of the national minorities of Anatolia, including the Kurds who represent an estimated 15 percent of the population and whose language, music and culture were banned for many years.

Kurdish Music

The bans on Kurdish music in Turkey have only been lifted in the last decade – largely due to EU pressure. You still won't hear it on TRT, but the state has long since lost its stranglehold on broadcasting, and now, walking down İstiklal Caddesi in Istanbul, you can hear Kurdish music blaring out of music shops and see groups in the nearby clubs. The most popular Kurdish artists in Turkey are the male singer **Ciwan Haco** and the young female vocalist **Aynur** (see chapter on Kurdish music). **Kardeş Türküler** (Songs of Fraternity) is an Istanbul-based group which draws on regional traditions, largely from eastern Turkey, and which frequently perform repertoire in Kurdish. The group was formed in the early 1990s at Bosphorus University in Istanbul with the ambition of performing songs from the various ethnic groups living in Anatolia – Turkish, Kurdish, Armenian, Laz, Georgian and so on. Many of the musicians come from different (and mixed) ethnicities and is one of the few groups that has successfully taken Anatolian folk music to an international audience.

Corazon/Intervista

Greek–Turkish Music

The Turkish audience has always been interested in **Greek** music, and in the pop market there can be found both co-operations between Turkish and Greek singers and Turkish covers of Greek songs. **Yeni Türkü**'s versions of Greek numbers were very popular in the 1980s (see below). Accordion player **Muammer Ketencioğlu**'s *Kumpanya* features the unique voice of **Ivi Dermancı**, an original Istanbul Greek. In a rare instance of a return to Turkey, Greek cantor **Nikiforos Metaxas** created the Bosphoros Ensemble; their joint effort with Greek group **Mode Plagal**, *Beyond the Bosphorus*, is worth seeking out. *Kemençe* virtuosos **Derya Türkan** and **Sokratis Sinopoulos**'s "Letter from Istanbul" project is a delicate, acoustic celebration of the joint musical heritage of Greece and Turkey, while Turkish art singer **Melahat Gülses** has released a CD of songs dedicated to Istanbul and Athens.

Jewish Traditions

The Jewish presence in Istanbul goes back several centuries, at least to 1492, when Sephardic Jews expelled from Spain were welcomed by Ottoman sultans who wanted to boost the industrial and financial infrastructure. They brought with them their language (**Ladino** or Judeo-Spanish) and their culture, including both secular songs (*romansas*) and devotional music. With time, they adapted the Turkish classical music style to their own heritage, and many became important composers and performers. Today, amateur and professional musicians still perform the traditional songs and there is even a pop group called **Sefarad**, who have revitalized and repopularized the style. **Janet and Jak Esim** are important exponents of this music, while the **Maftirim** project focuses on the connections between Jewish and Turkish sacred musics, with a group of Jewish cantors accompanied by *ney* and *kanun*.

Arabesk

Arabesk – Turkey's dominant popular music in the 1980s – draws on folk, classical and *fasıl* traditions, though it takes its name from its predominantly Arabic rather than Turkish melodies. Turkish nationalists made strenuous efforts to exclude Turkey's "Arab" history and cultural links, but most people at that time thought Arabesk simply represented Turkish music in its most basic and appealing form.

Arabesk is a working-class and to an extent outsiders' music which addresses everyday realities and problems, and the concerns of the poor and disenfranchised.

Oriental Roots

Arabesk has its roots in Egyptian 'oriental' dance music – **Raks Şarkı** or **oriyental**, often misleadingly known as 'bellydancing' music – which has been of enduring popularity in Turkey. It was introduced in the 1940s by **Haydar Tatliyay** (1890–1963), who had worked in Egyptian groups and on returning to Turkey set up a large dance orchestra as used in Egyptian film. When the Turkish state attempted to ban Arabic-language music and film in 1948, and began in earnest to establish a national alternative through the TRT, people voted with their radio dials, tuning to Radio Cairo.

Turkey's nascent recording and film industry subsequently invested heavily in recording versions of Egyptian hits, particularly those associated with Mohammed Abdel-Wahab, Umm Kalthum and the Lebanese-born star Farid al-Atrache.

But Arabesk is not simply derivative Egyptian music, and from the 1940s its songs addressed specifically Turkish problems such as rural–urban migration. Many popular films, particularly those of Baha Gelenbevi, began to deal with themes of rural life, accompanied by rural music, and urbanized rural genres began to appear in the cities and on record. **Diyarbakırlı Celal Güzelses** and

Corazon/Intervista

Orhan Gencebay

Bellydance star Üzel Türkbas

Malatyalı Fahri Kayahan were amongst the earliest to record popularized folk-based forms for an urban audience, drawing heavily on the musical styles and repertoires of the southeast. **Ahmet Sezgin** took this one step further, bringing urban and rural styles into a creative mix in the mid-1960s.

Arabesk Goes Big-Time

In the 1960s Turks bought into Anglo-American rock music, and some singers adopted elements into their music. The first figure of interest to do so was **Orhan Gencebay**, who was born in 1944 on the Black Sea coast and began his career with Ahmet Sezgin. His first solo recording, "Bir Teselli Ver" (1969), related to the classical form, but the sobbing intensity of the voice owed much to the *gazel*, and frank lyrics addressed the plight of the

lonely lover – a far cry from the heavy metaphors and archaic language of the classical song style. A more eclectic set of references, including rock and flamenco, was in evidence on his 1975 album *Batsın Bu Dünya*, and a creative and playful eclecticism has marked his career to date. He is also a composer and a film actor.

Despite Gencebay's colossal status, it is the voice which defines Arabesk aesthetics, and those of **İbrahim Tatlıses**, **Müslüm Gürses** and **Ferdi Tayfur** (all are also film actors) are the most significant. Their songs tell of self-pity and humiliation in the big city, experiences close to many Turkish hearts. **İbrahim Tatlıses** himself migrated from the impoverished southeastern town of Urfa, and many of his films and songs allude to his story. He has been a big star since the mid-1980s, with a series of albums featuring well-drilled orchestras, danceable tunes and his electrifying voice, heard to best effect in the rural *uzun hava* (long, semi-improvised pieces, accompanied by a solo *saz*) that appear on every CD. He even owns a nationwide chain of kebab shops that play his music exclusively. **Ferdi Tayfur**'s voice also has strong resonances with southeastern vocal styles, and his reputation similarly rests on his self-portrayal as a poor villager made good in the big city. Müslüm Gürses' older hits are mournful, fate-obsessed numbers inviting the listener to light another cigarette ("Bir Sigara Yak"), pour another glass ("Bir Kadeh Daha Ver") and curse the world ("Yeter Allahım").

Arabesk was legitimized by Özal's government, as part of a general relaxation of the official social codes introduced by Atatürk and "protected" by the military, and many Arabesk stars were quick to take advantage. Private FM radio and TV gave the music a new lease of life, and it is now possible to see classic Arabesk films from the 1970s on a more or less daily basis. Some younger stars are getting a look in, too. **Mahsun Kırmızıgül** has been the biggest Arabesk star of the new millennium – his "Sarı Sarı" was the market sensation of 2005 – but his style has evolved into a pop-influenced Arabesk, as has that of **İbrahim Tatlıses**. Singers with classical backgrounds, notably **Bülent Ersoy**, **Muazzez Abacı**, **Emel Sayin**, **Nese Karaböcek** and most recently **Muazzez Ersoy** and **Yılmaz Morgül**, continue to drift in and out of Arabesk.

Pop and Anatolian Rock

Rock and **pop** have leapt to great prominence since 1990. But they have long been influential. Turks have always made their own versions of international genres: tango was enormously popular from the 1930s to the 1950s; French *chanson* had Turkish exponents such as blonde bombshell **Ajda Pekkan** (who still performs); and Elvis Presley spawned a wave of imitators in the late 1950s, most notably **Erol Büyükburç**.

Somewhat away from the mainstream, a number of musicians began to try to reconcile Anatolian folk and Western rock. Most of these musicians were from the bourgeoisie, and despite the phenomenal difficulties involved in procuring instruments and recording, an Anadolu (Anatolian) Rock movement gathered pace. The music became increasingly politicized. After 1980's military coup, most of the groups promptly disbanded, and **Cem Karaca** (1945–2004) – who had worked with nearly every significant Anadolu rock band – fled to Germany, returning only in 1987.

Cem Karaca was the most interesting voice of the genre, combining rock histrionics with a cultivated *sanat* bel canto; live, his voice sounded capable of filling an entire auditorium with or without amplification. His songs combined a taste for highbrow literature with social realism. With his group **Dervişan** he recorded *Safinaz* in 1979, a kind of rock opera about a poor girl's struggle with honour and blood feuds. He has also superbly recorded the work of left-wing poet Nazım Hikmet (who died in exile in the Soviet Union) and Orhan Veli.

The group **Moğollar**, formed and reformed under Karaca's direction, has kept a political edge, alongside an uptempo stadium rock style. **Yeni Türkü**, inspired by the Latin American *nueva canción* movement, enjoyed great popularity amongst the intelligentsia towards the end of the 1980s for its versions of old Istanbul songs and Greek rembetika numbers. Also popular at this time was the austere figure of **Zülfü Livaneli**, best known outside Turkey for his work with Greek singer Maria Farandouri and composer Mikis Theodorakis and for the music to Yilmaz Güney's film *Yöl*.

Other established groups worth checking out include **Erkin Koray**, **MFÖ** (one of the few to survive the generals) and **Barış Manço**. Current bands drawing on indigenous styles and instruments as well as technological bric-a-brac and avant-garde inspirations are **Zen**, **Replikas** and **Baba Zula**. Popular mainstream rock acts with Turkish lyrics are **Mavi Sakal**, **Mor ve Ötesi**, **Duman** and **Kargo**.

Pop

At the heart of Turkey's resolutely mainstream indigenous pop scene is one figure: **Sezen Aksu**. She trained as a *sanat* singer in her native Izmir and her current prominence owes much to her partnership with the late **Onno Tunç**, an Armenian musician who embraced soul and jazz in the 1960s, and had the challenging task of overseeing Turkey's Eurovision Song Contest entries in the 1980s. Aksu's soulful voice, owing much to traditional Turkish urban music, and Tunç's elliptical, keyboard-based arrangements, made for a winning combination.

Sezen Aksu is still very popular, mainly for her love songs, and at her concerts the audience can sing the lyrics to each and every one by heart. She has released around twenty albums since 1975. After the premature death of Onno Tunç his brother Arto, a well-known percussionist on the global jazz scene, took charge as her arranger. He brought in the members of Night Ark – Ara Dinkjan and Marc Johnson – to compose, arrange and perform on her *Deliveren* album, one of the most interesting for its challenging musical backing.

Her CD releases are national media events. When *Işık Doğudan Yükselir* (The Sun Rises in the East) came out in 1995, evoking the cultural mosaic of Anatolia during the worsening of the crisis in the southeast of the country, the album's release was the first item on the TRT's evening news.

Aksu's "students" dominated the Turkish pop scene in the late 1980s and early 1990s. **Levent Yüksel**, a multi-talented instrumentalist and singer, produced carefully crafted CDs which connected quite explicitly with indigenous Turkish traditions and Turkish literature. Among the singers coming from Aksu's "conservatoire" are **Candan Erçettin** (who draws on a wide range of Balkan and Mediterranean styles, including French chanson), Eurovision winner **Sertab Erener**, the powerful **Işın Karaca** – currently the most exciting contribution to the scene – and teen idol **Tarkan**. Tarkan has crossed the border into the world market, with his song *Şımarık* (composed by Aksu) becoming popular in Europe as "Kiss Kiss".

In the last few years, a newer genre of pop has come to the fore, with driving rhythms and a melodic style inspired by folklore, but with a hedonistic attitude. **Mirkelam** made a big splash in the mid-1990s with his excellent *Her Gece*

Sezen Aksu

In Turkey, they call **Sezen Aksu** "The Goddess", "The Queen of Turkish music" and, in honour of her most successful album, "The Sparrow". The diminutive singer, songwriter and producer is Turkey's most celebrated pop star, a mould-breaker who combines Western musical tastes with a dedication to traditional music from Turkey and local cultures not always in harmony with her own.

In the four decades since Aksu's first single, "Come On, My Luck, Come to Me" (1976), and her first number-one hit, "Wish It Never Happened" (1978), she has sold in excess of 20 million records. Fabulously rich, with a portfolio including a nightclub and a Bosphorus-side recording studio, Aksu is unconventional, independent (she has had four husbands), fearless and outspoken (about environmental issues and Turkey's treatment of its minorities, especially Kurds and Armenians). Her audiences – women in *hijab*, girls with bare midriffs, stylish young couples, men with thick moustaches and youths in hip-hop gear – flock to hear this voluptuously beautiful woman whose songs resonate with their experiences.

Fatma Sezen Yıldırım grew up in the southern town of Izmir, where she studied agriculture, theatre, dance, music, sculpture and art. She travelled to Istanbul to sell "Sezen Aksu: singer-songwriter, *oud* and *saz* player", and landed a deal. "Come On, My Luck", her first broadcast on TRT, launched a string of hits. "Serçe", from 1978, is still requested today.

For three consecutive years during the early 1980s, Aksu was a finalist in the Eurovision Song Contest – an experience whose echoes can be heard occasionally in booming bass drums and a penchant for voice echo. Increasingly, her maturing lyrics reflected social change or were poetic love songs. The 1984 album *Sen Ağlama (Don't Cry!)*, produced during her long relationship with the Turkish-Armenian composer **Onno 'Tunç' Tunçboyaciyan**, included a controversial song about passionate love. Banned by TRT, it was inevitably a hit. When Onno died in a plane crash in 1996, Aksu withdrew for months; she still performs their duet "Tutuklu" (Still Captured) about lost love, and his talented daughter, Anya, plays violin in her band. The couple's song "Kavaklar" (1988), written by a poet later killed during a massacre of Armenian artists, uses the Anatolian *kavak* tree as a potent symbol of resistance. Aksu's fans are receptive to such subtle protest-pop and to collaborations with non-Turkish musicians.

On stage, Aksu is absorbing, emotionally demanding and intimate, with the slow drama, grace and assurance of an opera diva. Her versatile contralto reveals myriad textures and effortlessly soars to high registers, exploiting the lusciousness of the Turkish language; "Söylüyor" (1999) earned her the title "The Voice of Turkey". Her magnificent 35-piece "oriental" orchestra is built around a small Turkish rock band: *oud*, *darbuka*, *ney* flute and oriental violin working with electric guitar, keyboards, bass and drums. The bestselling album "The Sun Rises in the East" (1995) typically mixes classical and traditional arrangements, with Aksu bringing her idiosyncratic vocal style to bear on regional songs, popular urban dance genres and the religious repertoire.

The celebrated Turkish-German filmmaker Fatih Akin, whose award-winning documentary *Crossing the Bridge: The Sound of Istanbul* includes Aksu's moving tribute "Istanbul, Hatirasi" (Memories of Istanbul), declares: 'Sezen can express how you feel when you are unhappy in love; I always feel hugged when I see her!'

album, but these days the consistently big names are **Çelik**, **Hande Yener**, **Nilüfer**, **Serdat Ortaç**, **Rafet el-Roman** and **Mustafa Sandal**.

Turkish Rap in Germany

Rap music – already common among the large Turkish diaspora in Germany – arrived in Turkey itself with **Cartel**'s 1995 CD. The group's lyrics explicitly equate the Turkish and Black American

Corazon/Intervista

Cesa & his crew

ghetto experiences, sampling Anatolian sounds (*saz*, *zurna* and *davul*), parading the Turkish flag, and appropriating the hyper-macho posturing of their US models. They rap in Turkish, German, Spanish and English and are a multicultural group, though their message is very clear: that Turks in Germany should unite (a hand of brotherhood is extended to Kurds, Circassians and Laz) against German racism. Cartel galvanized debate in Turkey and received, disturbingly, a warm welcome from Turkish fascists on their Istanbul debut.

Cartel inspired a new wave of Turkish hip-hop which is today reaching a mass audience. Artists include Ceza, Karargah, Sagopa Kajmer and the Circassian rapper Sultana whose hit *Kuşu Kalkmaz*, with its explicit lyrics, was very controversial.

Other Turkish-German rappers, for example the Frankfurt-based **DJ Mahmut**, **DJ Volkan** and **KMR**, pursue a style which is simultaneously mellow and avant-garde, mixing German and Turkish in complex lyrics which are more about urban dislocation than racial conflict. **Aziza-A**, based in Berlin, raps on feminist issues. Arguments will continue to rage about what is and what is not Turkish; what is and what is not mere imitation; what is appropriately "political" and what is not. Turkish rap poses the question in stark terms, but also indicates the inventive dynamism that is taking this music forward into the 21st century.

With thanks to Sergül Aktan

DISCOGRAPHY Turkey

In Turkey, the leading label for folk and classical recordings is Kalan (*www.kalan.com*) which has released an unrivalled range of archive recordings of classical instrumentalists, contemporary folk and popular singers, *aşık* bards and the music of minority groups in Turkey. Doublemoon (*www.doublemoon.com.tr*) specializes in the most current fusion projects, while Ada's catalogue ranges from fringe rock to ethno-jazz and folk. In the US, Traditional Crossroads (*www.traditionalcrossroads.com*) has an excellent catalogue of archive and contemporary recordings, while small independent label Golden Horn (*www.goldenhorn.com*) has a well-selected catalogue with each record representing a specific field of Turkish music.

One of the best record shops in Istanbul is *Lale Plak*, Tünel, Galipded Caddesi No.1, 80050 Beyoğlu, Istanbul ((90) 212 293 7739). *Metropol*, on İstiklal Caddesi, functions as a headquarters of sorts for the new folk movement, and recently started its own label. You'll find announcements of performances there, the staff might not smile at you but will be helpful, and the selections are good – as are the prices (İstiklal Caddesi 140, tel. 0212 249 36 73).

Folk and Aşık

⊙ **Ashiklar: Those Who Are In Love**
Golden Horn, US

Featuring Ashik Mahsuni Serif, Musa Eroglu, Ashik Bahattin Kader, Ashik Nuri Kiliç and Ashik Ali. Recorded at the Haci Bektas festival and the houses of leading *aşık* during the production of a 1994 documentary movie, this is a lively, vibrant collection with a varied repertoire. The lyrics of Pir Sultan Abdal are well represented.

⊙ **Masters of Turkish Music Volumes 1–3**
Rounder, US

These three compilation CDs are fine historical introductions to Turkish music. Based on vintage recordings carefully restored without killing all the noise associated with 78rpm records, they feature most of the important genres and artists from the beginning of the recording industry to the 1960s. The focus is on the early recorded repertoire, however, so folk music is not as well represented as classical and *sanat*.

⊙ Saz
Kalan, Turkey

A compilation tracing examples of the various types of *saz* from Central Asia to Turkey and beyond to Greece. It features the Uzbek *dutar*, Tadjik *tambur*, Kyrgyz *komuz*, Kazakh *dombra*, Iranian *tanbur*, Azeri *saz* and various Turkish varieties including Ali Ekber Çiçek playing "Haydar" on the big divan *saz*. A useful and accessible survey with photos and a few notes in English by leading musicologist Melih Duygulu.

⊙ Song Creators in Eastern Turkey
Smithsonian Folkways, US

Four *aşıks* from Kars and Erzurum in northeastern Turkey recorded in *aşık* cafés in the early 1990s. Excellent notes about the singers, tradition and repertoire, with translations.

★ Turkish Village Music
Nonesuch/Explorer, US

There are plenty of field recordings of Turkish rural musics, but this is the best, recorded by ethnomusicologist Laxmi Tewari in two villages in northwest Turkey. The *aşık's* songs are heart-rending, and represent the repertoire as heard and performed in villages – a long way away from the TRT's idea of what it should sound like. The disc also contains good examples of *zurna* and *davul*.

⊙ Turquie: Aşık
Inédit, France

This is probably the best introduction to *aşık* music, featuring the celebrated Ali Ekber Çiçek and one of the few female *aşıks*, Nuray Hafiftaş, plus a spectacular *saz* solo from Arif Sağ. Good notes and translations.

⊙ Turquie: Musiques des Yayla
Ocora, France

Jerome Cler's excellent recordings from a mountain village in the southwest of the country. Instrumental dance tunes on various types of *saz* and violin predominate, ranging from the sprightly "Teke Zortlatması", representing the skipping of mountain goats, to the ponderous and macho "Zeybek".

Belkis Akkale

Akkale is a TRT (Turkish Radio) vocal artist specializing in the Alevi repertoire, though she is not herself from this community. She set the agenda for an entire decade of popular folk-music recording in the 1980s with "Türkü Türkü Türkiyem", featuring her characteristic earthy voice and driving *saz* rhythms.

⊙ Güvercin
Raks/Midas, Turkey

This 1986 recording contains perfect examples of Akkale's renditions of the popularized Alevi repertoire: poised, grave, and passionate in tone. Note the brief excursion to Azerbaijan in "Bu Gala Dasli Gala", characterized by a 6/8 rhythm unusual in western or central Anatolia.

Sabahat Akkiraz

This singer was brought up in the Alevi musical and cultural tradition, and is now one of the most vigorous exponents of folk music in Turkey, her concerts all over the country drawing wide attention.

⊙ Konserler
Akkiraz, Turkey

The first production of her own label, this combines a recording made live in London with a jazz orchestra with more traditional acoustic arrangements of songs from the *aşık* repertoire.

Aynur

This Kurdish singer already had two CDs and hundreds of concerts in the grassroots circuit under her belt when she entered the Kalan catalogue; her strong performance in the film *Crossing the Bridge* has won her a wider following abroad.

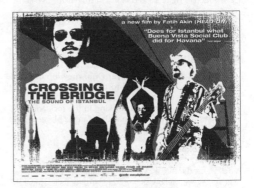

★ Nûpel

Kalan, Turkey

This album has the urgency of a live concert. The short opening – non-metric vocal improvisation followed by a rendition of a traditional song incorporating a heartfelt *ney* solo by Şenol Filiz – clearly establishes the set-up: voice centre-stage, accompanied by limited electronics, excellent instrumentalists and strong rhythms. Especially intense and satisfying are the arrangements of Şivan Perwer's "Nemire Lawik" and Erol Mutlu's new melodies for the poems "Suware" and "Eman Dilo".

Ali Ekber Çiçek

Çiçek is an *aşık* from Erzincan in eastern Turkey, famed for his singing and *saz* playing.

⊙ Haydar Haydar
Mega Müzik, Turkey

A collection of classic songs. Haydar is the name given to Ali, meaning the "lion of God".

Kardeş Türküler

The Kardeş Türküler project was born in 1993 out of Bosphorus University's Performing Arts and Folk Societies. It is a big group (a dozen singers and multi-instrumentalists), playing traditional tunes powered by percussion, passionately delineated by the vocal soloists, and enlivened with improvisations by musicians well aware of jazz and rock. The music has raised criticisms among folk purists, but the combination is uplifting. Their popularity in Turkey is huge, and their concerts in Istanbul are usually sold out. Their participation in the successful *Vizontele* movie further broadened their appeal, and their political relevance was boosted when radio and TV channels in Turkey refused to broadcast some of their songs.

⊙ Hemavaz
Kalan, Turkey

A well-researched selection of tunes from different cultures – Alevi, Kurdish, Armenian, Greek, traditional and contemporary Turkish – in arrangements that add bass and classic guitar, violin and accordion.

Latife

A singer from Radio Ankara, in the current style of popular folk singers, Latife maintains a low profile.

⊙ Latife
Ada, Turkey
Her first CD is a well-balanced, warm mixture of the traditional repertoire and carefully crafted modern arrangements. The presence among her instrumentalists of Erkan Oğur and Musa Eroğlu indicates her status among the older generations.

Erkan Oğur

Vocalist, guitarist and *saz* player Oğur grew up in eastern Turkey, where he listened to the local *aşık* as well as Jimi Hendrix on the radio. He studied *ud* before building himself a fretless guitar and working in the rock and folk scene. He often works in a duo with divan saz player Ismail Demircioğlu.

⊙ Gülün Kokusu Vardi
Kalan, Turkey
A delicate and rather ascetic CD of traditional songs from all over Turkey with fellow singer and instrumentalist İsmail H. Demircioğlu and other guest musicians. With exquisite instrumental playing, this is good listening even if you don't understand the lyrics (which are not translated). The title-track ("The Rose Had a Scent") regrets the lost riches of tradition.

★ Hiç
Kalan, Turkey
A very unusual album featuring instrumental versions of classic songs. Simply recorded with some of the best performers from the folk-music scene, this CD is especially attractive for non-Turkish listeners, as it focuses on the musical values and not on the words.

Talip Özkan

Born in 1939 in southwest Turkey, Özkan worked for many years at TRT before settling in France. He is not a traditional musician, but an intellectual and fine player who's mastered many of Turkey's different types of *saz*.

⊙ L'art vivant de Talip Özkan
Ocora, France
Eight great tracks covering different regional styles and instruments from the large *divan saz* to the small *cura bağlama*.

Arif Sağ

One of Turkey's most important *bağlama* players and a major innovator.

⊙ Davullar Çalınırken
Iber, Turkey
A striking album from 2005 in which Sağ concentrates on Anatolian rhythms, performing all the percussive parts as well. A memorable concerto for *bağlama* and orchestra with harmonic modulations far removed from the folk traditions. On this CD he stresses the rhythmic basis of Turkish music from different regions of Anatolia including *zeybek*, *çiftetelli* and *horon*.

Birol Topaloğlu

Born in Rize on the Black Sea in 1965, Topaloğlu is an engineer with no formal musical training who has learned *kemençe*, the local instrument.

⊙ Lazuri Birabape Heyamo
Kalan, Turkey
A very accessible album of vocalists from the Black Sea Laz minority, featuring Topaloğlu on *kemençe* and musicians from the popular Grup Yorum. The title-track is a well-known work song which sounds almost Bulgarian in this arrangement.

Aşik Veysel

Aşık Veyshel was born in 1894 in Sivrialan, Sivas province, and died there in 1973. He lost his sight at the age of seven in a smallpox epidemic which killed his two brothers. Contrary to prevalent *aşık* tradition, he did not have a mystic dream but was taught by local master *saz* players. In the 1920s and 30s, *aşık* lost their nomadic status and took on a more institutionalized role: telling the people in the villages about the new Republic, which embodied the social change they had traditionally requested. Veysel was "discovered" at the Aşık festival organized in 1931 in Sivas by the Society for the Preservation of Folk Poetry. He became a national institution, and his songs – mystical contemplations on the human condition – are still sung all over Turkey.

★ Aşık Veysel
Kalan, Turkey
The "definitive" Veysel collection, a great double-CD album with songs carefully reissued from the best available versions on vinyl, and fully annotated in English. "Kara Toprak" is exemplifies Veysel's poetry, which is fully rooted in village life but carries a universal message: 'I embraced so many, thinking them a friend/My true love is the black earth/In vain I wandered, exhausted myself for naught/My true love is the black earth.'

Classical and Sufi Music

⊙ The Bektashi Breaths
Cemre, Turkey
The Bektaşi are a Turkish sect who perform musical rituals and dances in which the hymns are called *nefes*, breaths. This is an extraordinarily powerful CD which exudes a real ritual solemnity and power. The melodies sigh expressively with an ensemble of *ney*, *kemençe*, *kanun*, *ud*, cello and drum.

⊙ Istanbul 1925
Traditional Crossroads, US
Despite the title, this covers the early years of the Turkish recording industry up to the 1950s. It features excellent examples of popular classical instrumentalists (Udi Hrant, Şükrü Tunar) as well as the precursors of Arabesk (Mahmut Celallettin, Kemani Haydar Tatlıyay).

⊙ Mevlana
Kalan, Turkey
This is a precious reissue of a classic recording of a complete suite (*ayin*) used by Mevlevi sufis for worship, composed by Dede Efendi (a key figure from the nineteenth century, who is considered to have brought Turkish classical music to perfection). The group reads like a who's who of Turkish *sanat* from the first half of the twentieth century, with Mesut Cemil on cello, Aka Gündüz Kutbay, Ulvi Erguner and Niyazi Sayin on *ney*, Cuneyd Orhon on *kemençe* and Sadettin Heper on *kudüm*. A reference recording.

⊙ Women of Istanbul
Traditional Crossroads, US
A companion selection to *Istanbul 1925*, this archival collection brings together the greatest female singers from the golden era of cabaret-style nightclubs (from 1920 to the mid-

1940s), including the great Müzeyyen Senar and Safiye Ayla. Excellent notes and photos.

Latif Bolat

While it's the Mevlevi music of the whirling dervishes that seems to have caught the imagination of audiences outside Turkey, the Sufi music that is most popular within the country is that linked to the Alevi-Bektaşi tradition. Born in Mersin but now resident in the US, *saz* player and singer Bolat is a great advocate of the music of Turkey's Sufi poets.

⊙ Gül: The Rose
Latif Bolat, US
A 2005 recording with a small acoustic ensemble that really brings the poetry of the Turkish mystics to life.

Mercan Dede

It may seem strange to include the club-oriented Mercan Dede alongside classical and Sufi musicians, but he cites Rumi as his principal inspiration, and the *ney* is a prominent part of his performances with live musicians, electronic beats and female whirler Mira Burke.

⊙ Su
Doublemoon, Turkey
With Mercan Dede it's the live experience that is most exhilarating, but this 2004 album with guests Sabahat Akkiraz, Dhafer Yousef and Susheela Raman is a fine disc.

Kudsi Erguner

The Erguner family tradition of *ney* playing started with Kudsi's grandfather Süleyman the elder. Since settling in Paris in 1975, Kudsi has become one of the most visible exponents of Turkish music abroad, working widely as a musicologist, publishing his own field recordings and performing. The sound of his *ney* can be heard on film soundtracks and albums with jazz musicians. He performs regularly in Turkey and his concerts in Aya Irini have been major musical events, with strong political overtones. For example, a 2004 concert featured two choirs, one of *muezzins* and one of Greek Orthodox monks.

⊙ Ferahfeza Mevlevi Ayini
Imaj, Turkey
The Mevlevi ritual composed by Ismail Dede for Sultan Mahmut II in 1839.

⊙ Islam Blues
ACT, Germany
Kudsi's delves into contemporary jazz, but keeps a distinctive spiritual quality.

⊙ L'Héritage Ottoman
Institut du Monde Arabe, France
Erguner's own ensemble – joined by some of the finest young Turkish classical music soloists – perform original compositions and a selection of classic instrumental pieces alternating solos and ensemble. Excellent liner notes in English by Erguner himself discuss structures, instruments and composers of Ottoman classical music.

★ Les passions d'Istanbul
Imaj, Turkey
An original suite composed by Erguner himself with a larger ensemble including vocal soloists from different traditions, this focuses on the multinational, multi-ethnic character of the city. Erguner now prefers to release energetic live recordings from concerts rather than more technically accomplished studio recreations.

Kudsi Erguner

Süleyman Erguner

Unlike his brother Kudsi, Süleyman chose to stay in Istanbul where he is now a *ney* soloist for the TRT ensemble as well as a *ney* instructor at Istanbul Conservatoire. He is also founder and leader of the Istanbul Mevlevi Ensemble, with which he performs regularly in Turkey and abroad.

WITH IHSAN ÖZGEN AND KORAY SAFKAN

⊙ Tende Cânım
Sera, Turkey
From the stately opening notes of the *ney*, building its *taksim*, this establishes itself as an extraordinary live recording that allows you to hear one of the contemporary masters of *ney* and *kemençe*. In a series of compositions from the classical and religious tradition, Ihsan Özgen also teaches at the Istanbul Conservatoire. The educated but soulful voice of Koray Safkan provides the vocal parts. Excellent notes in English by Erguner.

Bülent Ersoy

A singer in the *sanat* and Arabesk genres and a student of Müzeyyen Senar, Bülent underwent sex-change surgery in London in 1981, and spent many years abroad, unable to perform in Turkey. Since her return, Bülent has been associated primarily with the recording company Raks, which has done much to engineer the megastar status she enjoys in Turkey today.

★ Alaturka
Raks, Turkey
On this CD Bülent interprets popular classics from the 1880s to the 1950s and 60s. Conceived as a tribute to her mentor, Muzaffer Özpınar, this is definitely her best recording in recent years. It contains some *gazels* of scorching intensity, marking the comeback of this semi-improvised classical vocal genre.

Udi Hrant

One of the most important players and composers on the Turkish *ud*, Hrant (1901–78), from an Armenian family, was born blind and started out playing in cafés before making it onto the radio. He became one of the most popular performers in Istanbul's nighclubs and toured widely.

⊙ The Early Recordings Vol 1
Traditional Crossroads, US

This might seem a specialized disc of tracks from early 78s, but it includes some storming and touching performances (some including the celebrated Şükrü Tunar on clarinet) that leap out at you. Exemplary remastering and good notes, photos and translations of lyrics. There are two other volumes of later recordings on the same label.

Lalezar Ensemble

Founded in 1997 by *kanun* player Reha Sagbaş, the four-piece Lalezar Ensemble (*kanun, kemençe, ney/tanbur*, percussion) perform classical music of the Ottoman Period.

⊙ Music of the Sultans, Sufis and Seraglio
Traditional Crossroads, US

A four-CD series that gives an approachable and well-annotated introduction to the music. *Vol 1: Sultan Composers* includes music from the 17th–20th century, composed by the Sultans themselves – notably Selim III (1789-1808). *Vol 2: Music of the Dancing Boys* represents the harem entertainments of the köçek dancers. *Vol 3: Minority Composers* underlines the important contributions of Armenian, Greek and Jewish musicians in Ottoman music and *Vol 4: Ottoman Suite* is an example of an extended courtly suite.

Zeki Müren

Born in Bursa, Zeki Müren (1931–96) first came to public attention as an interpreter of the contemporary *sanat* through his radio concerts in the early 1950s. His repertoire, however, also included Turkish versions of tango, chanson and the songs of Arab singers such as Umm Kalthum and Farid el-Atrache. His fame was established by some eighteen musical films and by his live performances in Istanbul's *gazino* clubs, characterized by their elaborate decor and Müren's increasingly camp costumery.

⊙ Türk Sanat Müziği Konseri
Coskun Plak, Turkey

Remastered from the old HMV catalogue, this recording is a near-perfect example of Zeki's elegant mastery of the classical lyric style.

Münir Nurettin Selçuk

Born in Istanbul in 1900, Selçuk was dubbed "the man who put Turkish music in Western dress". He established the idea of the star vocalist in Turkish popular music in a concert given in Istanbul's French Theatre in 1930 but was famous primarily for his recordings, which ranged from light classical to tango.

⊙ Bir Özlemdir
Coskun Plak, Turkey

One of a series of reissues of old HMV recordings of the *bel canto* master of the Turkish classical style, *Bir Özlemdir* contains some of the enduring classics: "Aziz Istanbul", "Kalamış", "Endülüste Raks" (a Turkish view of flamenco), and an electrifying improvised *gazel*, "Aheste Çek Kürekleri".

Hamiyet Yüceses

Hamiyet was the singer of choice for the new songs by Turkish composers in the 1930s and 40s, especially Sadettin Kaynak, who gave her the name "Yüceses" (Gorgeous Voice) when the Republican government required everybody

to get a family name instead of the patronymic used in Ottoman times.

★ Makber
Istanbul, Turkey

This outstanding collection includes her magnificent recording of "Bakmıyor Çeşm-i Siyah Feryade" – a classic piece by Hacı Harif Bey to which she added a long improvised *gazel* section – and an intense interpretation of the Hafız Burhan piece "Her Yer Karanlık".

Fasıl/Gypsy Music

Kemani Cemal

Born in Thracian Turkey, the heartland of Turkish Roma music in 1928, Cemal learnt music from his father, specializing in the violin (*keman*). He has played in many of Istanbul's nightclubs and *gazinos*.

⊙ Sulukule: Roma Music of Istanbul
Traditional Crossroads, US

A splendid selection of instrumental numbers and songs which evoke the earthy character of urban Roma music. Good notes and translations of lyrics.

Klaus Wedding/World Netwerk

Burhan Öcal's Istanbul Oriental Ensemble

Istanbul Oriental Ensemble

This ensemble of Roma musicians, led by percussionist Burhan Öçal, is currently top of the pile as far as recordings are concerned. The line-up is the traditional one of clarinet, violin, *oud*, *kanun* and *darbuka* drums.

⊙ Gypsy Rum
Network, Germany
Fourteen tracks of tight instrumental playing. Emotional twists and lightning virtuosity will have you bellydancing – listen for the screaming shrieks from Fethi Tekayğil's violin. Once you've tried this, move on to their follow-up album, *The Sultan's Secret Door* (Network, Germany).

Mustafa Kandıralı

Born in Kandıra, this Gypsy clarinet player toured the USSR and USA as a band leader in the 1960s, and there had his formative encounter with jazz. His later improvisations could be compared to Benny Goodman for virtuosity and to Charlie Parker for audacity. Kandıralı's performances have a quiet radicalism to their melodic invention.

⊙ Caz Roman
World Network, Germany
This is the epitome of instrumental *fasıl*, including some of Turkey's best-known *fasıl* instrumentalists, Ahmet Meter (*kanun*), Metin Bükey (*ud*) and Ahmet Kulik (*darbuka*). The last section of dance tunes is from a live recording at a concert in Düsseldorf in 1984.

Selim Sesler

Born in 1957, clarinettist Sesler comes from the Thracian village of Keşan and is the most charismatic player of Turkish Gypsy wedding music. He features prominently in Fatih Akin's film Crossing the Bridge.

★ The Road to Keşan
Traditional Crossroads, US
Exemplary CD of wild Gypsy wedding music from Thrace with clarinet, violin, *cumbuş*, *kanun* and percussion. Exhilarating.

Laço Tayfa

Hüsnü Şenlendirici leads this group of Gypsy musicians from the Aegean Turkish town of Bergama, famous for its bands in which the classic *zurna* and *davul* are coupled with clarinet and snare drum. Hüsnü comes from a long lineage of trumpet and clarinet players, so much so that his family name means "those who celebrate". Laço Tayfa create an exciting fusion of Gypsy styles from Thrace and Asia Minor with the current forms of urban music.

⊙ Bergama Gaydasi
Doublemoon, Turkey
Also released as *Çiftetelli* on the Traditional Crossroads label, this is a collection of classic material from different cultural and musical areas of Turkey – Aegean *zeybek*, central Anatolian folk song, Gypsy wedding tunes – treated with an exploratory attitude which never loses touch with its popular roots. Driving rhythms and extended improvisations on unexpected instruments have made this a very successful album internationally.

Istanbul Jewish Music

Hadass Pal-Yarden

An Israeli singer and musicologist who moved to Istanbul in order to investigate the multifaceted Jewish traditions in Turkey. Her approach is passionate and deeply felt, and her research goes deep into the subject.

⊙ Yahudice
Kalan, Turkey
A labour of love, this is almost a book about Middle Eastern Jewish music with CD attached. The extensive notes in Turkish, English and Hebrew include details on all the printed and recorded sources. The performances reflect a maze of influences all over the eastern Mediterranean, and the finest musicianship. A rare combination of schooled erudition and true musical creation.

Arabesk

Orhan Gencebay

Gencebay was born in Samsun in northern Turkey in 1944 and trained in folk, classical and *sanat* music. He was associated with Arabesk's emergence as a popular genre addressing rural–urban migrant experience. Most of his early recordings accompanied musical films, and most can still be found on either cassette or CD.

⊙ Yalnız Deşilsin
Kervan, Turkey
This 1994 recording demonstrates Gencebay's unflagging and wide-ranging musical curiosity, taking in Middle Eastern, European and American popular and classical genres in a magisterial sweep. His own virtuosic *saz* playing, as ever, is to the fore. Listen out for the thunderous bellydance number "Gencebay Oriyentalı" and mock baroque overture "Nihavent Üvertür".

Müslüm Gürses

Gürses, like many Arabesk singers, is from Adana in the southeast of the country, but he has lived in Istanbul for many years, where he records, makes films and runs a *gazino*. His Arabesk has, for many of his critics, stood as an extreme manifestation of the lugubrious self-pity inherent in the genre, and his fans are drawn from the poorer and younger ranks of Turkey's urban proletariat.

⊙ Senden Vazgeçmem
Elenor Plak
A lush orchestra combining violins, a group of *bağlamas*, and a full "classical" Turkish music band backs Müslüm Baba in this recording of some popular songs from his repertoire, the despairing lyrics delivered with an intense vocal style full of melisma. The arrangements draw freely from European classical music and even country and western, while the tunes include an Azeri folksong and a special rendition of "Haydar, Haydar" with Ali Ekber Çiçek himself on *bağlama*.

İbrahim Tatlıses

Tatlıses' poverty-stricken life in Urfa in the far southeast of the country, his mixed Arab-Kurdish family background and his turbulent domestic situation are a matter of public mythology in Turkey today. His early recordings (many associated with films) alternated traditional folk and Arabesk; many have circulated widely outside Turkey as well.

⭐ **Fosforlu Cevriyem**
Emre, Turkey

This live recording is a rare chance to hear what Arabesk sounds like in the flesh, with some of Tatlıses' all-time favourites ("Beyaz Gül", "Kırmızı Gül", "Fosforlu Cevriyem", "Beyoğlu", "Yeşil Yeşil"), and some superb *uzun hava*. It was a huge hit in Turkey in 1990, and gives some sense of Tatlıses' phenomenal vocal presence.

Pop, Rock and Rap

⭐ **Made in Turkey**
Soulstar, Germany

Compiled by Turkish DJ and Açık Radyo programmer Gülbahar Kültür, this intriguing 2-CD collection from 2005 features a varied choice of Turkish performers, giving a good representation of what the current music scene in Istanbul perceives as relevant: classical and folk music, Anatolian rock, pop, rap, dance and electronica.

Sezen Aksu

Aksu trained in classical music in her native Izmir. She has dominated the world of Turkish pop since the mid-1970s, but her distinctive style emerged later through her collaboration with Onno Tunç. Since the early 1990s she has explored musics outside the Turkish popular mainstream, notably Anatolian folk genres and Balkan music.

⊙ **Deli Kızın Türküsü**
Tempa-Foneks, Turkey

Among the many Aksu albums, this is one of the more endearing, an intimate reading of songs titled after a lyric by Gülten Akın, a famous Turkish poetess. With love ballads, a traditional prayer, a Nazim Hikmet poem set to music by Onno Tunç and a children's rhyme, this 1993 album is a good example of her grasp of the musical trends then current.

⊙ **Işık Doğudan Yükselir/Ex Oriente Lux**
Foneks, Turkey

The release of this album made headline news in Turkey. Despite the hype, it is an intriguing CD, from the overblown orchestral opening (worked out with Onno Tunç) to the intimate and sparse style which characterizes all of Aksu's recent work. It makes playful reference to a variety of urban and rural Turkish genres, some self-consciously "authentic" in spirit, others in a more abstract and allusive style.

Cem Karaca

Born in Bakırköy in Istanbul in 1945, Karaca has been a leading figure in Turkish and "Anatolian" rock through his work with bands such as Apaşlar, Kardaşlar, Moğollar and Dervidan. His work became progressively more radical throughout the 1970s and he left Turkey in 1979, shortly before the military coup. But he returned in 1987, after a big public display of reconciliation with the liberal-rightist regime of Turgut Özal. Whilst (some would argue) his politics have lost their way, his music has lost none of its jagged intensity and literary intelligence.

⭐ **Cemaz ül-Evvel**
Kalan, Turkey

This is a retrospective of all of Karaca's major work with his early groups, particularly Apaşlar and Kardaşlar, and thus traces his experiments through a variety of Western pop and rock genres, and his emerging political radicalism. The story of Turkish highbrow rock, in its entirety, on one disc.

Ahmet Kaya

Since the early 1980s, Kaya has been one of the main figures associated with so-called "independent" (*özgün*) music, a guitar-oriented genre with radical aspirations, and much reference to indigenous traditional musics (especially that of the *saz*). Kaya is a Kurdish Jacques Brel, and the blend of *saz* and guitar with his deep, melancholy voice and political lyrics has an enduring appeal amongst many of the Turkish and Kurdish intelligentsia to this day.

⊙ **An Gelir**
Taç, Turkey

Plangent *saz* and up-tempo Halay dance numbers, radical in gesture, but social-realist Weltschmerz in content. Nothing that Kaya did subsequently lived up to the enormous vitality and lyricism of this early album.

Zülfü Livaneli

Livaneli is a composer, *saz* player and vocalist, born in the eastern Black Sea region. As a leftist intellectual he spent several years in exile in Sweden where he hooked up with the like-minded Greek composer Mikis Theodorakis. Since his return to Turkey he has been an important opinion maker and even ran for mayor of Istanbul. Recently he's been through a New Age phase, but his 1998 album *Nefesim nefesime* (Breath to Breath) showed him back on better form.

⭐ **Maria Farandouri Söylüyor**
Raks, Turkey

From the early 1980s, this is one of the great Turkish albums of all time: Maria Farandouri sings Livaneli. The beautiful melodies are exquisitely sung in fine arrangements; the songs are in Greek and Turkish, but are just as appealing if you understand neither.

Sultana

The even rhythm of the Turkish language suits rapping admirably, and on the scene – centred on Istanbul – there's a healthy share of female rappers such as Sultana.

⊙ **Çerkez Kız**
Doublemoon, Turkey

The best tracks reach back to the political traditions of folk music, but the scandal here was the song "The Bird Can't Fly" which criticized the performance of a lover who spends his energies outside the relationship – some Turkish males weren't too happy about it. The album stands out for the vocal performance and the energetic backing tracks.

Yeni Türkü

The group's name means "new song" and betrays the influence of South American groups like Inti Illimani and Greek musicians like Manos Laizos. Since the late 1970s their music has been characterized by fine instrumental arrangements featuring traditional Turkish instruments. The key musicians have been Derya Köroşlu (lead vocal and *saz*), Murat Buket (vocals and *ud*) and Selim Atakan (keyboard and guitar), but the group has now reformed with new members under Köröşlu. They have many excellent releases on BMG.

⊙ **Her Dem Yeni [New Every Time]**
BMG, Turkey

The greatest hits album with twenty of their songs. Excellent listening even if you don't speak a word of Turkish.

1 **SABA TAKSIM Aka Gündüz Kutbay and Niyazi Sayin** from *Masters of Turkish Music: Ney*
A rare example of *taksim* – improvised prelude – for two instruments, this recording allows you to hear side by side two masters of the *ney*.

2 **BAKMIYOR ÇEŞM-I SIYAH FERYADE Hamiyet Yüceses** from *Makber*
The agile but powerful voice of Yüceses, combining a classic tune with an extended vocal improvisation (*gazel*). A supreme example of classical Turkish music in its maturity.

3 **AHESTE ÇEK KÜREKLERI Münir Nurettin Selçuk** from *Bir Özlemdir*
This song demonstrates his deep knowledge of tradition and his ability to improvise vocal lines on a specific *makam*.

4 **HAYDAR HAYDAR Ali Ekber Çiçek** from *Haydar Haydar*
A song that was crucial in the establishment of the new "folk" scene – an initimate dialogue between voice and instrument.

5 **AGIT Sabahat Akkiraz** from *Konserler*
Among the current crop of Alevi-influenced singers Akkiraz stands out for her open approach. The acoustic accompaniment showcases her voice.

6 **KANTE KADIFE Hadass Pal-Yarden** from *Yahudice*
A Turkish melody – most probably from Urfa – which migrated all over the Mediterranean as love ballad, religious hymn and drinking song, acquiring words for all these purposes.

7 **ZAHID BIZI TAN EYLEME Erkan Oğur** from *Hiç*
This *nefes* (religious hymn from the Bektaşi Sufi order) in *Uşşak* mode features Oğur's liquid style on the small *kopuz* lute.

8 **ZIKIR Okay Temiz** from *Zikir*
The breathy sound of *ney* player Aka Gündüz Kutbay improvising over the rhythmic variations of Okay Temiz and a funky-jazz arrangement.

9 **ZÜLÜF Laço Tayfa with Kibariye** from *Hicaz Dolap*
Demonstrating the intricate connections within Turkish music, the Gypsy-fusion group from Bergama updates the classic song by Neşet Ertaş with vocalist and TV celebrity Kibariye.

10 **KÖROĞLU Grup Çığ** from *Mevsim*
The classic epic song in a rendition pairing the voice and *bağlama* of Musa Eroğlu with the electric guitars of young Ankara musicians Grup Çığ. Unlikely and fascinating.

Ethno-jazz

Burhan Öçal

This *darbuka* virtuoso doubles on stringed instruments and his projects are branching out from a celebration of Gypsy and *fasıl* traditions to fusion with rock-jazz.

⭐ **Groove alla Turca**
Doublemoon, Turkey
Öçal joins forces with ex-Ornette Coleman electric bassist Jamaladeen Tacuma, creating an exciting mix with his Istanbul ensemble and a group of adventurous jazzmen including trumpet supremo Jack Walrath. Natacha Atlas is the guest vocalist on some of the tracks.

Okay Temiz

With Don Cherry and Mongezi Feza, Okay Temiz was one of the early proponents of World Music, including in his percussion set not only Turkish drums and gongs but his own electrified version of *berimbau*.

⊙ **Zikir**
Ada, Turkey
One of the most successful fusions of jazz and Turkish music. The international group assembled by Temiz includes Aka Gündüz Kutbay on *ney*, D.D. Gouirand on soprano, Onno Tunç on bass, and Tuna Ötenel on piano.

PALM WORLD VOICES

SEE THE WORLD, HEAR THE WORLD, FEEL THE WORLD

Palm World Voices presents a series of speciality multimedia collections, inviting music lovers to completely immerse themselves in the vibrant imagery, history, culture, and terrain of musically rich areas of the globe.

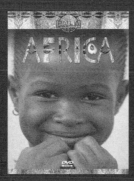

AFRICA
A continent rich in musical history, explored through a combination of classic and contemporary tracks with unique imagery of Africans at work, play and celebration

VEDIC PATH
An exploration of the magical Indian Sub-Continent through a mesmerising and unprecedented convergence of music, photography and film

BAABA MAAL
A gift set combining classic tracks from the Senegalese superstar with a compelling documentary film that traces his journey from the village of Podor near the Mauritanian border to a successful international recording career

MANDELA
The original film and soundtrack to the Oscar-nominated documentary, capturing the incredible spirit of one of the world's most fascinating people

SPIRIT
A collection of tranquil and meditative sounds from the Mediterranean Basin and Middle East, illustrated with atmospheric imagery from this often misunderstood region

BRAZIL (Coming Soon)
An exquisite package showcasing musical contributions from both classic and contemporary artists from a country seductive in both sound and landscape

Each Deluxe Multimedia Gift Set Contains:

www.palmworldvoices.com

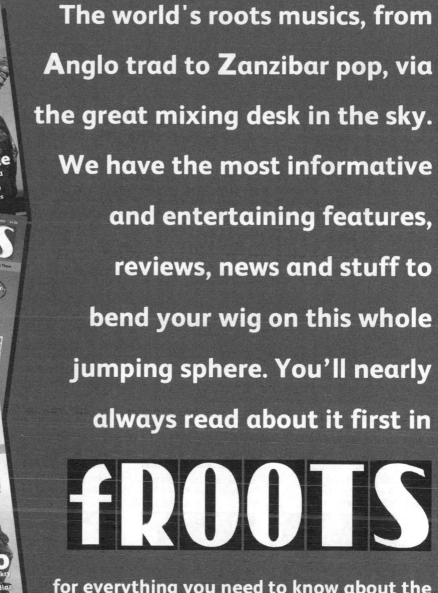

BBC RADIO 3
Passionate about world music

BBC RADIO

90-93 FM

BBC Radio 3 brings you the finest music from around the globe all year round.

Every year

The BBC Radio 3 Awards for World Music recognises and celebrates the very best in world music.

BBC Radio 3 broadcasts exclusively from WOMAD.

Every week

LATE JUNCTION - Monday to Thursday, 10.15pm

WORLD ROUTES - Saturday, 3pm

ANDY KERSHAW - Sunday, 10.15pm

Every day

For information on the world of music that BBC Radio 3 can bring you and to listen at your leisure go to bbc.co.uk/radio3

bbc.co.uk/radio3

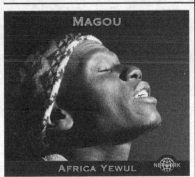

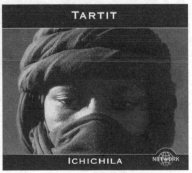

BEAUTIFUL TO LOOK AT

REALV

WORLD

WONDERFUL TO HEAR

REALWORLD RECORDS
THE SOUNDS OUR PLANET MAKES

WWW.REALWORLDRECORDS.COM

Listen Up!

"You may be used to the Rough Guide series being comprehensive, but nothing will prepare you for the exhaustive Rough Guide to World Music . . . one of our books of the year."
Sunday Times, London

ROUGH GUIDE MUSIC TITLES

Bob Dylan • The Beatles • Classical Music • Elvis • Frank Sinatra
Heavy Metal • Hip-Hop • iPods, iTunes & music online • Jazz
Book of Playlists • Opera • Pink Floyd • Punk • Reggae • Rock
The Rolling Stones • Soul and R&B • World Music Vol 1 & 2

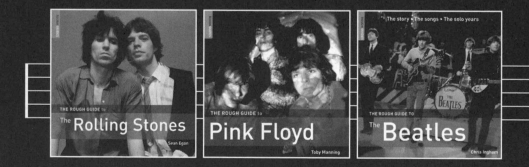

BROADEN YOUR HORIZONS

Index

A

Aakef, Tarek 476
Aatabou (Aâtabu), Najat 257, 262, 476
Aatigui, Aarab 251
Aba Shante 366
Ababio, Desmond 133
Abacı, Muazzez 606
Abadi, Ibrahim al- 398
Abafana Baseqhudeni 358
Abafana Bentutuko 358
Abate, Amelmal 110
Abatte 545
Abba, Cheikh ould 242
Abba, Dimi mint 242, 245
Abba, Jheich ould 242
Abba, Sidaty ould 241, 243
Abboud, Mihera bint 401
Abdal, Pir Sultan 598
Abdallah 199
Abdallah, Salum 420
Abdalwahab, Mohamed 255
Abdel Aziz el Mubarak Orchestra 399, 406
Abdel Gadir Salim's Merdoum Kings 399
Abdeletif, Alamin 104
Abdelkrim 252
Abdelli 23
Abdelmoghit, El Hadj 255
Abdelrahim, Osman 104
Abdel-Reheem, Shaaban 500, 501
Abd-el-Wahhab, Mohamed 410
Abdessamad, Sheikh Abdelbas-set 465
Abdoul Kabir & the Goumbe Goumbe Band 329
Abdu, Mohammed 511, 515
Abdulkareem, Idris 299
Abdullah, Abdul Majeed 511, 516

Abdullat, Omar 560, 562
Abeid Ba-Rajab, Shaib 410
Abeni, Queen Salawa 295
Abessolo, Alexis 121
Abeti 36
Abifuna, Tebifanana 432
Abioro, Chief 291
Abladei 128
Aboud Abdul, al- 476
Abou-Khalil, Rabih 576, 577
Abovian, Benik 486
Abrio, Augusto 70
Abua people 288
Abubakar, Tariq 405
Abyssinia Band 113
Abyssinia Infinite 114
Accentus 554
accordion 53, 201
Accra Orchestra 124
Acheampong, Nana 129
Achigo Stars 423
Achtouk, Raïs Lhoucine 251
Ackah, Jewel 129, 133
Açoreano 324
Adaweyah, Ahmed 500, 501
Addy, Mustapha Tettey 130, 134
Addy, Obo 130
Ade, King Sunny 296, 288, 290, 301
Adekunle, Prince 290
Adeniji "Heavy Wind" 298
Adeniyi, Kunle 298
Adepoju, Sikiru 298
Adewale, Segun 290
Adewale, Shina 290
Adjekum, Appiah 125
Adofo, J.A. 126, 133
Adonai Pentecostal Singers 442
Adu, Kofi 129
Adu, Sade 298
Adugna, Essoubalew 113
Afewerki, Abraham 105, 106

Africa Livre 156
Africa Musique 48
Africa No. 1 119
African All Stars 79
African Brothers 126
African Brothers 128
African Dope Records 370
African Express Band 212
African Fiesta 75, 77
African Gospel Acapella 189, 191
African Heroes 126, 133
African Inkspots 379
African Jazz 75, 77, 353
African Jazz & Variety 379
African Jazz Pioneers 383
African Music Society 394
African Revolutions Band 422
African Shrine 296
African Songs label 291
African Stars Band "Twanga Pepeta" 422
African Swingsters 378
Africando 36, 337, 340
Afrigo Band 431, 433
Afrika Revenge 455
Afrikan Show Boys 132
Afrikaner music 363
Afrisa 77
Afro, Teddy 111
Afro-beat 296
Afro-Celt Sound System 334
Afrodesia 291
afroma 212
Afro-Nationals 347, 348
Afro-Salseros de Senegal, Los 341
Afrosound 111
Afro-Succès 118
Afro-zouk 120
Aga, Alemu 112
Agbafoi Bukom 128
Agoromma, Adadam 133
Agorsor's Cultural Ensemble 132

Aguado, Berta 555
Ahenfo Band 130
ahidus 249
Ahlam 258, 512, 516
Ahmad, Zakaria 466, 470
Ahmadinejad, Mahmoud 527
Ahmed, Fethi Baba 13
Ahmed, Mahmoud 109, 110, 114
Ahmed, Rachid Baba 14, 17
Ahmed, Sherhabeel 403
ahouache 249
Aşık music 597
Aina 206
Aingo, George William 124
Air Fiesta 175
Aisha Kandisha's Jarring Effects
    257, 262, 477, 479
Aissar, Raïs M'Barek 251
Aissawa 254
Aïwa 478, 479
Ajaj, Nancy 402
Ajayi, Kunle 299
Aje, Alhaja Asanat Ejire Omo 295
Ajram, Nancy 502, 575, 577
Aka Kora, Bil 48, 50
Aka people 305
Akan Trio 126
Akarsu, Muhlis 598
Akatakyie 131
Akbal, Nilüfar 569
Akberov, Djanali 492
Akendengué, Pierre 118, 119,
    120, 121
Akiwumi, Diana 130
Akkale, Belkis 596, 609
Akkiraz, Sabahat 596, 609
Akli D 24, 25
Aksu, Sezen 606, 607, 614
Akyürek, Umut 600
al'Aïta 255
Âla, al- 251
Alade, Art 296
Aladokun, Rasaki 298
Alage, Jose 270
Alaji Frempong's Cubanos Fiesta
    126
Alake, Alhaja Chief Batile 295
Alakpéhanhou 39
Alal, Nayim 241
Alama, Ragheb 502, 575, 577
Alamu, Osman 399
Alariwo of Africa 297
Alaska 368, 371
Alaskar, Aşiq 490
Alayev Family 542
Alberstein, Chava 540, 541, 545
Alcalay, Liliana Treves 555
Aldik, Ali 592, 593
Alevi music 597, 598

Alevi-Bektasi Sufis 602
Alexandra All Stars 378
Alexandre, Bill 76
Algazi, Rabbi Isaac (Yitzhak) 556
Algazi, Yitzhak 553
Algeria (Kabylia) 22–26
Algeria (Rai) 5–21
Alhabib, Ibrahim Ag 282
Alhambra 555
Alhinho, Tété 68, 70
Ali, Farida Mohammed 534, 537
Ali, Khaled Mohammed 538
Ali, Mohammed 466
Ali, Mwanahawa 413
Alia Musica 554
Alice, Maria 65, 69
Aliyen, Mennina mint 242
Alizadeh Ensemble 529
Alizadeh, Hossein 485, 521, 522,
    528, 529
All Mighty 95
Allam, Djamel 23
Alleluya Band, The 214, 215
Allen, Arkin 478
Allen, Tony 298, 302
Almeida, Bluecky d' 37
Alnar, Hasan Ferit 603
al-Nasser, Tareq al- 560, 562
Alpha Music Shop 113
Alpha Waves 133
Altramar 555
Amado, Tony 31
Amadodana Ase Wesile 390
Amadou & Mariam 220, 234
Amala 297
Amampondo 371, 384
Amân, Mohammed 516
Amar, Jo 553
Amar, Mostafa 501
Amarfio, Sol 128
Amartichitt, Deye ould 243
Amartichitt, Ooleya mint 243, 245
Amatshitshi 358
Amayenge 439, 442
Amazones de Guinée, Les 142
Ambassadeurs du Motel, Les 226,
    228
Ambassel Music Shop 113
Amechi, Stephen 292
Amel, Latifa 255
Amenzou, Ahmed 253
Amenzou, Mohammed 253
Amin, Mohammed el 400, 405
Amina 411, 415
Amir, Kat Kut el- 501
Amir, Salim Ali 164, 168
Amirov, Fikrat 492
Amougou, Richard 57
Amour, Papa I' 164

Ampoumah 125
Ampoumah, T.O. "Jazz" 125
Anassua Jazz de Parakou 36
Anatolia 599
Anatolian rock 606
Andalibi, Jamshid 521
Andalous orchestras 251, 252
Andalusi de Tanger, Orquesta 263
Andon, Lavtaci 599
André, David 167
Androy, Vilon' 204, 206, 210
Andy 527
Angeles, Los 525
Angeles, Victoria de los 554
Angelo 95, 96
Anges Noires, Les 54
Angola 27–34
Angusha Band 179
Anjouan 164
Anka, Hadj Mohamed el 7
Ankere, Gual 106
Annabi, Amina 476, 479
Annusur 194
Anouar, Cheb 18
Ansah, Bob 126
Antibalas 297
António, Chico 266, 269, 270
Antsaly, Ny 200
Antwi, Kojo 130
Anwar, Mahmud 537
Aoreste, Sarah 555
apala 293
Apartment 22 478
Apollo 222
Appianing 125
Appleseed 366
Appollo people 92, 147
Aqili, Shadmehr 527
Arab World/Egypt (Classical)
    463–474
Araba, J.O. 290
Arabesque 475–480
Arabesque Moderne 477
Araibi, Hassan 195
Araimi, Salem al- 515
Araújo, Terezinha 68
Arboleras 556
Arcadius, John 37
Archach 256
Ardiess Posse 37
ardin 241
Arfawi, Latifa al- 502
Argan 258
Argov, Sasha 540
Argov, Zohar 542
Ari, Mosh Ben 544, 546
Arian 527, 530
Ariç, Nizamettin 569
Ariya Niteclub 296

Armede, Mary 110
Armenia 481–488
Armenian Kurdistan 567
Armenian Navy Band 484, 486
Armenian-Iranian Traditional Music
    Ensemble, Mihr 483
Army Squad 31
Army Strings, The 214
Aroeste, Sarah 556
Arom, Simha 310
Arssen, Mr 271
Art's Place 296
Arthur 366
Asafo-Agyei, Herman 129
Asante, Okyefema 130
Asante, Okyerema 133
Asare, Kwame 124, 125
Ashalay, Naa 132
Ashantis, The 175
Ashiedu Keteke 128
Ashiqeen, al- 582
Ashitey Jr, Nii Tei 132
ashoughs 484
aşık 597
Aşiq bard tradition 490
Aşkın, Cihat 603
Asmahan 468, 472, 593
Asmine Bande 164
as-Saadi, Hamid 534
as-Safi, Wodya 468
Assal, Salma Al 401, 405
Assar, Ali Reza 527, 530
Assefa, Tigist 113
assiko 53, 55
Assyrians 535
Astatqé, Mulatu 110, 114
Atari, Gali 542
Atatürk, Kemal 596
Athamy, Hussein al- 534
Atlan, Françoise 555, 556
Atlas, Natacha 477, 479, 502, 503
Atomic Advantage 420, 425
Atrache, Farid el- 468, 472, 593
Atraf 542
at-Tablawi, Sheikh Muhammad
    Mahmoud 465
Attar, Bachir 257, 477
Attar, Osama al- 515
Attieh, Rouwayda 591, 593
Attisso, Barthelemy 330
Atuwonuwu, Buchi 299
Atzmon, Gilad 545
Aures, Markunda 24
autoharp 360
Avis, Jeremy 311
Avraham, Bustan 586
Awa, Sid Ahmed Bekaye ould 242
Awad, Ibrahim 399
Awadi, Didier 338

Aweke, Aster 109, 110, 114
Axe Studios 291
Axim Trio 126
Ayal Mama 410
Ayalew Music Shop 113
Ayangil, Ruhi 599
Aydat 243
Ayi Soba, King 132
Ayinla, Kollington 294, 302
Ayissi, Chantal 57, 59
Ayla, Safiye 600
Aynur 569, 603, 609
Ayu people 290
Ayuba, Adewale 294
Azem, Slimane 23
Azerbaijan 489–494
Azibekian, Zaven 486
Aziza-A 478, 608
azmaris 111, 112
Azza 405
Azzdine 477

B

B, Jimmy (James Bangura) 347,
    349
B.A.N.T.U. 299
B'Iwaku, Abakobwa 317
B-29s, The 70
Ba, Djombolo 244
Baah, Papa 125
Baazra, Shekan 564
Baba 2010 297
Baba Zula 606
Baba, Ali 57
Baba, Granmoun 165
Babata 201
Babloom 414
Baby, Ras Natty 165
Babylon Festival 536
Babylonian Heritage Centre 535
Bacanos, Yorgo 599
Bachitta de Mascara, Cheikha 10
Backos 278, 279
Baco 164
Bada people 290
Badalian, Hovhaness 484
Badarou, Wally 36
Badema National 226
Badenya Les Frères Coulibaly 48,
    51
Badou, Jheich ould 243
Badwan, Qamar 560
Baffour, Kyerematen 125
Baga people 143
Bagayogo, Issa 233, 234

bağlama 596
Bahari, Asghar Ali 526
Bahrain 512
Bahula, Julian 369
Baitsile, Tsilo 45
Bajdoub, Hadj Mohammed 252
Baka Beyond 309, 310, 311
Baka Gbine, Orchestre 311
Baka people 57, 305
Bakgatla people 44
Bakheit, Abu Araki al- 401
Bakhtiari 524, 525
Bakirgian, Garbis 484
bakou 331
Bakshi of Khorasan 524
Baktagir, Göksel 599
Bakustik 493
Bala, Zwai 381
balaadi 561
balaban 564
Balabil 401
balafon 48, 53, 118, 134
Balete people 44
Balkan Beat Box 546
Balla et ses Balladins 142, 143, 149
Ballaké, Amadou 48
Ballet Djoliba 138, 143
Ballet Inganzo 314, 319
Ballet of Rwanda, National 314
Ballets Africains, Les 137, 138, 140,
    143, 149
Balogun, C.A. 290
Balogun, Lady 290
Baloi, Gito 271, 272
Baloyi, Francisco 361
Baluchistan 525
Balzac, Prince 49
Bambino, Sekouba (Diabaté) 137,
    141, 145, 146, 150
Bamogo, Jean-Claude 49
Bana 65, 69, 71
Bana Kadori 176
Bana Maquis 422, 427
Bana Ngenge 178
Bana OK 82
Banai, Ehud 542
Banai, Me'ir 542
Banda Azul 270
Banda Maravilha 28, 31, 32
Banda, Lucius 214, 216
Banda, Paul 214, 216
Banda, Rikki 438
Banda, Robson 451
Bangaladish, Hassouna 405
Bangura, Ansumana 347
Bangura, Ansumana 349
Bangura, James (Jimmy B) 347
Baniel, Nana ad 81
banjo 353

Bannerman, Alfred 130
Bannerman, Alfred Kari 129
Bantous de la Capitale 77, 85
Bantowbol 57
Bantu Group 423
Bantu Radio 355
Bantu-speaking people 352
Baobab Club 330
Baobab, Orchestra 329, 330, 339, 342
Baoulé people 92
Baqbou, Mustapha 254, 256
Bar, Essev 544, 547
Bar, Shlomo 543
Barad 527
Baranyanka, Eric 318
Barbarity 258
Barghouti, Thaer 583
Bari, Aliu 159
Baria, Yemane 105
Baro, Fodé 137, 144
Baro, Ronnie 337
Baroudi, Hamid 477
Barouh, Pierre 119
Barrister, Sikiru Ayinde 294, 296, 298, 302
Barrister, Wasiu Ayinde 294
Barros, Maria de 71
Barry 258
Barry, Amadou 148
Bartók, Béla 24
Barura Express 452
Basa-Basa 128
Basalama, Aliy Salum 413
Basement Platform 370
Bashier, Hussein 498
Bashir, Jamil 536
Bashir, Khidir 403
Bashir, Munir 535, 536, 538
Bashir, Omar 536
Basotho Dihoba 360
Bass, Kotto 57, 59
Bassline club 383
Bastos, Waldemar 29, 30, 31, 32
Batchiellilys, Annie-Flore 120, 121
Batlokwa people 44
Batonga Crew 449
Batswana people 44
batuco 63, 67
Bau 69, 71
Bawurera 164
Bax, Bery 493
Bayat, Zohreh 522
Bayete 372, 383
Bayler, Aygun 492
Bazanca, La 554
Bazmaouen, Raïs Ahmed 251
Beats , Black 127
Bébé, Granmoun 165

Bebey, Francis 53, 54, 59
Bedjil, Botango 179
Bedouin 559–562
Bedouin songs 536
Bekamby 200
Bekele, Bezunesh 110
Bekele, Hirut 110
Bekele, Tigist 111
Bekkas, Majid 258
Bekwara people 288
Bel, Mbilia 80
Bel, Mbilia 86
Belafonte, Harry 58, 380
Belaid, Hadj 251
Belarbi, Mohammed 10
Belkhayat, Abdelhadi 255
Bell, Nyanka 96
Bella Bella 80
Bella people 49
Bella, Uta 57
Belle Lumière 164
Bellow, Bella 40
belly-dancing 499, 602, 604
Bembeya Jazz 137, 141, 142, 143, 149, 155
Bembo, Gaby Lita 79, 86
Ben, Zehava 542, 546
Benayun, Amir 542, 546
Benchenet, Houari 13
Bendaoud, Djelloul 10
Bend-skin 57
Benfissa 12
benga 173, 175, 198
Bengi Trio 597
Benin & Togo 35–42
Benin people 288
Bennani, Khalid 255
Benros, Gardenia 65, 70
Bensaïd, Muhammad 253
Bensari, Larbi 6
Bensmir, Cheikh Hachemi 7
Benson, Bobby 292, 296
Benson, George 57
Beraki, Tséhaytu 105, 106, 107
Berber music 22–26, 249–264
Berber, Chleuh 251
Beriberi people 281
Bernard, Dikoume 55
Berrahal, Muhammad 253
Bessis, Sandra 555
Bessoso 101
Best, Adane 131
bey, ambasse 53
Bey, Hacı Arif 599
Bey, Tanburi Cemil 599
Beyene, Girma 109
Bhalo, Juma 411
Bhengu, John 361
Bhojpuri Boys 165

bhor 240
Bhundu Boys, The 451, 456
Bidan people 241
Bidaoui, Ahmed 255
Bidaoui, Bouchaïb el 255
Bidawia, Khadija el 255
Bidinte 157, 159
Big Beats 128
Big Gold Six Band 437
Big Pin 183
Biggy, Okatch 175
Bikindi, Simon 317
Bikoko, Jean 55
bikutsi 55
Bilac, Olavo 66
Bilal, Sidi 254
Bilé, Moni 55, 59
Bilenge Musica 179
Bill, Soum 98
Billé, Didier 94
Bilong, Conti 53
Bina, Sima 522, 524, 530
Binesh-Pajouh, Shahkar 527
bira 446
Birkin, Jane 477
Birra, Ali 110
Bissa people 49
Bisso na Bisso 85, 86
Bitasika 179
Bitonga people 266
Biyouma 477
Black Cabs, The 527
Black Daps 283
Black Mambazo 356, 357
Black Missionaries 214, 216
Black Muntu 441
Black Sea Turks 597
Black So Man 48, 49
Black Spirits, The 449
Black Star Musical Club 414
Black Stars 403
Black Styl 55
Black Umfolosi 454, 456
Black Velvet 542
Blakky 299
Blay-Ambulley, Gyedu 133
Blemabii 128
Blk Sunshine 215
Blondy, Alpha 92, 94, 96, 130
bloor 564
Blue Notes, The 382, 385
BMG44 338
Bnet Marrakech 16, 251, 262
Boana, Shao 206
Bobo people 49
Bobo, Paa 126
Bocoum, Afel 234
Bodo 204, 206
Boetie & Janice 277

Bokosi, Malume 213
Bolat, Latif 611
bolel 113
Boma Liwanza 178
Bona, Richard 53, 57, 58, 59
Bonchaka, Terry 131
Bonga 29, 31, 32
bongo flava 423, 424
Bongo Maffin 366, 371
Bongo people 305
Bongo, Alain 120
Bongo, Albert Bernard 120
Bonsu, Osei 125
Boo! 363
Booker T 455
Boom Shaka 366
Boombaya 128
Bopape, Rupert 354
Bori, Saadou 283, 284
Borochov, Israel 544
Bosman, Gloria 384
Botswana 43–46
Bouboul 203
Bouger-Musica International 179
Bouhadanna, Albert 259
Bourgogne, Moustapha 255
Bouskila, Shimon 542
Bouteldja, Belkacem 11
Boutella, Safy 476
Boven, Kas 50
Boyoyo Boys 358
Boys, The 527
Boyz of Butuburam, The 190, 191
Boziana, Bozi 79, 86
bozlak 598
Brahim, Khaled 12
Brako, Ben 129
Brand, Dollar 380
Brass Band, Gangbe 40
brass-band music 124
Brasse Vannie Kaap 369
Bridges, Bles 363
Briha, Rachid 258
Brillant, Ekambi 53
Bror 243
brosca 154
Brotherhood of Breath 382
Brothers Keepers 298
Brothers of Peace 368, 371
Brothers, Kafala 29
Brothers, Monrovia 189
Brou Félix, Anoman 92
Broulaye Sidibé , Allata 236
Brown Sugar 45
Brown, Andy 445, 455
Brown, James 79, 120, 347
broxa 154
Brozman, Bob 166
Bruce, King 127

Brulaye Sidibé, Allata 232
bubblegum music 364, 365
Bubi people 100
Buddha Bar 477
Buesh, Abdalla Saleh 410
Buika, Concha 101
Buk-Bak 131
Buk-Lu, Baron Ya 101, 102
Bukom 128
Bulawayo 453
Bulimundo 66
Bulu-bulu, Hanan 401
Bunzus 128
Bura'i, Awlad al- 405
burgher highlife 129
Burity, Carlos 31
Burlty, Carlos 33
Burkina Faso 47–51
Burma Jokers 126
Burroghr, Ali 512
Burstein, Mike 540
Burundi 313–320
Busheme 243
Bustan Abraham 544, 546
Buti Kubwa 425
Büyükburç, Erol 606
Bwaba 49
Bwiti religious music 118
Byrne, David 30, 476
Byron, Albert 317

C

C, Ray 424
Cabaço, André 271
Cabaço, João 269
Cabo Verde Show 65, 69
CAC (Christ Apostolic Church) 297
Cairo 466
Calendar, Ebenezer 346
Caluza, Reuben 371
calypso 127
Camara, Aboubacar Demba 141
Camara, Sayon 146
Camaroes, Los 56
Camayenne Sofa 143
Cameroon 52–61
Campbell, Ambrose 292, 298
Canada 129
Canar, Shani Ben 540, 544, 546
Cannibals, The 364
Canonge, Mario 58
Canta, Ballou 86
Cantata 126
Cape Coast Sugar Babies, The 124
Cape Province 378

Cape Verde 62–73
Cape Verdean Serenaders, The 70
Capo-Sound, Le 119
Carlito 83
Carlo Mombelli's Abstractions 383
Carlo Mombelli's Prisoners of
    Strange 384
Carlos, Zé 155, 156, 159
Carmichael, Stokely 380
Carril, Angel 554
Carstens, Nico 363
Cartel 608
Casamance region 336
Cassiya 165, 169
Castle Lager Big Band, The 386
Castro 131
Castro, Urbano de 29
cavacha rhythm 172
Cavaquim, Frank 65
cavaquinho 64
CDs 291
Cele 378
Cele, Willard 355
Çelebi, Ekrem 598
Çelik 608
Cemal, Kemani 612
CFPM (Centre for Musical Training
    and Promotion) 281
chaabi 7, 255
Chaheb, Lem 476
Chaka Chaka, Yvonne 364, 371
Chalamanda, Nathan 215, 216
Chali, Kris 439, 442
Challe, Claude 477
Chameleon 431
Chameleone 433
chamonge guitar 172
Chamou, M'toro 165, 168
Chantre, Teófilo 66
Chaoui people 24
Charamba, Charles 453
Charamba, Mai 453
chatta 564
Chauke, Thomas 362
Cheb Khaled 12, 14, 19, 476
Cheb Mami 14, 20
Cheb Mimoun 258
Cheb Sahraoui 18
Chebli 164, 168
Chechamba, Wyndham 214
Chege, Sam 184
Chehade Brothers, The 586
cheikhas 8
Chekara, Abdesadak 252
Chemical Brothers, The 476
Chemirani, Trio 529
Chenkula, Maua 424
Cher 482
Cherifa 23

Cherry, Neneh 333
Chewa people 213
Chewke, Hassan 534
Chhadeh, Abdullah 590, 591, 593
Chibadura, John 452, 453, 456
Chibite 425
Chicago 300
Chicago, Roy 292
Chicco (Sello Twala) 364, 365, 372
Chidzanja, Nankhoma 215
Chidzanja, Peter 216
Chief Chipoka Band, The 214
Chifre Preto 156
Chigamba, Tute 447
Chighaly, Jheich ould 243
Chighaly, Mohammed ould 243
Chihabi, Abou 164, 168
Chikuni Brothers, The 212
Chimbetu, Simon "Chopper" 445, 452
Chimbini, Phillipo 442
Chimedza, Albert 447
Chimombo, Overton 216
chimurenga 447
Chimvu Jazz 212, 217
Chinx, Comrade 448
Chiquitin 100
Chiquito 270
chirokbej 564
Chishala, PK 439
Chiskop 367
Chitipi Sounds 212
Chitsondzo, Roberto 270
Chiweshe, Ashton "Sugar" 449
Chiweshe, Stella 447, 456
Choc Stars 86
Chongo, Zaida 271
Chonguiça, Moreira 269
Chopi people 266
Choueikh, Mohammed ould Ded-
  dah ould 242
Choueikh, Nema mint 246
Christafari 299
Chtouki, Raïs Brahim 251
Chucunene 100
Chukwuma, Ali 293
Çiçek, Ali Ekber 596, 609
çifte telli 597
Çınar, Feyzullah 598
Çingene 602
Cissoko, Ba 137, 148, 150
Cissoko, Mammadou Lakras 146
Cissoko, Soundioulou 336
City Boys 126
Clash, The 476
Clegg, Johnny 363
Clement, Mily 200
Clotaire K 478, 576, 577
Club Mannenberg 383

Cobiana Djazz 155, 160
Coetzee, Basil 382
Coeurs Brisé, Les 85
Coffee House, The 111
Coffi Akoha, Ambroise 37
Cohen, Judith 555
coladeira 63, 65
Cold Castle National Jazz Festival
  380
Cole, Bob 126
Cole, Olofemi ('Doctor Oloh') Israel
  346
Cole, Peter 190
Coleman, Jaz 476, 479
Color Blu 455
Comöé, Soeurs 92
Comoros Islands 164
Conceição, Orlando da 269
concert parties 124, 126, 127
concertina 353
Condé, Emile 141
Confiance Jazz 56
Congo 74–90
Congolese OS Africa Band 178
Congolese rumba 53, 75, 76, 118,
  178, 437, 452
Cooder, Ry 225
Cool Crooners 455
Coopé, Maio 157
Coptic Christians 497
Copts 497
Cordas do Sol 71
Cori people 290
Corlea 381
Corneille 317, 319
Costa, Manecas 157, 158, 160
Côte d'Ivoire 91–98
Coupé-décalé 95
Cradick, Martin 309
Crann 120
cranning 121
Crazy GK 424
Crentsil, A.B. 129
Creole Sextet, The 70
Creole Vagabonds 70
Cuban Marimba 420
Culture Musical Club 409, 412, 415
Culture T 453
Cut'n'run 95
Cuttayen, Bam 165

D

D, Carlou 339
D'ablo, Pablo 277
d'Afrique, Omidi 277

D'Gary 201
D'Gary 208
d'Novas, Manuel 63
d'Oro, Denti 67
D'zirya, Fadila 7
Da De-Plow-MaTZ 423
Daande Lenol 334
Daara J 338, 340
Daasebre 131
Dabaghyan, Gevorg 484, 486
Dabany, Josephine 120
Dabany, Patience 120, 121
Dabiré, Gabin 48, 50
dabke 574, 581
Daccache, Laure 473
Dada de Fort Dauphin 204, 206
Dadasova, Brilliant 493
Daddy Zemus 441
Dadzie, Osofo 126
daf 564
Dagara people 49
Dagnon, Bako 221
Dahari, Yosefa 257
Dairo, I.K. 290, 291, 296, 297, 301
Dairo, Paul 291
Dakar All Stars 339
Dalal, Muhammed Qadri 590, 593
Dalal, Yair 535, 542, 543, 547
dalauna 581
Dama 198
Damara punch 277
Damari, Shoshana 540
Damba, Fanta 221, 226
Dambo de La Costa 100
Damciri, Hadj Mohammed 251
Damisa, Segun 298
Dan Gourmou, Prix 281
Dan people 92
Dana, Simphiwe 367, 372
dances 564
danço-congo 322
Dangana 283
Dania 477
Danialou, Sagbohan 36, 39
Dante, Alassane 281
Daoud, Salem 535
Dar, Yanar 494
Darhem, Mohammed 256
Dark City Sisters 357
Darko, George 129
Darwîsh, Sayed 468, 473
Dashiki 45
Dastan Ensemble 528
Daughters of Glorious Jesus 130
Daves, Yinka 300
Dawuni, Rocky 130
Daz Nundaz 423
DDC Mlimani Park Orchestra 420
de Mingongo, Luciana 86

Deaf Ears, The 212
Debaba 83
Debebe, Neway 110
Deborah 390
Decca, Ben 55
Dechaud 77
Decibel 455
DeCoque, Eugene 298
DeCoque, Oliver 293
Dede Korkut Ensemble 493
Dede, Amekye 130, 133
Dede, Mercan 601, 602, 611
Dedesse 200
Dee, Ragga 435
DeeDee's Disco 402
Deep Forest 312
Deep Horizon 449
Défense d'Ivoire Groupe 93
Degg J Force 3 149
Dekokaye, Didier 121
Delgado, Djoy 69
Delgado, Justino 156, 157, 160
Demba Djadje Ba, Samba 244
Dembo, Leonard 452, 453
Demirdelen, Selim 478
Demissie, Heywet 113
Demote 45
Dendenni, Ahmed ould 242
Dendenni, Luleide ould 243
Dendera Kings 452
Dendi people 281
dengbej 564
Denge, Irewolede 290
Deres, Zeray 104
Dermancı, İvi 604
Dervişan 606
Desert Rebelle 282
Dési et les Sympathiques 48
Desmali y su Grupo Dambo de la
    Costa 100
Destyn 166
Detta, Jolie 81
Devera Ngwena Jazz Band 452
Dewayon, Paul 78
dêxa 322
Diab, Amr 500, 501, 503
Diabaté, Abdoulaye 226, 234
Diabaté, Djanka 147
Diabaté, Ibro 145
Diabaté, Kassé Mady 230, 235
Diabaté, Kélétigui 221, 235
Diabaté, Lassana 226
Diabaté, Les Soeurs 152
Diabaté, Mama 145, 150
Diabaté, Naïny 221, 223
Diabaté, Papa 142, 147
Diabaté, Sékou 141, 142, 143, 147
Diabaté, Sekouba Bambino 137,
    141, 145, 146, 150

Diabaté, Sidiki 139, 140, 224, 235
Diabaté, Sona 145
Diabaté, Toumani 220, 225, 229,
    235
Diabaté, Zani 228
Diablo, El 166
Diablotins 118
Diakité, Benogo 233
Diallo, Ali 49
Diallo, Medouné 337
Diallo, Samba Miriam 244
Diamond Star 413
Diamono 332
Diarra, Kady 49
Dias, Liceu Vieira 28
Diawara, Jali Musa 146, 150
Diawara, Kadé 142, 145, 150
Díaz, Joaquín 554
Dibala, Diblo 82
Dibango, Manu 53, 54, 57, 58,
    59, 77
Dibo, Mandelbosh "Assabelew"
    113
Dieng, Fallou 337, 340
Diggs, Jimmy 189
Digital Bled 478
digital media 291
Digital Networks International 441
Dikongue, Henri 58, 59
Din, Hamza el 405
Din, Hamza el- 498, 504
Dindin, Tata 329, 343
Dinizulu, Princess Constance
    Magogo 367
Dinka Malual 406
Dinka people 402
Dino 269
Diop, Amadou Tamba 244
Diop, Wasis 340
Dioubaté, Oumou 137, 145, 146,
    150
Diouf, Papé 337
Dipoko, Sissi 57
disco 362
Disco, Kacky 121, 122
Dissidenten 256, 476, 479
District Six 378
Ditholwana 45
DJ Arafat 95
DJ Cool Para 414, 416, 424
DJ Jacob 95
DJ Rupture 478
Djaaka 271, 272
djambadon 154
Djamilla 23
Djantakan 40
Djédjé, Ernesto 54, 93
Djellal, Cheb 18
Djellal, Cheb 258

djembe 49, 134, 201
Djenia, Cheikha 10
Djerma people 281
Djiguiya 49
Djimera, Hawa 244
Djimi, Gnaore 93
Djindji, Dilon 267, 270, 272
Djob, Djim 70
Djoliba Percussions 233
Djombo, Super Mama 155, 158
Djongo Diffusion 48
Djorçon (Ernesto Dabó) 155
Djoro G 283
Djosinha 65
Djovana 271
Djungandeke, Théthé 83
Djurdjura 23
Dludlu, Jimmy 271, 368, 383
Docolma 157
Dogg, The 277
Dogo, Maty Thiam 337
Domby, Nick 48
Dominguez , Manuel 241
Domrane, Malika 23
Dona, Kodé di 66
Donkor, Kwadwo 128
doozela 565
dopé 93
Dorley, Molly 189
Dosol 206
Double M Sound 422
Doublemoon 478
Douce Parisette, La 139
Doukkali, Abdelwahab 255
Douleur 55
Doumbia, Amadou 228
Doumbia, Kokanko Sata 235
Doumbia, Mamadou 92
Doumbia, Nahawa 233, 235
Dowa Mbumba 213
Dowa Symphony 213
Dr Gyasi's Noble Kings 126
Dr J.B. and The Jaguars 200
Drakus, Gibraltar 57
Dramé, Adama 49
Dramé, Hawa 226
Dramé, Lalo Keba 336
DRC 75
Dream 502
Drive, The 383
Drum magazine 378
Drummers of Burundi, The 314,
    320
Duarte, Abilio 66
Dubale, Bertukane 113
Dubale, Enana 113
Dubale, Iyerusalem 113
Dubale, Yeshimebet 113
Dube and the Peace Soldiers 277

Dube, Joshua 449
Dube, Lucky 370, 372
Dudley, Anne 476, 479
duduk 483, 484, 485
Duggy-Tee 338
Duguri people 290
Duman 606
DuOud 478
duplicators 291
Durão, Eduardo 272
Dut, Nyankol Mathiang 402
Dutiro, Chartwell 449
Dyer, Steve 450
Dygo 214
Dzadzeloi 128
Dzoku-Kay 40

E

E.K.'s Band 127
E.T. Mensah's Tempos 125
Earthquake Band 447
East African Melody 413
East Coast 424
East-West Ensemble, The 547
Ebadi, Ahmad 521
Ebbo, Mr 424, 427
edongole talking drums 92
Edward Said National Conservatory of Music 585
Eelu 276
Efamba 101
Efé people 305
Efendi, Hammamizade Ismail 'Dede' 599
Efendi, Tatyos 599
Effiom, Peter 293
Efik people 288
efundula drums 276
efundula drums 276
Eggon people 290
Egypt (Classical) 463–474
Egypt (Popular/Street Music) 495–504
Egypt 80 297
Eide, Khalife ould 242, 246
Eide, Seddoum ould 242, 246
Eidel, Philippe 282
EIN 221
Ejagham people 288
Ejeagha, Mike 293
Ekemode, Orlando Julius 298
ekoda 118
Ekondo, Vickos 118, 121
Ekpeye people 288
Ekserciyan, Kemani Tatyos 484

Ekweza 118
Elahi, Ostad 525
Elanga, Maurice "Elamau" 56
Electra Music Shop 113
electric guitar 323
Elec-Trip 478
Elefteriades, Michel 573
Eleme people 288
Elemotho 278
Elenga, Jhimmy 76
Elenga, Zachery 76
Elimhlophe, Ihash' 361, 372
Elissa 502, 575
Elite Swingsters 379
Eliya, Ilana 542
Ellington, Duke 225
Elyas, Moh'd Ali 410
Emeneya, Kester 86
EMI 291, 354
Emilien, Jean 201
Emperor Orlando 431
Empire Bakuba 80
Engel, Héléne 555
Enigbokan, Soji 299
Eno, Brian 476
Enoch, "King" Michael 420
Ensemble Instrumental de la Radiodiffusion Nationale 142
Ensemble Instrumental de Labe 144
Ensemble Instrumental National 221, 227
Epémé, Théodore 57
epic songs 564
Equator Sound Band 175
Equatorial Guinea 99–102
Erçettin, Candan 606
Erener, Sertab 606
Erguner, Kudsi 599, 601, 611
Erguner, Süleyman 599, 611
Eric 278
Eric MC 40
Erimbity 206
Erisioni 508
Eritrea 103–107
Erkin, Ulvi Cemal 603
Erkomaishvili, Anzor 507
Erköse brothers 603
Eroğlu, Musa 598
Erraji, Hassan 258
Ersoy, Bülent 600, 606
Ersoy, Bülent 611
Ersoy, Muazzez 606
Ertaş, Muharrem 598
Ertaş, Neşet 598
Erzincan, Erdal 597
ESA 55
Escrocs, Les 230
Esfahani, Mohammad 527

Eshete, Alemayehu 110, 115
Eshete, Amha 109
Esim, Jak and Janet 553, 604
E-Sir 183
eskista 113
Espandar, Shir-Mohammad 530
Espoirs de Coronthie, Les 137, 148, 150
Essebsadija, Kheira 8
Essome, Jean Pierre 57
Essous, Jean Serge 77
Esta 547
Etche people 288
Ethio Stars 110
Ethio-jazz 110
Ethiopia 108–116
Ethiopian Army Band 109
Étoile 2000 331, 340
Étoile de Dakar 331, 340
Étoiles de Boulbinet, Les 148
Etran Finatawa 284
Everest Kings 181
Evergreen 542
Evora, Cesaria 29, 63, 64, 65, 67, 71
Evora, Grace 69
Excelsior Orchestra 124
Express Band, The 111
Extra Bongo 422
Extra Musica 85
Eyango, Prince 55
Eyoum, Nelle 53
Eyuphuro 270, 272

F

Fadela , Chaba 12
Fadl, Mahmoud 498, 504
Fahmi, Ibrahim 195
Fahnbulleh, Miatta 190
Fairuz 468, 573, 574, 575, 578
Fakhri, Sabah 468, 590, 593
Faki, Makame 412
Fakoly, Tiken Jah 92, 95, 98, 230
Fakrun, Ahmed 195
Faladey 299
Fall, Aminata 336
Fall, Papé 337
famadihana 202
Family Singers 453
Fan Fan, Mose Se Sengo 79, 86
Fan Thomas, Sam 61
Fang people 100
Fania All Stars, The 54
Fantaz, Sebit 399
Farabi, Abu Nasr al- 466
Farafina 48, 50

Farah, Khalil 398
Fâris, Mohammed bin 512
Farjum, Avshalom 544
Farka Touré, Ali 220, 225, 237
Farnatshi, Barraka El 477
Fashek, Majek 299
fasıl 602
Fasıl music 602
Faso Ambience 48
Fassie, Brenda 365, 372, 383
Fataki, Yousif 402
Fatako, Sekouba 148
Father Huddleston Band 380
Fathey, Ahmed 514, 518
Fatiha 24
Faudel 17, 19
Favaneva 40
Faya, Founy 49
Faye, Adama 331
Faye, El Hadji 331
Faye, Habib 331
Faye, Laminé 331, 336
Faytinga 106
Fekade, Abbebe 113
Fekkai, Myriam 7
Fellatiya, Aisha el 401
Feogasy 208
Ferghana 491
Ferhat 23
Ferka el-Masaya, el 503
Ferooz 423
Feruzi 76
Fes Festival of Sacred Music 250, 252
Festival in the Desert 282
Festival of Arabic Music 471
Feza, Mama 83
Fifth Floor 370
Finaçon 66, 67
Fishers of Men 453
Five Alive 182
Five Revolutions 439
Flores, Paulo 28, 31, 33
Fnaïre 258
Fodeba, Keita 140
Foe, Tanus 57
Foidjou, Said Omar 164
Fokkofpolisiekar 363
Fonda, Sah 284
Fools of Prophecy 544
Formah, Vicky 348
Forro language 322
Forward Kwenda 447
Four Brothers 451
Four Stars 80
Fourie, John 383, 385
Frah, Rakoto 201
Fraile, José-Manuel 554

Franco (Luambo Makiadi) 77, 78, 87
Frankel, Judy 555
Frantal, Tabu 178
Fredy, Jean 199
Frente Polisario 241
Frère, Ti 165, 169
Frères Djatys 92
Frères Guisses, Les 338
Freshlyground 369
Froiss, Pee 338
Fryo, Baba 300
Fuhais, al- 560
fuji 294
Fuji Chambers 296
Fulani people 288, 335
Fulani, Wodaabe 281
Fulbe people 49
funana 63, 65
funk 258
Funoun Palestinian Popular Dance Troupe, El- 582, 583, 584, 587
Futa Jallon 138

G

Gabon 117–122
Gabriel, Peter 332, 476
Gabrio, Don 277
Gacheru, Albert 177
Gadama, Richard 216
Gadir Salim, Abdel 406
Gaita, Ferro 66, 71
Galeta, Hotep Idris 385
Galinoma, Innocent 426
Galissa, Nino 157, 160
Gallo 353
Gama, Victor 31, 33
Gamal, Samia 469
Gambia, The 327
Gamlielit, Esther 540
Gangbe Brass Band 37
Gangue, Ousmane 244
Gangwe Mobb 423, 426
Gannirni, Aid el- 497
Gaon, Yehoram 540, 547, 553
Garagistes, Les 94, 97
Gari Kubwa 425
Gasparyan, Djivan 484, 485, 487
Gaston, Baba 79, 178
Gavrielov, Miki 542
gawlo 244
Gawlo, Coumba 336, 340
Gayflor, Princess Fatu 190, 192
Gazza 277
Gbessi-Zolawadji 39

Gbetuwai, Ngoh 347
Gebah, Zack 189
Gebre-Markos, Tsedenia 111
Gedassi, Avner 542
Geghard 482
Gencebay, Orhan 605, 613
General MD Shirinda & the Gaza Sisters 362
Génitaux, Les 93
George, Linda 535
George, Zakiya 535
Georgia 505–509
Georgian Voices 508
Geply, Twale 189
gesere 244
Gessesse, Tlahoun 109, 110, 115
Gewel, Fatou 340
Ghana 123–135
Ghana Trio 126
Ghanaba 127
Ghania, Maleem Mahmoud 262
Ghansah, Mary 130
gharnati 251, 254
Gharnati 253
Gharnati festival 250
Ghazal 526
Ghazaly, Nathem al- 468, 535, 537
Ghorwane 266, 270, 272
Ghulami, Najmeddin 569
Giddie, Tsholofelo 45
Gidigidi Majimaji 182, 184
Gil & the Perfects 69
Gilbert Matthews' Spirits Rejoice 383
Gilberto, João 57
Gisma 401
Gizavo, Regis 201, 202, 208
Glass and Grant 126
Glorious Band 442
Gnaoré, Dobet 92, 97
Gnaoua (Gnawa) 254
Gnawa (Gnaoua) 254
Gnawa Diffusion 257, 478
Gnawa Festival, Essaouira 250
Gnawa Impulse 257
Gnawa N'joum Experience 257
Gnawa Njoum 262
Gnawa Njoum Experience 478
Gnawi, Met'al 497
Gning, Madiodio 336
Godessa 369
Goge, Harouna 285
Gokana people 288
Golafruz, Rowshan 524
Gold Coasters, The 133
Gold, Nick 330
Golden Gospel Sounds 453
Golden Sounds Band 181, 184
Golden Star 414

Golden Star Taarab 416
gombe polyrhythmics 92
Gomi, Nacia 67
Gomis, Rudy 330
Gong 476
Good Women's Choir 297
Googoosh 526, 531
Goosen, Anton 363
Gora, Sekuru 447
gospel 130, 172, 189, 214,
 389–392
Gospel, South African 389–392
Gospel Musicians Union 130
Gospel Singers, Genesis 130
Gotani Sounds 214
goumbala 244
Gourgy, Filfel 534, 535, 537
Gourounsi 49
Govinal 57
Gramophone Company Ltd 353
Great Pekachi Band, The 439
Great Steady Bongo 347
Great WITCH 438
Greek–Turkish music 604
Green Arrows, The 451, 456
Greenwood Singers 189
Greisha, Bahr Abu 498
Grélo, Cheikha 10
Gronich, Shlomo 542
Groupe Kawtal, Le 57
Grup Çığ 597
Guayla 104
Guèbrou, Tsegué-Maryam 115
Guelewar 328
Guendil, Cheikha Kheira 10
Guennoun, Saïd 252
Guillaume, Toto 55
Guinea 136–152
Guinea, Mahmoud 254
Guinea-Bissau 153–162
Guinean Quintet 143
Guiné-Bissau, Juntos Pela 161
Guisse, Ousmane 244
Guitar, Mohammed 243
Gülay 596
Gulestan 569
Gulf States 510–518
Guliyev, Zahid 492
Gülses, Melahat 604
gumbe 154, 158
Gumbezarte 157, 160
Gumede, Sipho 369
Gürses, Müslüm 605, 613
Güzelses, Diyarbakırlı Celal 604
Gwangwa, Jonas 45, 380
GWM 423
Gyanfi, Sloopy Mike 130
Gyeli people 305
Gypsies 599, 602

H

H2O 37
Haastrup, Joni 298
Habboush, Sheikh Ahmed 592,
 594
Haco, Ciwan 569, 570, 603
Hadad, Sarit 542, 547
Haddab, Mehdi 478
Haddad, Diana 502
hadith, al- 399
hadra 254
Hadraoui, Touria 253
Hafez 521
Hafez, Abdalhalim 468, 471, 473
Hagopian, Richard 483, 487
Hagour, Boujemaa 256
Haile Selassie Theatre Band 109
Haja 199
Hajib 255
Hajibeyov, Uzeyir 492
Hakim 477, 500, 501, 503
Hakmoun, Hassan 257
halay dance 597
Half-Green records 199
Hallelujah Chicken Run Band 456
Hamada, Cheikh 7, 19
Hamadcha 254
Hamadi Ali Sy, Ali 244
Hamady Diop, Ousmane 244
Hamaida, Ali 501
Haman, Isnebo 60
Hambare, Baba ould 243
Hambare, Isselmou ould 243
Hambare, Mohammed ould 243
Hamdaouia, Hajja 255
Hamid, Cheb 14
Hamid, Hmaoui Abd el- 261
Hamid, Mehad 512, 516
Hamid, Sultan 512
Hamza Shakkur, Sheikh 592, 594
Hanana, Steve 276, 278
Hanifa 23
Hanine y Son Cubano 573
Hanmer, Paul 383, 385
Happy Stars 126
haqiiba 399
Haqim, Tariq Abdul 511
Haqq, Ahl-e 524
Harari 364, 382
Haratin music 243
Hardstone 182
Harem 478
harepa 360
Harlem Swingsters 378
Harmandian, Adiss 486
Harmattan 336
Harrachi, Dahmane El 7

Harris, Corey 225
Hart 182
Hart, Su 309
Hasni, Cheb 16, 19
Hassan Saba, Abol 521
Hassan, Ammar 586
Hassan, Cheb 17
Hassan, Dakhil 536
Hassan, Mariem 241, 247
Hassan, Mohamed 164, 168, 195
Hativeet, Habrera 542, 547
Hattar, Sakher 560, 561
Hausa people 281, 288
Hayedeh 526
Hayes and Harvey 190
Hayes, Howard 189
Hayots, Vostan 486
Haza, Ofra 476, 514, 542, 547
Hazolahy 204, 206
Heart Beat of Africa 431
Hébrail, Jean 38
Hedzolleh 128
Hefny, Ratibah al- 471
Helwani, Faisal 128
Hemsi, Albert 556
Henawy, Mayada el- 592, 594
Henry Sithole's Heshoo Beshoo
 Band 382
Henshaw, Inyang Nta 293
Hentsoa 206
Herman, Trevor 395
Hewale Sounds 132, 134
Heydari, Emran 491
Hezbollah 206
Higelin, Jacques 58
highlife 53, 124, 292
Hijas del Sol, Las 101, 102
Hi-Life International 129
Hill, Dan 356
Hillage, Steve 15, 476
hillbilly string bands 363
hip-hop 37, 40, 48, 49, 95, 230,
 258, 259, 277, 299, 339, 366,
 368, 490, 608
Hiplife 131
hiragasy 198
H-Kayne 258
Hlongwane, Jabu 391
Hodhodza Band 455
Hodi 526
Hodi Boys, The 175
Hohberg, Roland 270
Holmes, Jack 58
Homeirah 526
Honfo, Denagan Janvier 37, 41
Hooker, John Lee 225
Hope, Jimi 40
horn-playing 399
horon 597

Horoya Band, The 143, 145
Horoya Jazz 142
Hossein Banan, Gholam 521
Hotel, Bobby 296
Houari, Blaoui 10, 15
Houriyat, Bnet 251
house music 258
Houston 300
Houston, Thelma 120
Houzaiyan 168
Hovhannissyan, Varazdat 484
Hrant Kenkulian, Udi 484
Hrant, Udi 599, 611
Humberto, Jorge 71
Hunègn, Teberèh Tesfa 104
hungo 28
Huraish, Youssouf 534
Huraish, Yusuf 535
Husseïn, Haj 252
Hussein, Muha 249
Hussein, Salem 535
Hussein, Zuhur 535, 536
Hyacinthe, Jimmy 92

I

Ibani 288
Ibeba System 178
Ibrahim, Abdullah 380, 385
Ideal Black Girls, The 149
Idibia, 2Face 299, 303
Idir 23, 25
Idriss, Bahija 255
ieta 307, 308
Ifang Bondi 329, 343
Ifouta, Landry 121, 122
Igbo people 288
Igd el Djilad 401, 406
iggawen 240
Ihsas, Omar 399, 403
Ihya, Raïs 249
Ikalanga people 44
ikembe 314
Ikhwani Safaa Musical Club 409,
    416
ikinimba 314
Ikwerre people 288
Ililonga, Rikki 438
Ilyas, Mohamed 413
Imani Ngoma Group 426, 427
Imbizo 454
Imena 317
Imilonji Kantu Choral Society 391
Imitari 317
Impactus 4 277
Impala 317

Imperial Bodyguard Band 109
Imperial Hotel 111
Imvuselelo Yase Natali 390, 391
inanga 314
incantations, praise 276
İnce Saz 600
Indian Ocean 163–170
Infected Brain 258
Inganzo, Ballet 314, 319
Ingeli 317
Ingeli Pan-African Band 317
ingoma 314
inhore 314
iningiri 314
Innocent Versace 95
Inrzaf 256
Inspecta Haroun 424
Institut du Monde Arabe 515
International Library of African
    Music 394
International Orchestra Safari
    Sound 421
Internationale, Vivi l' 37
intifada uprising 582
Intik 18
IPCC 390, 391
Iran 519–532
Iranian Classical music 520
Iranian Pop 525, 526
Iraq 533–538
Iraqi Maqam Ensemble 537
Iraqi, Hatem al- 537
Isaac, Ismaël 95, 97
iscathamiya 360
Ishola, Haruna 291, 293, 301
Ishola, Museliu 293, 301
isikhwela jo 358
Iskander, Afifa 535
Iskander, Nouri 535
Iskandrani, Abdou el- 497
Islam 464
Ismail, Ahmed 497
Ismail, Shah 490
Ismaïlova, Sakine 492, 493
Isoko people 290
Israel 539–550
Israel Borochov's East-West En-
    semble 544
Israeli Andalusian Orchestra 540,
    547
Issa, Fatma 412
Istanbul Oriental Ensemble 613
Izanzaren 256
Izintombi Zezi Manje Manje 358
İzzet, Ali 598

J

J, Daara 338, 339
Jabali Afrika 183
Jabbar Kardyagdioglu Ensemble
    493
Jabbar, Pat 477
Jabr, Sadoun 537
Jacinta 555
Jafete, Alexander 269, 361
Jagoda, Flory 553, 556
Jaguar Jokers 126
Jagwa music 425, 426
Jah Wobble's Invaders of the Heart
    477
Jahlé 525
Jairos Jiri Sunshine Band 451
Jajouka, The Master Musicians
    of 261
jakwar 242
Jal, Emmanuel 402, 403
Jalikunda Cissokho 341
Jam Brothers 426
Jamhuri Jazz 420
Jamus 403
Jaojoby 199, 208
Jassar, Wael 575
Javdan, Parvin 522
Jaza, Tsy an- 201
Jaza'iriya, Warda al- 468, 471, 474
Jazz Dazzlers 380
Jazz Epistles 380, 386
Jazz Forces 378
Jazz Giants 212
Jazz Invitation 455
Jazz Kings 124
Jazz Maniacs 353, 378
Jazz, Mr T.O. 129
Jazz, South African 377–388
JBZ studio 92
Jedouane, Orchestre 255
jejy voatavo 201
Jeli 223, 224
Jelle 403
Je-luo 399, 403
Jesrawi, Mohammed Arif 566
Jet-Set 95
**Jewish music (Sephardic)
    551–558**
Jewish music in Iraq 535
Jewish music in Turkey 604
Jezar, Tahir 403
Jheich, Idoumou ould 243
Jhetto, Jheri 298
Jilala Brotherhood 254
Jilala, Jil 254, 256, 262
Jilaliate musicians 253
Jilani, Cheb 195

jit 451
jive 353, 354
JJC and the 419 Squad 298, 299, 303
JKT Taarab 414
Jobarteh, Amadou Bansang 329, 343
Jobarteh, Pa Bobo 329, 343
Jocker, Evoloko 79, 87
Jofabro Records 291
Joganah, Nitish 165
Joganah, Ram 165
Johannesburg 378
Johar, Abadi al- 511, 516
Johnson, Bob 126
Johnson, Dexter 341
Jojo, Ngalle 55
Jones, Hank 139
Jordan & Bedouin 559–562
Joseph & One 586
Joseph, Beti 56
Josiah, Tedd 182
Joubran, Samir 585, 587
Joubran, Trio 585, 587
Jourias, Ita 40
Jovens do Prenda, Orquestra os 28
Joviale Symphonie, La 139
Joy, Ti 65
Joyous Celebration 391
Ju/'hoansi people 277
Jubilee Singers 353
Jubran, Kamilya 585, 587
Jubran, Khaled 586
Judeo-Spanish 552
juju 290
Juka 324, 325
Julius, Orlando 296
Jully, Prince 175
Juluka 363
Juma, Issa 180
Juma, Peter Tsotsi 439
Junayd, Hamud al- 518
Jundi, Zein al- 594
Junior Mulemena Boys 439
Junior, Adam's 281, 283
Justin Vali Trio 205

K

K.K.'s No. 2 126
K10 (Kapa Dêch) 270, 273
Kaba, Achken 141
Kabaka of Buganda 431
Kabaka, Daudi 176
Kabalah 544
Kaban, Karim 566

Kabanda, Bernard 431, 434
Kabarira, Victor 317
Kabasele, Joseph 54, 78
Kabaselleh, Ochieng 175, 185
Kabbala 129
Kabelo 366, 368, 372
Kabir, Abdoul 329
Kabli, Abdel Karim el- 400, 406
Kabobo, K.K. 130
kabosy 201
Kabral, Bibinha 67
Kabrou 243
Kabylia 22–26
Kachaka, Victor 441
Kachamba, Daniel 212, 216
Kachamba, Donald 212, 216
Kadry, Salam 195
Kaf, Lo Rwa 165
Kafala Brothers, The 33
Kafeero, Paulo 431
Kahol 542
Kaïdan Gaskia 283
Kaifa, Ali "Ali Tango" 111
Kaira Trio, The 343
Kaiser, Henry 205
Kakadu 296
Kakaiku 125, 126
Kakhetia 506
Kakongo Sisters 178
Kakum Bamboo Orchestra 132
Kalabari people 288
Kalakuta Republic 296
Kalamashaka 182
Kalambya Boys 177
Kalhor, Kayhan 521, 526, 528, 567, 570
Kaliati, Elias 214, 216
Kalikawe, Justin 426
Kalimba 212
kalimba 53
kalindula 439
Kalle, Pepe 81, 87
Kaloudji, DJ 95
Kalthoum, Oum – see Kulthum, Umm
Kamal, Nouri 194
Kamaldine 146
Kamalengoni 232
Kamali, Mohammad Sedigh 525
kamancha 484
kamancheh 520, 565
Kamandi, Abbas 567
Kamaru, Joseph 177
Kamau, Daniel 'DK' 177
Kamba 177
Kamel, Sheikh al- 253
Kamkan 125
Kamkar, Ardavan 570
Kamkar, Hassan 567

Kamkars, The (family) 521, 525, 530, 567, 570
Kamwendo, Ethel 215, 216
Kan, Kouman 50
Kanda Bongo Man 81
Kandıralı, Mustafa 603, 613
Kandonga, Studio 270
Kangue, Emile 55
Kanji 442
Kantata 129
Kanté, Baba Galle 139
Kanté, Djessou Mory 147
Kanté, Facelli 137, 140, 142
Kanté, Jali Mamadou 140
Kanté, Kerfala 145
Kanté, Mama 142, 145
Kanté, Manfila 137
Kanté, Mory 137, 145, 146, 147, 150, 223
Kanuri people 288
Kanza, Lokua 58, 85
Kapa Dêch (K10) 270, 273
Kapa Negra 156
kapuka 183
Karaböcek, Nese 606
Karaca, Cem 606, 614
Karaca, Işın 606
Karaca, Kani 600
Karadahari 567
Kardeş Türküler 603, 609
Kargo 606
Karim, Adnan 570
Karoli, Saida 424, 426
Karoma 398
Kars 598
karşılama 597
Kasanda, Nicholas "Dr Nico" 77
Kasheba, Ndala 421, 423, 427
Kassa, Getatchew 109
Kassav 144
Kassé, Alioune 337
Kassé, Ndeye 337
Kassey, Mamar 283, 285
Kassy, Serge 95
Kasule, Sammy 431
Katembula, Jordan 443
Katitu Boys Band 178
Kaujeua, Jackson 277
Kaunda, Billy 214, 216
Kaunda, Kenneth 438
Kavango people 276
Kavari, Kakazona 278
Kay, Jon 129
Kaya 169
Kaya, Ahmet 614
Kayahan, Malatyalı Fahri 605
Kayamba Afrika 183
Kayirebwa, Cécile 317, 319
Kayla, Kamal 399

Kazimova, Aygün 493
Keita, Mamady 138, 150
Keita, Modibo 227
Keita, Salif 58, 144, 147, 220, 236
Keita, Sunjata 220
Kékélé 84, 87
Kel Tamashek 282
Kelani, Reem 585
Kélétigui et ses Tambourins 142, 143
Kelly, Joe 127
Kenya (Popular) 171–187
Kenya (Taarab) 408–417
Kenya, F. 126
Kenya, Lord 131
Kenyan tribal music 173
Kerkorrel, Johannes 363
Keser, Mustafa 600
Kesouani, Elie 535
Ketencioğlu, Muammer 604
Keyrouz, Sister Marie 576, 578
Kfoury, Wael 575, 578
Kgopo, Whyte 45
Khader, Cheb 258
Khafaji, Ibrahim 511
Khaldi, Cheikh 7
Khaled (Cheb) 12, 14, 19, 476
Khaleej, Shadl al- 513
khaleeji 510, 536
Khalifa, Marcel 576, 578
Khalil, Khalil Mohammed 514
Khalil, Wahida 535
Khalsoum, Oum – see Kulthum, Umm
Khalsoum, Oum (see Kulthum, Umm) 473
Khama, Mphoeng 45
Khan, Shujaat 526
Khana people 288
Khanmammadov, Haji 492
Khanyile, Jabu 368, 372, 384
Khatchaturian, Aram 482
Kheddam, Cherif 23
Kheira 17
Khezri, Hamid 530
Khiama Boys 452
Khoi people 352
Khoisan Bushmen 44
Khoury, Suhail 583, 586
Khumalo, Sibongile 367, 395
Kiamanguana, Verckys 79
Kibukosya, Suzanne 183
Kidjo, Angélique 36, 38, 41
Kidude, Bi 413, 416
kidumbak 412
Kiema, Kuela 277
Kiezos, Os 28
Kiflemariam, TeKle 106
Kiko Kids 174, 420

Kikuyu-speaking people 176
Kili, Houssaine 258, 262
Kilimambogo Brothers Band, Les 177
Kilimani Muslim School 416
Kilimanjaro 423, 427
Kill Point 148
Kilonzo, Kakai 173, 177, 185
Kiltir 166
Kilwa Jazz Band 420
Kimangu Boys Band 178
Kimbuteh, Jah 426
Kimono, Ras 299
Kinamatamikuluty 269
Kindi Ensemble, Al- 593
King MCs 338
King Star Brothers 360
King, Nana 131
King, Tunde 290
Kininike, Rasoa 201
Kinois, Les 178
Kippie's club 383
Kirimungu, Siragi 432
Kırmızıgül, Mahsun 605
Kirochi Sound 317
Kirusu 317
Kiteta Boys 178
Kituxi 28, 31, 33
kizomba 29
Kleptomaniaks 183
Klezmatics 541
Klezmer 540
KMR 608
Knar 483
Koala, Koudbi 49
Koezy 200
Kohinoor records 382
Koinyi, Ismael 403
Koïta, Ami 221, 236
Koïta, Moriba 224
Koité, Habib 220, 227, 236
Kol Oud Tof Trio 540, 548
Kola people 305
Kolosoyi, Antoine Wendo 76
Kolosoyi, Wendo 87
Koly, Amadou 244
Kombat, Faso 50
Kombuis, Koos 363
Komitas 482, 488
Konadu, Alex 126, 133
Konak, Volkan 597
Konaté, Famoudou 138, 150
Konaté, Papis 336
Konde, Fundi 174, 185
Kondombolos 277
Koné, Aïcha 92, 97
Koné, Babani 223
Koné, Tidiané 227
Konono No. 1 84, 87

Konteh, Alhaji Bai 329, 344
Konteh, Dembo 329, 344
Koode Pinal 244
Kooligan and Kalabash 455
kopla 552
Koppo 58
kora 220
Koranic recitation 464, 465, 511
Korankye, Osei 132
Korankye, Osei Kwame 125
Koray, Erkin 606
Korikima 297
Korkut, Dede 490
Kosal, Vedat 603
Kotoja 298
Kouyaté, Bala Faseke 223
Kouyaté, Bassekou 224
Kouyaté, Djeli Fode 146
Kouyaté, El Hadj Djeli Sory 137, 142, 151
Kouyaté, Famoro 143
Kouyaté, Kabine 145
Kouyaté, Kandia 220, 221, 222
Kouyaté, Kandia 236
Kouyaté, Kausu 329, 344
Kouyaté, Kemoko 143
Kouyaté, Modibo 223
Kouyaté, Mory Djeli Deen 137, 145, 151
Kouyaté, Ousmané 229
Kouyaté, Sekouba Kandia 145
Kouyaté, Sory Kandia 143, 151
Kouyaté, Tata Bambo 221, 223
Kozman Ti Dalon 166
Krama, Dade 129
krar 104
Kriolu language 154
Kriolu music 155
Krotal 58
Krushed and Sorted 370
Krutambull 206
K-Sim 39
K-Tino 55
Kuban, Ali Hassan 498, 504
Kubat 596
Kulna Sawa 594
Kulthum, Umm 255, 410, 464, 468, 469, 473, 476
Kumapim Royals, The 130
Kumasi Trio 125
Kumpanya 604
kundere 154
Kunene, Madala 369, 372
Kung people 277
Kurd, Mustafa al- 582
Kurdish Institute, Paris 567
Kurdish music 563–571
Kurds, Armenian 567
Kurds, Syrian 567

Kurds, Turkish 603
Kurdistani, Said Asghar 567
kussundé 154
Kusum Gboo 132
Kusun Ensemble 132
Kuti, Fela 288, 295, 296, 302, 347
Kuti, Femi 288, 296, 297, 302
Kuti, Seun 297
Kuwait 513
Kuwaiti, Daud al- 535
Kuwaiti, Saleh al- 535
Kuyateh, Jaliba 329, 344
Kwade, Obour 131
Kwade, Okonfo 131
kwaito 277, 366
Kwame 125
Kwanza Unit 423, 427
kwassa kwassa 213
kwela 175, 354, 355
Kxoe people 277

L

l'Abdin, Zein 411
La Réunion 165
Lacaille, René 166
Laço Tayfa 603, 613
Ladino 540, 552, 604
Lady JD 424
Ladysmith Black Mambazo 359,
    360, 372, 391, 454
Lágbájá 296, 297, 300, 303
Lahcen, Raïs Ajmaa 249
Lakal Kaney 283
Lalezar Ensemble 612
Lam, Kiné 336
Lamandier, Esther 555
Lamartine, Carlos 28, 29, 31, 33
Lamdaghri, Al-Thami 252
lamellaphone 432
Lamu 172, 411
Lando, Teta 31, 33
Landy 205
Langa Langa, Zaïko 75, 79, 90
Langa, Hortêncio 269
Langa, Pedro 270
langarm 277
Laobé, Fatou 336
Laope, Maxime 165
Las Ondas, Orchestra 36
Lassan, Lessa 179
Laswell, Bill 257, 477
Latanié, Grup 165
Latife 610
Latroup Kiltirel Nasyonal Sesel 167
Lawson, Cardinal Rex 292

Laz 597
Ldy-Paye, Won 189
Le Roux, Gabi 367
Lebanon 572–579
Lebrijano, Juan Peña 258, 263
Lecco, Armand Sabal 53
Lecco, Sabbal 57
Lefatshe, Chreiser Matlhoko 45
Lego 200
Leil, Abu 581
Lekanskills 299
lélé 244
Lélé, Granmoun 165, 166, 169
Lema, Ray 84
Lemchaheb 256
Lemvo, Ricardo 85
Lemzo Diamono 337, 341
Lenny, Mr. 183
Leoninos 323
Lerole, Aaron Jack 357
Letourdie, Jenny de 167
Levy, Gloria 552
Levy, Isaac 553, 556
Levy, Shem Tov 542, 548
Levy, Yasmin 540, 553, 556
Lewitová, Jana 555
Lex 299
Leyoad 241
Leza, B. 63, 65, 66
Lhoucine, Fatna bent 255
Liberia 188–192
Liberian Dreams 189
Libya 193–196
Lijadu Sisters 298
likanos 305
Lilanda, Maureen Lupo 442
Lilwal 283
Lima, Pepe 323, 325
limbindi 307
Linda, Solomon 358
Lindigo 166
Lindley, David 205
Lingala language 76
Linsan, Fatou 139, 148
Lions of Zion 370
Lipua Lipua 80
liquindi 307
Lisbon 159
Livaneli, Zülfü 606, 614
Living Fire Ensemble 569
Lô, Cheikh 337, 341
Lô, Ismael 332, 333, 341
Lô, Ndongo 337
Lobe Lobe 53
Lobe, Guy 60
Lobi people 49, 92
Lobi, Kakraba 134
Lobitos, Koola 295
Lobo, Ildo 65, 71

Lobo, Mirri 70
Lockwood, Didier 58
Logozo 37
lokanga 201
Loketo 82
Lolik 540
Longo, Nyoka 79
Longomba, Awilo 82
Longomba, Vicky 79
Longwe, John Selolwane 212
Loningisa records 78
Lopes, Carlos 34
Loramou, Nyanga 148
Lord's Resistance Army 433
Lorestan 525
Lotfi, Mohammad Reza 521, 528
Lotin, Eboa 55
Lougah, François 92
Louk, Haim 553
Loukili, Moulay Ahmed 252
Lounès, Matoub 23, 24, 25
Love Aquarius 214
love poetry, courtly 281
Love, M'Pongo 81
Lowe, Mass 329
Lubumbashi Stars, The 453
Luciana & Ballou Canta 86
Lucio, Mario 68, 72
Lucky Star Musical Clubs 415
Lucky Stars 213, 214
Luhya 176
Luisira 100
Lulendo 34
Lulus Band, The 177
Lumba, Daddy 129
Luna Loca 100
Lungu, Stonard 213
Lura 72
Luri 525
Lusaka Radio Band 437
Lushi, John 437
Lusófona, Cena 323
Lutaaya, Philly 431
Luzon, Eli 542

M

M.K. Group 423
M'Afriq 455
M'barek, Ammouri 256
M'Bomio, Louis 101
M'Rabati, Hamid 258
ma'luf 195
Maal, Baaba 327, 334, 341
Maalesh 164, 168
Mabah 40

Mabiaku, Dede 297
Mabulu 270, 273
Mabuse, Sipho "Hotstix" 364, 373
Machesa 45
Macheso, Alick 445, 452, 457
Machine-Gunners, The 437
Mack, Bunny 347
Mackjoss 118
Macucua, David 270
Madagascar 197–210
Madama, Etienne 119
Madani, Cheikh 7
Madfai, Ilham al- 537, 538, 560
Madiaga, Khar Mbaye 336
Madiko, Wes 58
Madlingozi, Ringo 384
Madosini 367, 373
Madrid 101
Madson Junior 50
Madunga, Ngal 100
Maekwana 267
Maele 101
Mafikizolo 368, 373
Maftirim 604
Magdy, Sohar 497
Magereza 413
Maghni, Mohammed 13
Maghribi, Samy el 259, 264
Magic Aliens 128
Magic System 49, 92, 94, 97
Magoola, Rachel 431, 434
Magubane, Cyril 382
Mahabou 164
Mahaleo 198
Mahasti 526
Mahber Theatre Asmara 104
Mahendere Brothers 453
Mahlasela, Vusi 369, 373
Mahlathini and the Mahotella
    Queens 358, 373
Mahmoud Music Shop 113
Mahmut, DJ 608
Mahola, Zolani 369
Mahotella Queens 358, 373
Mahube 450
Maiga, Boncana 145
Maiga, Mamadou 332
Maison Française 296
Majaivana, Lovemore 454, 457
Major E 455
Makaba, Alain 82, 88
Makala, Tshwatla 360
Makale 477
makam 598
Makasi, Duke 382
Makassy, Orchestra 79
Makasu 212
Makeba, Miriam 143, 379, 380, 386
Makhendlas 367, 373

Makhene, Motsumi 367
Makhona Tsohle Band 356
Makhoul, Sameer 548
Makiadi, Franco Luambo 78, 87
makondera 314
Makonnen, Ketema 110
makossa 53, 55, 100
makossa-soukous 57
Makuzeni, Siya 384
Makwela, Joseph 356
Mala, Afia 40
Malabo Dos 101
Maladé, Fou 339
Malaika 368, 381
Malapet, Nino 77
Malawi 211–218
Male, Cheri 101
Malhangalene Jazz Quartet 269
Mali 219–238
Malika 411, 416
Malomou, Seyni 137, 148
Malope, Rebecca 390, 392
maloya 165
Mama Djombo 160
Mami, Cheb 14, 20
Mamlê, Hama 567, 570
MAMU 179
Manatsa, Zexie 451
Manço, Barış 606
Mande 48, 137, 220, 223, 224, 327
Mande Senegambia 327
Manden 223
Mandenge, Jeannot Karl 55
Mandingo Griot Society 329
Mandinka people 224, 327, 336
Mandjeku, Dizzy 79
Mandoza 367, 373
Mané, Kaba 156, 157
Mané, Kaba 161
Manel, Zé 156, 157, 161
Manfila, Kanté 146, 151, 228
Manfred, Ebanda 53
mangambe rhythm 53
Mangwana, Sam 31, 79, 88
Manhattan Brothers 379, 380, 386
Manhenga, Dudu 455
Maninka 224, 226
Mankwane, Marks 356
Mann, C.K. 133
Manquina, Madosini 373
Mansaré, Mamady 146
Manuaku, Pepe Feli 79
Manyeruke, Machanic 453
Maoma Band 439
Mapangala, Samba 178, 185
Mapfumo, Thomas 447, 457
Mapulanga, William 437
Maputo Jazz 269
maqam 465, 466, 534, 537

Maquis de Maison Mère, Les 88
Maquis, Orchestre 79
marabi 353, 378
Marahati, Sanaa 253
Maraire, Chiwoniso 447
Maraire, Dumisani 447, 457
Marakesh 542
Maravillas de Mali, Las 228
Maraya, Dan 290
Marcos, Antonio 270, 273
Mardan, Ali 566
Maria, Zé 269
Mariko, Fati 281
maringa 346
Mario 78
Mark Fransman's Tribe 384
Maroantsetra, Lazan'i 200
Maroon Commandos 180
marovany 200
Marques, Djosa 65
Marrabenta 267
Marrabenta Star de Moçambique,
    Orchestra 269, 274
Mars 206
Marsalis, Brandford 58
Marshall, Wasiu Ayinde 294, 302
Martin, Messi 53
Martin, Messi Me Nkonda 56
Martins, Vasco 69
Marzia 569
Masaka 212
Masasu Band 439
Mascara 101
Masco, King 347, 349
Masekela, Hugh 380, 386
Masekini, Abeti 80
mashamba 276
Mashiyane, Spokes 354, 355, 373
Mashonaland 394
maskanda 361
Mason, I.E. 125
Masresha, Gennet 113
Massacreur 283
Massako military band 121
Massamba 317
Massengo, Edouard 175
Massi, Souad 23, 24, 25
Massukos 273
Master Musicians of Armenia 483
Master Musicians of Jajouka, The
    261
Master Musicians of Tanzania, The
    424, 429
Masters of Persian Music 526
Masucci, Jerry 54
Masuka, Dorothy 379, 380, 386,
    445, 454, 457
Masy, Madame 200
MaTA 104

Matafale, Evison 214, 216
Matavel, Lisboa 267, 270
Matavire, Paul 451
Matchatcha 82
Matéké, Benji 57, 60
Matevosian, Rouben 484
Mathosa, Lebo 367
Mathosa, Thembi 367
Matona, Issa 414, 416
Matovu, Moses 431
Matsheha, Tau Oa 360
Matumba, Cuthbert 354
Matumona, Defao 88
Maulidi Musical Party 411
Maulidi, Maurice 212
Maurice, Simporé 48
Maurin Poty, Charles 200, 206
Mauritania & Western Sahara 239–247
Mauritius 165
Mavi Sakal 606
mawal 499
Maxi 45
Maya, José Heredia 258
Mazee, Collela 175
Mazouz, Mourad 477
Mazuze, Ivan 269
Mazwai, Thandiswa 366, 367, 374
Mazzica 502
MB Papa Kado 439
Mbada, Kouchouam 57
mbalax 244, 330, 337
Mbalire, Frank 431
Mbande, Venancio 267, 274
Mbanga, Lapiro de 55, 60
Mbango , Charlotte 60
Mbappe, Etienne 53, 58
mbaqanga 354, 356, 378
Mbaraka Mwinshehe Mwaruka 427
Mbarga, Prince Nico 299
Mbassi, Coco 58, 60
Mbaye, Daro 336
MBC Band, The 212, 216
mbila 267
mbira 446
Mbira dze Nharira 447, 457
Mbolatina 205
Mboup, Assané 337
Mboup, Laye 330
MBS 18
Mbube 358
Mbuli, Mzwakhe 364, 374
mbumba 213
Mbuti people 305
MC Fata 339
MC Raï 478
MC Sultan 478
MC Wabwino 441

McAdoo, Orpheus 353
McClaren, Malcolm 358
McGregor, Chris 381, 386
mchiriku 425
Mchunu, Sipho 363
medh 243
Medina Band, The 111
Medina, Dina 69
Médioni, Maurice El 20
Médioni, Maurice el 10, 15
Medjo, Oncle 55
Meera 527, 531
Megastar Band, The 133
Mehari, Tesfai 106
Mehegan, John 380
Meidah, Arafate ould 242
Meidah, Malouma mint 242, 246
Meissonnier, Martin 476
Meiway 92, 93, 97
Mekoa, Johnny 378
Mekurya, Getachew 110, 115
Melanz Nasyon 166
Meles, Helen 104, 107
Melkon, Marko 484
Mellesse, Muluken 109, 110
Mellesse, Netsanet 110, 115
Melody 502
MELT Music (MELT 2000) 368, 383
Menad, Soubira bent 8
Mendes Brothers 65
Mendes Brothers, The 70
Mendes, Felício 324, 325
Mendes, Kalú 324, 325
Mendes, Ramiro 66
Mendi, Nha Gida 67
Mengisteab, Bereket 105
Mengrelia 506
Menguellet, Aït 23, 26
Menheim, Nicolas 337, 341
Mensah, E.T. 126, 292
Mensah, King 40, 42
Mensah, Kwaa 125
Menu, Kojo 125
Menu, Kwesi 125
Menwar, Lélou 165
Mercan Dede 478
Merhaba 104
Mesfin, Ayalew 110
Meshkatian, Parviz 521, 528
Messaoud, Bellemou 11, 20
Messaoudi, Malika 24
Metaphore Crew 284
Metaxas, Nikiforos 604
Meteku, Teshome 109, 110
Meter, Ahmet 599
Metronomes, The 44
Mevlevi music 596
Mevlevi sema 601
Meyde, Ahmedou ould 242

Meyde, Mahjouba mint 242
meyjana 581
Meyxana 490
Mêzel, Iness 23, 24, 25
MFÖ 606
Mhango Salvation Choir 215
Mhango, Griffen 212
Mhlanga, Louis 44, 383, 387
Mhlongo, Busi 368, 374
Miambo, Paulo 270
Miami 513, 517
Michael, Ben 217
Mighty Popo, The 318, 320
Mikaya people 305
Mikidache 164, 168
Mikoko Band 213
milhûn 251, 252
Milhûn festival 250
milhûn orchestra 252
Miliki 296
Millenium Sound Checks 215, 217
milo-jazz 346
Mimi 113
Mimoun, Cheb 258
Mindelo 323
Mingas 269
mipasho 414
Mireku 125
Mirkelam 606
Misiani, Daniel Owino 175, 185
Miski, Maruja 100
Miski, Yoli 100
Missal 331
Mista, Hassan 256
Mizdawi, Nasser 194
Mkandawire, Wambali 215, 217
Mkhitarian, Gor 486
Mkhize, Lindelani 391
Mkhize, Themba 367
Mlevu, Keith 438
Mlimani Park Orchestra 427
Mlotshwa, Jerry 356
Mmereki, Michael "Malombo" 45
Mntambo, Shaluza Max 384
Moanda, D.V. 79
Mode Plagal 604
Modjo, Isidore 57
Moeen 527, 532
Moeketsi, Kippie 378, 380
Moğollar 606
mohabelo 360
Mohamed "Tenge", Yusuf 411
Mohamed Senoussi, Cheikh 7
Mohamed, Famau 411, 416
Mohammed, Pops 368
Mohammed, Salimo 266, 269
Mohammed, Tayfa de Cheikh Sidi 262
Mohand, Si Mohand Ou 23

Moheli 164
Mohlala, Johannes 360
Moholo, Louis 382
Moholo, Solly 390, 392
Mokoena, Vuyo 390, 392
Mokonotela, Peter 356
Molatlhgegi, Peter 45
Molelekwa, Moses 367, 383, 387
Molema, Batho 44
Molosi, Skizo 45
Mombelli, Carlo 383, 384, 387
MoMo 257, 263
MOMO 478
Mona Mona 298
Mondlane, Chude 274
Mondo Music 441
mongongo 118
Monja 200, 206, 208
Monteiro, Kalú 70
Moodphase 5ive 369
Moore, Princess Hawa 189, 192
Moorish music 240
Mootseng, Boli 277
Mopero 83
Mor ve Ötesi 606
Moradi, Ali Akbar 525, 526, 530, 567, 570
Morais, Luis 65, 69
Morente, Enrique 258
Morgado, Mestre Geraldo 31
Morgül, Yılmaz 606
morna 63
Morocco 248–264
Morogoro Jazz 420
Morolong, Sebene 45
Morteza 526
Moruakgomo, Socca 44, 45
Moses, Afro 130
Moshe, Chaim 542
Moshe, Salman 535
Moss, Alfredo 45
Mossi people 49
Mossiliya al-Djazaïriya al- 18
Mostganmia, Cheikha Grélo 10
Motherlan 296
Mothupi, Buster 45
Mougahid, Ahmed 497
Moukhadrami, Ensemble el- 246
Moulay Ahmed Loukili de Rabat, Orchestre 260
Moultaka, Zad 576, 578
Moumouni, Yacouba 281
Moundanda, Antoine 88
Mounir, Mohamed 498, 504
Mount Sinai Choir 215, 217
Mouquet, Eric 310
Moussa, Kaboré 48
moussems 249, 250, 253
Mousset, Christian 166

Movers, The 354, 362, 374
Moxy, Matu 31
Moyo, Jonah 452
Moyo, Tongai 453
Moyyere, El Hajj 139
Mozambique 265–274
Mpale, Dennis 382
Mpharanyana 374
Mpharanyana and the Cannibals 364
Mpiana, J.B. 82, 88
mqashiyo 357
Mr II 429
Mrad, Said 478
Mrakadi, Yuri 477
Mrubata, McCoy 368, 384, 387
Msasa wa Chuma 425
Mseleku, Bheki 388
Mshoza 367
Msungilo, Peter 437
Mthenga, Stanley 217
Mtiebi 508
MTS Matassa 284
Mtukudzi, Oliver 445, 448, 449, 458
Mubarak, Abdel Aziz el 399, 406
Mucavel, José 270, 274
Muchena, Amai 447
Mudéjar 557
Mudeka, Patience 449
Mueni, Peris 178
mugham 491, 492
Muhabbet 598
Muhammad bin Fâris Ensemble 516
Muhandis, Majid al- 537
Muhirwa, Ciza 318
Mujuru, Ephat 447
Mukangi, Deyess 81
Mukasa, Hope 431
Mukenga, Filipe 31, 34
Muki 545
Mukwesha, Virginia 447
Mulangeni Sounds 214
Mulayya, Sadiqa al- 534
Mulemena Boys 438
Mulemena, Emmanuel 438
Mulemwa, Spuki 439
Muluk El Hwa 256, 263
Municipality Band, The 109
Munir, Ensaph 535
Munir, Mohammed 501
Murad, Leyla 468, 470
Murad, Selima 535
Murefu, Aimé 317
Müren, Zeki 600, 612
Muri ko Muchena 447
Murkus, Amal 548
Musica, Wenge 75, 80, 82, 90

Musical Messiahs 189
Musiciens du Nil, Les 497, 503
Musîki Cemiyeti, Üsküdar 600
Musi-o-tunya 437
Muson Centre, The 296
Mussodji 271
Mustafa Itri, Buhurizade 599
Mustafa-Zadeh, Aziza 492, 494
Mustafa-Zadeh, Vagif 492
Mutende Cultural Ensemble 442
Mutituni Boys Band 178
Mutsari, Jean 317
mutuashi 81
Mutuku, Henrie 183
Muungano Taarab 414
Muvi Posse 441
Muyah, Orchestra 347
Muyango 317
Muyinda, Evalisto 432, 434
Muyonga, Abdul 181
muziki wa dansi 419
Muzipasi 212
Mvelé, Jimmy Mvondo 57
mvet 100, 118
Mwachupa, Paul 174
Mwalale, Ndiche 212
Mwale, John 175
Mwambi, Peter 177
Mwana, Tshala 81, 88
Mwanafalsafa 424
Mwanahela 414
mwanaSegere 415
Mwandjani, Toto 200
Mwansa, John 439
Mwenda, Jean Bosco 76, 88, 175
Mwenda, Jean-Bosco 395
Mwilonje Jazz 176
MXO 368, 374
Myéné 119
Myra, Mercy 183
Mzuri label 411

N

N'Dour, Viviane 337
N'Dour, Youssou 147, 327, 330, 331, 341
N'gola Ritmos 28
N'Goma, Oliver 119, 120, 121
N'Guema, Hilarion 118, 122
N'kassa Cobra 156
Naab 478
Nabay, Ahmed Janka 348
Nachash, Hadag 545
Nafar, Tamer 545
Nagbe, Anthony 189

Nairobi City Ensemble 183
Naka, Ramiro 156, 157, 161
Nakibembe Xylophone Group 432
NAKOREX 133
Nama people 277
Namakau 442
namastap 277
Namba, Mthunzi 391
Namibia 275–279
Namibian National Cultural Festival 278
Namoko, Alan 212, 217
Nana, Hammadi ould 243
Nandujja, Annet 432
Nangalembe, Joseph 213
Nankana people 49
Nara 591
Narusib 278
Nasery, Abana Ba 184
Nash Didan 542, 548
Nashil Pichen Kazembe 439
Nasibov, Edalat 490, 493
Nasmy, Layla 499
Nasra 401
Nasri, Assala 591
Nasri, Assala 594
Nass el Ghiwane 255, 262
Nass el Hal 257
Nass Marrakech 258, 262
Nasser , Tania 583
Nasser, Rum al- 562
Nasty D 441
Natiembé, Nathalie 166, 169
National Authority, Palestinian 583
Native Funk Lords 131
Native Spirit 129
Natty Rebels 165
Nature, Juma 423, 428
Nawaz, Aki 477
Nawroz 564
Nazareth Orchestra, The 548
Nazé 569
Nazeri, Shahram 521, 529
Nazeri, Sharam 567
Ndaba, Canny 45
Ndau people 266
Ndebele 445, 454
Nder, Alioune Mbaye 337, 341
Ndere Troupe 431, 434
Ndiaye, Assané 337
Ndiaye, Baro 330
Ndingo Brothers Band 213
Ndioné, Marie Ngoné 337
Ndirande Pitch Crooners, De 212
Ndlazilwane, Victor 379
ndombolo 83
Ndoni people 288
Near Eastern Music Ensemble 585
Nedule, Papa Noel 77

Néfertiti 92
Negra, África 323, 325
negritude 327
Negro-Tropical 118
Neji, Sunny 293, 302
Nekatibeb, Fikreaddis 111
Néko, Ano 92, 97
Nekros 258
Nelly, Ochieng 175
Neto, Costa 271
Netos de Gumbé 161
Neves, Dulce 161
Nevrou, Isselmou ould 242
Nevrou, Mneitou mint 243
New African Shrine 296
New Black Eagles, The 456
New Scene 212
New York 300
Newroz, Nazé 571
ney 520
nganja rhythm 57
Ngatu 276
Ngcobo, Shiyani 374
Ngereza, John 180
Ngoh, Misse 55
Ngom, Moussa 332
ngombi 118, 307
Ngonguenha, Conjunto 31, 33
Ngosa, Matthew 442
Ngozi, Paul 439
Ngozi, Winston Mankunku 382, 388
Ngqawana, Zim 383, 388
Nguini, Vincent 57
Ngumuya, Allan 215, 217
Niang, Prosper 331
Nice, Mr 424, 427
Nickelos, Los 79
Nico, Dr. 36
Niger & Touareg 280–286
Niger, Abdallah du 282, 284
Nigeria 287–303
Night Ark 484
Night Star Musical Club 425
Nightingale, Tunde 290
Nil, Hanan an- 402, 403
Nile Beat Artists 432
Nile One 502
Nile, The 318
Nilüfer 608
Nimo, Koo 125, 132, 133, 134
Nin, Khadja 318, 320
Nina, Joe 366
Ning'anga, Kenneth 214, 216
Ninie 200
Njava 202
Njie, Mam Tamsir 329
Njohreur 57
Njung'wa Stars 177

Nkabinde, Simon "Mahlathini" 357
Nkasa, Joseph 213
Nkasa, Phungu Joseph 218
Nkengas, The 293
Nkhata, Alick 213, 437, 443
Nkolo Mboka 80
Nkosi, Ben 356
Nkosi, Isaac "Zacks" 378
Nkosi, West 374
Nkosi, Zacks 354, 388
Nkotti, François 55
Nkwanyane, Elijah 354, 378
Nnaddibanga, Gerald 431
Noa 542
Noel, Jean 201
Noel, Sofía 554
Nolo, Djo 83
Nondje 269
Notias 70
Noujoun el Khams 12
Nour Ensemble 529
Nouvelle Génération 82, 88
Nova, Sayat 484
Novas, Manuel de 65, 66
Nuba people 402
Nuba, The 195, 251
Nubenegra 241
Nubian music 498
Nujoom FM 502
Number One du Senegal 329
Nune 487
Nunes, Artur 28, 29
Nupe people 289
Nurettin Selçuk, Münir 600, 612
Nuta Jazz Band 420, 428
Nxumalo, Gideon 381, 388
Ny Sakelidalana 204
Nyachan 402
Nyama, Kwabena 125, 133, 134
nyambo 215
Nyambura, Queen Jane 177, 181
Nyame, E.K. 124, 125, 126, 127
Nyampinga 317
Nyanyagwa, Ras Innocent 426
Nyathi, Albert 454
nyatiti 173
Nyembe, Sparks 356
Nyika Club Band, The 174
Nyirenda, Angela 442
Nyirongo, Joyce 440
Nyolo, Sally 57, 60
Nzenze, John 176
Nzié, Anne-Marie 56, 60
Nzimande, Hamilton 354

O

O'Bryant, King 191
Obesere, Abass Akande 294
Obey Records 291
Obey, Ebenezer 290, 297, 301
obokano 172
Obra 126
Öcal, Burhan 603
Öçal, Burhan 615
Odeh, Sammy Needle 300
Odhiambo, Bruce 183
Odukoya, Ade Bantu 298
Ofarim, Esther 540
Ofojebe, Chuks 299
Ogada, Ayub 186
Ogba people 288
Ogene Super Band 293
Ogholi, Evi-Edna 299
Ogopa Deejays 183
Oğur, Erkan 485, 597, 610
Ohandja, Mama 56
O-Hum 527
OK Jazz 75, 77, 78
Okafor, Ben 299
Okai, Kobina 125
Okalla, Bob 126
Okosun, Sunny 297
Okri, Mike 298
Okrika people 288
Okukuseku 126, 129
Okulolo, Kenneth 298
Ol, al 542
Olaiya, Dr Victor 292, 296
Olaiya, Moses 290
Olajuyeybe, Chief 291
Olemba, Thierry 58
Oliver, Nel 36
Oliya Band 439
Olomide, Koffi 75, 82, 88
omaimbilo emanguluko 276
Oman 515
Omar, Yusuf 534
Omart Mapara, Robert 441
Ombale, Bimi 83
Omensah, Eddie 130
Omnyama, Mfaz' 361, 374
Omolo, Gabriel 186
Omoratly, Massaoud 536
Omoumi, Hossein 529
Omowura, Ayinla 293
omutibo 176
ondjongo 277
Ondo, Jimmy 120
Ongala, Remmy 422, 428
Ongaro, Sukuma bin 176
Onwenu, Onyeka 293
Onyina 125

Onyina's Royal Trio 126
Onyiya, Zeal 292
Oojami 478, 479
Opetum, Ndombe 79
Oran 6
Oranais, Saoud l' 6
Oranaise, Reinette l' 6, 7, 20
Orchestra Jazira 129
Orchestra Les Mangelepa 179
Orchestra Makassy 422, 427
Orchestra Maquis Original 422, 427
Orchestra Matimila 422
Orchestra Mazembe Academia 179
Orchestra Mberikwazvo 453
Orchestra Popolipo 180
Orchestra Safari Sound 421, 422
Orchestra Super Mazembe 176, 186
Orchestre Liberty 199
Orchestre M'Bala 119
Orchestre Maquis 79
Orchestre National de Barbés 477, 479
Orchestre Nationale A 226, 227
Orchestre Rivo-Doza 201
Orchestre Virunga 173, 178
Orchestre Virunga 185
Orient Expressions 478
Oriental Brothers 293
Oriental Music Ensemble 586, 587
Original Brothers 442
oriyental 604
orkes 363
Orozco, Carlos 158
Ortaç, Serdat 608
Oryema, Geoffrey 433, 435
Os Úntués 323
Osadebe, Chief Stephen Osita 293, 302
Osadebe, Obiajulu 298
Osborne, Jane 442
Osei, Teddy 128
Osho, Ignacio Blazio 36
Osibisa 128, 129, 437
Osiris 512
Osman, Khogali 398
Osukoya, Timi 297
Othmani family 282, 285
Othmani, Baly 282
Othmani, Khadija 282
Ottu Jazz Band 420
Ouachma, Cheikha el 10
Ouattara, Désiré 49
Oud, Iraqi 536
Oud, Israeli 543
Oudaden 256
Oudag Boereorkes 363

oudano 276
Ouédraogo, Georges 48
Oumar, Fadimata Walet 282
Ovahimba people 276
Owambo people 276
Owiyo, Suzanna 183, 186
Owusu, Felix 133
Oyiwane, Groupe 282
Özak, Müzaffer 600, 601
Özçimi, Sadrettin 599
Özgen, Ihsan 599
Özkan, Talip 597, 610
Öztürk, Okan Murat 597

P

Pa, Le Karma 87
Paasewe, E. Kaikpai 189
Pablo D'ablo O'outlaw 278
Paco, Celso 269
Paco, Frank 271
Padaud, Luckson 93
Paim, Eduardo 31
Pais, Sidónio 156, 157
Paix , L'Ensemble de la 576
Paledi, Livingstone "Dollar" 45
Palestinians 580–588
palm wine music 55, 124, 125, 346
Pal-Yarden, Hadass 540, 613
Pan African Orchestra 132
Panako 206
Pandi 77
Papa Fransua and Tropical Tune 277
Pape & Cheikh 338, 342
Papillon 57, 60
Parents du Campus, Les 94
Paris, Tito 65, 69
Parisa 521, 522
Parisian soukous 81
Paris-Tehran Project 529
Parlak, Erol 597
Parliament 370
Parra, Eliseo 554
Parrots 126
Paseli Brothers 212
Paseli, Barry 212
Pasharos Sefardíes 553
Pasharos Sefardíes, Los 557
Pat'Jaune 166, 169
Patengue 57
Patou, RX 40
Patria, Cuarteto 54
Patricia 277, 278
Paul, Mr 424
Payvar, Faramarz 521

Pazedi Jazz Band 269
Peace Band 438
Peacocks International 292
Pedi people 360
Pedro, Gnonnas 36, 337
Pekkan, Ajda 606
Pené, Omar 332, 342
pennywhistle jive 355
Pepa, Gina 271
Pepera, Kwesi 125
percussion, Afro-Cuban 127
Percussions de la Guinée, Les 138
Pereira, Celina 65
Perpignan, Joca 542
Perwer, Şivan 565, 571
Peters, Shina 290, 301
Petit Pays 57, 60
Pfumo, Fany 267, 361
Philharmonie Jazz 139
Philoé, David 167
Phiri, Dennis 213, 218
Phiri, Ray 364
Phiri, Saleta 212, 218
Phuka, Morson 212
Phuzekhemisi 361, 375
Phuzushukela 361
Picoby Band d'Abomey 36
Pierre, Amédée 93
Pili Pili 38
Piliso, Ntemi 378
Pillay, Lionel 383
Pina, Frank de 70
Pina, Zé Rui de 70
Pinado, Bob 130
Pino, Geraldo 296, 347, 349
Pioneer Jazz of Missira 227
Pipa, Moz 270
Pirattack, Tere 50
Pires, Guto 157
Piro, Ahmed 260
Plaatjie, Sol 353
Planets, The 432
Plange, Stan 133
Plantashun Boyz 299
pluriarch 119
pluriarcs 277
Police Band, Ethiopia's 109
Police Strings Band 214
Poliker, Yehuda 542
Polo, Marco 317
Polo, Sergeo 57
polyphonous multipart singing 173
polyphony, Georgian 506
Poopy 205
poro rhythm 92
Positive Black Soul 334, 336, 338, 342
Poussy, Moussa 281, 284

Pozo, Omanhene 131
praise incantations 276
praise singing (Nigerian) 297
Professeur T 121
Professional Uhuru Band, The 127
Professor Jay 424
Prophets of Da City 369
Public Image Ltd 476
puíta 322
Pukwana, Dudu 369, 381
Pulaar people 240, 244, 327, 334
Pulakena 278
Pure Magic 392
Puritans 453
Pygmy music 304–312

Q

Qantara 585
qanun 409, 591
Qasabgi, Mohammed al- 466, 470
Qasimov, Alim 490, 491, 492, 493
Qatar 513
qawaali 581
Quame, Nana 131
Quartier Latin 88
Quaye, Cab 129
Qubanchy, Mohammed al- 534, 537
Queen Jane 177, 181
Qundarchi, Rachid al- 534, 538

R

Raam Daan 333
Rabat 252
Rabelados Splash, Os 69
Rachabane, Octavia 384
Rachid 13
Racinetatane 165
Radio Moçambique, Grupo 269
Radio Zulu 359
Rafiatou, Fifi 40
Rafidain al- 534
Ragga Dee 431
Raharimala, Noro 199
Rahasimanana, Paul Bert 198
Rahbani, Asi 574
Rahbani, Mansour 574, 575
Rahbani, Marwan 575
Rahbani, Sabah 574
Rahbani, Ziad 574
Rai 5–21

Rai, Moroccan 259
Raices 554
Rail Band, The 147, 223, 227
Raina Rai 14
raïs 251
Raïs, Abdelkrim 252
Raitt, Bonnie 225
Rajery 200, 208
Rakoto Kavia 198
Rakotozafy 200, 209
raks sharki 499
Ralf 167
Rama, Sami 49
Ramanu, Daddy 347
Ramblers International Dance Band 127
Ramblers, The 133
Ramboatiana, Etienne 203
Ramdani, Abdallah 252
Ramilison 198
Ramogi, George 175
Ramos, Mariana 65, 72
Ramy, Ahmed 467
Ramzy, Hossam 476, 502
Randafison, Sylvestre 200
Randimbiarison, Ricky 199, 209
Randriamanantena, Donné 200
rap 37, 40, 48, 49, 95, 230, 258, 259, 277, 299, 339, 366, 368, 490, 608
Rapadio 338
RAS 95
Ras Mêlé 166
Rasai, Afsaneh 522
Rasha 402, 404, 406
Rasoanaivo, Hanitra 198
Rast 493
Rathebe, Dolly 379, 380
Ravelonandro, Zeze 200
Ravinala 206
raysat 251
Razafindramanga 198
Razazi, Naser 567, 569
Razbar Ensemble, The 569, 571
Razjwan, Naim 535
Real Elements 215
Real Estate Agents, The 370
Real Sounds 79, 453, 458
Rebel Moves 478
rebita 28
Reborn 258
Red Spots 127
Redda, Tewelde 104
Redda, Tewolde 110
Redsan 183
reggae 37, 94, 130, 213, 230, 299, 370, 426
Rego, El 36, 37
Rehavia, Hagai 542

Reichel, Idan 545, 548
Rejaf Jazz 402
Reliziana, Cheikha Zohra el 10
Remedies, The 299
Remedy, Eddy 299
Remitti, Cheikha 8, 9, 20
Rendall, Luis 66
Renegade Soundwave 476
Renovation Cha Cha 119
Replikas 606
Résistance DJ collective 95
Reşit Rey, Cemal 603
Reuben Caluza's Double Quartet 371
Réunion, La 165
revival , acoustic 84
Revolution 368, 375
Rhabbles, Helen 130
Rhino Band, The 174
Rhumba Japan International 179
Rhythm Aces 127
Ribocho, Mastho 101
Richard Band de Zoetele 56
Richo 278
Richy, Sita 100
riengo 121
Rifaat, Mohammed 465
Riho Ensemble 509
Ringo 368, 375
Riziki, Boina 164, 168
Rmiki, Ihsan 260
Robbie Jansen's Estudio 383
Roberts, Zack 189, 190, 191
Rochereau, Pascal Tabu 77
Rochereau, Tabu Ley 89
Rock'a Mambo 77
Rocket 104
Rockstone, Reggie 131, 134
Roger, Kaboré 48
Rogie, S.E. 347, 350
Roha Band, The 110
Roi Alokpon, Le 39
Roman, Rafet el- 608
romansas 552
Romeo, Elvis 100
Roots and Kulture 426
Roots, The 212, 214
Rossignol 77
Rossy 198
Rotana 502
Rouicha, Mohammed 257
Rowaishid, Abdallah al- 513, 517
Royal Band Thies & Dieuf Dieul 342
Royal Obonu Drummers 134
Royals, Kumapim 126
Ruby 502, 503
Ruggedman 299
Rujindiri, Maître de 317

Rum 560
rumba 53, 75, 76, 118, 178, 437, 452
Rumba Ray 82
Rumba-Sungura 452
Rumi, Jalal Edin 521
Rustavi Choir 507, 509
Ruz, Soley 165
rwaïs 251
Rwanda & Burundi 313–320
Ryco Jazz 79, 89
Rykiel, Jean-Philippe 229

S

Saaba 49
Saad, Siti bint 409
Sabá Miniambá 156
Sabannoh International 75 348
Saber, Ahmed 10, 11
Sabounyouma 49
Sabreen 582, 583, 587
Sacko, Fanta 221
Sadio, Bah 148, 151
Saeed, Samira 502
Safaa, Ikhwani 410, 412
Safari Sound 181
Safi, Nia 427
Safi, Wadi al- 573, 578
Sağ, Arif 597, 598, 610
Saga, Douk 95
Sagath, Racine 57
Saher, Kazim al- 537, 538
Sahraoui, Cheb 18
Sahraoui, Mohamed 14
Sahrawi people 241, 247
Said, Mokhtar al- 503
Said, Samira 255
Saiyidi 497
Saj, Daddy 348, 349
Saka, Fuat 597
Sakala Brothers 441
Sakhile 383
Şakı 492
Salala 204
Salama, Baba 241
Salamat 504
Salameh, Adel 585
Salameh, Adel 588
salegy 199
Saleh, Self Salim 413
Salem Tradition 166, 169
Salem, Christine 166
Salem, Fouad 537
Salfiti, Haddaji Rajih el- 581
Salim, Abdel Gadir 398, 399, 402

Salim, Abdel Gadir 399
Sall, Samba Diye 244
Saltiel, David 557
Sam, Bil de 146, 149
Sam, Jacob 125
Samaha, Carole 575, 579
Samaké, Sibiri 232, 236
Samba Demba Djadje Ba 244
Samban'goma 214
Sambat, Alexandre 119
Sambeco 164
Samite 435
Samputo 317, 319
Samuelin 100
Samuels, Ebenezer Kojo 189, 192
San people 277, 352
San, Ayse 566
Sana, Mama 200
Sanaa Taarab 414
Sanchez, Michel 310
Sandal, Mustafa 608
Sanders, Pharoah 262
sandiya 220
Sangaré, Amadou 232
Sangaré, Oumou 220, 236
Sankomota 383
Santiago, Black 36
santur 520, 565
sanza 118
São Tomé & Principe 321–325
Saozinha 65, 70
sapeur 95
Sapltwa 213
Saqati, Amira 258
Saqati, Amíra 477
Saramaya 49
Saran, Missia 146
Saravah 119
Sariyeva, Sevintch 492
şarkı 599
Şarkı, Raks 604
Sarr, Seydou 244
Sata, Kokanko 233, 235
Sattar, Ali Abdul 513
Saudi Arabia 511
Savuka 363
Sawaaba Sounds 128
Sawt El Atlas 258, 262
sax jive 354
Sayid, Omar 256
Sayin, Emel 606
saz 596
Schal Sick Brass Band 298
Seal 298
Seba, Marilou 57
Sebatta, Fred 431
Sebatunzi and Sentore 317
Sebbaduka, Christopher 431
seben 77

Sebsebe, Kuku 109, 110
Seck, Abdou Guité 337
Seck, Cheikh Tidiané 139, 229
Seck, Mansour 246, 334, 342
Seck, Ousmané 337
Seck, Papé 337
Seck, Thioné 333, 343
Sefarad 604
séga 165, 199
seggaemuffin 165
Segid, Atoweberhan 104
Séka, Monique 98, 146
Sekiri people 290
Sela, Eyal 540, 544, 549
Sele, Afande 429
Selim III 599
Selolwane, Blackie 44
Selorm Cultural Troupe 132
sem-enna-werq 110
Senar, Müzeyyen 600
Senegal & The Gambia 326–344
Sene-Rap 339
Senge 204
Senhaji, Orchestre 255
Şenlendirici, Hüsnü 603
Senoufo 49
Senoufo people 92
Şenses, Adnan 600
Senyatso, Duncan 45, 46
Sephardic music 551–558
Sephardic music, Moroccan 259
Sephum, Judith 384
Serakoeng, Baba Mokoena 369
Serenje Kalindula Band 439, 443
Serer polyphony 327
Seri, Gadi 542
Sería, João 323
Şerif, Mahsuni 598
Serpent Noir 95
Sesiyılmaz, Hafız Burhan 600
Sesler, Selim 603, 613
setar 520
Setona 401, 406
Set-son and the Mighty Dreads
    276, 279
Seychelles 166
Seydou 347, 350
Seymali, Nora mint 243, 246
Seymali, Sidi ould 243
Seyoum, Betsat 113
Sezgin, Ahmet 605
Sfatayim 542, 549
Sghir, Boutaïba 12
Sha'er, Aida al- 499
Sha'eri, Hameed al- 195, 196
shaabi 499
shababi 499, 501
Shabalala, Joseph 359

Shabazi, Shalom 476
Shadz o'Blak 182
Shaeri, Hamid el- 500, 501
Shahebrahimi, Amrollah 530
Shaheen, Simon 585, 588
Shahram 526
Shahrokh, Aziz 567
Shaikh, Khalid al- 512, 516
Shajarian, Mohammad Reza 521,
    522, 526, 529
Shakawe 45
Shakes Mgudlwa's Soul Giants 382
Shakila 414
Shalawambe 439
Shama Shama 80
Shamma, Naseer 536, 538
Shangaan people 360, 361
Shangara Jive 449
Shanuolu 291
Shar'abi, Boaz 542
Sharafyan, Vache 484
Sharif, Mahjoub 400
Shasha, Jethro 383
Shawki, Ahmed 467
Shawqi, Narzjes 535
Shaygiya, Um el Hassan el 401
Sheehama, Ras 278, 279
Sheer Sound 383
Shehan, Steve 282
Sheikhli, Najim al- 534
Shereen 502
Sherie, Ammar el- 476
Sheva 544, 549
Shibbeth, Salim 535
Shifty records 383
Shikamoo Jazz Band 429
Shikololo 277
Shiku 277
shimshal 564, 565
Shinyori Sisters 362
Shirati Jazz 175
Shoghaken Ensemble 483, 487
Shona 445
Shoukoukou 497
Showkey, Daddy 299, 303
Shuail, Nabil 513, 517
Shukri, Samir 542
Si Tony, Nkondo 56
Siamoux people 49
Siavash 527, 532
Sibalo, Brian 453
Sibanda, George 454
Sidi Bemol, Cheikh 24, 25
Sidibe, Balla 330
Sidibé, Coumba 232, 233
Sidibé, Kagbé 233
Sidibé, Lama 139, 148, 151
Sidibé, Sali 233
Sidibé, Yoro 232

Sierra Leone 345–350
Sika Sound 48
Silgee, Wilson "King Force" 378
Silva, Dany 69
Silva, José da 64
Simba Wanyika Original 180, 186
Simentera 68, 69, 72
Simon, Paul 359
Simonga 455
Simplice, Sery 92
Singh, Talvin 477
Sinopoulos, Sokratis 604
Sissoko, Babani 222, 224
Sissoko, Ballake 236
Sissoko, Banzoumana 226
Sissoko, Djelimady 224
Sista D 442
Sister, Yondo 81
Sisters With Attitude 348
Sithole, Jonah 449, 458
Sitson, Gino 58, 61
Siulapwa, Danny 443
ska 213
Skeleton 375
Skidmore, Alan 384
Skinner, Graham 437
Skizo 46
Skwatta Kamp 369
Skylarks, The 379, 380, 402
Slaoui, Houcine 255
Slimani, Ali 477
Smadj 478, 480
Small Poppy 40
Smockey 50
socopé 322
sodina 201
Soeurs Diabaté, Les 152
Soeurs Doga 49
Sofaa 50
Sofakolé, John 281
Soga 432
Sogo 132
Sojas, Wan Pot 348
Sokay, Naser 190
Solar System, The 95
Soleimani, Haj Ghorban 524, 530
Solo Dja Kabako 49
Solo Miral 199, 209
Solo, Bisso 57
Solo, Neba 230
Solomon Linda's Original Evening
    Birds 358
Solven Whistlers 356
Somo Somo 79
Somo, Mavuela 83
Songani Swing Stars 212
Songhai people 281
Soninke 240, 244
Sontonga, Enoch 353

Sooley, Baay 339
Sophiatown 378
Sorciers Noirs, Les 118
Sory, El Hadj Deli 137
Sotho people 352, 360
Sotho Sounds 360
Soubi 164, 168
Souiri, Abderrahim 252
soukous 75, 100
Soukous Stars 82
Soukous, Mbarga 56
Soul Brothers 362, 375
Soul, DJ Eric 318, 319
soulevé 118
Soum Bill 94
Soumah, Momo Wandel 139, 143, 146, 152
Sound of Africa CD series 394
South Africa (Gospel) 389–392
South Africa (Jazz) 377–388
South Africa (Popular Music) 351–376
Southern Africa Archives 393–396
Southern Freeway 450
Sow, Binta Laly 139, 148
Sow, Laye 338, 343
Sperança, Janota Di Nha 162
Sphinx, Les 118
Spielman, Udi 540
Spinto, Bally 92
Spirit of The People 447
Spirit, Hoba Hoba 258
Splash 364
spray money 300
Springbok Nudegirls 363
Ssempeke, Albert 432
SSP 31
Staati, Abdelaziz 255
Stan, Tohon 36, 37
Star Band 328, 330, 332, 341
STAR Records 291
Star, Razo 49
Star, Rigo 81
Stargazers 133
Station Master 126
Stella, Cella 37, 41
Stiger's Sister 45, 46
Stimela 364
Stones, Les 119
stranbej 564
Strit Band, Malabo 101, 102
Struggling Islanders 424
Stukas 79, 86
Stybar's Reggamuffin 426
Su, Ruhi 598
Sua people 305
Suade 132
Subliminal and the Shadow 545

Sudan 397–407
Sufi music 254, 403, 465, 496, 497, 564, 592, 601
Suku Troupe 128
Sukuma, Stewart 269, 274
Sukura, Aaron Bebe 132
sukuti 172
Suliko 508
Sultan Tunç 478
Sultan, Abu 581
Sultana 614
sumu 220
Sunai el Nagam 401
Sunai el Samar 401
Sunai Kordofani 401
Sunbati, Riyad as- 470
sungura 452
Sunni, Mustafa al 407
Sunny Alade Records 291
Sunset Boys 189
Supa Hi-Life Band, The 135
Super Band Ulanga 164
Super Biton de Segou 227
Super Boiro Band, The 142, 143
Super Bonkaney 283
Super Bunyore Band 176
Super Cayor de Dakar 343
Super Combo 347
Super Diamono 331, 342
Super Djata Band 228
Super Eagles 327, 328, 343, 344
Super Étoile de Dakar 331
Super Matimila 428
Super Mazembe, Orchestra 176, 186
Super Rail Band, The 236
Super Sabadaor, Le 341
Super Star de Ouidah 36
Superselection 144
Surfs, Les 198
Surgi 201
Şusa 492
Suso, Foday Musa 329
Suso, Jali Nyama 329, 344
Susso, Papa 344
Susso, Sambou 329
Suuf 343
Suzy 540, 557
Svanetia 507
Swahili music 178, 180, 266, 423
Swaleh, Zuhura 411
Swa-Ray Band, The 190
Swaray, Gebah 191, 192
Swede Swede 84, 89
Sweet Talks, The 130
swing 126
Syli National Orchestra 142
Syliphone 142
Syliphone Records 142

Sylla, Ibrahima 146, 222, 229, 334
Sylla, Maciré 148, 152
Syndicate 338
Syria 589–594
System Tazvida 453

T

T.P. Orchestre Poly-Rythmo 36, 41
Taabamrant, Raysa Fatima 251
Taarab 408–417
taa-rap 414, 424
Tabane, Phillip 382
Tabanka Djaz 70, 157, 162
Tabora Jazz 420
Tachinouit, Aicha 251
Taffetas 162
Tafiq, Tahir 566
Tagada 256
Tagoe Sisters 130
Tagtaaga, Hawa 403
Taha , Rachid 7, 16, 21, 476
Taha, Tasin 566
Tahihit, Fatima 251
taishokoto 409
Taiwo, Dele 291
Taj Mahal 225
tajwid 465
Takashi 132
Takfarinas 23, 26
taksim 599
Tala, André Marie 53, 57
Talai, Dariush 529
talking drums, edongole 92
Tall Mountaga 48
Tall, al 257
Tall, Cheikh Tidiane 336
Talsam, Hadia 401
tama 329
Tamashek 282
tambour 398
Tambours Gasy 206
Tamru, Ephrem 109, 110
Tananas 271, 383, 388
Tanara 542
tanbur 524, 565
Tanbura, el 503
Tandale Modern Taarab 415
Tandia, Demba 244
tandima 118
Tangier Orchestra 258
Tanoute, Imin 249
Tanrıyar, Seher 603
Tanza Musica 423
Tanzania & Kenya (Taarab) 408–417

Tanzania (Popular Music) 418–429
Tapha 332
tar 483, 520, 565
Tarab 590
Tarazi, Rima 583
Tarbas, Kamal 400
Tarbiat 282
Tarika 198, 199, 209
Tarkan 476, 606
Tarras 227
Tartit Ensemble 282, 285
tassou 331, 336
Tata Pound 230
Tatlıses, İbrahim 565, 605, 613
Tatliyay, Haydar 604
Tavares, Eugénio 63, 66
Tavares, Ira 158
Tavares, Norberto 70
Tawfik, Ehab 501
Tawfiq, Lamiya 535
Tawfiq, Walid 575, 579
Tawia, Kwadwo 125
Tayfur, Ferdi 605
TAZ Bolingo 81
Tazi, Ustad Massano 261
tbal 241
Tchakounte, Pierre Didi 53
tchamassi 53
Tchangou, Denis 53
Tchéka 72
Tchiloli 322
Tchink System 37
Tea Packs 542, 549
Teacher and his Afrikana 126, 133
Teal Record Company 437
Teal records 354, 355
Team of Makossa, National 55
Teanet, Peta 362
Techno Roman Project 478
Tedje 113
Tee-Jay, Abdul 347, 350
Tefera, Yared 116
Tejajlu Musical Group 189
Teka, Adaneh 113
Teka, Malefya 113
Tekbilek, Omar Faruk 478
Telouat 282
Temba, Abia 356
Temba, Ellison 354, 378
Tembo Brothers, The 452, 456
Temiz, Okay 603, 615
Temo 571
Tempos, The 127
Tesfahunegn, Tebereh 110
Tess, Faya 83
Tessema, Kassa 110
Teta 201

Tete Mbambisa's Soul Jazzmen 382
Têtes Brulées, Les 57
Tetma, Cheikha 7
Tetouan Orchestra 252, 258
Tetuila, Tony 291, 299
Thailo and Kapiye Duet 212
theatre, popular 322
Thekwane, David 354
Them Mushrooms 181, 187
Think Of One 257
Third Ear Band, The 476
Thomas, Pat 129
Thomas, Sam Fan 55
Thompson, Cindy 135
Thomson, Sarah 189
1001 Music Productions 269
Thu Zahina 79, 90
thumb-piano 432
Tiana 205
Tianjama 200, 209
TID (Top In Dar) 424
Tidawt 282
tidinit 240
Tikhu Vibrations 218
Tilipano 214
Tim & Foty 55
Timas, Lena 72
timbila 266, 267
Timbila Muzimba 269
tina 154
Tiná-Koia 156
Tinariwen 196, 282, 286
tinga 154
Tinkles, The 438
Tirikoti, Garikari 447
Titi 337
Titinha 65
Tiv people 290
Tiyamike 214
Tiyamike Band 218
Tjahe, Marcel 55
TKZee 366, 376
TMK 423
Tod One 283
Toe, Robert 189
Togo 35–42
Tohon & the Tchink System, Stan 41
Tokcan, Yurdal 600
Tokyo Ngoma 425
Tolno, Sia 137, 148
Tomas, Childo 271
Tombak 520
Tombo, Daniel 200, 209
Tontoh, Mac 128
Top, Yavuz 598
Topaloğlu, Birol 597, 610
Tosy 206

TOT (Tanzania One Theatre) 414, 416
Toteng, "Blind" 44
Toto , Gerald 58
Tôty 199
Touareg 280–286
Touareg de Fewet 196
Toulali, El Hadj Houcine 252, 261
Tounkara, Djelimady 221, 227, 229, 237
Touré Kunda 336, 343
Touré, Aladji 55
Touré, Daby 244, 246, 338
Touré, Sékou 140
Touré, Touré 244
Toussian 49
Tovo 200
Tracey, Hugh 213, 394
Trance music 254, 403, 465, 496, 497, 564, 592, 601
trane trekkers 363
Transglobal Underground 477, 502
Traoré, Boubacar 238
Traoré, Désiré 48
Traoré, Lobi 225, 227
Traoré, Moussa 227
Traoré, Rokia 226
Traoré, Rokia 238
Traoré, Seydou 232
Travadinha 65
Tribe 388
Trimo, Tino 162
Trio Feminino 28
Trois Filles de Baghdad , Les 8
Troubadour Records 354, 355
Troupe Lélé, La 166
TRT folk music 596
trumpeters, horn 53
Trutone records 354, 355
Trybesman 299
tsapika 198, 201
Tsâtagos, Lydia 277
Tshabalala, Bhekitshe 358
Tshabalala, Saul 358
Tshanda, Dan 364
Tsiboe, Nana 130, 135
Tsimihole 204
Tsinandali Choir 509
Tsisperi Trio 508
Tsitisibana 366
Tsonga people 266, 361
Tsotsi Kasumali, Stephen 437
Tubarões, Os 65, 72
Tube, Shem 176
Tucan, Trio 542
Tucan, Tucan 271, 274
Tuffour, Nana 133
Tuhami, Yassin al- 497

Tunar, Şükrü 599
Tunç, Onno 606
Tunçboyaciyan, Onno 'Tunç' 607
Tunsi, Bayram al- 467
Türkan, Derya 604
Turkey 595–615
Turkish classical music 598, 599, 600
Turkish folk 596, 597
Turkmani, Mahmoud 576, 579
Türkü, Yeni 604, 614
Turnbull, Colin 308
Tututu, Lukas 174
Twa people 305
Twahirwa, Hervé 317
Twala, Sello 'Chicco' 364, 365, 372
Twarab 164
Twenna, Naim 535
2wice 441
Twinkling Stars 413
2Face 291
2-Proud 423

U

UCAS Jazz Band 336
U-Cef 257, 263257, 263, 477, 478, 480
Udemba, Herbert 53
Udo, Peter 330
Uganda 430–436
Uhuru 133
Ukwu, Celestine 292
Umayri, Ensemble al- 513, 517
Umba, Tindika 179
Umbelina, Gilberto Gil 323
Umosen, Folake 299
umuduri 314
Unconditional Love 133
United Arab Emirates 512
University Highlife Band 133
Urithi Band 426
US Chicago House 366
Ushshâq, al- 252
Usman 256
ússua 322
Utakataka Band 453
uukorasa 276
Uwaifo, Victor 292
Uyoga 181, 187

V

Vakoka 206, 210
Valance, Holly 476
Vali, Justin 200, 210
Vali, Justin 205
valiha 200
Vall, Seymali ould Hamed 242
Vally, Rashid 382
Valozi people 276
Van Dúnem, Lourdes 28, 31
Vans, Andy 130
Vans, Bob 126
Vaovy 204
variété 164
Vee 45
Veli, Haci Bektas 602
Venhereque, Orlando 269
Verdi, Don 70
Verity, Ben Jah 49
Versatile Eight 126
Veterans, Les 56
Veve, Orchestre 79
Veysel, Aşik 598, 610
Vickey, G.G. 36
Victor, Patrick 167, 170
Victoria 80
Victoria Jazz 175
Victoria Kings 175, 187
Vieira, Nancy 65, 72
Vieira, Paulino 69
Vijana Jazz Band 420, 429
Viking, Nguza 421
Vilakazi, Strike 354
Vilon'Androy 201
viola 64
VIP 131
Virunga, Orchestre 79
Viry, Firmin 165, 169
Vital, John 167
Voice 384, 388
Voice of the Turtle 555, 558
Voices of Sepharad 555
Volcy, Jean-Marc 167, 170
Volkan, DJ 608
Voninavoko 204
Vox Africa 79
Vundumuna 178
Vüqar 490

W

Wadé, Seydina Insa 338, 343
Wagon Wheels, The 449
Wagosi wa Kaya 424

Wagué, Ali 139
Wahab, Mohammed Abdel 467, 468, 469, 470, 472, 476
Wahbe, Haifa 502
Wahby, Ahmed 10
Wahu 183
Wainaina, Eric 183, 187
waka 295
Wallias Band, The 110
Wameedd 585
Wanyika, Les 173, 180, 185
Wara 49
Warda (al- Jaza'iriya) 468, 471, 474
Wardi, Mohammed 398, 400, 407
Waro, Danyèl 166, 170
Warren, Guy (Kofi Ghanaba) 127, 129, 135
Was, Don 15
Washington DC 300
Wassa Afrika Dance Ensemble 132
Wassie, Etenesh 113
Wassika 283
Wassouf, George 590, 594
wassoulou 228
WassWong 283
Wassy, Brice 53, 61
Watan Musical Clubs, al- 414
watcha watcha 198, 199
Watt, Moussa 244
Watwani, Mahabouba el 164
Wax and Gold 110
Wazekwa, Felix 85
Wazenj Kijiwe 424
Wazimbo 269, 274
Weah, George Oppong 191
Wedy 40
Weich-Shahak, Shoshana 554, 555
Weird MC 297, 298
Weiss, Julien 590
Wemba, Papa 75, 79, 80, 89, 365
Wenge BCBG 82
Wenge Musica Maison Mère 82
Werrason 82
Wesley, Ebeny 55
West African Highlife Band 298
Western Diamonds, The 133
Western Jazz Band 420
Western Sahara 239–247
whirling dervishes 601, 602
White South African music 363
Whyte, Abu 347
Wildlife Society 370
Wilensky, Moshe 540
William, Fadhili 175
Williams and Marbel 126
Williams, E. Tonieh 191
Williams, Tunde 298
Williki, Orits 299
Winsé, Tim 48

Wisdom, Johnny 348
Wobble, Jah 477
Wolde, Teshome 110, 116
Wolof 240, 327
Wongary 283
Woody Woodpeckers, The 379
Worku, Asnaketch 110
Wossenatchew, Menelik 109
Wulomei 128
Wunmi 298
Wutawunashe, Jonathan 453
Wuzzi 49

X

Xalam 331, 343
Xan, Miryem 566
Xidimingwana 267
Xigutsa-Vuma 269
Xitende 269
X-Plastaz 424, 429
Xuman 338, 339
xylophone 92

Y

Yaakov, Ruth 554, 558
Yaba, Captain 135
Yahiatene, Akli 23
Yahyaoui, Majda 253
Yakar, Suzan 484
Yalley, Teacher 126
Yamoah 125, 126
Yankson, Papa 133
Yannatou, Savina 555, 558
Yaovi, Yaya 37
Yaşar, Necdet 599
Yeleen 50
Yellitare Lenal 244
Yemen 513
Yemenite songs 540

Yemna, Maâlma 7
Yener, Hande 608
Yeni Türkü 606
Yero, Petit 139, 148
Yesayan, Nune 486
Yèshiwork 113
Yiddish songs 540, 541
Yiriba 49
Yogo, Dindo 82
Yohannes, Seifu 110
Yom's, Tom 55, 61
Yopougon 94
Yoruba people 288
Yosefa 264, 549
Young Stars Modern Taarab 414
Young Stars Musical Club 417
Yüce, Abdullah 600
Yüceses, Hamiyet 600, 612
Yüksel, Levent 606
Yunasi 183

Z

Zafa 542, 550
Zagazougou people 92
Zahouani, Cheb 21
Zaida & Carlos Chongo 272
Zaïko Langa Langa Familia Dei 80
Zain, Mohammed 257
Zainaba 169
Zaïre 75
Zaita Musica 421, 423
zajal 581
zajaleen 581
Zakaria, Nicholas 453
Zakarian, Lucine 482
Zako, Sizwe 390
Zambia 436–443
Zam-rock 437
Zan'ani, Margalith 542
Zanda, Zoubna 49
Zande people 402
Zanzibar Stars Modern Taarab 413
Zap Mama 310, 312

Zaragoza, Rosa 554
Zaramo ngoma 414
zarb 520
Zarur, Yusuf 535
Zawinul, Joe 58
Zawose, Hukwe 424, 429
Zaydan, Ahmad 534
Zé, David 28, 29
Ze'ira, Mordechai 540
Zeca 270
Zêdess 48, 49
Zefira, Bracha 540
Zeidane, Sidi ould Ahmed 243
Zein Musical Party 411, 417
Zekri, Camel 242
Zele 57
Zelmat, Fadela 12
Zen 606
Zenawii, Levi Jesse 190
Zerrouki, Alloua 23
zeybek 597
Zeze 200
Zhakata, Leonard 445, 452
ziglibithy 93
zikr 496
Zimba, Atongo 132, 135
Zimbabwe 444–462
Zirak, Hassan 567
Ziryab 251, 534
Ziryab Trio 542, 550
zoblazo 92, 93
Zohar 478
Zoid, Karen 363
Zola 367, 376
Zomba Evening Birds, The 212
Zondi, Sam 390
zouglou 93
Zouk 119
Zrihan, Emil 259, 542, 550, 553
Zuhura & Party 417
Zula, Baba 478
Zulu Acapella 358
Zulu Ballad 440, 442
Zulu-Traditional 360
Zvakavapano, Fungisai 453
Zwai 366